Dedication

We dedicate this book to the ichthyologist Professor Dr. Werner Ladiges.
He has decisively contributed to promoting and deepen our knowledge of aquarium fishes and their biology. He was always there for us and other aquarists with valid recommendations and practical suggestions. Our sincere thanks to him again.

Hans A. Baensch
Dr. Rüdiger Riehl

Cover photos:

Title:	*Symphysodon aequifasciatus* Arend van den Nieuwenhuizen	
Back cover:	*Melanotaenia trifasciata* Hans-Joachim Richter	*Rivulus xiphidius* Lothar Seegers
	Apistogramma nijsseni Werner Schmettkamp	*Nymphoides humboldtiana* Kurt Paffrath
Page 3:	*Petitella georgiae* MERGUS-Archiv	

Publisher
Hans A. Baensch

Editors
Hans A. Baensch
Dr. Rüdiger Riehl

Translated and revised by:
Dr. Gero W. Fischer
Shellie E. Borrer

ISBN 1-890087-06-8 (U.S.A. only)
ISBN 3-88244-509-2 (For other countries)

First English Edition, 1993
Third English Edition, First Paperback Edition, 1997

Published in the United States by:
Microcosm Ltd., 2085 Shelburne Road, Shelburne, Vermont 05482

Distribution

USA:	Microcosm Ltd., 2085 Shelburne Road, Shelburne, Vermont 05482
Canada:	Rolf C. Hagen Inc., 3225 Sartelon Street, Montreal, Que. H4R 1E8
Great Britain:	Rolf C. Hagen (U.K.) Limited, California Drive, Whitwood Industrial Estate, Castleford WF10 50H, West Yorkshire, England
Australia:	Pet Pacific Pty Ltd., Unit C, 30 Skarratt Street, Auburn NSW 2144, P.O. Box 398, Rydalmere NSW 2116, Australia

Printed in Singapore

Hans A. Baensch　　Dr. Rüdiger Riehl

AQUARIUM ATLAS

Volume 2

Paperback Edition

Publishers of Natural History and Pet Books
Hans A. Baensch • Melle • Germany

Preface

The attentive reader will have noticed that Volume 1 was presented as a "single-volume, practical and modern book".
Originally, only one volume was planned. You, dear reader, have decided otherwise. The comments received were so numerous and so clearly in favor of a second volume that the authors had to grant the readers' wish. The result is presented here.
This volume turned out more extensive than the first. Of the roughly 5000 freshwater fish species suitable for the aquarium, only 1500 are presented in these two volumes. That is more than an aquarist could ever keep in his life, but interests are very variable and everyone's preference is not equal.
We have tried to present something for everyone, but we are aware that one can never present all that a individualist or specialist could wish for, even in two hefty volumes dealing with aquarium fishes and plants.
Some species reach importers only once and may not be seen again for years, sometimes even decades (!). Sometimes a species becomes extinct after the scientific description or first import. Environmental problems in the countries of origin may play a role in limiting imports.
Volume 2 of the Aquarium Atlas purposely does not go further into sophisticated and highly specialized hardware but rather into the breadth of the hobby. This allows us to give you more information on additional fishes and plants. Often the information on individual species is more extensive. This may occasionally interfere with the concept of side-by-side text and photo. We hope you will understand, but more information was one of the wishes of our readers.
We continue to ask for your input on the aquarium atlas. Only in that manner can this now two-volume, handy, modern work be kept up to date and on its aspired high level of standards.
Some additional comments:
Some perfectionists wish that the first volume would contain catfishes and the second cichlids. From a scientific point of view this may be apropos, but our reasoning is as follows.

The first volume is a self-contained work—nobody has to buy the second volume if the number of species in Volume 1 suffices.
In an edition conceived from the beginning as a multivolume set, one is aware of the fact that several volumes have to be purchased. However, that might not always be economically justifiable for the beginner. The publisher wanted to pay special attention to this point. That is why, for example, catfishes and cichlids can be found in both volumes.
We hope that this second volume provides you with as much information as you wish.

Hans A. Baensch Dr. Rüdiger Riehl

Melle/Düsseldorf, January 1997

Acknowledgments

This volume could not have been written without the help of numerous scientists and dedicated aquarists. This book is rich in special knowledge not previously found in other aquarium books.
Our special thanks go to
Dr. Gero Fischer and his wife Shellie,
Dr. Jacques Géry (Characins),
Gerhard Ott and Dr. Axel Zarske (Cyprinids),
Dr. Han Nijssen and Dr. Isaäc Isbrücker as well as Mike Sandford (Catfishes),
Manfred Meyer (Livebearers),
Dr. Jörg Vierke (Labyrinth Fishes),
Dr. Greenwood, Uwe Werner and Rainer Stawikowski (Cichlids),
Gunther Schmida (Australian Fishes),
and Kurt Paffrath (Plants).
The photographers of the more than 1000 color photographs share a large part of the success of this volume. They frequently contributed important information for the care of the different species.

Table of Contents

Lotus flower and fruit

More than 300 different plants are presently known for aquaria. Their nomenclature is quite secure, and with the exception of 12 species, all could be identified beyond a doubt. This assortment of aquarium flora is composed of 256 true species, 42 varieties and forms as well as two hybrids. These plants come from 80 genera and 46 families. To ease the finding of a specific plant, the species and genera are arranged in groups and subgroups based on growth characteristics. These are briefly explained below.

Group 1

Plants with Upright Stems

The common characteristic of these plants is the upright main axis with leaves arranged singly, paired or in whorls on the nodes. This group is comprised of 41 genera, 85 species with 18 varieties and forms as well as one hybrid. These are subdivided according to their different leaf arrangements.

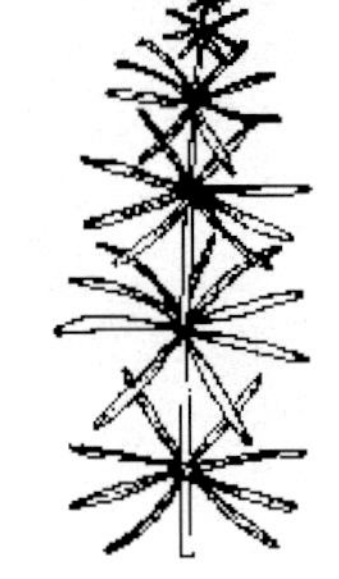

1.1. *Eusteralis*

Sub-Group 1

Leaves arranged in a whorl

Three or more leaves originate from a node at the same height around the stem. This sub-group includes the following genera:
Egeria, Elodea, Eusteralis, Hemianthus, Hydrilla, Hydrothrix, Limnophila, Myriophyllum, Nitella, Rotala.

Sub-Group 2

Opposing leaves

Two leaves on a node form a pair. Included in this sub-group are the following genera:
Althernanthera, Ammannia, Bacopa, Cabomba, Crassula, Didiplis, Gymnocoronis, Hydrotriche, Hygrophila, Ilysanthes, Ludwigia, Lysimachia, Micranthemum, Najas, Nesaea, Rotala, Shinnersia.

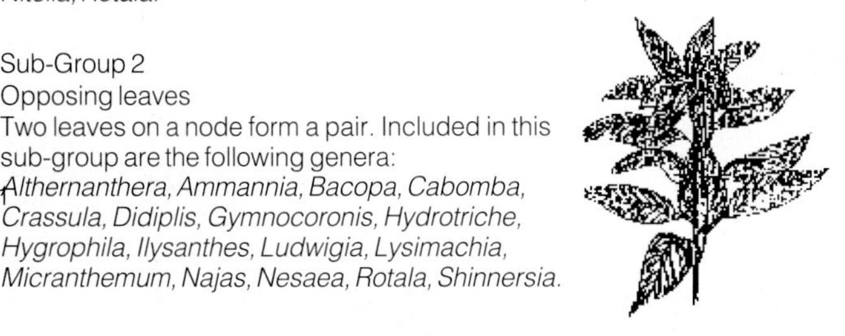

1.2. *Hygrophila*

Sub-Group 3

Alternating leaves

Single leaves originate from the node and are usually arranged in a spiral around the stem. The following genera fall into this sub-group:
Cardamine, Eichhornia, Fontinalis, Heteranthera, Houttuynia, Hydrocotyle, Lagarosiphon, Lobelia, Mayaca, Polygonum, Potamogeton, Proserpinaca (order *Hottonia*), *Saururus, Zosterella.*

1.3 *Lobelia*

Group 2
Plants with Leaves in a Rosette

The leaves grow upward from a thick root stock (rhizome) in the ground. These are very differently shaped, either with or without a petiole. In total, this group is comprised of 22 genera with 126 species and 24 varieties.

2.1. *Sagittaria*

Sub-Group 1
Narrow-leaved rosettes

Predominately tall forms with sessile, thin, ribbon- or thread-shaped leaves. This sub-group includes the following genera:
Acorus, Blyxa, Crinum, Eleocharis, Isoetes, Ranalisma, Sagittaria, Spiranthes, Vallisneria.

2.2 *Nuphar*

Sub-Group 2
Broad-leaved rosettes

Special characteristics are the roundish, usually cordate incised leaves and an often compact often compact growth form. This sub-group includes the following genera:
Anubias, Barclaya, Ceratopteris, Lagenandra, Nuphar, Nymphaea, Nymphoides, Ottelia, Samolus, Spathiphyllum.

2.3. *Echinodorus longiscapus* (round leaved)

Sub-Group 3
Amazon sword plants

Native to the American continent and variable in form. There are 47 species and 12 varieties. About 25-30 species can be kept in an aquarium. Their requirements and uses are varied.

2.3 *Echinodorus* (narrow-leaved)

Sub-Group 4
Aponogetons (*Aponogeton*)
Its 42 described species are distributed in Africa (15), Madagascar (11), southeast Asia (13) and Australia (4). 13 species and 3 varieties are more or less well suited for the aquarium. These are rapid growing plants that easily flower and fruit in an aquarium.

2.4. *Aponogeton*

Sub-Group 5
Cryptocorynes (*Cryptocoryne*)
This genus has over 60 described species and is widely distributed in southeast Asia. About 30 species are suited for aquarium cultivation in varying degrees. Their living requirements in an aquarium are usually higher than those of numerous other aquarium plants.

2.5. *Cryptocoryne*

Group 3

Creeping-shoot plants
This small group with 16 species from 10 genera is characterized by a creeping shoot with different shaped leaves. Some species can be fastened on stones or wood and will continue to grow there. The following genera are included in this group: *Bolbitis, Elatine, Glossostigma, Hydrocotyle, Lilaeopsis, Marsilea, Microsorium, Pilularia, Selliera, Vesicularia.*

3. *Hydrocotyle*

Group 4

Floating plants
Its 15 genera with 30 species can be divided into 3 biological types.
1. The genera producing totally submersed plants without roots: *Lemna, Utricularia* and *Riccia.*
2. Free floating plants with the top side of the leaf above the water or aerial leaves are grown by the genera: *Azolla, Ceratopteris, Eichhornia, Lemna, Limnobium, Pistia, Salvinia* and *Wolffia.*
3. Rooted plants with floating leaves: *Heteranthera, Hydrocleys, Nymphaea, Nymphoides* and *Trapa.*

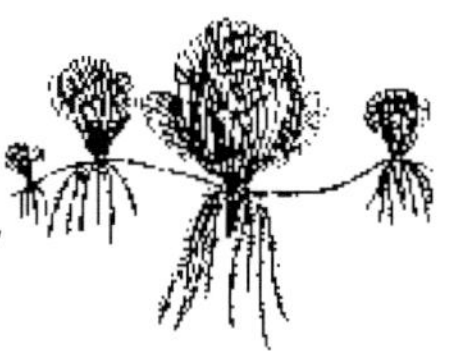
4. *Pistia*

Cryptocoryne cordata, pink vein variety. This plant, which is sought by specialists, has also been called "*Cryptocoryne siamensis rosanervus*".

The "Dutch plant aquarium" permits all that pleases. In the foreground are low-growing plants and the tall-growing slender ones are in the background. Such a tank places less emphasis on fishes; nevertheless, a lot of care is demanded.

Symbols used in the plant descriptions

D = Degree of Difficulty

This symbol indicates whether a species has basic or specific demands for successful growth. Degrees 1 or 2 are recommended for beginners. Plants in group 3 demand somewhat more experience. Those in group 4 depend on high quality (usually soft) water and should be considered only by experienced aquarists.

D: 1 Robust and adaptable species; also tolerates hard water and is content with less than optimal nutrient conditions. Light requirement is low to moderate, about 1 watt per 3-4 liters (1 gal) tank volume.
Propagation is usually without problems.
pH 6.0-8.0
Hardness up to 20° KH

D: 2 Robust and enduring species with somewhat higher demands on water quality. Light requirement is moderate to medium, about 1 watt per 2-3 liters ($^{3}/_{4}$ gal) tank volume.
Propagation very possible.
pH 6.0-7.5
Hardness up to 15° KH

D: 3 The species prefers soft to medium-hard water with balanced nutrients. However, it can remain healthy and grow in water of higher carbonate hardness with the addition of carbon dioxide. Light requirement is medium to high, about 1 watt per 1.5-2.0 liters ($^{1}/_{2}$ gal) tank volume.
Propagation not always easy.
pH 6.0-7.2
Hardness up to 10° KH

D: 4 The species has little adaptability and predominantly requires soft water. Usually has a high light requirement of about 1 watt per 1.5 liters ($^{2}/_{5}$ gal) of tank volume.
Propagation usually difficult.
pH 6.0-6.8
Hardness up to 4° KH

KH = Carbonate Hardness

The proportion of carbonate hardness in the water often determines the well-being of the plants. Very soft water, below 2° KH, is usually less suitable for plant growth. Decisive, however, is the adaptation of the plant to a certain hardness range. Some plants have to have soft water. Numerous plants, although they tolerate a higher carbonate hardness, are hampered in their growth when the pH rises or the carbon dioxide content of the water is too low.

The indications, made from experience, show the range most favorable for plant growth. Minor fluctuations are possible as many factors are interrelated. It is best not to combine plants with widely differing requirements.

pH = Reactivity of the Water

The acidity or alkalinity at which the plant grows best is noted. Most plants prefer the favorable range of 6.5-7.2. Deviations above or below are possible, but for certain species or genera it should not deviate too far from the suggested range. If problems in growth are noted, one can easily measure pH to determine if the error can be traced to inadequate reactivity.
Plants with widely differing preferences should not be planted in the same tank.

T = Temperature

The possible range in which the plant grows under normal conditions is indicated. The optimum is usually slightly above the middle value. In certain species, 2° C more warmth is possible, but because of increased respiration rates, more nutrients and more light than normal have to be provided.

AH = Aquarium Height

The symbol indicates the suitable aquarium height for the species. Tall plants and large rhizome plants, as well as rapid growing stalked plants, should be placed in aquaria which are as roomy and tall as possible. In shallow aquaria, such plants are out of place or have to be pruned too often. Plants that are low and of moderate height are suitable for any tank in regard to height, but the light-dimming effect of additional water above a short plant in a tall aquarium has to be considered. Small plants or small-leaved, stalked plants could receive too little light and languish if light intensity is not increased. For brevity, tank heights are grouped into three types.
AH = 1 Small aquaria up to 35 cm (14") in height.
AH = 2 Medium aquaria up to about 45 cm (18") in height.
AH = 3 Large aquaria above 45 cm (18") in height.

A group with presently 23 species and 3 varieties in 11 genera. A common characteristic is the thin main axis, which becomes buoyant. Three or more leaves are opposite at the node and form a whorl. Most are aquatic plants in their natural habitat. With strong illumination, hornwort, *Ceratophyllum demersum*, will flower in an aquarium. Its bloom is a small cluster with plain staminate flowers. Argentine acharis, *Egeria densa*, also grows in water but elevates its white flowers into the air so that they can be pollinated by insects. Among other things, this led to the separation of the genus *Elodea*, with its water-loving (hydrophyllic) blooms. *Myriophyllum tuberculatum* also flowers above the water surface, allowing its delicate spike to make use of the wind to transport the pollen to the stigma. *Rotala wallichii* can grow and flower as a swamp plant, but its inflorescence develops out of the water. The genus *Limnophila* shows several types of flower formations. *L. aquatica*'s whorled aquatic plant forms an aerial shoot with opposite, undivided leaves and large white and violet flowers. *Limnophila sessiliflora* develops an aerial shoot from the aquatic plant or grows as a bog plant. In the axile of the lobate aerial leaves sit single flowers. *L. indica* only flowers as a land form, and its aerial leaves are as finely divided as its aquatic form.

Egeria densa

Ceratophyllum demersum

Myriophyllum tuberculatum

Rotala wallichii

Limnophila sessiliflora

Limnophila aquatica

Limnophila indica

Ceratophyllum submersum LINNAEUS (1753) — Tropical Hornwort

Fam.: Ceratophyllaceae

Distribution: Almost cosmopolitan.
An undemanding water plant which remains healthy under almost any conditions. The main axis is green, slightly brittle, rootless with leaves in whorls of 6-12, up to 4 cm ($1^2/_3$") long, divided several times, forming 6-8 thin, soft tips with a sparsely thorned underside. Can be kept on the bottom with clamps to form loose bushes, but it is usually used as a floating plant. Meter long shoots and numerous lateral shoots create dense mats. It has been discovered to be a great help against black brush algae, probably using their subsistence from the water. Practice general regular thinning, particularly in small aquaria. Propagation: side-shoots and shoot segments.

D: 1, **KH:** 2-15, **pH:** 6.0-7.5, **T:** 18-30° C (64-86° F), **AH:** 1-3

Egeria najas PLANCHON (1849) — Slender-Leaved Elodea

Fam.: Hydrocharitaceae — Syn.: *Elodea najas*

Distribution: Brazil, Argentina
A group plant for taller aquaria and a floating plant for shallow tanks. The plants have elongated shoots with a maximum of four leaves arranged in whorls. The leaves are sessile, linear, acute, rarely slightly bent back, 2-4 cm ($^3/_4$"-$1^2/_3$") long and 2 mm ($^1/_{16}$") wide with coarse serration. Often confused with the similar *E. densa*, but its wider leaves are arranged in whorls of five leaves. Trim and replant the rapid growing shoots. Will also grow floating, forming dense bunches. Requires strong illumination or weak shoots with degenerate tips will result. Can be placed in the garden pond over the summer. Propagation: cuttings from lateral shoots, self-propagator.

D: 2, **KH:** 5-15, **pH:** 6.0-7.2, **T:** 20-24° C (68-75° F), **AH:** 2-3

Elodea canadensis MICHAUX (1803) — Canadian Elodea

Fam.: Hydrocharitaceae

Distribution: North America, introduced to other continents.
About 1865 it was brought to the European continent and there multiplied rapidly. Today, however, it occupies a normal place among the other aquatic vegetation. Mainly a coldwater plant that will tolerate higher temperatures for short periods of time. Thin, brittle main axis. Leaves are arranged in whorls of three (seldom 2-5), sessile, oblong, obtuse, up to 1 cm ($^1/_3$") long, 3 mm ($^1/_8$") wide, single-veined, somewhat bent back with a very finely serrated edge. Use in small groups under strong light. With excessive warmth the plants rapidly become spindly. In the outdoor pond it is undemanding, winter hardy and becomes extensively branched and completely submersed, forming beautiful, dense mats. In German waters only female plants are found. Propagation: cuttings from side-shoots.

D: 3, **KH:** 5-15, **pH:** 6.0-8.0, **T:** 10-20° C (50-68° F), **AH:** 1-2

Elodea nuttallii (PLANCHON) ST. JOHN (1920)

Fam.: Hydrocharitaceae

Distribution: North America
This plant does best in cool water, but it can be kept in higher temperatures for a limited time. It has a long, thin main axis that can be rooted in the substrate or natant. Normally, 3 leaves are in a whorl at each node, occasionally with 4 or 5 leaves. Blade is sessile, oblong, acute, 6-8 mm long ("-$^5/_{16}$"), 1 mm ($^1/_{32}$") wide, slightly twisted and curled with serrated edges. It's similar to *E. canadensis* but more delicate and not as brittle. Several cuttings form a loose group; do not plant as bunches but singly. Keep the vicinity clear to allow light penetration to the bottom. Prefers harder water. It is not often used in aquaria; a plant well suited for the garden pond. Propagation: cuttings, good self-propagator.

D: 2, **KH:** 5-15, **pH:** 6.0-8.0, **T:** 10-22° C (50-72° F), **AH:** 1-2

Ceratophyllum submersum

Elodea canadensis

Egeria najas

Elodea nuttallii

Eusteralis stellata (LOUREIRO) PANIGRAHI (1976)

Fam.: Lamiaceae Syn.: *Dysophylla verticillata, Ceficaulis, Eriocaulon*

Distribution: Tropical Asia, Australia
A decorative plant for small groups, but difficult to care for. Whorls of 5-14 leaves are borne on upright shoots. Aquatic leaves are thin-skinned, lanceolate, almost sessile, 3-7 cm (1 "-2 3/4") long, 3-5 mm (1/8"-3/16") wide, with a weakly dentate edge and an obtuse tip. The upperside is green to slightly brown, underside green or reddish. Aerial leaves are dark green, firmer, shorter with dentate edges. The shoot produces a terminal spike with small whitish blooms in several rows. A delicate plant whose limited growth requires soft water, a nutrient-rich environment and strong lighting. After a period of active growth, the tips deteriorate and don't form new leaves. Rooted plants, however, will grow new side-shoots from the leaf axil after a few weeks. Bushy plants result which should be pruned by pinching off all but a few of these side-shoots. These will develop better but follow the cycle of the main axis. The reasons for this are unclear since not all plants degenerate simultaneously. Propagation: cuttings of side-shoots.

D: 4, **KH**: 2-8, **pH**: 5.5-6.8, **T**: 22-28° C (72-82° F), **AH**: 1-2

Hydrilla verticillata (LINNAEUS fil.) ROYLE (1839)

Fam.: Hydrocharitaceae

Distribution: Almost cosmopolitan
A versatile, undemanding water plant that in nature occurs in dense stands on the bottom of waters. Main axis is thin and brittle with leaves in whorls of 3-9, sessile, lanceolate, 1-2.5 cm (1/3"-1.0") long, 2-4 mm (1/16"-3/16") wide, smooth, acute, serrate and dark green with a central vein that is often reddish. A different plant with curved-back, curled leaves is described as *H. verticillata* var. *crispa* CASPARY. *Hydrilla* grows under moderate light and adapts to a wide range of temperatures and hardnesses. It is, however, not easy to anchor the brittle shoots in the substrate; they will often break at the base and float again to the surface. Therefore, it is cultivated free-floating in the aquarium, creating loose mats. Var. *crispa* can grow in the open foreground. Short cuttings, placed at an angle, continue horizontally and form 10 cm (4") high, dense, profuse mats. Propagation: cuttings from side-shoots, self-branching.

D: 1, **KH**: 2-15, **pH**: 5.5-7.8, **T**: 15-30° C (59-86° F), **AH**: 1-3

Hydrothrix gardneri HOOKER fil. (1887)

Fam.: Pontederiaceae

Distribution: Brazil, in the state of Ceara.
This species is only distributed in a very limited area and became known in German aquaria around 1976. A graceful plant for loose groups with good adaptation to water values, but it is quite light requiring. The thin, erect, later floating axis grows to be 3 mm (1/8") thick. On the nodes, the leaves form apparent whorls, but they originate from superimposed short nodes as bunches of 10-25. The light green, thread-like leaves are 1 mm (1/32") wide, 2-5 cm (3/4"-2") long, with a pointed tip and a base that is slightly thicker and bent downward. The genus name refers to these leaves: *hydor* = water, *thrix* = hair. The flower shoot is emerse with two yellow, up to 8 mm (5/16") blooms with 6 petals whose tips are unequal. The shoots grow uncommonly fast, soon reaching the upper areas. There they bend and float below the water surface. With plenty of side-shoots, a large water surface is greened quickly. As a group in the visible area, trim regularly and replant. Propagation: cuttings from side-shoots, good self-propagator.

D: 2, **KH**: 2-12, **pH**: 5.5-7.5, **T**: 22-28° C (72-82° F), **AH**: 2-3

Eusteralis stellata

Hydrilla verticillata

Hydrothrix gardneri

Limnophila glabra (BENJAMINI) KERR (1950)

Fam.: Scrophulariaceae

Distribution: India
Finely structured water plant suited for the formation of small groupings in the foreground. 3-6, 1 cm (1/3") long leaves form whorls up to 2 cm (3/4") in diameter. The leaves are simple pinnate with the proximal leaflets rarely forked. Thin, flat tips are about 5 mm (3/16") long, 1 mm (1/32") wide and have a fine central vein. Imported for the first time in 1975; species name has not been confirmed by flowering cultured plants. It will tolerate hard water, does not degenerate in warm water, requires high light intensity and is best used for flat aquaria. Grows numerous side-shoots which can be encouraged by planting 15 cm (6") cuttings singly with some distance in between. This older group is trimmed when needed and occasionally renewed with the new tips. Can also float beneath the water surface. Propagation: cuttings, good self-propagator.

D: 2, **KH**: 2-15, **pH**: 6.0-7.2, **T**: 22-28° C (72-82° F), **AH**: 1-2

Limnophila heterophylla (ROXBURGH) BENTHAM (1835)

Fam.: Scrophulariaceae

Distribution: India, Pakistan, Ceylon, Indonesia, southern China, Japan
Superb group plant for the background or as a free-standing group in the middle of the aquarium. 5-13 leaves form 5 cm (2") whorls. Aquatic leaves are pinnate, segments opposite; lower segments are either pinnate or forked. The underside of the tips are slightly reddish, up to 2 mm (1/16") wide, not broadened distally. The last segment surpasses in length both tips underneath. *L. h. forma reflexa* has twisted leaf segments whose light underside is partially turned up. Aerial leaves are lanceolate, to 2 cm (3/4") long, serrulate, with short-stalked, axillary, single flowers that are white with a light purple striped throat. Most of the time the plant will not grow malformed even under low lighting conditions, but it should not be kept too warm. Rejuvenate older stands by removing the most vigorous tips and replanting the group. Remove all old specimens. Propagation: cuttings from side-shoots; when floating, an extraordinary self-propagator.

D: 1, **KH**: 2-12, **pH**: 6.0-7.2, **T**: 22-28° C (72-82° F), **AH**: 2-3

Limnophila indica (LINNAEUS) DRUCE (1923) — Indian Ambulia

Fam.: Scrophulariaceae — Syn.: *Limnophila gratioloides*

Distribution: Tropical Africa, southeast Asia, Australia
Several varieties of this widely distributed plant have been described. *L. indica* var. *indica* has whorls up to 5 cm (2") in diameter consisting of 6-12 leaves that are simple pinnate with forked lower segments. Tips are about 2 mm (1/16") wide, and the terminal segment surpasses both below by almost half of its length. *L. indica* var. *elongata* BENTHAM forms up to 7 cm (2 3/4") whorls with 8-10 leaves. These are structured hair-thin and are just 1 mm (1/32") wide. End segments also exceed the next significantly. Aerial leaves are variable, either lanceolate serrated or pinnate. Blooms are white, yellow, pink, or pale purple; the three-lobed lower labia has a larger central lobe. Can adapt well to diverse environmental conditions; the graceful variety has a higher light requirement. Cut shoots are said to exude fish toxins. It is probably a heart poison which is almost inactive in plants that have been in an aquarium for a while. Exercise caution in small tanks with sensitive fishes. Better to take cuttings outside the water, soak, thoroughly wash and then plant. Propagation: cuttings from lateral shoots.

D: 2, **KH**: 2-12, **pH**: 6.0-7.5, **T**: 22-28° C (72-82° F), **AH**: 2-3

Limnophila glabra

Limnophila heterophylla

Limnophila indica

Myriophyllum elatinoides GAUDICHAUD (1825)

Fam.: Haloragaceae

Distribution: South America, Mexico, Falkland, Tasmania, New Zealand
Group plant for cool to temperate aquaria with soft to medium-hard water. The axis is naked with 4 small grooves and 3-5 whorled leaves. Aquatic leaves grow up to 3 cm (1 ") long, wide, rhomboidal with 5-10 thread-like dark green segments on each side of the rachis, 5-15 mm (3/16"-2/3") long. Aerial leaves are incised at first then either oblong, entire or serrulate further down. Plant several cuttings as a loose row in the background of a tall aquarium. The plant grows quickly and soon reaches the water surface. Floating shoots provide green for the upper free zones of the aquarium. Grows numerous side-shoots that will shade its lower branches. The stands will need to be thinned so that the lower leaves are not shed. Propagation: cuttings, a good self-propagator.

D: 2, KH: 2-12, pH: 6.0-7.5, T: 15-22° C (59-72° F), AH: 2-3

Myriophyllum hippuroides NUTTAL ex TORREY et GRAY (1848)

Fam.: Haloragaceae Syn.: *Myriophyllum scabratum*

Distribution: North America, Mexico
Contrast plant for smaller groups in temperate or unheated aquaria. The main axis is sparsely branched, reddish, with 4-6 whorled leaves; on occasion, one leaf is located higher than the others. Submersed leaves grow up to 5 cm (2") long, very finely feathered, on both sides of the rachis are 6-10 thin segments, 5-25 mm (3/16"-1") long, which, with strong illumination, are reddish to brown-red, especially at the apex. General requirements fall in the median ranges; however, place the plants under the most light possible and provide sufficient room for larger specimens. Dirt accumulation on the dense whorls has to be avoided to prevent algae from growing on the leaves. Provide well-filtered water and adequate water movement. Propagation: cuttings from moderate side-shoots.

D: 2, KH: 2-15, pH: 6.0-7.5, T: 15-23° C (59-73° F), AH: 2-3

Myriophyllum verticillatum LINNAEUS (1753) Whorly Milfoil

Fam.: Haloragaceae

Distribution: Europe, Asia, Africa, America
A robust water plant for cool to temperate aquaria. The axis has whorls of 4-6 leaves. Aquatic leaves are 5 cm (2") long, numerously divided, and have 20 to 35 segments, 8-30 mm (5/16"-1 ") long, thread-like, slightly bent inwards with a hair-fine tip on both sides of the leaf. The flower head is emerse at the apex, up to 25 cm (9 3/4") long, with small, comb-like leaves. Blooms are pink. The relatively fast growing garlands are recommended for deeper aquaria; they grow well in soft to slightly hard water under intense illumination. A loose group will provide green for the background or sides in an aquarium. These plants can also grow natant. When the plant is left in a pond through the winter, it will not remain vegetative; instead, it will form winter buds that will germinate in the spring. Propagation: cuttings, good self-propagator.

D: 2, KH: 5-12, pH: 6.0-7.5, T: 15-22° C (59-72° F), AH: 2-3

Rotala wallichii (HOOKER fil.) KOEHNE (1880) Whorly Rotala

Fam.: Lythraceae

Distribution: Southeast Asia
A demanding species suitable for small groups. The main axis is thin with dense whorls of 10-13 leaves. Submerse leaves are sessile, almost thread thin, up to 2.5 cm (1") long, 1 mm (1/32") wide, single-veined and have a pointed tip. The upper side is sometimes brownish while the underside is usually reddish. In nature it is an amphibious water plant with broad emerse leaves and single flowers in the axils. It can grow for a while in hard water but will soon develop a degenerate form and die off. Prolonged growth is only obtained in soft water where the pH can fall. Under favorable conditions, the numerous side-shoots form many-branched loose groups. Light requirement is moderate. Do not transplant unnecessarily. Propagation: cuttings, good self-propagator.

D: 4, KH: 2-5, pH: 5.0-6.5, T: 22-30° C (72-86° F), AH: 1-3

Myriophyllum elatinoides

Myriophyllum verticillatum

Myriophyllum hippuroides

Rotala wallichii

This is an extensive group of 17 genera with 41 species and 15 deviating types or varieties. The common identifying characteristic is the erect main axis with 2 leaves per node, forming a pair. The blades are mostly lanceolate, seldom ovate, threadlike or pinnate. The genera *Cabomba, Hydrotriche* and *Najas* grow as true submersed plants. *Cabomba aquatica* grows a floating stem with ovate leaves and conspicuous yellow blooms. The remaining genera are swamp plants whose flowers only appear when the plant is emerse. For *Hygrophila corymbosa*, it suffices if the apex can grow above the water surface of an open aquarium. In the same manner, *Ludwigia repens* will flower on its stems which hang over the edge of the tank. *Bacopa caroliniana* requires a separate bog aquarium and bright daylight to develop its blue calyx. The same applies to the new genus, *Shinnersia rivularis*, with its small white composite flowers. In the same family, *Gymnocoronis spilanthoides* grows and flowers without problems in a window or a pond. *Ammannia gracilis* will flower and produce seeds regularly in a water-filled, shallow dish placed in a window sill. Since the plant produces seeds, propagation is easily possible. *Lysimachia nummularia*, called "Pfennigkraut" (= penny herb) in German, is a beautiful flowering plant whose creeping runners develop numerous golden yellow flowers in the yard.

Cabomba aquatica

Hygrophila corymbosa

Gymnocoronis spilanthoides

Lysimachia nummularia

Ludwigia repens

Shinnersia rivularis

Bacopa caroliniana

Ammannia gracilis

Alternanthera reineckii BRIQUET (1899)

Fam.: Amaranthaceae

Distribution: Brazil, Paraguay
This plant is seldom cultivated due to its moderate adaptation to submersed conditions and its demanding requirements. Aquatic leaves are lanceolate, flat, smooth, up to 3 cm (1 ") long and 1 cm (1/3") wide with both ends symmetrically pointed. The upper side of the leaf is green to olive-green with a reddish edge and is pink to dark red underneath. The emerse form has smaller leaves and dense, white, clusters of flowers in the leaf axils. Continuous growth in water is slow and requires a fertile, warm substrate. The high light requirement of 75 watts/100 l should be met, or elongated, small-leaved shoots will result. Leaves with good coloration are also light dependent. A nice optical effect can be achieved by a small group consisting of several loosely spaced plants placed in the bright center of a moderately tall aquarium. Propagation: cuttings, side-shoots after pruning. Note: here we are dealing with a variable species with several diverging growth forms; the form presented here is the type for the species. Another morph is presented in Volume 1, page 92, as *Alternanthera lilacina*; the following narrow-leaved morph is more common in aquaria.

D: 3, KH: 2-8, pH: 5.5-7.0, T: 22-28° C (72-82° F), AH: 1-2

Alternanthera reineckii "narrow-leaved type" BRIQUET (1899)

Fam.: Amaranthaceae

Distribution: Tropical areas of South America
The best representative of the group for aquaria. The plant shows good adaptation to aquaria life. Leaves are narrowly lanceolate, 5-10 cm (2"-4") long, 0.5-1 cm (3/16"-1/3") wide, with a prolonged base connected to a short petiole. The leaf tip is acute, the edge undulate, upperside olive-green to brown-red, underside wine-red. Aerial leaves are lanceolate, densely and short pilose on an uniformly pilose stem. The similar *A. sessilis* (Vol. 1, page 92) has a stem that has four pilose edges. With bright illumination, the plant remains more compact and better colored; iron fertilization will intensify leave coloration. A single robust specimen can be pleasing to the eye. In larger tanks, it is effective as an extended group arranged in terraces. Under favorable conditions, it is relatively fast growing, thereby necessitating regular pruning and replanting. Propagation: cuttings, side-shoots after pruning, self-branching, shoot-segments. Remark: another form of the species with larger leaves, up to 15 cm (6") long and 2 cm (3/4") wide is also known for aquaria.

D: 2, KH: 2-12, pH: 5.5-7.2, T: 24-30° C (75-86° F), AH: 2-3

Ammannia gracilis GUILLEMIN et PERROTTET (1830) Delicate Ammania

Fam.: Lythraceae

Distribution: Tropical Africa
An adaptive, quite fast-growing group plant. Submerged leaves are linear, sessile, slowly narrowing from the base to the long pointed tip and have a pinnately veined blade that is straight, flat and spread out. Leaf dimensions are variable; when unfavorable conditions exist (e.g., sand bottom, nutrient-poor water, moderate lighting), the leaves are usually only 7 cm (2 3/4") long and 6 mm (") wide. Under better conditions, the leaves are 10 x 1 cm (4" x 1/3"), optimally over 12 x almost 2 cm (4 3/4" x almost 3/4"). Coloration is olive-green to reddish. Aerial leaves are also variable; 3-15 cm (1 "-6") long and 1-2 cm (1/3"-3/4") wide, obtuse, green to reddish with red veins. In roomy aquaria, use a large group arranged in terraces by pruning the cutting at different heights. Attention should be given towards contrasts with other, lighter green plants and complementing the front plants with low growing species. With intense illumination and iron fertilization, the coloration becomes more intense. The plants are easily cultivated on the window sill, resulting in ample flowers with good fruit setting. Propagation: cuttings, side-shoots after pruning. Seedling cultivation is not difficult.

D: 2, KH: 2-15, pH: 5.5-7.5, T: 22-28° C (72-82° F), AH: 2-3

Alternanthera reineckii

Ammannia gracilis

Alternanthera reineckii narrow-leaved type

Bacopa floribunda (R. BROWN) WETTSTEIN (1891)

Fam.: Scrophulariaceae

Distribution: Tropical America, Java
A rarity for the experienced plant keeper. Leaves are lanceolate, 2-4 cm (3/4"-1 2/3") long, 2-4 mm (1/16-3/16") wide, dark green and entire. The base of the leaf is sessile and does not clasp the stem. The blade becomes gradually more slender and pointed towards the tip. The emerse form is more branched; aerial leaves are shorter and glandular pilose with several small, pale blue flowers borne in the leaf axils. Only moderate growth will occur in an aquarium and only for a short time under normal lighting conditions. Use at least 75 watts/100 l. Plant cuttings in small groups in intervals and totally free. Avoid unnecessary transplanting. The weak root system will develop better in coarse, loose sand. Coarse gravel is unsuitable. Propagation: cuttings, lateral shoots after pruning, moderate self-branching.

D: 4, **KH:** 2-10, **pH:** 6.0-7.0, **T:** 22-26° C (72-79° F), **AH:** 1-2

Bacopa lanigera (CHAMISSO et SCHLECHTENDAHL) WETTSTEIN (1891)

Fam.: Scrophulariaceae

Distribution: Brazil
This plant needs intense light and is recommended for the experienced connoisseur. Generally, it is rarely cultivated. The underside of the aquatic leaves are sparsely pilose, round-oval, up to 3 cm (1 ") long and 2.5 cm (1") wide, light green, obtuse and entire; seven branched green veins emerge from the wide overlapping base. Emersed stems are strongly pilose with aerial leaves that are covered with long hairs on the underside and have white, purple-veined, stalked, axillary flowers. A form with yellow-veined leaves exists, but it is unable to live in the water. There is a green form, but it needs strong illumination to achieve even slow growth. To guarantee that light will reach lower shoot areas, cuttings should be placed at least 3 cm (1 ") apart. Add CO_2 to hard water and fertilize with iron. At higher temperatures, growth is sparse and even more sensitive. Propagation: cuttings, side shoots are moderately formed.

D: 4, **KH:** 5-12, **pH:** 6.0-7.0, **T:** 20-24° C (68-75° F), **AH:** 1-2

Bacopa rotundifolia WETTSTEIN (1891) Round Bacopa

Fam.: Scrophulariaceae

Distribution: Southern USA
Growth and adaptation to aquatic life is poorly developed; therefore, it is seldom found in an aquarium. Leaves are roundish, up to 3 cm (1 ") long and 2.5 cm (1") wide. The stem and undersides of blade are pilose, and the base clasps the stem, often overlapping. Aerial leaves are almost round. Single, pale blue flowers with a white spot on the upper labia are found in the upper leaf axils of the emerse stem. The main condition for healthy growth is sufficient light (75 watts/100 l); in the shade, the stems remain thin and continuously develop smaller leaves. Adequate availability of iron is important as this plant evidently has a higher requirement than other aquarium plants. Stems are somewhat foamy; therefore, plant with care. With too much pressure it rots and, in consequence, will have inferior root formation. Coarse sand with the addition of clay will foment root formation and moderate growth. Propagation: cuttings, side-shoots after pruning, occasionally self-branching.

D: 3, **KH:** 2-10, **pH:** 6.0-7.2, **T:** 22-26° C (72-79° F), **AH:** 1-2

Bacopa floribunda

Bacopa rotundifolia

Bacopa lanigera

Cabomba caroliniana GRAY (1837) Green Cabomba

Fam.: Cabombaceae

Distribution: Northern South America to southern North America

The species has different varieties which differ in the division of their leaves. The type variety, *C. c.* var. *caroliniana*, is described in Vol. 1, page 94. The variety presented here is characterized by significantly fewer leaf divisions and continuously forming, 20-40 leaf tips, which widen towards the ends and become almost 3 mm (1/8") wide. It was described from cultivated plants, but it also occurs in nature. Position as a loose group in the middle area of the aquarium or in the background. This plant has a relatively low light requirement and grows well in harder water. Other requirements are similar to the nominate form. Propagation: cuttings, natant with side-shoots.

D: 2, KH: 2-12, pH: 6.5-7.2, T: 22-28° C (72-82° F), AH: 2-3

Cabomba pulcherrima (HARPER), FASSETT (1953)

Fam.: Cabombaceae Syn.: *Cabomba caroliniana* var. *pulcherrima*

Distribution: Florida

Coincides in habits to the type species *Cabomba caroliniana*. The main axis and leaf segments are reddish. Floating leaves are lanceolate with light pink flowers. Its position as an autonomous species is doubted by some authors. A beautiful contrast plant when placed between plants of different shapes. The color of the leaves is light dependent and only remains with very bright illumination (75 watts/100 l). In hard water, growth is poor and the addition of carbon dioxide will be necessary. Regular iron fertilization promotes coloration and growth. A loose sand bottom is preferred and minimal transplanting should be practiced. Propagation: cuttings, lateral shoots after pruning; a good brancher when growing floating beneath the water surface.

D: 3, KH: 2-8, pH: 6.0-7.0, T: 24-28° C (75-82° F), AH: 2

Crassula helmsii (KIRK) COCKAYNE (1930)

Fam.: Crassulaceae Syn.: *Tillaea helmsii*

Distribution: Australia, New Zealand

Delicate group plant with modest demands but high light requirements. It has a thin main axis and opposite leaves that are somewhat fleshy, sessile, needle-shaped, up to 1 cm (1/3") long and 1 mm (1/32") thick. Persevering swamp plant with creeping stems. In the axils, up to 3 mm (1/8") in size, are single flowers with 4 roundish white petals. In nature, it is permanently submersed in sections, but also easily cultivated in the emerse form. It shows good adaptation to water values and temperature as an aquatic plant but degenerates under low light. Less recommendable for deep tanks. Through its numerous lateral shoots, it creates a dense structure and provides a favorable aesthetic effect in a group. Propagation: cuttings, good self-propagator.

D: 2, KH: 2-15, pH: 6.0-7.5, T: 18-25° C (64-77° F), AH: 1-2

Hydrotriche hottoniiflora ZUCCARINI (1832)

Fam.: Scrophulariaceae

Distribution: Madagascar

A demanding water plant with moderate adaptability to aquarium conditions. The green main axis is naked, 3 mm (1/8") thick, and has slightly swollen nodes. Leaves are opposite, up to 5 cm (2") in size, made of up to 10-16 projecting, blunt, needle-shaped, light green segments. Two sessile leaves that are forked to the base give the impression of whorls. Stem and leaves are brittle and sensitive to pressure, so insert the stem into the prepared hole with care when planting. A loose sand bottom and soft water is recommended to encourage development. There seems to be little advantage to adding carbon dioxide. Use caution with large, fast swimming, rough fishes. Propagation: cuttings, moderate side-shoots.

D: 4, KH: 2-8, pH: 6.0-7.0, T: 22-26° C (72-79° F), AH: 1-2

Cabomba caroliniana

Crassula helmsii

Cabomba pulcherrima

Hydrotriche hottoniiflora

Hygrophila balsamica (LINNAEUS fil.) RAFINESQUE (1838) Balsam Hygrophila

Fam.: Acanthaceae

Distribution: Sri Lanka, India
Imported for the first time in 1978. It is said to be poisonous in its emersed form, so do not place it in small tanks with sensitive fishes. According to experience, the aquatic form either releases toxins to a limited extent, or not at all. A few specimens can be kept without problems in aquaria with a volume above 150 liter (40 gal). Aerial leaves are opposite, lanceolate, 3 cm (1 ") long by 1 cm (1/3") wide and serrate. The plant has short hairs and is glandular and sticky. The leaf axils have 3-5 short-stalked flowers with a bi-labiate corolla. The submersed leaves are pinnate (like *H. difformis*), reaching 10 x 5 cm (4" x 2") in size, but the leaf segments are only 2 mm (1/16") wide. Growth is light dependent and requires at least 65 watts (florescent lamp)/100 l (26 gal). With insufficient illumination, the leaves remain small, less divided and form short tips. A decorative plant that should be planted alone and in the midground of the aquarium. When considering a group, include good spacing. Propagation: cuttings, side-shoots after pruning.

D: 3, **KH:** 2-12, **pH:** 6.5-7.2, **T:** 22-28° C (72-82° F), **AH:** 2-3

Hygrophila corymbosa type "gracilis" Syn.: *Nomaphila stricta*

Submersed leaves are lanceolate, 10-15 cm (4"-6") long, 3-6 cm (1 "-2 1/3") wide with variable coloration of dark brown to medium green. Aerial leaves are pilose, lanceolate, up to 3 cm (1 ") long, 1 cm (1/3") wide, similar, but clearly more graceful than the type species. Blooms are irregularly developed or incomplete. When kept singly in a free area, the plant will grow uncommonly full with 25 x 6 cm (9 3/4" x 2 1/3") leaves. Best to grow in aquaria with at least 50 cm (20") water depth and strong illumination. It is typical for this variant that newly planted aerial shoots will initially grow brown-red leaves and then later green blades which can alternate with dark leaves. It is not clear what factors contribute to this phenomenon. Plants that are submerged for long periods will remain totally green. Propagation: cuttings, lateral shoots after pruning.

D: 1, **KH:** 2-15, **pH:** 6.0-7.5, **T:** 22-28° C (72-82° F), **AH:** 2-3

Hygrophila corymbosa type "crispa"

Aquatic leaves are narrowly lanceolate, 10-16 cm (4"-6 1/3") long, 1.0-1.5 cm (1/3"-2/3") wide, light green with both ends uniformly acute. Aerial leaves are pilose, lanceolate, up to 10 cm (4") long, 2 cm (3/4") wide with undulate to curled edges. Stamens are fertile. Full-grown plants reach up to 30 cm (12") in diameter. In smaller aquaria, only single specimens should be kept. It becomes a beautiful eye catcher when out in the open. In roomy aquaria, give individual plants in a group enough lateral space and unobstructed light. Propagation: cuttings from side-shoots.

D: 3, **KH:** 2-12, **pH:** 6.0-7.5, **T:** 22-28° C (72-82° F), **AH:** 2-3

Hygrophila balsamica

Hygrophila corymbosa type "crispa"

Hygrophila corymbosa type "gracilis"

Hygrophila corymbosa type "glabra"

Aquatic leaves are linear-lanceolate, 10-17 cm (4"-6¾") long, 2-4 cm (¾"-1⅔") wide, green and, under strong illumination, have a pink to brownish apex. Aerial leaves are nonpilose, broadly lanceolate, up to 10 x 5 cm (4" x 2") and dark green. It is almost like the type species but without hairs and similar to *H. stricta* (Vol. 1, page 98). The blooms have 4-6 stamens that are sterile. The best aquarium plant of all varieties of the species; barely shows acclimation problems, adapts well to different environmental conditions and is a positive part of the overall decoration. Shoots are relatively fast growing, making smaller tanks less suitable. A decorative group plant suitable for terracing in large aquaria. General light requirement is in the moderate range, but they are more reddish under strong illumination. Older leaves turn green. Propagation: cuttings, lateral shoots after pruning; a self-propagator in tall tanks.

D: 1, KH: 2-15, pH: 6.0-7.5, T: 22-28° C (72-82° F), AH: 2-3

Hygrophila corymbosa type "strigosa"

Aquatic leaves are linear-lanceolate, rather sword-like, bent, 20-27 cm (8" x 10⅔") long, 1.0-1.7 cm (⅓"-⅝") wide, light green with brownish cross-veins. The main axis of the terrestrial form has stiff, protruding setae. Aerial leaves are slender, up to 7 cm (2¾") long, 1.5 cm (⅔") wide and pilose. Flowers form in the leaf axils. The opposite axil usually has a leaf shoot. The robust plant reaches almost 50 cm (20") in diameter with its large leaves. Best to plant it alone in a tall aquarium where there is enough room to expand. Pay attention to the higher light requirement; with insufficient intensity or duration of illumination, the lower leaves drop off. Such plants become stunted and never reach their full size. The general requirements are within the conditions reigning in the aquarium. Group planting is possible, but it generally leads to fast upward growth which has to be pruned often and replanted. Propagation: cuttings, side-shoots after pruning.

D: 2, KH: 2-12, pH: 6.0-7.5, T: 22-28° C (72-82° F), AH: 3

Hygrophila difformis (LINNAEUS fil.) BLUME (1826) Indian Hygrophila
var. *folius variegatus Hortorum*

Fam.: Acanthaceae

Distribution: Southeast Asia
Submersed leaves are arranged similar to the green leaved nominate form (Aquarium Atlas Vol. 1, page 96). However, segments have a whitish or yellow middle stripe. Aerial leaves are 5 x 3 cm (2" x 1 "), undivided, incised, and also have a network of yellow veins. Discovered in 1975 in an Asian import. It is unclear if we are dealing with a mutation or if the coloration is viral in origin. Markedly high light requirement (100 watts/100 l); therefore, it is rarely cultivated in an aquarium. The leaves can turn totally green in the aquarium also. It is favorable to use GroLux or type 77 L-Flora lamps. As a rule, new striped leaves will grow from the base of a green plant. This is contingent on a well-rooted plant which can grow freely. Propagation: cuttings, lateral shoots after pruning (green), lateral growth from the stem base.

D: 4, KH: 2-10, pH: 6.0-7.2, T: 24-28° C (75-82° F), AH: 1-2

Hygrophila corymbosa type "glabra"

Hygrophila corymbosa type "strigosa"

Hygrophila difformis "white-green"

Hygrophila guianensis NEES ex BENTHAM (1845) Guiana Hygrophila

Fam.: Acanthaceae

Distribution: Northern South America

Difficult to acclimate to the aquarium and does not always grow satisfactorily in submersed culture. Aquatic leaves are 5-10 cm (2" x 4") long, 1.0-1.5 cm (1/3" x 2/3") wide with both ends acute and a round, green main axis. Aerial leaves are broadly lanceolate, 10-18 cm (4" x 7") long, 1-3 cm (1/3"-1 ") wide with a truncated tip. The upperside of the leaf is intense green with dark green veins. In the leaf axils are clusters of 3-7 blooms; corolla white, up to 1 cm (1/3") long, bi-labiate, five-lobed, slightly clefted laterally. In comparison to the emerse form, the water plant is degenerative and small-leaved. Aerial shoots tend to grow better in an aquarium than the specimens found in stores because they have usually been there for a while. Place in an open area in the aquarium, provide good lighting and give the group sufficient lateral space. Adapted shoots should not be unnecessarily transplanted and especially not soon after adaptation. Stunted forms will result which rarely produce normal growing plants later. Best kept in soft water. The general intense light requirement is 75 watts of florescent lighting for each 100 liters of tank volume. Propagation: cuttings, lateral shoots after pruning, let the sprout grow at least 15 cm (6"). The terrestrial form placed in a window sill will flower and seed well; therefore, seedling cultivation is possible.

D: 3, **KH**: 2-10, **pH**: 6.0-7.2, **T**: 22-28° C (72-82° F), **AH**: 1-2

Hygrophila lacustris (SCHLECHTENDAHL) NEES (1845) Lake Hygrophila

Fam.: Acanthaceae

Distribution: Tropical America

The acclimation of the emerse to the submerse form can be tricky. Once achieved, the plant presents no special problems and adapts well. The aquatic leaves are green, almost linear, short-stalked, 10-20 cm (4"-8") long and 0.5-1.0 cm ("-1/3") wide (about 20 times longer than wide). Aerial leaves are lanceolate, up to 8 cm (3") long and 1 cm (1/3") wide with clusters of 5-11 blooms in the axils; corolla white, up to 1.8 cm (3/4") long, bi-labiate, five-lobed, slightly clefted laterally. Grows leafy and compact due to the small internodal distances. Obtaining this dense growth requires good illumination; therefore, keep floating plants away from the area. A full, solitary plant results from the long leaves which is best placed in a free frontal area of the aquarium. The formation of a group is reserved for larger tanks; give the individual plants at least 15 cm (6") free space so that they do not push each other higher. Remove tips and replant before they reach the water surface and shed their aquatic leaves. Propagation: cuttings, side-shoots after pruning; pay attention to short lateral shoots in the leaf axils and cut the apex a few nodes above that point. Older plants grow robust lateral shoots close to the bottom that quickly grow into usable cuttings.

D: 2, **KH**: 2-12, **pH**: 6.0-7.2, **T**: 24-26° C (75-79° F), **AH**: 1-3

Hygrophila guianensis

Hygrophila lacustris

Hygrophila salicifolia (VAHL) NEES (1832)

Fam.: Acanthaceae Syn.: *Hygrophila angustifolia*

Distribution: South China, south India, Malaysia, Australia, Sri Lanka
Cuttings of the emersed plants, such as those offered through the trade, adapt without problems to aquatic life. Aquatic leaves are slender, lanceolate, almost sessile, 8-12 cm long (3"-4 3/4"), 0.7-1.0 cm ("-1/3") wide (about 12 times longer than wide), dark green and reddish at the tip of the main axis. Emersed leaves are lanceolate, up to 20 cm (8") long, 2 cm (3/4") wide with clusters of 7 blooms in the leaf axils. The corolla is up to 1.7 cm (3/4") long, whitish with light purple veins in the lower labia. Also called *H. angustifolia*, it was originally described as *Ruellia salicifolia*. In water, the aerial leaves remain alive for a long period, and if left undisturbed, soon grow a sufficiently long aquatic shoot. When planting the stems, which are often elongated, at least one leaf node should be buried. Stronger roots will develop from the node than from the internode of the axis. Maximum leaf length seems to be attained in soft water. At higher carbonate hardness the addition of CO_2 is recommended. Propagation: lateral shoots which develop after pruning, side-shoots from the main axis of older plants.

D: 1, KH: 2-15, pH: 6.0-7.2, T: 22-28° C (72-82° F), AH: 2-3

Lindernia parviflora

Fam.: Scrophulariaceae

Syn.: *ILysanthes parvifflora, Lindernia microcalyx* (incorrectly identified)

Distribution: Southeast Asia, Africa
Graceful stemmed plant suitable for small groups. Its thin stem has opposing, roundish leaves up to 7 mm (") in diameter. From the base of the leaf, which almost clasps the stem, 5 thin, longitudinal veins radiate. Edges of the leaf are slightly sinuate or serrate. There are single, axillary blooms, up to 7 mm (") long with white petals that are light violet on the bottom, bi-labiate in the front and five lobed. The 2 fertile stamens are on short filaments while the 2 sterile stamens are on longer filaments with blue tips. They are transformed into staminodes. Side-shoots create a dense stand, and the upward growing tips are regularly pruned. These can be used as new cuttings. In general, the plants place limited demands on substrate and water; however, it has a high light requirement of 60 watts/100 l. Under low illumination, the shoots easily turn spindly and will continuously grow smaller leaves. It is better suited for the shallow tank where the light requirement can be easier met. Propagation: cuttings, side-shoots from self-branching.

D: 3, KH: 2-15, pH: 6.0-7.5, T: 20-26° C (68-79° F), AH: 1-2

Ludwigia brevipes (LONG) EAMES (1933)

Fam.: Onagraceae

Distribution: Southeast coast of North America
This species is comparatively less adapted to being submersed than are others of the genus. Aquatic leaves are green to slightly reddish on both sides, up to 3 cm (1 ") long, 4 mm (3/16") wide, tip acute, base slender and stem-like. Aerial leaves grow up to 2.5 cm (1") long and 8 mm (5/16") wide. The blooms consists of four yellow petals (shorter than the sepals) borne singly on very short peduncles in the leaf axils. With high water temperatures, the shoots turn spindly and grow progressively smaller leaves; sufficiently bright illumination can partially compensate. Better suited for the aquarium that is cool or slightly heated and of moderate height. Good optical effect is achieved by planting in groups and pruning and replanting the high growing shoots regularly. The land form with its creeping runners is a good ground cover which spreads quickly in the bog aquarium. During the summer it can also be kept in the swamp part of a garden pond where it will flower decoratively. Propagation: cuttings, side-shoots after pruning, also obtained from self-branching.

D: 3, KH: 2-10, pH: 6.0-7.0, T: 18-22° C (64-72° F), AH: 1-2

Hygrophila salicifolia

Lindernia parviflora

Ludwigia brevipes

Ludwigia glandulosa WALTER (1788) — Glandular Ludwigia

Fam.: Onagraceae

Distribution: Southern USA
An attractive plant when planted as groups in the central area of the decoration. Aquatic leaves are lanceolate, short-stalked, up to 4.5 cm ($1^{3}/_{4}$") long and 1.3 cm (") wide, widest above the midpoint, more slender towards the base with a short tip that is acute or obtuse, olive-green, brownish and sometimes also reddish. Aerial leaves grow up to 2 cm ($^{3}/_{4}$") long, 5 mm ($^{3}/_{16}$") wide and can have single, stalked, axillary blooms. The flower has 4 bright yellow, slender, oval petals and longer sepals. The submersed plant is similar to *L. repens*, whose widest part of the leaf is about central. *L. glandulosa* is often sold but is usually unrecognized. Places higher than average demands on the living conditions in an aquarium, principally in regard to illumination. Provide an unobstructed location and keep floating plants away. Under favorable conditions, the plant is fast growing, forms a voluminous stand with its side-shoots and can also grow natant. The prostrate, terrestrial form grows well in the bog aquarium and can be kept in a pond during the summer. Propagation: cuttings, side-shoots after trimming, and numerous self-branchings on floating stems.

D: 2, **KH**: 2-12, **pH**: 6.0-7.2, **T**: 22-28° C (72-82° F), **AH**: 1-3

Micranthemum umbrosum (WALTER) BLAKE (1915)

Fam.: Scrophulariaceae — Syn.: *Micranthemum orbiculatum*

Distribution: Central America, southern USA
This plant can be used in the bog aquarium as a recumbent plant to form a bushy patch or as a foreground or free-floating plant in the aquarium. The main axis is thin with leaves that are thin, opposite, short-stalked, almost sessile, roundish, up to 5 mm ($^{3}/_{16}$") in size, entire and have up to 5 weak veins extending from the base. In the axils are whitish inconspicuous blooms. Under floating cultivation of the plant, dense clusters are formed from intense branching. Suitable for certain fish species as excellent spawning sites. Shoots planted in the substrate have a high light requirement but will create extensive mats in the foreground that can be kept low by regular pruning. The light green plant with its roundish leaves offers a good contrast in front of large-leaved vegetation. Cultivation as a whole is not difficult; however, exercise caution with snails and compounds containing acroflavin. Propagation: cuttings, good self-propagator, dividing the clusters.

D: 2, **KH**: 2-12, **pH**: 5.5-7.2, **T**: 24-30° C (75-86° F), **AH**: 1-3

Najas guadelupensis (SPRENGEL) MAGNUS (1870)

Fam.: Najadaceae — Syn.: *Najas microdon*

Distribution: Southern USA, Central America, South America
Floats close beneath the water surface or will root in the substrate. The main axis is thin, green and very brittle. The leaves are opposite with the third leaf higher than the others though they often appear to be in whorls. Blade is linear, up to 2 cm ($^{3}/_{4}$") long, 2 mm ($^{1}/_{16}$") wide, usually arched. Three brownish veins emerge from the base and one extends to the tip. Edges are sparsely serrulate; the half round base has 5-10 darker teeth. Rooted specimens form dense bunches with their numerous side-shoots. Planting is a problem, and stems planted with all care will often loosen and float to the top. *Najas* actually grow best natant where it branches heavily, forming an extensive mat with time. A beautiful loose decoration for the upper tank areas. It is not recommended to place these brittle plants in an aquarium with rough, fast swimming fishes. Propagation: cuttings, side-shoots, shoot segments, dividing of the mat.

D: 2, **KH**: 2-12, **pH**: 6.0-7.5, **T**: 22-28° C (72-82° F), **AH**: 1-3

Ludwigia glandulosa

Micranthemum umbrosum

Najas guadelupensis

Najas indica (WILLDENOW) CHAMISSO (1829)

Fam.: Najadaceae Syn.: *Najas kingii*

Distribution: Tropical Asia
Imported for the first time in 1952 as *N. kingii*, a synonym for *N. indica*; first described in 1801 as *Caulinia indica* by WILLDENOW. Leaves opposite or as three-part pseudowhorls, sessile, small, lanceolate, 2.0-3.5 cm (3/4"-1 1/3") long and up to 1 mm (1/32") wide. The leaf has a row of typically larger cells running along the central vein and 10-20 relatively coarse teeth at the edge. The wider base has a slight rectangular shape, no distinct edge towards the top and 7-10 fine teeth on the upper edge. Shoots are slightly brittle, making planting into the substrate somewhat difficult. Short shoots of about 10 cm (4") length planted individually with spacing are easier to anchor in the substrate. In a free location, the branched specimens grow with pleasing visual result. Robust fishes will break the shoots easily; handling in the aquarium must be done with care. *Najas* are, therefore, kept free-floating and form extensive but loose mats beneath the water surface. Propagation: cuttings, side-shoots, parts of shoots.

D: 2, KH: 2-15, pH: 6.0-7.5, T: 24-28° C (75-82° F), AH: 1-3

Nesaea pedicellata HIERN (1871)

Fam.: Lythraceae Syn.: *N. crassicaulis* (incorrect post identification)

Distribution: East Africa
An extremely difficult plant; when submersed, it grows well only under optimal conditions. Stems and leaves are deep red, lamina lanceolate, up to 5 cm (2") long, 5 mm (3/16") wide, with a cuspidate tip and slightly undulate edge. The broadest point of the leaf is in the upper half; from there the leaf uniformly narrows to terminate in a short stalk. The bog plant will produce a short-stalked false cyme that bears small blossoms with 4 tiny, pink petals (which quickly fall off, or occasionally do not develop) in the axils of the aerial leaves. Under bright light the leaves are deep red; in dim light they are olive-green. This conspicuous plant is best planted as a loose group open in the foreground. Continued growth is normally slow and dependent on light and soft water. You can often see that the shoots grow well in the beginning but then slack off and die. This is related to the moderate formation of roots. The situation improves with the addition of peat into the substrate. Propagation: cuttings, side-shoots through self-branchings.

D: 4, KH: 2-5, pH: 5.5-6.5, T: 22-27° C (72-81° F), AH: 1-2

Shinnersia rivularis (A. GRAY) R.M. KING et ROBINSON (1970)

Fam.: Asteraceae Syn.: *Trichocoronis rivularis*

Distribution: North Mexico
One of the newer aquarium plants which became known in Germany in 1981. Original description as *Trichocoronis rivularis* is by GRAY 1849; separated from *Trichocoronis* by the two British botanists KING and ROBINSON and placed in the new genus *Shinnersia*. Leaves are opposite, sessile with pinnate venation, up to 5 cm (2") long and 3 cm (1 ") wide, edge several times sinuate, tip rounded, obtuse, becoming more slender as it proceeds to the base and clasps the stem. The land plant has several flowers at the apex and on each recepticle up to 100 small, simple florets. The uncommonly rapid growing aquatic form first grows long internodes and later, close to the water surface, compact shoots with larger leaves. It will continue to grow floating, without breaking the water surface. Remove the strong tips and use them to form new loose groups. Sufficient light (75 watts/100 l/26 gal) and moderate high water temperatures are conditions for compact growth. Due to rapid growth and constant trimming, it is laborious to maintain. Propagation: cuttings, side-shoots after trimming, self-branchings.

D: 2, KH: 2-15, pH: 5.5-7.5, T: 20-25° C (68-77° F), AH: 2-3

Najas indica

Nesaea pedicellata

Shinnersie rivularis

The common characteristic of these 22 species of 14 genera is the upright stem with a single leaf at each node. Leaf shape is predominantly slender and rarely roundish. In their natural habitat, *Fontinalis, Heteranthera, Lagarosiphon, Potamogeton* and *Zosterella* are disseminated as aquatic plants. The narrow-leaved *Zosterella dubia*, also known by the synonym *Heteranthera graminea*, opens its six-petaled, yellow flowers close above the water surface. The plant has not been cultivated in an aquarium for a long time. The head of *Potamogeton crispus* is composed of conspicuous flowers. Over the summer, they grow in the garden pond. The sky blue water hyacinth, *Eichhornia azurea*, develops its decorative frayed-fringed blooms in the uncovered aquarium after growing large aerial leaves. A fast grower for the bog aquarium is the land form of *Hydrocotyle leucocephala* with its creeping runners and small umbels on long stalks. *Lobelia cardinalis* can grow out the top of a shallow aquarium, on a window sill or in the yard and develop large, deep red flowers. The related genera *Saururus cernuus* and *Houttuynia cordata* are winter hardy and, as a rule, only flower in an open pond, showing an upright or drooping spike.

Zosterella dubia

Eichhornia azurea

Hydrocotyle leucocephala

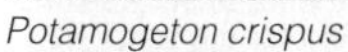
Potamogeton crispus

Saururus cernuus

Lobelia cardinalis

Houttuynia cordata

Eichhornia diversifolia (VAHL) URBAN (1832)

Fam.: Pontederiaceae

Distribution: Tropical South America
Decorative group plant with moderate adaptability. Main axis is upright and will later float beneath the water surface. Submersed leaves are alternate, in 2 rows, linear, sessile, up to 6 cm ($2^{1}/_{3}$") long, 6 mm (") wide, acute tipped and clasp the stem. Five fine, longitudinal veins originate from the base. Natant shoots have elliptical, stalked, floating leaves with 2 small, blue flowers in each axil. Demands intense illumination; therefore, cultivate in moderate water depth. Its relatively compact growth is achieved by planting in a loose group. When suitable conditions are provided, it is quite fast growing. The shoots can develop floating leaves, allowing it to grow natant when it reaches the surface. Propagation: cuttings from side-shoots, good self-propagator. Note: *E. natans* (BEAUVIS) SOLMS-LAUBACH, 1882 (Africa) is very similar. Aquatic leaves are wider; floating leaves larger and flowers occur singly. Requirements and uses are quite similar.

D: 3, **KH:** 2-10, **pH:** 5.5-7.5, **T:** 20-28° C (68-82° F), **AH:** 1-2

Houttuynia cordata THUNBERG (1874)

Fam.: Saururaceae

Distribution: East India, China, Korea, Japan
Demanding plant for intensely lit aquaria. Aquatic leaves are alternate, heart-shaped, pointed, 2-3 cm ($^{3}/4$"-1 ") in size with 5 longitudinal veins. The petiole has a sheath that has an extended tip (missing in the similar *Saururus cernuus*). Aerial leaves up to 10 cm (4") in size, sparsely pilose, often reddish; terminal spike, up to 3 cm (1 ") long with four white bracts. Requires at least 65 watts/100 l/26 gal of water. Allow enough space when planting cuttings and bury at least one node. Let the shoots grow to the water surface and then trim. Do not choose tips that are too short. Robust swamp plant for the bright bog aquarium. Grows in the garden pond and is winter hardy.

D: 4, **KH:** 2-10, **pH:** 6.0-7.2, **T:** 22-24° C (72-75° F), **AH:** 2

Lagarosiphon madagascariensis CASPARY (1881)

Fam.: Hydrocharitaceae

Distribution: Madagascar
Graceful group plant for middle areas in flat to moderately deep aquaria. Thin main axis, leaves alternate, sessile, dark green, up to 1.5 cm ($^{2}/_{3}$") long and 1 mm ($^{1}/_{32}$") wide, sticking straight out or occasionally slightly bent. Under intense illumination, the leaves form tight spirals, easily creating the appearance of whorls. In the axils are stalked single-sex flowers. They grow to 3 mm ($^{1}/_{8}$") in size, have 3 colorless petals and drift on the water surface. Male flowers have bushy stamens while female flowers have 6 fimbriate, white stigmas. Shoots branch on their own, and in time, form dense bushes. Thin the group occasionally and replace with fresh cuttings as needed. Good adaptation to water values but quite light demanding. It forms dense bunches when left free floating on the water surface. Propagation: cuttings from side-shoots, good self-propagator.

D: 2, **KH:** 2-10, **pH:** 6.0-7.2, **T:** 20-26° C (68-79° F), **AH:** 1-2

Eichhornia diversifolia

Lagarosiphon madagascariensis

Houttuynïa cordata

Potamogeton crispus LINNAEUS (1753)

Fam.: Potamogetonaceae

Distribution: Temperate cosmopolitan
Generally for an open pond or brightly lit coldwater aquaria; it will grow for a limited time in a moderately warm aquarium. It has an elongated, four-edged main axis. Leaves are alternate, sessile, up to 10 cm (4") long and 1.5 cm (2/3") wide, reddish or green. The edge is undulate to curly and serrulate. Stalked heads form above the water with 5-10 bisexual flowers. In higher water temperatures, the shoots become progressively thinner and die. If long cuttings found floating beneath the water surface are used, the period of growth will be longer. Clay is a better substrate than coarse sand. The medium-hard water should have circulation and regular exchanges. A recommendable submersed plant for the open water garden which can multiply extensively. Propagation: cuttings, removal of side-shoots.

D: 3, KH: 5-12, pH: 6.0-7.5, T: 12-20° C (54-82° F), AH: 1-2

Potamogeton gayi A. BENNET (1892)

Fam.: Potamogetonaceae

Distribution: South America
Rapid growing group plant for the background of tall aquaria. The main axis is thin, light green and elongated. Leaves are alternate, sessile, linear, up to 10 cm (4") long and 4 mm (3/16") wide with a needle-like tip. A prominent central vein emerges from the base with fine, often vague, veins on each side. Coloration is brownish or reddish under strong lighting, principally at the apex. Peduncle up to 6 cm (2 1/3") long and slightly thicker towards the top. The head is 1.5 cm (2/3") in size and bears a few tiny bisexual flowers without petals. Freshly planted cuttings require some time to take root and adapt, but they grow rapidly afterwards. Undemanding plant, well suited for the tropical aquarium. Runner-like shoots on the substrate transverse large areas of the aquarium and form upright stems at intervals. Propagation: cuttings, self-propagator, runners.

D: 1, KH: 2-12, pH: 6.0-7.5, T: 20-30° C (68-86° F), AH: 2-3

Potamogeton mascarensis CHAMISSO et SCHLECHTENDAHL (1827)

Fam.: Potamogetonaceae

Distribution: Macarene Islands, Madagascar
Known in the aquarium trade since 1977; the species name has not been confirmed with blooming cultured plants. Main axis is thin and slightly elongated. Leaves are alternate, linear, sessile, up to 10 cm (4") long and 3 mm (1/8") wide, tip cuspidate and, depending on the light, green to reddish. From the base, the central vein and two very fine side veins emerge. Similar to *P. gayi*, but it normally has five veins. Suitable species for the tropical tank; tolerates higher temperatures well, but it needs time to acclimate. Under bright illumination, the leaves are located in two uniform rows on the shoot. Because of the less rapid growth rate and the somewhat short leaf distances, the plant remains relatively compact. Plant cuttings singly and with lateral room. When sufficient free space is provided, a voluminous plant results because of the numerous side-shoots. Propagation: cuttings, side-shoots from self-branchings.

D: 2, KH: 2-15, pH: 6.0-7.5, T: 20-28° C (68-82° F), AH: 1-3

Potamogeton crispus

Potamogeton gayi

Potamogeton mascarensis

There are presently 31 species and 7 sub-species of 9 genera known. The common characteristic is a short, slender rhizome (or bulb) with narrow, elongated, sessile leaves. In their natural habitat, different environments are occupied. As true aquatic plants, *Blyxa* flower from a submersed shoot, opening their stalked bisexual flowers in the air. The closely related *Vallisneria* is dioeceous. The long-stalked, plain female blooms float on the water surface and are fertilized by numerous floating pollen sacs. These pollen sacs are formed on the short-stalked male inflorescence at the base of the male plant and float to the surface when ripe. *Crinum purpurascens*, a swamp plant in the wild, can, when half submersed in an aquarium, still develop large flowers on a long peduncle. *Isoetes setacea* does not flower, but produces spores on the wide leaf base from which new plants develop. The flowers of *Eleocharis minima* are similar to meadow grasses and develop outside the water. The various arrowheads form water or swamp forms. Among them, *Sagittaria lancifolia* will still flower in 30 cm (11$^{3}/_{4}$") water depth. Specialties for the garden pond flora include cultivated forms of *Sagittaria sagittifolia* that have large, full blooms.

Blyxa novoguineensis

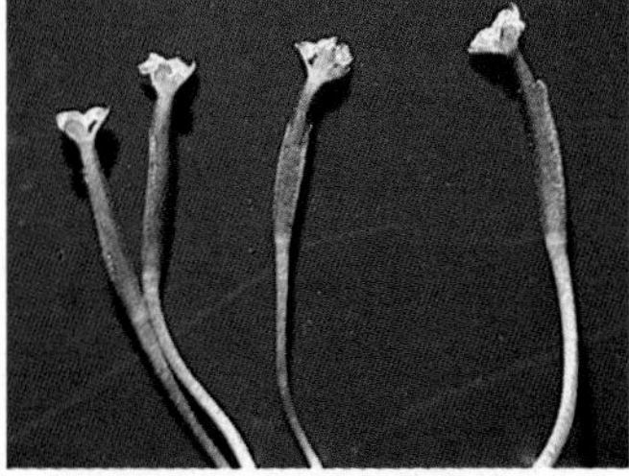

Vallisneria americana var. *biwanensis* ♀

Crinum purpurascens

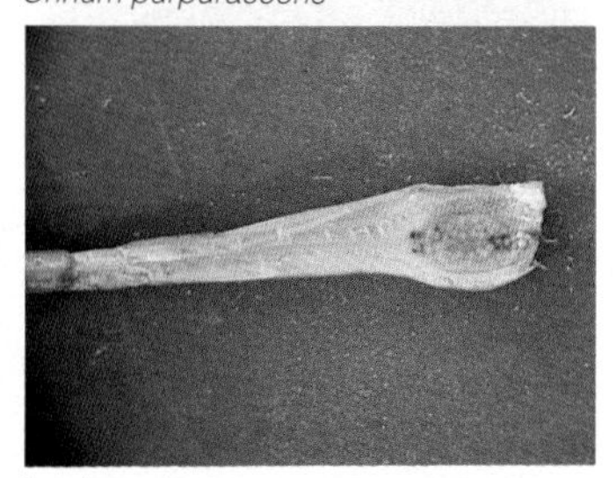

Isoetes setacea

Vallisneria americana var. *americana* ♂

Sagittaria lancifolia

Eleocharis minima

Sagittaria sagittifolia

Blyxa aubertii L. C. RICHARD (1814)

Fam.: Hydrocharitaceae

Distribution: Southeast Asia, India, Madagascar
A solitary plant for the middle areas of the aquarium that grows up to 40 cm (16") tall. Leaves are basal, linear, 20-40 (60) cm (8"-16"; 24") long, 0.5-1.5 cm (3/16"-2/3") wide, often reddish or olive-green. The lower third of the leaf has three distinct edges, becoming uniformly more slender towards the top and finishing in a hair-thin tip. Besides the dark midvein, there are several longitudinal side veins, 2 thereof being more pronounced. Flowers are long-stalked with 2 whitish-green tiny petals, 3 white stamens up to 1 cm (1/3") long and a short pistil with a small, three-rifted stigma. The fruit grows up to 2 cm (3/4") long underwater and is wrapped in a transparent sheath. Seeds have 8 rows of creases. The similar *B. echinosperma* has a different shaped seed. In general, this plant is moderately adaptable and is suitable for soft to medium-hard water. Higher carbonate hardness (up to 15° KH) is possible with the addition of CO_2. Use loose coarse sand as the substrate. Propagation: separate side-shoot at the rhizome with about 6 leaves. Fruits easily after self-pollination, but seedling cultivation is lengthy and not easy.

D: 3, **KH:** 2-10, **pH:** 5.5-7.2, **T:** 22-28° C (72-82° F), **AH:** 2-3

Blyxa echinosperma (CLARKE) HOOKER fil. (1888)

Fam.: Hydrocharitaceae

Distribution: India, Indonesia
A decorative solitary plant that, given time, will grow into a bushy specimen by producing several side-shoots. Leaves are basal, 30-60 cm (11 3/4"-24") long, 0.5-1.5 cm (3/16"-2/3") wide, usually entirely green, seldom olive-green or reddish. The leaf is occasionally slightly twisted and less angular and more half-rounded in the lower third with the tip terminating in a small slender point. Besides the darker central vein there are several lateral parallel veins with short cross-veins in between. The flower and fruit is similar to *B. aubertii* with the seeds notably thorned and having a 5 mm (3/16") long thorn-shaped projection at both ends. Can adapt to conditions in an aquarium relatively well, but grows better in water that is less hard. The aquarium form is usually weaker than the wild plants and reaches about 40 cm (16") height. Place in a free zone with undisturbed light access and use moderately coarse substrate. Normally somewhat sensitive when transplanting with less vigorous growth for a long time afterwards. Propagation: separate side-shoots at the rhizome, often seeds though self-pollination, seedling cultivation is difficult.

D: 3, **KH:** 2-10, **pH:** 5.5-7.2, **T:** 22-28° C (72-82° F), **AH:** 2-3

Blyxa japonica ASCHERSON et GÜRKE (1889)

Fam.: Hydrocharitaceae

Distribution: Bengal, Korea, Japan, Indonesia
This species is actually erroneously classified in this sub-group since it is a stemmed plant. The upright stem in nature reaches 50 cm (20") in height; however, in the aquarium it always remains extremely short with dense leaf spirals giving the impression of a rhizome plant. The leaves are arranged alternately and grow to be 3-5 cm (1 "-2") long and 3 mm (1/8") wide. Stalked bisexual flowers with white slender petals and ragged edges are found in the axils. The similar *B. novoguineensis* (Vol. 1, page 102) has longer leaves and stems as well as single-sexed flowers. Best cultivated in the foreground of a flat tank with very intense illumination. The plant is extremely difficult to grow and is rarely kept over longer periods of time in an aquarium. According to experience, culture is only possible in very soft water. In hard water with higher carbonate hardness, the plant routinely dies within a short time period. Robust specimens or fresh imports will develop blooms, but their short stalks will only reach the water surface of flat tanks. Propagation: separate side-shoots.

D: 4, **KH:** 1-3, **pH:** 5.5-6.5, **T:** 22-26° C (72-79° F), **AH:** 1

Blyxa aubertii

Blyxa echinosperma

Blyxa japonica

Crinum natans BAKER (1898)

Fam.: Amaryllidaceae

Distribution: Africa, various regions

A voluminous plant which can only be well kept in large and roomy tanks. The bulb grows up to 8 cm (3") in size and has a neck up to 15 cm (6") long and 3-5 cm (1 "-2") wide. Shortly above the bulb the leaves arch and form an extensive solitary plant. The flower is an umbel produced on a 80 cm (31") long peduncle with 3-5 fragrant flowers. The corolla has 6 small, white petals with stamens rising far above them. Rarely flowers in an aquarium. Its pattern of wide growth makes the plant difficult to integrate into the decoration. Generally, it is moderately adaptable, and fertile substrate and strong lighting are recommended. Shorter leaves and poor growth normally result in hard water. Medications or algicides containing acriflavin as the active ingredient are not tolerated. Propagation: daughter bulbs are seldom formed, separate when ready. Note: the species changes markedly and produces the following narrow-leaved variant. It, however, is not yet designated a variety.

D: 3, **KH:** 2-10, **pH:** 6.0-7.0, **T:** 25-30° C (77-86° F), **AH:** 3

Crinum natans BAKER (1898) (narrow-leaved type)

Fam.: Amaryllidaceae

Distribution: Camaroon

In nature this plant is permanently submerged; first specimens were found in 1974 in Camaroon in the Menge River and brought to Europe. The plant forms a tuber with a bulb-like projection instead of a bulb. Leaves are dark green, 50-100 cm (20"-39") long and about 3 mm (1/8") wide with a long, slender, pointed tip. To the side of the wide midrib run slim, extremely curly strips of the laminae. An excellent aquarium plant with good adaptation to various conditions. Medium bright light of 50 watt/100 liters seems more favorable than intense illumination. A large plant is created with long leaves whose blades are natant but don't break the surface. This can be quite decorative in a flat aquarium. Propagation: daughter shoots with about 6 leaves carefully separated from the rhizome.

D: 2, **KH:** 2-12, **pH:** 5.5-7.2, **T:** 24-28° C (75-82° F), **AH:** 2-3

Crinum purpurascens HERBERT (1837)

Fam.: Amaryllidaceae

Distribution: Brazil, western India

A rare aquarium plant that in nature normally grows as a robust swamp plant reaching almost 1 m (39") in height. The bulb grows up to 4 cm (1 2/3") thick with a neck of about 15 cm (6") long. Leaves are straight, firm and stiff, obtaining 30-60 cm (11 3/4"-24") length in the aquarium, up to 3 cm (1 ") wide with the lower leaf grooved, edge undulate and slowly narrowing towards the blunt tip. The leaf has up to 22 thin longitudinal veins, some of which extend to the tip. The midrib protrudes from the base. Flower formation can occur with submersed cultivation. On the robust stem above the water, 5-9 large, white flowers with purple-red stamens form. Shallow water is advantageous as long as higher hanging illumination (HQI lamps) provide enough free space for the development of the flowers. Cultivation is not particularly difficult, but growth in soft water is significantly better. Well-rooted specimens make several daughter bulbs, creating a dense bush. A full swamp plant for the bog aquarium or one suitable for 30 cm (11 3/4") of water depth. Propagation: separate daughter bulbs with 4-5 leaves.

D: 2, **KH:** 2-10, **pH:** 5.8-7.0, **T:** 22-28° C (72-82° F), **AH:** 2-3

Crinum natans (broad-leaved)

Crinum natans (narrow-leaved)

Crinum purpurascens

Eleocharis acicularis (LINNAEUS) ROEMER et SCHULTES (1817)

Fam.: Cyperaceae

Distribution: World wide, except tropics
Small groups should be placed at intervals throughout the area to be covered; in time, dense turf is formed from numerous lateral runners. Leaves are thread-like, 10-25 cm (4"-9³/4") long, 0.5-1 mm (¹/64"-¹/32") thick, laterally compressed and somewhat angular. The tip is long and thin without an adventitious bud. Land forms are 5-8 cm (2"-3") tall and can be used in bright bog aquaria. Different heights are found depending on conditions, thereby providing a variety of uses. With bright illumination and cool water, the plants are low; however, since growth is usually taller it is used decoratively in the middle ground of the aquarium. Occasionally transfer part of the dense stand to stimulate growth. Propagation: runners with numerous adventitious buds.

D: 2, KH: 2-15, pH: 5.8-7.5, T: 20-28° C (68-82° F), AH: 1-3

Eleocharis minima KUNTH (1837)

Fam.: Cyperaceae

Distribution: South America, Central America, tropical Africa
A group plant that requires intense light and soft water. Similar to *E. vivipara*. Leaves are thread-like, 20-30 cm (8"-11³/4") long and 1 mm (¹/32") thick. An adventitious plant is produced on the tip whose base is rarely opened in an arch. Sometimes several generations are grown above each other. The land form is shorter and also has adventitious plants on its sterile stems. Although the species originates from warm areas, it is slightly sensitive to excessive warmth. Therefore, the plant is better suited for the cooler tank. This plant can also be used in shallower tanks as it barely reaches 30 cm (12") height. Seldom cultivated and not as well suited to the aquarium as *E. vivipara*. Propagation: adventitious plants.

D: 3, KH: 2-8, pH: 6.0-7.0, T: 18-22° C (64-72° F), AH: 1-3

Isoetes flaccida SCHUTTLEWORT ex A. BRAUN (1846)

Fam.: Isoetaceae

Distribution: Florida, Georgia
Free standing solitary plant for the deeper aquarium. Leaves are like quills, dark green, rising straight from the base, 30-50 cm (11³/4"- 20") long, up to 3 mm (¹/8") thick. Cross section of the leaf is rectangular and slightly tapered, without hook-like setae at the tip (compare *I. setacea*). Besides the central vein, there are 2 very weak longitudinal veins and moderate cross venation. The leaves are not as brittle as other species, so they do not break as easily. Not overly demanding and healthy development can also be expected in harder water. A neutral to slightly acid pH is important. Can be kept in warmer water and is easier to maintain than the similar *I. setacea*. Propagation: raising spores is rarely successful.

D: 2, KH: 2-12, pH: 5.5-7.0, T: 20-27° C (68-81° F), AH: 2-3

Isoetes malinverniana CESATI et DE NOTARIS (1858)

Fam.: Isoetaceae

Distribution: Upper Italy (probably introduced from Asia)
Almost extinct in its native habitat. Leaves are quill-like, medium green, somewhat translucent, 30-80 cm (11³/4"-31") long, up to 2 mm (¹/16") thick, roundish to half-round in cross section, not angular, with a long, pointed tip. External leaves are bent sideways, then rise in a faint spiral. Under moderate light the spirals are little pronounced. Bright as well as slightly shaded locations are suitable. Medium-hard water is endured to 15° KH when CO_2 is added. Not as sensitive to transplanting, and, as a whole, less difficult to keep than several other species of the genus. Propagation: in the broadened base of the leaves, male and female spores are formed separately. These are mixed and placed on wet peat. Acclimate seedlings slowly to deeper water.

D: 2, KH: 2-10, pH: 5.5-7.0, T: 22-28° C (72-82° F), AH: 2-3

Eleocharis acicularis

Isoetes flaccida

Eleocharis minima

Isoetes malinverniana

Isoetes setacea LAMARCK (1789)

Fam.: Isoetaceae

Distribution: Southern France, Portugal, Corsica, Sardinia, Capri, Florida
Use alone in an open place with undisrupted light penetration. Leaves are quill-like, bright green, rise straight up from the base, 30-40 cm (11¾"-16") long, 1.5 mm (1/16") thick, young leaves have a rectangular cross section, later cylindrical to half-round. There are 3 longitudinal veins with distinct cross-veins between. The 5 mm (3/16"), hook-shaped, thin seta normally found on the tip are usually absent on leaves grown in aquaria. Water depth needs to be sufficient to cover the leaves, or they dry from the tip down and die. A brittle plant, so handle with care. Continuous elevated temperatures of a tropical tank are detrimental. Propagation: similar to *I. malinverniana*.

D: 4, KH: 2-8, pH: 5.5-6.8, T: 20-24° C (68-75° F), AH: 2-3

Ranalisma humile (KUNTH) HUTCHINSON (1936)

Fam.: Alismataceae Syn.: *Echinodorus humile*

Distribution: West Africa
A small genus with 2 species of amphibious bog plants. *Ranalisma* was included for a while in *Echinodorus*, but later separated. *R. humile* was first imported in 1965 from the Belgian Congo but has remained rare. In nature, it generally grows in its narrow-leaved aquatic form in extensive populations. Aquatic leaves are 5-10 cm (2"-4") long, 5 mm (3/16") wide, uniformly narrowing from the upper third down, but without forming a distinct petiole; usually only the central vein develops. The leaves of the emerse plant are typically ovate and stalked. From the axils emerge bisexual single flowers with three pale blue petals. Occasionally laying down and branched or with adventitious plants. Cultivate under bright illumination with ample nutrients in soft water; overall, this plant has reduced adaptation capabilities. Leaves are brittle. Situate in the bright foreground, providing sufficient room for daughter plants. Never keep together with snails or cleaner fishes; the leaves are delicate and eaten with pleasure. Propagation: elongate runners with daughter plants form a 10 cm (4") tall, loose group under favorable conditions.

D: 4, KH: 2-5, pH: 6.0-7.0, T: 24-28° C (75-82° F), AH: 1-2

Sagittaria graminea (ENGELMANN) SMITH (1894)

Fam.: Alismataceae Syn.: *Sagittaria platyphylla*

Distribution: Southern USA, West Java, Indonesia
This plant does not have a uniform nomenclature. The original description was done by ENGELMANN in 1867 as *S. g.* var. *platyphylla*. Categorized by SMITH in 1894 as an independent species and named *S. platyphylla*. BOGIN (1955) and RATAJ (1972) have placed the species again under the status of variety. In its native habitat, it has stalked, lanceolate aerial leaves. In submersed form it has phyllodia which lack a lamina, but the broadened stalk exercised its function. The drooping styles of the female flowers are typical for this variety. Submersed leaves are 20-30 cm (8"- 11¾") long, up to 2.5 cm (1") wide, narrowing to 2 cm (¾") at the bottom, tip cuspidate and rounded. At the base are 7-9 equally pronounced longitudinal veins with the central vein ending at the tip. A somewhat cumbersome aquarium plant that is best grouped loosely. Grows satisfactorily in hard water, endures poor temperatures and flourishes in nutrient rich substrate. Large specimens grown in shallow water will readily produce aerial leaves, necessitating sufficient water depth. Propagation: moderate runners with daughter plants.

D: 1, KH: 2-15, pH: 6.0-7.5, T: 20-28° C (68-82° F), AH: 2-3

Isoetes setacea

Sagittaria graminea

Ranalisma humile

Sagittaria graminea var. *weatherbiana* (FERNALD) BOGIN (1955)

Fam.: Alismataceae Syn.: *Sagittaria weatherbiana*

Distribution: USA, Australia
First described by FERNALD as *S. weatherbiana* (1935), but BOGIN placed the species into the group of *S. graminea* in his revision (1955). Very similar to *S. g.* var. *platyphylla*. Phyllodia up to 20 cm (8") long and 1.5-2.5 cm (2/3"-1") wide, narrowing slightly towards the bottom, with a tip that ends in a point. 5-7 longitudinal veins extend from the base with a more pronounced central vein. Interior veins terminate in the tip, cross-veins more distinct. This aquarium plant is not sensitive and adapts well to various conditions. With bright light and open placement the plant is lower growing and can be used in the foreground. With moderate illumination and dense positioning, the plant becomes a decorative, taller plant for the central area. Adult plants can grow aerial leaves, which can be suppressed by correspondingly deep water. With less than 12 hours of daily illumination, stalked leaves are more frequently develop. Propagation: moderate runners with daughter plants.

D: 1, **KH:** 5-15, **pH:** 6.5-7.5, **T:** 20-30° C (68-86° F), **AH:** 2-3

Sagittaria lancifolia LINNAEUS (1759)

Fam.: Alismataceae

Distribution: Central America, northern South America
A rare species which has probably been cultivated in Germany only since 1975. It is usually erroneously identified as *S. platyphylla*, and it is difficult to differentiate it from other *Sagittaria*. Aquatic leaves are ribbon-like with obtuse tips, up to 20 cm (8") long, 1.0-1.5 cm (1/3"-2/3") wide, with 5-7 longitudinal veins emerging from the base and a somewhat thicker central vein. The lamina is dark green or, with bright sunlight, reddish-brown with a redder tip. The aquarium form is weaker with acute, medium green leaves and a dark green edge. Aerial leaves can appear in 30 cm (11 3/4") water depth and are long-stalked and lanceolate. With exposure to sun, submersed plants can also bloom, producing 2-3 whorls of female flowers; male blossoms usually do not develop (in cultivated plants). Adapts to general aquarium conditions quite well, but demands sufficient lighting (50 watts/100 l) and fertile substrate. When placed in the open and loosely planted, low growing plants (up to 15 cm; 6") result. In shallow water, adult plants with aerial leaves can be trimmed. Propagation: runners with daughter plants.

D: 2, **KH:** 2-15, **pH:** 6.0-7.5, **T:** 22-28° C (72-82° F), **AH:** 2-3

Sagittaria sagittifolia LINNAEUS (1753)

Fam.: Alismataceae

Distribution: Europe, Asia
Generally grows as a robust swamp plant with typical, very variable, sagittate leaves. An excellent winter hardy swamp bush for the garden pool. Several varieties have been bred, some with beautiful large, full flowers. 30-200 cm (11 3/4"-79"), ribbon-like leaves are formed in deep water. These plants were previously called *S. s.* var. *vallisneriifolia*. Occasionally one can find short-leaved specimens with walnut-size tubers in the trade. Aquatic leaves are bright green, 20-30 cm (8"-11 3/4") long, 2 cm (3/4") wide with pointed tips and 7 longitudinal veins radiating from the base. Of these 7, the central vein is clearly more pronounced. There are numerous cross-veins. The plant is very buoyant, and it is difficult to anchor it without a bulb. A plant clamp can be of service until rooted. This light requiring plant is sensitive to high water temperatures; therefore, it is best to keep it in a cooler tank. Only for limited use in a tropical tank. Often grows long-stalked aerial leaves which are not always prevented by deeper water. Propagation: occasional side-shoots.

D: 3, **KH:** 2-15, **pH:** 6.0-7.5, **T:** 15-22° C (59-72° F), **AH:** 3

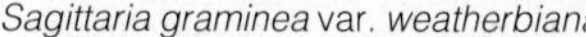

Sagittaria graminea var. *weatherbiana*

Sagittaria sagittifolia

Sagittaria lancifolia

Sagittaria subulata var. *gracillima* (WATSON) J.G. SMITH (1943)

Fam.: Alismataceae Syn.: *Sagittaria filiformis, S. lorata*

Distribution: North America, New Guinea
The species was described with several varieties, and differentiation is not always easy. Leaves of this variety are 30-60 cm (11 3/4"-24") long, 1-3 mm (1/32"-1/8") wide and normally have 3 visible veins and a tip elongated into a point. In an aquarium, it tends to produce small, white, natant single-sexed flowers. Often confused with *Vallisneria*, but it has serrulate edges while those of *Sagittaria* are entire. This upright group plant is useful for providing a lasting green for the sides or extensive areas of the background of tall aquaria. In shallow water, the leaves float decoratively beneath the water surface. Plant the initial specimens with lateral distance. After sufficient root growth, the acclimated specimens spread freely and grow numerous runners. These will also penetrate less lit sections and propagate there. Generally, not particularly demanding. Propagation: runners with chains of daughter plants.

D: 1, **KH:** 2-15, **pH:** 6.0-7.5, **T:** 22-28° C (72-82° F), **AH:** 3

Sagittaria subulata var. *kurziana* (GLÜCK) BOGIN (1955)

Fam.: Alismataceae Syn.: *Sagittaria kurziana*

Distribution: North America
Though this plant was once commonly found in aquaria, it is rarely cultivated today. Initially described as *S. kurziana* by GLÜCK, it can sometimes be found in the literature as *S. subulata* var. *natans*. Aquatic leaves are 30-50 cm (11 3/4"-20") long and 0.7-1.4 cm ("-2/3") wide. There are 3 longitudinal veins. The central vein terminates at the blunt tip while the 2 laterals end sooner at the entire leaf edge. Occasionally one can find a short-leaved potted bog plant in the trade. Male blooms have 6-9 stamens. Height of the plant in an aquarium is variable. When grown under dense and fertile conditions, growth is tall, making it suitable for larger aquaria with a corresponding water level. Moderate hardness and temperature are preferred. In sterile substrate, coarse gravel, or under strong illumination, it grows with shorter leaves and can be used in moderately tall tanks. This short-leaved form is almost indistinguishable from *S. s.* var. *subulata*. Propagation: runners with daughter plants in chains form copious stands.

D: 1, **KH:** 5-12, **pH:** 6.0-7.2, **T:** 24-28° C (75-82° F), **AH:** 1-3

Vallisneria americana MICHAUX (1803)

Fam.: Hydrocharitaceae Syn.: *Vallisneria spiralis* f. *tortifolia*
Distribution: Southeastern North America, West Indies
Decorative in central areas of the tank or in the foreground of tall tanks. Leaves are ribbon-like, twisted several times, 15-25 cm (6"-9 3/4") tall, 5-8 mm (3/16"-5/16") wide. The entire edge is serrulate and the tip acute. Known to the hobby since 1906, but erroneously described by WENDT (1952), creating the above synonym. The male flower with its single stamen, however, shows us that it belongs to the variable *V. americana*, whose 100 cm (39") tall variety is not yet cultured. It likes light but is otherwise quite undemanding. Because of its constant height, this species can be kept better in a shallow aquarium than the long-leaved *V. spiralis* or *V. asiatica*. The twisted leaves add an additional decorative element to the underwater garden. Due to good propagation, few plants placed at intervals are necessary as starters. Thin regularly and change placement on occasion. Propagation: runners with numerous daughter plants in chains.

D: 1, **KH:** 2-15, **pH:** 6.0-7.5, **T:** 22-30° C (72-86° F), **AH:** 1-3

Sagittaria subulata var. *gracillima*

Vallisneria americana

Sagittaria subulata var. *kurziana*

Vallisneria asiatica MIKI (1934)

Fam.: Hydrocharitaceae

Distribution: Temperate areas of Asia
Adaptive plant used to form groups in not overly shallow aquaria. Leaves are ribbon-like, smooth, not twisted, 40-60 cm (16"-24") long, up to 1 cm (1/3") wide (wild plants usually smaller and shorter), tip obtuse, edges of wild plants are serrulate; the aquarium form is only serrulate in the upper areas. Male flowers have one stamen. Imported more often since 1970, but usually classified as *V. spiralis*. It can be assumed that the Asian *Vallisneria* is cultured predominantly in aquaria and that *V. spiralis* has almost completely been displaced. When planted loosely and provided with strong illumination and cool water, growth tends to be more compact. Generally the leaves become over 40 cm (16") long and the large plants serve to green large areas in the background or the sides. In time, it grows profusely, creating dense stands which should be thinned periodically. Provide sufficient iron in the water; the plant seems to be poorly suited to very soft water. Propagation: runners form numerous daughter plants in series.

D: 1, KH: 5-12, pH: 6.0-7.5, T: 22-28° C (72-82° F), AH: 2-3

Vallisneria gracilis F.M. BAILEY (1889)

Fam.: Hydrocharitaceae

Distribution: Australia (Mulgrave River)
One of the few species endemic to Australia that has been known to aquarists since 1976. Group plant with good adaptation but needs more light than other species. Leaves are ribbon-like and not twisted. Leaves of the wild plants are to 10 cm (4") long and 2 mm (1/16") wide; cultured forms have 40 cm (16") long, 4 mm (3/16") wide leaves that are only serrated around the tip. Three inner longitudinal veins are clearly visible. The two outer veins in close proximity to the edge are very faint, cross-veins occasionally absent. Typically, the tip is clearly extended into a point. Male inflorescence up to 4 mm (3/16") in size are common in aquarium plants also. Due to the numerous water plants, there soon is dense growth which constantly spreads further. When thinning, remove about one half of the plants so that the remaining stay strong. The short leaves known from wild plants are only formed in cool, nutrient poor water. As a rule, it grows up to 40 cm (16") tall. Propagation: runners with numerous daughter plants.

D: 1, KH: 2-15, pH: 6.0-7.5, T: 20-30° C (68-86° F), AH: 2-3

Vallisneria neotropicalis MARIE VICTORIN (1943)

Fam.: Hydrocharitaceae

Distribution: Southern USA, Cuba
Used in aquaria since 1975; grows in nature on sandy bottoms in water up to 3 m (118") deep. Wild plants almost always have short, black-red leaves about 35 cm (14") long. In an aquarium, new leaves grow to a length of 150 cm (59") and a width of 3 cm (1 ") with an obtuse tip and serrated edge. Coloration is deep green to reddish with dark red strips running crosswise. The midrib is thicker than the remaining 4 longitudinal veins. Male flowers have 3 stamens. With its long leaves, it grows into a very voluminous plant which can only be used in a tall, roomy aquaria. Part of the leaf blades will float beneath the water surface, creating a decorative effect. General adaptation is good; hard water is tolerated without problems and a marked temperature flexibility makes care in unheated to tropical tanks possible. However, leaf coloration is light dependent. Propagation: runners with rapid growing daughter plants.

D: 2, KH: 2-15, pH: 6.0-7.5, T: 18-28° C (64-82° F), AH: 3

Vallisneria asiatica

Vallisneria neotropicalis

Vallisneria gracilis

A group with 20 species and 5 varieties from 10 genera. The common characteristic is a rhizome rooted in the substrate from which a more or less large leaf rosette emerges. In their natural habitat, *Barclaya longifolia* grows as a true water plant; therefore, it also flowers regularly in an aquarium. The genus *Nymphaea* normally grows floating leaves, but some species with short petioles are kept underwater in the aquarium. Water lilies, however, only flower when the floating leaves are allowed to develop. The red tiger lotus, *Nymphaea lotus*, is quite willing to bloom in an aquarium. *Nymphaea stellata* requires a roomy aquarium to bloom. Our photo illustrates the pink variety, *N. stellata* var. *rosea*. If *Nuphar* are to flower, they have to be grown in a larger open pond where they acquire a respectable size. The African swamp plants *Anubias barteri* and *Anubias gracilis* bear their characteristic spadix above the water in a bog aquarium. To the contrary, *Samolus parviflorus* will display its numerous small white flowers on long stalks in simple pots in a window sill.

Nymphaea lotus

Nymphaea stellata var. rosea

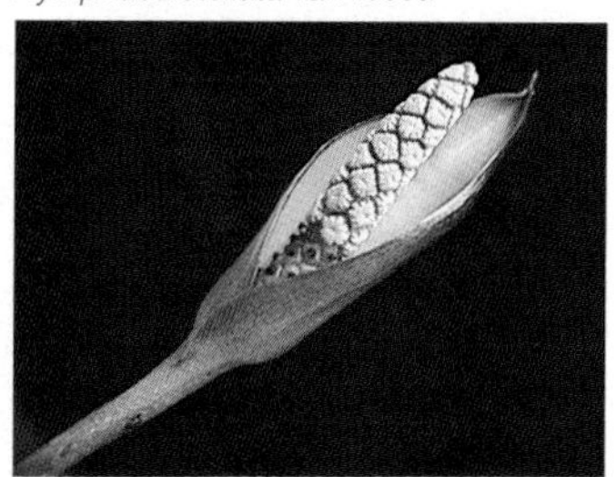

Anubias gracilis

Barclaya longifolia

Anubias barteri

Nuphar advena

Samolus parviflorus

Anubias barteri var. *barteri* SCHOTT (1860)

Fam.: Araceae

Distribution: Nigeria, Cameroon, Fernando Po
One of the best of the genus for the aquarium. It forms a compact rosette of rugged leaves. The creeping rhizome bears leaves that are oval-lanceolate in shape and have an acute tip and a rounded cordate base. The leaves are 15-20 cm (6"-8") long with an elevated midrib and 14 lateral veins on both sides that unite at the edge. The spadix is about 1.5 times as long as the white spathe and the male part grows 1.7 times as long as the female. Place at least the front part of the rootstock flat against the substrate. Plants planted too deep will easily deteriorate. Various water values are tolerated well and the minimum light requirement of approximately 30 watts/100 l is not particularly high. With bright light, however, the plant grows more compact and puts new leaves on faster. This strong, tough leaved species can be kept with robust fishes. The plant is well suited for the bog aquarium and will easily flower there. Propagation: the rhizome grows some side-shoots. The correspondingly long rootstock of an older plant can be cut 10 cm (4") behind the tip. Both pieces remain buried and the distal segment will develop a side-shoot. Remove at 10 cm (4") length and plant separately.

D: 1, **KH**: 2-15, **pH**: 6.0-7.5, **T**: 22-28° C (72-82° F), **AH**: 2-3

Anubias barteri var. *caladiifolia* ENGLER (1915)

Fam.: Araceae

Distribution: Nigeria, Cameroon, Fernando Po
A full, individual plant for the larger aquarium. It has an elongated rhizome with leaves that are oval-elliptical, acutely tipped, 10-20 cm (4"-8") long, 5-14 cm (2"-5 ") wide. Its heart-shaped base extends 2 cm (3/4") below the insertion of the petiole into the blade. A pair of side veins off the base of the midrib branch into the lobes of the base. This branching is not present in *A. b.* var. *barteri*. The flower spadix is 1.5 times longer than the white spathe; the male part is up to 2.5 times longer than the female segment. Although this species can be used in an aquarium, often it will not continue to grow satisfactorily. The newly planted specimen requires a longer acclimation time and should be allowed to root undisturbed. Only then is there a guarantee for healthy new leaves. Special attention has to be paid to the superficially placed rhizome, which under no circumstance should end up too deep in the substrate. It is important to place it in a free location with unobstructed light, whereby about 65 watts/100 l should be sufficient. In soft water, better results are obtained when the nutrient poor surroundings are enriched with aquarium plant fertilizer. Excessive temperatures cause older leaves to turn yellow and new laminae to have long stalks. The plant grows up to 40 cm (16") in a bog aquarium. Propagation: moderate formation of side-shoots at the rhizome. Separate the correspondingly long rootstock to encourage the formation of a lateral shoot.

D: 2, **KH**: 2-8, **pH**: 6.0-7.0, **T**: 22-26° C (72-79° F), **AH**: 2-3

Anubias barteri var. *barteri*

Anubias barteri var. *caladiifolia*

Anubias gracilis CHEVALIER ex HUTCHINSON (1939)

Fam.: Araceae

Distribution: Guinea, Sierra Leone

Leaf blades are triangular, 7-12 cm (2 3/4"-4 3/4") long and 4-7 cm (1 2/3"-2 3/4") wide with the widest point at the base. The midrib branches into the base lobes and there divides again into short lateral veins. The spathe is dark green outside, whitish inside and up to 3 cm (1 ") long. The spadix is somewhat shorter; the male part up to 4 times as long as the female segment. Like the other species of the genus, this species is offered in the trade as a bog plant. Though cultivated in Germany since 1980, the species has remained quite rare. The average aged specimen with about 4 leaves will adapt better to life in water than a larger plant. Even though the trasition to submersed life is eased because of its tough and durable leaves, it takes more time for the 30 cm (12") tall water plant to emerge from the emerse form. Growth of the plant is variable. This plant does not grow well everywhere; surely, a consequence of its living conditions. The capability to adapt to life in water is not particularly developed in this species. Soft water, moderate temperature, rich loose substrate and strong illumination can be considered favorable conditions. Emerse plants of a bog aquarium will grow better and produce flowers and fruit easily. Propagation: the rhizome rarely has side-shoots. Ripe seeds are easily obtained with bog culture; nevertheless, the rearing demands patience.

D: 3, KH: 2-8, pH: 5.8-6.8, T: 22-26° C (72-79° F), AH: 1-3

Anubias gilletii DE WILDEMANN et DURAND (1901)

Fam.: Araceae

Distribution: Tropical west Africa

The rhizome is 5 mm (3/16") thick, short and slightly branched. Leaf blades are variable in shape and size, 15-20 cm (6"-8") long, 5-13 cm (2"-5") wide with spear-shaped base lobes that are relatively short and extend out, forming a wide angle. The spathe is green and up to 3 cm (1 ") in size, while the spadix grows up to 3 cm (1 ") long with the male part equal in length to the female segment. Previously, it was erroneously identified as *A. hastifolia* ENGLER, 1839. This species has significantly longer base lobes. *A. gilletii* should be used as a robust solitary plant in a tall aquarium. In shallow water, aerial leaves will be produced easily. Normally sold as a land plant, and its conversion to submersed life is quite difficult. Initial growth is very hesitant but improves after sufficient root formation. Do not transplant rooted plants unnecessarily; this disturbance is badly tolerated and leads to stunted growth. Cultivation of well-rooted plants in a buried flower pot is recommended. Grows vigorously in a roomy bog aquarium. Needs high humidity, plenty of light and fertile substrate. Propagation: the swamp form flowers and fruits easily. Rearing of seedlings is possible but time consuming.

D: 3, KH: 2-10, pH: 6.0-7.0, T: 22-26° C (72-79° F), AH: 2-3

Anubias gracilis

Anubias gilletii

Lagenandra lancifolia (SCHOTT) THWAITES (1864)

Fam.: Araceae

Distribution: Sri Lanka
The habitus of this species is similar to narrow-leaved young plants of *L. ovata*. The leaves are lanceolate, 15-20 cm (6-8") long, 3-6 cm (1 -2 ") wide, entire with an acuminate tip and a acute base. The petiole is shorter or equal to the blade length. While the flower spike is similar to *L. ovata*, it differs in being less "warty" or grooved. Young plants are slow growing, allowing use in shallow water. However, well-rooted specimens will rapidly break the surface with their long-stalked leaves. Because of this, the plant is normally used in tall aquaria with strong illumination to keep the growth compact. These measures, together with occasional pruning, can keep the plant below the water surface. A recommendable plant for the bog aquarium, it reaches approximately 30 cm (12") in height and develops an interesting inflorescence. Propagation: side-shoots at the rhizome, but only on older, well-rooted specimens.

D: 2, **KH:** 2-15, **pH:** 6.0-7.8, **T:** 22-28°C (72-82°F), **AH:** 3

Lagenandra meeboldii (ENGLER) FISCHER (1931)

Fam.: Araceae

Distribution: Algalhatti, Tuppanad, Sri Lanka
This plant has egg-shaped, medium green, 12-15 cm ($4^{3}/_{4}$-6") long, 6-8 cm (2 -3 ") wide, thick leaves with an acute tip and a base that is rounded, acute or slightly cordate. The petiole is either shorter or equal to the blade length. Out of the midrib of the leaf, numerous side veins emerge. There is a brown variation of this plant that has not been declared a variety. This brown variation is outstanding for aquaria. The flower spike grows up to 8 cm (3 ") long and has an egg-shaped bottom. It is smooth or velvety on the outside and only opens a small amount. Though the plant grows slowly in the water, this is not necessarily a disadvantage. It is well suited for the aquarium. When choosing a land form of the plant, look for robust specimens. These will tend to adapt better to life under water. The leaves of the land form will drop off, but the rooted plant has ususally grown several new aquatic leaves 2 spaces by then. During the acclimation, do not transplant, or stunted growth can result. Excellent as a strong swamp plant in the bog or shore aquarium. Propagation: side-shoots of the rhizome.

D: 2, **KH:** 2-15, **pH:** 6.0-7.5, **T:** 22-28°C (72-82°F), **AH:** 2-3

Lagenandra ovata (LINNAEUS) THWAITES (1864)

Fam.: Araceae

Distribution: Sri Lanka
Principally the plant grows too large in an aquarium and routinely breaks the water surface. The blade is thick, lanceolate to narrowly ovate, up to 40 cm (16") long and 15 cm (6") wide with both ends pointed. The base converges on to the round petiole. The petiole is often as long or longer than the blade. Its flower spike is fleshy, dark purple, up to 10 cm (4") long and terminates into an elongated tip. The exterior is warty, little-opened and purple on the inside. Only for tanks taller than 60 cm (24"). Even here, pruning leaves and roots is necessary to keep the plant from growing out of the water. Infertile sand or cultivation in a restrictive pot can help hamper growth. Its tough leaves make it well suited for aquaria with rough cichlids. The swamp plant grows up to 100 cm (39") tall and can be used in roomy bog aquaria. Sometimes the plant has been considered poisonous (rhizome), but this error is due to confusion with a similar plant, *L. toxicaria*. Propagation: side-shoots at the rhizome, rhizome cuttings.

D: 3, **KH:** 2-15, **pH:** 6.0-7.8, **T:** 22-28°C (72-82°F), **AH:** 3

Lagenandra lancifolia

Lagenandra meeboldii

Lagenandra ovata

Nuphar japonica DE CANDOLLE (1821)

Fam.: Nymphaeaceae

Distribution: Japan, Hokkaido
This species is considered to be a variety of *N. lutea* by several authors. Its floating leaves and flowers are similar. The green, cylindrical rhizome grows 4 cm (1 2/3") thick. Relatively long-stalked medium to yellowish green aquatic leaves are 10-15 cm (4"-6") long, 8-15 cm (3"-6") wide with a deeply split base that results in wide spaced basal lobes, thereby creating a slightly triangular shape. Leaf tips are obtuse, and the edge is slightly undulate. A plant with brownish leaves is described as *N. japonica* var. *rubrotinctum*. This voluminous plant keeps its leaves well in an aquarium. When mature, it is better suited to a roomy tank that allows the stately leaves to open undisturbed. Low water hardness is preferred, but it will grow in hard water for a limited time. With sufficiently strong lighting (over 14 hours a day), floating leaves can be avoided; otherwise, they should be pinched off. Place the rhizome shallowly in the loose bottom; counteract buoyancy with a flat stone until rooted. Propagation: side-shoots on the rhizome are rare.

D: 2, **KH:** 2-12, **pH:** 6.0-7.5, **T:** 18-25° C (64-77° F), **AH:** 3

Nuphar lutea (LINNAEUS) J. E. SMITH (1808)

Fam.: Nymphaeaceae

Distribution: Europe, Mediterranean region, north Asia
Its rhizome is cylindrical and 5 cm (2") thick. Aquatic leaves are light to yellow-green, thin-skinned, shiny, up to 20 cm (8") long, 15 cm (6") wide, edge undulate, tip obtuse, base of the leaf split to the petiole. Floating leaves are long-stalked, somewhat thick, cordate and up to 30 cm (12") in diameter. Yellow, 5 cm (2") flowers are produce. A native winter hardy, floating leaved plant suitable for the larger, deeper garden ponds. For the aquarium, the short-stalked aquatic leaf form, which is the form the species usually over-winters in, is appropriate. Height is variable. Some specimens remain stubby while others have long petioles, growing taller. This can be a result of light intensity or water values. Though the plant is normally planted alone, provide sufficient spacing if used otherwise. Nutrient poor sand and plentiful light inhibit growth of floating leaves. Prior to planting, inspect the rhizome for damage, excising damaged sections and briefly air while keeping the leaves wet. Propagation: side-shoots on the rhizome are rarely formed.

D: 2, **KH:** 2-15, **pH:** 6.0-7.5, **T:** 18-25° C (64-77° F), **AH:** 3

Nymphaea x *daubenyana* Hortorum

Fam.: Nymphaeaceae

Distribution: cultivated cross
A result of a cross which was performed in 1863 by Professor Caspary in Königsberg. *N. micrintha* and *N. coeruae* are assumed to be the parents of the cross. Named after Professor Daubeny (Oxford) who successfully completed the cross in 1865. It only grows long-stalked, floating leaves which reach about 25 cm (9 3/3") in diameter. The front half of the leaf is usually entire while the base is sometimes serrate. The top of the leaf is green and the lower surface is pale green with occasional dark spots. A special characteristic is the adventitious plants that grow from the leaf base. The whitish yellow flower reaches a size of 15 cm (6") and remains open several days. This plant is rarely cultivated and is recommended for the roomy, brightly illuminated aquarium. Can be successfully kept in the aquatic section of a shore aquarium. To diminish the light blocking effect of the large floating leaves, their number can be reduce. This moderate reduction has hardly any influence on its willingness to flower. Propagation: removal of adventitious plants from the leaves; sometimes these will already have small flowers.

D: 2, **KH:** 5-12, **pH:** 6.0-7.5, **T:** 22-28° C (72-82° F), **AH:** 2-3

Nuphar japonica

Nuphar lutea

Nymphaea x daubenyana

Nymphaea lotus var. *rubra* LINNAEUS (1753)

Fam.: Nymphaeaceae

Distribution: East Africa, Madagascar, Southeast Asia
This water lily can exist in an aquarium for an extended period of time without floating leaves and adapts well. An excellent solitary plant that can provide a special accent. A variable species that has several submersed color morphs. *Nymphaea lotus* var. *viridis*, the green tiger lotus, has green leaves with dark red spots (see Atlas 1, page 116). *Nymphaea lotus* var. *rubra*, the red tiger lotus, has red leaves with dark red spots. In nature both varieties occur separately as well as together. Resulting crosses show different colored aquatic leaves, so aquarium plants are not always uniformly colored. Intensity of the coloration is sometimes light dependent. Adult specimens grow long-stalked floating leaves. These leaves grow to 20 cm (8") in size, are green and red speckled and coarsely serrate. These can be pinched without consideration and short-stalked aquatic leaves will grow again. If you desire the plant to flower, allow the floating leaves to develop. In consequence, stalked, pleasantly smelling white-yellow flowers about 10 cm (4") in size are grown. The blossoms are nocturnal and open on several consecutive days in the evening and close in the morning. Propagation: daughter plants on short runners, fruit formation is by self-pollination, seedling rearing.

D: 2, **KH**: 2-12, **pH**: 5.5-7.5, **T**: 22-28° C (72-82° F), **AH**: 2-3

Nymphaea stellata WILLDENOW (1799)

Fam.: Nymphaeaceae

Distribution: India
Useful water lily for an aquarium: under strong illumination a compact solitary plant with numerous short-stalked aquatic leaves forms. The tuber is cylindrical (pine cone shaped) and up to 2 cm (3/4") thick. Submersed leaves are 12 cm (4 3/4") in length, 8 cm (3") wide, have an obtuse tip and a deeply split base forming bluntly pointed basal lobes. The upperside of the leaf is brownish to pale pink with a few dark red blotches. The green (occasionally with red spots) 20 cm (8"), roundish floating leaves sit on a long petiole. It flowers above the water, displaying 7 cm (2 3/4") blooms with whitish, light pink or pale blue petals. Under weak illumination, the plant tends more towards floating leaves which can be pinched off for a while. This species will probably not live for long with only submersed growth. After some time of rapid leaf formation, the leaves are often shed and a vegetative hibernation is entered. The rhizome should be removed from the substrate, leaves and roots taken off, and left sitting on the substrate in the open for about 8 weeks. New, weaker aquatic leaves grow after planting. For flower development, the plant needs to be cultivated with floating leaves. Propagation: daughter plants on short shoots, separate cautiously with several leaves from the rhizome and plant separately.

D: 2, **KH**: 2-12, **pH**: 6.0-7.2, **T**: 22-28° C (72-82° F), **AH**: 2-3

Nymphaea lotus var. *rubra*

Nymphaea stellata

A large genus with 47 species and 12 varieties. The distribution area stretches from southern North America through Central America to extensive parts of South America. *Echinodorus* are predominantly amphibious bog plants; they partially resist longer flooding and then produce water forms. A few true water plants will sometimes produce degenerate bog forms. The cylindrical rhizome is strong. In smaller species, the rhizome is compressed and weaker. Leaves have a petiole and laminae. The laminae is usually lanceolate, linear, ovate or cordate. The requirements in an aquarium vary, but the medium ranges of light, temperature and water values are preferred. Cordate species tend to have long-stalked floating or aerial leaves. This can be avoided by using infertile sand substrate, confinement to a container and regular pruning. Due to relatively constant heights, Amazon swords can be used in a variety of ways. Small species can create a lawn with runners, establishing dense, flat growth in the foreground. Plants of medium height grow well in moderately tall tanks and higher growing voluminous plants are kept in roomy aquaria as individuals. In general, *Echinodorus* flower as bog plants. Various species grow long peduncles in the aquarium which sometimes flower above the water. These are pollinated with a small brush. The fruits are removed when they are brown and ripe, then stored dry for 3 months. Raising is done in a small, separate bog tank. With about 10 cm (3") in size, the young plants can be placed in an aquarium. Vegetative propagation is sometimes possible. Some species grow runners with daughter plants in chains which will root on their own. Larger plants occasionally form side-shoots on the rhizome or rhizome segments. Adventitious shoots on submersed peduncles are separated and planted or lowered with the peduncle to the substrate. Free placement and undisturbed growth are necessary for a healthy development.

Echinodorus andrieuxii, fruit

Echinodorus cordifolius, blossom

Echinodorus bleheri, adventitious shoots on a submersed peduncle

Echinodorus latifolius runners with daughter plants

Echinodorus angustifolius RATAJ (1975)

Fam.: Alismataceae

Distribution: Brazil

A small, amphibious bog plant. Aerial leaves are lanceolate, 10-15 cm (4"-6") long, up to 1 cm (1/3") wide with almost no petiole. Erect inflorescence grows up to 20 cm (8") tall, 2 or 3 whorls, flower up to 1.5 cm (2/3") in size, 6 stamens, rarely 12, green carpels, fruitlets 1.4 mm (1/16") in size with three lateral ribs. In its emerse form, the species is easily confused with *E. latifolius* who grows yellow carpels and distinctly stalked aerial leaves. The aquarium plant posses slender, ribbon-shaped leaves that are 20-40 cm (8"-16") long, 0.5-0.8 cm (1/4"-1/3") wide, long tipped, narrowing towards the base of the leaf, leaving almost no petiole. With less than 12 hours of daily illumination, however, the leaf is divided into petiole and lamina. Coloration is medium green and either solid or darkly striated. The midrib is distinct, but both lateral veins are faint. Its long leaves are similar to some slender leaved *Sagittaria* or *Vallisneria*, making it suitable to provide a green background or side. In acidified water, the plants do not develop well. Intense formation of runners can weaken the parent plant, thereby reducing growth markedly. After sufficient propagation, pinch off the runners. This will encourage growth of a multileaved rosette which develops shorter leaves under strong light. Propagation: elongated runners often grow in open water, anchor the offshoot with its stem to the bottom.

D: 2, **KH:** 5-12, **pH:** 6.5-7.5, **T:** 20-25° C (68-77° F), **AH:** 2-3

Echinodorus argentinensis RATAJ (1970) — Argentine Sword

Fam.: Alismataceae — Syn.: *E. grandiflorus* var. *ovatus*

Distribution: Brazil, Uruguay, Argentina

This plant is rarely imported and usually is identified incorrectly as *E. longistylis* although it has been known as an aquarium plant for sometime. Medium sized bog plant whose oval aerial leaves have a rounded base, acute tip, and are 15-25 cm (6"-10") long and 10-15 cm (4"-6") wide. Its inflorescence is 150 cm (59") tall, branched at the base, has 12-16 whorls, flowers up to 4 cm (1 2/3") in size, 24 stamens, fruitlets 3 mm (1/8") long with 3 glands arranged in one row. Aquatic leaves are dark green, small, egg-shaped or lanceolate, 15-20 cm (6"-8") long, 3-6 cm (1 1/4"-2 1/3") wide, firm, longer towards the tip, acute, shorter based, edge usually smooth. From the base emerge 5 or 7 longitudinal veins clearly visible from the lower surface of the leaf with the 3 inner veins ending in the tip. The petiole is sharply triangular and normally longer then the laminae. Leaves are sometimes very small (8 x 2 cm; 3" x 3/4") with an exceptionally long petiole, probably a hard water form. This is a wide reaching specimen plant, whose adult specimens reach almost 40 cm (16") diameter. Therefore, it requires open placement and sufficiently deep water. When the plants are placed in shallow tanks or under crowded conditions, long-stalked aerial leaves tend to develop above the water. Prune these until short-stalked leaves are grown again. Sometimes part of the older blades have to be removed. The robust species makes no particular demands and can be kept in acidic water; however, it is somewhat more light demanding when compared to other species of the genus. Propagation: unknown submersed, emersed with seeds.

D: 2, **KH:** 3-12, **pH:** 6.0-7.5, **T:** 22-28° C (72-82° F), **AH:** 2-3

Echinodorus angustifolius

Echinodorus argentinensis

Echinodorus aschersonianus GRAEBNER (1911) Ascherson's Amazon Sword
Fam.: Alismataceae

Distribution: Brazil, Paraguay, Uruguay, Argentina
Mid-sized bog plant with variable oval to lanceolate aerial leaves, up to 13 cm (5") long and 8 cm (3") wide, base usually cordate. The inflorescence is unbranched, prostrate, and rooted at the whorls. The flowers grow to 3.5 cm (1 1/3") and have 24-28 stamens, a fruitlet that is 2 mm (1/16") long and usually has 2-3 lateral glands (*E. a.* var. *nulliglandulosus*, RATAJ, 1970 has no glands). Aquatic leaves are dark green, 10-15 cm (4"-6") long, 3-5 cm (1 1/4"-2") wide and are variable in shape. They are either heart-shaped with obtuse or acute tip, or oval to almost lanceolate. Depending on the size of the leaf, 3 or 5 longitudinal veins emerge from the base. Leaf shape is obviously light dependent. With less than 12 hours illumination the leaf tends to be lanceolate with a wedge-shaped base; with longer duration, the leaf is wider, oval and cordate to roundish. It forms a single plant about 25-35 cm (9 3/4"-14") high. Can also be used in shallower tanks. With strong illumination or crowded conditions the plant tends to put on aerial leaves. Therefore, provide the correct amount of light (around 50 watts/100 l) and open placement. Propagation: the initially upright peduncle bends towards the bottom, forms roots and a few adventitious plants on 1 or 2 whorls. Evidently, this only happens with a daily illumination exceeding 12 hours.

D: 2, KH: 2-12, pH: 6.5-7.2, T: 22-28° C (72-82° F), AH: 2-3

Echinodorus bolivianus (RUSBY) HOLM NIELSEN (1976) Bolivian Sword
Fam.: Alismataceae Syn.: *E. austromoamericanus*

Distribution: South Brazil, Uruguay, Argentina
Small amphibious bog plant. Aerial leaves are lanceolate-ovate, 3-5 cm (1 1/4"-2") long, 0.5-1 cm (3/16"-1/3") wide, acute, but not pointed, and have a 2-3 cm (3/4"-1 1/4") petiole which is usually red at the base. Inflorescence up to 20 cm (8") long with 1-2 whorls, flower 1.5 cm (2/3") in size, 9 stamens, 8-12 carpels, fruitlets 1.3 mm (1/32") long with 3 lateral ribs. It is usually sold as *E. quadricostatus* (or *E. xingu*) which, however, does not have reddish stalked aerial leaves but does have distinct leaf stalks on the aquatic leaves. *E. isthmicus* and *E. latifolius* also grow similarly. Aquatic leaves are narrow-linear, light green, short-stalked, 7-12 cm (2 3/4"-4 3/4") long, 0.5-0.8 cm (3/16"-5/16") wide with both ends equally acute. Excellent decoration for the foreground of small to large aquaria; forms extensive mats about 10 cm (4") high. With time, it will grow quite dense, necessitating occasional thinning to maintain growth and prevent stunting. An undemanding small plant that adapts well to different living conditions of aquaria. 50 watts/100 l tank volume are sufficient to meet the moderate light requirement. Add iron fertilizer when yellow, sickly leaves appear. The addition of CO_2 is recommended in very hard water. Propagation: creeping runners form numerous chains of daughter plants which will take root on the bottom.

D: 1, KH: 2-15, pH: 5.8-7.5, T: 18-28° C (64-82° F), AH: 1-3

Echinodorus aschersonianus

Echinodorus bolivianus

Echinodorus grandiflorus (CHAMISSO et SCHLECHTENDAL) MICHELI (1881)

Large-Flowered Amazon Sword

Fam.: Alismataceae

Distribution: Central America to southern Brazil
This imposing bog plant is the largest species of the genus. The blade of the aerial leaf grows up to 40 cm (16") long, 35 cm (14") wide and is borne on equally long petioles. The lamina is cordate with an acute tip. The midrib, edge of the base, and the petiole have spines. The inflorescence attains 200 cm (79") length, is basally branched and has a warty peduncle. Flowers are 3.5 cm (1 1/3") in size, usually have 24 stamens (rarely 18), and 3.5 mm (1/8") long fruitlets with numerous sticky glands. Considered unsuitable for the aquarium because it regularly produces aerial leaves. Young plants can remain in the water for a while as long as tall leaves are repeatedly trimmed. Various varieties are described, and crosses with *E. longiscapus* and *E. macrophyllus* are known. These are probably better suited for aquaria. Aquatic leaves are oval, up to 15 cm (6") long and 8 cm (3") wide, base rounded to slightly cordate, tip short and pointed and 7 longitudinal veins emerge from the base. Provide a nice, roomy open aquaria so the leaves can expand above the water. Its emerged form is also useful in the larger bog aquarium. Propagation: submersed unknown—otherwise, seedling rearing.

D: 3, KH: 2-10, pH: 6.0-7.5, T: 22-24° C (72-75° F), AH: 3

Echinodorus uruguayensis ARECHAYALETA (1903) Horeman's Amazon Sword

Fam.: Alismataceae Syn.: *E. horemani*

Distribution: South Brazil, Uruguay, Chile, North Argentina
Grows predominantly submersed in slow flowing and relatively cool water. Aerial leaves are rare, ovate-oval, up to 15 cm (6") long and 9 cm (3 ") wide. The 30 cm (12") long inflorescence is first erect then prostrate, unbranched with 2-4 whorls. Flowers are 2 cm (3/4") in size carrying 18 stamens and a 1.5 mm (1/32") long fruitlet with lateral glands. Submersed leaves are dark green, parchment-like, hard, short-stalked, lanceolate, 25-35 cm (10"-14") long, 2-3 cm (3/4"-1 ") wide with a weakly undulate edge, elongated base and a bluntly pointed tip. The midrib is thicker at the base and has one pair of longitudinal veins emerging from it. The other pair of veins arises quite high out of the midrib. A dark red leaf variety is rarely imported and very expensive. In the closely related *E. osiris*, all side veins emerge from the base. The leaves do not break the water surface. Suitable for the background and makes an impressive plant in a roomy aquarium. This robust specimen plant places moderate demands and seems to prefer neutral to slightly alkaline water and nutrient rich substrate. A lot of warmth is detrimental; however, it can be temporarily kept in cool water. Propagation: lateral shoots on the rhizome segment.

D: 2, KH: 2-15, pH: 6.5-7.5, T: 20-25° C (68-77° F), AH: 2-3

Echinodorus quadricostatus FASSETT (1955) Central American Sword

Fam.: Alismataceae

Distribution: Central America, South America, West Indies
Small bog plant. Aerial leaves are lanceolate, stalked, 10-12 cm (4"-4 3/4") long, 4-7 mm (3/16"- ") wide and are quite tough. Inflorescence with 2 whorls, flowers 1 cm (1/3") in size with 9 stamens, black fruitlets, 2.3 mm (1/8") long with 3-4 lateral ribs. Aquatic leaves are short-stalked, narrowly linear, light green, 10-20 cm (4"-8") long, 5-7 mm (3/16"- ") wide, single-veined with clear cross-veins and an acuminate tip. The lower part of the petiole is half-round and laterally bent upward, distinguishing it from other species. This adaptive aquarium plant is healthy under almost all conditions, but it sometimes becomes stunted in hard water. The addition of CO_2 is advised. Similarly, the high iron requirements for this plant should be meet. With daughter plants, a voluminous stand occurs; by pinching off the runners, a specimen plant can grow numerous leaves. Attains a height of 10-20 cm (4"-8"). Use in the foreground. Propagation: creeping runners anchor their daughter plants in the substrate.

D: 2, KH: 2-15, pH: 6.0-7.2, T: 22-28° C (72-82° F), AH: 1-3

Echinodorus grandiflorus

Echinodorus uruguayensis

Echinodorus quadricostatus

Echinodorus opacus RATAJ (1970) Opaque Amazon Sword

Fam.: Alismataceae

Distribution: South Brazil

Originating from the Rio Grande do Sul, it grows as a small bog plants or, sometimes, in the relatively cool waters of about 18° C (64° F). Aerial leaves are 15 cm (6") long, 8 cm (3") wide with a rounded base and an acuminate tip. Flower and fruit are unknown. Additional details are found under *E. portoalegrensis*, a similar plant with curved aquatic leaves and an obtuse, slender base. Aquatic leaves of *E. opacus* are dark green, 8-12 cm long (3"-4³/4"), 4-6 cm wide (1²/3"-2¹/3"), elongate lanceolate, quite firm and stiff with a weakly rounded base. 5 longitudinal veins originate from the base and have marked cross-venation between. The blade is spread flat, entire, upright, forming a 10-20 cm (4"-8") tall solitary plant. As it does not grow out of the water, it is suitable for flat aquaria also. The formation of new leaves is moderate, followed by slow growth. Nutrient rich substrate and fertilization of the water encourages growth. Its demands towards water values are not particularly high, though it does require high light intensity. The plant does not tolerate transplanting well, demanding a long period to recuperate and resume growth. Therefore, do not transplant unnecessarily. Do not place the elongated and creeping rhizome close to or in the direction of the front glass since the leaves will later bunch up against it. Propagation: side-shoots from the separated rhizome piece.

D: 3, KH: 2-12, pH: 6.5-7.5, T: 20-28° C (68-82° F), AH: 1-2

Echinodorus maior, see Vol. 1, page 120

Echinodorus latifolius (SEUBERT) RATAJ (1975)
Fam.: Alismataceae Syn.: *E. magdalenensis*

Distribution: West Indies, Central America, northern South America
Short swamp plant, existing constantly submersed in some places. Aerial leaves are lanceolate, differentiated into petiole and blade, single-veined, up to 4 cm (1 2/3") long and 6 mm (") wide. Inflorescence is thin, up to 20 cm (8") long, becoming prostrate, usually 2 whorls, flowers up to 1.5 cm (2/3") in size, petals sloping downward in a typical fashion (for this plant), 8 stamens, yellow carpels, fruitlets up to 1.8 mm (1/16") long with 3 lateral ribs. Original description as *Alisma tenellum f. latifolium* SEUBERT, 1848. Rataj declared the form a species. *E. isthmicus* is a close relative (see *E. isthmicus* for special characteristics). Aquatic leaves are light green, linear to lanceolate, 5-15 cm (2"-6") long, 0.5-1.5 cm ("-2/3") wide, tip uniformly long pointed, base progressively narrows without forming a distinct petiole. Under short duration of illumination, the leaf is sometimes divided into petiole and blade. The leaf has a prominent midrib and two fine lateral veins which are occasionally absent. The aquarium form normally has shorter, more slender leaves, reaching 10 cm (4") in height. An excellent decoration for the foreground of small and large aquaria. General requirements are moderate and healthy growth is also possible in hard water. The extended runners constantly form new daughter plants, creating an extensive lawn-like stand which later grows exuberantly. So that the specimens do not compete and weaken each other, the lawn is sometimes thinned and annually rejuvenated. Propagation: runners with chains of daughter plants.

D: 1, **KH:** 2-15, **pH:** 6.5-7.5, **T:** 22-30° C (72-86° F), **AH:** 1-3

Echinodorus longiscapus ARECHAVALET (1903)
Fam.: Alismataceae Syn.: *E. grandiflorus* var. *longiscapus*

Distribution: South Brazil, Uruguay, Argentina
A small bog plant with ovate or cordate aerial leaves that are 9-11 cm (3 "-4 1/3") long, 7-8 cm (2 3/4"-3") wide and sometimes have an indistinct tip. The inflorescence is erect, up to 80 cm (31") long, unbranched with 3-9 whorls. Flowers grow to 4 cm (1 2/3") in size, have 20-24 stamens and fruitlets with 4 lateral ribs and 1-3 glands. The species bears a certain similarity to *E. cordifolius*. A recent, rare addition to aquaria. Aquatic leaves are roundish to ovate, short-stalked, 7-9 cm (2 3/4"-3 ") wide and have 9-11 longitudinal veins emerging from the base. Normally, coloration is totally green; sometimes the top of the leaf has red-brown spots. Adapts to the submersed form quite well, but lighting should not be too bright, and it should be kept in infertile bottom sand. The specimen reaches a height of 15-25 cm (6"-10"); however, it does not produce as many leaves as comparable species. Leaves should develop undisturbed and short-stalked; therefore, cultivate in the open. When crowded or provided with very weak light, long-stalked floating leaves are produced which become aerial leaves in shallow water. Prune until short-stalked submersed blades grow again. If this does not help, transplant and reduce its leaves. Propagation: submersed inflorescence are rare and have few adventitious plants.

D: 3, **KH:** 5-12, **pH:** 6.5-7.5, **T:** 22-28° C (72-82° F), **AH:** 2-3

Echinodorus latifolius

Echinodorus longiscapus

Echinodorus palaefolius (NEES & MARTIUS) McBRIDE (1931)

Fam.: Alismataceae

Distribution: Tropical South America
This variety is based on *E. ellipticus* var. *latifolius* MICHELI, 1881. Original description was as *Alisma ellipticum* MARTIUS, 1830. The designation was newly combined by RATAJ. This 100 cm (39") tall bog plant has ovate aerial leaves that grow to 25 cm (10") long, 15 cm (6") wide with an obtuse tip, rounded base and 9-11 longitudinal veins. The inflorescence is erect, simple or branched, up to 50 cm (20") tall with 1.5 cm (2/3") flowers with 12 stamens. The fruitlets have a curved point and 1 large lateral gland. The nominate form, *E. p.* var. *palaefolius*, was originally described as *Sagittaria palaefolius* NEES et MARTIUS, 1823 but changed to the genus *Echinodorus* in 1931. Part of the plants described as *E. ellipticus* belong to the species. These, as well as *E. palaefolius* var. *minus* (SEUBERT) RATAJ, 1971, are not yet cultivated. Aquatic leaves are lanceolate, 20-30 cm (8"-12") long, 3-4 cm (1"-1 2/3") wide, widest in the middle, both ends acute, with a petiole significantly shorter than the blade. Developing young leaves are reddish with red spots under strong lighting. 3 longitudinal veins originate from the base; they are easily seen from the underside. This is a medium-sized solitary plant that grows above the water surface in brightly lit shallow water. Through less intense light, nutrient poor sand substrate and open placement, that can be avoided. A demanding aquarium plant which is rarely cultivated. Propagation: submersed unknown, the emerse plant forms seedlings.

D: 3, KH: 2-10, pH: 6.5-7.2, T: 24-28° C (75-82° F), AH: 2-3

Echinodorus portoalegrensis RATAJ (1970)

Fam.: Alismataceae Syn.: *E. porto alegre* (nomen nudum)

Distribution: Brazil
A small amphibious bog plant. Growth in nature occurs in relatively cool waters of about 18° C (64° F). Aerial and aquatic leaves are similar. Since the flower and fruit are unknown, the classification into the section *Portoalegrensii* (with *E. opacus*) has to be regarded as provisional. A different grouping could result when the fruit and flowers are seen. It is suspected that both species are of equal origin and could possibly be regarded as the same species. Leaves are dark green, elongate to lanceolate, very rigid and firm, 8-12 cm (3"-4 3/4") long, 4-5 cm (1 2/3") wide, short-stalked, tip bluntly acute, more slender towards the base with 3-5 lighter green longitudinal veins extending from the base. The blade is bent up on the edges and arched downward along its length; the tips of older leaves almost touch the bottom. A low growing decoration for front and middle areas. To use the different growth form as an accent, place in a free area and do not plant other vegetation too close. Do not plant the rhizome tip towards the front glass (place parallel) or the plant's creeping rootstock will later become wedged against the glass. It has a very strong light requirement of at least 70 watts/100 l. In pure sand or coarse gravel, the plants usually remain degenerate. Propagation: lateral shoots from the separated rhizome segment.

D: 3, KH: 5-15, pH: 6.5-7.5, T: 22-28° C (72-82° F), AH: 1-2

Echinodorus palaefolius

Echinodorus portoalegrensis

Echinodorus macrophyllus (KUNTH) MICHELI (1881) Thorny Amazon Sword

Fam.: Alismataceae Syn.: *E. scaber*

Distribution: Venezuela to Brazil

Due to different geographic races, some plants can grow constantly submersed while others produce aerial or floating leaves more often. A vigorous bog plant for the aquarium. Aerial leaves are long-stalked, broadly ovate to cordate, base flap-like, tip narrowly edged and the stalk and base edges have thorns. The inflorescence is warty, erect, up to 200 cm (79") long, basally branched with 6-12 whorls. Flowers usually have 24 stamens and are 3 cm (1 1/4") in size. The spindle-shaped fruitlets grows up to 5 mm (3/16") long, 1 mm (1/32") wide and has 1-3 lateral glands. According to RATAJ, the older name, *E. muricatus* FASSETT, 1955, is wrong and is a synonym of *E. grandiflorus*. Confusion with *E. macrophyllus* is possible. Submersed leaves are olive-green, red speckled when young, 15-30 cm (6"-12") long, 10-20 cm (4"-8") wide, base cordate, round or weakly emarginate tip. The stalk, edge of the base and sometimes the main vein have short thorns. Of the 7-11 longitudinal veins, the 3-5 central ones end in the tip. Cultivate this plant, which can become quite large, under nutrient poor conditions and with moderate lighting. Prune floating leaves. Propagation: lateral shoots on the rhizome are rare.

D: 2, **KH:** 2-12, **pH:** 6.5-7.2, **T:** 24-28° C (75-82° F), **AH:** 2-3

Echinodorus subalatus (MARTIUS) GRISEBACH (1866)

Fam.: Alismataceae

Distribution: Central America, southern Brazil

Give this vigorous bog plant free placement in tall aquaria. Aerial leaves are lanceolate or elliptical, variable, 15-25 cm (6"-10") long, 3-10 cm (1 1/4"-4") wide, both ends acute with 7 red-brown, longitudinal veins emerging from the base. The lower petiole is winged. The inflorescence is erect, up to 70 cm (28") long, simple or branched. Flowers are 1.5 cm (2/3") in size and carry 12 stamens. Fruitlets are 2 mm (1/16") long and rarely have 2 glands and 1 rib. Larger bog plants with wide aerial leaves cannot be adapted to water. Young shoots with slender leaves are better suited for this purpose. The submersed form has linear leaves, 20-30 cm (8"-12") long, 1-2 cm (1/3"-3/4") wide, with both ends narrowed and normally only have a midvein. As a rule, the petioles are longer than the blade. In shallow aquaria, the long leaves regularly float beneath the water surface leaving only the stalks in view. Low carbonate hardness is important and use washed, coarse sand. Generally rare as an aquarium plant. Good for the larger bog aquarium. Propagation: submersed unknown, seedling rearing.

D: 4, **KH:** 2-8, **pH:** 6.0-7.0, **T:** 20-26° C (68-79° F), **AH:** 3

Echinodorus macrophyllus

Echinodorus subalatus

A beautyfully planted aquarium is very decorative.

These monocot water plants, sometimes existing with floating leaves or as bog plants, have 42 species distributed endemically on various continents. About 15 species are suitable for aquaria; for the remaining species, the strongly adapted requirements from their home ranges cannot be meet in an aquarium. Also, the water forms of the genus have 1 or 2 rest periods coinciding when shallow waters become dry. The dry period is survived with a buried tuberous rhizome. New growth is put out during the rainy season. Because Aponogetons also flower easily in an aquarium, their characteristics, together with the typical leaf shapes, can be used for species identification. Certain species only grow well in soft water (*A. loriae, A. madagascariensis, A. rigidifolius*). Others easily tolerate medium-hard water or grow well for extended amounts of time in hard water (*A. crispus, A. echinatus, A. ulvaceus, A. undulatus*). A weakly acidic pH is favorable, and some species endure values below pH 6.0. The tuber should be shallowly placed in clean, coarse sand or moderately sized gravel. Fresh imports grow well and produce numerous leaves over the short term, but growth is weaker later. After a period of vegetative growth, a pause usually follows, whereby the leaves die off leaving the healthy tuber which can resume growth after 2-3 months (leave in the ground and wait, remove, clean and place on the ground or store in sand in a plastic bag). Aponogetons will easily flower in an aquarium; the long peduncle holds 1 or several spikes above the water. There are numerous small bisexual flowers on the peduncle whose pollen can be transferred with a small brush or cotton swab. In self-sterile species, a second inflorescence is required. Self-pollination and cleistogamy are possible. After pollination, the fruits ripen in 6-8 weeks. The seeds then loosen from the peduncle, float 1-2 days on the water then sink to the bottom and germinate. Seedling rearing is done in shallow water and an open place. The adventitious plants produced by *A. stachyosporus* and *A. undulatus* on their peduncles are mentioned as a specialty.

Aponogeton, seed germination

Aponogeton stachyosporus

Aponogeton madagascariensis var. *guillotii*

Aponogeton, fruit

Aponogeton undulatus, adventitious plant

Aponogeton bernieranus (DECAISNE) HOOKER fil. (1883)

Fam.: Aponogetonaceae

Distribution: East Madagascar

The dark green blade is strongly waffled, 20-30 cm (8"-12") long, 6-8 cm (2 1/3"-3") wide with an acute or rounded base and an obtuse tip. 3 or 4 pairs of weak lateral veins branch from the midrib and cross-venation is indistinct. Tubers are roundish-elongate, smooth, up to 3 cm (1 1/4") thick. The inflorescence has 3-10 spikes up to 10 cm (4") long that carry fleshy white or pale pink flowers. In nature, the leaves become 120 cm (47") long and almost 10 cm (4") wide. Cultivated plants, however, always grow as smaller compact solitary plants. This extraordinarily difficult plant only lives for a short time in harder water, demanding soft water with little carbonate hardness; substrate should be free of calcium. Coarse gravel is detrimental for root development. After the resting period, the rhizome grows very few and markedly smaller leaves. Often there is no growth at all. Propagation: self-fertilizing inflorescence, abundant fruits, seedling rearing is especially difficult.

D: 4, **KH**: 1-3, **pH**: 6.0-6.8, **T**: 20-24° C (68-75° F), **AH**: 1-2

Aponogeton crispus THUNBERG (1781)

Fam.: Aponogetonaceae

Distribution: South and central India

Has a light green blade with translucent spots. Leaf measurements are variable; sometimes only 10 cm (4") long and 3 cm (1 1/4") wide but predominately 20-35 cm (8"-14") long and 3-5 cm (1 1/4"-2") wide. The base is short, pointed, rarely weakly rounded, tip obtuse to rounded. One pair of lateral veins emerges from the midrib; the others originate from the base. Floating leaves are brownish, 10-20 cm (4"-8") long, 2-5 cm (3/4"-2") wide with both ends acute or somewhat rounded. The inflorescence is simple, about 15 cm (6") long, white and loosely flowered. Sometimes similar to *A. ulvaceus* (without floating leaves, two-armed inflorescence) or *A. natans* with a distinct cordate base on the floating leaves. A decorative *Aponogeton* which usually grows extensively; therefore, cultivate as a specimen plant in a free place to allow it to achieve its potential. Growth perseveres in water that is up to medium-hard. With higher carbonate hardness, the addition of CO_2 helps remarkably. Occasional floating leaves can be removed without harming the plant. Observe the resting period, but the new shoot is usually weaker. Propagation: inflorescence is self-fertile, moderate fruiting, seedling rearing is unproblematic.

D: 2, **KH**: 2-12, **pH**: 6.0-7.5, **T**: 22-28° C (72-82° F), **AH**: 2-3

Aponogeton elongatus F. von MUELLER ex BENTHAM (1878)

Fam.: Aponogetonaceae — Elongated Swordplant

Distribution: North and east Australia

A variable species with several growth forms which can be clearly differentiated. The plant presented in Vol. 1, page 128 is called *A. e.* forma *latifolius*. We are dealing with the type species here. The blade is dark green to slightly brownish, 20-30 cm (8"-12") long, 1-2 cm (1/3"-3/4") wide, base somewhat elongated, tip weakly pointed, edge tightly undulate, sometimes curly with a short petiole. 5 longitudinal veins stretch from the base; the inner pair sometimes leans against the wide midrib and only separates from it in the upper half. The spike is simple, 10-20 cm (4"-8") long and yellow. With free placement and sufficiently strong illumination, a compact specimen plant evolves. Due to the relatively constant height of about 30 cm (12"), it is also suitable for smaller tanks. The general adaptation can be described as good. In hard water, growth is moderate and the life span is shorter. Observe a rest period. It is best to store the rhizome in damp sand. Propagation: spike is self-sterile, may also cross with other species, fruit production is modest, rearing seedlings is not easy.

D: 2, **KH**: 2-10, **pH**: 6.0-7.2, **T**: 22-26° C (72-79° F), **AH**: 1-3

Aponogeton bernieranus

Aponogeton crispus

Aponogeton elongatus forma *elongatus*

Aponogeton elongatus F. von MUELLER ex BENTHAM (1878)
forma *longifolius* VAN BRUGGEN (1969) Long-Leaved Swordplant

Fam.: Aponogetonaceae

Distribution: North and east Australia, northwestern Australia.
Although the general requirements are not demanding, this long-leaved form does not necessarily make a good aquarium plant. The light green to yellow-green blade is 40-60 cm (16"-24") long, up to 2 cm (3/4") wide, base elongated downward, tip short, pointed, and obtuse, edge slightly undulate. From the wide midrib, 2 pairs of weak side veins emerge and proceed to the tip. The petiole is elongated, often the same length as the blade. A 10 cm (4") long, simple yellow spike is produced. With its extremely long leaves, this form is suitable for the background of tall aquaria. Not recommended for aquaria of normal height as the leaves will lie less decorative and bent beneath the water surface. Repeated transplanting in succession can slow growth and lead to shorter leaves for a time. After sufficient root growth, however, they return to their original length. Through removal of the exterior leaves the impetuous sprouting can be kept in check. Propagation: spike self-sterile, fruiting is modest and seedling raising is difficult.

D: 2, **KH**: 2-15, **pH**: 6.0-7.5, **T**: 22-26° C (72-79° F), **AH**: 3

Aponogeton loriae MARTELLI (1897)

Fam.: Aponogetonaceae

Distribution: New Guinea, north Australia
Some authors assume that *A. loriae* does not represent a species but a morph of *A. elongatus*. However, the spathe of the inflorescence does not fall off (as with *A. elongatus*). It dries progressively and remains hanging on the base. The light green or sometimes light reddish blade is 10-25 cm (4"-9 3/4") long, 2-3 cm (3/4"-1 1/4") wide with both ends acute and a weakly undulate edge. The 2 pairs of lateral veins branch off the midrib at about the middle of the leaf. The tuber is round, smooth, light brown and up to 1 cm (1/3") thick. The spike is simple, about 10 cm (4") long, yellow-green, loosely flowered. An extremely rare species in the hobby and in nature. This small plant is well suited for the shallow aquarium. According to experience, cultivation is not very easy and remains confined to soft water. Although the species occurs in calcium containing waters in its natural biotope, growth in hard water is only moderately possible. The resting period is somewhat difficult to fulfill because the tuber rots easily. Propagation: inflorescence self-sterile, fruit formation is moderate, seedling rearing not always successful.

D: 4, **KH**: 2-8, **pH**: 6.0-7.0, **T**: 22-26° C (72-79° F), **AH**: 1-2

Aponogeton madagascariensis (Mirbel) VAN BRUGGEN (1968)
var. *guillotii* (HOCHREUTINER) JUMELLE (1936) Narrow-Leaved Laceplant

Fam.: Aponogetonaceae Syn.: *Aponogeton guilotii*

Distribution: Madagascar
The older literature identifies this plant erroneously as *A. bernierianus*. That is a different species without lattice structure. Nomenclature of this variety is quite extensive. The plant was first described in 1908 by HOCHREUTINER as *A. guillotii* then in 1936 by JUMELLE a as variety of *A. fenestralis*. Though VAN BRUGGEN does not recognize the variety, the author is not of this opinion. Leaves are narrowly lanceolate, dark green, up to 25 cm (9 3/4") long, 3 cm (1 1/4") wide with an elongated base, obtuse tip and a sinuate edge. 5-7 longitudinal veins are present with tightly spaced cross-veins. In between the venation, leaf tissue is missing, creating narrow slits. The inflorescence has 3-5 spikes up to 12 cm (4 3/4") long, pink and densely flowered. This narrow-leaved lace plant grows remarkably better than the broad-leaved main form (see Atlas, Vol. 1, page 130) in an aquarium. Especially notable is the adaptation to harder water and medium illumination intensities. This interesting plant has proven itself to be a good subject for the normal community tank. Propagation: inflorescence self-pollinating, numerous fruit, seedling rearing difficult.

D: 2, **KH**: 2-12, **pH**: 5.5-7.2, **T**: 22-26° C (72-79° F), **AH**: 2-3

Aponogeton elongatus forma longifolius

Aponogeton madagascariensis var. *guillotii*

Aponogeton loriae

Aponogeton natans (LINNAEUS) ENGLER et KRAUSE (1906) Drifting Swordplant

Fam.: Aponogetonaceae

Distribution: Sri Lanka, India, east Australia
Aquatic leaves are medium to dark green, short-stalked, 15-20 cm (6"-8") long, 2-3 cm (3/4"-1 1/4") wide, sometimes smaller (8 x 2 cm; 3" x 3/4"), base acute-rounded, tip with a short point, edge weakly sinuate. Out of the base emerge the midrib and 3 pairs of finer side veins. Floating leaves are lanceolate, 8-12 cm (3"-4 3/4") long, 2-3 cm (3/4"-1 1/4") wide with a cordate base. The tuber is smooth, light brown, roundish and 1-2 cm (1/3"-3/4") thick. Spikes are simple, up to 15 cm (6") long, densely flowered, reddish-purple or, less commonly, white. Apparently, there are hybrids (perhaps with *A. crispus*) whose aquatic leaves are more permanent and less floating leaves are grown. Flowers of these hybrids are sterile and bear pseudofruit without germinating seeds. In general, a difficult plant which is conditionally recommendable for the home aquarium. Often, a few crooked, short-lived aquatic leaves grow and then long-stalked floating leaves soon follow. As a rule, both leaf types are grown alternately and floating leaves predominate later. Addition of CO_2 to the water promotes the formation of short-stalked leaves. Propagation: inflorescence self-fertilizing, numerous seeds, rearing not easy.

D: 4, **KH:** 2-8, **pH:** 6.0-6.8, **T:** 22-26° C (72-79° F), **AH:** 1-3

Aponogeton rigidifolius VAN BRUGGEN (1962)

Fam.: Aponogetonaceae

Distribution: Sri Lanka
Blades are dark green to brownish, somewhat hard and brittle, 30-50 cm (12"-20") long, 2-3 cm (3/4"-1 ") wide, both ends acute, edge usually smooth, rarely weakly undulate. This species does not form a tuber but an elongated creeping rhizome instead. The inflorescence is simple, about 15 cm (6") long, whitish-green and densely flowered. A rarely cultivated aquarium plant with special requirements. Does not adapt to higher water hardness; growth is only possible in rain water or other soft water with a low overall salt content. The substrate should be of clean, coarse sand without additives or moderately coarse gravel. Insert the rhizome shallowly in a free location. However, light should not penetrate too intensely, about 50 watts/100 l suffice. The formation of new leaves is moderate. The species is delicate when transplanted and growth continues slowly for a long time. With unfavorable conditions, leaves soon become spotty and curl downward. Propagation: lateral shoots on the rhizome. Inflorescence self-sterile, few fruits, rearing hardly possible.

D: 4, **KH:** 1-3, **pH:** 5.5-6.5, **T:** 22-26° C (72-79° F), **AH:** 2-3

Aponogeton undulatus ROXBURGH (1832)

Fam.: Aponogetonaceae

Distribution: Malay Peninsula
It is uncertain if this is a species. VAN BRUGGEN, who is a specialist on *Aponogeton*, would like to place the plant as a variety of *A. undulatus*. The bright green blade is almost transparent, slightly brittle and fragile, 20-30 cm (8"-12") long, 1 cm (1/3") wide with an acute base and an obtuse tip. The leaf is strongly undulate and twists several times. Out of the wide midrib 2 pairs of weaker side veins emerge. The tuber is spherical, brown, smooth, up to 7 mm (") thick. Inflorescence is simple, about 8 cm (3") long, white or greenish, loosely flowered. The spathe does not fall off. The peduncle usually carries an adventitious plant in the aquarium. This is a difficult plant which is not usually kept in aquaria. Imports are also extremely rare because the species is not common in nature. According to experience, it only grows healthy for extended amounts of time in soft water. The high light requirement should be observed. Under less intense light, the leaves do not grow twisted but are almost flat. Propagation: remove the adventitious plant with a few leaves from the peduncle.

D: 4, **KH:** 1-5, **pH:** 5.5-6.5, **T:** 22-26° C (72-79° F), **AH:** 1-2

Aponogeton natans

Aponogeton rigidifolius

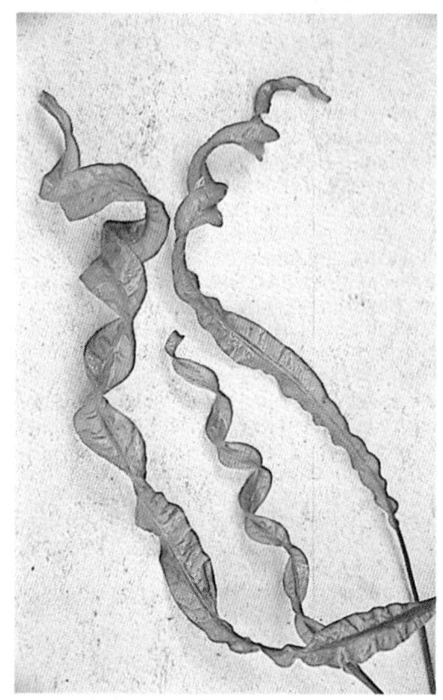

Aponogeton undulatus

In this group, there are over 60 species distributed in the Indomalayan area as perennial, amphibious bog and water plants. Some species of cryptocorynes inhabit the shores of sunny, mud bottomed, flowing waters. Many grow in small waters with sandy-gravel bottoms, often heavily shaded by tall shore vegetation. Still others live in swampy, slow-flowing waters. About 30 species are suitable for the aquarium, and include a number of problem plants. In general, there are about 20 relatively robust species. Soft water is usually preferred, but certain species tolerate higher carbonate hardness. A substrate temperature of 26-28° C (79-82° F) should, if possible, be provided (substrate heater). Cryptocorynes demand more attention in the aquarium, usually need a longer time to adapt and should not be transplanted frequently. Large changes in water values, temperatures, and illumination ought to be avoided; they usually lead to leaf damage and the feared cryptocoryne rot. Group planting is preferred. Those that are planted in a group usually grow better than those distributed singly. Propagation is accomplished through runners with one daughter plant, each creating an adapted and well-rooted specimen. Rate of propagation is species dependent. Submersed cryptocorynes are quite variable, making a description based on characteristics of aquatic leaves only a tentative method of species identification. Scientifically, cryptocorynes are identified following the characteristics of flower morphology; however, the formation of flowers is predominantly limited to land plants. Bog cultivation in a separate, shallow water aquaria is relatively uncomplicated with certain species. A few species also flower as water plants. Inflorescence have a standard morphology consisting of a peduncle, kettle, tube, and flag. The spadix proper is hidden in a kettle-like widening in the lower part. On the spadix base is a crown of female flowers; the male stamens are arranged in several circles above the female flowers. Above the kettle, the spathe narrows to a constricted tube whose length varies according to species and water level. On top of the duct is a flag that varies in shape, size, coloration and surface texture. Species specific characteristics result that are used in identification.

Cryptocoryne affinis, open kettle

Cryptocoryne affinis

Cryptocoryne albida

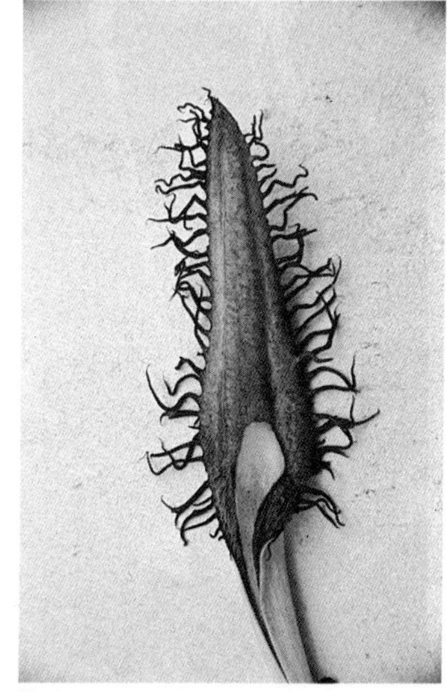
Cryptocoryne ciliata

Cryptocoryne beckettii

Cryptocoryne costata

Cryptocoryne walkeri, green

Cryptocoryne pontederiifolia

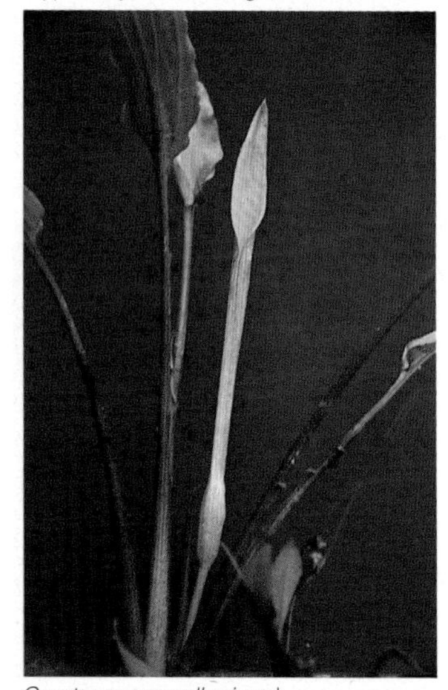

Cryptocoryne walkeri, red

Cryptocoryne purpurea

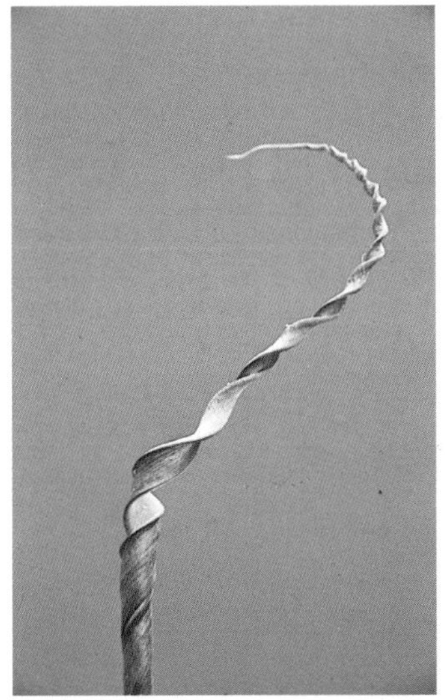
Cryptocoryne crispatula

Cryptocoryne undulata

Cryptocoryne spiralis

Cryptocoryne wendtii

Cryptocoryne albida PARKER (1931)

Fam.: Araceae

Distribution: Burma, Thailand
De Wit erroneously identified this species as a variety of *C. retrospiles*; the description as *C. korthausae*, by RATAJ, is not accepted. JACOBSEN determined that the species *C. costata* GAGNEPAIN (brown leaves) is identical to *C. albida*. This is a small bog plant with light green to brownish aerial leaves that are narrowly lanceolate, undulate edged, 5-13 cm (2"-5") long, 1.0-1.5 cm (1/3"-2/3") wide and have an acute base and tip. Spathe 7-10 cm (2 3/4"-4") long, flag 3-4 cm (1 1/4"-1 2/3") long, flat towards the back rolled crosswise, white with purple spots, throat equally colored, without collar. Aquatic leaves are slender, almost linear, 15-20 cm (6"-8") long, 0.5-1.0 cm (1/4"-1/3") wide, both ends evenly acute and green on both sides without striations. Because of its inconspicuous foliage, the plant is rarely cultivated. Adaptation to submersed life is moderate and only possible within a narrow range of living conditions. A moderate light intensity of 30 watts/100 l seems to be more important. Under stronger illumination, problems with growth are to be expected. They manifest themselves through curly leaf edges and constantly smaller leaves. In addition, cultivation over an extended amount of time is only possible in soft water with low carbonate hardness. An interesting plant for the connoisseur. Grows well and flowers easily in the bog aquarium. Propagation: moderate runner formation after good adaptation.

D: 4, **KH:** 2-6, **pH:** 6.0-6.8, **T:** 22-28° C (72-82° F), **AH:** 1-3

Cryptocoryne beckettii THWAITES ex TRIMEN (1885) Beckett's Cryp

Fam.: Araceae

Distribution: Sri Lanka
This was one of the first species of the genus used in aquaria. It was imported for the first time in 1906, but it is rarely cultivated. It is a small, amphibious bog plant in nature. Aerial leaves are elongate, oval, olive-green, 6-8 cm (2 1/3"-3") long, 2-3 cm (3/4"-1 ") wide with a pointed tip and a base that is often unequal (crooked). Spathe 8-10 cm (3"-4") long, flag 3-4 cm (1 "-1 2/3"), the lower edges jagged, yellow, throat and collar are purple. Well suited for the bog aquarium and quite willing to flower as a swamp plant. Aquatic leaves are lanceolate, 8-12 cm (3"-4 3/4") long, 2-3 cm (3/4"-1 ") wide, relatively short-stalked, smooth edged with a rounded to cordate base and a short pointed tip. The whole leaf is often bent slightly backwards. The upperside of the leaf is olive-green to brownish; the reverse side is red or green with a reddish tinge. Depending on density and light penetration, height in an aquarium is 10-15 cm (4"-6"), thereby making the plant ideally suited for the foreground. However, growth is relatively moderate, and adventitious plants are only grown by well adapted specimens. Due to short runners, the young plants grow close to the mother plant, forming a compact, leafy cluster. Sufficient warmth with nutrient-rich substrate noticeably stimulates growth. It has an intermediate light requirement of 50 watts/100 l. Propagation: moderate production of adventitious plants.

D: 2, **KH:** 2-15, **pH:** 6.5-7.5, **T:** 25-28° C (77-82° F), **AH:** 1-3

Cryptocoryne albida

Cryptocoryne beckettii

Cryptocoryne blassii DE WIT (1960) — Giant Cryp

Fam.: Araceae — Syn.: *C. kerrii*

Distribution: Thailand
It is suspected that this species is only a variety of *C. siamensis*. Rataj calls it *C. siamensis* var. *kerrii*, but JACOBSEN places it as a race of the *C. cordata* group. The same also applies to *C. siamensis*. In nature, this is a typical water plant which endures dry periods in a prostrate, stunted form. Spathe up to 8 cm (4") long, flag 3 cm (1 "), inclined, flat, shiny, yellow, throat without collar. Aquatic leaves are wide, ovate, sometimes having a tubercular structure, 10-15 cm (4"-6") long and 4-6 cm (1²/3"-2¹/3") wide. The upper surface is reddish-brown, occasionally greening and often has a dark design. Underside is dark red with blackish striations. A liked and sought after cryptocoryne that develops numerous large leaves when planted alone. Under favorable conditions, a multileaved group will grow with adventitious plants. In dense stands, longer stalks produce taller growth. However, significant problems occur in adapting plants from very soft water with low conductivity. Only after sufficient acclimation will these wild plants grow well with medium water hardness values. Patience is necessary. The fertile substrate should be well heated; coarse-grained material can be used. Propagation: adventitious plants, they can be quite numerous on well-rooted specimens.

D: 2, KH: 2-10, pH: 5.5-7.2, T: 25-28° C (77-82° F), AH: 1-3

Cryptocoryne bullosus BECCARI (1877) — Blistered Cryp

Fam.: Araceae

Distribution: Borneo
The more gibbous specimens of *C. affinis* are frequently offered under this name. However, they revert back to their typical leaf shape (whitish midrib) in an aquarium. The aquatic plant develops an emerse stunted form in nature. Spathe 4 cm (1²/3") long, flag 2 cm (³/4"), straight, purple, throat lighter without distinct collar. *C. scurrilis* DE WIT, 1962 probably belongs to this species; therefore, it should be named *C. bullosa* var. *scurrilis* RATAJ, 1975. Flag yellow with red throat. Aquatic leaves are broadly lanceolate, strongly bullate, 8-10 cm (3"-4") long, 3-4 cm (1 "-1²/3") wide with a slight cordate base and a gradually narrowing, blunt tip. Upperside of the leaf is dark green to blood red; underside is reddish but greening. The veins are paler, but the midrib remains reddish. A rare, sporadically imported, aquarium plant with special requirements and a narrow range of living conditions. According to experience, care demands very soft water and a low pH. The typical bullate leaf structure is maintained only with sufficient illumination. Even with good conditions—nutrient rich and loose bottom sand—growth is not perennial. The new leaves are consistently smaller until the plant finally stops developing after a more or less extended period of growth. Propagation: adventitious plants are rare.

D: 4, KH: 1-3, pH: 5.5-6.5, T: 24-28° C (75-82° F), AH: 1-3

Cryptocoryne blassii

Cryptocoryne bullosus

Cryptocoryne costata GAGNEPAIN (1941)

Fam.: Araceae Syn.: *C. hansenii*

Distribution: Thailand

The species has also been described as *C. retrospiralis* var. *costata* (GAGNEPAIN) DE WIT, 1966; it was then again named *C. hansenii* S.Y. HU, 1968. This small bog plant has lanceolate aerial leaves which become 9-11 cm (3 "-4$^1/_3$") long, 1.0-1.5 cm ($^1/_3$"-$^2/_3$") wide, pointed at both ends and have a weak undulate edge. The dark brown upperside of the leaf has a dark design. The spathe is 9 cm (3 ") long, flag 4 cm (1$^2/_3$"), wider than the tube, straight, smooth, top with a short tail and twisted, whitish with red spots, throat same color without collar. Submersed leaves are narrowly lanceolate, almost even edged, 10-12 cm (4"-4$^3/_4$") long, up to 1 cm ($^1/_3$") wide, taper towards the base and have a short pointed tip. Top is brown-red with a dark design; underside is light brown. Decorative low plant; suitable for the foreground of shallow, intensely illuminated tanks. Cultivation as an aquatic plant is quite difficult and can only be achieved in soft, slightly acid water. Slow leaf formation can be improved with rich, warm substrate. Maintaining this species as a bog plant in a bog or special aquarium has proven to be less problematic. It grows and propagates well; however, the development of flowers requires bright light and moderately high temperatures. Propagation: adventitious plants are slow and moderate growing in an aquarium.

D: 3, KH: 2-5, pH: 5.5-6.5, T: 25-28° C (77-82° F), AH: 1-2

Cryptocoryne ferruginea ENGLER (1879)

Fam.: Araceae

Syn.: *C. sarawacensis, C. pontederiifolia* var. *sarawacensis*

Distribution: Malaysia, Sarawak

Was described under the synonyms by JACOBSEN (1) and RATAJ (2) erroneously. JACOBSEN found flowering plants in their natural habitat and recognized it as the previously described *C. ferruginea*. The blade is wide, ovate-round, 6-8 cm (2$^1/_3$"-3") long, 3-5 cm (1 "-2") wide, slightly bullate with a sinuous edge, a pointed tip and a cordate base. Three pairs of lateral veins emerge from the midrib and two pairs originate from the base. In between are arched cross-veins that form a dark green pattern in young leaves. Aerial leaves are similar but have a pilose underside. Flower spathe is like *C. pontederiifolia*. A demanding aquarium plant for soft water with low pH. With higher carbonate hardness, new leaves emerge progressively smaller, making a displeasing degenerate form. Light requirement is average; nutrient-rich bottom sand is recommended. Plant in the foreground and let the plant grow undisturbed. A compact rosette will result. Allow for several specimens arranged in a loose group so the plants can develop undisturbed. Propagation: moderate development of adventitious plants.

D: 3, KH: 2-8, pH: 5.8-6.8, T: 24-26° C (75-79° F), AH: 1-3

Cryptocoryne costata

Cryptocoryne ferruginea

Cryptocoryne fusca DE WIT (1970)

Fam.: Araceae Syn.: *C. longicauda, C. tortilis*

Distribution: Borneo

Nomenclature for the plant is confusing. It was previously called *C. longicauda*, but then it was redescribed as *C. tortilis* by De Wit. The former *C. johorensis* is now *C. longicauda*. However, JACOBSEN determined that *C. tortilis* and *C. fusca* are the same species. This prostrate bog plant rarely grows submersed. Aerial leaves are ovate, 10-20 cm (4"-8") long, 6-15 cm (2¹/₃"-6") wide, somewhat fleshy, grass green with an irregular gibbous upper surface. Spathe 18-25 cm long, flag 10-15 cm, very slender, twisted corkscrew-like, open in a slender slit, inside warty, purple-red, throat similarly colored, without collar. Aquatic leaves broadly ovate, somewhat bullate, solid green, 10-15 cm (4"-6") long, 6-10 cm (2¹/₃"-4") wide with a slightly cordate base and an obtuse tip. The leaves are bent to the substrate, sometimes even lying on the ground, forming a uniform, flat rosette. To accentuate the distinctive growth pattern, the plant is cultivated singly in an open space. Strong illumination is detrimental, and according to experience, a value to 30 watts/100 l is totally sufficient in a small aquarium. Shade bright tanks with floating plants. The plant is delicate when transplanting and acclimating but has no other special problems. The upper layer of the substrate should be of medium gravel (3-5 mm; ¹/₈"-³/₁₆" diameter); provide warm substrate. Propagation: adventitious plants on older plants.

D: 3, KH: 2-12, pH: 6.0-7.2, T: 24-28° C (75-82° F), AH: 1-3

Cryptocoryne walkeri SCHOTT (1857), green Walker's Cryp

Fam.: Araceae Syn.: *C. legroi*

Distribution: Sri Lanka

This species, *C. lutea* and *C. walkeri* are quite similar. According to DE WIT, they are closely related and could be varieties of one species. RATAJ describes them as varieties of *C. walkeri* and calls this plant *C. walkeri* var. *legroi*. JACOBSEN also places the species into the group *C. walkeri* but without giving it variety status. This small bog plant grows near water courses. Aerial leaves are 10-15 cm (4"-6") long, 4-6 cm (1²/₃"-2¹/₃") wide, sometimes gibbous with an olive-green to dark green upper surface and a lower side that is usually red. Spathe 8-10 cm (3"-4") long, flag 3-4 cm (1 "-1²/₃"), erect, upper part somewhat bent back, edge downward bent, light yellow to greenish yellow, throat lighter with thin collar. Aquatic leaves are short-stalked, broadly lanceolate, 10-12 cm (4"-4³/₄") long, 2-3 cm (³/₄"-1 ") wide with a round to cordate base and a short pointed, often skewed tip. Upperside of the leaf is olive-green to brownish; underside is reddish. With its low growth, the species can be used as a small group in the foreground. It develops numerous durable leaves when planted alone, but growth is moderate. Submersed plants may occasionally develop an inflorescence, but the spathe remains closed. General acclimation is relatively good. The aquarium form does not develop many runners. This species is not particularly sensitive when transplanting and is less prone than others to leaf rot. Propagation: moderate formation of adventitious plants and only on sufficiently rooted mother plants.

D: 2, KH: 2-12, pH: 6.0-7.2, T: 22-28° C (72-82° F), AH: 1-3

Cryptocoryne fusca

Cryptocoryne walkeri, green

Cryptocoryne lingua BECCARI ex ENGLER (1879) Tongue-Shaped Cryp

Fam.: Araceae Syn.: *C. spathulata*

Distribution: Borneo

A simultaneously published, invalid name for *C. lingua* is *C. spathulata* BECCARI ex ENGLER, 1879. The description was based only on different shaped leaves, but the flowers of both "species" are the same. Small amphibious bog plant whose aquatic and aerial leaves are not markedly different. Spathe 7 cm (2³/₄") long, flag 4 cm (1²/₃"), dark purple, throat bright yellow, without collar, upper part tail-like elongate and laterally positioned. Leaves are elongate, shaped like a tongue, green, thick, fleshy, 3-5 cm (1 "-2") long, 1.5-2.5 cm (²/₃"-1") wide with a wedge shaped base, a short pointed tip and an even edge. 7 to 9 longitudinal veins emerge from the base without a clear midrib. Small plant for the foreground; however, it does not grow satisfactorily in an aquarium. Remains green for extended periods of time submersed but producing smaller leaves until it dies after a more or less extended growth period. With strong lighting (100 watts/100 l) and soft water, this negative reaction is delayed. Grows as a swamp plant in the bog aquarium, but it is a difficult plant there also. Requires rich, marshy substrate and bright light. Propagation: strong specimens sometimes grow adventitious plants.

D: 4, **KH:** 2-10, **pH:** 5.5-6.5, **T:** 22-26° C (72-79° F), **AH:** 1-2

Cryptocoryne longicauda BECCARI ex ENGLER (1879)

Fam.: Araceae Syn.: *C. johorensis*

Distribution: Malay Peninsula, Borneo, Johor

Flat growing bog plant. Aerial leaves are similar to submersed leaves but have small serrations. Spathe up to 25 cm (9³/₄") long, flag 15 cm (6"), straight, wine red, long-tailed, throat lighter colored with collar. Leaves are ovate, 10-12 cm (4"-4³/₄") long, 5-7 cm (2"-2³/₄") wide, dark green on both sides, rarely slightly bullate with a cordate base and a somewhat long pointed tip. The petiole is normally the same length as the blade; leaves are usually held upright. Previously called *C. johorensis*, but that name has been withdrawn. To distinguish it from the similar *C. fusca*, note its horizontal, wider, foveated leaves with shorter stalks. Depending on living conditions, the aquarium plant reaches a height of 15-20 cm (6"-8") and is suitable for the central areas of the decoration. This is a rare species with a limited capability of adapting to higher water hardness. Well acclimated and rooted specimens make several runners which develop their daughter plants near the mother plant. A decorative dense plant group develops. In regard to illumination, the plant's needs can be considered modest; exaggerated lighting is detrimental and can disrupt proper growth. Propagation: daughter plant production is satisfactory and growth is relatively fast.

D: 3, **KH:** 2-6, **pH:** 6.0-7.0, **T:** 24-28° C (75-82° F), **AH:** 1-3

Cryptocoryne lingua

Cryptocoryne longicauda

Cryptocoryne walkeri SCHOTT (1857), red

Fam.: Araceae

Distribution: Sri Lanka
According to RATAJ, this plant is *C. walkeri* var. *lutea*, not an autonomous species. JACOBSEN places the species into the *C. walkeri* group but without variety status. An amphibious bog plant. The aerial leaves are elongate-lanceolate, up to 10 cm (4") long, 2 cm (3/4") wide with a round base and a short pointed tip. The leaf edge is normally wavy and somewhat curled in the lower part. The upperside is dark green, and the underside is reddish. Spathe 8-12 cm (3"-4 3/4") long, flag 3.5 cm (1 1/3"), smooth, straight and yellow. Throat yellow with a very thin collar. Submersed leaves are lanceolate and more undulate towards the base. The blade is 8-12 cm (3"-4 3/4") long, 1-2 cm (1/3"-3/4") wide with a weakly rounded base and a slender, long pointed tip. The upper surface is dark green, and the lower side is lighter. The area around the protruding veins is often a light reddish color. It is a good decoration for the foreground due to its low growth. Solitary plants placed in the open grow many durable leaves, creating a decorative bush. In dense groups, growth is weaker and outer leaves are shed more often. Nutrient rich substrate significantly improves its growth rate. The light requirement of 30-50 watts/100 l is moderate. Adapts to harder water and rarely develops the feared leaf rot. Propagation: sparse runners, more numerous in well adapted and rooted specimens.

D: 2, **KH:** 2-15, **pH:** 6.0-7.5, **T:** 22-28° C (72-82° F), **AH:** 1-2

Cryptocoryne moehlmannii DE WIT (1979) Möhlmann's Cryp

Fam.: Araceae

Distribution: West Sumatra
This new species was only discovered in 1977 and is still quite rare in aquaria. Based on the easy adaptation and breeding, this is likely to change. Named after L. Möhlmann, a renowned breeder of cryptocorynes. Spathe up to 4 cm (1 2/3") long, flag 2 cm (3/4"), pointed, angled, purple, warty, throat equally colored, smooth, collar present. Submersed and emersed leaves are almost equally shaped. The petioles grow to 10 cm (4") long. The lamina is broadly lanceolate, 8-12 cm (3"-4 3/4") long, 4-5 cm wide with weakly undulant edges and a cordate base. Three pairs of lateral veins originate from the base and two pairs from the midrib. Both sides of the leaf are uniform green, occasionally slightly gibbous. The similar *C. pontederiifolia* has a reddish underside, a somewhat gibbous blade and a longer, drawn out tip. This compact solitary plant grows numerous leaves and a voluminous rosette results, creating a focus for the mid area of the aquarium. Grows well when its requirements are met; thrives in soft to medium-hard water under strong illumination. With higher carbonate hardness, the plant benefits from the addition of CO_2. However, it has problems in very hard water. Propagation: adventitious plants readily develop.

D: 2, **KH:** 2-10, **pH:** 6.0-6.8, **T:** 25-28° C (77-82° F), **AH:** 1-3

Cryptocoryne walkeri, red

Cryptocoryne moehlmannii

Cryptocoryne parva DE WIT (1970) Tiny Cryp

Fam.: Araceae

Distribution: Sri Lanka
DE WIT described the species based on cultivated plants discovered in a larger stand of *C. willisii*. It was later found in nature, but the plant is not common. The tiny bog plants grow at the edge of small flowing waters, totally submersed in parts in a small copse. Aerial leaves are dark green, 2-3 cm (3/4"-1 ") long, up to 0.3 cm (1/8") wide with both ends obtuse. Spathe is up to 2.5 cm (1") long, flag 1 cm (1/3"), somewhat twisted, warty, dark purple, throat lighter with a thin collar. Aquatic leaves are narrowly lanceolate, 2-3 cm (3/4"-1 ") long and usually only to 0.2 cm (1/16") wide. The petiole is often longer than the blade and insignificantly narrower. Both sides are green, and the base and tip are acute. This "lawn" plant rarely grows taller than 2 cm (3/4") in an aquarium, thereby remaining significantly smaller than any other similar plant of the genus. Because of its low growth, the plant is ideal for the foreground, but its high light requirement will make its distribution in the aquarium trade sparse. The substrate should be clean, coarse sand with a nutrient rich sublayer. In its submersed state, this species is very similar to *C. willisii* which will surely be preferred due to its hardiness. A rewarding endeavor for the plant hobbyist interested in specialties. Propagation: daughter plants on short runners; production is quite satisfactory with well acclimated mother plants.

D: 3, **KH:** 2-10, **pH:** 6.0-7.0, **T:** 25-28° C (77-82° F), **AH:** 1-2

Cryptocoryne pontederiifolia SCHOTT (1863)

Fam.: Araceae Syn.: *C. sulphurea*

Distribution: Sumatra, Borneo
The species was erroneously redescribed as *C. sulphurea* DE WIT, 1976. A robust bog plant whose aerial leaves deviate insignificantly from the aquatic form. Shows a slight similarity to *C. ciliata* and *C. moehlmannii*. Spathe is up to 12 cm (4 3/4") long, flag about 9 cm (3 "), bright yellow, smooth. Throat is somewhat lighter and without a collar, the "tail" up to 5 cm (2") long. Leaves are broadly ovate, 8-12 cm (3"-4 3/4") long, 3-5 cm (1 "-2") wide, long tipped, with a cordate base and a smooth, bowl-like edge. The upper surface is green, slightly gibbous; underside is normally light pink between the main veins. 7 longitudinal veins emerge from the base. Both inner veins grow along the midrib for 2-3 cm (3/4"-1 "). Long leaf stalks develop on plants grown in weak light, making the plant relatively large and suitable for the middle areas or the sides. With sufficient illumination and free placement, a more compact form occurs. As with all cryptocorynes, repeated transplanting is detrimental and plants repeatedly disturbed tend to degenerate. General acclimation is quite good and medium water hardness is tolerated. With higher carbonate hardness, the addition of CO_2 is recommended; the plant reacts extraordinarily. Propagation: daughter plants are quite numerous after sufficient acclimation.

D: 2, **KH:** 2-10, **pH:** 6.0-7.2, **T:** 22-26° C (72-79° F), **AH:** 2-3

Cryptocoryne parva

Cryptocoryne pontederiifolia

Cryptocoryne schulzei DE WIT (1972) Schulze's Cryp

Fam.: Araceae

Distribution: Malay Peninsula, Johor
The plant was discovered in 1970 by Professor Dr. Schulze and named after him. Has remained quite rare, but it is probably being grown in aquaria without it being recognized. Small, amphibious bog plant that grows near water courses. Aerial leaves have longer stalks, an 8-10 cm (3"-4") long and 2 cm (3/4") wide blade that is predominantly green with a dark green cross design. Spathe 7-9 cm (2 3/4"-3 ") long, flag about 2.5 cm (1"), straight, warty, with a "tail", inside yellow, throat purple, collar darker. Aquatic leaves are lanceolate, 5-7 cm (2"-2 3/4") long, 1.5-2.0 cm (2/3"-3/4") wide with a faintly undulating edge, a rounded base and a short arched, pointed tip. The top of the leaf is brownish to deep red with dark cross figurations; lower side is light brown. The leaves tend to be green with a dark midrib and a slight design when very dim light is used. The foreground plant grows to a height of about 10 cm (4"), but it can grow taller in dense groups. With its colored leaves, the small, solitary plant serves as a effective contrast among other short, green plants. Evidence has shown that the light should not be too strong, below 50 watts/100 l. If needed, provide shade with a thin cover of floating plants. The remaining needs can be easily met. The plant can be also grown in harder water (with the addition of CO_2). Propagation: moderate production of adventitious plants and only on mother plants acclimated over longer periods of time.

D: 2, **KH:** 2-12, **pH:** 6.0-7.2, **T:** 24-28° C (75-82° F), **AH:** 1-3

Cryptocoryne spiralis (RETZIUS) FISCHER ex WYDLER (1830) Spiral Cryp

Fam.: Araceae

Distribution: India
This 40 cm (16") tall bog plant grows for extended periods of time in water in its native habitat. Aerial leaves are linear, up to 25 cm (10") long, 1.5 cm (2/3") wide, light green, with a few dark cross-veins, a broad midrib and slender side veins. Spathe is about 15 cm (6") long, almost without tube, flag up to 13 cm (5") long, twisted, terminating in a point, inside has warty cross channels, purple, without throat, without collar. Aquatic leaves are almost linear, 10-20 cm (4"-8") long, 0.5-0.8 cm (1/4"-1/3") wide with both ends pointed and narrowing uniformly, edge weakly undulate or smooth. Upperside is brown-red with dark striations, sometimes also green; underside is lighter with reddish edges. The fuller solitary specimen plant generally reaches about 20 cm (8") height but usually remains shorter in an open place. When planted in a group, the plants tend to grow taller. The strong, extensive root system indicates that a fertile substrate is required. The bottom should be loosely structured and not be made of coarse gravel. Grows best in soft to medium-hard water; grows satisfactorily in very hard water when CO_2 is added. Can easily be cultivated as a bog plant, flowering regularly and growing numerous adventitious plants which grow in aquaria without problems. Propagation: the aquarium form grows daughter plants only as an exception.

D: 3, **KH:** 2-12, **pH:** 5.8-7.2, **T:** 24-28° C (75-82° F), **AH:** 1-3

Cryptocoryne schulzei

Cryptocoryne spiralis

Cryptocoryne crispatula ENGLER (1920)

Fam.: Araceae

Distribution: Vietnam

The opinions of what species the plant belongs to are divergent. DE WIT calls the plant *C. retrospiralis* var. *tonkinensis*. JACOBSEN places the species as a race of *C. crispatula*. Has been found in flowing water of the Baatai River at the foot of Mount Bavin of Balansa in Tonkin. An amphibious water plant that develops a small land form with tough aerial leaves during droughts. Depending on water level, the spathe will be 10-25 cm (4"-10") long, flag 5 cm (2"), the front twisted like a corkscrew, inside light olive-green to soft pink, dark speckled, throat the same color, without collar. Aquatic leaves are linear 15-20 (40) cm (4"-8" (16")) long, 0.3-0.6 (1.0) cm (1/8"-1/3" (1/3")) wide. An extremely narrow-leaved variation with dark green to reddish brown and spotted grass-like blades is pictured. The species is rarely offered in the trade and is one of the special varieties of aquarium flora. With its very slender, inconspicuous leaves, this cryptocoryne is not particularly noticeable and will only keep the interest of specialty plant breeders. According to experience, soft water is recommended and the illumination can be in the 50-70 watts/100 l range. Decorative as a loose group in the central areas of the aquarium. The optical effect can be improved with contrasting plants. Do not transplant unnecessarily. Propagation: moderate formation of daughter plants.

D: 3, **KH:** 2-8 **pH:** 5.5-6.8, **T:** 24-28° C (75-82° F), **AH:** 1-3

Cryptocoryne undulata WENDT (1955) — Undulate Cryp

Fam.: Araceae — Syn.: *C. willisii, C. axelrodii*

Distribution: Sri Lanka

The original description as *C. willisii* ENGLER ex BAUM, 1909 is a homonym already published in 1908 for *C. nevillii*. Although WENDT states the color of the flag incorrectly, the description remains valid because, according to JACOBSEN , a particular species was clearly intended. Therefore, the description by RATAJ as *C. axelrodii* (1975) is invalid. Small, amphibious bog plant, aerial leaves are medium green, lanceolate, 8-12 cm (3"-4 3/4") long, 1-2 cm (1/3"-3/4") wide with a base that is usually rounded and a pointed tip. Spathe is 8-12 cm (3"-4 3/4") long, flag 3 cm (1 1/4"), twisted, pale brown, throat whitish, collar darker with bright upper rim. Aquatic leaves are narrowly lanceolate, 8-12 cm (3"-4 3/4") long and 0.5-0.8 cm (1/4"-1/2") wide. Both ends of the leaf are tapered; the tip is pointed; the edge is wavy to curly; both sides are deep red and the upperside has a dark slanted design. With weak illumination, the leaves become green and the rhizome often grows vertical, stilt-like into the water column. A group plant that can grow 10-20 cm (4"-8") high, depending on density. Generally adapts well, and strong lighting produces deep red plants with excellent contrast effect. Through intense propagation, an extensive stand develops which should be thinned periodically. The plant easily develops leaf rot when water, light or temperature change significantly over a short time. However, if the healthy rhizomes remain undisturbed in the substrate, new leaves are grown. Propagation: numerous, rapid growing adventitious plants.

D: 1, **KH:** 2-15, **pH:** 5.5-7.5, **T:** 22-28° C (72-82° F), **AH:** 1-3

Cryptocoryne crispatula

Cryptocoryne undulata

Cryptocoryne wendtii DE WIT (1958), brown — Wendt's Cryp

Fam.: Araceae

Distribution: Sri Lanka
Was imported for the first time to Germany about 1970. Small amphibious bog plant possessing aerial leaves that are 6-8 cm (2 1/3"-3") long, 1-2 cm (1/3"-3/4") wide, olive-green to red-brown with fine reddish veins, a rounded base and a pointed tip. Leaf texture is somewhat gibbous at times. Spathe is 5-7 cm (2"-2 3/4") long, flag 2-3 cm (3/4"-1 1/4") long, erect, slightly twisted, purple, throat dark violet, collar darker. Aquatic leaves are 8-12 cm (3"-4 3/4") long and 0.8-1.2 cm (1/3"-1/2") wide. The lamina narrows uniformly towards the tip, has a short, pointed tip and a rounded base. The broadest part of the leaf is near the base. The edge is thin and tightly undulate but is almost smooth under weak light. Upperside is deep red to brown-red with a dark black-green cross pattern; lower side is red to brown. Although the leaves are less colored under weaker light, they do not become totally green. Depending on density and light penetration, height is 10-20 cm (4"-8"). Therefore, the plant can be placed as a group in the foreground or middle areas. This species is less sensitive when transplanting and usually continues to grow speedily and adapts well to a variety of conditions. The most favorable light value is 50 watts/100 l. Through numerous adventitious plants, a dense stand results which is occasionally thinned. A beautiful contrast against other light-green plants. To differentiate this variety from the following, pay attention to the widest part of the leaf and the length to width ratio of the blade. Propagation: adventitious plants grow quite well.

D: 1, KH: 2-15, pH: 6.0-7.2, T: 25-28° C (77-82° F), AH: 1-3

Cryptocoryne wendtii DE WIT (1958) (var. *krauteri* RATAJ, 1975) — Krauter's Cryp

Fam.: Araceae

Distribution: Sri Lanka
This variety was imported occasionally in 1955 with the nominate form (*C. w.* var. *wendtii*, see Aquarium Atlas Vol. 1, pages 136-137). A low growing amphibious bog plant. Aerial leaves are oblong, 10-12 cm (4"-4 3/4") long, 2.0-3.5 cm (3/4"-1 1/3") wide with a short pointed base, an undulate edge and a blade that has a slightly gibbous texture. Upperside is either olive-green, red-brown or pink. Spathe is 7-9 cm (2 3/4"-3 1/2") long, flag 2-3 cm (3/4"-1 1/4"), erect, slightly twisted, purple, throat dark violet, collar darker. Aquatic leaves are 10-15 cm (4"-6") long, 2-3 cm (3/4"-1 1/4") wide with a rounded base, a short pointed tip and a densely undulate to curly edge. The blade is widest at the middle. The coloration is olive-green to deep red with a clear, dark cross design on the upperside and a brown lower side. Note the similarity to variety *jahnelii*. The submersed leaf shape is only slightly different from the nominate type. The difference lies mainly in its dark coloration which is maintained under moderate light. The acclimation to various water values is good and the formation of adventitious plants is fast and numerous. In a loose stand, the plants grow to a height of about 15 cm (6"). When planted denser, it grows longer stalks and reaches a height of 30 cm (12"). Because of its susceptibility to leaf rot, short term marked changes in light intensity and water values should be avoided. Not particularly sensitive when transplanted and quickly resumes rapid growth. Propagation: numerous, fast growing adventitious plants.

D: 2, KH: 2-15, pH: 6.0-7.5, T: 22-30° C (72-86° F), AH: 1-3

Cryptocoryne wendtii, brown

Cryptocoryne wendtii (var. *krauteri*)

Cryptocoryne wendtii DE WIT (1958) (var. *nana* RATAJ, 1975)

Fam.: Araceae Syn.: *C. wendtii* var. *minima*

Distribution: Sri Lanka

Imported for the first time in 1963 under the above named synonym. Small bog plant whose aerial leaves are 3-5 cm (1¼"-2") long, 1.0-1.5 cm (⅓"-⅔") wide with a blunt to somewhat rounded base, green upperside with a faint design and an olive-green underside. Spathe 4-5 cm (1⅔"-2") long, flag 1.5 cm (⅔"), erect, slightly twisted, purple, throat dark violet, collar darker. Aquatic leaves are lanceolate, 4-6 cm (1⅔"-2⅓") long, 0.8-1.2 cm (⅓"-½") wide, with a round or slightly cordate base, a long pointed tip and an undulate edge. Coloration of the upperside is dark green to brown-red, depending on light intensity. The cross design is faint or nonexistent; the veins are mostly reddish or pink; the stalk is of equal length or shorter than the blade. With a height of 6-10 cm (2⅓"-4"), this variety is excellent for the foreground. These plants are not especially sensitive and acclimate well when transplanted. Due to numerous short runners, a thicket develops with time. This can be kept loose by removing plants and using them to expand the group. Care is best achieved under medium-strong light of 50 watts/100 l. Under weak illumination, the plants remain loose, become longer stalked, are often solid green and are no longer representative of the species. Cannot always be readily differentiated from the variety below. As a distinguishing feature, pay special attention to the either mostly absent or only faintly present cross-design on the leaf of the var. *nana*. Propagation: numerous, rapid growing adventitious plants.

D: 2, **KH**: 2-12, **pH**: 6.0-7.2, **T**: 22-28° C (72-82° F), **AH**: 1-3

Cryptocoryne wendtii DE WIT (1958) (var. *rubella* RATAJ, 1975)

Fam.: Araceae Syn.: *C. rubella*

Distribution: Sri Lanka

Became known in 1963 when it was imported as *C. rubella*. Small bog plant with aerial leaves that are 5-7 cm (2"-2¾") long, 1.5-2.0 cm (⅔"-¾") wide and have a brown-green to red-brown upperside with a dark pattern. Spathe up to 5 cm (2") long, flag up to 1.8 cm (¾"), erect, somewhat twisted, purple, throat dark violet, collar darker. Submersed leaves are lanceolate, 4-6 cm (1⅔"-2⅓") long, 0.8-1.0 cm (⅓") wide with a short pointed base and tip and an undulate edge. On the olive-green to weakly reddish-brown upperside is a distinctly darker cross design; underside of the leaf is light brown. All main veins are green, rarely light pink. This variety is exceptionally well-suited as a foreground plant, especially for shallow tanks. With its numerous daughter plants on short runners, a compact group is formed which, if possible, should be kept separate and in the open. An excellent contrast results between other light green foreground plants. To maintain the typical "*rubella*" pattern, sufficiently strong illumination is required. If it is too low, the leaves are less intensely colored and look dirty green-brown. Acclimation to hard water is good, but medium carbonate hardness values are preferred. Also note the similar variety *nana*; both forms are not always easily distinguished. Propagation: numerous daughter plants.

D: 2, **KH**: 2-15, **pH**: 6.0-7.2, **T**: 22-28° C (72-82° F), **AH**: 1-3

Cryptocoryne wendtii (var. *nana*)

Cryptocoryne wendtii (var. *rubella*)

Small group with 16 species from 10 genera. The common characteristic is a creeping ground shoot with roots. Position and shape of the leaves are very different. In their natural habitat they are predominately bog plants, but some live in the splash areas or in the water for extended periods of time. With the exception of Java moss, *Vesicularia dubyana*, which develops sporophores on thin stalks underwater, the other species flower in the air. The tiny four-leaf clover, *Marsilea exarata,* also belongs to the amphibious ferns. At the base of the petiole are small sporophores that have both male and female spores. In some areas the fruits of the four-leaf clover may serve as meager nourishment for the natives. The umbelliferous flowers of *Lilaeopsis brasiliensis* are tiny; they grow among the dense leaf cushion of the hardy land form which can be kept on the window sill. The multitude of small white flowers growing from the plant mat in *Glossostigma elatinoides* are interesting. The small stigma shows a movement mechanism which favors pollination through insects. The erect inflorescence with several whorls of small white flowers is typical for *Hydrocotyle verticillata*. These grow numerously from the axils of the petioles on the ground, form dense bunches and are present during most of the summer. The land form prospers in the bog aquarium, the window sill or the pond during the warm part of the year.

Vesicularia dubyana

Glossostigma elatinoides

Lilaeopsis brasiliensis

Marsilea exarata

Hydrocotyle verticillata

Bolbitis heteroclita (PRESL) CHING (1934) — Chinese Waterfern

Fam.: Lomariopsidaceae

Distribution: Northeast Himalaya to southern China, Malaysia to New Guinea
The suitability of this fern for submersed life became known in 1975. A useful bog fern for the larger bog aquarium; the shoot can float in the water and develop its leaves in the air. The greenish-brown, creeping rhizome is up to 1 cm (1/3") thick with black-brown roots. Leaves are alternate, stalked, 20-80 cm (8"-31") long with 1-4 pairs of lateral pinna. The terminal pinna grows up to 20 cm (8") long, 7 cm (2 3/4") wide, and often has a slender, tail-like appendage over 20 cm (8") long in the land form. Lateral pinna are shorter and narrower, 10-17 cm (4"-6 2/3") long and 2-4 cm (3/4"-1 2/3") wide. The edge is undulate and is sometimes dentate at the tip. From the midrib, 16-18 pairs of lateral veins branch almost horizontally; the leaf is fairly bullate in between. The aquatic form remains smaller and develops only one pair of lateral pinna. The rhizome will have to be fastened to a stone or wood at first. Later, it will attach itself with new roots. Growth is generally moderate, and new leaves take relatively long periods of time to develop. Best placed in roomy aquaria with water that is not too hard. Young shoots can be cultivated for a time in smaller receptacles. Not necessarily an ideal aquarium plant. Propagation: dividing the shoot, lateral shoots, and adventitious plants on the leaves.

D: 3, **KH:** 2-10, **pH:** 5.5-6.8, **T:** 22-26° C (72-79° F), **AH:** 2-3

Glossostigma elatinoides WIGTH et ARNESS (1836)

Fam.: Scrophulariaceae

Distribution: Southeast Australia, New Zealand, Tasmania
An unusually low growing decoration for the foreground. It almost never reaches 1 cm (1/3") in height and can grow very dense. The green creeping shoot has short roots and grows opposite, spatulate, up to 0.8 cm (5/16") long and 0.3 (1/8") cm wide leaves. Their base narrows into a long petiole roughly equal in length to the blade. The tip is obtuse and very faintly indented. A thin midrib is present; lateral veins are missing. In the axils of the aerial leaves are short-stalked, single flowers. The crown is 0.3 cm (1/8") in diameter, white, with 5 petals and 4 stamens. The species is easily confused with *Elatine macropoda*. Identification is only possible by the greenish flowers. The same is also valid for *G. diandra* with two stamens per bloom. In water it is probably not creeping but erect. A few shoots distributed evenly at the prospective site is a sufficient start. Plant them horizontally in the upper layer of the substrate and not vertically (as with other stalked plants). Coarse-grained sand is the preferred substrate material. When planted in coarse gravel, the tender roots cannot take hold and the plants wane. The shoots continue growing recumbent, constantly forming new lateral shoots. Offer sufficient light (60-70 watts/100 l) and do not shade the site. Also suitable for hard water if CO_2 is added. Propagation: removal of lateral shoots.

D: 2, **KH:** 2-12, **pH:** 6.0-7.2, **T:** 22-28° C (72-82° F), **AH:** 1-2

Bolbitis heteroclita

Glossostigma elatinoides

Hydrocotyle verticillata THUNBERG (1798) Whorled Umbrella Plant

Fam.: Apiaceae

Distribution: Southeastern North America, Central America
Thin creeping main shoot with alternate leaves. The petioles are up to 15 cm (6") long and attached underneath to the center of the leaf. Blade is peltate, circular, up to 3 cm (1 ") in diameter, often with a white dot in the center, with the veins radiating to the emarginate edge. The axil of the petiole has several inflorescence with small white flowers in whorls of three, 5-7 whorls superimposed. In comparison, the similar *H. vulgaris* has singular whorls. With its deviating leaf shape, *H. verticillata* is one of the preferred plants for the aquarium and is used in the foreground or the central areas. Not particularly demanding. The determinate for good submersed growth is an illumination of about 70 watts/100 l. Therefore, if at all possible, do not use floating plants which block the light. This leads to long-stalked, less decorative specimens. Although the species tolerates warm water better than *H. vulgaris*, extreme high temperatures should be avoided. With undisturbed development, dense, tiered leaf groups are grown. Suitable for the bog aquarium and the shores of the garden pond in the summer. Propagation: removal of side-shoots.

D: 2, **KH:** 5-12, **pH:** 6.0-7.5, **T:** 20-25° C (68-77° F), **AH:** 1-2

Lilaeopsis brasiliensis (GLAZIOU) AFFOLTER (1985)

Fam.: Apiaceae

Distribution: Australia, New Zealand
A decorative, low plant for the foreground. Adapts well to various water values, temperatures and substrates. The thin, prostrate shoot grows stalked, alternate leaves. The lanceolate blades are 3-10 cm (1 "-4") in length, 0.3-0.5 cm (1/8"-3/16") wide with an obtuse tip and a base that tapers to the petiole. Next to the midrib are several thin side veins; a few horizontal cross-veins reach the weakly incised edge. In the axils are small umbels, usually with 3 pink flowers. The aerial leaves are significantly more slender and reach 0.3 cm (1/8") in width, are acute and only have a mid-rib. *Lilaeopsis* is often confused with *Echinodorus tenellus* and was distributed under the name of "false tenellus" for a while. The grass-like dwarf amazon sword, however, grows a rosette at ground level and runners with daughter plants. *L. novea-zelandiae* is cultivated in its land form and sold in small pots or cups. The plant adapts well to submersed live if planted shallow. New shoots branch extensively and soon form a lawn-like stand. The high light requirement has to be met (about 70 watts/100 l), or the plants degenerate. Avoid light-blocking surface vegetation. Propagation: removal of side-shoots.

D: 2, **KH:** 2-15, **pH:** 6.0-7.2, **T:** 20-28° C (68-82° F), **AH:** 1-3

Hydrocotyle verticillata

Lilaeopsis brasiliensis

Marsilea exarata A. BRAUN (1870) Four-Leaf Clover

Fam.: Marsileaceae

Distribution: Australia

A low-growing plant for the foreground of shallow, well-lit aquaria. The species has been sold since 1977 and is usually offered as *M. crenata*. However, the small fern can be positively identified as a different species based on the fruiting land plant. The sporangia, found in the leaf axils, are 0.3 cm (1/8") long, laterally flattened, pilose and have a pointed tip. On both sides are 8 shallow ribs. The upper edge has 2 short teeth; the upper tooth is pointed, and the lower is bent back. The sparsely pilose, multilobed aerial leaves reach 1.2 cm (") in size, are somewhat lighter green in the center and sit on 5-10 cm (2"-4") petioles. Sold as bog plants in small pots. Plant the bunches shallow. The tips soon produce short-stalked leaves. During the transition phase, these are still vaguely four-lobed. The final aquatic leaf is single-lobed, oval-ovate, up to 0.5 cm (3/16") in size on a 2 cm (3/4") petiole. A good aquarium plant under suitable conditions but somewhat demanding. Under high carbonate hardness the leaves remain very small and growth will halt with insufficient lighting. The leaves tend to yellow on older shoots. This is delayed in soft water with a low pH. The submersed form is rather sensitive to transplanting and only hesitantly overcomes the shock. Propagation: removal of side-shoots with several leaves.

D: 3, **KH**: 2-10, **pH**: 6.0-7.0, **T**: 22-26° C (72-79° F), **AH**: 1-2

Pilularia americana A. BRAUN (1863)

Fam.: Pilulariaceae

Distribution: America, from Arkansas to Chile

In the tropics, subtropics and temperate areas, 6 species are distributed as amphibious small ferns in wet or moist areas that temporarily dry up. Rarely found in nature. Distribution is frequently local and disjunct. The thin creeping shoot grows alternate, quill-shaped leaves—on the land form, 4-8 cm (1 2/3"-3") long and up to 0.1 cm (1/32") thick. *P. americana* adapts better to aquatic life than other species and also resists higher temperatures, but it becomes spindly in excessive temperatures. First used in 1920 for aquaria, but it disappeared soon afterwards, and to this day, it is only raised as a curiosity. Reasons for this are likely to be the high demands and its inconspicuous, grass-like appearance. The land form adapts to submersed life immediately. The submersed leaves become thread thin and, depending on temperature and light intensity, 12-25 cm (4 3/4"-9 3/4") long. The creeping shoot continues to grow above the ground, always producing new leaves and side-shoots, creating a loose mat. Cultivation is best in the bright foreground with about 75 watts/100 l. In harder water, the addition of CO_2 markedly improves growth. Loose, coarse sand is recommended as substrate.

D: 3, **KH**: 2-8, **pH**: 5.5-6.8, **T**: 22-25° C (72-77° F), **AH**: 1-2

Marsilea exarata

Pilularia americana

The 30 species of 15 genera encompass diverse plants. *Utricularia* grow totally submersed, producing an elongated shoot with graceful divided leaves. *Utricularia aurea,* like the other species, lifts its inflorescence from the aquatic shoot into the air. Dense mats of *Utricularia gibba* grow like flowering floating islands in an aquarium. However, only the long-leaved, tropical variety is capable of flowering. *Pistia stratiotes* is a free-floating plant; intense illumination is needed to develop the small blooms in the leaf axils. The same applies to the water hyacinth, *Eichhornia crassipes*, which can only form its tall inflorescence in open tanks. Plants with long-stalked floating leaves rooted in the substrate require strong illumination, but the leaves become damaged if the clearance between the cover and the water surface is too hot. The development of blooms is influenced in this manner also. A plant that will almost certainly flower is the livebearing water lily, *Nymphaea x daubenyana*, with its large, white, yellow centered flowers. *Nymphoides* regularly develops fuzzy blooms from the petioles, whereby the orange colored *Nymphoides kirkii* are very rare.

Pistia stratiotes

Nymphoides kirkii

Utricularia gibba

Utricularia aurea

Nymphaea x daubenyana

Azolla caroliniana WILLDENOW (1810) Water Velvet

Fam.: Azollaceae

Distribution: Temperate North America to northern South America
The best known species of the genus for aquaria. Plants are up to 2 cm (3/4") long and wide with 3-5 dense, laterally placed branches. Not all branches are rooted. The upper leaf flap is elongate-rhomboid or roundish, up to 1 mm (1/32") in size with a transparent edge. The leaves are medium green in color; they have a reddish tinge in strong light. The small, floating fern is sensitive to heat and condensation on its leaves. Under suitable conditions and intensive light, propagation is quite intense, and densely spreading stands impede light penetration to the plants below. Therefore, you should thin regularly. Use to shade small, coverless breeding aquaria. Partially introduced into southern Europe and Asia. Grows well in the outdoor pond, is quite hardy there and occasionally lives through mild winters. Propagation: isolation of the lateral branches.

D: 2, KH: 2-12, pH: 6.0-7.2, T: 18-24° C (64-75° F), AH: 1-3

Azolla pinnata R. BROWN (1810)

Fam.: Azollaceae

Distribution: Australia, Java, Africa
Free floating fern with moderate adaptation. The plant attains a length of 3 cm (1 "), is usually triangular and branched panicle-like. Lower side branches are loose with secondary shoots; branches in the front are denser and unbranched. The upper leaf flaps are scale-shaped, up to 1 mm (1/32") in diameter and sometimes lie on top of each other like roof shingles. *A. pinnata* var. *africana* DESVAUX, a tropical African variety, is smaller, up to 1.5 cm (2/3") long and is less laterally branched. Hard water is unsuitable, and the air space above the water should not be overheated from strong illumination. Falling drops and condensation are detrimental; therefore, incline the cover glass and provide slight movement with less humid air. An uncovered tank with suspended illumination is recommended. It can also be cultivated outdoors in sunny locals. Propagation: removal of lateral branches.

D: 3, KH: 2-10, pH: 6.0-7.0, T: 20-24° C (68-75° F), AH: 1-3

Heteranthera reniformis RUIZ et PAVON (1789)

Fam.: Pontederiaceae

Distribution: Tropical America, subtropics
In general, a rarely cultivated aquarium plant. Main shoot grows horizontal in a swamp or natant on the water surface. Leaves are alternate with fleshy stalks, upright in the bog or floating in the water. Blade reniform to cordate, 5-10 cm (2-4") wide, 3-5 cm (1 -2") long, curvinervate and medium green. Axillary inflorescence are made of 4-8 small, light blue flowers with 6 slender pointed petals. Used as a free floating plant in the aquarium. It is without special requirements in regard to water values and temperature, but it has a high light requirement. This is a beautiful, undemanding, intensely branched swamp plant for the bog aquarium. During the warmer time of the year, it can also be placed in the shallow shore of the outdoor garden pond. Propagation: remove side-shoots.

D: 3, KH: 2-15, pH: 6.0-7.5, T: 18-28° C (64-82° F), AH: 1-3

Azolla caroliniana

Azolla pinnata

Heteranthera reniformis

Hydrocleys nymphoides (WILLDENOW) BUCHENAU (1868)

Fam.: Limnocharitaceae

Distribution: Tropical South America
A rooted rhizome plant with stalked, floating leaves. Blade is roundish, up to 10 cm (4") in size, smooth, shiny, somewhat fleshy, with 7 longitudinal veins and hair-fine cross-veins. The lower side around the midrib is thickened and sponge-like. The blooms are up to 6 cm (2¹/3") in size, have 3 roundish, yellow, deciduous petals and flower above the water. The plant was more common in aquaria before, but now, it is seldom cultivated and is a true rarity. A reason for this is surely the modern aquarium set-up which precludes a view of the water surface. Suitable for shallow tanks with 30 cm (12") water depth and intensive light. If deeper tanks are used, the plants only produce floating leaves, no flowers. Best planted in free-standing, uncovered aquaria. In a bog aquarium, the shoot roots in the shallow shore section and grows stalked leaves into the aquatic part. Propagation: runner-like lateral shoots with daughter plants.

D: 3, **KH:** 2-12, **pH:** 5.5-7.2, **T:** 22-28° C (72-82° F), **AH:** 1-2

Lemna gibba LINNAEUS (1753)

Fam.: Lemnaceae

Distribution: Europe, North America, Africa, Australia
Its leaves are ovate, symmetrical, 0.2-0.5 cm (¹/16- ") long, with a shiny green upperside and a lower side that is thickened like a belly. The blades are rather coarsely structured, spongy, colorless and do not have a clear center keel. This species is infrequently found in nature. As a rule, it occurs together with *L. minor* and usually floats as small groups among larger stands of *L. minor*. Typical plants only result with ground contact and nutrient-rich substrate. Plants floating freely in an aquarium will barely show species typical characteristics, and the humped underside will be totally flat. The undemanding floating plant soon forms a dense stand which needs to be regularly thinned to avoid light blockage. Propagation: daughter plants grow in the T-shaped joints. They remain connected for a time but later separate.

D: 1, **KH:** 2-15, **pH:** 5.5-7.5, **T:** 10-30° C (50-86° F), **AH:** 1-3

Lemna trisulca LINNAEUS (1753)

Fam.: Lemnaceae

Distribution: Europe, Asia, North America, Australia
Close beneath the water surface, the loose mats of interconnected plants float. Leaves are light green, elongated, acute, up to 1 cm (¹/3") long and 0.5 cm (") wide with 3 veins and 3 grooves. Crosswise blades are interconnected by short stalks and form forked larger colonies. In nature, mats may form on the bottom. Can grow well in an outdoor pond. Little used as an aquarium plant, but it is suitable and, like the other species, it adapts well. Higher temperatures are tolerated over extended periods of time with strong illumination, but generally for cold water. The shallow floating mats form a decorative, loose greening of the upper tank zones. Less disturbing and can be reduced without problems. Propagation: branches, dividing of the mats.

D: 2, **KH:** 5-15, **pH:** 5.5-7.5, **T:** 10-25° C (50-77° F), **AH:** 1-3

Hydrocleys nymphoides

Lemna gibba

Lemna trisulca

Nymphoides indica (LINNAEUS) O. KUNTZE (1891)

Fam.: Menyanthaceae

Distribution: Tropical America, circum tropical
Separated single leaves, which are placed on the water to flower, are normally found in the trade. The blade is round to cordate, 10-20 cm (4-8") in size, often wider than long. Upperside is shiny dark green; lower side is slightly glandular uneven, sometimes reddish. Beneath the attachment to the blade are a number of peduncled 2 cm ($^{3}/_{4}$") flowers growing from the leaf stalk. The flower's 5 white petals are slender, densely pilose, with a yellow spot at the base. As a rule, a young plant is grown from the leaf after the flower. It is acclimated slowly to deeper water levels and is planted in fertile substrate. It is rapid growing and forms an extensive leaf canopy which constantly flowers. To provide enough light for the bottom plants, old leaves and new shoots need to be removed regularly. Propagation: after flowering, several leaves emerge from the same place at the stalk. A new plant is formed as a lateral shoot.

D: 2, **KH:** 1-15, **pH:** 5.5-7.2, **T:** 22-30° C (72-86° F), **AH:** 2

Salvinia cucculata ROXBURGH ex BORY (1828/33)

Fam.: Salviniaceae

Distribution: Tropical southeast Asia
A free floating plant with a high light requirement. The plant has a horizontal main shoot and floating leaves. These are short-stalked, almost sessile, strongly cupped, round to cordate, up to 1.1 cm (") long, 1.3 cm ($^{2}/_{3}$) wide, obtuse, and not indented. Upperside is warty with very dense, felt-like, single bristles that are pointed forward and arranged in uniform rows. Even in bright daylight, the typical cup shape is not maintained. New leaves are flatter and only the base is slightly turned up. The aquarium plant usually has considerably smaller leaves, requires strong light, and is sensitive to high humidity and heat. Used in aquaria since 1979, but infrequently imported and rarely cultivated. Very similar to *S. sprucei*. Propagation: isolation of side-shoots.

D: 4, **KH:** 2-10, **pH:** 6.0-7.0, **T:** 18-24° C (64-75° F), **AH:** 1-3

Salvinia minima BAKER (1886)

Fam.: Salviniaceae

Distribution: Southern Brazil
This relatively new species was first imported in 1979 but is usually overlooked or confused. The thin natant main shoot has opposing floating leaves. The blade is roundish, light green, short-stalked, 5-9 mm ($^{3}/_{16}$-$^{3}/_{8}$") long, 4-7 mm ($^{3}/_{16}$- ") wide with a slightly cordate base. Upperside is not warty but sparsely pilose with paired bristles in uniform rows. Cultivation in aquaria is not without problems; it requires soft water, does not tolerate strong heating of the air space and is sensitive to condensation. Better kept in a free standing open tank with high hanging light fixtures. In nature, it forms a swamp form during low water. It grows emersed in wet peat in the bright bog aquarium. Propagation: under suitable conditions numerous side-shoots may separate and grow independently.

D: 4, **KH:** 2-10, **pH:** 6.0-6.8, **T:** 22-25° C (72-77° F), **AH:** 1-3

Nymphoides indica

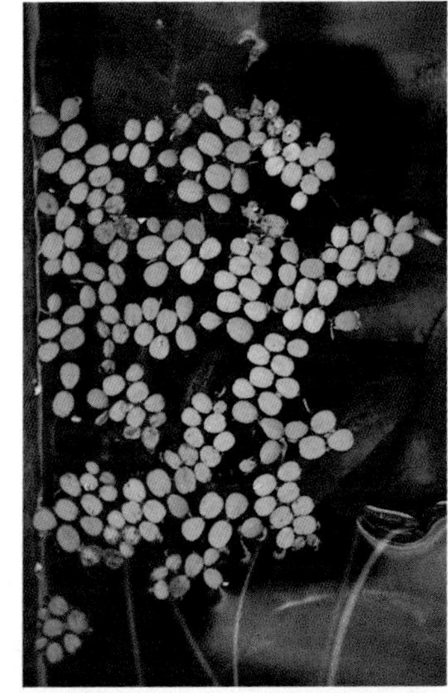

Salvinia minima

Salvinia cucculata

Salvinia rotundifolia WILLDENOW (1810)

Fam.: Salviniaceae

Distribution: Tropical South America
A well suited, small, floating aquarium plant that poses no particular problems. On the thin natant main shoot the leaves are floating, opposite, round-oval, up to 0.7 cm (") in size, usually as long as wide, with an obtuse tip, without a clear indention. The upperside is warty, loosely or densely pilose, with two short, light bristles on each papillose projection. Degenerate *S. auriculata* has a similar appearance; however, that species has 4 bristles emerging from each papilla. This fern resists hard water better than other species, is less sensitive and adapts well to varied living conditions. Dense vegetation is formed rapidly through numerous lateral shoots; the opportune thinning will prevent the plants below from being shaded out. Propagation: lateral shoots separate and form separate independent individuals.

D: 2, **KH:** 2-15, **pH:** 6.0-7.5, **T:** 18-25° C (64-77° F), **AH:** 1-3

Salvinia sprucei KUHN (1884)

Fam.: Salviniaceae

Distribution: Amazon basin
This species, which is new for aquaria, was first imported in 1980 and is often confused with *S. cucculata*. The natant main shoot has short-stalked, round to cordate, extremely cupped floating leaves. The leaves are up to 1.5 cm long (2/3"), 2.5 cm (1") wide and have a shallow cleft. The upper surface is free of papillose projections, densely pilose, with single, straight upward projecting, randomly distributed bristles. This species adapts well to varying living conditions, endures higher temperatures, grows without problems in covered aquaria and shows almost no damage from condensation. Light requirement is very high. The aquarium form has smaller leaves that are only moderately cupped. Growth is rapid and very dense; light-blocking mats are formed. Thin regularly. The dense, hanging, divided roots provide protection for young fish. Propagation: lateral shoots separate and grow independently.

D: 1, **KH:** 2-15, **pH:** 5.5-7.5, **T:** 22-30° C (72-86° F), **AH:** 1-3

Trapa natans LINNAEUS (1753) Water Chestnut

Fam.: Trapaceae

Distribution: Temperate and cold zones.
Though it is rarely cultivated in an aquarium, it can be accomplished under favorable conditions. A dense rosette of stalked, deltoid, dentate leaves floats on the water surface, alternately emerging off an elongated main shoot which can reach 5 meters (5.5 yd) length in nature. Blade is up to 5 cm (2") in size, held on a thickened, inflated petiole. The submersed nodes have hair-fine, pinnate aquatic leaves. The small axillary flowers produce horned edible fruits. Within this very difficult species, the variety *bispinosa* is apparently better suited for the aquarium. Needs very soft, slightly acid water with low carbonate hardness as well as intense illumination of at least 75 watts/100 l (26 gal) for 14-16 hours daily. Do not cultivate free floating, but anchor the main shoot in the substrate. Nonrooted plants show degenerate growth patterns and quickly die. *T. maximowiczii* (perhaps a form of *T. natans*) probably grows better in an aquarium. Leaves have a dark brown base. Propagation: runner-like lateral shoots.

D: 4, **KH:** 2-4, **pH:** 6.0-6.8, **T:** 22-26° C (72-79° F), **AH:** 1-3

Salvinia rotundifolia

Salvinia sprucei

Trapa natans

Utricularia minor LINNAEUS (1753)

Fam.: Utriculariaceae

Distribution: Europe, north Africa
A decorative surface plant for unheated to temperate aquaria. The thin, elongated main shoot grows up to 50 cm (20") long and is moderately branched. Leaves grow flat, up to 2 cm (3/4") in size, forked several times, forming a roundish periphery with 10-20 very fine, thin tips. The small catch bladders, usually on the lower part of the leaves, trap and digest small aquatic insects. Corresponding to the natural conditions, bog lakes or shallow bog swamps, the water should be nutrient poor and acid. It can then grow exuberantly and green large areas of water. Propagation: lateral shoots and shoot segments.

D: 3, **KH**: 2-8, **pH**: 5.5-6.5, **T**: 18-22° C (64-72° F), **AH**: 1-3

Utricularia neglecta LEHMANN (1828)

Fam.: Utriculariaceae

Distribution: North and west Europe, north Africa
Rarely maintained in an aquarium, but it is excellently suited and adapts well. The main shoot is up to 100 cm (39") long and intensively branched. Leaves consist of 4 parts and are up to 5 cm (2") in size, flat, usually compound pinnate with numerous, slightly flattened, thin tips. Up to 80, 2 mm (1/16") capture bladders sit in several rows on the leaf, trapping and digesting small water insects. The species varies a lot and exhibits several growth forms. Higher temperatures are not detrimental; quick growing and can green a large area of water in a few months. Propagation: lateral shoots, shoot segments, leaf cuttings.

D: 1, **KH**: 2-15, **pH**: 6.0-7.5, **T**: 18-28° C (64-82° F), **AH**: 1-3

Utricularia vulgaris LINNAEUS (1753)

Fam.: Utriculariaceae

Distribution: Europe, north Africa
This species is not easy. It is best grown under moderate temperatures. The main shoot is elongate and up to 200 cm (76") long. The leaves consist of 4 lobes up to 8 cm (3") long, 6 cm (2 1/3") wide and are repeatedly forked with numerous thread-thin tips. A full-grown leaf sports more than 100, 5 mm (3/16") capture bladders. This plant is totally unsuitable for breeding tanks since fry are also caught. For a limited time it will also grow in harder water under higher temperatures. In cold water or outdoors, the plant dies towards the fall and forms winter buds. These should be stored in a cool, frost-free environment. They will germinate later. Propagation: lateral shoots and shoot segments.

D: 3, **KH**: 2-10, **pH**: 5.5-7.0, **T**: 15-22° C (59-72° F), **AH**: 1-3

Wolffia arrhiza (LINNAEUS) HORKEL ex WIMMER (1857)

Fam.: Lemnaceae

Distribution: Almost cosmopolitan
This genus of 7 species contains the smallest known flowering plants. The bodies are round-oval or ovate, about 1 mm (1/16") in size, light and grass green or slightly reddish under strong light. The species are difficult to distinguish. Propagates massively in nature; harvested and eaten in Thailand as vegetables. Rare in aquaria because the tiny plants are eaten by many fish species. Nutrient rich water is preferred. Higher water hardness is not detrimental, but growth is very light dependent. Propagation: numerous daughter shoots.

D: 3, **KH**: 2-15, **pH**: 6.0-7.5, **T**: 15-25° C (59-77° F), **AH**: 1-3

Utricularia minor

Utricularia neglecta

Utricularia vulgaris

Wolffia arrhiza

Various factors influence the healthy growth of plants in an aquarium. If water plants do not grow satisfactorily, the causes have to be sought and errors remedied. Possible sources of errors are problems in the basic furnishings of the aquarium, such as substrate, illumination and temperature. If only certain species show poor growth, the provided conditions are probably not suitable. A possible cause may be unfavorable water values, perhaps excessive water hardness, elevated pH or insufficient lighting. The choices of species can be adapted to the prevailing living conditions, but this criterion for selection is quite complicated and often costly. A more favorable method is to use growth aids to improve water quality, a result of fertilizing with iron, nutrients and CO_2. Some companies offer these mixtures.

Iron and Plant Growth

The source of degenerate growth of aquarium plants is often a disturbance in the iron cycle. For the synthesis of the green pigment of plants (chlorophyll) which is the key to photosynthesis, available iron is essential. Traces suffice, because it has not been identified as a component of chlorophyll but as a catalyst for its formation. It serves a similar purpose for the building of cellular plasma, perhaps acting as an oxygen transporter. Iron deficiency causes pale, yellow leaves, often with glassy parts. Iron chlorosis impedes carbohydrate synthesis, and even in presence of other nutrients, the plants can literally starve. The demands towards iron content in water vary with species. For slow growing plants, a relatively small amount of iron is sufficient, but rapid growing species usually demand higher concentrations.

Iron in the Water

Comparisons of tropical waters with municipal water supplies show large differences in regard to the iron content. Tropical creeks with plant growth often contain more than 1 mg iron per liter (1 ppm). City water, by contrast, normally contains less than 0.1 mg/l iron, or it can even be totally absent. Sometimes aquarium plants are content with small quantities of iron, specially under moderate light, low temperatures, or if slow growing. For these conditions, the iron requirement can usually be met by regular water changes. This method, however, restricts the choice of plants to undemanding species. As a rule, only ferrous (Fe^{++}) iron is available for aquatic plants. In combination with water, however, iron goes over to the ferric (Fe^{+++}) form and becomes unavailable. Quantitatively, iron may be present in sufficient amounts but still be inadequate for plant nutrition. Certain species can chelate the iron in a species-specific form and thereby keep it available. These various factors help explain the phenomenon of yellowish plants and healthy plants occurring in an aquarium simultaneously.

Fertilizing with Iron

Available iron in the water can be made into a soluble form with an artificial chelator (such as EDTA) and, through it, remain available to plants. This indirect fertilization is only successful if there is actually iron in the water. It is better to use one of the special iron fertilizers available in aquarium stores. Dosage in hard water (above 10° KH) is 1 g/100 l and 0.5 g/100 l in soft water. Maintenance dosage is half that amount weekly. After partial water exchanges, replace according to the quantity of water removed. Avoid overfertilization because too much iron competes for other nutrients, e.g., adversely affects the absorption of manganese. This leads to its own problems with the plants. About 0.5 mg active iron per liter of water is considered adequate and not detrimental. Measurements can be taken with tests available from Hach and other companies (e.g., Brustmann, Aqua-Control, Test FE Iron in Germany).

Advantages of Iron Fertilization

- Iron fertilization produces working chlorophyll. Plants can adapt better to tank conditions.
- Through specific improvements, other nutrients available in excess can be better taken advantage off.
- A few days after the addition of iron, chlorotic plants show significantly more intense green leaves.
- Cultivating plants with different requirements simultaneously becomes possible.
- The content of total soluble salts in the water is raised less than when nutrient fertilizers are added. Special very soft and electrolyte poor water for sensitive fishes maintains its desired low conductivity.

Nutrients and Plant Growth

Nutrients are necessary for plant growth. Nitrogen, phosphorus, potassium, calcium, magnesium, iron, sulfur, carbon, hydrogen and oxygen are the macronutrients. These are found in all plants in larger quantities and are the building blocks of the plant body. Microelements such as iodine, manganese, zinc or copper, although required, are only needed in trace amounts. Nutrients accomplish certain functions for plant life:

- Nitrogen is involved in protein synthesis.
- Phosphorus promotes, among other things, the formation of flowers.
- Potassium is part of protoplasm synthesis.
- Calcium acts as a detoxicant for the plant body.
- Iron makes the synthesis of chlorophyll possible.
- Sulfur is a component of protein synthesis.
- Carbon is the base component of carbohydrates.
- Hydrogen (water), among other things, serves as transport medium of nutrients.
- Oxygen is the motor of all life functions.

Nutrients and Deficiency Symptoms

If one of these nutrients is missing from the water, deficiency symptoms appear in plants. Several factors are usually involved, and the symptoms cannot always be catalogued clearly.

- Nitrogen deficiency produces yellow leaves, whereby older leaves become yellow first. Sometimes they also become reddish through the formation of anthocyanin.
- Phosphorus deficiency provokes early leaf loss and the formation of anthocyanin. Small areas die within the leaves.
- Potassium deficiency manifests itself as yellow spots on the leaves, followed by withered parts on the tips and leaf edges. Begins on older sections of the plant.
- Calcium deficiency causes damage to the apical cells of shoots and leaves, which later die off. Younger leaves often have yellow edges.
- Iron deficiency leads to yellow leaves, first on the growing tips. The yellow areas are often surrounded by a network of somewhat greener veins.
- Magnesium deficiency appears as yellow spots, first on older leaves, later on younger leaves.
- Sulfur deficiency produces yellow leaves. Younger ones yellow first. Red coloration due to anthocyanin is possible.
- Manganese deficiency manifests itself as yellow spots between the leaf veins; these parts later die off and leave small, elongated holes behind. Also occurs as a consequence of overfertilization with iron which interferes with manganese absorption.

Nutrients in the Water

All nutrients have to be available in a balanced form. If certain nutrients are present in excess, they can interfere with the absorption of others. Reciprocal antagonists are, for example, iron with manganese or calcium with potassium. In the wild, the plant is confronted with relatively nutrient poor water, but principally without nutrient gaps. The continuous water exchange in flowing creeks and the large water volume guarantee a constant level of nutrients. In an aquarium, numerous plants grow in a small volume of water. Soon, nutrient deficiencies occur. Regular water exchanges can compensate for the nutrient use, but certain salts will form insoluble components and will not be available to the plants. Nutrients are only absorbed in ionized forms and with certain chelated complexes maintaining the substances available for the plants. Such chelating agents are formed in the aquarium (moderately) through the natural organic load of the water after the decomposition of metabolites resulting from feeding. Therefore, overly clean water does not promote plant growth and result in "starting difficulties" after a new tank set-up.

Fertilizing with Nutrients

A sure solution to the problem are nutrient fertilizers for water plants which are offered in aquarium stores. However, some preparations have a deficient iron content. Additional iron fertilization is then indicated.

- Nutrient fertilizers only work conditionally and according to the environment of the tank.
- Only use special preparations for water plants; fertilizers for terrestrial plants are ineffective in an aquarium.
- Test fertilizer with half the dosage and observe the plant reaction. Positive results are larger new leaves and faster plant growth.
- Small additions over shorter intervals are more effective than large sporadic doses of fertilizer.
- Use nutrient fertilizer moderately; more does not help more but is almost always detrimental.
- Stay within dosage recommendations; EDTA containing preparations produce skeleton damage in sensitive fishes if overdosed.
- Not every fertilizer is necessarily positive. This depends on the prevailing conditions in the tank. Use a different preparation if the effect was insufficient. However, first remove prior unused nutrient fertilizer with a water exchange.

Advantages of Nutrient Fertilization

The utilization of fertilizers is dependent on water characteristics. Through the addition of fertilizer, meager growth can be influenced to the better. Nutrient fertilizers offer significant advantages when cultivating water plants and are a good building block towards optimal plant growth.

- In water with low levels of dissolved salts, the nutrient climate is improved and the disadvantages of low nutrient salt levels are compensated.
- In water with an adverse nutrient climate, plant nutrition can be achieved through fertilization alone, for example, in deionized water.
- The nutrients are bound to nutrient carriers and remain available. Hereby, the nutrition of the plant is assured.
- In the same aquarium, under the same conditions, more plants species with varying requirements can be kept. Due to the increased choice of species, the decoration can be enhanced.

Carbon Dioxide Fertilization

Carbon is the base element in the organic matrix. During photosynthesis, plants use gaseous carbon with the help of chlorophyll, warmth and water to elaborate organic compounds. The initial compound (starch) reaches the areas of utilization and storage in a soluble form (dextrose). Through combination with nutrient salts, organic substances for cell construction are synthesized at growth points. In rhizomes, tubers or fruits, starch is usually stored as proteins. An adequate supply of carbon dioxide is, therefore, an important condition for plant growth. The carbon cycle in water is quite complicated, and the water plants meet their requirements in various ways. The uptake of free (uncombined) carbon dioxide is preferred because of the lower energy requirement. With declining CO_2 levels, pH rises and growth is continuously more difficult.Therefore, certain ranges of carbonate hardness will considerably limit the choice of aquarium plants.

Carbon Dioxide in the Water

Atmospheric carbon dioxide (CO_2) is present in small amounts in the water as carbonic acid (H_2CO_3). The principal component is carbon dioxide, like in the air. In contact with the air, water absorbs about 0.03% carbon dioxide. The values rise through the contact with the substrate because bacteria and roots produce CO_2 through their activities. The respiratory products from fish and plants are additional natural sources of CO_2. In soft water or with undemanding waters, this is adequate for certain species. However, it is not always the case that there is constantly sufficient carbon dioxide in aquarium water. To maintain calcium in solution, a certain amount of free carbon dioxide is needed. Above 10° KH the values rise considerably, and the following table (after K. Horst, Das perfekte Aquarium) provides an overview of the values with which bicarbonates are maintained in solution. These values fluctuate with temperature (25° C for the following values).

Carbonate Hardness (° KH)	Free CO_2 mg/l
1	0.01
2	0.11
3	0.41
4	0.96
5	1.88
6	3.24
7	5.18
8	7.25
9	10.96
10	15.10
11	19.10
12	25.60
13	33.40
14	41.60
15	51.20
16	61.80
17	73.90
18	88.10
19	104.30
20	120.50

Dissolved carbon dioxide constantly equilibrates with the lower carbon dioxide concentration in the air. Therefore, CO_2 in the water can decrease and reach 0. Constant aeration with an airstone shortens the gas exchange to several days. In such tanks, plants rarely grow well, and the options are usually limited to robust species that can assimilate bicarbonates. Sub-mersed plants initially meet their carbon requirement from the free carbon dioxide, which takes less energy. When the free CO_2 is used up, they use bound carbon from the bicarbonates. This process is more energy dependent. During bicarbonate assimilation, CO_2 is dissociated from the calcium in the plant leaf and the calcium is subse-quently released from the upperside of the leaf. Typical white pustules are formed, and sometimes the whole leaf is covered by deposits.

Fertilizing with Carbon Dioxide

CO_2 is difficult to exactly quantify in water and, for aquaria, there are no simple and cost effective measuring instruments. One is dependent on complicated and expensive methods and estimations. Quantitative CO_2 content is not a reference for deficient or sufficient values because its effectiveness is bound to carbonate hardness. In soft water, about 10 mg/l free CO_2 usually is sufficient for good plant growth. In hard water, the same content is more or less deficient. Therefore, carbon dioxide will need to be added more frequently at higher carbonate hardnesses. Sometimes, small additions will already improve the growth of plants. A bicarbonate-carbonic acid equilibrium is optimal, but is difficult to reach at high hardnesses. The aquarium hobby has different apparatuses to add CO_2 using different techniques and ranges of activity. The following apparatuses are mentioned with a short description.

CO_2 Devices

CO_2 Optimat (Tetra)

A combination of cylinder with pressure reducer and diffusion pipe. Gas reaches a reserve pipe with a gas permeable membrane inside the aquarium through an air hose. The containers are regularly refilled and several diffusers can be placed in parallel. For small to medium aquaria and moderately hard water. For larger aquaria there is the CO_2-System from Tetra.

Automatic Carbonic Acid Fertilizer ZEO (Reiß)

In a special container, CO_2 is produced by the addition of hydrochloric acid on marble. Gas reaches small containers with gas permeable membranes in the water through a hose. For small aquaria and soft water. Because of the use of hydrochloric acid, use with caution.

Floramat (Sander)
System consisting of cylinder, reducer and reaction bottle. Through a connection to a membrane pump, water flows through the container where it is enriched with CO_2. The reaction container is regularly refilled. For small to mid-sized aquaria and moderately hard water.

CO_2-System (Dupla)
System consisting of rechargeable CO_2 bottle, pressure reducing valve and a reaction container connected to the water pump of the aquarium filter. Water cascades through the reaction container which is automatically replenished with CO_2. A relatively maintenance-free system and also recommended by the manufacturer for large set-ups and hard water. Can be regulated according to need.

CO_2 Vario (Dennerle)
A spray chamber is fastened in an aquarium and is continuously supplied with CO_2. It is connected to canisters or rechargeable large bottles with a pressure reducer. The apparatus is connected to a power filter, where the water is sprayed into the reactor filled with gas and returned to the tank enriched. Also recommended for large aquaria with hard water.

Advantages of CO_2 fertilization
Numerous aquaria are being provided with additional CO_2 and aquarists are employing this method more and more as an effective means to further plant growth. Fertilizing with carbon dioxide offers significant advantages.

- pH values are maintained in the advantageous neutral to slightly acid range, and larger oscillations are avoided.
- The absorption of this macronutrient is eased for all plants, and general growth is encouraged.
- Through improved growth, roots are also grown faster, and transplanted plants continue growing better.
- Stronger illumination becomes possible so light requiring plants grow. Problem plants which normally require soft water will now grow in hard water.
- The more extensive choice of species allows for diverse aquarium decoration.

Typical iron chlorosis on *Echinodorus maior*, leaf and leaf veins are yellow or whitish, leaf tissue is glassy and brittle.

Chlorosis on *Echinodorus amazonicus*. However, the veins are green, so we are probably dealing with manganese deficiency. Excessive nitrogen content of the water often produces similar deficiency symptoms.

Excessive iron fertilization on *Echinodorus argentinensis*. The leaf tissue is whitish, the veins remain green, the tissue later falls out, and the leaf develops holes. The high iron content probably leads to a disruption of manganese uptake. With sufficient and balanced nutrition, plants grow healthy.

Small white spots on a leaf of *Cryptocoryne wendtii* show the beginnings of calcium deposits. The result of bicarbonate assimilation under low carbon dioxide conditions.

This leaf of *Bolbitis heudelotii* shows a dense white calcium deposit as a symptom of advanced bicarbonate assimilation.

Iron deficiency in *Echinodorus maior*

Manganese deficiency in *E. amazonicus*

overfertilization of *E. argentinensis*

Beginning calcium deposits on *C. wendtii*

Extensive calcium deposits on *B. heudelotii*

My plants do not grow. What is the reason? Such questions can usually only be answered after an exhaustive examination of the aquarium conditions. Certain disturbances appear slowly, and over time, growth is halted in the entire aquarium. However, often only certain species are affected. Such growth problems of the aquarium flora often do not display uniform symptomatology, making inferences as to their causes quite difficult.

Errors in the Substrate

External symptoms of problems originating from the substrate are degenerate, black, rotting roots and unhealthy growth. The following factors have to be checked.

- Texture: very fine (below 1 mm, 1/32") materials or mixtures of different sized materials compact with time. When testing for hardness, the finger should enter with relative ease.
- Additives: compost, potting soil, peat and other organic components do not belong into the aquarium substrate.
- Muddiness: organic wastes (feces, feed) sink into very coarse material (above 5 mm, 3/16"). This decomposing mud consumes oxygen, forms poisonous hydrogen sulfide and hinders root growth. Therefore, "vacuum" the substrate regularly.
- Temperature: a cold substrate hinders healthy plant growth. There should not be a temperature difference of more than 2° C.
- Age: the substrate becomes worn out with age, therefore exchange every 3 years.

Errors in Temperature

Excessive internode length and small leaves are usually a symptom of too much heat for stalked plants. An imbalance between temperature and light intensity can also be the case. Higher temperatures require more light; otherwise, the plants become excessively long. High temperatures are detrimental in conjunction with nutrient poor water because metabolism is stimulated. Complete fertilizer can help. Low temperatures hinder growth of tropical plants. Stratification due to insufficient water circulation or an excessive gradient between water and substrate are also detrimental. Plants with markedly different temperature requirements should not be cultivated together.

Errors in Lighting

Indications of deficient lighting are excessive leaf intervals, dropping of lower leaves, small blades, quick growing, slender stalks and pale-green leaves. Do not combine plants that have diverse light requirements. Excessive illumination is detrimental when the nutrient levels become deficient. Fertilization helps in those cases. The most common mistakes in lighting are:

- Inappropriate light quality emitted from fluorescent tubes.
- Deficient reflection of the light.
- Insufficient intensity.
- Insufficient daily duration.
- Old fluorescent tubes.

Errors in Choosing Plants

Because the requirements of plants vary, there can be good growers, moderate growers and total failures under similar aquarium conditions. Besides the errors committed in temperature and lighting, the requirements of the species in regard to water values need to also be considered. Plants which require soft water seldom grow well in high carbonate hardness. Species with little potential of adaptation are best avoided under certain conditions. The same goes for the pH-value; plants with differing requirements should not be cultivated together. The species should be chosen with regard to the present conditions. This is not always simple. Applicable descriptions can be found in the plant biographies.

Errors in Maintenance

Incorrect practices during regular care, as well as during planting and transplanting of plants, often leads to leaf loss. Consequences are retarded growth, continued degeneration or subsequent die off. This is avoided by following the basic rules of skillful plant care:

- Pay attention to healthy and well growing specimens.
- Do not use plants that are too large or weak.
- Cut roots correctly.
- Avoid strong pressure when planting.
- Pay attention to the correct planting depth.
- Do not plant cuttings in bunches.
- Maintain correct distances within a group.
- Prune and replant cuttings at the correct time.
- Thin out dense stands regularly.
- Do not transplant rooted plants over the short term.

Disorders in Nutrition

Growing problems in plants due to wrong or insufficient nutrition are difficult to identify. Deficiency symptoms are not always specific because it may be several problems producing the result. The main problems are briefly explained again. Iron deficiency manifests itself through yellowish leaves and a hard brittle leaf bud. Nutrient deficiency leads to general stunting, severely slowed growth and small leaves with pale coloration. The reasons are varied. Overfertilization can also hamper growth of plants. Carbon dioxide deficiency causes stunting, reduced height and the die off of certain species. In the chapter on additives for better plant growth, these disorders are explained in detail.

Poisonous Substances

The definition of poison is not very easy. Some normally harmless substances act as poisons under certain conditions. Copper, zinc or boron are trace nutrients, but turn into dangerous poisons with increasing concentrations.
Substrate poisons are a consequence of anaerobic bacterial activity in times of oxygen deficiency. Hydrogen sulfide is an extremely powerful poison and deadly even in small quantities. Telltale signs are black roots and black areas in the substrate.
Treatment poisons are the ingredients contained in preparations used against fish diseases, algae, water snails or hydra. These are commonly substances which kill the protoplasm of plant cells. This is usually a consequence of denatured proteins or disruption of respiration which is a function of the plasma. The opportune water exchange dilutes the poisons, shortens their effectiveness and checks plant damage.

Brown spots which later become holes. A result of chemical algae control on *Echinodorus macrophyllus*. This type of damage usually occurs some time after the use of algicides.

Due to absent or insufficient water changes, small brown spots, later turning into holes, appear on *Hygrophila*. They are more common on old leaves that are simultaneously receiving insufficient light. Probably a result of a nitrogen oversaturation.

Typical *Hygrophila polysperma* leaves eaten by fish from the edges.

Snail feeding on a leaf of *Hygrophila corymbosa*. The irregular holes with sharp edges are typical.

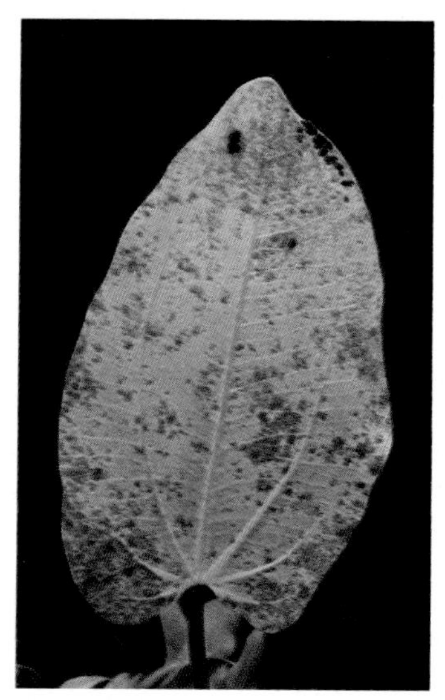

Algicide damage

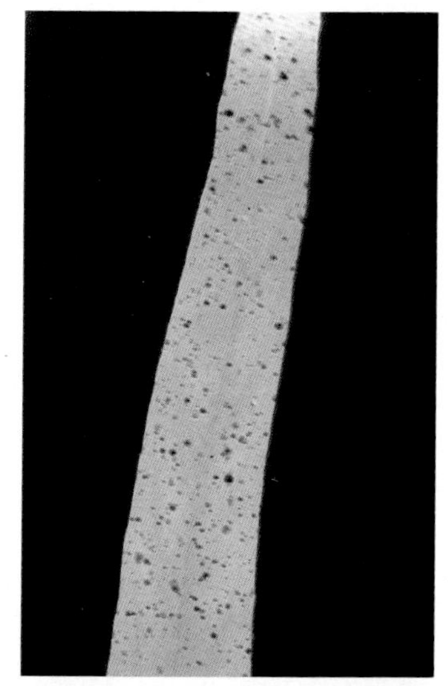

Damage from old water

Eaten by fish

Eaten by snails

Problems with Algae

In the plant kingdom, algae are classified as lower plants. Through chlorophyll, algae are autotrophs. They live mostly submersed and are either unicellular, colonial, filamentous or leaf-like growths. Propagation is accomplished via division, spores, conjugation or fertilization. The algae which occur in aquaria belong to the following groups.

Blue Algae *Cyanobacteria* are named after their own pigment, phycocyanin, which gives them the black, blue-green or brownish coloration. Many blue algae have an external slime layer, and the common filamentous organisms can oscillate for locomotion. About 2000 species live in water or on land.

Diatoms *Bacillariophyceae* are unicellular, brownish plants with a silica shell made of two matching halves. This is why they feel rough. They live on the bottom of shallow waters; in the ocean, they are a significant part of the plankton.

Green Algae *Chlorophyta* are either unicellular or form simple, sometimes branched filaments. More than 13000 species are known; they planktonic, grow attached or live out of the water.

Red Algae *Rhodophyta* are predominantly marine inhabitants; some genera also live in freshwater. Initially, they form claw-like or cup-like holdfasts. Red algae can be separated from green algae by placing them in acetone or alcohol. The green pigment is extracted; the red component remains. Green algae become colorless.

In an aquarium, algae are not only ugly, they directly damage higher plants by removing nutrients and carbon dioxide from the water. Generally, algae have the advantage when conditions are not equilibrated for higher plants, and living conditions for certain algae improve as a rule. Therefore, massive amounts of algae in an aquarium can also be viewed as poor plant growth. Due to the various requirements of different algae, this is not always the case. Some algae are not identified correctly by the aquarists which creates problems in its control. In the following overview, the algae are not only described but are also pictured for easier recognition.

Diatoms

Bunch algae

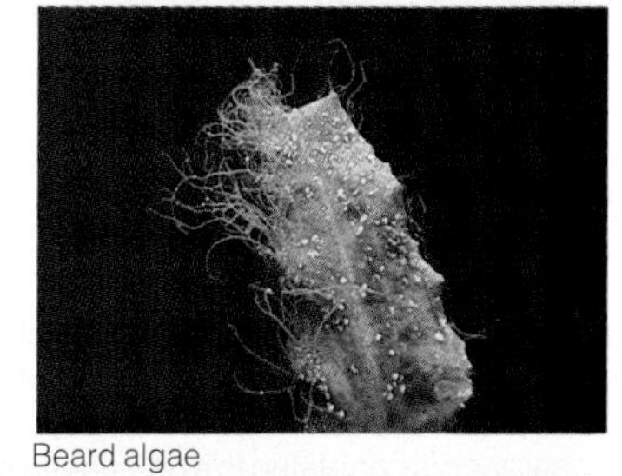
Beard algae

Cluster algae

Blue algae

Blue Algae

Description: *Oscillatoria* and other genera. These algae grow as greasy skin-like coverings that are ordinarily a blue-green color. The water acquires a typical musty odor.

Occurrence: Blue-green algae usually start on the bottom and cover everything with an amorphous layer. Plants are literally smothered. There are numerous reasons for their occurrence. Many species utilize organic compounds and their appearance is correlated to a deterioration of aquarium water quality. Additional reasons are: exposure of aquaria to strong sunlight, rotting substrate, excess feed, too few water exchanges, overfertilization or high nitrate levels.

Control: pH-values below 6.0 are usually not tolerated. Cleaner fishes, such as the black molly, are not always effective, as the algae are refused because of their bitter taste. Occasionally apple snails are a solution. Often the algae grow faster than the animals consume them. Chemical control is possible; the treatment is accelerated and shortened if the tank is kept dark for the initial 48 hours. Total darkness for 4-6 days or several total water changes can make the aquarium unsuitable for blue-greens.

Diatoms

Description: Erroneously also called brown algae. Its growth type is amorphous and seldom thread-like. Adheres strongly to plants and rocks, but also forms loose coverings. They feel rough to the touch.

Occurrence: Most diatoms prefer pH-values above 7.5 in the aquarium. Because they need dim light to live, they are not a problem in well-lit aquaria.

Control: Cleaner fish and snails usually feed on diatoms. Chemical measures can also be taken. Increase lighting intensity and duration for the tank.

Description: *Oscillatoria* and other genera.

Cluster Algae

Description: Green algae, usually from the genus *Ulothrix*. Light green, thin, occasionally slimy filaments which lie on the substrate and form tangled clusters and connected mats later. They do not attach.

Occurrence: Usually introduced with new plants. Conditions similar to filamentous algae.

Control: Collect or vacuum regularly; sometimes they disappear after a period of exuberant growth or at least are reduced. Cleaner fish offer partial help (*Ancistrus, Plecostomus*). Use preparations against filamentous algae.

Beard Algae

Description: Red algae from the genus *Compsopogon*. Relatively thick threads up to 15 cm long, little branched, dark to black green. Adhere very firmly to leaves and can almost not be removed without causing damage.

Occurrence: Usually introduced through new plants. Colonize actively growing plant parts closer to light, but they are not necessarily light dependent. Hard water with CO_2 deficiency and high pH seems to be a favorable condition, but they also appear in soft water. High nitrate content promotes growth. Under strong infestation, dense upward growing beards result, causing significant plant damage.

Control: Due to the firmly attached threads, mechanical removal leads to leaf damage. Infested plants or parts are best removed to contain the growth. New growth can be controlled by cleaner fish. Preparations against filamentous algae are possible, but the control usually must be repeated. Addition of CO_2 into the water provides successful control, whereby the calcium-carbonic acid equilibrium has to be maintained for 6-8 weeks. The filaments will shrink and die off. As a rule, beard algae are not a problem in aquaria that add CO_2.

Green Bunch Algae

Description: Green algae from the genus *Pithophora*. Moderately attached form that grows numerous, irregularly branched, light green threads from the attachment point. Forms bunches 2-3 cm tall.

Occurrence: Mostly colonizes dead material such as wood and stones but also tough-leaved plants. Intensive illumination, aquatic fertilizer and the addition of CO_2 encourage growth.

Control: Only detrimental with heavy infestation levels. Siamese algae eaters control spreading. Bunches are easily removed. Preparations against filamentous algae help.

Green Spot Algae

Description: A tiny green algae; forms light green, 3 mm (1/8"), round, very firmly attached spots. Colonizes on glass and hard-leaved plants.
Occurrence: Usually emerge during the break-in period of a new tank, when water conditions are not stable or when water conditions deteriorate. Not very damaging but ugly and stubborn.
Control: Often disappears after water conditions stabilize. Use cleaner fishes and snails. Algicides are ineffective.

Black Spot Algae

Description: Red algae on very short threads; colonizes and forms dark, almost black, roundish spots. The spots are about 5 mm in size and are firmly connected to the leaf's outer cuticle. Usually starts at the leaf edges, eventually colonizing the entire blade as irregular, interconnected spots.
Occurrence: Not bound to particular water conditions; light also seems secondary. Multiplies fast and colonizes neighboring plants. With strong infestation the leaves die off and young shoots decay.
Control: Extremely difficult; therefore, remove affected leaves and plants immediately. Cleaner fishes and chemicals have no effect. Ramshorn snails can help by grazing on the tough mats.

Pelt Algae

Description: Green algae of the genus *Oedogonium*. Single unbranched strands grow densely next to each other. They are light green, very thin, unbranched single filaments that are strongly fastened to the epidermis of the leaf and stems. On the upperside of the leaf, a pelt-like lawn grows, varying from 2-20 mm (1/16-3/4") in height, depending on species.
Occurrence: Active growing parts are preferred, and almost all occurring plants are infested. Dense growth leads to leaf die off. It seems that water with a high organic load (high nitrate levels) leads to more growth. Other water values and illumination seem to be of little importance. Propagation is uncommonly fast, and neighboring plants will be infested.
Control: Mechanical removal damages the leaves. Absolute cleanliness of the tank and regular water exchanges hamper growth. Short-thread forms are grazed by ramshorn snails, Planorbidae and Siamese algae eaters. However, long filaments and slimy forms are avoided. Promptly remove infested leaves or plants. After an extensive period of fast growth, the algae seem to slow down. Preparations against filamentous algae can be used but must be applied twice to be effective against this robust algae.

Black Brush Algae

Description: Red algae from the genus *Audouinella*. From one attachment point, numerous infrequently branched, black-green, very thin threads grow. They form 5-20 mm (3/16-3/4) tall, brush-like, very well attached bushes. Short and long thread forms exist.
Occurrence: Practically on all objects in the aquarium, including the plants. Multiplies rapidly from spores and colonizes other plants. Often begins on the plant edges. Many brushes together can form a pelt-like mat. Covered leaves die off. Water enriched with organic acids and lower pH values offer favorable conditions. At higher carbonate hardnesses, the calcium deposits on the leaves offer a good substrate.
Control: Cleaner fishes and snails only graze the short forms. Mechanical removal damages the leaves. The long threaded forms react to the addition of CO_2 in the water. Brushes detach after 2-3 months and drift free close to the substrate and can be vacuumed up. If constant CO_2 fertilization is provided, one hardly has to worry about brush algae infestations. Short brush algae are resistant. Preparations against filamentous algae must be applied repeatedly.

Green Spot Algae

Pelt Algae

Black Spot Algae

Black Brush Algae

Filamentous algae

Filamentous Algae

Description: Usually a green algae from the genus *Spirogyra*. Forms branched bunches of long, light green, thin filaments.

Occurrence: Of all the algae, their requirements are the closest to higher plants. Good conditions must prevail for their occurrence. Usually more common under intense illumination. Quite rapid growing, particularly annoying but less damaging with the exception of competition between them and aquarium plants for nutrients. The aesthetic appearance of the aquarium is disrupted and delicate plants can suffocate under the dense webbing.

Control: Preparations to control filamentous algae are possible but dangerous due to the aquarium plants. Cleaner fish occasionally eat younger groups but are usually still an ineffective control measure. Best to wrap the threads around a rough piece of wood to mechanically remove them. Sometimes they disappear on their own.

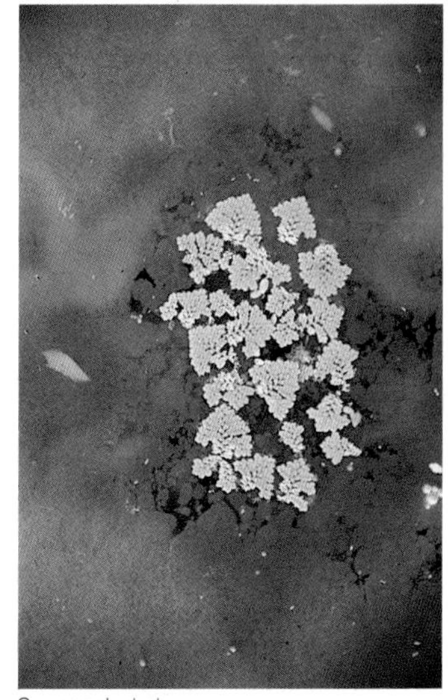
Suspended algae

Suspended Algae

Description: Green algae of the genus *Volvox* and others. Water turns green and becomes opaque later. Microscopic suspended algae which appear in large numbers and form dense cohesive colonies (spheres) are the causative agent.

Occurrence: Commonly introduced with pond food. Very high light intensity and surplus nitrogen or too much nutrient fertilizer encourages growth.

Control: Large water exchange. Put the tank in total darkness for 3 days and add algicides. Can be killed with UV light.

Algae Prevention

Certain groups of algae can be provisionally avoided with preventative measures. Prophylactic measures are: good living conditions for aquarium plants, moderation in fish load, moderate feeding, regular water changes, and siphoning organics from the substrate. By changing the pH values into unfavorable ranges for certain algae, one is in danger of producing a favorable range for other groups of algae.

Cleaner Fish and Snails

Certain aquarium fishes are known as algae cleaners. Fishes which take vegetable supplement but leave the aquarium plants undisturbed are suitable. Cleaner fishes graze only flat or filamentous forms of algae. Only blue algae and diatoms are cleaned by livebearers (black molly, platies, sailfin mollies and swordtails). Kissing gourami, Siamese algae eaters and loaches can be used. Against filamentous algae, fish with an inferior rasping mouth, such as *Ancistrus dolichopterus, Oto-*

cinclus vittatus and *Hypostomus* are recom-mended. The Siamese algae eater (*Crossocheilus siamensis*) cleans especially well. Apple snails graze on blue algae. Ramshorn snails can rasp spot algae and short pelt algae.

Chemicals

The various preparations (algicides) act against smear and/or filamentous algae. A few medications are named here. Tetra Algicid is a fast acting preparation against smear algae. Tetra-Algetten acts slowly and releases its active ingredient over several weeks into the water. Initially, the concentration rises slowly and, because of the missing shock, plant damage is less. Stubborn blue algae are controlled and the growth of filamentous algae is hampered.

Protalon 707, added to the water over a period of 7 days, is used against a variety of filamentous algae but is somewhat critical with blue algae.

With fast acting preparations, there is the danger that many plants in the tank will reduce their effectiveness before the algae are completely eliminated. A booster dose (½ dosage) applied 3 days later is recommended. One generally has to contend with plant damage after the addition of algicides, and the extent depends on the medication. Different plant species will react differently. With appropriate application, the little damage sustained is usually inconsequential, but, for example, *Vallisneria* are always strongly affected. After chemical algae control, a significant water exchange is advised to remove toxins from the water.

Ever since the 10th edition of Linné's (Linnaeus) work "Systema naturae"[1] (1758), every animal and plant is identified by two names. The first identifies the genus; the second identifies the species. With this "binomial nomenclature", every organism has its specific place in the system and can be catalogued. This work is performed by taxonomists. But before one can catalogue an animal—such as our fishes—it has to be identified. One has to try to determine its scientific name.
This report should provide guidelines for the aquarist on how to proceed systematically when he tries to identify a fish on his own.

How we identify our fishes

The identification of fishes usually is done on alcohol-preserved specimens. Determining[2] the fish immediately raises the question of what family does the fish belong to. For this, the origin of the fish can be very indicative: a fish from Australia cannot be a cichlid and a fish from South America can never be a *Botia* or a *Rasbora*. When the family question has been cleared, the genus needs to be determined next—this is markedly more difficult than identifying the family. In complex families with many genera, this task can become very time consuming and almost impossible to accomplish without the aid of specialized literature. Because the pertinent literature is distributed throughout the world, often in several languages, procurement and, frequently, translations are difficult and time consuming. Once the genus is determined, one has arrived at the rockiest road, the determination of the species. For this, even more specialized literature is required. Sometimes nothing but the original description of the species will do. Has one obtained the needed literature—often interlibrary loans can take months. The body of the fish is measured and the various indices[3] are established. We now have arrived at the technical phase of the determination. I would like to now list these measurements and indices in numerical order. Completeness cannot be guaranteed because characteristics which are only present in a single family have not been taken into consideration.

[1] Carl von LINNÉ (LINNAEUS), Swedish naturalist, born May 13, 1707 in Rashult, died January 10, 1778 in Uppsala. After studying medicine and natural sciences, research and study expeditions took him to Lappland, the Netherlands, Great Britain and France. After this, he was initially doctor in Stockholm, became president of the Academy of Science of Stockholm in 1737, the founding of which he had promoted, professor for anatomy and medicine in Uppsala in 1741, 1742 of botany, 1747 personal physician of the King; Linné designed the botanical garden and erected a museum of natural history.
Linné established the foundations of the botanical technical language still valid today by naming the parts of plants in a clear manner. He created the method of diagnosis. In other words, the description which always looks for and identifies the parts of a plant in a specific order. He strictly followed the binomial nomenclature which gives every plant a Latin double name, consisting of genus and species. The abbreviation L. following such plant and animal names tells us that he was the original describer and gave it the name. LINNÉ united the genera in classes and orders. LINNÉ's system was published in 1735 and was based on the differences of the sexual organs of plants (sexual system). At the same time, LINNÉ tried for the rest of his live to establish a plant system based on their habitus. He also published animal and mineral systems.
Principal works: Systema Naturae (1735; in the last edition by LINNÉ 1766-1768 in Volume 1, The Animals, Volume 2, Plants, Volume 3, Minerals, reprinted 1963); Genera Plantarum (1738); Materia Medica (1749-1763); Philosophia Botanica (1751, reprinted 1966); Species Plantarum, 2 volumes (1753, reprinted in 1966).
[2] Determination: In systematics, the identification of plants and animals by comparison with related forms or with the aid of keys.
[3] Indices: Relative values of various measurements.

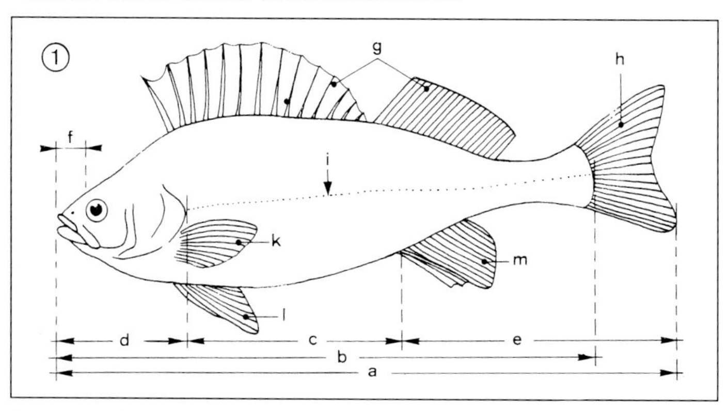

Illustration 1: Some measurements of a fish.

a)Total Length, b) Body Length, c) Body, d) Head, e) Tail, f) Snout, g) Dorsal Fins, h) Caudal Fin, i) Lateral Line, k) Pectoral Fins, l) Pelvic Fins, m) Anal Fins.

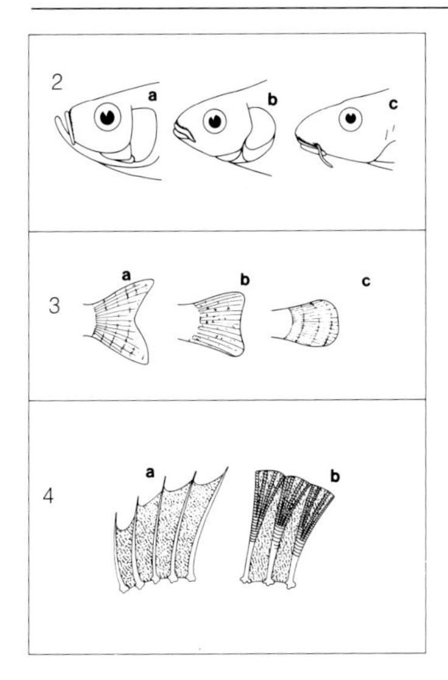

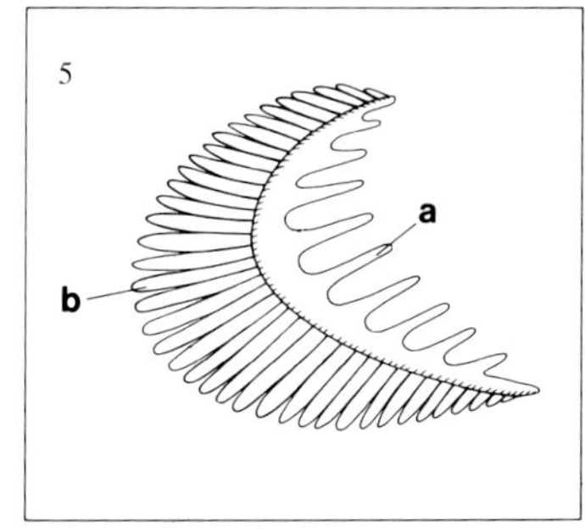

Illustration 2 (upper left): Shape of the mouth: a superior (or dorsal); b terminal; c inferior (or ventral).
Illustration 3 (middle left): Tail fin shapes: a forked; b concave; c rounded.
Illustration 4 (lower left): Fin rays: a hard rays (spines); b soft rays.
Illustration 5 (right): Gill arch: a gill rakers; b lamellae
Drawings: A. Bleichner

Measures and Numbers (of External Features)

All measurements are in millimeters (1 inch = 25.4 mm).

1. Total length: The distance between the tip of the snout to the end of the tail fin (illustration 1).
2. Body length (Standard length): The distance from the tip of the snout to the base of the tail (ill. 1).
3. Body height: From the base of the dorsal fin to the base of the ventral (pelvic) fin.
4. Head length: Distance from the tip of the mouth to the posterior edge of the operculum (ill. 1).
5. Head width: The widest part of the head. It is measured with a caliper.
6. Snout length: The distance from the tip of the snout to the anterior edge of the eye (ill. 1).
7. Eye diameter.
8. Interorbital width (width between the eyes): Also measured with a caliper.
9. Caudal Peduncle length: Distance from the base of tail fin to the posterior base of the anal fin.
10. Caudal Peduncle height: Usually the lowest part of a fish.

11. Snout to base of the pectoral fin.
12. Snout to base of the dorsal fin.
13. Snout to base of the pelvic fin.
14. Snout to base of the anal fin.
15. Shape of forehead: For exeample, is it straight, curved inward (concave) or curved outward (convex)?
16. Shape of the mouth: superior, terminal, inferior (ill. 2).
17. Number of scales across: The number of scales from the highest part of the fish to the lowest. Often given as: 4/1/8 which means: 4 = scales above the lateral line, 1 = the lateral line itself, 8 = scales below the lateral line.
18. Scales lengthwise: Preferably the central scale line, it can be the lateral line, but does not have to be.
19. Lateral line (Linea lateralis): The line of scales which has pores. The lateral line does not always have to be straight. It can be curved, incomplete or missing altogether.
20. Number of scales around the caudal peduncle.
21. Position of the cranial pores (important in the genus *Apistogramma*).
22. Fin rays: Hard rays and soft rays. The formula III/14 indicates the presence of 3 hard rays and 14 soft rays. Hard rays are always undivided, while soft rays are divided (ill. 4).
23. Length of the hard rays. Which is the longest?
24. Length of the soft rays. Which is the longest?
25. Shape of the tail fin. Forked, concave or rounded (ill. 3).
26. Longest ray of the tail fin: For example, the following formula for the tail fin (4/8/8/4) means: 4 upper support rays, 8 rays down to the middle, 8 rays from the middle down and 4 support rays on the bottom.
27. Pectoral fin formula: Usually one hard ray or only soft rays.
28. Pelvic fin formula: Usually two or three hard rays, otherwise, only soft rays.

Numbers 22 to 24 refer to the dorsal and the anal fins.

Measurements and Numbers (of Interior Characteristics)

29. Gill rakers: Number, shape, position, etc. (ill. 5).
30. Dentition: Which bones are toothed? How many teeth are there? What do they look like? Are they mono-, bi-, tri- or polycuspid? Are canines present?

Indices

31. Body height within total length: 3.8 to 4.3, for example, means that body height is contained in the total length 3.8 to 4.3 times. The smaller number comes from adult fish because those are usually deeper bodied than juveniles. Consequently, the number is smaller. Juveniles have the larger number.
32. Body height into standard length.
33. Head length into total length.
34. Head length into standard length.
35. Eye width (diameter) into head length.
36. Eye diameter into snout length.
37. Head width into head length.
38. Snout length into head length.

Both internal characteristics (gill rakers and teeth)— we have to remember this well—are the most reliable indicators at the moment for a correct identification. The concerted values of all measurements and numbers then result in a correct identification.
Only after securing all numbers and measurements for the specimen in question should they be compared to the literature. If one does not adhere to this basic rule, one is easily subjectively influenced, which often leads to erroneous identifications. In closing, I would like to say that the gathering of counts and relationships of points 1 to 38 takes at least six to eight hours. We need a dissecting scope and a microscope. Because the determination always occurs on preserved specimens which look more or less gray-brown, the living color of the specimen plays a secondary role. Whether a fin shows three or four spots is usually trivial in fish identification.

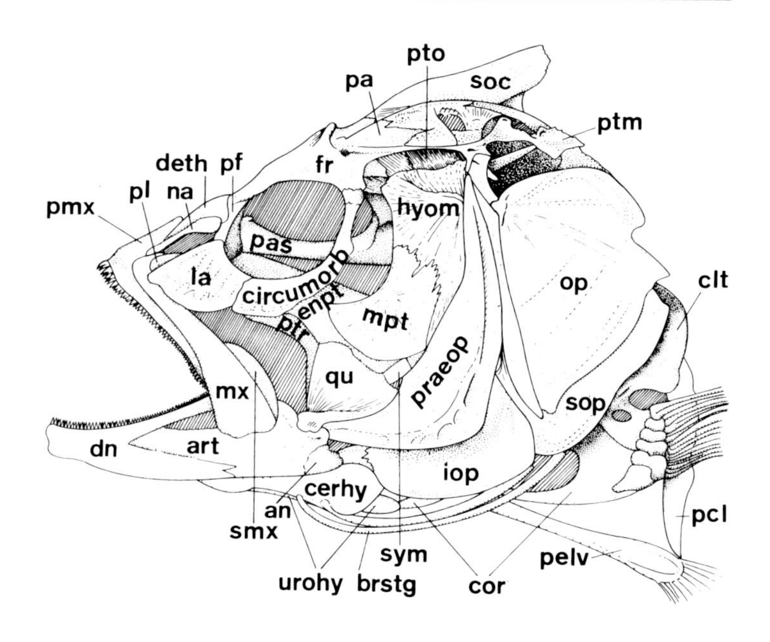

Scull bone of a perch-like fish

Plate of the "Skull"

The figure shows an idealized skull of a perch-like fish. The common names are given as far as they are named. A number of bones only occur in certain systematic groups of fishes. For this reason, not all occurring skull bones of a fish can be shown in the present drawing. The vomer (plowshare) cannot be seen on the drawing.
an = Angular, art = Articular, brstg = Branchiostegal rays, cerhy = Ceratohyal, circumorb = Suborbitals, clt = Cleithrum, cor = Coracoid, deth = Dermethmoid, dn = Dentary (bone of the lower jaw that has teeth), enpt = Epipterygoid, fr = Frontal (forehead), Hyom = Hyomandibular, iop = Interopercular, la = Lacrimal, mpt = Metapterygoid, mx = Maxilla (upper jaw), na = Nasal (nose bone), op = Operculum (gill cover), pa = Parietal, pas = Parasphenoid, pelv = Pelvic (fin), pcl = Postcleithrum, pf = Prefrontal, pl = Palatine, pmx = Premaxilla (lower jaw), praeop = Preoperculum, ptm = Posttemporal, pto = Pterotic, ptr = Pterygoid, qu = Quadrate, smx = Supramaxilla, soc = Supraoccipital, sop = Subopercular, sym = Symplectic, urohy = Urohyal.

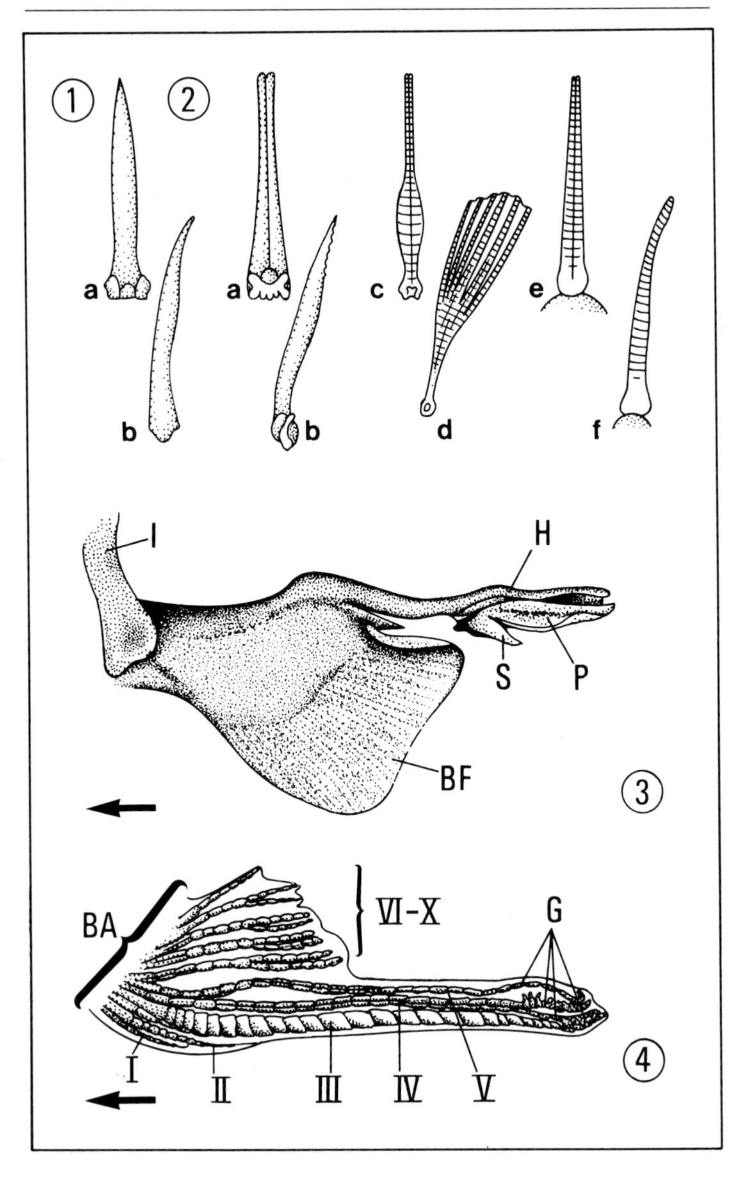

1
2
a
b
a
b
c
d
e
f
I
H
S
P
BF
3
BA
VI-X
G
I
II
III
IV
V
4

Plate of “Fin Rays and Modifications”

Fig. 1:
Frontal view of the spine (a) and lateral view (b). Spines are always uniform, undivided and not articulated, usually smooth and pointed.

Fig. 2:
Shapes of soft rays. All soft rays, also undivided and unarticulated ones, are easily distinguishable from hard rays (spines) when seen from the front. Soft rays are always made up of a left and right half which are joined, while spines are always uniform. a, c, e = front views, b, d, f = lateral views.
a + b. Undivided and totally unarticulated soft ray. Note the division into left and right halves (a).
c + d. Fan-like divided, more or less completely articulated soft ray.
e + f. Undivided, more or less articulated soft ray.

Fig. 3:
Ventral view of one half of the male organ of the shark *Heterodontus francisci*. Pictured is the left modified ventral fin which, the same as the right one, forms a pterygopodium. BF = Ventral fin, H = Hook, I= Ischiopubic cartilage, P= Pterygopodium, S= Spur. The arrow points towards the head.

Fig. 4:
The anal fin modified into a gonopodium in a livebearer (*Heterandria formosa*, Fam. Poeciliidae). This anal fin is subdivided into 3 segments; a) an anterior, greatly reduced fin segment (rays I + II), b) a middle, functional copulation segment (= gonopodium, rays III-V) and c) a posterior, normal fin segment (rays VI-X). Ray III is the main support of the gonopodium. BA = base of the anal fin, G = gonopodium. The arrow points towards the head.

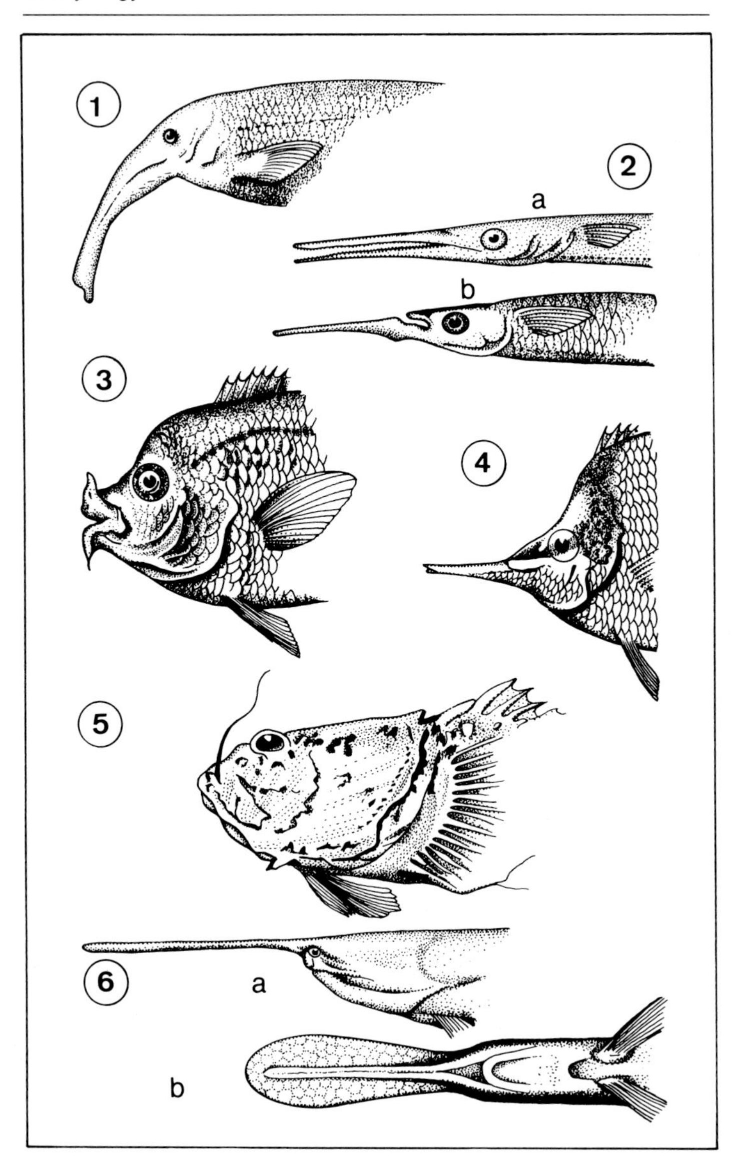
1
2
a
b
3
4
5
6
a
b

Plate of "Mouth Structures"

Fig. 1:
Elongation of the snout of an elephant-nose (Fam. Mormyridae, *Gnathonemus elephas*). The animals work the soft substrate with their trunk-like mouth in search of food.

Fig. 2:
Elongation of the snout of needlefishes (Fam. Belonidae, a) and half-beaks (Fam. Hemiramphidae, b). a) Upper and lower jaws are equally elongated. For example: *Strongylura longirostris*. b) Only the lower jaw is elongated. Example: *Hyporhamphus unifasciatus*. Representatives of the halfbeaks with an elongated lower jaw, which is fixed while the upper jaw moves (big exception among fishes!).

Fig. 3:
Extremely fleshy lips, an adaptation to the feeding habit (aufwuchs feeder (= biocover feeder)). Example: *Cichlasoma labiatum.*

Fig. 4:
Elongation of the snout of a longnosed butterfly fish, (*Forcipiger longirostris*) Fam. Chaetodontidae. This fish is also adapted for its feeding habits. The fish use this snout like a pair of tweezers to pick at corral polyps and other invertebrates.

Fig. 5:
Barbel-like appendage on the upper jaw of *Uranoscopus tosae.*

Fig. 6:
Rostrum of a paddlefish (*Polyodon spathula*) in a) side and b) ventral view. The function of this structure is presently unknown.

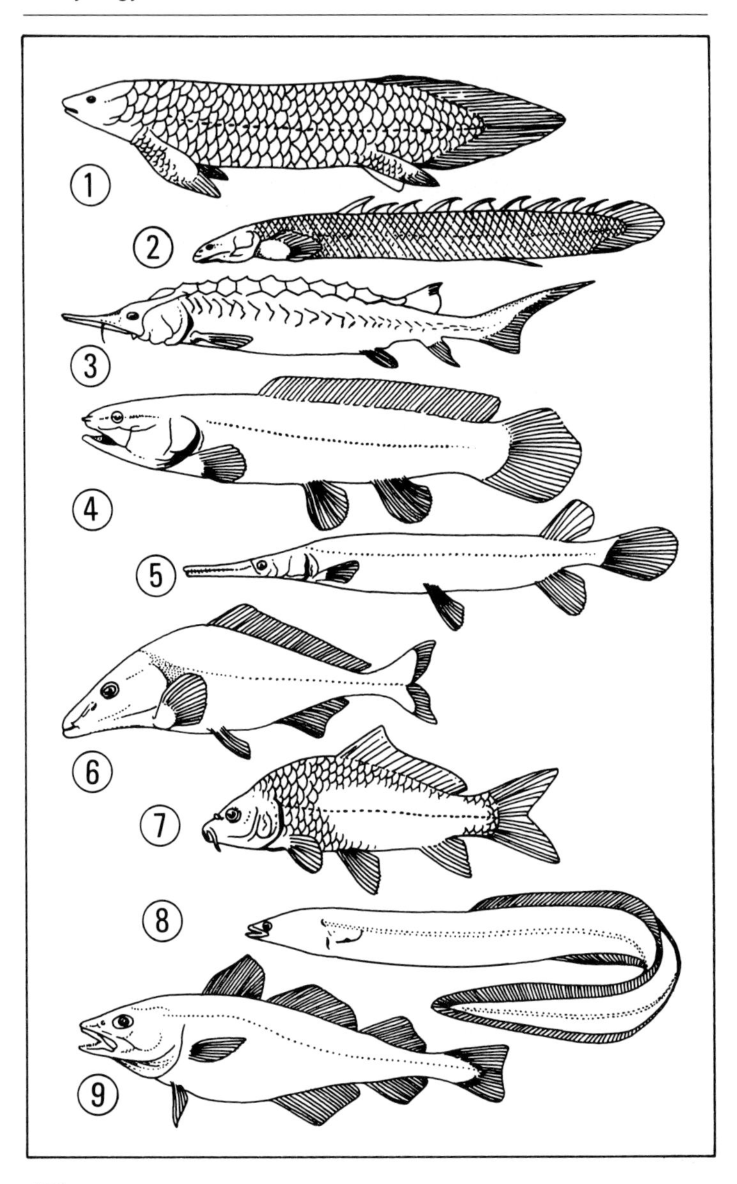
1
2
3
4
5
6
7
8
9

Plate of "Body Shapes I"

Fig. 1:
Australian lungfish (*Neoceratodus forsteri*), sub-class Dipnoi. Note the paired fins. They are composed of a strong, externally scaled shaft with anterior and posterior finned fringes.

Fig. 2:
African lobe-finned fish (*Polypterus senegalus*, Fam. Polypteridae). The dorsal fin is composed of numerous, individual lobes.

Fig. 3:
Sturgeon (*Acipenser oxyrhynchus*, Fam. Acipenseridae). Sturgeons sport bone plates on their sides and have an asymmetrical (heterocercal) tail fin.

Fig. 4:
Mud fish (*Amia calva*, Fam. Amiidae). The deeply split jaws betray this fish as being a predator.

Fig. 5:
Longnose gar (*Lepisosteus osseus*, Fam. Lepisosteidae). Gars belong to the ambush predators, who are easily identified by the posterior location of the dorsal and anal fins. Together with the tail fin, they compose the propulsion unit of the fish.

Fig. 6:
Mormyrus caballus (Fam. Mormyridae). This representative of the elephant-nose fishes has only a slightly elongated snout (like an elephant trunk).

Fig. 7:
Carp (*Cyprinus carpio*, Fam. Cyprinidae). Carp and other carp-like fishes have a "typical" fish shape.

Fig. 8:
European eel (*Anguilla anguilla*, Fam. Anguillidae). Eels have a snake-like shape, no ventral fins and dorsal, caudal and anal fins that form a continuous fin fringe.

Fig. 9:
Gadus morhua (Fam. Gadidae). The single barbel on the lower jaw is typical for cod. In addition, many cod have a three-part dorsal fin and a two-part anal fin.

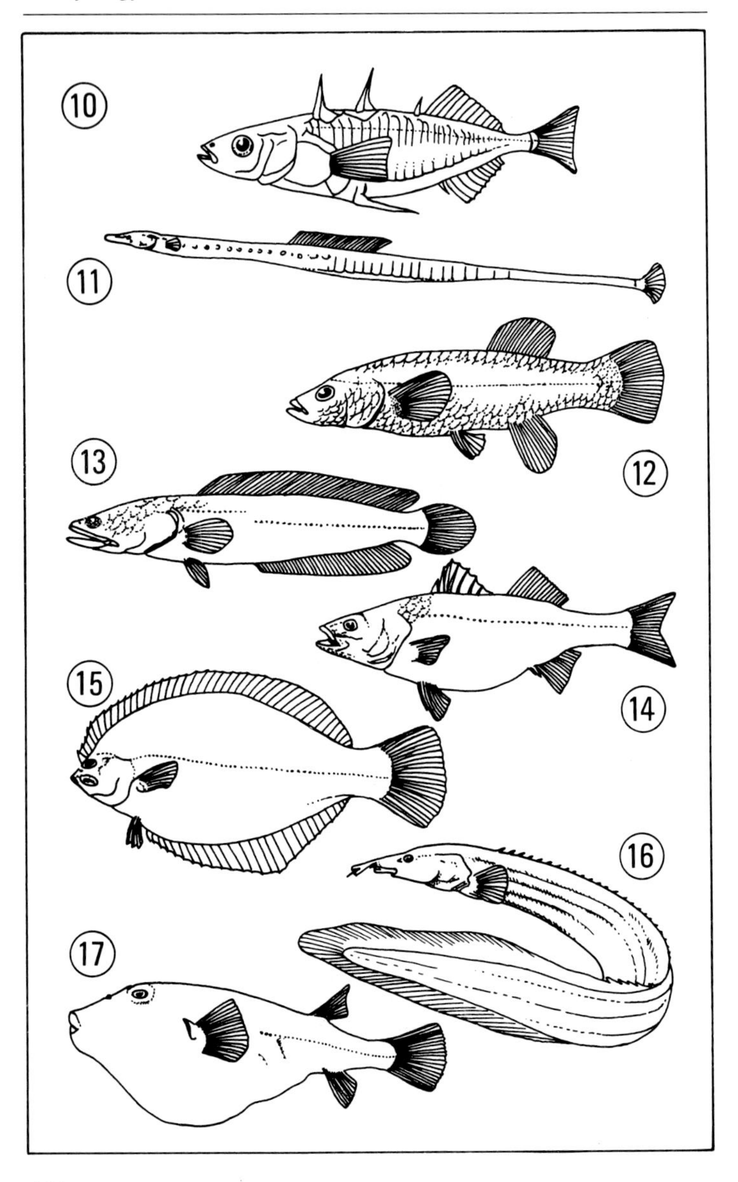
10
11
13
12
15
14
16
17

Plate of "Body Shapes II"

Fig. 10:
Three-spined stickleback (*Gasterosteus aculeatus*, Fam. Gasterosteidae). The animals have bone plates on the sides of the body. The first three rays of the dorsal fin are separate.

Fig. 11:
Pipefish (*Pseudophallus starksi*, Fam. Syngnathidae). The animals have developed an appropriate body shape for their life in seaweed. Even more extreme is the adaptation of sea horses to their biotope.

Fig. 12:
Killifish (*Fundulus majalis*, Fam. Cyprinodontidae). Many killies have a body with a totally circular cross-section.

Fig. 13:
Snakehead (*Channa striata*, Fam. Channidae). Ambush predators with a deeply split mouth. The unpaired fins of the fish constitute the propulsion unit.

Fig. 14:
Roccus saxatilis (Fam. Serranidae). Typical representative of the perch-like fishes. These generally have a two-part dorsal fin with hard rays anterior and soft rays posterior.

Fig. 15:
Flat fish (*Pseudopleuronectes americanus*, Fam. Pleuronectidae). These fishes are well adapted to their life on the bottom. They are dorsoventrally flattened. One half of the body becomes the bottom, the other the top. The eyes move to the upper half.

Fig. 16:
Spiny eel (*Mastacembelus maculatus*, Fam. Mastacembelidae). Eel-like fishes with a peculiarly elongated rostrum and an inferior mouth.

Fig. 17:
Puffer (*Sphoeroides maculatus*, Fam. Tetraodontidae). Puffers differ strongly from the "typical" fish shape. Locomotion is achieved mainly through the pectoral fins.

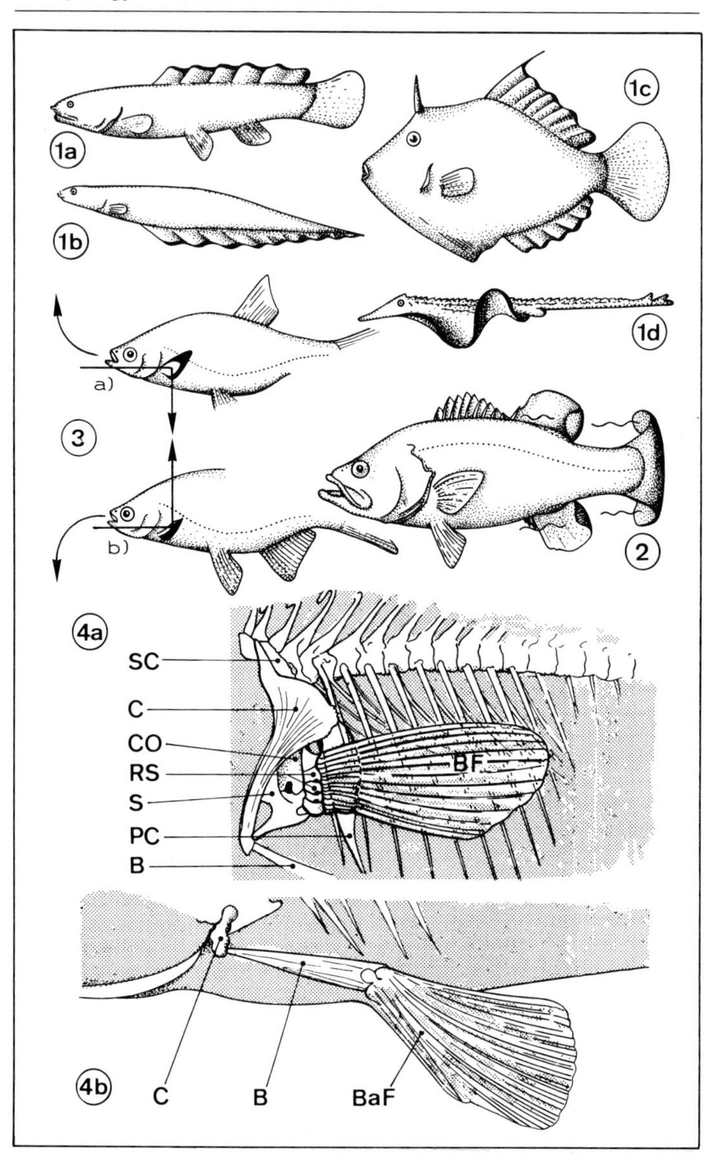
1a
1b
1c
1d
3
a)
b)
2
4a
SC
C
CO
RS
S
PC
B
BF
4b
C
B
BaF

Plate of "Locomotion in Fishes"

Fig. 1:
Unusual modes of locomotion with fins in fishes.
a) With the dorsal fin. It is elongated and forms a wavy (undulating) fringe. Example: bowfin (*Amia calva*).
b) With the anal fin. Most fishes with this type of locomotion have no dorsal fin, or it is greatly reduced. Examples: knife fishes (Fam. Notopteridae), electric eels (Fam. Electrophoridae).
c) With dorsal and anal fin. Both fins are elongated and can be moved singly or together. Example: trigger fish (Fam. Balistidae).
d) With the pectorals. These are often strongly elongated in rays and provide thrust with an undulating movement. Example: freshwater sting ray (Fam. Paratrygonidae).

Fig. 2:
The figure shows the use of the unpaired fins (dorsal, tail and anal fins) in the locomotion of large mouth bass (*Micropterus salmoides*). These three fins serve to control direction, as well as to stabilize the fish.

Fig. 3:
The position of the pectoral fins while swimming of a "normal" fish (Fam. Cyprinidae). a) Swimming upward, b) diving. The curved arrows indicate the change in direction. The angled arrows show the vectors of the acting forces.

Fig. 4:
Skeleton of the paired fins (pectoral and pelvic fins) of a perch (*Perca fluviatilis*). a) Shoulder with pectoral fin, b) pelvis with ventral fin.
B = Basipterygium, BaF = Pelvic fin, BF = Pectoral fin, C= Cleithrum, CO = Coracoid, PC = Postcleithrum, RS = Radius, S= Scapula, SC = Supracleithrum.
Since many bones have no common name, they were omitted altogether.

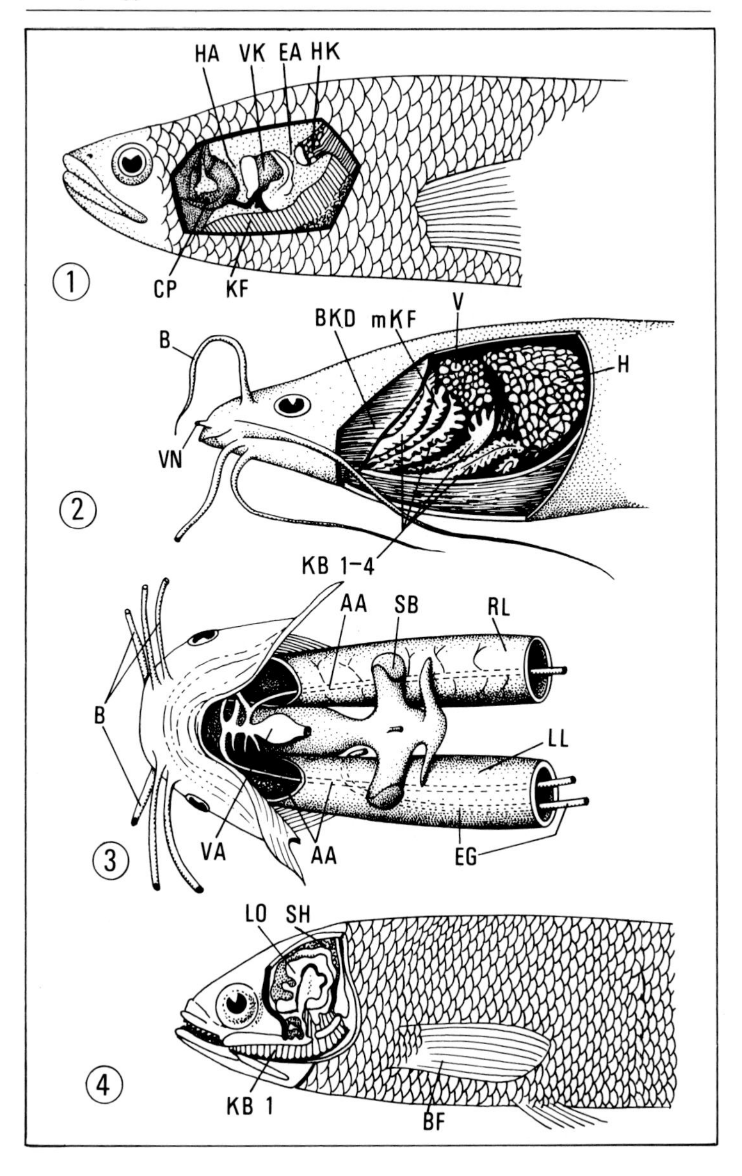
HA
VK
EA
HK
1
CP
KF
BKD
mKF
V
B
H
VN
2
KB 1–4
AA
SB
RL
B
LL
VA
AA
EG
3
LO
SH
4
KB 1
BF

Plate of "Accessory Respiratory Organs"

In the following fishes, the accessory respiratory organs represent the organisms' adaptation to air breathing. Although the majority of gas exchange is still handled by the gills, these fishes would still die after several hours if they were deprived of atmospheric air, even in good water.

Fig. 1:
Head of a snakehead (*Channa* sp.) with removed operculum. Snakeheads use the open space above the gills as an additional breathing organ. It is also called a labyrinth, as in anabantids. However, both labyrinths have evolved completely independent. CP = Connection with the pharynx (throat), EA = Hypophysis of the 1st gill arch, HA = Hypophysis (bony growth) of the hyomandibular, HK = Posterior chamber, KF = Gill filaments of the 1st arch, VK = Anterior chamber.

Fig. 2:
Head of a walking catfish of the genus *Clarias*. The operculum has been removed. These catfishes have an accessory breathing organ in the shape of a short breathing sac which only reaches the shoulder line. Projections of the 2nd and 4th gill arches reach into it. The walls of the chamber, as well as the projections, are derivatives of those spread gill filaments and are richly vascularized. B = Barbels, BKD = Base of the operculum, H = Posterior branched extensions, KB 1-4 = Gill arches 1-4, mKF = Modified gill filaments, V = Anterior branched extensions, VN = Anterior nostril.

Fig. 3:
Ventral view of the Asian stinging catfish, *Heteropneustes fossilis*, with opened gill and abdominal areas. The same as *Clarias* sp., *H. fossilis* also has an accessory breathing organ. However, in this fish, the breathing sac encloses the gills and are blind sacs on both sides of the column far posterior. These blind sacs are also richly vascularized. AA = Afferent artery, B = Barbels, EG = Efferent (removing) vessels, LL = Left air sac, RL = Right air sac, SB = Swim bladder in bone capsule, Va = Ventral aorta.

Fig. 4:
Head of a climbing perch (*Anabas* sp.) with an opened labyrinth. The labyrinth organ is made up of a dorsal enlargement of the gill chamber above the 4th gill arch. Three or more sinuate bone lamellae covered by a mucus membrane are located in this cavity. The membrane is richly vascularized. When the mouth is opened, the labyrinth is in contact to the oral cavity. BF = Pectoral fin, KB1 = 1st gill arch, LO = Labyrinth, SH = Suprabranchial cavity (labyrinth cavity).

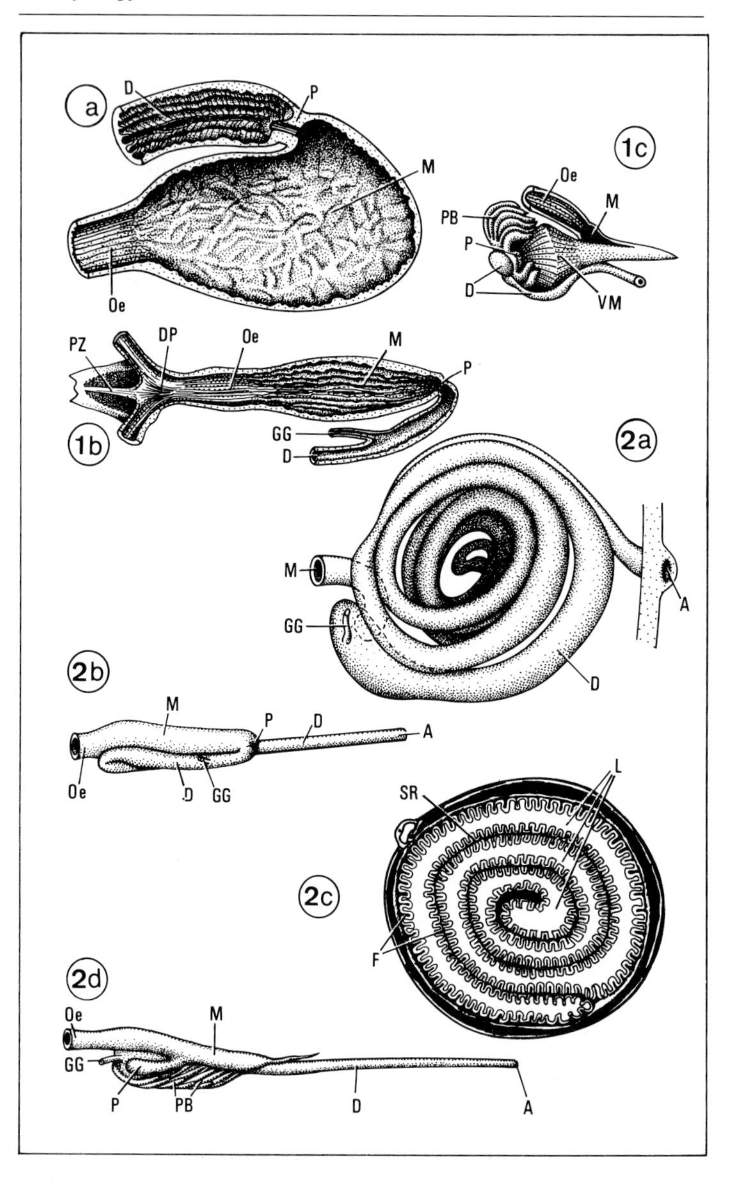
a
D
P
M
Oe
1c
Oe
M
PB
P
D
D
VM
PZ
DP
Oe
M
P
1b
GG
D
2a
M
GG
A
D
2b
M
P
D
A
Oe
D
GG
L
SR
2c
F
2d
Oe
M
GG
P
PB
D
A

Plate of "Intestines"

Fig. 1:
Changes in shape, appendages and coatings of the anterior segment of the digestive tract. a) The omnivorous European catfish (*Silurus glanis*). b) The carnivorous/piscivorous pike (*Esox lucius*). c) The detritovorous mullet (*Mugil cephalus*). D = Intestine, DP = Opening to the ductus pneumaticus (= the connection between swim bladder and intestine), GG = Bile duct, M = Stomach, Oe = Esophagus, P = Pylorus, PB = Pyloric caeca, PZ = Pharyngeal teeth, VM = Muscular stomach.

Fig. 2:
Changes of the intestine in length and other characteristics in carnivorous and herbivorous fishes. a) Wound up intestine of the herbivorous catfish *Loricaria* sp. b) Straight intestine of the carnivorous/piscivorous pike (*Esox lucius*). c) Spiral valve of the carnivorous/piscivorous shark (*Scyliorhinus* sp.) in cross-section. d) Straight intestine with caeca of the carnivorous/piscivorous perch *Perca fluviatilis*.
A = Anus, D = Intestine, F = Mucosa folds, GG = Bile duct, L = Lumen, M = Stomach, Oe = Esophagus, P = Pylorus, PB = Pyloric caeca, SR = Spiral valve.

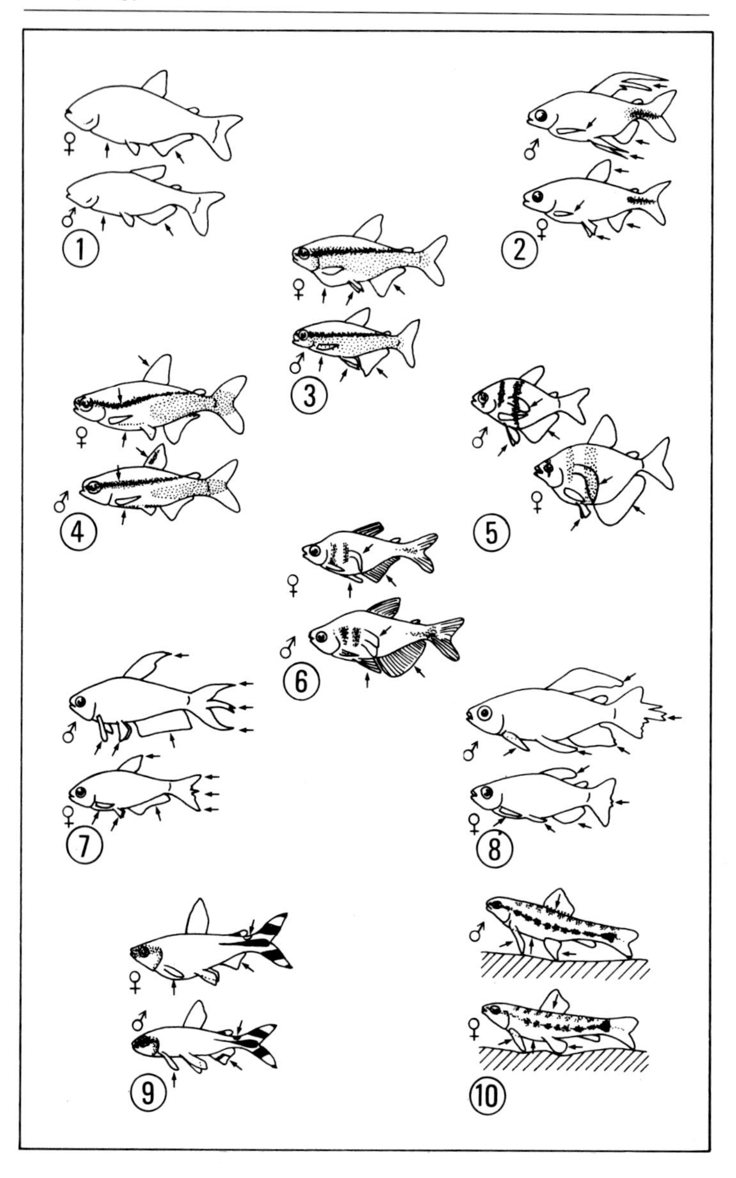

♀
♂
1
♂
♀
2
♀
♂
3
♀
♂
4
♂
♀
5
♀
♂
6
♂
♀
7
♂
♀
8
♀
♂
9
♂
♀
10

Plate of "Sexual Differences in Characins"

Fig. 1:
Blind cave tetra (*Astyanax fasciatus mexicanus*). ♂ is more slender, anal fin is convex; ♀ with plumper abdomen, anal fin is concave.

Fig. 2:
Long-finned characin (*Brycinus longipinnis*). ♂ longer, slimmer. Thread-like elongated dorsal fin, elongated ventral fins and convex anal fin. ♀ plumper without elongated fin rays and the anal fin is either straight or concave.

Fig. 3:
Cardinal tetra (*Paracheirodon axelrodi*). ♂ slimmer, ventral line almost straight, anal fin straight or vaguely indented; ♀ fuller, stomach never indented, anal fin indented.

Fig. 4:
Neon tetra (*Paracheirodon innesi*). ♂ more slender, stomach straight or slightly indented; ♀ fuller, stomach convex.

Fig. 5:
Black tetra (*Gymnocorymbus ternetzi*). ♂ smaller with the end of the swim bladder rounded and finishing high in the body cavity; ♀ thicker and fuller. Swim bladder ends pointed and reaches down to the anal opening.

Fig. 6:
Yellow tetra (*Hyphessobrycon bifasciatus*). ♂ more slender, anal fin straight, swim bladder rounded. ♀ fuller, and anal fin concave, swim bladder pointed.

Fig. 7:
Emperor tetra (*Nematobrycon palmeri*). ♂ larger, with longer dorsal and anal fins, central rays of the tail fin are elongated. ♀ is smaller with normal finnage.

Fig. 8:
Congo tetra (*Phenacogrammus interruptus*). ♂ larger, dorsal fin longer, anal fin and center of caudal fin are elongated in a rag-like fashion. ♀ smaller, fins normal.

Fig. 9:
False rummy nose tetra (*Petitella georgiae).* ♂ smaller, more slender with a white and dark design on the anal fin. ♀ longer, fuller without design on the anal fin.

Fig. 10:
Banded darter tetra (*Characidium fasciatum*). ♂ smaller, thinner, better developed fins, dots on the base of the dorsal fin; ♀ larger and fatter, base of dorsal fin without dots.

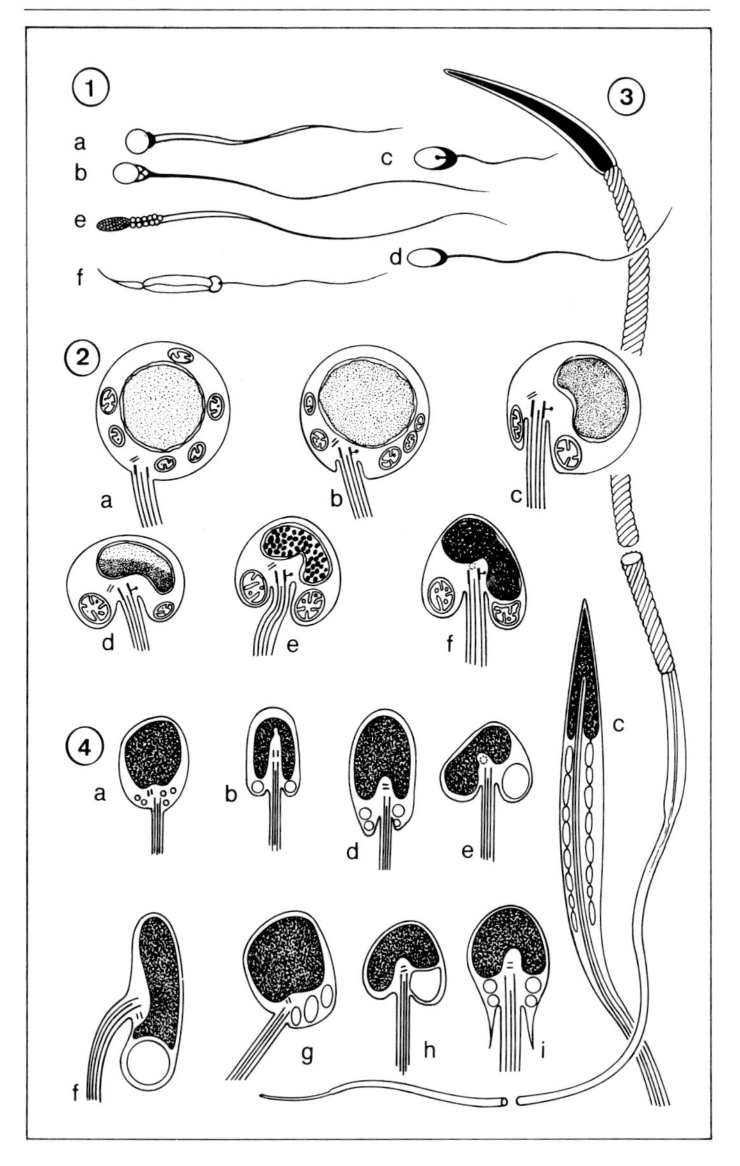
1
a
b
c
e
d
f
2
a
b
c
d
e
f
3
c
4
a
b
d
e
f
g
h
i

Plate of "Sperm"

Fig. 1:
Differences in the sperm shape of some teleosts.
a) Pike (*Esox lucius*). The three segments of the sperm (head, middle piece, tail or flagellum) are clearly defined. b) Atlantic herring (*Clupea harengus*), c) Rainbow trout (*Onchorhynchus mykiss*), d) Sea trout (*Salmo trutta trutta*), e) Guppy (*Poecilia reticulata*), f) Eel (*Anguila anguila*).

Fig. 2:
Spermatogenesis (formation of sperm cells) of the teleost, *Parapristipoma octolineatum* (Fam. Pomadasyidae).
a) A young spermatid (pre-sperm stage) with a large, centrally located nucleus and mitochondria in the cytoplasm. b) Migration of the centrioles and rotation of the nucleus. The axial filament is now tangent to the nucleus. c) The nucleus becomes indented and the mitochondria migrate around the centrioles. d-f) Transformation of the nucleus: the spermatid turns into spermatozoon capable of fertilization (f).

Fig. 3:
A sperm of the butterfly fish *Pantodon buchholzi* (Fam. Pantodontidae). The nucleus (black) is elongated; the screw-like middle piece is also greatly elongated. It follows a short windowed region (exception!) and the long flagellum (tail).

Fig. 4:
The figure shows the diverse appearance of the heads of some teleost spermatozoa.
a) *Epiplatys spilargyreius* (Fam. Cyprinodontidae), b) *Balistes forcipatus* (Fam. Balistidae), c) *Poecilia reticulata* (Fam. Poeciliidae), d) *Hemichromis fasciatus* (Fam. Cichlidae), e) *Boops boops* (Fam. Sparidae), f) *Ophiblennius atlanticus*, g) *Scartella cristata* (both Fam. Blenniidae), h) *Periophthalmus papilio* (Fam. Gobiidae), i) *Sarotherodon niloticus* (Fam. Cichlidae).

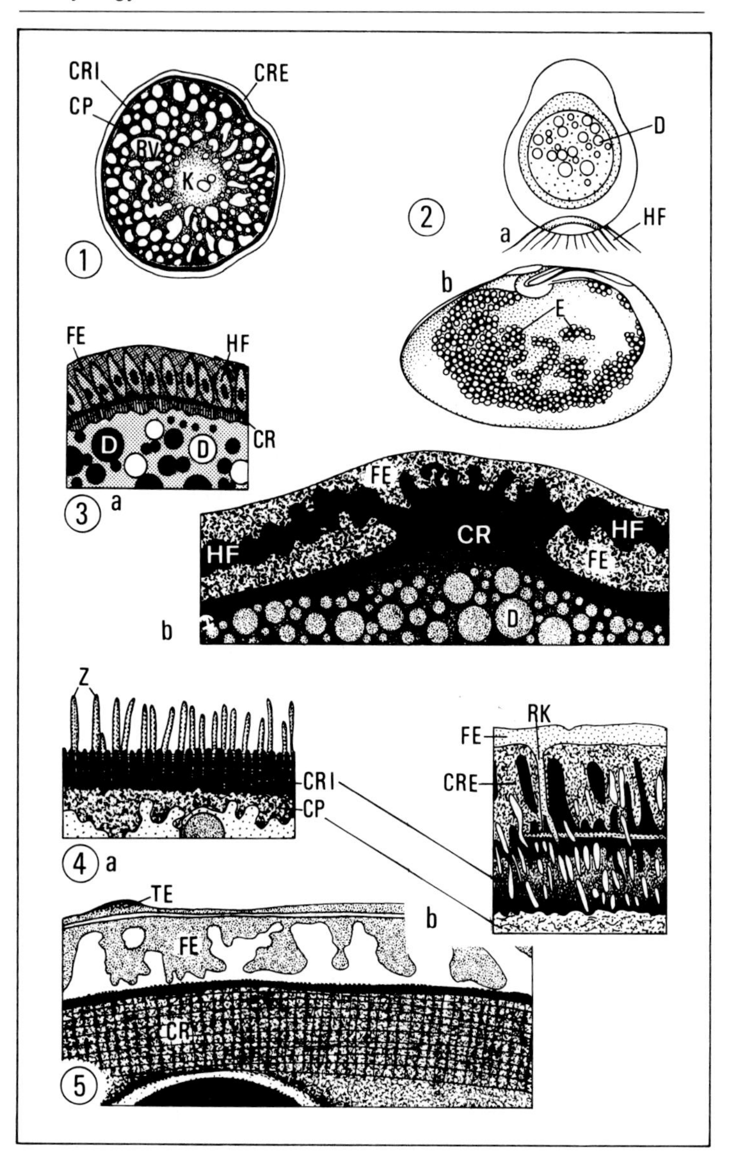
CRI
CRE
CP
RV
K
1
D
2
HF
a
b
E
FE
HF
CR
D
D
3
a
FE
CR
HF
HF
FE
D
b
Z
CRI
CP
4
a
RK
FE
CRE
b
TE
FE
CR
5

Plate of "Egg Cells and Eggs"

Fig. 1:
Structure of a fish egg (oocyte) at the late state II under a light microscope. The nucleus (K) is centrally located. The oocyte is filled mostly by cortical granules (RV). In between the granules is the cytoplasm (CP). The egg membrane (= Cortex radiatus) has already differentiated into an external (= Cortex radiatus externus) and an internal (= Cortex radiatus internus) component.

Fig. 2:
a) Pear-shaped egg of the goby, *Pomatochistus minutus*.
b) The figure shows a spawn of this fish on the open shell of the sand mussel, *Mya arenaria*. The eggs stick with the aid of adhesive threads. These threads of goby eggs are always on the pole of the egg. D = Yolk, E = Eggs, HF = Threads.

Fig. 3:
Egg membrane of the goby, *Pomatochistus minutus*, under a light microscope. a) Adhesive threads, in cross-section. The threads are only in direct contact with the egg membrane at the pole; there are no other areas of contact. These threads are formed by epithelial follicle cells which are triangular to trapezoidal in cross-section. b) Attachment site of the adhesive threads on the pole of the egg at the egg membrane. According to electron microscopic studies, the threads are part of the egg membrane (of the cortex radiatus externus). CR = Cortex radiatus, D = Yolk elements, FE = Follicular epithelium, HF = Adhesive threads.

Fig. 4:
Electron microscope sections of the egg membranes of bottom spawning freshwater fishes. The egg membranes of these fishes are always relatively thick (10-70 μm). a) Gudgeon (*Gobio gobio*). The outside of the egg membrane is differentiated into villi. They are a part of the Cortex radiatus externus and fasten the egg to a substrate. b) Loach (*Noemacheilus barbatulus*). Here the villi are embedded in a matrix. Both are mainly composed of polysaccharides which become sticky in contact with water (when spawning). CP = Cytoplasma, CRE = Cortex radiatus externus, CRI = Cortex radiatus internus, FE = Follicular epithelium, MA = Matrix, RK = Radial microvillus, Z = Villi.

Fig. 5:
Segment of the egg membrane of *Trigla* sp. The eggs are planktonic which is why neither adhesive threads nor villi are present. BM = Basal membrane, CP = Cytoplasm, CR = Cortex radiatus, FE = Follicular epithelium, TF = Theca folliculi.

The Amazon at Manaus, a place to capture angelfish and discus.

Symbols used in the illustrated fish section:

Fam.: = Family
Sub-Fam.: = Sub-family
Syn.: = Synonym = named the same
In the systematics of animal names, only the name of the original describer is valid. Subsequent descriptions of the same species using another name create so called synonyms.
Hab.: = Habitat; the natural region of origin.
F.I.: = First imported. With many species it is interesting to know how long the species has been known in the hobby.
Sex: = Differences between the sexes.
Soc. B.: = Social behavior.
M: = Conditions recommended for maintenance. Following the indications for pH and degrees German total hardness (dGH), there are often values in parentheses. These values are considered optimal for the species.
B: = Breeding. Indications under this heading are meant merely as a guideline. Complete breeding accounts should be obtained from fish journals or relevant specialty books.
F: = Feeding.
S: = Special observations.
T: = Temperature.
L: = Final length of the adult fish. A value in parenthesis refers to a possible length in an aquarium.
A: = Recommended aquarium length.
R: = Water region preferred by the fish in an aquarium: t = top, m = middle, b = bottom.
D: = Degree of difficulty. For explanations refer to page 203 (Volume 1).

F: (Feeding)

At each fish description under this heading are the abbreviations: C, H, L, O. These stand for:

C = Carnivore = meat/fish-eater
H = Herbivore = plant/vegetable eater
L = Limnovore = aufwuchs/detritus eater
O = Omnivore = eats some of everything
D: 1 = species for the beginning hobbyist.
D: 2 = species for novices with some basic knowledge.
D: 3 = species for advanced hobbyists
D: 4 = species for experts and specialists.
H = Herbivore; Ch = Water chemistry; C = Carnivore; S = Size

* Detailed explanations can be found in Vol. 1, page 200.

Fam. Petromyzontidae (Lampreys)

The body of these fish-like species is naked and eel-like. The nasal orifice is not connected to the mouth. On each side are seven gill openings. The tongue is covered with teeth and functions as a rasp. Many lampreys are predators or parasites on fishes. Larvae differ in several aspects from the adult. The larvae was described as *Ammocoetus*. The animals live partially in saltwater and partially in freshwater. Some species migrate back and forth. According to STERBA, the life cycle of lampreys can be divided into the following clearly defined stages. Embryonic period, larval period, transformation (metamorphosis), feeding period and reproductive period. Lampreys occur in North and South America, Europe and north Asia as well as north Africa, southern Australia and New Zealand.

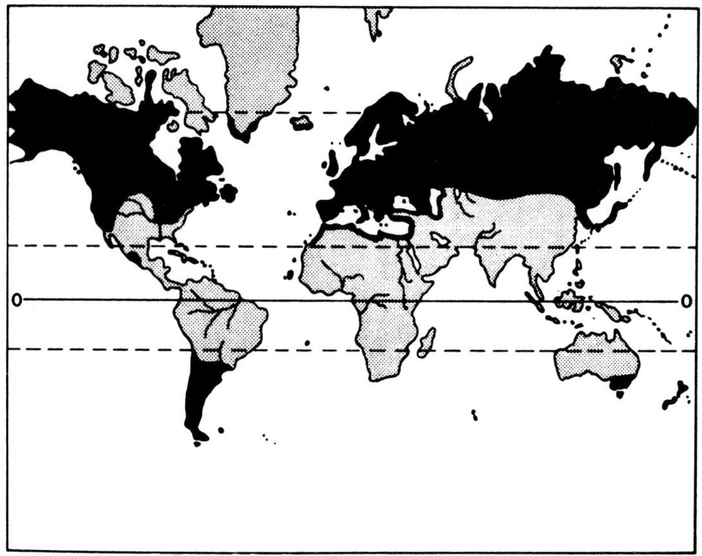

Distribution of the Petromyzonidae

Lampetra planeri (BLOCH, 1784)
Lamprey

Syn.: *Petromyzon planeri, P. branchialis.*

Hab: Europe; from Ireland and France to the upper course of the Volga. Mainly in the North and Baltic Sea region.

Fl.: Native to Germany.

Sex: During the spawning season, the anal region of the ♀ is distinctly swollen and rust red.

Soc.B.: A bottom dweller that lives buried. It is twilight- and night-active. Predator.

M: Fine-grained sand where the animals can burrow; some stones as hiding places; no plants are necessary. Clear, medium-hard (around 10° dGH), neutral (pH around 7.0) water. Sensitive to higher temperatures. *Lampetra planeri* is a fish for the specialist. Best kept in a species tank.

B: Has not been successful in an aquarium. The spawning season in nature is from March to June. After spawning, the fish quickly die off. The larvae are called *Ammocoetus* and metamorphose after about four years into sexually mature animals.

F: The species is either predatory or parasitic on fish flesh and young.

S: Adults lack a functional intestine. The larvae (*Ammocoetus*) have neither a sucking mouth nor eyes. These two characteristics differentiate them from the adult.

T: 4-16° C (coldwater fish), L: 19 cm, A: 80 cm, R: b, D: 4
39-61° F (coldwater fish), 7 ", 31",

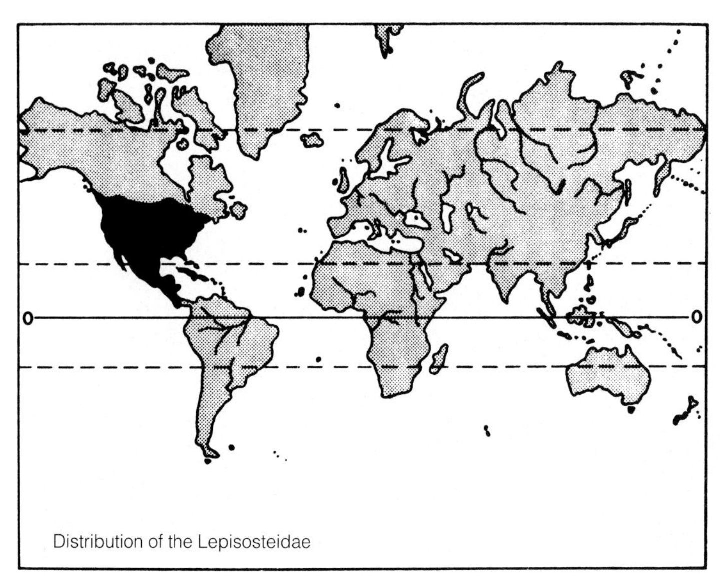

Distribution of the Lepisosteidae

Fam. Amiidae (Bow Fin)
This family reached its summit during the Mesozoic Era (Jurassic and Cretaceous periods). Today it is represented by a single species which has a series of primitive anatomical features. The animals have round scales and their mandibles cannot move forward.

Fam. Ceratodontidae (Australian Lungfishes)
The family only has a single species (*Neoceratodus forsteri*). The body is covered with thin, large scales. There is only one lung sac, and it has interior folds. The paired fins are fleshy-lobed. The vomer of these fishes has teeth. These fish only occur in Australia.

Fam. Lepisosteidae (Gar Pikes)
The gar pikes exclusively inhabit North and Central America. They have an elongated body with a long snout. The body has a dense layer of ganoid scales, providing armor. The mandibles are heavily toothed. Gar pikes are predatory freshwater fishes which have existed since the Cretaceous period. The swim bladder serves as an accessory breathing organ. Dorsal and anal fins are posteriorly (ambush predator) located. Presently there are seven species.

Fam. Polydontidae (Paddlefishes)

A small family of sturgeon-like fishes which possess a very long snout. They differ from other sturgeon-like fishes by the absence of lateral bony plates. Their skin is smooth; ganoid scales can only be found on the caudal peduncle. Today's representatives have two barbels. There are two recent species: *Polyodon spatula* in North America and *Psephurus gladius* in the Jang-tse-kiang River of China.

Fam. Pristidae

This family is characterized by a shark-like body shape and an overly developed rostrum shaped like a saw. These fishes are closer related to rays than to sharks. They differ from saw sharks (Fam. Pristiophoridae) by the missing barbels, the position of the gill openings and the dentition of the saw. In saw fishes, all teeth are about the same size, but in saw sharks, small and large teeth alternate. Saw fishes are large fishes with the largest representatives reaching almost 8 m (25 ft). They inhabit tropical and subtropical seas. Some species enter freshwater or live there permanently, for example, a species from Lake Nicaragua in Central America and the species from north Australia, presented on page 220.

Descriptions of the other families in this group can be found in Volume 1, page 206.

Scaphirhynchus platorhynchus (RAFINESQUE, 1820)
Shovelnose Sturgeon

Syn.: *Acipenser platorhynchus, A. cataphractus, Scaphirhynchus cataphractus, S. rafinesquei.*

Hab.: North America; area of influence of the Mississippi. The species lives only in freshwater; it does not migrate to the sea.

F.I.: Unknown.

Sex: None known.

Soc. B.: The animals are peaceful and will not disturb other fish.

M: As noted under *Acipenser sturio.*

B: Breeding in an aquarium has thus far not been accomplished. In the wild the breeding season is from April to June. The sturgeon migrates into rocky bottomed tributaries to spawn.

F: C; predominantly insect larvae and other benthic invertebrates.

S: The genus *Scaphirhynchus* can be differentiated from the genus *Acipenser* by a flattened snout, a long tail base covered by bony plates and a missing spiracle. Besides *S. platorhynchus,* there is the much rarer species, *S. albus*, which also occurs in the Mississippi region.

T: 10-20° C (coldwater fish), L: 150 cm, A: 300 cm, R: b, D: 4
50-68° F (coldwater fish), 59", 118",

Amia calva LINNAEUS, 1766
Bowfin, American Mudfish

Syn.: *Amia canina, A. centiginosa, A. cinera, A. marmorata, A. occidentalis, A. ocillicauda, A. ornata, A. piquotii, A. reticulata, A. subcoerulea, A. thompsonii, A. viridis, Amiatus calvus.*

Hab.: North America; drainage area of the Mississippi; Lake Huron and Erie.

F.I.: 1891 by Max von dem Borne, Berneuchen, Germany.

Sex: ♂ with black and yellow framed ocellus at the base of the tail; ♀ without the ocellus and usually somewhat larger.

Soc. B.: Solitary predator; practices brood care (patriarch family).

M: Only keep in large tanks. Provide hiding places of stones and roots (rockwork). Gravel bottom, densely planted edges with coldwater species. Use cold, neutral (pH 7.0) and medium-hard (10° dGH) water. Can be kept with equally sized fish, but best kept alone.

B: Not yet accomplished in an aquarium. In the wild the breeding season is in May and June. The ♂♂ build a nest of plant fragments in the plant thicket. The fish spawn at night and are very prolific (up to 70,000 eggs). The young hatch after about one week and are guarded by the ♂ up to a length of 10 cm (4").

F: Hefty live foods: fish, crustaceans, snails and earthworms. Beef pieces are also accepted after the fish become accustomed to them. The species is a voracious eater.

S: The swim bladder of *Amia calva* sports a lung-like structure which allows the fish to breath air. In the wild the fish may spawn next to each other creating breeding colonies.

T: 15-20° C (coldwater fish), 59-68° F (coldwater fish), L: ♂ 55 cm, ♀ 75 cm, ♂ 22", ♀ 30", A: from 120 cm, from 47", R: b, D: 4 (S, C)

Neoceratodus forsteri (KREFFT, 1870)
Australian Lungfish

Syn.: *Ceratodus forsteri, C. miolepis.*

Hab.: Australia; Queensland, in the Bennet and Mary rivers. Due to intentional releases, the species is now found in many parts of Queensland. The fish is found exclusively in freshwater.

F.I.: Unknown.

Sex: None known.

Soc. B.: A sluggish, predatory bottom dweller.

M: The mature size of the fish limits its suitability to public aquaria. For normal aquaria, only juveniles are appropriate. No demands are placed on water make-up. A fish for specialists, if at all obtainable.

B: Not yet achieved in captivity. In the wild *Neoceratodus forsteri* does not practice brood care. Eggs have a diameter of approximately 7 mm (") and are covered by a gelatinous layer, similar to frog eggs. The eggs are laid on water plants. The hatching fry do not have exterior gills.*

F: Fish, snails, aquatic invertebrates. The species can also be trained to accept cut up meat.

S: Compared to other lungfishes the lung-breathing or dual-breathing (gills and lungs) of *Neoceratodus forsteri* are the least developed. In well-oxygenated waters, the fish only breathe over the gills. In contrast to African and American lungfishes, *Neoceratodus forsteri* never burrows into the mud. The fish dies when the water dries up.

* Egg and larvae are pictured on page 208.

T: 22-28° C, L: 180 cm, A: over 150 cm, R: b, D: 4 (S)
72-82° F, 71", over 59",

Lepidosiren paradoxa FITZINGER, 1836
American Lungfish

Syn.: *Lepidorsiren articulata, L. dissimilis.*

Hab.: Central South America: Brazil, Paraguay; in swamps. A freshwater fish.

F.I.: 1928.

Sex: None known.

Soc. B.: Relatively quiet and predatory fish. They practice brood care (patriarch family).

M: Not suitable for a normal aquarium because of its size; however, juveniles can be kept without problems. Provide dense vegetation and numerous hiding places with roots and stones. Though the animals are sensitive to chlorine, they are otherwise undemanding towards water conditions. The species needs warmth. Keep together only with equally large or larger fishes.

B: Has not been accomplished in an aquarium. In the wild, tunnels are dug to lay the eggs within. Spawn and larvae are guarded by the ♂. The larvae breathe with feather-like external gills.

F: Live foods (fish, snails, earthworms). The species will also eat meat strips.

S: In the wild the species is capable of surviving droughts by hiding in the mud. Ducts are dug in the ground, into which the fish retreats. Afterwards the duct is closed with mud balls. The fish have a lung which evolved from the swim bladder. During the breeding season the lung is not used for breathing, so *L. paradoxa* does not come up to the surface for air. During this time the fish breathe exclusively with their gills and richly-branched, thread-like appendages, which are formed during the breeding season on the extremities.

* A juvenile is pictured on the next page.

T: 24-28° C, L: 125 cm, A: 100 cm, R: b, D: 4 (S)
75-82° F, 49", 39",

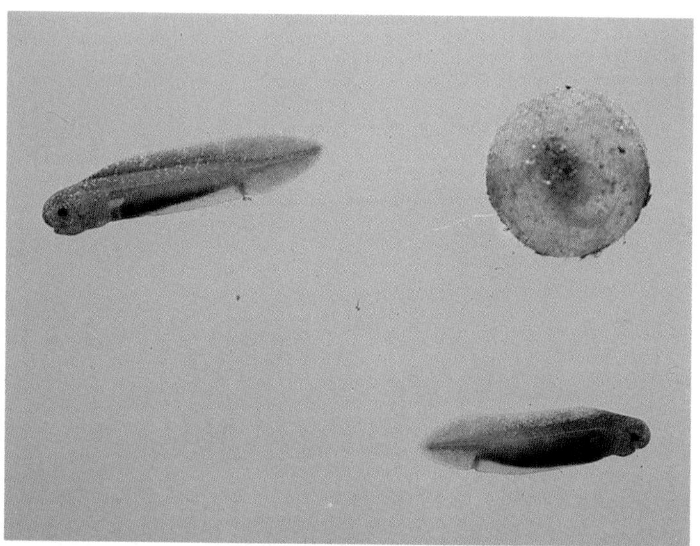

An egg and larvae of *Neoceratodus forsteri*

Lepidosiren paradoxa, juv.

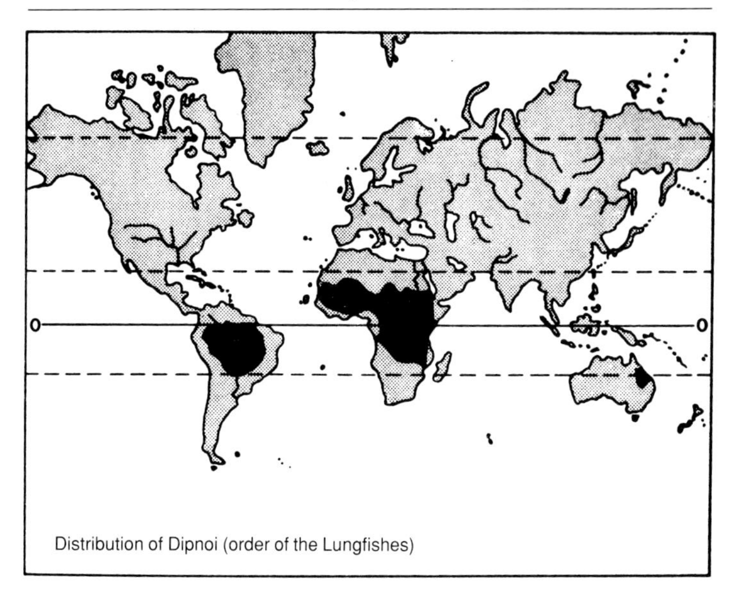

Distribution of Dipnoi (order of the Lungfishes)

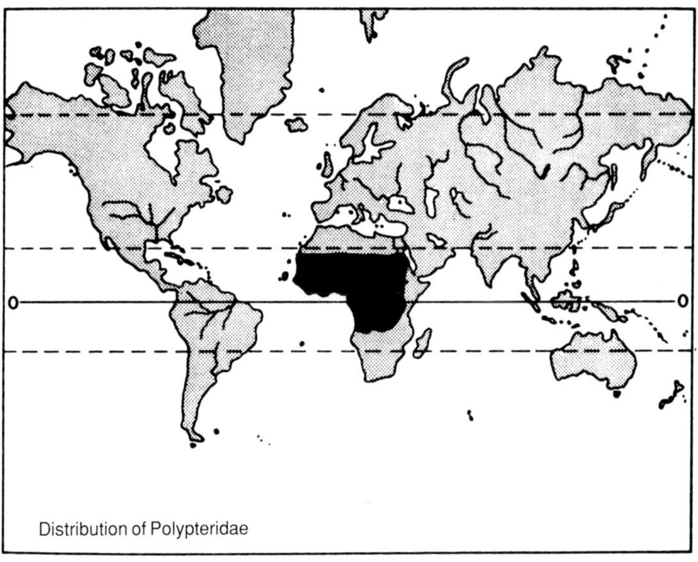

Distribution of Polypteridae

Lepisosteus oculatus WINCHELL, 1864
Spotted Gar

Syn.: *Lepidosteus oculatus, Lepisosteus productus.*

Hab.: North America; USA, Great Lakes, along the Mississippi and the Gulf of Mexico from western Florida to Corpus Christi.

F.I.: Unknown.

Sex: None known.

Soc. B.: A solitary, predacious fish.

M: As listed under *Lepisosteus osseus*. It is recommended that only juveniles be kept.

B: Due to its size, it has not occurred in an aquarium.

F: C; hefty live foods of any kind; after a certain size, fish are eaten almost exclusively.

S: All *Lepisosteus* species are predators representing the ambush predator type. The fish lurk, waiting for prey in a manner similar to the pike (*Esox lucius*). The prey is ambushed by a lighting fast attack. Dorsal and anal fins are located far back and together with the tail fin serve as the "propulsion unit".

T: 12-20° C (coldwater fish), **L:** 125 cm, **A:** 120 cm, **R:** m, t, **D:** 4 (S, C)
54-68° F (coldwater fish), 49", 47",

Lepisosteus osseus (LINNAEUS, 1758)
Longnose Gar

Syn.: *Esox osseus, E. viridis, Lepisosteus bison, L. clintonii, L. gavialis, L. gracilis, L. huronensis, L. leptorhynchus, L. lineatus, L. longirostris, L. loricatus, L. oxyurus, L. otarius, L. semiradiatus, L. treculii, Macrognathus loricatus, Sarchirus argenteus, S. vittatus.*

Hab.: North America; Great Lakes and rivers from Vermont southward to the Rio Grande del Norte.

F.I.: 1909 by the Berlin Aquarium.

Sex: None known.

Soc. B.: Solitary predator. They lie in wait, as do pikes, for their prey.

M: Only temporarily suitable as juveniles (size!). Gravel bottom, dense planting with coldwater species. Hiding places made with stones and roots. Provide an open area for swimming. These animals are sensitive to high temperatures (not over 20° C; 68° F). Use clear, oxygen-rich water,which should be medium-hard (10-15° dGH) and neutral (pH 7.0). Best kept singly.

B: The species has not been bred in captivity because the animals grow too large. In the wild, *Lepisosteus osseus* spawns from March to May. Eggs are adhesive and stick to any surface. Juveniles grow rapidly.

F: Hefty live foods (fish, earthworms). Beef. Smaller individuals will also eat insects (cockroaches, mealworms, etc.).

S: *Lepisosteus osseus* has two sub-species, *L. osseus osseus* (LINNAEUS, 1758) and *L. osseus treculii* (DUMERIL, 1865). The latter has smaller eyes and inhabits the Delaware and Ohio rivers. The swim bladder of *Lepisosteus* species can function as an accessory breathing organ.

T: 12-20° C (coldwater fish), **L:** 150 cm, **A:** from 100 cm, **R:** m, t, **D:** 4 (S)
54-68° F (coldwater fish), 59", from 39",

Lepisosteus oculatus

Lepisosteus osseus

Lepisosteus platostomus RAFINESQUE, 1920
Spotnose Gar

Syn.: *Cylindrosteus agassizi, C. bartoni, C. castelnaui, C. productus, C. rafinesquei, C. zadocki, Lepisosteus albus, L. grayi, L. latirostris, L. platystomus.*

Hab.: North America; USA, Great Lakes region including rivers west and south thereof.

F.I.: 1910.

Sex: No external differences known.

Soc. B.: Lone, predatory behavior. It is an ambush predator (compare *Esox lucius*).

M: Follow recommendations for *Lepisosteus osseus.*

B: Not yet successful in captivity.

F: C; hefty live foods of any kind (earthworms, fish), also crustacean, mussel and fish meat; beef in pieces.

S: *Lepisosteus platostomus* differs from *L. osseus* by the following morphometric data (values for *L. osseus* in parenthesis): body length is 3.5 (3) times that of the head length, length of the body is 8 times the height (12 times), anal fin has 8 rays (9) and the lateral line has 56 scales (62). In addition, *L. platostomus* has a significantly shorter snout.

T: 10-18° C (coldwater fish), L: 60 cm, A: 100 cm, R: m, t, D: 2
50-64° F (coldwater fish), 24", 39",

Lepisosteus tristoechus (BLOCH & SCHNEIDER, 1801)
Alligator Gar

Syn.: *Esox tristoechus, Atractosteus lucius, Lepidosteus berlandieri, L. manjuari, L. viridis, Lepisosteus manjuari, L. spatula, Litholepis tristoechus.*

Hab.: America: southern USA, Cuba and northern Mexico. The species inhabits fresh and brackish water, will often enter pure seawater.

F.I.: 1915.

Sex: None known.

Soc. B.: Predatory loner.

M: As indicated for *Lepisosteus osseus.* Only juveniles are suitable to be kept in an aquarium (size!).

B: Not yet realized in an aquarium and is probably not possible because of its size.

F: C; hefty live foods of any kind, specially fish.

S: The lateral line of *Lepisosteus tristoechus* has 60 scales. *L. tristoechus* is the most warmth requiring gar species.

T: 18-23° C, L: over 300 cm, A: from 150 cm, R: m, t, D: 3 (S, C)
64-73° F, over 118", from 59",

Lepisosteus platostomus

Lepisosteus tristoechus

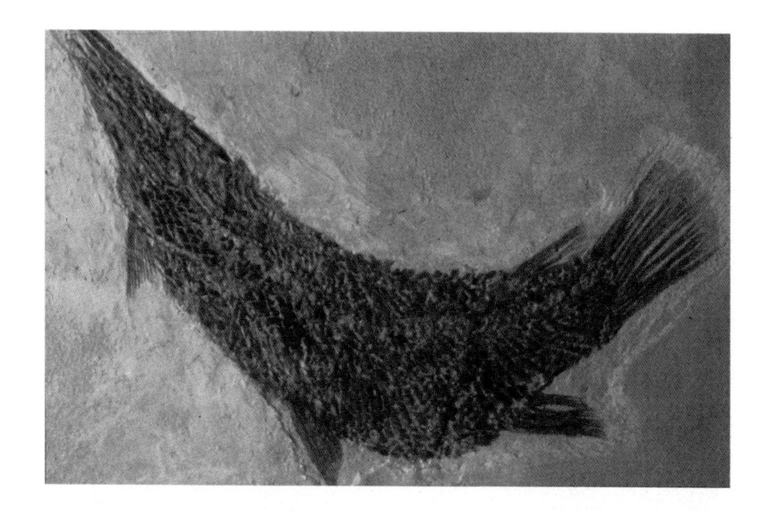

Class:	Osteichthyes
Sub-Class:	Actinopterygii
Super-Order:	Holostei
Order:	Lepisosteoidea
Family:	Lepisosteidae

Lepisosteus cuneatus of the Eocene epoch in Wyoming, USA.

Here we are dealing with a pike-like fish with a notoriously long snout. The tough, almost armor-like scales belong to the placoid-type, that is, above the bone-like basal segment lies a shiny layer similar to dentine. The dorsal fin is located far back, almost opposite the anal fin. The caudal fin is irregular. For the first time one can find *Lepisosteus* in the upper Cretaceous period, about 100 million years ago. Close relatives still live today. These are known as gar pikes (see preceding pages) and live in shallow, often weed choked waters from southern Canada to Central America. They can reach up to 3 m (118") in length. Because of their crocodile-like appearance, they are also called caiman fishes. Fossils of these fishes are also confirmed for Europe and Africa.

Polyodon spathula (WALBAUM, 1792)
Paddlefish

Syn.: *Squalus spathula, Acipenser lagenarius, Planirostra spathula, Platirostra edentula, Polyodon folium, Procerus maculatus, Spatularia reticulata.*

Hab.: North America: USA, Mississippi River and its tributaries; also in Lake Erie.

F.I.: Unknown.

Sex: None known.

Soc. B.: A peaceful, active, plankton feeder that schools during the breeding season.

M: Keeping this "original" fish is reserved for large public aquaria and specialists due to its diet and large size. Decorate the tank as for *Acipenser sturio*.

B: Not yet achieved in an aquarium. In nature the animals spawn, depending on geographic latitude, between February and May. The species forms sizable schools during the spawning season. Spawning occurs in river beds and lakes on sandy or rocky bottoms and can occur in shallows. The larvae of *P. spathula* has a short snout and 2 well developed barbels.

F: C; extreme zooplankton feeder (planktonic crustaceans, to a minor extent also insect larvae).

S: *Polyodon spathula*, with a length of about 2 m (2.2 yd) and a weight of up to 75 kg (165 lb), is the largest freshwater plankton feeder. The fish swims with its mouth wide open and filters planktonic organisms with the aid of its long, dense gill rakers. The function of the elongated snout is unknown.

T: 10-18° C (coldwater fish), L: 200 cm, A: 300 cm, circular tank, R: m, D: 4 (dietary requirements)
50-64° F (coldwater fish), 79", 118", circular tank,

Polypterus delhezi BOULENGER, 1899
Armored Bichir

Syn.: None (?).

Hab.: Africa: Zaire, upper and middle Zaire River.

F.I.: 1953.

Sex: No definite ones known.

Soc. B.: Intolerant and aggressive to conspecifics. Usually peaceful towards equal sized fishes of other species. The species is predatory.

M: As indicated for *Polypterus palmas*.

B: Not yet reproduced in an aquarium.

F: As listed under *P. palmas*.

S: None.

T: 26-28° C, **L:** 35 cm, **A:** 100 cm, **R:** m, b, **D:** 3-4
79-82° F, 14", 39",

Polypterus palmas AYRES, 1850
Marbled Bichir

Syn.: None.

Hab.: Africa: Guinea, Sierra Leone, Liberia, Zaire.

F.I.: 1953.

Sex: The anal fin of the ♂ is twice as wide at the base as that of the ♀ and, during reproduction, serves as a sexual organ.

Soc. B.: The animals are usually peaceful towards other species. Among themselves aggressions can occur. Predator.

M: Provide an aquarium with a large surface area, relatively shallow water (30 cm, 12") and hiding places of stones and roots. Vegetation should be sparse, leaving free swimming room. Substrate of sand or fine gravel. Water medium-hard (around 10° dGH) and pH around 7.0. Best kept in a species tank.

B: The species has only sporadically been bred in captivity. A successful breeding report was given by HARTL (1981): DATZ **34**, 334-337. The trigger for the courtship seems to have been the regular 14 day interval water exchanges. The ♂ begins the courtship, and after some time, both partners perform a full-fledged marriage dance. At the end of courtship, the ♂ encloses the anal fin and opening of the ♀ with its pocket-like spread anal fin. Accompanied by strong shivering of both partners, up to 5 eggs and sperm are expelled into the fin pocket of the ♂. After about 20 seconds, the pair separates, the eggs are scattered and sink to the bottom. This spawning process is repeated several times in different parts of the aquarium. The parents do not disturb the eggs which are 2 mm (3/32") in diameter. The larvae hatch after four days and are free-swimming after another six days. They then have a length of 1 cm (3/8") and are fed *Artemia* nauplii.

F: C; almost exclusively live foods; also eat fish and crustacean meat.

S: Above a length of 15 mm (5/8") the developing external gills can be recognized.

T: 26-28° C, **L:** 30 cm, **A:** 100 cm, **R:** m, b, **D:** 3
79-82° F, 12", 39",

Polypterus delhezi

Polypterus palmas

Polypterus senegalus CUVIER, 1829
Senegal Bichir, Cuvier's Bichir

Syn.: *Polypterus arnaudii, P. senegalensis.*

Hab.: Africa, White Nile up to Lake Albert, Lake Rudolf and Lake Chad, Senegal, Gambia, Niger.

F.I.: 1953.

Sex: No sure ones known.

Soc. B.: Among themselves they are quite quarrelsome and aggressive fishes. Often there is fighting. The animals are pronounced predators.

M: As listed under *Polypterus palmas.*

B: No reports are available about successful aquarium breeding.

F: As mentioned for *P. palmas.*

S: None.

T: 25-28° C, L: 30 cm, A: 100 cm, R: m, b, D: 3-4
77-82° F, 12", 39",

Potamotrygon motoro (MÜLLER & HENLE, 1841)
Ocellated Freshwater Stingray

Syn.: *Taeniura motoro, Ellipesurus motoro, Paratrygon dumerilii, P. motoro, Potamotrygon dumerilii, Raja motoro, Taeniura dumerilii, T. henlei, T. mülleri, Trygon dumerilii, T. henlei, T. mülleri.*

Hab.: South America: Brazil, Paraguay, Uruguay.

F.I.: Cannot be established exactly. Probably around 1970.

Sex: ♂ has claspers on the pelvic fins.

Soc. B.: Peaceful, relatively mobile bottom dweller. The species is ovoviviparous.

M: The tank should have a large surface area and shallow water (30 cm; 12"). Provide a sandy bottom layer 10 cm (4") thick, allowing the animals to burrow; perhaps floating plants should be added. Leave plenty of free swimming space. Water not too hard (up to 10° dGH) and slightly acid (pH about 6.5). Best kept in a species tank.

B: No reports of successful aquarium breeding are known.

F: C; live foods and other foods of animal origin (*Tubifex*, earthworms, mosquito larvae, shrimp and fish meat, strips of beef heart).

S: The feeding habits are interesting to observe. To ingest the food, the ray lies on the bottom covering the prey totally. It then blows a water jet into the bottom, whirling the bottom up. This is then sucked up, the food consumed and the sand expelled.

T: 24-26° C, L: 30 cm wide, A: 100 cm, R: b, D: 3
75-79° F, 12", wide 39",

Pristis microdon (LATHAM, 1794)
Northern Sawfish

Syn.: *Squalus microdon.*

Hab.: Southeast Asia and Australia; the species inhabits the ocean from India and Sri Lanka (Ceylon) to Queensland and New South Wales, Australia. However, the fish also enters freshwater and is found up to 400 km (250 miles) inland.

F.I.: Heiko Bleher attempted the first import into Germany in 1983. Of ten fish, seven arrived alive at the Berlin Aquarium.

Sex: The pelvic fins of the ♂ are modified into a copulative organ.

Soc. B.: Almost nothing is known about the social behavior of *P. microdon*. It is known that ♂♂ use their saw, that can be as long as 180 cm (71"), during fights over a ♀.

M: The maintenance of *P. microdon* is reserved for large public aquaria.

B: Has not occurred in an aquarium and, because of its size, probably not possible in captivity. This fish is a livebearer that has few young (barely over 20). The saw teeth of the young are soft and flexible and are covered by a membrane which protects the mother before and during delivery.

F: C; live foods: fish and benthic invertebrates.

S: The saw is used primarily to dig in the mud. But it has also been observed that by swinging the saw back and forth they can injure and kill fishes which are subsequently eaten. Not an aquarium fish. Only because of the large interest of aquarists for rays has the species been introduced here for the first time in an aquarium book.

T: 24-26° C, **L:** 5 m, **A:** from 150 cm, **R:** b, **D:** 4 (S)
75-79° F, 5.5 yd, from 59",

Protopterus a. annectens (OWEN, 1839)
African Lungfish

Syn.: *Lepidosiren annectens, L. tobal, Rhinocryptis annectens, Protopterus anguilliformis, P. annectens.*

Hab.: Africa; from Senegal to Nigeria, in Lake Chad, from Zaire to Zambia and Mozambique; in freshwater swamps.

F.I.: 1910.

Sex: None known.

Soc. B.: A predatory fish. Antagonistic and quarrelsome towards conspecifics as well as heterospecifics. Guards the spawn, patriarch family.

M: Provide muddy bottom, dense vegetation; water level does not need to be high (25 cm; 10"). No demands are placed on water chemistry. Only young specimens are suitable for the home aquarium. Keep alone.

B: Has not been bred in an aquarium.

T: 25-30° C, L: 65 cm, A: 100 cm, R: b, D: 2
77-86° F, 26", 39",

F: Live foods; fish, tadpoles, snails, earthworms, insect larvae.

S: The lungs of these animals acquire a special significance during the dry season. When the water dries up the animals burrow into the mud, curl up and exude mucus. This solidifies and coats the tunnel. In the proximity of the mouth is a hole that allows the fish to breathe with lungs. In these mud cocoons the four to six month long dry season is survived. Then the rains begin, the summer sleep of the buried animals ends, and they leave the capsule unharmed.

Rio Manicoré, Brazil. Bamboo thicket, brown peat water, pH 5.4, hardness below 1. Many small tetras, *Corydoras*, cichlids and *Exodon paradoxus* can be found here.

Catoprion mento (wimple piranha)

Alestes nurse (RÜPPELL, 1832)
Nurse Tetra

Syn.: *Myletes nurse, Brachyalestes rüppellii, Myletes guile, Alestes senegalensis, Chalceus guile, Brachyalestes nurse, Alestes rüppellii, A. erythropterus.*

Hab.: Africa, from the Nile to the Niger.

F.I.: 1911.

Sex: The ♂ is clearly distinguishable by its concave anal fin; the anal fin of the ♀ is straight.

Soc. B.: A peaceful, schooling fish which is only suitable as a juvenile for the community aquarium. Adults can only be kept in large display tanks.

M: An adaptable species which occurs in the most varied biotopes. Needs a large tank with ample swimming space and dense vegetation at the edges. Water: pH 6.0-7.8, hardness to 30° dGH.

B: Not successful in an aquarium. In nature the fish spawn among the grasses of flooded river banks.

F: O; omnivore, large flake food, any large live food, frozen food.

S: Older animals have pink caudal and dorsal fins.

T: 23-27° C, **L:** 25 cm, **A:** 150 cm, **R:** m, **D:** 4 (S), otherwise 1
73-81° F, 9³/4", 59",

Bryconaethiops microstoma GÜNTHER, 1873
Filament Tetra, Small-Mouthed Featherfin Tetra

Syn.: *Bryconaethiops yseuxi.*

Hab.: Lower Zaire, Stanley Pool, in fast flowing headwaters and rapids.

F.I.: 1973 by Heiko Bleher, Frankfurt.

Sex: Not exactly known. The ♀♀ are said to be plain with shorter dorsal fins. See **S.**

Soc. B.: A peaceful loner. Best kept alone or in small groups.

M: The animals only inhabit fast flowing waters. They can jump several meters (yards) so cover the tank well. Water: pH 6.0-7.5 and hardness to 18° dGH (8° dGH). Provide structures of stones and roots and ample light for algae growth. Since these fish are skittish, care should be taken when working on the tank, especially while cleaning. The half not being cleaned should be well covered. The species prefers oxygen-rich, clear, fast flowing water, thereby requiring a strong filter.

F: H, L; omnivore in an aquarium, flake food, small live foods and frozen food. Algae! Higher plants are not accepted.

S: Only imported in small numbers. The attractive ♂♂ with their extended dorsal fins sometimes reach the trade. The plain ♀♀ have not come to Germany (because ♂♂ and ♀♀ are considered different species by the native collectors?).
Full-grown specimens appear totally different from juveniles. The dorsal fin of mature ♂♂ has thread-like elongations that reach the tail fin. Juveniles are silver; adults are almost black.

T: 24-28° C, **L:** 15 cm, **A:** 120 cm, **R:** m, t, **D:** 2
75-82° F, 6", 47",

Alestes nurse

Bryconaethiops microstoma

Hydrocynus goliath BOULENGER, 1898
African Tiger Fish, Wolf Tetra Sub-Fam.: Hydrocyninae

Syn.: *Hydrocyon goliath*, but it can be easily confused with *H. vittatus*.

Hab.: Zaire River, Africa.

F.I.: Unknown.

Sex: Not distinguishable on live juveniles.

Soc. B.: Juveniles can be kept together when well fed. Otherwise only keep with larger fish that can defend themselves. Should be kept alone when larger than 18 cm (7").

M: Needs show aquaria with stones and roots. Provide strong filtration. Anchor plants well. Water values: pH 6.5-7.5 and hardness up to 25° dGH. Cover the tank.

B: Not possible in an aquarium.

F: C; meat, fish. These beasts are almost insatiable.

S: The teeth of this fish are similar to those of a dog; they have an overbite. This allows large chunks of flesh to be torn from other fish. A well-liked sports fish. The record stands at 1.32 m (51") and 38 kg (84 lb). Hands off! The species is only listed here to warn the ignorant. Six species are known in the genus.

T: 23-26° C, L: 40 cm in aquaria, 150 cm in wild, A: 250 cm, R: all, D: 4 (S, C)
73-79° F, 16" in aquaria, 59" in wild, 98",

Micralestes humilis BOULENGER, 1899
African Redfin Tetra Sub-Fam.: Alestinae

Syn.: *Brycinus humilis, Rhabdalestes septentrionalis.*

Hab.: Togo, Ghana between Alera and Kumasi, Zaire River, Samtesi River, Chad (Africa).

F.I.: 1977, Heiko Bleher, Frankfurt.

Sex: ♂ more slender, anal fin longer and more curved.

Soc. B.: A peaceful, gregarious schooling fish. Suitable for any larger community tank.

M: The fish are quite undemanding and are satisfied with almost any aquarium that has well-filtered water. Water: pH 6.5-7.5 and hardness up to 25° dGH (10° dGH).

B: No reports are available.

F: O; flake food of any kind, frozen food, any kind of live food.

S: The species is hard to distinguish from *Micralestes stormsi*. Since the pictured fish was caught in Ghana, the given species name is relatively certain.

T: 23-27° C, L: 12 cm, A: 120 cm, R: m, D: 1
73-81° F, 4 3/4", 47",

Hydrocynus goliath

Micralestes humilis

Belonophago tinanti POLL, 1939

Needle Fin-Eater Sub-Fam.: Ichthyborinae

Syn.: None.

Hab.: Lower Congo (Stanley Pool), Africa.

F.I.: Not known.

Sex: Not yet described.

Soc. B.: These animals will even eat the fins of conspecifics (see picture). Nonactive fishes which lurk in hiding places waiting for their prey to swim by. They will then dart out and seize their victim. Not for the community tank.

M: Needs a well-planted aquarium with dark substrate. Cover the water surface with floating plants and provide branch work out of wood or bamboo. Water: pH 5.8-7.0 and hardness up to 15° dGH. Perform regular water changes with the addition of a good conditioner to keep the water low in nitrates.

B: Up to now there is nothing known.

F: C; while young, insect larvae and small fish, when older they primarily eat the fins of other fish.

S: A rarely imported species. It should, however, find few fanciers. This sub-family has occupied a very interesting and original feeding niche, but not one suitable for the aquarium.

T: 24-26° C, **L:** 20 cm, **A:** 120 cm, **R:** all, **D:** 4
75-79° F, 8", 47",

Distichodus notospilus GÜNTHER, 1867

Sub-Fam.: Distichodinae

Syn.: None.

Hab.: Southern Cameroon to Angola, Africa.

F.I.: Not sure.

Sex: Unknown.

Soc. B.: Usually a peaceful fish, but can become quarrelsome towards conspecifics (similar to red-tail sharks).

M: If several individuals of the species are kept, the tank should be arranged with roots and stones in a manner that allows territories to be outlined. The best suited plants are Java fern, *Anubias* and moss. Water values: pH 6.5-7.2 and hardness up to 18° dGH. A strong filter to provide a current is recommended.

B: Not successful.

F: H, O; small animals are omnivorous. They prefer *Daphnia* and vegetable foods (Tetra Conditioning Food, TabiMin, etc.). From 10 cm (4") length, the animals like large flakes and vegetable foods like lettuce, chickweed, peas, boiled beans (canned) and others.

S: The species is very similar to *D. noboli*, but the tips of the caudal fin are pointed (see Vol. 1, page 226).

T: 23-27° C, **L:** 15 cm, **A:** 150 cm, **R:** b, **D:** 3
73-81° F, 6", 59",

Belonophago tinanti

Distichodus notospilus

Nannocharax parvus

PELLEGRIN, 1906

African Broad-Band Darter

Syn.: None. Confuse with *Nannocharax ansorgii.*

Hab.: Niger to Ogove.

F.I.: Unknown.

Sex: ♂ more slender than ♀. When viewed from above the two body bands of the ♂ appear straight, on the ♀ they appear curved.

Soc. B.: A peaceful fish that can be kept in a small school. The droll animals pursue each other from time to time, then disappear in small hiding places which should be provided. Well suited to a community tank with not overly robust species.

M: Stone and root decoration should be provided rather than tough plants. Provide lots of light for algae growth. Water: pH 6.5-7.5, hardness to 25° dGH.

B: Otto GARTNER gives an extensive report in "Aquarium heute" (Today's Aquarium) 4/1986 about the successful breeding of *N. parvus.* With daily feedings of "bite size" live foods, the young achieve a length of 25 mm (1") in 70 days.

F: H, O; flake food from the bottom, tablets, algae.

S: According to GÉRY (1977), the species is a possible synonym of *N. ansorgei.* MAYLAND (1979) doubts this. In his opinion, the habitats are too far apart. In addition, there are differences in finnage. It is interesting to note the great similarity to the genus *Characidium.* If one does not know the original habitat, most *Nannocharax* (African) cannot be distinguished from a *Characidium* (South American) with the naked eye. However, the African genus has ctenoid scales (see Vol. 1, page 164) while its South American cousin has cycloid scales. Two sub-orders are known: *N. parvus* and *N. parvus maculatus* POLL & LAMBERT, 1959.

T: 22-26° C, **L:** 5 cm, **A:** 60 cm, **R:** b, **D:** 1-2
72-79° F, 2", 24",

Neolebias trilineatus

BOULENGER, 1899

Three-Lined Neolebias

Syn.: *Nannaethiops tritaeniatus, Rhabdacetiops trilineatus.*

Hab.: Zaire basin, Africa.

F.I.: 1949.

Sex: ♂ with reddish spots; on the ♀ these are paler.

Soc. B.: A peaceful schooling fish that can be combined with other tranquil African characins. However, its colors show much better in a species tank.

M: Substrate of fine sand or dark, fine gravel. Water values: pH 6.2-7.2 and hardness to 15° dGH. Use only a few plants in order to preserve plenty of free swimming space. Quality lighting (e.g., mercury vapor spot lights) is recommended.

B: Place breeders in pairs in a 50 l (13 gal) tank with fine-leaved plants or perlon fibers (Eheim: green, coarse filter fibers). They will lay 150-250 eggs that will hatch after 24-36 hours; feed microscopic pond organisms or infusoria cultured from banana peels.

F: C, O; fine flake food; FD and varied live foods.

S: None.

T: 23-26° C, **L:** 5 cm, **A:** 60 cm, **R:** all, **D:** 2
73-79° F, 2", 24",

Nannocharax parvus

Neolebias trilineatus

Paraphago rostratus BOULENGER, 1899

Striped Fin-Eater

Syn.: None.

Hab.: Congo basin (Zaire), Africa.

F.I.: Unknown.

Sex: Not known.

Soc. B.: A predatory loner which can only be kept with larger bottom dwelling catfish (*Hypostomus*, etc.).

M: Provide a densely planted aquarium with some open space to hunt in. We suggest a pH 6.0-7.0 and hardness up to 12° dGH.

B: Not successful in an aquarium thus far.

F: C; large live foods, small fish, pieces of fish fins.

S: The upper mandible can also move. This ability allows the fish to use its snout like a pair of scissors and sever fins off its tankmates.

T: 23-26° C, L: 18 cm, A: 80 cm, R: all, D: 4
73-79° F, 7", 31",

Hepsetus odoe (BLOCH, 1794)
African Pike-Characoid

Syn.: *Xiphorhamphus odoe, Xiphorhynchus odöe, Hydrocyonoides cuvieri, Sarcodaces odoe, Salmo odoe.*

Hab.: Tropical Africa with the exception of the Nile basin.

F.I.: 1913.

Sex: Unknown.

Soc. B.: Predator. Can only be kept with much larger fish or conspecifics.

M: Only suitable for exhibition aquaria. The fish easily injure themselves within the constraints of home aquaria and then die. Water values are not critical; pH 6.0-7.5, hardness up to 18° dGH. Provide strong filtration.

B: Not possible in an aquarium. In nature a free-floating bubble nest is built (similar to labyrinth fish). The eggs are guarded by either one or both of the parents.

F: C; chunks of meat, fish. Small specimens will also accept *Tubifex* and other live foods.

S: In STERBA one can still find the species listed under the closely related south African family Ctenoluciidae. A good tasting food fish which will fight on a fishing pole like the European pike.

T: 26-28° C, L: 70 cm, A: 1000 l, R: m, D: 4 (C), weights up to 4 kg
79-82° F, 28", 263 gal,

Pseudanos gracilis (KNER, 1859)
Four-Spotted Headstander
Sub-Fam.: Anostominae

Syn.: *Schizodon gracilis, Anostomus gracilis.*

Hab.: Orinoco, Rio Negro, Rio Guaporé; Brazil, South America.

F.I.: Unknown.

Sex: Not externally distinguishable.

Soc. B.: Usually a peaceful schooling fish. Lively but very shy. Territorial fights may occur between conspecifics of different sizes. Only associate them with small, peaceful species.

M: This species is quite demanding. It needs soft water with 2-8° dGH and prefers a pH not higher than 7. Peat filtration and a strong current are conditions for its well-being. The fish live mostly in rocky crevices in rapids of large creeks.

B: Not yet successful.

F: C, O; tablet food with freeze-dried components, small live foods. Algae mats with small crustaceans.

S: The species is rarely imported and up to now often confused with *A. trimaculatus* (see Vol. 1, page 237).

T: 24-26° C, L: 14 cm, A: 100 cm, R: b, m, D: 3
75-79° F, 5½", 39",

Leporellus vittatus (VALENCIENNES, 1849)
Leporellus
Sub-Fam.: Leporellinae

Syn.: *Leporinus vittatus, L. maculifrons, L. pictus, Leporellus timbore, Leporinodus vittatus, Salmo cagoara.*
There are at least 6 species which are likely to be identical and only represent local races (GÉRY, 1977).

Hab.: Amazon basin, Orinoco and Paraná, South America.

F.I.: Uncertain.

Sex: ♀ with fuller abdominal line.

Soc. B.: Peaceful, lively fish that prefer to be kept in small schools. Will associate with gentle species without problems.

M: Should be kept similar to darter tetras; clear, not too warm, oxygen-rich water that must closely reflect the origin of the fish. A good average value is pH 6.0-6.5, hardness up to 12° dGH.

B: No reports as of yet. A worthwhile endeavor for committed breeders.

F: L, H; food particles are preferably picked from plant leaves and the bottom. It can be aufwuchs or remains of flake, tablet, FD and frozen foods. Planktonic feeds are preferred.

S: The widely distributed but rare species is possibly a synonym of *Leporellus pictus* KNER, 1859. Different local races vary as can be seen from the 2 pictures. While the related Anostominae have a superior mouth, it is slightly inferior or terminal in Leporellinae. This explains the different swimming positions of the two. *Leporellus* swim almost horizontal, while *Anostomus* almost always swim with the head down. *Anostomus* live primarily in vertical crevices in rapids. There it can feed off the vertical walls with its upward pointing mouth. *Leporellus* lives more in the plains and feeds on stones and vertical walls. *Leporellus* occupies a niche which *Anostomus* could not.

T: 22-25° C, L: 12 cm, A: 100 cm, R: b, D: 2-3
72-77° F, 4¾", 39",

Pseudanos gracilis

Leporellus vittatus; an additional picture on page 237.

Fire clearing in Brazil. The creek stopped the fire.

Leporinus desmotes FOWLER, 1914

Black and Yellow Leporinus, Trunk Leporinus

Syn.: None.

Hab.: Rupuruni River, Guyana, Amazon basin, South America.

F.I.: Since it is often confused with *Leporinus fasciatus* and its sub-species, it cannot be determined.

Sex: Not recognizable from the exterior.

Soc. B.: With the exception of Java fern and Java moss it is not suited for planted aquaria. A schooling fish which can be kept singly. Will not disturb other fish.

M: They need a sunny or well lit roomy aquarium. The fish waste away without aufwuchs. Current from a strong filter is desirable but not necessary as long as water is exchanged frequently (1/3 every 2-3 weeks). Water: pH 6.5-7.2, hardness 5-18° dGH.

B: Not known.

F: L, H; algae, vegetable flake food, TabiMin. Blanched lettuce, chickweed, fruits. Young plant shoots! *Tubifex*. Frozen food, *Daphnia*.

S: The only species of the sub-genus *Myocharax*. The inferior mouth with some horizontally protruding teeth identifies and distinguishes the species from *L. fasciatus*. Very rare!

T: 22-26° C, L: 18 cm, A: 120 cm, R: m, b, D: 2-3
72-79° F, 7", 47",

Leporellus vittatus

Leporinus desmotes

Leporinus friderici (BLOCH, 1794)

Frideric's Leporinus

Syn.: *Salmo friderici, Curimatus acutidens, C. frederici, Leporinus acutidens, L. megalepis.*

Hab.: Fast flowing tributaries of the Amazon, Guyana, South America.

F.I.: 1913.

Sex: During spawning season the ♂ has dark, brick-red pectoral and pelvic fins.

Soc. B.: A peaceful schooling fish that can be kept with large cichlids, piranhas and other relatively peaceful large fish. This fish is shy, diurnal and a plant eater.

M: Large tank with strong water movement. Provide roots or *Philodendron* roots as cover. Water values: pH 5.6-7.2, hardness up to 18° dGH. Peat filtration is desirable but not necessary. It is interesting to note that in their natural habitat these fish have little access to plants and, during the dry season, feed solely on fallen fruits and leaves of fallen trees.

B: Probably not possible in an aquarium.

F: H, O; plants, omnivore. Fruits, leaves. Small specimens appreciate flake food and tablets.

S: One of the most numerous and largest South American characins which, because of its size and herbivorous nature, is not an aquarium fish. Appropriate care of this species is only possible in large display aquaria.

T: 23-26° C, **L:** 50 cm, **A:** 200 cm, **R:** m, b, **D:** 2-4 (S, H)
73-79° F, 20", 79",

Leporinus "maculatus" not MÜLLER & TROSCHEL, 1846

Spotted Leporinus

Syn.: None, the species is not exactly defined.

Hab.: The Guianas, Amazon region in deep, clear creeks.

F.I.: 1934.

Sex: ♂ more slender and slightly smaller.

Soc. B.: Peaceful schooling fish suitable for the community aquarium. A plant eater.

M: Water: pH 6.0-7.2, hardness up to 10° dGH. Peat filtration. Requires a high performance, large volume filter which will also provide needed surface currents. Provide roots (*Philodendron*) or thin cane as cover and ample free swimming space. Try to provide a species tank to encourage successful reproduction. Dark substrate, perhaps beech leaves.

B: A successful coincidental spawn and rearing of the young has occurred in Japan. The eggs were randomly scattered throughout the aquarium. The act of spawning is said to be similar to barbs. Remove parents after spawning.

F: H, O; vegetable flake food, tablets, peas, lettuce, but also live foods (*Daphnia*).

S: One of the most beautiful *Leporinus* species. Unfortunately it is rarely offered in the trade. There are at least 4 *Leporinus* species with a spotted design similar to the one pictured here. Until there is a much needed taxonomic revision they will all be assigned to the "*maculatus*" group. It can already be predicted that the name *maculatus* will probably have to be withdrawn.

T: 22-26° C, **L:** ♂ 18 cm, ♀ 20 cm, **A:** 150 cm, **R:** m, b, **D:** 2
72-79° F, ♂ 7", ♀ 8", 59",

Leporinus friderici

Leporinus "maculatus"

Leporinus octofasciatus STEINDACHNER, 1915
Red-Finned Leporinus, Eight-Banded Leporinus

Syn.: None.

Hab.: Santa Catarina, Brazil.

F.I.: Uncertain.

Sex: Unknown.

Soc. B.: Sometimes quarrelsome towards conspecifics, otherwise suitable for the community aquarium. Fish larger than 3 cm (1 ") are not disturbed.

M: Provide a long tank with suitable tough vegetation. Stones and roots are needed to establish territories, and a strong filtration system is required to achieve good water currents. pH 5.6-7.0; hardness up to 15° dGH.

B: Has not occurred in an aquarium thus far.

F: H; fruits, lettuce, FD tablets, large live foods.

S: None

T: 23-26° C, **L:** 22 cm, **A:** 180 cm, **R:** m, b, **D:** 3
73-79° F, 8^3/4", 71",

Leporinus pellegrini STEINDACHNER, 1910
Pellegrin's Leporinus, Belted Leporinus

Syn.: None.

Hab.: The Guianas, upper Amazon.

F.I: Uncertain.

Sex: Unknown.

Soc. B.: A peaceful, schooling fish that will nibble on young plants. Keep together with all peaceful species.

M: A tank well-planted with tough species (e.g., Java fern, Java moss). Provide strong lighting to encourage an algae cover and a large filter for strong water movement. pH 5.8-7.5; hardness up to 15° dGH.

B: Has not been reproduced. See *L. "maculatus"*, page 238.

F: H, O; vegetable flakes, FD foods and frozen foods. Mashed frozen peas.

S: Pellegrin's leporinus continues causing confusion due to erroneous information in the aquarium literature. The situation did not improve after the publication of Géry's book "Characoids of the World", because his work is incorrectly translated by renown authors, confusing identification again. The fish pictured here is *L. pellegrini*, identified by Géry himself.

T: 25-26° C, **L:** 12 cm, **A:** 150 cm, **R:** m, **D:** 2
77-79° F, 4$^3/_4$", 59",

Leporinus octofasciatus

Leporinus pellegrini

Schizodon fasciatus SPIX & AGASSIZ, 1829
Banded Schizodon

Syn.: None.

Hab.: Amazon basin, South America.

F.I.: 1907.

Sex: None known.

Soc. B.: Suitable for large, unplanted community tanks. Conspecifics are usually pursued.

M: Spacious tank with stone and root structures. Large volume filter. No special demands are placed on the water; pH 5.5-7.5 and hardness to 25° dGH.

B: Hardly possible in an aquarium because of its size.

F: H: omnivore, specially plant foods, fruits, lettuce, chickweed, mashed peas, large flakes.

S: Fishes of this genus are appreciated food fish in their native land. Not suitable for the home aquarium. The genus is similar to *Leporinus* in appearance, but has a totally different dentition.

T: 22-28° C, L: 40 cm, A: 200 cm, R: b, m, D: 4 (S)
72-82° F, 16", 79",

Aphyocharax dentatus (EIGENMANN & KENNEDY, 1903)
False Bloodfin

Syn.: *Bryconamericus dentatus, Hemibrycon dentatus.*

Hab.: Paraguay basin; northern South America, from Rio de Janeiro to Bogatá (Colombia).

F.I.: Uncertain.

Sex: ♂ more slender (photo), ♀ is very full during the breeding season. ♂ has a hook-shaped anal fin.

Soc. B.: Quick, lively schooling fish of the upper water strata. Some animals possibly nip tankmates' fins.

M: Hardy species, suitable for the larger community tank. Only juveniles should be kept in smaller tanks up to 80 cm (31") in length. pH 6.0-7.6 and hardness to 25° dGH. Edge vegetation with plenty of free swimming room. Strong lighting and filtration are desirable.

T: 15-22° C, L: 12 cm, A: 80 cm, R: t, m, D: 2
59-72° F, 4 3/4", 31",

B: Will spawn in schools at the water surface. Egg scatterers. Breeders should be removed after spawning since they will eat the eggs.

F: C, O; flake food, hefty live foods, frozen foods, FD foods. Well fed animals will not nip fins.

S: Cover the tank well since the species likes to jump. If well maintained they can live over 10 years.

Aphyocharax paraguayensis EIGENMANN, 1915
White-Spot Tetra

Syn.: *Aphyocharax nattereri, A. agassizi (?).*

Hab.: Rio Paraguay basin, South America.

F.I.: In larger numbers in 1983 by Heiko Bleher, Kelsterbach; before, often as by-catches, mostly as the genus *Hyphessobrycon.*

Soc. B.: A peaceful schooling fish. Do not place with large cichlids, etc., or the fish will disappear one by one.

M: Unproblematic to keep. A tolerant fish (as are many from the Paraguay basin). Water: pH 6.0-7.8, hardness to 25° dGH (better 15° dGH). A dark substrate is advantageous but not absolutely necessary.

B: Otto BÖHM (1986) gives a report on its aquarium breeding in the magazine Aquarium heute (Today's Aquarium) **4** (2): 13-15. The 70 l (18 gal) aquarium had very soft, acid water (2° dGH; pH 5.5). The characins spawned in a large clump of Java moss. Since the fry could eat newly hatched brine shrimp nauplii from the beginning, they were easily reared.

F: O; fine flake food, *Artemia*, any small live food, frozen and freeze-dried natural foods.

S: In a short time the species has earned a place in the trade. It represents a pretty and easily cared for contrast fish in the community aquarium. This fish is said to occasionally feed on scales of other fish.

T: 22-27° C, 72-81° F, **L:** 4 cm, 1 2/3", **A:** 60 cm, 24", **R:** all D: 1-2

Aphyocharax rathbuni EIGENMANN, 1907
Rathbun's Bloodfin

Syn.: *Aphyocharax stramineus.*

Hab.: Rio Paraguay, South America.

F.I.: Unknown.

Sex: ♂ with white tipped fins (dorsal, pelvic and pectorals).

Soc. B.: Peaceful schooling fish. Suitable for almost any community tank without rough, quarrelsome or predatory tankmates.

M: As most fish from the Paraguay basin, the species is not choosy. In the wild it has to adapt to ever changing conditions. Depending on the season, temperature and other water values are subject to significant fluctuations. Water hardness to 20° dGH and a pH of 6.0-7.5. Subdued light, perhaps a floating plant cover, is advantageous for the species' well-being.

B: Use soft water with a peat extract added. Intense feeding with black mosquito larvae and/or FD foods should ripen the pairs. They spawn between fine-leaved plants, moss, etc., in aquaria over 50 cm (20") length.

F: C, O; omnivore. Insect larvae, FD foods, flake food, frozen food (mosquito larvae).

S: There are different color forms, which, in part, are not yet described.

T: 20-26° C, 68-79° F, **L:** 5 cm, 2", **A:** 60 cm, 24", **R:** m, t, **D:** 2

Aphyocharax paraguayensis

Aphyocharax rathbuni, ♂ top ♀ bottom

Brycon melanopterus (COPE, 1871)
Sickle-Band Brycon

Syn.: *Megalobrycon melanopterum, Brycon siebenthalae.*

Hab.: Widely distributed in the Amazon region, South America.

F.I.: Has not been imported into Europe. USA 1980.

Sex: Unknown.

Soc. B.: Young animals are easily kept in schools in a community aquarium. Quite peaceful, rapid swimmers. Larger fish over 15 cm (6") will sometimes eat smaller fish.

M: A high capacity filter is required for maintenance. The fish reach the size of trout, eat accordingly, and need the space of a fish in a creek. pH 6.0-7.5 and hardness to 20° dGH.

B: Not yet described.

F: C, O; flake food, large live foods, frozen foods.

S: Magnificent schooling fish for the large aquarium or show tank. It does not, however, belong in the home aquarium.

T: 22-26° C, **L:** 18 cm and over, **A:** 200 cm, **R:** m, **D:** 2-3
72-79° F, 7" and over, 79",

Bryconops affinis (GÜNTHER, 1864)

Syn.: *Creatochanes affinis, C. melanurus, Bryconops melanurus, Tetragonopterus affinis.*

Hab.: Rio Sao Francisco, west Brazil (South America).

F.I.: 1913 by Wilhelm Eimeke, Hamburg.

Sex: Not yet known.

Soc. B.: A peaceful, lively schooling fish while young. Adults are quarrelsome among themselves and must be kept separate.

M: Provide a large, long, clear tank with plenty of oxygen. A surface fish which can be associated with *Leporinus*, large catfishes and cichlids. Through its energetic activity it can "liven up" such tanks. pH 5.5-7.5 and hardness to 20° dGH.

B: Will scatter its eggs between feathery plants. High fecundity. The young are fast growing and can be raised on *Artemia* and flake food.

F: C, O; while young, flake food, FD foods, live foods such as black mosquito larvae and fruit flies are accepted. Full-grown individuals require larger live foods such as worms and small fish.

S: Based on its appealing appearance and its liveliness, this fish should be imported more often.

T: 22-28° C, **L:** 12 cm, **A:** 80 cm, **R:** t, m, **D:** 3 (C)
72-82° F, 4 3/4", 31",

Brycon melanopterus

Bryconops affinis

Triportheus albus COPE, 1872
Yellow-Finned Hatchetfish

Syn.: *Chalcinus albus, Ch. knerii.*

Hab.: Rio Ambyiacu, Rio Tocantins, Brazil; in swamps and flood plains, South America.

F.I.: About 1968.

Sex: ♀ with a fuller stomach area during the spawning season. Barely noticeable in an aquarium.

Soc. B.: Magnificent fast swimmers, peaceful towards other fish. However, will eat fry. The animals hunt alone or in schools for insects that fall to the water surface after their "mating dance" (LÜLING, "Südamerikanische Fische und ihr Lebensraum," E. Pfriem Verlag).

M: Very oxygen demanding. It is closely related to the herring and, like the herring, almost always in motion. Usually a shy fish. The tank needs to be covered well since the fish is a good jumper. Water: pH 5.2-7.0 (6.5); hardness to 15° dGH. Frequent water changes, peat filtration.

B: Scatters its eggs among plants (usually terrestrial) during the rainy season. Nothing is precisely known.

F: C, O; flake food, FD foods of all kinds, in nature it is an insectivore.

S: This is the type species for the genus. It can jump several meters and suspend itself with the aid of its large pectoral fins. These fish are the primary prey of such fishes as *Osteoglossum, Boulengerella, Exodon* and others.

T: 22-28° C, L: 11 cm, A: 120 cm, R: t, D: 3-4 (C)
72-82° F, 4 1/3", 47",

Triportheus pictus (GARMAN, 1890)
Colored Hatchetfish

Syn.: *Chalcinus pictus.*

Hab.: Amazon basin, South America.

F.I.: Unknown.

Sex: ♂ more elongated, ♀ fuller.

Soc. B.: A lively, peaceful fish that is best kept in a group of 3-8 animals.

M: An aquarium with a large surface area is important because the fish are sensitive to low oxygen. Water values are not as critical as cleanliness. pH 5.8-7.2 and hardness to 15° dGH. Once acclimated the animals are easily kept. Cover the tank to prevent the fish from literally "flying" out.

B: Not yet bred.

F: O; omnivore, flake food of any kind, frozen foods.

S: The species is often confused with the previously discussed fish as well as the next. The black design on the head and pectorals of juveniles (*T. albus*), and the underside of the caudal peduncle and the upper caudal fin lobe (*T. rotundatus*) is probably responsible. What juvenile *T. pictus* look like could not be ascertained.

T: 22-28° C, L: 16 cm, A: 150 cm, R: t, m, D: 2-3
72-82° F, 6 1/3", 59",

Triportheus albus

Triportheus pictus

Triportheus rotundatus (SCHOMBURGK, 1841)
Black-Winged Hatchetfish

Syn.: *Chalceus rotundatus, Chalcinus brachypomus, Ch. guentheri, Ch. muelleri, Ch. trifurcatus, Triportheus guentheri.*

Hab.: The Guianas; Guanoco, Venezuela, South America.

F.I.: Unknown.

Sex: ♀ fuller through the ventral area.

Soc. B.: A peaceful, shy, lively schooling fish.

M: A large, flat sunny tank with some surface cover. Needs sparse vegetation along the edges and a lot of free swimming space. Water: pH 6.0-7.5 and hardness up to 18° dGH.

B: Not yet described.

T: 24-27° C, L: 15 cm, A: 150 cm, R: t, m, D: 2
75-81° F, 6", 59",

F: O; fruits, insects, especially mosquitoes and their larvae. Omnivorous in an aquarium. Flake food, frozen food.

S: Since the fish likes to jump, cover the tank well.

Acestrorhynchus falcirostris (CUVIER, 1819)

Dog Characin, Amazon Cachorro

Syn.: *Hydrogon falcirostris, Xiphoramphus falcirostris, Xiphorhynchus falcirostris.*

Hab.: Amazon basin, Orinoco, Guyana, Rio Ucayali (Peru), South America.

F.I.: 1913.

Sex: Not known.

Soc. B.: Vicious predator which can only be kept with conspecifics of equal size, larger robust cichlids, *Leporinus*, piranhas or similar fishes.

M: Provide a large tank with some cover. Peat brown water or floating plants on of the surface. Otherwise the fishes become shy and nervous, darting back and forth in the aquarium, often injuring the tip of their snout. Water values, depending on origin, should be soft to medium-hard 5-18° dGH, pH 5.2-7.2. Strong filtration.

T: 24-28° C, L: 40 cm, A: 150 cm, R: all, D: 4 (C)
75-82° F, 16", 59",

B: Not possible in an aquarium.

F: C; fish, meat, large insect larvae.

S: Quite a good food fish, which quickly takes a lure (spoon). The meat is somewhat soft, but quite tasty. Caution is needed when keeping this fish in an aquarium. It will sometimes attack a hand. Not an aquarium fish. Hands off!

Charax gibbosus (LINNAEUS, 1758)

Glass Headstander

Syn.: *Salmo gibbosus, Epicyrtus gibbosus, Cynopotamus gibbosus, Epicyrtus macrolepis, Anacyrtus gibbosus, A. macrolepis, Characynus gibbosus.*

Hab.: Guyana, Amazon basin, Rio Paraguay, South America.

F.I.: Around 1910.

Sex: The ♂ is yellowish during the breeding season, otherwise wax colored. ♀ somewhat larger and rounder through the ventral area.

Soc. B.: A calm, peaceful species that appreciates not being disturbed by livelier fish. Small fish under 4 cm (1²/3") may be considered food. It will nibble on young plant shoots, but only during food shortages.

M: Places no demands on water conditions. pH 6.0-7.5 and hardness to 25° dGH. The fish prefer warmer temperatures of about 25° C (77° F) and above to prevent them from becoming more lethargic than normal. A thicket of harder plants (giant *Vallisneria*) is needed for their well-being.

B: Breeding becomes possible in a tank longer than a meter (39"). After intense courtship, the eggs are loosely scattered among plants. Larvae hatch after about 30 hours and require plentiful fine pond plankton for rearing.

F: O; but primarily live foods, frozen foods and sometimes vegetable flake foods.

S: Despite its dangerous appearance the species is also suitable for the tranquil community tank. Finds few followers because of its plain appearance.

T: 24-27° C, L: 15 cm, A: 120 cm, R: m, D: 2
75-81° F, 6", 47",

Cynopotamus argenteus (VALENCIENNES, 1837)

River Dog, Silver Dentudo

Syn.: *Hydrocyon argenteus, Anacyrtus argenteus, Charax argentea, Cyrtocharax argenteus.*

Hab.: Rio Paraguay, Paraguay (South America).

F.I.: 1982 by Heiko Bleher, Frankfurt.

Sex: External characteristics are not described.

Soc. B.: A predator which can only be kept with animals over 8 cm (3") in length. Not suitable for the normal community tank.

M: Decoration is not important to this species. Both a planted aquarium and a rocky landscape are suitable. Not particular concerning its care as long as it is not being starved. If live fish cannot or will not be fed, then tablets can be tried. A planted tank with cover and free swimming room for hunting is needed. A pH of 6.0-7.2 and a hardness up to 15° dGH is suitable.

B: Has not been bred.

F: C; predator; large live foods, later pieces of fish and meat. With training it will accept tablets or pellets.

S: The German common name, "river dog" (Flußhund), is a translation of its Latin genus name.

T: 20-24° C, L: 12 cm, A: 80 cm, R: all, D: 4 (C), otherwise 2
68-75° F, 4³/4", 31",

Charax gibbosus

Cynopotamus argenteus

*Mimagoniates lateralis**
NICHOLS, 1913

Tenuis Tetra

Syn.: *Coelurichthys lateralis, C. inequalis, C. tenuis* (♀).

Hab.: Southeast Brazil, Paraguay, northern Argentina, South America.

F.I.: 1907 by Oscar Kittler, Hamburg.

Sex: The dorsal fin of the ♀ is rounded while that of the ♂ is higher and more pointed. The anal fin of the ♂ reaches beyond the base of the caudal fin (elongated into a point), on the ♀ it ends in a rounded tip at the middle of the caudal peduncle.

Soc. B.: A peaceful schooling fish. This species is suited to cooler community aquaria.

M: Because these fish originate in fast flowing rivers of hilly regions, they are difficult to maintain. The edges of the river are shaded by trees. Water is clear, slightly peat brown and oxygen-rich.
These conditions can only be met in a slightly heated (cooled in the summer) home aquarium when special attention is paid to these points. pH 5.5-6.5 and a hardness to 4° dGH. Provide dim lighting but a strong current and meticulous cleanliness.

B: T: 24° C (75° F). There is internal fertilization. After intense courtship and unflagging attempts to embrace, the sperm package is transferred to the ♀. If fertilization is successful the female can deposit fertilized eggs at a later time, even weeks later. The eggs are preferentially deposited on the underside of water plants or grass roots. The larvae are difficult to raise because of their small size. The finest pond plankton is mandatory for the limited success of rearing the fry.

S: Much has been reported about this species under the name *"Mimagoniates barberi."* This is a totally different species, however, which has yet to be imported. See Vol. 3, page 120, for text of *C. microlepis*.

* The previous name *Coelurichthys tenuis* is a synonyme and discribes the female of *C. lateralis*. Both taxa have now been placed into the genus *Mimagoniates*.

T: 19-22° C, **L:** 5 cm, **A:** 80 cm, **R:** t, **D:** 3-4 (Ch)
66-72° F, 2", 31",

Mimagoiates microlepis "Joinville"

Mimagoniates lateralis

Gephyrocharax valencia EIGENMANN, 1920
Mountain Minnow Tetra, Valencia Tetra

Syn.: None.

Hab.: Lake Valencia in Venezuela, South America.

F.I.: 1932 by Otto Winkelmann, Hamburg-Altona.

Sex: The anal fin of the ♂ is longer at the middle; the anal fin of the ♀ is even and slightly concave. ♀ is plumper.

Soc. B.: A peaceful, agile species which is best kept in schools. ♂♂ are sometimes "impolite" towards tankmates. These encounters, however, never result in injury.

M: An undemanding species which places few conditions on water chemistry. pH 6.0-7.5 and hardness to 25° dGH.

T: 23-28° C, **L:** 5 cm, **A:** 60 cm, **R:** all, **D:** 1
73-82° F, 2", 24",

B: As with the swordtail characin, there is internal fertilization. 28° C (82° F). ♀♀ spawn without ♂♂ on fine-leaved plants. The fry hatch after 36 hours and are free-swimming after 3 days. In 3 months the fish have grown to 4 cm (1 2/3"). At this time the sexes can be identified. Raise the young with a variety of micro foods, *Artemia*, TetraMin Baby Food, Liquifry.

F: O; flake food.

S: See **B.** Fertilization by the ♂ is almost unnoticeable during an impressive courtship. Later, the ♂ does not participate in the spawning.

Pterobrycon myrnae BUSSING, 1974
Blotched Arrowhead Tetra

Syn.: None.

Hab.: Costa Rica; Pacific flatland tributaries, Central America.

F.I.: 1973 by Dr. Stanley Weitzman to the USA. 1983 to Germany.

Sex: Soft, elongated pelvic fin rays, which are pointed towards the ♀ during courtship. ♂ with black spreadable "paddle scales" at the shoulder area. The black coloration disappears after courtship.

Soc. B.: Because of the interesting courtship behavior, the species should have a tank without disturbances. A peaceful species that energetically chases conspecifics outside of the spawning season.

M: The animals were kept for 2 years (after sexual maturity) under normal aquarium conditions by Dr. Weitzman. Water hardness was 15° dGH with a pH of 6.0-7.0. Provide the aquarium with dim lights, dark substrate and a moderate amount of plants. Possibly peat filtration. This species is sensitive to diseases. However, after acclimation it is quite hardy.

T: 23-26° C, **L:** 7 cm, **A:** 80 cm, **R:** m, **D:** 2
73-79° F, 2 3/4", 31",

B: Though breeding has not been accomplished, the courtship is spectacular in itself.

F: C, O; flake food, insects and insect larvae, FD and frozen foods.

S: There are two double-scales behind the head of the ♂. During courtship these are spread, acting as an attractant or stimulator. In addition, the ♂ secretes a scent from a gland at the base of the tail.

Gephyrocharax valencia

Pterobrycon myrnae ♂

Phenagoniates macrolepis (MEEK & HILDEBRAND, 1913)
Barred Glass Tetra

Syn.: *Roeboides macrolepis, Phenagoniates wilsoni.*

Hab.: Southern Panama, small, fast flowing creeks of the Rio Tuyra, Central America.

F.I.: 1983 by Heiko Bleher, Frankfurt.

Sex: Unknown.

Soc. B.: Lives as an aggressive loner or in small groups. The animals can seriously injure each other. Other species are not disturbed.

M: Water values in nature are as follows; pH 6.4-6.6, hardness approximately 4° dGH, µS[20]175. The species live in shaded headwaters. A tank with strong filtration is a necessity. Frequent water changes, 2/3 every 14 days, and the addition of a water conditioner are recommended. Cover the tank well; the fish will jump.

B: Has not been successful.

F: C; live foods of all kinds, especially small flies, frozen foods.

S: A magnificent species which can sometimes be kept in a school. However, suddenly, i.e., when an individual has been removed from the group, they injure themselves so badly that within a short time the entire group will have destroyed itself (verbal communication, Heiko Bleher, Frankfurt).

T: 22-24° C, **L:** 6 cm, **A:** 80 cm, **R:** m, **D:** 3-4
72-75° F, 2 1/3", 31",

High plains of east Brazil, Rio Candindé: characins, livebearers and some cichlids live in this desolate landscape.

Flooded pool at St. Joâo de Patos, east Brazil (Para). Millions of small fish live in this water remnant after the rainy season.

Astyanax zonatus EIGENMANN, 1908
Diamond Tetra, False Kennedy's Tetra

Syn.: *Poecilurichthys zonatus.*

Hab.: Rio Paraguay, Paraguay (where the photographed animals were caught!). According to the literature, this species occurs at the upper Amazon (South America).

F.I.: 1981 by Heiko Bleher, Frankfurt.

Sex: ♂ more slender and somewhat larger than the ♀.

Soc. B.: Peaceful schooling fish with good qualities for a community aquarium.

M: An undemanding species. It is a true fish for the beginner. The shining red eyes of adult fish are in strong contrast to the silver body, which shines bluishj or golden depending on the angle of the lighting. Soft water is advantageous but not necessary. pH 6.5-7.8. Provide plenty of free swimming room.

T: 20-25° C, L: 8 cm, A: 80 cm, R: m, D: 1
68-77° F, 3", 31",

B: Breeds in schools among clusters of plants. Use a breeding trap or remove the parents after spawning. The very small fry require the finest pond plankton.

F: C, O; flake food, frozen food, FD foods and small live foods.

S: It is sometimes traded as *Moenkhausia comma* which is a different genus and species. See page 284.

Axelrodia stigmatias (FOWLER, 1914)
Pepper Tetra*, White-Star Tetra

Syn.: *Hyphessobrycon stigmatias, Axelrodia fowleri.*

Hab.: Amazon basin, South America.

F.I.: 1984 by Heiko Bleher, Frankfurt. Certainly as by-catch before then.

Sex: ♀ is fuller during spawning season. The white markings on the dorsal and anal fins are more intense on the ♂.

Soc. B.: Very peaceful schooling fish, but only conditionally suitable for the community tank because of its sensitivity.

M: Peat filtration! Soft, brown water up to 8° dGH; pH 5.5-6.5. Dark substrate, e.g., lava. Associate with fishes such as checkerboard cichlids, neons and *Corydoras*. A partial cover of floating plants is recommended. The fish show their beauty only in subdued light.

T: 22-26° C, L: 3 cm, A: 60 cm, R: m, D: 2-3
72-79° F, 1 ", 24",

B: Not described yet. It should be possible with extremely soft water. The breeders will have to be conditioned with black mosquito larvae.

F: C, O; fine flake food, FD-Menu, live *Artemia, Cyclops.*

S: *In German the common name pepper tetra is suggested because the fish is covered with tiny black dots, appearing as though sprinkled with black pepper.

Bryconops caudomaculatus (GÜNTHER, 1864)
Red Cross Tetra

Syn.: *Creatochanes caudomaculatus.*

Hab.: Guyana, middle Amazon, Colombia, South America.

F.I.: 1933.

Sex: ♂ with pointed, extended caudal fin lobes; ♀ is more rounded.

Soc. B.: When small it is a harmless schooling fish that can be kept with equally sized or other peaceful species. From 8 cm (3") on it becomes aggressive towards smaller fish. Can be kept with *Hypostomus*, larger cichlids, etc.

M: Needs a well-filtered tank, preferably 120 cm (47") long or longer, with abundant oxygen and current and well-planted in parts. Water: pH 6.5-7.5, hardness to 25° dGH.

B: Has not taken place in an aquarium. Scatters its eggs in schools. Prefers to reproduce during the rainy season, and therefore during the annually occurring floods.

F: C, O; flake, FD and frozen foods.

S: One of the most commonly imported species of the genus. Nevertheless, not a hit among the characins.

T: 23-26° C, **L:** 13 cm, **A:** 120 cm, **R:** t, m, **D:** 2-3
73-79° F, 5", 47",

Bryconops caudomaculatus, juv.

Bryconops caudomaculatus ♂

Bryconops caudomaculatus ♀

Bryconops melanurus (BLOCH, 1795)
Tail-Light Tetra

Syn.: *Creatochanes melanurus, Tetragonopterus melanurus.*

Hab.: Eastern Brazil, Rio Sao Francisco system, South America.

F.I.: ?

Sex: ♂ more slender, ♀ rounder through the ventral area.

Soc. B.: Very active peaceful schooling fish as a juvenile—well suited for larger community tanks with soft water. Full-grown specimens are not quite as peaceful.

M: Requires larger aquaria with current and high oxygen content. Peat filtration. Nitrate-free water with a pH between 5.6 and 6.8 and hardness up to 10° dGH. Sand bottom and plenty of light. Open swimming space and some cover of roots or plants reaching the water surface.

B: Has not been accomplished in an aquarium. Egg scatterer. Extremely soft water (<4° dGH). T: 28° C (82° F).

F: C, O; insects and their larvae, flake food, frozen and freeze-dried mosquito larvae, brine shrimp, etc.

S: One of the most beautiful species of the genus *Bryconops*. Unfortunately, it is seldom imported.

T: 23-26° C, 73-79° F, **L:** 10 cm, 4", **A:** 120 cm, 47", **R:** t, **D:** 2-3

Cheirodon affinis (MEEK & HILDEBRAND, 1916)
Black-Base Tetra

Syn.: None (?).

Hab.: Costa Rica, Panama, Central America.

F.I.: 1983 by Heiko Bleher, Frankfurt.

Sex: There is distinct sexual dimorphism in this genus. Usually ♂♂ are smaller than ♀♀. ♂ has distinctly thickenend rays in the anterior region of the anal fin and small hooks used to cling to the ♀ during the sexual act. The base of caudal fin has a wedge-like appendage which also has fine barbs.

Soc. B.: Fast, peaceful schooling fish. Suitable for any community tank.

M: Needs a relatively cool aquarium with strong filtration (current) and good movement of the water surface. In nature the pH is approximately 6.5; in the aquarium the values can be higher, up to 7.5. Hardness to 12° dGH. They become timid if the lighting is too strong.

B: Not yet bred.

F: C, O; flake food, FD-Menu, frozen food, small live foods.

S: *Cheirodon affinis* occurs in Panama, *Cheirodon terrabae* (BUSSING, 1967) in Costa Rica. Neither fish can be distinguished from a photograph. The pictured fish was caught in Panama.

T: 22-24° C, 72-75° F, **L:** 4.5 cm, 1 3/4", **A:** 60 cm, 24", **R:** m, **D:** 2

Bryconops melanurus

Cheirodon affinis

Cheirodon galusdae EIGENMANN, 1927

Chile Tetra

Syn.: None.

Hab.: Central Chile, South America.

F.I.: 1981 by Dr. Busse, Bonn.

Sex: ♀ noticeably fuller when ripe.

Soc. B.: Peaceful schooling fish, gentle and shy. Best kept in a species tank.

M: Use a well-filtered, small, species tank with current. Can be kept outside during the summer. Fine, dark substrate with swimming room at the filter discharge. pH 6.5-7.2 and hardness to 15° dGH.

B: Not successful.

T: 18-22° C, **L:** 6 cm, **A:** 70 cm, **R:** b, m, **D:** 3
64-72° F, 2 1/3", 28",

F: C; insect larvae, small flies, tablet food, FD food.

S: Chile has three *Cheirodon* species: *Cheirodon pisciculus* (northern Chile), *Cheirodon australe* (southern Chile) and the species presented here.

Cheirodon kriegi SCHINDLER, 1937

Three-Spot Tetra

Syn.: None.

Hab.: Rio Paraguay basin, upper Guaporé River, Brazil (South America).

F.I.: Unknown since it is usually not recognized.

Sex: ♀ fuller in the ventral area.

Soc. B.: Very peaceful, lively schooling fish which fits well in a community aquarium.

M: Clear, well-filtered water with a slight current. pH 6.0-7.2 and hardness up to 15° dGH. The illumination should not be too intense, so that these plain animals stand out better.

T: 24-27° C, **L:** 5 cm, **A:** 80 cm, **R:** m, **D:** 2
75-81° F, 2", 31",

B: Like other tetras, an egg scatterer among plants. See *C. piaba*, page 269.

F: C, O; flake food of any kind. FD and frozen foods.

S: The black spot above the anus is similar to the pregnancy patch exhibited by the livebearers. Some authors identify females by it. However, *MM* also have the spot and is not related to spawning ripeness.

Cheirodon galusdae

Cheirodon kriegi

Cheirodon kriegi

Cheirodon kriegi (?)

Odontostilbe piaba LÜTKEN, 1874
Piaba Tetra

Syn: *Cheirodon calliurus, C. jaguaribensis, C. macropterus, C. micropterus, C. piaba.*

Hab.: Across Brazil from Rio Paraguay to Rio Sao Francisco, South America.

F.I.: 1911 by Albert Mayer, Hamburg.

Sex: ♂ slimmer and has a longer swim bladder which can be seen against the light. ♂ with strongly concave anal fin, almost straight on the ♀.

Soc. B.: Very peaceful species suitable for the community aquarium that doesn't contain rough fishes.

M: A robust schooling fish. Due to its wide area of origin, it can have different requirements. pH 6.0-7.5 and hardness to 25° dGH. During the acclimation period, peat extract and/or a water conditioner (i.e., AquaSafe) is advantageous.

B: Breeding the species is normally easy, as long as one has well fed pairs available. Place two ♂♂ with one ♀. Approximately 200 eggs are deposited and fertilized in between fine plants after vigorous chasing. The larvae hatch after 5 days, hang suspended (if left undisturbed) another 4 days among the plants and then search for food. Rearing with *Artemia* nauplii, pond plankton, finest ground flakes (recommendation: Tetra Ruby or Tetra FD-Menu), Liquifry Red or similar foods poses few problems. Parents should be removed.

F: O; flake food, fine live foods, almost any frozen food and FD food.

S: The species is easily confused with *Cheirodon kriegi*. The ♂♂ of that species have tiny hooks on the base of the tail which aid in embracing the ♀ during spawning.

T: 20-27° C, L: 5 cm, A: 70 cm, R: m, D: 2
68-81° F, 2", 28",

Creagrutus beni EIGENMANN, 1911
Benny Tetra

Syn: None.

Hab.: Lake Valencia in Venezuela, Bolivia, upper Amazon (Peru). Rio Tocantins, Brazil, South America.

F.I.: 1932 by Otto Winkelmann, Hamburg.

Sex: As an exception, here the ♀♀ are more colorful and (as usual) fuller. ♂ is plain.

Soc. B.: Peaceful, almost gentle, active schooling fish which is well suited for the normal community aquarium.

M: A typical representative of the "tetra" sub-family. Requirements are similar to *Hemigrammus* or *Hyphessobrycon* which the species can easily be combined with. Provide a few plants and adequate swimming space. Bright light. Maybe peat filtration could be of benefit, though not a necessity. Water: pH between 6.0-7.2; hardness up to 20° dGH (10°).

B: The fish has a short-term ability to store sperm. A ♀ can, if fertilization occurred earlier, deposit fertilized eggs. 50-70 eggs are laid which hatch 24-28 hours later (26° C; 79°F). The fry are free-swimming after 3 days and take any food of suitable size, usually off the bottom.

F: O; flake, FD, tablet and frozen foods.

S: According to GÉRY, the species name is not certain. It seems that two species or sub-species are imported and traded under the same name.

T: 22-26° C, **L:** 8 cm; in Venezuela only 4.5 cm, **A:** from 40 cm, **R:** m, **D:** 1-2
72-79° F, 3", in Venezuela only 1 3/4", 16",

Gymnocorymbus socolofi GÉRY, 1964
Socolof's Tetra

Syn: None.

Hab.: Upper Rio Meta, Colombia (South America).

F.I.: To the USA in 1963.

Sex: Not yet described.

Soc. B.: A lively schooling fish when young. Older animals become more sedate and colorless.

M: A dark tank bottom, strong filtration and plants offering hiding places will encourage the brighter colors which come from healthy fish. Water: pH 5,5-7,5 and hardness to 20° dGH.

B: Not yet described, but bred several times in the USA on "Socolof's" fish farm in Florida.

F: O; besides plants, flake food with plenty of vegetable food.

S: Named after the US fish breeder Ross Socolof. Juveniles up to 3 cm (1") in length have orange-red (unpaired) fins and are a desirable beginner fish.

T: 23-27° C, **L:** 5.5 cm, **A:** 70 cm, **R:** m, **D:** 2
73-81° F, 2", 28",

Creagrutus beni ♀

Gymnocorymbus socolofi

Hemigrammus boesemani GÉRY, 1959

Boeseman's Tetra

Syn: None.

Hab.: The Guianas and upper Amazon, South America.

F.I.: Certainly often as by-catches. 1983 by Heiko Bleher, Frankfurt.

Sex: End of the swim bladder is pointed on the ♂ and much more rounded on the ♀.

Soc. B.: Peaceful, nimble, schooling fish. Does well in a densely planted community tank.

M: Keep in an aquarium that is - densely planted and free swimming area. It enjoys standing in a plant thicket. Subdued light (floating plant cover) or peat filtration/peat extract will aid in showing the shiny longitudinal band along its body. Water: pH 5.8-7.4 and hardness to 16° dGH.

B: As with other *Hemigrammus* species.

F: C, O; flake food, FD-Menu, frozen food and fine live foods.

S: Was previously considered a subspecies of *Hemigrammus micropterus*.

T: 23-26° C, **L**: 4.5 cm, **A**: 60 cm, **R**: m, t, **D**: 2
73-79° F, 1ʃ", 24",

Hemigrammus guyanensis GÉRY, 1959

Red-Dot Tetra, Guyana Tetra

Syn: None.

Hab.: In headwaters of French Guyana (South America). In the lower courses of the rivers it is replaced by *H. ocellifer*.

F.I.: Unknown.

Sex: Against the light, the pointed lower end of the ♂'s swim bladder can be seen. In the ♀ it is partially covered. Therefore, it appears round.

Soc. B.: Peaceful schooling fish well suited for the cooler community aquarium. During food shortages tender plant shoots are nibbled on.

M: Should be kept in a small school. Single individuals wane. Water: pH 6.0-7.2, hardness to 18° dGH. Moderate lighting with a dark substrate and a strong filter current. Peat filtration is an advantage but not a necessity.

B: Scatters its eggs among plants.

F: C, O; small live foods (*Artemia, Cyclops*), Bosmina (perhaps frozen). Flake food of any kind.

S: None.

T: 20-24° C, **L**: 4 cm, **A**: 60 cm, **R**: m, t, **D**: 1-2
68-75° F, 1 2/3", 24",

Hemigrammus boesemani

Hemigrammus guyanensis

Hemigrammus schmardae (STEINDACHNER, 1882)
Schmard Tetra

Syn: *Tetragonopterus schmardae, Hemigrammus melanochrous, H. proneki.*

Hab.: Upper Rio Negro in Brazil, South America.

F.I.: Unrecognized as by-catch and uncertain

Sex: ♂♂ more slender; ♀♀, at least when ripe, are easily distinguishable by the full abdominal area.

Soc. B.: Very peaceful schooling fish. Keep in a community tank with equal natured fish.

M: Well-planted tank with $^1/_3$ as swimming space in the front. pH 5.8-7.2. Hardness to 10° dGH, up to 18° dGH outside of breeding time. Use a substrate as dark as possible. Regular water changes every 3-4 weeks ($^1/_3$-$^1/_2$).

B: Darken the aquarium with floating plants and peat water. When you are dealing with full-grown individuals and ripe ♀♀ (rounded abdomen) illuminate the tank strongly in the morning or expose the tank to morning sun. After a stormy courtship, the animals press together and spawn among plant bunches (moss). The parents should be removed afterwards to prevent them from consuming eggs and young.

F: C, O; flake food, FD food, some frozen food (Bosmina, *Cyclops*), *Artemia* nauplii.

S: None.

T: 24-27° C, **L:** 5 cm, **A:** 60 cm, **R:** m, **D:** 2
75-81° F, 2", 24",

Hemigrammus stictus refer to page after next.

Hemigrammus vorderwinkleri GÉRY, 1963
Vorderwinkler's Tetra

Syn: None.

Hab.: Rio Negro, Brazil (South America).

F.I.: Unknown.

Sex: ♂ has a more distinct hook-shaped anal fin and more pronounced white scales on the ventral side.

Soc. B.: Quick, peaceful schooling fish. Well suited to be kept together with neons, dwarf cichlids, etc.

M: It prefers the environment of the neon; peat filtered, soft water. Lots of free swimming room with sparse vegetation in the background to serve as a cover.

B: Scatters its eggs in a school. Best to place pairs in breeding aquaria that are 50 cm (20") long. Rain water and a good water conditioner (i.e., Duplagen, AquaSafe), possibly combined with a peat extract, should be added. After strong chasing, the eggs are released randomly among plant groups.

F: C, O; flake food, FD foods and fine live foods (*Artemia*).

S: The species is very similar to *H. schmardae*. It differs in the shape of the spot on the tail base and in the number of scales along the lateral line. *H. vorderwinkleri* has 29-30 and *H. schmardae* has 30-34.

T: 23-27° C, **L:** 4 cm, **A:** 60 cm, **R:** m, **D:** 2
73-81° F, 1$^2/_3$", 24",

Hemigrammus schmardae

Hemigrammus vorderwinkleri

Hemigrammus stictus (DURBIN, 1903)
Red-Base Tetra

Syn: None.

Hab.: The Guianas; Amazon region; Rio Meta, Colombia (South America).

F.I.: Uncertain, since imported as little noticed by-catch.

Sex: ♂ more slender than ♀. Our upper photo shows a ♀, the lower, a young ♂ with the anterior part of the anal fin distinctly more elongated.

Soc. B.: Peaceful, brisk schooling fish, well suited for the community tank.

M: An African cichlid tank would not be ideal even though the fish is durable. A better option is an Amazon tank with *Echinodorus*, *Heteranthera* and floating ferns.

T: 23-27° C, L: 6 cm, A: 80 cm, R: m, D: 2
73-81° F, 2 1/3", 31",

Soft, peat filtered water with a pH between 6 and 7 and a hardness up to 10° dGH is preferred. Dark gravel substrate.

B: T: 26° C (79° F). Soft, slightly acid, peat filtered water. Spawning occurs among plant bushes or moss. The eggs are adhesive for a time. Since the parents often eat the eggs; they should be removed. The larvae hatch after one day and soon require the finest pond plankton. Starting on the 5th day, the fry will accept *Artemia*, TetraMin Baby Food or Liquifry Red.

F: C, O; flake food, FD-food, frozen food as mosquito larvae, Daphnia; *Artemia* as livefood.

S: The animals will only show their beautiful color in soft water with a low nitrate level.

Flooding in the Rio Xingu, Brazil! At this time nothing can be caught. The herbivorous fish now have a full plate. For many species this marks the beginning of the breeding season since there is an abundance of food.

Hemigrammus stictus ♀, adult

Hemigrammus stictus ♂

Hyphessobrycon metae EIGENMANN & HENN, 1914

Rio Meta Tetra, Purple Tetra

Syn: None.

Hab.: Rio Meta, Colombia, South America.

F.I.: Probably only after 1970.

Sex: ♀ clearly fuller and taller than the ♂.

Soc. B.: Timid, peaceful schooling fish. A subject for the community aquarium with gentle fishes. Keeping them in a small species tank is recommended, however.

M: This precious fish demands attention for its keep. Peat filtration or addition of peat extract, soft water of about 4-8° dGH, subdued light and tranquil, peaceful tankmates are required for successfully maintaining them. In addition, the water needs to be low in nitrates which can only be achieved by filtering through an ion exchanger or regular water changes ($^2/_3$ every 4 weeks) and a low biomass.

B: Low fecundity, perhaps comparable to the cardinal tetra. Needs a breeding tank with peat filtered soft water (below 4° dGH) and a pH of 5.8-6.2. Clumps of fine-leaved plants. The fish dive into them following a vigorous courtship. After spawning the parents need to be immediately removed. Rear with only the finest pond plankton.

F: C, O; any live food of appropriate size, FD foods, flake foods.

S: It is possible that the three species, *Hephessobrycon loretoensis*, *H. metae*, and *H. peruvianus,* belong to a single species (local races or subspecies (written communication Dr. GÉRY, 1984). At least *H. peruvianus* and *H. metae* appear to be very similar in coloration. Besides, *H. metae* and *H. loretoensis* are close relatives.

T: 22-26° C, L: 5 cm, A: 60 cm, R: m, D: 2-3
72-79° F, 2", 24",

Picture on the right page: side arm of a river at Leticia (Colombia). Here tens of thousands of aquarium fishes are caught and held in open oil barrels.

Hyphessobrycon reticulatus ELLIS, 1911
Netted Tetra

Syn: None.

Hab.: Southeast Brazil; La Plata basin (South America).

F.I.: 1932; uncertain because this tetra has had little attention until now.

Sex: Unknown.

Soc. B.: Agile, active schooling fish, suitable for the community tank with appropriate decoration (tough plants). Not suitable to be combined with smaller species because the animals are said to be "quarrelsome and aggressive" (according to STERBA).

M: A very hardy species that can endure quite a bit. An interesting change for the connoisseur. It knows how to stand its ground in a cichlid tank with bullies. Water: pH 6.0-8.0 and hardness to 30° dGH (12° dGH).

B: Not yet described. Should be similar to other *Hyphessobrycon*.

F: O; flake food, Daphnia, frozen food, tender plants!

S: The largest *Hyphessobrycon*. The species is similar to a *Astyanax* (e.g., *A. ribeirae*, under whose name it is traded in the US). With the exception of two species, according to GÉRY (1977), all *Hyphessobrycon* belong in other genera. It remains to be seen if this popular genus will be named differently. In this century hardly an ichthyologist will dare to touch it.

T: 15-25° C, **L:** 8 cm, **A:** 100 cm, **R:** m, t, **D:** 2-3
59-77° F, 3", 39",

Hyphessobrycon socolofi WEITZMAN, 1977
Socolof's Cherry-Spot Tetra, Lesser Bleeding Heart

Syn: None.

Hab.: Rio Negro, Brazil (South America).

F.I.: Not known, since the species was traded under a wrong name for a long time.

Sex: In full-grown animals the ♂♂ are somewhat larger and the dorsal is bluer; on the ♀ the tip of the dorsal is red. The posterior part of the anal fin of the ♀ is red, on the ♂ it is blue throughout.

Soc. B.: Peaceful schooling fish. At least 6 individuals should be kept together. Best to associate with quiet bottom dwellers, small cichlids or other characins.

M: Use a dark tank with floating plant cover, heavily peat filtered water or peat extract. Dim lighting and dark bottom. Water: pH 5.8-7.0; hardness to 10° dGH. Good biological filtration and regular partial water changes of $^1/_3$ every 3-4 weeks.

B: Feed breeders well on live/frozen foods. The ♀ should have a well-rounded abdomen. Breeding tanks from 50 cm (20") length. Use one pair. T: 27° C (81° F), soft water to 4° dGH, pH around 6.0. Scatters its eggs among plants; use a breeding mesh.

F: C, O; flake food, FD food, frozen foods.

S: This species is imported more often than the close relative *H. erythrostigma*. The species is sometimes sensitive to bacterial attack. That is why only well acclimated animals should be bought. See the picture also in Vol. 1, page 213.

T: 23-27° C, **L:** 4.5 cm, **A:** 80 cm, **R:** m, **D:** 2-3
73-81° F, $1^3/_4$", 31",

Hyphessobrycon reticulatus

Hyphessobrycon socolofi, ♂ bottom, ♀ top

Megalamphodus roseus GÉRY, 1960
Golden Phantom Tetra

Syn: None.

Hab.: Maroni river system in the Guianas, South America.

F.I.: 1978 by a Dutch Pater; 1984 through Westaquarium, Bad Lauterberg, Germany.

Sex: ♂ has a smaller shoulder spot and more white in the dorsal fin. See picture: ♀ above, ♂ below.

Soc. B.: Peaceful schooling fish, which is a special decoration for any community tank.

M: pH 6.0-7.8 (6.8); hardness to 30° dGH, less is better. A lot of light and plant growth, free swimming space in the front. Do not associate with small or large predators. Dark substrate. Good filter maintenance (low nitrate in the water, below 20 mg/l). The addition of peat extract promotes its well-being.

B: Has already been bred; should be as with other species of the genus. See Vol. 1, page 298.

F: C, O; fine flake food, FD foods, *Artemia*, black mosquito larvae.

S: One of the most beautiful new imports of the last years. A wonderful contrast to the neon and cardinal.

T: 23-27° C, **L:** 3 cm, **A:** 60 cm, **R:** m, **D:** 2
73-81° F, 1", 24",

Megalamphodus (sp. ?) or bred

Syn: Partially uses the names *M. sweglesi* or *M. rogoaguae.*

Hab.: ?

F.I.: After 1970.

Sex: ♂ has a larger dorsal fin, usually without black; ♀ has a red-black dorsal fin.

Soc. B.: Peaceful schooling fish.

M: Somewhat easier than *M. sweglesi* but somewhat harder than *M. megalopterus.* pH approximately 6.5, hardness to 10° dGH.

B: Is it a bred species?

F: C, O; flake food, FD foods, fine live foods.

S: The most beautiful *Megalamphodus* species, at least the most gorgeously red colored one. It should finally receive a name.

T: 23-27° C, **L:** 4 cm, **A:** 60 cm, **R:** m, **D:** 2-3
73-81° F, $1^2/_3$", 24",

Megalamphodus roseus, ♂ bottom, ♀ top

Megalamphodus (sp. ?) or bred

Moenkhausia ceros
EIGENMANN, 1908

Ceros Tetra

Syn: None.

Hab.: Rio Ucayali, Peru (South America).

F.I.: 1983 through Heiko Bleher, Frankfurt. As by-catch earlier?

Sex: ♀ fuller and with a rounded swim bladder; pointed in the ♂.

Soc. B.: In the wild it associates with angelfish, *Mesonauta festiva*, *Ctenobrycon hauxwellianus*, *Hemigrammus ocellifer*. In an aquarium the fish will provide much joy as a peaceful, lively schooling fish.

M: As with the following species.

B: Breeding in an aquarium has not been described. It should be similar to the other *Moenkhausia* or *Hemigrammus*.

F: C, O; in the aquarium, flake, FD and frozen foods. In nature the fish also feed in shallow shores on the blood of slaughtered *Arapaima*.

S: None.

T: 24-28° C, **L:** 6 cm, **A:** 70 cm, **R:** m, t, **D:** 1-2
75-82° F, $2^1/_3$", 28",

Moenkhausia comma
EIGENMANN, 1908

Comma Tetra

Syn: *Moenkhausia coma* (Typographical error by STEINDACHNER).

Hab.: Lower Amazon from Belem to Para, South America.

F.I.: 1963.

Sex: ♂ more slender through the stomach area; ripe ♀♀ are plump.

Soc. B.: Schooling fish when young; mature animals outline territories in large aquaria. Associate with all robust species; peaceful.

M: A large tank with dark substrate is suggested. Use groups of taller grouped plants (swords) to define territories when keeping several pairs. Water: 6.0-7.5, hardness to 18° dGH.

B: As for *Hemigrammus* species. Breeding tanks 60 cm (24") long with single pairs, plant bundles and soft water. Feed the breeders heavily with mosquito larvae (live). The eggs hatch after 60 hours. Parents remain with the fry.

F: C, O; flake food (large flakes), frozen food.

S: Specially during spawning time, it is a magnificent species, no less so than *Moenkhausia pittieri*.

T: 23-28° C, **L:** to 8 cm, **A:** 120 cm, **R:** m, **D:** 2
73-82° F, to 3", 47",

Moenkhausia ceros

Moenkhausia comma

Moenkhausia copei (STEINDACHNER, 1882)
Cope's Moenkhausia

Syn: *Tetragonopterus copei.*

Hab.: Amazon basin and Guianas.

F.I.: Uncertain; since there are seldom reports about plain by-catches.

Sex: The anal fin of the ♂ is more curved than the ♀'s.

Soc. B.: Peaceful schooling fish, suitable for the "demanding" community aquarium. Always keep a small school!

M: The species likes a tank darkened with a floating plant cover and peat filtration. Water: pH 5.8-7.2; hardness to 15° dGH. When the water conditions suit the species, the animals display a violet and golden shimmering beauty, which enthuses every connoisseur.

B: Egg scatterer in a school or in pairs. The eggs are expelled among fine-leaved plants as is typical for tetras. Remove parents after spawning. Raise the young with finest pond plankton.

F: C, O; flake food, frozen and freeze-dried natural food. Once a week feed live *Artemia* nauplii.

S: None.

T: 22-26° C, L: 6.5 cm, A: 60 cm, R: m, D: 2-3
72-79° F, $2^2/_3$", 24",

Rio Sumidoro, Mato Grosso, Brazil (headwaters of Rio Xingu). In this El Dorado of water plants many fish feel at home. On the plant leaves one can find thousands of *Otocinclus*; in the deep hollows of the creek *Corydoras*. *Moenkhausia phaenota* and *Hyphessobrycon vilmae* live together here.

Moenkhausia lepidura (KNER, 1859)
Half-Mast Flag Tetra

Syn: *Tetragonopterus lepidurus.*

Hab.: The Guianas, entire Amazon basin.

F.I.: Uncertain.

Sex: ♂ with anteriorly wider anal fin (photo); on the ♀ it is concave.

Soc. B.: Peaceful, very active schooling fish. Well suited for the community tank.

M: This species is a strong swimmer and wants a lot of room. An undemanding fish that accepts almost any type of water. pH 5.5-7.8; hardness up to 30° dGH. Cover the aquarium well!

T: 22-28° C, L: 8 cm, A: 120 cm, R: m, t, D: 1
72-82° F, 3" 47",

B: Not yet described, but should be similar to other *Moenkhausia*. Scatters eggs among plants or perlon. As soon as ripe ♀♀ can be distinguished, provide the aquarium with sun or strong illumination in the morning. Will eat their spawn.

F: C, O; flake food, frozen food. A vegetable diet (e.g., Tetra Conditioning Food) should be added if plant shoots are nibbled on.

S: One of the most common characins of South America. It is used as bait. Several sub-species have been described.

Moenkhausia melogramma EIGENMANN, 1903
Golden-Glass Tetra

Syn.: None.

Hab.: Upper Amazon (Colombia).

F.I.: Surely unknowingly as a by-catch years ago.

Sex: ♂ with pointed, pulled down swim bladder; ♀ with blunt, round swim bladder and ventral area.

Soc. B.: Peaceful, schooling fish well suited for a soft water community aquarium.

M: Densely planted tank with peat filtration and extremely soft water; pH 5.8-6.8 and hardness up to 6° dGH. After acclimation higher values are tolerated. Provide the aquarium with a dark bottom and clear, well-oxygenated water.

T: 23-27° C, L: 4.5 cm, A: 60 cm, R: m, D: 2-3
73-81° F, 1∫", 24",

B: Scatters eggs in a plant thicket; soft water, peat filtration. T: 23° C (73° F). Set-up as with *Hemigrammus* species.

F: C, O; flake food, FD, frozen food.

S: A rarely imported species that does poorly and appears plain in an intensely lit, hard water aquarium.

Moenkhausia lepidura ♂

Moenkhausia melogramma, ♂ bottom, ♀ top

Moenkhausia phaenota FINK, 1979
Black and Gold Moenkhausia

Syn: None.

Hab.: Creeks in the Mato Grosso, Brazil, e.g., Rio Sumidoro (South America).

F.I.: 1975 by Hans Baensch, Melle, Germany.

Sex: ♀ rounder and fuller and about cm larger than the ♂.

Soc. B.: Peaceful schooling fish, suitable for the well-oxygenated and maintained community tank. The animals live together (sympatrically) with *Otocinclus* sp. and *Hyphessobrycon vilmae*.

M: Densely planted tanks with a lot of free swimming room in the front third of the tank. pH in nature (Rio Verde, Mato Grosso) is 5.8, hardness below 1° dGH, temperature 23° C (73° F), water depth 30cm to 1.50 m (12-60"). It lives in the shallow areas of the creek with dense plant growth of a still unidentified (?) water plant, which is pictured in its biotope on page 287.

B: Not yet described. Probably spawns in a group among plants. Care and rearing should be similar to *Hemigrammus* species.

F: C, O; flakes, fine live food. Any type of frozen food. In the wild the fish eagerly ate flake food.

S: The species was supposed to be named *M. baenschi* by GÉRY in tribute to Dr. Ulrich Baensch. It was then discovered that the species was already known in the USA, that the description of the species was in progress. A pity actually, Dr. Baensch would have deserved the honor. One of the smallest *Moenkhausia* which in a school has a behavior similar to the cardinal, but forms looser groups. When danger threatens, these fish quickly flee into dense vegetation of their native waters. The native waters of the cardinal rarely contain plants.

T: 23-26° C, **L**: 4,5 cm, **A**: 60 cm, **R**: m, **D**: 2-3
73-79° F, 1ʃ", 24",

Moenkhausia simulata EIGENMANN & PEARSON, 1929
Mimik Moenkhausia

Syn: *Astyanax simulata*.

Hab.: Rio Pachitea, upper Amazon, South America.

F.I.: Probably has not been imported into Europe.

Sex: ♀ fuller and stouter, ♂ with a more pronounced concave anal fin.

Soc. B.: Peaceful, lively schooling fish, well suited to the community tank.

M: Desires a tank with sunlight and a lot of free swimming space. Plant heavily along the edges and provide a dark bottom. Regular water changes every 3 weeks of $^{1}/_{3}$-$^{2}/_{3}$ should be performed with the addition of a good water conditioner.

B: Not yet described. Should be similar to other *Moenkhausia* or *Hemigrammus*.

F: C, O; flake food, hefty live foods such as *Gammarus*, FD foods. Rarely eats tender plant shoots (only when hungry).

S: The genus is very similar to *Astyanax*. *Moenkhausia* is distributed more in the central Amazon region and the Guianas while *Astyanax* is found in the border regions thereof. The scaled caudal fin of *Moenkhausia* (*Astyanax*'s is unscaled) is suspected to have played a role in the colonization of certain water regions since similar indications are found for the genera *Hemigrammus* and *Hyphessobrycon*, as well as *Knodus* and *Bryconamericus* (from GÉRY, 1977).

Knodus: Caudal fin scaled, central Amazon.

Bryconamericus: Caudal fin naked, regions on the edge of the Amazon from northwest South America to northern Panama.

The species resembles *Pseudochalceus* (*Hollandichthys*) *multifasciatus*, which formerly was a well known aquarium fish—also for the unheated aquarium, see page 293.

T: 24-27° C, **L**: 6 cm, **A**: 80 cm, **R**: m, **D**: 2
75-81° F, 2$^{1}/_{3}$", 31",

Moenkhausia phaenota

Moenkhausia simulata

Piabucus dentatus (KOELREUTER, 1761)
Toothed Piabuco Tetra

Syn: *Trutta dentata, Characinus argentinus, C. piabuca, Piabuca argentina, Salmo argentinus.*

Hab.: The Guianas, middle and lower Amazon (South America).

F.I.: 1912 by W. Eimeke, Hamburg.

Sex: Not yet described.

Soc. B.: Peaceful schooling fish. It should always be kept with sufficiently large fish that can stand their ground when foraging. Sometimes quarrelsome among themselves.

M: Large tank with strong lighting and a few planted corners. Part of the surface should be covered with floating plants. Places few demands on water conditions: pH 6.0-7.5; hardness to 18° dGH. Well-filtered water with some current.

B: Not yet bred.

F: C; accepts all types of live foods such as Enchytraea, *Tubifex* and mosquito larvae, which will primarily be taken from the bottom. Frozen food, FD tablets.

S: A plain, but interesting and enduring charge. It was previously classified under the sub-family Iguanodectnae. The new discovery of *Iguanodectes geisleri* from Rio Negro made a new classification necessary because the species represents an exact connection to the true characins (Tetragonopterinae).

T: 20-25° C, **L:** 18 cm, **A:** 150 cm, **R:** m, b, **D:** 2
68-77° F, 7", 59",

Pseudochalceus multifasciatus (EIGENMANN & NORRIS, 1901)
Multi-Lined Tetra

Syn: *Tetragonopterus multifasciatus, Pseudochalceus affinis, P. perstriatus, Hollandichthys multifasciatus.*

Hab.: Southeastern Brazil around Sao Paulo, Porto Alegre, Santa Catharina (South America).

F.I.: 1906 by O. Kittler, Hamburg.

Sex: ♂ more slender, ♀ with fuller ventral area. The anterior section of the anal fin of the ♂ is concave, the ♀'s is almost straight. The fish in the photograph is a ♀.

Soc. B.: Schooling fish; sociable in its youth. Older specimens tend to be quarrelsome, bite and are even considered predatory to small fish. Can live with larger catfish, cichlids, *Leporinus*, etc.

M: A large tank with plenty of swimming room and dense vegetation in a corner. A lot of light and strong filtration are suggested. Water: pH 6.0-7.5; hardness up to 20° dGH.

B: Possible in a large aquarium over 150 cm (59") long. Scatters eggs among plants. 26° C (79° F). Remove parents after spawning. Raise on infusoria and from the 5th day on, *Artemia* and TetraMin Baby Food.

F: C, O; omnivore, although predominantly large live food; large flakes, FD and frozen foods.

S: Lovely, interesting fish which can be kept in a garden pond during the summer. Small ponds need to be covered at night to help insulate them against the cold.

T: 16-23° C, **L:** 12 cm, **A:** 120 cm, **R:** m, **D:** 2-3
61-73° F, 4∫", 47",

Piabucus dentatus

Pseudochalceus multifasciatus ♀

Thayeria ifati GÉRY, 1959
Half-Striped Penguin

Syn: None.

Hab.: Maroni river system in French Guyana and Surinam (South America).

F.I.: Unknown.

Sex: ♀ fatter in the pelvic region. The first rays on the anal fin are white on the ♂, transparent on the ♀.

Soc. B.: Peaceful species which should always be kept in small groups of 3-8 individuals. Single specimens waste away.

M: It should only be associated with small docile fish. A well-planted aquarium with a nitrate level below 30 mg/l is required. pH 6.0-7.2; hardness to 12° dGH.

T: 23-28° C, L: 5 cm, A: 60 cm, R: m, D: 2-3
73-82° F, 2", 24",

B: Not described yet, but surely spawns among plants like *Hemigrammus* species.

F: C, O; flake food, FD food, small live food.

S: This genus is only differentiated from *Hemigrammus* because of its mode of swimming, otherwise the two genera are anatomically equal. The slanted swimming position combined with the black line serve to camouflage the fish in an unusual manner. Enemies do not recognize it as a fish, therefore not as prey.

Characidium sp. aff. *fasciatum*
a) Rio Negro Darter Tetra, b) Peru Darter Tetra

Syn.: None.

Hab.: a) Rio Negro, b) Peru.

F.I.: 1983 by Heiko Bleher, Frankfurt.

Sex: Not described.

Soc. B.: Usually several animals can be kept together. The association with other fish poses no problems.

M: Clear, moving water free of turbidity. pH, depending on origin, 5.6-7.5 (6.0); hardness to 10° dGH. Coarse gravel substrate with rocks, $^{2}/_{3}$ free of plants and the other $^{1}/_{3}$ densely planted. The fish enjoys sitting on elevated ground where it supports itself with its pectoral, pelvic and tail fins.

B: Successful with some species. The difficulty lies in obtaining a compatible pair of the same species. See Vol. 1, page 314.

F: C, O; omnivore, but primarily benthic insect larvae. In an aquarium the fish will pick the finest feed remnants off the bottom. FD-Menu, frozen food, Tetra Tips.

S: The pictures only convey the beauty and variation within the genus. A precise species description can only be given after a revision is made. See also Vol. 1, page 314. The species from Peru is new and does not possess an adipose fin.

T: 22-24° C, L: 8-10 cm, A: 100 cm, R: b, D: 2
72-75° F, 3-4", 39",

Characidium sp. aff. *fasciatum* a)

Characidium sp. nov. from Peru, Peruvian darter tetra b)

Biotope of *Characidium*, Rio Verde, Mato Grosso, Brazil.

Elachocharax georgiae GÉRY, 1965

Dwarf Darter Tetra

Syn.: None.

Hab.: Brazil, Rio Negro, Rio Madeira system in small tributaries and flood plain puddles, which, nevertheless, need to have an affluent.

F.I.: Only a few specimens to date. 1975 to Germany by Hans Baensch, Melle, Germany.

Sex: Not known.

Soc. B.: Very gregarious species. Several hundred young and adult animals can live together in a 1 m² (1 yd²) puddle of 10 cm (4") depth.

M: The fish should be kept in a species tank or with calm, peaceful dwarf cichlids, killies or perhaps labyrinth fish. Provide a densely planted tank with gravel and flat stones to rest on. Water: pH 5.4-6.8; hardness to 8° dGH. Frequent water exchanges with peat extract added.

B: In the wild an exponential population explosion can occur while these fishes are isolated from their predators in puddles.

F: C; finest live food (*Artemia*), *Cyclops*, young water fleas. But also Tetra Tips and FD-Menu.

S: A cute species still awaiting the aquarist.

T: 24-30° C, **L:** 3 cm, **A:** 40 cm, **R:** b, **D:** 2-3
75-86° F, 1 ½", 16",

Odontocharacidium aphanes WEITZMAN & KANAZAWA, 1977
Green Dwarf Darter Tetra

Syn.: *Klausewitzia aphanes.*

Hab.: Rio Moiocu (Tapajos system), Brazil (South America).

F.I.: To date, only one preserved specimen by Hans Baensch, Melle, Germany.

Sex: None known.

Soc. B.: Peaceful species with a small territory that trespassing conspecifics are chased out of. In nature it is found with discus, *Anostomus, Osteoglossum* (only hunts in open water), cichlids and *Nanostomus.*

M: The fish occur under floating plants (*Eichhornia*). During flooding, the floating plant islands are frequently carried downstream and subjected to changing water conditions. The fish shown here came from a 30-50 m (32-54 yd) wide, 1 m (1.1 yd) deep river. The water was peat brown and had a pH of 5.8; hardness 0, T: 26° C (79° F) (Sept. 12, 1975).

T: 24-28° C, **L:** 4 cm, **A:** 40 cm, **R:** t, **D:** 3
75-82° F, 1 2/3", 16",

B: Not known.

F: C; small crustaceans and water insects which are picked from between plant roots and the undersides of leaves.

S: A lively, handsome species which will find friends once it is imported.

Boulengerella lateristriga (BOULENGER, 1895)
Striped Pike Characin

Syn.: *Xiphostoma lateristriga.*

Hab.: Rio Negro, Rio Urubu, Brazil (South America).

F.I.: Unknown.

Sex: None known.

Soc. B.: The animals hunt alone or in groups on the water surface. They can only be kept with considerably more massive (tall-bodied), calm fishes, such as some large cichlids and catfishes.

M: The fish are shy and need a spacious tank with dense plant growth as cover. Part of the surface should be covered with floating plants. Peat filtration with surface movement. Oxygen demanding. Water: pH 5.2-6.8, hardness to 10° dGH. Make regular water changes of 1/3- every 14 days adding a water conditioner (e.g., AquaSafe). Attention should be given towards maintaining low nitrite and nitrate levels.

B: Has not been accomplished in an aquarium.

F: C; insects and their larvae, caterpillars, small fish. In most cases imported specimens are injuried in transport and will not easily accept feed. Purchase only fish which feed well.

S: *B. lateristriga* (sub-genus *Boulengerella*) differs from *B. lucia* (sub-genus *Spixostoma*) primarily by the lateral line. The former has an incomplete lateral line while in the latter (*B. lucia*) it is complete.

T: 23-27° C, L: 40 cm, A: 150 cm, R: m, t, D: 3-4 (S)
73-81° F, 16", 59",

Boulengerella lucia (CUVIER, 1817)
Cuvier's Pike Characin

Syn.: *Hydrocynus lucius, Hydrocyon lucius, Xiphostoma lucius, Xiphostoma cuvieri, Hydrocynus cuvieri, Boulengerella cuvieri, Xiphostoma longipinne, Hydrocynus longipinnis, Xiphostoma ocellatum, Hydrocynus ocellatum, Xiphostoma oseryi, Spixostoma lucia, Boulengerella ocellatus.*

Hab.: The Guianas, Amazon region (South America).

F.I.: 1935.

Sex: Has not been described.

Soc. B.: A sociable surface predator similar to *B. lateristriga*.

M: The species needs lots of room. The width of the aquarium should be at least 60 cm (24"). The animals easily injure the tip of their upper snout which is made of a soft fleshy appendage. Injuries of this nature are incurable, and in most cases, the animals die of infection. Water: pH 6.0-7.2, hardness to 15° dGH; otherwise similar to the previous species.

B: Not possible in an aquarium.

F: C; large water insects, crickets, fish. The animals can be trained to eat fish meat and sometimes tablet foods.

S: Only suitable for larger show aquaria. These are very interesting and long-lived charges.

T: 23-27° C, **L:** 60 cm, **A:** 200 cm, **R:** m, t, **D:** 3-4 (S)
73-81° F, 24", 79",

Ctenolucius beani (FOWLER, 1907)

Syn.: *Belonocharax beani, Luciocharax beani, Ctenolucius hujeta beani.*

Hab.: Central and South America: Panama and Colombia.

F.I.: Uncertain. The nominal form, *C. h. hujeta*, was already imported in 1905.

Sex: Not known.

Soc. B.: Keep singly or in pairs. Equal sized juveniles can be kept together. Only keep with fish of at least half its length.

M: Needs a well-planted large tank with cover provided in the background. The fish are shy and sensitive. The snout tips are susceptible to injury and infection. Diseased animals are usually not treatable. One should only acquire totally healthy, small individuals with a maximum length of 15 cm (6"). Water: pH 5.5-7.0; hardness to 15° dGH. Peat filtration or the addition of peat extract. Cover the aquarium well and handle it with care.

B: Probably not possible in an aquarium.

F: C; the fish hunt on the water surface. Small individuals accept insects and larvae; large specimens chiefly feed on fish.

S: The genus is very similar to the African genus *Hepsetus*.

T: 23-26° C, **L:** 30 cm, **A:** 200 cm, **R:** m, t, **D:** 3
73-79° F, 12", 79",

Ctenolucius hujeta hujeta (VALENCIENNES, 1849)
Hujeta Pike Characin, Slant-Nosed Gar

Syn.: *Luciocharax insculptus, Xiphostoma hujeta, Ctenolucius hujeta.*

Hab.: Central and South America; Panama, Colombia and Venezuela.

F.I.: 1905; reintroduced in 1979 (?).

Sex: In aquarium populations ♂♂ are generally smaller than the ♀♀. During spawning, the ♂♂ are noticeably slimmer, the anal fin is larger, the outside fin rays are clearly shorter with the middle rays the longest. The edge of the anal fin is not straight but frayed. The anal fin of the ♀ is triangular, the outer fin rays are longer and the edge of the anal fin is straight.

Soc. B.: Depending on its care, it is either very shy or, in the presence of slight water movement, an actively swimming predator;

Boulengerella lucia

Ctenolucius beani

the animals usually hunt in small groups in the upper water layers.

M: In water from 5 to 22° dGH and a neutral pH, care and breeding is possible without problems. Vegetation on the sides and the background; leave free swimming space. Dim the light using a loose cover of floating plants. Good water circulation is important because it contributes to the overall well-being. Current makes the animals notoriously active swimmers. Change half of the aquarium water once or twice per week. Associate only with equal sized fish (predator!) or best kept in a species tank. When working on the aquarium do not move too fast, the animals are skittish and can injure themselves.

B: 25-28° C (77-82° F). A detailed account was written by SOMMER (1982) in Aquarienmagazin 16 (6): 370-377. Breeding set-up in pairs or also possible with extra ♂♂. Courtship begins with the ♂♂ chasing each other through the tank, followed by swimming in parallel, displaying with extended fins, turning in circles and biting. The ♀ is also chased initially. It follows dorsal courtship swimming and quick parallel swimming between ♂ and ♀ close beneath the water surface. Originating from this phase, ♂ and ♀ lift the back third of their bodies out of the water after a strong tail swing. Under strong quivering, eggs and sperm are released. During this phase, the ♂ claspes the ♀'s stomach in the region of the genital papilla with his larger anal fin. Due to continued tail beating and the re-entry of the tail into the water, a part of the spawn and air bubbles are whirled on the water surface. The interval between individual spawning acts initially was two to three minutes. In the last hour of the overall spawning ritual, the interval increased by six to eight minutes. Spawning lasted close to 3 hours. The spawn is not sensitive and develops in soft or hard water equally well. At a water temperature of about 27° C (81° F) the larvae hatch after 20 hours. Eggs number over 1000; large ♀♀ should lay between 2000 and 3000 eggs. The young can be fed after 60 hours with rotifers, *Cyclops* or *Artemia* nauplii. Raising the young is easy when feeding generously 3 times per day; otherwise, they are cannibalistic. Perform frequent water changes.

F: Any live food, mainly fish, large insects and their larvae and crustaceans. *Tubifex* and Enchytraea are not liked, especially by older animals. The type of feed is decisive for the growth rate. The fish has a huge appetite.

S: *C. hujeta hujeta* should barely get longer than 20 cm (8").

T: 22-25° C, 72-77° F, L: up to 70 cm, usually much smaller, up to 28", usually much smaller, A: from 100 cm, from 39", R: t, m, D: 4 (C)

Ctenolucius hujeta hujeta

Steindachnerina elegans (STEINDACHNER, 1874)
Elegant Curimata

Syn.: *Curimata elegans.* The exact species identification is not certain, but it is probable that it belongs to the *Curimata elegans* group.

Hab.: Rio Araguaya at Arauna, central Brazil (South America).

F.I.: 1983 through Heiko Bleher, Frankfurt, Germany.

Sex: Not yet described.

Soc. B.: Peaceful, lively schooling fish, which will nibble on tender plant shoots. Associate with calm cichlids.

M: Soft water up to 8° dGH, pH 5.5-6.8. Darkened tank with dark substrate. Peat extract. The fish are shy and pale with intense lighting. Plastic plants are suggested; however, Java moss and Java fern are also well suited.

B: Not bred.

F: H, O; vegetable flakes, water fleas, lettuce, tablet food.

S: Only imported in limited numbers. The habitat is a great distance from Brazilian export stations.

T: 24-27° C, L: 10 cm, A: 100 cm, R: m, b, D: 2-3
75-81° F, 4", 39",

Cyphocharax spilurus (GÜNTHER, 1864)

Diamond-Spot Curimata

Syn.: *Curimata spilura.*

Hab.: Widely distributed throughout South America.

F.I.: Uncertain.

Sex: ♀ has a much rounded pelvic line (photo to the right), ♂ with a more compressed ventral keel.

Soc. B.: Peaceful schooling fish for large community tanks with tough plants. A good tankmate for catfish and larger cichlids.

M: Decorate the tank with roots and stones, plastic plants and Java fern. With copious feedings of vegetarian foods, tough plants are not bothered. Water: pH 6.0-7.8; hardness to 25° dGH. Provide a moderately dark substrate, strong filtration and a sunny place (for algae growth).

T: 20-28° C, **L:** 9 cm, **A:** 100 cm, **R:** m, **D:** 2
68-82° F, 3 ", 39",

B: Probably has not yet been reproduced in an aquarium. Spawning occurs in flood plains after the onset of the rainy season.

F: H, O; primarily vegetable food. Flake food, tablet food, *Daphnia.*

S: Not a fish which will establish itself in the aquaria.

Curimatopsis macrolepis (STEINDACHNER, 1876)

Shiny-Scaled Curimata

Syn.: *Curimatopsis macrocephalus.*

Hab.: Colombia, upper Rio Meta, South America.

F.I.: Uncertain.

Sex: ♂ is laterally flatter; ♀ is round through the ventral area. With advancing age the ♂ becomes more compact with a taller caudal peduncle. The ♂ is usually more colorful.

Soc. B.: Peaceful species, well suited for the community aquarium. A small school should be kept.

M: The fish needs coarse sand for their well-being. They like to search through it for edible matter, not clouding the water excessively with its activity. Soft water with a pH of 6.5 is preferred; higher values to 7.5 and a hardness of 25° dGH are tolerated.

T: 22-26° C, **L:** 6 cm, **A:** 80 cm, **R:** b, **D:** 2
72-79° F, 2 1/3", 31",

B: Spawning occurs in pairs or a in school among fine-leaved plant bunches. A small increase in tank temperature, lowering the hardness to 4-8° dGH and the addition of peat extract and fresh water all contribute to the fish's willingness to spawn. The rearing of the larvae on pond plankton is initially difficult. After 10 days TetraMin Baby Food, Liquifry, egg yolk and *Artemia* are accepted.

F: H; algae, plants.

S: The similar species *Curimatopsis crypticus* VARI, 1982 inhabits the Rio Negro. It is therefore important to determine its origin in order to identify the species.

Cyphocharax spilurus

Curimatopsis macrolepis

Semaprochilodus theraponura (FOWLER, 1906)
Flag-Tailed Prochilodus

Syn.: *Prochilodus amazonensis, Prochilodus theraponura.*

Hab.: Middle and upper Amazon; Ambiyacu (Peru). In larger rivers (South America).

F.I.: 1910.

Sex: Unknown.

Soc. B.: Peaceful schooling fish.

M: Like the previous species this is not a good aquarium fish, but an appreciated food fish.

B: Unknown.

F: H, L: vegetable foods and small plankton of any kind.

S: Only juveniles up to approximately 12 cm (4∫") are attractively colored. The pictured fish is over 20 cm (8") long.

T: 23-26° C, **L:** 35 cm, **A:** 150 cm, **R:** m, b, **D:** 3
73-79° F, 14", 59",

Fam.: Curimatidae — Curimatas

Potamorhina altamazonica (COPE, 1878)

Syn.: *Semitapicis altamazonica, Curimata altamazonica, Curimatus altamazonicus.*

Hab.: Amazon region, Rio Paraguay (South America).

F.I.: 1984 by Heiko Bleher, Frankfurt/Main, Germany.

Sex: Unknown.

Soc. B.: Peaceful towards other fishes. Plant eater. Swift schooling fish.

M: A tank with Java moss and Java fern is possible, otherwise perhaps plastic plants. The species loves currents and clear water. pH 6.0-7.5, hardness up to 18° dGH. Provide strong lighting for algae growth.

B: Not yet reproduced.

F: H; small specimens like flake food. Larger specimens of over 10 cm (4") length can be fed raw peas (frozen), spinach, chickweed and unsprayed lettuce leaves. Planktonic live foods such as *Daphnia* and *Cyclops* are also appreciated.

S: In their natural habitat they are food fish. It is possible that the species also feeds on suspended algae (filter feeder). Although the young have teeth, the adults do not. Different diets for the different life stages are likely.

T: 22-26° C, **L:** 18 cm, **A:** 150 cm, **R:** m, **D:** 4 (H)
72-79° F, 7", 59",

Semaprochilodus theraponura

Potamorhina altamazonica

Hoplias malabaricus (BLOCH, 1794)

Common Trahira, Tiger Tetra

Syn.: *Esox malabaricus; Synodus malabaricus, S. tareira, S. palustris; Erythrinus trahira, E. macrodon, E. microcephalus, E. brasiliensis; Macrodon guavina; Macrodon trahira; Macrodon tareira, M. auritus, M. teres, M. patana; Macrodon ferox; Macrodon intermedius; Macrodon malabaricus; Hoplias microlepis* (not *Macrodon microlepis* GÜNTHER, 1864).

Hab.: Middle and northern South American rivers, lakes and ditches.

F.I.: 1895 by the Triton Aquarium Club, Berlin.

Sex: ♂ more slender, with a ventral line that is almost straight. On the ♀ it is convex. See also the pictures.

Soc. B.: Dedicated predator. Should be kept alone.

M: Large tank with strong filtration. Use stones, roots and tough well rooted plants as decoration. Water, depending on origin, soft to hard (4-25°dGH). pH of 6.0-8.0 (7.0).

B: Not possible except in large show aquaria.

F: C; live fish, fish meat, beef heart. Juveniles accept sinking tablet food after acclimation. Caution—larger specimens bite.

S: Due to a special additional breathing organ, the fish can survive in the worst living conditions. Some specimens are said to move over land when conditions deteriorated too much. They can store air and moisture.

T: 20-26° C, L: 50 cm, A: 200 cm, R: b, m, D: 4 (C)
68-79° F, 20", 79",

Hoplias malabaricus ♂

Hoplias malabaricus ♀

Bivibranchia protractila EIGENMANN, 1912
Silver Sandsucker

Syn.: None.

Hab.: South America; Rio Tocantins, Rio Negro, Rio Branco (Brazil), and Venezuela in sandy river shore areas.

F.I.: Unknown.

Sex: Unknown.

Soc. B.: Quite a peaceful species, but because of its diet it should be kept with its own kind.

M: Fine, 1-2 mm (1/32"-1/16") sand as substrate. The animals like to dig a lot, sifting the sand for something edible. Fine-leaved plants are not suitable due to suspended matter. Good filtration and current are necessary. Water values: pH 5.5-7.5; hardness to 25° dGH.

T: 22-28° C, **L:** 25 cm, **A:** 180 cm, **R:** b, **D:** 4
72-82° F, 9¾", 71",

B: Unknown.

F: L; smallest live foods, however, also decaying plant matter (detritus). Leftover flake food. FD-Menu, FD tablets.

Hemiodopsis gracilis (GÜNTHER, 1864)
Slender Hemiodus

Syn.: *Hemiodon gracilis.*

Hab.: Amazon, Rio Sao Francisco, Brazil, Guyana, South America.

F.I.: 1935.

Sex: Not yet known.

Soc. B.: Shy, fast and peaceful schooling fish. Quite suitable for the larger community aquarium.

M: Needs a lot of oxygen and requires some attention during acclimation. 4-6 weeks later the fish is more tolerant. Peat filtration. Large volume filter. Water: pH 5.8-7.2 (6.8); hardness 4-15° dGH. Provide plenty of swimming room.

T: 23-27° C, **L:** 16 cm, **A:** 150 cm, **R:** m, b, **D:** 2-3
73-81° F, 6⅓", 59",

B: Has not been successful.

F: L, O; plankton and aufwuchs. Flake food, pellets. Water fleas and other small live foods.

S: This is the most commonly imported hemiodus species, but still a rare guest in our aquaria.

Bivibranchia protractila

Hemiodopsis gracilis

Hemiodopsis sterni GÉRY, 1964
Stern's Hemiodus

Syn.: None.

Hab.: Upper Rio Juruena in the Mato Grosso, Brazil.

F.I.: Approximately 1970.

Sex: Not known exactly.

Soc. B.: Peaceful schooling fish, which can damage a planted aquarium. Lively, nimble swimmer that enjoys other fast swimmers as tankmates. Other quiet fish would be irritated by the constant activity.

M: Use Java moss, Java fern and maybe plastic plants, roots and rocks as decoration. Peat filtered water with a pH of 5.8-7.0; hardness to 12° dGH. The animals need a slight current and a lot of oxygen. Algae should only be removed from the front glass of the aquarium. Nitrate below 10 mg/l. Frequent water changes and good filtration are needed for successful maintenance.

B: Has not been accomplished.

F: H, O; preferably algae and tender plants, water fleas, frozen food, flake food (vegetal), tablet food.

S: The species should be imported more often.

T: 22-26° C, **L:** 12 cm, **A:** 100 cm, **R:** b, **D:** 3
72-79° F, 4ʃ", 39",

Hemiodus orthonops EIGENMANN & KENNEDY, 1903
Paraguay Hemiodus

Syn.: None.

Hab.: South America; Rio Paraguay, the southern most distribution area of the family.

F.I.: Uncertain due to continuous confusion with similar species, see **S**.

Soc. B.: Peaceful schooling fish, suitable for the community tank with robust plants and fishes.

M: As for the previously mentioned species of the family. Water: pH of 6.5-7.5 (7.0), hardness to 15° dGH.

B: Not known.

F: L, O; plankton feeder, water fleas, *Artemia,* frozen food, FD-Menu.

S: The overview of the design patterns within the family represents the species with a dot and no middle line, as shown in the picture. Actually, both *H. orthonops* and *H. unimaculatus* differ from the pattern depending on origin. The species is hard to identify from a picture. *H. orthonops* has 90 scales along the lateral line, while *H. unimaculatus* only has 60-72. The animals pictured at the bottom right could also be adult *H. orthonops*.

T: 22-26° C, **L:** 16 cm, **A:** 150 cm, **R:** b, m, **D:** 2
72-79° F, 6 1/3", 59",

Hemiodus orthonops

Hemiodopsis sterni

Hemiodus orthonops

Hemiodus unimaculatus (BLOCH, 1794)
Single-Spot Hemiodus

Syn.: *Salmo unimaculatus, Anisitsia notatus, Anodos notatus, Hemiodus crenidens, Hemiodus microcephalus.*

Hab.: Rio Negro, Brazil; the Guianas, Orinoco system (South America).

F.I.: Perhaps in 1912 by Kropac, Hamburg, as *H. semitaeniatus.*

Sex: Not distinguishable from external features.

Soc. B.: Quick, strong, schooling fish for the community tank with robust cichlids or other characins. The fishes are shy under intense light and like to jump.

M: Current loving animals which predominately live above rocky substrates. Decorate with rock structures. Water: pH 5.5-7.5, depending on origin; hardness up to 20° dGH.

B: Has not been successful.

F: L, O; in the aquarium any fine feed is accepted, especially freeze-dried foods, frozen foods and live *Daphnia*. Vegetable flakes.

S: The most widely distributed species of the family. The design is very variable. Normally only a dot is visible on the side (similar to *H. orthonops*). Presently the genus *Hemiodus* (previously *Anisitsia*) consists of only two species. The main difference to *Hemiodopsis* lies in the scales. *Hemiodus* has larger scales in the ventral area than the sides or the dorsal area. In *Hemiodopsis* all scales are relatively the same size (within each species). This is not always applicable to juveniles of *Hemiodus*. The identification of the fish on the picture is doubtful. BLOCH (1794) called the fish "Le capelan", the chaplain.

Continued on page 317

Rio Moioçu (Tapajos system, Brazil). In this peat brown water, the hunter *Osteoglossum* is abundant. Brown discus occur 500 km (300 mi) south of the Amazon! *Klausewitzia* sp. inhabit the roots of the floating islands of *Eichhornia*. *Hemiodopsis* sp., two *Anostomus* species, *Nannostomus* and larger cichlids are also inhabitants of such fish paradises.

Hemiodopsis argenteus

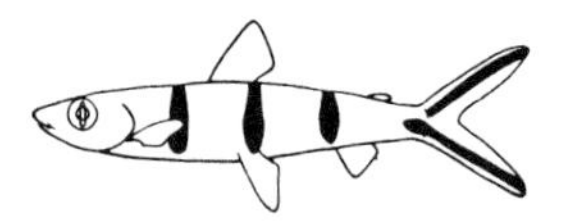

Hemiodopsis q. quadrimaculatus

Hemiodopsis fowleri

Hemiodopsis quadrimaculatus vorderwinkleri

Hemiodopsis goeldii

Hemiodopsis rodolphoi

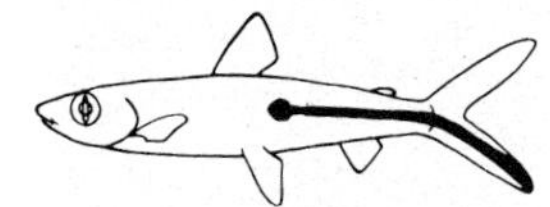

Hemiodopsis gracilis

Hemiodopsis semitaeniatus

Hemiodopsis huraulti

Hemiodopsis sterni

Hemiodopsis immaculatus

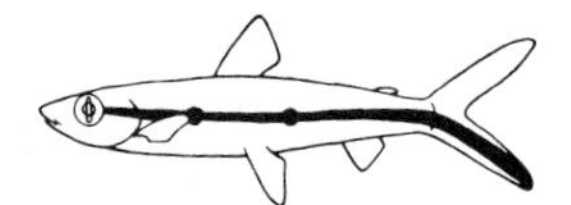

Hemiodopsis ternetzi

Hemiodopsis microlepis

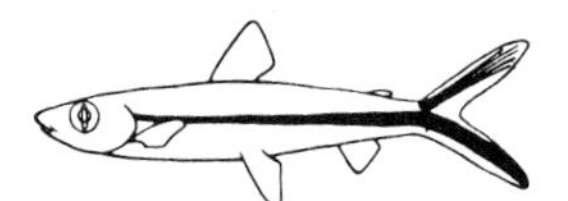

Hemiodopsis thayeria

Hemiodopsis parnaguae

Hemiodus orthonops

Hemiodus unimaculatus

Argonectes longiceps

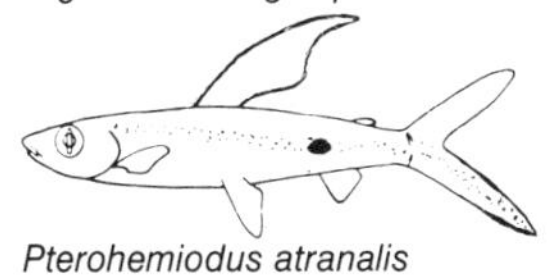

Pterohemiodus atranalis

Its common name, "single-spot hemiodus", does not separate it enough from other species.
The larger pelvic scales characteristic of *Hemiodus* can be clearly distinguished.

T: 23-26° C, **L:** 18 cm, **A:** 150 cm, **R:** m, **D:** 3
73-79° F, 7", 59",

Design patterns of *Hemiodopsis* and related genera.
Sketches out of BÖHLKE (1955), modified after GÉRY (1977).

High water marks on a river arm of the Rio Madeira, Brazil.

Parodon affinis STEINDACHNER, 1879

Paraguay Darter Tetra

Syn.: *Parodon paraguayensis.*

Hab.: La Plata, Parana, Paraguay basin (South America).

F.I.: 1984 by Heiko Bleher, Frankfurt. Imported earlier as unrecognized by-catch.

Sex: Not described.

Soc. B.: A peaceful schooling fish of rocky bottomed small creeks. In the aquarium several specimens can swim around in small circles for hours. This hardly disturbs the other fishes.

M: The species loves current and oxygen saturated water. Good filtration and water low in nitrite/nitrate are necessary for growth. The green algae preferred as food only grow in very clean, unpolluted water. pH 6.0-7.2; hardness up to 15° dGH; after acclimation, 25° dGH are also tolerated. Changing 1/3 of the water twice a month is recommended. Use stones and coarse gravel as substrate material and strong illumination for algae growth.

T: 22-26° C, **L:** 6 cm, **A:** 80 cm, **R:** b, **D:** 2
72-79° F, 2 1/3", 31",

B: Not known.

F: L, H; algae, aufwuchs, TabiMin, small live food and any fine flake food, especially vegetable food.

S: While this species belongs to the sub-genus *Apareiodon*, the species *Parodon pongoensis*, presented in Vol. 1 on page 330, belongs to the sub-genus *Parodon*. Some ichthyologists separate the sub-family Parodontinae from the family Hemiodidae and create a separate family. Much speaks in favor of this, since the living habits of both groups are quite different. *Parodon* are bottom dwellers with an inferior mouth, flat, wide chest and well developed paired fins. With the paired fins the fish can "walk" on the bottom. Dentition is also very different. Because a regrouping of *Parodon* under its own family is not yet scientifically "official", we list them here under Hemiodidae.

Parodon suborbitalis VALENCIENNES, 1849

Green-Banded Darter Tetra, Big-Nose Darter Tetra

Syn.: *Parodon hilarii, P. nasus.*

Hab.: Bolivia, Venezuela, Colombia (South America).

F.I.: 1982 by the Christ, Hamburg.

Sex: Only ripe ♀♀ can be distinguished by the fuller abdomen.

Soc. B.: Peaceful schooling fish as a juvenile. Older specimens show a faint territorial behavior and sometimes chase weaker animals away from the food. Outside of feeding time, they like to swim together or chase each other without ever inflicting injury. A lively species, which is well suited for any larger community tank.

M: The animals prefer clear water with a current and large-leaved plants to rest on. A bottom dwelling life in fast flowing habitats can be deduced from the jerky swimming motions. While swimming, the head is always kept at an upward angle of 70°. Keep the tank well covered.

B: Has not been done.

F: H, O; algae, vegetable flake food, FD and frozen foods.

S: A appreciative species which is sure to find broad distribution. It is as useful as *Crossocheilus* (formerly *Epalzeorhynchos*) *siamensis*, but less sensitive. In its native habitat it is called the tobacco fish. This fish is the type species of the genus. It is a fast growing fish. I had two specimens of 10 cm (4") length and two of only 5 cm (2") length. Within two months the small ones had reached the length of the larger individuals.

T: 23-26° C, **L:** 12 cm, **A:** 100 cm, **R:** m, b, **D:** 1
73-79° F, 4∫", 39',

Parodon affinis

Parodon suborbitalis

Copella vilmae GÉRY, 1963
Rainbow Copella

Syn.: None; "*Copella vilmai*" = incorrectly written.

Hab.: South America; Igarapé Preto (upper Amazon), at Tabatinga, Brazil.

F.I.: 1963.

Sex: The dorsal fin of the ♂ is more elongated than that of the ♀. ♂ is more colorful. The picture shows two ♂♂.

Soc. B.: A peaceful species. In the wild the adults and the young swim in close proximity of each other.

M: The species is an extreme soft water fish: pH of 4.5-5.2; hardness of 0.2° dGH! After a slow acclimation, slightly higher values will also be tolerated. Provide peat filtration, dark substrate and a lot of cover with roots.

B: Provide mosquito larvae to induce ripening. Actual breeding is still unknown.

F: C, O; flake food, feed a variety of live and frozen foods.

S: The species is very similar to *Copella compta* of the upper Rio Negro which has fewer scales along the lateral line and fewer predorsal scales.

T: 23-25° C, **L:** 6.5 cm, **A:** 80 cm, **R:** m, t, **D:** 3-4 (Ch)
73-77° F, 2²/₃", 31",

Lebiasina multimaculata BOULENGER, 1911
Multi-Spotted Lebiasina

Syn.: None.

Hab.: Northwest Colombia, South America.

F.I.: Because of the similarity of several species, the date is uncertain.

Sex: ♂ more colorful and slender.

Soc. B.: The species is a small predator, similar to the large trahiras. Only associate with fish of at least half the body length of this species.

M: An undemanding fish sometimes found in oxygen-poor backwaters. The animals can also endure in almost dried up, oxygen-poor waters. The swim bladder is used as a second breathing organ. Water: pH 6.0-7.8; hardness to 25° dGH. Provide hiding places with wood and plants.

B: Not yet reproduced in an aquarium.

F: C; coarse live food, frozen foods such as mosquito larvae, mysids and adult *Artemia.*

S: Most species (14) of the genus lack an adipose fin, but also within a species there are both individuals with and without an adipose fin. The animal in this picture does not have one, the animal in Vol. 1, page 336 does have one. About 10% of the species presented here have an adipose fin.

T: 23-27° C, **L:** 7 cm, **A:** 80 cm, **R:** m, **D:** 3
73-81° F, 2ʃ", 31",

Copella vilmae ♂♂

Lebiasina multimaculata

♂ bottom, ♀ top

Nannostomus digrammus FOWLER, 1913

Twin-Stripe Pencilfish

Syn.: None.

Hab.: Lower and middle Amazon. Rio Madeira, Brazil; Guyana.

F.I.: Until now only as unrecognized by-catch.

Sex: ♀ with full ventral area (top fish in the photo). The anal fin of the ♂ is broader (see S).

Soc. B.: Peaceful, quiet schooling fish, which should only be kept in a species tank or with a few delicate species.

M: A problematic fish which is usually starving since suitable foods are not available in the holding/catch stations. Because of this, the fish will have to be fed well at first. They require a dark and peaceful tank, densely planted in parts and plants on the water surface also. Clear, peat filtered water with some movement. pH 5.8-6.8; hardness to 6° dGH. Dark substrate. Cover the tank well because the fish jump.

B: Very difficult. Because of the difficulty in providing the smallest food, the young often die within a few hours.

F: C; finest live foods, *Artemia*, FD-Menu. Best fed 1-2 hours before turning off the light. The animals only like to eat at dusk.

S: Easily confused with *N. bifasciatus* (Vol. 1, page 342). Differences: *N. digrammus* has an adipose fin, no lateral line, anal fin rays III, 8. *N. bifasciatus* has no adipose fin, some scales with lateral line pores, anal fin III, 9. The anal fin of ♂ *N. digrammus* has a rag-like widening, but that of *N. bifasciatus* does not.

T: 24-26° C, L: 4 cm, A: 50 cm, R: m, t, D: 3
75-79° F, 1 2/3", 20",

Rio Tapajos, Brazil

Pyrrhulina brevis brevis STEINDACHNER, 1875
Short-Lined Pyrrhulina

Syn.: None.

Hab.: South America; Rio Negro at Manaus, Brazil.

F.I.: 1910 by the Blumenthal Co., Hamburg.

Sex: The ♂ has a more elongated upper caudal fin lobe, both are the same length in the ♀. The ♂ has fire-red pelvic and anal fins, also the caudal peduncle and the caudal fin are partially colored. In the ♀ they are yellowish and not framed in black.

Soc. B.: Normally a peaceful species which only becomes quarrelsome during spawning. Association with small catfish (*Corydoras*) and many armored catfish as well as dwarf cichlids is possible.

M: Cover the tank well, because the animals are sometimes skittish and will jump out. Cover 1/3 of the water surface with floating plants. Keep at least half the tank void of larger plants. Peat filtration, little current. Water: pH 5.2-6.8; hardness up to 8° dGH.

T: 24-28° C, **L:** 9 cm, **A:** 80 cm, **R:** t, **D:** 2-3
75-82° F, 3", 31",

B: Little is known. Spawning is said to occur on flat stones or large plant leaves. Only use one pair, since ♂♂ are quarrelsome at this time.

F: C, O; flake food, FD foods, frozen food, fine live foods.

S: There are a number of sub-species widely distributed throughout South America:

P. brevis australe, La Plata region, Paraguay.

P. brevis lugubris from the upper Amazon and Rio Meta, Colombia.

Pyrrhulina brevis brevis

Pyrrhulina brevis, melanistic form

Pyrrhulina laeta (COPE, 1871)

Half-Lined Pyrrhulina

Syn.: *Holotaxis laetus, Pyrrhulina semifasciata, P. melanostoma, P. maxima.*

Hab.: The Guianas (?), central Amazon (South America).

F.I.: 1910 through Fritz Mayer, Hamburg.

Sex: The upper tail fin lobe is more elongated in the ♂ that the ♀.

Soc. B.: These animals should be kept in a small school or in pairs in a species tank. At spawning time the ♂♂ are quite quarrelsome.

M: The species needs hiding places made of densely planted areas, but also a free water surface as swimming and hunting room. Use peat filtration or peat extract. Water: pH 5.8-7.0; hardness 2-8° dGH. Weak filtration with some surface movement. Dark substrate. A dimmer for dusk feeding is recommended.

B: No reports about a successful spawn have been filed. *P. laeta* is closely related to *P. brevis*. After a possible spawn, the parent fish should be removed.

F: C, O; in nature, insects landing on the water surface are the main diet. Frozen, flake food.

S: The species name is not completely certain, because the holotype is missing the anterior half of the body, including the head!

T: 23-27° C, **L:** ♂ 8 cm, ♀ 7 cm, **A:** 60 cm, **R:** m, t, **D:** 2-3
73-81° F, ♂ 3", ♀ 2ʃ", 24",

Pyrrhulina rachowiana MYERS, 1926

Eye-Line Pyrrhulina, Red-Spotted Pyrrhulina

Syn: *P. filamentosa* (not C. & V.), *P. brevis* (not STEINDACHNER), *P. australis* (not EIGENMANN & KENNEDY).

Hab.: Argentina in the lower Paraná and La Plata at Rosario de Santa Fé (South America)

F.I.: 1906 by Köppe and Siggelkow, Hamburg.

Sex: The top lobe of the caudal fin is longer in ♂♂, all fins are larger than in ♀♀.

Soc. B.: Can be kept together with suitable, somewhat robust, but not predatory fishes. At spawning time the animals need to be placed in pairs into a prepared breeding tank; otherwise, they will attack their tankmates.

M: The least sensitive species of this type. Cover the tank well. A 15 l (4 gal) tank is already enough to keep a single pair. Dense vegetation should be provided as cover for the often persecuted ♀. Water: pH 6.0-7.8; hardness up to 20° dGH!

B: T: 24° C (75° F). 50-200 eggs are deposited and fertilized on broad-leaved plants during several spawning acts, which together last about 30 minutes. The eggs are fanned and guarded by the ♂. After 20 hr the eggs fall from the spawning substrate and hatch 10 hr later. At first the young are only 2 mm (1/16") long and feed after the 4th day on fine rotifers and infusoria. From the 10th day forward TetraMin Baby Food, Liquifry and *Artemia* can be given. From then on the raising is nonproblematic. The parents should be removed after spawning, or better, the leaves with eggs should be placed in a jar underwater and transferred to a rearing tank with 10-15 cm (4"-6") water.

F: O; flake food and any kind of small live foods.

S: According to GÉRY (written communication) the animals pictured here could also be *P. eleanorae* FOWLER, 1940. A final identification can probably only be made on preserved material.

T: 15-22° C, **L:** 5 cm, **A:** 60 cm, **R:** m, t, **D:** 1-2
59-72° F, 2", 24",

Pyrrhulina laeta

Pyrrhulina rachowiana

Catoprion mento (CUVIER, 1819)
Wimple Piranha

Syn.: *Serrasalmus mento, Mylesinus macropterus.*

Hab.: South America; Guyana, southern Amazon region (Mato Grosso).

F.I.: 1958 through Heiko Bleher, Frankfurt.

Sex: Not known.

Soc. B.: Keep alone or with specimens of equal size. Younger animals are still quite amiable; older animals feed on scales of other fishes from below.

M: The author has observed the species in its natural habitat in the Mato Grosso: pH 5.4!; hardness immeasurable (0°). The large creek empties south into the Madeira system and has a depth between 50 cm (20") and 3 m (3.3 yd). Strong current. Only in the deeper regions can a diver manage the current. There, at a depth of 1.80 m (71"), the wimple piranhas stand in schools. They are about 15 cm (6") long. Nearby are 30 cm (12") *Leporinus*. Fallen trees and bushes provide shelter.

B: Probably not possible in an aquarium, perhaps in extremely large tanks.

F: C; scale-eater, but also live foods and fish flesh.

S: This is the type species of the genus and the only one in the sub-family. A very expensive fish ($150—and more), which in the long run can only be kept in well maintained, large aquaria.

T: 23-26° C, **L:** 15 cm, **A:** 200 cm, **R:** m, **D:** 4 (C)
73-79° F, 6", 79",

Colossoma brachypomus (SPIX, 1829)
Silver Pacu

Syn.: *Myletes bidens, Colossoma mitrei, Myletes edulis, Reganina bidens, Myletes brachypomus, Colossoma bidens, Piaractus brachypomus.*

Hab.: Upper Amazon.

F.I.: 1964 through Dr. Lüling, Bonn, Germany.

Sex: Not known.

Soc. B.: Gregarious, peaceful fish which is not suitable for the standard aquarium because of its size.

M: Large aquarium without plants. Java fern could be tried, it will probably not be eaten. I have never had a fish that has eaten it. Water: pH 4.8-6.8 (6.0); hardness up to 15° dGH. Plenty of current with a large sized filter.

B: Not possible in an aquarium.

F: H, O; eats plants, fruits, oats, etc. Juveniles also like flakes, frozen and live food.

S: The species is like *Colossoma macropomum* (Vol. 1, page 350)(formerly *C. oculus*), an appreciated food fish of the natives. They catch individuals up to 25 kg (55 lb) in weight, mostly with a spear. Contrary to related species, the adipose fin has no rays. The species is also shy in nature and flees from divers. The author could not approach them closer than 3 m (3.3 yd). Other fish found with them were (Mato Grosso) *Corydoras, Leporinus* of 40 cm (16") length, and other large fish. As juveniles their coloration mimics *S. natteri* thereby probably protecting them quite well.

T: 23-28° C, **L:** 45 cm, **A:** 200 cm, **R:** all, **D:** 4 (S)
73-82° F, 18", 79",

Catoprion mento

Colossoma brachypomus

Metynnis hypsauchen fasciatus AHL, 1931
Striped Metynnis

Syn.: *Metynnis fasciatus.*

Hab.: South America; Amazon basin.

F.I.: Not ascertainable.

Sex: ♂ with longer, hook-like anal fin.

Soc. B.: Peaceful schooling fish which can be combined with similar species. When kept correctly, they are nimble lively swimmers which quickly cruise through the tank.

M: The species does best in soft water with strong filtration over peat. The water can be deep brown. In any case, dim light is preferred. Under strong light the fish are shy and grow slowly. A long tank with plenty of swimming space is recommended. pH 4.8-6.5, after acclimation also up to 7.5. Well covered tank.

B: 28° C (82° F). Darken breeding tank, perhaps peat filtration, very soft water. After a pair or school are ripe, illuminate the tank again. Place some floating plants or moss on the surface. Some animals eat the spawn, so remove the eggs. The eggs hatch after 3 days and after another 5 need fine live food (infusoria and others). Raising the young successfully is easiest in well-planted tanks with lots of green algae.

F: H; vegetable flakes, lettuce, chickweed, but also any live food.

S: The status of this sub-species is not certain. Although the vertically barred animals are higher backed than *M. hypsauchen* and the tail fin is taller and more slender, the sub-species is nevertheless considered *M. hypsauchen* and *M. fasciatus* a synonym thereof. But because even exterior distinguishing characteristics exist, here we follow the opinion that it is at least a sub-species of *M. hypsauchen* (compare Vol. 1, pages 352-3).

T: 23-26° C, **L:** 14 cm, **A:** 150 cm, **R:** all, **D:** 3 (H)
73-79° F, 5 ", 59",

Myleus rubripinnis luna (VALENCIENNES, 1849)
Moon Redhook

Syn.: *Myleus luna, Tetragonopterus luna, Myloplus luna.*

Hab.: South America; central Amazon.

F.I.: Cannot by ascertained.

Sex: ♂♂ show their splendid colors only when mature. During the spawning season they are clearly more intensely colored than ♀♀. ♂ has a bi-lobed anal fin (photo).

Soc. B.: Quite peaceful schooling fish which can be kept with other fish as long as they are not too small (above 5 cm, 2" in length).

M: This species is demanding and requires attention to its feed and water quality. Peat filtration or peat extract and soft water (6° dGH) are desired. pH 5.8-6.8. Good water turnover because the species has a high oxygen requirement. Use only older, large plants. Best to use Java moss or fern or plastic plants. Sandy bottom, which is often searched for something edible. Nitrate-free water is important, otherwise the animals decline.

B: Large tank over 150 cm (59"). Strong lighting, dark substrate. 27-29° C (81-84° F). Soft water up to 4° dGH. Bunches of plants on the water surface, some tall plants in the background.

F: O; vegetable flakes, any live food. Frozen food. Spinach, lettuce, etc. Fruits. Fairy shrimp.

S: This is the most beautiful of the silver dollar species, but unfortunately is only very rarely offered and then usually in very poor condition. The animals are often starved for weeks while they are kept in the net enclosures of the collecting stations.

T: 23-25° C, **L:** 12 cm, **A:** 120 cm, **R:** m, **D:** 3-4
73-77° F, 4∫", 47",

Metynnis hypsauchen fasciatus

Myleus rubripinnis luna ♂

Myleus schomburgkii (JARDINE, 1841)
Black-Barred Myleus

Syn.: *Tetragonopterus schomburgkii, Myletes palomet, Myloplus schomburgkii, Mylesinus schomburgkii.*

Hab.: South America; Rio Negro, Rio Xingu, Rio Araguaia (Brazil); Orinoco, Rio Apure (Venezuela).

F.I.: Not yet imported into Europe.

Sex: ♂'s anal fin is bi-lobed and elongated; ♀'s anal fin is wider but shorter at the tip. Dorsal fin of the ♂ is more pointed and elongated.

Soc. B.: Lively schooling fish, well suited for the community tank without plants.

M: Needs a large aquarium with a sand bottom and stone and root decorations. Tender plants have to be avoided. Java moss and fern and large *Echinodorus* are suitable. For this type of fish, plastic plants can be recommended. Peat filtration with a large filter producing a strong current is important. Water: pH 5.0-7.0; hardness to 10° dGH.

B: Has not occurred yet due to the lack of imported animals.

F: H, O; fruit such as peach, pumpkin, mango, melon, avocado, etc. Plants, lettuce, chickweed, frozen peas. Detritus; the animals work the bottom sand and sieve finest food items out. Live food, flake food.

S: A fish known for a long time to science. However, it either has not or has rarely been kept in an aquarium.

T: 23-27° C, **L:** 12 cm, **A:** 150 cm, **R:** m, **D:** 2-3
73-81° F, 4¾", 59",

Serrasalmus calmoni STEINDACHNER, 1908
Tail-Light Piranha, Dusky Piranha

Syn.: *Serrasalmus bilineatus, S. coccogenis.*

Hab.: Lower Amazon, Guyana and Venezuela (South America).

F.I.: Unknown.

Sex: Only recognizable in animals over 2 years old. ♂ darker bodied with a black vertical band on the tail fin and a higher build. The anal fin of the ♂ is more curved than the ♀'s.

Soc. B.: Peaceful schooling fish suitable for community tanks with fish more than 4 cm (1⅔") long. When hungry (vacation time) plants are eaten!

M: A quite unproblematic fish which adapts to all water conditions and grows fast in large aquaria as long as it is liberally fed. Large aquaria and strong filtration are desirable; otherwise, the animal's health declines. Cleaning the filter at least every 2-3 months or sooner is recommended, or the fins, particularly the caudal fin, rapidly rot away. After filter maintenance, the fins quickly heal. The species seems to be very regenerative. It prefers clear water, a lot of light and can be kept even in hard water with African cichlids. Water: pH 6.5-7.8; hardness 4-25° dGH.

B: Group spawner among plants. More specific information is not available.

F: O; any kind of flake food, live food, frozen food; but specially plant food (Tetra Conditioning Food, etc.).

S: Although the species belongs to the "true" *Serrasalmus* species, that is, to the sub-genus *Serrasalmus*, it does not belong to the true piranhas. The species is susceptible to fin rot. Treat it with Tetra FungiStop and/or Chloramphenicol (3-6 g for 500 l; 130 gal water).

T: 23-28° C, **L:** 15 cm, **A:** 120 cm, **R:** m, **D:** 1-2
73-82° F, 6", 47",

Myleus schomburgkii

Serrasalmus calmoni

Serrasalmus notatus LUETKEN, 1874

Shoulder-Spot Piranha

Syn.: None.

Hab.: Venezuela, Guianas, Orinoco region (South America).

F.I.: Unknown.

Sex: ♂♂ have a stouter head and a more slender body than the ♀♀.

Soc. B.: This schooling fish is a predator. Sometimes only the fittest survives. Caution when working in the water.

M: A large tank with a high-capacity filter is suggested. Water soft (up to 10° dGH) and slightly acid (pH 5.8-7.2). Plants are only bothered during spawning. It is best to plant them in pots at that time. A large spawning pit is dug.

B: See Vol. 1, page 356. The juveniles of the morph (?) presented here already have the black shoulder spot (see also Vol. 1, back cover).

F: C; fish flesh and any large live food, including live fish. Some animals do not notice fellow tankmates as long as they are sufficiently fed.

S: *(sp. nov.?). This species has two color morphs. One has a black spot behind the operculum (Orinoco and Guianas) and a red anal fin. The other morph lacks the spot and has a dark anal fin (Vol. 1, page 357). It is the opinion of the authors that these are two species or sub-species. The specimens without the spot are distributed throughout the Amazon region and loose the red coloration of the fins and chest with age. The juveniles of *S. natteri* have many small spots on the body. The juveniles of the morph presented here have the black spot immediately and the red chest and fins do not fade with age. This species has been considered as Synonym from *S. nattereri*.

T: 22-27° C, **L:** 28 cm, **A:** 180 cm, **R:** all (m), **D:** 3-4
72-81° F, 11", 71",

Serrasalmus ternetzi STEINDACHNER, 1908

Diamond Piranha

Syn.: Offered in the trade as "*S. brandti*", but this is a different species from Rio Sao Francisco.

Hab.: Rio Paraguay, Paraguay, South America.

F.I.: Uncertain.

Sex: Not known.

Soc. B.: Schooling fish which is suitable for the unplanted community aquarium with fish over 8 cm (3") length. Plant eater.

M: Provide a large aquarium decorated with plastic plants, roots and stones. Fine gravel substrate. Because of the large amount of food taken, large amounts of excreta result. Filtration needs to be correspondingly generously dimensioned. Water: pH 6.0-7.2; hardness up to 15° dGH.

B: Has not yet occurred, but should be similar to *S. natteri*. Vol. 1, page 356. Several individuals are needed for successful breeding.

F: H; fruits, frozen peas, chickweed, lettuce, blanched or frozen spinach. Juveniles also like water fleas, frozen food, flake food, etc.

S: A rarely imported but impressive species.

T: 20-25° C, **L:** 25 cm, **A:** 150 cm, **R:** all, **D:** 4 (H)
68-77° F, 9ʃ", 59",

Serrasalmus notatus

Serrasalmus ternetzi

Barbus barbus, the type species of the genus *Barbus*, see page 364.

Erimyzon sucetta (LACÉPÈDE, 1803)
Lake Chubsucker

Syn.: *Cyprinus sucetta, Erimyzon goodei, Myxostomus campbelli, M. kennerlyi, M. tenue.* For ***E. sucetta oblongus:*** *Cyprinus oblongus, Catostomus fasciolaris, C. gibbosus, Labeo elegans, Myxostoma claviformis, M. oblongum.*

Hab.: North America; eastern North America up to the Midwest, from southern New York to Florida, westward to Texas, north to Minnesota, Michigan and Wisconsin.

F.I.: Sporadically kept in Europe. The exact date of import is unknown.

Sex: No definite external characteristics are known. The ♀ is fuller during the spawning season.

Soc. B.: Peaceful schooling fish. Its behavior is similar to the European *Gobio gobio.*

M: Sandy substrate with some stones. Use native coldwater plants and clear, clean water that is medium-hard (up to 15° dGH) and neutral to weakly alkaline (pH 7-7.5). Provide a weak current. House with other native coldwater species (*Notropis* and *Catostomus* species).

B: Has not been reproduced in an aquarium. Although the fishes are still spawning at the beginning of July, the main spawning season is in March or April. During the two week spawning period one ♀ lays up to 20,000 eggs. At 20° C (68 °F) egg development takes 6-7 weeks.

F: All types of live foods (small crustaceans, mosquito larvae, *Tubifex*, Enchytraea, earthworms). After an acclimation period, the fish also accept flake and tablet food.

S: Two sub-species of *Erimyzon sucetta* are known. *E. sucetta sucetta* (LACÉPÈDE, 1803) and *E. sucetta oblongus* (MITCHILL, 1815). Since the fishes are good jumpers, cover the tank well. Juveniles can be clearly differentiated from adults by a wide black band extending from the base of the tail to the tip of the snout. Adults either lack the band or it is dissolved into spots. These spots sometimes form vertical stripes.

T: 4-20° C (coldwater fish), L: 25 cm, A: 100 cm, R: b (m), D: 2-3
39-68° F (coldwater fish), 9¾", 39",

Pangio anguillaris (VAILLANT, 1902)

Eel Loach

Syn.: *Acanthophthalmus vermicularis, Cobitophis anguillaris, C. perakensis, Acant(h)ophthalmus anguillaris.*

Hab.: Southeast Asia; Thailand, Lake Borapet, Mae Nam Ping River at Chiang Mai; northern Borneo, Tawau district, Kalabakan, Sungei Marikut (surely distributed more widely but because it is difficult to catch, it is probably often overlooked).

F.I.: Uncertain (have been offered in Germany, like other species, as "silver eels"); the first report with a picture was by U. Essmann (1987) in TI 79 (The animals were acquired in 1980).

Sex: Unknown.

Soc. B.: Not an overly shy fish; however, when working around the aquarium, it quickly disappears in a hiding place. It appears hesitantly for feed, then stays visible for some time. Can also be observed during the day. Not a loner! Day- and night-active!

M: Despite its sensitive appearance, it is a very adaptive and robust fish. Bottom of fine sand. Offer plenty of hiding places of stones, clay fragments, bamboo pipes, etc. A well-planted tank is recommended.

B: No known successes. Irregular hour- or day-long restlessness (independent of day or night) has been observed, but no ventral fullness could be determined in relation to it. However, the restlessness seems to be correlated to improving water conditions (under poor water conditions the animals are visible less often).

F: O; *Tubifex*; microworms are relished; flake food is readily eaten from the bottom.

S: Cannot be confused with other single-colored loaches, since it is extremely slender and lengthy. Coloration is (due to its wide distribution?) variable.

T: 24-26° C, 75-79° F, **L:** 6.5 cm, 2 2/3", **A:** 40 cm, 16", **R:** b, **D:** 1

Pangio pangia (HAMILTON, 1822)

Cinnamon Loach

Syn.: *Cobitis pangia, Cobitis cinnamomea, Pangio cinnamomea, Acant(h)ophthalmus pangia.*

Hab.: South Asia; India (northeast Bengal), Burma.

F.I.: Uncertain, but recognized about 1978 with certainty.

Sex: Unknown.

Soc. B.: Since the species lives a reclusive life, little is known about its behavior.

M: Because this retiring species lives in the fine bottom mud of its native creeks and lakes, soft, peaty substrate is recommended. Use dimmed lights, or the species will live concealed. Although the species is shy and sensitive to vibration, it will come out when it senses food.

B: Nothing is known about a successful aquarium spawn.

F: O; worms (*Tubifex*), small insect larvae, noodles, detritus, flake food.

S: *Pangio pangia* is an infrequently imported and kept single-colored loach.

T: 23-25° C, 73-77° F, **L:** 6 cm, 2 1/3", **A:** 50 cm, 20", **R:** b, **D:** 1

Pangio anguillaris

Pangio pangia

Pangio semicinctus (FRASER-BRUNNER, 1940)
Half-Banded Loach — Sub-Fam.: Cobitinae

Syn.: *Acanthophthalmus semicinctus.*

Hab.: Southeast Asia; Malay Peninsula.

F.I.: Uncertain, probably before 1914.

Sex: The second pelvic fin ray is thickened on the ♂♂, the fins are somewhat larger and the coloration is redder; ♀♀ are thicker and have a whitish-yellow base coloration.

Soc. B.: Dusk- and night-active loner which hides during the day.

M: Prefers a soft bottom that can be covered by a thin layer of mulm or peat and a dense planting of fine-leaved plants. Only use the latter in the absence of mulm; hiding places of roots and stones. Use floating plants to reduce the light. Soft (around 5° dGH), peat-acidic (pH around 6) water. The species needs warm water.

B: It seems that it has not been successful in an aquarium.

F: Predominantly live foods of all types (mosquito larvae, *Tubifex*, Enchytraea, small crustacea). Sometimes flake food will be accepted after training.

S: The importer of this species is unknown. *Pangio semicinctus* probably came to Germany through North America and Holland. The Swiss ichthyologist Maurice Kottelat (1987, Jap. J. Ichthyology **33**, 368-375) discovered that the genus *Acantophtalmus* VAN HASSELT, 1823 is an earlier synonym of *Gobitis* LINNAEUS, 1758 and, therefore, not valid. *Acanthophthalmus* BLEEKER, 1859 is an erroneous version of that name. The fish which, until now, were commonly called *Acantophthalmus* have been placed in the genus *Pangio* BLYTH, 1860.

T: 26-30° C, 79-86° F, **L:** 8 cm, 3", **A:** 50 cm, 20", **R:** b, **D:** 2

Botia eos TAKI, 1972
Sun Loach — Sub-Fam.: Botiinae

Syn.: None.

Hab.: Southeast Asia; Laos and Thailand: Mekong River and tributaries, Bung Borapet, Mae Nam Chao Phraya system; above mud and sand substrate. There are large seasonal water level variations in this habitat.

F.I.: Probably around 1960.

Sex: No external ones known.

Soc. B.: In nature the animals school and swim in middle and lower water strata. *Botia eos* is a peaceful loach.

M: Similar to *Botia lecontei.*

B: A successful spawn in captivity has not described. It seems *Botia eos* migrates in the wild. During the rainy season from May to August the fish migrate into small tributaries; they can even be found on flooded areas. At the beginning of the dry season, the animals return to the main river channels.

F: C; live food of any kind: small crustaceans, mosquito larvae, worms (*Tubifex,* Enchytraea).

S: According to ZARSKE (1982, Aquarien Terrarien **29**, 58-61) *Botia eos* has been repeatedly imported, but often confused with *Botia modesta* BLEEKER, 1864 and *B. lecontei* FOWLER, 1937. The broad (10-11 rays) dorsal fin (see picture) is one of the distinguishing features of this fish.

T: 24-28° C, 75-82° F, **L:** 6 cm, 2⅓", **A:** 70 cm, 28", **R:** b, m, **D:** 2-3

Pangio semicinctus

Botia eos

Botia beauforti SMITH, 1931
Beauforti's Loach

Syn.: None.

Hab.: Southeast Asia; Thailand, Laos; in flowing waters.

F.I.: Date uncertain. Imported by Tropicarium, Frankfurt/Main.

Sex: External sexual differences are unknown.

Soc. B.: Quite quarrelsome but, nevertheless, a shy, nocturnal fish. Other fish (of the same and different species) are attacked from its hiding place.

M: Furnish the tank with a bottom of soft, fine sand because the species will dig. Use tough plants planted in pots or secured with stones to protect them from being dug up. Soft (5° dGH) and slightly acid (pH 6-6.5) water. The species needs warm water.

B: Has not been successful in an aquarium.

F: O; live food of any kind, algae and flake food. Tablet food is especially liked.

S: *Botia beauforti* is divided into 2 subspecies: *Botia beauforti beauforti* SMITH, 1931 and *B. beauforti formosa* PELLEGRIN & FANG, 1940. The latter is from Laos and has not been introduced into the aquarium hobby.

T: 26-30° C, **L**: 25 cm, **A**: 100 cm, **R**: b, m, **D**: 2
79-86° F, 9¾", 39",

Botia lecontei FOWLER, 1937
Le Conte's Loach, Red-Finned Loach

Syn.: None.

Hab.: Southeast Asia; east Thailand, Laos.

F.I.: 1955 by the Tropicarium Co., Frankfurt/Main.

Sex: No discernible features.

Soc. B.: *Botia lecontei* is a peaceful loach. The animals are evening- and night-active. They are poor swimmers.

M: Provide the aquarium with a bottom of fine, soft sand, heavily planted resistant plants, and some hiding places made with stones and roots. Water not too hard (8° dGH) and slightly acid (pH 6.0-6.5). Exchange 10% of the water weekly; without it, the species soon wastes away. Provide subdued light (floating plants). The animals can be kept in a community aquarium.

B: No reports on a successful aquarium spawn are yet available.

F: C; live foods of any kind (small crustacea, *Tubifex*, Enchytraea, mosquito larvae).

S: *Botia lecontei* and *Botia modesta* were, and still are, easily confused. *B. lecontei* is more slender and the juvenile crossband at the caudal peduncle seems to remain as a spot in mature adults.

T: 24-28° C, **L**: 15 cm, **A**: 100 cm, **R**: b, **D**: 2-3
75-82° F, 6", 39",

Botia beauforti

Botia lecontei

Botia striata RAO, 1920

Zebra Loach

Syn.: *"Botia weinbergi"* (fictitious name!).

Hab.: Asia; southern India. The animals often inhabit muddy, oxygen-poor waters.

F.I.: 1953 by the Tropicarium Co., Frankfurt/Main.

Sex: None known.

Soc. B.: The animals are peaceful, inoffensive and quite lively. They live in small groups.

M: Needs a well-planted aquarium and soft substrate to burrow into. Provide tubes and cracks close to the bottom as hiding places. No special demands are placed on the water composition. Always keep a group, never singly. Associate with *Pangio* species or *B. morleti* (syn. *Botia horae*). *Botia striata* can also be kept in a community tank.

B: No reports on successful breeding are available.

F: O; essentially anything edible is accepted (live foods, frozen foods, flake food, vegetable food, detritus).

S: None.

T: 23-26° C, **L:** 10 cm, up to 6 cm in an aquarium, **A:** 60 cm, **R:** b, **D:** 1-2
73-79° F, 4", up to 2 1/3" in an aquarium, 24",

Fam.: Balitoridae
Sub-Fam.: Nemacheilinae

Lefua costata (KESSLER in PRZHEVAL'SKII, 1876)

Lefua

Syn.: *Diplophysa costata, Elxis coreanus, Lefua andrewsi, L. pleskei, Noemacheilus dixoni, Octonema pleskei.*

Hab.: Asia; Soviet Union and North China (Amur basin, Sedanka, Sunfun and Tumen rivers), Korea and Mongolia.

F.I.: Not yet imported into Germany.

Sex: Still unknown (?).

Soc. B.: The social behavior of *Lefua costata* has not been described.

M: As recommended for *Noemacheilus dorsalis.*

B: Has probably not been bred in an aquarium.

F: O; live foods of any kind.

S: The genus *Lefua* is characterized by eight barbels. Besides *Lefua costata* there two other species in Japan: *Lefua nikkonis* on Hokkaido and *L. echigonia* on Hondo (Honshu). This is the type species of the genus.

T: 18-22° C, **L:** 10 cm, **A:** 80 cm, **R:** b, **D:** 3
64-72° F, 4", 31",

Botia striata

Lefua costata

Lepidocephalus thermalis (VALENCIENNES, 1846)
Indian Stonebiter, Lesser Loach

Syn.: *Cobitis thermalis, Lepidocephalichthys thermalis.*

Hab.: India; Malabar Coast, southern India and Sri Lanka (Ceylon). In flowing or clear, cool, stagnant waters.

F.I.: 1954.

Sex: No external features known.

Soc. B.: Nocturnal, bottom dwelling fishes which burrow and remain hidden in the substrate for extended periods of time.

M: Needs a substrate of dark, fine-grained gravel or sand and some larger, flat stones placed directly on the substrate. Plant the sides and background loosely with medium-hard to hard species (e.g., cryptocorynes). Provide a strong current in the tank. Water should be soft (around 5° dGH) and slightly acid to neutral (pH 6.5-7.0); replace 1/5 of the water weekly. Best kept in a species tank.

B: Nothing is known about the reproductive behavior and breeding of *L. thermalis* in an aquarium.

F: O; the animals take almost any kind of food: mosquito larvae, *Tubifex*, Enchytraea; frozen food, rolled oats, carrots; flake and tablet foods. Food is only taken from the bottom.

S: The genus *Lepidocephalus* has four pairs of barbels; *Noemacheilus* only has three.

T: 22-24° C, **L:** 8 cm, **A:** 80 cm, **R:** b, **D:** 2-3
72-75° F, 3", 31",

Leptobotia mantschurica BERG, 1907
Manchurian Loach

Syn.: *Leptobotia hopeiensis.*

Hab.: Asia; Soviet Union and China: Amur basin, the basin of Ussuri and Sungari, Liao He River.

F.I.: Has not yet been imported into Germany.

Sex: Still unknown.

Soc. B.: No reports are available.

M: As listed for *Nemacheilus dorsalis.*

B: Probably has not been reproduced in an aquarium.

F: O; live foods of any kind.

S: The genus *Leptobotia* is comprised of several species, most of which are native to China.

T: 16-20° C, **L:** 22 cm, **A:** 100 cm, **R:** b, **D:** 3
61-68° F, 8 3/4", 39",

Lepidocephalus thermalis

Leptobotia mantschurica

Misgurnus anguillicaudatus (CANTOR, 1842)
Chinese Weatherfish

Syn.: *Cobitis anguillicaudata, Cobitichthys enalios, Cobitis bifurcata, C. maculata, C. pectoralis, C. rubrispinis.*

Hab.: Asia; parts of Siberia (Amur region), China, Korea, Hainan and Japan. The species inhabits waters with muddy bottoms.

F.I.: 1913.

Sex: Not recognizable with certainty; usually the 2nd ray of the ♂'s pelvic fin is thicker.

Soc. B.: A sedentary, peaceful, nocturnal bottom dweller.

M: Soft bottom cover; native potted coldwater plants (the species digs!). Hiding places of rock and roots. Likes subdued light. They will require good filtration to handle the debris stirred up when the animals dig. No special demands are placed on the composition of the water. A report on this species is given by RIEHL (1972): DATZ **25**, 1-2.

B: Possible, but successes have thus far been accidental.

F: O; live foods of any kind, flake food, and part vegetable matter.

S: The species likes to burrow itself into the substrate (mud) so that only the head sticks out. Some authors consider *Misgurnus anguillicaudatus* only a sub-species of *Misgurnus fossilis*. According to these authors there is the typical European form (*M. fossilis fossilis*) and the spotted Asian form (*M. fossillis anguillicaudatus*).

T: 10-25° C, L: 50 cm, are sexually mature from 10 cm, A: 100 cm, R: b, D: 1-2
50-77° F, 20", are sexually mature from 4", 39",

Fam.: Balitoridae
Sub-Fam.: Nemacheilinae

Acanthocobitis urophthalmus (GUENTHER, 1868)
Eye-Spot Loach

Syn.: *Noemalcheilus urophthalmus.*

Hab.: India, Mae Khlong, Ganges, Chidwin, Irrawady, Sitang, Salween, Sri Lanka (India, Thailand and China).

F.I.: 1903.

Sex: ♂ has a definite groove under the eye.

Soc. B.: Territorial; four animals (♂♂?) can barely cohabitate in a 100 x 30 cm (39" x 12") aquarium. Fast swimmers.

M: Easy to keep, no special demands are made. Hiding places (caves, roots, plant thickets) increase the prosperity of the animals. *A. urophthalmus* leaves other fish alone as long as they don't have long appendages. Therefore, do not combine them with angelfish or gouramis.

B: Has been successful in England. Use a tank of 50 x 16 x 16 cm (20" x 6 1/3" x 6 1/3") to spawn; pH 7.2, hardness around 8° dGH, 25° C (77° F). The species spawns in plant thickets by indisciminately spreading 100-150 sticky eggs. The larvae hatch after 36 hours and are free-swimming after the third day. Feed with *Artemia* nauplii the first week. Microworms, strained *Daphnia* and fine flake food were fed afterwards. One hundred juveniles were raised successfully.

F: O; all types of live foods, frozen food, supplementary vegetal feedings, freeze-dried and flake foods. Wild caught fish had many beetles (Coleoptera) in their stomach.

S: *A. botia* is a very beautiful loach which will have orange-red fins when properly cared for.

T: 24-26° C, L: 8 cm, A: 100 cm, R: m, b, D: 1
75-79° F, 3", 39",

Misgurnus anguillicaudatus

Acanthocobitis urophthalmus

Triplophysa dorsalis (KESSLER, 1872)
Gray Loach

Syn.: *Cobitis dorsalis, Diplophysa dorsalis, D. kungessana, Nemacheilus dorsalis, Noemacheilus kungessanus, N. dorsalis.*

Hab.: Asia; Soviet Union (Amudar'ya basin, upper and middle Syrdar'ya, Issyk-Kul' Lake, Ili basin, Talas and Chu basins).

F.I.: Not yet imported into Germany.

Sex: No external signs are known or described.

Soc. B.: Nothing is known.

M: Requires a roomy tank with a fine sand or gravel bottom. Provide some hiding places and refuges. Good aeration and perhaps a weak current should be provided. There are no reports on water values (pH, dGH), but medium-hard water (15° dGH) with a neutral pH (7.0) should be fine.

B: Has probably not occurred in an aquarium. In the wild the species spawns from mid-April to mid-June.

F: O; live foods of any kind, especially worms but also small crustacea and sowbugs.

S: TURDAKOV, 1946 has described the sub-species *Nemacheilus dorsalis kafirnigani* from the Kafirnigan River. It can be distinguished from the nominal form by its shorter caudal peduncle.

T: 18-22° C, **L:** 13 cm, **A:** 80 cm, **R:** b, **D:** 3
64-72° F, 5", 31",

Nemacheilus fasciatus KUHL & VAN HASSELT, 1823
Barred Loach, Spot-Fin Loach

Syn.: *Cobitis fasciata, Namachilus fasciatuss, Noemacheilus fasciatus.*

Hab.: Indonesia; Sumatra, Borneo, Java; also on small neighboring islands.

F.I.: 1914.

Sex: No sure ones known. ♀ is fuller; see picture.

Soc. B.: Territorial twilight- and night-active bottom fish. It will often energetically defend its territory against conspecific and heterospecific intruders.

M: Needs a soft bottom and some large, flat stones placed directly on the bottom. Lightly plant sides and background with medium-tough to tough plants. Water should be moderately hard (up to 12° dGH) and slightly acid to neutral (pH 6.5-7.0). A weekly exchange of 1/5 of the aquarium water and subdued lighting, perhaps dimmed with floating plants, are needed. *N. fasciatus* does not need excessive warmth.

B: Has not yet spawned in an aquarium.

F: Live food of any kind (small crustaceans, aquatic insect larvae, *Tubifex*, Enchytraea). Flake food is not readily accepted.

S: The fish are somewhat sensitive to transfers.

T: 22-24° C, **L:** 9 cm, **A:** 80 cm, **R:** b, **D:** 2
72-75° F, 3", 31",

Triplophysa dorsalis

Nemacheilus fasciatus

Nemacheilus selangoricus, ♂ top, ♀ bottom

Nemacheilus selangoricus DUNCKER, 1904
Kuiper's Loach

Syn.: *Nemachilus kuiperi, N. trans-lineatus, Botia selangorica, Noemacheilus selangoricus.*

Hab.: Indonesia; island of Belitung (= Billiton), Malaysia.

F.I.: 1957.

Sex: The ♂ has slender, pointed pectoral fins, and the upper lobe of the caudal fin is elongated. Pectoral fins of the ♀ are rounded. The ♀ is fuller and has a thicker stomach.

Soc. B.: A lively, diurnal loach which establishes a territory and is often quarrelsome.

M: Needs a soft bottom and a few larger, flat stones placed directly on the bottom. Lightly plant the sides and background with medium-hard to hard plants (cryptocorynes). Water not too hard (up to 10° dGH) and slightly acid to neutral (pH 6.5-7.0). Perform weekly 20% water exchanges. Subdued lighting. Do not keep with peace-loving fishes.

B: Has not yet been successful in an aquarium.

F: C, O; live food of any kind: insect larvae, small benthic crustaceans, *Tubifex*, etc. Flake and tablet foods are also accepted.

S: WICKLER (1959): Z. Tierpsychol. **16**, 410-423 observed the following details about *Nemacheilus selangoricus*: the caudal peduncle of both sexes has three to six specially large scales above and below the lateral line. Underneath the scales is an organ which swells noticeably during fights. If two fish are fighting, they lay next to each other and strongly beat at each other with their tails.

T: 23-25° C, **L:** 7.5 cm, **A:** 70 cm, **R:** b, **D:** 2
73-77° F, 3", 28",

Nemacheilus notostigma BLEEKER, 1864
Fighting Loach

Syn.: *Nemachilus notostigma, Noemacheilus notostigma.*

Hab.: South Asia; Sri Lanka (Ceylon).

F.I.: Probably only after 1980.

Sex: ♂♂ have a considerably larger upper caudal fin lobe.

Soc. B.: The species is relatively aggressive, quarrelsome and territorial. The animals should be kept in a large species tank with plenty of hiding places.

M: As mentioned for *Nemacheilus botia*. Provide many hiding places. It's undemanding towards water values though the water should be clean and clear.

B: In a densely planted 120 l (32 gal) tank, *N. notostigma* spawned with the following water values: 22° C (72° F); pH 6.8-7.2; 4° dKH, 9° dGH; < 0.05 mg N/l (measured as NO_2^-). Within one month the loaches spawned at least twice, because juveniles of 5-10 mm (1/4"-1/3") and 20-25 mm (3/4"-1") length were observed simultaneously. Feed: the dense stands of *Ceratopteris* developed infusoria (stimulated by Protagen-Granulate), serving as the larvae's first food. Later they can feed on *Artemia* nauplii or *Cyclops*. Because they also feed on aufwuchs, they don't need to constantly swim in food. In this manner over 20 juveniles were raised to a length of 25 mm (1") (from February to mid-May). Data given by Gerhard Ott (Date: 5.16.1984).

F: O; nevertheless, they should be fed predominantly with live foods of all kinds.

S: While fighting, the animals try to grasp the adversaries' pectoral fins. Even though the species has a toothless mandible, fin injuries do occur.

T: 22-24° C, **L:** 8 cm, **A:** 80 cm, **R:** b, **D:** 2-3
72-75° F, 3", 31",

Nemacheilus selangoricus

Nemacheilus notostigma

Triplophysa stoliczkai (STEINDACHNER, 1866)
Stoliczka's Loach

Syn.: *Cobitis stoliczkae, C. elegans, C. uranoscopus, Noemacheilus cueljuensis, N. dorsonotatus, N. fedtschenkoae, N. lhasae, N. stenurus, N. stoli, Nemacheilus stoliczkai, Nemachilus stoliczkai.*

Hab.: Asia; Soviet Union and China. In the mountainous regions of the rivers in the basin of Lake Aral and Balkhash and the Indus, Tarim He, Hwang He, Yangtze and Brahmaputra rivers. Also in the upper Amudar'ya, Zeravshan, Kashka-Darya, upper Syrdar'ya, Chu basin and the tributaries of Lake Issyk-Kul', as well as in the Tibetian Lake Uukunor.

F.I.: Not yet imported into Germany.

Sex: The first three to six rays of the pectoral fins of ripe ♂♂ are enlarged.

Soc. B.: No reports are available.

M: See recommendations for *Nemacheilus dorsalis.*

B: Has probably not been accomplished in an aquarium.

F: O; live foods of any kind.

S: Besides the nominal species of *Nemacheilus stoliczkai,* the sub-species *N. stoliczkai elegans* KESSLER, 1874 and *N. stoliczkai uranoscopus* KESSLER, 1874 have also been described.

T: 16-20° C, **L:** 15 cm, **A:** 80 cm, **R:** b, **D:** 3
61-68° F, 6", 31",

Nemacheilus strauchi (KESSLER, 1874)
Spotted Thick-lipped Loach

Syn.: *Diplophysa strauchi, D. papilloso labiata, Noemacheilus strauchi.*

Hab.: Asia; Soviet Union (Lake Balkhash, Sassyk-kul', Alakol', Ili River and Lake Zaysan) and China (Tarim basin).

F.I.: Has not been imported into Germany.

Sex: ♂♂ have a flatter head and body, a more slender caudal peduncle, a lower dorsal fin and grow larger.

Soc. B.: Nothing is known.

M: Similar to *Nemacheilus dorsalis.*

B: Has probably not been bred in an aquarium. In the wild the animals spawn from April to June. The species has up to 3 spawning periods, with four or more day intervals. Up to 47,000 eggs can be laid on plants and gravel.

F: O; live food of any kind, especially molluscs (snails and small mussels) which are sucked out of their shells.

S: The nominal form *Nemacheilus strauchi strauchi* (KESSLER, 1874) and the subspecies *N. strauchi ulacholicus* (BERG, 1905) of Lake Issyk-Kul' (Soviet Union), have been described.

T: 18-22° C, **L:** 25 cm, **A:** 100 cm, **R:** b, **D:** 3
64-72° F, 9¾", 39",

Triplophysa stoliczkai

Nemacheilus strauchi

Schistura notostigma (BLEEKER, 1863)

Syn.: *Nemacheilus notostigma, Noemacheilus notostigma.*

Hab.: Asia; representatives of the genus *Schistura* occur in India as well as Japan, Korea, north and south China (with the exception of the Yang-tse-Kiang) and the Amur area.

F.I.: Uncertain, because it usually is not recognized as a separate genus. Animals are needed for identification!

Sex: None known.

Soc. B.: Territorial, dusk- and night-active bottom dweller.

T: 22-24° C, 72-75° F, L: variable, A: 80 cm, 31", R: b, D: 2

M: See *Acanthocobitis urophthalmus*, page 348.

B: Has not been successful in captivity.

F: C, O; predominantly live foods of any kind (small crustaceans, aquatic insect larvae, *Tubifex*, Enchytraea), flake and tablet foods.

Barbus jae ♀, Zaire, wild caught, for text, see page 368.

Schistura notostigma

Schistura sp.

Acanthorhodeus asmussi (DYBOWSKI, 1872)
Russian Bitterling

Syn.: *Devario asmussi.*

Hab.: Asia; Soviet Union (Amur basin: middle and lower Amur River, Ussuri River, Lake Khanka), west and south Korea.

F.I.: The species has not been imported into Germany.

Sex: The ♂ is more colorful during the spawning season (courtship coloration). ♀ has a long ovipositor.

Soc. B.: Gregarious, peaceful fish. This species cares for its young.

M: As listed under *Acheilognathus chankaensis.*

B: There are no described successes in western literature. It is probably similar to *Rhodeus sericeus amarus* (compare Vol. 1). In nature *Acanthorhodeus asmussi* deposits its eggs in the mantle of the mussel *Cristaria plicata.* Up to 1,000 eggs are deposited in small piles. The larvae have a small head and an elongated body covered with small scales. As soon as they hatch, they crawl apart and distribute in the mussel's mantle. This peculiarity is probably due to the low oxygen levels they would have been subjected to if they would have remained in the mounds the eggs were originally deposited in.

F: H, O; predominantly plant matter (lower aquatic plants), also live foods and vegetable flake food.

S: The ovipositor of the ♀ *Acanthorhodeus asmussi* extends 12-16 cm (4 3/4"-6 1/3") during the spawning season.

T: 18-22° C, **L:** 16 cm, **A:** 90 cm, **R:** m, b, **D:** 2-3
64-72° F, 6 1/3", 35",

Acheilognathus chankaensis (DYBOWSKI, 1872)

Syn.: *Devario chankaensis, Acanthorhodeus asmussi sungariensis, A. chankaensis.*

Hab.: Asia; Soviet Union (Lake Khanka, middle Amur and Sungari rivers).

F.I.: Not yet into Germany.

Sex: ♂ has courtship coloration during the spawning season; ♀ has a long ovipositor.

Soc. B.: A lively, peaceful, gregarious fish which cares for its young.

M: Needs a bottom of fine sand; dense back and edge vegetation; leave enough swimming room. Water medium-hard (15° dGH) and a pH of about 7. Always keep several individuals. Combining with other peaceful species is possible.

B: No reports are available in the west. Breeding biology is similar to the German bitterling (compare Vol. 1). The eggs are deposited in the mantle of a mussel where they develop.

F: H, O; predominantly vegetable foods, including vegetable flakes.

S: BERG (1949): The Freshwater Fishes of the USSR, Vol. 2, expresses the suspicion that *Acheilognathus chankaensis* is not a true species, but perhaps a cross between *Acanthorhodeus asmussi* and *Rhodeus sericeus.*

T: 18-22° C, **L:** 11 cm, **A:** 80 cm, **R:** m, b, **D:** 2-3
64-72° F, 4 1/3", 31",

Acanthorhodeus asmussi

Acheilognathus chankaensis

Tor soro (VALENCIENNES in CUVIER & VALENCIENNES, 1842)
Large-Scaled Barb
Sub-Fam.: Cyprininae

Syn.: *Barbus soro, Labeobarbus soro.*

Hab.: Southeast Asia; Indonesia (Sumatra), Java, Thailand.

F.I.: Uncertain.

Sex: No external ones known.

Soc. B.: Not a pronounced schooling fish. The fish prefer to remain within sight of each other under different cover (branches, large leaves).

M: Large, densely planted aquaria are recommended for this shy species. Only placid species are suitable tankmates for this timid species. Floating plants will help to alleviate this characteristic.

B: No reports are available.

F: O, H; also likes vegetable matter.

S: In nature the fishes grow nearly 1 m. They're very tame.

T: 22-26° C, L: >50 cm, A: 200 cm, R: b, m, D: 3
72-79° F, > 20", 8047",

Alburnoides taeniatus (KESSLER, 1874)
Striped Tailor
Sub-Fam.: Abraminae

Syn.: *Alburnus taeniatus, Squalalburnus taeniatus.*

Hab.: Asia; Soviet Union, in the waters of the Aral region, in the Amudar'ya from the delta to the estuary of the Kafirnigan; in the Syrdar'ya from the Naryn and Kara-Darya to Kzyl-orda and in the Chu River. The species prefers slow flowing and standing waters

F.I.: Has not been imported.

Sex: Ventral line of the ♀ is more convex during the spawning season.

Soc. B.: A surface oriented schooling fish which avoids waters with strong currents and usually lives in densely vegetated lakes and bays.

M: Use a sandy substrate and provide dense side and background vegetation of coldwater species, leaving some swimming space. The aquarium should be well-aerated and filtered. Water up to 20° dGH and pH neutral to slightly alkaline (7.0-7.7).

B: No breeding reports are known to us. In the wild the species spawns in June and July. The fish attain sexual maturity during the second year.

F: C, O; live foods of all kinds, predominately zooplankton and mosquito larvae; also flake food.

S: *Alburnoides taeniatus* distinguishes itself from other representatives of the genus by its longer and denser gill rakers.

T: 10-20° C (coldwater fish), L: 9 cm, A: 70 cm, R: t, m, D: 2
50-68° F (coldwater fish), 3 ", 28",

Tor soro

Alburnoides taeniatus

Barbichthys nitidus SAUVAGE, 1878
"Siam Highfin Shark" (trade name), Sucker Barb

Syn.: None.

Hab.: Southeast Asia; Malay Peninsula and Thailand.

F.I.: ?

Sex: Still unknown.

Soc. B.: Nothing known. It is probably similar to *Leptobarbus* species.

M: Similar to *Leptobarbus hoevenii*, page 394. Only young specimens are suitable for an aquarium.

B: Has not been accomplished in captivity.

F: O; live foods of any kind, frozen food and flake food.

S: A pretty fish, but too large for the normal aquarium.

T: 23-26° C, **L:** 30 cm, **A:** 120 cm, **R:** m, **D:** 2-3
73-79° F, 12", 47",

Barbus ablabes (BLEEKER, 1863)

Syn.: *Puntius ablabes, Barbodes ablabes, Barbus spurelli, Enteromius ablabes, E. potamogalis.*

Hab.: West Africa: Ivory Coast, Gambia, Senegal, Niger, Burkina Faso (Upper Volta), Chad.

F.I.: Could not be determined.

Sex: ♂ more slender; ♀ much plumper during the spawning season with a more convex ventral line.

Soc. B.: Lively, peaceful, schooling fish.

M: As stated for *Barbus barilioides* or *B. jae.*

B: The first breeding report is given by J. PALICKA (1986) in the magazine "Das Aquarium" **20** (203): 240-243. Use a 10-12 l (2.6-3.1 gal) aquarium. Water with a temperature of 25-27° C (77-81° F), not harder than 8° dGH and a pH of about 6.7 is needed. Well aged water is important for breeding. Since the fish eat their spawn, efficient breeding will demand a breeding trap. Spawning occurs after extended courtship in open water. With each act, four to ten eggs are released which fall to the bottom. No plants are necessary as spawning substrate. Up to 500 sticky, 1 mm (1/32"), transparent eggs are released. At 27° C (81° F), development takes 28 hours. After about four days, they are free-swimming. Raising them is easy; first feed pulverized food, then feed larger particles.

F: C, O; predominantly live foods of all types (mosquito larvae, small crustaceans, *Tubifex*, Enchytraea), also flake food.

S: Several different morphs and populations of *Barbus ablabes* are known.

T: 23-25° C, **L:** 11 cm, **A:** 100 cm, **R:** all, **D:** 2-3
73-77° F, 4 1/3", 39",

Barbichthys nitidus

Barbus ablabes

Barbus barbus (LINNAEUS, 1758)
River Barb, Barbel

Syn.: *Cyprinus barbus, Barbus fluviatilis.*

Hab.: Europe: from France to the Memel; in the Thames and some other rivers in England; in the Danube and side rivers. The species is not found in Iceland, Ireland, Scotland, Denmark and Scandinavia.

F.I.: Indigenous to Germany.

Sex: ♂♂ have white spots during the spawning season; the ♀♀ are much plumper during spawning season.

Soc. B.: Sedentary, twilight-active, schooling fish. During the spawning season the fish migrate upstream. The animals overwinter as large groups in quiet, river segments of moderate depth.

M: Provide sand or gravel substrate and shelter out of roots and/or stones. Plant coldwater plants along the edges, leaving some swimming space. Needs medium-hard (12-15° dGH) and neutral to slightly alkaline (pH 7.0-7.5) water. Always keep in groups of at least six animals.

B: Has not yet occurred in an aquarium. In nature the fish form large schools (May-July) and migrate upstream. They spawn on rocky and coarse gravel bottoms of creeks. The eggs will stick to the stones at first and then fall down between them. The eggs will take 10 to 15 days to develop while hidden between the stones.

F: O; live food of any kind, frozen, freeze-dried, vegetable, flake and tablet foods.

S: *Barbus barbus* is the principal fish of the Epipotamons (= headwater of the cyprinid region = barb region) in German waters. Several sub-species have been described in Europe, from France, Yugoslavia and Greece. Its eggs are slightly poisonous.

T: 10-24° C (coldwater fish), L: 90 cm, A: 100 cm, R: b, D: 2
50-75° F (coldwater fish), 35", 39",

Barbus barilioides BOULENGER, 1914
Blue-Barred Barb

Syn.: *Barbodes barilioides, Capoeta bariliodes, Puntius barilioides.*

Hab.: Africa; Angola, northern Rhodesia (Zimbabwe), Zambia and southern Zaire (Province of Shaba = present day Katanga).

F.I.: 1963.

Sex: The ♂ is more slender; ♀ usually fuller and, according to STERBA, young ♀♀ are ink red.

Soc. B.: Very lively swimming fishes. If the tank is too intensely lit, the fish remain shy and timid. It is a peaceful, schooling fish and maintaining it individually accentuates its shyness.

M: Requires a dark substrate of lava or basalt. Plant densely on the sides and background with nondelicate leaved vegetation. Decorate with roots leaving free swimming space. At least seven individuals should be kept. Water; soft (around 6° dGH) and slightly acid (pH 6.0-6.5). Suitable for the community tank.

B: Breeding this species can sometimes be tricky. Use the water values stated above. Best to use a prearranged breeding tank. A well-planted set-up is very important. When the fish get into the mood, spawning will take place in the dense plant bunches. ♀♀ deposit several hundred eggs. The parent fish should be immediately removed because they readily eat their own eggs. At 26° C (79° F) the eggs hatch in approximately 40 hours and hang from the glass and the plants. Three to four days later they are free-swimming. Initial feedings should consist of infusoria, later with *Artemia* nauplii.

Continued page after next.

Barbus barbus

Barbus barilioides

Continuation of *B. barilioides:*

F: O; live foods of any kind, especially small crustaceans, mosquito larvae and *Tubifex*; frozen food, plant food (spinach, tips of water plants), flake food.

S: *Barbus barilioides* is easily distinguishable from other representatives of the genus by its coloration and markings.

T: 20-26° C, L: 5 cm, A: 80 cm, R: b, m, D: 1-2
68-79° F, 2", 31",

Barbus bimaculatus (BLEEKER, 1864)

Two-Spotted Barb, Red-Striped Barb

Syn.: *Gnathopogon bimaculatus, "Barbus bicaudatus"* (trade name), *Puntius bimaculatus.*

Hab.: South Asia: Sri Lanka (Ceylon). The species inhabits standing and flowing waters from sea level to the headwaters in the mountains; Kerala, India.

F.I.: 1957.

Sex: ♂ is more slender with a dark red longitudinal stripe from the base of the tail to the operculum; ♀ with or without a faintly visible band.

Soc. B.: Peaceful, quite shy, schooling fish. They remain timid even in large aquaria.

M: Supply a dark bottom of lava or sand; densely planted edges and background. Does not need deep water (20 cm; 8"). Provide roots as decoration and leave a lot of open swimming room. Use medium-hard (15° dGH) and slightly acid (pH 6.5) water. Always keep at least six animals.

B: 24-26° C (75-79° F); breeding is possible in small tanks (25 l; 6.6 gal). A detailed breeding report is given by GABRIEL & ELIAS (1981): DATZ 34, 422-425. Furnish the breeding tank with Java moss and *Myriophyllum*. Set up with two ♂♂ and two ♀♀. Water should be softer (to 10° dGH) and slightly acid. Spawning follows an unflagging courtship by the ♂♂. Spawning occurs in bursts among the plants (3-4 eggs per act), up to a total of 400. Remove parents immediately as they will eat the spawn. At 25° C (77° F) the larvae hatch in 24 hr. Feed with nauplii, TetraMin Baby Food and Protogen-Granulate. The young are sensitive to water pollution.

F: O; live food (*Cyclops*, water fleas, mosquito larvae, *Tubifex*), frozen food, flake food.

S: *Barbus bimaculatus* is very fecund for its size.

T: 22-24° C, L: 7 cm, A: 80 cm, R: b, m, D: 2
72-75° F, 2¾", 31",

Barbus binotatus VALENCIENNES, 1842

Spotted Barb

Syn.: *Puntius binotatus.*

Hab.: Southeast Asia: Malaysia, Indonesia, Philippines. Occurs in creeks, rivers and lakes. Not rare anywhere.

F.I.: 1907 by Vereinigten Zierfischzüchtereien at Conradshöhe, Berlin.

Sex: ♂ more slender, ♀ is disproportionately fat during the spawning season.

Soc. B.: Lively peaceful schooling fish.

M: As listed under *Barbus stoliczkanus*, page 376. Always keep at least six to eight individuals. The species needs warmer temperatures. Keep together with other *Barbus* species of the same size.

Continued the page after next.

Barbus bimaculatus, ♂ bottom, ♀ top

Barbus binotatus

Continuation of *B. binotatus:*

B: 25-28°C (77-82° F); use a breeding tank that is densely planted, but not too small. Set up with one ♂ and two ♀♀. The water should be weakly acidic (pH 6.0-6.5) and not too hard (to 12° dGH). Breeding usually occurs in the morning hours. The fish will eat their spawn; therefore, use pebbles or a plastic screen to protect the eggs. Remove the parents after spawning is complete. *B. binotatus* is very productive. Feed the young with *Artemia* nauplii.

F: O; a nonproblematic omnivore: live foods of all types, frozen food, scraped meat, vegetable foods, flake and tablet foods.

S: *Barbus binotatus* is not a very attractive barb. For this reason it has remained a rare aquarium guest.

T: 24-26° C, **L:** 18 cm, max. 12 cm in an aquarium, **A:** 80 cm, **R:** b, m, **D:** 1-2
75-79° F, 7", max. $4^3/_4$" in an aquarium, 31",

Barbodes pierrei SAUVAGE, 1880
Pale Barb

Syn.: *Puntius daruphani, Barbodes daruphani, Barbus daruphani, Puntius pierrei.*

Hab.: Thailand, Laos, Yunnan, Cambodia, Southern Vietnam.

F.I.: Unknown.

Sex: The ♀ is clearly thicker during the spawning season with a convex ventral line.

Soc. B.: Peaceful, lively schooling fish.

M: The substrate should be dark (lava). Provide dense side and back vegetation; decorate with some roots; leave some free swimming room. No special demands are placed on the make-up of the water (hardness 15° dGH, pH around 7.0); regular partial water changes. Suitable to be kept in a community aquarium.

B: Probably not very difficult, but no reports are available.

F: O; live foods of any kind, vegetal foods, also flake food.

S: *Barbodes pierrei* has four barbels, about 27 scales on the lateral line and 14 scales at the narrowest part of the tail.

T: 22-25° C, **L:** 45 cm, **A:** 100 cm, **R:** m, **D:** 2
72-77° F, 18", 39",

Barbus jae BOULENGER, 1903
Jae Barb, Puntius Jae

Syn.: None.

Hab.: Africa; western part of central Africa in the area of the inland plateau of south Cameroon and north Gabon.

F.I.: About 1970.

Sex: The ♂♂ are more beautiful and intensely colored.

Soc. B.: Peaceful, lively schooling fish.

M: Use dark substrate (lava) and low water. The aquarium does not need to be large. Always keep a group of at least six animals. Plant the tank with *Anubias* and *Crinum* species. Strongly lit tanks are not appreciated; the colors are best at twilight. Dim the light with floating plants. Water should be very soft (1-5° dGH) and acid (pH 5.5-6.0).

B: 24-26° C (75-79° F); breeding is not very difficult but not particularly productive. Use peat filtered water with a slightly acid pH (6.0). Breeding with pairs leads to mediocre results.

Continued on page 370.

Barbodes pierrei front, *Barbus schwanefeldi* back

Barbus jae ♂, Zaire, wild caught, photo of ♀ on page 356

Continuation *B. jae.*:

Better results are obtained by using two ♂♂ with two or three ripe ♀♀. A glass lattice, spawning mop, or peat fibers safeguard the eggs from the parents. Yields up to 70 young are possible. The eggs are small (0.7-1.2 mm; 1/64"-1/32") and hatch after 36 hr; the larvae become free-swimming after a total of six days. Feed the young with *Artemia* nauplii and Liquifry.

T: 21-25° C, L: 4 cm, A: 50 cm, R: b, (m), D: 2
70-77° F, 1 2/3", 20",

F: O; live foods of all kinds (*Cyclops*, grindal worms, mosquito larvae, *Artemia* nauplii); flake food is also accepted.

S: None.

Barbus janssensi

Janssen's Barb

POLL, 1976

Syn.: None.

Hab.: Africa; drainage area of the Zaire (Congo) River, Shaba Province, Zaire.

F.I.: Unknown.

Sex: ♂ smaller, with two clear dark spots on the dark longitudinal stripe on the body sides. ♀ is larger and the two spots are more vague (the picture shows two ♂♂).

Soc. B.: Peaceful, active schooling fish.

T: 24-26° C, L: 10 cm, A: 100 cm, R: b, m, D: 2
75-79° F, 4", 39",

M: Large, densely planted tanks that still preserve enough swimming space are preferred. Water values similar to other African *Barbus* species.

B: Has not been bred.

F: O; live foods of any kind, flake food.

S: *Barbus janssensi* is seldom imported and seems to be uncommon in its native habitat.

Barbus leonensis

Sierra Leone Barb

BOULENGER, 1915

Syn.: *Barbus salessei.*

Hab.: West Africa; Sierra Leone, Gambia, Niger, Chad.

F.I.: ?

Sex: No external ones known. ♀♀ are probably significantly plumper during the spawning season.

Soc. B.: Active, very peaceful schooling fish.

T: 22-24° C, L: 3 cm, A: 50 cm, R: b, m, D: 2
72-75° F, 1 ", 20",

M: Similar to *Barbus jae.*

B: No reports on a successful breeding are available.

F: O; live foods of any kind, frozen and flake food.

S: *Barbus leonensis* has only been sporadically imported into Germany. With a length of 3 cm (1 ") this fish is one of the smallest *Barbus* species.

Barbus janssensi

Barbus leonensis

Barbus lineatus DUNCKER, 1904
Striped Barb

Syn.: None.

Hab.: Malay Peninsula, southwest Malaysia (Johor), parts of Indonesia.

F.I.: 1934 by the Härtel Company, Dresden.

Sex: ♂ is clearly slenderer with a more noticeable line design; ♀ is much fuller with a higher back and paler lines.

Soc. B.: A peaceful, agile swimmer and a somewhat timid schooling fish.

M: Dark substrate (lava); tank with dense planting and many hiding places; floating plants to dim the light. Decorate with bogwood roots. Always keep a small school (8 or more). Water up to 12° dGH and a pH of 6.0-6.5; peat filtration. Associate with *Danio* and *Brachydanio* species.

T: 21-24° C, **L:** 12 cm, **A:** 80 cm, **R:** m, b, **D:** 2
70-75° F, 4 3/4", 31",

B: 25-26° C (77-79° F); soft (2-5° dGH), acid (pH 5.5-6.5) and shallow (20 cm; 8") water. Dense vegetation, dark substrate and a detritus layer are suggested. After intense courtship, spawning takes place among the plants. During spawning, feed the fish with Enchytraea. The species is very productive; remove the parents after spawning is complete. The larvae hatch after 24-30 hours. Raising the young is easy.

F: O; live food, vegetal food, freeze-dried foods, flake food.

S: *Barbus lineatus* is possibly a morph of *Barbus fasciatus* (JERDON, 1849) without barbels. Also see Vol. 1, page 384.

Barbus lineomaculatus BOULENGER, 1903
Dotted-Line Barb

Syn.: *Barbus lineomaculatus* var. *quadrilineatus.*

Hab.: Africa; Kenya, Tanzania, Zaire (Province Shaba = formerly Katanga).

F.I.: 1925.

Sex: No externals signs known; ♀♀ are probably fuller during the spawning season.

Soc. B.: Nothing known. In all likelihood, this fish is also a peaceful schooling fish.

T: 22-25° C, **L:** 8 cm, **A:** 80 cm, **R:** b, m, **D:** 2
72-77° F, 3", 31",

M: See *Barbus barilioides.*

B: Probably has not been reproduced in captivity.

F: C; in the wild mainly insects and insect larvae are eaten.

S: *Barbus lineomaculatus* is closely related to *Barbus greenwoodi* POLL, 1967, from Angola.

Barbus lineatus, bottom ♂, top ♀

Barbus lineomaculatus

Barbus narayani

HORA, 1937

Syn.: *Puntius narayani.*

Hab.: Southern Asia.

F.I.: Unknown.

Sex: Distinct differences in coloration have not been described; however, the ♀♀ can be easily identified by the fuller body.

Soc. B.: Peaceful schooling fish well suited for a community tank with related species.

M: Demands are similar to related species from the same geographic area (*Barbus nigrofasciatus*, s. Bd. 1, Seite 392). Large, well-planted aquaria with plenty of swimming space and nu-merous hiding places are best for *B. na-rayani.* If kept singly or with too much light, the species is shy. For this reason use some floating plants and keep a school.

B: Has not been successful.

F: O; live foods of any kind, but also flake food and supplemental vegetal foods (algae, lettuce).

S: A little known, rarely imported species.

T: 22-26° C, **L:** 6 cm (?), **A:** 70 cm, **R:** b, m, **D:** 2
72-79° F, 2¹/₃" (?), 28",

Barbus phutunio
Dwarf Barb

(HAMILTON, 1822)

Syn.: *Cyprinus phutunio, Systomus leptosoma, S. phutunio, Puntius phutunio.*

Hab.: Southeast Asia: east India from Bengal to the southern tip. The animals inhabit small, slow flowing and standing waters.

F.I.: 1906 by Paul Matte, Lankwitz, Germany.

Sex: ♂ is more slender, with a distinct spot design on the sides of the body, ventral fins reddish; ♀ is fuller, spot design much fainter, ventral fins yellow.

Soc. B.: Very peaceful, active schooling fish. The animals are undemanding, but turn shy, timid and lazy. The ♂♂ fight among themselves without resulting serious injury.

M: As recommended for *Barbus bimaculatus.* The fish should always be kept in a school of conspecifics or associated with other small, lively cyprinids. The species is suitable for community tanks.

B: 24-26° C (75-79° F); use densely planted breeding tanks. Spawning occurs like with other *Barbus* species. Usually takes place in the morning in upper water regions among the plants. The eggs hang on the plants. The parents should be removed immediately, since they eat the spawns. The larvae hatch, depending on temperature, after 30-40 hours, and become free-swimming in another two to three days. Feed *Artemia* nauplii and sieved small crustaceans.

F: O; live food of all kinds, vegetal food, supplemental animal food (shrimp, scraped meat, etc.), flake food.

S: *Barbus phutunio* tends to waste away when kept in an aquarium.

T: 22-24° C, **L:** 5 cm, **A:** 60 cm, **R:** all, **D:** 1-2
72-75° F, 2", 24",

Barbus narayani, a ♂

Barbus phutunio

Barbus stoliczkanus
Stoliczka's Tic-Tac-Toe Barb

DAY, 1871

Syn.: *Barbus ticto stoliczkanus, Puntius stoliczkanus.*

Hab.: Southeast Asia: eastern Burma and the river region of the Irawadi. Northern Thailand.

F.I.: In 1925 by the "Platy-Tischrunde" Hamburg.

Sex: The ♂ is more slender with a blood red dorsal fin that has a black spot or black dots and is edged in black along the top. ♀ has a more convex ventral line, a reddish dorsal fin and does not have black markings.

Soc. B.: Very lively, active and peaceful schooling fish. ♂♂ will fight out of jealousy, but there are never injuries.

M: Use a soft substrate with a cover of mulm, dense edge and background vegetation, some roots as decoration; leave plenty of free swimming space. Water should be slightly acid (pH around 6.5) and not overly hard (up to 12° dGH).

T: 22-26° C, **L:** 6 cm, **A:** 60 cm, **R:** all, **D:** 1-2
72-79° F, 2 1/3", 24",

Associate with other *Barbus, Brachydanio, Danio* and/or *Rasbora* species. Always keep a group of at least 6 animals.

B: 24-26° C (75-79° F); breeding is not difficult. The breeding tank should be densely planted with fine-leaved plants. Partial water exchanges foster ripeness. The ♂♂ can be placed one or two days before into the breeding tank; the ♀ is put in a few hours prior to the intended breeding time. Spawning usually occurs in the morning. The eggs are laid as the bodies press together in the darkest corner among the plants. Remove the parents soon thereafter since they will eat the spawn. Several hundred eggs are laid which hatch 30-36 hours later, and the larvae are free-swimming a few days afterward. Feed the young with the finest feed (infusoria, rotifers, small nauplii).

F: O; undemanding: live, freeze-dried, frozen and vegetable foods. Flake and tablet foods.

Barbus toppini
Toppin's Barb

BOULENGER, 1916

Syn.: *Barbus umbeluziensis.*

Hab.: Africa; from the Umsunduzi River in Natal (South Africa) northward to Lake Chilwa, Malawi.

F.I.: 1981 (?).

Sex: ♂♂ are smaller and more slender with nodules on the snout; ♀♀ are larger and fuller.

Soc. B.: Peaceful, lively, schooling fish.

T: 22-26° C, **L:** 4 cm, **A:** 60 cm, **R:** m, b, **D:** 2
72-79° F, 1 2/3", 24",

M: Follow recommendations for *Barbus barilioides.*

B: No reports concerning a breeding success are available.

F: O; live food of any kind, any small replacement foods, flake food.

S: *Barbus toppini* is related to *B. barnardi* and *B. macrotaenia.* It has an incomplete lateral line and a pair of short barbels.

Barbus stoliczkanus

Barbus toppini

Barbus vittatus (DAY, 1865)
Sub-Fam.: Cyprininae

Syn.: *Puntius vittatus, Puntius sophore.*

Hab.: Southern India; in creeks, pools and rice paddies. Usually found in schools.

F.I.: 1904 by Mr. Köppe and K. Siggelkow, Hamburg.

Sex: ♂♂ are usually more slender and smaller than ♀♀.

Soc. B.: An undemanding, peaceful and gregarious fish. *B. vittatus* is calmer than other *Barbus* species. Juveniles live in dense schools, but adults are usually solitary.

M: Soft substrate with a lot of detritus; plant the edges with hardy vegetation, leaving plenty of free swimming space. No special demands are placed on the water; however, soft (to 10° dGH) and slightly acid (pH around 6.5) water is preferred.

B: 23-25° C (73-77° F); best to use one ♂ and two ♀♀. Provide a 20-30 l (5-8 gal) tank; soft to medium-hard (8-15° dGH) and slightly acid (pH 6-6.5) water. Requires a bottom of coarse gravel or plastic mesh to protect the eggs from being eaten. Actual spawning is preceded by an elaborate courtship and several false matings. About 300 sticky eggs are laid on the water plants. Remove the parents directly after spawning is completed. The young hatch in little more than one day and are raised with finest foods.

F: O; live food of any kind, flake food, lettuce, algae, etc.

S: Older specimens remain for a short time among the plants, twitching their fins. This is characteristic behavior for this species.

T: 20-24° C, L: 6 cm, A: 50 cm, R: m, D: 1-2
68-75° F, 2 1/3", 20",

Chela caeruleostigmata (SMITH, 1931)
Blue Hatchetfish
Sub-Fam.: Cultrinae

Syn.: *Laubuca caeruleostigmata, Chela mouhoti.*

Hab.: Southeast Asia; central Thailand, in the Menam Chao river system, Cambodia.

F.I.: Uncertain. The species was only positively identified in 1981.

Sex: The ♀♀ are thicker than the ♂♂.

Soc. B.: Peaceful schooling fish that likes to swim.

M: Needs ample, dense vegetation along the edges and the back of the tank; leave a lot of swimming room. Provide clear water with exchanges of 20% every 2 weeks. Water values: hardness 5-12° dGH, pH 6.5-7.0. *Chela caeruleostigmata* can be associated with *Brachydanio* species and is also suitable for the community tank.

B: 26-28° C (79-82° F). Water characteristics as mentioned above. The animals spawn at twilight. Water level of 10-15 cm (4"-6"); plant thickets of fine-leaved plants. 2 ♂♂ with 1 ♀. The ♀ should be placed in the set-up one to two days prior to the introduction of the ♂♂. The ♂ embraces the ♀, causing 30-40 eggs to be released. Many matings occur. The parents will not disturb the spawn. At 24° C (75° F) the fry hatch after approximately 24 hours and are free-swimming after an additional three to four days. Feed *Artemia* nauplii.

F: O; undemanding; live food of any kind (black mosquito larvae and insects blown onto the water surface*), vegetarian foods, flake food.

*Needed to bring the fish into spawning condition.

S: A few years ago *Chela caeruleostigmata* was erroneously named *Chela laubuca* or *Laubuca laubuca*. The genus *Chela* belongs to the sub-family Cultrinae which was separated from Abraminae in 1947.

T: 24-26° C, L: 6 cm, A: from 70 cm, R: t, m, D: 2
75-79° F, 2 1/3", from 28",

Barbus vittatus

Chela caeruleostigmata

Chela dadyburjori MENON, 1952
Dadyburjor's Hatchetfish, Orange Hatchetfish

Syn.: None.

Hab.: Southern India, Kerala.

F.I.: Cannot be determined due to repeated confusion with *Oxygaster* and *Laubuca* species.

Sex: ♂♂ more slender than ♀♀.

Soc. B.: Delicate schooling fish which only feels secure in a school of a dozen or more fishes. Marked surface fish.

M: Often described as frail. However, in an established aquarium, the species lives several years. The species depends on floating foods. Use the tank arrangement recommended for *Chela caeruleostigmata*.

B: Has been accomplished several times. The animals spawn among loose vegetation close to the water surface. *Ceratopteris, Nitella, Salvinia, Riccia* bundles and algae are suitable spawning mediums.

F: C; floating insects are a necessity for breeding. *Drosophila*, mayflies, mosquitoes, mosquito larvae; no worms!

S: The species name is often misspelled (*dadiburji, daduborjori*). It was named in honor of Sam Dadyburjor, a collaborator of the describer. Therefore, *Ch. dadyburjori* is the correct spelling.

T: 22-24° C, **L:** 4 cm, **A:** 60 cm, **R:** t, **D:** 3
72-75° F, 1 2/3", 24",

Chela fasciata SILAS, 1958
Striped Chela

Syn.: None.

Hab.: Southeast Asia; southern India, Annamalai River at the foot hills of the Annamalai Mountains close to Vannathurai.

F.I.: Definitely in 1980 by Avifauna, Krusaa/Denmark. Earlier photos exist, but the fish had been misidentified.

Sex: Presumably the ♀♀ are fuller bodied than the ♂♂.

Soc. B.: Schooling fish which should be kept in groups of at least six individuals. The species is rather shy. Keeping it with more outgoing species such as *Danio* and *Rasbora* species may help to counteract this behavior.

M: *Ch. fasciata* can be kept without problems in a community tank with smaller or equal sized fishes. Water up to about 12° dGH, pH around 7.0. Side and background vegetation conveys security to the fishes. They will then display themselves close to the water surface.

B: Unknown; presumably similar to *Chela caeruleostigmata*.

F: O; the species also accepts flake food. To keep the species healthy over extended periods of time, mosquito larvae (live or frozen) should be offered. Food is taken from the water surface.

S: The animals belong in the sub-genus *Allochela*. A very similar species, *Chela maassi* WEBER & DE BEAUFORT 1916, is known from Sumatra.

T: 22-26° C, **L:** 6 cm, **A:** 70 cm, **R:** t, m, **D:** 2
72-79° F, 2 1/3", 28",

Chela dadyburjori

Chela fasciata

Danio regina FOWLER, 1934
Queen Danio Sub-Fam.: Rasborinae

Syn.: None (?).

Hab.: Southeast Asia; southern Thailand, northern Malaysia.

F.I.: Unknown.

Sex: ♂ more slender and intensely colored; ♀ fuller and paler.

Soc. B.: Lively, active and peaceful schooling fish.

M: As described for *Chela caeruleostigmata.*

B: No reports about a success in an aquarium are available. Breeding is probably similar to *D. aequipinnatus* (compare Vol. 1, page 417).

F: O; live foods of any kind (mosquito larvae, *Tubifex*, water fleas, *Cyclops*), vegetable food (algae), flake food.

S: A black spot at the top of the gill slit is characteristic of *Danio regina* (see picture). The species is very similar to *D. aequipinnatus*, but as a whole, it is a higher backed fish.

T: 23-25° C, L: 13 cm, A: 80 cm, R: all, D: 2
73-77° F, 5", 31",

Eirmotus octozona SCHULTZ, 1959
Eight-Banded False Barb Sub-Fam.: Cyprininae

Syn.: None.

Hab.: Southeast Asia; Indonesia, Borneo.

F.I.: 1958.

Sex: ♂ more slender with reddish unpaired and ventral fins; ♀ much fuller during the spawning season with yellowish unpaired and ventral fins.

Soc. B.: Relatively quiet, undemanding and peaceful schooling fish.

M: Needs a tank with a dark substrate (lava, basalt) with densely planted sides and background, leaving enough open swimming room; use plants that are not too coarse and some floating ones to dim the light. Water to 12° dGH and around neutral (pH 7.0); perform regular water exchanges. Always keep a school of at least 6 individuals. House with other small and peaceful cyprinids.

B: No reports are available.

F: O; all types of small live food, plant food (algae), also flake food.

S: *Eirmotus octozona* is characterized by a large quantity of sensory pores in the head region and an incomplete lateral line. *Eirmotus* is a monotypic genus.

T: 24-26° C, L: 5 cm, A: 60 cm, R: b, D: 2
75-79° F, 2", 24",

Danio regina

Eirmotus octozona

Crossocheilus reticulatus FOWLER, 1934
Spotted Flying Fox Sub-Fam.: Garrinae

Syn.: None.

Hab.: Southeast Asia; Thailand.

F.I.: None known.

Sex: None known.

Soc. B.: No information available; assumably like other *Crossocheilus* species (see Vol. 1, pages 418-420).

M: Prefers a fine sand bottom; hiding places made of roots and stones; dense vegetation in parts; soft (around 5° dGH) and slightly acid (pH 6.5) water. Partial water changes (weekly one quarter of the tank volume) fosters the well-being of the species. Well-aerated tank.

B: Not yet accomplished in an aquarium.

F: H, O: aufwuchs; but also supplemental foods of animal origin, flake food.

T: 23-25° C, **L:** 14 cm, **A:** 100 cm, **R:** m, b, **D:** 1
73-77° F, 5 ", 39",

Esomus malayensis (no photo) AHL, 1923
Malayan Flying Barb Sub-Fam.: Rasborinae

Syn.: *Nuria danrica* var. *malayensis, Nuria malayensis.*

Hab.: Southeast Asia; Thailand, Malay Peninsula, in flowing and standing waters (lakes, pools, rice paddies).

Sex: ♂ is more slender with an almost straight ventral line; ♀ has a full, round ventral line. ♀♀ grow larger than ♂♂.

Soc. B.: Actively swimming fish which only form loose schools, if at all. The animals often claim a small territory and chase other fish away.

M: Provide long tanks with room to swim; dense edge vegetation; the swimming area divided with large plants. Water soft to medium-hard (5-12° dGH) and slightly acid to neutral (pH 6.5-7.0). Suitable for the community tank.

B: 24-28° C (75-82° F); arrange the breeding tank as for *Brachydanio* species (plenty of delicate plants, maximum water level 20 cm (8"), fresh water). Spawning usually occurs in sunny mornings among the plants. Each mating produces up to 50 eggs. The entire sequence lasts 60 to 90 minutes. Up to 700 eggs are laid. Feed the breeders while spawning, and remove them when spawning is complete. The fry hatch after 24 hours and can be reared with live and flake foods.

F: O; the animals are undemanding omnivores which take live food of any kind as well as vegetable fare and flake food.

S: The young are very sensitive against fluctuations in temperature, pH and hardness. The species grows very rapidly and is mature after 10-12 weeks.

T: 21-25° C, **L:** 8 cm, **A:** 70 cm, **R:** t, **D:** 1-2
70-77° F, 3", 28",

Crossocheilus reticulatus

Esomus malayensis? Probably *Esomus thermoicos*

Garra lamta (HAMILTON, 1822)

Syn.: *Cyprinus lamta, Discognathus lamta.*

Hab.: South Asia: India, Pakistan, Nepal.

F.I.: Could not be determined.

Sex: No external ones known.

Soc. B.: There is no information. It is probably similar to *Crossocheilus* species.

M: Follow recommendations for *Epalzeorhynchos coatesi.*

B: Not bred in an aquarium.

F: O; live foods of all kinds, but also accepts frozen, plant and flake foods.

S: None.

T: 24-26° C, **L:** 20 cm, **A:** 90 cm, **R:** b, (m), **D:** 2-3
75-79° F, 8", 35",

Garra cambodgiensis (TIRANT, 1834)
Siamese Stone-Lapping Fish

Syn.: *Cirrhina cambodgiensis, Garra spinosa, G. taeniatops, G. taeniata, G. fasciacauda.*

Hab.: Southeast Asia; Thailand, western Malaysia, Cambodia, Vietnam, Laos; Yunnan (China).

F.I.: 1967 (?).

Sex: None known.

Soc. B.: No information is available. It is probably similar to *Crossocheilus* species.

M: As listed for *Epalzeorhynchos coatesi.*

B: Breeding of *Garra cambodgiensis* has not been accomplished in an aquarium.

F: O; live food of all kinds, frozen, freeze-dried, vegetable (algae, lettuce) and flake foods.

T: 24-26° C, **L:** 15 cm, sexually mature at 7 cm, **A:** 100 cm, **R:** b, (m), **D:** 2
75-79° F, 6", sexually mature at 2 3/4", 39",

Garra lamta

Garra cambodgiensis, juv.

Garra cambodgiensis, adult

Epalzeorhynchos munensis (H.M. SMITH, 1934)

Syn.: *Labeo munensis*

Hab.: Southeast Asia; Thailand.

F.I.: 1953.

Sex: See Vol. 1, page 422.

Soc. B.: Territorial loner. They are often antagonistic among themselves, but normally peaceful towards heterospecifics.

M: Do not keep in excessively small tanks. The aquarium should have fine sand as a substrate and hiding places of roots and stones. Arrange the plants in a way so that the animals can claim territories without being in direct sight of their neighbors; offer plenty of free swimming room. Water soft to medium-hard (to 15° dGH) and around neutral (pH 7.0).

B: Has been successful in individual cases, but so far, these have been coincidences.

F: C, O; live foods of all kinds, freeze-dried food, vegetables (algae, lettuce, spinach), vegetable flakes.

S: The species pictured here was often identified as *Epalzeorhynchos erythrurus* (see also Vol. 1, page 422).

T: 22-26° C, **L:** > 50 cm, **A:** 200 cm, **R:** b, m, **D:** 2
72-79° F, > 20", 80",

Labeo forskalii RÜPPELL, 1853
Plain Shark

Syn.: None (?).

Hab.: Africa; in the drainage area of the Nile and the Blue Nile.

F.I.: 1935.

Sex: The first and last ray of the dorsal fin are elongated on the ♂.

Soc. B.: Aggressive and quarrelsome among themselves but peaceful towards heterospecifics. Larger specimens become loners that defend a territory.

M: Requires large tanks with sand substrate, and a few hiding places made with roots and stone plates. Plant the tank densely and in such a way as to allow the fish to form territories without being in direct sight of their neighbor. Leave some open swimming room. Water up to medium-hard (12-15° dGH) and around neutral (pH 7.0). Larger specimens are only conditionally suitable for the community tanks.

B: No information on a successful spawn is available. Spawning is probably only possible in large tanks.

F: O; live foods of any kind, freeze-fried and frozen foods, vegetable foods (algae, lettuce, spinach), flake food.

S: ELIAS (1972) reports in "Aquarienmagazin" **6**, 14 that *L. forskalii* "nibbles" on tankmates at night, thereby slightly injuring them.

T: 18-25° C, **L:** 35 cm, up to 20 cm in an aquarium, **A:** 120 cm, **R:** b, m, **D:** 2
64-77° F, 14", up to 8" in an aquarium, 47",

Epalzeorhynchos munensis

Labeo forskalii

Labeo parvus BOULENGER, 1902
Small Shark

Syn.: *Labeo walkeri, L. chariensis, L. obscurus, L. toboensis.*

Hab.: West Africa: Senegal, Mali, Niger, Burkina Faso (Upper Volta), Tschadsea.

F.I.: Cannot be determined.

Sex: No certain ones known.

Soc. B.: Very unsociable towards conspecifics as well as heterospecifics. Not a fish for the community aquarium.

M: See *Labeo variegatus.*

B: Breeding has not been successful in an aquarium.

F: O; live foods (insects and their larvae, small crustacea, worms of all kinds), plant foods (algae, lettuce), frozen foods, flake and tablet foods.

S: Rowdy.

T: 23-25° C, **L:** 45 cm, **A:** 100 cm, **R:** b, (m), **D:** 3
73-77° F, 18", 39",

Labeo variegatus PELLEGIN, 1926
Variegated Shark, Harlequin Shark

Syn.: *Labeo cyclorhynchus.*

Hab.: Africa; Zaire, upper Zaire River, Stanley Pool; Ogowe-River.

F.I.: Uncertain.

Sex: No sure ones known.

Soc. B.: The species is highly aggressive. It should therefore only be kept with fishes able to defend themselves.

M: Large, densely planted tanks; some roots as territory markers and shelter. Good aeration; water values are secondary, but extremes should be avoided.

B: The species has yet to be reproduced in an aquarium.

F: O; nonproblematic omnivore. The animals have large appetites.

S: None.

T: 21-27° C, **L:** 30 cm, **A:** 100 cm, **R:** b, m, **D:** 2
70-81° F, 12", 39",

Labeo parvus

Labeo variegatus

Labiobarbus leptocheila (VALENCIENNES in CURVIER & VALENCIENNES, 1842)
Long-Finned Shark

Syn.: *Dangila leptocheila.*

Hab.: Southeast Asia: Burma and Thailand.

F.I.: Uncertain.

Sex: Unknown. ♀♀ are probably fuller during the spawning season.

Soc. B.: Actively swimming, peaceful schooling fish.

M: As noted for *Labiobarbus festivus.*

B: Has not yet occurred in an aquarium.

F: O; live foods of all kinds, vegetable foods (lettuce, spinach, algae). Flake food.

S: Representatives of the genus *Labiobarbus* have a large dorsal fin consisting of 26 to 28 soft rays. No spines are in the dorsal fin. *Labiobarbus leptocheila* has 39 or 40 lateral line scales.

T: 24-26° C, L: 25 cm, A: 120 cm, R: m, b, D: 2-3
75-79° F, 10", 47",

Labiobarbus festivus (HECKEL, 1843)
Signal Barb, Festive Apollo Shark

Syn.: *Cyrene festiva, Dangila burmanica* (not DAY), *D. festiva.*

Hab.: Southeast Asia: Kalimantan (Borneo).

F.I.: Uncertain.

Sex: Unknown; ♂♂ are perhaps more slender and stronger colored than the ♀♀.

Soc. B.: Shy, active schooling fish.

M: The species needs large tanks. Moderate illumination and dense vegetation are recommended. Initially the fish are very shy; therefore, some hiding places (roots, stones) should be offered. Good filtration and regular water changes.

B: No reports concerning a successful spawn are known.

F: O; live food (bloodworms, *Tubifex*, water fleas, aquatic insects); vegetable foods (lettuce). The animals also feed on tender plants. When hungry, they accept flake food.

S: The genus name *Dangila* VALENCIENNES 1842 has been used for about one hundred years. SMITH (1945) discovered that the older genus name *Labiobarbus* VAN HASSELT, 1823 had been either overlooked or ignored. However, according to the laws of nomenclature, the older name has priority.

T: 24-26° C, L: 20 cm, A: 120 cm, R: m, b, D: 2-3
75-79° F, 8", 47",

Labiobarbus leptocheila

Labiobarbus festivus

Leptobarbus hoevenii (BLEEKER, 1851)
Red-finned Cigar Shark

Syn.: *Barbus hoevenii.*

Hab.: Southeast Asia; Thailand, Indonesia (Sumatra, Kalimantan/Borneo). The species inhabits freshwater.

F.I.: ?

Sex: No external ones known.

Soc. B.: Lively, quite peaceful schooling fish.

M: Because of its mature size, only juveniles are suitable for normal aquaria. It can only be kept in large aquaria. Substrate of sand or fine gravel. Dense side and background vegetation; perhaps some roots as decoration; leave some swimming space free. No special demands are placed on water quality. Hardness to 12° dGH and a pH around neutral (pH 7.0). *L. hoevenii* is a fish for large show aquaria.

B: Nothing known.

F: O; nonproblematic: live food of any kind, frozen food, crustacean meat and beef, vegetable foods, flake and tablet food.

S: The genus *Leptobarbus* differentiates itself from the other genera of Cyprinidae, among other things, by the wide head, four well developed barbels, spoon-shaped pharyngeal teeth arranged in three rows (5, 3, 2) and a continuous lateral line which extends to the lower part of the caudal peduncle.

T: 23-26° C, **L:** 50 cm, **A:** 120 cm, **R:** m, **D:** 3 (S)
73-79° F, 20", 47",

Leptobarbus melanotaenia BOULENGER, 1894

Syn.: None.

Hab.: Southeast Asia; Kalimantan (Borneo). The animals only live in freshwater.

F.I.: ?

Sex: No external ones known.

Soc. B.: Similar to *Leptobarbus hoevenii.*

M: As mentioned for *L. hoevenii.*

B: The species has not been bred.

F: O; live food of all kinds, vegetable food, crustacean meat, flake and tablet food.

S: *Leptobarbus melanotaenia* differs from *L. hoevenii* by having more scales vertically between the middle of the back and the middle of the stomach (5.5-1-4.5 vs. 4.5-1-3.5). In addition, all ages of *L. melanotaenia* have a black longitudinal band. Such a band only exists in juvenile *L. hoevenii*, disappearing with age.

T: 23-26° C, **L:** 25 cm, **A:** 100 cm, **R:** m, **D:** 2-3
73-79° F, 10", 39",

Leptobarbus hoevenii, adult

Leptobarbus hoevenii, juv.

Leptobarbus melanotaenia, juv.

Microrasbora erythromicron ANNANDALE, 1918
Cross-Banded Dwarf Rasbora, Emerald Dwarf Rasbora

Syn.: None.

Hab.: South Asia; Burma, in Lake Inlé and surrounding waters.

F.I.: 1978.

Sex: ♂ more intensely colored, thinner; ♀ paler, body strongly convex.

Soc. B.: Very peaceful, lively schooling fish.

M: Dense edge and background vegetation to help overcome its shyness. Use sand as substrate, some roots for decoration and leave lots of free swimming space. Water medium-hard to hard (10-25° dGH) and around neutral (pH 7.0). In water that is too soft, the colors fade and the fish becomes susceptible to disease. Best kept in a small group. It is possible to house them with other small, peaceful species.

B: Not difficult. The animals like to press against the plants while spawning; Java moss is especially appreciated. Rearing the young is accomplished with the finest foods (infusoria, rotifers, etc.). The spawn is more productive if the parents are removed upon completion.

F: O; small live foods of any kind, flake food.

S: *Microrasbora erythromicron* differs from *M. rubescens* by the number of lateral line scales (21-25 vs. 29-32). In addition, the pectoral fins of *M. rubescens* reach all the way back to the base of the ventral fins. In *M. erythromicron* the pectoral fins barely reach the base of the ventral fins.

T: 21-25° C, L: 3 cm, A: 50 cm, R: m, b, D: 3
70-77° F, 1 ", 20",

Microrasbora rubescens ANNANDALE, 1918
Reddish Dwarf Rasbora, Red-Lined Dwarf Rasbora

Syn.: None.

Hab.: South Asia; Burma, in Lake Inlé and surrounding water.

F.I.: 1962.

Sex: The ♂ is more slender and intensely colored; the ♀ is fuller and paler.

Soc. B.: Very peaceful, lively schooling fish.

M: Follow recommendations for *Microrasbora erythromicron.*

B: Parallels *M. erythromicron.* When the young are fed with suitably small foods, rearing is not particularly difficult.

F: O; finest live food, flake food.

S: *Microrasbora rubescens* is the type species for *Microrasbora.* Representatives of the genus lack barbels.

T: 21-25° C, L: 3 cm, A: 50 cm, R: b, m, D: 3
70-77° F, 1 ", 20",

Microrasbora erythromicron

Microrasbora rubescens

Notropis bifrenatus (COPE, 1866)
Shiner

Syn.: *Hybopsis bifrenatus, Hemitremia bifrenata.*

Hab.: North America; USA, from Massachusetts to Maryland, eastern Canada. The species is not numerous.

F.I.: ?

Sex: ♂♂ have larger fins.

Soc. B.: Very peaceful schooling fish.

M: As mentioned for *Erimyzon sucetta*. Always keep a school of at least eight animals.

B: As far as we know, the species has not been bred in Europe.

F: C, O; live food of all kinds (small crustaceans, mosquito larvae, *Tubifex*, Enchytraea), but also flake food.

S: None.

T: 6-20° C (coldwater fish), **L:** 5 cm, **A:** 60 cm, **R:** m, **D:** 2
43-68° F (coldwater fish), 2", 24",

Notropis hypselopterus (GÜNTHER, 1868)
Sailfin Shiner

Syn.: *Leuciscus hypselopterus, Alburnus formosus, Cliola hypseloptera, Notropis metallicus, Photogenis grandipinnis.*

Hab.: North America; USA, southern Georgia, Alabama and Florida.

F.I.: 1900 by H. Stüve, Hamburg.

Sex: The ♂♂ are more slender and colorful, with a black tipped dorsal fin; ♀♀ are somewhat plumper, paler and do not have a black tipped dorsal.

Soc. B.: Very peaceful, lively schooling fish.

M: *Notropis hypselopterus* should always be kept in a small school of at least six individuals. pH should not be above 7.0 (neutral). Leave lots of room for swimming.

B: As far as we know, *N. hyselopterus* has not been bred in Europe.

F: O; predominantly fine live food of any kind (small crustacea, mosquito larvae, *Tubifex*, Enchytraea, grindal worms). The animals also take flake food.

S: The fish are gorgeously colored during the breeding season.

T: 6-20° C (coldwater fish), **L:** 6 cm, **A:** 60 cm, **R:** m, **D:** 2
43-68° F (coldwater fish), 2 1/3", 24",

Notropis bifrenatus

Notropis hypselopterus

Osteochilus melanopleura (no photo) (BLEEKER, 1852)

Syn.: *Rohita melanopleura.*

Hab.: Southeast Asia; Indonesia (Kalimantan/Borneo, Sumatra), Malaysia, Thailand.

F.I.: Unknown.

Sex: Unknown. The ♀♀ are probably fuller during the spawning season.

Soc. B.: Active swimmer, agile and peaceful schooling fish.

M: Dark substrate of fine-grade material (ground lava). The substrate should be well washed, because the fish work the ground for food. Requires dense edge and background vegetation; create hiding places of roots and/or stones. Enough free swimming space should remain available. Water soft (5-8° dGH) and slightly acid (pH around 6.5). Twenty-five percent weekly water exchanges should be performed. Combine with species that place similar demands.

B: It seems breeding has not yet been successful in an aquarium, because corresponding reports are missing.

F: O; live food of all kinds, vegetable supplement, frozen food, but also flake food.

S: *Osteochilus melanopleura* is one of the largest species within the genus, probably the largest. We are seeking for a photo. Who can have?

T: 22-26° C, **L:** 40 cm, **A:** 120 cm, **R:** m, b, **D:** 3 (S)
72-79° F, 16", 47",

Cirrhinus macrosemion (FOWLER, 1935)

Syn.: *Osteochilus macrosemion.*

Hab.: Southeast Asia; central Thailand.

F.I.: Unknown.

Sex: No external ones known.

Soc. B.: Lively and peaceful species, which forms groups or schools.

M: As recommended for *Osteochilus melanopleura.*

B: There are no reports about a successful spawn.

F: O; live food of all kinds, plant food, flake food.

S: *Cirrhinus macrosemion* is characterized by its nostril barbels, two rows of large pores on the front of the snout and approximately 44 short gill rakers on the anterior arm of the first gill arch.

T: 22-26° C, **L:** 22 cm, **A:** 100 cm, **R:** m, b, **D:** 2-3
72-79° F, 8 3/4", 39",

Cirrhinus molitorella, Vol. 3, page 250

Osteochilus microcephalus?

Parachela maculicauda (H.M. SMITH, 1934)
Glass Barb

Syn.: *Chela maculicauda.*

Hab.: Southeast Asia; Thailand, Indonesia (Sumatra, Borneo, Java).

F.I.: 1929.

Sex: ♀♀ are fuller, at least during the spawning season; there are no differences in pigmentation.

Soc. B.: Peaceful and lively schooling fish.

M: Use recommendations for *Chela* species.

B: No reports about a successful spawn are available.

F: C, O; live food of all kinds, but also freeze-dried food, frozen and flake food.

T: 24-26° C, L: 14 cm, A: 100 cm, R: m, D: 2-3
75-79° F, 5", 39",

River in Sarawak, northern Borneo. This is home to *P. oxygastroides* and many other ornamentals.

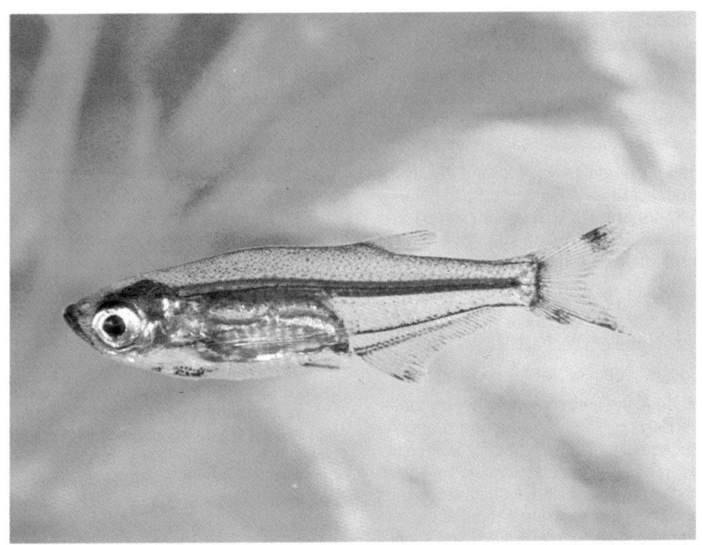

Parachela maculicauda

Paralaubuca typus (no text)

Rasbora argyrotaenia (no photo) (BLEEKER, 1850)
Black-Edged Rasbora Sub-Fam.: Rasborinae

Syn.: *Leuciscus argyrotaenia, L. cyanotaenia, L. schwenkii, Opsarius argyrotaenia, Rasbora buchanani* (not BLEEKER), *R. vaillanti, Parluciosoma argyrotaenia.*

Hab.: Southeast Asia; Thailand, Malaysia, Indonesia (Java, Sumatra, Kalimantan = Borneo) and Philippines (Busuanga and Palawan islands). The species is said to also occur in China and Japan.

F.I.: 1913, then again in 1970.

Sex: ♂ smaller and more slender, with an almost straight ventral line.

Soc. B.: Peaceful, lively schooling fish.

M: Keep the animals in long, roomy tanks, densely planted along the edges and the background, leave space for swimming; perhaps floating plants should be added to dim the light. Sandy substrate; several bogwood roots for decoration. Water medium-hard (around 10° dGH) and slightly acid to neutral (pH 6.5-7.0). Always keep a school; association with other lively fishes is possible.

B: Breeding is easy. In several ways it resembles *Rasbora daniconius*. A detailed breeding report is offered by LÜBECK (1972): Aquarien Terrarien **19**, 262-263. The species is very productive; two thousand offspring from one set-up are not rare.

F: O; live food of any kind, vegetable foods, also flake and tablet food.

S: Several sub-species and local morphs of *R. argyrotaenia* are known. The best known is *Rasbora argyrotaenia everetti* BOULENGER, which occurs in the Philippines. It differs from *R. a. argyrotaenia* (BLEEKER, 1850) by its relatively smaller eye, more slender body and a higher number of lateral line scales and pectoral fin rays.

T: 20-26° C, **L:** 12 cm, **A:** 100 cm, **R:** m, t, **D:** 1
68-79° F, 4 3/4", 39",

Lagowskiella czekanowskii (DYBOWSKI, 1869)
Czekanowski's Dace Sub-Fam.: Leuciscinae

Syn.: *Phoxinus strauchi, P. sublaevis, P. czekanowskii.*

Hab.: Asia; Soviet Union, in the rivers which flow into the Artic Ocean; from the Kara River to the Kolyma, Amur basin.

F.I.: Has yet to be imported into Germany.

Sex: Difficult to determine; ♀♀ grow larger and thicker.

Soc. B.: Lively, peaceful schooling fish which can be kept with other coldwater fishes.

M: Needs a bottom of coarse sand or gravel; some stones for decoration. Provide long tanks with plenty of swimming space;edge and background plantings of appropriate coldwater species. Fresh water (clear and clean), good oxygenation; medium-hard to hard (10-20° dGH) water with a pH between 7.0 and 7.5 is suggested.

B: In western magazines there are no reports dealing with successful breeding in an aquarium. Reproduction is probably not very difficult and similar to *Phoxinus phoxinus* (compare Vol. 1).

F: C; live food: insect larvae, small crustacea, fairy shrimp, *Tubifex* and Enchytraea.

S: Several sub-species of *Lagowskiella czekanowskii* have been described. This is a very close relative of the swamp dace, *Phoxinus percnurus*. It differs from *P. percnurus* by its more elongated body.

T: 16-20° C, **L:** ♂ 6 cm, ♀ 9.5 cm, **A:** 80 cm, **R:** t, m, **D:** 2
61-68° F, ♂ 2 1/3", ♀ 3 3/4", 31",

Rasbora cephalotaenia, page 412/413

Lagowskiella czekanowskii

Rhodeus ocellatus (KNER, 1867)
Hong Kong Bitterling
Sub-Fam.: Rhodeinae

Syn.: *Pseudoperilampus ocellatus, P. lighti, Rhodeus wangkinfui.*

Hab.: East Asia; China, Taiwan (Formosa).

F.I.: Cannot be determined.

Sex: ♂ is significantly more colorful at spawning time; ♀ has an ovipositor during the spawning season.

Soc. B.: Gregarious, lively, peaceful fish which cares for its spawn.

M: Use fine sand on the bottom, dense vegetation and maintain open swimming space. Water not too hard (10-15° dGH) and about neutral (pH 7.0).

B: A successful spawn was reported by Andreas Schneider, Rüsselsheim, Germany (written communication): the set-up consisted of one ♂, five ♀♀ and a number of freshwater mussels. In a larger tank more ♂♂ can be used, but it has to be taken into account that they claim territories. Many hiding places (dense vegetation, stones) are necessary for the set-up. A ♂ chooses a mussel, it then draws attention by displaying and showing intense spawning coloration. If a ♀ comes, he circles her and gently pushes the ♀. Unwilling ♀♀ are bitten. The ♀ deposits her eggs into a mussel with the ovipositor. The ♂ then fertilizes the eggs. Three to four eggs develop in the mussel. Later, the young are expelled by the mussel. If the mussel is disturbed too early, immature embryos are expelled which cannot yet survive. The following values were measured in the aquarium: 22° dGH, pH 7.8, temperature 19-24° C (66-75° F).

F: O; live foods of any kind; frozen, vegetable, and flake foods.

S: The spawning behavior of *Rhodeus ocellatus* is similar to the native German bitterling *Rhodeus amarus* (see Vol. 1, page 442).

T: 18-24° C, L: 12 cm, A: 70 cm, R: m, b, D: 2-3
64-75° F, 4 3/4", 28",

Pseudorasbora parva (SCHLEGEL, 1842)
Sub-Fam.: Gobioninae

Syn.: *Leuciscus parvus, Fundulichthys virescens, Fundulus virescens, Leuciscus pusillus, Micraspius mianowskii, Pseudorasbora altipinna, P. depressirostris, P. fowleri, P. monstrosa, P. pusilla.*

Hab.: Introduced 1961 in Romania (Ialomita River), it spread in the Danube upstream to Austria. Found 1970 in Hungary (Balaton). In the CSFR in the rivers Tisza, Chlaba and Ilpa. In Thüringen in the White Elster at Gera. Even found in the Teutoburger Forrest and in the Rhein.

F.I.: Unknown.

Sex: No sure differences in coloration are known. Sexually mature ♂♂ display nodules below the eyes and around the mouth, and in addition, they are larger than the ♀♀.

Soc. B.: Peaceful schooling fish which, despite its different origin, can be kept together with similar European species. The ♂♂ guard the spawn.

M: Needs large, roomy aquaria with a lot of free swimming space. Dense side and back vegetation appeals to the animals. No special demands are placed on the water (hardness to 15° dGH, pH around 7.0).

B: No information on a successful aquarium spawn is available. In nature the spawning season stretches from May to August, depending on origin. One ♀ spawns several times per season. The eggs are attached to stones. They are guarded by the ♂. A ♀ lays up to 3000 cylindrical eggs that measure about 1.4 x 1.8 mm (1/16"). At temperatures of 15-18° C (59-64° F) they hatch after 12 days, at 21-23° C (70-73° F) in 5-7 days. After another five days the egg sac is absorbed and the young feed on plankton.

F: O; live food of any kind, frozen food, flake food.

S: A plain, rarely imported fish.

T: 14-22° C, L: 11 cm, A: 80 cm, R: m, b, D: 2
57-72° F, 4 1/3", 31",

Rhodeus ocellatus

Pseudorasbora parva

Pseudorasbora pumila MIYADI, 1930
Sub-Fam.: Gobioninae

Syn.: None.

Hab.: Asia; Japan: northern and central Hondo.

F.I.: Probably not yet imported into Germany.

Sex: Little difference; ♂♂ grow somewhat larger.

Soc. B.: Similar to *Pseudorasbora parva*.

M: As indicated for *P. parva*.

B: No reports are available for a successful aquarium spawn in Europe. The reproductive biology is likely to be similar to *P. parva*.

F: O; live foods of all kinds. Frozen, freeze-dried and flake foods.

S: Besides the nominal form *Pseudorasbora pumila pumila* MIYADI, 1930, the subspecies *P. pumila uchidai* OKADA & KUBOTA, 1957 has also been described. It occurs in central Hondo. *P. pumila* is very similar to *P. parva*, but is smaller and has an incomplete lateral line.

T: 15-20° C, **L:** ♂ 8 cm, ♀ 7 cm, **A:** 70 cm, **R:** b, m, **D:** 2
59-68° F, ♂ 3", ♀ 2³/₄", 28",

Opsaridium zambezense (PETERS, 1852)
Zambesi Barilius
Sub-Fam.: Cyprininae

Syn.: *Leuciscus zambezensis, Barilius boweni, B. neavii, B. peringueyi, B. stephensoni, B. stevensoni, B. zambezensis.*

Hab.: Africa; upper Kasai Zambesi, Okovango, Pungwe, Limpopo and Buzi river systems and south to the Pongolo River.

F.I.: Unknown.

Sex: No sure ones known. ♀♀ are fuller during spawning season.

Soc. B.: Active swimming, peaceful schooling fish.

M: Substrate of sand or fine gravel; edge and background vegetation; use long aquaria with plenty of swimming room. Hardness 8-12° dGH, pH slightly acid to neutral (pH 6.5-7.0). The animals should always be kept in a school (six or more specimens). Cover the tank well, as the animals are good jumpers.

B: No reports are yet available about a successful spawn in an aquarium.

F: C; live food of all kinds, especially floating foods; flake food.

S: This species can easily be identified by its large mouth.

T: 24-26° C, **L:** 16 cm, **A:** from 120 cm, **R:** m, t, **D:** 2
75-79° F, 6¹/₃", from 47",

Pseudorasbora pumila

Opsaridium zambezense

Rasbora axelrodi BRITTAN, 1976
Axelrod's Rasbora

Syn.: None.

Hab.: Indonesia; Sumatra.

F.I.: 1976 (1977).

Sex: ♂♂ are more intensely and splendidly colored.

Soc. B.: Peaceful, lively schooling fish.

M: Follow suggestions for *Rasboroides vaterifloris* (see on page 422). *Rasbora axelrodi* is only conditionally suitable for the community aquarium! Associate only with species of equal size and temperament.

T: 23-26° C, L: 3 cm, A: 50 cm, R: m, D: 2
73-79° F, 1 ", 20",

B: Surely possible, but no reports are yet available.

F: Small live foods of all kinds, flake food.

S: *Rasbora axelrodi* is one of the few *Rasbora* species that lack the entire lateral line. It differs from the others by its brilliant and unique coloration.

Rasbora brittani AXELROD, 1976
Brittan's Rasbora

Syn.: None.

Hab.: Southeast Asia; Malaysia, in Johore River; Sumatra.

F.I.: Uncertain; probably only after 1980.

Sex: ♂ more slender; ♀ fuller, with a more convex ventral line.

Soc. B.: Lively, peaceful schooling fish.

M: Needs a long tank with a dark bottom of fine sand, dense side and background vegetation and plenty of free swimming space. Water slightly acid (pH 6.0-6.5) and up to medium-hard (12° dGH); perhaps peat filtration. Keep together with fishes having similar demands.

T: 23-26° C, L: 6 cm, A: 70 cm, R: m, t, D: 2
73-79° F, 2 1/3", 28",

B: No reports about a successful spawn in an aquarium are yet available. Probably similar to *Rasbora trilineata* (compare Vol. 1).

F: O; live foods of any kind, freeze-dried, frozen and flake foods.

S: *Rasbora brittani* can be distinguished from all other *Rasbora* species by its precaudal spot which is outlined in orange.

Rasbora axelrodi

Rasbora brittani ♀

Rasbora caudimaculata VOLZ, 1903
Greater Scissortailed Rasbora

Syn.: *Rasbora dorsimaculata, R. layangi.*

Hab.: Southeast Asia; Indonesia (Sumatra). Malaysia, Thailand; also in Kalimantan (Borneo).

F.I.: 1961 (?).

Sex: ♂ more slender with a yellowish anal fin, tips of the caudal fin lobes distinctly white; ♀ fuller, plain.

Soc. B.: Very active, peaceful schooling fish.

M: As recommended for *Rasbora rasbora*. An ample aquarium is needed because of its liveliness. No special demands are placed on the water values. Suitable for the community tank. Well covered tank, since they are good jumpers.

T: 20-26° C, **L:** 12 cm, **A:** 100 cm, **R:** t, m, **D:** 2
68-79° F, 4¾", 39",

B: No detailed breeding reports are available. Reproduction is probably similar to other *Rasbora* species from the same general area.

F: O; live food of any kind, plant food, flake food.

S: According to BRITTAN (1954), *Rasbora caudimaculata* belongs together with *R. trilineata* STEINDACHNER, 1870 and *R. dorsiocellata* DUNCKER, 1904 in the *caudimaculata* group. The predominant characteristic of the species in this group is the fainter dark lateral band, the anterior edge of the dorsal fin exactly above the center of the base of the pelvic fin and the occurrence of striking dark designs on dorsal and caudal fins.

Rasbora cephalotaenia (BLEEKER, 1852)
Porthole Rasbora

Syn.: *Leuciscus cephalotaenia, Rasbora tornieri, Parluciosoma cephalotaenia.*

Hab.: Southeast Asia; western Kalimantan (Borneo), eastern Sumatera (Sumatra), Bangka, Belitung, Malay Peninsula. The species inhabits flowing (lotic) and standing (lentic) waters.

F.I.: 1959 by Toni Dunker, Hilden, of Sumatra.

Sex: ♂♂ are much more slender; ♀♀ have a strongly convex ventral line.

Soc. B.: Peaceful, spirited schooling fish.

M: Best kept in long, shallow tanks (from 20 cm; 8"). Provide a sandy bottom, dense side and background vegetation as resting places. Leave lots of free swimming space since the fish is an avid swimmer. Medium-hard (10-15° dGH) and slightly acid (pH 6.0-6.5) water. Use peat filtration to acidify the water. Always keep six or more individuals.

B: 25-26° C (77-79° F); soft (around 5° dGH) and slightly acid (pH 6.5) water. Breeding is best accomplished in a separate 30-40 l (8-10 gal) tank. Plant the tank with fine-leaved species (*Vesicularia, Cabomba, Myriophyllum*, etc.). After passionate chasing, the fish lay their eggs (usually around 100) among the plants. Remove the parents after the eggs are laid since they will eat the spawn. Depending on temperature, the eggs hatch after 24 to 48 hours. Infusoria and micro food are given initially; after one week *Artemia* nauplii can be fed. Frequent partial water changes of a fifth to a quarter total volume every one to two days are advantageous.

F: O; live foods (small crustaceans, mosquito larvae, *Tubifex*, grindal worms), minced crustacean meat, some vegetable foods; flake food is also taken.

Continued on page 414.

Rasbora caudimaculata

Rasbora cephalotaenia

Rasbora daniconius (HAMILTON, 1822)
Golden-Striped Rasbora

Syn.: *Cyprinus daniconius, Opsarius daniconius, Rasbora neilgherriensis, Rasbora zanzibariensis, Parluciosoma daniconius.*

Hab.: Asia: Thailand, Burma, western part of India, Sri Lanka (Ceylon).

F.I.: 1910.

Sex: ♂♂ are more slender, smaller, with a yellowish or reddish stomach: ♀ stronger, larger, whitish stomach, fins transparent to yellowish.

Soc. B.: Peaceful, lively schooling fish. Associate with other *Rasbora*, *Brachydanio* or small *Barbus* species. Never keep less than 6-10 individuals. Single specimens waste away.

M: Needs a medium sized aquarium with dense vegetation to offer the fishes numerous hiding places while preserving swimming room. The fish like direct sunlight. Easy to keep.

B: Relatively easy, successful in pairs as well as schools. Comparatively productive. Do not use a breeding tank that is too small(at least 50 x 25 x 25 cm; 20" x 10" x 10"). If the tank is too small, the nondeveloping eggs and "left over" sperm spoil the water. Water up to 12° dGH, pH around 7. The fish spawn in the early morning hours among fine-leaved plants close to the water surface. The young hatch after 3 to 4 days and are already relatively large. Feed after another 3 days with *Cyclops* nauplii. Growth is quite fast. Frequent water changes further their well-being and hereby contribute to fast development.

F: C, O; live foods: *Cyclops*, *Daphnia*, mosquito larvae as well as flake food.

S: Relatively plain species which is rarely kept. In the latter years probably only the smaller sub-species *R. daniconius labiosa* MUKERJI, 1935 has been cultivated. In comparison to the nominal form, it has fat, fleshy lips, a more slender, mostly cylindrical body, smaller round fins and a reduced lateral line (L. lat. 23 to 31 instead of 30 to 33).

T: 24-26° C, **L:** 10 cm, 6 cm for *R. daniconius labiosa,* **A:** 80 cm, **R:** t, m, **D:** 1
75-79° F, 4", 2 1/3" for *R. daniconius labiosa,* 31",

Continuation of *Rasbora cephalotaenia*:

S: According to BRITTAN (1954): A revision of the Indo-Malayan freshwater fish genus *Rasbora*, pages 153-157, *Rasbora cephalotaenia* belongs to the "*einthovenii*" group. Other members include the following species: *Rasbora einthovenii* (BLEEKER, 1851), *R. tubbi* BRITTAN, 1954 and *R. jacobsoni* WEBER & DE BEAUFORT, 1916. All species of this group have a complete lateral line.

T: 22-24° C, **L:** 14 cm, usually smaller in an aquarium, **A:** 100 cm, **R:** t, m, **D:** 2
72-75° F, 5 ", usually smaller in an aquarium, 39",

Rasbora daniconius daniconius

Rasbora daniconius labiosa or *Rasbora caverii*?

Rasbora einthovenii (BLEEKER, 1851)
Long-Band Rasbora

Syn.: *Leuciscus einthovenii, Rasbora cephalotaenia* (not BLEEKER), *R. vegae.*

Hab.: Southeast Asia; west Malaysia, Singapore, Sumatra, Borneo, Bangka, Belitung; in flowing and standing waters.

F.I.: 1909 by "Vereinigten Zierfischzüchtereien" in Conradshöhe by Berlin.

Sex: ♂ more slender and somewhat smaller; ♀ with fuller body and strongly convex ventral line. Outside the spawning season the sexes are practically indistinguishable.

Soc. B.: Active swimmers and peaceful schooling fish.

M: Tank with fine sand as substrate; dense side and rear vegetation, lots of free swimming space. Provide hiding places of plants and bogwood roots. Well covered tanks, because the fish are good jumpers. Use water values recommended under B. An undemanding fish suitable for the community tank with other peaceful fishes.

B: 25-28° C (77-82° F); water slightly acid (pH 6.0-6.5) and soft (around 5° dGH). Breeding tank with dense vegetation. The ♀ initiates the courtship. Spawns among plants, similar to *Brachydanio* species. The young hatch after 36 hours and are fed *Artemia* nauplii.

F: O; live foods of all kinds (mosquito larvae, small crustacea, *Tubifex*). The fish also eat flake food.

S: The closest relatives of *Rasbora einthovenii* are *Rasbora jacobsoni* WEBER & DE BEAUFORT, 1916 and *Rasbora cephalotaenia* (BLEEKER, 1852).

T: 22-25° C, L: 8,5 cm, but usually smaller, A: 60 cm, R: t, m, D: 1-2
72-77° F, 3 1/3", but usually smaller, 24",

Rasbora paviei TIRANT, 1885

Syn.: None.

Hab.: Southeast Asia; Malayan Archipelago.

F.I.: Unknown.

Sex: ♂ slenderer, somewhat smaller and more intensely colored. ♀ has a stronger convex ventral line and is much fuller during the spawning season.

Soc. B.: Active, peaceful schooling fish.

M: As recommended for *Rasbora rasbora.* The animals should be offered ample, well-planted aquaria which offer plenty of free swimming space. Suitable for the community tank.

B: 26-28° C (79-82° F); probably spawned successfully in an aquarium, but no reports are yet available.

F: O; live foods of any kind, vegetable and flake foods.

T: 22-25° C, L: 6 cm, A: 80 cm, R: m, t, D: 2
72-77° F, 2 1/3", 31",

Rasbora einthovenii

Rasbora paviei

Rasbora rasbora (HAMILTON, 1822)
Ganges Rasbora

Syn.: *Cyprinus rasbora, Leuciscus rasbora R. buchanani.*

Hab.: South and southeast Asia; northern India, Burma. The area of distribution is located in the Ganges region and in Burma.

F.I.: 1913.

Sex: ♂ more slender. ♀ with stronger curved ventral line.

Soc. B.: Peaceful, lively schooling fish.

M: Densely planted tank; leave plenty of swimming space; perhaps floating plants to dim the light. Strong sunlight should be avoided. Some roots for decoration, soft bottom (sand with a layer of mulm). Water not too hard (10° dGH) and weakly acid (pH 6.0-6.5). Perform regular water changes (a quarter of the volume every week). The species is suitable for the community tank.

B: No reports about a successful spawn are available, however, it is likely to be similar to other *Rasbora* species from the same area.

F: O; live foods of all kinds, freeze-dried, frozen, flake foods.

S: *Rasbora daniconius* is the only species with comparable morphometric values to *R. rasbora*. *R. rasbora* has only 1 or 1 scales between the lateral line and the base of the ventral fins and 12 rows of scales around the caudal peduncle, while *R. daniconius* has 2 or 2 and 14, respectively.

T: 20-25° C, **L:** 10 cm, **A:** 80 cm, **R:** all, **D:** 2
68-77° F, 4", 31",

Rasbora reticulata WEBER & DE BEAUFORT, 1915
Net Rasbora

Syn.: None.

Hab.: Southeast Asia; western Sumatra and on the island Nias, which is located off the west coast of Sumatra. Habitats from Indochina are very doubtful.

F.I.: 1974 by Edith Korthaus, Hagen (Dahl).

Sex: ♂ more slender; ♀ is more rounded in the ventral region during the spawning season.

Soc. B.: Peaceful, lively schooling fish.

M: Follow suggestions for *Rasbora rasbora* or *Rasbora cephalotaenia*.

B: After active pursuit, spawning occurs among plants.

F: O; live food of appropriate size, vegetable foods, flake food.

S: Due to its isolated distribution it is not easy to classify the relationship of *Rasbora reticulata*. BRITTAN (1954) considers it probable that the species is a descendent of the *trifasciata* group. Also see "Das Aquarium" 7/74.

T: 22-26° C, **L:** 6 cm, **A:** 70 cm, **R:** m, t, **D:** 2
72-79° F, 2⅓", 28",

Rasbora rasbora

Rasbora reticulata

Rasbora sumatrana (BLEEKER, 1852)
Sumatran Rasbora

Syn.: *Leuciscus sumatranus, Rasbora aurotaenia, R. cheroni, R. cromei, R. calliura, R. hosii, R. lateristriata* var. *trifasciata* (not POPTA), *R. paviana, R. sumatrensis, R. trilineata* (not STEINDACHNER).

Hab.: Southeast Asia; Malay Peninsula, Kalimantan (Borneo), Thailand.

F.I.: ?

Sex: ♂♂ are more slender.

Soc. B.: Lively, peaceful schooling fish.

M: Keeping the species in an aquarium is nonproblematic. Follow the recommendations made for other large *Rasbora* species.

B: Unknown thus far.

F: O; live foods of all kinds, vegetable supplement, frozen food, flake food.

S: The systematic relationships of the *sumatrana-elegans* group within the genus *Rasbora* are not yet definite.

T: 23-25° C, **L**: 13 cm, **A**: 100 cm, **R**: t, m, **D**: 1
73-77° F, 5", 39",

Rasbora gracilis KOTTELAT, 1991
Black-Striped Rasbora

Syn.: *Rasbora agilis* (non AHL), *Rasbora taeniata* (non AHL).

Hab.: Southeast Asia; west Malaysia, Sumatra and Belitung.

F.I.: 1913 by Scholze & Pötzschke Co., Berlin.

Sex: ♂ with an almost straight abdomen, tail fin yellowish-red; ♀ rounder, a mat orange tail fin.

Soc. B.: Peaceful, lively schooling fish.

M: As indicated for *R. cephalotaenia*. Fresh additions of water every once in a while helps keep *R. gracilis* healthy. Always keep a school, or they become shy. Some floating plants to dim the light. Best kept with other *Rasbora* and *Barbus* species.

B: 25-28° C (77-82° F); breeding tank with low water level (15 cm; 6") and floating plants to dim the light. Water not too hard (up to 10° dGH) and slightly acid to neutral (pH 6.5-7.0); additions of fresh water. Spawning usually occurs several days after being placed in the breeding tank. *Rasbora gracilis* does not pursue the ♀♀ excessively. Remove parent fish after spawning has been completed. The young hatch after 36 hr and are fed finest micro food or ground flake food.

F: O; live foods, flake food, freeze-dried foods and vegetable supplements (algae).

S: According to BRITTAN (1954), *Rasbora chrysotaenia* and *Rasbora pauciperforata* are the closest relatives of *R. gracilis*.

T: 22-24° C, **L**: 7 cm, **A**: 60 cm, **R**: m, t, **D**: 1-2
72-75° F, 2¾", 24",

Oreichthys sp. (no text)

Rasbora sumatrana, adult

Rasbora gracilis

Rasboroides vaterifloris (DERANIYAGALA, 1930)

Singhalese Fire Barb, Orange Finned Barb

Syn.: *Rasbora vaterifloris.*

Hab.: Southeast Asia; Sri Lanka, in the Kaluganga River.

F.I.: 1936 by Werner Ladiges, Hamburg.

Sex: ♂ more slender, nicer colored and with orange or reddish fins; ♀ fuller, with yellowish fins.

Soc. B.: A peaceful, active swimmer which forms loose schools.

M: Dark substrate; dense vegetation consisting of cryptocorynes and some fine-leaved plants; free swimming room should be available. Water soft (up to 5° dGH) and slightly acid (pH around 6.5). Needs warmth. Associate with *Rasbora* species which have similar demands.

T: 25-29° C, **L**: 4 cm, **A**: 50 cm, **R**: m, **D**: 3
77-84° F, 1²/₃", 20",

B: 26-30° C (79-86° F); not very easy; heavily planted breeding tank. The ♂ strongly pursues the ♀♀. Spawning occurs in the plant thicket. Lower the water level after spawning to 15 cm (6"). The young hatch after 36 hours and are then fed with micro food or crumbled flake food.

F: O; live foods of any kind, vegetable supplements, flake food.

S: *Rasbora vaterifloris* has the shortest lateral line of any *Rasbora* species. There are only 3 or 4 lateral line scales on each side.

Rasbora vulgaris (?)

Syn.: None.

Hab.: Southeast Asia; so far the species is only known from the island of Labuan, which is located a few miles off the coast of northern Borneo (Kalimantan).

F.I.: Probably only after 1970.

Sex: ♂ more slender; ♀ is thicker, especially during the spawning season, with a strongly convex ventral line.

Soc. B.: Peaceful, active schooling fish.

M: As indicated for *Rasbora cephalotaenia.*

B: Has not yet been bred in an aquarium.

F: Live foods of all kinds, vegetable supplements (algae). Frozen and flake foods.

S: *Rasbora vulgaris* is very rare. It is related to the *Rasbora pauciperforata* group

T: 22-26° C, **L**: 6 cm, **A**: 60 cm, **R**: m, t, **D**: 2
72-79° F, 2¹/₃", 24",

Rasboroides vaterifloris

Rasbora vulgaris (?)

Rhinichthys cataractae (VALENCIENNES, 1842)
Longnose Dace

Syn.: *Gobio cataractae, Argyreus nasutus, Ceratichthys cataractae, Leuciscus nasutus, Rhinichthys marmoratus, R. nasutus.*

Hab.: North America; in northeast USA from New England to Virginia and Wisconsin, eastern Canada. The fish inhabits clear and fast flowing waters.

F.I.: Unknown, it has probably not been imported into Germany.

Sex: No external ones known.

Soc. B.: They are not pronounced schooling fishes. However, they are always moving.

M: Use coarse gravel on the tank bottom with stones of varying sizes as shelters and hiding places; aquaria with a large base (from 120 x 50 cm; 47" x 20"). The water does not need to be deep (20 cm; 8"). Plant current-loving, coldwater plants sparsely. Produce a strong current with a pump. If possible, simulate a small waterfall. Water cold and clear, pH around 7 and medium-hard (10-15° dGH). Always keep several individuals (at least 6).

B: As far as we know, it has not been accomplished in an aquarium.

F: Live foods (mosquito larvae, small crustacea, *Tubifex*, Enchytraea, small earthworms), crustacean meat (shrimp) and also flake food on occasion.

S: Two sub-species of *Rhinichthys cataractae* have been described: *R. cataractae cataractae* (VALENCIENNES, 1842) and *R. cataractae dulcis* (GIRARD, 1856). This sub-species has a more western distribution.

T: 4-16° C (coldwater fish), **L:** 10 cm, **A:** 120 cm, **R:** b, **D:** 3
39-61° F (coldwater fish), 4", 47",

Sawbwa resplendens ANNANDALE, 1918
Nacked Microrasbora

Syn.: None.

Hab.: South Asia; Burma, in Lake Inlé and the surrounding swamps.

F.I.: 1962.

Sex: The ♂ is red through the head and tail fin area. This coloration is missing on the ♀.

Soc. B.: Peaceful, lively schooling fish.

M: Dense edge and background vegetation. Bottom of gravel or sand, leave free swimming space. Water around neutral (pH 7.0) and medium-hard to hard (10-25° dGH). In soft water the colors fade and the fish become sensitive. Best kept in a small school. Keep together with other small peaceful species.

B: Similar to *Microrasbora* species. The young are very small and initially need finest foods (infusoria, rotifers, etc.). Other than this, it is not difficult to breed.

F: O; small live food of all kinds, flake food.

S: The body is totally naked (no scales).

T: 21-25° C, **L:** 4 cm, **A:** 50 cm, **R:** m, b, **D:** 3
70-77° F, 1⅔", 20",

Rhinichthys cataractae

Sawbwa resplendens ♂ bottom, ♀ top

Crossostoma tinkhami HERRE, 1934
Funkien Hillstream Loach

Syn.: *Formosiana tinkhami.*

Hab.: East Asia; China, Fukien Province (Fuching-ksien, Chung-an-ksien).

F.I.: Unknown.

Sex: None known.

Soc. B.: Not known, probably similar to *Pseudogastromyzon cheni*, page 430.

M: As recommended for *Pseudogastromyzon cheni.*

B: Thus far, there are no reports dealing with a successful aquarium spawn.

F: C, L; "aufwuchs", small live food, *Artemia*, frozen bloodworms, algae.

T: 22-24° C, L: 10 cm, A: 100 cm, R: b, D: 3-4
72-75° F, 4", 39",

S: *Crossostoma tinkhami* is very similar to *Crossostoma fascicauda* FANG, 1935. It differs from the latter (among other things) by five transverse bands on the tail fin.

Gastromyzon punctulatus INGER & CHIN, 1961
Spotted Hillstream Loach

Syn.: None.

Hab.: Southeast Asia; Indonesia, Kalimantan (Borneo), Baleh River, Rajang Basin, Province of Sarawak.

F.I.: Uncertain.

Sex: Unknown.

Soc. B.: Little is known. WICKLER has analyzed some behaviors. He thought he was observing *Gastromyzon borneensis*, but in all likelihood the animals he was observing were *Gastromyzon punctulatus*.

M: Like other Homalopterides.

B: Unknown.

T: 23-25° C, L: 5 cm, A: 60 cm, R: all, D: 2
73-77° F, 2", 24",

F: O; aufwuchs, however, the species also takes supplemental feed.

S: For those who would like to deal with these fishes more in depth, we recommend a publication by Tyson R. Roberts, 1982: Proceedings of the Californian Academy of Science **42** (2): 497-524.

Crossostoma tinkhami

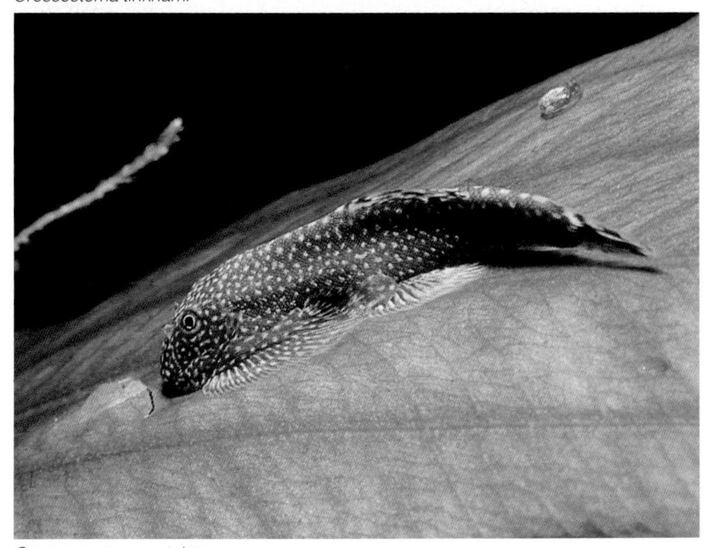

Gastromyzon punctulatus

Glaniopsis multiradiata (no photo) ROBERTS, 1982

Syn.: None.

Hab.: Southeast Asia; Kalimantan (Borneo). The holotypes were collected Oct. 11, 1971 at Arur Dlan, Sungai Padapur and Baram Basin, close to Bario/Province Sarawak.

F.I.: Unknown.

Sex: Unknown.

Soc. B.: Little known, but one can assume that the species behaves similarly to small Gastromyzoninae species.

M: It is necessary to experiment in the maintenance of this species. It is surely not wrong to base the testing on the experiences with *Gastromyzon punctulatus*.

B: Unknown; has not been successful in captivity.

F: O; an aufwuchs feeder which, surely like other Gastromyzoninae species, needs appropriately sized supplemental feed of animal origin.

S: None.

T: 22-24° C, 72-75° F, **L:** 6 cm, 2 1/3", **A:** 60 cm, 24", **R:** all, **D:** 2-3

Homaloptera orthogoniata VAILLANT, 1902
Saddled Hillstream Loach

Syn.: None.

Hab.: Southeast Asia; Indonesia (Kalimantan = Borneo, Sumatra), Thailand.

F.I.: Uncertain; 1969 (?).

Sex: Unknown.

Soc. B.: The animals will perform exhibition battles. Other fishes are completely ignored.

M: The care of this species is easier than often indicated. In the aquarium it is not markedly rheophilous (current-loving). The animals can be kept for years in the following water: pH 7.0, 9° dGH, 6.5-7.0 mg O_2/l at 24° C (75° F). Every 2 to 3 weeks exchange a quarter to a third of the aquarium water. *H. orthogoniata* loves large, flat stone surfaces. Because the animals move clumsily about, robust plants are recommended.

B: So far unknown.

F: O; aufwuchs, blood worms (also frozen) are specially relished.

S: None.

T: 20-24° C, 68-75° F, **L:** 12 cm, 4 3/4", **A:** 100 cm, 39", **R:** b, m, **D:** 3

Liniparhomaloptera disparis, page 430

Homaloptera orthogoniata

Liniparhomaloptera disparis (LIN, 1934)
Broken-Band Hillstream Loach

Syn.: *Homaloptera disparis, Parhomaloptera disparis. Praeformosiana* sp. cf. *intermedia* (old trade-name).

Hab.: China; Tu-yuen-hsien region, south Kweichon. Hong Kong, southern Canton.

F.I.: Unknown.

Sex: Unknown.

Soc. B.: Behaves like other Homalopterides, peaceful towards heterospecifics and generally also towards conspecifics.

M: Probably similar to *Gastromyzon* species.

B: Unknown.

F: O; vegetable and animal aufwuchs feeder.

S: None.

T: 22-24° C, L: about 5 cm, A: 60 cm, R: b, m, D: 2-3
72-75° F, about 2", 24",

Pseudogastromyzon cheni LIANG, 1942
Chinese Hillstream Loach

Syn.: None.

Hab.: East Asia; south China, Fukien Province.

F.I.: Unsure, initially the fish were erroneously identified as *Gastromyzon borneensis*.

Sex: Unknown, some animals have a red fringe on the dorsal fin. Perhaps these are ♂♂.

Soc. B.: Peaceful among themselves. The species performs harmless but interesting pseudo-fights in the feeding area. Other fishes are totally ignored.

M: Even though the animals originate from flowing waters, they are not markedly rheophilous (current-loving). One should always acquire several individuals, even though they are not really a schooling fish.

T: 20-25° C, L: 5 cm, A: 70 cm, R: all, D: 2
68-77° F, 2", 28",

No special demands are placed on water chemistry. Gerhard OTT gives the following values: 5° KH, 7-9° dGH, pH 6.5-7.5. The temperature in OTT's tank fell accidentally to 15° C (59° F). The animals were not harmed.

B: Nothing is known about a successful spawn.

F: O; aufwuchs feeder which also likes blood worms and *Tubifex*.

S: *Pseudogastromyzon cheni* is an interesting species which, phylogenetically, is closely related to *Gastromyzon* species from Borneo. Of those, it seems that only *Gastromyzon punctulatus* has been imported so far and was falsely traded as *Gastromyzon borneensis*.

Liniparhomaloptera disparis

Pseudogastromyzon cheni

Acanthicus adonis, see page 502

Ageneiosus brevifilis VALENCIENNES, 1840
Guyana Slopehead Catfish

Syn.: *Ageneiosus inermis, Ageneiosus dawalla, Ageneiosus sebae, Pseudageneiosus brevifilis, Hypophthalmus dawalla.*

Hab.: Surinam, Guyana, Amazon basin (South America).

F.I.: Probably imported for the first time in 1986.

Sex: During the breeding season, the ♂ develops an elongated, S-shaped dorsal fin spine; one pair of upper maxillary barbels elongate considerably; the first rays of the anal fin enlarge. ♂ and ♀ are barely distinguishable outside the spawning season.

Soc. B.: By no means an unsociable species, but it should only be kept with larger, robust species. There are day- and night-active individuals. Most animals, however, search for food during the night. Can be kept with equal sized conspecifics.

M: Hiding places should be provided. Actually, the fish can not be kept adequately in an aquarium due to their large mature size and active lifestyle. Water: pH 6.4-7.8; hardness up to 20° dGH.

B: The eggs are fertilized internally with the modified anal fin of the ♂. A few days later the ♀ deposits the eggs, without the presence of a male, in the plants. Aquarium breeding has probably not been successful.

F: C; a pure carnivore/piscivore whose hunger is hard to satiate in an aquarium. Almost any larger live foods are eaten (fairy shrimp, earthworms, etc.). Beef heart and fish flesh are taken after the fish are accustomed to them.

S: An appreciated food fish in their natural habitat. Due to its attractive shape the species will always find some demand. It is best to avoid this fish.

T: 22-24° C, L: 45 cm, A: 200 cm, better longer, R: b, m, D: 4 (S)
72-75° F, 18", 79", better longer,

Arius seemani GÜNTHER, 1864

West American Shark Cat, Jordan's Catfish

Syn.: *Tachisurus seemani, Arius "jordani", Hexanematichthys seemani.*

Hab.: Pacific rivers of California and Mexico down to Colombia.

F.I.: Starting in 1980.

Sex: Externally unrecognizable. On mature animals over 30 cm (11³/4") long, the ♀ has a fuller abdomen and lighter fins.

Soc. B.: A relatively peaceful species that gets along with larger cichlids.

M: A freshwater fish which often enters brackish waters of the Pacific. Provide good filtration with adequate current. Small animals have few demands and accept any tank. Larger specimens over 12 cm (4³/4") become restless and require plenty of swimming space (migration drive). Provide caves for hiding, dark substrate and subdued lighting. Water values depend on the origin: pH 6.8-8.0; hardness 8-30° dGH.
Addition of salt: 2% = 200 g/100 l (200 g/26 gal) of aquarium water.

B: Mouthbrooder; the few, very large eggs are incubated by the ♂. Reproduction in an aquarium has not been successful.

F: O; omnivore, but prefers insect larvae. Frozen foods: mosquito larvae, *Tubifex*. After training, tablet foods such as TabiMin and Tetra Tips are accepted; however, flake food is preferably taken from the water surface.

S: A pretty, lively catfish when young. However, the colors fade with age and progressively larger aquaria with an increased salt content become necessary.

T: 22-26° C, L: 35 cm, A: 100 cm later larger, R: b, m, D: 3
72-79° F, 14", 39" later larger,

Hexanematichthys graeffei (KNER & STEINDACHNER, 1866)

Berney's Shark Cat

Syn.: *Arius berneyi, A. graeffei, Hexanematichthys berneyi.*

Hab.: Brackish and freshwaters flowing into the Gulf of Carpentaria (North Australia). Lakes and rivers of New Guinea.

F.I.: 1982 by Heiko Bleher, Frankfurt, Germany.

Sex: Not described.

Soc. B.: Day-active schooling fish which can easily be associated with large cichlids or similar fishes.

M: Needs a large aquarium with plenty of swimming space. Sufficiently strong filtration; a turnover rate of at least twice per hour should be achieved. pH 7.5-8.2; hardness 18-30° dGH.

B: Not yet known. In other species of the genus, the ♂♂ incubate the eggs for a while. Pairing occurs during the Australian summer (Nov./Dec.).

F: C; strict carnivore. Live foods of any kind, beef heart, frozen live foods. After training, FD tablet food (perhaps halved).

S: The picture shows a 15 cm (6") long juvenile.

T: 24-26° C, L: 25 cm, A: 150 cm, R: b, m, D: 2
75-79° F, 9³/4", 59",

Arius seemani

Hexanematichthys graeffei

Bunocephalus verrucosus verrucosus (BLOCH, 1794)
Tall Banjo Catfish

Syn.: *Agmus lyriformis, Bunocephalichthys verrucosus, verrucosus.*

Hab.: Amazon basin, in forest creeks and ditches (South America).

F.I.: 1967 by Heiko Bleher, Frankfurt.

Sex: ♀ clearly plumper at times.

Soc. B.: A delightfully peaceful and gentle fish which can even be kept with the smallest of tankmates. Perhaps young fry are an exception. The fish prefer to lie all day among large-leaved plants (Amazon swords, *Echinodorus*).

M: Unlike some banjo cats (*Bunocephalus*), the species does not burrow. Therefore, it can also be kept with small-leaved plants (in addition to some broad-leaved ones). Dark gravel bottom; water: pH 6.8-7.5; hardness 9-18° dGH.

B: Unknown. Could be similar to the genera *Platystacus, Bunocephalus*, etc.

F: C, O; tablet food. Live food such as *Tubifex*, water fleas and bloodworms.

S: A catfish which should receive more attention despite its plainness. *Bunocephalus* differs from *Dysichthys* primarily by the wider and higher anterior body. The related *Bunocephalus verrucosus scabriceps* is very difficult to distinguish from the presented species. Both genera can be distinguished by the grainy skin of *Bunocephalus verrucosus scabriceps* and the smooth skin of *Dysichthys*.

T: 20-24° C, L: 8 cm, A: 60 cm, R: b, D: 1
68-74° F, 3", 24",

Dysichthys knerii (STEINDACHNER, 1882)
Kneri's Banjo Catfish

Syn.: *Bunocephalus knerii.*

Hab.: Amazon and tributaries, specially in slowly flowing edge-waters with trees.

F.I.: Cannot be determined (see S).

Sex: Not known.

Soc. B.: Very peaceful species. Small fishes are considered as prey. Inactive. Most of the time the fish lies buried in the sand or quietly on a plant leaf. Associate with all quiet species.

M: Provide the dark, shaded places the fish love—or they will burrow into the sand during the day. Gravel substrate and alkaline water values are to be avoided. Who can provide a species tank with (beech/oak) leaf litter? Water: pH 5.8-7.0; hardness up to 15° dGH (8° dGH). Broad-leaved plants (*Echinodorus*, etc.).

B: Reports stating that the eggs are carried on the body of the ♀ are based on a confusion with *Platystacus cotylephorus*. Banjo cats of the genera *Bunocephalus* and *Dysichthys* place their eggs into a shallow depression made in the sand. There, one of the parent fish guards the eggs. So far breeding is mostly a coincidence.

F: C, O; tablet foods based on FD components, insect larvae, *Tubifex*, small fishes.

S: The species predominantly lives in leaf litter in its native habitat and is almost invisible therein. In the trade the species is often confused with *D. coracoideus*. See Vol. 1, page 454.

T: 20-25° C, L: 8 cm, A: 80 cm, R: b, D: 1
68-77° F, 3", 31",

Bunocephalus verrucosus verrucosus

Dysichthys knerii

Platystacus cotylephorus BLOCH, 1794
Mottled Whiptailed Banjo Catfish

Syn.: *Aspredo cotylephorus.*

Hab.: Estuaries of larger rivers in Surinam and Amazonia, South America.

F.I.: Around 1978 to England.

Sex: ♂♂ are sometimes more intensely colored (not on our picture) and have a longer dorsal fin spine. In contrast, the ventral fins of the ♀♀ are wider than the ♂♂'s.

Soc. B.: Peaceful species which may consider young fry as food, but besides this it can be associated with even the smallest fishes.

M: The fish spends most of the day buried in the ground. Therefore, the bottom should not be too coarse or have sharp edges. A corner of sand (of the aquarium) has to be provided for the fishes. It can be kept in freshwater as well as in brackish water (density 1.010). This results in a pH range of 6.8-8.2 and a hardness of 12-35° dGH! The species is found in nature with four eyes (*Anapleps*).

B: Not successful yet in an aquarium. In nature it has been observed that the female sticks the eggs to her soft abdomen skin after spawning is complete. Within a short time, short stalks develop between the skin, which has returned to its hardened state, and the eggs. These stalks only disappear after the eggs have hatched.

F: C, O; mostly an insectivore, but one who also likes tablet foods (TabiMin, Tetra Tips, etc.). *Gammarus* (fairy shrimp), mosquito larvae (including frozen) should represent the main food in the aquarium.

S: The species is also offered as *Asperdo asperdo* in the trade. Our pictures show a ♂ as well as a ♀. Normally the contrast in the coloration is reversed.

T: 22-25° C, L: 25 cm, A: 100 cm, R: b, D: 2
72-77° F, $9^3/_4$", 39",

Playtstacus cotylephorus ♂

Playtstacus cotylephorus ♀

Auchenipterichthys longimanus (GÜNTHER, 1864)
Spotted Woodcat

Syn.: *Auchenipterus longimanus.*

Hab.: Middle and lower Amazon, as well as southern tributaries (Peru, Brazil), South America.

F.I.: Unknown.

Sex: The ♂ develops a thickened urinogenital pore out of the first rays of the anal fin during the spawning season. In addition, the hard fin rays become noticeably elongated.

Soc. B.: A comparatively peaceful species which, occasionally considers smaller fishes up to neon size as food. Associate with conspecifics and/or larger catfishes or cichlids.

M: Predominantly active in the twilight hours. Depending on the number of individuals, one or more caves are needed which sometimes are inhabited by several individuals. Water: pH 6.0-7.2; hardness to 18° dGH.

B: Has not been successful in an aquarium. The ♂ fertilizes the eggs internally before they are deposited by the ♀.

F: C, O; all kinds of flakes, tablet foods. Use live insect larvae to ripen the animals for breeding.

S: None.

T: 20-23° C, L: 15 cm, A: 120 cm, R: b, m, D: 2
68-73° F, 6", 47",

Flooded pool by Belém, Brazil.

Auchenipterichthys longimanus ♂

Auchenipterichthys longimanus ♀

Auchenipterichthys thoracatus (KNER, 1858)

Midnight Catfish, Zamora Woodcat

Syn.: *Auchenipterus thoracatus, Auchenipterus thoracicus, Trachycorystes coracoideus.*

Hab.: Upper Amazon and southern tributaries (Peru at Iquitos), South America.

F.I.: 1969 by Heiko Bleher, Frankfurt.

Sex: Same as *T. taeniatus* (page 446). Main pectoral and dorsal fin spines more pronounced in the ♂ and longer than those of the ♀. Anal fin of the ♂ is straight, ♀ slightly convex.

Soc. B.: Normally a nocturnal species which is kept in smaller groups. Can be associated with fishes about half its length.

M: Use a well-planted tank with large roots. Drill holes into the roots corresponding to the size of the fish. The fish hold fast therein with the help of their dorsal and pectoral fin rays. They can then be lifted out of the aquarium without complications. Since they usually entangle hopelessly in a net, capture only with a glass. Water: pH 6.5-7.2; hardness 7-16° dGH.

B: Internal fertilization. Has not been bred in an aquarium.

F: C, O; insectivore. Tablets and flakes are readily accepted. Flakes eaten from the water surface are the nutritional basis in aquarium maintenance.

S: The species is easily identified by its "raven-beak appendage" immediately below the pectoral fins.
The picture does not do justice to the beauty of these animals. The back is velvet blue with light, yellowish dots along the lateral line. The half-moon in the tail fin is a shiny, bright yellow.

T: 20-24° C, L: 11 cm, A: 100 cm, R: t, m, D: 2
68-75° F, 4 1/3", 39",

Auchenipterus nuchalis (SPIX, 1829)

Mustache Woodcat, Demerara Woodcat

Syn.: *Hypophthalmus nuchalis, Auchenipterus dentatus, Euanemus colymbetes, Auchenipterus demerarae, Auchenipterus ambyiacus, Ceratocheilus osteomystax, Euanemus nuchalis, Euanemus dentatus, Auchenipterus osteomystax.*

Hab.: Widely distributed in the estuary areas of larger South American rivers. From the Essequibo River to the Rio Paraguay and the La Plata basin.

F.I.: 1976 to England.

Sex: The ♂ has the genital papilla anteriorly on the anal fin, as is typical for the family. The maxillary is markedly more developed in the ♂ than in the ♀ (picture). The ♀ sports some sharp-edged scales between the dorsal and the adipose fin, which are missing in the ♂. The ♀ is more compact and has a longer head than the ♂. Because of these differences, ♂♂ and ♀♀ were considered different species for a long time.

Soc. B.: Dusk and night-active species which is mostly quiet and relatively peaceful. The association with fishes that are too small (neon size), however, is not recommended. The small fishes disappear one after the other. Maintain in pairs. Best to keep two pairs in a species tank.

M: Provide rock and root cover as hiding places for the day. Plant thickets are also suitable for this purpose. Good water turnover is appreciated by the animals. Water: pH 6.7-7.2; hardness 7-16° dGH; differing values are also tolerated.

B: Nothing is known. Fertilization is internal.

F: C, O; feed shortly before turning off the lights. Almost all flakes and tablets (Tetra Tips, etc.) are accepted. Mosquito larvae, *Gammarus*, *Mysis* and other frozen foods are, however, preferred.

S: While feeding, the ♂ extends its barbels at a 90° angle to the body axis. This gave it the name *A. osteomystax* (see Syn.); *mystax* = mustache. The bony barbel of the ♂ is undoubtedly a secondary sexual characteristic.

T: 20-22° C, L: 15 cm, A: 120 cm, R: b-t, D: 2-3
68-72° F, 6", 47",

Auchenipterichths thoracatus

Auchenipterus nuchalis

Parauchenipterus galeatus (LINNAEUS, 1766)
Starry Woodcat

Syn.: *Silurus galeatus, Auchenipterus maculosus, Auchenipterus immaculatus, Auchenipterus puncatus, Auchenipterus robustus, Auchenipterus glaber, Auchenipterus galeatus, Parauchenipterus paseae, Pimelodus galeatus, Euanemus maculosus, Trachycorystes glaber, Trachycorystes galeatus, Trachycorystes robustus, Trachycorystes jokcannae.*

Hab.: Widely distributed in all of northern South America down to Peru.

F.I.: 1970 by Heiko Bleher, Frankfurt.

Sex: ♂ has a slightly concave anal fin; slightly convex in the ♀. The first rays of the anal fin form the urinogenital organ of the ♂.

Soc. B.: Since they are sometimes quite stormy, the fish should not be put in a planted aquarium. Can only be combined with large fishes.

M: Growth is very fast. Therefore, only buy the fish if a sufficiently large aquarium with its equipment is available. Roots with Java moss, perhaps also Java fern, are fitting decoration. Caves for hiding should be provided. Water: pH 6.0-7.5; hardness to 18° dGH.

B: Internal fertilization. Nothing is known about aquarium breeding.

F: C, O; tablet foods, pellets, live foods of all kinds, also fishes.

S: The colors of the animals vary considerably due to its vast distribution range. The skin is very slimy, allowing the fish to slip out of the hand.

T: 20-24° C, L: 20 cm, A: 120 cm, R: b, D: 2-3
68-75° F, 8", 47",

Swamp in the Amazon jungle.

Parauchenipterus galeatus ♂, juvenile

Parauchenipterus galeatus, adult

Pseudauchenipterus nodosus (BLOCH, 1794)
Yellow Woodcat, Black Tailband Catfish

Syn.: *Silurus nodosus, Arius nodosus, Auchenipterus nodosus, A. furcatus, Felichthys nodosus, Pseudauchenipterus nigrolineatus, P. guppyi, Euanemus nodosus.*

Hab.: The Guianas, Venezuela, Trinidad, Amazon (South America).

F.I.: After 1970, before as by-catch.

Sex: ♂ has the urinogenital opening at the anterior end of the anal fin; therefore, it is somewhat convex. Anal fin of the ♀ is shorter and straight. Pelvic fins of the ♂ are pointed; round in the ♀. During the spawning season the hard rays of the ♂ severely lengthen, and in addition, the dorsal fin ray curves into a S-shape.

Soc. B.: Smaller fishes may be considered food during nocturnal foraging. Therefore, they should only be associated with large catfishes or characins.

M: The species lives in estuaries, which is why a density of 1.006 to 1.008 is well tolerated. They also live in pure freshwater. pH 6.5-8.0; hardness up to 30° dGH.

B: Has not been successful in an aquarium.

F: C, O; preferably meat (heart) and live foods. Tablet foods and trout pellets are also accepted after training. The body of *P. nodosus* is covered by a thin slime layer. Therefore, do not associate with fishes which (not always with bad intentions) bump into them, such as loaches, algae eaters or cichlids.

S: The genus is characterized by the long barbels which are missing on other driftwood catfishes. The extended distribution of the species leads to variations in coloration and design. The picture shows a juvenile. The dark coloration of the caudal fin disappears with age.

T: 20-25° C, **L:** 20 cm, **A:** 150 cm, **R:** b, m, **D:** 2-3
68-77° F, 8", 59",

Trachelyopterichthys taeniatus (KNER, 1857)
Striped Woodcat

Syn.: *Trachelyopterus taeniatus.*

Hab.: Upper Amazon (Solimoes) and tributaries, Brazil; South America.

F.I.: Could not be determined.

Sex: The first rays of the anal fin of the ♂ form a gonopodium.

Soc. B.: Lives secluded, relatively peaceful. Do not place larger individuals with small fishes (neons). Nocturnal.

M: Part of the tank should have a floating plant cover. Provide a cave of suitable size. Water: pH 5.8-7.2; hardness up to 15° dGH.

B: Fertilization is internal. During mating, the ♂ embraces the ♀ so that the anal fin ray is located close to the anus of the ♀. Afterwards, the eggs are deposited on a previously cleaned place.

F: C; insects and their larvae, frozen foods. Flake foods with freeze-dried components.

S: This species does not have an adipose fin, although most representatives of the family do have one. The genus is monotypic (only has one species).

T: 20-25° C, **L:** 15 cm, **A:** 100 cm, **R:** b, m, **D:** 2-3
68-77° F, 6", 39",

Pseudauchenipterus nodosus, juvenile

Trachelyopterichthys taeniatus

Auchenoglanis occidentalis (VALENCIENNES, 1840)
Giraffe-Nosed Catfish

Syn.: *Pimelodus occidentalis, Oxyglanis sacchii.*

Hab.: Widely distributed in tropical Africa. Lower Nile to the Blue Nile; Niger, Congo, in lakes Chad, Tanganyika, Mweru and Bangwelu.

F.I.: 1909 by Paul Matte, Lankwitz; 1974 again by Heiko Bleher, Frankfurt.

Sex: Not described yet.

Soc. B.: Mostly diurnal catfish, specially at feeding time. It is quite peaceful, but should not be kept with smaller fishes. Good companions are *Distichodus* and *Ctenopoma* species.

M: To protect the barbels, the substrate should not contain any sharp edges. During feeding it sifts through the sand, making fine-leaved plants unsuitable. Water: pH 6.5-7.8; hardness up to 28° dGH.

B: Not known.

F: O; tablet foods (TabiMin and similar foods), left over flake food. Any live food, frozen foods, FD feeds.

S: The species accepts even the smallest aquaria. Nevertheless, the fish should not be cramped.

T: 21-25° C, L: 45 cm, A: 150 cm, R: b, D: 2
70-77° F, 18", 59",

Bagrus docmac (FORSSKÅL, 1775)
Nile Catfish, Hog catfish

Syn.: *Silurus dacmak, S. bajad* (Not FORSSKÅL), *Porcus docmac.*

Hab.: Nile, lakes Victoria, Chew Bahir (Lake Stefanie) and Kainji, Sagan River (Africa).

F.I.: 1936.

Sex: Not yet described.

Soc. B.: Not a fish for the community aquarium because small fish are always eaten. Usually night- and twilight-active. During the day the fish only appears because of its immeasurable appetite.

M: Very undemanding species. pH 6.5-8.2; hardness up to 30° dGH. Offer lots of free swimming space. Plants are not eaten but are easily dug up. Needs a sandy bottom with a large cave for hiding. Tough, well-rooted plants, perhaps in pots.

B: Not known.

F: C, O; juveniles like tablet food and *Tubifex*. Later they require hefty live foods: fish and earthworms. In their natural habitat the young are insectivores.

S: Not a proper aquarium fish, although it is easy to maintain when young. The German common name, Nile catfish, is probably not descriptive enough. Close to one hundred catfishes live in the Nile. That is why a new name is suggested (Syn. *Porcus* = hog). Good food fish.

T: 21-25° C, L: 60 cm, A: 150 cm, R: b, D: 3-4 (S)
70-77° F, 24", 59",

Auchenoglanis occidentalis

Bagrus docmac

Mystus bocourti (BLEEKER, 1864)
King Bagrid
Sub-Fam.: Bagrinae

Syn.: *Heterobagrus bocourti, Prajadhipokia rex.*

Hab.: Southeast Asia; Thailand.

F.I.: 1977.

Sex: Not known.

Soc. B.: They hide during the day. Can only be kept together with fishes that are too large to be swallowed (above 10 cm; 4" length). Not suitable for the community tank.

M: 3-5 specimens should be kept. These require a lot of room to swim and forage. Sandy substrate and hiding places. Only plant the background. Plants are not damaged. Large filter with good water turnover. Water pH 6.5-7.2; hardness 10-20° dGH.

B: Not known.

F: C; some young animals accept tablet food. Later, beef heart, earthworms and small fish are fed.

S: Not really a predator. Small fish are only occasionally eaten (when the occasion is propitious).

T: 22-25° C, L: 18 cm, A: 200 cm, R: b, D: 3
72-77° F, 7", 79",

Leiocassis siamensis REGAN, 1913
Asian Bumblebee Cat
Sub-Fam.: Mystinae

Syn.: *Leiocassis albicolaris, L. albicollis, L. bicolor.*

Hab.: Thailand, Cambodia.

F.I.: 1937.

Sex: Unknown.

Soc. B.: Loner, defends a territory, dangerous for small fish.

M: As with many catfishes, this one shuns the light. Nocturnal. Provide large tanks with few plants. In keeping with its natural biotope, a flower pot or coconut shell as a cave underneath stones or bogwood roots should be added. pH 6.0-8.0; hardness 4-25° dGH.

B: Not known. The related species, *L. brashnikowi*, spawns on the ground among roots. The ♂ guards the nest. Young hatch after about three days and become free-swimming after seven.

F: Live foods, tablet foods, also flake foods (large).

S: Emits croaking sounds. Can cause significant injury with its hard pectoral fin ray. Do not capture with a net, but use a glass container.

T: 20-26° C, L: 20 cm, A: 100 cm, R: b, D: 2-3
68-79° F, 8", 39",

Mystus bocourti

Leiocassis siamensis

Lophiobagrus cyclurus (WORTHINGTON & RICARDO, 1937)
Tanganyika Catfish, African Bullhead

Syn.: A revision of the genus is in progress.

Hab.: Endemic to Lake Tanganyika, Africa.

F.I.: About 1978 to England.

Sex: Not known.

Soc. B.: Predominantly a nocturnal catfish which is readily kept in groups of 4-6 specimens. The species does not seem to be territorial. Can be kept with fishes that are not too small, but see **S**.

M: Lots of shelter; substrate partially of sand for rooting. Hard water of 15-25° dGH; pH 7.5-8.0. Keep with Tanganyika cichlids.

B: The eggs are laid in roomy caves or shelters. They are 2 mm ($^1/_{16}$") in Ø, milky and very sticky. Keeping the spawning pair alone is recommended. Otherwise, the eggs could be eaten by the parents if disturbed. The larvae hatch after 4-5 days and become pigmented after an additional 5. The young should be raised in a separate tank without the parents. Initially Liquifry and *Artemia* are offered, later finely grated earthworms and sieved flake food.

F: C; primarily insect larvae and occasionally small fishes. Happily accepts tablet foods and pellets.

S: Terrorized specimens can produce a secretion which kills other fish (in an aquarium) (according to Pierre Brichard in "Fishes of Lake Tanganyika", TFH Publications). Animals bred in England, including the breeders, did not show this behavior, not even towards other fish species when provoked.

T: 23-26° C, **L:** 10 cm, **A:** 100 cm, **R:** b, **D:** 3
73-79° F, 4", 39",

Mystus nigriceps (CUVIER & VALENCIENNES, 1830)
Antenna Bagrid

Syn.: *Mystus micracanthus.*

Hab.: Widely distributed in Asia. However, reports are available only from India and Burma.

F.I.: Unknown.

Sex: Not known.

Soc. B.: Quite sociable species which, however, considers small fishes as prey. Tankmates should not be smaller than $^3/_4$ the length of *M. nigriceps*. Nocturnal.

M: Requires plenty of room for swimming and for the long barbels. Provide hiding possibilities. Sparse vegetation, perhaps floating plant cover or a dimmer for evenings. Water of any quality.

B: Not known.

F: C, O; tablet foods, pellets, worms, insects and their larvae, frozen foods and flake food remains.

S: The pectoral fin rays are long and pointed. Use caution with hand and net. The thorns can, even though not actually poisonous, result in blood poisoning because of their foreign protein.

T: 22-25° C, **L:** 15 cm, **A:** 120 cm, **R:** b, **D:** 2-3
72-77° F, 6", 47",

Lophiobagrus cyclurus

Mystus nigriceps

Hemibagrus nemurus (VALENCIENNES, 1839)
Asian Red-Tailed Catfish

Syn.: *Bagrus nemurus, Mystus nemurus, Hemibagrus hoevenii, Macrones nemurus.*

Hab.: Malaysia, Thailand, Sumatra, Singapore, Java in fresh and brackish waters.

F.I.: About 1975.

Sex: Not known.

Soc. B.: A extreme predator which attacks anything in the aquarium, even the hand of the aquarist. Only keep together with very large tankmates or equally sized conspecifics.

M: The imported animals all seem well acclimated to freshwater, which is why they can also be kept at a hardness of 10-25° dGH, pH 7.0-8.2. The species jumps readily and well when it is disturbed or provoked. Therefore, the aquarium has to be well covered. Robust plants.

B: Not known.

F: C; fish and, after habituation, large earthworms or beef heart. In the wild small specimens take even ants as feed.

S: The largest animals come from Sumatra. Smaller in other areas.

T: 22-25° C, L: 60 cm, A: 200 cm, R: b, D: 4
73-79° F, 4", 39",

Aspidoras albater NIJSSEN & ISBRÜCKER, 1976

Syn.: None.

Hab.: Rio Tocantins and tributaries, Brazil; South America.

F.I.: Not known.

Sex: Not described.

Soc. B.: Peaceful fish which does best when kept in groups of 6-8 fishes. The species is very similar to *Corydoras* and can, as such, be associated with almost all, including smaller fishes.

M: The species requires sand substrate to root. It is very similar to *Corydoras* species in regard to maintenance. pH 6.0-7.3; hardness up to 20° dGH. Mainly diurnal. A corner of the aquarium should be densely planted to provide cover.

T: 22-24° C, L: 4 cm, A: 60 cm, R: b, D: 2
72-75° F, 1 2/3", 24",

B: Not yet described.

F: C, O; flake and tablet foods, feed remains. Small live foods of any kind. Freeze-dried *Tubifex*. This species should not be kept with overly voracious feeders because it will get the short end.

S: The difference between the genera *Corydoras* and *Aspidoras* is that the latter has two fontanels instead of one.

Aspidoras menezesi NIJSSEN & ISBRÜCKER, 1976

Syn.: None; in the trade sometimes as *Aspidoras poecilius* which, however, is another species.

Hab.: Rio Salgado river system, Brazil; (South America).

F.I.: 1978.

Sex: The ♀♀ are rounder during the spawning season. Other differences are not known.

Soc. B.: Very peaceful, quiet, even almost motionless fish. It should only be kept with other gentle species.

M: The species is not suited for the large community tank. It disappears there. Smaller, well-planted tanks with dark substrate, strong filtration and surface movement are well suited. The species is oxygen needy. Water: pH 6.0-7.0; hardness up to 12° dGH. Perhaps peat filtration.

B: Not yet successful, but should be similar to small *Corydoras*.

F: Live food is preferred. Flake and tablet foods are also accepted.

S: There are at least 9 species in this genus. For differences from *Corydoras*, see *Aspidoras albater* (previous page).

T: 21-24° C, **L:** 4,5 cm, **A:** 50 cm, **R:** b, **D:** 2-3
70-75° F, 1 3/4", 20",

Aspidoras pauciradiatus (WEITZMAN & NIJSSEN, 1970)
False Corydora, Blotch-Fin Aspidoras

Syn.: *Corydoras pauciradiatus, "C. U6".*

Hab.: Rio Araguaia, Brazil; South America.

F.I.: Around 1970 to England, presumably not till 1985 to Germany.

Sex: Not known.

Soc. B.: Peaceful schooling fish for the species tank or to be associated with gentle characins and dwarf cichlids. Not suitable for the "normal" community aquarium.

M: Like *Corydoras*. Cover tank with floating plants. pH 6.0-7.2; hardness up to 12° dGH. Well-filtered, oxygen-rich water and current are conditions for its well-being.

B: Has not been bred in an aquarium.

F: L, O; small live foods, Tetra Tips, Tetra FD-Menu.

S: A delicate and difficult species that requires a lot of attention for its care.

T: 22-25° C, **L:** 3,5 cm, **A:** 60 cm, **R:** b, **D:** 3
72-77° F, 1 1/3", 24",

Aspidoras menezesi

Aspidoras pauciradiatus

Brochis multiradiatus (ORCES-VILLAGOMEZ, 1960)
Hog-Nosed Brochis

Syn.: *Chaenothorax multiradiatus.*

Hab.: Upper Napo River, Ecuador (South America).

F.I.: Around 1974.

Sex: Not yet described.

Soc. B.: Peaceful species which likes to dig; therefore, it can only be kept in tanks with well-rooted or potted plants.

M: The bottom should consist mainly of coarse grained sand to allow the fish to root. Sharp edged gravel is to be avoided, because the long barbels are damaged. However, these also deteriorate under poor water conditions. Water exchanges of 1/2-2/3 every 2-3 weeks with the addition of a water conditioner are recommended. Water: pH 6.0-7.2; hardness up to 15° dGH. The species needs water movement and room to swim.

B: The species has been bred, but no description was given in the English report.

F: L, C; flake foods (alternating staple and vegetable food). Freeze-dried *Tubifex*, mosquito larvae. Live foods or frozen mosquito larvae should be given once a week.

S: Until now only two *Brochis* species were known. *B. multiradiatus* differs from *B. splendens* (Vol. 1, page 458) by the greater number of dorsal fin rays and a longer snout. In November 1983, *Brochis britskii* was described by NIJSSEN & ISBRÜKKER.

T: 21-24° C, 70-75° F, **L:** 8 cm, 3", **A:** 80 cm, 31", **R:** b, **D:** 2

Corydoras ambiacus COPE, 1872

Syn.: *Corydoras grafi, C. melanistius longirostris.*

Hab.: Rio Ambiyacu, Peru (South America).

F.I.: Before 1952.

Sex: No differences in coloration are known. ♀ fuller through the ventral area.

Soc. B.: Peaceful species which likes to swim in small groups.

M: Peat filtration, filter current. Dark, sandy substrate. Water: pH 6.0-7.0; hardness up to 10° dGH.

B: No breeding reports are available. It should be possible to breed the species in extremely soft water. Who has suitable breeding pairs available?

F: C, O; tablet foods and flake food remains; live foods (*Daphnia* and mosquito larva), frozen and freeze-dried foods.

S: The species belongs to the *Corydoras punctatus* group. *C. ambiacus* is the closest related and the most similar to *C. agassizii*. However, the species presented here has a shorter head. The species is also often confused with *C. delphax* and *C. leucomelas*.
Pattern differences in the dorsal fin are good indicators for the species.

T: 21-24° C, 70-75° F, **L:** 6 cm, 2 1/3", **A:** 60 cm, 24", **R:** b, **D:** 2

Brochis multiradiatus

Corydoras ambiacus

Corydoras atropersonatus WEITZMAN & NIJSSEN, 1970
Masked Cory

Syn.: None.

Hab.: Ecuador, South America.

F.I.: Around 1978.

Sex: Only possible during the spawning season when the ♀ is fuller.

Soc. B.: Very peaceful, diurnal species which is best kept in a small school in a species tank or together with other gentle fishes or larger, peaceful, nocturnal catfishes (*Hypostomus, Pecoltia*).

M: The fishes root readily. Therefore, the substrate needs to be of fine sand with a partial mulm layer and never of rough-edged gravel. Soft water of 4-8° dGH, pH 6.0-7.0. Provide good filter maintenance and current-rich water. Nitrates are rarely tolerated. Peat filtration is advantageous.

B: Not yet reproduced, even by experienced *Corydoras* breeders.

F: C, O; tablet foods, flakes and frozen foods.

S: The species is very similar to *C. sychri*, WEITZMANN, 1960. Aquarium Atlas Vol. 1, page 474.

T: 21-24° C, L: 4.5 cm, A: 60 cm, R: b, D: 3
70-75° F, 1 3/4", 24",

Corydoras caudimaculatus RÖSSEL, 1961
Tail-Spot Cory, Big-Blotch Cory

Syn.: None.

Hab.: Upper Rio Guaporé, Brazil (at the border to Bolivia); South America.

F.I.: To the USA in 1959, to Germany in 1982 by Heiko Bleher.

Sex: Not known.

Soc. B.: An attractive species similar to *C. guapore*, but somewhat more robust and sedate. Well suited for the community tank.

M: Like *C. guapore*, but even more tolerant towards water conditions. Nevertheless, not a species for the beginner! Clear, nitrate-free, well-filtered water with regular water exchanges every 3-4 weeks and filter maintenance are recommended. pH 6.5-7.5; hardness up to 22° dGH. If no nitrate-free water is available, beginners are to be dissuaded from keeping this fish.

B: Because of the lack of imported animals, it is little bred. Where are the specialists who reproduce this species for the trade? STERBA shows pictures of the species from KNAACK. According to them, the ♀♀ carry the eggs after spawning in the ventral fins, which act as a pouch.

F: O; easily nourished with tablet foods (Tetra Tips or TabiMin—or similar). Naturally, no small live food is refused.

S: The species is stouter than *C. guapore*. Otherwise the two are very similarly patterned.

T: 22-26° C, L: 6 cm, A: 60 cm, R: b, D: 2
72-79° F, 2 1/3", 24",

Corydoras atropersonatus

Corydoras caudimaculatus

Corydoras delphax NIJSSEN & ISBRÜCKER, 1983
Delfax Cory

Syn.: None.

Hab.: Rio Inirida system, Colombia (South America).

F.I.: Unknown since the species is often confused with *C. leucomelas* and *C. ambiacus*.

Sex: ♀♀ are stockier and rounder in the ventral area when full-grown.

Soc. B.: Peaceful and hardy species suitable for any community aquarium.

M: A nondemanding species that has minimal water quality needs. If the aquarium is livable for other fish, then *C. delphax* will have no problems. However, the water should not be too hard (up to 25° dGH).

T: 21-24° C, **L**: 6 cm, **A**: 50 cm, **R**: b, **D**: 1
70-75° F, 2", 20",

B: Follows other *Corydoras*.

F: O.

S: The Latin name means "young pig" in reference to its feeding customs.

Corydoras ehrhardti STEINDACHNER, 1910
Ehrhardt's Corycat

Syn.: *Corydoras meridionalis*.

Hab.: South Brazil, state of Parana, Jaragna, mountain streams at Joinville, Brazil.

F.I.: About 1970 by K. H. Lüling.

Sex: ♂ more slender and elongate than the ♀.

Soc. B.: Typical for the genus.

M: Similar to other members of the genus, but a cooler tank with strong filtration to provide current should be used.

B: Not reported.

T: 19-22° C, **L**: 7 cm, **A**: 50 cm, **R**: b, **D**: 2-3
66-72° F, 2 3/4", 20",

F: C, O; predominantly insect larvae in nature. In the aquarium the fish is an omnivore.

S: Very similar to *Corydoras paleatus*. However, the body is slimmer, the dark pigmentation more pronounced and *Corydoras ehrhardti* attains a somewhat larger size.

Corydoras delphax

Corydoras ehrhardti

Corydoras guapore KNAACK, 1961
Guapore Cory

Syn.: None.

Hab.: Rio Guaporé, Brazil (South America).

F.I.: 1959 to USA, 1982 by Heiko Bleher to Germany.

Sex: Not known.

Soc. B.: An active, nimble species always in search of something edible. Conditionally suitable for the community tank (temperature).

M: Because of the level of their activity (along the lines of *C. hastatus* and *C. pigmaeus*), offer a good current by means of a strong filter and lots of free swimming space. pH 6.5-7.2; hardness 5-18° dGH.

B: No reports are yet available.

F: C, O; tablet and flake foods, frozen and freeze-dried live foods. Mosquito larvae, *Daphnia* and Enchytraea.

S: An attractive species.

T: 21-24° C, 70-75° F, **L:** 5 cm, 2", **A:** 60 cm, 24", **R:** b, **D:** 2-3

Corydoras haraldschultzi KNAACK, 1962
Harald Schultz's Cory

Syn.: None.

Hab.: Rio Tocantins, Rio Araguaia, upper Rio Guaporé, central Brazil (South America). The latter habitat is given by STERBA (however, this is more applicable to *C. sterbai*).

F.I.: 1959.

Sex: ♀ stouter and fuller at spawning time.

Soc. B.: Peaceful, gregarious species.

M: Similar to other *Corydoras*. Offer plenty of free swimming room and current. Peat filtered water is advantageous. A large tank of over 100 l (26 gal) volume with a strong filter and nitrate-free water is necessary.

B: As with many species, breeding occurs during the dark time of the year (winter). Soft, peat-filtered water with a pH around 6.0; hardness below 10° dGH. 1-2 ♀♀ and 3-5 ♂♂ are used. Feeding with hearty live foods (mosquito larvae) and freeze-dried foods.

F: C, O; specially benthic insect larvae. Flake and tablet foods are readily taken.

S: Many questions have arisen over whether or not this fish is a true species. Confusion with *C. sterbai* has occurred constantly. The pictures of both species in this book, however, clearly show the differences: *C. haraldschultzi* has a light body and head with dark spots, dots and lines. *C. sterbai* is exactly the opposite: here the body and head are dark with light dots and lines. The coloration of the fins also differs: the pictures speak for themselves. See page 481.
The pectoral and ventral fins are a strong orange color in full-grown specimens.

T: 24-28° C, 75-82° F, **L:** 7 cm, 2 3/4", **A:** 60 cm, 24", **R:** b, **D:** 2

Corydoras guapore

Corydoras haraldschultzi

Corydoras julii — STEINDACHNER, 1906

Juli Corycat

Syn.: None.

Hab.: Lower Amazon around Belem, Brazil (South America).

F.I.: Unknown; constantly confused with *C. trilineatus*.

Sex: Not recognizable.

Soc. B.: A peaceful fish which likes to school with other corys.

M: Needs a lots of free swimming room on the bottom, which should be sand. Few demands are made of the water: pH 6.5-7.8; hardness up to 20° dGH. Plant loosely with *Echinodorus* and *Vallisneria*; fine-leaved plants such as *Cabomba* are also suitable. Regular water changes every 2-3 weeks are advocated.

T: 23-26° C, **L:** 5 cm, **A:** 50 cm, **R:** b, **D:** 1
73-79° F, 2", 20",

B: No reports are yet available.

F: O; feed remains of all kinds, specially tablets and flake food. *Daphnia* and mosquito larvae.

S: The species is commonly confused with *C. trilineatus* which has a more banded pattern on the head. In *C. julii* it is more dotted, in addition to the species being smaller and stouter. The definite taxonomic situation still needs to be resolved by specialists. It is said that the species is (almost) not offered in the trade; however, a Frankfurt importer annually brings thousands into Germany. Compare photo Volume 1, page 467!

Corydoras leopardus — MYERS, 1933

Leopard Corycat

Syn.: *Corydoras funelli.*

Hab.: Coastal area around Maracaña (north of Belem), Brazil, South America.
C. julii occurs about 500 km (310 mi) west thereof in the region of the mouth of the Amazon.
It has to be pointed out that the picture shows a fish from **Peru**. The photograph was identified by specialists as *C.* cf. (similar to) *leopardus*. The true *leopardus* from east Brazil has more numerous and smaller dots which are partially arranged in lines. Therefore, the species pictured here could be a new species or sub-species!

F.I.: Probably under a different name. An exact date cannot be determined anymore.

Sex: ♀♀ fuller and stouter.

Soc. B.: Peaceful, robust and active species for the community aquarium with otherwise calm inhabitants.

M: Quite an undemanding species. Water: pH 6.5-7.5; hardness up to 20° dGH. During water exchanges care has to be taken to remove the chlorine. Perhaps a good water conditioner should be added. Otherwise like other *Corydoras*.

B: No breeding reports are available. Breeding should not deviate much from other *Corydoras*. Because the species is rarely imported, suitable breeders are naturally in short supply.

F: C, O; flake food, tablet foods; small live foods.

S: According to STERBA, the species is, at the most, a sport of *C. julii*. The longer snout, however, clearly distinguishes *C. leopardus* from *C. trilineatus* and *C. acrensis*.

T: 20-25° C, **L:** 7 cm, **A:** 50 cm, **R:** b, **D:** 1-2
68-77° F, 2 3/4", 20",

Corydoras julii

Corydoras leopardus

Corydoras leucomelas EIGENMANN & ALLEN, 1942
False Spotted Cory, Blackfin Cory

Syn.: *Corydoras caquetae.*

Hab.: Colombia, Peru (South America).

F.I.: Unknown.

Sex: The ♂♂ have more pointed and elongated pectoral fins. ♀♀ stouter than the ♂♂.

Soc. B.: An ideal companion for small characins, dwarf cichlids and other peaceful species.

M: pH 6.2-7.2; hardness up to 12° dGH.

B: Not yet bred.

F: L, O.

S: None.

T: 22-26° C, L: 4.5 cm, A: 50 cm, R: b, D: 1-2
72-79° F, 1 3/4", 20",

Corydoras macropterus REGAN, 1913
Sailfin Cory, Long-Finned Cory

Syn.: *Corydoras bertoni.*

Hab.: Brazil at Sao Paulo, South America.

F.I.: 1912 by Albert Mayer, Hamburg.

Sex: ♂♂ have more developed bristles forming "sideburns". Dorsal and pectoral fins are significantly larger than in the ♀♀.

Soc. B.: Peaceful species, suitable for the cooler community tank. The species should be kept in a small school. Do not keep together with "fin nibblers" (e.g., tiger barbs).

M: Little demanding species which, however, can be sensitive during acclimation. The somewhat more oxygen-needy animals easily suffer from excessively warmth. Water: pH 6.5-7.5; hardness up to 18° dGH.

B: Not yet successful.

F: O; tablet and flake foods. Live foods of all kinds.

S: The species rather resembles *C. barbatus* and smaller ♀♀, *C. paleatus.* The picture shows a ♂. With its appearance and customs, the species does not fit into the genus.

T: 18-21° C, L: 10 cm, A: 80 cm, R: b, m, D: 1-2
64-70° F, 4", 31",

Corydoras leucomelas

Corydoras macropterus ♂

Corydoras melanistius brevirostris
Spotted Corycat, Black Sail Cory

FRASER-BRUNNER, 1947

Syn.: *Corydoras wotroi.*

Hab.: Orinoco River in Venezuela (South America).

F.I.: Unknown.

Sex: ♀ is rounder during the spawning season.

Soc. B.: A polite *Corydoras* which does not fit well into a community tank with ill-behaved gluttons.

M: Fine-grained dark substrate. Perhaps a corner of mulm to root in. A back corner separated by dense plant growth or pebbles is suitable for this purpose. It should be arranged so that the water entering the filter comes from this corner. This way the coarse mulm will automatically collect in this corner. The fine mulm will be sucked up and filtered out. Water: pH 6.0-7.8; hardness up to 25° dGH (10°).

B: The species has been repeatedly bred in an aquarium.

F: C, O; food remains, tablet foods, trout chow, etc. Every so often frozen foods and/or smaller live foods should be offered.

S: The original description of this species was done on an aquarium specimen. The exact habitat was not known. This is why NIJSSEN & ISBRÜCKER (1967) described the species as *C. wotroi* anew. Later the identity was discovered and *C. wotroi* became a synonym.

T: 20-24° C, L: 6 cm, A: 60 cm, R: b, D: 1
68-75° F, 2 1/3", 24",

Corydoras melanotaenia
Green Gold Cory, Blackband Cory

REGAN, 1912

Syn.: None.

Hab.: Rio Meta basin, Colombia (South America).

F.I.: Not known.

Sex: The ♂ is more slender than the ♀.

Soc. B.: Peaceful species which should be kept in a species tank because of its rarity.

M: Like other *Corydoras*.

B: Typical for *Corydoras*: the eggs are adhesive and are preferentially adhered to broad leaves. T: 23-25° C (73-77° F), pH 6.5-7.2; hardness up to 17° dGH. The larvae hatch after 5 days and are raised on fresh *Artemia* nauplii. More than 150-180 eggs are laid in several courtship and spawning episodes.

F: C, O; flake food, tablets and all kinds of food remains.

S: The yellow coloration of the caudal fin has given the species its name. It is otherwise quite similar to *C. aeneus* besides minor deviations in body measurements. Its distribution, however, is much more restricted than that of *C. aeneus*.

T: 20-23° C, L: 6.5 cm, A: 60 cm, R: b, D: 2
68-73° F, 2 2/3", 24",

Corydoras melanistius brevirostris

Corydoras melanotaenia

Corydoras ornatus

NIJSSEN & ISBRÜCKER, 1976

Ornate Cory

Syn.: None.

Hab.: Tributaries of the Rio Tapajos, Amazonia (South America).

F.I.: About 1980 to England.

Sex: No visible external differences.

Soc. B.: Peaceful species that lives in small to larger schools. It occurs together with the black cichlid, *Cichlasoma arnoldi*.

M: Clear, well-filtered water with extremely low hardness (below 2° dGH) and a pH of 5.8 are values from its natural habitat. In the aquarium the animals are more tolerant. A good water conditioner should be used with water exchanges. The species is very nitrite/nitrate sensitive.

B: Breeding has already been successful in England. Unfortunately, no data are known to us.

F: O; any food remains on the bottom.

S: The species has already been presented in Vol. 1, page 471.

T: 23-26° C, 73-79° F, **L:** 6 cm, 2 1/3", **A:** 60 cm, 24", **R:** b, **D:** 2

Corydoras orphnopterus

WEITZMAN & NIJSSEN, 1970

Spotfin Cory

Syn.: *Corydoras orphonopterus*.

Hab.: Lower Rio Bobonaza, Pastaza river system, Ecuador (South America).

F.I.: 1984 by Heiko Bleher, Frankfurt/M.-Kelsterbach, Germany.

Sex: No external characteristics known.

Soc. B.: A peaceful species which should not be maintained with tiger barbs, angelfish or others that may have a fondness of nibbling on its long barbels.

M: Pay special attention to the substrate; it should be made of fine to coarse sand, for sharp-edged quartz is unsuitable. Otherwise the species is undemanding. Water: pH 6.5-7.5; hardness up to 20° dGH. Good filtration.

B: Not yet known.

F: C, O; mosquito larvae are probably the closest to its natural diet. Tablet foods (Tetra Tips) are accepted after habituation, but flake food is more readily taken (FD-Menu, etc.).

S: Because of its specially accentuated long snout, the German common name trunk corycat (Rüsselpanzerwels) is suggested.

T: 20-24° C, 68-75° F, **L:** 5.5 cm, 2 1/4", **A:** 50 cm, 20", **R:** b, **D:** 1-2

Corydoras ornatus

Corydoras orphnopterus

Corydoras panda NIJSSEN & ISBRÜCKER, 1971

Panda Cory

Syn.: None.

Hab.: Peru; in the Ucayali river system, South America.

F.I.: 1976 by Alfred Hanrieder, Scheinfeld.

Sex: The ♀♀ are somewhat larger and fuller. The sexes differ in shape.

Soc. B.: Very peaceful species; suitable for the smallest tank with small characins and dwarf cichlids.

M: This small species could almost be counted as a dwarf cory. They require well-filtered, oxygen-rich water with an exchange every 3-4 weeks.

B: FOERSCH (1984) reports an initial breeding experience with *Corydoras panda* in DATZ **37**, 41-44. The spawning occurred in a 30 l (8 gal) tank without a substrate. The tank was furnished with a bunch of Java moss and two clay pots as hiding places. The breeders were fed *Daphnia* and *Tubifex*. Every few days a third of the water was exchanged. It was medium-hard (16° dGH) with a temperature of 22-24° C (72-75° F). The clutch was small and was composed of adhesive, 1.5 mm (1/16"), light yellow eggs. Development takes 4.5 days at 25° C (77° F), then the 7.5 mm (5/16") long larvae hatch, still carrying a clearly visible yolk-sac. It is absorbed after one and a half days. The young are quite active swimming and very timid. They are fed with *Artemia* nauplii, micro food and minced grindal worms.

F: L, O; aufwuchs in the algae lawn and substrate, small worms, FD tablets and leftover flake food.

S: The name is derived from the spot pattern which is similar to that of a panda.

T: 20-25° C, 68-77° F, L: 4.5 cm, 1 3/4", A: 60 cm, 24", R: b, D: 2-3

Corydoras polystictus REGAN, 1912

Many-Spotted Cory

Syn.: *Corydoras virescens*, *"C. vermelinhos"* (trade name).

Hab.: Eastern tributaries of the Rio Guaporé (Mato Grosso, Brazil); South America.

F.I.: 1955.

Sex: The ♂ is thinner and has a straight ventral line; ♀ has a rounded belly.

Soc. B.: Peaceful species which should be kept in a school of 5-8 animals. A good species to combine with gentle characins and cichlids.

M: Current generated by a pump or a strong filter. Fine sandy bottom. Water: pH 6.2-7.5; hardness up to 18° dGH. As low a nitrate content as possible, up to 30 mg/l. Frequent water changes, every 3-4 weeks 1/3 of the tank volume. Use peat extracts or a good water conditioner. Plants are not harmed.

B: At spawning time the species shows "jumping" motions according to STERBA. The breeding tank should be shallow (20 cm; 8") and large (100 x 40 cm; 39" x 16"). Clear, well-filtered water. Several ♂♂ with few ♀♀.

F: O; tablet and flake foods. Any kind of small live foods. Frozen and freeze-dried foods.

S: A beautiful species which is somewhat similar to *C. punctatus* (Vol. 1, page 471), but because of the regular dots and the absence of other patterns, it is easily distinguished. Despite its wide distribution, this beautiful species is rarely found in the trade.

T: 22-28° C, 72-82° F, L: 4 cm, 1 2/3", A: 60 cm, 24", R: b, D: 1-2

Corydoras panda ♂

Corydoras polystictus

Fish catching station at Iquitos. The fish are held in halved oil barrels.

Corydoras robineae BURGESS, 1983
Flagtail Corycat

Syn.: None.

Hab.: Drainage of the upper Rio Negro (Rio Aiuana). South America.

F.I.: 1983 to USA; first import to Europe in 1977.

Sex: Not yet known.

Soc. B.: Probably peaceful like all smaller corys. In general its behavior is more sedate than that of other cory species.

M: According to the habitat of this new catfish, peat filtered soft water should be the most favorable. pH 5.6-7.0; hardness up to 15° dGH.

B: Difficult; see TFH, Dec. 1995.

F: C, L; tablet foods, flake food remains, small worms and mosquito larvae.

S: The species is quite similar to *Dianema urostriata* (Aquarium Atlas, Vol. 1, page 476) in appearance but has 6 barbels while *D. urostriata* only has four.

T: 23-26° C, L: about 4 cm, A: 60 cm, R: b, D: 2-3
73-79° F, about 1 2/3", 24",

Corydoras septentrionalis GOSLINE, 1940
Southern Green Cory

Syn.: None.

Hab.: Colombia; tributary of the Rio Meta (South America).

F.I.: 1975 by Heiko Bleher, Frankfurt.

Sex: No obvious ones.

Soc. B.: Species tank; can easily be associated with other fish of tropical mountain streams.

M: A current-loving fish from headwaters. Use dark sand or broken lava as substrate. Likes to root. pH 6.0-7.5; hardness up to 18° dGH.

T: 20-23° C, L: 5.5 cm, A: 60 cm, R: b, D: 2
68-73° F, 2 1/4", 24",

B: No reports are yet available.

F: O, L; the species readily roots through the sandy bottom and layers of mulm in search of something edible. Tablet foods and worm-like foods.

S: Similar to *Corydoras acutus* (Vol. 1, page 460), however, the dark spot on the anterior part of the dorsal fin is missing.

Corydoras simulatus WEITZMAN & NIJSSEN, 1970
Masquerade Cory

Syn.: None.

Hab.: Colombia (Amazon drainage area).

F.I.: Unknown; it is sometimes imported together with *C. metae*.

Sex: Not known; ♀ probably plumper and more robust, ♂ more slender.

Soc. B.: Peaceful bottom dweller. Suitable for the community tank with good water conditions.

M: In contrast to the opposing picture, the species should be kept on coarse sand. The fish prefers flowing, clear water. Therefore, a good, frequently cleaned filter (every 4-6 weeks) is recommended. Plant as desired. Water: pH 6.2-7.5; hardness up to 20° dGH.

T: 20-25° C, L: 5.5 cm, A: 60 cm, R: b, D: 1-2
68-77° F, 2", 24",

B: No proof that it has been bred.

F: O; tablet food, flake food remains. A leftover devourer which likes to root. Worms and mosquito larvae are delicacies.

S: The species lives sympatrically (together) with *C. metae*.

Corydoras septentrionalis

Corydoras simulatus

Corydoras steindachneri ISBRÜCKER & NIJSSEN, 1973
Steindachner's Cory

Syn.: None.

Hab.: Paranagua, south Brazil (South America).

F.I.: Uncertain.

Sex: The ♂♂ have a more elongated dorsal fin and are more slender than the ♀♀.

Soc. B.: Nimble, peaceful species, best kept in a species tank or an aquarium with decoration fitting a stream fish.

M: If wild caught specimens can be obtained, an acclimation time and the addition of a water conditioner with water exchanges every two weeks is recommended. Aquarium bred specimens are usually quite robust. Water: pH 6.0-7.2; hardness up to 15° dGH

B: The animals in the trade these days are probably all bred in an aquarium. Breeding is in a manner typical for the genus.

F: C, O; flake food with freeze-dried components, frozen food (bloodworms), *Artemia*.

S: The species looks like a cross between *Corydoras macropterus* (the tall dorsal) and *Corydoras paleatus*.

T: 22-26° C, L: 6 cm, A: 60 cm, R: b, D: 1-2
72-79° F, 2 1/3", 24",

Corydoras sterbai KNAACK, 1962
Sterba's Cory

Syn.: See S.

Hab.: Upper Rio Guaporé, Brazil.

F.I.: 1960.

Sex: ♂ somewhat more slender. ♀ stouter.

Soc. B.: Peaceful species best kept in a small school. Tankmates should be upper and midwater dwelling species.

M: Bottom soft and, if possible, dark. Soft, clear water with some current. The tank should not be planted too densely and offer plenty of free swimming space.

B: Like other *Corydoras* species? No breeding reports are yet available.

F: O; all kinds of tablet and flake foods. Occasionally live food, e.g., *Daphnia*, *Tubifex* and Enchytraea.

S: The species is usually considered to be *C. haraldschultzi*, but that is a different species.

T: 21-25° C, L: 8 cm, A: 80 cm, R: b, D: 1-2
70-77° F, 3", 31",

Hoplosternum littorale (HANCOCK, 1828)
Clay Hoplo, Cascudo
Sub-Fam.: Callichthyinae

Syn.: *Callichthys laevigatus, Hoplosternum laevigatum, Callichthys littoralis, C. subulatus, Hoplosternum stevardii.*

Hab.: Widely distributed in South America, from Argentina in the south to Trinidad (Central America) in the north.

F.I.: Could not be determined (1959?).

Sex: During the spawning season the first ray of the pectoral fin of the ♂ is strongly turned upward. This has often been considered an abnormality.

Soc. B.: Quite peaceful bottom dweller which, as a full grown specimen, will sometimes consider smaller fishes as prey.

Continued page 482.

Corydoras steindachneri

Corydoras sterbai

Continuation of *H. littorale*

The animals like to root, not to say they sometimes dig.

M: An aquarium with fine-leaved plants is not suitable because the plants fill with mulm. In contrast, larger *Echinodorus* plants in pots are a suitable decoration. A mulmy sand corner is important for rooting. Strong filtration. Caves as hiding places, darken the surface with floating plants.

B: The ♂ builds a bubble nest and guards the larvae for several days. The ♀ is chased away. The larvae hatch after 3 days and should be fed small live food (e.g., *Artemia*). However, the young also accept flake food particles, tablet food, (TabiMin—crumbled tablets) and freeze-dried foods—in short, they graze the substrate for edibles. It has not been determined if the parents cannibalize on the young. Depending on the observations, first the ♀, and then perhaps the ♂, should be removed from the breeding tank. For the breeding set-up, the parents are to be provided with plenty of live foods (*Tubifex*, *Daphnia*, frozen bloodworms).

F: O; worms, tablet foods, leftover food. Plants are not eaten but often uprooted (see **Soc. B.**).

S: HOEDEMANN (1952) described the sub-species *H. littorale dailliy* from Surinam. Unfortunately, whether or not this is still a valid sub-species could not be determined. As long as it is valid, *Hoplosternum littorale littorale* would also be a sub-species.
Juveniles are quite attractively colored, adults are a quite monotonous yellow/gray color (clay colored). This is why this common name is suggested here.

T: 18-26° C, **L:** 23 cm, **A:** 100 cm, **R:** b, **D:** 1-3, depending on size.
64-79° F, 9", 39",

Hoplosternum pectorale (BOULENGER, 1895)

Pepper and Salt Hoplo, Spotted Hoplo

Syn.: *"Hoplosternum magdalenae", Callichthys pectoralis, Hoplosternum pectoralis.*

Hab.: Rio Magdalena in Brazil, South America.

F.I.: Uncertain because almost always identified as *H. thoracantum.*

Sex: ♂ has more developed pectoral fins.

Soc. B.: Mostly a peaceful species. During the spawning season, the ♂♂ are very aggressive. Several animals can be kept in large tanks. The fish develop pronounced territorial behavior.

M: Densely planted tanks and some free swimming room above the plants. Diurnal species, well suited for the community tank when kept individually. Water: pH 5.8-7.8; hardness up to 25° dGH (10°). Sandy bottom. The species digs.

B: A bubble nest is built either among plant parts beneath larger floating leaves or in caves. Water depth should only be 20 cm (8"). The ♂ courts intensively. After spawning, the ♀ should be removed. The ♀ places the eggs in a pouch, which is created between the body and the pectoral fin when the ♂ wedges the ♀'s body into a curve. From this pouch the eggs are adhered to the bubble nest. Hatching occurs after 4-5 days. T: 26-28° C (79-82° F), soft water to 5° KH. Rear in an algae tank with *Artemia* and fine micro food, TetraMin Baby Food and/or Liquifry. Always siphon out the food remains.

F: O; leftover foods of all kinds.

S: Animals of the coloration pictured here are often called *H. magdalenae*. However, today this has to be considered a synonym of *H. thoracatum*.

T: 20-22° C, **L:** 12 cm, **A:** 80 cm, **R:** b, **D:** 1-2
68-72° F, 4¾", 31",

Hoplosternum littorale

Hoplosternum pectorale

Channallabes apus (GÜNTHER, 1873)
Eel Catfish

Syn.: *Gymnallabes apus.*

Hab.: Zaire (Congo) and Angola, Africa.

F.I.: 1956, then again in 1974 by Heiko Bleher, Frankfurt.

Sex: Not known.

Soc. B.: A reclusive fish which sometimes is not seen for months. Nocturnal. Only associate with larger fishes which cannot be eaten.

M: A species which is content with any aquarium water. pH 6.5-7.8; hardness up to 25° dGH. Hiding places have to be offered. The species likes to remain buried during the day in a sandy bottom.

B: Has probably not yet been attempted.

F: C; tablet foods (any quantity), pieces of beef heart. Any kind of larger live foods.

S: *Channallabes apus* has very rudimentary pectoral fins, and the ventral fins are missing entirely.

T: 22-25° C, L: 30 cm, A: 120 cm, R: b, D: 3
72-77° F, 11¾", 47",

Clarias angolensis STEINDACHNER, 1866
Angola Walking Catfish

Syn.: *Clarias gabonensis.*

Hab.: West and central Africa; Niger system to Angola, also in brackish water.

F.I.: 1910 by the Vereinigten Zierfischzüchtereien Berlin-Conradshöhe, Germany.

Sex: ♀ has a clearly fuller ventral area.

Soc. B.: Loner, only associate with fish longer than 1/3-1/2 of its body length. Nocturnal.

M: Hides during the day and needs a cave among rocks or roots as hiding places. Best to plant robust, strongly rooting species or floating plants. Subdued lighting. pH 7.0-9.0; hardness 15-40° dGH.

B: Not yet.

F: C; small fish, fish flesh (thawed fish sticks, cleaned of batter), earthworms, freeze-dried fairy shrimp, etc. Juveniles up to 15 cm (6") also take tablet food readily, flake food remains and frozen foods.

S: The species is aided by a facultative accessory breathing organ to endure extended periods of time on land, thereby allowing it to wander about over land during the night in search of food or other living areas. Albino forms are in the trade.

T: 23-28° C, L: 35 cm, A: 120 cm, R: b, D: 3-4 (S)
73-82° F, 14", 47",

Channallabes apus

Clarias angolensis

Clarias cavernicola TREWAVAS, 1936
Blind Cave Walking Catfish

Syn.: None.

Hab.: Algumas cave in Nordotavi (Namibia), Africa.

F.I.: Up to now only imported for public aquaria (i.e., Berlin).

Sex: Not known.

Soc. B.: Peaceful among themselves, but only suitable for a species tank.

M: Similar to the species below, however, the tank can be kept almost totally dark.

B: No reports dealing with a successful spawn are yet available.

F: C, O; a species which in nature feeds primarily on insects (moths, etc.). In an aquarium, table food and meats are accepted.

S: Not a fish for the hobbyist. Although a rare fish, it has no attraction (besides as oddity) for the aquarist.

T: 15-25° C, 59-77° F, **L:** 25 cm, 9¾", **A:** 150 cm, 59", **R:** b, **D:** 3

Clarias gariepinus (BURCHELL, 1822)
African Walking Catfish

Syn.: *Silurus gariepinus.*

Hab.: South Africa, widely distributed throughout tropical Africa, Asia Minor.

F.I.: 1984 by L. Seegers.

Sex: The ♂♂ have partially red fin tips during the spawning season. The genital papilla is more pointed in the ♂♂ than in the ♀♀.

Soc. B.: Only keep in a species tank. The species is a glutton like a shark.

M: The species is a bully. It can break 4 mm (3/16") glass panes! Cover the tank well, because the animals readily "take off" and then dry up on the floor. No demands whatsoever are placed on water conditions.

B: Not possible in an aquarium. Perhaps by stripping the eggs and sperm. ♀♀ over 50 cm (20") in length produce 50,000-150,000 eggs. Pairing occurs at night, usually after heavy rains. No care of the spawn.

F: C; pisci- and insectivore. In nature it mainly consumes young cichlids. The species hunts in groups in schools of other fish.

S: This animal should be removed from the importers list. The animals eat excessively, specially fish, to achieve their fast rate of growth. Lately, some partial albino specimens were imported. Stay away!

T: 20-26° C, 68-79° F, **L:** 80 cm, 31", **A:** 250 cm, 98", **R:** b, **D:** 4 (S)

Clarias cavernicola

Clarias gariepinus

Clarias lazera (BURCHELL, 1822)

Syn.: *Silurus gariepinnis, Macropteronotus charmuth, Heterobranchus anguillaris* (not L.), *Clarias syriacus, Clarias capensis* (not C. & V.), *Clarias orontis, Clarias macracanthus, Clarias xenodon, Clarias longiceps, Clarias silurus gariepinnis,* and others.

Hab.: Nile and widely distributed in tropical west Africa.

F.I.: Not known.

Sex: Both sexes have a genital papilla similar to cichlids; long and pointed in the ♂ and round in the ♀. However, this is only visible during the spawning season.

Soc. B.: A very predatory nocturnal fish. Associate only with conspecifics or other very large fishes able to defend themselves. Even juveniles may already be aggressive.

M: The tank has to be well covered, because the fish like to get out and then will dry up in the room. The species tolerates any, even bad, water and survives even in waters devoid of oxygen as long as they are not too hard (less than 20° dGH). Sensitive to salt water. pH 6.5-8.0; hardness 5-28° dGH.

B: Fish breeding establishments achieve the best breeding results by manually stripping the eggs and sperm. To spawn naturally (including an aquarium), a cold freshwater flood (rainy season) should be imitated.

F: C, O; omnivore, but prefers foods of animal origin. Meat, fish; juveniles take tablet foods, adults after habituation also accept carp and trout pellets.

S: The species can travel across land when the habitat is drying up. An accessory breathing organ (bag-like pouch in the gill cavity, with tufted protuberances), makes it possible for the animals to endure several hours without water.
Food fish. No incentive for the aquarium hobby. The dorsal and pelvic fin rays can,

T: 19-27° C, L: 90 cm, A: 200 cm, R: b, m, D: 4 (C)
66-81° F, 35", 79",

Anadoras grypus (COPE, 1871)
Dusky Doradid

Syn.: *Doras grypus*.

Hab.: Amazon basin, South America.

F.I.: 1970. As "*A. hancockii*", surely already earlier.

Sex: Not yet described.

Soc. B.: Loner. In larger tanks with sufficient hiding places, several individuals can be maintained, each of which will establish its own territory. Tankmates should only be larger cichlids and characins, e.g., *Prochilodus* and *Leporinus*. Smaller fish could be eaten.

M: Water: pH 6.2-7.2; hardness up to 15° dGH.

T: 22-26° C, L: 15 cm, A: 120 cm, R: b, D: 2
72-79° F, 6", 47",

B: Not known. Perhaps like *Amblydoras hancockii* (Vol. 1, page 482). Bubble nest beneath plant leaves.

F: C, O; tablet foods. Frozen foods. *Tubifex*. *Gammarus*. Small snails. The species can also be maintained for extended periods of time on tablet food.

S: The species is often confused with *Amblydoras hancockii*. However, *A. hancockii* has a serrated dorsal fin ray. It is smooth in *A. grypus*. The fontanel is D-shaped. The lateral bone plates are smaller than on *Amblydoras*.

Continuation of *Clarias lazera*:

although not really poisonous, inflict painful injuries because of their foreign protein. Only catch with plastic containers.

Clarias lazera seems to be a synonym to *Clarias gariepinus*.

Astrodoras asterifrons (HECKEL, 1855)
Helmet Doradid

Syn.: *Doras asterifrons.*

Hab.: Middle Amazon (Solimoes) and Bolivia; South America.

F.I.: 1914.

Sex: The ♂ has a longer dorsal fin ray.

Soc. B.: A species that lives in seclusion and is often not noticed for weeks. It can be housed without reservations with small fish.

M: The elongated pointed dorsal and pelvic fins, as well as the spines along the lateral line, can easily get entangled in a coarse meshed net or injure the hand of a captor. Therefore, it is best to catch the fish with a cup or other plastic container (chase in). Otherwise the fish is unproblematic and very long-lived. pH 6.5-7.8; hardness up to 20° dGH.

B: Not yet known.

F: O; leftover flake food, tablet foods, any kind of live foods as long as it is not too large; especially *Tubifex* and *Gammarus*.

S: The common name is derived from the bony shield on its head.

T: 20-25° C, **L:** 10-12 cm, **A:** 100 cm, **R:** b, **D:** 1
68-77° F, 4"-4¾", 39",

Hassar notospilus (EIGENMANN, 1910)
Black-Finned Doradid

Syn.: *Hemidoras notospilus, Hemidoras onestes, Hassar orestis.*

Hab.: Guianas, South America.

F.I.: After 1975.

Sex: ♂ has an elongated dorsal fin ray. ♀ has a more rounded ventral area. The pelvic fins are more developed in the ♀.

Soc. B.: Very peaceful small catfish which is best kept together with small characins, dwarf cichlids or small labyrinth fishes. Larger fish cause unease, even if they are not aggressive. It seems that *Hassar* recognizes larger fish only as enemies. If residing with such tankmates, it becomes reclusive and very shy.

M: The bottom has to be soft. Under no circumstances should sharp-edged gravel be used. The finely branched barbels are constantly in the search of food in the substrate. Only in very darkened aquaria does the fish eat during the day. Sufficient hiding places, e.g., dense vegetation in the background, have to be provided. Very sensitive to Ich. Copper containing preparations should be applied at half the dosage.
Water: pH 6.5-7.0; hardness up to 20° dGH, clear, biologically pure water is a condition for successful maintenance of the species. Peat filtration or the regular addition of peat extract is recommended along with a good water conditioner for water exchanges.

B: Not yet bred.

F: C, O; leftover food, tablet foods (Tetra Tips or similar, FD-Menu). Small live foods, especially small worms and *Daphnia*.

S: The species is initially very shy. Sudden unusual movements in front of the tank should be avoided.

T: 21-25° C, **L:** 7.5 cm, **A:** 100 cm, **R:** b, **D:** 2-3
70-77° F, 3", 39",

Astrodoras asterifrons

Hassar notospilus

Leptodoras linnelli

EIGENMANN, 1912

Syn.: *Leptodoras acipenserinus, Hemidoras linnelli.*

Hab.: Northern South America: Colombia, Brazilian Amazon, South America. Rare.

F.I.: 1978 by Heiko Bleher, Frankfurt. USA 1980.

Sex: Not known. Probably like *Hassar notospilus* (page 490).

Soc. B.: Gregarious species, but it should be kept together with fish of at least 7 cm (2³/4") length.

M: Use a large surface area, shallow aquarium with a gravel bottom and alternating mulm corners or sand bottom. Sparse vegetation in the background. Medium to strong current. Oxygen-rich water which must be free of nitrite/nitrate. pH 5.8-7.0; hardness up to 18° dGH. Provide hiding places beneath roots or in crevices between stones.

B: Because so few individuals have been imported, it has not been bred.

F: L, C; primarily benthic insect larvae. Frozen foods, mosquito larvae and fairy shrimp. Flake and tablet foods are probably possible. Nothing is yet known about it.

S: The picture shows a juvenile. Adults are taller built and have branched barbels, similar to *Synodontis*.

T: 18-22° C, L: 21 cm, A: 150 cm, R: b, D: 2-3
64-72° F, 8¹/3", 59",

Liosomadoras oncinus, see next page

Opsodoras leporhinus

(EIGENMANN, 1912)

Syn.: *Hemidoras leporhinus.*

Hab.: Middle Amazon, Bolivia and Peru (Iquitos); South America.

F.I.: 1972 by Heiko Bleher, Frankfurt, Germany.

Sex: Not known.

Soc. B.: This conspicuous species should be kept as a small group in a species tank. Do not associate with other, overly small species. Do not keep with fin nipping species (tiger barbs). Combine with peaceful fishes roughly the same size.

M: The species is nitrate sensitive. A mature biological filter is therefore a condition for its well-being. The fish likes to stand in a weak current. Ich considers the fish especially attractive. All medication should be applied at half the recommended dosage. In a darkened aquarium (floating plant cover) the fish will search for food as along as live food is offered. Water: pH 6.5-7.0; hardness up to 20° dGH.

B: Not known.

F: C; *Tubifex*, *Daphnia*, *Cyclops*, occasionally Enchytraea. After acclimation, flake and tablet foods are also eaten.

S: A sensitive fish which requires a lot of attention.

T: 22-25° C, L: 8 cm, A: 100 cm, R: b, D: 3
72-77° F, 3", 39",

Leptodoras linnelli

Opsodoras leporhinus

Liosomadoras oncinus (JARDINE, 1841)
Jaguar Catfish

Syn.: *Arius oncina, A. oncinus, Liosomadoras morrowi.*

Hab.: Rio Ucayali, Peru; Rio Xeruiuni, Rio Negro, Brazil; South America.

F.I.: 1968 by Heiko Bleher, Frankfurt.

Sex: ♂ has the urogenital papilla at the anterior edge of the anal fin. ♂ more brightly colored.

Soc. B.: Twilight-active, gregarious fish which is suitable for the community aquarium. Can be kept with fishes over 5 cm (2") long.

M: The species requires soft, strongly acid water. pH 4.8-6.8; hardness 0° to 12° dGH. Peat filtration. Tough vegetation using *Echinodorus* species, roots and large stone constructions as hideouts.

B: Eggs are fertilized internally, similar to the genus *Auchenipterus,* and are immediately thereafter expelled. The species has not been bred in an aquarium.

F: C; live foods of all kind, fish. Juveniles prefer *Tubifex* and *Gammarus* (fairy shrimp).

*S: The species is very close to the genus *Auchenipterus* and should be placed there. However, the criteria for classification into the family would have to be changed (armored body from the cranium to the dorsal fin for doradids, but not for auchenipterids). *L. oncinus* does not have these bony plates.

T: 20-24° C, L: 25 cm, A: 120 cm, R: b, D: 2-3
68-75° F, 10", 47",

Liosomadoras oncinus, juvenile

Liosomadoras oncinus

Opsodoras stuebelii (STEINDACHNER, 1882)

Syn.: *Oxydoras stubeli, Hemidoras stubeli.*

Hab.: Rio Marañón, Brazil.

F.I.: 1971 by Heiko Bleher, Frankfurt as "*Acanthodoras spinosissimus* var."

Sex: Not yet described.

Soc. B.: Very peaceful catfish which can even be kept with neons and similar fish. 3-4 fish should be kept together.

M: The species prefers twilight, a lot of hiding places and dark substrate. In tanks that are too bright, it often cannot be seen for months. It is then forgotten. This is why this species is not a beginners fish, even though it is easily kept and hardy. Darkening the water with peat filtration or the addition of Tetra Blackwater Extract or similar products is appreciated. Sand bottom and a corner of mulm aid in keeping the fish healthy and happy.

B: Not known.

F: O; flake food remains, tablet foods. All kinds of small live foods.

S: An unobtrusive, reclusive species. Something for the "twilight-active" aquarist.

T: 22-25° C, **L:** 12 cm, **A:** 100 cm, **R:** b, **D:** 1-2
72-77° F, 4 3/4", 39",

Pseudodoras niger (VALENCIENNES, 1811)
Black Doradid

Syn.: *Doras niger, Doras humboldti, Oxydoras niger, Corydoras edentatus, Rhinodoras niger, Rhinodoras prionomus, Rhinodoras teffeanus.*

Hab.: Amazon region, Rio Purus, Rio Sao Francisco, Brazil; Peru (South America).

F.I.: 1970 by Heiko Bleher, Frankfurt, Germany.

Sex: Not yet described.

Soc. B.: A notoriously peace-loving, large catfish. It is best kept with 2 or 3 conspecifics. One can even combine with platys, peaceful cichlids or a school of larger characins. However, if the species feels harassed, it wildly beats its tail. Even larger stones can be thrown against the aquarium pane, breaking it. Therefore caution should be used when capturing and when combining with very large fish, i.e., cichlids.

M: In a large tank the species is easy to care for. They will not thrive in tanks under 2 m (79") in length. An undergravel filter should not be used since the fish constantly roots in the substrate for something edible. A large mechanical and good biological filter (at least 15% of the tank volume) are a necessity. Few demands are placed on the water as long as it is not polluted. pH 6.0-7.8; hardness to 25° dGH.

B: Not known.

F: O; specimens of 25 cm (10") in length can easily consume 500 TabiMin tablets per week! In nature detritus, worms, fruits and seeds have been found in the stomach.

S: In a show aquarium the animals may have a place. In the home aquarium it is only for specialists who grant the species a giant tank. The fish have an extraordinarily well developed sense of taste and smell.

T: 21-24° C, **L:** 80 cm, **A:** 150-250 cm, **R:** b, **D:** 2-4 (S)
70-75° F, 31", 59"-98",

Opsodoras stuebelii

Pseudodoras niger

Pterodoras granulosus (VALENCIENNES, 1811)
Common Bacu

Syn.: *Doras granulosus, Doras maculatus, Doras murica, Doras muricus.*

Hab.: Widely distributed in almost all larger rivers of South America.

F.I.: Unknown.

Sex: Not known.

Soc. B.: Nocturnal catfish which is not really a predator, but "by mistake" and out of hunger it will also eat fishes of suitable size. Large cichlids, catfish and larger characins can be tankmates without problems. In nature the animals migrate seasonally in large schools.

M: Adaptive species. However, alkaline water with a pH above 7.5 causes skin and eye cloudiness. Provide sparse vegetation with Java fern or moss. Other plants are eaten during food shortages. Large caves of stone. Use a darkened aquarium or place the tank in a room without much daylight.

B: Not known.

F: O; in nature, snails, water plants and fruits are eaten. In the aquarium, tablet foods are preferred.

S: The picture is from the Berlin Aquarium. Valued food fish.

T: 20-24° C, L: 90 cm, A: 200 cm, R: b, D: 4 (S)
68-75° F, 35", 79",

Rhinodoras dorbignyi (KROYER, 1855)
Fog Doradid

Syn.: *Doras dorbignyi, D. nebulosus, Oxydoras dorbignyi.*

Hab.: South Brazil and Paraguay, South America.

F.I.: 1980.

Sex: Not known.

Soc. B.: Smaller animals up to 12 cm (4^3/4") in length are well suited for the community tank. Larger animals can prey at night on smaller fish on the substrate. Nocturnal.

M: Species requires soft water up to about 10° dGH, pH 6.5-7.0. A greater number of hideouts should be offered, especially when several specimens are cared for. Peat filtration. Requires frequent water changes with the addition of a water conditioner. Plants are not eaten, but fine-leaved plants should not be used because of its fondness of digging. Do not use sharp-edged gravel or the barbels suffer and thereby the entire fish.

B: Not described.

F: C, O; acclimated animals like tablet foods and food remains. Otherwise *Tubifex* and fly maggots, which one can easily raise oneself outside in the summer in rotting meat or fish (in your own garden).

S: The species is rapid growing under good care. This should be considered at the time of purchase, so that the fish is provided with a large enough home.

T: 20-25° C, L: 17 cm, A: 150 cm, R: b, D: 2
68-77° F, 6^3/4", 59",

Pterodoras granulosus

Rhinodoras dorbignyi

Heteropneustes fossillis (BLOCH, 1794)
Asian Stinging Catfish

Syn.: *Silurus fossilis, Clarisilurus kemratensis, Heteropneustes kemratensis, Silurus singio, Saccobranchus fossilis, S. singio.*

Hab.: Widely distributed in India, Sri Lanka?, Thailand, Burma.

F.I.: 1891 by Dr. Schad of Treptow by Berlin.

Sex: ♂ has a thinner ventral line, ♀ stockier.

Soc. B.: An aggressive fish which likes to prey on smaller tankmates. Nocturnal; rarely mobile during the day. Can be kept with barbs over 12 cm (4³/4") in length, etc. The species likes to live with conspecifics; therfore, a species tank is recommended.

M: Provide several hiding and resting places. These are sought during the day and must be available. Plant only with nondelicate, larger species (giant *Vallisneria*, Java fern). Water: pH 6.0-8.0; hardness up to 30° dGH. Good filtration.

B: Has occurred in an aquarium. The 2 mm (¹/16") eggs are laid in a cluster in previously fanned out gravel pits. Eggs and juveniles are guarded by the parents. Rear with *Artemia, Daphnia.*

F: C, O; small specimens like tablet food. Later, the hardy appetite must be appeased with heart, fish flesh, mealy worms, etc.

S: The pectoral fin rays of the species are poisonous; therefore, use caution when catching.
Perhaps the imported and also repeatedly bred specimens of this genus that have appeared on the market are *Heteropneustes microps*, a clearly smaller (to 25 cm; 10") and, consequently, easier kept species. From the outside *H. microps* and *H. fossilis* are very similar. The only distinguishing characteristic between the species is that the anal and caudal fins of *H. fossilis* are separated by a deep notch, continuous in *H. microps*. *H. microps* has only been found in a small region in Sri Lanka.

T: 21-25° C, **L:** 50 cm, **A:** 150 cm, **R:** b, **D:** 4 (C)
70-77° F, 20", 59",

Heteropneustes microps (GÜNTHER, 1864)
Small Asian Stinging Catfish

Syn.: *Saccobranchus microps.*

Hab.: South Asia; Sri Lanka (Ceylon). The species occurs in fresh and brackish water.

F.I.: Not sure, because the species has usually been kept as *Heteropneustes fossilis.*

Sex: ♂ is thinner. ♀ stockier and fuller in the ventral area.

Soc. B.: Follow recommendation for *H. fossilis.*

M: As indicated for *H. fossilis.* Both species are very adaptive in regard to water composition. Because of their length and related food intake, a good filter and regular water exchanges are recommended, especially for *H. fossilis.*

F: C, O; tablet foods, large flakes, animals over 10 cm (4") in length accept small earthworms, appreciate bloodworms, *Tubifex*, etc.; fish!

S: In *Heteropneustes microps* the anal fin is joined to the tail fin, and the dorsal fin has 8 rays. Contrary to this, the anal and tail fin of *H. fossilis* are distinct and the dorsal fin has 6-7 rays.

T: 22-26° C, **L:** 16 cm, **A:** 100 cm, **R:** b, **D:** 3
72-79° F, 6¹/₃", 39",

Heteropneustes fossilis

Heteropneustes microps

Acanthicus adonis

ISBRÜCKER & NIJSSEN, 1988

Syn.: None.

Hab.: Tributary of the Amazon at the Brazilian border to Peru, South America. According to the literature, however, it has a much wider distribution. It is said to also occur by Xeberos in Peru, in the Rio Branco of the Brazilian state of Pará, and even in the Guianas. It has been confirmed in these three localities at least twice, according to leading ichthyologists. But it is probably rare throughout its range. Perhaps the various localities are related to seasonal migrations?

F.I.: 1983 by Heiko Bleher, Frankfurt-Kelsterbach, Germany.

Sex: Not known.

Soc. B.: Peaceful species which should not be kept with fishes that are too lively and restless. A species tank is recommended, perhaps house them with small characins. In any case not together with any potential spawn eaters, as a breeding success of this species would be an aquaristic sensation.

M: A tank as large as possible with current. Rockwork with caves and crevices. Intense illumination for algae growth. Background vegetation is possible since it is not a plant eater. Dark substrate. Water: pH 6.0-7.0; hardness 5-12° dGH. Peat extract and a good water conditioner for water changes are recommended.

B: Not known. The animals seem to migrate during the spawning season. The animals could not be found a second time at the original locality.

F: H, L; algae, tablet foods and small live foods.

S: It may be a different species pictured in Vol. 3, page 361 (only available in German at this time).

T: 23-27° C, **L:** 100 cm, **A:** 120 cm, **R:** b, **D:** 3
73-81° F, 39", 47",

Ancistrus sp.
Bristlenose Catfish*

(VALENCIENNES, 1840)

Syn.: *Loricaria plecostomoides, Hypostomus temminckii, Plecostomus aculeatus, Hypostomus schneideri, Xenocara temminckii, Ancistrus cirrhosus* (not VALENCIENNES), *A. dolichopterus* (not KNER), *A. temminckii.*

Hab.: French Guiana, Surinam, north Brazil, perhaps even to Peru, South America.

F.I.: ?

Sex: Adult ♂♂ have tentacle-like bristles along the mouth and the anterior head region. The bristles are shorter and hardly branched in the ♀.

Soc. B.: A peaceful species outside the spawning season. During the spawning season the ♂♂ develop marked territoriality. All fins and mouth spines are spread to impress. It is possible that fighting ♂♂ entangle themselves with their mouth spines making it hard to separate them.

M: Bogwood roots and stones should form caves. Water current is preferred. Intense illumination for algal development. Water slightly acid and medium-hard up to 25° dGH.

B: The orange, sometimes amber eggs are generally deposited on wood overhangs and guarded by the ♂ for about 10 days. During this time the ♂ has a camouflage coloration for protection. Rarely can the young be raised in a community tank. That is why several newly hatched fry should be reared separately in a rearing tank. Feeding is accomplished with peeled mashed peas that are passed through an *Artemia* sieve. The species is easy to breed. Spawning occurs every few weeks, chiefly during the winter months (the shorter days with less light signal the beginning of the rainy season to the fish). If one is in possession of a mature pair, a major water exchange (3/4) in November will initiate spawning.

F: H; peas (frozen ♦ thawed ♦ mashed). Pea skins are usually eaten the following day, after they have soaked. Vegetable flakes, tablet food. Sporadically, frozen mosquito larvae.

Continued on page 504.

Acanthicus adonis, below *Pseudacanthus* sp.

Ancistrus sp.

Continuation of *Ancistrus* sp.:

S: * This name is not identifying for the species because other catfishes of the family have very similarly developed bristles on the upperside of the mouth. The picture shows a juvenile which is much lighter colored than normal because it is located on a light substrate. The light tail fin tips disappear with age and become unavailable as identifying characteristics.

T: 21-24° C, L: 12 cm, A: 70 cm, R: b, D: 1
70-75° F, 4 3/4", 28",

Chaetostoma sp.

Sub-Fam.: Ancistrinae

Syn.: None.

Hab.: Mountain streams of Colombia.

F.I.: About 1977.

Sex: In some species the ♂♂ develop "tentacles" on the pectoral fins during the spawning season.

Soc. B.: The behavior of *Chaetostoma* is very similar to larger *Hypostomus* (previously *Plecostomus*). However, *Chaetostoma* occurs in mountain streams while *Plecostomus* originates from larger waters at lower elevations. *Chaetostoma* is a peaceful genus, but it can prey on hatched larvae and smallest fishes. Some animals develop territorial behavior towards conspecifics.

M: Use a well-filtered and aerated tank with coarse gravel substrate. Caves of stones or roots. Otherwise follow suggestions for *Hypostomus.*

B: Not known.

F: H, O; normally eats algae and aufwuchs, but it will accept tablet foods, flake food remains, lettuce leaves, spinach (frozen is best) and mashed peas as substitute foods. Glassworms and *Tubifex* are also occasionally taken.

T: 20-22° C, L: 10 cm, A: 100 cm, R: b, D: 2-3
68-72° F, 4", 39",

Cochliodon cochiliodon (KNER, 1854)

Cochliodon Catfish

Sub-Fam.: Hypostominae

Syn.: *Hypostomus cochliodon, Cochliodon hypostomus, Loricaria melanoptera, Plecostomus cochliodon, Panaque cochliodon.*

Hab.: Rio Cuiaba, Rio Jangada, Rio Paraguay, Paraguay, South America.

F.I.: 1969 by Heiko Bleher, Frankfurt, for the Berlin Aquarium.

Sex: Not known.

Soc. B.: One of the most peaceful, even lovable, representatives of the catfish family. The species is even inoffensive towards the smallest fishes.

M: Contrary to other loricariids, this species is also active during the day as long as enough vegetable food is available. (Some nocturnal catfish do not eat during the day, even if they are starving, e.g., *Sturisoma*). Acclimation is not always easy; the species is more demanding towards water quality then similar species of the genus, and it requires somewhat more attention. Maintain it only with very quiet species, i.e., with species that do not represent feed competitors (characins, small cichlids). *Cochliodon* requires oxygen-rich, slightly acid water (6.3-7.2); hardness up to 10° dGH during acclimation, later up to 18°. An aquarium full of algae is advantageous.

B: Not bred yet in an aquarium.

F: H; use tablet foods as the daily ration, then satiate 1-2 times per week with frozen (mashed) peas, lettuce, spinach and chickweed.

S: Unfortunately a species rarely offered in the trade. Shouldn't some hobbyists get together to attempt breeding? The publisher will mediate the addresses of interested owners.

T: 21-24° C, L: 15 cm, A: 80 cm, R: b, D: 2-3
70-75° F, 6", 31",

Chaetostoma sp. (in the trade *C. thomasi*)

Cochliodon cochliodon

Hypostomus plecostomus (LINNAEUS, 1758)

Pleco — Sub-Fam.: Hypostominae

Syn.: *Acipenser plecostomus, Loricaria plecostomus, Loricaria flava, Hypostomus guacari, Plecostomus plecostomus, P. guacari, Plecostomus bicirrhosus, P. flavus, Plecostomus brasiliensis, P. boulengeri, P. seminudus.*

Hab.: Northern South America.

F.I.: Not known; there has been constant confusion with other species of the genus.

Sex: Not known.

Soc. B.: Young specimens can be kept in small aquaria together with all species. Above 15 cm (6") the animals begin to develop territorial behavior. 2-3 animals can be kept in a 250 liter (65 gal) aquarium. Plants are never eaten but occasionally uprooted.

M: The species is very enduring even in tanks not well maintained. It grows fast. In 8 months two fish grew from an initial 15 cm (6") to 22 cm (8^3/4") in length. For small aquaria this species becomes too big! *Pecoltia* or *Chaetostomus* should be chosen instead. pH 6.2-8.2; hardness up to 28° dGH. Good filtration because of large amounts of feces. Tough plants, large caves as hiding places.

B: Bred in large quantities in Singapore and Hong Kong in ponds. A spawning pit is fanned out on a steep bank.

F: H, O; omnivorous in the aquarium. Can be fed tablet foods (Tetra TabiMin preferred), flake food remains as well as peas, lettuce and spinach. Algae in the aquarium don't stand a chance. Blue algae are not consumed.

S: The "*Plecostomus*" is one of the hardiest and enduring of all catfishes. It should not be left out of any larger community tank. Of the over 100 *Hypostomus* species, many more than 50 are spotted to a greater or lesser degree. If the pictured animal is indeed *H. plecostomus* is unknown.

T: 20-28° C, L: 28 cm, A: 120 cm, R: b, D: 1-2
68-82° F, 11", 47",

Chaetostoma sp. (GÜNTHER, 1864)

Bulldog Catfish — Sub-Fam.: Ancistrinae

Syn.: None.

Hab.: Upper Amazon region.

F.I.: About 1980.

Sex: Not known.

Soc. B.: Peaceful bottom dweller which is often seen during the day. Can also be housed with other small fish.

M: Can also be kept in smaller aquaria. Water: pH 6.0-7.5; hardness up to 15° dGH, strong filtration, perhaps additional aeration. If the room is heated during the winter, an aquarium heater may be unnecessary. Illuminate well to promote algae growth.

B: No reports are yet available.

F: O; omnivore in an aquarium: tablet foods, flake food remains, algae, frozen mashed peas. Frozen live foods such as mosquito larvae.

S: A rarely imported but appealing small catfish. *Chaetostomus* catfishes can easily be distinguished from the closely related *Hypostomus* catfishes by the longer head and the distinctly broader sucker mouth. At present, 39 descriptions in the genus are known. A classification of the pictured species is probably not possible without a revision of the genus. The species has been traded as *"Hypostomus wuchereri"*.

T: 20-24° C, L: 25 cm, A: 120 cm, R: b, D: 2-3
68-75° F, 9^3/4" 47",

Hypostomus plecostomus

Chaetostoma sp.

Otocinclus flexilis — COPE, 1894
Imitator Sucker Catfish

Syn.: *Otocinclus fimbriatus, O. arnoldi.*

Hab.: Rio Grande do Sul, Brazil, South America.

F.I.: 1905.

Sex: ♂ more slender than ♀.

Soc. B.: Very appealing, gentle and peaceful species. Can be kept in an aquarium together with almost all smaller species. Loner.

M: The species loves well-planted tanks with shading at the surface. All plants are possible, but broad-leaved ones such as *Echinodorus* are preferred. It likes to graze algae from the leaves. Water: pH 6.5-7.8; hardness 2-25° dGH.

B: Quite easy with a matched pair. The ♂ dances around the ♀, frequently touching the head region. Then the ♀ is totally embraced and approximately 50 yellow/greenish eggs are laid in an upper corner of the aquarium. The larvae hatch after 3-4 days and are raised with *Artemia* and spinach.

F: H, L; green algae which are grazed from any substrate with its dentate sucker mouth. Tablet food (evenings!), blanched lettuce but also flake food (Tetra Conditioning Food) and small live foods are eagerly taken.

S: None.

T: 20-25° C, 68-77° F, L: 6 cm, 2 1/3", A: 50 cm, 20", R: all, as long as plants are present, D: 1

Microlepidogaster notata — (EIGENMANN & EIGENMANN, 1889)
Marked Otocinclus

Syn.: *Hisonotus notatus, Otocinclus maculicauda, Otocinlcus notatus.*

Hab.: Around Santa Cruz, southeast Brazil, South America.

F.I.: Around 1974 to Europe.

Sex: Not known.

Soc. B.: A very withdrawn loner. An ideal companion fish for all delicate characins in a small aquarium.

M: Because of the large-leaved plants on which the species likes to live, the minimum tank length of 50 cm (20") should actually be larger (about 1 m; 39"). Current and clean water are indispensable for good plant growth. This is where *Otocinclus* feels most at home. Water: pH 6.5-7.5; hardness up to 20° dGH.

B: Not known. Some animals periodically gain markedly in girth, prompting the caretaker to think he is dealing with a ripe ♀. The next morning these animals are slender again but without signs of fertilization or, worse, eggs.

F: H, L; omnivore in the aquarium. Vegetable flakes, tablet foods and pellets. Lettuce, peas, live foods like *Daphnia* and *Tubifex*.

S: Sometimes the species can be problematic in its acclimation. Therefore, place only in well established tanks. It is possible that the fish in the photograph belongs to a new, perhaps still to be established, genus.

T: 22-24° C, 72-75° F, L: 4 cm, 1 2/3", A: 50 cm, 20", R: all, D: 2

Otocinclus flexilis

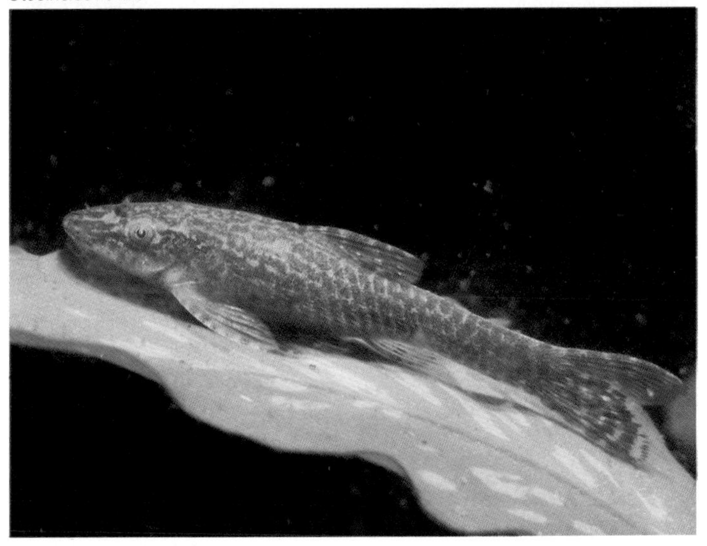

Microlepidogaster notata

Otothyris lophophanes (EIGENMANN & EIGENMANN, 1889)
Brown Otocinclus
Sub-Fam.: Hypoptopomatinae

Syn: *Otothyris canaliferus*.

Hab.: Southeast Brazil; imported from Rio de Janeiro, South America.

F.I.: Sporadically with *Otocinclus* species, e.g., *O. affinis* or *Paratocinclus maculicauda*.

Sex: Indistinguishable outside the spawning season. Shortly before spawning the genital papillae can be seen. It is more pronounced in the ♀.

Soc. B.: Peaceful species, well suited for the densely planted community aquarium. Only associate with delicate species.

M: Requires an extremely well-filtered and well-planted aquarium with strong illumination for growth of green algae. Only the front pane should be cleaned. Low fish density to maintain a low nitrate level. Good biological filtration. Slight current. Water: pH 6.0-7.0; hardness up to 15° dGH (10°).

B: Eggs are attached to plant leaves but also on the glass. Raise only in a rearing tank with plenty of algae. The larvae hatch after about 3 days at 24° C (75° F) and after another 3 days search the surroundings for feed. Feed with pond plankton, perhaps Liquifry Green, planktonic algae. After 10 days, feed with *Artemia*, TetraMin and *Cyclops*.

F: H, O; algae, plant fare (Tetra Conditioning Food or similar). Mashed peas without skin. *Cyclops, Artemia*. If possible, the algae should not be grazed by a strong feed competitor (other larger loricariids).

S: The genus is presently being revised by Dr. Britski.

T: 20-24° C, L: 4 cm, A: 50 cm, R: all, as long as plant leaves are present, D: 2
68-75° F, 1 2/3", 50",

*Panaque suttonorum** SCHULTZ, 1944
Blue-Eyed Plecostomus
Sub-Fam.: Ancistrinae

Syn.: *Panaque suttoni*.

Hab.: The Guianas in clear mountain streams?, Colombia, South America. Rare!

F.I.: 1975 through Heiko Bleher, Frankfurt. In larger numbers from 1979.

Sex: Not known.

Soc. B.: Peaceful species which likes peace. Therefore, only associate with other quiet fishes or keep in a species tank, perhaps with *Peckoltia*.

M: The large sucker mouth identifiesfishes from rapids. The species really occurs only in oxygen-rich, higher mountain streams. It is, therefore, best to offer the species a shallow aquarium with a strong current, large surface area, coarse pebbles as substrate and some large caves under tree roots. Water: pH 6.2-7.5; hardness 4-15° dGH.

B: Not likely in the aquarium, but large-scale experiments have been initiated.

F: H, O; in nature mainly algae and aufwuchs. In the aquarium flake food remains, tablet foods, frozen peas (thawed!), algae, cucumbers and TabiMin are eaten.

S: An interesting charge which, despite its inconspicuousness, always enchants with its blue eyes.
Meanwhile, several hundred animals are imported per month (1983). A renowned importer receives the animals from Colombia. Statements from American importers who claim to receive the animals from Guyana are to be doubted.
*Pers. Information from Dr. I.J.H. ISBRÜCKER, 1996.

T: 20-24° C, L: 18 cm, A: 100 cm, R: b, D: 3
68-75° F, 7" 39",

Otothyris lophophanes

Panaque suttonorum

Parotocinclus maculicauda (STEINDACHNER, 1877)
Redfin Otocinclus Sub-Fam.: Hypoptopomatinae

Syn.: *Hisonotus maculicauda.*

Hab.: South America, southeast Brazil south of Rio de Janeiro, in rivers not deeper than 1.5 m (59").

F.I.: Not known.

Sex: Not yet exactly known. It seems that some specimens do not have the nice red markings on their fins. However, it is uncertain whether this indicates sexual dichromatism. More specimens are needed!

Soc. B.: Very peaceful species. It can be kept with the smallest characins, etc. To keep it with larger, too robust fishes is not recommended. If possible, a small group should be kept.

M: The animals spend most of their time on plant leaves. Broad-leaved *Echinodorus* species are preferred. Very high oxygen requirement, therefore, avoid elevated temperatures. Surface movement from the filter is desired. Water: pH 6.0-7.0; hardness 5-15° dGH. Lots of light for algae growth.

B: Not known.

F: H; algae on plant leaves are preferably grazed. Flake food and tablet food are rarely accepted.

S: The genus *Parotocinclus* is comprised of 12 species and is differentiated from *Otocinclus* by the presence of an adipose fin. *Otocinclus* lacks the adipose fin. The similarly colored species *Otocinclus maculipinnis* does not have an adipose.

T: 22-24° C, **L:** 4.5 cm, **A:** 60 cm, **R:** m, among plants, **D:** 2
72-75° F, 1$^3/_4$", 24",

Peckoltia brevis (LA MONTE, 1935)
Spotted Pecoltia Sub-Fam.: Ancistrinae

Syn.: *Hemiancistrus brevis.*

Hab.: Rio Purus and Rio Jurua, west Brazil, South America.

F.I.: About 1970.

Sex: ♂♂ have well developed spines (not soft as with *Sturisoma*) on the pectoral and dorsal fin rays.

Soc. B.: Nocturnal, very peaceful species. Well suited for almost any community tank. No territorial behavior. The fish wane when associated with excessively aggressive cichlids or other catfishes.

M: Somewhat nitrate sensitive (maximum 30 mg/l). Well-planted aquarium with plenty of hiding places of roots. Caves are cohabited with other fishes without difficulty. pH 5.8-7.8 (6.8); hardness up to 28° dGH (after acclimation), better is 15° dGH. Peat extract or filtration is advantageous but not necessary. In a newly established tank and during water exchanges, it is necessary to add AquaSafe or a similar product. Good filtration with slight current.

B: T: 24° C (75° F), very soft, fresh water. Eggs are laid in caves underneath roots or stones. Parents guard the spawn and the young for about 10 days. Rear the young in an algae tank with the smallest vegetable flake food, ground peas (young!).

F: H, L; in the aquarium it is easily fed almost any kind of flake food or tablet food (especially Tetra TabiMin or similar product). Algae are grazed but are not a necessity. Provide mashed peas without skin 2-3 times a month.

S: A lasting species which over the years leads a quite inconspicuous life. In tanks well shaded with floating plants, the animals will leave their hiding places during the day when all is quiet. The species is usually considered to be a *Chaetostoma* but has a significantly wider sucker mouth. The animals have very sensitive eyes. Through poor water conditions and/or injuries sustained from rough tankmates, the eyes fungus much easier than they do in other catfishes. Blind animals are incurable but still live for years.

T: 22-26° C, **L:** 9 cm, **A:** 80 cm, **R:** b, **D:** 2-3
72-79° F, 3 " 31",

Parotocinclus maculicauda

Peckoltia brevis

Liposarcus anisitsi (EIGENMANN & KENNEDY, 1903)

Snow King Sailfin Pleco

Syn.: *Ancistrus multiradiatus* var. *alternans, Pterygoplichthys alternans, P. juvens, P. anisitsi.*

Hab.: Rio Paraguay, Brazil and Paraguay, South America.

F.I.: Around 1970.

Sex: Not known.

Soc. B.: Requires a tank generously furnished with roots and stones, forming a roomy cave appropriate for the size of the fish. Protect individual plants against uprooting with fist-sized stones. Relatively undemanding in regard to water values: 6.5-8.2; hardness up to 25° dGH. Good filtration and water turnover. Under oxygen deficient conditions, these catfishes can surface to take air for temporary oxygen supplementation through the intestine.

M: In the USA (Florida) this species is bred in large quantities in ponds with a steep clay slope. The sailfin digs tunnels of up to 1 m (39") in depth and 7 cm (2³/4") in diameter close to the water level. In this cave the partners spawn. The ♂ guards the egg cluster until the larvae hatch. In an aquarium, breeding has not been successful. Compare also Volume 3, page 382 (in German).

F: H; tablet foods (TabiMin, Tetra Tips) are eagerly taken. To satiate, mashed (frozen) peas, lettuce, chickweed, etc., are a necessity. In nature the species is an algae and aufwuchs eater.

S: The aforementioned species is only rarely imported because of its large mature size and the fact that imports from its natural habitat rarely reach Germany. The species can easily be distinguished from other sailfins by its characteristic pattern.

T: 21-24° C, L: 42 cm, A: 150 cm, R: b, D: 2
70-75° F, 17", 59",

Pterygoplichthys sp., Peru

Liposarcus anisitsi

Liposarcus anisitsi in its cave during the dry season (above water!)

Pterygoplichthys duodecimalis VALENCIENNES 1840

Syn.: *Hypostomus duodecimalis, Ancistrus duodecimalis.*

Hab.: Rio Sao Francisco and tributaries, east Brazil, South America.

F.I.: Only as by-catch so far.

Sex: Not sufficiently known.

Soc. B.: Peaceful species which, however, could consider young fishes on the bottom at night as prey.

M: With sufficient vegetable matter (algae), a very long-lived species. In poor water conditions it can still survive with intestinal respiration. Water: pH 6.2-7.8; hardness up to 25° dGH. Few or robust plants because the fish sometimes like to root in the substrate for food.

T: 22-30° C, L: 50 cm, A: 200 cm, R: b, D: 1
72-86° F, 20", 79",

B: Probably not possible in an aquarium because of its size. Breeds in Brazilian lowland swamps which flood during the rainy season.

F: O; any vegetable fare, algae and organisms living therein. Tablet foods and frozen peas. This species of catfish can overeat on tablet food.

S: An appreciated protein source in Brazil (tail).

Glyptoperichthys punctatus (GÜNTHER, 1864)
Spotted Sailfin Pleco

Syn.: *Ancistrus punctatus, Loricaria punctata, Chaetostomus punctatus, Pterygoplichthys punctatus.*

Hab.: Venezuela, upper and middle Amazon, South America.

F.I.: Probably imported for years as *Plecostomus* (*Hypostomus*), but never recognized.

Sex: Not known.

Soc. B.: Loner or in pairs. Two specimens of the same sex display weak territorial behavior. Slight pursuit defense reactions always end peacefully and are of short duration when there is room to escape for the weaker animal. Otherwise, the weaker animal is constantly disturbed when trying to feed.

T: 22-26° C, L: 18 cm, A: 120 cm, R: b, D: 1-2
72-79° F, 7" 47",

M: Always provide at least one cave per animal. A clay pipe (drainage pipe) is well suited. Caves made of bogwood are more decorative. The tank can easily be greened up with Java moss. Plants are not damaged but should not be placed too densely, allowing the armored catfish to swim in between.

B: No reports of successful breeding are yet available.

F: H, L; tablet foods (Tetra Tips or similar). Flake food remains and lots of vegetable matter in the form of algae, mashed small (uncooked) peas.

S: The species is quite similar to *Liposarcus multiradiatus* but has a flatter dorsal fin.

Pterygoplichthys duodecimalis

Glyptoperichthys punctatus

Rineloricaria lanceolata (GÜNTHER, 1868)
Lanceolate Whiptail Catfish

Syn.: *Loricaria lanceolata, Loricariichthys lanceolatus.*

Hab.: Rio Paraguay, South America.

F.I.: 1925 by the company Scholze and Pötzschke, Berlin.

Sex: Full-grown ♂♂ are easily distinguished by their bristle rimmed head and pectoral fin edges. ♀♀ lack this "beard".

Soc. B.: Peaceful species best kept in pairs. Two animals of the same sex can also be kept in an aquarium over 1 m (39") long. The species should not be kept with individuals which are too rough.

T: 20-24° C, L: 13 cm, A: 80 cm, R: b, D: 2-3
68-75° F, 5", 31",

M: As stated for *Sturisoma barbatum.*

B: The species spawns in caves (hollow tree trunks). Pipes of 5-7 cm diameter (2"-2^{3}/4") are well-suited in an aquarium.

F: C, O; small live foods of any kind, FD foods, flake foods.

S: The species is active at twilight and at night.

Sturisona aureum (STEINDACHNER, 1900)
Giant Whiptail, Golden Whiptail

Syn.: *Loricaria aureum.*

Hab.: Colombia, South America.

F.I.: 1975.

Sex: ♂♂ have thorns or tentacles on the sides of the mouth. In ♀♀ these are lacking. (compare photos pages 519 and 521)

Soc. B.: Extremely peaceful, very sedentary species which has to kept in a species tank or together with inactive fishes.

M: The fishes exclusively place themselves into the strongest current. Clear water with few pollutants is preferred: nitrite 0; nitrate up to 25 mg/l. pH 6.5-7.8; hardness up to 18° dGH. Only nocturnal! Caves, however, are either not sought or are relinquished to stronger fishes.

T: 22-26° C, L: 22 cm, A: 100 cm, R: m, D: 2-3
72-79° F, 8^{3}/4" 39",

B: See page 520.

F: H, O; exclusively nocturnal. Algae, algae, algae! with aufwuchs. As a substitute food, mashed (frozen) peas and glassworms can be offered.

S: A very interesting fish as a change from the ordinary, but its nutrition requires lots of attention.

Rineloricaria lanceolata

Sturisoma aureum ♀

Town pool with thousands of *Pterygoplichthys* which are eaten (East Brazil).

Sturisoma aureum

B: The species has been bred several times. The author BAENSCH made these personal observations on breeding. The breeding season is during winter, between October and February. In the middle of October '84 the first spawn of about 100 eggs of 2.5 mm (1/16") diameter was observed. After 6 days (at 28° C; 82° F) the first larvae hatched and were immediately free-swimming, attaching themselves with their tiny sucker mouth to plant leaves, or preferably, to the aquarium glass. The length of the larvae was 7-8 mm (5/16"). Dorsally they have a rhomboidal design and two crossbands on the caudal peduncle. The body base coloration is black. The animals can already achieve an incredible speed to escape when disturbed. Otherwise, they often sit for hours in one place. Three days after hatching the yolk sac is absorbed and feeding must begin. This is when problems commence.

The juveniles feed during the day and partially during the night. Adults only feed at night. As feed I gave: frozen mashed peas, hard boiled egg yolk, *Bosmina* and *Tubifex*. Everything was passed through an *Artemia* sieve of 0.14 mesh size. *Artemia* nauplii were not accepted. It was even observed how 3 day old nauplii, which came into the proximity of the head region of the small catfishes, made them flee. The young catfish prefer to graze the glass for something edible. There should be an algae and bacteria lawn as a result of high light intensity. I have often fed infusoria (banana leaf culture). I cannot say whether or not these were accepted.

Filtration consisted of an air pump and a foam filter (Tetra Billi). I rinsed the filter cartridge in the aquarium despite its dirt. Microscopic analysis showed the filter to contain huge amounts of infusoria. After 4 weeks the strongest juveniles have reached a length of 20-22 mm (3/4") and are now beyond the initial feeding difficulties. They should be feed twice daily with foods of vegetable (peas) as well as animal origin. The adults spawn every 2-3 weeks, but the number of eggs per spawn progressively diminishes. Initially the spawns have 100, maximum 200, eggs. Later spawns only number 30-50 eggs.

A thorough breeding account which deviates in part from my observations can be found in DATZ 7/84, page 242-243.

Sturisoma aureum ♂; guards the spawn

Sturisoma barbatum (KNER, 1854)
Long-Nosed Whiptail

Syn.: *Loricaria barbata, Oxyloricaria barbata.*

Hab.: Rio Cajuba, Paraguay (South America).

F.I.: About 1974.

Sex: ♂ with bristles on the side of the mouth and head. Absent on the ♀. The ♀ is more stout.

Soc. B.: Very peace-loving species which, despite its size, can be associated with even the smallest fishes.

M: The species should only be kept in moderately stocked tanks, since it has a high oxygen requirement. Strong water turnover and a large capacity filter (well maintained!) are conditions for successful care. Water: pH 6.4-7.2; hardness up to 15° dGH. Voluminous decoration with roots and strong plants (which can support the fish).

B: Not yet described, but should be similar to *S. panamense.*

F: H, L; algae, peas (best without skin), occasionally glassworms. Flake and table foods are rarely taken.

S: Diurnal species, which is rare for this genus.

T: 20-22° C, L: 25 cm, A: 140 cm, R: b, D: 2-3
68-72° F, 9 3/4", 55",

Photo on left:
Rio Purus, western Brazil, the home of many armored catfishes.

Sturisoma nigrirostrum FOWLER, 1940
Black-Nosed Sturisoma

Syn.: *Sturisoma brevirostre.*

Hab.: Northern tributary of the Solimoes (middle Amazon), Brazil, South America.

F.I.: By Heiko Bleher, Frankfurt, 1973.

Sex: As with other *Sturisoma*: ♂ with a "beard".

Soc. B.: Peaceful like other *Sturisoma.*

M: Good filtration with strong current. Intense light for algae growth. Low tank density to guarantee low nitrate levels. Water: pH 6.0-7.0; hardness up to 15° dGH.

B: "Handbuch der Welskunde" FRANKE (1985) gives a detailed breeding account. Refer to the following text page.

F: H; well washed lettuce, perhaps blanched and sliced; mashed peas, algae!

S: *Sturisoma* fasts from time to time for 1-2 weeks. The fish are very restless during this time (desire to migrate?). If they remain undisturbed, they will resume feeding by themselves.

T: 25-30° C, L: 24 cm, A: 120 cm, R: b, m, D: 2
77-86° F, 9 1/3", 47",

Sturisoma sp.
Panama Sturisoma

Syn.: None.

Hab.: Not known.

F.I.: Around 1973 to Europe.

Sex: ♂ has bristles on the sides of the head. Number and length of these bristles increases before the spawning time. ♀♀ have a deeper body and are stouter.

Soc. B.: Very gentle species which delights the caretaker through its liveliness and peacefulness. Can be kept in a well-planted tank together with all nonaggressive tankmates. Diurnal.

M: As the two previously mentioned species, but somewhat more robust. Water: pH 6.5-7.2, hardness up to 25° dGH.

B: The ♂ hits the ♀ softly to stimulate her. About 100 transparent adhesive eggs are deposited either on plant leaves or, more commonly, on a glass pane. The ♂ guards the spawn and cleans it occasionally. The eggs hatch (depending on temperature) after 7-9 days. The young eat newly hatched *Artemia*, well minced lettuce and young, mashed peas. Neither temperature nor hardness seem to influence breeding, but plentiful vegetarian fare and oxygen-rich water seem to be important. In DATZ 2/82 David Allison (England) gives a detailed breeding report.

F: H; algae, peas, lettuce, occasionally *Tubifex* are appreciated.

S: A specially attractive catfish which does not leads a seclusive life.

T: 20-22° C, L: 17 cm, A: 120 cm, R: b, D: 2
68-72° F, 6 3/4", 47",

Sturisoma nigrirostrum, juv.

Sturisoma sp. ♂

Continuation of page 524

This catfish, identified by experts as *Sturisoma rostratum* (SPIX 1829), is really *Sturisoma nigrirostrum*. According to FRANKE (written communication) we are dealing here with a ♂ which was injured in transport (during capture?) ora result of a deformity. FRANKE successfully bred *St. nigrirostrum* with this animal and its normal sub-adult offspring are pictured on the top of the preceding page. The upward-bent rostrum, therefore, was not expressed. Unfortunately it could not be settled if the description of *Sturisoma rostratum* by Spix in 1829 was also based on an animal with a similar abnormal rostrum.

Breeding differed somewhat from the previously described *Sturisoma aureum*: the eggs were deposited on the bottom (glass—no sand) at a rate of 5-7 every 20 minutes, until a total of 100-120 were laid. The ♂ lies over the spawn and fans it. The larvae hatch after five days at 26-28° C (79-82° F) and start feeding on the third day. Frozen *Cyclops* nauplii and live red rotifers were given. After a month lettuce, tablet food, *Tubifex* and flake food are already accepted. To improve the hatching rate, the eggs should be incubated in a hatching dish with methylene blue and two daily water changes. Non hatching eggs are aided by pipetting and releasing the eggs to fall on the water surface. The author, BAENSCH, hastened the hatching of the larvae or the freeing from the egg membrane by siphoning the eggs with a hose (5 mm; 3/16 i.d.). At the other end the larvae already emerged freed. They had been freed by the high flow velocities inside the hose.

*Chiloglanis paratus** CRASS, 1960

Syn.: None.

Hab.: Tropical Africa, from the Nile to Cameroon.

F.I.: Unknown.

Sex: Full-grown ♀♀ can be recognized by the round ventral area.

Soc. B.: Peaceful species suited for the cooler community tank.

M: While *Synodontis* species usually inhabit the lower sections of African streams, the related *Chiloglanis* colonize the headwaters. They can often be found in fast flowing waters (rapids). One species (*Chiloglanis neumanni*) occurs in Lake Malawi and is occasionally imported with cichlids from there. They prefer well-filtered, oxygen-rich water with pebbles as substrate. Provide abundant light for algae growth. Water: pH 6.0-7.2; hardness up to 15° dGH. There is a report in DATZ 11/84.

B: Not known.

F: H, O; algae, aufwuchs, insect larvae, flake food.

S: *Species determination is not confirmed. The genus is made up of a dozen similar species. Pectoral and dorsal fin rays are pointed and cause painful wounds; therefore, only catch the fish with a glass.

T: 20-24° C, **L:** 8 cm, **A:** 100 cm, **R:** b, m, **D:** 2-3
68-75° F, 3", 39",

Hemisynodontis membranaceus (HILAIRE, 1809)
Membrane Synodontis

Syn.: *Pimelodus membranaceus, Synodontis guentheri, Synodontis membranaceus.*

Hab.: Nile basin, Chad, Niger, Senegal, Gambia, Volta River (Africa).

F.I.: Not known.

Sex: No external ones known.

Soc. B.: Considering the size, this is a relatively quiet and peaceful representative. However, associating with smaller species is not recommended.

M: Sparse vegetation consisting of robust potted plants. Water: pH 6.8-7.2, hardness up to 25° dGH. Generously dimensioned filter because the animals are insatiable and require a lot of feed.

B: Not yet known.

F: C, O; more a planktivore than a predator. Therefore, provide *Daphnia*, mosquito larvae and flake food. Frozen food is a good substitute.

S: Contrary to popular believe, most "synodontis catfishes" do not swim upside down. This species does, so the dorsal area is lighter in color than the ventral area.

T: 22-25° C, L: 30 cm, A: 200 cm, R: b-t, D: 2-3
72-77° F, 11¾", 79",

Mochokiella paynei HOWES, 1980
Payne's Synodontis

Syn.: None.

Hab.: Kassawe nature preserve in Sierra Leone, Africa.

F.I.: To England in 1978.

Sex: Only distinguishable with ripe ♀♀. They are ventrally rounder.

Soc. B.: Primarily a diurnal species, specially when there is something to eat.

M: An enduring species which, however, cannot do without a regular water exchange every 3-4 weeks. The nitrate level has to remain below 40 mg/l. This is not guaranteed with all tap water (e.g., Cologne). So measure nitrate or inquire at the water works. Free swimming space, otherwise undemanding.

B: Has not been bred.

F: C; insectivore, but also flake and frozen feed, FD foods.

S: One of the few synodontis catfishes also to be recommended to the beginner.

T: 22-24° C, L: 7 cm, A: 50 cm, R: b, D: 1
72-75° F, 2¾", 20",

Hemisynodontis membranaceus

Mochokiella paynei

Synodontis acanthomias BOULENGER, 1899

Black-Spotted Dusky Synodontis

Syn.: *Synodontis pfefferi, S. depauwi, S. omias* (not GÜNTHER).

Hab.: Congo (Zaire) basin, Africa.

F.I.: Not known.

Sex: Not yet described.

Soc. B.: Do not keep in an aquarium that is heavily stocked. Develops territorial behavior that becomes more prevalent with age. Small fishes are considered prey, even though the species is not a predator.

M: Use a large aquarium with powerful filtration. Plants should be in pots. A dark substrate is preferred. No special demands are placed on water quality: pH 6.5-8.0; hardness up to 25° dGH.

B: Not known.

F: O; from trout pellets and flake food of any kind, up to beef heart and mosquito larvae.

S: The special identifying characteristic of this species are the spiny, backwards bent hooklets on the shoulder bone.

T: 22-24° C, **L:** 40 cm, **A:** 200 cm, **R:** b, **D:** 2-3
72-75° F, 16", 79",

Synodontis afrofisheri HILGENDORF, 1888

Syn.: *Synodontis "atrofisheri".*

Hab.: Nile basin, in lakes Victoria, Nabugabs, Kioga and Ihema; also in the Congo basin; Africa.

F.I.: About 1976.

Sex: Not known.

Soc. B.: Peaceful species which can be kept successfully with fast swimmers such as *Brycinus longopinnis* or *Phenacogrammus interrruptus* (Congo tetra). Not an upside-down swimming catfish.

M: Not very demanding. The species tolerates wide ranges of pH and hardness, but large fluctuations should be avoided. pH 6-8; hardness 5-25° dGH.

B: Unknown, the same as for almost all upside-down catfishes (except *Synodontis nigriventris*). Why is this? First, a large aquarium is needed. Second, a pair which forms out of a group, perhaps one that has been in our care for several years. Nutrition plays a very important role in *Synodontis* species. Snails and insect larvae are usually the natural foods. These foods contain substances (this is proven- but little known) which other feeds, especially flake and tablet foods, cannot contain. The drying process destroys the traces of these vitamins (made up in part of trace substances not yet investigated). I only am aware of this from conversations with my father (Dr. U. Baensch), who never published his work in this subject, however.
Breeding of *Synodontis* will remain a secret until these substances can be specifically added to the aquarium food, or the food given by the hobbyist more resembles what is found in nature. Since many of the *Synodontis* species will disappear from the price lists of importers because of export restrictions, the methodical research into breeding these fish will be prerequisite for their continued presence in our aquaria.

F: C; in nature, the diet consists primarily of insect larvae and snails.

S: None.

T: 22-26° C, **L:** 12 cm, **A:** 120 cm, **R:** b, **D:** 1-2
72-79° F, 4 3/4", 47",

Synodontis acanthomias

Synodontis afrofisheri

Synodontis brichardi POLL, 1959
Brichard's Synodontis

Syn.: None.

Hab.: Lower Zaire River (Congo) in rapids and below water falls, Africa.

F.I.: Since about 1970.

Sex: Not known.

Soc. B.: Mostly a peaceful fish, twilight-active. Small fishes are pursued if they sleep on the bottom. Slight territorial behavior.

M: The water should have a high oxygen content and a strong current. Large, flat pebbles with a 10-15 cm (4"-6") diameter serve as resting places. Hiding places out of roots. Swimming room in the foreground. Plants are not bothered, but they should be well-rooted before the fish are added. pH 6.2-7.5; hardness up to 20° dGH (10°).

B: Has not yet been successful in an aquarium.

F: C, O; tablet, frozen and freeze-dried foods. Live mosquito and other larvae could bring the fish into breeding condition.

S: A flat species well adapted to rapids, like *S. ornatipinnis*. Despite its origins of rapid currents, it is a very enduring species which can be kept for extended periods of time, even in moderately aerated tanks. *S. brichardi* seems capable of slightly adhering to objects or the glass of the aquarium and moving while sucking.

T: 22-25° C, L: 15 cm, A: 120 cm, R: b, D: 2
72-77° F, 6", 47",

Synodontis brichardi, juvenile

Synodontis brichardi, adult

Synodontis camelopardalis POLL, 1971
Panther Synodontis

Syn.: None.

Hab.: Congo basin, Zaire River, Lake Victoria (Africa).

F.I.: Around 1976.

Sex: Not known.

Soc. B.: A quite peaceful species which appreciates its peace. Can be kept together with smaller fishes such as *Nannaethiops unitaeniatus*.

M: The species has a high oxygen requirement, but it is not overly particular towards the other water values. Strong surface current and regular substrate and filter cleaning are necessary. pH 6.0-7.5; hardness 5-25° dGH. The fish are often lazy and can "scald" themselves on an over-dimensioned heater. Only use vertical rod heaters. Avoid sharp objects in the tank. The fish ram them without apparent reason. Provide a floating plant cover and a sufficiently dark hiding place.

B: As with other *Synodontis*, unknown.

F: C, O; tablet foods, sometimes snails, all kinds of feed remains. Primarily frozen foods.

S: Sudden movements in front of the aquarium and turning the light on in the evening are to be avoided. The species is very skittish.

T: 22-26° C, L: 12-15 cm, A: 100-150 cm, R: b, D: 1-2
72-79° F, 4 3/4"-6", 39"-59",

Synodontis clarias (LINNAEUS, 1758)
Red-Tailed Synodontis*

Syn.: *Silurus clarias, S. callarias, Pimelodus synodontis, Synodontis macrodon.*

Hab.: Nile, Chad basin, Senegal, Gambia and Niger rivers (Africa).

F.I.: Not known.

Sex: Cannot be differentiated from the exterior.

Soc. B.: Keep older specimens singly or in pairs. Can show territoriality.

M: No reports are available; its wide area of natural distribution indicates an adaptable species. Give it a generously dimensioned filter and regular water changes. Water, depending on capture site: pH 6.5-7.5; hardness up to 18° dGH

B: Not known.

F: O; from algae in the aquarium to insect larvae (in nature). Possibly the algae are only searched for insect larvae. Frozen mosquito larvae should be the best aquarium food. In addition, feed large flakes (TetraRuby), brine shrimp and other crustaceans (mysids, etc.). This is the only way to maintain the healthy red coloration of the tail fin. If it becomes pale, the animals are not being fed correctly.

S: * The name is proposed because of the conspicuous red tail fin. This feature is not found in other *Synodontis*.

T: 21-24° C, L: 20 cm, A: 150 cm, R: b, m, D: 2
70-75° F, 8", 59",

Synodontis camelopardalis

Synodontis clarias

Synodontis congicus POLL, 1971
Congo Synodontis, Domino Synodontis

Syn.: None.

Hab.: Zaire River and tributaries, Stanley Pool, Africa.

F.I.: Not known.

Sex: Not visible.

Soc. B.: Juveniles can be kept in a group. Older individuals are less tolerant of conspecifics if they don't have enough room. 60-80 cm (24"-31") tank length is needed for each individual of 12 cm (4³/4") length. Otherwise, there are constant quarrels.

M: Plants are not really possible because the species digs constantly. Giant *Vallisneria* or other tough vegetation planted in pots covered with coarse pebbles can be tried. Water: pH 6.2-7.2; hardness 5-15° dGH. Darkened tank with caves as hiding places.

B: Not likely in an aquarium because of the lack of information on its natural living conditions.

F: C, O; its natural food is benthic insect larvae. In the aquarium any substitute such as tablet foods (Tetra Tips) is accepted.

S: The number of dots varies from individual to individual, which is the reason to name this fish "domino synodontis" in Germany.

T: 22-25° C, **L:** 18-22 cm, **A:** 180 cm, **R:** b, m, **D:** 2-3
72-77° F, 7"-8³/4", 71",

Synodontis contractus VINCIGUERRA, 1928
Big-Nosed Upside-Down Catfish

Syn.: *Synodontis davidi.*

Hab.: Congo region (Stanley Pool) at Kinshasa, Africa.

F.I.: To Germany in 1980.

Sex: Unknown.

Soc. B.: Very peaceful, two or more specimens can be kept.

M: Very similar in behavior to *S. nigriventris*, also almost always swimming upside-down. However, this fish is darker, taller built and remains smaller. Needs a dark tank with a lot of overhanging roots, stones and broad-leaved plants (*Anubias, Echinodorus*). The undersides of leaves are preferentially searched for food. Once acclimated, the species is easy to maintain. pH 6.2-7.2; hardness 4-15° dGH

B: Not known. Perhaps similar to *S. nigriventris*. See Vol. 1, page 506.

F: C, O; insect larvae, FD tablets, frozen foods.

S: Only reaches 7 cm (2³/4") in length, probably making it the smallest "synodontis catfish".

T: 22-25° C, **L:** 7 cm, **A:** 100 cm, **R:** m, t, **D:** 1-2
72-77° F, 2³/4", 39",

Synodontis congicus

Synodontis contractus

Synodontis courteti PELLEGRIN, 1906
Dotted Synodontis

Syn.: None.

Hab.: Lake Chad and Niger basin, Africa.

F.I.: 1980.

Sex: Not known.

Soc. B.: Full-grown specimens are loners that can only be kept with large, robust fish (cichlids, large catfish). Juveniles are almost entirely diurnal and constantly in search of food. This restlessness carries over to the other tankmates.

M: Do not touch; the pectoral rays can cause painful injuries. Capture with a cup, not a net. Water: pH 6.5-8.0; hardness up to 25° dGH (12°). Large tank with a well dimensioned cave as hideout. Robust plants. Sand and mulm bottom to root around in. The illumination should be dimmed in the evening. Lot of free swimming space, free water surface, good filtration.

B: Not to be expected in an aquarium.

F: C, O; omnivore as a juvenile; specially insect larvae, tablet foods, pellets. Frozen foods: mosquito larvae, brine shrimp, shrimp, *Tubifex* (well purged). Small fish.

S: Despite the attractive coloration as a juvenile, it is not really an aquarium fish (mature size).

T: 22-26° C, **L:** 25 cm in aquaria, else larger, **A:** 180 cm, **R:** b, **D:** 3
72-79° F, 9 3/4" in aquaria, else larger, 71",

Synodontis eburneensis DAGET, 1964
Ivory Synodontis*

Syn.: *Synodontis dageti.*

Hab.: Volta River, Sassandra and Bandama basin, Ivory Coast (Africa).

F.I.: Not known.

Sex: Not distinguishable from the exterior.

Soc. B.: Moderately peaceful but should not be placed together with other *Synodontis* species. Small fishes are probably considered prey; therefore, caution is in order.

M: The species is not demanding if it is furnished with a sufficiently roomy aquarium with moderate filtration and slightly acid to neutral water. Overstocked aquaria are to be avoided because it makes the fish restless, which in turn infects its tankmates.

B: Not known.

F: O; insect larvae, such as mosquito larvae are preferred. Flake and other dry foods are the staple diet of trained individuals which accept them readily.

S: * The name is derived from its natural habitat.

T: 22-25° C, **L:** 16 cm, **A:** 150 cm, **R:** b, **D:** 2
72-77° F, 6 1/3", 59",

Synodontis courteti

Synodontis eburneensis

Synodontis filamentosus BOULENGER, 1901
Filamentous Synodontis

Syn.: *Synodontis augierasi.*

Hab.: Nile basin, Chad, Niger, Volta (Africa).

F.I.: Unknown.

Sex: None known. It is possible the extended dorsal filaments are indicative for ♂♂.

Soc. B.: Keeping singly is recommended. The animals are aggressive towards conspecifics as well as heterospecifics and will defend their territory energetically.

M: Not a choosy species. It accepts almost all water conditions. pH 6.0-7.5; hardness to 25° dGH. Use strong filtration. Use firmly rooted or potted plants.

B: Has not been successful.

F: O; from flake food and tablets to earthworms.

S: None.

T: 21-24° C, L: 17 cm, A: 150 cm, R: b, D: 2-3
70-75° F, 6 3/4", 59",

Synodontis longirostris BOULENGER, 1902
Long-Nosed Synodontis

Syn.: *Synodontis ovidius.*

Hab.: Zaire River (Congo basin), Africa.

F.I.: 1974 by Heiko Bleher, Frankfurt.

Sex: Not known.

Soc. B.: Not as rude and aggressive as other "synodontis" catfishes. The species can and should be kept in a small school. Nevertheless, do not keep with very small fishes which could be considered prey. Not territorial.

M: The fish is suitable for the community tank when young. They require a large swimming area. Fine sand and mulm bottom for rooting is necessary for its well-being. Water: pH 6.2-7.5; hardness 8-18° dGH. Use only tough, large-leaved, well rooted plants since the species searches the bottom for feed.

B: Not likely in an aquarium.

F: C, O; prefers benthic insect larvae and worms. *Tubifex*, small earthworms. In the aquarium tablet foods, pellets, frozen foods.

S: The species is a specialized bottom feeder which can be easily deduced from its long snout.

T: 21-24° C, L: 45 cm! A: 200 cm, R: b, D: 2-4 (S)
70-75° F, 18"!, 79",

Synodontis filamentosus

Synodontis longirostris

Synodontis multipunctatus BOULENGER, 1898

Cuckoo Synodontis, Multi-Spotted Synodontis

Syn.: None.

Hab.: Lake Tanganyika, tributaries of the Malagarasi River, Tanzania (Africa).

F.I.: Unknown.

Sex: Not known.

Soc. B.: An attractive and peaceful fish when young. 3-5 juveniles can be kept together. Adults are solitary fish but do not exhibit marked territorial behavior. Day and twilight active. Do not keep with fishes that are too small. Ideal companion for east African lake cichlids.

M: As expected from its origin, the species likes hard water between 15 and 35° dGH with a high proportion of carbonate hardness. Perhaps some salt (1/2-1 teaspoon per 10 l; 2.5 gal of water) should be added. Stone decoration with caves. Clear water with constant water values. Avoid nitrates.

B: Not much is yet known, but it probably also exhibits cuckoo behavior, specializing on a certain cichlid species as does *S. petricola*.

F: C, O; tablet food, pellets, snails, live foods of all kinds. An insectivore in nature.

S: It has been reported (from observations in the wild) that the eggs of Tanganyikan *Synodontis* species (3 species = *S. multipunctatus, S. petricola, S. eurystomus*) are taken up and incubated in the mouth of cichlids of the genus *"Haplochromis"*. *Synodontis multipunctatus* is very similar to *S. petricola* but differs by the larger eye diameter, fewer and larger spots on the body and a shorter, rounder mouth.

T: 21-25° C, 70-77° F, **L:** 12 cm, 4 3/4", **A:** 120 cm, 47", **R:** b, m, **D:** 2-3

Synodontis nigrita VALENCIENNES, 1840

Black Synodontis

Syn.: *Hemisynodontis nigrita, Synodontis ornatus* (not BOULENGER, 1920), *S. fascipinna*.

Hab.: Nile basin, Niger, Senegal River, Gambia River, Ghana and Nigeria (Africa).

F.I.: 1951.

Sex: Are not known.

Soc. B.: Although peaceful, this restless loner may, on occasion, disturb tankmates with its barbels. If there are several animals of the same species or genus kept together in a tank, the larger animals sometimes forcibly chase the smaller animals away. Only young specimens are suitable for the community tank.

M: The skin of the species is very thin and prone to injury. Therefore, decorations should be rounded. The species likes to rest on an elevated piece of root or stone. Such a place gives it a feeling of security. Sandy or mulmy substrate. Tender plants will be eaten when the animals lack sufficient food. No special demands are placed on water composition. The species is sensitive to fresh tap water. pH 6.0-7.5; hardness 4-15° dGH. The tank requires a strong filter to cope with the turbidity generated by the catfish.

B: Probably has been successful several times but often declared offspring of *S. nigriventris*, since young specimens of *S. nigrita* also swim upside-down.

F: O; fine to coarse live foods and vegetable fare. Flake and tablet foods.

S: The species was presented erroneously in the German edition of Vol. 1, page 504 with a picture of *S. schoutedeni*. With the 4th German edition this error was corrected. Here is the true *S. nigrita*. *S. schoutedeni* is presented again on page 550.

T: 21-26° C, 70-79° F, **L:** 16 cm, 6 1/3", **A:** 120 cm, 47", **R:** b, m, **D:** 2

Synodontis multipunctatus

Synodontis nigrita

Synodontis njassae KEILHACK, 1908
Njassa Synodontis

Syn.: *Synodontis zambesensis* (BOULENGER, 1898); *S. zambesensis* PETERS, 1852 is a valid species.

Hab.: Lake Malawi (previously Lake Nyassa), Africa.

F.I.: Unknown.

Sex: Not known.

Soc. B.: Suitable for association with Malawi cichlids. In overpopulated tanks, the species tends to be aggressive. Likes to chase smaller fishes without eating them.

M: As with Malawi cichlids. Water: pH 7.5-8.2; hardness 20-30° dGH and above.

B: Has not yet been successful. Perhaps *S. njassae* also spawns together with cichlids?

F: O; from flake foods to almost all types of live foods.

S: The body pattern is very similar to *S. longirostris*; however, the head shape is very different.

T: 20-23° C, L: 12 cm, A: 100 cm, R: b, D: 2
68-73° F, 4 3/4", 39",

Synodontis nummifer BOULENGER, 1899
Penny Synodontis

Syn.: None.

Hab.: Lower Zaire River, Stanley Pool, Africa.

F.I.: Probably not until 1960.

Sex: Not known.

Soc. B.: Older specimens of the species defend their territory. Do not associate with smaller species or other *Synodontis* species. The exceptional case is when very large tanks are used, allowing the fish to evade each other. Nocturnal, restless species. Juveniles are also diurnal.

M: Water: pH 6.4-7.2; hardness up to 18° dGH. Perhaps slight peat filtration. Large stone caves, etc., as divisions of territories. Sparse, tough vegetation. Round pebbles and sand bottom (the pictured gravel is wrong because it is too sharp).

B: Not yet successful in an aquarium.

F: C, O; worms, insects and larvae. The juveniles like tablet food, pellets and left-over flake food.

S: The species is very similar to *S. notatus* (Aquarium Atlas Vol. 1, page 506). It can be especially distinguished by the size of the adipose fin. In *S. nummifer,* it is about twice as long as the adipose of *S. notatus*.

T: 22-25° C, L: 20 cm, A: 150 cm, R: b, D: 2-3
72-77° F, 8", 59",

Synodontis njassae

Synodontis nummifer

Synodontis ornatipinnis BOULENGER, 1899
White-Barred Synodontis

Syn.: None; trade name: *S. "zebra"*.

Hab.: Africa, Zaire River, Zaire (Congo) mostly in rapids.

F.I.: Since 1970.

Sex: Unknown.

Soc. B.: Not a species for the community tank. Small fish are hunted and eaten. Strongly territorial towards conspecifics and others. Keep only 1 fish for each meter (39") of aquarium. Nocturnal.

M: According to the native waters of this species it needs turbulent, well-filtered water and a dark gravel bottom. Do not use an undergravel filter because the fish dig. Use tough, better yet, potted plants. Light dimmer for evening observation. pH 6.5-7.5; hardness up to 18° dGH. Water filtered over peat could be beneficial.

B: Not described.

F: C, O. The species is primarily an insectivore; snails are sometimes eaten. In the aquarium tablet food, frozen food and small worms.

S: The picture shows an especially well marked juvenile. With age the design changes, giving rise to several cross-bands.

T: 22-25° C, **L:** 22 cm; in aquaria approx. 15 cm, **A:** 150 cm, **R:** b, m, **D:** 2-3
72-77° F, 8 3/4" in aquaria approx. 6", 59",

Synodontis petricola MATTHES, 1959
Even-Spotted Synodontis, Cuckoo Synodontis

Syn.: None.

Hab.: Northern part of Lake Tanganyika.

F.I.: Approximately 1980.

Sex: No external signs known.

Soc. B.: Quiet, peaceful species which could, however, consider fishes smaller than 4 cm (1 ") as prey. It is best to associate it with larger Tanganyika cichlids or in groups of 4-6 of the same species.

M: Requires hard, slightly alkaline water with a pH between 7.5 and 8.2; hardness 15-35° dGH. Hardness can easily be raised with gypsum. One corner of the tank bottom should consist of fine sand so the fish may "work" the bottom without damage to its barbels.

B: As with *Synodontis multipunctatus* (Cuckoo breeding behavior together with cichlids of the genus "*Haplochromis*"), see page 542.

F: C, O; insect larvae, but also flakes and FD tablets.

S: The species resembles *S. multipunctatus*, but resembles *S. polli* (previously *S. eurystomus*) more. See Volume 3, page 406.

T: 22-25° C, **L:** 10 cm, **A:** 100 cm, **R:** b, m, **D:** 2
72-77° F, 4", 39",

Synodontis ornatipinnis

Synodontis petricola

Synodontis pleurops BOULENGER, 1897

Big-Eyed Synodontis, Forked-Tail Synodontis

Syn.: None.

Hab.: Africa; upper Zaire River, Zaire (Congo) basin.

F.I.: Unknown. The species was surely imported prior to 1970 but remained unrecognized.

Sex: Not known.

Soc. B.: Peaceful species which can also be kept with smaller species. Juveniles are often diurnal.

M: The fish like a lot of free swimming space, a slight water current and soft, slightly acid water (pH 6.0-7.0; hardness up to 10° dGH). After acclimation they tolerate other conditions. 1/3 ot the tank volume should be exchanged every 3-4 weeks. Peat filtration is possible but not essential. Offer hiding places with roots and large leafed plants.

B: Not yet described.

F: C, O; insect larvae and small snails. Tablet foods (TabiMin). For a change offer vegetable flakes and/or frozen mashed peas.

S: The marble design usually disappears with age.

T: 22-26° C, **L:** 20 cm, **A:** 150 cm, **R:** b, m, **D:** 1-2
72-79° F, 8", 59",

Synodontis robbianus SMITH, 1873

Spotfin Synodontis, Red-Brown Synodontis

Syn.: None.

Hab.: Gold Coast, Niger river delta, Africa.

F.I.: Not known.

Sex: No external ones known.

Soc. B.: Quite peaceful representative of the genus. Can be kept together with small fishes above 4 cm ($1^2/_3$") in length. The species does not develop territorial behavior.

M: An ideal fish for the community aquarium. Darken the water slightly with peat extract or a floating plant cover. pH 6.0-7.8; hardness 10-25° dGH. A corner of the tank should have a sand bottom.

B: Not yet described.

F: C, O; insect larvae and flake food.

S: None.

T: 21-24° C, **L:** 13 cm, **A:** 100 cm, **R:** b, **D:** 1
70-75° F, 5", 39",

Synodontis pleurops

Synodontis robbianus

Synodontis schall (BLOCH & SCHNEIDER, 1801)
Schall's Synodontis

Syn.: *Silurus schall, Synodontis arabi, Hemisynodontis schall, Leiosynodontis maculosus, Pimelodus schall, Synodontis clarias, S. maculosus, S. smithii.*

Hab.: The species has a large distribution area in the freshwaters of Africa. From the Nile basin to Senegal. Lakes Rudolf, Stephanie, Victoria and Chad.

F.I.: 1935.

Sex: Not known.

Soc. B.: Juveniles are often quarrelsome, even among themselves, so only keep one animal with other larger and robust fishes. Twilight- and night-active. Older animals often search restlessly for food during the day.

M: Large tank with strong filtration. Caves. No demands are placed on the water: pH 6.0-8.0; hardness up to 30° dGH. Avoid sharp gravel least the barbels are damaged and the animals waste away. Tough plants!

B: Has not yet occurred in an aquarium.

F: C; small animals are omnivores: tablet foods, pellets and leftover flake food. Larger animals over 15 cm (6") in length accept earthworms, fish meat, beef heart, live fishes and snails.

S: The species is best reserved for large public aquaria. Juveniles have a more beautiful design than the monotonous gray adult.

T: 22-26° C, L: 41 cm, 25 cm in aquaria, A: 150 cm, R: b, m, D: 3
72-79° F, 16", 10" in aquaria, 59",

Synodontis schoutedenti DAVID, 1936
Vermiculated Synodontis

Syn.: *Synodontis depauwi.*

Hab.: Middle Zaire region, Zaire River (Congo), Africa.

F.I.: 1951.

Sex: Are not known.

Soc. B.: Peaceful loner which may disturb some tankmates with its barbels and restless swimming habits. If several animals of the same species or genus are kept together, the larger animals may forcibly chase the smaller animals away. Not suitable for the community tank.

M: Large tanks with sandy to mulmy substrate. Tender plants may be eaten if the food is inadequate. The animals like to rest during the day on vertical roots and stones. No special demands are placed on water composition. The species is sensitive to fresh tap water. pH 6.0-7.5; hardness 4-15° dGH. The tank requires a strong filter to cope with the turbidity generated by the catfish.

B: Not known.

F: O; fine to coarse live foods and vegetable fare. Flake and tablet foods.

S: The species was already presented in the German Vol. 1, 4th edition. Erroneously, however, it is called *S. nigrita* in editions 1-3. An English paper by David Sands calls the species *S. greshoffi*, SCHILTHUIS, 1891. This species has a similar design but with significantly weaker contrast coloration. Because of its yellowish ventral side and reddish base coloration, it is one of the most attractive upside-down catfishes.

T: 22-26° C, L: 14 cm, A: 100 cm, R: b, m, D: 2-3
72-79° F, 5 ", 39",

Synodontis schall

Synodontis schoutedeni

Brachyrhamdia imitator MYERS, 1927
False Cory — Sub-Fam.: Pimelodinae

Syn.: None.

Hab.: Venezuela (Canno dè Quiribana), probably also Colombia, South America.

F.I.: Around 1975.

Sex: None known.

Soc. B.: Should not be kept with small tetras or with young; these will be preyed upon. Diurnal. In its natural habitat it likes to swim with *Corydoras*. See **S**. Schooling fish.

M: Maintain in large, flat aquaria with current. Alternate sand and gravel substrates. Provide plants along the edges and free swimming space. If possible, keep in a species tank and/or with *Corydoras*. The middle and upper strata can be occupied by peaceful tetras, labyrinth fishes, etc., but the bottom should be solely for this fish. Perhaps nocturnal, peaceful catfishes can also be kept with this fish. Water: pH 6.0-7.5; hardness to 18° dGH.

B: Has not been described.

F: C, O; tablet foods supplemented with live foods such as bloodworms (frozen or freeze-dried), *Tubifex*. All insect larvae.

S: The Latin name "*imitator*" is derived from the schooling behavior of the species with *Corydoras* (e.g., *C. blochi blochi, C. m. melanistius*). It is not exactly known why the fish follows this behavior or what advantages it derives. It would be interesting to know what observations the aquarist can make towards this relationship. Keep a small school of the aforementioned fishes!

T: 21-25° C, **L:** 7.5 cm, **A:** 60 cm, better100 cm for a school, **R:** b, **D:** 1-2
70-77° F, 3", 24", better 39" for a school,

Hemisorubim platyrhynchos (VALENCIENNES, 1840)
Spotted Shovelnose Catfish — Sub-Fam.: Sorubiminae

Syn.: *Platystoma platyrhynchos, Silurus gerupoca.*

Hab.: South America: Surinam, Venezuela, Amazon and tributaries down to the Paraguay basin, in deeper parts of the rivers.

F.I.: Around 1972.

Sex: Not known.

Soc. B.: Twilight-active predator which likes to rest among roots and stones on an elevated place during the day. With the exception of armored catfishes, doradids and conspecifics, all fish under 8 cm (3") length are in danger. A good addition for the "community tank" of the specialist. Large *Pimelodus, Hoplosternum thoracantum, Osteoglossum,* etc., are ideal companions.

M: Provide a large aquarium with a corresponding filter. Needs hiding places for the daytime and floating plants (not for *Osteoglossum,* which hunts on the surface). Peat filtration (not condition). Water: undemanding; pH of 6.0-7.8; hardness to 25° dGH. Good oxygen availability is vital, therefore the low temperature.

B: Not possible to duplicate in an aquarium. Nothing is known.

F: C; fish, occasionally earthworms and larger live foods.

S: Juveniles or half-grown specimens have a larger lower tail fin lobe than the upper. Both lobes are the same size in adults. *H. platyrhynchos* is easily distinguishable from all other pimelodids. On the one hand by the body design (large spots on the sides) and on the other hand by its protruding lower jaw. In all other shovelnose catfishes, the upper jaw is longer!

T: 20-22° C, **L:** 35 cm, **A:** 150 cm, **R:** b, m, **D:** 3-4 (C)
68-72° F, 14", 59",

Brachyrhamdia imitator

Hemisorubim platyrhynchos

Sciades pictus (MÜLLER & TROSCHEL, 1849)
Sailfin Pimelodid Sub-Fam.: Sorubiminae

Syn.: *Bagrus pictus, Leiarius longibarbis, L. pictus, Sciades longibarbis, Sciadeichthys pictus.*

Hab.: Amazon and its tributaries, South America.

F.I.: Around 1960.

Sex: Not known.

Soc. B.: Predator, usually restlessly searching during the day. The long antennae may disturb other fish. Best kept alone or with "giants" such as *Osteoglossum* and others. Loner, conspecifics are chased away.

M: Needs a well covered tank (see S). Keep tank dark (floating plants). Strong filtration. Water: pH 6.2-7.5; hardness up to 18° dGH. Large caves for cover. Robust plants.

B: Has not been attempted.

F: Live fishes, large earthworms.

S: The aquarium needs to be large enough to avoid the barbels on both sides of the head from being stimulated at the same time; otherwise, the fish suffers of claustrophobia and will attempt to forcefully escape the aquarium.

Typical juvenile coloration (picture) disappears with age. The animals turn a dirty brown with dark spots and blots, and the light coloration of the juveniles almost completely disappears. Not a fish for the home aquarium. The tips of the forked caudal fin are round when juvenile and elongated and pointed in adults.

T: 22-26° C, L: 60 cm, A: 200 cm, 60 cm width, R: b, D: 4 (S)
72-79° F, 24", 79", 24" width,

Microglanis iheringi GOMES, 1946
South American Bumblebee Catfish Sub-Fam.: Pimelodinae

Syn.: None.

Hab.: Venezuela and Colombia, South America.

F.I.: Unknown; often confused, see S.

Sex: Not described.

Soc. B.: Quiet, nocturnal, peaceful guy who only occasionally considers young offspring resting on the bottom (newborn livebearers) as nourishment. An ideal addition for the well arranged community tank. Associate with *Corydoras* and tetras, not with predatory, nocturnal catfishes.

M: Well-filtered and biologically impeccable water of 10-18° dGH; pH between 6.5-7.5. Plant generously and provide room for swimming and feeding with a sand substrate.

B: Not yet bred.

F: C, O; tablets, flake food, FD foods, frozen foods. Any small live foods such as *Daphnia* and mosquito larvae. In nature the species consumes insects and their larvae.

S: The species is often confused with *M. poecilus*. They are the easiest to distinguish by a spot at the base of the caudal fin: almost square with *M. iheringi*, and a triangle whose tip points towards the head in *M. poecilus*.

T: 21-25° C, L: 6 cm, A: 60 cm, R: b, D: 1-2
70-77° F, 2 1/3", 24",

Sciades pictus

Microglanis iheringi

Perrunichthys perruno (no photo)

SCHULTZ, 1944

Reticulated Pimelodid

Syn.: None.

Hab.: South America: Venezuela, Rio Negro, Brazil.

F.I.: Unknown.

Sex: Not known.

Soc. B.: Severe predator that can only be kept with large cichlids such as *Astronotus ocellatus*, large characins such as *Leporinus* over 10-15 cm (4"-6") or with conspecifics.

M: Requires a large tank and a few plants in the background. Stone and root shelters. Perhaps floating plant cover. Strong filter which can handle the excrement that accumulates from its large appetite. Water: pH between 5.8-7.2; hardness up to 15° dGH.

B: Has not been described.

F: C; meat and fish, smaller animals accept frozen foods, any live foods.

S: None.

T: 21-25° C, **L:** 60 cm, **A:** 200 cm, **R:** b, **D:** 3-4 (S)
72-86° F, 20", 79",

Phractocephalus hemioliopterus

(BLOCH & SCHNEIDER, 1801)

Redtail Catfish

Syn.: *Silurus hemiliopterus, Phractocephalus bicolor, Pirarara bicolor.*

Hab.: South America; Amazon, Rio Negro; Venezuela and Guyana, in deeper river pools.

F.I.: Around 1970.

Sex: Not known.

Soc. B.: Marked predator that can only be kept with other large fish (i.e., large cichlids or other large catfish). Loner? Nothing is known about keeping several animals simultaneously. Older specimens are almost motionless and lurk motionless for prey.

M: Needs a huge tank with plenty of room to swim and hunt in. Large cave as hiding place. Peat filtration, soft and slightly acid water. pH 5.5-6.8; hardness up to 10° dGH. Only use large, robust plants since smaller ones are hopelessly buried.

B: Not possible in an aquarium.

F: C; fish. Do not overfeed. Imported animals are often emaciated.

S: The red colored tail fin secrets a substance which colors hands an intense red on contact. A fish only suitable for public show aquaria. At the time of purchase, it should already be known where it will be housed.
Phractocephalus is a monotypic genus; it only has a single species.

T: 20-26° C, **L:** to 60 cm, **A:** 200 cm, **R:** b, **D:** 4 (C)
68-79° F, to 24", 79",

Leiarius marmoratus

Phractocephalus hemioliopterus

Pimelodella gracilis (VALENCIENNES, 1840)
Slender Pimelodella

Syn.: *Pimelodus gracilis, Pimelodella taeniophora, Pimelodus taeniophorus, Rhamdia gracilis, Silurus dundu.*

Hab.: Northern west Brazil, Rio Ucayali, Amazon, Rio Tabatinga; South America.

F.I.: 1895 by P. Nitsche, Berlin.

Sex: None known.

Soc. B.: Suitable for large, dark community tanks. However, the other fishes should not be smaller than 8 cm (3"). Otherwise a peaceful, nocturnal species.

M: Caves made of roots or stones. Floating plant cover. Use a light dimmer to observe the animals at night. Not very demanding towards water values: pH 6.5-7.8; hardness 5-20° dGH

B: Has not been successful in an aquarium.

F: O; leftover foods, tablet foods, frozen foods. Small fish which are not very actively pursued.

S: The species differs from the very similar *P. vittata* by a significantly larger upper caudal fin lobe.

T: 20-24° C, L: 17 cm in aquaria, 30 cm in nature, A: 120 cm, R: b, D: 2-3
68-75° F, 6 3/4" in aquaria, 12", in nature 47"

Pimelodella lateristriga (MÜLLER & TROSCHEL, 1849)
Striped Pimelodella

Syn.: *Pimelodus lateristrigus, Pimelodus lateristriga, Pseudorhamdia lateristriga, Rhamdia lateristriga.*

Hab.: Eastern Amazon basin; specially from Rio Sao Francisco to Rio de Janeiro (Atlantic tributaries), South America.

F.I.: 1908.

Sex: Not yet described.

Soc. B.: Not a suitable fish for the community aquarium; small fishes disappear one after the other.

M: Easily kept in aquaria decorated in the manner typical for the catfishes of this genus: hiding places made of roots, sparse vegetation, a lot of free swimming space and a sand substrate.

B: Has not been reproduced in an aquarium.

F: C, O; younger specimen accept tablet foods and trout pellets, later only fish and meat. Beef heart, large insect larvae (from where?), small fishes.

S: The species is easily confused with *P. gracilis* which, however, has an enlarged upper tail lobe. Fast growing species; the mature size should be considered from the beginning. Dorsal and pectoral fins are poisonous! Only capture with a glass!

T: 20-24° C, L: 20 cm, A: 120 cm, R: b, D: 2-3
68-75° F, 8", 47",

Pimelodella gracilis

Pimelodella lateristriga

Pimelodus albofasciatus MEES, 1974
White-Striped Pimelodus

Syn.: None.

Hab.: Guyana and Surinam, South America.

F.I.: 1973 by Dr. Lüling, Bonn.

Sex: None known.

Soc. B.: The fishes defend their territory in a peaceful manner. Keep singly in aquaria less than 1.50 m (59") long. Only keep with larger fishes.

M: Easy to keep since so few demands are placed on water values. If possible, it should be soft and slightly acid, but other values are also tolerated. Nitrate, however, makes the barbels rot. After a water exchange (with AquaSafe or similar), these regenerate within a week.

B: Not known.

F: C; live foods, earthworms, small or frozen fish. Small specimens occasionally take tablet food.

S: The hard fin rays are poisonous. Pain can last up to 24 hours and may be accompanied by numbness. The animals can live over 10 years. In an aquarium one animal grew in that time from 5 cm (2") to 22 cm (8 3/4") length. Half of that growth occurred in the first year.

T: 22-25° C, **L**: 25 cm, **A**: 150 cm, **R**: b, **D**: 3 (see **S**)
72-77° F, 10", 59",

Pimelodus maculatus LACÉPÈDE, 1803
Spotted Pimelodus

Syn.: *Pimelodus clarias, P. rigidus, Piramutana blochii, P. macrospila, Pseudorhamdia piscatrix, Silurus clarias, S. callarias, S. lima.*

Hab.: Velhas River in Brazil. The pictured specimen, however, comes from the Rio Paraguay, Asunción, Paraguay, South America.

F.I.: Imported in 1895 by Paul Nitsche to Berlin as *P. clarias.*

Sex: None known.

Soc. B.: Twilight- and night-active species. Relatively peaceful but do not keep with fishes smaller than 6 cm (2 1/3"). With plenty of food the animals also come out of hiding during the day.

M: The pectorals are serrated, danger of injury. Capture the animals with a glass, not with the net. Sparse ground vegetation. Soft substrate. Provide sufficient caves and hiding places. A large diameter pipe, closed on one side, the open end pointed at the observer, has been successfully employed. Water: pH of 6.8-7.8; hardness 5-20° dGH.

B: Has not been successful.

F: C; tablet food, leftover flake food for smaller specimens. Animals over 12 cm (4 3/4") in length are given earthworms, insect larvae, whole Tetra Tips, trout pellets and small fish.

S: One of the most beautiful pimelodids which, unfortunately, is only rarely offered in the trade. Earlier authors place *P. maculatus* as a synonym to *P. blochi* VALENCIENNES, 1840. Both are distinct species. *P. maculatus* is spotted and *P. blochi* is striped longitudinally.

T: 20-24° C, **L**: 26 cm, **A**: 120 cm, **R**: b, **D**: 2-3
68-75° F, 10 , 47",

Pimelodus albofasciatus

Pimelodus maculatus

Pimelodus ornatus
Ornate Pimelodus

KNER, 1857

Syn.: *Megalonema rhabdostigma, Pseudorhamdia ornatus, Silurusmegacephalus.*

Hab.: Surinam, Guyana and Paraguay, South America.

F.I.: 1976.

Sex: Not known.

Soc. B.: Diurnal, restless catfish, constantly searching for food. Can be associated with fishes of the mid and upper water strata as long as they are not too small (over 6 cm; 2 1/3" in length). Other bottom dwellers should be nocturnal to avoid disturbing each other.

M: The species needs a lot of swimming room. Provide a sand and mulm bottom at the feeding area. A large power filter should provide current. Plants are not damaged, but they should be well rooted before introducing the catfish. Water: pH 6.5-7.2; hardness up to 18° dGH. The barbels degenerate under poor water conditions (nitrate). Improve through water exchanges! Barbels will regenerate after 5-10 days.

B: Breeding not described.

F: C, O; tablet food for smaller specimens. Later, earthworms, *Gammarus* and any other large live foods.

S: Do not keep with angelfish; they consider the barbels irritating and become shy.

T: 24-25° C, **L:** 28 cm, **A:** 150 cm, **R:** b, **D:** 3
75-77° F, 11", 59",

Pimelodus pictus
Angelicus Pimelodus

STEINDACHNER, 1876

Syn.: None.

Hab.: Mitu, Colombia, South America.

F.I.: 1968 to USA.

Sex: Not known.

Soc. B.: Peaceful catfish which can be kept alone or in small groups. Nocturnal. Will not disturb even small fish.

M: In dimly illuminated aquaria, this beautiful species will feed even during the day. Peat filtration. Soft water with a pH of 5.8-6.8. Roots and structures creating caves, floating plant cover. Good filtration with a slight current.

B: Not yet described.

F: O; tablet foods, leftover flake food, frozen or freeze-dried feeds. Any live foods of suitable size.

S: The nomen *Angelicus pimelodus* is somewhat misleading, since the African species *Synodontis angelicus* is colored exactly the opposite: black with white spots. The species was imported in 1968 as *"Pimelodella angelicus"* (fictitious name). The hard pectoral fin rays are strongly serrated which can lead to injuries. Specimens captured with a net hopelessly entangle themselves. Therefore, use a glass or suitable plastic container to capture them.

T: 22-25° C, **L:** 11 cm in aquaria, longer in nature, **A:** 80 cm, **R:** b, **D:** 2
72-77° F, 4 1/3" in aquaria, longer in nature, 31",

Pimelodus ornatus

Pimelodus pictus

Platystomatichthys sturio (KNER, 1857)
Sturgeon Catfish
Sub-Fam.: Sorubiminae

Syn.: *Platystoma sturio, Sorubim mena.*

Hab.: The entire Amazon basin.

F.I.: Not known.

Sex: Not yet described.

Soc. B.: Will not bother each other. Combining with larger fishes (10 cm; 4" length) also does not cause problems. Smaller fishes, however, are easily considered prey. Several animals can be kept together or singly.

M: This species demands a soft substrate. They dig and root, making a strong filter essential. Fine-leaved plants soon die from the mulm. pH should be between 6.0-7.5. Hardness up to 18° dGH. The tank must **be at least** twice the barbel length in width, otherwise the fish feel crowded and wane.

B: Not possible in an aquarium. Full-grown animals require a tank of 1.20 m (47") width and 3 m (118") length. If the fish will breed there is uncertain.

F: C; worms! *Tubifex*, small earthworms and Enchytraea for juveniles. Specimens over 20 cm (8") in length accept almost any carnivorous nourishment. Fish.

S: The sturgeon-like upward turned snout is interesting; it makes it possible for the fish to find the finest food organisms in the substrate. Most imports are half starved when they reach the trade. These animals are to be specially pampered. The long (over body length) maxillary barbels have a blood red point roughly in the center. Its purpose is unknown.

T: 21-25° C, L: 40 cm, A: 120 cm, R: b, D: 3-4 (S)
70-77° F, 16", 47",

Pseudopimelodus raninus raninus (VALENCIENNES, 1840)
Frog Marbled Catfish
Sub-Fam.: Pimelodinae

Syn.: *Pimelodus raninus, Batrachoglanis raninus, Pseudopimelodus acanthochira.*

Hab.: Wide spread in Surinam, French Guiana, Brazil, Peru and Paraguay, South America.

F.I.: 1894.

Sex: Not described

Soc. B.: Gregarious fish which does best in groups of 2-3. Do not associate with small fishes (neons) or overly large fishes (predators). The species has a very sedate lifestyle and does not like to be disturbed, especially during the daytime. It can sometimes be enticed to emerge from its hiding place with food.

M: Soft water up to 10° dGH and slightly acid 6.0-7.0, is the most fitting for the animals. Hiding places and subdued lighting need to be provided.

B: Not yet reproduced in an aquarium.

F: C; predominately an insectivore. In the aquarium tablet foods (Tetra TabiMin or similar) and flake food are readily accepted. Every once in a while live food (*Gammarus*) should be provided. However, fish of more than half its body length are also eaten.

S: Very seclusive species which is often not seen for weeks.

T: 21-25° C, L: 10 cm, A: 100 cm, R: b, D: 1-2
70-77° F, 4", 39",

Platystomatichthys sturio

Pseudopimelodus raninus raninus

Pseudopimelodus zungaro bufonius (VALENCIENNES, 1840)
Black Banded Marbled Catfish

Syn.: *Pimelodus bufonius, Pimelodus charus, Pseudopimelodus bufonius, Pseudopimelodus charus, Pseudopimelodus zungaro, Cephalosilurus bufonius, Zungaro zungaro, Zungaro bufonius, Zungaro charus.*

Hab.: Venezuela, Colombia, Guyana, Surinam and east Brazil, South America.

F.I.: About 1970.

Sex: Not known.

Soc. B.: Nocturnal, quiet loner which likes to consider small, resting fish as prey when swimming past. Otherwise peaceful.

M: Not a species for the well planted aquarium as it will dig a lot at night. Best suited are floating plants and those that attach to roots and stones (Java moss). Water: pH 6.5-7.2; hardness up to 18° dGH.

B: Not yet described.

F: C; meat such as mealworms, heart, snails, fish.

S: The disproportionately large, deeply forked caudal fin gives the fish its characteristic appearance. The species grows fast.

T: 20-24° C, L: 18 cm, A: 120 cm, R: b, D: 2-3
68-75° F, 7", 47",

Rhamdia guatemalensis (GÜNTHER, 1864)
Guatemala Rhamdid

Syn.: *Pimelodus boucardi, P. cinerascens* (not GÜNTHER), *P. godmani, P. guatemalensis, P. petenensis, P. wagneri, Rhamdia bransfordi, R. depressa, R. oaxacae, R. scrificii, R. wagneri.*

Hab.: Central America, in pacific tributaries from southern Mexico down to Colombia, perhaps even continued into Amazonia.

F.I.: 1981 and 1983.

Sex: Unknown.

Soc. B.: Agile species that likes to swim, knows how to avoid attacks of aggressive fish and even steals the feed or the young from the most resolved cichlids. Juveniles are quarrelsome in the aquarium. Heterospecifics have to be equal in size.

M: Undemanding, does not place any special requirements on the water which, however, should not be very hard (pH around 7.0). Likes hiding places made of stones and roots, not too bright. The natural environment of this catfish is a rock bottom with partial mud and gravel. Wood and leaves can always be found.

B: Has not yet been successful in an aquarium.

F: Voracious omnivores which immediately notice any feed given and who excitedly feel for something edible with their barbels as they nervously dart about the tank.

S: Young specimens are easily confused with *Pimelodella chagresi* (STEINDACHNER). Those catfish remain smaller.

T: 22-28° C, L: 28 cm, A: 120 cm, R: b, D: 2
72-82° F, 11", 47",

Pseudopimelodus zungaro bufonius

Rhamdia guatemalensis

Neosilurus argenteus (ZIETZ, 1896)
Silver Eel-Tailed Cat

Syn.: *Plotosus argenteus.* The species is probably identical to *Porocheilus obbesi* (WEBER, 1913) which, however, only reaches 10 cm (4") in length and inhabits north Australia.

Hab.: Interior of Australia.

F.I.: Not known.

Sex: None known.

Soc. B.: Small individuals are lasting aquarium inhabitants.

M: The species loves hard water (20-40° dGH) and a high pH (7.5-8.2)! Otherwise the species is unproblematic. If possible, give the fish a dark tank with caves of stone or roots.

B: Not known.

F: C, O; flake foods, live foods of any kind.

S: As in other members of the family, the dorsal fin ray is poisonous.

T: 5-30° C, L: 20 cm, A: 100 cm, R: m, b, D: 2-3
41-86° F, 8", 39",

Neosilurus ater (PERUGIA, 1894)
Black Tandan

Syn.: *Lambertia ater, Copidoglanis ater, Lambertichthys ater sepikensis.*

Hab.: New Guinea and north Australia, in freshwater rivers.

F.I.: Unknown.

Sex: None known.

Soc. B.: Juveniles up to 18 cm (7") are peaceful schooling fishes. With increasing length, fish under 6 cm (2[1]/3") are in danger of being eaten.

M: Large tank with stone decoration. Coarse gravel substrate. The species digs occasionally, but in general plants, are respected. Nevertheless, put small stones around the base of the plants.

B: Not yet reproduced in an aquarium.

F: C, O; tablet foods, pellets (carp and trout). Live foods of any kind.

S: The photo shows a fish of about 10 cm (4") length with its typical silver juvenile coloration.

T: 22-30° C, L: 50 cm, A: 150 cm, R: m, b, D: 2
72-86° F, 20", 59",

Neosilurus argenteus

Neosilurus ater

Neosilurus glencoensis (RENDAHL, 1922)
Yellow Fin Tandanus

Syn.: *Tandanus glencoensis.*

Hab.: Coastal waters of northwestern to northeastern Australia. Only in freshwater. Very numerous in parts.

F.I.: 1985 by J. Clasen.

Sex: None known.

Soc. B.: Lively, peaceful schooling fish that is very shy when maintained alone. Well suited for the community tank with larger fish.

M: Undemanding species which likes a densely planted background and an open foreground for swimming. pH 6.8-8.0; hardness up to 30° dGH. Substrate of coarse gravel and decorations of stone.

B: Unknown.

F: C, O; flake and tablet foods, any live foods.

S: The yellow fringe on the fins disappears with age.

T: 22-28° C, **L:** 20 cm, **A:** 100 cm, **R:** m, **D:** 1-2
72-82° F, 8", 39",

Tandanus tandanus (MITCHELL, 1838)
Dewfish

Syn.: *Plotosus tandanus.*

Hab.: Tweed River south of Brisbane to Sidney; southern region of the Murray-Darling river basin, Australia.

F.I.: Could not be determined.

Sex: After one year the sexes can be distinguished. The ♂ has a triangular urogenital pore and the ♀ has a cylindrical pore.

Soc. B.: Gregarious predators.

M: Like the preceding species.

B: In the Australian spring/summer (November,December) a bowl-like depression 2 m (79") in diameter is fanned out of the gravel bed of a creek. The eggs are non-adhesive, have a diameter of 3.2 mm (1/8") and hatch in about 7 days.

F: C; omnivore. Principally shrimp and mussels in coastal areas.

S: The hard fin rays of the dorsal and the pectorals can inflict painful injuries.

T: 5-25° C, **L:** 90 cm, **A:** 200 cm, **R:** m, b, **D:** 4
41-77° F, 35", 79",

Neosilurus glencoensis, juveniles

Neosilurus glencoensis

Tandanus tandanus

Eutropiellus buffei GRAS, 1960

Swallow-Tail Glass Catfish*

Syn.: *Eutropius buffei, Eutropiellus vandeweyeri.*

Hab.: Freshwater rivers of Nigeria, Cameroon and probably Gabon and Zaire, Africa.

F.I.: Unknown.

Sex: ♀♀ are fuller in the ventral area, appearing heavier. However, this only applies to well acclimated individuals.

Soc. B.: Diurnal schooling fish. Very peaceful, even towards the smallest species. Keep at least 6 individuals together.

M: Offer a lot of free swimming space. Strong filtration motivates the swimming activity of the fishes. Under poor water conditions the animals stay hidden or move around the bottom. Water: pH 6.5-7.2; hardness up to 18° dGH. Avoid larger fluctuations; therefore, make regular exchanges of 1/3 to 2/3 with conditioned tap water.

B: Breeding has been successful at 22-26° C (72-79° F). The set-up should consist of 2 ♂♂ and 1 ♀. Usually during the morning hours about 100 white eggs are scattered among the plants. Remove the parents. The larvae hatch after 3 days and can be fed newly hatched *Artemia* nauplii. The young are fast growing.

F: C, O; mainly eats insect larvae. In the aquarium, especially bloodworms (also frozen), *Daphnia* and *Cyclops*; however, flake food and freeze-dried foods are also accepted. The species requires varied foods.

S: The species is often called *E. debauwi*, even though that species is almost never available in the trade. The external differences are as follows:

E. buffei

1. Underneath the black stripe along the lateral line and through the tail fin, there is a second black stripe which is interrupted around the anus.
2. The caudal fin lobes have black tips which are **rounded.**
3. The adipose is transparent.

E. debauwi

1. The second stripe is missing, but the center stripe is the same.
2. No black dots or designs on the tips of the caudal fin, which are **pointed.**
3. The forward edge of the adipose is dark.

* This name is a suggestion of the authors because the tail fin distinguishes it from *E. debauwi*.

T: 22-27° C, L: 8 cm, A: 120 cm, R: m, D: 1-2
72-81° F, 3", 47",

Parailia congica BOULENGER, 1899

African Glass Catfish*

Syn.: *Parailia longifilis.*

Hab.: Zaire, Africa (Stanley Pool).

F.I.: 1955.

Sex: Not known.

Soc. B.: Peaceful, often shy, schooling fish which may consider young and small tankmates as food. Diurnal. Should be kept in a school of 4-6 animals.

M: A species which sometimes does not adapt easily to aquarium conditions. The water should be very clear and well aerated. Even low nitrate levels (below 30 mg/l) are detrimental. pH 6.5-7.4; hardness up to 18° dGH.

B: Not yet successful.

F: C, O; after acclimation, flake food (TetraMin or similar) is easily taken. However, *Daphnia* and mosquito larvae (frozen) should be given 1-2 times per week.

Eutropiellus buffei

Parailia congica

S: There is another African glass catfish *(Parailia pellucida)* which has an adipose. Neither should be confused with *Kryptopterus bicirrhis*, the Indian glass catfish. It has 1 pair of barbels, while *Parailia* has 4 pairs.

˙Both species of African glass catfishes have the same common name in German as well as in English, even though they belong to different subgenera. This is why a new name has been suggested (Nile glass catfish) for the latter.

T: 23-26° C, L: 9 cm, A: 80 cm, R: m, b, D: 2
73-79° F, 3 ", 31",

Parailia pellucida (BOULENGER, 1901)
Nile Glass Catfish, African Glass Catfish

Syn.: *Physailia pellucida, Parailia congica* (non BOULENGER).

Hab.: Headwaters of the Nile.

F.I.: 1927 by Vereinigten Zierfischzüchtereien Conradshöhe of Berlin.

Sex: Not known.

Soc. B.: Friendly schooling fish which has to have conspecifics for its well-being. Diurnal. Can be associated with small, quiet bottom dwelling and labyrinth fishes.

M: The species demands a lot of free swimming space, maybe a partially covered water surface. Clear water with some current is appreciated. Water: pH 6.5-7.2; hardness: 5-15° dGH.

B: Not yet known.

F: C; small live foods such as *Artemia*, mosquito larvae, Enchytraea, also occasionally flake food. FD tablets are well accepted after acclimation.

S: The Indian glass catfish *Kryptopterus* has a dorsal fin; it is absent in both African glass catfishes.

T: 25-28° C, L: 15 cm, A: 80 cm, R: m, D: 3
77-82° F, 6", 31",

Platytropius siamensis (no photo) (SAUVAGE, 1883)
False Siamese Shark

Syn.: *Pseudeutropius siamensis, Nemasiluroides furcatus.*

Hab.: Thailand.

F.I.: Not known.

Sex: The ♂ has a fleshy hump just in front of the anus (SMITH, 1945).

Soc. B.: A diurnal catfish which considers smallest fish (i.e., *Rasbora maculata)* as food. Otherwise quite peaceful. Maintaining several specimens corresponds to its natural habits.

M: At least 4-6 specimens of this schooling fish should be kept. The large eyes of the animals are easily injured, especially since the fishes are skittish. Sudden movements in front of the aquarium should be avoided. The aquarium should not be decorated with sharp edged objects.

B: Not yet known.

F: C, O; good quality flake food, *Daphnia*, mosquito larvae (also frozen), *Tubifex*. In nature it is an insectivore.

S: The species is more free-swimming than bottom oriented, in contrast to other catfishes. The genus was established by HORA.

T: 21-25° C, L: 20 cm, A: 120 cm, R: m, b, D: 2
70-77° F, 8", 47",

Parailia pellucida

Pseudeutropius brachyopterus (?)

Kryptopterus cryptopterus (BLEEKER, 1851)

Syn.: *Silurus cryptopterus, Kryptopterus micropus, Cryptopterus cryptopterus, Cryptopterus micropus.*

Hab.: Thailand, Sumatra and Borneo (Southeast Asia), Malaysia, Cambodia, Laos, Vietnam.

F.I.: ?

Sex: Are not known.

Soc. B.: Day-active, usually peaceful fish which may consider fish smaller than 4 cm (1 2/3") as prey. Otherwise a slow moving fish which should only be kept with quiet tankmates.

M: The species requires a lot of space and light. Floating plants on 1/3-1/2 of the water surface provides cover to hunt in the open water.

B: Has not been successful in an aquarium. In nature the animals breed in June/July. Water: pH 6.8-7.8; hardness up to 18° dGH.

F: C; insect larvae, frozen foods, but also large flakes and tablet food particles, small earthworms.

S: In Thailand the species is highly appreciated smoked.

T: 22-25° C, **L:** to 20 cm, **A:** 100 cm, **R:** b, m, **D:** 3
72-77° F, to 8", 39",

Kryptopterus macrocephalus (BLEEKER, 1858)

Striped Glass Catfish

Syn.: *Kryptopterichthys macrocephalus, Cryptopterus macrocephalus.*

Hab.: Borneo and Sumatra, Southeast Asia, Malaysia, South Thailand.

F.I.: 1950.

Sex: Not known.

Soc. B.: The species is not as peaceful as *K. bicirrhis* (Vol. 1, page 514). It prefers the open water. Small fish such as *Rasbora urophthalma* or *R. maculata* can easily be eaten. Otherwise this species is tolerant. Larger fish over 5 cm (2") in length are good tankmates.

M: Water values: pH 6.5-7.4; hardness 10-20° dGH. The water should be very well-filtered but not fast moving. Plant and stone hideaways are needed.

B: Not known.

F: C, O; primarily an insectivore (surface feeding), but also flake and tablet foods.

S: When stationary, the fish's tail fin is downward. When moving, the fish is horizontal.

T: 22-26° C, **L:** 11 cm, **A:** 80 cm, **R:** m, t, **D:** 1, 2
72-79° F, 4 1/3", 31",

Kryptopterus cryptopterus (?)

Kryptopterus macrocephalus

Ompok eugeneiatus (VAILLANT, 1893)
Borneo Glass Catfish

Syn.: *Callichrous eugeneiatus, Silurodes eugeneiatus.*

Hab.: In fresh, flowing waters in Sumatra and Borneo.

F.I.: About 1970 as by-catch of more common species.

Sex: Not distinguishable from the exterior. The length of the dorsal my be a distinguishing characteristic of the gender, possibly also of age.

Soc. B.: A restless schooling fish which is only at ease with conspecifics. It may be possible to associate it with other glass catfishes. Housing with aggressive fishes is not recommended; the animals become shy and waste away. After acclimation the fish are no longer shy, but accustomed to the caretaker.

M: The fish are very sensitive. The extremely long barbels and extremely thin skin are easily injured. Therefore, capturing them with a net is dangerous to the animals. Use a glass cup and drive them in singly. Clear, well-filtered, oxygen-rich water are mandatory for successful care. pH 6.5-7.0; hardness 7-16° dGH.

B: Not yet bred.

F: C; live foods of any kind, frozen foods; occasionally full-grown animals additionally take smaller fish. After adaptation, flake food is also accepted.

S: The animals appear to be swimming upside-down because of their high body cavity. The long dorsal ray and the absent adipose are identifying characteristics. The African glass catfish, *Physalia pellucida*, has an adipose but is missing a dorsal.

T: 20-24° C, **L:** 18 cm, **A:** 150 cm, **R:** m, **D:** 3
68-75° F, 7", 59",

Wallago attu (BLOCH & SCHNEIDER, 1801)
Helicopter Catfish

Syn.: *Silurus attu, Silurus boalis, Silurus asotus, Silurus mulleri, Silurus ruallagoo. Callichrus macrostomus, Wallago russellii, Wallagonia attu.*

Hab.: Java, Sumatra, Thailand, India, Burma, Sri Lanka (Ceylon).

F.I.: About 1970 to Europe.

Sex: Not known.

Soc. B.: Predator that will eat anything smaller than itself. Only as a juvenile can it be put with much larger fishes.

M: The large fishes are not only fast swimmers, they also jump well. Therefore, cover the large aquarium well. Otherwise few demands are made. Because of the large feed intake, a good large volume filter is required.

B: In nature the fish leave the deeper water regions and enter the shallow water to spawn. Probably impossible to breed in an aquarium.

F: C; only juveniles are content with tablet food, beef heart and similar foods. Larger fish demand living fish!

S: Not an aquarium fish. Why such a giant is sporadically offered in the trade is not understood. The species has been included here as a novelty (to warn prospective buyers).

T: 22-25° C, **L:** 90 cm, **A:** 4 m, **R:** b, m, **D:** 4 (C)
72-77° F, 35", 157",

Ompok eugeneiatus

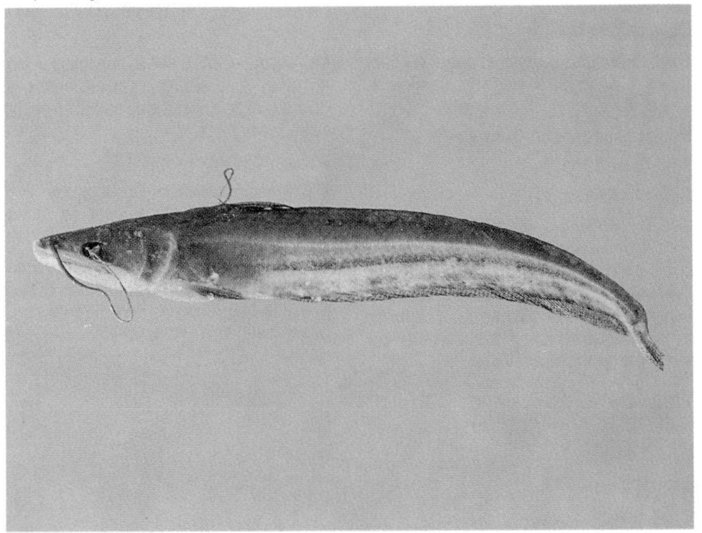

Wallago attu

Bagarius yarellii (HAMILTON, 1822)
Freshwater Shark

Syn.: *Pimelodus bagarius, P. platespogon, Pachypterus luridus, Pimelodus carnaticus, Bagarius buchanani, Pimelodus yarellii.*

Hab.: India, Burma, Thailand, Vietnam, Sumatra, Borneo, Java.

F.I.: To England in 1974.

Sex: No certain characteristics known.

Soc. B.: Should only be kept in a species tank with equal sized conspecifics. The fish are usually nocturnal and appreciate quiet during the day.

M: Depending on origin (mountain stream or river) the final size and temperature requirements vary. Animals from mountain regions are preferred, but because they live in rapids, they require lots of oxygen. Good filtration with current is probably necessary for juveniles. Larger animals withstand hard water, even the addition of salt (density 1.006). Water: pH 6.5-7.8 (7.0); hardness for juveniles up to 12° dGH, after acclimation up to 30° dGH.

B: Not known. Who wants to breed this demon, anyway?

F: C; bad predator, even eats scales from tankmates. Small animals up to 20 cm (8") in length take insects and their larvae, later only fishes.

S: Not an aquarium fish. At the turn of the century there were even reports of 2 m (79") long animals being caught. Weight more than 150 lbs or 65 kg.

T: 18-25° C, **L:** 100 cm, large specimens up to 200 cm!!, **A:** 200 cm, **R:** b, m, **D:** 3-4 (C)
64-77° F, 39", large specimens up to 79"!!, 79",

Gagata cenia (HAMILTON, 1822)
Clown Catfish

Syn.: *Pimelodus gagata, P. cenia, Gagata typus, Callomystax gagata, Hemipimelodus cenia.*

Hab.: India (Bengal), Burma.

F.I.: About 1970.

Sex: Not described.

Soc. B.: A peaceful species which can be kept with smaller animals. Best kept in a small school. Perfect companion for other river fishes such as *Tanichthys albonubes* (white cloud), *Homaloptera zollingeri* or similar fishes which prefer current and relatively cool temperatures.

M: As stated. pH 6.8-7.2; hardness up to 15° dGH. Use a strong filter to create a good current. Keep a long section free for swimming.

B: Has not been successful.

F: C; insectivore which also takes other live foods and can be well cared for with tablet food (Tetra Tips FD) and flake food.

S: Mistakenly called *Microglanis parahybae* in the aquarium literature. Therefore, the fish appears from time to time under that name in the trade.

T: 20-22° C, **L:** 7 cm, **A:** 100 cm, **R:** b, **D:** 1-2
68-72° F, 2 3/4", 39"

Bagarius yarellii

Gagata cenia

Nothobranchius patrizii, ♂ top ♀ bottom

The Killifish Genera* and the Sub-Families They Belong to:

Sub-Family Aphaniinae
- Aphanius
- Valencia

Sub-Family Cyprinodontinae
- Cyprinodon
- Jordanella and Garmanella

Sub-Family Fundulinae
- Fundulus
- Profundulus
- Adinia
- Chriopeoides
- Cubanichthys
- Lucania

Sub-Family Orestiatinae
- Orestias

Sub-Family Procatopodinae
- Aplocheilichthys
- Procatopus
- Lamprichthys

Sub-Family Rivulinae
- Adamas
- Aphyosemion
- Diapteron
- Roloffia
- Fundulosoma
- Nothobranchius
- Epiplatys and Pseudepiplatys
- Pachypanchax
- Aplocheilus
- Cynolebias
- Austrofundulus
- Rachovia
- Pterolebias
- Rivulus

*Only genera represented in the Aquarium Atlas are listed here.

Adamas formosus HUBER, 1979

Syn.: None.

Hab.: West Africa, Congo, western Congo basin.

F.I.: Probably initially in the '60's to the USA by Brichard. However, certainly imported in 1978 by Huber to France.

Sex: The ♀♀ are less brightly colored and plain; the body circumference is comparatively large with good feeding; the caudal peduncle is more slender.

Soc. B.: A peaceful, rather shy fish which prefers to live alone or in small schools at the water surface.

M: *A. formosus* is difficult to maintain. The water should be soft and slightly acid with a constant supply of small (live) foods. Because of the diminutive size of the fish, smaller aquaria are recommended. The fish are to be kept either in a species tank or together with very small fish species, for example, with *Aphyoplatys duboisi* or *Pseudepiplatys annulatus*. Perhaps it can also be kept with very small barbs or characins.

B: Breeding is not easy, primarily because of their small size. The fish are set up in pairs or a trio (1 ♂, 2 ♀♀) in a small aquarium (5-10 l; 1.3-2.5 gal) with spawning substrate (peat fiber, perlon). The water has to be soft and slightly acid. The fish are continuous spawners which only deposit a few eggs at a time over an extended period. These can be collected, the whole spawning substrate transferred to another aquarium, or the parent fish can be transferred after about 2 weeks. After hatching, the tiny juveniles have to be fed with paramecium. Growth is slow and the species is not very productive.

F: C; small live foods, preferably nauplii of *Artemia salina* and sieved pond plankton.

S: The fish have a silver spot made of 2-3 scales on the head. Its function is still unclear.

T: 22-24° C, L: 2.5-3 cm, A: 30-50 cm, R: t, D: 4
72-86° F, 1"-1 ", 12"-20",

Aphanius (*Kosswigichthys*) *asquamatus* (SÖZER, 1942)
Naked Turkish Killifish
Sub-Fam.: Cyprinodontinae

Syn.: *Kosswigichthys asquamatus.*

Hab.: Turkey, Hazer-Gölü, a bitter lake in east Anatolia. The animals prefer shore areas.

F.I.: ?

Sex: The ♂♂ are more colorful. The ♀♀ are somewhat shorter and stouter.

Soc. B.: According to observations by KOSSWIG, the fish are found in schools close to shore in the open water of the Hazer-Gölü (Gölü = lake). In the aquarium, the fish are gregarious and peaceful. They are extraordinarily curious and explore all changes in the aquarium in detail.

M: The fish should be kept in hard, alkaline water. A species tank is recommended, but the animals can also be kept with other small nontropical Cyprinodontinae.

B: Breeding is easy; the fish spawn at 22-25° C (72-77° F) on a perlon mop. Therefore, best to place a trio in a 10 l (2.5 gal) breeding tank and collect the eggs regularly. In a breeding dish—perhaps add acriflavine—they hatch after about 8-12 days. Initially feed with paramecium. After a few days, they can be fed with *Artemia salina* nauplii. Growth is slow.

F: C, O; live foods, also frozen and flake foods.

S: The fishes do not have true scales. Only some individuals show remnants of scales. The independent genus *Kosswigichthys* was previously placed in Fundulinae because of dentition. Because this character, as well as the scale reduction, does not represent a sufficient grouping (dividing) characteristic, today *Kosswigichthys* is at best considered a sub-genus of *Aphanius*.

T: 10-25° C, L: 4 cm, A: 50 cm, R: t, m, b, D: 2-3
50-77° F, 1 2/3", 20",

Aphanius dispar (RÜPPELL, 1828)

Mother of Pearl Killie

Syn.: *Lebias dispar, Cyprinodon dispar, Cyprinodon aerebejensis, Cyprinodon desioi, Cyprinodon eilensis, Cyprinodon cilensis, Cyprinodon hammonis, Cyprinodon lunatus, Cyprinodon stoliczkanus.*

Hab.: Coastal areas of the Indian Ocean, Red Sea, Persian Gulf from Somalia in the south around the Arabian Peninsula, up to Kutch in west India, also in the Dead Sea and a few oasis of the eastern Sahara.

F.I.: 1904 by Hans Stüve, Hamburg.

Sex: The ♀♀ are smaller and rounder than the longer ♂♂. Their coloration, especially of the fins, is simpler, and the caudal fin does not have the beautiful yellow stripes. The fins are also smaller.

Soc. B.: *A. dispar* are peaceful and tend to form groups and schools, particularly as juveniles. Full-grown ♂♂ are more territorial, but this is not extreme when compared to other species of the genus. *A. dispar* distinguishes itself by its special liveliness and its restless swimming.

M: Corresponding to their distribution, from pure freshwater all the way to hypersaline, water with high salt content and a high evaporation rate, these fishes are very salt tolerant and actually halophilic. Therefore, they should by all means receive salt. The dosage depends on the origin of the fish, but if you do not know exactly, pure sea water will not be detrimental. If kept in freshwater, hard water is recommended.

B: To breed, the temperature should be about 24-28° C (75-82° F) and a spawning mop or perlon fiber should be offered as spawning substrate. The hatching young should be offered *Artemia salina* nauplii immediately.

F: O; live foods, flake food; if possible also provide filamentous algae.

T: 16-26° C, L: 7 cm, A: 80-100 cm, R: m, D: 3-4
61-79° F, 2 3/4", 31"-39",

Aphanius mento (HECKEL, 1843)

Orient Killie

Syn.: *Lebias mento, Lebias cypris, Aphanius sophiae mentoides, Aphanius sophiae similis, Aphanius cypris alexandri, Aphaniu cypris boulengeri, Aphanius cypris orontis.*

Hab.: From southern Turkey towards the east, including the region of Euphrates and Tigris, to the Persian Gulf and southward to Israel to the Dead Sea.

F.I.: Fall of 1910 by Vereinigte Zierfischzüchtereinen in Conradshöhe, Berlin, Germany.

Sex: The coloration of the sexes is so different that, upon discovery, the ♀ was described as a different species, *Lebias cypris*. Depending on origin, the ♂♂ are more or less blue-black with bright dots and lines. The ♀♀, in contrast, have dark brown to black spots on a light brown-gray background; their fins are faintly brown to translucent.

Soc. B.: The ♂♂ are, again depending on origin, moderately to strongly aggressive against each other and ♀♀. They es-tablish territories, and the dominant ♂ has the most intense coloration. In aquaria that are too small, fishes of aggressive strains can kill each other.

M: The fish should be kept in overdimensioned aquaria. They are not choosy regarding water and temperature, but it should tend towards hard. According to VILLWOCK, the addition of a dash of magnesium sulphate ($MgSO_4$) as well as a minor addition of iodine (solution of Lugol) is beneficial. They have been kept outside successfully during the summer.

B: Breeding is best attempted in the regular tank, where the strongest ♂♂ have territories. The ♂♂ constantly spawn with ♀♀ on a wool mop or perlon bunch; in nature, they spawn on an algae mat. The spawning substrate is then exchanged every week, or the eggs have to be collected. They are transferred to brooding bowls. The young hatch after 8-10 days and immediately feed on *Artemia* nauplii.

F: O; live foods as well as frozen and dry foods. Green algae are also important.

T: 10-25° C, L: 5 cm, A: 80 cm, R: m, D: 2-3
50-77° F, 2", 31",

Aphanius dispar

Aphanius mento "Kirk Göz"

Aphyosemion arnoldi (BOULENGER, 1908)

Arnold's Killie

Syn.: *Fundulus arnoldi*.

Hab.: West Africa, Nigeria, western Niger delta near Sapele and Warri.

F.I.: 1905 by W. Schroot, Hamburg.

Sex: The ♂♂ are very colorful. On blue to violet background, they show numerous red dots and spots. The dorsal and anal fins are orange and have red longitudinal stripes or rows of spots at the edges and close to the body. The tail fin is trilobed. Both the upper and lower lobes are separated from the red spotted central lobe by a red stripe. The ♀♀ are a uniform brown with dark brown spots on the body and the fins; they are stouter and have rounded fins.

Soc. B.: Peaceful species, only the ♂♂ are somewhat aggressive among each other or towards ♂♂ of related species.

M: A species tank with a dark substrate, preferably peat, is recommended. Roots with Java fern or moss can be distributed throughout the aquarium as decoration. The lighting should be somewhat subdued. Generous feedings with live foods are important.

B: The reproduction of *A. arnoldi* is not easy. Strong and healthy breeders are important. The species is a continuous bottom spawner and a seasonal fish. Use breeders well fed with a varied diet. Place 1 ♂ and 2-3 ♀♀ in a 10-15 l (2.5-4 gal) tank which is furnished with a layer of peat. The breeders remain there for 1 week while being sparingly fed. Later, the fish are removed, the water decanted and the peat is pressed and left to dry slightly on a newspaper before being stored in a plastic bag (with identification!). After about 2-3 months the peat is placed in an appropriate tank and fresh water is added. The young, which hatch within 24 hours, will immediately feed on nauplii of *Artemia salina*.

F: C; live food, worms are liked but should be given sparingly.

S: *A. arnoldi* occupies a special place within the genus *Aphyosemion* in regard to body measurements and egg structure.

T: 22-25° C, L: 5 cm, A: 50 cm, R: b, m, D: 3-4
72-77° F, 2", 20",

Aphyosemion aureum RADDA, 1980

Gold Killie

Syn.: None.

Hab.: West Africa, southern Gabon, in small and fast-flowing creeks of the mountains of the Du-Chaillu-Massif.

F.I.: 1980 by Hofmann and Pürzl to Austria.

Sex: The ♂♂ are quite colorful, the body is pink to light brown, the fins are golden (name!) and the dorsal and anal fins have either a slender or broad stripe towards the body. The tail fin is framed in red on the top and bottom. The ♀♀ are a monotonous brown with transparent, rounded fins which lack the elongation found on the ♂♂.

Soc. B.: Peaceful and somewhat shy killifish.

M: We recommend a well-planted tank. When plants grow well, water quality is also well suited for the fish. The tank should not be overdimensioned, or the fish are rarely seen because of their reclusive lifestyle. Soft to medium-hard and, preferably, slightly acid water of a moderate temperature (18-22° C; 64-72° F) is suitable. Perform frequent water changes.

B: Breeding is recommended in a separate 10-12 l (2.5-3 gal) tank. Set up for a substrate or adhesive spawner. However, a permanent set-up with a wool mop or similar substrate is recommended. The eggs are regularly collected and developed in brooding containers with the slight addition of acriflavine. The young hatch after about 18-20 days and immediately eat *Artemia* nauplii.

F: C; all live foods of appropriate size.

S: The crosses with *Aphyosemion punctatum* indicate that *A. aureum* is probably only a color morph of that species.

T: 18-22° C, L: 5 cm, A: 50 cm, R: b, m, D: 2-3
64-72° F, 2", 20",

Aphyosemion arnoldi

Aphyosemion aureum

Aphyosemion bamilekorum RADDA, 1971

Bamileke Killie

Syn.: None.

Hab.: West Africa, west Cameroon, highland creeks northwest of Bafoussam.

F.I.: 1971 by Radda to Vienna, Austria.

Sex: Not always easy to determine because ♂♂ of this species are not as colorful as others. Full-grown ♂♂ have elongated dorsal and anal fins. The base coloration is brown-green, occasionally tinted blue. Over this lays a red-brown net design, the fins are spotted and dotted. In ♀♀, the red-brown net design over a brown background is faint, and the spots on the rounded fins are absent.

Soc. B.: A peaceful and rather timid, small species.

M: This small fish should be maintained in a moderately sized species tank. Decorate as described for *A. arnoldi*. Additionally, peat fiber bunches can be offered where the ♀♀ can hide.

B: The set-up should suit a bottom spawner like *A. arnoldi*, even though they will also spawn on a wool mop. The combination of difficult breeding and lack of appeal to most aquarists (deficient coloration) constantly places the fish in danger of becoming extinct in captivity. After the addition of water (storage time of the peat about 3-4 weeks), the hatching young should receive infusoria during the first days.

F: C; live foods which must correspond to the small size of the fish.

S: *A. bamilekorum* has been placed with *A. bualanum* and *A. exiguum* in the subgenus *Kathetys*.

T: 18-22° C, 64-72° F, **L:** 4 cm, 1 2/3", **A:** 40 cm, 16", **R:** b, m, **D:** 3

Aphyosemion calliurum (BOULENGER, 1911)

Red-Seam Killie

Syn.: *Haplochilus calliurus, Panchax vexillifer.*

Hab.: West Africa, coastal areas of southern Benin through southern Nigeria into southwest Cameroon.

F.I.: January 1908 by Siggelkow, Hamburg, Germany.

Sex: The ♂♂ are markedly more colorful than the smaller and uniformly colored ♀♀ which only have a number of red dots in common with the ♂♂. In addition, the fins of the ♀♀ are rounded while those of the ♂♂ are elongated.

Soc. B.: Peaceful fish which is occasionally somewhat aggressive towards ♂♂ of their own species and other *Aphyosemion* species, but usually only until a pecking order is established.

M: Dense vegetation and a dark substrate are recommended. The decoration can be a beautiful plant aquarium following the "Dutch" example. Water should be soft to medium-hard and slightly acid, perhaps peat filtered. Tankmates should be chosen from smaller *Aphyosemion*, e.g., the *bivittatum* group. Other small and not excessively active fishes are also appropriate.

B: The animals are plant and bottom spawners. One ♂ and two ♀♀ can be set up either with peat substrate or a wool mop. When using peat substrate, the eggs are handled similar to bottom spawners (*Aphyosemion robertsoni*), i.e., store dry 3-4 weeks. Otherwise, remove the eggs regularly from the wool mop and place them in bowls with a small amount of acriflavine for further development. After 2-3 weeks the young hatch and immediately feed on *Artemia* nauplii.

F: C; live foods; after adaptation also frozen foods and beef heart with the occasional dry foods.

S: *Aphyosemion ahli* is probably only a strain of *A. calliurum*, which has additional populations that have proven not to interbreed successfully among each other.

T: 24-26° C, 75-79° F, **L:** 5 cm, 2", **A:** 50 cm, 20", **R:** b, m, **D:** 2

Aphyosemion bamilekorum

Aphyosemion calliurum, wild caught "Funge, Cameroon"

Aphyosemion cameronense (BOULENGER, 1903)
Cameroon Killie, Powder Blue Killie

Syn.: *Haplochilus cameronensis, Panchax microstomus, Panchax escherichi.*

Hab.: West Africa, inland plateaus of southern Cameroon, equatorial Guinea (= Rio Muni) and north Cameroon in numerous different morphs.

F.I.: 1968 (?) by Scheel from equatorial Guinea (= Rio Muni).

Sex: The ♂♂ are very colorful with much variation, depending on the natural distribution. Characteristic for all *A. cameronense* morphs, however, is a red band extending approximately from the pectoral fin to the caudal fin along the ventral side. All forms have a variable number of rows of red dots on their sides.

Soc. B.: This peaceful species is quite skittish.

M: *A. cameronense* is surely one of the most sensitive *Aphyosemion* species. The water should be soft and slightly acid (pH 6.5). The tank should be well-planted and is probably best decorated as described for *A. arnoldi*.

B: In the described strain from the Rio Ecucu, reproduction was not very difficult. The animals spawned in a wool mop and the young ate *Artemia* nauplii after hatching.

F: C; live foods. Corresponding to the sensitivity of the fish, they should only be feed the best live foods and as few worms as possible.

S: Several sub-species have been described of *A. cameronense* who belong to the sub-genus *Mesoaphyosemion*: *A. c. halleri, A. c. haasi* and *A. c. obscurum*.

T: 18-22° C, 64-72° F, **L:** 5 cm, 2", **A:** 50 cm, 20", **R:** m, b, **D:** 4

Aphyosemion caudofasciatum HUBER & RADDA, 1979
Tail Stripe Killie

Syn.: None.

Hab.: West Africa, south of the Congo (= Congo Brazzaville), waters of the rain forest of the Batéké in the near or far surroundings of Zanaga, Lékomou Province.

F.I.: August 1978 by J. Buytaert and W. Wachters to Belgium.

Sex: The ♂♂ are intensely colored. The ♀♀ are only olive-brown with small red-brown dots on the body and also on the otherwise colorless fins.

Soc. B.: An active and thoroughly peaceful killifish which can occasionally be aggressive towards ♂♂ of *Aphyosemion* species, especially those of its own, while establishing a social hierarchy.

M: Water should be soft to medium-hard, slightly acid and not too warm. To create hiding places and—in the species tank—also spawning sites, bushes of peat fibers are added.

B: Can be bred with a continuous set-up in a species tank. The young are picked out, even though they are not pursued by the parents when well fed. Experience has shown that temperatures above 22° C (72° F) diminish spawning activity.

F: C; live foods; after adaptation perhaps also dry and frozen foods.

S: *A. caudofasciatum* is very close to *A. ogoense*. Some populations of *A. ogoense* have the beginnings of a vertical caudal stripe, while individuals of *A. caudofasciatus* are missing such a stripe. Despite this, it can be said at this time that *A. caudofasciatum* is a true species.

T: 18-22° C, 64-72° F, **L:** 5 cm, 2", **A:** 50 cm, 20", **R:** m, b, **D:** 2-3

Aphyosemion cameronense

Aphyosemion caudofasciatum

Aphyosemion christyi (BOULENGER, 1915)

Christy's Lyretail, Spotfin Killie

Syn.: *Haplochilus christyi, A. castaneum, A. decorsei, A. margaretae* (?), *A. schoutedeni.*

Hab.: In the entire Congo basin including the Ubangui, Africa.

F.I.: 1949 from Leopoldville (= Kinshasa) into Belgium.

Sex: The ♂♂ are colorful and, depending on origin of the strain, very variable. In general, a yellowish to yellow-green or bluish base coloration predominates. On this base are numerous red dots. The fins are long, drawn out and normally have a red stripe on the upper and lower edges. The ♀♀, in contrast, are brown with small red-brown dots at the intersection of the scales. The fins are round and usually transparent.

Soc. B.: These are peaceful, retiring, small statured fish.

M: A somewhat sensitive species, as are all representatives of the *A. elegans* group. Water should be soft (up to about 10° dGH) and slightly acid (pH 6-6.5); however, water values are not that important under otherwise favorable conditions (e.g., food). A species tank is preferred, but the species can also be kept with other small fishes.

B: The animals may be more regarded as adhesive spawners than bottom spawners; the division is fluid. Breeding should be performed in a small (10 l; 2.5 gal) separate tank. A spawning substrate of either perlon or peat fibers should be offered. Hatching occurs after 12-16 days. When peat fibers are used, the substrate containing the eggs can be stored moist in a plastic bag for about 3 weeks then placed in a small tank with water. The young immediately eat small *Artemia* nauplii; additionally, feeding infusoria can only be advantageous during the first days.

F: C; all kinds of live foods of appropriate size.

S: *A. christyi* has numerous morphs within its large distribution area which have to be kept pure. *A. castaneum*, a synonym of *A. christyi*, is the type species of the genus *Aphyosemion.*

T: 20-24° C, **L:** 5 cm, **A:** 50 cm, **R:** b, m, **D:** 3
68-75° F, 2", 20",

Aphyosemion cinnamomeum CLAUSEN, 1963

Cinnamon Killie

Syn.: None.

Hab.: West Africa, west Cameroon, drainage area of the upper Mungo River from Badouma to Manyemen.

F.I.: 1960 by Clausen to Denmark.

Sex: The ♂♂ are dark blue to almost black on the body and have yellow edged fins. Contrary to this, the ♀♀ have the typical brown to brown-gray coloration of all *Aphyosemion* ♀♀. In addition, their fins are barely colored and translucent.

Soc. B.: *A. cinnamomeum* is quite robust and likes to subdue smaller *Aphyosemion* species. Singly kept, older ♂♂ can turn into tyrants towards other *Aphyosemion* species. When kept with totally different fish, for example, small African barbs, there are hardly any problems. When housed with other killifish, only correspondingly vigorous species should be chosen.

M: Simple to care for; water should be soft to medium-hard and slightly acid and frequently changed (each or every other week).

B: As with other *Aphyosemion* species.

F: C; live foods, possibly frozen and flake foods every once in a while, also beef heart.

S: *Aphyosemion cinnamomeum* belongs to the *A. gardneri* group of the sub-genus *Paraphyosemion* and is very similar in color to the sibling species *A. celiae* which belongs to the *A. calliurum* group (sub-genus *Mesoaphyosemion*).

T: 22-24° C, **L:** 5 cm, **A:** 80 cm, **R:** t, m, b, **D:** 2-3
72-75° F, 2", 31",

Aphyosemion christyi, "Bangui, central Africa"

Aphyosemion cinnamomeum, wild caught, west Cameroon

Aphyosemion coeleste — HUBER & RADDA, 1977

Sky Blue Killie

Syn.: None.

Hab.: West Africa, southeastern Gabon and Congo (Congo = Brazzaville), in creeks of the Batéké highlands.

F.I.: 1977 by Huber and Radda.

Sex: ♂♂ are very colorful with a blue body (name!) and red-yellow fins. ♀♀ have a brownish base coloration with essentially transparent fins which are more rounded than the ♂♂'s.

Soc. B.: Peaceful and somewhat shy species which leads a secluded life.

M: A somewhat more difficult and sensitive species to keep. Needs soft to medium-hard, slightly acid water. Not overly suited for a community tank but, if done, combine with peaceful and not too robust species, including fishes other that killies.

T: 18-22° C, 64-72° F, **L:** 5 cm, 2", **A:** 50 cm, 20", **R:** m, b, **D:** 3

B: Can be treated as a plant or bottom spawner. That is, with a perlon spawning mop and removing the eggs or above a layer of peat which is dried after about a week (see *A. arnoldi*). *A. coeleste* is not particularly fertile.

F: C; live foods, very few or no worms.

S: Several strains are known from Gabon and Congo which differ in design and coloration pattern. The strains should be kept pure and only passed on with their corresponding habitat identification (e.g., "G 15" = Gabon, locality 15). It can not be excluded that—as it has been proven in other *Aphyosemion* species—fish from differing habitats cannot be indefinitely crossed and that such strains become extinct when foreign fish are crossed in.

Aphyosemion cognatum — MEINKEN, 1951

Red-Spotted Lyretail

Syn.: None.

Hab.: West Africa, southwest of Zaire, distant surroundings of Kinshasa.

F.I.: 1950 (by Brichard?) through Aquarium Hamburg from Zaire.

Sex: The base coloration of the ♂♂ is red-brown, anteriorly somewhat lighter. On this base coloration are numerous red spots which are uniform in some populations, but they become denser posteriorly in other populations. The dots cover the body and the yellowish fins. The ♂♂ have drawn out fins framed in red on the top and bottom and often have a blue or blue-white rim at the top of the dorsal and caudal fin. The ♀♀ are brown with red-brown dots over the body. Their fins are rounded with red dots.

T: 20-24° C, 68-75° F, **L:** 5 cm, 2", **A:** 50 cm, 20", **R:** b, m, **D:** 3

Soc. B.: Like *A. christyi*, this is a shy and peaceful fish. At the most, the ♂♂ fight for social position.

M: Like *A. christyi*.

B: Follow recommendations for *A. christyi*.

F: C; live foods of appropriate size.

S: *A. cognatum*, like *A. christyi*, belongs in the *elegans* group in the sub-genus *Aphyosemion* of the same named genus. The more strains that reach us, the more difficult it becomes to optically divide the described species. Newer papers attempted to define the phenotype of *A. cognatum* in relation to related species (*A. schioetzi, A. christyi*) by the presence of a blue-white edge on the upper dorsal and tail fins. However, this is not a divisionary criterion because the types did not have a light edge.

Aphyosemion coeleste

Aphyosemion cognatum "Madimba, Zaire"

Aphyosemion congicum (AHL, 1924)

Blacktail Killie

Syn.: *Panchax congicus, Aphyosemion melanopteron.*

Hab.: West Africa, southwestern Zaire, south of the Congo River. Both the description of *A. congicum* as well as the available specimens of *A. melanopteron* are without an exact origin and only listed as from "Congo". In 1982, however, Pürzel and Radda were able to collect the species again in the southwest part of Zaire.

F.I.: 1968 (by Brichard?) to the USA.

Sex: The ♂♂ have a yellow-brown body coloration that tends towards green; the anal and caudal fins are yellow. Over this base coloration, the body and fins are dotted red. The dorsal fin can be totally black or only black on the upper edge. The tail fin is black on the upper and lower edges. The ♀♀ are brown to gray-brown with almost colorless, rounded fins.

Soc. B.: A distinctly peaceful, rather shy, small killifish.

M: Soft to medium-hard, acid water. Care for the fish either in a species tank or with other small fishes, including other killifish. The animals are sensitive to deteriorating water quality, requiring regular water changes.

B: *A. congicum* can be set up as an adhesive or bottom spawner; the first method is preferred. Keep a trio (1 ♂ and 2 ♀♀) in a 10 l (2.5 gal) tank, feed well and perform regular water changes.

F: C; live foods, but few worms.

S: *A. congicum* belongs to the *A. elegans* group, that is, to the sub-genus *Aphyosemion* of the same named genus.

T: 20-24° C, **L:** 4.5 cm, **A:** 50 cm, **R:** b, m, **D:** 2-3
68-75° F, 1 3/4", 20",

Aphyosemion elegans (BOULENGER, 1899)

Elegant Lyretail

Syn.: *Haplochilus elegans.*

Hab.: Equatorial west Africa, Zaire and Congo (= Congo Brazzaville).

F.I.: In the '60's by Lambert from Boende, Zaire.

Sex: The elongated ♂♂ are distinguished by their colorfulness and drawn out fins. Base coloration is yellow, but there are populations in blue. On this background are numerous dense red dots which, particularly at the posterior end, can fuse together to form vertical bars. The dorsal fin is distally yellow, proximally red, as is the upper lobe of the caudal fin. The inferior lobe is colored exactly opposite. The anal fin, as well as the central portion of the tail fin, have large red spots on a yellow background. The ♀♀ are gray-brown with small red dots and have almost transparent, rounded fins. They are smaller than the ♂♂.

Soc. B.: Shy, peaceful and sensitive small species which, at the most, should be kept together with smaller killifishes.

M: Keep in a small tank with soft and slightly acid water, abundant vegetation (*Anubias barteri* forma *nana*, Java moss, Java fern) and diffused lighting. The water must be in perfect condition and clear.

B: A difficult to breed and not very productive fish whose spawning basically follows *A. congicum*. The most favorable method involves letting the animals spawn in a dense spawning mop of artificial wool and collect the eggs, as described for *A. congicum*. The newly hatched young initially require infusoria.

F: Small live foods of all kinds, as varied as possible. No prepared diets.

S: *A. elegans* belongs in the sub-genus *Aphyosemion* of the same named genus. The species can be distinguished from related species, despite its variability, by the slender and elongated body shape.

T: 20-24° C, **L:** 4.5 cm, **A:** 40 cm, **R:** m, b, **D:** 4
68-75° F, 1 3/4", 16",

Aphyosemion congicum

Aphyosemion elegans

Aphyosemion gabunense gabunense RADDA, 1975
Gabon Killie

Syn.: None.

Hab.: West Africa, northwest Gabon, east of Lambarene.

F.I.: 1972 by Bochtler and Herzog.

Sex: The ♂♂ are very colorful and have rows of red dots on a blue-green body. The fins are more green and have a red fringe. The ♀♀ are brownish, and the red dots are faint. The fins are rounded and green-brown and also have small red dots. See picture.

Soc. B.: Very peaceful and suitable for the community tank. Not a shy species.

M: Water should be soft to medium-hard and slightly acid to slightly alkaline. It is recommended to maintain the fish in a well-planted tank following the "Dutch" example, so the fish can be well appreciated.

B: Rearing is not very difficult. The young also eat pulverized dry food (not to be fed exclusively).

F: C; live foods, after adaptation dry foods are accepted.

S: Of the three forms described as sub-species, the nominate form of *A. g. gabunense* deviates the most and, compared to the others, is also the most difficult to keep and breed. It is possible that both other forms deserve to be separated as autonomous species, *A. marginatum marginatum* and *A. marginatum boehmi*. However, additional collec-tions would be necessary before this could be done.

T: 22-25° C, **L:** 5 cm, **A:** 50 cm, **R:** m, b, t, **D:** 2-3
72-77° F, 2", 20",

Aphyosemion gabunense boehmi RADDA & HUBER, 1977
Boehm's Killie

Syn.: None.

Hab.: West Africa, northwestern Gabon, south of Lambarene.

F.I.: January 1976 by Bochtler and Gaspers.

Sex: As in both other sub-species, the ♂♂ are more colorful than the ♀♀, which are similar in all three sub-species. In comparison to *A. g. marginatum*, ♂♂ of *A. g. boehmi* also have yellow on the fins, but the base coloration is more brown-blue and not as green, and the anal fin and lower tail fin are missing the outer broad, red band. The top and bottom edges of the tail fin are not as parallel as in *A. g. marginatum* but more V-shaped.

Soc. B.: Like the sub-species *A. g. marginatum*. Though peaceful, it is not as shy as the nominate species.

M: Similar to *A. g. gabunense*.

B: As for *A. g. gabunense*. This is the most fecund and easiest to breed sub-species.

F: Like *A. g. gabunense*.

S: Refer to the nominate species.

T: 22-25° C, **L:** 4.5 cm, **A:** 50 cm, **R:** m, b, t, **D:** 2
72-77° F, 1 3/4", 20",

Aphyosemion gabunense marginatum RADDA & HUBER, 1977

Syn.: None.

Hab.: West Africa, northwestern Gabon, north of Lambarene.

F.I.: August 1976 by Huber and Radda.

Sex: The body coloration is similar to the nominate species. Base color is more green, the upper and lower fringes of the fins are red followed proximaly by a yellow stripe. Again, the ♀♀ are a unicolor brown with small red dots and rounded, almost colorless fins.

Soc. B.: Like the nominate form, a peaceful species, perhaps not as retiring.

M: Follow recommendations for *A. g. gabunense*.

B: Similar to *A. gabunense gabunense*, but this form is more productive and reproduction is easier.

F: Like *A. gabunense gabunense*.

S: See the nominate species.

T: 22-25° C, **L:** 4.5 cm, **A:** 50 cm, **R:** m, b, t, **D:** 2
72-77° F, 1 3/4", 20",

Aphyosemion gabunense gabunense

Aphyosemion gabunense boehmi

Aphyosemion gabunense marginatum

Aphyosemion herzogi bochtleri RADDA, 1975
Herzog's Killie

Syn.: *Aphyosemion bochtleri.*

Hab.: West Africa, northern Gabon, Ivindo/Ogowe basin.

F.I.: 1972 by Bochtler and Herzog.

Sex: The ♂♂ are explicitly colorful. Red dots are spread over the blue or yellowish body base coloration, uniting anteriorly into lines. The fins show dots and lines running along the fin rays. The type initially described as *A. bochtleri* (see picture) gives an overall impression of blue; the one described as *A. herzogi* is more yellow. There are intermediate individuals. The ♀♀ of both forms are a uniform brown with rounded, almost transparent fins and only a small amount of red design on the body.

Soc. B.: A peaceful, more retiring, shy species which attempts to jump out of the aquarium or dives into a soft substrate (peat) when a threat is perceived.

M: As described for *A. cameronense*; however, care is not quite as difficult.

B: Also in regard to breeding, see *A. cameronense.*

F: C; all kinds of live foods.

S: *Aphyosemion herzogi* is the valid name for both species originally described by RADDA as independent species *A. herzogi* and *A. bochtleri* in the same publication. Collection of intermediate forms by J. Pap and A. Brosset, France, and crossbreeding experiments of Brosset, demonstrated that both forms belong to one species. Because *A. herzogi* was described before *A. bochtleri* (page priority), the former is valid.

T: 18-22° C, **L:** 5 cm, **A:** 50 cm, **R:** b, m, **D:** 4
64-72° F, 2", 20",

Aphyosemion fallax AHL, 1935
Kribi Lyretail

Syn.: *Aphyosemion kribianum, A. schwoiseri.*

Hab.: West Africa, southwestern Cameroon, waterholes of a swamp area southeast of Kribi.

F.I.: December 1974 by A. Radda.

Sex: The ♂♂ are brownish-blue-purple on the flanks with large red dots and spots. The dorsal fin and the upper third of the caudal fin are red-brown to greenish with numerous red spots. The anal fin and the lower part of the tail fin are yellow-orange to greenish with a few dark red spots. The anterior anal fin rays and the upper and lower caudal fin rays are elongated. The ♀♀ are reddish-brown and also have red-brown dots. Their fins are not elongated.

Soc. B.: The species is peaceful towards other fish and rather shy. ♀♀ not in spawning condition and submissive ♂♂ can be bitten to death when the aquarium is too small; therefore, transport the fish singly in bags. The ♂♂ can also become aggressive towards other *Aphyosemion* species.

M: In relation to maintenance and breeding, the species can be compared to the better known and closely related *A. sjoestedti*, but *A. fallax* is more retiring and lives more secluded. It is likely that when it is kept in an appropriate species tank with diffuse lighting, one will not always be able to see it.

B: *A. fallax* is a typical bottom spawner. Breeding is accomplished in a separate tank (about 15-20 l; 4-5 gal) with peat substrate as for *A. arnoldi.* Because the fishes are larger and more robust, they should be observed closely and separated if the ♂ becomes too aggressive towards the ♀♀ after spawning. With strong pairs, one could also make short set-ups under constant supervision, each lasting only 1 or 2 hours a day.

S: *A. fallax*'s closest relative is *A. sjoestedi.* It is said that intermediate forms have been found.

T: 22-26° C, **L:** 9 cm, **A:** 100 cm, **R:** b, m, **D:** 3-4
72-79° F, 3 ", 39",

Aphyosemion herzogi bochtleri

Aphyosemion fallax

Aphyosemion labarrei POLL, 1952
Red-Streaked Killie, Labarre's Aphyosemion

Syn.: None.

Hab.: West Africa, southwestern Congo (= Congo Brazzaville) and contiguous Zaire. The central distribution area is probably north of the Congo River.

F.I.: 1956 (by Brichard?) to the USA and from there to Europe by Scheel.

Sex: The ♂♂ are multicolored with a whitish-blue background that often has a greenish tinge. Over this lies a dark red design of spots. The edges of the fins tend to be almost black towards the outside. The ♀♀ are a simple brown with some small red dots. In addition, their fins are rounded and the total length is less than that of the ♂♂.

Soc. B.: Peaceful fish who can become somewhat aggressive towards conspecific ♂♂ or those of other *Aphyosemion* species, especially if no social order has been determined or the tank is too small and does not offer an opportunity for retreat.

M: This fish, the same as all species of the sub-genus *Mesoaphyosemion*, should be kept in medium tanks with soft to medium-hard and slightly acid water. Keep *A. labarrei* either in a species tank or with equal sized killifishes of the tropical rain forest, or with others of the same size who are peaceful and not excessively active. Provide dense vegetation in part of the tank to allow the fishes to retreat.

B: Possible as a plant spawner with a wool mop or as a bottom spawner over peat. The former method has proven more advantageous with *A. labarrei*. The eggs are collected from the spawning substrate and transferred to a hatching jar. The young hatch, depending on temperature, after 12-14 days and immediately feed on *Artemia salina* nauplii.

F: C; live foods; after adaptation also frozen foods.

S: *A. labarrei* is probably the southern most representative of the *Aphyosemion ogoense* species-group.

T: 22-24° C, **L:** 5 cm, **A:** 60 cm, **R:** m, b, **D:** 2-3
72-75° F, 2", 24",

Aphyosemion lamberti RADDA & HUBER, 1977
Lambert's Lyretail

Syn.: *Aphyosemion christyi* (not BOULENGER).

Hab.: Equatorial west Africa, central Gabon, south of Ayem to Booué, Ogowe drainage.

F.I.: January 1976 by Bochtler and Gaspers.

Sex: The ♂♂ are blue to blue-green with numerous red spots on the the body and fins. The fins, whose tips are elongated, are edged in red on top and bottom. The ♀♀ have a brown-gray base coloration with fine red-brown dots in the intersecting points of the scales. The fins are rounded, transparent and also have fine red-brown dots.

Soc. B.: A peaceful and reclusive species.

M: Like *A. congicum*. However, *A. lamberti* is somewhat more robust.

B: Like *A. congicum*, but breeding is somewhat easier and the species is more productive. Within the *A. elegans* group, this species is the easiest to breed.

F: C; live foods of any suitable size and occasionally dry food.

S: This is the most northwestern known representative of the *A. elegans* group, that is, of the sub-genus *Aphyosemion* within the same named genus.

T: 18-22° C, **L:** 5 cm, **A:** 50 cm, **R:** m, b, **D:** 2-3
64-72° F, 2", 20",

Aphyosemion labarrei

Aphyosemion lamberti

Aphyosemion louessense (PELLEGRIN, 1931)

Louesse's Killie

Syn.: *Haplochilus lujae louessensis.*

Hab.: West Africa, southern Congo (= Congo Brazzaville).

F.I.: 1964 by Brichard and Roberts.

Sex: ♂♂ are colorful with elongated fins. Depending on the population, the base color is blue to blue-violet, occasionally greenish with yellow fins. The body has red dots which sometimes run together. In the unpaired fins, specially the caudal fin, red lines run along the fin rays. The ♀♀ are brownish with rows of small red dots, and the fins are more or less translucent and rounded.

Soc. B.: As in all *Aphyosemion* species, the ♂♂ are somewhat aggressive among themselves and towards other species. Otherwise, the species is peaceful and can be associated with small rivulines and other small and not too active fishes.

M: Maintenance follows most *Aphyosemion* species: soft to medium-hard and slightly acid water. Keep the fishes in a species tank or in a community as described under Soc. B. Decoration should include dense vegetation or other places to retreat. Do not keep too warm.

B: Possible to breed as a plant or bottom spawner. However, it is more advisable to set the species up as a plant spawner. Provide a wool mop in the breeding tank, as well as 1 ♂ and 2 ♀♀ which should be fed well. The eggs are collected regularly from the wool mop and placed in brooding containers for development. The young hatch after 12-14 days. They immediately feed on *Artemia salina* nauplii.

F: C; live foods; after adaptation, frozen food.

S: The present strains such as "RPC 24", (RPC = Republic Populaire du Congo), "RPC 31", "RPC 33" must be kept pure, not crossbred, and always passed on with correct information on their origin. See also *A. coeleste*.

T: 18-22° C, L: 5 cm, A: 50 cm, R: m, b, D: 2-3
64-72° F, 2", 20",

Continuation of *A. escherichi:*

A mop of perlon wool, Java moss, green perlon cotton or peat fibers are suitable spawning substrates. The eggs can be collected from the substrate and developed in brooding dishes. When peat fibers are used as substrate, they can also be stored humid in a plastic bag, and water added after 3 weeks. If left in water, the young hatch after 10-14 days. They immediately eat *Artemia salina* nauplii. Supplementary feeding of paramecium during the first days is recommended.

F: C; small live food.

S: This species is closely related to *A. striatum* and belongs in the sub-genus *Mesoaphyosemion*.

T: 22-24° C, L: 5 cm, A: 50 cm, R: b, m, D: 2-3
72-75° F, 2", 20",

Aphyosemion louessense "RPC 24"

Aphyosemion louessense "RPC 31"

Aphyosemion maculatum RADDA & PÜRZL, 1977

Spotted Killie

Syn.: None.

Hab.: West Africa, north Gabon.

F.I.: December 1975 by Pürzl and Radda.

Sex: The ♂♂ are more colorful with dark red dots and spots on a blue-white base. They are larger than the ♀♀ and have more elongated fins. The ♀♀ have small red dots on the flanks on a brown-gray base. Their fins are more or less translucent and rounded.

Soc. B.: Peaceful, rather shy species which needs areas to retreat to and which should not be associated with larger *Aphyosemion* species.

M: *A. maculatum* is a demanding and sensitive fish. It should only be kept in a species tank, even though it is possible to keep it together with equal sized *Aphyosemion* and other peaceful, not too large or active fishes. Slightly acid and soft to medium-hard water should be provided at moderate temperatures.

B: The species is difficult to breed, as is the case with most members of the *A. cameronense* group. Often the eggs—usually not many anyway—are not fertilized. The reasons for this difficulty are not yet known. The fish should be treated as adhesive spawners, the eggs regularly collected from a spawning mop and transferred into a brooding dish to develop within 12-14 days. Breeding as a bottom spawner is possible. The young immediately accept *Artemia salina* nauplii.

F: C; live foods excluding worms.

S: *A. maculatum* belongs to the *A. cameronense* group within the sub-genus *Mesoamphyosemion*.

T: 18-22° C, **L:** 5 cm, **A:** 50 cm, **R:** m, b, **D:** 4
64-72° F, 2", 20",

Aphyosemion escherichi AHL, 1924

Syn.: *Panchax escherichi, Aphyosemion simulans, A. microphtalmum.*

Hab.: Equatorial west Africa, coastal lowlands from northern Gabon to Congo (= Congo Brazzaville).

F.I.: July 1913 as *Haplochilus cameronensis* by the Vereinigte Zierfischzüchtereien in Conradshöhe through Wolmer, Hamburg, Germany.

Sex: The ♂♂ are more colorful than the ♀♀, but this species as a whole is not as colorful as related species. Within the species, the northern strain, described as *A. simulans*, is somewhat more colorful than the southern. All ♂♂ have red dots or rows of dots along the body on a blue-gray, dorsally brown, background. The fins are a somewhat more intense red and can have bright red stripes along the edges. Though the ♀♀ are inconspicuous, they can also have a red dot design similar to that found in the ♂♂. The fins, however, are translucent, and the body's base coloration is more brown.

Soc. B.: Peaceful fish.

M: Does not need a large aquarium. The water should tend to be soft (up to 10° dGH) and slightly acid (pH around 6.0-6.5). Well-planted aquarium with dark substrate (peat) with roots and peat fibers to provide hiding and spawning sites. Keep in a species tank or with other cyprinodontids, e.g., *Aplocheilichthys, Epiplatys* species. Can also be kept with other small fishes (*Barbus jae*, etc.).

B: Can be bred as a plant or bottom spawner; the former is superior. In a spawning tank (about 5-10 l; 1.3-2.5 gal) one trio is stocked and well fed.

Continued on page 606.

Aphyosemion maculatum

Aphyosemion escherichi

Aphyosemion mimbon HUBER, 1977

Syn.: None.

Hab.: West Africa, northern Gabon.

F.I.: 1976 by Huber.

Sex: As with all killifishes, here too, the ♂♂ are more colorful than the ♀♀. They have a blue to blue-green base coloration with dark red blotches and spots. In contrast, the ♀♀ are brown with sporadic red dots, their fins rounded.

Soc. B.: A peaceful and rather shy species which should not be combined with larger species.

M: A difficult to maintain fish, especially in regard to food. This requires much attention. Water values are soft to medium-hard at the most. pH should be slightly acid. Only use a species tank.

B: Breeding is extremely difficult, and the population has been at the edge of extinction every since its introduction into the aquarium hobby. In principle, it corresponds to *A. maculatum* (see there). The reasons for the lack of breeding success are still unclear. Also see *A. cameronense*.

F: C; live foods, no worms.

S: *A. mimbon* belongs to the *A. cameronense* group within the sub-genus *Mesoaphyosemion*. This is probably only a color morph and therefore a synonym of *A. maculatum*.

T: 18-22° C, **L:** 5 cm, **A:** 50 cm, **R:** m, b, **D:** 4
64-72° F, 2", 20",

Aphyosemion bitaeniatum AHL, 1924
Multicolored Lyretail

Syn.: *Fundulopanchax multicolor, Fundulus bivittatus* (not LÖNNBERG), *Aphyosemion bivittatum multicolor, A. multicolor.*

Hab.: West Africa, from Togo through Benin to and including the mouth of the Niger in Nigeria, principally coastal lowlands.

F.I.: September 1908 from Warri, Nigeria, by the Siggelkow Co., Hamburg, Germany.

Sex: The ♂♂ are very colorful. The extremely extended dorsal fin can reach to the end of the tail fin and is red-brown with dark red dots and lines and is characteristic for the species. Two horizontal dark stripes run along the body, varying in intensity depending on strain and mood. The base color of the body is red-brown, tending towards rainbow colors dorsally. ♀♀ are brown and also show the horizontal dark stripe along the body. Their fins are not elongated, and they are smaller than the ♂♂.

Soc. B.: Among themselves and towards related species, the ♂♂ can become aggressive, but are otherwise peaceful.

M: Follow recommendations for *A. calliurum*.

B: As indicated for *A. calliurum*; however, the species is more of a plant or adhesive spawner.

F: C; live foods, rarely will dry food be accepted.

S: Together with other species of the group, *A. bitaeniatum* belongs to the sub-genus *Chromaphyosemion*. Strains of this species are not always well defined when compared to *A. splendopleure* and *A. volcanum*.

T: 22-24° C, **L:** 5 cm, **A:** 50 cm, **R:** b, m, **D:** 2-3
72-75° F, 2", 20",

Aphyosemion mimbon

Aphyosemion bitaeniatum

Aphyosemion bitaeniatum

Aphyosemion ocellatum HUBER & RADDA, 1977
Shoulder-Spot Killie

Syn.: None.

Hab.: Equatorial west Africa, creeks of the inland plateau of southern Gabon, Migoto-Ogoulou system, southwestern slope of the Du-Chailu-Massif.

F.I.: August 1976 by Huber and Radda.

Sex: The ♂♂ have a blue-violet body color, brown dorsally. The fins are yellow-orange with a dark violet to black edge. The dark violet spot behind the base of the pectoral fin is distinctive. The ♀♀ are brownish and have transparent and rounded fins.

Soc. B.: As for *A. coeleste*, however, this fish is more timid. When disturbed, the animals easily jump out of the water or, if available, dive into a soft substrate.

M: See *A. coeleste*.

B: Follows *A. coeleste*, but this species is even less fecund.

F: C; live food.

S: *A. ocellatum* has various strains. For more information, refer to *A. coeleste*.

T: 18-22° C, 64-72° F, L: 5 cm, 2", A: 50 cm, 20", R: m, b, D: 3-4

Aphyosemion ogoense ogoense (PELLEGRIN, 1930)
Broken-Striped Killie

Syn.: *Haplochilus lujae* var. *ogoensis*.

Hab.: Equatorial west Africa, Batéké highland of southern Gabon and southern Congo (= Congo Brazzaville).

F.I.: Various strains at the end of the 70's by different travelers.

Sex: The ♂♂ are very colorful but differently colored, depending on strain. Base coloration is an intense blue to blue-yellow with (usually 4) longitudinal rows of red dots. These may run together and form strong red areas along the back. The fins are usually elongated at the top and bottom with red stripes running in the direction of the fin rays. In contrast, the ♀♀ are uniformly brown with a fainter red dot design; their fins are rounded.

Soc. B.: Like *A. louessense*.

M: Similar to *A. louessense* and *A. ogoense pyrophore*.

B: As with *A. louessense*. The animals should be set up as adhesive spawners.

F: C; live foods, dry foods are often taken also.

S: See also *A. ogoense pyrophore*. There are numerous different color and habitat strains of *A. ogoense*. The yellow morph, later described as *A. ogoense ottogartneri*, has been known to the hobby since 1961, although under the incorrect name of "*A. lujae*". Between this yellow morph and the blue morph (see picture) are intermediates, and the fish captured at "Malinga" (see picture) is an intermediate between the two, but it also simultaneously bridges to *A. louessense*. Because of the aforementioned reasons, the different morphs have to be maintained pure and only passed on with the correct habitat or population identification.

T: 18-22° C, 64-72° F, L: 5 cm, 2", A: 50 cm, 20", R: b, m, D: 2-3

Aphyosemion ocellatum, Gabon

Aphyosemion ogoense ogoense "Malinga"

Aphyosemion ogoense pyrophore HUBER & RADDA, 1979

Syn.: None.

Hab.: West Africa, southern Gabon and southern People's Republic of Congo (= Congo Brazzaville).

F.I.: 1978 by J. Buytaert and W. Wachters.

Sex: ♂♂ are more colorful. Depending on strain, they have a yellow or blue base coloration. Over this, the anterior body has three longitudinal stripes that dissolve into dots posteriorly. On the posterior part of the body are vertical stripes which may disintegrate into rows of dots. The tail fin has red stripes in the direction of the rays. The ♀♀ have a brown base coloration that has a similar red design as that found in ♂♂; however, the rows are more disseminated into dots. The fins show somewhat more color than those of other *Aphyosemion* ♀♀, but they are also rounded.

Soc. B.: Throughout a peaceful and recommendable sub-species which is only somewhat aggressive towards conspecific ♂♂ or those of other *Aphyosemion* species.

M: The fish can be kept in a species tank or with other killifishes; however, one should not choose other species out of the *Aphyosemion ogoense/louessense* group, but rather totally different, not overly large species. Combining with totally different and not too large or active fishes is possible. The water should be soft to medium-hard and slightly acid. The tank should be well-planted with a dark substrate. Use moderate water temperatures.

B: Like *A. louessense*, this sub-species is preferably set up as a plant spawner. The eggs are collected and brooded in a breeding dish.

F: C; live foods, with as few worms as possible.

S: As already stated for other species, the different strains of *A. o. pyrophore* should be identified and passed on with the proper description of origin. *A. o. pyrophore*, initially described as an autonomous species, is a sub-species at best, but it is probably only a strain of *A. ogoense* since the delimitation against other populations is not clear.

T: 18-22° C, **L:** 5 cm, **A:** 50 cm, **R:** m, b, **D:** 2-3
64-72° F, 2", 20",

Aphyosemion ogoense pyrophore "RPC 18"

Aphyosemion ogoense ogoense

Aphyosemion ogoense pyrophore (GHP 23/80)

Aphyosemion pascheni (AHL, 1928)
Gray Killie

Syn.: *Panchax (Aphyosemion) pascheni.*

Hab.: Equatorial west Africa, southern Cameroon, coastal lowlands east of Kribi.

F.I.: March 1972 by Dr. A. Radda and companions.

Sex: ♂♂ are gray-blue, dorsally gray-brown, ventrally lighter with red-brown dots which merge together into longitudinal lines and spread to the dorsal and upper caudal fin. The lower tail and anal fin have a white-blue outline which is separated from the middle of the fin by a red stripe. The ♀♀ are yellow-brown with small dark red dots on the sides of the body which can also be found in the dorsal and upper tail fin. The fins are rounded.

Soc. B.: Peaceful, quite shy and leads a secluded life.

M: As with *A. calliurum.*

B: Similar to *A. calliurum.*

F: C; live food.

S: Belongs to the *A. calliurum* group of the sub-genus *Mesoaphyosemion*, and *A. calliurum* is its closest relative.

T: 22-25° C, **L:** 5 cm, **A:** 50 cm, **R:** b, m, **D:** 3
72-77° F, 2", 20",

Aphyosemion primigenium RADDA & HUBER, 1977

Syn.: None.

Hab.: West Africa, southwest Gabon.

F.I.: 1976 by Huber and Radda.

Sex: The ♂♂ are colorful and have four horizontal lines of red dots on a blue or blue-green background which, depending on strain, more or less merge. The yellow dorsal and anal fins have a red band proximal and distal to the body. The tail fin shows an arched, red band; the interior is a yellow-green with red spots. The ♀♀ are smaller and brownish. They sport rows of small, dark red dots; the fins are smaller, colorless and rounded.

Soc. B.: Throughout a peaceful fish which, at the most, can become somewhat aggressive towards the ♂♂ of the same or related species.

M: Soft to medium-hard and slightly acid water, well-planted tank with dark substrate. Perhaps decorate with randomly placed roots. Keep in a species tank together with other Rivulinae or with totally different, not overly large or aggressive fishes. Water temperature not too high.

B: Breed as a plant-spawner, but it is also possible as a bottom spawner. The former is preferred. See the recommendations for *Aphyosemion calliurum.*

F: C; live foods, after acclimation also frozen foods.

S: *A. exigoideum* is probably only a strain, at the most a sub-species of *A. primigenium.* Both populations are contiguous, the morphological values correspond, and newer collections produced animals that are phenotypic intermediates. *A. primigenium* belongs in the *A. striatum* group of the sub-genus *Mesoaphyosemion.*

T: 18-22° C, **L:** 5 cm, **A:** 50 cm, **R:** m, b, **D:** 2-3
64-72° F, 2", 20",

Aphyosemion pascheni

Aphyosemion primigenium

Aphyosemion rectogoense RADDA & HUBER, 1977
Silver-Yellow Killie

Syn.: None.

Hab.: Southeast Gabon, west Africa.

F.I.: 1976 by Huber and Dr. A. Radda.

Sex: ♂♂ are more colorful than ♀♀. The ♂♂ have dense rows of red dots on a blue-green body; the fins are very elongated. On the unpaired fins is a red design on a yellow background. The ♀ is usually smaller, brownish with pale red dots, which also appear on the otherwise colorless fins. These are not elongated but rounded.

Soc. B.: Peaceful and active fish. The ♂♂ may be moderately aggressive towards each other.

M: Maintain either in a species tank, together with other Rivulinae or with totally different small fishes. The water should be soft to medium-hard (at the most) and slightly acid. The tank can be well-planted; this would also provide retreats for the fish. The general impression of the set-up should be somewhat subdued (floating plants). A dark substrate helps. Don't forget the water exchanges.

B: The fish will spawn in plants or on the bottom in a layer of peat (see *Aphyosemion calliurum*). More advantageous for this species, however, is the continuous set-up using a spawning mop, and regularly transferring the eggs to a hatching dish. The young, which hatch after 2 weeks, immediately accept *Artemia salina* nauplii.

F: C; live food of any kind.

S: *A. rectogoense* is the most northwestern representative of the *A. elegans* group and the sub-genus *Aphyosemion*.

T: 20-24° C, **L:** 5 cm, **A:** 50 cm, **R:** m, b, **D:** 2-3
68-75° F, 2", 20",

Aphyosemion robertsoni RADDA & SCHEEL, 1974
Robertson's Killie

Syn.: None.

Hab.: West Africa, annual swamp in the rubber plantation in Ekona, west Cameroon.

F.I.: 1973 by Dr. A. Radda, Dr. J. Scheel and travel companions.

Sex: The more colorful ♂♂ have a design of red blotches and dots on a blue to blue-green body. These dots can merge posteriorly to form slanted stripes. These are numerous in the dorsal fin but scarce in the anal fin. The tail fin has a red horizontal band on the top and bottom with red dots in between. The caudal fin is tri-lobed. The much smaller ♀♀ are brown and show a red-brown dot design which can also form slanted bands posteriorly. The fins are clear, slightly brownish with dark dots and rounded.

Soc. B.: Overall a peaceful killifish with annual spawning behavior. Possible to keep with additional robust *Aphyosemion* species or other small fishes.

M: The fish should not be kept in a tank which is brightly decorated or situated, but rather one with a dark substrate and soft to medium-hard water. Pleasing vegetation simultaneously offers the fish hiding places, specially when several ♂♂ are kept.

B: 24-26° C (75-79° F); the fish are bottom spawners; therefore, 1 ♂ and 2 ♀♀ are set up with a peat substrate in a 10 l (2.5 gal) tank. The set-up lasts one week and should be closely observed. The ♂♂ become aggressive towards ♀♀ that are not ripe and can chase them to death. The fish are fed well but not excessively with live foods, preferably mosquito larvae or glassworms. After one week, the breeders are removed, the water poured off and the peat pressed dry, dried a little and stored (well identified) for 8-10 weeks. Subsequently place the egg-containing peat in an aquarium and add fresh water. The young usually hatch soon and can immediately be fed *Artemia* nauplii. Continued rearing is easy with appropriate live foods.

Continued on page 620.

Aphyosemion rectogoense

Aphyosemion robertsoni

Continuation of *Aphyosemion robertsoni*:

F: C; live food of all kinds. After acclimation, frozen foods, including beef heart are eaten.

S: *Aphyosemion filamentosum* is so rich in variations that the question arises whether or not *A. robertsoni* is just another of its local strains. Several concurrences of both morphs seem to indicate such a situation.

T: 21-24° C, L: 6 cm, A: 50 cm, R: m, b, D: 2-3
70-75° F, 2 1/3", 20",

Aphyosemion rubrolabiale RADDA, 1973

Red-Lipped Killie

Syn.: None.

Hab.: West Africa, southwestern Cameroon, swampy rain forest.

F.I.: February/March 1972 by Dr. A. Radda.

Sex: Similar to *A. robertsoni*. The yellow-brown ♂♂ have a red dot design which is stronger on the dorsal fin and fainter on the anal fin. The tri-lobed caudal fin has a red longitudinal stripe which separates a yellow edge on the lower lobe, and sometimes also on the upper one, from the central area which also has red dots. ♀♀ are smaller and have the same coloration as those of *A. robertsoni*; on the light brown body is a red-brown dot design which can also be found in the fins.

Soc. B.: Same as *A. robertsoni*. A peaceful fish towards other species. Potentially aggressive only among its own ♂♂ and those of related species.

M: Like *A. robertsoni*.

B: Similar to *A. robertsoni*.

F: C; live foods, also frozen food and beef heart.

S: Closely related to *A. filamentosum*, representing the yellow morph of the blue *A. robertsoni*. Several habitat strains have been collected which also differ in their chromosomal number: the strain "Mungo Delta" has n = 20, the strain from "Mbonge" n = 22. In comparison, *A. robertsoni* has n = 21 chromosomes.

T: 21-24° C, L: 6 cm, A: 50 cm, R: m, b, D: 2-3
70-75° F, 2 1/3", 20",

Aphyosemion schluppi RADDA & HUBER, 1978

Schlupp's Killie

Syn.: None.

Hab.: Equatorial west Africa, Congo (= Congo Brazzaville), in creeks and rivers of the rain forest in the mountains of the Province of Lékoumou.

F.I.: August 1978 by J. Buytaert and W. Wachters.

Sex: Not always easy to distinguish. The ♂♂ are somewhat more colorful than the ♀♀, and their fins are more elongated. They have an ochre to orange body coloration, and the scales on the sides have red-brown edges. The fins are orange. The ♀♀ have a gray-brown base coloration and their fins have less color.

Soc. B.: Very peaceful fish.

M: A dark tank with dark substrate and Java moss, Java fern or *Anubias barteri* forma *nana* is recommended. Needs soft to medium-hard (up to about 15° dGH) and slightly acid water at a moderate temperature (18-22° C; 64-72° F). Keep like *A. thysi*.

B: Like *A. thysi*. Animals are not aggressive towards each other, and the young are hardly pursued, allowing *A. schluppi* to be kept in a continuous set-up. The newly hatched young are skimmed from the aquarium and transferred to a rearing tank. Keep temperatures in the low range.

F: C; live foods of all kinds and small quantities of worms.

S: This species has also several habitat strains (RPC 18, 27, 28, 29) which should remain pure and be passed on with the correct information on origin.

T: 18-22° C, L: 4 cm, A: 50 cm, R: m, D: 2
64-72° F, 1 2/3", 20",

Aphyosemion rubrolabiale

Aphyosemion schluppi

Aphyosemion spoorenbergi BERKENKAMP, 1976
Spoorenberg's Killie

Syn.: None.

Hab.: West Africa, exact habitat is unknown; it is probably located in the border region of southeast Nigeria/west Cameroon.

F.I.: March 1974 by the Roelofs Co., Amsterdam as a commercial aquarium import from Cameroon.

Sex: The ♂♂ are quite colorful and have a blue-green body with numerous red spots which turn into a zig-zag design towards the tail. The upper and lower edges of the tail fin are elongated and yellow, followed by a red band; the center of the fin is yellow-green with a red spot design. The dorsal and anal fins are also yellow-green with strong and weak red spotting respectively.

Soc. B.: A robust species from the *A. gardneri* group, but this species is more shy and reclusive than *A. gardneri*.

M: *Aphyosemion spoorenbergi* is a recommendable killifish because the species is robust and not very sensitive. Any water values are fine as long as they are not extreme. Dense vegetation and dim illumination are advantageous. Because these fish are somewhat shyer than other *A. gardneri* types and easier to get along with, one can stock them denser. In this manner, they can be seen more often out of the plants.

B: Breeds as an adhesive or bottom spawner as described for *A. calliurum*. However, the species is one of the larger of this type; hence a correspondingly larger rearing and breeding aquarium is needed. The eggs develop in about 2 to 3 weeks and the young immediately accept *Artemia salina* nauplii. Breeding is similar to *A. gardneri* but somewhat more difficult.

F: C; live food of any kind, after adaptation frozen and dry feeds are accepted, also beef heart.

S: Within the sub-genus *Paraphyosemion*, *A. spoorenbergi* is probably positioned between *A. gardneri* and the *A. traudeae* forms.

T: 20-24° C, **L:** 8 cm, **A:** 80 cm, **R:** b, m, **D:** 2-3
68-75° F, 3", 31",

Aphyosemion thysi RADDA & HUBER, 1978
Thys' Lyretail

Syn.: None.

Hab.: Equatorial west Africa, Congo, creeks and rivers of the Louesse system in the hills of the Niari and Lékoumou provinces in tropical rain forests.

F.I.: In July/August 1978 by J. Buytaert and W. Wachters.

Sex: ♂♂ are larger with elongated unpaired fins and a blue to yellowish-green body with red vertical stripes. The fins are more or less mottled and striated in the direction of the rays. The ♀♀ are uniformly olive-brown with some red-brown dots which continue over into the otherwise colorless unpaired fins.

Soc. B.: Peaceful, somewhat shy killifish which can be kept either in a species tank or with other small fishes (killifishes, small characins, etc.) in a well-planted, not necessarily large tank.

M: Like other species of the inland plateau of the Congo and Gabon, these animals should not be kept at high temperatures. 18-22° C (64-72° F) is sufficient. The aquarium should be provided with a peat bottom and bogwood, and should be dim and planted with Java fern, Java moss and other plants. As long as wild caught fish are not kept, the water can be soft to medium-hard and should be slightly acid (pH 6.0-6.5). Frequent water changes are very much recommended. Cover!

Continued on page 624.

Aphyosemion spoorenbergi

Aphyosemion thysi, wild caught, "RPC

Aphyosemion thysi continued:

B: *A. thysi* is a continuous spawner. In a well-planted species tank, which is not densely stocked, the hatching young can be skimmed off and a few can also grow in the presence of the parents. A specific breeding set-up is more productive. Here the eggs are removed regularly, either individually or with the spawning substrate (peat fibers or a spawning mop can be used). If the eggs are collected singly, artificial fibers are recommended; otherwise, peat fibers are preferred. The eggs can be stored with moist peat for three weeks in a plastic bag. Cool (16° C; 61° F) fresh water is then added, or if they were collected singly, they are hatched in water with acriflavine or Cilex which takes about 2-3 weeks. The young immediately accept *Artemia salina* nauplii. *A. thysi* grows relatively slow. After 6-7 months, the young begin to develop their color.

F: C; small live foods of any kind; frozen food after adaptation. Flake food is rarely accepted.

S: *A. thysi* also has several habitat strains (RPC 6, 9, 20, 22) which should not be crossed and should only be passed on with their correct origin information.

T: 18-22° C, L: 4 cm, A: 50 cm, R: b, m, D: 3
64-72° F, 1 2/3", 20",

Aphyosemion wachtersi RADDA & HUBER, 1978

Wachter's Killie

Syn.: *Aphyosemion wachtersi mikeae.*

Hab.: Equatorial west Africa, southern (People's Republic) Congo. Only 2 habitats are known, RPC 30 and RPC 19. The latter strain (see photo) was described as the sub-species *A. w. mikeae*. The habitats are located in Komono (19) and Zanaga (30).

F.I.: August 1978 by J. Buytaert and W. Wachters.

Sex: The ♂♂ are colorful. From top to bottom their sides reflect the following colors: brown, green, blue and orange. This is overlaid by a row of red dots which merge posteriorly into a central band. The typical animal from habitat 30 has an orange band, narrow or absent on the top and broad on the bottom, on all unpaired fins. This band is separated from the body by a red stripe. The dorsal and interior caudal fins have blue or green dots on a red background. The ♀♀ are a uniform brown and have red dots on the body. The colors of the ♂ are often faintly shown. Their fins are smaller and rounded.

Soc. B.: Peaceful species. At the most, the ♂♂ become aggressive towards each other.

M: As with *A. thyse.*

B: Similar to *A. thyse*, however, it is recommended to remove the eggs from the breeding tank.

F: C; all kinds of live foods.

S: *A. wachtersi* is very closely related to *A. buytaerti*. The described sub-species *A. w. mikeae*, in a certain sense, mediates between the two. Both forms belong to the sub-genus *Mesoaphyosemion*.

T: 18-22° C, L: 4 cm, A: 50 cm, R: b, m, D: 3
64-72° F, 1 2/3", 20",

Aplocheilichthys johnstoni continued:

F: C; small live food, *Artemia salina* nauplii are relished, also flake food.

S: Belongs within the genus to the subgenus or species group *Micropanchax*. Much of what has been described in the literature as *A. johnstoni* is likely not to be that species, but some undescribed species that have been referred to by that name.

T: 18-26° C, L: 5.5 cm, A: 80 cm, R: m, t, D: 2-3
64-79° F, 2 ", 31",

Aphyosemion thysi "RPC 9"

Aphyosemion wachtersi

Aplocheilichthys antinorii (VINCIGUERRA, 1883)
Black Lampeye

Syn.: *Haplochilus antinorii, Haplochilichthys antinorii, Micropanchax antinorii.*

Hab.: Northeast Africa, Ethiopia, Lake Abiyata, Lake Langano.

F.I.: July 1982 by T. Schulz.

Sex: Difficult to determine. The ♂♂ are comparatively more slender, elongated and smaller. When feeling well, their coloration is significantly darker to almost black with iridescent body sides. The ♀♀ are anteriorly fuller and more brownish.

Soc. B.: Though a schooling fish, each member needs sufficient room, or stress and biting occurs. This species can be considered semi-pelagic and will swim nervously around the aquarium. Towards other fishes, they are very peaceful.

M: Difficult to keep. Requires a comparatively large tank. Not a fish for a conventional community tank. Specially sensitive towards unappropriate water conditions. Prolonged care of the fish has not yet been achieved.

B: They have spawned in Java moss in a breeding aquarium. The eggs are very large and the young are quite thin and long, incapable of eating newly hatched brine shrimp nauplii; they require smaller foods. The young are pronouncedly pelagic and move with a snaking motion in the water. The fish are so sensitive that, to this point, none have been raised.

F: C; small live foods of any kind, especially *Artemia salina.*

S: The species occupies a special place within the large number of very different *Aplocheilichthys* species and probably does not belong in this genus.

T: 18-22° C, L: 4 cm, A: 50 cm, R: m, t, D: 4
64-72° F, 1 2/3", 20",

Aplocheilichthys johnstoni (GÜNTHER, 1893)
Johnston's Lampeye

Syn.: *Haplochilus johnstonii, Haplochilichthys johnstoni, Micropanchax johnstoni, Aplocheilus johnstoni.*

Hab.: Southern Africa from Malawi and Tanzania to South Africa, the basin of Lake Malawi, Shrie River, drainage area of the Sambesi and Kafue, drainage area of the Chobe, Limpopo and Olifants rivers.

F.I.: ?

Sex: The ♀♀ are corporally fuller than the somewhat larger and more slender ♂♂. The ♂♂ have larger fins, a livelier coloration and tend more towards a blue-green. The coloration of the ♀♀ is grayer and duller. There are several strains within this species' large distribution area; they differ in coloration.

Soc. B.: Peaceful schooling surface fish.

M: Needs a large tank; nonextreme water values are secondary. Temperature, according the origin of the strain, is 18-26° C (64-79° F). Do not keep with unduly larger fishes. Housing with small cichlids in a large Malawi aquarium is possible. Plant according to taste, but the surface needs to remain partially uncovered. Somewhat sensitive towards suboptimal water values, starts to sway.

B: Breeding is not difficult. Spawning will take place on an artificial mop hung into the aquarium. Of course, a separate spawning tank with a spawning mop, Java moss or perlon webbing as spawning sites is also recommendable. It is best to collect the eggs and rear them in a brooding dish. The young hatch after about 10-14 days and should be fed paramecium initially and then *Artemia salina* nauplii.

Continued on page 624.

Aplocheilichthys antinorii

Aplocheilichthys johnstoni

Aplocheilichthys katangae (BOULENGER, 1912)
Katanga Lampeye

Syn.: *Haplochilus katangae, Haplochilichthys katangae, Micropanchax katangae, Haplochilus carlislei, Aplocheilichthys carlislei.*

Hab.: Southern central to south Africa; south Zaire to South Africa; upper Lualaba, Kasai and Lulua drainage areas, Sambesi, Cunene, Cubango and Cuando drainages in Angola, Chobe River, Okavango, Luapula River, drainage area of the Lake Bangweulu, rivers of South Africa to Natal.

F.I.: Fall 1937 by Roloff out of east Africa.

Sex: The ♂♂ are yellowish with a black-brown stripe from the base of the pectoral fin to the caudal peduncle. The stomach is white. The fins are intense yellow. The ♀♀ have a more slender caudal peduncle and are fuller anteriorly. The coloration is not as intense as in the ♂♂, the black band is narrow, and the fins are transparent.

Soc. B.: A peaceful fish which likes to live in schools.

M: The fish require soft water, pH 6.5-7.5. The tank can be well-planted, but it should offer open areas. Though it can be associated with smaller fishes, a species tank is recommended. A dark substrate shows the colors better.

B: The animals are plant or adhesive spawners. A spawning mop can be hung into the aquarium (see *A. johnstoni*), but here too, a separate breeding tank is more beneficial. See *A. johnstoni.*

F: C; small live foods, *Artemia salina* nauplii are much recommended. Will sporadically accept flake food.

S: Belongs in the sub-genus or genus group *Lacustricola.*

T: 20-28° C, **L:** 4 cm, **A:** 50 cm, **R:** t, m, **D:** 3-4
68-82° F, 1 2/3", 20",

Aplocheilichthys meyburgi MEINKEN, 1971
Meyburg's Lampeye

Syn.: *Micropanchax ericae* (?).

Hab.: Central Africa, shore regions of Lake Victoria.

F.I.: September 1968 by Dr. G. Meyburg.

Sex: The coloration of the ♂♂ is livelier. A black and a red morph exist. The former is possibly independent and identical to *Micropanchax ericae.* The ♂♂ of the red morph have tomato red fins with black edges and a bronze colored body with a hint of a dark longitudinal band. The black morph has smoke black fins and a greenish body. The ♀♀ of both forms have smaller, rounded fins and are paler as a whole with an anteriorly fuller body. The caudal peduncle is more slender.

Soc. B.: These fishes are basically peaceful and live in loose schools and groups; however, every animal reserves some free space. If this buffer zone is violated or nonexistent, as in the case of excessively small aquaria, the fish bite each other, resulting in injury. This is especially valid during prolonged transport, so pack individually!

M: In relation to their small size, the fishes require a comparatively large aquarium because of the aforementioned reasons. In an appropriate aquarium, the animals form a decorative loose school. The background should be densely planted, while the foreground should be open. Water not too hard (up to 8° dGH), pH 6.5-7.5. The association with smaller fish is possible, specially with those that prefer lower water strata.

B: As with *A. johnstoni*, the animals are plant or adhesive spawners. The eggs are pressed between the threads of a spawning mop.

F: C; small live food, specially *Artemia salina* nauplii or similar small food.

S: *A. meyburgi* belongs in the genus group or sub-genus *Lacustricola.*

T: 22-26° C, **L:** 3 cm, **A:** 60 cm, **R:** m, t, **D:** 3-4
72-79° F, 1", 24",

Aplocheilichthys katangae

Aplocheilichthys meyburgi

Austrofundulus limnaeus SCHULTZ, 1949
Venezuelan Killie

Syn.: *Austrofundulus transilis limnaeus, Austrofundulus stagnalis, Austrofundulus myersi.*

Hab.: Northern South America from Guyana through Venezuela to Colombia.

F.I.: ?

Sex: The ♂♂ are larger and more colorful than the ♀♀. Their fins are more elongated, the top and bottom of the tail fin have wimples. The "*myersi*" strain does not have an elongated caudal fin.

Soc. B.: Despite their bullish appearance, this is a peaceful species. The fishes tend to live alone.

M: Best kept in a species tank, although a community set-up is possible. Arrange a dark tank with dark substrate (peat) and diffuse illumination, allowing the colors to come out better. Water values are secondary as long as they are not extreme. The decoration can be done with bogwood and Java moss or fern. *Anubias barteri* forma *nana* can also live well under low lighting conditions.

B: The fish are seasonal bottom spawners. Therefore, they should be provided with a thick layer of peat. It suffices if one half of the aquarium is laid 5 cm (2") deep with boiled peat, separated with a plastic strip. A plant anchored in the peat gives protection to a pursued ♀. One ♂ and 2 ♀♀ are placed in the set-up for one week and fed well. The fish like to dive into the peat layer, but this is not necessary. If the layer is too thin, spawning occurs anyway. Remove the fishes and the water afterwards, and place the previously pressed and somewhat dried peat into a plastic bag. Store, depending on temperature, for 3-6 months. The first fresh water can be added after this time. The young are removed with a pipette, the peat is redried after 2 days and later water is added anew. The young immediately accept *Artemia salina* nauplii and grow rapidly.

F: C; live food, worms are liked, beef heart is also accepted, but flake food is not.

S: THAPHORN and THOMERSON (1978) united *A. myersi* with *limnaeus*, which up to then was considered a sub-species of *A. transilis*, into the one species *A. limnaeus*. Despite their quite different appearance, this was done because intermediate forms are said to exist. They differentiate a total of 4 strains up to now; however, only the two pictured have reached us in Germany.

T: 22-26° C, 72-79° F, L: 8 cm, 3", A: 60 cm, 24", R: m, b, D: 3

Austrofundulus limnaeus

Austrofundulus limnaeus "Type myersi"

Nothobranchius furzeri continued from page 662:

Frequent partial water changes are advantageous.

B: The fishes are bottom spawners, continuous spawners and seasonal fishes. The breeding set-up should be in a separate tank. Fill the bottom with boiled peat. The ♂♂ pursue very actively; therefore, a short set-up with strong individuals is recommended. Bring the fish together for a few hours under supervision, or there is the danger that spent ♀♀ are bitten to death. Remove the peat afterwards and let it dry some on newspaper, then place in a plastic bag (don't forget the identification) and store at 25° C (77° F) for about 12 weeks. Higher temperatures are better, so the storage time is shortened. At lower temperatures, the storage time is significantly longer, often 7 months and more. After storage, place the peat in an aquarium and add fresh water. The hatched young immediately feed on *Artemia salina* nauplii. While rearing (warm!), change the water often and feed copiously. The peat can be redried for awhile after the first infusion.

F: C; coarse live foods of all kinds, worms are also liked.

S: The species'closest relative is *N. orthonotus,* which has also been found together with *N. furzeri.* The ♂♂ have strongly developed conspicuous yellow gill membranes.

T: 23-30° C, L: 6 cm, A: 60 cm, R: m, b, D: 2-3
73-86° F, 1 1/3", 24",

Procatopus aberrans continued from page 668:

An ideal aquarium has dense, well established plant growth, CO_2 fertilization and is sparsely stocked. Decorate with roots, ornamental cork and the like. Good aeration is necessary, even if it increases CO_2 consumption. The addition of table salt (1 teaspoon/10 l; 2.5 gal) is recommended.

B: *Procatopus* species are crevice and continuous spawners. Spawning may also occur in a show tank, for example, in the filter slits and similar, where it may be possible to collect the eggs. In a breeding tank, which allows for a better yield, FOERSCH got good results using pumice with grooves filed into it. Plastic pot scrubbers, grooved cork and similar materials with holes, crevices and slits have also been successfully used. The relatively large eggs hatch after about 2 weeks. Growth is not fast.

F: C; all types of live foods, also flake food. If possible, avoid *Tubifex.* Even full-grown animals appreciate *Artemia salina* nauplii.

S: Today the three certain *Procatopus* species, *P. aberrans, P. similis* and *P. nototaenia* are polymorphic and variable. This has led to the numerous descriptions of species and sub-species which are not all recognized today. In addition, the genus *Procatopus* is closely related to the genus *Plataplochilus* from Gabon and Congo.

T: 24-26° C, L: 6 cm, A: 60 cm, R: t, m, D: 2-3
75-79° F, 2 1/3", 24",

Rachovia maculipinnis continued from page 672:

Development takes 6-7 months at 22-23° C (72-73° F). The young immediately eat *Artemia salina* nauplii and grow quickly.

F: C; live food.

S: Initially the species was described by WEIBEZAHN. After RADDA (DATZ, **17** (2): 39-41, 1964) mentioned the name of the fish, probably in the belief that the description by WEIBEZAHN had occurred, the latter withdrew his paper in anger. However, because RADDA 1964 expressly credited the first description to WEIBEZAHN, the latter should be considered the first describer, as has been suggested by TAPHORN and THOMERSON (1978).

T: 22-27° C, L: up to 8 cm, A: 60 cm, R: m, b, D: 3-4
72-81° F, up to 3", 24",

Cubanichthys pengelleyi
Jamaican Large-Scaled Killie

FOWLER, 1939
Sub-Fam.: Cubanichthyinae

Syn.: *Cyriopeoides pengelleyi.*

Hab.: In crystal clear headwaters of Jamaica.

F.I.: Unknown.

Sex: The ♀ is smaller and plainly colored. The body stripe is more slender but more intense than the ♂'s.

Soc. B.: Peaceful species which is best kept in a species tank. It displays its behavior better there than in a community tank.

M: Since the animals are rarely imported, it should be thoughtfully cared for in a species tank. The animals are quite undemanding. Water: pH 7.2-8.0; hardness 6-15° dGH. Plant with *Elodea* and *Myriophyllum.* Strong filtration and regular water changes.

T: 23-25° C, 73-77° F, L: 6 cm, 2 1/3", A: 70 cm, 28", R: all, D: 2

B: During courtship, the ♂ dances around the ♀. The eggs are deposited on fine-leaved plants and stones (adhesive spawner). The diameter of the eggs is 1.3 mm (1/16"). The larvae hatch after about 14 days and can be raised with newly hatched *Artemia* nauplii.

F: C, O; flake food is rarely accepted immediately. Acclimate with any live food, later with frozen food.

S: A killifish that should receive more attention. Unfortunately, the species is not long-lived (2-3 years).

Cubanichthys cubensis (EIGENMANN, 1902)
Cuban Minnow
Sub-Fam.: Cubanichthyinae

Syn.: *Fundulus cubensis.*

Hab.: Western Cuba, Pinar del Rio, Habana, Batabano.

F.I.: Initially into the USA in 1932 and shortly thereafter to Germany.

Sex: The ♂♂ are more colorful and have longitudinal stripes made of red dots on the body. The ♀♀ do not have this design; therefore, a dark longitudinal stripe becomes visible from the mouth to the caudal peduncle. The ♂'s stripe is overlaid by the aforementioned design. The fins of the ♀♀ are rounder and less colored.

Soc. B.: Peaceful fish which likes to live in groups.

M: Well-planted and bright tank, water values are secondary, up to medium-hard water is preferable, pH around neutral. A species tank is preferred, but association with smaller livebearers is possible.

B: In large, densely planted species tanks, sufficient young are allowed to grow alongside the parents. However, breeding in a separate tank is recommended. Java moss serves as a spawning medium. Temperature 25-30° C (77-86° F). The eggs can be collected, or left in the breeding tank and the parents removed after 1 week. The period of development, depending on temperature, is 8-12 days. The initial feeding should be with paramecium. Growth is initially slow.

F: C, O; all kinds of live foods of suitable size. In addition, flake food may be accepted.

S: The only species of the genus. Reports of 8 cm (3") seem to be false. So far, only 4 cm (1 2/3") could be confirmed.

T: 23-28° C, L: 4 cm, A: 50 cm, R: b, m, t, D: 2-3
73-82° F, 1 2/3", 20",

Cynolebias adloffi AHL, 1922
Adloff's Pearlfish, Banded Pearlfish
Sub-Fam.: Rivulinae

Syn.: None.

Hab.: Southeast South America, coastal plains of northern Uruguay and southeastern Brazil. Center is around Porto Alegre.

F.I.: 1921 by Adloff, Porto Alegre, Brazil.

Sex: The ♂♂ have a blue-green to brownish body with 9-12 vertical dark crossbars. The fins may have lighter spots and dots. The ♀♀ are light and dark brown mottled and have two black spots, one on the top and one at the base of the tail fin. Their fins, in comparison to the ♂♂, are shorter, more transparent and have fewer fin rays.

Soc. B.: A peaceful, solitary fish. It is possible the ♂♂ have territories, but this is not evident in an aquarium. The ♂♂ will occasionally become aggressive towards non-ripe ♀♀ in overly small breeding tanks.

M: Like *Cynolebias viarius*, best in a species tank.

B: The same as *Cynolebias viarius*. *C. adloffi* is also a seasonal fish and bottom diver. At higher temperatures, the egg-containing peat is ready for the addition of water after 6-8 weeks. Somewhat more sensitive than *C. viarius*.

F: C; live food, sometimes flake food.

S: A deep bodied species classified in the species group around *C. bellottii* and *C. viarius*.

T: 20-24° C, L: 5 cm, A: 50 cm, R: m, b, D: 2-3
68-75° F, 2", 20",

Cubanichthys cubensis

Cynolebias adloffi

Cynolebias boitonei (DE CARVALHO, 1959)
Brazilian Pearlfish

Syn.: *Simpsonichthys boitonei.*

Hab.: South America, Brazil, wider vicinity of the capital, Brasilia, D. F.

F.I.: 1964 to Denmark.

Sex: The ♂♂ are colorful with a red-brown body that darkens posteriorly. Anteriorly are light vertical bars which posteriorly change to bands of light-blue luminous dots, then to irregular dots at the caudal peduncle. The dorsal and anal fin are lyre-like elongated. The ♀♀ are plain reddish-brown with light vertical bands and 1-3 black dots on the sides of the body. The fins are smaller and colorless.

Soc. B.: Peaceful and a rather solitary fish. Particularily the ♂♂ are very lively.

M: Like *Cynolebias viarius*, but smaller tanks can be used. A species tank is preferred. In nature, *C. boitonei* is often found with *Rivulus punctatus* and, occasionally, with various characins.

B: An annual species which does not necessarily need to dive into the substrate to spawn; thinner peat layers are sufficient. Otherwise like *Cynolebias viarius*. The ♂♂ court the ♀♀ with a butterfly-like dance. Injured ♀♀ due to pursuing ♂♂ have not been observed. Storage time for the eggs is about 8 weeks.

F: C; live foods of corresponding sizes.

S: The fish used by CARVALHO to describe the species did not have ventral fins (see also photo). For this reason, he placed the species into a new genus. Today it has been shown that this characteristic can be found on other fishes of different genera and that it cannot be used to characterize a genus. In addition, populations of *Cynolebias boitonei* with ventral fins have been found.

T: 20-24° C, L: 4 cm, A: 50 cm, R: m, b, D: 3
68-75° F, 1 2/3", 20",

Cynolebias cheradophilus
VAZ-FERREIRA, SIERRA-DE-SORIANO & SCAGLIA-DE-PAULETE, 1964
Fine-Scaled Pearlfish

Syn.: None.

Hab.: Southern South America; coastal areas of eastern Uruguay, Departamento Rocha, between La Paloma and Aguas Dulces.

F.I.: Summer of 1980 by K. Fraga, Monetevideo and A. Rehm, Salzburg.

Sex: The ♂♂ are larger and somewhat more colorful.

Soc. B.: Peaceful fish.

M: As described for *C. viarius*, which the fish is found together with in puddles. Additionally, there were found *C. luteoflammulatus* and *Cynopoecilus melanotaenia*, and sometimes *Charax gibbosus*, *Cheirodon interruptus*, *Curimata* sp., *Acestrorhamphus jenynsii*, *Fitzroyia lineata* and *Phalloceros caudomaculatus*. The floor of the puddle consists of rotting leaves, feces of grazing animals and remains of decaying branches. In an aquarium, a peat bottom is recommended. Water soft (0.5-8° dGH), pH up to 8.9. The temperature fluctuates from about 4° C (39° F) in the southern winter to 40° C (104° F) in the summer when the pond dries up. 18-25° C (64-77° F) is recommended.

B: Like *C. viarius*. The peat layer should be about 6 cm (2 1/3") deep; storage time of the peat at 24-26° C (75-79° F) is about 3 months (values by REHM: DKG-Journal, **13** (11): 165-170, 1981)

F: C; live foods of all kinds depending on the size of the fish, including earthworms and beef heart.

S: The species has only been found in a single seasonal puddle 12 m (13 yd) long and 1.5 to 3.2 m (1.6-3.5 yd) wide. The question arises if urgent protection methods should not be implemented.

T: 18-25° C, L: 8 cm, A: 80 cm, R: b, m, D: 3
64-77° F, 3", 31",

Cynolebias boitonei

Cynolebias cheradophilus

Cynolebias heloplites HUBER, 1981 (?)

Syn.: *Cynolebias antenori* (?) see **S.**

Hab.: Eastern South America, east Brazil, State of Ceará and Rio Grande del Norte.

F.I.: October 1972 by S. Sellers to the USA; June 1973 by Dr. F. Fröhlich to Germany.

Sex: The ♂♂ are light brown and progressively darken towards the dorsum and posterior and have a hint of lighter vertical stripes on the dark fins. The body has small, bright iridescent spots; these are larger on the dark fins. The anal fin has a black edge with an orange band on the inside that gradually turns dark brown towards the body. The fins are elongated. The smaller ♀♀ are medium brown and have 1 to, usually, 3 black spots close together in the center of the body. Their fins are mostly transparent, not elongated, smaller and have fewer fin rays.

Soc. B.: Peaceful fish.

M: Maintain like *Cynolebias viarius* but warmer. According to G. C. Brasil, who caught the strain available in the hobby, the animals were found in typical temporary pools around Fortaleza. Water 10-55 cm (4"-22") deep; water temperature 27-30° C (81-86° F); pH between 7.0-7.1; dGH 3°. The vegetation consisted of *Nymphaea* and *Echinodorus*; other fishes were not found. The majority were ♀♀.

B: Like *Cynolebias viarius*, but higher temperatures are recommended. Storage time of the peat at high temperatures (about 30° C; 86° F) is about 3 months, at lower temperatures (about 23° C; 73° F), about 7 months.

S: The name is disputed. Animals of this species were already available in 1952 to MYERS, who named them *Cynolebias antenori*, but his description did not meet the requirements of the international nomenclature rules (nomen nudum). Because of this, HUBER 1981 described the fish anew. Meanwhile, some aquarium reports about the fish using the name *C. antenori* appeared which are partially considered valid descriptions of the fish because they comply with the rules, even though the authors did not intend a description. The article debated is by TULIPANO (Killi Notes of the Amer. Killif, Assn., **6** (11): 23-24, 1973). The nomenclature commission would now have to be requested to decide if the fish is to be called *Cynolebias antenori* TULIPANO, 1973 or *Cynolebias heloplites* HUBER, 1981. No assessment can be made here; either of the two names may be valid in the future.

T: 25-30° C, **L:** 5 cm, **A:** 50 cm, **R:** b, m, **D:** 3
77-86° F, 2", 20",

Cynolebias viarius
VAZ-FERREIRA, SIERRA-DE-SORIANO & SCAGLIA-DE-PAULETE, 1964
Blue-Banded Pearlfish

Syn.: None.

Hab.: Southeastern South America, coastal plains of Uruguay.

F.I.: 1976.

Sex: ♂♂ are more colorful than ♀♀ and have very variable striping on the body. The body color is light brown to light blue with darker blue to brown stripes. The fins are dotted. The smaller ♀ is spotted on a brownish background, and the fins are mostly colorless and transparent with dark dots.

Soc. B.: Peaceful seasonal fish and a bottom diving, continuous spawner. The ♂♂ are normally peaceful towards the ♀♀, but they can kill unripe ♀♀ in tanks that are too small and lack hiding places.

M: The water values should be medium (dGH about 6-15°, pH 6.5-7.5); nevertheless, they are not sensitive in this regard. The bottom should be of peat that the fish can penetrate when spawning. A dish with peat in a community tank is usually accepted and sought to spawn.

Continued on page 640.

Cynolebias heloplites

Cynolebias viarius

Perform regular water changes. Decoration can be with bogwood roots on which Java moss or Java fern is fastened. A species tank is very much recommended.

B: Breeding in a display tank has already been described; however, a specific breeding set-up is more productive. For this purpose, a 10 l (2.5 gal) tank is furnished with peat; the water can have the values mentioned above. The previously well fed animals (1 ♂, 2-3 ♀♀) are moderately fed and left in the set-up for one week. Then the animals are removed, the water poured off, and the peat well-pressed. The peat is placed on a layer of newspaper to dry further and subsequently placed in a plastic bag. After about 3 months, fresh water and the egg-containing peat are put in an aquarium. The young hatch after a few hours. After a day, the young are removed with a pipette and the peat can be dried anew for possible stragglers. The offspring immediately feed on *Artemia salina* nauplii and grow fast.

F: C; live foods, worms are liked.

S: *Cynolebias viarius* belongs to a species group which also contains *C. n. nigripinnis*, *C. n. alexandri* and *C. bellotti*.

T: 18-23° C, L: 6 cm, A: 60 cm, R: m, b, D: 2-3
64-73° F, 2 1/3", 24",

Diapteron abacinum (HUBER, 1976)

Syn.: *Aphyosemion abacinum*.

Hab.: Equatorial west Africa: eastern Gabon and western Congo (= Congo Brazzaville) in the Ivindo basin.

F.I.: One ♂ by Huber in 1976. Later several specimens by Heinemann and Lenz.

Sex: The ♂♂ are more colorful. They have a red body with vertical rows of blue scales. The more intense red fins also show these rows which can dissolve into irregular dots. There is a dark orange stripe on the anal and lower tail fin, occasionally also found on the upper tail fin. The edge of the tail fin is blue-white. The ♀♀ are smaller, their anterior body is more roundish, the caudal peduncle is more slender and the fins have less color and are rounded. The body coloration is more brown and the blue scales are barely present.

Soc. B.: Essentially peaceful fishes, but ♂♂ can become quite aggressive towards each other, particularly in tanks that are too small. Other ♂ killifishes are also threatened, but they escape as soon as the strength of the adversary is recognized. A solitarily living animal.

M: Best to keep them in a species tank densely planted with Java moss. Water should be soft (up to 10° dGH), slightly acid (pH 6-7) and not too warm. The decoration can be with bogwood roots.

B: Possible in a species tank. As long as the parents are well fed, there will always be some young which can be skimmed off. Because the fish are not very prolific anyway, this is the best tried method. The set-up in a species tank is possible; the eggs are collected and transferred to develop in a brooding dish. Acriflavine is useful against fungus. The young hatch after 10-14 days and must initially be fed paramecium. When skimming the young from the species tank, this step can be omitted because the young always find enough aufwuchs (rotifers, etc.) on the Java moss. However, to be on the safe side, some infusoria can be fed additionally.

F: C; small live food, often *Artemia salina* nauplii should also be fed. Flake food is not accepted.

T: 18-22° C, L: 4 cm, A: 50 cm, R: b, m, D: 3-4
64-72° F, 1 2/3", 20",

Flood or rain water puddle (central Brazil). Such waters are the home of killifishes, catfishes and characins. At 36° C (97° F), characins begin to die—the catfishes still survive. The killies have spawned long ago.

Diapteron abacinum

Epiplatys barmoiensis SCHEEL, 1968
Barmoi Panchax

Syn.: None.

Hab.: West Africa; Sierra Leone, Liberia. *E. barmoiensis* has also been exported from Nigeria (see photograph). These animals do not develop the long pectoral fins of comparable animals from Liberia.

F.I.: 1965 by E. Roloff from Sierra Leone.

Sex: The ♂♂ are larger and comparatively more slender. Their fins are more elongated, specially the tail and anal fins. The fins as a whole have a more pronounced design and are more colorful, even though the entire fish is not very colorful. The ♀♀ are anteriorly fuller and have transparent fins that are more rounded.

Soc. B.: A fish that prefers to swim alone, less often in schools, at the water surface. Harmless to equal-sized fishes.

M: Use a large tank with a tight fitting lid (!) distant from the water surface. The animals like to jump, particularly for blown-in live food, and would otherwise sustain injuries. Water should be soft to medium-hard, pH slightly acid to neutral. The tank can be densely planted, but should have some open areas, including the surface. The fish is suitable for the community aquarium with fishes that are not too active or too large; it is somewhat sensitive.

B: Should not be bred in a small aquarium. Several spawning mops can be provided for spawning and as cover. The eggs can be collected regularly and placed in a hatching jar to develop. The young hatch after about 10-14 days and immediately feed on *Artemia salina* nauplii.

F: C; live food, specially surface foods such as *Drosophila, Ephestia* and similar.

S: Despite the significantly differing chromosomal set indicated by SCHEEL (1968), the species is quite likely to be a relative of *Epi-platys bifasciatus*.

T: 24-27° C, **L:** 7 cm, **A:** 80 cm, **R:** t, m, **D:** 3
75-81° F, 2¾", 31",

Epiplatys berkenkampi NEUMANN, 1978
Berkenkamp's Panchax

Syn.: None.

Hab.: West Africa: central Gabon.

F.I.: 1976 by Bochtler.

Sex: ♂♂ are more colorful; in particular, they show a more intense red. Every scale possesses a red spot on a brown background. There are 5 faint—during fright more pronounced—cross stripes on the ventral side of the body. The fins are an orange rust-red. The ♀♀, which are not as intensely colored, have more transparent and rounded fins, specially the anal and tail fin.

Soc. B.: As all *Epiplatys*, a solitary, lurking fish which prefers the upper water regions, but will also frequent the middle regions. Housing with other fishes is possible.

M: Darker aquaria help bring out the colors. Cover part of the surface with floating plants. A dark substrate and diffuse lighting enhance the effect. Water should be soft (up to 10° dGH) and slightly acid. Do not keep with overly active fishes; otherwise, the animals might attempt to jump out. Cover glass!

B: Like *E. barmoiensis*. Breeding this species is not easy either.

F: C; any live food which can be tackled. Sometimes floating flake food is eaten, but it is not particularly liked.

S: This species belongs to the closer circle of the *E. sexfasciatus* group and links it to the *E. multifasciatus* group.

T: 20-24° C, **L:** 6 cm, **A:** 60 cm, **R:** t, m, **D:** 3-4
68-75° F, 2⅓", 24",

Epiplatys barmoiensis

Epiplatys berkenkampi

Epiplatys bifasciatus (STEINDACHNER, 1881)

Two-Striped Panchax

Syn.: *Haplochilus bifasciatus, Epiplatys ndelensis, Epiplatys steindachneri, Epiplatys taeniatus.*

Hab.: West and central Africa: from Senegal and Gambia to the upper Nile in savanna biotopes of the Sahel region, southward into the coastal savannas of Ghana, Togo and Benin.

F.I.: (?) to Denmark in 1959.

Sex: Not always easy to determine. In comparison, ♂♂ are usually more colorful and often have very nice drawn out fins, especially the anal and central region of the caudal fin. On the ventral half of the body above the light stomach, there is a dark, then a light band that ranges from the operculum to the caudal peduncle. The dorsal half is darker. Overlaying this are slanted lines, or a net pattern created by scales outlined in red. The unpaired gray-green fins have red dots. The ♀♀ are somewhat paler and notably fuller and lighter in the anterior region.

Soc. B.: A very timid fish that likes to jump. It should either be kept in a species tank or with *Aplocheilichthys normani*, its companion in nature.

M: Needs large and densely planted tanks with open areas, as indicated for *E. barmoiensis*. The fish are especially sensitive to vibrations. This has to be considered when deciding where to place the tank. Even after weeks of acclimation, the animals lose little of their timidity and remain hidden in the plants. For successful care, the water values are of secondary importance.

B: Large, low density species tanks allow some young fish to grow, but successful breeding will only be achieved with a single pair in a separate breeding tank. Java moss or a spawning mop should be contained therein, the eggs collected and then incubated in a brooding container with acriflavine. The young immediately feed on *Artemia salina* nauplii. Rearing is not difficult.

F: C; live foods of all kinds, especially food that falls on the water, such as insects, etc.

S: None.

T: 23-27° C, **L:** 5 cm, **A:** 60 cm, **R:** t, **D:** 2-3
73-81° F, 2", 24",

Epiplatys chaperi spillmanni ARNOULT, 1960

Spillmann's Panchax

Syn.: *Epiplatys spillmanni.*

Hab.: West Africa. Ivory coast.

F.I.: 1960 by Arnoult to France.

Sex: The ♂♂ are more colorful and, on average, grow somewhat larger. Their fins are larger, specially the tail fin which may have a wimple on the lower edge, and the ventral fins can be elongated. The ♀♀ are rather compact, the fins barely have a design and the anal fin is especially rounded.

Soc. B.: A peaceful surface fish which lives alone or in small loose schools. Only significantly smaller tankmates are considered prey.

M: Like *E. barmoiensis*. However, this subspecies is not as timid or sensitive and is well suited for a community tank. This species also jumps, so cover the tank! The water should be lightly acid and up to medium-hard, but the fish is not choosy in this regard and will tolerate diverging values.

B: Similar to *E. bifasciatus*, but simpler. Use of a spawning mop for this purpose is also advantageous. The eggs are collected from there and, depending on temperature, the young hatch after 14 days and immediately accept *Artemia salina* nauplii.

F: C; live foods of any kind. Food blown onto the water surface, such as insects, is especially appreciated.

S: *Epiplatys chaperi spillmanni* is one of the three described sub-species of the nominate form *Epiplatys chaperi chaperi*, which should not be confused with *E. dageti*. The other two sub-species are *E. chaperi sheljuzhkoi*, whose adult ♂♂ only have one distinct crossband behind the pectoral fin and no pronounced bands on the posterior body, and *E. c. schreiberi* from Kumasi, which is more blue-violet and normally has 4 wider crossbands posteriorly. The nominate form and *E. c. schreiberi* lack the stripe behind the pectoral fins.

T: 23-27° C, **L:** 7 cm, **A:** 60 cm, **R:** t, m, **D:** 2-3
73-81° F, 2", 24",

Epiplatys bifasciatus

Epiplatys chaperi spillmanni

Epiplatys etzeli BERKENKAMP, 1975
Etzel's Panchax

Syn.: None.

Hab.: West Africa, southern Ivory Coast.

F.I.: 1974 by H. Brachet and Dr. V. Etzel.

Sex: The ♂♂ have a yellowish-olive body with one dark, slanted bar behind the pectoral fin and 4 slanted half-bars on the posterior of the body. The ventral fins are wimpled. The ♀ are fainter colored with rounded, colorless fins and a more rounded anterior body.

Soc. B.: Similar to *E. chaperi spillmanni*, but the animals are somewhat more aggressive towards each other and, in front of other fishes and disturbances, very timid.

M: Like with *E. barmoiensis*. In nature the species inhabits weedy shores. Therefore, a densely planted aquarium is recommended. The animals are as shy as *E. bifasciatus* and flee heedlessly through the aquarium during disturbances, requiring a well covered aquarium. In presence of a soft substrate (peat), the fish dive into it during disturbances. The species is, therefore, not as well suited for a community tank; a species tank is the preferred choice.

B: Like *E. barmoiensis*. However, the fish is more bottom oriented and will also spawn on peat fibers in shallow aquaria. The peat can be stored moist for three weeks until water is again added. Eggs left in the water will hatch after about 14-18 days. Feeding can commence immediately with *Artemia salina* nauplii.

F: C; live food of all kinds.

S: The species is closely related to the *E. chaperi* group.

T: 23-27° C, **L:** 5 cm, **A:** 60 cm, **R:** t, m, **D:** 3
73-81° F, 2", 24",

Epiplatys grahami (BOULENGER, 1911)
Graham's Panchax

Syn.: *Haplochilus grahami, Epiplatys nigromarginatus.*

Hab.: West Africa: coastal regions of south Benin through Nigeria to Cameroon, entering the distribution area of *E. ansorgii* and *E. singa*.

F.I.: 1905 by Schroot, Hamburg, Germany and distributed as *Haplochilus spilargyreius*.

Sex: The ♂♂ have a metallic green base coloration with rows of red-brown dots that change from a strong red anteriorly to black towards the posterior. Slanted, dark crossbands are more or less visible depending on the mood. The ♀♀ are fuller anteriorly and have rounded, transparent fins; they are smaller and the cross stripes are more numerous and pronounced.

Soc. B.: Like *Epiplatys chaperi spillmanni*, a surface oriented fish which is also well suited for the community tank.

M: Like *Epiplatys barmoiensis*; however, the species is less problematic in its care, and water values are of secondary importance.

B: Similar to *Epiplatys bifasciatus*, breeding is uncomplicated and the eggs are best removed and placed in brooding dishes. Here, too, the fish immediately eat *Artemia salina* nauplii.

F: C; all types of live foods. Flake food sprinkled on the water surface is also accepted.

S: Forms a species group together with *E. ansorgii* and *E. singa*. The populations evidently overlap, and the question arises whether or not they all belong to one species.

T: 23-28° C, **L:** 6 cm, **A:** 60 cm, **R:** t, m, **D:** 2-3
73-82° F, 2 1/3", 24",

Epiplatys etzeli

Epiplatys grahami

Epiplatys huberi RADDA & PÜRZL, 1981

Hubert's Panchax, Green-Bellied Panchax

Syn.: None.

Hab.: Equatorial West Africa: southern Gabon and southern Congo (= Congo Brazzaville), in waters of the rain forest of the hilly and mountainous terrain of the Du-Chaillu-Massif.

F.I.: July 1980 by O. Hofmann and E. Pürzl.

Sex: The ♂♂ have a very colorful yellow-green coloration on the underside of the body and the fins, and a brown upper body. The sides have red dots. 5-6 blue-black strips are faintly visible, especially on the lower side of the body. Two of these stripes extend to the anal fin. The ♀♀ are smaller, not as iridescent, but more matte. The body stripes are more pronounced, and the rounded fins are more transparent.

Soc. B.: The animals like to stand alone or in groups close to the water surface. They are beautiful and peaceful, and in addition, they are not an especially sensitive fish.

M: Like *Epiplatys barmoiensis*; however, the animals are not as shy and are definitely suitable for the community aquarium. Water values should be slightly acid and soft.

B: Like *Epiplatys bifaciatus*, but the following method has also proven suitable: peat fibers are hung into the aquarium from the edge (fastened with the aquarium cover) where the fishes eagerly spawn. The peat with the eggs is removed after a few days and stored in a closed plastic bag. Water is added after barely 3 weeks. All young hatch simultaneously. Rearing is nonproblematic and the young immediately feed on *Artemia salina* nauplii.

F: C; all live foods which can be handled.

S: The species belongs to the *Epiplatys multifasciatus* group and is very closely related to *E. multifasciatus*.

T: 18-22° C, **L:** 5.5 cm, **A:** 60 cm, **R:** t, m, **D:** 2-3
64-72° F, 2 ", 24",

Epiplatys mesogramma HUBER, 1980

Syn.: None.

Hab.: Central Africa: Central African Republic, ditch on the road from Mbaika to Mongoumba, presently only known from the type locality.

F.I.: May 1977 by J. P. Gaudemard to France.

Sex: The ♂♂ are more colorful, and the fins are more elongate. On a blue-gray background, every scale on the side has a red dot; a red design becomes apparent anteriorly. About 6 crossbands are on the lower half of the body, 2 of which extend onto the anal fin. The tail fin has red stripes in the direction of its rays. The colors of the ♀♀ are not very attractive; the fins are rounded and more transparent.

Soc. B.: Like *Epiplatys huberi*; however, it is a more retiring and sensitive fish.

M: As indicated for *Epiplatys barmoiensis*. Water should be slightly acid and soft (up to 8° dGH). Maintenance in a species tank is more recommendable than in a community tank.

B: Like *Epiplatys huberi*, but the species is more sensitive and more difficult to reproduce.

F: C; all types of live foods.

S: The species belongs in the *Epiplatys multifasciatus* circle.

T: 20-24° C, **L:** 5.5 cm, **A:** 60 cm, **R:** t, m, **D:** 3-4
68-75° F, 2 ", 24",

Epiplatys huberi

Epiplatys mesogramma

Epiplatys roloffi ROMAND, 1978
Roloff's Panchax

Syn.: *Epiplatys olbrichtsi* (not POLL, 1941).

Hab.: West Africa: Liberia, drainage of the St. Paul River.

F.I.: 1971 by E. Roloff.

Sex: The ♂♂ are light to reddish-brown with darker scale edges which form a net design. Depending on the mood, the body has a prominent dark band from the mouth to the caudal peduncle with vertical crossbands above it which are equally mood dependent. The fins are edged in black; the dorsal and tail fin have an additional white narrow fringe on top and bottom. On the ♀♀, the dark crossbands on the body are more distinct and occur on a body that is browner and has less intense coloration. The fins are rounded and, with the exception of faint spots, transparent.

Soc. B.: Like all *Epiplatys* species, a single or, at the most, group living peaceful fish which only considers very small tankmates as prey. Occasionally the ♂♂ are quarrelsome towards each other.

M: Like with *Epiplatys barmoiensis*. Fishes acclimated in larger tanks are not at all shy and are very attractively colored. The water values are not very important.

B: As with *Epiplatys barmoiensis*; however, the animals can also be bred in the manner described for *E. huberi*. The young hatch after about 14 days and immediately feed on *Artemia* nauplii. Growth is rapid.

F: C; all kinds of live foods of corresponding size.

S: *Epiplatys roloffi* belongs in the *Epiplatys fasciolatus* species group.

T: 22-25° C, **L:** 7 cm, **A:** 80 cm, **R:** t, m, **D:** 2-3
72-77° F, 2 3/4", 31",

Epiplatys ruhkopfi BERKENKAMP & ETZEL, 1980
Ruhkopf's Panchax

Syn.: *Epiplatys coccinatus* (?).

Hab.: West Africa: Liberia, Kaningalitown.

F.I.: December 1978 by Dr. V. Etzel.

Sex: The body of the ♂ is brown, changing to blue and blue-violet towards the stomach. The dorsal fin is brown-green as is the caudal fin which shows a bluish edge. The anal fin is striped from the inside out: narrow blue, wide red-brown, narrow light green, dark brown edge. The ♀♀ are dark gray-brown and lighter towards the stomach. The posterior lower body half shows narrow dark slanted bands. The fins are rounded and mostly transparent.

Soc. B.: Active and peaceful towards fishes of the same size. A peaceful and beautiful species.

M: As indicated for *Epiplatys barmoiensis*. The species is not very sensitive and, correspondingly, the water values are not very important either.

B: Follow recommendations for *Epiplatys barmoiensis*. The eggs are easily collected and hatched in a brooding dish with acriflavine added. The young hatch after about 2 weeks and immediately feed on *Artemia salina* nauplii.

F: C; live foods of any kind, including some coarser fare. In addition, flake food is also accepted.

S: The species belongs in the *Epiplatys fasciolatus* group.

T: 22-26° C, **L:** 8 cm, **A:** 80 cm, **R:** t, m, **D:** 2-3
72-79° F, 3", 31",

Epiplatys roloffi

Epiplatys ruhkopfi

Epiplatys sangmelinensis (AHL, 1928)
Sangmelina Panchax

Syn.: *Panchax nyongensis, Panchax zenkeri, Aplocheilus sangmelinensis.*

Hab.: West Africa: inland plateau of southern Cameroon and northern Gabon.

F.I.: 1966 by Dr. J. Scheel to Denmark.

Sex: The ♂♂ have drawn out dorsal and anal fins. The base color is gray, turning red-brown dorsally. Every scale is marked with a brown to red spot. The fins have a more yellowish, often also bluish, base color with a red-brown dot design. The fins of the ♀♀ are more rounded and transparent, the body is less colorful in general, and the animals are usually smaller then the ♂♂.

Soc. B.: In general, a peaceful fish. The ♂♂ may occasionally be aggressive towards each other, especially in smaller tanks or towards new fish.

M: The species is somewhat sensitive. The fish need perfect water with low to, at the most, medium-hardness (less than 10° dGH) and slight acidity (pH 6-6.5). A traditional community tank is not recommended for this fish. Housing with *Aphyosemion* species or egg-laying toothcarps may be more appropriate. Dense background vegetation is recommended for cover.

B: Breeding this fish is expressly difficult. The fish are adhesive spawners which lay their eggs on plants or a spawning substrate such as a perlon mop. The young hatch after 10-14 days. The greatest difficulty is to entice the fish to spawn. Varied food is, therefore, a necessity. Some experiences have shown that the fish always spawned at a certain age (about 1 year). It is interesting to note that *Aphyosemion cameronense*, which occurs in the same distribution area, has similar breeding difficulties. It is possible that some yet unknown environmental factors act on both species similarly.

F: C; live foods. Take care when feeding worms.

S: Judging from the three types, *Panchax zenkeri* is identical to *Panchax sangmelinensis*, so the first name should have priority (page priority because both were described in the same scientific article). However, since its first description in 1928, more than 50 years have passed in which the former name has not been used, so it keeps the name *Epiplatys sangmelinensis*, and *Panchax zenkeri*, although older, is a synonym.

T: 20-24° C, 68-75° F, **L:** 5 cm, 2", **A:** 60 cm, 24", **R:** t, m, **D:** 4

Epiplatys sexfasciatus sexfasciatus GILL, 1862
Six-Barred Panchax

Syn.: *Haplochilus infrafasciatus.*

Hab.: West Africa: coastal regions of southern Togo through Benin, Nigeria, Cameroon, equatorial Guinea to northwest Gabon.

F.I.: 1905 by H. Schroot, Hamburg, from the mouth of the Niger.

Sex: The ♂♂ of the different sub-species are generally more colorful. Their fins are larger and partially elongated. The most common base color is a bronze-brown, and often a red to red-brown spot can be found on every scale of the lower body region. About 6 more or less pronounced slanted bars are on the lower body half. The fins are yellow to bronze colored. The ♀♀ are paler; the crossbars are clearer; the anterior body is fuller; the fins are smaller and less colorful.

Soc. B.: Lively fish. The ♂♂ are sometimes rather quarrelsome, especially against each other or when they are kept alone in an aquarium. Otherwise they are appreciative charges for a community tank with roughly equal sized fishes.

M: A quite undemanding species. Can be cared for in an aquarium like *E. barmoiensis*, but it will also be content with less favorable conditions. The water values are also of secondary importance.

B: Reproduction is easy. Following the method described for *E. barmoiensis* and *E. huberi*, the eggs can be collected from the spawning medium or stored in a peat

Continued on page 654.

Epiplatys sangmelinensis, south Cameroon

Epiplatys sexfasciatus, pair, "south Nigeria"

set-up. If no suitable material is available, the fish will spawn in a community aquarium, even on the filter or on the bottom in the corners, but no young grow up under these conditions. Offspring grow relatively quickly; the newly hatched fry immediately feed on *Artemia salina* nauplii.

F: C; live foods of any kind, occasionally flakes.

S: Presently 3 sub-species or population groups are recognized besides the nominate species: *Epiplatys sexfasciatus togolensis, E. s. rathkei* and *E. s. baroi.*

T: 22-26° C, L: 8 cm, A: 80 cm, R: m, t, D: 2-3
72-79° F, 3", 31",

Fundulus chrysotus (GÜNTHER, 1866)

Golden Topminnow, Golden Ear

Syn.: *Haplochilus chrysotus, Micristius chrysotus, Zygonectes chrysotus, Zygonectes henshalli, Fundulus arlingtonia, Fundulus kompi.*

Hab.: North America: southeastern USA, Florida, Georgia, South Carolina, Alabama, Tennessee, Missouri, Arkansas, Mississippi, Louisiana, Texas.

F.I.: 1904 by H. Stüve, Hamburg, Germany.

Sex: ♂♂ have a livelier coloration and are very variable. The ♀♀ are pale brown with transparent fins and, instead of the red-brown dots, have silver iridescent scales. There is a partially melanic form with black spots on both sexes.

Soc. B.: Social, active fishes. Single ♂♂ sometimes turn rather aggressive.

M: Well-planted, large tank. A heater is not absolutely necessary. Seasonally varying temperatures are perhaps advantageous. The temperatures should not be too low since the species likes some warmth. It is beneficial for the tank to receive sunlight. A species tank is recommendable.

B: Animals spawn on fine-leaved plants, algae bunches or artificial fiber mops. The fishes are continuous spawners which lay several eggs over an extended period of time; these should be collected for a good yield. The young hatch after about 10-12 days and immediately eat *Artemia salina* nauplii.

F: C, O; live foods of all kinds, frozen and dried foods.

S: Golden ear used to be a known and liked aquarium fish, but it was displaced by tropical species. The species belongs to the sub-genus *Zygonectes.*

T: 18-25° C, L: 7 cm, A: 80 cm, R: m, b, D: 3
64-77° F, 2 3/4", 31",

Fundulus cingulatus VALENCIENNES, 1846

Banded Topminnow

Syn.: *Zygonectes rubrifrons, Zygonectes auroguttatus, Fundulus cingularis.*

Hab.: North America; southeast USA, coastal areas from Carolina to Texas.

F.I.: November 1910 by C. Siggelkow, Hamburg, Germany, as *Fundulus rubrifrons.*

Sex: ♂♂ are olive-green with bluish sides that have numerous narrow, olive colored crossbands. At the intersection of the scales are red dots. The anal fin is tinged blue or red-brown; dorsal and caudal fins are red-brown with darker dots. ♀♀ are olive-green with less design on the body. Fins are reddish transparent, smaller and more rounded.

Soc. B.: As with *F. chrysotus.*

M: Similar to *F. chrysotus* but somewhat more warmth-loving. Water soft and slightly acid.

B: Like with *F. chrysotus.* The animals become brighter red during the spawning season.

F: C, O; especially live food but also frozen and dry foods.

S: The species is closely related to *F. chrysotus* and belongs to the same sub-genus, *Zygonectes.*

T: 20-25° C, L: 7 cm, A: 80 cm, R: m, D: 3
68-77° F, 2 3/4", 31",

Fundulus chrysotus, wild caught, Sarrasota, Florida, USA

Fundulus cingulatus

Fundulus diaphanus (LE SUEUR, 1817)

Banded Killie

Syn.: *Hydrargira diaphanus, Hydrargira multifasciatus, Fundulus extensus.*

Hab.: North America; southern Canada to Carolina, westward to and including the Mississippi region.

F.I.: 1905.

Sex: The ♂♂ are olive to blue-gray with numerous darker vertical stripes on the sides of the body. The fins are usually colorless to greenish. The ♀♀ are more gray; the vertical body stripes are darker, finer and not as numerous.

Soc. B.: Gregarious living fishes that seem to be peaceful towards other fishes.

M: Maintenance is probably very possible in larger and densely planted tanks. Not suited for a community aquarium. The species is mainly found in freshwater but also occurs in seawater. This should probably be taken into account for its maintenance, but the origin of the strain needs to be known. The pictured fish were kept successfully during the summer in a small garden pond with the addition of salt and were overwintered in a frost-free room.

B: Under the described conditions, the fish spawned in the garden pond; some young were found in the fall which had grown up alongside the parents.

F: C, O; every live food of corresponding size and also frozen and flake foods.

S: *Fundulus diaphanus* belongs in the sub-genus *Plancterus*. Besides the nominate form, the sub-species *Fundulus diaphanus menona* exists.

T: 10-25° C, **L:** 10 cm, **A:** 100 cm, **R:** m, b, **D:** 4
50-77° F, 4", 39",

Fundulus grandis BAIRD & GIRARD, 1853

Gulf Killifish

Syn.: *Fundulus floridensis, Fundulus pallidus.*

Hab.: North America; USA and Mexico, from northeastern Florida (Matanzas River) to the south around the peninsula of Florida, and along the Gulf of Mexico to the Laguna de Tamiahua south of Tampico, also on the northern coast of Cuba. Mostly in brackish water, also in seawater. In the southern habitat it also exists in freshwater, e.g., the drainage area of the Rio Conchos by Galeana and Linares.

F.I.: 1908 by Vereinigten Zierfischzüchtereien in Conradshöhe, Berlin, Germany, as *Fundulus pallidus.*

Sex: The ♂♂ are olive-brown with numerous metallic iridescent spots on the sides and the fins. Beautiful specimens show an intensive yellow to orange belly, especially during the spawning season. The ♀♀ are a uniform pale olive-green, the fins are mostly transparent, and posteriorly, dark vertical stripes are visible.

Soc. B.: The peaceful, very active fishes occur in loose groups and schools in nature. In small aquaria there exists the danger that the ♂ will pursue the ♀ too much. The fish can become tame in captivity.

M: An undemanding and easily kept species, especially the freshwater forms from the southern range. Water values are of secondary importance. Water chemistry of one habitat in northern Mexico (Rio Pablillo): air: 24° C (75° F), water: 24.5° (76° F), 6400 μsiemens, 17.0° dGH, 11.5° KH, pH 8.95. Among others, the following fishes were found: *Astyanax mexicanus, Cichlasoma carpintis, Poecilia sphenops.*

B: The animals spawn on plants and peat fibers as well as wool mops, but they will eat their spawn. The ♂♂ strongly pursue the ♀♀. Development of the eggs at 18-20° C (64-68° F) takes 12-14 days.

F: C, O; live foods of all kinds and also frozen and flake foods.

S: The species belongs in the sub-genus *Fundulus* of the same named genus. The sub-species *Fundulus grandis saguanus* has been described from north Cuba. The differentiation between *Fundulus grandis* and *F. heteroclitus* is not easy. If the origin of the fish is unknown, it can only be distinguished by the mandibular pores of preserved specimens. The coloration of both species is the same.

T: 22-26° C, **L:** up to 15 cm (?), **A:** 80 cm, **R:** m, b, **D:** 2
72-79° F, up to 6" (?), 31",

Fundulus diaphanus

Fundulus grandis

Fundulus lineolatus (AGASSIZ, 1854)
Line Topminnow

Syn.: *Zygonectes lineolatus, Zygonectes craticula, Zygonectes zonifer.*

Hab.: North America, USA; Florida to North Carolina in slow-flowing water.

F.I.: ? 1972 by Böhm and Häfelin to Vienna, Austria.

Sex: The ♂♂ have a silver body with thin horizontal lines that are intersected by 11-15 wide, vertical crossbars which terminate at the stomach in a point. In contrast, the ♀♀ have 7-8 dark longitudinal stripes, and the vertical crossbars are only faintly present.

Soc. B.: In nature, the young are found in schools. Full-grown fish prefer to form pairs. The fish is peaceful and rather shy and retiring in an aquarium. A species tank is recommended.

M: Like other *Fundulus* species. The tank should be densely planted around the edges and have open areas in the center. In nature, the fish are always caught in the open water near plants. Water values are not significant, pH should be about neutral (6.8-7.5), softer water is preferred and the temperature should not rise above 27° C (81° F). Lower temperatures in the winter could be advantageous.

B: Plant spawner. Eagerly spawns on artificial fiber mops, even when they are lying on the bottom of the aquarium. The eggs are very large and should be collected; otherwise, the parents will eat them. In addition, the eggs are light sensitive and should not be stored at a temperature above 24° C (75° F). The relatively large young hatch after 14-16 days and immediately feed on *Artemia salina* nauplii.

F: C, O; foods of all kinds, including frozen and flake foods, though live food is preferred.

S: *Fundulus lineolatus* belongs in the subgenus *Zygonectes* with the closely related *F. blairae, F. dispar, F. escambiae* and *F. nottii* into the *Fundulus nottii* species group.

T: 18-24° C, **L:** 7 cm, **A:** 60 cm, **R:** m, u, b, **D:** 3-4
64-75° F, 2¾", 24",

Fundulus zebrinus JORDAN & GILBERT, 1882
Zebra Topminnow

Syn.: *Plancterus zebra, Plancterus kansae, Fundulus kansae, Hydrargyra zebra, Fontinus zebrinus.*

Hab.: North America; southeast USA, Texas, New Mexico, South Dakota, drainages of the Brazos, Colorado, Pecos, Red, and Arkansas rivers.

F.I.: ? 1972 by O. Böhm to Vienna, Austria.

Sex: Depending on the origin of the strain, the ♂♂ have an olive to red-brown body, a number of light stripes of varying widths and an occasional dark spot behind the operculum. The fins are an olive-brown to a beautifully intensive red, but the tail fin is usually not as colorful. The ♀♀ have a simpler color and the fins are mostly transparent and smaller.

Soc. B.: Peaceful fish; if possible, maintain several animals together. The fish will always remain somewhat timid.

M: Undemanding fish which is to be kept like other *Fundulus*, but hard water with a pH above 7.0 is recommended.

B: Simple to breed; the fish spawn on Java moss or a spawning mop. The eggs can be collected and developed in a rearing bowl. The young immediately feed on *Artemia salina* nauplii.

F: C, O; all kinds of live foods, frozen and flake food.

S: Two species, *zebrinus* and *kansae*, were recognized earlier, and depending on author, they were once placed in the genus *Fundulus* then again into the autonomous genus *Plancterus*. MILLER (1983) proved, however, that all fish belong to one species which is called *zebrinus* and can be placed in the sub-genus *Plancterus* of the genus *Fundulus*.

T: 20-25° C, **L:** 6 cm, **A:** 60 cm, **R:** b, m, **D:** 2-3
68-77° F, 2⅓", 24",

Fundulus lineolatus

Fundulus zebrinus

Garmanella pulchra — HUBBS, 1936

Yucatan Pubfish

Sub-Fam.: Cyprinodontinae

Syn.: *Jordanella pulchra.*

Hab.: Freshwater, brackish and saltwater in the coastal areas of the Yucatan Peninsula in Mexico, to Corozal, Belize.

F.I.: 1972 by Dr. F. Fröhlish from the USA to Germany, into the USA by R. Goldstein who caught them on the island of Cozumel, Mexico.

Sex: ♂♂ are silver with a dark brown back and thin vertical bands on the sides. The ♀♀ are more simply colored. The fins are mostly colorless. The lateral dark body spot is more pronounced than in the ♂♂. In addition, ♀♀ are smaller.

Soc. B.: Peaceful towards other fish. However, in tanks that are too small, the ♂♂ soon become aggressive towards ♀♀ or other ♂♂. Like most Cyprinodontinae, they have territories.

M: A salt content of 6-7 g/l (23-27g/gal) is recommended. Salt tolerant plants must be chosen. The aquarium must be furnished with stones and other decorative articles, so that the center of the spawning territory has a bunch of filamentous algae or perlon wool as spawning substrate and separate hiding places for nonripe ♀♀.

B: The breeding aquarium should be outfitted as described above. After spawning, the eggs are collected and stored in brackish water. They soon turn white and seem fungused. The young hatch after about 10-14 days and live on the bottom at first. They immediately eat *Artemia salina* nauplii and need vegetable matter as additional nourishment. After about 2 months, they begin to show their colors, and they are sexually mature after 6 months.

F: O; all kinds of live foods; such vegetable fare as filamentous algae, cooked lettuce, etc.; also flake food.

S: In 1981 PARENTI placed *pulchra* into the genus *Jordanella*, thereby eliminating the monotypic (having only 1 species) genus *Garmanella*. This action has been strongly opposed; therefore, the use of *Garmanella* is continued here.

T: 22-28° C, L: 5-6 cm, A: 80 cm, R: b, m, D: 3
72-82° F, 2-2 1/3", 31",

Hypsopanchax stictopleuron — (FOWLER, 1949)

Sub-Fam.: Aplocheilichthyinae

Syn.: *Epiplatys stictopleuron, Hypsopanchax silvestris, Hylopanchax silvestris.*

Hab.: West Africa; Congo and Ivindo basin in Gabon, Congo and Zaire.

F.I.: ?

Sex: The ♂♂ are a beautiful metallic blue with a greenish sparkling tinge. The large scales of the anterior body create a net design. Pectoral and ventral fin tips are a strong yellow, and the remaining fins are blue. The ♀♀ have a roundish anterior body, a slender caudal peduncle, paler body coloration and transparent fins.

Soc. B.: Swims in loose groups or schools.

M: Up till now only single specimens could be imported. These animals were so weakened by the lengthy transport that they did not survive long. The fish are quite sensitive and require soft (up to 5° dGH) and slightly to strongly acidic (pH 5-6) water. A dense edge of vegetation as well as dim illumination should be beneficial.

B: Though there are no concrete experiences available, breeding will not be easy and should, in principle, correspond to that of *Procatopus* species.

F: C; small live foods.

S: HUBER (Rev. fr. Aquariol.: 1982) determined that *Hylopanchax silvestris* is a synonym for *stictopleuron* and placed the species into the genus *Micropanchax*. The former might be accurate, but *Micropanchax* is only a complex within today's *Aplocheilichthys* species group, from which *stictopleuron* differs. Therefore, it should remain in the genus *Hylopanchax* created by POLL and LAMBERT.

T: 20-24° C, L: 3.5 cm, A: 40 cm, R: m, t, D: 4
68-75° F, 1 1/3", 16",

Garmanella pulchra

Hypsopanchax stictopleuron

Nothobranchius cyaneus SEEGERS, 1981
Blue Notho

Syn.: None.

Hab.: East Africa; southern Somalia, northeastern Kenya.

F.I.: 1962 by Leaky to the USA, but it became extinct. 1980 by K. Lung to Germany.

Sex: The ♀♀ are a monocolored gray-brown. Some populations have dark horizontal, V-shaped, faint patterns on the posterior body. The ♂♂ are blue to blue-green; some individuals have a reddish tinge and a dark gray pattern. The populations vary considerably in design and coloration patterns.

Soc. B.: *N. cyaneus* is a seasonal fish and a bottom spawner. The ♂♂ can sometimes be aggressive towards unripe ♀♀ and chase them to death in small tanks.

M: As indicated for *N. furzeri*. The animals are quite active. The water values can vary from soft to hard and are of subordinate importance; however, higher temperatures are preferred. A species tank is advised.

B: Similar to *N. furzeri* and *N. jubbi*. The species is not as aggressive as *N. furzeri*, and the animals can be left set up for a somewhat longer period, as described for *N. jubbi*.

F: C; live foods of all kinds; worms are also liked.

S: In recent times new collections have been done in Somalia and Kenya. It was determined that the area of distribution of *N. cyaneus* is connected to that of *N. jubbi* in the north. In the transition area, both forms were found together as well as intermediate forms. It is, therefore, unclear whether both forms are independent species or if *N. cyaneus* is a sub-species or only a synonym to *N. jubbi*. It is interesting to note that some populations of *N. cyaneus* in their natural biotope fled during danger not into the bottom ground, as is typical for *Nothobranchius* species, but jumped out of the water and fled in this manner over several meters distance; an unusual behavior pattern for *Nothobranchius* species which has been observed in populations of Somalia as well as Kenya.

T: 24-26° C, better higher, **L:** 5 cm, **A:** 60 cm, **R:** b, m, t, **D:** 2-3
75-79° F, better higher, 2", 24",

Nothobranchius furzeri JUBB, 1971
Furzer's Notho

Syn.: None.

Hab.: East Africa; east Zimbabwe, Gona-re-Zhou Reservation on the border of Mozambique, drainage area of the Limpopo River.

F.I.: 1969 by R. E. Furzer to England and the USA, 1973 by Dr. W. Foersch to Germany.

Sex: The ♂♂ have a light gray body with each scale edged in dark brown, creating a net pattern on the body. The anal fin is red-brown and marbled light gray; the dorsal fin and the inner region of the tail fin are dark brown with a light gray design. On the tail fin there is a terminal black band then a yellow, occasionally reddish, vertical stripe proximally. The ♀♀ are light brownish-gray and show no particular design on the body. ♀♀ are smaller and have translucent fins.

Soc. B.: Not always a peaceful fish. The ♂♂ are occasionally aggressive against each other, against heterospecific ♂♂ and also towards unripe conspecific ♀♀.

M: The animals are best kept in a species tank or with similar sized charges in a community tank. The general impression should be rather dark, for example, well-planted and with a peat bottom. Decorate with bogwood roots. Water soft to medium-hard (4-15° dGH) and slightly acid (pH 6.5-7).

Continued on page 632.

Nothobranchius cyaneus

Nothobranchius furzeri

Nothobranchius janpapi WILDEKAMP, 1977
Jan Pap's Notho, Topwater Fire Killie

Syn.: None.

Hab.: East Africa; Tanzania, in seasonal waters of the Ruvu and the lower Rufiji drainages.

F.I.: 1976 by R. Wildekamp and travel companions.

Sex: The ♂♂ are distinctly more colorful with a blue body and a red net design. Anal fin is orange; the dorsal fin is green with red dots and fringed in blue; the caudal fin is transparent green with narrow orange lines along the fin rays. The smaller ♀♀ are a monotonous gray-brown; the fins are more rounded and transparent.

Soc. B.: Small peaceful fish. Only ♂♂ may become aggressive towards each other and carry out fights to establish social hierarchy.

M: This small species should only be kept in a species tank or together with small *Nothobranchius* species. Water values are of secondary importance.

B: The fishes are bottom spawners. Therefore, a 15 l (4 gal) tank with a layer of peat is used. After being fed very well, 2-3 ♀♀ and 1 ♂ are put into the aquarium. After 1 week, the animals are removed. The damp peat is put for 2-3 months into a plastic bag. Then water is added to a small tank. After 24 hours, the hatched young are pipetted out. These are very small and must be initially fed with paramecium until they are able to eat *Artemia salina* nauplii.

F: C; live foods in accordance to their small size.

S: Due to its somewhat deviating behavior and several body characteristics, *N. janpapi* belongs to the sub-genus *Aphyobranchius*. It is interesting that the species in its habitat has always been found together with *Nothobranchius melanospilus*, a very large species, as well as a third species of medium size such as *N. lourensi* or *N. eggersi*.

T: 23-30° C, **L:** 3.5 cm, **A:** 50 cm, **R:** b, m, t, **D:** 3-4
73-86° F, 1 1/3", 20",

Nothobranchius jubbi WILDEKAMP & BERKENKAMP, 1979
Jubb's Notho

Syn.: *Nothobranchius neumanni* (not HILGENDORF, 1905).

Hab.: East Africa; coastal region of southern Kenya and the immediate northern region of Somalia south of Kisimaio.

F.I.: 1962 by Leaky to the USA.

Sex: As in all *Nothobranchius*, the ♀♀ are a single-colored gray-brown; those of some populations of *N. jubbi* have a faint, dark, horizontal V-shaped pattern on the posterior body. The ♂♂ are blue-gray with a slight reddish tinge and have a dark gray pattern. The tail fin is red.

Soc. B.: Peaceful species; however, the ♂♂ can be aggressive towards each other.

M: As indicated for *N. furzeri*. *N. jubbi* is a robust, vigorous species.

B: As indicated for *N. furzeri*; however, the species is not as aggressive, allowing the set-up to continue longer. Best to use a trio, that is, 1 ♂ and 2 ♀♀. Either exchange the fish after 2 days, negating the necessity of food, or use a longer continuous set-up where feeding must consist of varied but sparse live foods. After 1-2 weeks decant the water and remove the peat.

F: C; live foods of all kinds, especially worms.

S: In the northern range, *N. jubbi* was found with *N. cyaneus*; intermediate forms, possibly crosses between the two, could also be discovered. It is possible that *N. cyaneus* is only a sub-species or a synonym of *N. jubbi*.

T: 24-26° C, better higher, **L:** 5 cm, **A:** 60 cm, **R:** b, m, **D:** 2-3
75-79° F, better higher, 2", 24",

Nothobranchius janpapi, wild caught, Tanzania, Rufiji

Nothobranchius jubbi

Nothobranchius microlepis (VINCIGUERRA, 1897)

Syn.: *Fundulus microlepis.*

Hab.: East Africa; coastal areas of eastern Kenya and southeast Somalia.

F.I.: February 1979 by Dr. R. Haas to the USA.

Sex: Full-grown ♂♂ are beefy and tall. The body is blue-gray, and some strains have a crossband pattern. The fins are intensely colored; the tail fin and the ventral fins are rimmed in black. A vertical dark line runs through the eye, as is commonly seen in the South American genus *Cynolebias*. The ♀♀ are brown-gray and smaller; their fins are transparent. The dark band through the eye is fainter.

Soc. B.: As with *N. furzeri.*

M: A species tank is recommended. As the animals get strong and large, a correspondingly sized tank must be provided. Otherwise, maintenance parallels *N. furzeri.*

B: Like with *N. furzeri.* The species does not seem to be very fecund.

F: C; hardy live foods of all kinds, especially worms.

S: Because of the peculiar shape, the small and numerous scales (name!) and the black line through the eye, *N. microlepis* deviates from other known *Nothobranchius* species and occupies a special position.

T: 23-30° C, **L:** 6 cm, **A:** 60 cm, **R:** m, b, **D:** 3
73-86° F, 2 1/3", 24",

Nothobranchius orthonotus (PETERS, 1844)
Dusky Notho

Syn.: *Cyprinodon orthonotus, Hydrargyra maculata, Fundulus mkuziensis.*

Hab.: Southeast Africa: South Africa, Mozambique, Malawi.

F.I.: ?

Sex: The ♂♂ are colorful; additionally, there is a certain variability within the species depending on the strain. Most ♂♂ have a gray base coloration, whereby every scale is more or less wide, edged in red to red-brown, forming a net pattern which becomes denser posteriorly and dorsally. The fins are spotted to solid colored in the same hue. The edges of the anal and dorsal fins are white. The population from the Krüger National Park has a light green part in the dorsal and anal fins that varies in width. The ♀♀ are light brown with small dark brown spots posteriorly.

Soc. B.: The ♂♂ can become quite rabid towards the ♀♀, especially when they are not ripe. Transport the animals singly! They are harmless to fishes of roughly the same size.

M: This very robust and lively *Nothobranchius* species should, if possible, be kept in a species tank. A layer of peat is recommended. Decorate with bogwood and Java fern or Java moss. ♂ and ♀ should be kept separate if the tank is not sufficiently large. Water chemistry is secondary; it can be slightly acid or basic (6.5-7.5) and low to medium-hard (up to 15° dGH).

B: Like *Nothobranchius furzeri.* Due to the aggressive nature of the ♂♂, a set-up of short duration is recommended.

F: C; live foods of all kinds, especially worms. The fish are hardy eaters and require a lot of food.

S: Krüger National Park, South Africa, had eggs and fish of this species stocked by helicopter in ponds and elephant watering holes for mosquito control.

T: 23-30° C, **L:** up to 9 cm, **A:** 70 cm, **R:** b, m, **D:** 2-3
73-86° F, up to 3 ", 28",

Nothobranchius microlepis ♂

Nothobranchius orthonotus

Nothobranchius patrizii (VINCIGUERRA, 1927)
Patrizi's Notho, Red-Tailed Turquoise Notho Sub-Fam.: Aplocheilinae

Syn.: *Fundulus patrizii.*

Hab.: East Africa: northern coastal areas of eastern Kenya in the drainage areas of the Tana River and the southeastern coastal areas of Somalia to the north.

F.I.: February 1979 by Dr. R. Haas to the USA, from there to Europe.

Sex: The ♂♂ have a blue body with a net design, formed by brown edges of the scales, that extends into the dorsal and anal fin. Especially the dorsal fin is strongly marbled. The tail fin to the caudal peduncle is a luminous red. The ♀♀ are brown and have a delicate pattern of horizontal Vs on the posterior body made by darker edges on the scales.

Soc. B.: Generally a peaceful and active fish. *Nothobranchius* species usually occur in waters void of other fishes. They should be kept in a species tank in captivity. Nevertheless, housing them with not too active and similar sized fishes is possible.

M: Similar to *Nothobranchius furzeri*. Provide hiding places for the ♀♀ so they are not constantly chased by the ♂♂ in the display aquarium. Instead, it is preferable to keep the sexes separate.

B: Like with *Nothobranchius fuzeri*; however, *N. patrizii* is not as aggressive towards ♀♀ so that a longer breeding setup (about 1 week) becomes possible. One can also use a large tank and introduce a flat bowl (about 5 cm (2") deep) of boiled peat. In this otherwise unfurnished tank, a larger number of ♂♂ and ♀♀ are kept; best results are obtained if the majority are ♀♀. The animals will spawn in the peat which can be exchanged weekly. The peat, as is customary for all *Nothobranchius* species, is dried and water can be added after 8-12 weeks if warmer storage temperatures are used.

F: C; live foods of all kinds.

S: This is the northern most known *Nothobranchius* species of the east African coastal areas. It has special appeal due to its beautiful, large unpaired fins.

T: 23-30° C, **L:** 5 cm, **A:** 60 cm, **R:** b, m, **D:** 2-3
73-86° F, 2", 24",

Procatopus aberrans AHL, 1927
Green Lampeye Sub-Fam.: Aplocheilichthyinae

Syn.: *Procatopus roseipinnis, P. nigromarginatus, P. gracilis, P. plumosus, P. andreaseni.*

Hab.: West Africa: Nigeria and west Cameroon.

F.I.: 1957 by Clausen and Scheel of Denmark.

Sex: The ♂♂ show—especially posteriorly—a metallic blue-green to blue uniform shine that may, depending on strain, also reach into the unpaired fins. Beautiful specimens have fins that are intensely red distally. The fins have a pattern or red-brown dots. The tail fin is vertically cropped and occasionally has a wimple on the top and bottom. In addition, the caudal fin is usually edged in white on the bottom. ♀♀ are smaller, paler and the fins are usually colorless and transparent.

Soc. B.: A peaceful fish which prefers to live in schools and should be maintained in this manner. Despite its schooling behavior, individuals need some free space. If two animals are kept very close together over an extended amount of time, e.g, in a plastic bag for transport or delivery, they can injure or even kill each other.

M: The fish can be cared for in sparsely stocked community tanks as long as their requirements are met. They are very sensitive to poor water quality which can lead to fish tuberculosis, poor health and death.

Continued on page 632.

Nothobranchius patrizii

Procatopus aberrans

Procatopus similis AHL, 1927

Nigerian Lampeye

Syn.: *Procatopus abbreviatus, P. glaucicaudis, P. lacustris.*

Hab.: West Africa: coastal plains in southeastern Nigeria and west Cameroon.

F.I.: 1966 by Scheel to Denmark.

Sex: The uniform metallic green-blue body of the ♂♂ of this species is similar to that of *P. gracilis*. This coloration is warmer in *P. similis* than in *P. aberrans*. The fins are usually yellowish to, less commonly, reddish. Proximally, they are red to red-brown spotted, usually in a double row, with the spots occasionally merged into bands. ♀♀ are smaller with less color and transparent fins.

Soc. B.: Like *P. aberrans*; a schooling fish which is usually peaceful. Also see *P. aberrans*. Single ♂♂ can become somewhat quarrelsome towards tankmates.

M: As with *P. aberrans*.

B: Parallels *P. aberrans*. The species is not quite as easy to breed. In this regard and also in appearance, it is more similar to *P. nototaenia*.

F: C; live foods of all kinds.

S: Like *P. aberrans* and *P. nototaenia*, this species also has the characteristic thorn-like appendage on the lower operculum typical for the genus.

T: 24-26° C, **L:** 7 cm, **A:** 60 cm, **R:** t, m, **D:** 3
75-79° F, 2 3/4", 24",

Profundulus punctatus (GÜNTHER, 1866)

Syn.: *Fundulus pachycephalus, Fundulus oaxacae, Profundulus balsanus, Profundulus scapularis.*

Hab.: Central America: Pacific slopes from Rio Papagayo in the state of Guerrero in southeastern Mexico down into southern Guatemala, as well as the Atlantic slopes from the upper Rio Coatzacoalcos drainage, Oaxaca, Mexico, over the Rio Chiapa basin to Guatemala.

F.I.: March 1932 by Dr. R. Oeser from the west coast of Guatemala.

Sex: During the spawning period, the general coloration of the ♂♂ becomes a more intense yellow. In contrast, the ♀♀ have a paler body color; especially the stomach is lighter and the fins have less color. The stomach is rounder.

Soc. B.: Peaceful fish; it likes to live in loose groups.

M: Undemanding, can be well maintained in a community aquarium. In nature the animals occur in fast flowing mountain creeks; therefore, it likes to jump. Provide a well-fitted cover! Water values are of subordinate importance; alkaline water of medium hardness, the kind also found in its biotope, is preferred. The species lives together with *Poeciliopsis gracilis, Poeciliopsis fasciata* and *Poecilia sphenops* in a habitat in Chiapas, southern Mexico.

B: Breeding is easy. The animals lay their eggs on plants, such as Java moss. From there they can be collected. In the display tank, the parents eat their spawn, but some young always grow up if maintained in a species tank because the parents largely ignore hatched young. According to experience, the fishes have spawning seasons during which they spawn spontaneously after the addition of freshwater.

F: C, O; live foods of all kinds as well as frozen and flake food.

S: Though very recommended, the species is infrequently kept because of its moderately attractive colors.

T: 22-26° C, **L:** 8 cm, **A:** 60 cm, **R:** m, t, b, **D:** 2
72-79° F, 3", 24",

Procatopus similis

Profundulus punctatus

Rachovia brevis (REGAN, 1912)

Magdalena Stop-Finned Killie

Syn.: *Rivulus brevis, Rachovia splendens.*

Hab.: South America; north Colombia and northwest Venezuela, in the drainage area of the Rio Magdalena and neighboring Atlantic tributaries east of Lake Maracaibo.

F.I.: 1906 by H. Stüve to Germany.

Sex: Usually the ♂♂ are larger and more colorful than the ♀♀. They have elongated fins and the morph described as *R. splendens* is quite beautifully patterned and colored. In general, the species is quite variable. The ♀♀ are, in contrast, plain, fuller bodied and have a thinner caudal peduncle. The body is gray-brown with little design; the fins are rounded and brownish transparent.

Soc. B.: The fish are rather solitary and do not show any particular social order.

M: Maintenance is similar to *Cynolebias* species. The water should have pH values around neutral or slightly below with soft to medium hardness (up to 15° dGH). The show tank should have a soft, dark bottom. Peat is recommended. Additionally, the tank can be decorated using bogwood with plants like Java moss, Java fern or *Anubias* tied to it. The fish can also be kept in a "normal" planted tank. House with not too active and equal or smaller fishes. A species tank is better.

B: Breeding follows the proven method of *Cynolebias* species. The fish, best is a trio, are stocked into an aquarium with a 4-5 cm (1 2/3"-2") peat layer and are fed live foods moderately but regularly. The fishes are bottom spawners but do not always dive into the substrate. After about 1 week, the peat is removed and dried. FOERSCH achieved the best results with 5 months storage at 22° C (72° F). Other experiences showed good results at higher temperatures with a shorter storage time. Perhaps individual experiences have to be made on one's own. After storage, fresh water is added to the egg-containing peat. The young immediately feed on *Artemia salina* nauplii. They grow rapidly and soon mature. The life expectancy of this species is about 3/4 to 1 years.

T: 22-26° C, 72-79° F, **L:** up to 8 cm, up to 3", **A:** 60 cm, 24", **R:** m, b, **D:** 3-4

Rachovia maculipinnis (WEIBEZAHN in RADDA, 1964)

Venezuelan Spot-Finned Killie

Syn.: *Pterolebias maculipinnis.*

Hab.: South America; savanna regions of the Rio Apure drainage in Venezuela.

F.I.: 1966 by Häfelin to Vienna, Austria.

Sex: The ♂♂ are more colorful than the smaller ♀♀ and have a greenish to yellowish brown body which turns brown dorsally. The scales are edged in brown; the anal fin is brown and green marbled. The dorsal fin has black and light dots on the posterior base which can merge to form one larger spot. Occasionally, beautiful specimens will have a red band on the top of the marbled caudal fin. In general, the animals are very variable and can show deviating color and design patterns. The ♀♀ are light brown to gray colored.

Soc. B.: This species evidently lives a solitary life without a particular recognizable social order. The ♂♂ are often aggressive towards each other in small tanks.

M: Similar to *R. brevis*. The fish should be kept in a species tank or maybe with fishes of similar ecological demands and size. However, do not put it in the usual hodge podge of fishes.

B: Like *R. brevis*. When a thick layer of peat is available, they dive into the substrate; they will also spawn in a thin layer of peat.

Continued on page 632.

Rachovia brevis

Rachovia maculipinnis

Rachovia stellifer (THOMERSON & TURNER, 1973)

Syn.: *Rivulus stellifer.*

Hab.: South America; Venezuela, state of Cojedes, at Caño Benito, between El Pao and El Baul.

F.I.: 1981 through the USA to Germany.

Sex: The ♂♂ have a brown to gray body which becomes lighter towards the belly. White to silver iridescent scales are distributed over the body. The anal fin has a black fringe followed by a white stripe. The dorsal is light and dark marbled in the colors of the body. The ♀♀ are smaller and have no stripes on the anal fin. The upper base of the caudal fin has one or more black dots.

Soc. B.: Similar to *R. brevis*; however, the ♂♂ are more quarrelsome, both towards each other and towards the ♀♀.

M: Like *R. brevis.* Maintenance in a species tank is necessary; in nature, the animals occur alone or with *R. maculipinnis*, but they are rarer than the latter and are always found alone at the edge of seasonal pools. Water values should be medium-hard at the most and have a neutral pH.

B: Like *R. brevis*. The ♂♂ are very rough towards the ♀♀; therefore, hiding places in the breeding tank are needed. A short set-up of a few hours under close supervision is probably better. The species is either not very productive or a high egg loss occurs during storage, so that the yield until now has only been moderate.

F: C; hardy live food.

S: *Rachovia stellifer* was originally described as a *Rivulus* species while pointing out the special seasonal character of the fish. This fish was the only *Rivulus* species with seasonal characteristics. After reassigning it to the genus *Rachovia*, it still exhibits peculiarities. It is somewhat more slender than the other *Rachovia* species and the black dot on the caudal peduncles of the ♀♀ is a *Rivulus* characteristic. Although the species clearly belongs to the genus *Rachovia* in regard to body shape and seasonal behavior, it is still a link to the *Rivulus genus* in certain ways.

T: 22-27° C, **L:** up to 7 cm, **A:** 60 cm, **R:** m, b, t, **D:** 4
72-80° F, up to 2³/₄", 24",

Rivulus agilae HOEDEMAN, 1954
Agila Rivulus

Syn.: *Rivulus manaensis.*

Hab.: South America; Guyana, Surinam and French Guiana.

F.I.: 1952 to the Netherlands.

Sex: The ♂♂ are quite colorful. Generally they are reddish brown over a blue-green base and red towards the posterior, intensely so in certain strains. The fins are marbled yellowish and red-brown. The tail fin is usually edged in yellow on the top with an intense red to red-brown inner area that turns yellow ventrally terminating on the bottom with a black edge of variable width. The throat and the belly are cream colored. The ♀♀ show a similar but paler body color and have rounder, more transparent fins.

Soc. B.: Peaceful species; however, the ♂♂ need a certain space where their aggressions are displayed and rivals are expelled. It is not clear whether this is a true territory. However, this aggressive behavior is not always open and directly visible to the observer. Often an animal deteriorates and eventually dies while the superior rival prospers. Hiding places and sufficiently large tanks are necessary.

M: The fish prefer soft to medium-hard water which is slightly acid. Maintenance in a community tank with smaller and not too lively fishes is possible. Flat, wide aquaria are preferred since the fish prefers shallow waters in nature.

Continued on page 678.

Rachovia stellifer

Rivulus agilae

Rivulus amphoreus HUBER, 1979

Syn.: None.

Hab.: South America; Surinam, in the area around Julianatop, a mountain region up to 1000 meters (3280 ft) in height, about 120 km (75 mi) south southwest of Paramaribo.

F.I.: 1978 to the Netherlands.

Sex: The ♂♂ have a bronze to greenish colored body; numerous red-brown spots which flow together are distributed over the body. The back is dark brown and the belly is lighter. The anal fin is the color of the body with small red-brown dots and is lighter at the base; the dorsal and tail fin become solid brown distally and then reddish gold-brown, often with a bright fringe. The ♀♀ are lighter colored than the ♂♂. The dorsal and tail fin also have dots and spots. Anteriorly they are fuller and the caudal peduncle is more slender. At the base of the tail fin is a *Rivulus* spot.

Soc. B.: Ordinarily peaceful, but comparatively a large, strong fish; this has to be considered when choosing potential tankmates.

M: Basically like *R. agilae*. However, the animals like more oxygen in the water, making aeration recommendable. Other water values play a secondary role. Medium hardness and a slightly acid to alkaline pH (6.5-8.0) are recommended. Caring for this fish is possible in a sparsely stocked community tank. A cover glass is absolutely necessary. Regular partial water changes should be performed.

B: In contrast to maintenance and care, breeding this species is not easy; that is probably the reason that is not often found in aquaria. A 15-20 l (4-5 gal) breeding tank as described for *R. agilae* with a continuous set-up is recommended. STENGLEIN achieved good success when he used a wool mop above an airstone as spawning substrate. Eggs are collected and put in a brooding dish for development. The young immediately eat *Artemia salina* nauplii and are slow growing. After about 1 year the fishes are sexually mature.

F: C; hardy live foods of all kinds and also worms.

S: None.

T: 20-26° C, 68-79° F, **L:** 7 cm, 2³/₄", **A:** 60 cm, 24", **R:** t, m, **D:** 3-4

Rivulus brasiliensis (HUMBOLDT & VALENCIENNES, 1821)
Half-Banded Rivulus

Syn.: *Fundulus brasiliensis, Haplochilus brasiliensis, Rivulus dorni.*

Hab.: South America; southeastern Brazil, surroundings of Rio de Janeiro.

F.I.: 1923 as *Rivulus dorni.*

Sex: The ♂♂ have a shining blue-green body. Every scale is edged in brown anteriorly. These edges become wider dorsally so that the fish becomes darker; the back is totally brown; there are 6-8 crossbars posteriorly. The anal fin is green and lighter proximally with a brown pattern posteriorly. Dorsal and caudal fins are green with a brown spot pattern. The spatula shaped tail fin is whitish-blue on top and edged in black on the bottom. The ♀♀ are smaller, rounder anteriorly and have rounded, less colored fins. A *Rivulus* spot is absent.

Soc. B.: The fish are solitary and do not form groups or schools. The ♂♂ seem to have a territory; at least they keep each other at a distance.

M: Like *R. agilae*. The species is somewhat sensitive and not for beginners. This is the reason they are not often found in the hobby although the animals have beautiful colors. A species tank is recommended; it is possible to maintain it with smaller, sedate characins or similar fishes.

Continued on page 678.

Rivulus amphoreus

Rivulus brasiliensis

Continuation of *Rivulus agilae* from page 674:

Like all *Rivulus* species, *R. agilae* prefers to live at the water surface and likes to jump. Therefore, a tightly fitting cover is necessary. The aquarium should have areas of dense vegetation that can serve as hiding places.

B: Breeding this species is not without its problems. For this purpose the fishes need to be placed in a separate breeding aquarium. A spawning web of artificial fibers (brown is best) or peat fibers, hanging into the water from the edge of the aquarium, are used as a spawning site. Some bunches of peat fibers are placed on the bottom to serve as hiding places. The eggs, which are quite large, are regularly collected and placed in a brooding dish with acriflavine to develop. Otherwise, the peat fibers are removed with the eggs, wrung out, stored for 3-4 weeks in a plastic bag, and then new water is added. The young immediately feed on *Artemia salina* nauplii but grow slowly. The species is not very productive.

F: C; live food which should not be too big.

S: Several color strains are known which can look very different and should only be passed on with the correct information on origin.

T: 22-27° C, L: 5 cm, A: 40 cm, R: t, m, D: 3-4
72-81° F, 2", 16",

Continuation of *Rivulus brasiliensis:*

The animals prefer a species tanks with peat mats where they will hide so that only the head sticks out. The fish like to jump and are accomplished at it. A tightly closing cover is extremely important and should be closed immediately, even if only leaving for a very short time.

B: Breeding is extraordinarily difficult, and the species is not very productive. The fish only reaches sexual maturity after about 1 year. The breeding tank should be furnished as described for *R. agilae*, and the use of peat fibers which hang down from the tanks edge (clamp under cover glass) is preferred. The fish like to hide within the peat and spawn in its upper regions. It is removed, examined for the presence of eggs, and stored dry for 3-4 weeks. Occasionally the developmental state can be checked. Fresh water is then added and the fish immediately feed on *Artemia salina* nauplii. Even experienced breeders are happy when a few young hatch after the addition of water.

F: C; all kinds of live foods of corresponding size.

S: *Rivulus brasiliensis* is the first known and described *Rivulus* species; however, for a long time the description could not be matched with any particular fish, although a good drawing is included.

T: 20-24° C, L: 6 cm, A: 50 cm, R: t, m, b, D: 4
68-75° F, 2 1/3", 20",

Rivulus caudomarginatus SEEGERS, 1984

Band-Tail Rivulus

Syn.: *Rivulus ocellatus* (not HENSEL, 1868).

Hab.: South America; southeastern Brazil, surrounding areas of Rio de Janeiro.

F.I.: 1906 by Köhler.

Sex: The ♂♂ have a contrasting light and dark gray pattern; the fins of full-grown ♂♂ have strong yellow-gray and black fringes, especially in the caudal fin (name!). The ♀♀ do not have these fringes on the fins. In young animals which have not colored up (below about 4 cm; 1 2/3" in length), the sexes can barely be distinguished.

Soc. B.: A peaceful and relatively shy species. Only dominant ♂♂ display their colors optimally. Otherwise like *R. brasiliensis*.

M: The animals need large aquaria; they are best kept in a species tank. Hiding places, for example, peat fibers, should be available. The fishes prefer to remain close to be bottom. Only when sufficient cover is available will they venture into higher regions. An aquarium cover is necessary, or the fish will jump out of the tank. Soft to medium-hard and slightly acid water is preferred. The substrate should be dark.

B: Breeding is similar to *R. brasiliensis* but more productive. However, the fish takes a long time to color up. The newly hatched young initially stay just below the water surface and immediately eat *Artemia salina* nauplii.

F: C; all kinds of live foods, as varied as possible. Worms are easily accepted but should not be fed too often.

S: The species does not seem to be very common in nature. It was previously thought to be *Rivulus ocellatus* and was occasionally imported under that name.

T: 20-24° C, L: 6 cm, A: 50 cm, R: t, m, b, D: 4
68-75° F, 2 1/3", 20",

Rivulus cryptocallus SEEGERS & HUBER, 1981

Iridescent Rivulus, Martinique Rivulus

Syn.: None.

Hab.: Central America; Lesser Antilles, Martinique and St. Lucia.

F.I.: 1973 to France.

Sex: The ♂♂ are very variable depending on their origin. The body is blue-green to reddish-brown. The back is reddish-brown, and the belly is lighter. The scales often have reddish dots so that, especially posteriorly, a longitudinal striation is created. Often the fins are the color of the body, but they can also be either totally or only edged in bronze and framed with a narrow dark fringe. The ♀♀ are more brownish with a light belly. The fins have a faint pattern. At the top of the base of the caudal fin, rarely at the bottom, is a *Rivulus* spot (every now and then up to three).

Soc. B.: Like all *Rivulus* species, there is no marked schooling behavior. *Rivulus cryptocallus*, however, can be easily kept in larger numbers, especially when enough hiding places are available.

M: Basically like *R. agilae*, but care of the species is totally unproblematic and feasible in a community tank. No demands are placed on water composition. The fish like to hide in plants, algae bunches or bunches of peat fibers placed below the water surface. This species is an accomplished jumper, aiming at the smallest hole present in the cover.

B: Nonproblematic. The young hatch after 2-3 weeks and can immediately be fed *Artemia salina* nauplii.

F: C; live foods of all kinds and also frozen and flake food.

S: *Rivulus cryptocallus* is especially well suited to provide an introduction to the genus *Rivulus* and offer first experiences in care and reproduction.

T: 22-26° C, 72-79° F, **L:** 8 cm, 3", **A:** 60 cm, 24", **R:** t, m, b, **D:** 2

Rivulus geayi VAILLANT, 1899

Chevron Rivulus

Syn.: *Rivulus strigatus.*

Hab.: South America; coastal areas of Surinam through French Guiana south to the mouth of the Amazon in Brazil.

F.I.: 1910?

Sex: The ♂♂ are significantly redder than the ♀♀ and highly variable depending on origin. Usually the body is blue-green to brownish, becoming brown dorsally. Anteriorly there are horizontal rows of smaller and larger dots; towards the posterior are vertical rows or red crossbands. The anal fin is yellowish to orange; the dorsal fin is the color of the body and is intensely spotted red to brown. The tail fin is a yellow to greenish color with red to brown spots. The lower tail fin has a yellow stripe which can frame the entire fin. A strain with the origin PK 15 from French Guiana is a very beautiful morph with red and blue irregular spots on the body, deviating significantly from the normal pattern. The ♀♀ have a light brown base coloration with irregular dark brown spots; the spotting also extends into the fins which are smaller than those of the ♂.

Soc. B.: As with *R. agilae.*

M: As with *R. agilae*, but this species is more sensitive and requires more warmth. Only keep in a species tank.

B: Very problematic and difficult. Principally like *R. agilae*, but the fish is even less productive and the offspring are predominately ♂. Breeding is obviously often very dependent on luck and chance.

F: C; good live foods of all kinds. If possible, feed mosquito larvae and few worms.

S: One of the most beautiful *Rivulus* species which is closely related to *R. agilae.* The strains imported up to now differ considerably in coloration, depending on natural habitat.

T: 24-28° C, 75-82° F, **L:** 5 cm, 2", **A:** 50 cm, 20", **R:** t, m, b, **D:** 4

Rivulus cryptocallus

Rivulus geayi

Rivulus ocellatus HENSEL, 1868
Marbled Rivulus

Syn.: *Rivulus marmoratus.*

Hab.: From Florida in the north through the Bahamas, Cuba, Grand Cayman, Jamaica, Yucatan, Guadeloupe, Aruba, Curaçao and Bonaire, Venezuela (Maracaibo) south to Brazil (Rio de Janeiro). Only in the narrow coastal areas, and relatively rare and sporadic there.

F.I.: Probably in 1973 by Dr. F. Fröhlish from the USA to Germany.

Sex: No ♀♀ have been found, but rather hermaphrodites and ♂♂ which either immediately become sexually mature as pure ♂♂ (primary ♂♂) or, after they were initially hermaphrodites, they develop into functional true ♂♂ (secondary ♂♂). Hermaphrodites are marbled light and dark gray-brown; the ♂♂ have red-brown (secondary ♂♂) to orange (primary ♂♂) spots. The transformation to secondary ♂♂ can be experimentally influenced to a certain degree.

Soc. B.: Solitary, reclusive fishes which can lie outside the water in a damp atmosphere, e.g., sticking onto the cover glass or vertically on the aquarium pane. Associate only with fishes that are not too active. A species tank is better.

M: Very varied experiences have been made with *R. ocellatus*. Water values can be varied. Offspring could be obtained from either soft and slightly acid or medium-hard (about 16° dGH) and alkaline (pH 7.5) water. According to their origin, the fishes are salt tolerant (euryhaline) or, even to certain degree, salt-loving (halophile). Quite a bit of salt should be added if they cannot be kept successfully in normal water.

B: A hermaphrodite is kept, perhaps with a ♂, in a separate tank; feed it well, also with larger foods like water insects, and offer a spawning site such as wool webbing. Check regularly. The fishes often spawn sporadically; usually only a few eggs are laid over a certain period of time. These are collected and developed in a brooding dish. A trace of acriflavine can be added to the water. The hatched young immediately feed on *Artemia salina* nauplii.

F: C, O; live foods of all sizes as long as they can be mastered.

S: If the described morphs *R. marmoratus* and *R. marmoratus bonairensis* represent autonomous and distinguishable sub-species as *R. ocellatus marmoratus* and *R. ocellatus bonairensis,* or if these names represent synonyms of *R. ocellatus,* still has to be investigated.

T: 18-24° C, 64-75° F, **L:** 5 cm, 2", **A:** 40 cm, 16", **R:** t, m, b, **D:** 3-4

Rivulus ornatus GARMAN, 1895
Ornate Rivulus

Syn.: None.

Hab.: South America; central Amazon basin in Brazil and Peru.

F.I.: ? end of the 60's.

Sex: The ♂♂, depending on native habitat, are quite variable in color. The body has a reddish to greenish tone, turning brown dorsally. Red-brown to red dots are distributed over the body. The unpaired fins are yellow-green to blue-green. The caudal fin and occasionally the anal fin show red-brown to red dots, mainly at their base. The dorsal fin has a red to brown stripe parallel and close to the body. The tail fin is nearly circular. The ♀♀ are not as colorful and more brownish. Anteriorly they are fuller; the caudal peduncle is more slender and the fins are smaller.

Soc. B.: Like *R. agilae.* Explicitly peaceful fishes which hardly pursue even the smallest young of its own species.

Continued on page 684.

Rivulus ocellatus, wild caught, Guadeloupe

Rivulus ornatus

Continuation of *Rivulus ornatus:*

M: Possible in small tanks of even 5 l (1.3 gal) and more. Because of the small size of the fish, a species tank is definitely recommended. The fish are nonproblematic and productive; this is certainly accurate for a strain imported in 1981 from the Padre Isla at Iquitos, Peru. The water should be soft to medium-hard with a neutral pH. The tank can be planted with Java moss, where the fish also like to spawn.

B: Also possible in small tanks. The most advantageous is a continuous set-up where several animals are cared for in a tank well endowed with Java moss. Because the parents do **not** pursue the young, these can be skimmed from the surface with a teaspoon and raised separately. However, one can also collect the eggs which will hatch 2-3 weeks later. The most advantageous is the first method. The young can be left in the breeding tank until they can eat *Artemia salina* nauplii. This occurs soon after hatching because the eggs, and therefore the young, are very large in comparison to the diminutive size of the adults. *Artemia* should also be put in the breeding tank for the parents.

F: C; small live food, corresponding to the small size of the animals. Occasionally crumbled flake food.

S: This could be the smallest known *Rivulus* species.

T: 24-28° C, **L:** 3 cm, **A:** 30 cm, **R:** t, m, b, **D:** 2-3
75-82° F, 1 1/4", 12",

Rivulus punctatus BOULENGER, 1895
Spotted Rivulus

Syn.: None.

Hab.: South America; northern Argentina, Paraguay, Bolivia and Brazil, the drainage areas of the upper Rio Paraguay, Rio Guaporé, Rio Paraná, north to Brasilia and surroundings.

F.I.: ? 1960 to the USA.

Sex: Not always easy to determine. This species also has several different habitat strains. The ♂♂ usually have a yellowish-brown to greenish-brown body which is lighter ventrally. Above the central line, which is sometimes marked by a dark band, the body is darker. Horizontal V-shaped crossbands which are open posteriorly with the tip on the lateral line are, depending on strain, less (western) or more (eastern, especially around Brasilia) distinct. The entire body is covered by red and brown dots which are also found in the fins; these dots are an intense dark brown in the tail fin, forming a marble pattern in western strains and vertical bars in the eastern population. The ♀♀ are similarly colored and often, but not always, have a *Rivulus* spot. They have a rounder belly.

Soc. B.: Like that of *Rivulus agilae*.

M: Similar to *Rivulus agilae*. Maintenance and care are not difficult, and it is also possible in community aquaria sparsely stocked with smaller fish. Nevertheless, a species tank is preferred. The fish like to lie on or between floating plants, even out of the water. Cover glass!

B: Like *Rivulus agilae*. Breeding difficulty is not the same for all strains. The western strain from Argentina, Paraguay and Bolivia obviously breed easier than the eastern forms from the surroundings of Brasilia.

F: C; small live food in accordance to the small size of the fish. Often flake food is additionally taken.

S: The eastern forms of *R. punctatus* were repeatedly confused with the similarly colored *R. zygonectes* because of its striped tail fin. Its stripes, however, are fewer and wider. In addition, a distinct, dark band goes from the mouth, below the body center to the lower caudal peduncle.

T: 22-26° C, **L:** 4 cm, **A:** 40 cm, **R:** t, m, b, **D:** 3
72-79° F, 1 2/3", 16",

Rivulus sp. aff. *holmiae*

Rivulus punctatus

Rivulus roloffi TREWAVAS, 1948

Roloff's Rivulus

Syn.: None.

Hab.: Central America; Haiti, Dominican Republic between Santo Domingo and Puerto Plata.

F.I.: 1938 by E. Roloff.

Sex: The ♂♂ are blue-green on the sides and undersides, turning yellowish towards the belly and brown towards the back. Dark spots may become stronger towards the tail and appear as a band. Behind the pectorals is a metallic blue-green spot. The fins are proximally bronze color and distally translucent; the anal fin has a dark brown to black edge. The ♀♀ are brown, and the band on the sides of the body is more pronounced. The fins are colorless. A *Rivulus* spot is absent.

Soc. B.: Similar to *R. agilae*.

M: Follow recommendations for *R. agilae*. Water values are of secondary importance as long as they are not extreme. A species tank is recommended. Provide floating plants as hiding places for ♀♀.

B: Like with *Rivulus agilae*. The species is not very productive. Breed in a separate tank with Java moss or use a spawning mop as the spawning medium. It is best to collect the eggs and develop them in a brooding dish. The young hatch after 2-3 weeks and are small. They should be fed infusoria. After about half a year, the fish are sexually mature.

F: C; live food of all kinds, especially insects that will float on the water surface, e.g., *Drosophila*; occasionally flake food.

S: None.

T: 20-26° C, **L:** 5 cm, **A:** 50 cm, **R:** t, m, b, **D:** 3-4
68-79° F, 2", 20",

Rivulus santensis KÖHLER, 1906

Santos Rivulus

Syn.: None.

Hab.: South America; southeast Brazil, coastal area from around Rio de Janeiro to north of Florianapolis.

F.I.: 1904 by Hesdörfer as *Rivulus elegans* (not STEINDACHNER, 1880).

Sex: The ♂♂ have a cinnamon colored body which becomes lighter to whitish towards the belly and medium brown towards the back. Posteriorly it changes to green. The unpaired fins are green to bronze colored; the anal fin is proximally a bright whitish color and edged in black. The inside of the tail fin is green to bronze colored and, depending on population, black on the bottom edge and possibly on top. The ♀♀ are light and dark brown as well as green spotted; the belly is whitish. The fins are brown and the tail fin is marbled dark brown. Usually a *Rivulus* spot is present.

Soc. B.: Peaceful species, similar in behavior to *R. agilae*.

M: The species is undemanding in its care. Water values are of secondary significance. Average values are recommended. The tank should be well-planted, and floating plants are especially recommended. The animals enjoy lying between and on them. Do not forget a cover glass. This species also jumps well and accurately.

B: Like with *R. agilae*. The experiences obtained in breeding this species have been varied. Once, over 100 young were obtained in one set-up (method as described for *R. agilae*). Other experienced *Rivulus* keepers had difficulties and occasionally had no success at all. The solution possibly lies in feeding with various live foods. The hatched young are easy to raise, immediately accept *Artemia salina* nauplii and grow quite rapid for a *Rivulus* species.

F: C; live food of all kinds, as varied as possible; the fish also accepts flake food.

S: In an unpublished thesis paper P. de SOUZA SANTOS FILHO determined that there are two populations of *R. santensis*: a northern population group between Rio de Janeiro and Santos that shows black edges on the top and bottom of the tail fin, and a southern population that deviates somewhat and only has a black fringe on the lower edge.

T: 20-26° C, **L:** 5 cm, **A:** 50 cm, **R:** t, m, b, **D:** 3-4
68-79° F, 2", 20",

Rivulus roloffi

Rivulus santensis, ♂ top ♀ bottom

Rivulus tenuis (MEEK, 1904)

Mexico Rivulus

Syn.: *Cynodonichthys tenuis, Rivulus godmani, Rivulus hendrichsi.*

Hab.: Central America: from southern Veracruz through southern Mexico over Belize and Guatemala to Honduras along the Atlantic slope of the Andes.

F.I.: Spring 1909 by Vereinigten Zierfischzüchtereien Conradshöhe, Berlin, Germany.

Sex: The ♂♂ are colored very differently according to habitat. The pictured fish shows an aquarium strain which, according to the design pattern, probably originated from the southern range. The population of the type locality El Hule (today Papaloapam) has a reddish base color with intense red to red-brown dots. The operculum has a bright blue spot. The anal fin is yellow and the dorsal fin is bronze. The inside of the tail fin is reddish followed distally by a dark semi-circular band (black on the bottom) which in the upper fin area borders on a yellow fringe and a broad yellow to red fringe on the bottom. The ♀♀ are simpler and brownish colored; the tail fin is marbled brown with a *Rivulus* spot at its upper base.

Soc. B.: As indicated for *R. agilae*. At a locality by Papaloapam, Oaxaca, Mexico, hundreds of *Rivulus tenuis* were found among the grass in a flooded swamp around a pool. However, it is not a schooling or gregarious species.

M: An undemanding beautiful species. Water values are not important. The locality mentioned above at 10:30 a.m.: air temperature: 30° C (86° F), water temperature: 31° C (88° F), KH and GH immeasurable (too low), pH 6.75, 850 µS. Therefore, even if harder water is tolerated without problems, slightly acid and soft water in a densely planted aquarium with floating plants should be used. The latter provides the fish with a resting area on the water surface. The fish can also be kept in a community tank with not overly large tankmates. Do not forget the cover glass!

B: As with *R. agilae*, but *R. tenuis* is significantly less problematic and more productive. The eggs can be collected or induced to develop "dry" with peat. The young can immediately be fed *Artemia salina*.

F: C; live food of all kinds, preferably insects that float on the water surface, like *Drosophila*. Worms are also liked.

S: The different strains should only be passed on with their proper identification.

T: 22-28° C, **L:** 6 cm, **A:** 50 cm, **R:** t, m, **D:** 2-3
72-82° F, 2 1/3", 20",

Continuation of *Apyhosemion* [*Roloffia*] *geryi* from page 692:

S: According to a decision of the Nomenclature Commission, the name *Roloffia* is invalid and to be replaced by *Callopanchax*. The type species for the genus is *occidentalis*; therefore, the name applies primarily to larger species. For smaller species, the name *Archiaphyosemion* RADDA, 1977 would be available if one considers it as an independent genus; otherwise, *Aphyosemion* would have to be applied. However, here the name *Roloffia* will be maintained for aquaristic reasons. Furthermore, the decision of the Nomenclature Commission has been appealed, but a final decision has not been reached. But since the smaller species do differ markedly from the genus group around the fish described as *Aphyosemion occidentale*, the use of the name *Archiaphyosemion* has to be anticipated.

T: 22-26° C, **L:** 5 cm, **A:** 50 cm, **R:** m, b, **D:** 2-3
72-79° F, 2", 20",

Rivulus tenuis

Rivulus tenuis ♀

Rivulus uroflammeus uroflammeus BUSSING, 1980

Flame-Tail Rivulus

Syn.: None.

Hab.: Central America: southwestern Costa Rica, drainage area of the Rio Grande de Terraba and the Rio Coto at an elevation between 570 and 1100 m (1870 and 3600 ft).

F.I.: 1981 by T. Schulz.

Sex: The ♂♂ are quite colorful, anteriorly reddish brown, ventrally blue-gray. Red dots become more numerous posteriorly and merge so that the caudal peduncle is brick red. The tail fin has a black semicircular band on the inside, followed on the outside by a yellow to blue-white broad fringe. The anal fin is approximately the color of the body and becomes yellowish with red-brown dots distally; the edges are black. The dorsal fin is proximally white-yellow with red-brown spots and distally white-yellow. The ♀♀ are spotted gray-brown on a light brown base. Their fins are marbled brown. A *Rivulus* spot is present, but not always clearly defined.

Soc. B.: As for *R. agilae* and *R. tenuis.*

M: As *R. tenuis.*

B: Parallels *R. agilae* and *R. tenuis.*

F: C; live foods of all kinds, also prefers worms.

S: Besides the nominate form *R. uroflammeus uroflammeus*, the sub-species *R. uroflammeus siegfriedi* has also been described. The latter is not as beautifully red posteriorly; the tail fin is edged in yellow, and the inner black band is missing. Surely the species is closely related to *R. tenuis.*

T: 22-26° C, **L:** 6 cm, **A:** 50 cm, **R:** t, m, b, **D:** 2-3
72-79° F, 2 1/3", 20",

Rivulus xiphidius HUBER, 1979

Blue-Stripe Rivulus

Syn.: None.

Hab.: Northern South America; coastal areas of Surinam and French Guiana.

F.I.: 1976 to France.

Sex: The ♀♀ are smaller than the ♂♂; they lack the blue and orange color and have a dark gray to black longitudinal band instead.

Soc. B.: A solitary, timid fish which lives in seclusion, especially in unaccustomed surroundings (newly arranged aquarium). Only keep with delicate, peaceful fishes, such as small characins, small *Corydoras*, etc., but a species tank is definitely preferable.

M: A dark arrangement with dense vegetation to subdivide the tank. Specially recommended plant: Java moss. Water soft and slightly acid (up to 6° dGH, pH 6-6.5). Frequent water changes. Not too large an aquarium or you won't find the animals again. Difficult and somewhat sensitive fish which requires some experience as well as a lot of attention and serenity.

B: Should be attempted in smaller tanks of 4-5 l (1 gal). Best accomplished in pairs or 1 ♂ and 2 ♀♀. Decoration is not necessary; Java moss or peat fibers hung into the water from the aquarium edge act as spawning substrates and also provide cover for the ♀. The animals are continuous spawners. Either remove the parents after 14 days and skim the hatching young as they appear, or set the fish up only for 1 week using peat fibers as substrate, storing the peat for three weeks, then adding water. Feed the young initially with infusoria and then switch to *Artemia salina* nauplii.

F: Live food of all kinds; caution with worms, the species is sensitive. Glassworms are best.

S: *Rivulus xiphidius* is an exception among *Rivulus* species in its care and breeding because of its sensitivity. In this regard, it is more comparable to members of the *Diapteron* genus.

T: 22-25° C, **L:** 4 cm, **A:** 30-40 cm, **R:** m, b, t, **D:** 4
72-77° F, 1 2/3", 12-16",

Rivulus uroflammeus uroflammeus

Rivulus xiphidius

Aphyosemion etzeli [formely *Roloffia*] BERKENKAMP, 1979
Etzel's Killie

Syn.: *Roloffia etzeli.*

Hab.: West Africa; Sierra Leone, District of Port Loko.

F.I.: 1975 by Dr. V. Etzel and W. Kessel.

Sex: The ♂♂ are more colorful than the ♀♀ and have a greenish base coloration that turns brown towards the dorsal. Over this are a number of red dots which unite posteriorly to form slanted bands. The dorsal and anal fin are spotted red on a greenish base; the dorsal fin has a yellow edge and a red band towards the body. The tail fin has wide yellow fringes on top and bottom followed by a red band and a coarsely marbled green and red central area. There is a semicircular red band along the base of the caudal fin. The ♀♀ are medium brown, dorsally dark brwon. Dark brown, slanted bands can be found posteriorly. The fins are brownish and rounded.

Soc. B.: These are peaceful fishes; only the ♂♂ will become aggressive towards each other. The association with smaller peaceful fishes is possible.

M: A species tank rather than a community tank is preferred. In any case, it should be decorated rather dark (peat bottom) to better display the colors of the fish. Water should be acid (pH 5.5 to 6.5) and soft; higher pH values and harder water are possible but not favorable for breeding. Vegetation should be dense in areas, perhaps with Java moss. Further decoration can be with bogwood roots.

B: In principle, breeding can follow methods used for smaller *Aphyosemion* species.

F: C; live food, flake food is rarely accepted.

S: The species is very closely related to *Roloffia roloffi*, and many authors only consider it a strain thereof. For genus determination, also refer to *Roloffia geryi.*

T: 22-28° C, **L:** 5 cm, **A:** 50 cm, **R:** m, b, **D:** 2-3
72-82° F, 2", 20",

Aphyosemion geryi [formely *Roloffia*] (LAMBERT, 1958)

Syn.: *Aphyosemion guineense geryi, A. roloffi geryi, Roloffia geryi.*

Hab.: West Africa; coastal areas from Gambia to Sierra Leone.

F.I.: One ♀ in 1962 by Roloff from Sierra Leone; 1965 both sexes.

Sex: The ♂♂ vary, depending on their origin. In general, southern populations have stronger colors. The ♂♂ are brown to greenish with a pattern of red-brown to lively dark red dots which unite into a zigzag line along the side; crossbands or a net design are formed posteriorly. The unpaired fins usually have a drawn out yellow fringe (top and bottom on the tail fin). It is not always present on the anal fin. A red band follows, and the inner area of the fins have red spots in a flame design on a yellow-brown to blue-brown background. The ♀♀ are light brown with a dark brown pattern. The fins are mostly free of designs and rounded.

Soc. B.: Parallels *R. etzeli.*

M: This species is easy to care for. Basically like *R. etzeli.*

B: Breeding can be accomplished similar to *R. etzeli.* The northern populations from Gambia should be set up with peat fibers; they have a stronger annual character.

F: C; live food; worms should be avoided if possible.

Continued on page 689.

Aphyosemion [*Roloffia*] *etzeli*

Aphyosemion [*Roloffia*] *geryi*, pair

Aphyosemion guineensis [formely *Roloffia*] (DAGET, 1954)

Guinea Roundfin Killie

Syn.: *Roloffia guineensis.*

Hab.: West Africa; Guinea, Sierra Leone, Burkina Faso, Mali and Ivory Coast.

F.I.: 2 ♀♀ were collected in 1962 by E. Roloff, 1965 both sexes anew from Sierra Leone.

Sex: The ♂♂ are a dark brown with a violet sheen. The ♀♀ have a brown base color that is lighter towards the belly and darker towards the back; without distinct design. The fins are rounded and brownish opaque. Only the dorsal fin has reddish brown dots.

Soc. B.: The fishes are very timid and live secluded, preferably close to the bottom. They are not gregarious but maintain a larger distance around themselves. The ♂♂ can be quite quarrelsome towards each other. Towards other fish, they are very shy.

M: The species is not suitable for a community tank. It requires an aquarium with plenty of cover, e.g., dense plant growth (Java moss), decorative materials such as peat fibers, or boiled beech tree leaves. The water should be clear and oxygen rich; good aeration and frequent water changes are beneficial. Water values: soft to medium-hard (up to 12° dGH), pH slightly acid, about 6.5.

B: Contrary to their appearance, these fish are not marked bottom spawners, but, given the possibility, they will spawn on Java moss, a mop or peat fibers in upper water strata. Breeding is recommended in a separate 10-15 l (2.5-4 gal) spawning set-up using a trio. The ♀♀ have to be provided with hiding places because they are strongly chased by the ♂♂. During courtship, the ♂♂ clearly become darker. The eggs can be collected; their development, depending on temperature, takes 2-3 weeks. The hatched young immediately accept *Artemia salina* nauplii. They are full-grown after about eight months.

F: C; live food, worms are also liked.

S: The species deviates from other members of the genus in many points. It represents a relic form and is the type for the sub-genus *Archiaphyosemion* described by RADDA. Ecologically it also occupies a special position since it can be found higher in the mountains than other Rivulinae.

T: 18-23° C, **L:** 9 cm, **A:** 60 cm, **R:** b, m, **D:** 3
64-73° F, 3 ", 24",

Aphyosemion jeanpoli [formely *Roloffia*] BERKENKAMP & ETZEL, 1979

Syn.: *Roloffia melantereon* (not FOWLER, 1950), *Roloffia jeanpoli.*

Hab.: West Africa; north Liberia.

F.I.: 1976 by A. Guignard and G. Schmitt to France.

Sex: The ♂♂ are blue-green, turning brown dorsally. A more or less distinct longitudinal band made of individual brown spots extends over the body to the base of the tail. The greenish dorsal fin is marbled in brown; the blue-green anal fin has a black fringe. The tail fin is marbled like the dorsal fin and has a white-blue fringe on the top and bottom. The ♀♀ are brownish; the band of spots is also red-brown like that of the ♂♂. The fins are predominantly colorless and rounded.

Soc. B.: Similar to *R. guineensis*. *R. jeanpoli* is also a timid species which should be kept in a species tank.

M: As with *R. guineensis*, but use higher temperatures. Here, too, the aquarium should be densely planted and have rather soft, slightly acid water values.

B: Like *R. guineensis*, this species is also easier to spawn as a plant spawner. The eggs should be collected and hatched in a brooding dish. The young hatch after about two weeks and immediately feed on *Artemia salina* nauplii.

F: C; live food such as *Cyclops*, *Daphnia*, *Tubifex* and all mosquito larvae, occasionally also flake food.

T: 22-28° C, **L:** 5 cm, **A:** 50 cm, **R:** b, m, **D:** 3
72-82° F, 2", 20",

Aphyosemion [*Roloffia*] *guineensis* ♂

Aphyosemion [*Roloffia*] *jeanpoli* ♂

Aphyosemion maeseni [formely *Roloffia*] (POLL, 1941)
Maeseni's Killie

Syn.: *Roloffia maeseni.*

Hab.: West Africa, west Ivory Coast, northwest Liberia and southeast Guinea.

F.I.: November 1971 by E. Roloff from Salayeo, northwest Liberia.

Sex: The ♂♂ are more colorful with a more intense green and a stronger design. The ♀♀ are brown or greenish-brown. Their fins are more rounded. The young are often very difficult to classify.

Soc. B.: Peaceful, rather shy fish that lives a secluded life.

M: As with all *Roloffia* species, soft to medium-hard water (4-12° dGH) is needed. Neutral to rather alkaline water is preferred for *R. maeseni.* Slightly acid water is also possible, but the pH has a proven influence on the willingness to breed and the proportion of sexes in the young. Tank decoration should be dark, only then will the colors show optimally. A species tank is recommended; otherwise, the fish are not sufficiently appreciated. Can be housed with killifishes, such as *Aplocheilichthys normani* or other small *Roloffia* species.

B: Like *R. etzeli*, it can either be bred as bottom or plant spawner. Best with peat fibers like *R. etzeli.* The species is not very productive. The young feed immediately on *Artemia salina* nauplii and do not grow especially fast.

F: C; live food of all kinds; occasionally flake food, but it is not accepted by all animals.

S: The species lives in the same area as the similar sibling species *R. viridis.* See there.

T: 20-24° C, L: 5 cm, A: 50 cm, R: m, b, D: 2-3
68-75° F, 2", 20",

Aphyosemion petersii [formely *Roloffia*] (SAUVAGE, 1882)
Peters' Killie

Syn.: *Haplochilus petersii, Roloffia petersii, Epiplatys petersi,* and others.

Hab.: West Africa; coastal areas of the southeastern Ivory Coast and of southwestern Ghana.

F.I.: Early fall of 1952 by L. Sheljuzhko from the Ivory Coast to Germany.

Sex: ♂♂ have a brownish to olive colored body on which, depending on strain, numerous red, bronze and also blue-green dots can be found. Posteriorly, dark crossbands become apparent. The dorsal fin has a white-blue or yellow fringe distally; the anal fin is either totally white-blue, yellow or approximately the body color with a whitish or yellowish band. The edge is brown. The caudal fin is body colored on the inside; it has yellow band that is narrow on the top and wider on the bottom. The ♀♀ have a paler body, but they are usually colored like ♂♂. The more rounded fins are brown to reddish brown. The colors of the ♂♂'s fin edges are faint or totally absent in ♀♀.

Soc. B.: Like *R. guineensis*; however, it is a lively peaceful fish. Not as shy and reclusive.

M: The aquarium should be set up as for *R. etzeli*: densely planted background, dark, perhaps peat bottom, possibly some boiled beech leaves, soft to medium-hard, slightly acid to neutral water.

B: Like *R. guineensis,* but the species is more warmth loving since it is a coastal fish. It should be set up as an adhesive spawner; more eggs were found in the upper part of the wool mop.

F: C; mainly live foods of all kinds, including floating insects (*Drosophila*) and worms. Rarely flake food.

S: This is the eastern most *Roloffia* species. It is quite isolated in regard to its habitat and some other characteristics.

T: 23-28° C, L: 5 cm, A: 50 cm, R: b, m, t, D: 2-3
73-82° F, 2", 20",

Aphyosemion [*Roloffia*] *maeseni*

Aphyosemion [*Roloffia*] *petersii*

Aphyosemion schmitti [formely *Roloffia*] ROMAND, 1979
Schmitt's Killie

Syn.: None.

Hab.: West Africa; east Liberia.

F.I.: 1977 by Romand and Schmitt to France.

Sex: The ♂♂ are very colorful. The base color is blue-green and turns red-brown towards the back. The body is covered with numerous red dots. The dorsal and anal fins have either a narrow yellow and blue edge or only a blue edge; a a red stripe follows proximally. The interior area of the spatula-shaped tail fin is blue with many small red spots on the fin membrane; above and below is a red stripe followed by a very narrow white stripe and a wide yellow fringe. The ♀♀ are brown with faint red-brown dots. The tail fin is especially rounded, and all fins have red-brown dots.

Soc. B.: Lively, peaceful and somewhat timid fish. Can be housed with similar fishes. The ♂♂ are occasionally somewhat aggressive towards each other.

M: Like *R. etzeli.* Water soft to medium-hard and slightly acid. Values in the wild: 23-24° C(73-75°F), hardness: 1-2° dGH, pH 6-6.5. However, deviating water values are also tolerated. If necessary, a peat bottom and a peat filter can be used to lower the water values. The species jumps well and readily. Do not forget the cover!

B: As with *R. etzeli*, the eggs of this species can either be collected or stored in peat. The eggs are laid on all areas of the mop, although somewhat more frequently on the upper areas. The young immediately feed on *Artemia salina* nauplii.

F: C; varied live foods of all kinds; floating insects and worms are also liked, but the latter should be fed sparingly.

S: The species is closely related to *Roloffia liberiensis.*

T: 22-24° C, **L:** 6 cm, **A:** 60 cm, **R:** b, m, **D:** 2-3
72-75° F, 2 1/3", 24",

Aphyosemion viridis [formely *Roloffia*] LADIGES & ROLOFF, 1973
Green Killie

Syn.: *Aphyosemion viride.*

Hab.: West Africa, southeast Guinea, northwest Liberia.

F.I.: November 1971 by E. Roloff from Salayeo, northwest Liberia.

Sex: The ♂♂ have a uniform blue-gray-greenish body, covered with a faint pattern of small red dots. Contrary to this, the ♀♀ are olive-brown, and their rounded fins are nearly transparent.

Soc. B.: Timid, somewhat sensitive fish that lives secluded.

M: As indicated for *R. maeseni.* A species tank is recommended.

B: Similar to *R. maeseni* but more a bottom spawner.

F: C; all kinds of live foods; dry food is not accepted.

S: The species lives in the same distribution area (sympatrically) as the sibling species, *R. maeseni*, and even occurs in the same place (syntope). However, both seem to have somewhat differing ecological demands. *R. viridis* should be more seasonal than *R. maeseni.*

T: 20-24° C, **L:** 6 cm,. **A:** 50 cm, **R:** b, m, **D:** 3-4
68-75° F, 2 1/3", 20",

Aphyosemion [*Roloffia*] *schmitti* ♂

Aphyosemion [*Roloffia*] *viridis* ♂

Valencia letourneuxi (SAUVAGE, 1880)
Corfu Minnow

Syn.: *Fundulus letourneuxi, Valencia hispanica* (not CUVIER & VALENCIENNES, 1846), *Valencia hispanica letourneuxi.*

Hab.: Southeast Europe; Corfu and opposite coastal mainland areas from southern Albania to the Lauros system in Greece.

F.I.: End of August 1979 by Baun from Corfu to Germany; October 1979 by Labhart from the Greek mainland to Switzerland.

Sex: The ♂♂ are brown, dorsally darker and ventrally becoming lighter to yellowish. The sides have a blue-green metallic sheen with 6-8 brown strips alternating with metallic blue crossbands posteriorly. The fins are light yellowish-brown with dark brown dots. Above the pectoral fins is a more or less pronounced dark gray spot. ♀♀ are pale and light brown; the belly is often silver, and the fins are mostly transparent.

Soc. B.: In nature, the fish is found in loose formations, usually outnumbered by the exotic *Gambusia affinis*. In the aquarium, they are usually loosely associated, peaceful fishes. Can be kept with other fishes.

M: The fish should be kept in large aquaria; a heater is not necessary. An outside aquarium or a small garden pool is even more appropriate. Water values according to LABHART (DKG-JOURNAL, **12** (10): 145-151, 1980) in its natural habitat: 34° dGH, 8° KH, pH 7.7. The furnishing of the aquarium: sandy bottom with dense background and edge vegetation, possibly *Sagittaria* or *Vallisneria* species and *Myriophyllum* as well as *Elodea*.

B: BAUN kept the fish (wild caught) in an outdoor tank of Eternit and, beginning in June, could collect 10-15 eggs daily from fine-leaved water plants and roots of bog plants.

The young hatched after 16-20 days and were very slow growing. It is probable that keeping them outdoors is very advantageous, as has been shown for the related *Valencia hispanica*. The change in temperature over the year (cool during the winter and warm for the summer) may be needed to breed them successfully. Rearing the young is easy since they immediately feed on *Artemia salina* nauplii.

F: C, O; live food of all kinds; possibly also vegetable fare; filamentous algae should also be offered; flake food is readily eaten.

S: The closest relative is *Valencia hispanica* from the east coast of Spain. How it came to this disjunct distribution pattern is still unclear. However, based on newest investigations, it is certain that *V. letourneuxi* and *V. hispanica* represent separate species.

T: 15-24° C, in winter down to 10° C, **L:** 6 cm, **A:** 80 cm, **R:** m, t, b, **D:** 2
59-75° F, in winter down to 50° F, 2⅓", 31",

Xiphophorus helleri, red population from Rio Playa Vicente, Mexico. See page 764.

Jenynsia lineata (JENYNS, 1842)
Broken-Stripe Livebearer

Syn.: *Lebias lineata, Lebias multidentata, Poecilia punctata, Cyprinodon lineatus, Cyprinodon multidentatus, Fitzroyia multidentatus, Xiphophorus heckeli.*

Hab.: Coastal Atlantic waters of south-eastern Brazil and northern Argentina, South America.

F.I.: 1905 by Hans Stüve, Hamburg, Germany.

Sex: ♂ is smaller, thinner and has a gonopodium. ♀ is fuller through the ventral area.

Soc. B.: A pugnacious and quarrelsome species that is not suitable for the community aquarium. Cannibalistic.

M: The species is very susceptible to fish diseases, especially fish tuberculosis. Meticulous cleanliness of the tank and the breeders are essential. The addition of table salt, 1-2 heaping teaspoons (5-10 g) per 10 l (2.5 gal) of water, has proven beneficial. Oxygen needy. In summer, the species may be kept in a garden pond because it tolerates temperatures to 12° C (54° F).

B: A well cared for ♀ can produce 10-40, 10 mm (1/3") long young every 6 weeks. After fertilization, the ♀ should be placed alone in a densely planted tank. Remove the ♀ after spawning because she pursues the young intensively.

F: O; flake food, algae, freeze-dried and frozen live foods. Lots of live food.

S: The genital opening of the ♀ is either to the right or left of the center of the body. During fertilization, the gonopodium of the ♂ can only be bent either to the right or the left. When making pairs, it has to be considered that only right-sided ♂♂ are combined with left-sided ♀♀ or vice versa.

T: 18-23° C, L: ♂ 4 cm, ♀ 10 cm, A: 100 cm, R: m, D: 3
72-79° F, ♂ 1 2/3", ♀ 4", 39",

Ameca splendens MILLER & FITZSIMONS, 1971
Butterfly Goodeid

Syn.: None.

Hab.: Rio Ameca, Rio Teuchitlán, Jalisco, Mexico, Central America.

F.I.: About 1975 by H. Entlinger (through the USA).

Sex: Dorsal fin of the ♂ is larger; the anal fin forms an andropodium. ♀ is paler in coloration and lacks shining scales; instead it has spot and black band designs. The tail fin of the ♂ has a black/yellow edge.

Soc. B.: Peaceful towards all other fish. Strong rivalry and momentary territoriality may be exhibited among ♂♂. Its natural habitat is shared with many other toothcarps: *Chapalichthys, Goodea, Skiffia, Zoogone-ticus, Xenotoca.*

M: Provide a dark gravel bottom and alternate larger rocks with dense vegetation. Needs a lot of light (algae growth!), good filtration with strong water turn over. pH 6.5-7.5; dGH to about 18°, better is 5-10°.

B: Breeding is not especially difficult. The gestation period is 55-60 days. 5-30 young are born which are already about 2 cm (∫") long. The fish are born with a 6 mm (") long "umbilical cord". It falls off within 24-36 hr. Rear with TetraMin Baby Food, *Artemia*, algae.

F: H, O; vegetable fare, algae, vegetable flakes (Tetra Conditioning Food). Live food and frozen plant and animal fare are readily taken. Provide a lot of variation.

S: Like all goodeids, this species needs to be packed singly when transported for an extended amount of time; otherwise, it can lead to injuries or death, even if dark bags or containers are used.

T: 26-32° C, **L:** ♂ 6-8 cm, ♀ 7-12 cm, **A:** 80 cm, **R:** b, m, **D:** 1
79-90° F, ♂ 2 1/3-3 1/3", ♀ 2 3/4-4 3/4" 31",

Chapalichthys encaustus (JORDAN & SNYDER, 1900)
Side-Spot Goodeid

Syn.: *Characodon encaustus.*

Hab.: Lake Chapala and Rio Grande de Santiago, Jalisco, Mexico.

F.I.: 1914 (one specimen); 1981 by Ivan Dibble, England.

Sex: ♀ has a pregnancy spot, less colored than the ♂.

Soc. B.: A rough species, fish up to half its length can be collectively attacked and eaten. They are peaceful among themselves but will pursue young.

M: Planted tank with dense floating plant cover, weak filtration with a slight current. Medium water values: pH 7.0-7.8; 10-20° dGH.

B: Not very fertile. Only about 10 young of about 1.5 cm (2/3") length are born; the ♀ never looks pregnant. Temp. 25-28° C (77-82° F). Use a well-planted breeding tank of 50-60 cm (20"-24") length!

F: C, O; flake food, tablet food, frozen food, freeze-dried natural foods. Once to twice a week, live food.

S: Fins are generally transparent; however, they may sometimes be yellow.

T: 20-28° C, **L:** ♂ 6 cm, ♀ 8 cm, **A:** 70 cm, **R:** m, t, **D:** 2
79-82° F, ♂ 2 1/3", ♀ 3 1/3", 28",

Laguna de Cuitzeo, Michoacan, Mexico.
Habitat of goodeids and *Chirostoma* species.
The shallow lake is milky opaque and full of grass mats in the shore areas. In these waters, *Chapalichthys encaustus* occur in the millions. Goodeids are sold dry in the local markets.

Characodon lateralis GÜNTHER, 1866
Rainbow Goodeid

Syn.: None.

Hab.: Central America; Ojo de Agua de San Juan, Durango; Los Berros, Durango, Mexico. Headwaters of smaller rivers.

F.I.: By Ivan Dibble, England.

Sex: ♂ is more beautifully colored, smaller, and has longer ventral fins.

Soc. B.: Peaceful species; suitable for combining with smaller fishes.

M: Requires a tank with algae, plenty of light, strong filtration, frequent water changes, dark substrate and planted zones with fine-leaved species (*Ceratophyllum*, *Elodea*, *Vallisneria*). A section of the aquarium should offer protection with floating plants. Water should be soft to moderately hard: 2-10° dGH, pH 6.8-7.3. The species gets sick easily, particularly with fish tuberculosis. Therefore, keep everything meticulously clean.

B: Breeding is not very productive. The ♀♀ have a gestation period of about 55 days and give birth to 5-20, 1 cm (1/3") long young. Usually five times more ♂♂ than ♀♀ are born. The young become sexually mature at an age of about 5 months. Rear with algae and *Artemia* in a densely planted breeding tank.

F: H, O; algae and live foods such as mosquito larvae and *Artemia*. Feed a varied diet! Vegetable flakes are readily taken.

S: A species at the verge of extinction whose propagation in an aquarium would be worthwhile.

T: 18-27° C, **L:** ♂ 3.5 cm, ♀ 5 cm, **A:** 60 cm, **R:** b, m, **D:** 3
64-81° F, ♂ 1 1/3", ♀ 2", 24",

Girardinichthys multiradiatus (MEEK, 1904)

Syn.: *Characodon multiradiatus*.

Hab.: Upper course of the Rio Lerma, Mexico, Central America.

F.I.: 1978 by Dr. Radda, Vienna, Austria.

Sex: ♀ has a fuller belly; ♂ has an andropodium that is only faintly recognizable.

Soc. B.: Too little is known about suitable tankmates for the species. According to other goodeids, a peaceful temperament can be assumed.

M: If kept too warm, it becomes very sensitive towards ectoparasites. Well-filtered, clear, cool water is a prerequisite for the successful care of the species. pH 6.0-7.5; hardness up to 15° dGH. A well-planted species tank is recommended.

B: Gestation time of the ♀♀ is about 55 days; one ♀ births 10-30 young of 1 cm (1/3") length. The young are barely noticed by the adults.

F: C; live food, specially mosquito larvae. Crustaceans (*Gammarus*), flake and frozen food.

S: Almost a cold water fish! During the summer, the species can be kept in a garden pond. The animals' design can be quite variable.

T: 12-20° C, **L:** ♂ 3.5 cm, ♀ 5 cm, **A:** 50 cm, **R:** m, **D:** 3
54-68° F, ♂ 1 1/3", ♀ 2, 20",

Characodon lateralis ♂

Girardinichthys multiradiatus

Ilyodon lennoni MEYER & FOERSTER, 1983
Lennon's Goodeid

Syn.: None.

Hab.: Arroyo Chacamero Altamirano, Mexico, Central America.

F.I.: 1981 by Manfred Meyer, Bad Nauheim, Germany.

Sex: ♂ is more intensely colored and recognized by its divided anal fin (andropodium).

Soc. B.: A peaceful species which should be kept in a species tank to assure its propagation.

M: The fish's natural habitat has the following characteristics: pH 8; hardness 15° dGH, 10° KH. Shallow, gravely or pebbly river segments which almost dry up during the dry season, alternating with deeper washed out gorges. In the remaining pools, large quantities of filamentous algae form during the dry season; seemingly the only nourishment of the fish during that time.

B: Breeding is accomplished in aquaria of 100 l (26 gal) or more. The ♀♀ give birth about every 2 months to between 15 and 40, 1 cm (1/3") long young. Rear with an algae mat, plankton, TetraMin Baby Food or Liquifry Green. After 4-5 months, the young are sexually mature.

F: O, H; algae (in nature predominantly filamentous algae), vegetable fare (Tetra Conditioning Food or similar), but also animal matter: flake food (TetraMin), frozen foods.

S: This species was named after the murdered ex-"Beatle", John Lennon. It is somewhat unusual that an animal species is described scientifically in such a way, but the original describer, Mr. Meyer, wanted to honor the peace-loving and peace-proclaiming musician. The species is threatened by extinction.

T: 24-30° C, L: ♂ 6.5 cm, ♀ 8 cm, A: 80 cm, R: m, b, D: 2-3
75-86° F, ♂ 2 2/3", ♀ 3", 31",

Ilyodon whitei (MEEK, 1904)
Balsas Goodeid

Syn.: *Goodea whitei, Balsadichthys whitei.*

Hab.: Tributaries of the Rio Balsas; Rio Cuautla, (Yautepec), Mexico, Central America.

F.I.: 1979 by the gentlemen Hinz, Weil and Daul to Germany.

Sex: The ♂♂ are significantly more colorful than the ♀♀. In addition, they are recognizable by their copulation organ, the andropodium.

Soc. B.: A peaceful species with all the good qualities for a "normal" community aquarium. Its rarity, however, obliges the hobbyist to treat the species with special attention. Therefore, use a species tank.

M: Like *I. lennoni.*

B: Similar to *I. lennoni.*

F: O; but predominantly algae and live foods in nature. Algae only serve as substitute food. In an aquarium: flake food of all kinds and frozen foods.

S: It is a shame that this fish either does not or only rarely appears in the trade. Persons interested in livebearers turn to the Gesellschaft der Lebendgebärenden Zahnkarpfen (Germany) or to the ALA (American Livebearer Association).

T: 20-26° C, L: ♂ 6 cm, ♀ 7 cm, A: 70 cm, R: m, D: 2
68-79° F, ♂ 2 1/3", ♀ 2", 28",

Ilyodon lennoni ♂

Ilyodon whitei ♂

Xenoophorus captivus (HUBBS, 1924)
Green Goodeid

Syn.: *Goodea atripinnis* (not JORDAN, 1880), *Goodea captiva, Xenoophorus erro, Xenoophorus exsul.*

Hab.: Central America; Mexico, see **S.**

F.I.: After 1970 by G. Entlinger, Hamburg, Germany.

Sex: ♂ has larger dorsal and anal fins, and the rows of scales are a brighter blue than those of the ♀.

Soc. B.: Peaceful species which does not bother young. Because of the importance of reproduction, a species tank is recommended, although the fishes are suitable to combine with other fishes.

M: Little demanding species. Fresh water every 8-14 days (1/3 of the tank): the addition of a water conditioner, e.g., AquaSafe, is recommended. Water: pH 7.0-7.8; hardness 10-25° dGH. Dark substrate. Well-planted tank. Do not place the tank in too much light.

B: 10-30 young are born approximately every 55 days. They are 18 mm (3/4") long. Through inbreeding, the animals have become smaller and less fertile. Carefully choosing large animals and crossing with foreign strains are important for the perpetuation of the species. Rear in an algae tank with *Artemia*, TetraMin Baby Food, Liquifry. Finely ground Tetra Conditioning Food can be fed from the 3rd week.

S: On the lower animal (♂), the typical fertilization organ (andropodium) of goodeids can clearly be recognized as a divided anal fin. The species is on the verge of extinction in nature! Three types are differentiated: type *captivus*: headwaters of the Rio Panuco, at Jesus Maria, San Luis Potosi. Type *erro*: Rio Santa Maria del Rio, San Luis Potosi. Type *exsul*: Aqua des Medio, between Venado and Montezuma.

T: 18-26° C, **L**: ♂ 5 cm, ♀ 6 cm, **A**: 60 cm, **R**: all, **D**: 2
64-79° F, ♂ 2", ♀ 2 1/3, 24",

Xenotaenia resolanae TURNER, 1946
Resolana Goodeid

Syn.: None.

Hab.: Central America; Rio Resolana, western Autlan, Mexico. In small tributaries with dense algae growth.

F.I.: 1981 by Ivan Dibble, England.

Sex: ♂ has an andropodium. A full-grown dominant ♂ is more intense yellow than ♀♀ and smaller ♂♂.

Soc. B.: According to MILLER (1975), the species occurs with *P. chica, Poeciliopsis turneri* and *Ilyodon xantusi.* The species should not be combined with equal sized fish; otherwise, it will engage in quarrels (harmless). Small fishes are ignored.

M: As for *Ilyodon lennoni* (page 708). Well-planted tank of *Ceratophyllum* (hornwort), which grows exuberantly in the natural habitat.

B: Providing algae as food is very important for the breeding set-up and rearing. Every 2 months, 10-30 young of 12 mm (") length are born and reach sexual maturity by the 4th month.

F: H; algae, plant fare, small live foods (*Cyclops*).

S: None.

T: 22-25° C, **L**: ♂ 4 cm, ♀ 5 cm, **A**: 60 cm, **R**: m, **D**: 2
72-77° F, ♂ 1 2/3", ♀ 2, 24",

Xenoophorus captivus ♂ bottom

Xenotaenia resolanae

Xenotoca eiseni (RUTTER, 1896)

Red-Tailed Goodeid

Syn.: *Characodon eiseni, Xenotoca variata* (not BEAN, 1887).

Hab.: Rio San Leonel, Rio Tamazula, Rio Grande de Santiago; Mexico, Central America. In clear mountain streams as well as in polluted roadsides ditches.

F.I.: About 1967 by Kurt Jacobs, Munich, Germany.

Sex: ♂ is clearly more colorful; caudal peduncle is orange, posterior body steel blue. ♀ is stouter with a full belly and a plain yellow/gray/green coloration.

Soc. B.: This species occasionally nibbles on the fins of other fishes. I have not had this experience with several generations. Furthermore, these animals are one of my least demanding, peaceful tank inhabitants. I keep them together with *Epalzeorhynchus siamensis*, cichlids, large nocturnal and day-active catfishes, *Corydoras* and a puffer in a 500 l (130 gal) tank which is densely planted with only giant *Vallisneria*. The catfishes either dug up or covered all other plants. Water: pH 7.5-8.0; hardness 18-25° dGH. Strong filtration (Eheim large canister). The filter output discharges over the middle brace of the tank to enrich with oxygen. The tank is not covered and is illuminated with 3 Dupla mercury vapor lamps of 125 watts.

B: Either use a large tank with dense floating plant cover, allowing some young to grow, or a breeding tank with a breeding box. The ♀♀ give birth about every 60 days to 10-50 young of about 15 mm (2/3") length.

F: O; algae, flake food, any small live food. Frozen foods of all kinds.

S: A species which can be kept in a small garden pond in the summer. At least a partial algae cover should remain in the pond. Tiny insect larvae inhabit these algae, providing valuable nourishment. With suitable temperatures (e.g., summer of 1983, Germany) several hundred young can be raised from 1 pair. The animals live about 5 years and take 2 years to become sexually mature.

T: 15-32° C, **L:** ♂ 6 cm, ♀ 7 cm, **A:** 100 cm, **R:** b, m, **D:** 1-2
59-90° F, ♂ 2 1/3", ♀ 2 3/4, 39",

Xenotoca variata (BEAN, 1887)

Syn.: *Characodon variatus, C. ferrugineus.*

Hab.: Rio Santa Maria, Rio Grande de Santiago, tributaries of the Rio de la Laja, Rio Lerma basin; Mexico, Central America.

F.I.: By G. Entlinger, Hamburg, Germany, through the American Livebearers Association (ALA).

Sex: The dark band along the lateral line is more pronounced in ♀♀; it fades dorsally and ventrally in the ♂. Caudal fin of the ♂ is dark with a yellow fringe; the ♀'s tail is colorless to slightly yellow.

Soc. B.: Best with other livebearers and catfishes which can exploit the vegetable feces-remains. Peaceful species.

M: All the natural habitats are either grown over or full of algae. If sufficient plant components are not fed, even larger plant shoots are eaten. Therefore, only use very tough plants such as Java fern and Java moss in a community tank. Water quality is not of great importance: pH 6.5-7.6; hardness: 5-25° dGH. Strong filtration because of the copious appetite. Strong illumination. With the exception of the front pane, algae growth is desired on all panes.

B: About 15 mm (2/3") long young (20-40) are born every 2 months.

F: H; algae, plant flake food, blanched spinach and lettuce, mashed frozen peas, chickweed. TabiMin tablet food. But also live food, e.g., *Daphnia.*

S: The species is very variable in coloration, which is referred to in the Latin name.

T: 20-27° C, **L:** ♂ 6 cm, ♀ 7 cm, **A:** 80 cm, **R:** m, t, **D:** 2-3
68-81° F, ♂ 2 1/3", ♀ 2 3/4, 31",

Xenotoca eiseni ♂

Xenotoca variata, ♂ top, ♀ bottom

Zoogoneticus quitzeoensis (BEAN, 1898)

Gold-Edged Goodeid

Syn.: *Platypoecilus zuitzeoensis.*

Hab.: Rio Grande de Santiago, Jalisco; Lago de Cuitzeo, Michoacan, Mexico, Central America.

F.I.: 1981 by Ivan Dibble to England, 1982 from there to Germany.

Sex: The ♂ has a golden/orange fringe on the dorsal and anal fins.

Soc. B.: The species is very peaceful and quite suitable to associate with small fishes when their special requirements are met.

M: The animals must always be kept warm; otherwise, they become ill, especially with fish tuberculosis. Provide frequent water changes (every 14 days) with the addition of AquaSafe. pH 6.5-7.2; hardness: 5-15° dGH. Densely plant in the background and leave a long swimming space in the front. In nature, the fish is found with *Skiffia bilineata* and *Goodea atripinnis.*

B: After 55 days, usually not more than 15 young of 10 mm (1/3") length are born. Rear under meticulously clean conditions with the smallest live foods: infusoria, later *Artemia* which are vitamin enriched through nutrition. The young are sexually mature after 4-5 months as long as they have been feed copiously.

F: C, O; predominately small live foods, but also flake food like FD-Menu and Tetra Conditioning Food for variety.

S: None.

Continuation of *Alfaro cultratus*:

F: C; live foods of all kinds, FD mosquito larvae, flake food.

S: The ventral side of this species has a knife-like keel (name!). This keel is formed by two closely stacked rows of scales at the posterior end of the body.

T: 25-28° C, L: ♂ 3.5 cm, ♀ 4.5 cm, A: 80 cm, R: m, t, D: 3
77-82° F, ♂ 1 1/3", ♀ 1 3/4, 31",

Alfaro cultratus (REGAN, 1908)
Knife-Edged Livebearer

Syn.: *Petalosoma cultratum, Petalurichthys cultratus, Alfaro acutiventralis, Petalosoma amazonum, Petalurichthys amazonum, Alfaro amazonum.*

Hab.: Central America; from Nicaragua through Costa Rica to west Panama, in clear creeks and streams of the Atlantic drainage.

F.I.: 1910 by Karl Zeller, Magdeburg, Germany.

Sex: ♂ has a gonopodium and elongated ventral fins which serve to stimulate the head region of the ♀ during pairing rituals.

Soc. B.: The species is sometimes skittish. Contrary to other authors, the opinion here is that the species is quite suitable for some community tanks with *Priapichthys, Phallichthys amates, Rivulus,* and other not too delicate, soft water species.

M: Shallow, planted tanks with a lot of swimming space in the lower and mid areas of the tank. According to its natural habitat of fast-flowing waters, the tank should have good filtration with a good turnover (current). pH values of 6.5-7.3 are tolerated the best. The water should be soft (maximum hardness 8° dGH). Water exchanges every 2-3 weeks (1/3) are recommended because the species is sensitive to bacterial attack. Perhaps Rivanol (see Vol. 1) or General Tonic by Tetra should be added.

B: Gestation lasts about 24 days. The young are especially sensitive to bacterial attack. Ten to thirty 8 mm (5/16") long young are born every time. These must be fed small live food (*Artemia*). At about 6 months of age, the animals become sexually mature.

Continued on the left page.

T: 24-28° C, L: ♂ 6 cm, ♀ 8 cm, A: 70 cm, R: m, b, D: 2-3
75-82° F, ♂ 2 1/3", ♀ 3, 28",

Alfaro huberi (FOWLER, 1923)

Syn.: *Priapichthys huberi, Furcipenis huberi.*

Hab.: Central America; southern Guatemala, Honduras and Nicaragua, on the Atlantic side.

F.I.: 1977 by E. Schlosser, Austria. Prior to this, some animals came from the USA (?).

Sex: ♂ with gonopodium. Coloration of both sexes is equal.

Soc. B.: Not a much kept aquarium fish as of yet. Should be like *Alfaro cultratus.*

M: The following values were collected in its natural habitat (3-6 m wide river): 20-80 cm (8"-31") deep, crystal clear water, pH 8.0, 5° dGH, conductivity 180 µS. In aquaria, *Vallisneria*, open swimming space, lots of light, good water turnover and frequent partial water changes are recommended. Use AquaSafe and General Tonic. The latter at the dosage.

B: Juveniles are even more sensitive than *A. cultratus.* This species has yet to be successfully raised. Meticulous cleanliness of the rearing tank is recommended.

F: C; small live foods.

S: The knife-like keel scales on the posterior underside of the body are either not, or not on all animals of this species, as pronounced as in the previous species.

T: 26-29° C, L: ♂ 5 cm, ♀ 7 cm, A: 70 cm, R: b, t, D: 4
79-84° F, ♂ 2", ♀ 2¾", 28",

Brachyrhaphis episcopi (STEINDACHNER, 1878)
Bishop

Syn.: *Gambusia episcopi, Priapichthys episcopi, Gambusia latipunctata.*

Hab.: Central America; canal zone of Panama by Obispo, central Panama on both sides of the ocean in quiet water areas.

F.I.: 1911 by Arthur Rachow, Hamburg, Germany.

Sex: The ♂ is more colorful and has a gonopodium.

Soc. B.: A peaceful fish, but not for the community tank. This timid species is easily oppressed there and doesn't get its rights. Put 3-5 pairs in a species tank or associate with very docile species.

M: Following the conditions in the wild, pH 8.0, hardness 4° dGH, conductivity 225 µS. Maintenance should not be very difficult. Nevertheless, it is rare to either successfully keep the species alive for a prolonged period of time or to breed it. Sandy substrate, mulm and good plant growth contribute to its well-being. Caution with live food because diseases are easily brought in.

B: Not very productive. The parents rarely pursue the young. Well-planted, quietly placed, larger breeding tanks of at least 100 l (26 gal) volume are recommended. After about 28 days of gestation, 10-20 young are born. Raising with small aufwuchs organisms is not easy. *Artemia* is only a makeshift feed. Try it in the summer with algae covered stones from a garden pond. Juveniles are susceptible to intestinal diseases and bacteria. The most meticulous cleanliness!

F: C; black mosquito larvae for breeding; otherwise, other small live and frozen foods, occasionally flake food.

S: One of the most beautiful livebearers.

T: 25-30° C, L: ♂ 3.5 cm, ♀ 5 cm, A: 80 cm, R: m, t, D: 3-4
77-86° F, ♂ 1⅓", ♀ 2, 31",

Alfaro huberi

Brachyrhaphis episcopi, ♂ bottom ♀ top

Brachyrhaphis hartwegi ROSEN & BAILEY, 1963

Syn.: None.

Hab.: Southern Guatemala (Pacific side at Retalhuleu), Pacific tributaries in Mexico (Rio Chiapas), Central America.

F.I.: 1977 by E. Schlosser, Austria.

Sex: See photo.

Soc. B.: A pronounced cannibal. If possible, associate only with conspecifics.

M: Well-planted tanks with hiding places of stone, strong filtration and frequent additions of fresh water are needed to keep it healthy. pH 7-7.5, hardness up to 5° dGH, conductivity to about 100 µS.

B: Difficult because of the procurement of feed. Only animals fed young fishes produced surviving fry. After 28 days of gestation, one ♀ gives birth to 10-20 young. A small breeding tank of 25 l (6.5 gal) is sufficient. Use a good spawning box!

F: C; live food, specially mosquito larvae and live young fish. Offer variation with frozen foods, flake and FD tablet foods.

S: None.

T: 25-28° C, **L:** ♂ 2.5 cm, ♀ 5 cm, **A:** 60 cm, **R:** **D:** 3-4
77-82° F, ♂ 1", ♀ 2", 24",

Brachyrhaphis rhabdophora (REGAN, 1908)
Regan's Bishop

Syn.: *Gambusia rhabdophora, Priapichthys olomina, Brachyrhaphis olomina, Panamichthys tristani, Plectrophallus tristani.*

Hab.: Atlantic and Pacific rivers in Costa Rica, Central America.

F.I.: 1975 from England.

Sex: ♂ has a gonopodium and is elongated; ♀ is stout with a bullish appearance.

Soc. B.: Should be maintained in a species tank because the species is aggressive towards smaller fishes. In contrast, it is often dominated by larger fishes. Keep in pairs or in a group of few ♀♀ and several ♂♂.

M: The water conditions in the wild are: creeks 3-6 m (3-6.5 yd) wide and approximately 30 cm (12") deep; pebbles. pH around 8.0, hardness to 8.5° dGH.

B: Young ♀♀ at an age of 4-5 months are placed together with smaller ♂♂. Older, larger ♀♀ are very aggressive towards the ♂♂ and cannibalistic towards the young. Breeding boxes are not accepted; undeveloped eggs and young are aborted. Dense plants in the breeding tank bring the best chance for success. Live food is a necessity for a successful breeding set-up. If possible, feed young fish or black mosquito larvae. Gestation lasts about 28 days. The species produces 10-30 young of about 7 mm (") length. Raise with the smallest live food (*Artemia*) and algae aufwuchs.

F: C, O; live and flake foods of all kinds.

S: The species has elongated strains in various regions. The populations of the Rio Javilla in Canas are not elongated.

T: 25-28° C, **L:** ♂ 4 cm, ♀ 6 cm, **A:** 60 cm, **R:** b, t, **D:** 2
77-82° F, ♂ 1²/₃", ♀ 2¹/₃, 24",

Brachyrhaphis hartwegi

Brachyrhaphis rhabdophora ♂

Carlhubbsia kidderi (HUBBS, 1936)
Straw Widow

Syn.: *Allophallus kidderi, Aulophallus kidderi.*

Hab.: Rio Champotén, Mexico; Rio San Pedro de Mártir, El Petén; Rio de la Pasión and Alta Vera Paz, Guatemala, Central America.

F.I.: 1977 by E. Schlosser, Austria.

Sex: The ♂ has a long gonopodium. No difference in coloration.

Soc. B.: A peaceful species which can also be kept in a community tank. Natural companion fishes are other livebears, characins and cichlids.

M: In nature, the species occurs in areas void of aquatic plants as well as in well-planted shore areas. The animals tolerate harder water up to 20° dGH quite well; pH 7.0-7.8. Conductivity (water in nature) about 500 µS. Good filtration, subdued light and regular water exchanges are desirable conditions for successful care.

B: Wild imports were initially easy to breed. After the third generation, however, the offspring died off. On average, every 24 days 15-60 young are born. ♀♀ are capable of breeding from the 4th month on. Large, quiet, well-planted tanks and frequent offerings of live food are needed for reproduction.

F: C; small live foods, occasionally flake and frozen foods.

S: On the sides of the body are 6-12 darker vertical stripes. The back of the dorsal fin has a dark spot which, according to SCHLOSSER, is framed in yellow in a population collected in Guatemala.

T: 27-30° C, **L:** ♂ about 4 cm, ♀ about 5 cm, **A:** 60 cm, **R:** m, **D:** 3
81-86° F, ♂ about 1 2/3", ♀ about 2", 28",

Cnesterodon carnegiei HASEMAN, 1911
Carnegie's Millionsfish

Syn.: *Cnesterodon decemmaculatus* (not JENYNS, 1843).

Hab.: South America, Rio Iguassú, Serrinba Paraná, Brazil; Uruguay, Argentina in smaller quiet creeks, ditches and lagoons.

F.I.: 1899 by Paul Matte, Berlin, Germany (as *C. decemmaculatus*).

Sex: See photo: ♂ is smaller and has a gonopodium.

Soc. B.: Very peaceful species which doesn't even pursue its own young.

M: An undemanding species which can be kept in the smallest containers (about 2 l; 2 qt). Sufficient light for algae growth and moderate filtering should still be provided. pH 6.5-8.0; hardness 5-25° dGH.

B: A small, algae covered breeding tank with dense vegetation should be available. Only 24 days of gestation; 5-15 young of about 2.5 mm (1/8") length are born. Raise with micro foods.

F: O; small flake foods of all kinds, e.g., Tetra FD-Menu; algae, small live food (*Artemia*).

S: The species is one of the few livebearers that occur south of the Amazon. It and *Heterandria formosa* are some of the smallest fish species. The species can be kept in a small garden pond in the summer.

T: 18-26° C, **L:** ♂ 2 cm, ♀ 3.5 cm, **A:** 40 cm, **R:** m, t, **D:** 1-2
64-79° F, ♂ 3/4", ♀ 1 1/3", 16",

Carlhubbsia kidderi

Cnesterodon carnegiei

Flexipenis vittatus HUBBS, 1926
One-Band Mosquitofish

Syn.: *Gambusia vittata.*

Hab.: Central America, Mexico; Rio Panuco basin from Ciudad to Veracruz.

F.I.: 1979 by Dr. A. Radda, Austria.

Sex: The ♂ is more colorful and clearly recognized by the gonopodium. The ♀ is larger and has a dark pregnancy spot.

Soc. B.: Peaceful gregarious fish which can be readily associated with other livebearers or characins, small cichlids and others. In nature, the species lives predominately with *Gambusia atrora, Poecilia mexicana, Xiphophorus variatus, X. montezumae* and *X. pygmaeus.*

M: The species prefers clean flowing water. Therefore, good filtration with regularly changed filter material is recommended. The species does not place any demands on vegetation. Ludwigia are found in its natural habitat. Water: pH 6.5-7.8; hardness to 20° dGH.

B: Gestation in the ♀♀ lasts about 28 days. About 15-30 young, which already have a length of 10 mm (1/3"), are born. The breeders only pursue the young if they have not been fed sufficiently. Rear with *Artemia* and finely sieved flake food 6-8 times daily.

F: C, O; small flake food (Tetra Menu and FD-Menu), *Artemia*, vegetable fare for variation (Tetra Conditioning Food, etc.).

S: The species is very similar to *Gambusia atrora.*

T: 24-28° C, **L:** ♂ 4.5 cm, ♀ 6 cm (mostly smaller), **A:** 50 cm, **R:** all, **D:** 2
75-82° F, ♂ 1 3/4", ♀ 2 1/3" (mostly smaller) 20",

Gambusia affinis (BAIRD & GIRARD, 1853)
Mosquitofish

Syn.: *Heterandria affinis, H. patruelis, Gambusia speciosa, G. patruelis, G. humilis, G. gracilis, Zygonectes inurus, Z. patruelis, Z. speciosa, Z. brachypterus, Z. gracilis.*

Hab.: Rio Medina and San Antonio River, Texas, USA.

F.I.: Around 1900; not exactly determinable because has often been confused with *G. holbrooki.*

Sex: ♂ is smaller and has a gonopodium; ♀ has a pregnancy spot.

Soc. B.: Gregarious fish which can kept with conspecifics or in a community tank. Cannibalistic towards young.

M: An undemanding fish that can be adapt to almost all water conditions. pH 6.0-8.5; dGH to 35°. Dense planting. Good filtration.

B: Keep more ♂♂ (full-grown!) than ♀♀ together. Gestation takes about 24 days. 10-60 young are born which are pursued and eaten by the ♀. Therefore, a spawning box or dense vegetation should be used in the breeding tank. Temperature about 24° C (75° F). Mulmy substrate should be avoided to prevent young from choking therein. Rear with *Artemia, Cyclops,* TetraMin Baby Food.

F: Mosquito larvae, other small live foods, *Artemia*, but also flake foods of all kinds with freeze-dried components, algae.

S: See Vol. 1, page 590, where *G. holbrooki* is described. Unfortunately, there, as in many other publications, the picture was mixed up. Only starting with the 4th German edition (fall 1983) is the correct picture of *G. holbrooki* shown.
Both sub-species are and were very important in malaria control.

T: 18-24° C, **L:** ♂ 4 cm, ♀ 6.5 cm, **A:** 60 cm, **R:** m, t, **D:** 1
64-75° F, ♂ 1 2/3", ♀ 2 2/3, 24",

Flexipenis vittatus

Gambusia affinis

Gambusia marshi MINCKLEY & CRADDOCK, 1962
Pellucid Mosquitofish, Salado Mosquitofish

Syn.: None.

Hab.: Central America: northeastern Mexico; Rio Sabinas de Coahuila, Rio Salado de los Nadadores, Rio Salado, Coahuila.

F.I.: 1980 by Meyer, Müller and Vogel, Germany.

Sex: ♂ is elongated with gonopodium; ♀ is deeper-bodied (especially during gestation).

Soc. B.: A peaceful species which can also be kept in a community tank of nonquarellsome species. Use a species tank for breeding.

M: Because the species inhabits such varied biotopes as narrow ditches and wide river beds, a great latitude for its care can be assumed. Exact aquaristic recommendations are missing. Suggestion: well-planted tank, perhaps with algae and weak filtration. Plenty of light. Water should have a pH of 6.5-8.0; hardness 5.0 to 25° dGH.

B: Initial births often yield many more ♀♀ than ♂♂; it balances out later. Only well developed, full-grown ♀♀ should be used for breeding. These give birth to 5 to 60 young of 6-7 mm (") length after a gestation of 28 days. Raise with *Artemia*, Liquifry Green, TetraMin Baby Food, micro food and algae aufwuchs.

F: O; from algae to any live food. Flake and tablet foods are readily taken. Offer variation with Tetra Conditioning Food and FD-Menu.

S: Some animals have more black pigmentation than others.

T: 22-26° C, **L:** ♂ 3.5 cm, ♀ 6 cm, **A:** 60 cm, **R:** m, t, **D:** 2
72-79° F, ♂ 1 1/3", ♀ 2 1/3, 24",

Gambusia puncticulata yucatana (REGAN, 1914)
Yucatan Spotted Mosquitofish

Syn.: *Gambusia yucatana.*

Hab.: Southern Mexico (Yucatan), Central America to Panama.

F.I.: 1912 by Hopp, Hamburg, Germany.

Sex: ♂ is smaller and easily recognized by the gonopodium.

Soc. B.: Unfortunately, a quite unsociable fish which pursues not only conspecifics but also fry and many smaller tankmates. The fins of calm large species are often damaged. Keep in a species tank.

M: Densely planted tanks with plenty of cover, such as roots and larger stones, are required to protect the ♀♀ from the rough and insistent ♂♂. The addition of salt at 1 teaspoon per 10 l (2.5 gal) of water is advantageous for breeding and its well-being. pH 7.5-8.3, dGH 15-30°. Plant with *Vallisneria*, perhaps Java fern. *Philodendron* roots.

B: For breeding, several ♂♂ are stocked with 1-2 ♀♀. Densely planted tanks increase chances of success. The addition of salt is required (see **M**); otherwise, the young easily suffer from bacterial attack. Gestation is about 24 days. Between 10 and 30 young of 10 mm (1/3") length are born. Raise with *Artemia* and the smallest flake foods (TetraMin Baby Food).

F: C, O; predominately all types of live foods; however, flake food is always readily accepted.

S: The nominate form, *G. p. puncticulata*, only occurs on the islands of Cuba, Bahamas, Jamaica and Cayman.

T: 22-28° C, **L:** ♂ 5.5 cm, ♀ 8 cm, **A:** 80 cm, **R:** m, **D:** 3
72-82° F, ♂ 2 1/4", ♀ 3", 31",

Gambusia marshi ♂

Gambusia puncticulata ♂

Gambusia puncticulata yucatana ♀

Gambusia regani HUBBS, 1926
Regan's Mosquitofish

Syn.: None.

Hab.: Rio Forlón, Rio Tamesi, Mexico, Central America.

F.I.: By Dr. A. Radda, Austria.

Sex: There is no difference in coloration. However, as in all livebearers, the ♂ can be easily recognized by its gonopodium.

Soc. B.: A peaceful species which can be kept in a suitable community tank. In nature, it usually lives alone and is rarely found with other species.

M: Little has become known about this plain livebearer species. Maintenance corresponds to other, less demanding species. At birth the young are already 1 cm (1/3") long. The animals primarily occur in ponds, pools, and shallow shore areas of various water bodies. It is rarely found in flowing water. pH 6.5-7.9; hardness to 25° dGH. Weak filtration.

B: The ♀♀ become sexually mature at 3 months. 10-20 young are born after a gestation of 24 days. Raise with smallest pond plankton, later *Artemia*; there are few difficulties in a separate breeding tank.

F: L, O; primarily small live foods or small flake foods 5-6 times daily.

S: The species was discovered in 1903 by Mr. Forlón, but not described until 1926.

T: 21-28° C, **L:** ♂ up to 3.5 cm, ♀ 4 cm, **A:** 50 cm, **R:** m, t, **D:** 2
70-82° F, ♂ up to 1 1/3", ♀ 1 2/3, 20",

Gambusia sexradiata HUBBS, 1936
Tropical Mosquitofish

Syn.: *Gambusia nicaraguensis sexradiatus, G. n. nicaraguensis.*

Hab.: Northern Belize (previously British Honduras), north Guatemala, Rio Nautla, Mexico, Central America.

F.I.: Not determinable.

Sex: Barely differ in coloration. ♂ is more slender and elongated. ♀♀ are deeper (about twice as deep as ♂♂).

Soc. B.: A peaceful species that can be combined with other species. In nature the species lives together with characins, cichlids, and other livebearers (*Xiphophorus maculatus, C. kidderi, P. fairweatheri, B. belizanus*).

M: Needs a well-planted tank with a floating plant cover, a dark bottom and weak filtration. Exchange the filter medium regularly. pH 6.5-7.8; hardness up to 18° dGH.

B: Breeding is easy. Every 28 days between 10 and 35 young are born. These are only approximately 5 mm (3/16") long. The animals are already sexually mature from the 4th month.

F: O; flake foods of all kinds, plant fare. FD food, frozen live foods.

S: Contrary to other gambusia which also penetrate brackish waters, this species only occurs in pure freshwater. This species is a "tough cookie". It could even be caught in waters contaminated with crude oil.

T: 22-26° C, **L:** ♂ 3 cm, ♀ 6.5 cm, **A:** 50 cm, **R:** m, t, **D:** 2
72-79° F, ♂ 1 ", ♀ 2 2/3, 20",

Gambusia regani ♂

Gambusia sexradiata ♀

Girardinus falcatus (EIGENMANN, 1903)
Sickle Girardinus

Syn.: *Glaridichthys falcatus, G. atherinoides.*

Hab.: River, lake and swamps of central and west Cuba.

F.I.: 1935 by Fritz Mayer, "Roßmäßler", Hamburg, Germany, through New York.

Sex: ♂ is smaller than the ♀ and has a gonopodium.

Soc. B.: A peaceful fish which can be kept together with all peaceful species in a well-planted tank.

M: The fish tolerate any type of tank. In nature it occurs in shallow, fast-flowing creeks with rocky bottoms as well as in swampy areas. The species likes free swimming room in part of the tank and good vegetation in the other.

B: In a species tank, breeding and rearing are easy. Gestation averages 25 days. 10-40 young with a length of 8 mm (5/16") are born. Feed the young with *Artemia* and Liquifry Green.

F: O; flake food, algae, frozen food, live foods of all kinds.

S: When the light hits the fish just right, its eyes shine light blue. The common name is based on the sickle-shaped curvature of the ♂'s gonopodium.
The species has been kept for over 10 years in the (East) Berlin Aquarium.

T: 24-30° C, **L:** ♂ 4.5 cm, ♀ 7 cm, **A:** 60 cm, **R:** m, **D:** 2
75-86° F, ♂ 1 3/4", ♀ 2 3/4, 24",

Heterandria bimaculata (HECKEL, 1848)
Spotted Tail Mosquitofish

Syn.: *Xiphophorus bimaculatus, Poecilioides bimaculatus, Pseudoxiphophorus bimaculatus, Pseudoxiphophorus pauciradiatus, Gambusia bimaculata, Gambusia (Pseudoxiphophorus) bimaculata, Pseudoxiphophorus bimaculatus bimaculatus, Pseudoxiphophorus bimaculatus taeniatus, Pseudoxiphophorus bimaculatus peninsulae, Pseudoxiphophorus reticulatus.*

Hab.: Through North America (Rio Nautla), along the coast of the Gulf of Mexico to Honduras, Central America.

F.I.: 1909 by Carl Siggelkow, Hamburg, Germany.

Sex: The ♂ is easily recognized by the 30 mm (1 ") gonopodium. Coloration of the ♂ and ♀ is almost equal.

Soc. B.: Largely a quiet fish which can be kept together with larger, robust species. However, it is also reported to be a quarrelsome animal, especially ♀♀. Young fish up to 2 cm (3/4") in length are readily hunted.

M: Because of the most varied origins (mountain streams at an elevation of 2500 m (8200 ft) down to brackish water areas at sea level!), knowledge of the source of the animals is important for their care. Actually, a general recipe can not be given. Tolerable median values for all strains could be water with a pH of 7 and a hardness between 10 and 15° dGH. Good vegetation while maintaining free swimming space is important for the animals.

B: Breeding can be very productive. Twenty to 110 young of about 15 mm (2/3") are born every 6-8 weeks. The parents should be removed immediately from the breeding tank. During the first 4 weeks, the young are slightly sensitive to bacteria. The normal dosage of General Tonic every 8-10 days is helpful . The young grow at different rates and can be cannibalistic. Therefore, offer numerous hiding places. Java moss is fitting.

F: C; larger live foods of all kinds, large flakes, tablet foods, fish sticks.

S: Depending on their origin, they can have totally different colors. The mountain stream strains are usually brownish and paler than the lowland strains.

T: 20-28° C, **L:** ♂ 7 cm, ♀ up to 15 cm, **A:** 100 cm, **R:** m, t, **D:** 3-4
68-82° F, ♂ 2 3/4", ♀ up to 6", 39",

Girardinus falcatus ♂

Heterandria bimaculata, ♂ bottom ♀ top

Limia dominicensis (VALENCIENNES, 1846)

Dominican Limia

Syn.: *Poecilia dominicensis* (Homonym).

Hab.: Santa Domingo, Haiti by Port au Prince and Jeremie.

F.I.: Ultimately in 1976 to Austria by Arnold Bimüller. Imported in 1914 as *Limia caudofasciatus*, a synonym of *Limia melanogaster*.

Sex: ♀♀ have clearly pronounced crossbars. The pectoral, dorsal and tail fins are intensely orange in the ♂. The ♂♂ have longer ventral fins than the ♀♀, and their body is more elongated.

Soc. B.: A peaceful appealing toothcarp that is suitable as a companion of correspondingly gentle species.

M: Provide a well-planted, well-oxygenated tank with good water turnover. Give regular water changes using AquaSafe. pH 6.0-7.2; hardness up to 20° dGH. In its natural biotope, dense vegetation in the water shades the habitat.

B: Sexual maturity is achieved at approximately 4 months of age. Gestation lasts about 24 days, and ♀♀ give birth to between 15 and 50, 6 mm (") long young. A ♀ can only be bred 3-4 times; thereafter, it is nearly infertile. Raise with plankton and TetraMin Baby Food.

F: O; flake foods, algae, live food (frozen).

S: RIVAS (1978) again separates the genus previously grouped into *Poecilia*.

T: 22-26° C, **L:** ♂ 3 cm, ♀ 4.5 cm, **A:** 60 cm, **R:** m, **D:** 1-2
72-79° F, ♂ 1 ", ♀ 1$^{3}/_{4}$", 24",

Limia perugiae (EVERMANN & CLARK, 1906)

Perugia's Limia

Syn.: *Platypoecilus perugiae, Poecilia perugiae.*

Hab.: Dominican Republic; Haiti.

F.I.: 1948 by E. Roloff, Karlsruhe, Germany.

Sex: Full-grown ♂♂ have an orange chest; in ♀♀ and young ♂♂, it is white. The gonopodium is black. ♀♀ have the genus-typical limia spot on the dorsal fin.

Soc. B.: Housing them with smaller cichlids and other livebearers, e.g., guppies, corresponds to its natural habitat.

M: Actually, the species is hardy and long-lived. However, the young only grow to full size and beauty under excellent water conditions. Regular, generous water exchanges every 14 days (the tank volume) and the slight addition of salt are very growth promoting. Water: pH 6.8-7.5; hardness up to 30° dGH.

B: The species is only productive in a densely planted tank of 200 liters (53 gal) and more. Every 24 days, 10-100 young of about 7 mm (") length are born. Only the largest ♀♀ should be used as breeders.

F: O; plant fare and live food. The animals should be allowed to satiate themselves. Flake food needs to be administered at least 5-6 times daily because it cannot be given "in advance". An automatic feeder is very helpful under these circumstances, provided the individual servings can be small enough.

S: There are two, different sized strains: the one described here and a smaller one in which the ♂♂ only reach 4 cm (1^{2}/3") and the ♀♀ 5 cm (2"). It may be an independent species. RIVAS (1980) calls it *Limia tridens* (HILGENDORF, 1889).

T: 24-28° C, **L:** ♂ 7 cm, **A:** 120 cm, **R:** m, t, **D:** 1-2
75-82° F, ♂ 2$^{3}/_{4}$", 47",

Limia dominicensis, ♂ bottom ♀ top

Limia perugiae ♂

Limia zonata (NICHOLS, 1915)

Syn.: *Heterandria zonata, Poecilia zonata.*

Hab.: Samaná Peninsula, Dominican Republic.

F.I.: Not exactly known.

Sex: The ♂ is easily recognized by its gonopodium.

Soc. B.: A peaceful species which is well suited for a small community aquarium of gentle tankmates.

M: Requires a well-planted aquarium with a lot of light. Dark gravel or sand substrate. Water: pH 6.8-7.5; hardness: 5-18° dGH. Provide good filtration and regular water exchanges of 1/3 every 3-6 weeks, depending on tank size and stocking density. Add a good water conditioner.

B: Every 30-40 days, 12-30 young of approx. 7 mm (¼") are born. Raise with micro food, *Artemia*, TetraMin Baby Food, Liquifry or egg-yolk.

F: O; flake food, FD-Menu, algae, small live foods.

S: The species is closely related to *Limia heterandria*.

T: 22-25° C, **L:** ♂ 3.5 cm, ♀ 4.5 cm, **A:** 60 cm, **R:** m, t, **D:** 2
72-77° F, ♂ 1⅓", ♀ 1¾", 24",

Phallichthys amates pittieri (MEEK, 1912)
Iridescent Widow

Syn.: *Poecilia pittieri, Poeciliopsis pittieri, Phallichthys pittieri, Poeciliopsis isthmensis, Phallichthys isthmensis.*

Hab.: Mountain streams to elevations of 1200 m (3900 ft) in Costa Rica and northern Panama, Central America.

F.I.: 1906 by W. Schroot, Hamburg, Germany.

Sex: ♂ more slender and easily differentiated by its gonopodium.

Soc. B.: Long-lived in a well-planted community tank with peaceful tankmates. Full-grown ♀♀ pursue of their own and other fish.

M: Well-filtered water with a current. Plentiful vegetation. Gravel bottom. pH 6.2-7.5; hardness up to 20° dGH.

B: Every 28 days, 10-50 young are born. Only one ♂ is born for every 10 ♀♀. A large breeding box is needed for spawning; a roomy aquarium of at least 50 liter volume (13 gal) is required to raise the young.

F: O, H; an omnivore which prefers algae and other vegetable fare.

S: In Vol. 1 of the Aquarium Atlas, the nominate species *P. a. amates* is described on page 594.

T: 20-24° C, **L:** ♂ 6 cm, ♀ 8 cm, **A:** 80 cm, **R:** m, **D:** 2
68-75° F, ♂ 2⅓", ♀ 3", 31",

Limia zonata ♂

Phallichthys amates pittieri, ♂ bottom ♀ top

Phallichthys fairweatheri ROSEN & BAILEY, 1959
Fairweather Widow

Syn.: None.

Hab.: Rio Hondo, New River; British Honduras, Rio de la Pasión, Rio San Pedro de Mártir. Tabasco, Mexico, Central America.

F.I.: 1977 by E. Schlosser, Vienna, Austria.

Sex: The ♂♂ have a very long gonopodium. The anus of the ♀ has a black spot pattern.

Soc. B.: ♂♂ are very quarrelsome among themselves. It is, therefore, best to keep only one ♂ with several ♀♀ in a community tank. In nature the fish occurs together with *Poecilia gilli, Gambusia sexradiata, Carlhubbsia kedderi, Phallichthys fairweatheri,* tetras, catfishes, needlefishes and cichlids.

M: A species tolerant towards water quality. Nevertheless, good filtration and current should be offered. Plant the tank and provide a slightly mulmy substrate. Food is readily picked from the mulm. Water: pH 6.5-8.0; hardness 15-25° dGH.

B: Very small young (15-30) of 5 mm (3/16") length are born every 24 days under good conditions. The young are sensitive to diseases. 5 g of table salt per 10 l (2.5 gal) of water and the addition of General Tonic at half the dosage insures a better success in rearing.

F: O; flake food, tablet food, algae, any small live foods.

S: Healthy, dominant ♂♂ have an orange caudal spot that makes them very attractive.

T: 22-29° C, **L:** ♂ about 3 cm, ♀ about 4 cm, **A:** 60 cm, **R:** m, b, **D:** 2
72-84° F, ♂ about 1 ", ♀ about 1 2/3", 24",

Phallichthys quadripunctatus BUSSING, 1979
Four-Spot Widow

Syn.: None.

Hab.: Central America; eastern Costa Rica (2 tributaries of the Rio Sixaola, km (1/3 mi) northeast of Chase).

F.I.: 1980 by Dr. A. Radda, Vienna, Austria.

Sex: ♂ is clearly smaller and has a gonopodium.

Soc. B.: In nature the species lives together with killifishes (*Rivulus*), *Phallichthys tico, P. amates pittieri, Alfaro cultratus.* A peaceful, undemanding species which lives secluded in the dense vegetation.

M: In its natural waters, the depth is only 10-50 cm (4"-20") and the bottom is sandy to rocky bottom. Temperatures can oscillate between 20 and 40° C (68 and 104° F)! Little else is known about the natural water values. Neutral water with a pH of about 7.0 and a hardness up to 12° dGH are agreeable values in an aquarium.

B: Very easy. Even in small tanks this species propagates very well. The adults do not pursue the young. They are easily raised with small foods.

F: O; small live foods such as *Artemia, Cyclops* and finely crumbled flake food, e.g., FD-Menu.

S: The species is not distributed in the trade and is only available through specialist breeders, i.e., the Deutsche Gesellschaft für Lebendgebärende Zahnkarpfen (German Livebearers Association).

T: 20-30° C, **L:** ♂ 2.5 cm, ♀ 3.5 cm, **A:** 40 cm, **R:** m, b, **D:** 1
68-86° F, ♂ 1", ♀ 1 1/3", 16",

Phallichthys fairweatheri ♂

Phallichthys quadripunctatus ♂

Phalloptychus januarius (HENSEL, 1868)
Barred Millionsfish

Syn.: *Girardinus januarius, Poecilia januarius, Girardinus iheringii, G. zonatus.*

Hab.: Rio de Janeiro, Brazil; Rio Chicu, Argentina; eastern Paraguay and Uruguay in lagoons, South America.

F.I.: 1907 by Curt Siggelkow, Hamburg, to Germany

Sex: ♂ is clearly more slender with a long gonopodium.

Soc. B.: A gregarious fish which sometimes occurs in the thousands (name!). Maintaining it with guppies, *Poecilia vivipara, Jenynsia lineata*, cichlids and tetras is in accordance with its natural habitat.

M: The barred millionsfish prefers lagoons to flowing waters. Dr. BODART found the species on a sand bank of the Lago de Freitas. No high demands are placed on water quality. Even polluted waters are inhabited by the species. pH 6.8-8.0; hardness up to 25° dGH. Aquaria with algae and the garden pond in the summer offer a correct habitat for the species.

B: Partially very productive. Due to the high rate of propagation, massive numbers can occur in nature. Usually every 24 days, 10-30 young are born. Unfortunately, the species is especially susceptible to a persistent species of Ich. It can be cured with a reliable Ich medication (active ingredient malachite green) at a slight overdose (20%). Raise with any small flake or live food.

F: O; FD-Menu, Tetra Conditioning Food, etc.

S: In nature, a few fish have black speckles.

T: 20-25° C, **L:** ♂ 3 cm, ♀ 4.5 cm, **A:** 60 cm, **R:** m, t, **D:** 1
68-77° F, ♂ 1 ", ♀ 1³/₄", 24",

Poecilia chica MILLER, 1975
Dwarf Molly

Syn.: None.

Hab.: Rio Maravasco (State of Jalisco), Rio Purificación, Rio Cuetzmala, Mexico, Central America.

F.I.: 1979 by Mr. Hinz and Manfred Meyer to Germany.

Sex: The ♂ is more splendidly colored and has a gonopodium. Dominant ♂♂ are almost completely black.

Soc. B.: A peaceful fish which is well suited for tanks with delicate species.

M: Do not use overly bright tanks, but ones with a floating plant cover and free swimming space. Dark bottom of sand, pebbles and rock fragments. Water: pH 6.5-7.5; hardness to 10-20° dGH. Slight water turn over. ¹/3 water exchange with the addition of a good conditioner every 4-6 weeks. Nitrite and nitrate levels have to be kept low with a good biological filter (large capacity).

B: Good breeding success can be obtained in aquaria with an algal bloom. The young take the unicellular algae as nourishment. A similar result can be achieved by feeding the finest flake food (TetraMin Baby Food) or Liquifry Green. Through strong aeration in the rearing tank, the feed is kept in suspension—the fish are "standing" in their feed. An hour after every feeding, the water should be exchanged.
With good feeding, every 30 days 30-50 young of 6 mm (") length are born. These become sexually mature in 4 months.

F: H, O; herbivore: algae, plant flake food, TabiMin. Small live foods (*Artemia*).

S: None.

T: 23-26° C, **L:** ♂ 3 cm, ♀ 5 cm, **A:** 60 cm, **R:** b, m, **D:** 1-2
73-79° F, ♂ 1¹/₄", ♀ 2", 24",

Phalloptychus januarius, ♂ top ♀ bottom

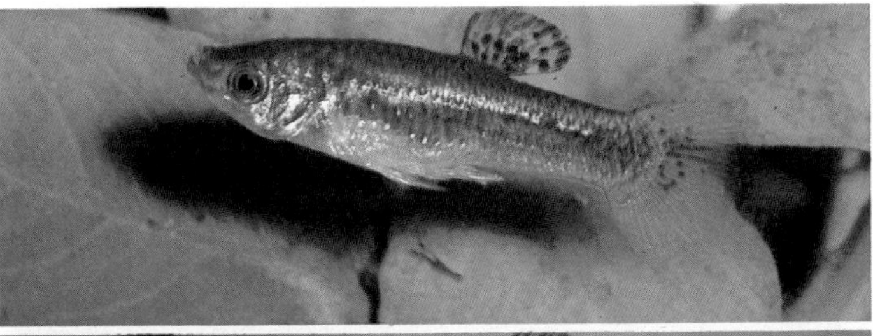

Poecilia chica, ♂ top ♀ bottom

Poecilia latipinna (LESUEUR, 1821)
Sailfin Molly

Syn.: *Mollienisia latipinna, Gambusia lineolata, G. matamorensis, G. poecilioides, Limia lineolata, L. matamorensis, L. poecilioides, Poecilia lineolata, P. multilineata.*

Hab.: South Virginia, Carolina, Florida, Texas. In brackish coastal waters; even in the sea.

F.I.: 1902 by Hans Stüve, Hamburg, Germany.

Sex: ♂ has a gonopodium and a distinctly larger dorsal fin. ♀ has a pregnancy spot.

Soc. B.: Peaceful species well suited for the community tank with larger fishes and hard water. Their own young and those of other fishes are pursued.

M: Add 2-3ppt table salt. Use tough plants such as Java fern, *Sagittaria, Vallisneria* and *Anubias*. Tender plant buds are grazed if insufficient algae and plant flake foods are offered. Some floating plants in a corner promote the coincidental rearing outside the breeding tank. The animals have a strong appetite; they need good filtration.

B: Requires a spawning box in a larger (60 cm; 24") breeding tank. Either plant the tank as dense as possible or provide a dense algae mat. Every 60-70 days 10-60 young which are already 12 mm (") long are born.

F: H, O; omnivore, especially algae. Any smaller live foods. Vegetable plant food.

S: The species is often confused with *P. velifera* (Vol. 1, page 604). After acclimation, the species can be kept in a marine tank. Very variable in its coloration. Black and albino animals exist. The hybrid is specially resistant.

T: 20-28° C, **L:** ♂ 10 cm, ♀ up to 12 cm, **A:** 120 cm, **R:** m, t, **D:** 2
68-82° F, ♂ 4", ♀ up to 4 3/4", 47",

Poecilia mexicana mexicana STEINDACHNER, 1863
Mexico Molly, Shortfin Molly

Syn.: *"Poecilia sphenops".*

Hab.: North Mexico to Colombia including certain Caribbean Islands in fast-flowing freshwaters, rarely in standing water or seawater.

F.I.: 1907 by J. Thumm, Dresden, Germany.

Sex: ♂ is a colorful blue to brown, sometimes black. ♀ plain. ♂ has a gonopodium.

Soc. B.: Peaceful fish; nice associates for nonpredatory species in a "hard water tank". *P. latipinna, Gambusia affinis* and *Limia vittata* are found sympatrically with the species.

M: The species requires hard water with 20-30° dGH. Add salt at 2-5 g/l (7.5-19 g/gal). A water turnover rate of 1-2 times the tank volume per hour should be strived for.

B: 28 days after fertilization, the ♀ gives birth to 30-80 young of about 8 mm (5/16") length. The animals become sexually mature after 7-12 months. Raise with pond plankton and, later, *Artemia*.

F: H; algae and plant food (e.g., Tetra Conditioning Food or similar), TabiMin tablet food.

S: There is also the sub-species *P. mexikana limantouri.*
1963 the species was placed as a synonym to *P. sphenops*. 1971 SCHULTZ & MILLER demonstrated that this is indeed an independent species.

T: 23-28° C, **L:** ♂ 7 cm, ♀ 8.5 cm, **A:** 100 cm, **R:** m, t, **D:** 1-2
73-82° F, ♂ 2 3/4", ♀ 3 1/3", 39",

Poecilia latipinna ♂

Poecilia mexicana mexicana ♂

Micropoecilia picta REGAN, 1913
Variegated Mollie

Syn.: *Poecilia picta.*

Hab.: South America; Rio Demarara in (British) Guyana, Trinidad, Brazil in coastal waters.

F.I.: 1939 by Mr. Griem of "Aquarium Hamburg" as *Micropoecilia parae.*

Sex: Clearly distinguishable: ♂ is more colorful; ♀ has a typical black spot in the upper 1/3 of the body.

Soc. B.: Although very peaceful, this fish needs a species tank to satisfy its special water requirements.

M: The species appreciates a 0.5 % addition of **sea salt**! A true brackish water fish but with the ability to live in freshwater. Special attention must be paid to the illumination. The light should come gently from the front so that the bright iridescent colors can be clearly appreciated. Dark substrate. Tough water plants. Water: pH 7.5-8.2; hardness 20-40° dGH.

B: Very varied experiences. Both very good experiences and difficulties are reported. The reasons for these various experiences are unknown. Perhaps vitamin additions to the feed would help. Provide the breeders with small mosquito larvae and *Drosophila*.

F: C; predominately small live foods, FD-Menu, FD tablets.

S: This is one of the most beautiful livebearers, and it should receive more attention. At first glance, it looks like a guppy. There is a whole range of different color strains. However, the base colors yellow, gold, and black are always present in the ♂♂.

T: 26-28° C, L: ♂ 3 cm, ♀ 5 cm, A: 50 cm, R: m, t, D: 2-3
79-82° F, ♂ 1", ♀ 2", 20",

Poecilia latipinna x *P. sphenops*, bred lyretail strain (*Poecilia mexicana*?)

Micropoecilia picta ♂, aquarium strain

Micropoecilia picta, wild coloration, ♂ top ♀ bottom

*Poecilia reticulata** PETERS, 1859

a) Wild Guppy Population Mexico,
b) Wild Guppy Population Peru
c) Wild Giant Guppy, Mexico.

Syn.: See Vol. 1, page 598.

Hab.: a) Upper photo: Mexico,
b) Middle photo: Peru,
c) Bottom photo: Mexico.

F.I.: c) 1982 by M. K. Meyer, Bad Nauheim and L. Wischnath, Berlin, Germany.

Sex: The ♂ has a gonopodium and is more intensely colored than the ♀.

Soc. B.: A peaceful schooling fish, but breeders will pursue their newborns.

M: Wild guppies are not as undemanding as some might believe. Clear, flowing water, mostly soft, depending on habitat also harder (Peru). The pH must be in accordance with the place of origin. Since most guppies available to the trade are bred specimens coming from Singapore, Hong Kong or other Asian countries (sometimes also from Florida), these are more adaptable. Those who are interested in buying wild imports to breed or to cross with bred specimens need to contact the Gesellschaft für Lebendgebärende Zahnkarpfen (Livebearers Association), the Deutsche Guppy-Gesellschaft (German Guppy Association) or the ALA (American Livebearer Association).

B: See Vol. 1, page 598.

F: C, O; omnivore but prefers mosquito larvae and *Artemia*. Provide a lot of variation in its food.

*S: 1993 by M. K. MEYER: Zool. Abh., Mus. Tierk., Dresden, 47, 10: Genus *Poecilia*, sub-genus *Lebistes*.

T: 22-28° C, L: a) ♂ 3-4 cm, ♀ 6 cm, b) ♂ 3.5 cm, ♀ 5-6 cm, c) ♂ 6-8 cm, ♀ 5-6 cm,
72-82° F, a) ♂ 1 1/4"-1 2/3", ♀ 2 1/3", b) ♂ 1 1/3", ♀ 2"-2 1/3", c) ♂ 2 1/3"-3", ♀ 2"-2 1/3",
A: 60 cm, R: t, m, D: 2
24",

Wild Guppy, Mexican population

Wild Guppy, Peruvian population

Giant Guppy, wild caught; Mexico

Poecilia vivipara (BLOCH & SCHNEIDER, 1801)

Syn.: *Poecilia surinamensis, Mollienisia surinamensis, Poecilia unimaculata, Poecilia unimaculata, Neopoecilia holacanthus, Poecilia holacanthus.*

Hab.: Still-water areas, brackish lagoons around Rio de Janeiro, Curaçao, Bonaire, Venezuelan Islands, Trinidad, Martinique, west Venezuela to Argentina to Rio de la Plata.

F.I.: 1904 by Christian Brüning, Hamburg, Germany. 1870 by Captain Perry for the Zoological Garden of Hamburg, Germany.

Soc. B.: A peaceful species which amasses in huge numbers in some places. Well suited for the community tank.

M: Use shallow tanks with a sandy bottom. Vegetation is secondary. Water: pH 7.0-8.2; hardness 10-40° dGH. Needs a low concentration of table salt, 1 teaspoon per 10 l (2.5 gal) of water.

B: Sometimes over 100 young of approximately 6 mm (") length are born every 28 days. Sexual maturity is already attained after 3-4 months. Raise with TetraMin Baby Food, *Artemia* and algae (bloom).

F: C, O; flake foods of all kinds, algae, small live foods.

S: None.

T: 26-28° C, **L:** ♂ 5 cm, ♀ 7 cm, **A:** 50 cm, **R:** b, m, **D:** 1
72-79° F, ♂ 2", ♀ 2¾", 24",

Poeciliopsis baenschi MEYER, RADDA, RIEHL & FEICHTINGER, 1985
Baensch's Mosquitofish

Syn.: None.

Hab.: Creek at El Tuito, Jalisco, Mexico, Central America.

F.I.: 1984 by Dr. A. Radda, Vienna, Austria.

Sex: The ♂ is smaller than the ♀ and has a gonopodium.

Soc. B.: The species is isolated in nature, that is, no other fish species is present. The parents pursue their young.

M: The fish inhabit fast flowing creeks. Therefore, a strong filter and good oxygenation are recommended. The water in its natural habitat was as follows: pH 6.5, hardness 2° dGH, conductivity 90 µS.

B: Not productive, see *P. latidens*.

F: C, O; predominantly live food, but also flake food.

S: A quite small livebearing species which is unlikely to become widespread in the trade. It belongs to the *P. latidens-fasciata* complex, but differs by its dentition (demonstrated by RIEHL [1984] with the aid of an electron microscope) and gonopodium.

T: 18-24° C, **L:** ♂ 2.5 cm, ♀ 3.0 cm, **A:** 40 cm, **R:** all, **D:** 3
64-75° F, ♂ 1", ♀ 1 ", 16",

Poecilia vivipara ♂ bottom ♀ top

Poeciliopsis baenschi, see page 748 for an additional picture

Poeciliopsis gracilis (HECKEL, 1848)
Porthole Livebearer

Syn.: *Gambusia heckeli, Xiphophorus gracilis, Girardinus pleurospilus, Heterandria pleurospilus, Poeciliopsis pleurospilus, Poecilistes pleurospilus, Poecilistes pleurospilus pleurospilus, Heterandria lutzi, Girardinus lutzi, Poeciliopsis lutzi, Priapichthys letonai.*

Hab.: Atlantic and Pacific tributaries in southern Mexico, Guatemala and Honduras, Central America.

F.I.: 1913 by Arthur Rachow and Fritz Mayer, Hamburg, Germany.

Sex: The ♂ is smaller than the ♀ and has a gonopodium.

Soc. B.: Very peaceful fish. Suitable for community tanks inhabited by not overly rough fishes.

M: Needs a darkened tank with a floating plant cover or broad-leaved *Echinodorus*. The fish likes to stand under the leaves. No exceptional demands are placed on water quality: pH 6.5-7.8; hardness to 25° dGH. Dark gravely substrate, partially covered with either mulm and/or algae. Good water turnover and regular filter maintenance.

B: Three months after birth, the first animals are already sexually mature and, within 1 month, give birth to 10-50 young. Breeding in large species tanks with algae is the most successful method.

F: O; omnivore which appreciates a lot of variety in its menu: flake food of all kinds, FD-Menu, algae, *Artemia*.

S: The species is widely variable. The fish have 4-11 eye-sized spots along the lateral line. Some animals in the Rio Orcones near Arriaga have a continuous band pattern similar to the *P. fasciata* that occurs there, but it disappears in its offspring.

T: 24-28° C, L: ♂ 3.5 cm, ♀ 6 cm, A: 80 cm, R: all, D: 1-2
75-82° F, ♂ 1 1/3", ♀ 2 1/3", 31",

Poeciliopsis hnilickai MEYER & VOGEL, 1981
Chiapas Mosquitofish

Syn.: None.

Hab.: Creek 3-5 m (3.3-5.5 yd) wide and shallow with 1.20-1.80 m (47"-71") deep holes at Ixtapas, Chiapas, Mexico, Central America.

F.I.: 1980 by Vogel, Müller and Meyer to Germany.

Sex: The ♀♀ have small black dots around the anus which are less intense in the ♂♂. ♂ is smaller and has a gonopodium.

Soc. B.: Peaceful schooling fish best kept in groups of 6-8 animals. A slender, fast swimmer recommended for large community tanks. In nature, the species lives with *Profundulus*.

M: Provide clear, moderately circulating, slightly acid to neutral water. pH 6.8-7.2; hardness 6-18° dGH. The tank should have dark substrate and intense illumination. Vegetation is not needed (as in nature), but of course, it is not detrimental as long as sufficient swimming space remains available.

B: Single pairs sometimes do not reproduce. Therefore, a school is necessary for breeding purposes. At 10 weeks of age, the offspring can already produce young of their own. Gestation requires 28-35 days.

F: O; flake foods of all kinds, freeze-dried and frozen live foods. *Artemia*.

S: None.

T: 24-28° C, L: ♂ 3.5 cm, ♀ 5 cm, A: 80 cm, R: b, m, D: 2
75-82° F, ♂ 1 1/3", ♀ 2", 31",

Poeciliopsis gracilis

Poeciliopsis hnilickai

Rio de Salina, Chiapas, Mexico. Habitat of *Poeciliopsis hnilickai*

Poeciliopsis baenschi, ♀ left ♂ right

♂

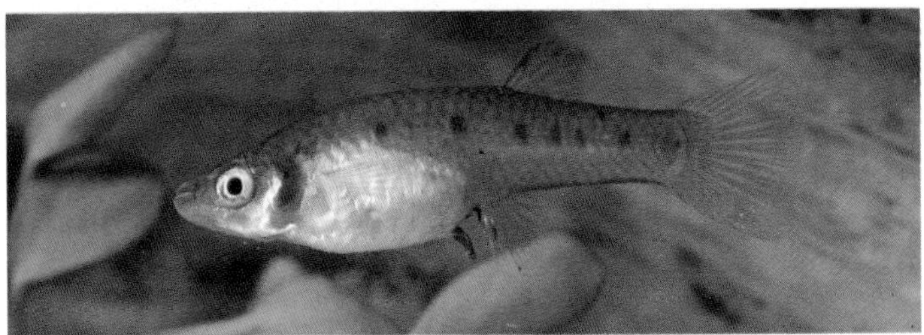

♀

Poeciliopsis latidens (GARMAN, 1895)

Syn.: *Glaridodon latidens, Glaridichthys latidens.*

Hab.: Pacific coastal regions from Rio del Fuerte to San Blas, Nayarit, Mexico, Central America.

F.I.: 1977 by Hans Kröger, Hamburg, Germany.

Sex: The ♂ is smaller and has a gonopodium.

Soc. B.: Quarrelsome towards conspecifics; explicitly cannibalistic towards its young.

M: Slightly saline water is preferable. Two teaspoons of iodine-free table salt or, better, sea salt per 10 l (2.5 gal) water. Lots of light for plentiful algae growth. Perhaps *Vallisneria* should be planted. Water: pH in nature, 8.0; hardness: KH and dGH 2.3.

B: Breeding appears to be difficult. Every 28 days between 8 and 25 young may be born. Only rarely do ♀♀ breed in an aquarium. Since the parents are so cannibalistic, it is important to remove the parents immediately following birth. Raise with algae, TetraMin Baby Food and *Artemia*. Dense vegetation of Java moss and a surface cover of water fern may protect some of the young.

F: H, O; algae, flake food (at least 4 times daily) given in smallest portions, additionally *Artemia* or *Cyclops* 1-2 times daily.

S: None.

T: 23-26° C, L: ♂ 4 cm, ♀ 5 cm, A: 50 cm, R: all, D: 3
73-79° F, ♂ 1 2/3", ♀ 2", 20",

Poeciliopsis viriosa MILLER, 1960
Viriosa Livebearer

Syn.: None.

Hab.: Central America; Rio Coluedor, Rio Ameca basin, Rio Mocorito, Mexico. In quiet waters up to an elevation of 1000 m (3280 ft).

F.I.: 1976 by Herrn Schreiber, Lüdenscheid, Germany.

Sex: ♂ has a long gonopodium.

Soc. B.: Mostly a peaceful species, but it readily considers smaller fishes a food item. Found with cichlids and *Astyanax fasciatus* in nature.

M: Needs moderately moving, clear water. Good filter maintenance (cleaned every 3-6 weeks) is required. pH 6.5-7.2; hardness 3-10° dGH. Dark substrate made of coarse gravel and rock fragments. Slight edge vegetation. Floating plant cover for the young. Regular water exchanges with a good water conditioner.

B: Not easy, the fish is very sensitive towards parasite infestation. Rivanol or General Tonic usually help. At 10 day intervals, 6-15, 7 mm (") long young are born. Raise in a densely planted tank with the smallest live foods (*Artemia*).

F: C, O; omnivore, but prefers small live foods. Flake food, FD-Menu.

S: Dominant, full-grown ♂♂ have a black coloration at the anal region which often reaches to the base of the tail fin.

T: 24-26° C, **L:** ♂ 3 cm, ♀ 6 cm, **A:** 60 cm, **R:** t, m, **D:** 2-3
75-79° F, ♂ 1¼", ♀ 2⅓", 24",

Priapella compressa ALVAREZ, 1948
Slap-Sided Blue-Eye

Syn.: None.

Hab.: Central America; Rio Grijalva, Chiapas, Rio Usomadinta system, Tabasco, Mexico. In fast flowing creeks and tributaries that flow to the Atlantic.

F.I.: Unknown.

Sex: ♂ is more slender and clearly recognizable by the gonopodium.

Soc. B.: A peaceful species, does not even pursue its own brood (when well fed). The animals are very shy, so one should approach the tank with caution.

M: Use a long shallow tank with a very good filter current. Likes sparse edge vegetation and a lot of free swimming space. The bottom should be sand or round pebbles; otherwise, there is a danger of injury. Sometimes the fish dart around like crazy in the aquarium. Water soft and neutral: hardness 5-15° dGH; pH 6.8-7.2. For water changes, add AquaSafe.

B: Breeding is only successful when sufficient hardy live foods, especially black mosquito larvae, have been fed. When well ripened, the breeding pair is transferred into a breeding tank (densely planted).

F: C; insects such as *Drosophila* and mosquito larvae, but also vegetable flake food and FD-Menu.

S: Cover the tank tightly: the species jumps well. In nature it can jump 30 cm (12") out of the water to capture flying insects.

T: 24-28° C, **L:** ♂ 3.5 cm, ♀ 5 cm, **A:** 100 cm, **R:** all, **D:** 3
75-82° F, ♂ 1⅓", ♀ 2", 39",

Poeciliopsis viriosa ♂

Priapella compressa, ♂ top ♀♀ bottom

Priapichthys festae (BOULENGER, 1898)

Festa Livebearer

Syn.: *Poecila festae, Pseudopoecilia festae, Poecilia fria, Pseudopoecilia fria, Priapichthys fria.*

Hab.: Ecuador by San Vicente and Santa Elena (Rio Chico Chone) in coastal areas, South America.

F.I.: 1977 by Dr. A. Radda, Vienna, Austria to Europe.

Sex: The dorsal and tail fin is yellow-orange in full-grown ♂♂. The fins on the ♀♀ are colorless. ♂ have a long gonopodium.

Soc. B.: Very peaceful species. Will not eat its offspring.

M: An explicit hard water fish which can stand a conductivity between 400 and 3000 µS[20] (measured in nature). The sparse vegetation has to be chosen accordingly. Water: pH 7.5-8.2; hardness 15-35° dGH and higher. Aged water is best tolerated; therefore, make infrequent water changes.

B: The species has a 28 day gestation period; normally only 3-7, 5 mm (3/16") long young are born. The breeding tank should only be 20-30 l (5-8 gal). Raise only with live food.

F: C; small live foods such as *Artemia, Cyclops*; FD-Menu.

S: None.

T: 21-30° C, L: ♂ 3.5 cm, ♀ 4.5 cm, A: 50 cm, R: m, t, D: 1-2
70-86° F, ♂ 1 1/3", ♀ 1 3/4", 20",

Quintana atrizona HUBBS, 1934

Black-Barred Livebearer

Syn.: None.

Hab.: Central America; Cuba, in a limited area close to Havanna. The animals inhabit smaller standing waters and stagnant shore regions of rivers. This species is endemic to Cuba.

F.I.: 1935 by Fritz Mayer, Hamburg, Germany, through F. H. Stoye, New York.

Sex: ♂ is smaller with a gonopodium; ♀ is larger and has a pregnancy spot.

Soc. B.: Peaceful fish, somewhat timid and, at the same time, curious.

M: This small fish can even be kept in very small tanks (45 x 25 x 20 cm; 18" x 10" x 8") without aeration or filtration. In overly large aquaria the animals tend towards dwarfism (compare DOKOUPIL (1982): Aquaria 29: 178-181). Water should be medium-hard (12-15° dGH), slightly acid (pH 6.8). Every 10-14 days exchange 1/3 of the water. Plant the tank with fine-leaved species. Does best in a species tank.

B: 26-28° C (79-82° F). Only easy in the first two generations; then it becomes progressively more difficult. Adult fish do not pursue the young. DOKOUPIL (1982) uses small aquaria furnished only with a bunch of a *Vesicularia* species and some *Riccia* on the surface. Gestation lasts 28-45 days at 26-28° C (79-82° F); the maximum number of young is 35. All young are born within 4 hours at the most. If the three main factors of small space, sufficient food and temperatures above 24° C (75° F) are met, the animals become sexually mature within 3-4 months. It can happen that among 50 offspring, only 1 sex is represented. This lopsided sex ratio could be temperature dependent; do not keep too warm!

F: The fish eat relatively little. They have to be, especially in larger tanks, feed 6-8 times daily. Feed with micro worms, grindal worms and chopped *Tubifex*, as well as vegetable flake food. The animals do not like *Artemia*.

S: It is said that the English breeder Jack Hems crossed *Quintana atrizona* with *Xiphophorus maculatus* prior to the Second World War and supposedly obtained salmon pink offspring. Surprisingly, the crosses were fertile even though the parents came from separate genera. *Q. atrizona* can be kept for several weeks in artificial seawater without problems.

T: 24-28° C, L: ♂ 2 cm, ♀ 4 cm, A: 50 cm, R: all, D: 4
75-82° F, ♂ 3/4", ♀ 1 2/3", 20",

Priapichthys festae ♂

Quintana atrizona, ♂ bottom ♀ top

Scolichthys greenwayi ROSEN, 1967
Big-Spot Mosquitofish

Syn.: None.

Hab.: Upper courses of the Rio Chixon, Rio Salinas, Rio Salba, Alta Verapaz, Guatemala, Central America.

F.I.: 1977 by E. Schlosser, Vienna, Austria.

Sex: The ♂ is more slender through the ventral area, has a gonopodium and is more intensely colored than the ♀. The lower posterior third of the body is notably violet hued in the ♂.

Soc. B.: The species can be easily combined with other fishes, specially livebearers, e.g., *X. helleri* and dwarf cichlids. Small tetras and young are not bothered either. *Heterandria obliqua* was found as a companion in its natural habitat.

M: The fish lives in the shady rain forest. The tank should not be too bright. A floating plant cover in part of the aquarium provides a good screen. The water can be moderately hard to 10° dGH. pH can fluctuate between 7.0 and 8.0.

B: Every month the ♀ gives birth to 10 to 30 young which can easily be raised on the usual fry foods, *Artemia*, etc.

F: O; flake food, plant food, tablet food, *Artemia*.

S: The pictured design shows one spot on the ♂ and two on the ♀. Up to 5 spots can be along the side of the body.

T: 22-26° C, **L:** ♂ 3.5 cm, ♀ 5 cm, **A:** 50 cm, **R:** m, t, **D:** 2
72-79° F, ♂ 1 1/3", ♀ 2", 20",

Xenophallus umbratilis (MEEK, 1912)
Shade Livebearer

Syn.: *Gambusia umbratilis, Brachyrhaphis umbratilis, Poeciliopsis maculifer, Neoheterandria umbratilis.*

Hab.: Southeastern Costa Rica in several tributaries of the Atlantic, e.g., Guapilis, Limón; Central America.

F.I.: 1980 by Dr. A. Radda, Vienna, Austria.

Sex: The dorsal fin of the ♂ is somewhat larger than that of the ♀ and is yellow-orange with a black fringe in full-grown ♂♂.

Soc. B.: Very peaceful fish which can readily be kept with conspecifics and other gentle species. Young are not eaten.

M: The animals are found together with *Brachyrhaphis holdridgei* in shaded, 1-3 m (39"-118") wide, shallow waters. Dr. Radda (1980) obtained these values from its natural habitat (2/23/1980, 9:30 a.m.): 22.2° C (72° F), conductivity 120 μS^{20}, pH 7.2; dGH 3°. Therefore, the fish should be offered soft, neutral water. Dimmed illumination or floating plants are beneficial. Dark gravel substrate. Sparse vegetation along the edges.

B: The animals are sexually mature after the 3rd or 4th month. Every month 15-50 young of approximately 8 mm (5/16") length are born. Raise on micro food, egg yolk, *Artemia* and, preferably, algae lawn.

F: O; fine flake food such as FD-Menu; grindal worms fed on vitamin mash or Tetra Conditioning Food; *Artemia*, TabiMin.

S: The tip of the gonopodium is clearly divided.

T: 22-26° C, **L:** ♂ 4 cm, ♀ 6 cm, **A:** 60 cm, **R:** m, t, **D:** 2-3
72-79° F, ♂ 1 2/3", ♀ 2 1/3", 24",

Scolichthys greenwayi, ♂ top ♀ bottom

Xenophallus umbratilis ♂

Xiphophorus alvarezi ROSEN, 1960
Blue Swortail

Syn.: *Xiphophorus helleri alvarezi.*

Hab.: Rio Usumacinta basin, Chiapas, southern Mexico, Central America.

F.I.: 1980 by Lothar Wischnath, Berlin, Germany.

Sex: The ♂'s lower tail fin ray is elongated into a sword, and he has the familiar gonopodium. The ♀ is fuller, and the pregnancy spot can be recognized at about 4 weeks of age. This pregnancy spot is important in selecting unfertilized ♀♀ for species-pure breeding.

Soc. B.: This species should be kept in a densely planted tank with about 1/3 free swimming space in the foreground. In smaller tanks always keep only 1 ♂ and several ♀♀ together. The ♂♂ are quarrelsome among themselves. The blue swordtail is suitable for a community tank, but should not be associated with other *Xiphophorus* to keep the species pure.

M: Corresponding to its natural habitat, the fish require a large volume filter and a current, especially on the water surface. The water should either be nitrite free or very low in nitrites (below 20 mg/l); otherwise, the ♂♂ are easily stunted and the ♀♀ are often infertile. In regard to water values, the species is quite tolerant; pH can be between 7.2 and 8.1 and the hardness between 10-20° dGH. As soon as the fishes are accustomed to certain water conditions, those water values should remain relatively constant. At water exchanges and especially when newly adding the fish, a good water conditioner, i.e., AquaSafe, should be used.

B: Not difficult, but in most cases few young (20-30, rarely 50) are produced with very large ♀♀. The breeding tank should have many hiding places and, if possible, floating plants. Raising of the young is accomplished with the smallest live foods; easiest in a tank full of algae.

F: O; this swordtail can only reach its full size through varied nutrition consisting of a lot of live food and plant containing flake foods (Tetra Conditioning Food). The best and most constant nutrition is offered by Tetra Tips, which are pressed to the glass in the morning and evening in a quantity according to the number of fishes. With them, the fishes can satiate themselves regularly.

S: The species can live 3-4 years and is sexually mature after 1 year. *X. alvarezi* distinguishes itself from *X. helleri* by 2-3 red central lines.

T: 25-28° C, L: ♂ 6 cm, plus sword, ♀ 6-8 cm, A: 50 cm, R: t, m, D: 2
77-82° F, ♂ 2 1/3", plus sword, ♀ 2 1/3"-3", 20",

Xiphophorus andersi MEYER & SCHARTL, 1979
Atoyac Platy

Syn.: None.

Hab.: Endemic to the Rio Atoyac near Finca Santa Anita, Veracruz, Mexico, Central America.

F.I.: 1979 by Manfred Meyer, Bad Nauheim, Germany.

Sex: ♂♂ have a gonopodium and a sickle-shaped elongation of the lower tail fin rays.

Soc. B.: The species can be kept in a community tank, but a species tank is more appropriate because of difficulties in its maintenance. Keep only one dominant full-grown ♂ with several ♀♀ and young. Its newborns and those of other species are strongly pursued.

M: Provide sufficient hiding places of dense vegetation or roots for weaker animals. Good filtration with a surface current is necessary. Water: pH 7.5; hardness 10-25° dGH.

Continued on page 760.

Xiphophorus alvarezi

Xiphophorus andersi

Xiphophorus clemenciae ALVAREZ, 1959

Gilded Swordtail

Syn.: None.

Hab.: Rio Sarabia, Rio dos Semillas, Rio Coatzacoalcos basin, Oaxaca, Mexico, Central America.

F.I.: 1978 by H. J. Schröder, Munich.

Sex: In the ♂ the lower rays of the tail fin are elongated into a sword; from the 2-3 month of age the gonopodium is formed. Young ♀♀ can be recognized by their tiny pregnancy spot after about 4 weeks.

Soc. B.: ♂♂ are often quarrelsome among themselves. In contrast to other swordtails, the young are barely pursued if adults are fed a varied diet. To keep the species pure, it should only be kept in a species tank if possible, but under no circumstances with other *Xiphophorus* species.

M: The fishes are sensitive to deteriorating water conditions, specially due to overfeeding and poor filter maintenance, i.e., an increase of the nitrate content. The filter should work biologically, having a large volume and a good water turnover. Do not put the species in a newly set-up aquarium, but one at least 3-6 months old. Water: pH 7.2-8.0; hardness 3-10° dGH. Needs dense edge vegetation and plenty of free swimming space in the front, dark gravel substrate with sand in between.

B: Extremely difficult. In very good water, full-grown ♀♀ give birth every 24-28 days to 10-15, sometimes to 25, young. The parents have to be removed, or the young transferred to an established tank with algae. Small live foods are necessary for rearing, the easiest is *Artemia*. Food remains have to be siphoned out half an hour after feeding. It has to be fed 6-8 times per day or twice daily with live food.

F: C, O; all kinds of smaller live foods, (especially mosquito larvae), FD foods, flake food.

S: This very rare and sensitive swordtail species is only known and kept by specialists. Successful maintenance and breeding are contingent upon good knowledge of water chemistry and the procurement of food.

T: 22-26° C, **L:** ♂ 3.5-4 cm + a 1.5-3 cm sword, ♀ 4-5 cm, **A:** 50 cm, **R:** t, m, **D:** 4
72-79° F, ♂ 1 1/3"-1 2/3" + a 2/3"-1 1/4" sword, ♀ 1 2/3"-2", 20",

Xiphophorus cortezi ROSEN, 1960

Cortez Swordtail

Syn.: *Xiphophorus montezumae cortezi.*

Hab.: Rio Axtla and other southern tributaries of the Rio Panuco system in Hidalgo and San Luis Potosi, Mexico, Central America.

F.I.: 1964 by the State Zoological Institute in Hamburg, Germany.

Sex: The ♂♂ have a short, sickle-shaped sword and a gonopodium. The ♀♀ are fuller and have a pregnancy spot.

Soc. B.: A quite peaceful species suitable for community tanks, however, not with other platys or swordtails. This would definitely lead to deterioration of the species and, in the end, an extinction of the true wild form.

M: Needs a well-planted tank, a strong filter and a lot of water current for its well-being. The water should turn over 2-3 times per hour; therefore, a 60 l (15 gal) tank should be provided with a filter rated at 200 l/hour (50 gal/hr). It also has to be considered that after 2-3 weeks the rate of flow-through decreases diametrically with the degree of fouling of the filter. Water: pH 7.5-8.2; hardness 5-20° dGH.

B: Every 4-5 weeks between 10 and 30 young are born; these are raised the easiest with *Artemia* and finest sieved flake food (Tetra Conditioning Food or TetraMin Baby Food).

F: O; varied feeding with vegetable flake foods and *Artemia*; mosquito larvae, *Cyclops* and *Daphnia*; freeze-dried and frozen foods.

Continued on page 760.

Xiphophorus clemenciae ♂

Xiphophorus cortezi, race with short sword

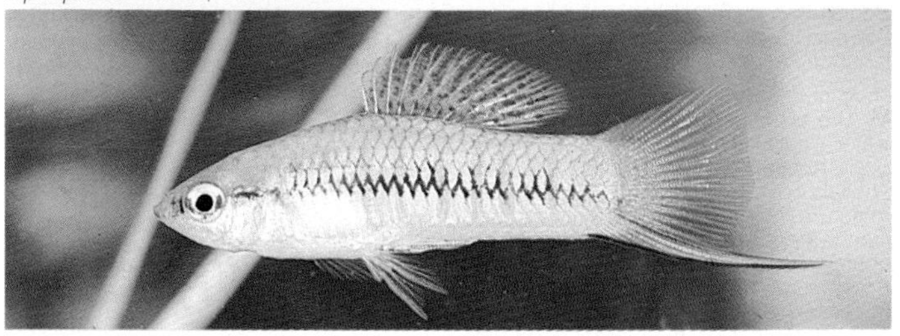

Xiphophorus cortezi, race with long sword.

Continuation of *Xiphophorus andersi from page 756*

B: It is quite difficult and requires thorough water management; namely, biological filtration through gravel or foam cartridges. Breeding tanks full of algae are best. The number of young fluctuates between 10 and 40. Rearing is best accomplished with *Artemia* and an algae stand which can be grown on glass panes under intense illumination.

F: H, O; vegetable flakes, FD feeds, freeze-dried and frozen live food, mosquito larvae and *Cyclops*.

S: It seems that the species will become extinct in nature without human intervention. It can only be found in a 2-3 km (1.2-1.9 mi) segment of the Rio Atoyac. The discoverer, E. Hnilicka, Puebla, Mexico, found the species in 1979, and he is of the opinion that it could be a remnant of an extinct species.

T: 24-28° C, **L:** ♂ and ♀ 4-4.5, sword 1-2 cm, **A:** 50 cm, **R:** b, m, **D:** 3
75-82° F, ♂ and ♀ 1$^2/_3$"-1$^3/_4$", sword $^1/_3$"-$^3/_4$", 20",

---

Continuation of *Xiphophorus cortezi:*

S: *X. cortezi* is the only swordtail species with an upward bent sword tip. Otherwise, this is only found in sword platys. There is a large range of variation within the species. Some animals have a spotted upper body area and dorsal fin, and others have a vertically striped lateral line. There are also differences in the thickness of the black band along the lateral line and in the lengths of the swords, as can be seen in the photos on the preceding pages.

T: 24-28° C, **L:** ♂ 4-5 cm + sword of 1-2 cm, ♀ 5-6 cm, **A:** 50 cm, **R:** m, b, **D:** 2
75-82° F, ♂ 1$^2/_3$"-2" + sword or $^1/_3$"-$^3/_4$", ♀ 2"-2$^1/_3$", 20",

---

Xiphophorus couchianus (GIRARD, 1859)

Monterrey Platy

Syn.: *Limia couchiana.*

Hab.: In headwaters, small rivers and ponds of the Rio San Juan system (Rio Grande basin) in the Huasteca Canyon by Santa Catarina and by Monterrey, Nuevo Leon, Mexico, Central America.

F.I.: 1979 by H. J. Schröder, Munich, Germany.

Sex: No differences in coloration. The ♂ is thinner and has a gonopodium.

Soc. B.: An extremely peaceful species, however, due to its rarity and difficult maintenance, it should only be cared for in a species tank.

M: The animals place high demands on water quality. The water must be absolutely nitrate-free and crystal clear. The animals are susceptible to fungus attack. In nature they apparently have very constant water conditions. The water must be chemically controlled at least once a week. A well "run in" tank with a biological filter is necessary to care for this problematic species. Water: pH 7.5-8.1; hardness 15-20° dGH. I would try a slight addition of table salt at about teaspoon per 10 l (2.5 gal) of water, General Tonic at half the recommended dosage every 4 weeks, and water exchange every 8 days with AquaSafe added.

B: It is very difficult. The young must be raised with the smallest live foods, especially *Artemia,* which have previously eaten algae, later with other types of sieved live foods.

F: C, O; varied nutrition based on disease-free live foods or frozen foods and alternating with vegetable flake foods. Perhaps TabiMin tablets.

S: This species was last caught in April of 1962 by American scientists, and because of its rarity in its habitat, it was placed in the Washington Species Protection Act Appendix 2 as a threatened animal species. Since this collection trip, the fish have not been seen in their natural habitat and are considered extinct in nature. There are

Continued on page 762.

Xiphophorus couchianus

Xiphophorus couchianus "Apodoca"

Continuation of *Xiphophorus couchianus:*

only reduced stocks in the tanks of a few specialists. Although the species is quite plain, it is a praise worthy endeavor to continue to propagate it, and eventually, with the help of specialists, to release it once again in its natural habitat as long as it still exists as such (drained by changing the course of the river or a lowering of the water table).

T: 27-30° C, **L:** ♂ 3-4 cm, ♀ 4-6 cm, **A:** 50 cm, **R:** m, t, **D:** 4
81-86° F, ♂ 1 -1 2/3", ♀ 1 2/3"-2 1/3, 20",

Xiphophorus evelynae ROSEN, 1960
Puebla Platy

Syn.: *Xiphophorus variatus evelynae.*

Hab.: Rio Teculutla system, Puebla, Mexico, Central America.

F.I.: 1980 by M. Meyer, Bad Nauheim, Germany.

Sex: The ♂ has a gonopodium, as do all members of the Poeciliidae, and it is more colorful.

Soc. B.: A very peaceful species well suited for the community tank void of other swordtails or platys. Note, this species is also very rare and has to remain pure.

M: Full-grown specimens need a lot of free swimming space in an aquarium that is as long as possible. It should be well-planted. Provide biological filtration with a water turnover of 1-2 times per hour. Except for the front pane, the algae should remain on the glass. Good algae growth should be encouraged through appropriate lighting.

B: Reproduction is not difficult. The young grow best in a breeding tank full of algae with the addition of finely ground vegetable flake food, mashed small frozen peas without skin, Liquifry and *Artemia* 2-3 times per week.

F: O; flake food, FD foods, frozen food and vegetable flake food.
The ♂♂ of this colorful species usually need 12-15 months to color up. Both sexes reach 2-3 years of age.

T: 22-27° C, **L:** ♂ 4 cm, ♀ 6 cm, **A:** 70 cm, **R:** t, m, b, **D:** 2
72-81° F, ♂ 1 2/3", ♀ 2 1/3, 28",

Xiphophorus gordoni MILLER & MINCKLEY, 1963
Gordon's Platy

Syn.: *Xiphophorus couchianus gordoni.*

Hab.: By Santa Tecla, Cuatro Cienegas basin, Coahuila, Mexico, Central America.

F.I.: 1980 by Lothar Wischnath, Berlin, Germany.

Sex: As the aforementioned species.

Soc. B.: Because of its difficult care, this timid but peaceful species should only be kept in a species tank.

M: The species is extremely warmth requiring and prefers to live in temperatures above 30° C (86° F), even up to 35° C (95° F). At temperatures below 28° C (82° F), the species becomes quite predisposed to disease. The tank should be well-planted. Good filtration with a calm water surface, partial water exchanges with the addition of a good water conditioner, and correct water values (pH 7.5-8.1, hardness 10-25° dGH) should be provided.

B: The ♀♀ normally only give birth to 5-15, sometimes 25, young of 6 mm (") length. The fish should be reared in a tank with algae and provided with *Artemia*, pond plankton and finely ground vegetable flakes.

F: Primarily with small live foods and vegetable flake food.

S: In its very small distribution area, this species is already endangered. It is probably being strongly decimated by companion fishes like gambusia and cichlids. The animals live in spring holes and small creeks, often in only 10-20 cm (4"-8") of water. There the temperature rises occasionally above 32° C (90° F). Those who keep the species should pass it on to other interested and experienced aquarists for propagation; otherwise, it will again disappear from the picture as so many other aquarium fishes before it.

T: 28-32° C, **L:** ♂ 2.5-3.5 cm, ♀ 3-4 cm, **A:** 50 cm, **R:** b, m, **D:** 4
82-90° F, ♂ 1"-1 1/3", ♀ 1 "-1 2/3", 20",

Xiphophorus evelynae ♂

Xiphophorus gordoni ♂

Xiphophorus helleri HECKEL, 1848
Belize Swordtail

Syn.: *X. helleri guentheri.*

Hab.: Rio Belize, close to the city of Belize, Belize, Central America.

F.I.: Unknown.

Sex: Like the following *Xiphophorus* species.

Soc. B.: The ♂♂ are less quarrelsome towards each other than are other populations.

M: Needs a densely planted tank with a pH of 7.5-7.8; hardness 4.0-15° dGH. Good water movement.

B: Breeding is usually difficult and very dependent on water composition. Nitrate-free water is essential. This population only has 10-25 young per spawn.

F: Like the following populations.

S: This is the smallest *Xiphophorus helleri* population. Since 1949, no catch data or biotope notes have been available. The spots of this population are larger, and the sword is shorter than in the following population from Rio Atoyac. There, the spots are smaller and denser, and the sword is significantly longer in relation to body length which is clearly visible in the photograph.

T: 24-28° C, L: ♂ + ♀ 4-5 cm, sword 2-3 cm, A: from 50 cm, R: t, m, b, D: 3
75-82° F, ♂ + ♀ 1 2/3"-2", sword 3/4-2 , from 20",

Xiphophorus helleri HECKEL, 1848
Atoyac Swordtail

Syn.: Very difficult to determine since the animals have been imported, if at all, under the most varied trade names. The spotted green form, for example, was called Montezuma swordtail. Today, we know that is a totally different species.

Hab.: Rio Atoyac, Veracruz, Mexico; Central America. Here one can find green swordtails with an especially long sword (endemic population) together with green-black spotted—long sword, red unspotted and red spotted. The latter two are color sports.

F.I.: Green population: by G. Daul, Berlin 1979. Green spotted, red spotted and red unspotted variations: 1980 by Lothar Wischnath, Berlin, Germany.

Soc. B.: Like the other *X. helleri.*

M: Depending on the size of the animals, place in tanks 50-80 cm (20"-31") long or larger. Provide dense plant growth, plenty of free swimming space, good filtration and water movement. pH 7.5; hardness 4-15° dGH.

B: This one is unproblematic, like the bred forms. Atlas Vol. 1, page 606.

F: O; flake food, Tetra FD-Menu and especially TetraTips, frozen food.

S: According to present knowledge, no *Xiphophorus* biotope has such differently colored animals living together without interbreeding, but of course, new natural crosses are not to be excluded.

T: 24-28° C, L: Quite varied. ♂ incl. sword 5-10 cm, ♀ 8-12 cm, A: from 50 cm, R: m, b, D: 1-2
75-82° F, Quite varied. ♂ incl. sword 2"-4", ♀ 3"-4 3/4", from 20",

Xiphophorus helleri HECKEL, 1848
Five Striped Swordtail

Syn.: None.

Hab.: Endemic to Rio Sontecomapan, Veracruz, Mexico, Central America.

F.I.: 1979 by Lothar Wischnath, Berlin, Germany.

Sex: Like other *helleri.*

Soc. B.: The ♂♂ are less quarrelsome than are most other *helleri* populations.

M: As recommended previously.

B: Like in other *helleri*, it is difficult.

F: As stated earlier.

S: The Rio Sontecomapan is a 35 km (22 mi) long drainage of Lake Catemaco. At the exit of the lake is a biotope limit so that the populations of the lake and the rivers cannot mix.

T: 24-28° C, L: ♂ + ♀ 8-12 cm, sword 6-10 cm, A: from 70 cm, R: m, b, D: 2
75-82° F, ♂ + ♀ 3"-4¾", sword 2⅓"-4", from 28",

Xiphophorus helleri HECKEL, 1848
Yucatan Swordtail

Syn.: None.

Hab.: In the eastern coastal tributaries, creeks and ponds in northwestern Yucatan, Mexico, and northeast of Campeche, Mexico, Central America.

F.I.: 1978 by G. Daul, Berlin, Germany.

Sex: As previously.

Soc. B.: As previously.

M: Like before, but hardness 4-20° dGH. The population is very sensitive to nitrates, making breeding sometimes difficult.

B: Occasionally difficult.

F: O; live foods of all kinds, flake food, frozen food, FD food.

S: A splendid, slender *helleri* population. Only the dominant ♂♂ have a beautiful red coloration below the lateral line. In weaker ♂♂, the red coloration only appears when they occupy the dominant position through age or removal of the previously reigning ♂. Can reach 3-4 years of age.

T: 24-28° C, L: 9 cm A: from 70 cm, R: m, b, D: 4
75-82° F, 3" from 28",

Xiphophorus helleri HECKEL, 1848
Catemaco Swordtail, Brass Swordtail

Syn.: None.

Hab.: Endemic to Lake Catemaco, Veracruz, Mexico, Central America.

F.I.: 1978 by F. Anders, Gießen, Germany.

Sex: Like other *helleri.*

Soc. B.: The ♂♂ are extremely quarrelsome, resulting in intense biting between equal aged ♂♂. Offspring are intensely pursued.

M: Several animals can be kept in a large tank with lots of hiding places provided by dense vegetation and stone and root edifications. Only keep one ♂ with about two ♀♀ in small tanks. Water make-up as before.

B: It is difficult and only succeeds with nitrate-free conditions and very good meals of live foods, e.g., mosquito larvae and TetraTips for the breeders. The young require *Artemia* and small pond plankton. The parents have to be removed. The water in the rearing tank should be well-filtered and provide a current. When feeding with plankton, the filter is, of course, turned off.

F: As the aforementioned *helleri.*

S: One of the most splendid *helleri* populations. The animals are rarely sexually mature prior to 15 months and reach an age of 3-4 years.

T: 24-28° C, L: ♂ 8-12 cm, ♀ 8-12 cm, sword 5-7 cm A: from 70 cm, R: m, b, t, D: 3
75-82° F, ♂ 3"-4¾", ♀ 3"-4¾", sword 2"-2¾"" from 28",

Xiphophorus helleri HECKEL, 1960
Oaxaca Swordtail

Syn.: None.
Hab.: Rio del Reyon, Oaxaca, Mexico, Central America.
F.I.: 1980 by Lothar Wischnath, Berlin, Germany.

F: Like the other *helleri* from the Rio Atoyac.
S: This slender *helleri* population has vertical banding on some animals, which crosses the lateral line.

T: 24-28° C, L: ♂ + ♀ 5-7 cm, sword 3-4 cm A: from 70 cm, R: t, m, b, D: 1-2
75-82° F, ♂ + ♀ 2"-2¾", sword 1"-1⅔" from 28",

Xiphophorus helleri, speckled, wild form from Rio Belize, Belize

Xiphophorus helleri, red, nonspeckled; Rio Atoyac

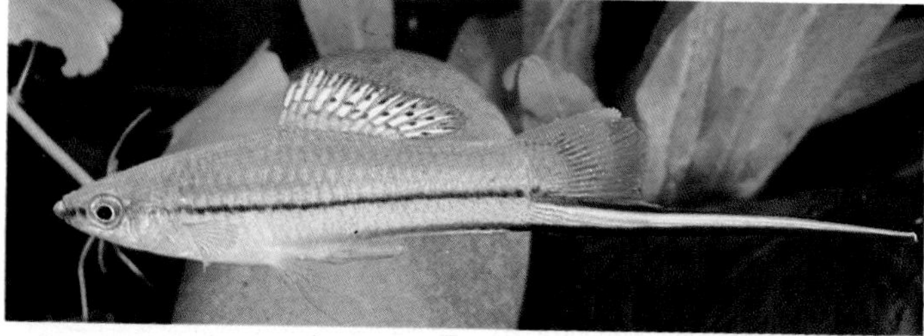

Xiphophorus helleri, Atoyac Swordtail

Xiphophorus helleri, Five-Striped Swordtail

Xiphophorus helleri, speckled; Rio Atoyac

Xiphophorus helleri, Yucatan population

Xiphophorus helleri, population from Rio del Reyon

Xiphophorus helleri, Brass Swordtail

Xiphophorus helleri HECKEL, 1848
Green Swordtail

Syn.: None.

Hab.: From Rio Nautla in Veracruz, Mexico, southward to Belize and Honduras, Central America.

F.I.: This population was first imported 1909 by W. Schroot, Hamburg, Germany.

Sex: As in other *helleri*.

Soc. B.: It differs with capture locality. The ♂♂ are often extremely bellicose. Its young, especially newborns, are usually pursued.

M: The requirements of the various populations are in part very different, depending on the water conditions of the various habitats. If two or more ♂♂ are to be kept, sufficient hiding places have to be provided. Provide 40 cm (16") tank length for each ♂. Hardness 3-30° dGH, depending on origin. pH 7.5-8.2; in every case a well-planted tank with good water turnover should be provided.

B: It varies from easy to difficult, depending on the populations. The number of young fluctuates correspondingly between 20 and 100.

F: O; plenty of live foods, flake food, Tetra Conditioning Food as variation. TetraTips and frozen mosquito larvae as staple food.

S: ROSEN (1979) extensively revised the systematics of *Xiphophorus*, making some important changes.
The previously recognized subspecies *X. helleri helleri*, *X. helleri strigatus* and *X. helleri guentheri* were withdrawn.

T: 22-28° C, L: ♂ 4-14 cm, depending on population sword 3-12 cm, ♀ 5-14 cm,
72-82° F, ♂ $1\frac{2}{3}$"-5 ", depending on population sword 1 -$4\frac{3}{4}$, ♀ 2"-5 ",
A: from 70 cm, R: m, b, t, D: 1-4, depending on population
from 28",

Biotope of *Xiphophorus helleri* "Atoyac". Creek to the Rio Atoyac, Arroyo Caiba.

Xiphophorus helleri

Biotope of *Xiphophorus helleri*, Rio Sontecomapan

Xiphophorus maculatus (GÜNTHER, 1866)
Gray Platy

Syn.: *Platypoecilus maculatus.*

Hab.: Rio San Juan, Veracruz, Mexico, Central America.

F.I.: Unknown.

Sex: As the previously stated.

Soc. B.: As the previously stated.

M: As before. pH 7.5-7.9, hardness 5-15° dGH.

B: As the previously mentioned.

F: As before.

S: The black spots are specially pronounced in ♂♂.

T: 24-28° C, 75-82° F, L: ♂ 3-4 cm, ♂ 1"-1 2/3", ♀ 4-6 cm, ♀ 1 2/3"-2 1/3", A: from 50 cm, from 20", R: t, m, D: 1

Xiphophorus maculatus (GÜNTHER, 1866)
Jamapa Platy, Variegated Platy

Syn.: *Platypoecilus maculatus.*

Hab.: Rio Jamapa and its small tributaries, Veracruz, Mexico, Central America.

F.I.: Unknown.
All other recommendations for care of this population can be taken from the previous.

S: In contrast to the previous species, the spots and dots are arranged and sized differently in this population.

T: 24-28° C, 75-82° F, L: ♂ 3-4 cm, ♂ 1"-1 2/3", ♀ 4-6 cm, ♀ 1 2/3"-2 1/3", A: from 50 cm, from 20", R: t, m, D: 2

Biotope of *Xiphophorus maculatus*. Pond at Veracruz, Mexico.

Xiphophorus maculatus, Gray Platy, Rio San Juan

Xiphophorus maculatus, Variegated Platy, Rio Jamapa

Xiphophorus maculatus (GÜNTHER, 1866)
a) Black Platy
b) Belize Platy
c) Red-Eyed Platy

Syn.: *Platypoecilus maculatus.*

Hab.: a) Swamps at the edge of the Rio Papaloapan, Veracruz, Mexico.
b) Swamps at the edge of the mouth of the Rio Belize, Belize.
c) Mouth of the Rio Belize.

F.I.: 1980 by L. Wischnath, Berlin, Germany.

Sex: Like the nominate form.

Soc. B.: All peaceful. Suitable for community tanks with peaceful species.
Don't keep together with other populations of *Xiphophorus* or their bred forms!

M: a) pH 7.0-7.8; hardness: 10-20° dGH.
b) pH around 7.5; hardness: 4-15° dGH.
c) pH 7.0; hardness: 4-6° dGH. Prone to fungal infections. All: planted tank with little water movement. As little nitrate as possible.

B: a) Sensitive towards fungal infections. Use FungiStop or General Tonic at the dosage to acclimate.
b) Easy.
c) Only possible in nitrate-free, aged water with a mature biological filter. *Artemia* are necessary for rearing. Warm, soft water, peat filtration.

F: a) O; b) O; c) H, O.

S: a) ♂ is always black; ♀ is gray.
b) This population is variable in coloration.
c) Both sexes have red eyes (lens); they are therefore not albinos.

T: all 24-30° C, L: a) ♂ 4 cm, ♀ 5 cm, b) ♂ 4 cm, ♀ 6 cm, c) ♂ 3 cm, ♀ 4 cm,
all 75-86° F, a) ♂ 1²/₃", ♀ 2", b) ♂ 1²/₃", ♀ 2¹/₃", c) ♂ 1 ", ♀ 1²/₃",
A: all from 50 cm, R: all, D: a) 3, b) 1, c) 4
all from 20",

Xiphophorus maculatus, Black Platy, Rio Papaloapan

Xiphophorus maculatus, Belize Platy, Rio Belize

Xiphophorus maculatus, Red-Eyed Platy, Rio Belize

Xiphophorus milleri ROSEN, 1960

Catemaco Platy

Syn.: None.

Hab.: Endemic to Lake Catemaco, Veracruz, Mexico, Central America.

F.I.: 1963 by the Zoological Institute of Hamburg, Germany.

Sex: The ♂ is clearly smaller and has a gonopodium. The underside of the posterior body is black spotted. The ♀ clearly has a fuller stomach and a pregnancy spot. Both sides of the caudal peduncle have only a black line; the spots are mostly absent.

Soc. B.: A peaceful species. Suitable for the community tank. Housing with the *Xiphophorus helleri* population of Lake Catemaco is recommended. There is no danger of a cross. In general, *helleri* and platys very rarely cross.

M: The species has a high oxygen requirement; therefore, a water turnover of 2-3 times per hour is required. The aquarium should have dense vegetation and a smooth bottom to facilitate the removal of the oxygen consuming mulm layer. Water: pH about 7.5; hardness 4-15° dGH. The water must be biologically beyond reproach, i.e., free of nitrate. Weekly monitoring with test kits available in the trade is required. Also check nitrate levels of your tap; if that is the case, it would have to be removed using an ion exchanger available in the trade to remove the nitrate.

B: Normally very difficult, and only successful under the best water conditions. The young are raised with *Artemia*. The young only number 3 to 8, maximum 10.

F: O; small flake food, specially FD-Menu. As variation, Tetra Conditioning Food and other on vegetable based flake foods. Try TetraTips. Once a week offer *Artemia* or other small live food.

S: These animals live in the shallow surge areas of the shores of Lake Catemaco as long as there is strong algae and plant growth. The fishes find their nourishment on the bottom among these plants. The animals reach 2 to 3 years of age.

T: 24-28° C, **L:** ♂ 2.5-3-3.5 cm, ♀ 3-4.5 cm, **A:** from 50 cm, **R:** b, m, **D:** 4
75-82° F, ♂ 1"-1 "-1 1/3", ♀ 1 "-1∫", from 20",

Xiphophorus montezumae JORDAN & SNYDER, 1900

Tailspot Montezuma Swordtail

Syn.: None.

Hab.: Northern tributaries of the Rio Panuco system in San Luis Potosi, Mexico, Central America.

F.I.: Not known.

Sex: ♂♂ have a sword and gonopodium. ♀ has a faint pregnancy spot and is somewhat larger than the ♂.

Soc. B.: Peaceful species. The ♂♂ only fight among themselves in tanks that are too small and sparsely planted. The fishes can be combined with other species, even platys, but not with other *Xiphophorus*; this would lead to undesired crosses.

M: According to its origin, a strong water turnover of 3-4 times per hour is required. Dense vegetation. Water: pH 7.5-8.2; hardness 5-20° dGH. Needs a bright tank placement and a dark bottom.

B: Not difficult. Every 4-5 weeks 15-30 young about 8 mm (5/16") long are born. Plankton and *Artemia* are necessary to raise the young. The breeding tank needs hiding places and a dense vegetation. Remove the parents after spawning. The ♂ should perhaps be removed after fertilization.

F: O; black mosquito larvae are specially important for growth and ripening of the parent fish. Outside of the spawning time, feed with all types of flake foods and TetraTips.

S: A very beautiful species; ♂♂ often have a pink sword. The species was already presented in Vol. 1, page 612. This picture, however, shows the tailspot variety.

T: 24-28° C, **L:** ♂ 5.5-6 cm, ♀ 6.5-7 cm, **A:** from 50 cm, **R:** m, b, **D:** 3
75-82° F, ♂ 2 "-2 1/3", ♀ 2 1/3", from 20",

Xiphophorus milleri

Xiphophorus montezumae, tailspot variety

Xiphophorus nigrensis ROSEN, 1960
Black Swordtail

Syn.: *Xiphophorus pygmaeus nigrensis.*

Hab.: Rio Choy and Rio Coy of the Rio Panuco system, San Luis Potosi, Mexico, Central America.

F.I.: 1964 by the Zoological Institute of Hamburg, Germany.

Sex: In ♂♂ the lower tail fin rays are elongated to a greater or lesser degree into a sword. The form from Rio Choy has a long sword while that of the Rio Coy has a short sword. In that same river is also a swordless morph. In ♂♂ the lower tail fin rays are only slightly elongated. These ♂♂ are yellow and the ♀♀ are black/gray.

Soc. B.: A quite peaceful *Xiphophorus* species. In well-planted tanks, several ♂♂ can be kept together. The weaker ♂♂ must be able to hide. However, quarrels do not lead to any injuries. The species is best kept alone since it possibly could be oppressed by other fishes. Keep with gentle tetras or dwarf cichlids as long as the water conditions are suitable for all.

M: The fish likes a strong water turnover and a well-planted aquarium. It has a high oxygen requirement; therefore, the surface of the aquarium has to be in constant movement, and between the water surface and the cover glass or the hood, there must be sufficient room for air to enter. The water should have a pH of about 7.5 (plus or minus 0.3) and a hardness to 25° dGH.

B: About every 4 weeks 15 young are born which can be raised with *Artemia* and pond plankton. A tank full of algae (green algae) with a mature filter is very advantageous.

F: C, O; feeding should predominantly consist of small live food, frozen live foods like mosquito larvae, *Daphnia* or bosmids.

Continued on page 778.

Xiphophorus nigrensis, long sword

Xiphophorus nigrensis, short sword

Xiphophorus nigrensis, yellow form

Continuation of *Xiphophorus nigrensis*:

In addition, daily or every other day, depending on the size of the animals, crumbled vegetable flake food is given to supply the required fiber for digestion.

S: These fish are actually quite hardy but are very sensitive to higher water temperatures. In contrast, they tolerate temperatures down to 22° C (72° F) for a longer time. Achieving the desired maintenance temperature of 24-25° C (75-77° F) is not difficult with today's thermostats. Note the variation of this species. Our three photographs show all three forms of this swordtail.

T: 24-25° C, L: ♂ about 4 cm, ♀ 4.5-5.5 cm, A: from 50 cm, R: t, m, D: 3
75-77° F, ♂ about 1²/₃", ♀ 1∫"-2 ", from 20",

Xiphophorus pygmaeus HUBBS & GORDON, 1943
Dwarf Swordtail

Syn.: None.

Hab.: Rio Axtla, Rio Moctezuma system in the Rio Panuco drainage area by San Luis Potosi, Mexico, Central America.

F.I.: 1963 by the Zoological Institute of Hamburg, Germany.

Sex: The ♂'s gonopodium is clearly visible; in contrast, the normal sword of swordtails is only suggested.

Soc. B.: A very peaceful species which can even be kept with other *Xiphophorus* species since apparently no interbreeding occurs.

M: The species likes current and oxygen-rich water. A large volume filter for nitrate removal is advantageous. The fish immediately react with clamped fins to poor water conditions; at that point a washing of the filter medium, a partial water exchange of ¹/3 to and the addition of a good water conditioner becomes imperative. The tank can be more or less densely planted, whereby ¹/3 of the foreground should remain free for swimming. The bottom can be made up of sand or gravel; mulmy corners are to be avoided and feed remains should always be removed. Water: pH 7.2-7.8; hardness 5-18° dGH.

B: It is only successful with excellent water quality. The breeding tank has to be planted especially dense. A floating plant cover of water fern makes it possible for the young to escape from the pursuit of other fishes or the parents (rare). Rearing is accomplished with the smallest live foods, for example, *Artemia*.

F: C; small live foods, FD-Menu, partially TetraTips, freeze-dried and small frozen types of live foods are a significant part of good nourishment. Once a day, crumpled vegetable flake food can be given to add fiber to the menu.

S: The yellow ♂ morph has been imported to Germany by Mr. Lothar Wischnath. The offspring of these ♂♂ are always yellow; in nature this color morph has few chances of survival. Supposedly old ♂♂ of the normal morph also turn yellow.

T: 24-26° C, L: ♂ up to 3.5 cm, ♀ up to 4 cm, A: from 50 cm, R: m, b, D: 3-4
75-79° F, ♂ up to 1¹/₃", ♀ up to 1²/₃", from 20",

Xiphophorus pygmaeus, yellow morph (only ♂)

Xiphophorus pygmaeus, normal coloration

Xiphophorus variatus x couchianus
Yellow Hybrid Platy

Syn.: *Xiphophorus roseni.*

Hab.: Arroyo Chapultepec, Nuevo León, Mexico, Central America.

F.I.: 1980 by Lothar Wischnath, Berlin, Germany.

Sex: The ♂♂ are easily recognized by their gonopodium.

Soc. B.: A peaceful species which can be kept in a community tank, but if possible, not with other platys or swordtails.

M: The fish prefers shaded areas and little water movement. Therefore, large and broad-leaved *Echinodorus* or a partial cover of floating plants is advantageous to their well-being. The water can have a pH between 7.5 and 8.1, and the hardness should be between 10 and 25° dGH.

B: It is not difficult. Successful rearing is achieved with TetraMin Baby Food or Liquifry, and *Artemia* 2-3 times a week. Some young also grow up in the floating plant cover without special attention; 20-40 are born.

F: C, O; flake foods of all kinds, frozen and freeze-dried foods, all flake foods. Once in a while offer live food if it is available. Feeding with live food, however, is not a requirement.

S: This fish was only discovered in 1980 by Erich Hnilicka, Puebla, Mexico, while searching for *Xiphophorus couchianus*. MEYER (1983) determined that this species, originally described as *X. roseni*, is a natural hybrid between *X. variatus* and *X. couchianus*.

T: 24-30° C, **L:** ♂ + ♀ 3.5-5 cm, **A:** from 50 cm, **R:** m, **D:** 1
75-86° F, ♂ + ♀ 1 1/3"-2", from 20",

Xiphophorus signum ROSEN & KALLMAN, 1969
Comma Swordtail

Syn.: *Xiphophorus helleri signum.*

Hab.: Rio Chajmaic, Río de la Pasión basin, Alta Verapaz, Guatemala, Central America.

F.I.: 1980 by M. Schartl, Gießen, Germany.

Sex: ♂ has a gonopodium and a short, very characteristic sword which has a wider outline in the upper half and a narrower outline in the lower. The picture opposite very clearly shows the differences of the sexes and the design. The ♂ often develops very late.

Soc. B.: Unfortunately, the ♂♂ are very quarrelsome. Many hiding places have to be offered in small tanks if more than one large ♂ is kept.

M: Tanks should be well-planted and have a large volume powerful filter. Careful monitoring of the biological make-up of the water is required weekly. This fish does not tolerate nitrites or nitrates in the water; therefore, pay special attention to the water supply. The nitrate should be below 5 mg/l in the water source. The pH can fluctuate between 7.2 and 8.0 and the hardness between 10 and 20° dGH, but constant values within these ranges are desirable.

B: It is difficult. Pregnant ♀♀ give birth every 4-5 weeks to 20-40 young.

F: C, O; the species prefers small live foods. As variation, crumpled TetraTips and Tetra Conditioning Food should be offered.

S: This very sensitive swordtail species deserves special attention. Presently, only some small stocks exist with specialists. Reproduction is especially difficult because the ♂♂ develop so late. After some time, a deficit of ♂♂ appears in the still very reduced stocks. The animals become sexually mature after about 1 year and can reach an age of 3-4 years.

T: 24-28° C, **L:** ♂ + ♀ 5-8 cm, sword 5-7 cm **A:** from 50 cm, **R:** t, m, **D:** 4
75-82° F, ♂ + ♀ 2"-3", sword 2"-2 3/4", from 20",

Xiphophorus variatus x couchianus

Xiphophorus signum

Xiphophorus variatus (MEEK, 1904)

Platy Variatus, as a bred form, see Aquarium Atlas Vol. 1, page 614.

Syn.: *Platypoecilus variatus, X. variegata,* (fantasy name).

Hab.: Atlantic tributaries south of Rio Soto la Marin, Tamaulipas, Mexico, south to Rio Nautla in Veracruz, Mexico, Central America.

F.I.: 1931 by Seaman Conrad of Hamburg, Germany.

Sex: The ♂ is clearly recognized by its gonopodium and the usually stronger colors; the ♀ has a pregnancy spot darker than the skin.

Soc. B.: A very peaceful species that is especially well suited for the community tank without competitors for algae. The association of the wild strain, see our photos on the right hand page, with other *Xiphophorus* is not recommended because it leads to unwanted crosses.

M: The fish prefer a densely planted tank with a moderate water turnover (to 1 per hour). Modest demands are placed on water quality. pH between 7.3 and 8.1, and the hardness can fluctuate between 4 and 25° dGH. When fish are transferred from one extreme into another, that is, low hardness in the show tank and then again high hardness with new water, a good water conditioner has to be added to the new water so that the fish do not suffer shock. This species of toothcarp endures even low temperatures, sometimes below 10° C (50° F), when, of course, it should not be fed then. Densely planted, slightly algae covered, sparsely populated tank.

B: It is not difficult. Place the ♀ into a spawning box shortly before spawning and remove thereafter. Besides quality feeding, hardly any attention has to be given to the young. Naturally the water should not be polluted by excessive food. Algae are especially important.

F: O; the fish are omnivorous, whereby 1/3 of the diet should be of animal origin and 2/3 of vegetable origin.

S: As the name of the species already expresses, there are many color variations, even in its natural biotope. Offspring of wild caught animals are almost never consistent in color and split strongly into several color sports. The species can be crossed with swordtails under favorable conditions; the offspring are sterile.

T: 22-28° C, L: ♂ 4-6 cm, ♀ 5-7 cm, A: from 50 cm, R: t, m, b, D: 1-2
72-82° F, ♂ 1 2/3"-2 1/3", ♀ 2"-2 3/4", from 20",

Xiphophorus variatus, Rio Axtla

Xiphophorus variatus, Rio Nautla

Xiphophorus variatus, Rio Axtla

Biotope of *X. xiphidium*; Rio Purificación, Mexico.

Xiphophorus xiphidium x *X. variatus*, a natural hybrid from Rio Soto la Marina. This one was described as *X. kosszanderi*.

X. xiphidium, Rio Purificación

Xiphophorus xiphidium (HUBBS & GORDON, 1932)

Sword Platy

Syn.: *Platypoecilus xiphidium.*

Hab.: Tributaries of the Rio Soto la Marina system, Rio Purificación, Rio Santa Engracia, Tamaulipas, Mexico, Central America. (Each of the three mentioned river systems harbors a different population.)

F.I.: Population from the Rio Purificación by F. Mayer, Hamburg, Germany, 1933.

Sex: The ♂ has a gonopodium and a short sword and is more intensely colored than the ♀.

Soc. B.: A peaceful species suitable for almost every community tank without other *Xiphophorus* species. If this species is associated with other, also bred, forms of swordtails and platys, it can easily lead to unwanted crosses. One should strive to keep the species pure.

M: The fishes like strong currents with good plant growth. They should only be stocked into a new tank when it has been biologically "run in" with an established filter and/or substrate. The water should have a pH of 7.5, plus or minus 0.3, and a hardness between 5 and 20° dGH. Despite the rich plant growth, enough free swimming space should remain for this active species.

B: Breeding is most successful in water below 10° dGH. The young should be feed twice daily with *Artemia*; 2-4 additional feedings can consist of sieved flake food, for example, TetraMin Baby Food or finest Tetra Conditioning Food.

F: C; flake and live foods with a high protein content, frozen and freeze-dried live foods. 2-3 times a week vegetable flake foods are readily accepted.

S: In Vol. 1 of the Aquarium Atlas the species was presented on page 615. The picture in the 3rd and 4th edition show the coloration of the Rio Santa Engracia population. At the top of the page, one can see the population presently known as *X. xiphidium* from Rio Purificación and bottom left, the population from Rio Soto la Marina.

T: 22-26° C, L: ♂ + ♀ 3-5 cm, A: from 50 cm, R: m, D: 3
72-79° F, ♂ + ♀ 1"-2", from 20",

Biotope of *Xiphophorus andersi*, *X. helleri*; Rio Atoyac.

Biotope of *X. milleri*; Lake Catemaco.

Parosphromenus filamentosus, see page 807 for text.

Microctenopoma congicum (BOULENGER, 1887)
Congo Ctenopoma

Syn.: *Anabas congicus, Ctenopoma congicum.*

Hab.: Lower Zaire (Stanley Pool), coastal waters of western Africa. Ogowe River at Lambarene, Ubangi River (largest northern tributary of the Zaire).

F.I.: 1912 by Kuntschmann, Hamburg, Germany.

Sex: ♂ has pointed, elongated fins; they are more rounded in the ♀.

Soc. B.: Normally a peaceful species which, in contrast to other climbing perches, can be kept in a community tank.

M: The species is found together with *M. ansorgei* (Vol. 1, page 620) in the same distribution area (Chioango at Landana). *M. congicum*, however, is not as demanding as the other species. Water: pH 6.8-7.8; hardness up to 25° dGH. A well-planted, not too bright aquarium is appropriate.

B: A bubble nest is built by the ♂ beneath overhanging roots or below broad plant leaves. Depending on the temperature, the larvae hatch after 24-30 hours. Raise with plankton.

F: C, O; flake food alternating with frozen food, and every once in a while offer some live food.

S: Often confused in the aquarium literature with other climbing perches, e.g., *M. fasciolatum, M. nanum* and *C. oxyrhynchum*.

T: 23-27° C, **L:** 8.5 cm, **A:** 100 cm, **R:** m, t, **D:** 2
73-81° F, 3 1/3", 39",

Microctenopoma damasi (POLL, 1939)
Pearlscale Ctenopoma

Syn.: *Anabas damasi, Ctenopoma damasi.*

Hab.: Eastern Uganda, Lake Edward, Africa.

F.I.: 1968 by Berns and Peters, Tübingen, Germany.

Sex: The ventral fins of the ♂ are clearly elongated and reach beyond the anus. In the ♀, the fins are elongated but do not reach past the anus. ♂ more colorful and darker.

Soc. B.: Peaceful, brood caring species. Because of its specialty, only keep in a species tank or with very docile species.

M: Use a densely planted species tank with lots of shelter. Floating plant cover. The animals live in seclusion, especially when they feel disturbed. The animals mostly stand among the plants. The hiding place is only left to take air. The animals are among the plants and much more active during the spawning season. Water: pH 6.5-7.5; hardness up to 15° dGH. Peat filtration. Regular water exchanges of 1/3 every 14 days (AquaSafe!).
The animals are sexually mature after 8 months and are ripened with live food, water exchanges and an increase in temperature.

B: A bubble nest is built usually among the plant leaves. After a strong embrace of the pair, the eggs rise into the nest. Eggs floating to the sides are collected and spit into the nest. This is guarded a few hours by the ♂. Afterwards, the ♂ observes the nest from some distance. After 36 hours (28° C; 82° F) the first larvae hatch and are free-swimming after an additional 48 hours. Pond plankton and fine, pulverized flake food (FD-Menu or similar) should be offered sparingly, but 5-8 times daily. After about 4 days, one can continue the feedings with *Artemia* without problems.

F: C, O; flake food, FD-Menu, frozen food. Small live foods.

S: This rare and beautiful species deserves special attention. While VIERKE (1978) writes that the larvae already take atmospheric air after the 10th day, RICHTER (1979) mentions that the 7.7 mm (5/16) long larvae do this between the 37th and 45th day.

T: 26-30° C, **L:** ♂ 7 cm, ♀ 6 cm, **A:** 80 cm, **R:** m, t, **D:** 3
79-86° F, ♂ 2 3/4", ♀ 2 1/3", 31",

Microctenopoma congicum

Microctenopoma damasi

Ctenopoma multispinis PETERS, 1844
Many-Spined Ctenopoma

Syn.: *Anabas multispinis, Spirobranchus smithii, Anabas rhodesianus, Anabas vermayi, Ctenopoma multispine.*

Hab.: Southeast Congo region, Zambia, Mozambique, Zimbabwe (Rhodesia), Okotango River and Lake Ngami (Botswana), Namibia (Southwest Africa) and Angola; Africa.

F.I.: 1935 a specimen; April of 1972 by D. Schaller, Munich, Germany.

Sex: ♂ has spiny areas.

Soc. B.: A species which likes to swim and requires a lot of room. Associate only with robust species, because *C. multispinis* is aggressive and bites. Equal-sized conspecifics, *Anabas testudineus* and *C. nigropannosum* are suitable tankmates.

M: Large tank with a dark bottom. Not too bright. Roots and stone structures. Water: pH 6.0-7.5; hardness 5-20° dGH.

B: The species was first bred in 1975 by Dr. Foersch. After an intense courtship, the ♀ is embraced by the ♂. For this, the thorny areas behind its eyes and on the caudal peduncle play a prominent role. Several thousand eggs rise to the surface because of their oily exterior. No brood care is practiced. The parents should either be removed after spawning, or the eggs carefully transferred to a rearing tank containing the same water (eggs skimmed off). Raise with *Artemia*.

F: C, O; omnivore.

S: Like *Anabas testudineus*, this species is also capable of moving over land; usually it buries into the mud of drying waters in order to survive the drought.

T: 24-27° C, **L:** 16 cm, **A:** 150 cm, **R:** m, t, **D:** 2-3
75-81° F, 6 1/3", 59",

Ctenopoma nigropannosum REICHENOW, 1875
Two-Spotted Ctenopoma

Syn.: *Anabas nigropannosus, Ctenopoma ashbysmithii, C. gabonense.*

Hab.: Delta of the Niger and mouth of the Zaire (Congo), Central Africa.

F.I.: 1933.

Sex: ♂ has a spiny area behind the eyes; it is lacking on the caudal peduncle of this species.

Soc. B.: A rough, unsociable species, unsuitable for community tanks. Perhaps it could be kept either with large cichlids, large catfishes or other large perches.

M: Species tank with roots and stones. Java fern. Gravel bottom. No demands are placed on water conditions.

B: Has not yet been performed in an aquarium. The parents do not guard their young.

F: C, O; omnivore, even water plants.

S: There is a great similarity to *Anabas testudineus*. This species is unimportant to the hobby.

T: 24-27° C, **L:** 17 cm, **A:** 180 cm, **R:** m, t, **D:** 4
79-86° F, 6 3/4", 71",

Ctenopoma multispinis

Ctenopoma nigropannosum

Sandelia bainsii CASTELNAU, 1861
Bain's Perch

Syn.: *Anabas bainsii, Spirobranchus bainsii, Ctenopoma microlepidotum.*

Hab.: South Africa at the cities of East London, King Williams Town, Grahams Town.

F.I.: 1973 by D. Schaller, Munich; very rare since there is obviously no interest.

Sex: Not described.

Soc. B.: Only keep with equal sized robust fishes, individually or as a pair. Extraordinarily aggressive.

M: Needs a large tank with a strong filter current. The fish can tolerate just about any water conditions. pH 6.8-8.0; hardness: 10-30° dGH. Coarse gravel as substrate. Plant roots need to be well anchored, e.g., in pots. During the summer the species can surely be easily kept in a garden pond as long as sufficient feed is available.

B: Has not yet occurred in an aquarium. Reproduction should be similar to *Sandelia capensis.*

F: C; predator; any substantial live food. After acclimation, also tablet food and trout pellets.

S: The genus is geographically very distant from other climbing perches. It lives in the southern most range of the anabantids. The closest climbing perch relatives live over 1000 km (620 mi) north.

T: 18-22° C, **L:** 21 cm, **A:** 150 cm, **R:** m, **D:** 2-3
64-72° F, 8 1/3", 59",

Sandelia capensis (CUVIER & VALENCIENNES, 1831)
Cape Perch

Syn.: *Spirobranchus capensis, Anabas capensis.*

Hab.: From the rivers Langerlei, Elands, Camtoos, Couritz to the Colga River northeast of Cape Town, South Africa.

F.I.: 1973 by D. Schaller.

Sex: Not known, but during the spawning season the ♀ is ventrally fuller.

Soc. B.: Keep in a species tank with several animals or combine with robust cichlids and catfishes; but then only one pair or an individual should be kept.

M: As the preceding species.

B: The animals can already be sexually mature in 1 year at a length of only 5 cm (2"). The fish are open spawners. The ♀ is embraced by the ♂ during spawning. The eggs adhere to plants and stones. The ♂ guards the small, 1 mm (1/32) eggs. After 35 hours (at 24° C; 75° F) the larvae hatch and are free-swimming on the third day. Raise with the smallest pond plankton, after 8 days, *Artemia.*

F: C, O; tablet foods, large flakes, pellets. Any live food of suitable size. Frozen food.

S: None.

T: 18-22° C, **L:** about 15 cm, max., 21.6 cm, **A:** 150 cm, **R:** m, t, **D:** 2-3
64-72° F, about 6", max., 8 ", 59",

Sandelia bainsii

Sandelia capensis

Betta anabatoides BLEEKER, 1850
Pearly Betta

Syn.: None.

Hab.: South Borneo (not rare). All other mentioned localities probably refer to other *Betta* species.

F.I.: March 1978 by the Foerschs, Mrs. Korthaus and Mr. Hanrieder.

Sex: ♀ with somewhat longer fins and more intense designs.

Soc. B.: Mouthbrooder which can be associated with other fish as long as they are not too small. ♂♂ establish territories among themselves without biting skirmishes. For breeding purposes, keep only one pair in the tank.

M: LINKE (1980) gives some specific values for the indigenous waters of this species: slightly brown water (iron and humic acids) with a water hardness to 1° dGH. The species should tolerate up to 5° dGH without problems. pH 4.5-4.8, with acclimation, values between 4.8 and 6.0 could also be possible. Conductivity is 5-30 microsiemens. The peat filter needs to produce only a small current. The fish prefer to inhabit weedy shores.

B: Spawning behavior is quite similar to *Betta picta*. The larvae hatch after about 80 hours (at 26° C; 79° F). 8 days later the ♂ spits the fry out close to the water surface. The fry immediately go in search of food and there is no further brood care.

F: C, O; flake food, FD-Menu, frozen food, every 2-3 days provide hearty live food.

S: None.

T: 27-30° C, **L:** 10-12 cm, **A:** 80 cm, **R:** m, t, **D:** 3
81-86° F, 4-4 3/4", 31",

Betta edithae VIERKE, 1984
Edith's Betta

Syn: *Betta anabantoides, B. taeniata.*

Hab.: Numerous in all of south Borneo.

F.I.: March 1978 by Mrs. Edith Korthaus, Dr. W. Foersch and A. Hanrieder.

Sex: ♂♂ at the small size of 4 cm (1 ") already display a blue-black fringe on the anal and the lower half of the caudal fin. ♀♀ are smaller and show no iridescent spots. During the breeding season they show a clearly fuller stomach.

Soc. B.: Quite peaceful and, in aquaria over 80 cm (31") long, several pairs can be kept. However, for breeding they should be kept in pairs.

M: Needs a well-planted tank with floating plants to reduce light. Provide the tank with moderate filtration and dark substrate. pH 6.5-7.5; hardness to 10° dGH. Cover the tank well; the fish is a good jumper!

B: Mouthbrooder (♂). For breeding purposes the pH must be below 7 and the hardness below 10° dGH; otherwise, the ♂ will not carry the brood to term. Mating occurs usually on the ground. The ♂ embraces the ♀ which deposits the eggs in the U-shaped body and anal fin. Afterwards, she picks up the eggs and spits them toward the ♂. After 10 days the fry emerge from the father's mouth. The fry should then be separated from the adults and initially fed micro foods.

F: C, O; flake foods, mosquito larvae, small earthworms, FD foods.

S: Interestingly, unknown fighting fish are often first misidentified as *B. taeniata*. This also happens to *B. edithae*. Most reports in the aquarium literature dealing with *B. taeniata* actually refer to *B. edithae*.

T: 24-28° C, **L:** 7.5 cm, **A:** 50 cm, **R:** all, **D:** 3
75-82° F, 3", 20",

Betta anabatoides

Betta edithae

Betta foerschi VIERKE, 1979
Foersch's Betta

Syn.: None.

Hab.: Mentaya River system in southern Borneo (250 km; 155 mi northwest of Benjarmasin) at the edge of a jungle creek with cola-colored water.

F.I.: Dr. Walter Foersch, Ms. Edith Korthaus and A. Hanrieder brought this new species back in March 1978 from a collection trip.

Sex: The previously held belief that the ♂♂ have two golden bands on the operculum while the ♀♀ are red cannot be maintained. The sexes can only be distinguished during the courtship and spawning season when the ♀ has a fuller belly. The dorsal and anal fin of the ♂ is wider and, to a greater extent, elongated into a tip.

Soc. B.: Mouthbrooder. Peaceful, timid fish, only suitable for a species tank or to keep with sedate catfishes. In the same habitat *Parosphromenus parvulus* (and *Sphaerichthys acrostoma*) can be found.

M: Provide a well-planted tank without disturbance by larger fishes or environment. Water: pH 4.6-6.0; hardness below 4° dGH. Peat filtration. Use great care during water exchanges and other aquarium hygiene activities. The fish is sensitive towards fluctuating water conditions. From these it easily develops diseases.

B: Builds a bubble nest, probably similar to *B. splendens*. Hiding places for the ♀ are necessary because the species is distinctly aggressive among themselves. Use peat filtration for water conditioning. Feed parent fish with live foods such as *Cyclops* and *Daphnia*; shortly before the breeding set-up, feed with Enchytraea. After the eggs are laid, the ♂ broods them in his mouth for about 10 days. The released young are then about 7 to 8 mm (5/16") long and immediately accept *Artemia* nauplii.

F: C; small live foods, FD-Menu, *Artemia*, small frozen foods.

S: Unfortunately, the species could not be further distributed after its first import.

T: 24-26° C, **L:** 6.5 cm, **A:** 50 cm, **R:** m, t, **D:** 3-4 (C)
75-79° F, 2 2/3", 20",

Betta macrostoma REGAN, 1910
Brunei Beauty

Syn.: None.

Hab.: Northwest of Borneo (Sarawak, Brunei) in headwaters.

F.I.: 1980 to USA by Dr. Axelrod, 1984 to Germany by Schulz.

Sex: ♀ is plain. ♂ is a beautiful red with a black chin and a tomato-red cheek spot.

Soc. B.: Omnivore which should only be kept in species tanks due to its rarity. Lies in wait to ambush water insects and small fishes. Keep ♂♂ singly.

M: Use well-planted tanks with hiding places made of roots. Filter over peat. Large water turnover, since current is appreciated. Water: pH 6.5-7.5; hardness up to 10° dGH. Cover the tank well. Frequent water exchanges: every 14 days 1/3 of the tank volume with the addition of a good water conditioner. When feeding live foods it has to be considered that they do not come out of fish ponds. An introduced disease has devastating consequences. Avoid water with nitrates.

B: Has not been bred in Europe. Reproductive behavior as with *B. picta* and *B. pugnax*; however, the ♀ does not spit the eggs towards the ♂, but transfers them directly into the mouth of the ♂ after a synchronization of the mouth movements. Raising of the young as for *B. unimaculata*. The exporters only send ♂♂; ♀♀ are retained to prevent reproduction. This practice is also exercised by some breeders in Germany with rainbow fishes.

F: C, O; coarse live foods of all kinds, earthworms. However, in the aquarium also flake food (large) and whole or, better, halved food tablets.

S: One of the most splendid fighting fishes which has just recently been imported to us (Germany).

T: 24-26° C, **L:** 11 cm, **A:** 60 cm, **R:** m, t, **D:** 3-4 (C)
75-79° F, 4 1/3", 24",

Betta foerschi ♂

Betta macrostoma ♂

Betta picta (VALENCIENNES, 1846)
Painted Betta

Syn.: *Panchax pictum, Betta trifasciata, Pseudobetta picta, Betta rubra.*

Hab.: Indonesia; the islands of Java, Sumatra, Bangka, Biliton. In puddles and mountain streams up to 1600 m (5250 ft).

F.I.: 1932 by Steyn, Amsterdam.

Sex: The anal fin fringe of the ♂ is broader than the ♀'s. The ♀ has a dot design on the anal fin (only in animals coming from Sumatra!) which is not found in ♂♂. ♂♂ are somewhat larger.

Soc. B.: Mouthbrooding species; ♂ carries the eggs in the mouth (see **B**). Peaceful species which can be kept in a well-planted community tank. The fish live secluded.

M: A larger species tank of 80 l (21 gal) or more stocked with 2-3 pairs is preferable to stocking with several other fish species if one wishes to observe the fish and its spawning. Water: not critical, pH 6.5-7.5; hardness up to 22° dGH.

B: VIERKE in Aqu. Mag. 7/81 gives the first comprehensive report. It is only reproduced in excerpts here: pairing usually in the afternoon. Initially the territory is vehemently defended against intruders by both partners. Later only by the ♀. Pairing usually occurs directly on the bottom in an open place. After about 1 hour of pseudopairing, true spawning with egg release takes place. Here, the U-shaped, bottom lying ♂, embraces the ♀ which releases its eggs into the bowl formed by the body and anal fin of the ♂. The ♀ takes the eggs and spits them towards the ♂ until he has them stowed in a throat sack. Afterwards, additional pairings occur over several hours. The ♂ eats the eggs which it cannot accommodate. In this manner it can endure a fast of 10-14 mouthbrooding days. Carefully transfer the ♂ into an extra tank (chase underwater into a glass and transfer therein). The father does not pursue the young; nevertheless, a separation is indicated. Newly released young are 7 mm (") long and immediately feed on *Artemia* nauplii. The young grow rapidly. Breeding is relatively easy.

F: C, O; FD feeds, frozen food, *Artemia*. Any small live foods, especially to condition the animals for breeding.

S: This peaceful and simple to maintain species is especially recommended for the beginner. There are 3 morphs: the 2 types from Java and Sumatra as well as an independent species very similar to *B. picta* (*B. rubra*?). RICHTER (1981) divides *Betta* species into 2 genera. Mouth-brooding species should from now on belong to the genus *Pseudobetta*, while bubble nest builders should remain in the old genus *Betta*. His proposal has many good points, but it seems not to be enough for other specialists to accept RICHTERs proposal. This is why this book has been left as usual, and the genus *Betta* has not been split.

T: 22-24° C, occasionally to 16° C, **L:** 5.5 cm, **A:** 40 cm, **R:** all, **D:** 1
72-75° F, occasionally to 61° F, 2 ", 16",

Betta taeniata REGAN, 1910
Banded Tetra

Syn.: *Betta trifasciata, Betta macrophthalma.*

Hab.: Northwest Borneo (Sarawak).

F.I.: 1982 by H. Linke, Berlin, Germany.

Sex: Fin rays of the ♂♂ are elongated.

Soc. B.: Several ♂♂ and ♀♀ can be kept in larger tanks, since this species is relatively peaceful. Because of its rarity, the association with other species is not recommended, but is possible.

M: The animals are undemanding towards water quality. pH 6.5-7.8; hardness 5-18° dGH. Provide moderately to well-planted tanks with roots and rock work as hiding places. Likes to jump. Cover the tank well!

B: Similar in almost all details to *B. pugnax*; Vol. 1, page 630.

F: C, O; flake food, FD food, frozen live food. Preferred food: earthworms!

Continued on page 800.

Betta picta

Betta taeniata

Continuation of *Betta taeniata*:

S: As with *B. edithae* and *B. pugnax*, reproduction is difficult because the father usually eats the brood after 1-3 days.

T: 23-26° C, 73-79° F, **L:** 8 cm, 3", **A:** 60 cm for a pair, 24" for a pair, **R:** b, t, **D:** 3-4

Betta unimaculata (POPTA, 1906)

One-Spot Betta

Syn.: *Parophiocephalus unimaculatus, Betta ocellata.*

Hab.: Southeast Asia; Bongon, Howong, and Kajan rivers in northern Borneo (Kalimantan). In headwaters and small pools; especially in current-rich areas but also in drainage ditches.

F.I.: April 1980 by Horst Linke, Berlin, Germany.

Sex: ♂ is more colorful; it has on a single isolated shiny scale on each side of an otherwise matte upper head region (see photo). ♀ is fuller during the spawning season.

Soc. B.: Full-grown ♂♂ are aggressive towards conspecifics in nature. In small natural ponds, only one adult always swims together with a few young. They like to hide under floating leaves. In aquaria the fish engage in harmless pseudofights which may lead to injuries among fish of equal strength.

M: An undemanding species which can either be kept in a species tank or in a community tank with a few docile but robust fishes. Provide hiding places and a dark cover with floating plants. Needs a dark bottom and places no special demands on water quality. Water: pH 6.5-7.5, hardness 10-20° dGH, temperature of around 24° C (75° F). Despite the low values at the natural habitat, the fish prove very sensitive in aquaria with soft water. Perhaps the animals were at that natural habitat only by accident.

B: Besides *B. picta*, this is the easiest mouthbrooding fighting fish species to breed. The ♀♀ do not help transfer the spawn. The young are released after 9 days (at 25° C; 77° F) and are about 6 mm (2/3") long (according to VIERKE). They immediately eat *Artemia* nauplii.

F: C, O; flake food (large), FD feeds, *Artemia*. Live food of all kinds, preferably earthworms!

S: Cover the tank well; the species readily jumps and jumps well. It is said that it even transverses waterfalls 5 m (5.5 yd) high by jumping up the lateral water spray areas (on land!). A large *Betta* species which can still live in small puddles of only 60 cm diameter (water depth 15 cm)(23" diameter; 6" depth).

T: 21-25° C, 70-77° F, **L:** 12 cm, 4 3/4", **A:** 70 cm, 28", **R:** m, t, **D:** 2-3

Colisa lalia

Red Dwarf Gourami, Sunset Gourami

Syn.: Bred form.

Sex: The picture shows two ♂♂; ♀♀ are paler.

Soc. B.: A peaceful species which can be kept in pairs in a species tank or together with other gentle fishes. In larger community tanks, the animals wane or live retired in a plant thicket (if present).

M: Soft, peat filtered water. Cover one corner of the surface with floating fern. Dark substrate. Regular water changes every 2-3 weeks (1/3-1/2) with a good water conditioner.

B: Like with *Colisa sota*, Vol. 1, page 634.

F: C, O; flake food, FD feeds, any small live foods.

S: Not a very long-lived fish (2-3 years); nevertheless, it is a colorful jewel. Something for connoisseurs.

T: 25-28° C, 77-82° F, **L:** 5 cm, 2", **A:** 60 cm, 24", **R:** m, t, **D:** 2

Betta unimaculata

Colisa lalia

A picture-perfect ♂ of *Macropodus ocellatus*

♀ front (light), ♂ back

Macropodus ocellatus (CANTOR, 1842)

Syn.: *Polyacanthus paludosus, P. opercularis, Macropodus ctenopsoides.*

Hab.: Korea and eastern China, Vietnam.

F.I.: By MATTE 1893, then in 1913 by Carl Siggelkow, Hamburg. Not again until 1983!

Sex: ♂ has a large orange tail fin and strong blackish vertical stripes on the head and anterior body regions. ♀ weaker patterned and somewhat smaller. ♂ has pointed elongated dorsal and anal fins; on the ♀ these tips only reach to the middle of the tail fin.

Soc. B.: Less aggressive than many *M. opercularis*. Single animals can be kept with catfishes, larger cichlids and larger tetras. However, pairwise care is recommended.

M: Use a well-planted tank. Variable temperatures: in the summer and for breeding up to 30° C (86° F), to overwinter cooler (not colder than 5° C; 41° F!). Can easily be kept in a small garden pond during the summer. Because it is presently a rare fish, hardly anyone will do that. Water: pH 6.0-7.5; hardness 5-25° dGH. Part of the tank should be covered with floating plants.

B: Reproduction corresponds to *M. opercularis*, but is less productive. See Vol. 1, page 638.

F: C, O; flake food, live foods of all kinds, FD food, frozen food.

S: After not receiving any Chinese fishes for decades it has finally been again possible to import this interesting labyrinth fish. In 1939 this species was crossed with *Macropodus opercularis*. The ♂♂ offspring were sterile, but the ♀♀ were fertile.

T: 15-22° C, L: 8 cm, A: 60 cm, R: m, t, D: 2-3
59-72° F, 3", 24",

Sphaerichthys acrostoma ♂, melanistic coloration

Sphaerichthys acrostoma VIERKE, 1979

Black-Tailed Chocolate Gourami

Syn.: None.

Hab.: Southern, central Borneo (Mentaya River) 250 km northwest of Banjarmasin at the edge of the flooded jungle rivers in low reeds.

F.I.: 1978 by Dr. W. Foersch, E. Korthaus and A. Hanreider.

Sex: ♂ has lighter gray body. The slanted bands behind the eye and on the throat are darker in the ♀. ♂ has a slender, light, longitudinal band from the base of the anal fin, and usually also through the longitudinal body axis, to the caudal peduncle. The ♂ has a somewhat convex throat; ♀'s is concave. In the ♀ the bands behind the eye and on the throat are darker and broader; black to dark red. Ripe ♀: base of the anal fin and posterior longitudinal band are an intense black, and the posterior quarter of the body is light.

Soc. B.: Similar to *Sphaerichthys osphromenoides,* but not quite as shy. Quiet, peaceful and somewhat more active. Combine only with very quiet fishes or, better, keep it in a species tank.

M: Leave some swimming room. Dark bottom. Peat filtration is desirable. Water: pH 5.0-7.5; hardness 4-8° dGH. As with all labyrinth fishes, the water level beneath the cover pane has to be sufficiently low.

B: Unknown. Probably a mouthbrooding species similar to *S. o. osphromenoides.* In this sub-species the animals spawn in the familiar manner of labyrinth fishes, but over the bottom. The ♂ takes the white eggs, which sink to the bottom, into her mouth and broods them.

F: C; live foods of all kinds; also *Drosophila* flies. Grindal worms are readily taken.

Sphaerichthys acrostoma ♂

S: The species has not been imported again after its discovery. A second collection trip by A. Hanrieder (1979) was unsuccessful. Dr. Foersch reported (written communication) that the water was slightly in 1978, but strongly acidic in 1979. The animals either emigrated or have become extinct at the collection site. Text after Dr. Foersch (1983).

T: 24-26° C, **L**: 9 cm, **A**: 70 cm, **R**: m, t, **D**: 3-4 (C)
75-79° F, 3 ", 28",

Sphaerichthys selatanensis (VIERKE, 1979)
Thin-Barred Chocolate Gourami

Syn.: *Sphaerichthys osphromenoides selatanensis*.

Hab.: Southeastern Borneo (Benjarmasin).

F.I.: Around 1970.

Sex: ♂♂ have a white fringe on the anal fin and are larger. The ventral area of ♀♀ is significantly fuller during spawning season.

Soc. B.: Peaceful species which can be housed with gentle tetras and small catfishes. However, ♂♂ can become very aggressive among themselves, necessitating large show tanks.

M: Needs a shallow aquarium with as large as possible surface area. Dense vegetation. Part of the tank should have floating plants. Water: pH 5-6.5; hardness 2-4° dGH. The water should be free of nitrates and peat filtered. Can be slightly brown. Every 3 weeks regular water exchanges of 1/3. Use peat extract and/or a good water conditioner.

B: One pair can be set up in a 40 cm (16") breeding tank. Breeding activity should be similar to *S. o. osphromenoides*. After the spawning act the ♂ takes the eggs off the bottom and into his mouth for about 14 days.

F: C; small live food (*Cyclops, Artemia*). Frozen food, flake food.

S: Contrary to *S. osphromenoides*, the ♂♂ carry the eggs in their mouth (Vol. 1, page 644).

T: 25-30° C, L: 5 cm, A: 100 cm, R: m, b, D: 3-4 (C)
77-86° F, 2", 39",

Parosphromenus filamentosus VIERKE, 1981

Spike-Tailed Licorice Gourami

Syn.: None.

Hab.: Southeast Borneo, region around Banjarmasin. In slowly flowing waters. Not rare.

F.I.: 1979 by Mr. Hanrieder and Hudoro.

Sex: Can only be positively identified during courtship and pairing season when the ♂ is significantly more colorful. Otherwise ,the ♂ is somewhat larger and has a slightly more elongated tail fin ray and dorsal fin than the ♀.

Soc. B.: Very peaceful, calm species that leads a seclusive life. The ♂ spends a lot of time in its spawning cave. Only associate with gentle tetras and *Corydoras* or dwarf barbs. Best to give them their own tank.

M: The fish require opportunities for concealment. These are best created with flat stones. When necessary, a flashlight shows the observer the interior of the cave. Plant with *Cryptocorynes*. Partially cover the water surface with floating plants. Water: pH 6.5-7.2; hardness up to 15° dGH. Conductivity to 200 µS. Slight filtration. Regular water exchanges of 1/3 every 2 weeks.

B: Cave spawner. The ♂ builds a bubble nest under a plant leaf (rare) or below the ceiling of a stone cave. The cave should be well protected against incoming light. After an impressive courtship, several pairings occur every 10 minutes. Only a few milky opaque eggs are released each time. In total, about 50. The ♂ spits the eggs underneath the bubble nest, where they adhere. For brooding, they should be transferred into an aerated rearing tank (all glass aquarium or similar) which has the same water values as the breeding tank. Eggs and larvae should be checked daily for fungus attack. After the young are free-swimming, some water ferns (*Ceratopteris*) are placed into the rearing tank. Feed infusoria and *Artemia* after 3 days. These feedings must be alternated with smallest pond plankton (bosmids, *Cyclops*).

F: C, O; small live foods for breeding. Small flake foods with FD components, more rarely, frozen foods are also taken.

S: The species can be easily distinguished from other dwarf gouramis: the middle tail fin rays of both sexes always protrude 4 mm (3/16"). See also the title picture of the chapter, page 787. An exhaustive report can be found in Aqu. Mag. Volume 5/82.

T: 21-28° C (24° C), L: 4 cm, A: 40 cm, R: m, t, D: 3
70-82° F (75° F), 1 2/3", 16",

Parosphromenus paludicola TWEEDIE, 1952
Pallid Licorice Gourami

Syn.: None.

Hab.: In the eastern Malaysian Peninsula, north up to south Thailand in small flowing waters of the swamp forest.

F.I.: May 1977 by P. and T. Nagy, Salzburg, Austria.

Sex: ♂ has more elongated ventral fins.

Soc. B.: Calm, timid and delicate species. Peaceful. Best kept in pairs in a (breeding) tank.

M: Soft, peat filtered water. LINKE (1980) described a water body by Kuala Brang: pH 5.5; hardness: KH and GH each less than 1. Conductivity 6 μS^{20}. T: 26° C (79° F). Shaded shore areas. The fish occur in densely vegetated waters that are sometimes only 5 cm (2") deep in parts. Small tanks without substrate (for the ease of cleaning) with Java moss and Java fern are suggested. Use a foam cartridge filter.

B: Set up in pairs. Spawning behavior and raising parallels *P. filamentosus*.

F: C, O; smallest live foods, especially *Artemia*.

S: Like all licorice gouramis, the species is very sensitive.

T: 25-27° C, L: 3.7 cm, A: 40 cm, R: m, b, D: 4 (C)
77-81° F, 1 ", 16",

Parosphromenus parvulus VIERKE, 1979
Pygmy Licorice Gourami

Syn.: None.

Hab.: Southern Borneo from the Kapuas system to the drainage area of the Mentaya River system (250 km; 155 mi northwest of Benjarmasin). Shore areas of jungle creeks among grass and dead vegetation.

F.I.: By Dr. Foersch, E. Korthaus and A. Hanrieder, 1978.

Sex: Fins of the ♀ are colorless; the ♂'s fins have a slight dark tinge with a light edge.

Soc. B.: Peaceful, very timid species which is best cared for in a species tank.

M: pH 4.8-5.5; hardness to 5° dGH (2-3°). Peat filtration or the addition of peat extract. Meticulous cleanliness of the tank is necessary. Otherwise, the sensitive animals quickly become diseased. A small tank without substrate is recommended (paint the bottom pane black or adhere a dark carton from the outside). Java fern tied to a root is sufficient as vegetation.

B: Has not been possible because of the scarcity of imported live animals, but it is probably like *P. filamentosus*.

F: C, O; smallest live foods, FD-Menu, *Artemia*.

S: Smallest known labyrinth fish species.

T: 23-26° C, L: 2.7 cm, A: 40 cm, R: m, t, D: 4 (C)
73-79° F, 1", 16",

Parosphromenus paludicola

Parosphromenus parvulus ♂

Swamp region of an Amazon creek that floods during the rainy season. The trees have been burned to clear the land. Nevertheless, there is a rich fish fauna: dwarf cichlids, tetras, *Mesonauta festivus*.

Hemichromis cristatus, pair with young, see page 914.

Acarichthys heckelii (MÜLLER & TROSCHEL, 1848)

Thread-Finned Cichlid

Syn.: *Acara heckelii, A. subocularis, Aequidens subocularis, Geophagus thayeri.*

Hab.: South America; Guyana, Brazil (Amazon and its tributaries), Peru.

F.I.: Unknown.

Sex: The ♀♀ are somewhat fuller at spawning time.

Soc. B.: Territorial; the animals are relatively quiet and peaceful. A strong bond forms between the breeding partners. Cave spawner; patriarch-matriarch family.

M: Offer a roomy tank. Build some caves out of stones, provide plenty of shelter and hiding places out of roots. The roots can extend up to the water surface; leave free swimming space. Water composition does not seem to be important. In nature the animals inhabit acid, soft water; however, they have bred in water with a hardness of 18° dGH. Regular partial water exchanges are important.

B: 26-28° C (79-82° F); a successful aquarium spawn was reported by BARAN (1981): DCG-Informationen **12**, 185-190. After a sometimes intense courtship, spawning occurs in a cave. Normally the spawn is laid on the ceiling of the cave. The white eggs are always laid in groups of 5-6 with free spaces in between; there are several hundred eggs. Larvae hatch after about 3 days and become free-swimming after an additional 3. They then have a length of about 4 mm (3/16). The ♀ stays in the cave, and the ♂ defends the opening of the cave and the territory. Feed the young with *Artemia* nauplii, crumbled flake food and egg yolk.

F: O; live foods of all kinds (aquatic insects and their larvae, *Gammarus*, freshwater isopods, large *Daphnia*, *Tubifex*, earthworms, etc.); after acclimation, the animals also accept beef heart, shrimp and tablet food.

T: 23-26° C, **L:** 20 cm, **A:** 120 cm, **R:** b, m, **D:** 2-3
73-79° F, 8", 47",

Acaronia nassa (HECKEL, 1840)

Big-Eyed Cichlid

Syn.: *Acara nassa, A. cognatus, A. rostratus, A. unicolor, Acaropsis nassa, A. rostratus, Centrarchus cyanopterus.*

Hab.: South America; Guyana, Brazil, Bolivia; in quiet areas among plants.

F.I.: 1909 by Carl Siggelkow, Hamburg, Germany.

Sex: Dorsal and anal fins of the ♂ are elongated to a point; coloration is more intense and brilliant. Dorsal and anal fins of the ♀ are either rounded or pointed, but never elongated; ♀♀ remain smaller.

Soc. B.: Territorial; *A. nassa* is intensely predaceous. Sometimes the species is rough; the animals only get along among themselves when each animal can claim a cave of its own. According to other keepers, the animals get along splendidly. The species does not dig and leaves plants in peace. Open spawner. Nuclear family with intense spawn and brood care.

M: Offer the fish roomy tanks; dense vegetation with large leaves and densely growing species; stone caves, some roots and a gravel or sandy bottom. The species needs warmth. Water up to medium-hard (12-15° dGH) and neutral (pH 7.0). Associate only with same sized fishes (predator!).

B: No detailed reports dealing with successful spawns are yet available. Dr. Lore FOTH was successful for the first time in 1939. Her report, however, does not deal with breeding, but with intelligence tests performed.

F: C; almost only live foods (fish, crustaceans, water insects). After a more or less extended acclimation period, the species also accepts tablet food and flake food.

S: The mouth of *Acaronia nassa* is very protrusile.

T: 25-28° C, **L:** 25 cm, **A:** 120 cm, **R:** b, (m), **D:** 3
77-82° F, 10", 47",

Acarichthys heckelii

Acaronia nassa

Aequidens coeruleopunctatus (KNER & STEINDACHNER, 1863)
Blue-Point Flag Cichlid

Syn.: *Acara coeruleopunctata.*

Hab.: South and Central America; from northwest Ecuador northward over Panama up into southern Costa Rica.

F.I.: Probably not until 1981, but it could not be maintained through breeding.

Sex: ♂ is larger with more developed finnage; ♀ is fuller and more rounded.

Soc. B.: Territorial, pair forming; robust but not a particularly aggressive species. The animals only dig during spawning time. Nuclear open spawner.

M: Territorial fish best kept in pairs; tank decoration should be rich in hiding places, and it can also be planted. Medium-hard (15° dGH), neutral (pH 7.0) water is preferred.

B: Open spawner which spawns on solid substrates; spawns are large.

F: O; undemanding omnivore.

S: *Aequidens coeruleopunctatus* looks very similar to *Aequidens pulcher* but has smaller scales, a smaller head and shorter fins; in addition, the species always has XV dorsal fin rays instead of XIV-XV. In comparison to *Aequidens sapayensis*, *Ae. coeruleopunctatus* has a smaller eye and a shorter caudal peduncle.

T: 22-27° C, L: 15 cm, A: 80 cm, R: b, m, D: 2
72-81° F, 6", 31",

Aequidens diadema (HECKEL, 1840)

Syn.: *Acara diadema.*

Hab.: South America; upper Rio Negro (towards the border to Venezuela) in jungle rivers with a lot of wood.

F.I.: ?

Sex: Sexes are difficult to distinguish, only with certainty by the shape of the genital papillae. In slightly larger ♂♂, it is pointed. Blunt in ♀♀.

Soc. B.: Territorial, pair forming. Quiet and peaceful species, even somewhat timid occasionally. It should not be associated with overly robust cichlids. Larvophile mouthbrooder; nuclear family.

M: No special demands are made; use water that is not too hard (up to 15° dGH) with a pH of 7.0. Shelter-rich decoration out of roots, etc. Dense vegetation is also recommended.

B: 26-28° C (79-82° F); larvophile mouthbrooder, initially lays a large spawn on a hard substrate like open spawners. The larvae hatch after about 2 days and are taken into the mouth where brooding continues. Both partners participate in mouthbrooding. The young are free-swimming after about 8 days, but for a time, they are admitted back into the mouth when threatened.

F: O; omnivore without particular demands; however, hardy nourishment should not be lacking.

S: The species seems very close to *Aequidens pallidus* and *Ae. metae*. The latter species, however, has a pronounced, interrupted opercular bar and is said to be an open spawner.

T: 23-28° C, L: up to 25 cm (?), A: 120 cm, R: b, m, D: 2-3
73-82° F, up to 9¾" (?), 47",

Aequidens coeruleopunctatus

Aequidens diadema

Aequidens pallidus (HECKEL, 1840)

Pale Flag Cichlid

Syn.: *Acara pallidus, A. pallida.* The species has been traded and cared for up to now as *"Aequidens duopunctatus"*.

Hab.: South America; Rio Negro.

F.I.: ?

Sex: Sexes are very difficult to distinguish, and it is probably only possible by the genital papillae. It is pointed in the ♂ and blunt in the ♀.

Soc. B.: Territorial and pair forming. A markedly quiet and peaceful fish, even timid and shy considering their size. They react to every disturbance with a color change. When scared as a consequence of the caretaker, the animals may dart around the tank in fear or even jump out of the water.

M: There are no special demands. Water not too hard (to 15° dGH) and neutral (pH around 7.0). Plants are possible; decoration rich in hiding places with roomy shelters is advised.

B: Probably not yet successful in captivity. It is possible the animals are larvophile mouthbrooders like *Aequidens diadema*. Depending on their mood, the animals show various color schemes and gleam with beautiful colors during courtship.

F: O; should receive hardy foods (beef heart, tablet food, frozen food).

S: The designs on individuals can vary in this species. On one side of the body, 2 spots can appear (photo). This is an exceptional case. A great similarity exists between this fish and the more ochre colored *Aequidens diadema*. However, the anal fin and the lateral spot are somewhat farther back in the greenish *Ae. pallidus*, the lines on the operculum are finer and the eye is red.

T: 23-28° C, **L:** ♂ up to 30 cm, **A:** 120-150 cm, **R:** b, m, **D:** 2-3
73-82° F, ♂ up to 12", 47"-59",

Aequidens sapayensis (REGAN, 1903)

Sapayo Cichlid

Syn.: *Acara sapayensis.*

Hab.: South America; Ecuador; the animals occur in the Rio Sapayo.

F.I.: 1978.

Sex: Very difficult to distinguish; elongated fins are not a definite criterion; ♂♂ become larger; ♀♀ appear fuller.

Soc. B.: Territorial; in its youth it is an active, not too aggressive, fish. But the animals become more sedate and somewhat more aggressive with age. Plants in their spawning territory are bothered the most. Open spawners; nuclear family with true pair formation.

M: Provide a substrate of sand or small gravel, some flat stones and refuges made of roots. The edges and background of the tank can be densely planted. Animals do not place any special demands on water. Does well with a hardness up to 12° dGH and a pH of about 7.0. Associate with other South and Central American cichlids.

B: 26-28° C (79-82° F); water as indicated above. Breeding is easily possible after a harmonizing pair evolves from a group of juveniles. The territorial requirements of *Ae. sapayensis* are not exaggerated, even during the spawning time. The animals search for a suitable spawning substrate (flat stone) and clean it carefully. Around the stone some pits are dug. The ♀ is more active in these preparations than the ♂. Without major courtship, the fish spawn on the stone. Up to 400 small eggs are laid. At 26° C (79° F) the larvae hatch after about 4 days and are free-swimming after an additional 3-4 days. The fry are put into one of the pits by the ♀ and transferred several times daily. The ♂ secures the spawning territory. The young are cared for by both parents. Feed the young with *Artemia* nauplii and crumbled flake food.

F: O; hardy live foods of all kinds; meat, beef heart, shrimp, tablet food, flake food.

S: *Aequidens sapayensis* is a representative of the *Aequidens rivulatus* group. *Aequidens coeruleopunctatus* is its closest relative.

T: 24-26° C, **L:** ♂ up to 20 cm, ♀ smaller, **A:** 100 cm, **R:** b, m, **D:** 2-3
75-79° F, ♂ up to 8", ♀ smaller 39",

Aequidens pallidus

Aequidens sapayensis ♂

Bujurquina vittata (HECKEL, 1840)
Half-Banded Cichlid

Syn.: *Acara vittata, Aequidens paraguayensis, A. vittatus, Astronotus vittatus.*

Hab.: South America; Brazil and northern Argentina (by Catamarca); upper Amazon, Rio Ucayali and tributaries (Peru).

F.I.: Around 1970.

Sex: Mostly a sexually monomorph species; ♂ has more elongated fins; ♀ is smaller and rounder.

Soc. B.: Territorial and peaceful cichlid, the fish will not attack plants. Larvophile mouthbrooder with nuclear family.

M: As indicated for *Aequidens sapayensis.*

B: A successful reproduction was reported by STAWIKOWSKI (1982): DATZ **35**, 284-287. The name *Aequidens paraguayensis* used by STAWIKOWSKI has meanwhile been identified as a synonym of *A. vittatus.* The animals are larvophile mouthbrooders. Spawning is not preceded by an intensive courtship, and the eggs are laid on more or less horizontal leaves of an *Echinodorus.* Spawning is typical for open spawners. A spawn consists of about 200 whitish to brownish colored (camouflaged) eggs. Care of the spawn until it is taken into the mouth of the parents follows the customs of open spawners. Alternately, the ♂ and ♀ hover over the eggs and fan oxygen-rich water towards the eggs with their pelvic fins. After about 36 hours the ♀ takes the eggs into her mouth and the developing larvae are chewed out of their shells. Afterwards, both parents participate in larval care. The larvae are transferred from partner to partner at irregular intervals. Each parent's "carrying period" becomes progressively shorter as the moment of free swimming nears. Two days after the young can actively swim, the attentiveness and caring intensity of the parents diminishes markedly.

F: O; live foods of all kinds; shrimp, beef heart, flake food.

S: *Aequidens vittatus* is very similar to *Aequidens mariae*; however, the body band is only intense to a lateral spot and the head has a less rounded profile.

T: 23-26° C, L: 15 cm, A: 100 cm, R: b, m, D: 2-3
73-79° F, 6", 39",

Bujurquina vittata

Bujurquina vittata

Apistogramma bitaeniata PELLEGRIN, 1936
Two-Striped Dwarf Cichlid

Syn.: *Apistogramma klausewitzi, A. kleei,* perhaps *A. sweglesi.*

Hab.: South America; central Amazon around the city of Leticia (Colombia).

F.I.: 1961.

Sex: The ♂♂ are significantly larger than the ♀♀ and have a much lighter base coloration.

Soc. B.: Territorial and relatively peaceful, the ♂♂ are polygamous (create a harem); therefore, always keep 1 ♂ with several ♀♀ (3-4). The ♂ defends a main territory which contains the subterritories of the ♀♀. Cave spawner with paternal-matriarch family.

M: See Vol. 1, page 674.

B: Not unproblematic, more difficult than in many other *Apistogramma* species. 27-29° C (81-84° F); soft (to 8° dGH) and slightly acid to neutral (pH 6.5-7.0) water. The animals are cave spawners. The eggs are either laid on the wall or the ceiling of the cave. Up to 100 eggs are laid, usually fewer. The ♀ guards and cares for the spawn and brood. Egg development takes about 3 days. In an additional 5 days, the young are free-swimming. They immediately accept *Artemia* nauplii.

F: C; live foods of all kinds. The animals can hardly be, if at all, trained to nonmoving feed.

S: *Apistogramma bitaeniata* is sensitive to polluted water. It belongs to the *Apistogramma agassizii* group. In the past years a scientifically undescribed species has appeared in the hobby that looks very similar to *A. bitaeniata*; however, among other things, it does not have dorsal fin membranes. In Germany it has been named Glanzbinden-Apistogramma (iridescent-banded apistogramma). The color morph pictured here is usually called *A. kleei.*

T: 26-28° C, **L:** ♂ 6 cm, ♀ 4.5, **A:** 80 cm, **R:** b, **D:** 3-4
79-82° F, ♂ 2 1/3", ♀ 1 3/4", 31",

Apistogramma caetei KULLANDER, 1980
Caete Dwarf Cichlid

Syn.: None.

Hab.: South America; Brazil, Rio Caete and Rio Apeu region.

F.I.: 1982 in larger numbers, prior as single specimens.

Sex: Sexual dimorphism; ♂ is larger with a blue shine on the body and sporadic red markings on the opercula; ♀ is smaller with a gray or yellow (coloration during brood care) body.

Soc. B.: A territorial, peaceful and infrequently digging dwarf cichlid. The ♂♂ tend to form harems but maintaining in pairs is also possible. Cave spawner; paternal-matriarch family.

M: Needs planted tanks with places to hide among clay pot fragments, roots, etc. Shelters are occupied by ♀♀ as spawning caves. Provide a fine-grained, dark bottom. Neutral (pH 7.0), medium-hard (around 10° dGH) water.

B: 23-30° C (73-86°F); slightly acid to neutral (pH 6.5-7.0) and medium-hard (10° dGH) water. The spawns of up to 200 eggs are deposited on the cave ceiling. The ♀ guards the spawn and the larvae; the ♂ defends the superterritory where several ♀♀ can have their spawning territories. Occasionally the ♂ participates in guiding the free-swimming young.

F: C; small live foods such as *Cyclops, Daphnia* and mosquito larvae.

S: *Apistogramma caetei* has a dark spot below the body band and immediately in front of the oval spot at the caudal peduncle. This spot distinguishes it from the closely related species *Apistogramma geisleri* and *Apistogramma* sp. (Wangenflecken = spotted-cheek apistogramma). The tail fin, which is entirely transversed by vertical rows of dots, is also a distinguishing characteristic. In 1911 HASEMAN erroneously identified *A. caetei* as *Apistogramma taeniata.*

T: 23-30° C, **L:** ♂ 6 cm, ♀ 4 cm, **A:** 50 cm, **R:** b, **D:** 3
73-86° F, ♂ 2 1/3", ♀ 1 2/3", 20",

Apistogramma bitaeniata

Apistogramma caetei

Apistogramma commbrae (REGAN, 1906)
Corumba Dwarf Cichlid

Syn.: *Heterogramma commbrae, H. corumbae.*

Hab.: South America; Brazil and Paraguay, Rio Paraguay from Asuncion to Corumba.

F.I.: Already at the beginning of this century.

Sex: Slight sexual dimorphism. The ♂ is somewhat larger than the ♀, has reddish spots on the operculum and a more pronounced design on the tail fin.

Soc. B.: A peaceful, territorial dwarf cichlid that does not harm plants. If several ♀♀ are present, the ♂ normally spawns with only one ♀. Cave spawner; paternal-matriarch family with tendency towards a nuclear family.

M: Needs a well-planted tank with numerous small caves for the ♀♀ to occupy as the center of their spawning territory. Fine-grained bottom and neutral (pH 7.0), medium-hard (10° dGH) water are best.

B: 23-28° C (73-82° F); follow water values listed above. Spawns are relatively small, up to 80 eggs. The ♀ lays the eggs on the ceiling of the cave and guards the eggs and larvae alone until free-swimming; the ♂ defends the outer territory. After the young are free-swimming, the ♂ often participates in guiding them. Occasionally the parents have real quarrels over the offspring; each guards part of the school.

F: C; small live foods such as *Cyclops*, *Daphnia*, etc.

S: *Apistogramma commbrae* is notorious for its large spot on the caudal peduncle, where the longitudinal band terminates. This characteristic differentiates it from all presently known species in the hobby. Young *Apistogramma commbrae* can sometimes be finicky feeders.

T: 23-28° C, **L:** ♂ 5 cm, ♀ 3.5, **A:** 40 cm, **R:** b, **D:** 3
73-82° F, ♂ 2", ♀ 1 1/3" 16",

Apistogramma eunotus KULLANDER, 1981
Blue Cheek Dwarf Cichlid

Syn.: None.

Hab.: South America; Peru, Rio Ucayali region.

F.I.: 1981 by several members of the Deutschen Cichliden Gesellschaft.

Sex: Pronounced sexual dimorphism; the ♂♂ are significantly larger, have an orange caudal fin, more developed fins, and a blue-green sheen on the scales. The ♀♀ are smaller and gray, or yellow with black contrasts (while caring for young).

Soc. B.: Territorial, peaceful dwarf cichlid that seldom digs. The ♂♂ tend to form harems and control a superterritory inclusive of several small female territories. Cave spawner; paternal-matriarch family.

M: Needs an aquarium with plenty of hiding places and a fine-grained dark bottom. Dense plant groups and free swimming areas should alternate. Neutral to slightly alkaline (pH 7.0-7.5), medium-hard (around 10° dGH) water is suggested.

B: 23-30° C (73-86° F); medium-hard water with a pH up to 7.5 is totally agreeable for breeding. A cave spawner, the ♀ lays up to 100 eggs and guards them and then the larvae alone while the ♂ defends the superterritory which can contain several ♀ spawning territories. Even after the young are free-swimming, the ♂ seldom participates in guiding the young.

F: C; live foods; mosquito larvae, *Daphnia*, *Cyclops*.

S: *Apistogramma eunotus* belongs together with *Apistogramma moae* into a group of several *Apistogramma* species native to the Peruvian Amazon region which only differ by a few characteristics. The species of this group are usually erroneously called *Apistogramma amoena* in the hobby.

T: 23-30° C, **L:** ♂ 8.5 cm, ♀ 5 cm, **A:** 50 cm, **R:** b, **D:** 3
73-86° F, ♂ 3 1/3", ♀ 2", 20",

Apistogramma commbrae

Apistogramma eunotus ♂

Apistogramma eunotus ♀

Apistogramma gephyra KULLANDER, 1980

Mottled Dwarf Cichlid, Red-Edged Dwarf Cichlid

Syn.: None.

Hab.: South America; Brazil, from Rio Negro by Manaus to Santarem on the Amazon.

F.I.: Numerous specimens in 1982. Single individuals were already in Germany.

Sex: Marked sexual dimorphism; ♂♂ are larger, more colorful, have more elongated dorsal and anal fins and a slightly lanceolate tail fin; ♀♀ are smaller, gray, or yellow with black markings at spawning time.

Soc. B.: Territorial and peaceful towards other fishes. Does not bother plants. This species can be kept and raised in pairs, though the ♂♂ tend towards polygamy in larger tanks. Cave spawner; paternal-matriarch family.

M: Needs a well-planted aquarium with a fine-grained dark bottom. Offer hiding places in the form of caves which are accepted by the ♀♀ as spawning sites. Provide acidic, soft water (pH 5.5-6.0; hardness less than 5° dGH).

B: 23-30° C (73-86° F); use water as indicated under **M**; this fish is a cave spawner. The ♀♀ guard the eggs (up to 120) and larvae while the ♂ defends the outer territory. After the young are free-swimming, the ♂ will participate in their guidance and eventually take over the care of the school so that the ♀ is free to spawn again.

F: C; small live foods: water fleas, mosquito larvae and *Cyclops*.

S: *Apistogramma gephyra* is very closely related to *Apistogramma agassizii*. Clear differences are the less developed fins, the narrow red fringe on the dorsal fin, the somewhat narrower band along the body, and a different aggression coloration. *A. gephyra* belongs to the *Apistogramma* species which practice jaw locking. There are several color morphs that have different colored tails (white, orange-white, orange).

T: 23-30° C, **L:** ♂ 6 cm, ♀ 4 cm, **A:** 50 cm, **R:** b, **D:** 3-4
73-86° F, ♂ 2 1/3", ♀ 1 2/3", 20",

Apistogramma gibbiceps MEINKEN, 1969

Yellow-Checked Dwarf Cichlid

Syn.: None.

Hab.: South America; Brazil, in the Rio Negro region.

F.I.: ?

Sex: Clear sexual dimorphism; ♂ is larger and has two drawn out tips on the tail fin; ♀ is smaller and has a round to cropped tail fin.

Soc. B.: Territorial, peaceful cichlid which hardly digs. The ♂♂ are rather monogamous and usually only one ♀ is accepted. Cave spawner; paternal-matriarch family.

M: Fine, dark sand or lava as the substrate; dense planting of the tank; hiding places of stone and roots which are close to the bottom; leave free swimming space. *A. gibbiceps* is very demanding towards water composition. The water should be very soft (to 3° dGH), humus acidic (pH 5.0-6.0), warm (about 28° C; 82° F). Under suboptimal water values, the colors fade and the animals do not live long. Best kept in a species tank.

B: Not simple since the larvae are very sensitive after hatching. The ♂♂ are predominately monogamous and usually only accept one ♀. Well conditioned ♀♀ produce up to 200 eggs. The ♀ guards and cares for the eggs while the ♂ does not actively participate in brood care, although he stays close to the cave. The larvae hatch after 2-3 days and are free-swimming after an additional 4-6 days. Rear the young with plankton, microorganisms and *Artemia* nauplii.

F: Live foods of all kinds: mosquito larvae, small aquatic insects, water fleas, *Cyclops*, *Artemia*, *Tubifex* and some Enchytraea.

S: The species name, *gibbiceps*, comes from gibbus = hump, lump and ceps (= cephalus) = head and is referring to the hump on the forehead of the holotype.

Continued on page 826

Apistogramma gephyra

Apistogramma gibbiceps

Continuation of *Apistogramma gibbiceps*:

This, however, is not present in live specimens and was a result of poor preservation, making the species name somewhat misleading.

T: 27-29° C, L: ♂ 8 cm, ♀ 6 cm, A: 60 cm, R: b, D: 4
81-84° F, ♂ 3", ♀ 2 1/3", 24",

Apistogramma hongsloi KULLANDER, 1979

Red-Lined Dwarf Cichlid

Syn.: None.

Hab.: South America; Colombia, Rio Vichada and Rio Meta (Orinoco basin).

F.I.: 1975 by Dr. Fröhlich, Lübeck, Germany.

Sex: Marked sexual dimorphism; ♂ is larger and more colorful with a red spot at the base of the caudal fin and elongated dorsal fin membranes; ♀ is smaller, grayish, yellow with contrasting black when breeding.

Soc. B.: A peaceful, territorial dwarf cichlid which rarely digs. The ♂♂ spawn with several ♀♀ in larger tanks. Keeping in pairs with other fishes is also possible in smaller aquaria. Cave spawner; paternal-matriarch family.

M: Make a planted aquarium rich in hiding places and provide a fine-grained dark bottom. Acid, soft water (pH 5.5-6.0; hardness under 5° dGH). When associated with smaller surface fishes, *A. hongsloi*, like all *Apistogramma* species, becomes more self-confident.

B: 23-30° C (73-86° F); use water values indicated above. Cave spawner, the ♀ cares for the 60-90 eggs while the ♂ secures the superterritory, where several ♀♀ can have their spawning territories, against other tankmates.

F: C; small live foods of all kinds. The animals do not accept flake food easily.

S: *Apistogramma hongsloi* ♂♂ differ from all other *Apistogramma* ♂♂ by having the caudal peduncle spot in red. In selected animals, this can extend to a red line above the anal fin. Based on differing body coloration, one can distinguish an orange and a blue morph. It is very difficult to distinguish these ♀♀ from *Apistogramma macmasteri* ♀♀; unwanted crosses have occurred.

T: 23-30° C, L: ♂ 7.5 cm, ♀ 4.5 cm, A: 50 cm, R: b, D: 3-4
73-86° F, ♂ 3", ♀ 1 3/4", 20"

Apistogramma hippolytae

Empress Dwarf Cichlid, Two-Spotted Dwarf Cichlid KULLANDER, 1982

Syn.: None.

Hab.: South America; Brazil, Lago Manacapuru at the Amazon and middle Rio Negro.

F.I.: 1980.

Sex: Sexual dimorphism: the ♂♂ become larger and have a bluish sheen on the scales; it is absent in smaller ♀♀. The tips of the ventral fins are more elongated in the ♂. The tail fin is round and slightly cropped in both sexes.

Soc. B.: A peaceful, plant friendly, dwarf cichlid which establishes its territory around a spawning cave. The species can be kept in pairs; sometimes the ♂♂ spawn with several ♀♀ (harem). Cave spawner; paternal-matriarch family.

M: Provide densely planted tanks with fine substrate and caves as hiding places. Neutral (pH 7.0) and medium-hard (around 10° dGH) water are sufficient for maintenance.

B: 23-30° C (73-86° F); slightly acid, medium-hard water (pH 6.5; hardness around 10° dGH); cave spawner with spawns up to 200 eggs. Eggs and larvae are guarded by the ♀ until free-swimming while the ♂ defends the outer territory. After the young are free-swimming, the ♂ often participates in guiding them.

F: C; live foods such as mosquito larvae, *Cyclops* and water fleas.

S: *Apistogramma hippolytae* distinguishes itself by a spot on the body which reaches from the lateral body band to the dorsal fin.

T: 23-30° C, L: ♂ 6.5 cm, ♀ 4.5, A: 50 cm, R: b, D: 3
73-86° F, ♂ 2 2/3", ♀ 1 3/4", 20",

Apistogramma hongsloi

Apistogramma hippolytae

Apistogramma hippolytae

Apistogramma iniridae KULLANDER, 1979
Thread-Finned Dwarf Cichlid

Syn.: None.

Hab.: South America; Colombia, Rio Inirida region (Orinoco basin).

F.I.: Mid '70's.

Sex: Pronounced sexual dimorphism; the ♂ is larger, more colorful, with a long round to lanceolate caudal fin, a tall dorsal fin whose elongated membranes are fused above the rays and thread-like elongated ventral fins. The ♀ is smaller with a round tail fin, no elongated membranes on the dorsal fin and short pelvic fins.

Soc. B.: A peaceful, dwarf cichlid which establishes its territory around a spawning cave. The ♂♂ usually only spawn with one ♀. They will not harm plants. Cave spawner; patriarch-maternal family.

M: Needs a heavily planted tank decorated with bogwood and coconut shells. Do not use an overly coarse-grained dark substrate. Associate with smaller surface fishes. Soft, acid water (hardness less than 5° dGH; pH 5.5-6.0).

B: 23-30° C (73-86° F); water values as indicated above. Cave spawner whose ♀♀ deposit between 80 and 100 eggs on the ceiling of a cave. The ♀ guards the eggs and larvae while the ♂ secures the outer territory. After the young are free-swimming, they are sometimes guided by both parents. Polygamous tendencies are little pronounced in *A. iniridae* ♂♂.

F: C; live food (*Cyclops*, water fleas, mosquito larvae).

S: *Apistogramma iniridae* belongs to the *Apistogramma pertensis* group. The species distinguishes itself by a spot design below the body band which is especially visible in combative or courting animals. *A. iniridae* is very sensitive to strong fluctuations in water chemistry.

T: 23-30° C, **L:** ♂ 7.5 cm, ♀ 4.5 cm, **A:** 50 cm, **R:** b, **D:** 4
73-86° F, ♂ 3", ♀ 1³/₄", 20",

Apistogramma nijsseni KULLANDER, 1979
Panda Dwarf Cichlid, Nijsseni's Dwarf Cichlid

Syn.: None.

Hab.: South America; Peru, lower Rio Ucayali by Jenaro Herrera.

F.I.: 1981 by Patrick de Rham, Lausanne, Switzerland

Sex: Pronounced sexual dimorphism. ♂ has a beautiful blue sheen, a slightly lanceolate tail fin with reddish fringe and is larger than the ♀; the ♀ has an unusual black and yellow coloration. The body background is yellow through the center of the body and the caudal peduncle has a broad black band. The entire opercular region, the anterior part of the dorsal fin, and the ventral fins are also tar black.

Soc. B.: A peaceful, territorial dwarf cichlid which only feels at home in a well-planted aquarium. The social behavior is probably similar to other *Apistogramma* species. However, no other suggestions can be given.

M: Needs a sufficiently planted tank with a dark fine-grained bottom. Provide hiding places with bogwood roots, coconut shells, etc. Acid, soft water (pH 5.5; hardness less than 5° dGH) seems to be necessary for maintenance.

B: *Apistogramma nijsseni* has not been successfully bred in Germany.

F: C; live food; *Cyclops*, water fleas and mosquito larvae.

S: Its distribution seems to be limited to a relatively small region in the vicinity of Jenaro Herrera, where interestingly, it seems that several fish species are endemic.

T: 23-30° C, **L:** ♂ 6.5 cm, ♀ 4 cm, **A:** 50 cm, **R:** b, **D:** 3-4
73-86° F, ♂ 2²/₃", ♀ 1²/₃", 20",

Apistogramma iniridae

Apistogramma nijsseni ♂

Apistogramma pertensis (HASEMAN, 1911)

Net Dwarf Cichlid, Amazon Dwarf Cichlid

Syn.: *Heterogramma taeniatum pertense.*

Hab.: South America; Brazil, Rio Negro by Manaus, Amazon from Manacapuru to Santarem.

F.I.: Single specimens have been imported since the beginning of this century, in larger numbers since 1980.

Sex: Sexual dimorphism; ♂ is larger and has a tall, sail-like dorsal fin with all the membranes fused above the rays with the exception of the first three; long ventral fins. The ♀♀ are smaller with shorter ventral and dorsal fins.

Soc. B.: A territorial dwarf cichlid, ideal to house with smaller fishes. Will not harm plants. The ♂♂ often only spawn with one ♀. Cave spawner; paternal-matriarch family.

M: Use aquaria with hiding opportunities, plant groups and free swimming space. Provide a dark fine-grained bottom. Acid, soft water (pH 5.5; hardness less than 5° dGH) is suggested.

B: 23-30° C (73-86° F); water values as indicated above. The ♀ adheres up to 120 eggs to the cave ceiling and guards spawn and larvae while the ♂ defends the outer limits of the territory. After the young are free-swimming, the ♂ will sometimes help guide the young. Other ♀♀ are usually not noticed by the ♂ after the first has spawned.

F: C; live foods (mosquito larvae, water fleas and *Cyclops*).

S: *Apistogramma pertensis* is often confused with the species known in the hobby as *Apistogramma meinkeni* which has been more frequently imported in the latter years, many times even together with *A. pertensis*. The caudal fin of *A. meinkeni* is asymmetrical, with the upper lobe somewhat longer than the lower (round in *A. pertensis*). The spot on the caudal peduncle is oval and vertically extended (small and round in *A. pertensis*) and more than 3 dorsal rays are exposed.

T: 23-30° C, 73-86° F, **L:** ♂ 6.5 cm, ♂ 2 2/3", ♀ 4.5, ♀ 1 3/4", **A:** 50 cm, 20", **R:** b, **D:** 3-4

Apistogramma regani KULLANDER, 1980

Regan's Dwarf Cichlid

Syn.: None; however, *Apistogramma regani* was erroneously identified by HASEMAN (1911) as *Apistogramma ortmanni* and by MEINKEN (1971) as *Apistogramma borellii.*

Hab.: South America; Brazil, Rio Negro and the Amazon region close to Manaus.

F.I.: Unknown.

Sex: Undeveloped sexual dimorphism; the ♂♂ become larger and have larger fins.

Soc. B.: A peaceful, territorial dwarf cichlid which does not disturb plants. No specific indications can be made about social behavior and breeding since *A. regani* presently has only been imported singly, and ♂♂ and ♀♀ have never been kept at the same time. However, in this aspect it should not differ much from other species in the *regani* group (see *Apistogramma caetei*, page 820).

M: Planted aquarium with hiding places close to the bottom. Use a fine-grained dark substrate. Slightly acid, soft water (pH 6.5; hardness around 5° dGH) is appropriate.

B: Not yet successful in captivity; see also under **Soc. B**.

F: C; live foods like mosquito larvae, water fleas and *Cyclops*.

S: *Apistogramma regani* distinguishes itself by having intensely colored crossbands which are usually faint in other species of the genus. With these, the fish appears cross striped. In certain moods, however, only a narrow longitudinal band and an oval, vertically drawn out spot on the caudal peduncle are apparent.

T: 23-30° C, 73-86° F, **L:** ♂ 7 cm, ♂ 2 3/4", ♀ 4.5 cm, ♀ 1 3/4", **A:** 50 cm, 20", **R:** b, **D:** 3-4

Apistogramma pertensis

Apistogramma regani ♂

Apistogramma viejita KULLANDER, 1979
Viejita Dwarf Cichlid

Syn.: None.

Hab.: South America; Colombia, Rio Meta area around Puerto Gaitan (Orinoco basin).

F.I.: Unknown.

Sex: Strong sexual dimorphism. ♂♂ are larger with elongated fins. ♀♀ are smaller and gray without young, but they are yellow with a contrasting black design when caring for a brood. The throat area from the ventrals to the lower lip is jet black.

Soc. B.: Territorial, plant-loving dwarf cichlid; it behaves peacefully towards other fish. Can be maintained in pairs. In larger aquaria, the ♂♂ tend to polygamy and spawn with several ♀♀. Cave spawner; paternal-matriarch family.

M.: Well-planted aquarium with dark, fine substrate. Create caves as spawning sites for the ♀♀. Use soft (below 5° dGH) and acid (pH around 5.5) water.

B.: 23-30° C (73-86° F); strongly acidic (pH around 5.0) water for breeding. Cave spawner; the ♀♀ cares for the eggs (up to 100) and larvae alone. Even after the young are free-swimming, no guidance by the ♂ has been observed. In spacious aquaria the male defends a large territory where several ♀♀ have spawning territories.

F.: C; small live foods of all kinds. The species accepts almost no flake food.

S: Male *A. viejita* are known in several color morphs. Both variants show olive-yellow dorsal regions and a yellow tail fin as well as a reddish fringe in the soft rays of the dorsal. Additionally, one of the forms displays an orange-yellow ventral region and a red-framed caudal fin. This variant can also have red spots on the operculum. This red form was first imported in 1982 by HORST LINKE (Berlin) and can easily be confused with *Apistogramma macmasteri*. *A. viejita* is often attacked by single-celled ectoparasites after being moved or a water exchange.

T: 23-30° C, **L**: ♂ 7.5 cm, ♀ 4 cm, **A**: 50 cm, **R**: b, **D**: 4
73-86° F ♂ 3", ♀ 1", 20",

Apistogrammoides pucallpaensis MEINKEN, 1965
T-Bar Dwarf Cichlid

Syn.: None.

Hab.: South America; Peruvian Amazon drainage. The type series was caught near the city of Pucallpa in the Ucayali.

F.I.: 1976.

Sex: Sexual dimorphism; ♂♂ grow larger and have a beautiful blue sheen, longer fin tips and a brighter caudal fin design. ♀♀ are smaller with black and yellow contrast.

Soc. B.: Peaceful, plant-loving dwarf cichlid which only demands a small territory. ♂♂ almost exclusively spawn with one ♀. Cave spawner; paternal-matriarch family with a tendency towards a nuclear family.

M: *A. pucallpaensis* can also be kept in small, well-planted aquaria which have enough hiding places. Fine-grained, dark substrate and acidic, soft water (pH around 5.5; hardness below 5° dGH) are recommended. Wild caught fish are very sensitive to fluctuations in water values. However, availability is almost exclusively limited to tank raised specimens.

B: 23-30° C (23-86° F); slightly acid, soft water (pH about 6.0, hardness below 5° dGH). The spawns consist of approximately 80 eggs and are usually deposited on the ceiling of a cave. Sometimes vertical substrates are chosen. ♀♀ guard the spawn and the young. The ♂ guards the outer territory, but he is also tolerated in the immediate vicinity without directly participating in the care of eggs and larvae.

Continued on page 834.

Apistogramma viejita

Apistogrammoides pucallpaensis ♂

After the young are free-swimming, the ♂ often participates in guiding them.

F: C; small live foods such as *Cyclops*, water fleas and small mosquito larvae.

S: *Apistogrammoides pucallpaensis* is very closely related to the representatives of the genus *Apistogramma*. The higher number of anal fin rays (7-9; 3, as an exception 4 or 6, in *Apistogramma*) and the different coloration of the longitudinal band are distinguishing characteristics. The longitudinal band of *Apistogrammoides* forms a horizontal T. Initially, *Apistogrammoides* fry are very small and must be fed with smallest *Artemia* nauplii or infusoria.

T: 23-30° C, L: ♂ 4.5 cm, ♀ 3 cm, A: 40 cm, R: b, D: 3-4
73-86° F, ♂ 1 ʃ", ♀ 1 " 16 "

Aristochromis christyi TREWAVAS, 1935

Syn.: None.

Hab.: Africa; Malawi (endemic).

F.I.: ?

Sex: The ♂ has a beautiful blue breeding dress.

Soc. B.: The animals are piscivores. A mouthbrooder with matriarch family (?).

M: Follow recommendations for *Cyrtocara* species from Lake Malawi.

B: The species has probably not yet been bred in an aquarium.

F: C; live food of all kinds. From a certain size on, it feeds almost exclusively on fishes.

S: The genus *Aristochromis* is monotypic so far, that is, it has only one species.

T: 24-26° C, L: 25 cm, A: 120 cm, R: b, m, D: 3 (C)
75-79° F, 9¾", 47",

Astatotilapia martini (BOULENGER, 1906)

Syn.: *Tilapia martini, Haplochromis martini.*

Hab.: Africa; Victoria (endemic). The holotype was caught in Uganda by Bunjako. The species is distributed throughout the lake but is not numerous in any part. The animals were caught above sandy and muddy bottoms.

F.I.: 1978 by the company Struck.

Sex: In courting ♂♂, the dorsal and tail fin are blackish, anal and pelvic fins are lighter; in ♀♀ and juvenile ♂♂, all fins are yellow.

Soc. B.: Territorial; the animals are quite aggressive in defending their territories. Plants are usually left alone. An ovophile mouthbrooder, it does not form pair bonds; matriarch family.

M: As indicated for *Haplochromis obliquidens*. To date, *Astatotilapia martini* as only been imported sporadically.

B: The species has not yet been bred in an aquarium.

F: O; live food, frozen food, freeze-dried food, shrimp, meat and flake food.

S: *Astatotilapia martini* is endemic to Lake Victoria. Specimens from Lake Edward, which had been identified as *Tilapia martini* (see synonym), turned out to be *Psammochromis schubotzi* (BOULENGER, 1914) (Syn.: *"Haplochromis" schubotzi*) under closer scrutiny.

T: 24-26° C, L: 13 cm, A: 100 cm, R: b, m, D: 2
75-79° F, 5", 39",

Aristochromis christyi

Astatotilapia martini

Aulonocara baenschi MEYER & RIEHL, 1985
Yellow Regal Cichlid, Baensch's Peacock

Syn.: None.

Hab.: Endemic to Lake Malawi, Africa.

F.I.: 1984 by Horst Dieckhoff, Herten, Germany.

Sex: ♂ is a brighter blue/yellow; ♀ is a single-colored black-brown. See photos on pages 836, 837, 841, 847.

Soc. B.: Quite a peaceful species suitable for most community tanks.

M: Use tough plants which tolerate harder water (from 10-30° dGH), pH 7.2-8.2 (7.8). Plants such as *Anubias, Cryptocoryne balansae, Sagittaria, Vallisneria,* etc. can be used. The substrate should be coarse gravel and pebbles. Use roots as territorial delimiters and perform water exchanges of about 1/3-1/2 every 3 weeks.

T: 22-26° C, **L:** 10 cm, **A:** 80 cm, **R:** all, **D:** 1-2
72-79° F, 4", 31",

B: The breeding pairs must be well conditioned (mosquito larvae, etc.). Mouthbrooder. The ♀♀ immediately take the eggs and sperm into their mouth after spawning (egg spot method).

F: C, O; in the aquarium, the species is an omnivore but does not touch plants. In the wild, all kinds of live foods are eaten. Flake food, frozen blood worms. The pharyngeal bone structure indicates that these animals are snail eaters in nature.

S: At least 3 color morphs occur. The blue-yellow is the most commonly bred (photo lower right).

Aulonocara baenschi, Marleri morph

Aulonocara baenschi, (nominate form), new yellow regal, from Nkoma/Benga

Aulonocara baenschi, blue-yellow morph, Chipoka

Aulonocara maylandi TREWAVAS, 1984

Mayland's Peacock, Sulphurhead Peacock

Syn.: None.

Hab.: Africa; Malawi, by Mankanjila Point (endemic).

F.I.: Probably in 1982.

Sex: Distinct sexual dichromatism; the ♂♂ are much more colorful than the plain ♀♀; the anal fins of the ♂♂ have egg spots.

Soc. B.: Territorial, but still quite peaceful. The species is appropriate for most community tanks. Mouthbrooder with maternal family.

M: Tank with rockwork that provides many crevices and caves as hiding places. Plant tough species which tolerate harder water (*Anubias, Vallisneria, Sagittaria*, etc.). Bottom of coarse gravel or pebbles. Some roots or stones should be added as territorial divisions. Needs water that is medium-hard to hard (10-30° dGH) and alkaline (pH 7.5-8.5). Regular water exchanges (1/3 every 2 weeks).

B: 24-28° C (57-82° F); water values as indicated above. The animals are mouthbrooders. Up to 50 eggs are laid by the ♀ and taken into her mouth where they are fertilized by the "egg spot" method. Raising the young is not difficult. Feed them *Artemia, Cyclops*, small *Daphnia* and ground flake food.

F: C, O; omnivore; live foods of any kind, frozen and freeze-dried food, flake and tablet foods.

S: Two color morphs are known: sulfur head and the blue orchid. The latter is rarer. Young, dominant ♂♂ already have a shiny blue hump on the forehead which becomes lighter with increasing age until it appears almost white. This morph has rarely been bred in Germany. The yellow sulfur head is often found in the trade.

The blue orchid is now concidered a new species: *Aulonocara kandeensis* TAWIL & ALLGAYER, 1988.

T: 22-26° C, **L:** 12 cm, **A:** 100 cm, **R:** all, **D:** 1-2
72-79° F, 4 3/4", 39",

Aulonocara maylandi ♂, sulfur head, Eccels Reef

Aulonocara kandeensis ♂, TAWIL & ALLGAYER, 1988; blue orchid, Kande Island;

Aulonocara maylandi ♀

Underwater picture, Lake Malawi

Mbenji Island, Lake Malawi. *Aulonocara stuartgranti* occurs here.

Lake Malawi looks like as a giant aquarium to the diver

Aulonocara baenschi ♀

Aulonocara stuartgranti MEYER & RIEHL, 1985
Grant's Peacock

Syn.: None.

Hab.: Endemic to Lake Malawi, Africa.

F.I.: 1984.

Sex: Clearly distinguishable from the pictures on page 843.

Soc. B.: A peaceful species which is suitable for community tanks.

M: As with *A. baenschi*.

B: Mouthbrooder. Fertilization follows the egg spot method. Raise the young on flake food and *Artemia*.

F: C, O; omnivore, flake food, any live foods.

S: The species is named in honor of Stuart GRANT. He collects and exports fishes of Lake Malawi and has earned special merits with the investigation of new species and capture areas.

T: 22-26° C, **L:** 10 cm, **A:** 120 cm, **R:** all, **D:** 1-2
72-79° F, 4", 47",

Lake Malawi, Africa; Mbenji Island from the air

Aulonocara stuartgranti ♂, picture of typical coloration

Aulonocara stuartgranti ♀

Aulonocara stuartgranti ♂, blue regal, Mbenji Island, Lake Malawi

A Lake Malawi collector examines a new cichlid species that awaits identification in Germany.

Aulonocara korneliae, MEYER, RIEHL & ZETZSCHE, 1987, blue-gold

Aulonocara hueseri, MEYER, RIEHL & ZETZSCHE, 1987, white top

Haplochromis sp., Jaro, Lake Malawi

Haplochromis sp., Jaro, head study

Aulonocara baenschi ♂, Usisya morph. The similarity in color with the opposite *Haplochromis* is amazing. However, *Haplochromis* has a significantly larger mouth than *Aulonocara*.

Aulonocara baenschi ♀, Usisya morph

Bujurquina vittata on page 818

Crenicichla semifasciata HECKEL, 1840

Syn.: *Batrachops semifascitatus.*

Hab.: South America; Paraguay, Uruguay, Argentina; Rio Paraguay, Rio de la Plata.

F.I.: 1983 in larger numbers, before only as by-catch.

Sex: ♀ normally has 2 rows of dark spots in the hard-rayed part of the dorsal fin and sometimes has small spots on the base of the scales.

Soc. B.: Young are quarrelsome and jealously feed among themselves; it is recommended to keep the species in pairs. *B. semifasciatus* is usually indifferent towards species with deviating shapes. In general, the species is more retiring than the larger *Crenicichla* species.

M: The species likes roomy caves and hiding places; the tank should not be too bright. Water not overly hard (to 12° dGH), pH around 7.0.

B: The sexes can be differentiated from 10-12 cm total length. The species has probably not yet been bred in an aquarium, but it should be a cave spawner, as are *Crenicichla* species, with direct care of the brood by the ♀.

F: O; undemanding omnivores which are probably less specialized than pike cichlids with their deeply cut mouth. The species appreciates hardy live and substitute foods (beef heart, frozen food).

S: *Batrachops semifasciatus* can be considered one of the most blunt-snouted pike cichlids.

T: 23-27° C, **L:** 27 cm, **A:** 120 cm, **R:** b, m, **D:** 3-4 (C)
73-81° F, 10²/₃", 47",

Chaetobranchopsis orbicularis, juv.

Crenicichla semifasciata ♂

Crenicichla semifasciata ♀

Caquetaia kraussii (STEINDACHNER, 1879)
Krauss' Cichlid

Syn.: *Petenia kraussii, Astronotus kraussii, Cichlasoma kraussii.*

Hab.: South America; Colombia and Venezuela (Amazon and Orinoco region, Lake Valencia, where the species was introduced in 1960).

F.I.: Not known. In 1983 some specimens reached Germany anew through the Netherlands from the USA.

Sex: The ♂♂ become larger and have elongated dorsal and anal fins; the genital papilla is pointed. The genital papilla of the ♀♀ is blunt.

Soc. B.: Territorial; during breeding, the species is aggressive and quarrelsome, but towards conspecifics as well as heterospecifics during this time. An open spawner with a nuclear family; the young are well guarded.

M: Decorate the tank with roots and stones, forming as many hiding places as possible; well-rooted robust plants (*Sagittaria, Vallisneria*, large *Echinodorus* and cryptocorynes) can be used on the sides and background. Housing with other robust American cichlids and catfishes is possible. Always remember that the species is a piscivore.

B: 24-28° C (75-82° F); the chemical makeup of the water is not very important. The water can be soft and slightly acid to medium-hard and slightly alkaline. Open spawner which spawns on previously cleaned substrates. A spawn consists of several hundred eggs; the larvae are transferred to earlier dug pits.

F: C, O; live foods of all kinds, small fishes are especially relished; also freeze-dried foods, tablet and flake foods.

S: Besides *C. kraussii*, KULLANDER (1983) places the species *C. spectabilis, C. myersi* and, tentatively, *C. umbrifera* into the genus *Caquetaia*.

T: 22-27° C, **L:** 25 cm, **A:** 120 cm, **R:** m, b, **D:** 2-3
72-81° F, 9¾", 47",

Chaetobranchopsis orbicularis STEINDACHNER, 1875
Two-Striped Cichlid

Syn.: *Chaetobranchus bitaeniatus.*

Hab.: South America; Amazon; nothing more specific is known.

F.I.: 1934 Aquarium Hamburg imported a *Chaetobranchopsis* species under the name of *Chaetobranchopsis bitaeniatus*. Since the differentiation of the species *C. bitaeniatus, C. australis* and *C. orbicularis* seems to be difficult, it cannot be said with certainty if the cichlid imported in 1934 was really *C. bitaeniatus*.

Sex: None known.

Soc. B.: Territorial and very sedate, the fish is peaceful towards conspecifics as well as heterospecifics; plants are not disturbed.

M: Decorate the tank with roots and plants, providing many hiding places, since the animals appreciate dark shelters.

B: Nothing known.

F: C; a feeding specialist: filtering planktivore. The species can only be kept alive with small live foods (*Artemia, Daphnia*, etc.), but only for a short period of time.

S: The genera *Chaetobranchopsis* and *Chaetobranchus* have often been confused in the aquarium literature. The *Chaetobranchus* species are also filter feeders which "inhale" small live foods with their protrusile mouth.
Picture of a juvenile is shown on page 848.

T: 23-27° C, **L:** 12 cm, **A:** 80 cm, **R:** m, b, **D:** 4, feeding specialist
73-81° F, 4¾", 31",

Caquetaia kraussii, adult ♂ with young

Chaetobranchopsis orbicularis, adult ♂

Chaetobranchus flavescens HECKEL, 1840
Red-Eye Cichlid

Syn.: *Chaetobranchus bruneus, Ch. robustus, Chromys ucayalensis, Geophagus badiipinnis.*

Hab.: South America; Guyana, Brazil, Peru and Bolivia.

F.I.: Probably already in 1934.

Sex: Full-grown ♂♂ have elongated dorsal and anal fins and usually grow larger than ♀♀.

Soc. B.: Territorial; other social aspects of this species are essentially unknown.

M: As with *Chaetobranchopsis orbicularis.*

B: No reports are yet available about a successful aquarium spawn. LOWE-McCONNELL (1969): J. Linn. Soc. **48**, 271-272, suspects that *Ch. flavescens* is a mouthbrooder. This suspicion, however, still requires proof. In the wild, the spawning season seems to be limited to the rainy season.

F: O; live foods of all kinds, frozen food, beef heart, shrimp, flake food.

S: The long, thin gill rakers indicate that *Chaetobranchus flavescens* is a plankton feeder.

T: 24-26° C, **L:** 28 cm, **A:** 100 cm, **R:** b, m, **D:** 3
75-79° F, 11", 39",

Chalinochromis brichardi POLL, 1974

Syn.: None.

Hab.: Africa; northeast Lake Tanganyika (Burundi, northern Tanzania) and in the south (Zambia), endemic. The animals are absent from the central east coast. The species inhabits the rocky shores and prefers depths between two and ten meters.

F.I.: 1973.

Sex: With age, the ♂ develops a more or less pronounced frontal hump, are usually larger, and the black spot in the dorsal fin is dark black and sharply delineated; the ♀, in contrast, always has a diffuse spot.

Soc. B.: Territorial cichlids which, as a rule, are sedate and plant friendly. Sometimes the animals can become very aggressive. A strong bond exists between ♂ and ♀. These are cave spawners with a nuclear family.

M: Rockwork with as many crevices and caves as possible for hiding places; plant the tank with tough-leaved species. *Ch. brichardi* can also be kept in a large community aquarium. Associate with other cichlids from the rocky areas (*Julidochromis, Lamprologus, Petrochromis, Telmatochromis, Tropheus*).

B: 26-28° C (79-82° F); water 6-15° dGH, pH 7.2-9. Breeding is rarely successful. Successes are usually only with bred specimens which are accustomed to conditions in captivity. Cave spawner. The eggs are usually adhered to the ceiling of a cave or the wall of a rock crevice. The eggs number to 120, hatch in 2-4 days, and the fry are free-swimming in 8-10 days. The fry are very small (3 mm; 1/8") and are fed *Artemia* nauplii. They do not form a school by the parents. The young usually stay within the territory of the parents which intensely defend it against intruders.

F: Difficult with new imports because usually only live foods (*Daphnia, Cyclops, Mysis*) are accepted. However, adaptation to flake food is possible.

S: Until recently, the genus *Chalinochromis* was considered monotypic. Meanwhile, two additional scientifically undescribed *Chalinochromis* species have been found by M. FAINZILBER at the central east coast. In contrast to *Ch. brichardi*, they have black longitudinal stripes on their sides.

T: 24-27° C, **L:** 15 cm, usually smaller, **A:** 60 cm, **R:** m, b, **D:** 2-3
75-81° F, 6", usually smaller, 24",

Chaetobranchus flavescens

Chalinochromis brichardi

Chilotilapia rhoadesii BOULENGER, 1908

Syn.: None.

Hab.: Africa; Lake Malawi (endemic). It primarily lives over sandy substrates.

F.I.: An exact date can not be established.

Sex: Clear sexual dichromatism; ♂ is more colorful and intensely colored; ♀ paler.

Soc. B.: Territorial ♂♂ are occasionally very aggressive towards conspecifics. An ovophile mouthbrooder; maternal family.

M: Structure the aquarium with individual larger stones and tough plants; provide some hiding places. A rocky shore should not be imitated; however, provide the fish with an extensive sandy bottom. Associate with *"Haplochromis"* species which have similar demands.

B: 26-28° C (79-82° F); water between 7-20° dGH and pH 7.2-8.6. If possible, keep two ♂♂ with a larger group of ♀♀. Courtship and spawning behavior similar to "*Haplochromis*" species from Lake Malawi.

Continued on facing page.

Chromidotilapia batesii (BOULENGER, 1901)

Bate's Chromidotilapia

Syn.: *Pelmatochromis batesii.*

Hab.: West Africa; in equatorial Guinea and southwest Cameroon (Kienke color morph). The animals normally inhabit slightly brownish rain forest rivers of varying sizes. The Eseka color morph also occurs in southwest Cameroon. It inhabits small flowing waters in the northern drainage area of the Nyong River.

F.I.: 1913.

Sex: Differentiation of the sexes is not very easy in the Kienke color morph. Sexually mature ♀♀ have a fuller stomach, and during courtship, the ventral region is wine red. In contrast, the Eseka color morph has clear sexual dimorphism (dichromatism). The ♂♂ are larger and have numerous small dark dots on the dorsal, tail, and anal fins; in ♀♀, these dots are lacking, and they have a shining metallic chrome- yellow band on the dorsal fin.

Soc. B.: Territorial; the species is peaceful and does not damage plants. It can become aggressive towards conspecifics, but it barely notices cichlids of other genera. Spawns in caves and takes the larvae which hatch after about 3 days into its mouth. Larvophile mouthbrooder; patriarch-matriarch family.

M: Keep in roomy aquaria (from 130 x 50 x 50 cm; 51" x 20" x 20"). Use small-grained gravel as substrate; build caves out of stones with a horizontal surface as the roof of the cave. Decorate with roots. Use plants from west Africa (*Anubias, Nymphea lotus, Bolbitis heudelotii*). LINKE recommends a heater which acts from below (e.g., a substrate heater). The water should be soft and low in calcium (1-5° dGH) as well as slightly acid (pH 6.5). However, it is also possible to keep it in harder water. Every 1 to 2 weeks exchange of the water. 12 hours of illumination (tropical day!). In larger tanks they can be kept with other west African cichlids and/or larger labyrinth fishes or characins.

B: Water values as indicated above. Reproduction and brood care of *C. batesii* differ from other *Chromidotilapia* species since *C. batesii* is a larvophile mouthbrooder. Spawning usually occurs on the ceiling of a cave. The eggs, up to 100, are immediately fertilized by the ♂. After the eggs are laid, the ♀ cares for the spawn while the ♂ defends the territory. At a temperature of 25° C (77° F) the larvae hatch after barely 3 days and are taken into the mouth of the ♀. There they remain until free-swimming. Afterwards, both parents care for and guard the young for about 6 weeks. Feed the young with *Artemia* nauplii, micro foods and TetraMin Baby Food.

F: Hardy live foods like small crustaceans (*Gammarus, Asselus, Artemia, Daphnia magna*), mosquito larvae, *Tubifex*, Enchytraea and small earthworms; flake food and tablet food.

S: *Chromidotilapia batesii* occurs in two color morphs: 1. Kienke color morph, named after the Kienke River system in southern Cameroon, and 2. the Eseka color morph, named after a locality in southwest Cameroon.

T: 24-26° C, **L:** 12 cm, **A:** 130 cm, **R:** b, m, **D:** 2-3
75-79° F, 4 3/4", 51",

Chilotilapia rhoadesii

Chromidotilapia batesii

The ♀♀ are ovophile mouthbrooders. The young are released from the mouth of the mother for the first time after about 3 weeks. Feed the young with small crustacea and crumbled flake food.

F: A specialized molluscivore that crushes snail shells with its blunt teeth. The species can be adapted to any common substitute food. Feed hardy foods (insect larvae, earthworms, cut shrimp, cut meat, tablet food).

S: The genus *Chilotilapia* is closely related to the genus *Chromidotilapia* but differs by the dentition which is made up of 5 rows, each with blunt, broad molars.

T: 23-28° C, L: 23 cm, A: from 120 cm, R: b, m, D: 3
73-82° F, 9", from 47",

Chromidotilapia linkei STAECK, 1980
Linke's Chromidotilapia

Syn.: None.

Hab.: West Africa; western Cameroon, in the Mungo River and its drainage area. The animals prefer shallows.

F.I.: 1977 by Horst Linke, Berlin, Germany.

Sex: Clear sexual dichromatism. The ♀ has a metallic chrome-yellow longitudinal band in the hard-spined part of the dorsal fin, and the opercular spot is surrounded by a light blue area; the ♂ is without this longitudinal band and lacks the light blue area around the opercular spot.

Soc. B.: Territorial, even outside of the spawning season. Peaceful cichlid which can be combined with other fishes. They do not disturb water plants. Ovophile mouthbrooder; nuclear or patriarch-matriarch family with a close partner bond; intensive brood care by both parents.

M: Needs large aquaria with fine-grained, not too light colored gravel as substrate. Provide hiding places, caves of stone and a cover of roots. Generous lateral and background vegetation with *Anubias* species, *Nymphea lotus* and *Bolbitis heudelotii*. The plants should be set in groups; 12 hours illumination (tropical day!). Water soft (around 3° dGH) and neutral to slightly alkaline (pH 7.0-7.5). A slight water current is needed. Every 1-2 weeks regularly exchange 1/3 of the tank volume. House with other cichlids (*Pelvicachromis* and *Pelmatochromis* species), large labyrinth fishes and characins.

B: 26-28° C (79-82° F); water values as indicated above; spawning has also occurred in harder water (15° dGH). Breeding of a well matched pair is not difficult. The animals spawn on a hard substrate and the eggs are immediately taken into the mouth of the ♀. Both parents participate in brooding the eggs and defending the spawning territory. If danger is present, the ♂ takes eggs into his mouth during spawning; if there is no danger, the ♀ takes all the eggs into her mouth when spawning is complete. In the former case, the ♂ places all eggs again on the spawning site or in its immediate vicinity towards the end of spawning, and the ♀ then immediately takes them into her mouth. The eggs are yellow and oval and number to 150. The ♀ now retires and is protected by the ♂. After 7 days, the eggs or larvae are transferred to the ♂. He keeps them for a similar amount of time in his mouth. After barely 2 weeks, the free-swimming young are released from the mouth of the ♂. The parents care for the young for about 3-4 weeks. Feeding is best done with *Artemia* nauplii. According to LINKE & STAECK (1981), the average number of young per spawn is limited to 20-25 animals.

F: Hardy live foods of all kinds (*Gammarus, Daphnia magna,* mosquito larvae, Enchytraea, *Tubifex*, small earthworms); flake food and tablet foods are also readily taken.

S: *Chromidotilapia linkei* is characterized by a light blue iris and a large dark spot on the opercula; in ♀♀ the spot is surrounded by a light blue area.

T: 24-27° C, **L:** 10 cm, **A:** 120 cm, **R:** b, m, **D:** 2-3
75-81° F, 4", 47",

Cichla ocellaris BLOCH & SCHNEIDER, 1801
Peacock Bass

Syn.: *Acharnes speciosus, Cichla argus, C. atabapensis, C. monoculus, C. orinocensis, Crenicichla orinocensis, Cychla argus, C. flavo-maculata, C. trifasciata.*

Hab.: Northern South America; Venezuela, Guyana, Brazil, Peru, Bolivia; the species inhabits almost all larger water bodies there. They are also raised in ponds as food fish.

F.I.: 1912 by Wilhelm Eimeke, Hamburg, Germany.

Sex: Older ♂♂ have a nuchal hump; otherwise, the sexes are only distinguishable during the spawning act. *Cichla ocellaris* is monomorphic.

Soc. B.: Territorial; in nature the animals are rapid swimmers, but in an aquarium they are usually sedate and wait motionless for prey. The species does not dig or molest plants. Open spawner; nuclear family.

Continued on page 858.

Chromidotilapia linkei ♀

Cichla ocellaris

Continuation of *Cichla ocellaris*:

M: Needs large tanks with a sand or gravel bottom. Provide some cover with stones and roots as well as a few flat stones as spawning substrates. Edges and background can be planted. The species is quite adaptive; it does not place any special demands on water chemistry. Keep in a species tank because of its predatory lifestyle.

B: 26-28° C (79-82° F); no reports are yet available about successful breeding in an aquarium. Water values play a subordinate role. The fish are sexually mature from 20 cm (8"). In nature the eggs are adhered to a hard substrate in a pit in shallow water. Larger ♀♀ have spawns with over 10000 eggs. Parents guard the young over 1 month. The young can already be 5 cm (2") long at that point.

F: C; live foods of all kinds. The animals are pronounced predators which, from a certain size on, live almost exclusively from fish.

S: Because of its size, *Cichla ocellaris* is only suitable as a juvenile for most aquarists. The most important characteristic of the genus *Cichla* is a deep indentation separating the hard spines from the soft rays of the dorsal fin. The genus contains two additional species: *Cichla intermedia* MACHADO-ALLISON, 1971 and *C. temensis* HUMBOLDT, 1833.

T: 24-27° C, L: 60 cm, A: 120 cm, R: b, m, D: 3-4 (C)
75-81° F, 24", 47",

Caquetaia kraussi, juv.

Cichlasoma altifrons (KNER & STEINDACHNER, 1863)
Hi-Head Cichlid

Syn.: *Heros altifrons, Astatheros altifrons, Astronotus altifrons.*

Hab.: Central and northern South America; Costa Rica, Panama, Colombia.

F.I.: 1981.

Sex: ♂ is larger, has a more intense blue component in the coloration, and a steeper forehead.

Soc. B.: Territorial and forms pairs; very pugnacious towards additional conspecifics. They are constantly chased around, but are bitten less often. Open spawners; nuclear family.

M: The bottom should not be too coarse, and it should never be sharp. Provide open hiding places and sufficient swimming space. Plants are not molested. The water should be rich in oxygen, clear and medium-hard (around 10° dGH), pH around 7.0.

B: 25-27° C (77-81° F); open spawner which spawns on hard substrates.

F: This species, which is placed in the section *Amphilophus* (= detritivore) of the genus *Cichlasoma*, lives close to the bottom and digs like the eartheaters, searching for edible matter. This behavior extends to an aquarium even though the animals accept any common feed. The "pouting" fleshy lips leads one to suspect that the fish is a feeding specialist.

S: Excited animals display the juvenile coloration of 5 broad crossbands on a light background with a spot on the caudal peduncle.

T: 23-27° C, L: 22 cm, A: 120 cm, R: b, m, D: 2
73-81° F, 8 3/4", 47",

Cichlasoma alfari MEEK, 1907
Pastel Cichlid

Syn.: *Astatheros lethrinus, Cichlasoma alfaroi, C. bouchellei, C. lethrinus, Copora alfari, Parapetenia alfari.*

Hab.: Central America; Nicaragua (Atlantic drainage of the Rio San Juan), Costa Rica (Atlantic and Pacific side; particularly numerous in the south), Panama (Rio Guarumo, Bocas del Toro Province); in clear, often fast-flowing waters.

F.I.: 1980.

Sex: The ♀ has a dark spot of varying intensity on the 7-12 dorsal fin rays and a tendency towards pronounced contrast coloration; the ♂♂ become larger and have a boxy forehead.

Soc. B.: Although the species appears gracious with its pastel colors, it has the ability to dominate. An elegant, actively swimming species which should be kept in pairs. The animals dig a lot. Open spawners; nuclear family.

M: Use coarse substrate and provide numerous hiding places. Water should be slightly acid to neutral (pH 6.5-7.0), hardness 2-10° dGH.

B: A typical open spawner that tends to choose vertical substrates. The ♀ dominates in caring for the brood. The larvae hatch after 70-76 hours at 23° C (73° F) and a pH of 7.0; the young are free-swimming after 240 hours. The bottom is initially swirled up by the parents to "feed the young".

F: O; undemanding omnivore.

S: *Cichlasoma alfari* is an extremely variable species despite its narrow distribution area. It can show deviations in body height, length of the caudal peduncle and dorsal fin as well as variations in color. Differences even appear within the same river system.

T: 23-27° C, **L:** 22 cm, **A:** 120 cm, **R:** b, m, **D:** 2-3
73-81° F, 8¾", 47",

Cichlasoma atromaculatum REGAN, 1912
Rust-Belly Cichlid

Syn.: None.

Hab.: Central and South America; Pacific area of Panama (San Blas Province), western Colombia (Atrato and San Juan basin).

F.I.: Probably in 1977.

Sex: The ♂♂ usually grow larger. ♀♀ have a dark spot on the dorsal fin (?).

Soc. B.: Territorial, the fish are quarrelsome towards hetero- and conspecifics. Open spawner; nuclear family.

M: Use an aquarium with sand or gravel bottom, hiding places of stones or roots, some spawning stones, and edge and background plantings. The species is extremely sensitive towards sudden changes in water hardness and pH; even large animals can die a few minutes after being transferred. Very clear water, up to medium-hard (12° dGH) and slightly alkaline (pH around 7.5) is suggested.

B: 25-27° C (77-81° F); water values as above. Breeding parallels other open spawning cichlids from Central and South America. The eggs are laid on a previously cleaned, hard substrate. Spawns are large (often over 1000 eggs). Spawn and young are cared for by both parents. The young should be fed with *Artemia* nauplii and small, sieved crustacea.

F: O; live foods of all kinds (mosquito larvae, water fleas, earthworms, Enchytraea, *Tubifex*), freeze-dried food, shrimp, beef heart, flake food.

S: A typical characteristic of *Cichlasoma atromaculatum* are 3 dark spots in the posterior body region: one on the base of the soft-rayed part of dorsal, one on the soft-rayed part of the anal fin, as well as a 3rd on the upper half of the base of the tail fin. Systematically, *C. atromaculatum* occupies an intermediate position between the Amphilophus and Parapetenia sections of *Cichlasoma*.

Cichlasoma atromaculatum ♀

T: 23-25° C, **L:** 25 cm, **A:** 100 cm, **R:** b, m, **D:** 3
73-77° F, 9¾", 39",

Cichlasoma alfari, high backed morph

Cichlasoma atromaculatum ♂

Cichlasoma bifasciatum (STEINDACHNER, 1864)
Red-Spotted Cichlid

Syn.: *Cichlaurus bifasciatus, Astronotus bifasciatus, Cichlasoma bifasciatum.*

Hab.: Central America; Mexico and Guatemala, Rio Usumacinta basin.

F.I.: Probably in 1978 by Thomas Schulz.

Sex: Barely pronounced outside the spawning season; the ♀ has a somewhat darker coloration on the lower head and body region while caring for the spawn; in addition, the ♂ grows a few centimeters larger than the ♀.

Soc. B.: Territorial; the species can become quite aggressive and quarrelsome towards conspecific and heterospecific fishes (especially while caring for the young). Open spawner that forms a nuclear family; good parents to the numerous young.

M: Decorate the tank with as many hiding places as possible, using numerous roots and stones. Vegetation is not possible; the animals are pronounced herbivores. Use flat, smooth stones as substrate. Combining with other robust Central American cichlids and catfishes is possible.

B: 24-27° C (75-81° F); the water chemistry is secondary. The water can be soft and slightly acid to medium-hard and slightly alkaline.
Open spawner who lays the eggs on previously cleaned smooth stones. A spawn is composed of about 500 eggs; the larvae are transferred into earlier dug pits.

F: H, O; vegetable fare (lettuce, spinach, vegetable flake food), live foods of all kinds, freeze-dried tablet and flake foods.

S: This species is occasionally confused with *Cichlasoma melanurum* (GÜNTHER, 1862).

T: 22-27° C, **L**: 25 cm, **A**: 120 cm, **R**: m, b, **D**: 2
72-81° F, 9 3/4", 47",

Cichlasoma bimaculatum (LINNAEUS, 1758)
Twin-Spot Cichlid

Syn.: *Labrus bimaculatus, Acara bimaculata, A. gronovii, A. marginata, A. margarita, A. punctata, Astronotus bimaculatus, Centrarchus cyanopterus, Chromis taenia, Cichla bimaculata, Cichlasoma taenia, Cichlaurus bimaculatus, Heros bimaculatus, Perca bimaculata, Sciaena bimaculata.*

Hab.: Northern South America; from east Peru to the Guianas (but not found in the Magdalena basin).

F.I.: ?

Sex: Sexual monomorph; the ♂♂ become slightly larger.

Soc. B.: Sedate, relatively peaceful species which, although territorial and should be kept in pairs, is rather retiring when housed with similar sized cichlids.

M: A robust, undemanding species which tolerates vegetation. Offer the animals many hiding places created with stones and roots. Water not too hard (up to 15° dGH) and around neutral (pH 7.0).

B: 25-27° C (77-81° F); a fertile open spawner with strong pair formation and intensive brood care. Corresponding to the absent sexual dimorphism, the eggs, larvae and young are cared for by both parents equally; the young are hardy and rapid growing.

F: O; undemanding omnivore.

S: Although the species is the type species for the genus *Cichlasoma*, the fish looks very similar to *Aequidens tetramerus* (HECKEL, 1840). That species, on the other hand, is the type species for the genus *Aequidens*! The important distinguishing characteristic is the unscaled base of the dorsal and anal fin of *Ae. tetramerus*. The fish known as *"Aequidens portalegrensis"*, and initially described by HECKEL (1840) as *Acara dimerus*, is the closest relative of *C. bimaculatum*. *C. bimaculatum* has 4-6 anal fin rays. *"Ae. portalegrensis"* only has 3, so meanwhile they have been recombined into *Cichlasoma dimerus*.

T: 22-27° C, **L**: 20 cm, **A**: 120 cm, **R**: b, m, **D**: 1-2
72-81° F, 8", 47",

Cichlasoma bifasciatum

Cichlasoma bimaculatum

Cichlasoma citrinellum (GÜNTHER, 1864)
Midas Cichlid

Syn.: *Heros citrinellus, H. basilaris, Cichlasoma basilare, C. granadense, Erythrichthys citrinellum.*

Hab.: Central America; southern Mexico, Nicaragua (lakes Nicaragua, Managua and Xiloa), Costa Rica (in the Atlantic tributaries of the Costa Rica River and Cuba River), Honduras.

F.I.: Probably after 1970.

Sex: Large ♂♂ have a distinct cephalic hump and longer fins. Genital papillae of the ♂♂ are conical; wider and half-lobed in the ♀♀.

Soc. B.: Territorial, the species forms pairs. The animals are relatively quarrelsome, but they are definitely bellicose at spawning time. They dig a lot at this time. Open spawner, nuclear family with pronounced brood care behavior.

M: Needs roomy tanks with free swimming space and hiding places of stones and roots. The rockwork has to be based on the bottom of the aquarium. If not, there is danger of collapse because of the animal's digging. Plants can be waived. The chemical water values do not have an important role in the care of this cichlid.

B: 24-28° C (75-82° F); *Cichlasoma citrinellum* can be bred in soft, acid or hard, alkaline aquarium water. They are not choosy concerning their spawning substrate. Spawning occurs on horizontal, slanted or vertical hard substrates. A typical open spawner with spawns of several hundred to over 1000 eggs. The larvae hatch after 3 days. These are placed in pits and are free-swimming after an additional 5 days.

F: O; hardy live foods (mosquito larvae, earthworms, snails, fishes), beef heart, shrimp, tablet and large flake food.

S: *Cichlasoma citrinellum* has a yellow and a gray morph. The young of *C. citrinellum* eat a mucous secretion produced by the skin of the parents.

T: 22-25° C, L: 30 cm, A: 120 cm, R: b, m, D: 1-2
72-77° F, 11¾", 47",

Cichlasoma coryphaenoides (HECKEL, 1840)
Chocolate Cichlid

Syn.: *Acara coryphaenoides, Cichlasoma coryphaenoides, C. arnoldi, Chuco axelrodi, Heros coryphaenoides, H. niger.*

Hab.: South America; in current-rich parts of the Amazon and Rio Negro and their tributaries.

F.I.: 1911.

Sex: Older ♂♂ a have distinct cephalic hump. Dorsal and anal fins of the ♂ are usually more elongated and pointed.

Soc. B.: Territorial, the animals are bellicose and quarrelsome. They do not disturb plants, but dig a lot. Open spawner with a nuclear family.

M: As for other *Cichlasoma* species from South America.

B: No reports have yet been filed about successfully breeding this fish in an aquarium. Breeding reports about the species usually refer to *Hypselecara temporalis*.

F: C; hardy live foods of all kinds, cut meat and heart, large flakes and tablet foods.

S: The species has a marked ability to change colors and design: young and subadult animals can have a "comma shaped", black lateral spot over a red-brown base coloration; they can be dark-brown/ochre-yellow vertically striped; and they can have a lemon yellow "forehead spot" on a dark brown to dark gray base coloration (depending on the mood of the animal).

T: 22-25° C, L: 25 cm, A: 120 cm, R: b, m, D: 2
72-77° F, 9¾", 47",

Cichlasoma citrinellum

Hypselecara coryphaenoides

Cichlasoma dovii (GÜNTHER, 1864)

Dow's Cichlid, "Lagunero"

Syn.: *Heros dovii, Astronotus dovii, Cichlasoma dowi, Parapetenia dovii.*

Hab.: Central America; eastern Honduras, Nicaragua, Costa Rica.

F.I.: ?

Sex: ♀ is smaller with a blunt snout and lacks a hump. The body has a black-brown band and stripe design on a yellowish-gray base and a line on the operculum; ♂ has fine, dark dots on body and fins and a violet sheen as the base color. Snout and fins are greenish-blue.

Soc. B.: Territorial, forms pairs; an extremely robust, bellicose species which dominates without compromise. Open spawner; nuclear family.

M: Furnish the aquarium with a coarse bottom and securely based rockwork to offer many hiding possibilities for the ♀. Decorating with tough plants is possible. Water neutral (pH 7.0), hardness up to 20° dGH. Cool water sedates the temperament of the animal.

B: 25-28° C (77-82° F); open spawner which spawns on sufficiently dimensioned substrates. The animals mature after about 15 months and a body length of 20 cm (8"). Even young ♀♀ produce over 1000 eggs. Raising the young is easy.

F: C; these specialized predators should sometimes receive hardy live foods (fish, earthworms). They also accept substitute foods (beef heart, shrimp, krill, tablet food).

S: *Cichlasoma dovii* has several morphs. Even orange-red individuals are known from Lake Nicaragua and Rio Puerto Viejo

T: 22-28° C, 72-82° F, **L:** ♂ 70 cm, ♂ 28", ♀ 50 cm, ♀ 20", **A:** from 150 cm, from 59", **R:** b, m, **D:** 3-4 (C)

Cichlasoma festae (BOULENGER, 1899)

Red Terror

Syn.: *Heros festae.*

Hab.: South America; western Ecuador; the species inhabits the Guayas River system. The animals predominately inhabit the shores.

F.I.: Around 1980.

Sex: Sexual dichromatism occurs from 10 cm (4") length. ♂♂ have a number of sky blue dots on the unpaired fins; dorsal and ventral fins are not dark black. ♀♀ do not have dots on the unpaired fins, and the hard-rayed part of the dorsal fin and the pelvic fins are pitch black.

Soc. B.: Territorial; the species is very aggressive and quarrelsome. The animals are predators and dig during spawning time. Open spawner; nuclear family.

M: If not kept in a roomy tank, the fish will stop growing early. Hiding places, caves and shelter of stones and roots should be available. Since *C. festae* digs, stone structures should always be very stable by basing them on the bottom pane of the aquaria. Use a thick layer of fine-grained gravel for substrate. Provide neutral (pH around 7), medium-hard water (up to 15° dGH). Perform regular water exchanges (every 2 weeks 1/3 of the tank). Best kept in a species tank.

B: *C. festae* prefers to spawn on hidden substrates. Offer the animals flat stone plates located under rockwork and/or roots. Part of the spawning preparations is a digging phase during which several deep pits are dug. The hatched larvae are placed in the pits. Spawning occurs after the preparations are finished and an extensive courtship. A hard substrate is used where the adhered eggs are fertilized by the ♂. Up to 3000, I-type eggs are laid; the eggs of *C. festae* are larger than most *Cichlasoma* eggs. The ♀ guards the spawn while the ♂ defends the territory. At 26° C (79° F) the larvae begin to hatch after a good 3 days. They are freed from the egg shells by the mouth of the ♀ and deposited into one of the prepared pits where the ♀ continues to guard them. After 5-6 days,

Continued on page 868.

Cichlasoma dovii

Cichlasoma festae

Cichlasoma festae

Continuation of *Cichlasoma festae*:

the young are free-swimming and are guarded by both parents. Feed the young with *Artemia* nauplii, *Cyclops*, sieved water fleas and crumbled flake food.

F: C; live foods of all kinds; small fish, insects, insect larvae, snails, worms, *Gammarus*; chopped meat, krill, flake and tablet foods.

S: *Cichlasoma festae* belongs to the *Cichlasoma* section *Parapetenia*, whose members are all meat and fish eaters. Representatives of this section are, for example, *Cichlasoma managuense, C. octofasciatum, C. salvini* and *C. trimaculatum.*

T: 26-28° C, L: 50 cm, A: 150 cm, R: b,
79-82° F, 20", 59",
D: 3 (C)

Continuation of *Cichlasoma friedrichsthalii*:

all kinds, freeze-dried food, tablet and flake food.

S: The species has been imported in Germany under the name *Cichlasoma managuense* and has long been maintained under this name.

T: 22-28° C, L: up to 25 cm, A: from 100 cm,
72-82° F, up to 9 3/4", from 39",
R: m, b, D: 1-2

Cichlasoma friedrichsthalii (HECKEL, 1840)
Friedrichsthal's Cichlid

Syn.: *Astronotus friedrichsthalii, Cichlosoma friedrichsthalii, Parapetenia friedrichsthalii, P. multifasciata.*

Hab.: Central America; Mexico, Guatemala, Honduras, Belize, Costa Rica, Nicaragua. Differently colored habitat variants exist.

F.I.: It seems questionable that the animals imported in 1914 by A. Mayer from Progresso were indeed the species *C. friedrichsthalii.*

Sex: ♂♂ are larger and darker in color; in the population present (aquarium) in Germany, the ♀ is intensely yellow colored, and the ♂ varies in his base color between light gray, violet and blue hues, but it can also become almost black.

Soc. B.: A sedate and peaceful open spawner which forms strong pairs; it is territorial and guards the hundreds of offspring well.

M: Needs decorations of roots and stones to provide hiding opportunities for inferior animals (important during the brood care period) and smooth stones for spawning substrates. The aquarium can be planted along the background and sides since *C. friedrichsthalii* is a carnivore and is uninterested in plants. Water values as for other *Cichlasoma* from Central America.

B: 24-28° C (75-82° F); an open spawner with a nuclear family; a spawn can be comprised of several hundred eggs; the ♀ cares for the eggs, larvae and the young; the ♂ secures the territorial borders. The young are placed into the previously dug pits. Temperature and water values play a subordinate role for successful reproduction (as long as they are within the normal ranges).

F: As a representative of the Parapetenia section of *Cichlasoma*, the animals are actually carnivores and piscivores. In the aquarium they are omnivores: live food of

Continued on facing page.

Cichlasoma labiatum (GÜNTHER, 1864)

Red Devil

Syn.: *Heros labiatus, Cichlasoma erythraeum, C. lobochilus.*

Hab.: Central America; Nicaragua, in lakes Nicaragua, Managua and Xiloa.

F.I.: 1976 (?).

Sex: ♂♂ grow larger than ♀♀. The ♂ has a pointed genital papilla. The ♀ has a blunt genital papilla.

Soc. B.: Territorial, these robust and aggressive cichlids are occasionally very rude towards conspecifics and heterospecifics. The animals are pronounced diggers. Open spawners; patriarch-matriarch family.

M: As indicated for *Cichlasoma citrinellum* or *C. nicaraguense.* No special demands are placed on water values.

B: 25-27° C (77-81° F). The animals are typical open spawners; however, they prefer to spawn on inclined substrates. The spawns consist of numerous (600-700), transparent, amber-yellow eggs. The immediate brood care is the responsibility of the ♀. At 25° C (77° F) the larvae hatch after about 3 days. They are unable to swim and are transferred often. After an additional 5-7 days, the young are free-swimming. They are nourished with *Artemia* nauplii. After about 2-3 weeks, the young can "graze" the parent's skin as an additional food source.

F: O; greedy omnivore: live foods of any kind, frozen food, beef heart, fish flesh, flake and tablet foods.

S: *Cichlasoma labiatum* and *Cichlasoma citrinellum* differ little in their morphometric values. This has lead to discussions on their systematic status. In contrast, the distribution areas are different. *Cichlasoma labiatum* only occurs in the above mentioned lakes of Nicaragua. *C. citrinellum* can be found from Costa Rica to Nicaragua. *C. labiatum* shows a strong polychromatism.

T: 24-26° C, **L:** 25 cm, **A:** 120 cm, **R:** b, **D:** 3
75-79° F, 9¾", 47",

Cichlasoma synspilum ♀, text on page 880

Cichlasoma trimaculatum continued (from page 882):

open. The "loose" spawns can be comprised of more than 1000 eggs. The ♀ takes over guarding the spawn; the ♂ secures the territory. Larvae hatch after 72 hours at 28° C (82° F); they are placed in pits and are free-swimming after an additional 92 hours. Both parents intensively care for and guide the young. Feed the young with *Artemia* nauplii.

F: O; live foods, vegetable fare, frozen food, shrimp, beef heart, flake food, tablet food.

S: Young *Cichlasoma trimaculatum* have a similar appearance to juvenile *Cichlasoma salvini* in submissive coloration.

T: 21-30° C, **L:** ♂ 36 cm, ♀ 25 cm, **A:** 150 cm, **R:** b, m, **D:** 2-3 (C)
70-86° F, ♂ 14", ♀ 9¾", 59",

Cichlasoma longimanus (GÜNTHER, 1869)

Longfin Cichlid

All information refers to the Pacific population from Costa Rica!

Syn.: *Astronotus longimanus, Astatheros longimanus, Cichlasoma popenoei.*

Hab.: Central America; the species occurs in various geographic races: 1. In Atlantic tributaries of the Rio Aguan in Honduras to Rio Priuzapolka in north Nicaragua; 2. In Pacific tributaries from Arroyo Agua Caliente in Guatemala to the Rio Bebedero system in Costa Rica; 3. In the basin of the large lakes of Nicaragua.

F.I.: 1981, private collections made by H. G. Breidohr, B. Weber and U. Werner.

Sex: The ♂ is larger, usually lighter colored with a beautiful brass sheen. The ♀ tends to be dark colored.

Soc. B.: Territorial fish that forms pairs. The animals are relatively peaceful towards other cichlids; they lack the ability to dominate and do not have large space requirements. Open spawner; nuclear family.

M: A soft muddy substrate is the preferred habitat of these bottom oriented fishes. They do not eat plants but will dig them up in the course of spawning preparations. The aquarium should offer some hiding places and an open, moderate-grained sandy area. Particular demands on the water are not placed; in their natural habitat, the water is warm (26-28° C; 79-82° F) and soft (about 5° dGH) with a pH around 7.0.

B: This is an open spawner with a strong brood care instinct and a great passion for digging. The spawns are extensive and the fry hatch after 50 hours at 26° C (79° F); the young are free-swimming after 146 hours.

F: O; the species, which is part of the *Amphilophus* (= detritivore) section, can be considered an omnivore in the aquarium; however, worms seem to be a special delicacy.

S: The different populations reach various sizes: Pacific populations are said to reach a standard length of 18 cm (7") and Honduras populations to about 11 cm (4 1/3"). The species does not form a cephalic hump. The species name is derived from the long pelvic fins (*longimanus* = with long hands).

T: 24-28° C, 75-82° F, L: 22 cm, 8 3/4", A: 120 cm, 47", R: b, m, D: 2

Cichlasoma maculicauda (REGAN, 1905)

Black Belt Cichlid

Syn.: *Astatheros maculicauda, Astronotus parma, Chuco globosum, Ch. manana, Cichlasoma fenestratum* var. *parma, C. globosum, C. manana, C. nigritum, C. parma, Heros parma.*

Hab.: Central America; southern Mexico, Guatemala, Belize, Costa Rica (Atlantic coast), Panama (canal zone).

F.I.: 1912 by C. Siggelkow, Hamburg. Towards the end of WWI the species became extinct in Germany. A renewed import from Aquarium Hamburg occurred in 1934; anew at the end of the 70's by aquarists.

Sex: The ♂ is larger, more splendidly colored, has a slight cephalic hump and a pointed genital papilla; in the ♀, the genital papilla is blunt.

Soc. B.: Territorial, the fish can be quite aggressive towards conspecifics as well as heterospecifics (particularly while caring for the young). Open spawner with nuclear family; good care of the numerous brood.

M: Decorate the tank with many roots and stones as rich in hiding places as is practical; vegetation is not possible because the animals are express herbivores. Provide flat, smooth stones as spawning substrates. House with other robust Central American large cichlids and large catfishes.

B: 23-27° C (73-81° F); the chemical composition of the water is secondary. The water can be soft and slightly acid to medium-hard and slightly alkaline. An open spawner on flat, previously cleaned stones. One spawn consists of up to 600 eggs; the larvae are placed in previously dug pits.

F: H, O; vegetable fare (lettuce, spinach, vegetable flake foods), live foods of all types, freeze-dried food, tablet food and flake food.

S: Because of its extensive distribution area, several different color morphs exist.

T: 22-27° C, 72-81° F, L: 30 cm, 11 3/4", A: over 120 cm, over 47", R: m, b, D: 3

Cichlasoma longimanus

Cichlasoma maculicauda

Cichlasoma nicaraguense (GÜNTHER, 1864)

Spilotum, Nicaragua Cichlid

Syn.: *Heros nicaraguensis, Cichlasoma balteatum, C. spilotum.*

Hab.: Central America; Nicaragua (lakes Nicaragua and Managua) and Costa Rica (Rio San Juan basin).

F.I.: 1976 (?).

Sex: ♂♂ have dark edged scales in the posterior body region and a dark design on the vertical fins; ♀♀ have a beautiful golden metallic hard-rayed dorsal fin and are generally more intensely colored. ♂♂ grow larger and develop a slight cephalic hump.

Soc. B.: Territorial; *C. nicaraguense* is a relatively peaceful and reserved fish. The animals dig during the spawning season and eat soft-leaved plants. Open spawners; patriarch-matriarch family.

M: Needs caves and hiding places of stones or slanted stone plates. Decorate with some roots and a sandy or fine-grained gravel bottom. The tank can be planted since they only occasionally nibble on plants. No special demands are placed on the water; water medium-hard (10-15° dGH) and neutral to weakly alkaline (pH 7.0-8.0).

B: 26-28° C (79-82° F); the reproduction of *C. nicaraguense* differs from that of other *Cichlasoma* species. *C. nicaraguense* is the only known pit-spawning species who produces nonadhesive eggs. The spawn consists of roundish, 2 mm (1/16"), transparent eggs which are not adhered to a wall or the ceiling of a cave, but lie as a loose conglomeration on the floor in the backmost corner of the cave. Development of the eggs takes about 3 days at 26° C (79° F). After an additional 4-5 days, the young are free-swimming. A clear division of duties can be observed between ♂ and ♀; the ♀ cares for egg and larvae while the ♂ defends the outer territory. Feed the young with *Artemia* nauplii.

F: O; in nature, the species is a molluscivore; in the aquarium, all normal cichlid foods are accepted: live foods, beef heart, fish flesh, vegetable flake food, tablet food.

S: *Cichlasoma nicaraguense* crossbreeds with *C. nigrofasciatum*. There are hybrids with adhesive eggs as well as those whose eggs are nonadhesive. The crosses are fertile to at least the 4th generation. *C. nicaraguense* has several geographic color morphs.

T: 23-27° C, 73-81° F, L: ♂ up to 25 cm, ♂ up to 9¾", A: 120 cm, 47", R: b, D: 2

Cichlasoma septemfasciatum ♀, see page 878.

Cichlasoma nicaraguense

Cichlasoma nicaraguense

Hoplarchus psittacus (HECKEL, 1840)

Parrot Cichlid

Syn.: *Acara psittacum, Astronotus psittacus, Cichlaurus psittacus, Heros psittacus, Hoplarchus pentacanthus, Pomotis fasciatus, Cichlasoma psittacus.*

Hab.: South America; Brazil, Rio Negro, Rio Orinoco, Rio Padauri.

F.I.: Probably around 1975-1977 (?).

Sex: The sexes are very difficult to distinguish; differences in coloration cannot be used as a reference for sexual determination; it is almost always the result of current mood, social position, etc.; finnage also does not allow a safe sexual determination. The genital papilla is pointed in the ♂ and blunt in the ♀.

Soc. B.: Territorial and have a "personal space" requirement. The animals are aggressive and quarrelsome in tanks that are too small and offer too few hiding places. Open spawner with a nuclear family; good care of the numerous young.

M: Decorate the tank with lots of convoluted roots and stones to provide as many hiding places as possible. The edge and background can be planted with hard well-rooted plants (*Sagittaria, Vallisneria,* large *Echinodorus* and cryptocorynes). Can be associated with other robust South American cichlids as well as large catfishes.

B: 26-28° C (79-82° F); soft, acid water (around 5° dGH and pH 5.5-6.0). An open spawner which likes to spawn under a "protective roof". Spawns are large and are comprised of several hundred eggs. The larvae are placed in previously excavated pits (?).

F: O; live foods of all types, freeze-dried, tablet and flake foods.

S: The intense red chest and belly coloration described by HECKEL has not yet been observed on living aquarium specimens. Large wild caught ♂♂ (Rio Negro), however, have it regularly. Breeding this cichlid has been successful only one time in Germany.

T: 24-28° C, L: 35 cm, A: from 150 cm, R: m, b, D: 2-3
75-82° F, 14", from 59",

Continuation of *Cichlasoma sajica* from page 878:

C. sajica is evolving from the not, or only little, specialized open spawner to the specialized cave spawner. The animals almost always (if available) spawn in caves. The eggs are quite small, whitish to brownish transparent (camouflage coloration), and number up to 300. The larvae hatch in 3 days at 26° C (79° F), and the fry are free-swimming in an additional 5-7 days. Primarily the ♀ is in charge of brood care; the ♂ takes care of territorial defense. Sometimes the roles are reversed. Raising the young has its problems since usually only one part of the spawn grows normally. The majority stagnate in growth. Feed with *Artemia* nauplii.

F: O; undemanding omnivore.

S: *C. sajica* should not be kept with *C. nigrofasciatum* or its relatives who may interbreed. The species name *sajica* is an acronym for **Sa**lvador **Ji**menez **Ca**nossa, director of the Library of Congress of Costa Rica.

T: 23-26° C, L: ♂ 22 cm, ♀ 17 cm, A: 80 cm, R: b, m, D: 2
73-79° F, ♂ 8 3/4", ♀ 6 2/3", 31",

Hoplarchus psittacus, juv.

Hoplarchus psittacus, wild caught ♂, Rio Negro, Brazil

Cichlasoma sajica BUSSING, 1974
T-Bar Cichlid

Syn.: None.

Hab.: Central America; Costa Rica. The species occurs in rivers.

F.I.: 1976 by Daniel Fromm to the USA, 1979 to Germany.

Sex: ♂♂ grow markedly larger and develop a steep forehead with age. The tips of the dorsal and anal fin are elongated, forming an arch towards the inside that frames the caudal fin. The genital papilla is pointed. The ♀♀ are considerably smaller, and their genital papilla is blunt.

Soc. B.: A territorial, pair forming cichlid. A relatively peaceful, sometimes shy fish which does not molest plants. The species digs at spawning time. Cave spawner; nuclear family or in transition to a patriarch-matriarch family.

M: Tank with a sandy bottom; hiding places of stones and roots; perhaps plant the edge and background with tough species. No high demands are placed on water composition by *C. sajica*. Water to medium-hard (15° dGH) and neutral (pH 7.0). Best to associate with other Central American *Cichlasoma* species (not with relatives of *Cichlasoma nigrofasciatum*; see under **S**).

B: Around 26° C (79° F); reproduction is not difficult, but there are sometimes problems. Water values as indicated above.

Continued on previous page.

Cichlasoma septemfasciatum REGAN, 1908
Cutter's Cichlid

Syn.: *Cichlasoma cutteri.*

Hab.: Central America; Costa Rica. The species occurs in different colored strains. It inhabits fast flowing, clear rivers and creeks as well as quiet side arms and remnant pools. Its habitat is characterized by rocky areas and large accumulations of leaf litter.

F.I.: 1963 to the USA by William Bussing, again in 1976 by Daniel Fromm. Wild fish were imported into Germany in 1981 by U. Werner, H. G. Breidohr and B. Weber.

Sex: Clear sexual dimorphism is present. The ♂♂ grow larger, are taller and have longer fins. Both sexes differ in their coloration. Photo of ♀ on page 874.

Soc. B.: Territorial, a relatively peaceful cichlid which does not disturb plants. Open spawner with tendency towards cave spawner; nuclear family with intense brood care. According to STAECK (1980): Das Aquarium **14**, 18-21, patriarch-matriarch family.

M: Needs a tank a with sandy bottom, hiding places of stones and roots, and maybe edge and background vegetation of tough species. Water not too hard (up to 15° dGH) with a pH of 7.0. House with other cichlids and/or characins and gobies.

B: 26-28° C (79-82° F); water values as indicated. *C. septemfasciatum* is an open spawner with a tendency towards shelter spawning; caves (if present) are usually used. Intensive brood care of the spawn by the ♀. According to WERNER, the larvae hatch at 27° C (81° F) in 72-80 hours and are free-swimming after 180-200 hours. The young are intensively cared for by both parents. Feed with *Artemia* nauplii and sieved small crustacea.

F: O; undemanding omnivore which eats live foods of all kinds, frozen food, shrimp, beef heart and also flake food.

S: *C. septemfasciatum* occurs in different race/color morphs. In addition, there is a oligomelanotic pink color. Oligomelanotic fish have normal pigmented eyes but have a strongly reduced or absent ability to produce melanin in other body areas. Some ichthyologists, for example, ASTORQUI, consider *C. septemfasciatum* a synonym of *Cichlasoma spilurum.*

T: 24-26° C, **L:** ♂ 12 cm, ♀ 8 cm, **A:** 100 cm, **R:** b, **D:** 2
75-79° F, ♂ 4¾", ♀ 3", 39",

Cichlasoma sajica ♂

Cichlasoma septemfasciatum ♂

Cichlasoma sieboldii (KNER & STEINDACHNER, 1864)

Siebold's Cichlid

Syn.: *Heros sieboldii, Cichlasoma punctatum* (not LINNAEUS), *C. terrabae, Herichthys underwoodi, Paraneetroplus sieboldii.*

Hab.: Central America; especially on the Pacific coast of Costa Rica down to Panama (also in central Panama), more exact—in the systems of Rio Esquinas, Rio Grande de Terraba and Rio Chiriqui del Tire.

F.I.: 1981, private collections by H. G. Breidohr, B. Weber and U. Werner.

Sex: ♀ is smaller and has more contrasts and a black hard-rayed section of the dorsal fin, or the dorsal fin has a black spot.

Soc. B.: An agile and active species from fast-flowing waters; holds its own against larger cichlids.

M: A typical biotope aquarium for this species would contain a uniform rubble area of smooth stones so that numerous hiding possibilities are created. A strong filter should imitate flowing water. Water soft to medium-hard (5-15° dGH), pH around 7.0, not too warm.

B: The species prefers to spawn in shelters. The eggs are large, roundish, not as numerous but still transparent. The spawning cave is expanded by both partners; the ♀ dominates in all spawning preparations and in direct care of the brood which is executed very intensively. The larvae hatch after 48 hours at 28° C (82° F), in 60 hours at 25° C (77° F). The young are free-swimming after 168 or 276 hours, respectively. Brood care coloration is white-gray with intense black contrasts. The white-green eyes sparkle out of the face mask.

F: H, O; the species belongs to the herbivore/algivore Theraps of the genus, but it will accept any usual foods.

S: The Swedish ichthyologist Sven O. Kullander considers *Cichlasoma sieboldii* a *Paraneetroplus* species. The fish seems to be especially sensitive to attack by *Hexamita.*

T: 23-25° C, **L:** 25 cm, **A:** 120 cm, **R:** b, m, **D:** 2-3
73-77° F, 9³/₄", 47",

Cichlasoma synspilum HUBBS, 1935

Redheaded Cichlid

Syn.: *Cichlasoma hicklingi, Cichlaurus hicklingi.*

Hab.: Central America; Atlantic coast of Guatemala from Rio Usumacinta basin to Belize (Belize River and Rio San Pedro de Martir).

F.I.: 1975 (?).

Sex: No sexual dichromatism; the sexes cannot be distinguished by color. Old ♂♂ develop a cephalic hump. Photo of ♀ on page 871.

Soc. B.: Territorial, the animals are sedate and quite peaceful towards heterospecifics despite their size. Among themselves the animals are aggressive and quarrelsome. The species digs during the spawning season and chews and eats plants. Open spawner; nuclear family.

M: Use sand and fine-grained gravel as substrate. The background decoration should have hiding places of stones and stone plates (slate) and some bogwood roots. Plants should be waived. Regular partial water exchanges are important. No special demands are placed on the water. Use values for Central American cichlids, medium-hard (to 15° dGH) and neutral to slightly alkaline (pH 7.0-7.5).

B: 26-28° C (79-82° F); reproduction can be problematic. Mature animals cannot be associated without further ado. The encounter often ends in death for the weaker individual. The best possibility to produce a harmonious breeding pair is to acquire a small group (6-8) of equal young. Sexual maturity is reached at a length of 10 cm (4"). Prior to spawning, the animals have a courtship and clean the spawning substrate. Eggs number over 1000. The larvae hatch after 3-4 days; after an additional 4-5 days, they are free-swimming. Both parents guide the young. Feed the young with crustacean nauplii, sieved small crustacea and small flake foods (TetraMin Baby Food).

F: O; hardy eaters which consume any live foods, shrimp, meat, beef heart, frozen food, vegetable fare, flake and tablet foods.

S: The intensive coloration of the animals depends on a varied diet. The animals remain pale under monotonous feeding regimes. Some English ichthyologists consider *C. synspilum* a synonym of *Cichlasoma melanurum.*

T: 24-28° C, **L:** 35 cm, **A:** 150 cm, **R:** b, m, **D:** 3
75-82° F, 14", 59",

Cichlasoma sieboldii

Cichlasoma synspilum ♂, ♀ on page 871

Cichlasoma tetracanthus (CUVIER & VALENCIENNES, 1831)

Cuban Cichlid

Syn.: *Acara tetracanthus, A. fusco-maculata, Chromis fusco-maculatus, Heros nigricans, H. tetracanthus, Parapetenia nigricans, P. tetracantha.*

Hab.: Central America; Cuba, Lagunas Castellanos, in swamps, lakes and ponds; also in brackish water.

F.I.: 1931 by the W. Eimeke Co., Hamburg, Germany.

Sex: The ♂♂ grow larger; colorwise, the sexes can barely be distinguished outside of courtship and brood care. While caring for their brood, the ♀♀ are noticeable due to their deep black ventral region and black vertical bands on a silver, white body; these patterns are less contrasting in the ♂♂.

Soc. B.: Territorial, but not particularly aggressive (neither towards conspecifics nor heterospecific fishes). The species does not harm plants outside of spawning. Open spawner with nuclear family; good pairing and parental care for the numerous young.

M: Provide some hiding places of rockwork and roots (especially important during spawning time for weaker, unpaired individuals and conspecifics without territories); needs flat smooth stones as spawning substrate. Keep with equal sized cichlids and catfishes.

B: 23-27° C (73-81° F); the chemical makeup of the water is secondary (soft and slightly acid to medium-hard and slightly alkaline). Open spawner; prefers to spawn on previously cleaned stones. A spawn is made up of up to 600 eggs. The larvae are placed in previously dug pits.

F: C, O; live foods of all kinds, freeze-dried food, tablets and flakes.

S: Five sub-species have been described for *C. tetracanthus* which differ morphologically, colorwise and by their natural habitat: *C. tetracanthus torralbasi* (EIGENMANN, 1902), *C. t. griseus* (EIGENMANN, 1902), *C. t. latus* (EIGENMANN, 1902), and *C. t. cinctus* (EIGENMANN, 1902). Additionally, the species *C. nigricans* described by EIGENMANN (1902) from Cuba is nowadays either considered an additional sub-species or a synonym of *C. tetracanthus* by many authors. The same also applies to *C. ramsdeni* described in 1938 by FOWLER from Jamaica and Cuba.

T: 20-27° C, 68-81° F, **L:** 25 cm, 9¾", **A:** from 80 cm, from 31", **R:** m, b, **D:** 1

Cichlasoma trimaculatum (GÜNTHER, 1866)

Three-Spot Cichlid

Syn.: *Heros trimaculatus, Cichlasoma cajali, C. centrale, C. gordonsmithi, C. mojarra.*

Hab.: Central America; from Laguna Coyuca (Mexico) down to Rio Lempa (El Salvador). The animals primarily occur in lakes, less often in rivers.

F.I.: 1972 (?).

Sex: The ♂♂ grow significantly larger than the ♀♀. Otherwise, the species is monomorphic. The ♀♀ are fuller and have a dark spot on the hard rays of the dorsal fin which can already be recognized in juveniles of 6 cm (2⅓"). Usually they are darker or have a more contrasting coloration. They react to the courtship of the ♂♂ with a striped design consisting of 5-7 vertical bands.

Soc. B.: Territorial, the animals are very aggressive towards conspecifics and have the capability to tyrannize other tankmates; one of the most aggressive cichlids! The animals dig a lot during the spawning time. Open spawners with a true pair bond; nuclear family.

M: Offer large or largest aquaria; use sand and/or gravel substrate. Provide hiding possibilities through large rocks and roots. Vegetation should be waived since the plants are bitten off. The animals dig a lot. Good filtration is necessary. No special demands are placed on water composition. Keep in a species tank or associate with cichlids of the same caliber.

B: 26-30° C (79-86° F); breeding is easiest with young pairs. ♀♀ are sexually mature from 8-10 cm (3"-4"), the ♂ from 12-14 cm (4¾-5 "). The animals dig a lot during spawning. After extensive courtship and vehement conflicts, spawning occurs on a previously cleared, hard substrate in the

Continued on page 871.

Cichlasoma tetracanthus

Cichlasoma trimaculatum

Cichlasoma umbriferum MEEK & HILDEBRAND, 1913
Umbriferum

Syn.: *Cichlaurus umbrifer.*

Hab.: Central America and northern South America; from Panama in the Pacific river systems of Rio Tuyra, Rio Atrato, down to the Magdalena basin of Colombia.

F.I.: 1975 to the USA, from there probably to Holland and Germany.

Sex: ♀♀ have an olive base coloration with a row of spots on the sides of the body to the caudal peduncle, as well as black and bluish tones on the body and fins. ♂♂ shine a sky blue to blue-green and have a wine red lower head and shiny blue dots on the sides of the body; unpaired fins are filamentous.

Soc. B.: Develops its aggressive behavior towards conspecifics when young, but it is mostly indifferent towards other cichlids before sexually maturity is attained. Sexually mature specimens are bellicose; sexual partners show clear encounter rituals in which the ♀ signals submission through a slanted to vertical upward head position.

M: Needs a coarse bottom, well based rockwork and roots. Since the animals are intense diggers, plants should be waived. Water medium-hard (up to 15° dGH), pH around 7.0.

B: ♀♀ are sexually mature at about 10 cm (4"), ♂♂ from about 15 cm (6"). Open spawner with a strong division of labor according to the dimorphism. Direct brood care is performed by the ♀. Eggs are numerous and the larvae hatch after about 72 hours at 28° C (82° F)(pH and dGH of about 7). The young are free-swimming after an additional 6 to 7 days and grow very rapidly.

F: *C. umbriferum* is a highly specialized representative of the *Parapetenia* section; therefore, it is an active predator. The greedy feeders will accept just about any substitute feed (pellets, meat, shrimp, worms) in the aquarium.

S: *C. umbriferum* is likely to be one of the largest cichlids of all. The actual beauty of this active, elegant fish only becomes apparent after 20-30 cm (8"-11 3/4") length.

T: 23-27° C, L: to 80 cm?, A: from 150 cm, R: b, m, D: 3-4 (C)
73-81° F, to 31"?, from 59",

Cichlasoma urophthalmus (GÜNTHER, 1862)
Eight-Banded Cichlid

Syn.: *Heros urophthalmus, Astronotus troscheli, A. urophthalmus, Heros troscheli, Parapetenia urophthalma.*

Hab.: Central America; Mexico, Belize, Honduras, Guatemala, Nicaragua (according to A. Ufermann).

F.I.: 1913 by Siggelkow and Kropac, Hamburg, Germany.

Sex: ♀ has a black spot on the dorsal fin; ♂ is more colorful and larger; genital papilla in the ♂ is pointed, blunt in the ♀.

Soc. B.: Territorial, but not particularly aggressive (neither towards conspecifics nor heterospecifics). Does not damage plants. Open spawner with nuclear family; good care of the numerous brood.

M: Some hiding places provided by rockwork, roots and plants; add flat, smooth stones as spawning substrate. No major demands are placed on the water composition. It is possible to associate it with smaller sedate fishes.

B: 23-27° C (73-81° F); chemical make-up of the water is secondary (soft and slightly acid to medium-hard and slightly alkaline). An open spawner, spawns on stones or roots which have been previously cleaned. A spawn is comprised of up to 600 eggs. The larvae are deposited in previously dug pits.

F: C, O; live foods of all types, freeze-dried, tablet and flake foods.

S: 11 sub-species, which differ morphologically, in color and by their origin (one sub-species has adapted to a life void of light in subterranean cave waters), have been described of *Cichlasoma urophthalmus*: *C. u. urophthalmus, C. u aguadae* HUBBS, 1936, *C. u. alborum* HUBBS, 1936, *C. u. amarum* HUBBS, 1936, *C. u. cienagae* HUBBS, 1936, *C. u. conchitae* HUBBS, 1936, *C. u. ericymbae* HUBBS, 1938, *C. u. mayorum* HUBBS, 1936, *C. u. trispilum* HUBBS, 1935, *C. u. troscheli* (STEINDACHNER, 1867) and *C. u. zebra* HUBBS, 1936.

T: 20-27° C, L: 20 cm, A: 80 cm, R: m, b, D: 1-2
68-81° F, 8", 31",

Cichlasoma umbriferum

Cichlasoma urophthalmus

Crenicichla johanna HECKEL, 1840

Red-Finned Pike Cichlid, Gray Pike Cichlid

Syn.: *Crenicichla johanna* var. *carsevennensis, C. obtusirostris, Cychla brasilensis* var. *johanna, C. fasciata.*

Hab.: South America; Brazil, Guyana, Paraguay, Peru and Venezuela.

F.I.: ?

Sex: Fringe of the ♀'s dorsal fin is dark, light proximally; they may have a reddish or cream colored ventral region when ripe.

Soc. B.: Territorial and demands a roomy shelter (root or stone cover of a larger pit). It usually indifferent towards fishes which do not qualify as food and don't initiate quarrels. Cave spawner with nuclear family (?).

M: Maintain in a large aquarium with caves, roots and tough vegetation. It is recommended to house the species with differently shaped, robust cichlids. Bright illumination is not appreciated by *Crenicichla.* Water up to 20° dGH and pH around 7.0.

B: The species has probably not been bred, but it is surely a cave spawner with polar eggs. Because of the slight sexual dimorphism, it can be expected that both partners care equally for the brood.

F: Since the species is a predator in nature, at least some hardy live foods (fish, worms) should be given. Frozen foods (beef heart, shrimp, krill) and compressed feeds (tablet food, pellets) are also accepted.

S: *Crenicichla johanna* is possibly a synonym of *Crenicichla strigata.*

T: 23-26° C, **L:** more than 35 cm, **A:** from 150 cm, **R:** b, m, **D:** 3-4 (C)
73-79° F, more than 14", from 59",

Crenicichla lepidota HECKEL, 1840

Two-Spot Pike Cichlid, Comb Pike Cichlid

Syn.: None; but the species has often been confused with *Crenicichla saxatilis.*

Hab.: South America; Brazil and Bolivia.

F.I.: Not known; usually reaches Europe as by-catch.

Sex: ♂ is larger, more olive-gray and has body spots that are surrounded by areas of shiny scales; its fins are larger, elongated and drawn-out, and the dorsal lacks the white design. ♀ is smaller, rounder and has a more pronounced metallic sheen; the belly is faintly reddish or orange, and the dorsal fin has a black-white pattern.

Soc. B.: Territorial, aggressive within the species but indifferent towards differently shaped cichlids.

M: Like other *Crenicichla* this species does not place special demands on the water, but it should not be too hard (up to 12° dGH, pH about 7.0). Maintain the animals in tanks with plenty of hiding places and roomy shelters. The tank should not be overly bright.

B: ♀♀ become sexually mature at about 14 cm (5 "); ♂♂ mature at about 18 cm (7"). The species usually spawns on the ceiling of a roomy cave. The eggs are whitish and hang from their pole. The young hatch on the 4th or 5th day, depending on temperature (24-28° C; 75-82° F). The young are free-swimming after day 11 to 13. Corresponding to the distinct sexual dimorphism, the ♀ performs direct brood care more or less alone, while the ♂ secures the territory and only becomes directly involved when the young are free-swimming.

F: *Crenicichla lepidota* is a pronounced predator which greatly appreciates bite-size feeder fish. Worms, beef heart, fairy shrimp and krill are also accepted. Adaptation to tablet food is possible.

S: There seem to be several different color morphs, but also within one morph there are differences in coloration.

T: 23-28° C, **L:** ♂ up to 45 cm, ♀ smaller, **A:** 120 cm, **R:** b, m, **D:** 3-4 (C)
73-82° F, ♂ up to 18", ♀ smaller, 47",

Continuation of *Cyathopharynx furcifer* (page 888):

S: The animals are extremely sensitive to transport. Several distinctly different color morphs exist, but only the ♂♂ vary.

T: 24-26° C, **L:** 20 cm, **A:** 120 cm, **R:** b, m, **D:** 3
75-79° F, 8", 47",

Crenicichla johanna ♀

Crenicichla lepitoda

Crenicichla semifasciata on page 848

Crenicichla wallacii REGAN, 1905

Slender Pike Cichlid

Syn.: None.

Hab.: South America; Guyana, Brazil.

F.I.: Probably for the first time in 1980.

Sex: ♀ is fuller during spawning time.

Soc. B.: A territorial cichlid which is harmless to other medium sized cichlids. They do not disturb plants. Cave spawner; probably a paternal-matriarch family.

M: Needs a gravel or sandy bottom and hiding places built of stones, stone plates and roots. The animals love dense edge and background vegetation. Water up to 20° dGH and a pH that is about neutral (pH 7.0). House with other medium sized cichlids or keep in a species tank.

B: The first report about a successful spawn was given by J. FREYHOF (1986) in DCG-Information 17(1): 11-15. FREYHOF considers extreme water values as the key to success: deionized water with a conductivity of 10-15 µS and peat filtration down to a pH of 4.5. Spawning occurred in a coconut shell. After 11 days, the ♀ reappeared for the first time with about 150 fry. These were 7 mm (") long and milky white. The parents only guard the young, they do not guide them. The young have a big appetite and are fast growing. They are first fed *Artemia*, later *Cyclops*.

F: C; live foods of all kinds: mosquito larvae, earthworms, small fish; fish meat and beef heart.

S: *Crenicichla wallacii* differs from the closely related *Crenicichla nana* by longer dorsal rays; differs from *C. notophthalmus* by having more teeth, a larger eye, longer dorsal rays and the absence of an ocellus on the dorsal fin between the 16th and the 20th hard ray.

T: 24-27° C, L: 15 cm, A: 90 cm, R: b, m, D: 3-4 (C)
75-81° F, 6", 35",

Cyathopharynx furcifer (BOULENGER, 1898)

Furcifer

Syn.: *Paratilapia furcifer, Cyathopharynx grandoculis, Ectodous foae, Ophthalmotilapia foae, Tilapia grandoculis.*

Hab.: Africa; Lake Tanganyika (endemic). The species is widely distributed in the lake. It inhabits the sandy shore area or the transition zone from sandy to rocky littoral zone.

F.I.: Probably in 1958 together with *Ophthalmochromis ventralis*.

Sex: Well developed sexual dimorphism; ♂ has a shining blue body and long drawn out pelvic fins; ♀ is a plain gray-green color without elongated pelvic fins.

Soc. B.: Territorial, spawning pits are energetically defended against conspecifics; otherwise, the animals are not particularly aggressive. The species digs in the sand for food. Specialized ovophile mouthbrooder; matriarch family.

M: Maintain *C. furcifer* in a tank that is as roomy as possible. Provide a bottom of thick sand; put rockwork riddled with caves and niches in the background; some flat stones; vegetation can be waived. Good filtration. Water medium-hard to hard (12-20° dGH) and moderately alkaline (pH 7.5-9.0).

B: 26-28° C (79-82° F); successful reproduction was first reported by KOZIOL (1982) in Buntbarsche Bulletin no. 90: 2-7. The ♂ builds a crater shaped pit (diameter 25-30 cm; 9¾-11¾") in the sand. If a sufficiently large sandy area is not available, it transports sand to a horizontal stone until a bowl-like nest is made. After extensive courtship, the ♀ deposits one or two eggs into the pit and then takes them into her mouth. Now the ♀ snaps at the spade-shaped ends of the ♂'s ventral fins. The sperm enters her mouth and fertilizes the eggs in this manner. This procedure is repeated until the ♀ has deposited the up to 25 eggs. Hatching period is about 3 weeks at 26° C (79° F); the young are then released for the first time from the mother's mouth. Feed the young with *Artemia* nauplii.

F: In nature, microorganisms and zooplankton are eaten. Once the animals are accustomed to the aquarium, all types of foods, from living to flake food, are accepted.

Continued on page 886.

Crenicichla wallacii

Cyathopharynx furcifer

Cynotilapia afra (GÜNTHER, 1893)
Dogtooth Cichlid

Syn.: *Chromis afra*.

Hab.: Africa; Lake Malawi (endemic). Preferred habitat is the rocky coast. However, the animals are not found directly above the substrate, but in the open water where they feed on planktonic crustacea.

F.I.: 1973.

Sex: Distinct sexual dichromatism. ♂♂ are a light to turquoise blue with 7 lateral, black crossbands; anal fin has 3 or 4 egg spots. ♀ is a plain dove blue to slate gray.

Soc. B.: Territorial, the animals are quite quarrelsome and bellicose among themselves. Aggressions are usually limited to the spawning time. The presence of heterospecific fishes dampens the intraspecific aggressions. The species does not bother tough plants. Mouthbrooder; matriarch family.

M: Needs rockwork with many caves and cracks suitable for hiding and robust vegetation. Best to keep one ♂ with several ♀♀. Associate with *Pseudotropheus* and/or *Melanochromis* species.

B: 25-27° C (77-81° F), water up to 15° dGH and slightly alkaline (pH 8-8.5). Use 1 ♂ with 2-3 ♀♀. *C. afra* is an agamic mouthbrooder, does not form pair bonds. Matriarch family, the ♀ cares for and raises the young alone. The young are released from the mouth after about 20 days. With good feeding, the animals reach sexual maturity after 6-8 months.

F: Live foods of all kinds, especially small crustacea (*Cyclops, Daphnia, Artemia*). Flake food is also accepted.

S: *Cynotilapia afra* can easily be confused with *Pseudotropheus zebra*. Both species can be differentiated by the color of the dorsal fin and their dentition. *Cynotilapia afra*: the dark crossbands enter the dorsal fin, and the teeth of the outer row are monocuspid. *Pseudotropheus zebra*: the dorsal is single-colored and has no black design. The outer teeth are bicuspids. There is a second species: *Cynotilapia axelrodi* BURGESS, 1976.

T: 23-27° C, 73-81° F, L: 12 cm, 4 3/4", A: from 100 cm, from 39", R: m, b, D: 2

Cyprichromis microlepidotus (POLL, 1956)
Small-Scaled Slender Cichlid

Syn.: *Limnochromis microlepidotus*.

Hab.: Africa; Lake Tanganyika (endemic). The species obviously prefers a very special type of rocky zone. It has been found where there are large boulders with numerous vertical crevices.

F.I.: 1975.

Sex: Marked sexual dichromatism; during the spawning season the ♂ has a black throat and is darker colored.

Soc. B.: Peaceful towards heterospecific fishes; within the species, there is strong rivalry demeanor, without injuries incurring. The animals school. During the spawning period the ♂♂ are very aggressive. The animals do not bother plants or dig. Free spawning ovophile mouthbrooders; matriarch family.

M: Large aquaria are needed to successfully care for this species. These lively swimmers have to be offered sufficient swimming space. The animals prefer the upper 1/3 of the water column; for this reason, they can be associated with many other cichlids. Always keep in schools of at least 6 animals. Cover the tank well since the animals will jump out of the water during courtship. Water hardness 10-18° dGH, pH 7.5-8.5.

B: 24-26° C (75-79° F); the species has already been bred in an aquarium. The spawning behavior is very similar to that of *Cyprichromis leptosoma* (see Vol. 1). The ♂ develops a deep black throat a few hours to a few days prior to spawning; it is very colorful and becomes very aggressive. Courtship and spawning activity occur close below the water surface. The mature ♀ stands with the head slanted downward and is approached by the ♂ from above. The ♀ now lays 1 egg. This falls along the almost vertically standing ♀ and is taken into her mouth. This process is lightning fast. Fertilization of the eggs

Continued on page 892.

Cynotilapia afra

Cyprichromis microlepidotus

Continuation of *Cyprichromis microlepidotus*:

occurs when the ♀ snaps at the ♂'s **ventral** fins. There are about 25 eggs, and they are brooded in the mouth of the ♀ for 26 to 29 days at 27° C (81° F). They are then released from her mouth. Continued brood care does not occur. The young form a school in open water and eat *Artemia* nauplii (compare EYSEL 1982: DCG-Informationen **13**(8): 153-158).

F: C; prefers suspended foods (plankton): water fleas, *Cyclops*, glassworms; suspended flake food.

S: The ♂♂ of *Cyprichromis microlepidotus* are polychromatic. One part has a black/blue tail fin, while it is dirty yellow in the other part. *Cyprichromis microlepidotus* differs from the other 2 *Cyprichromis* species by its uncommonly large number of notoriously small scales (species name!).

T: 23-25° C, **L**: 14 cm, **A**: 120 cm, **R**: t, **D**: 3
73-77° F, 5", 47",

Paracyprichromis nigripinnis (BOULENGER, 1901)
Black-Fin Cichlid

Syn.: *Paratilapia nigripinnis, Limnochromis nigripinnis, Cyprichromis nigripinnis.*

Hab.: Africa; Lake Tanganyika (endemic). The animals occur singly within schools of *Cyprichromis microlepidotus*.

F.I.: 1975.

Sex: Marked sexual dichromatism. The ♂ has several horizontal, light blue pin-stripes on the sides. The dorsal fin and the top and bottom of the caudal fin are fringed in light blue; anal fin is black. The ♀ is without pin-stripes; the edge of the dorsal fin is dark blue, the tail fin is not edged in blue; first pelvic fin ray is a strong yellowish color, anal fin yellow.

Soc. B.: *P. nigripinnis* is peaceful towards other species. Among themselves there is constant rivalry without serious consequences. The species lives almost exclusively as a schooling fish in the open (pelagic). Only for actual spawning is the bottom sought. Ovophile mouthbrooder; matriarch family.

M: As indicated for *Cyprichromis microlepidotus*. Additionally some flat stones should be placed in the tank as spawning substrates.

B: A rare event. SCHRAML (1981): DCG-Informationen **12** (7): Cichliden von A-Z, indicates that *P. nigripinnis* spawns on a hard substrate (stones). From there the eggs are taken into the mouth by the ♀.

F: C; suspended foods is preferred (water fleas, *Cyclops*, glassworms). The fish can also be trained to take flake food.

S: *P. nigripinnis* is a mouth-brooder while the other two *Paracyprichromis* species are open spawners.

T: 23-25° C, **L**: 10 cm, **A**: to 100 cm, **R**: t, (m), **D**: 3
73-77° F, 4", to 39",

Protomelas annectens REGAN, 1922
Chunky Hap

Syn.: *Haplochromis annectens, Cyrtocara annectens.*

Hab.: Africa; Lake Malawi (endemic). The animals inhabit medium depths close to the shore, preferably 1 cm (1/3") above the bottom. The species is relatively rare.

F.I.: 1978 (?).

Sex: Clear sexual dimorphism; the ♂♂ are more splendidly colored (blue coloration), and dorsal, anal and pelvic fins are strongly elongated in full-grown ♂♂. In addition, ♂♂ grow larger.

Soc. B.: Very peaceful cichlid that shows very little aggression towards other fishes or plants. The animals are only territorial at spawning time. *P. annectens* does not root at the bottom, but sand is taken into its mouth and worked through. Agamic, ovophile mouthbrooder; matriarch family.

M: As indicated for *Protomelas electra*. House with *Cyrtocara moorii, Copadichromis boadzulu, C. borleyi, Protomelas electra* or with *Aulonocara* and *Trematocranus* species.

Paracyprichromis nigripinnis ♂

Protomelas annectens ♂

B: 26-28° C (79-82° F); no reports of a successful spawn are available. It is probably similar to *Cyrtocara moorii*. (AQUARIUM ATLAS, Vol. 1, page 718)

T: 24-26° C, L: 20 cm, A: 100 cm, R: b, D: 2
75-79° F, 8", 39",

F: L, O; live food, mosquito larvae are especially relished. The animals also eat frozen food, scraped meat, flake and tablet foods.

Copadichromis boadzulu (without photo) (ILES, 1960)

Syn.: *"Haplochromis hinderi"* (trade name!), *H. boadzulu, Cyrtocara boadzulu.*

Hab.: Africa; southern Lake Malawi (endemic). The species has been found at White Rock, Boadzulu Island, and Namalenji Island. The animals are inhabitants of the rocky littoral zone and prefer a water depth of 10-20 m (11-22 yd).

F.I.: 1977.

Sex: Well developed sexual dimorphism. The ♂♂ are beautifully colored and have elongated anal and dorsal fins; the ♀♀ are silvery-gray, and anal and dorsal fins are not as pointed.

Soc. B.: A relatively peaceful cichlid which is only territorial at spawning time. The animals are avid swimmers. They do not dig or molest plants. Agamic, ovophile mouthbrooder; matriarch family.

M: As with *Copadichromis borleyi.*

B: As indicated for *C. borleyi.*

F: O; live foods of all types, frozen food, freeze-dried and flake foods.

S: *C. boadzulu* is a zooplankton feeder of the utaka group.

T: 24-26° C, **L**: 15 cm, **A**: 100 cm, **R**: m, b, **D**: 2-3
75-79° F, 6", 39",

Copadichromis borleyi (ILES, 1960)

Syn.: *"Haplochromis granderus"* (trade name!), *H. borleyi, Cyrtocara borleyi.*

Hab.: Africa; Lake Malawi (endemic). The animals occur in the rocky littoral zone.

F.I.: About 1975 (?).

Sex: Marked sexual dichromatism. ♂ are much more colorful and have extremely elongated pelvic fins that are white to bluish on the anterior edge. In old ♂♂, the pelvic fins can reach the back edge of the anal fin, egg spots; ♀ is plain gray and has 3 black spots on the sides.

Soc. B.: Relatively peaceful cichlids which are only territorial at spawning time. The animals claim a territory in a rocky area and place the spawning site in the center. As a rule it is the top of a horizontal stone or rock.

M: Provide rockwork with many hiding places. Plants can also be used since *C. borleyi* does not harm them. One should insure that enough free swimming space remains available. Mouthbrooder; matriarch family.

B: 26-28° C (79-82° F); water about 15° dGH and slightly alkaline (pH 8-8.5). Reproduction in a community tank is possible. Agamic mouthbrooder; 1 ♂ with several ♀♀. A flat horizontal stone plate is the preferred spawning substrate. Courtship parallels other *Copadichromis* species; fertilization of the eggs is by the egg spot method. The development of the approx. 60 eggs and larvae takes about 20 days at 26° C (79° F). The young are relatively large when they leave the mouth of the mother. Rearing of the young is done in a matriarch family. Feed with sieved small crustacea or crumbled flake food.

F: Live foods of all kinds (*Daphnia, Artemia, Cyclops, Tubifex, Drosophila* larvae, etc.). Flake food and frozen food are also eaten.

S: *C. borleyi* belongs to the utaka cichlids. These temporarily inhabit the near shore areas of the open water zone and are specialized zooplankton feeders with a protrusile mouth. The utaka group is comprised of about 16 species.

T: 24-26° C, **L**: 15 cm, **A**: from 100 cm, **R**: m, b, **D**: 2-3
75-79° F, 6", from 39",

Protomelas taeniolatus var. ♂

Copadichromis borleyi ♂

Copadichromis borleyi ♀

Placidochromis electra (BURGESS, 1979)
Deepwater Hap

Syn.: *"Haplochromis jahni"* (trade name!), *H. electra, Cyrtocara electra.*

Hab.: Africa; Lake Malawi (endemic). The species lives above sandy bottoms around the island of Likoma.

F.I.: 1978.

Sex: Marked sexual dimorphism; ♂♂ are much more colorful (blue coloration) and grow larger.

Soc. B.: *Placidochromis electra* is an extremely sedate and peaceful charge which can be associated without difficulty with conspecifics and heterospecific cichlids. The fish do not bother plants. They are only territorial at spawning time. Agamic, ovophile mouthbrooder; matriarch family.

M: Decorate the aquarium with a background of rockwork with many hiding places and cover, some plant groups as side vegetation, fine sand as substrate which the fish can "work" in the search of food, and free swimming space. Medium-hard to hard (12-20° dGH), moderately alkaline (pH 7.5-9.0) water. Associate with other *Placidochromis* species which have similar demands.

B: As with other *Protomelas* species of Lake Malawi. About 50 relatively small (diameter 2.5-3 mm; 1/16"-1/8") eggs are laid. At 28° C (82° F), the ♀ broods the eggs for about 18 days in her mouth.

F: O; live foods of all kinds, freeze-dried, frozen, tablet, and flake foods.

S: *Placidochromis electra* is similar in behavior and appearance to *Cyrtocara moorii* (AQUARIUM ATLAS, Vol. 1, page 718).

T: 24-26° C, L: ♂ to 16 cm, ♀ smaller, A: 100 cm, R: b, m, D: 2
75-79° F, ♂ to 6 1/3", ♀ smaller, 39",

Placidochromis milomo juv. (page 900)

Placidochromis electra ♂

Placidochromis electra ♀

Protomelas fenestratus (TREWAVAS, 1935)
Fenestratus

Syn.: *Haplochromis fenestratus, Cyrtocara fenestratus.*

Hab.: Africa; Lake Malawi (endemic). The only known habitat lies in the southwestern part of the lake at the Maleri Island group. The animals inhabit the near rocky shore zone and prefer depths between 3 and 6 m (3-7 yd).

F.I.: Probably after 1978.

Sex: Distinct sexual dichromatism. The ♂ is splendidly colored; ♀ is an inconspicuous gravel-gray to silver with a pattern of 9-12 crossbands and 2 dark longitudinal stripes.

Soc. B.: They are territorial, very peaceful, but lively, cichlids. The species does not bother plants. Mouthbrooder; matriarch family.

M: Rock structures of large stones and rocks with many caves and crevices, and a sandy bottom. Plant with low growing species which do not restrict swimming space. Combine with peaceful species such as small *Protomelas* or *Aulonocara* and *Trematocranus.*

B: 24-26° C (75-79° F); water as for other Lake Malawi cichlids. Breeding is possible in a community tank. Maintain 1 ♂ and 2-3 ♀♀. Courtship and spawning behavior is similar to other *Protomelas* species of Lake Malawi. The animals are agamic mouthbrooders; the ♀ cares for the young. After about 20 days at 26° C (79° F), the young are released for the first time from the mother's mouth. Feed the young with *Artemia* nauplii and crumbled flake food. The young grow rapidly.

F: Live foods of any kind that are not too large (crustacea, mosquito larvae, *Tubifex*); frozen and flake foods are also taken.

S: There are at least five cichlids whose ♀♀ show the colors listed under **Sex**, but whose males are totally different. The colors of *Protomelas taeniolatus* TREWAVAS, 1935 (AQUARIUM ATLAS, Vol. 3, page 782) are very similar to *P. fenestratus* in both sexes.

T: 22-26° C, **L:** 14 cm, **A:** from 100 cm, **R:** b, m, **D:** 2
72-79° F, 5 ", from 39",

Nimbochromis fuscotaeniatus (REGAN, 1922)
Fuscotaeniatus

Syn.: *Haplochromis fuscotaeniatus, Cyrtocara fuscotaeniatus.*

Hab.: Africa; southern Lake Malawi (endemic). The species inhabits the rocky shore area, but it also occurs above sandy substrates.

F.I.: Unknown.

Sex: Marked sexual dichromatism. The ♂♂ are considerably more colorful, and they have more elongated ventral, anal, and dorsal fins.

Soc. B.: Only territorial at spawning time. The animals are aggressive and predatory. They rarely bother plants. Agamic, ovophile mouthbrooder; matriarch family.

M: As indicated for *Protomelas fenestratus.* Combine with similar sized fishes, particularly with other *Nimbochromis* species.

B: No reports are yet available on a successful aquarium spawn. Presumably, it is similar to other *Nimbochromis* species (*N. linni, N. polystigma*). AQUARIUM ATLAS, Vol. 1, page 716/718.

F: C; hearty live foods of all kinds (insects, crustacea, earthworms, fish).

S: *Nimbochromis fuscotaeniatus* is similar to *N. polystigma,* but not as deep-bodied.

T: 24-26° C, **L:** 25 cm, **A:** 120 cm, **R:** b, m, **D:** 3 (C)
75-79° F, 9 3/4", 47",

Protomelas fenestratus ♂ top, ♀ bottom

Nimbochromis fuscotaeniatus

Placidochromis johnstonii (GÜNTHER, 1893)
Johnston's Hap

Syn.: *Chromis johnstonii, Tilapia johnstonii, Haplochromis sexfasciatus, H. johnstonii, Cyrtocara johnstonii.*

Hab.: Africa; Lake Malawi (endemic). The species inhabits extensive *Vallisneria* lawns of sandy littoral zones.

F.I.: 1958 (?).

Sex: Pronounced sexual dichromatism. Mature ♂♂ are extraordinarily colorful and have an anal fin with egg spots; ♀♀ are a plain yellow-gray to green-beige color.

Soc. B.: Territorial; it is peaceful and will not bother young fishes. Sometimes feeds on tender plant shoots. Mouthbrooder; matriarch family.

M: Needs rockwork with caves and crevices as hiding places; furthermore, the rocks should subdivide the aquarium; bottom of coarse sand or fine gravel. Only tough vegetation, e.g., dense stands of giant *Vallisneria*. Put with other *Placidochromis* species or with *Pseudotropheus* and *Labeotropheus* species.

B: 26-28° C (79-82° F); water values as with other *Placidochromis* species from the lake. Breeding is possible in a community aquarium, but a separate breeding tank should be used because of the poor chances of survival for the young. The ♂♂ make a spawning pit in the center of their territory. Courtship and spawning behavior corresponds to that of other specialized east African mouthbrooders. Eggs are relatively numerous (up to 120). At 26° C (79° F) the young are released from the mother's mouth after 18 days for the first time. They are still protected and cared for by the ♀ after their release. At night they return to the safety of the mother's mouth. Feed the young with *Artemia* nauplii and micro food.

F: O; live food of all kinds: water fleas, *Cyclops, Artemia,* insect larvae; crustacean and fish meat; flake and tablet foods.

S: To maintain the brooding instinct, the ♀ seems to require the presence of other fishes to induce a certain level of stress.

T: 24-26° C, 75-79° F, **L:** 17 cm, mostly smaller, 6²/₃", mostly smaller **A:** from 100 cm, from 39", **R:** b, m, **D:** 2-3

Placidochromis milomo (OLIVER, 1989)
Big-Lip Hap, Super VC 10

Syn.: *Melanochromis labrosus, Haplochromis labrosus, Cyrtocara labrosus, C. milomo.*

Hab.: Africa; Lake Malawi (endemic). The only known habitat is the rocky shores of the Mbenji Islands, located in the southwestern part of the lake.

F.I.: 1973 (?).

Sex: Clearly defined sexual dichromatism in adults. In ♂♂, the upper half of the head is a metallic sky blue, and the lower half is turquoise. ♀♀ lack this coloration.

Soc. B.: A quite robust fish which can maintain its ground in front of aggressive tankmates. Ovophile mouthbrooder; matriarch family.

M: Provide a tank furnished with rocks that create caves and niches, delineating various territories. Vegetation is not essential; tough and resistant plants are usually not harmed. Plants which grow on the stone structures (*Anubias* species, Java fern, *Microsorium pteropus*) are best because the free swimming space is not further diminished. The water should be medium-hard to hard (10-20° dGH) and have a pH between 8.0-8.5. Associate with other *Placidochromis* species and with strong mbuna cichlids.

B: 26-28° C (79-82° F); breeding is best accomplished in a community tank. The breeding set-up consists of 1 ♂ with 2-3 ♀♀. Spawning and egg fertilization is similar to other *Cyrtocara* of Lake Malawi. The animals are specialized mouthbrooders which raise their brood in a matriarch family. Development of eggs and larvae to the point of first release takes roughly 20 days at 26° C (79° F). The relatively large young can be fed sieved large crustacea or crumbled flake food. The picture of juvenile animals in Vol. 1, page 715 shows a different species and genus: *Melanochromis labrosus.*

Continued on page 902.

Placidochromis johnstonii

Placidochromis milomo ♂

Continuation of *Placidochromis milomo*:

F: O; live foods of all kinds (small fish, *Tubifex*, small earthworms, mosquito larvae), flake and tablet foods.

S: *Placidochromis milomo* belongs to the "lip cichlids" which have very enlarged lips, often with a hook-shaped appendage. The thickened lips have a high density of sensory cells and probably serve as a tactile organ to sense food.

T: 23-26° C, **L**: 15 cm, **A**: 120 cm, **R**: b, m, **D**: 2
73-79° F, 6", 47",

Otopharynx ovatus (TREWAVAS, 1935)

Syn.: *Haplochromis ovatus, Cyrtocara ovatus.*

Hab.: Africa; southern Lake Malawi (endemic). The animals inhabit the medium depths of waters near shore.

F.I.: 1981 (?).

Sex: ♂♂ are significantly more colorful with a beautiful blue coloration.

Soc. B.: Nothing is yet known about its social behavior. The species is probably a ovophile mouthbrooder with matriarch family.

M: As indicated for *Protomelas electra* or *P. fenestratus*. Water neutral to moderately alkaline (pH 7.0-8.5) and medium-hard to hard (12-20° dGH). Do not keep the animals in water that is overly soft and acid.

B: Not yet reproduced in an aquarium.

F: C; live food, flake food (large flakes).

S: The species is closely related to *Nimbochromis venustus*.

T: 24-26° C, **L**: 20 cm, **A**: 100 cm, **R**: b, m, **D**: 2-3
75-79° F, 8", 39",

Ctenopharynx pictus (TREWAVAS, 1935)

Syn.: *Haplochromis pictus, Cyrtocara pictus.*

Hab.: Africa; Lake Malawi (endemic). The species occurs above rocky bottoms near sediment areas. The animals inhabit depths of 2-30 m (2-33 yd).

F.I.: Probably only after 1980.

Sex: Marked sexual dichromatism; ♂ more colorful.

Soc. B.: According to present observations, the animals are not territorial. Agamic, ovophile mouthbrooder; matriarch family.

M: Use values given for *Otopharynx ovatus*.

B: No reports are yet available dealing with a successful reproduction.

F: C, O; live foods of all kinds (*Daphnia*, *Cyclops*, *Artemia*), also crustacean and fish meat as well as tablet and flake food.

T: 24-26° C, **L**: 13 cm, **A**: 100 cm, **R**: b, m, **D**: 2-3
75-79° F, 5", 39",

Otopharynx ovatus ♂

Ctenopharynx pictus

Trematocranus placodon (REGAN, 1922)

Snail-Crusher Hap

Syn.: *Haplochromis placodon, Cyrtocara placodon.*

Hab.: Africa; Lake Malawi (endemic). The species is numerous above sandy bottoms with *Vallisneria* stands throughout the lake.

F.I.: 1981 (?).

Sex: Color sexual dimorphism; the ♂♂ grow somewhat larger and are more colorful.

Soc. B.: Territorial, the animals are more or less aggressive, especially toward conspecifics. The ♂♂ build large, often deep pits into the sandy bottom which are kept meticulously clean. The species does not bother plants. Agamic, ovophile mouthbrooder; matriarch family.

M: Use tanks with large surface area, dense lateral and background vegetation with species of *Vallisneria*, some hiding places made of stones and roots, and a thick layer of sand on the bottom. As for all Lake Malawi cichlids, hard, slightly alkaline water is preferred (hardness up to 25° dGH, pH 7.0-8.5). Associate with similar sized cichlids from the Lake.

B: 26-28° C (79-82° F); use the water values listed above; otherwise it is similar to other species from Lake Malawi. The ♀♀ brood up to 100 young in a throat sac.

F: O; predominately live foods (mosquito larvae, snails, earthworms, etc.). However, the animals can also be fed meat, frozen food and flake food without problems.

S: *Trematocranus placodon* is a pronounced feeding specialist in its natural habitat. The animals are molluscivores which can effortlessly grind up snails and small mussels between their strong jaws and millstone-like pharyngeal teeth.

T: 24-26° C, L: 25 cm, A: 120 cm, R: b, D: 2
75-79° F, 9³/₄", 47",

Champsochromis spilorhynchus (REGAN, 1922)

Syn.: *Haplochromis longipes, H. spilorhynchus, Cyrtocara spilorhynchus.*

Hab.: Africa; Lake Malawi (endemic).

F.I.: About 1972.

Sex: There is distinct sexual dichromatism when the fish is breeding. In brooding ♀♀, the entire lower half of the body, the anal fin and large parts of the tail fin are deep black.

Soc. B.: The animals are only territorial during spawning. These are pronounced piscivores which live off of small fishes. Plants are not eaten. Agamic, ovophile mouthbrooder; matriarch family.

M: Similar to *Protomelas fenestratus*. Furnish the tank as indicated under *C. fenestratus*. Because of the predatory nature of *C. spilorhynchus*, only associate it with similar sized, robust cichlids.

B: Nothing has been reported in the aquarium literature. In the wild it was observed that during danger, the ♀ readmits her young into the mouth. At a length of barely 2 cm (³/4"), the young numbered over 100 (see STAECK, 1976: Das Aquarium **10**, 439).

F: C; live foods of all kinds; when the fish reach a certain size, they almost exclusively eat fish.

S: The fish is well adapted to a predatory lifestyle with its elongated, almost torpedo-like, body. The mouth is broadly cut and dotted with teeth which can even be seen with the naked eye.

T: 24-26° C, L: 30 cm, A: 120 cm, R: b, D: 4 (C)
75-79° F, 11³/₄", 47",

Trematocranus placodon

Champsochromis caeruleus

Champsochromis spilorhynchus ♀, ♂ page 912

Etroplus suratensis (BLOCH, 1790)

Banded Chromide, Green Chromide

Syn.: *Chaetodon suratensis, Ch. caris, Etroplus meleagris.*

Hab.: Asia; coast and mouth of rivers in India (Malabar, Coromandel, Orissa) and Sri Lanka (Ceylon). The animals inhabit brackish waters but also enter freshwater and pure seawater.

F.I.: 1905.

Sex: The species is sexually monomorphic; the animals are identical in coloration, body shape and finnage. It may be that old ♂♂ grow larger.

Soc. B.: Territorial, the animals are quite aggressive and quarrelsome among themselves, especially at spawning time. *E. suratensis* eats plants. Open spawner; nuclear family.

M: Provide large tanks with a sandy bottom, some hiding places and caves of stone; some brackish water resistant roots for decoration. Plants are possible as long as they tolerate brackish water. Brackish water (2-3 tablespoons of sea salt per 10 l; 2.5 gal of water). *E. suratensis* can also be maintained in freshwater after an acclimation period; however, the water should be hard and alkaline. House with *E. maculatus* which inhabits the same biotopes and has similar demands.

B: 26-28° C (79-82° F); also possible in freshwater. The fish are sexually mature from a length of roughly 15 cm (6"); spawning occurs in the open or in a shelter. Eggs are numerous and adhere on the end; they hatch after about 36 hours. After 7 additional days, the young are free-swimming. The young have a dark band extending around the center of the body during the first week. Afterwards, they are monocolored silver until the stripes appear. Parents caring for their brood develop a black throat and chest.

F: O, H; live foods of any kind, also vegetable fare (blanched lettuce or spinach); large flakes and tablet food.

S: WYMEN & WARD (1972): Copeia no. 4: 834-838, described a cleaning symbiosis between *Etroplus maculatus* and *E. suratensis*. *E. maculatus* was the cleaner, *E. suratensis* the recipient. Details are found in SCHOENEN (1980): DCG-Informationen 9(10): 197-200.

T: 23-26° C, **L:** to 46 cm, **A:** 130 cm, **R:** m, b, **D:** 3
73-79° F, to 18", 51",

Geophagus acuticeps HECKEL, 1840

Sparkling Geophagus

Syn.: *Satanoperca acuticeps, Geophagus cauticeps* (typographical error!).

Hab.: South America; in the entire Amazon basin. The species occurs in quiet waters with a sandy bottom.

F.I.: 1913 by Wilhelm Eimeke, Hamburg, Germany.

Sex: ♂ has an elongated dorsal and anal fin.

Soc. B.: Territorial, usually a peaceful and harmless cichlid which does not bother even smaller tankmates. The species likes to dig. Open spawner (?); nuclear family.

M: Provide the aquarium with a sandy or gravel bottom, roomy caves and hiding places and shelter of stones and roots. If the tank is planted, tough, well-rooted species should be used. Add flat stones as spawning substrate. Because the animals dig, good filtration is necessary. Water to medium-hard (12-15° dGH) and slightly acid (pH about 6.5). The species requires warmth.

B: 26-28° C (79-82° F); no recent breeding reports of this fish are available. According to reports from around 1900, *G. acuticeps* is an open spawner and both parents care for spawn and young.

F: O; live foods of all types (insect larvae, *Tubifex*, Enchytraea, small crustacea); beef heart, shrimp, flake and tablet foods.

S: After a revision by GOSSE (1975), *Geophagus acuticeps* is a true species and not a synonym of *G. daemon*.

T: 24-26° C, **L:** 25 cm, **A:** 120 cm, **R:** b, **D:** 2-3
75-79° F, 9¾", 47",

Etroplus suratensis

Geophagus acuticeps

Geophagus daemon HECKEL, 1840

Three-Spotted Eartheater

Syn.: *Satanoperca daemon, Geophagus daemon.*

Hab.: South America; Orinoco and Amazon region, Rio Negro.

F.I.: 1975.

Sex: Sexes are difficult to distinguish when young. The first 4 or 5 soft rays of the dorsal fin are extremely elongated and extend beyond the tail fin in older ♂♂.

Soc. B.: Territorial; outside of spawning season, it is also amiable to conspecifics. The animals are usually sedate and peaceful. The species digs a lot. The help of aquarists is still needed to answer whether the species is an open spawner or a mouthbrooder.

M: Needs a bottom of fine sand and well-rooted tough plants for the sides and background. Arrange some flat stones and rocks as hiding places. Soft (5-10° dGH) and moderately acid (pH around 6.0) water. The species requires warmth. At temperatures below 27° C (81° F), the fish are susceptible to disease. Do not associate with species which are aggressive or voracious feeders.

B: There are no reports of a successful aquarium spawn.

F: O; live foods of all kinds, shrimp, frozen food, also flake and tablet foods.

S: *Geophagus daemon* is very similar, especially as a juvenile, to *G. acuticeps*. *G. daemon* has 2 dark spots on its sides, while *G. acuticeps* has three (not counting the spot on the base of the tail fin).

T: 27-30° C, **L:** 30 cm, **A:** 120 cm, **R:** b, **D:** 2-3
81-86° F, 11 3/4", 47",

Gephyrochromis moorii BOULENGER, 1901

Syn.: *Christyella nyassana.*

Hab.: Africa; northern Lake Malawi (endemic). The animals live predominately above sandy bottoms where it "plows", searching for nourishment.

F.I.: 1976 (?).

Sex: It is still unclear if there is sexual dichromatism, as in so many other mbuna cichlids.

Soc. B.: Exact descriptions of the social behavior of this species are not yet available. Probably a mouthbrooder with a matriarch family.

M: Arrange rockwork in the background of the tank to form caves and crevices. Sides can be planted. Bottom of fine sand; leave free swimming space. Water should medium-hard to hard (10-20° dGH) and in the alkaline range (pH 7.1-8.5). Associate with other mbuna cichlids with similar demands.

B: Nothing is yet known about a successful spawn.

F: C, O; predominately live foods of all kinds (aquatic insects and their larvae, small crustacea, *Tubifex*, Enchytraea), crustacean meat (shrimp), frozen food, also flake and tablet foods.

S: The genus *Gephyrochromis* is closely related to the genus *Pseudotropheus*, but its representatives are not as rock oriented.

T: 24-26° C, **L:** 12 cm, **A:** 100 cm, **R:** b, m, **D:** 2
75-79° F, 4 3/4", 39",

Geophagus daemon

Gephyrochromis moorii ♂

Gephyrochromis moorii ♀

Gymnogeophagus gymnogenys (HENSEL, 1870)

Squarehead Geophagus

Syn.: *Geophagus gymnogenys, G. bucephalus, G. labiatus, G. pygmaeus, G. scymnophilus.*

Hab.: South America; southern Brazil, Uruguay and Argentina.

F.I.: 1900 by J. Reichelt, who obtained the animals from the French breeder Jennet.

Sex: Older ♂♂ have a frontal hump and are larger than the ♀♀.

Soc. B.: Not much known, probably similar to *Geophagus brasiliensis.*

M: The tank decoration should be as convoluted as possible using many roots. Edge and background vegetation of hard, well-rooted plants is possible (the fish are "eartheaters"!!), i.e., *Sagittaria, Vallisneria,* large *Echinodorus* and cryptocorynes. Use a bottom of fine-grained sand so the animals can "work" it in search of something edible.

B: These are probably open spawners with nuclear families comparable to *Geophagus brasiliensis* and *Gymnogeophagus rhabdotus.*

F: O; hardy live foods of all kinds, beef heart, shrimp, flake and tablet foods.

S: The species had disappeared for decades from German aquaria. Only recently have single animals reappeared in the trade.

T: 21-24° C, **L:** 25 cm, **A:** 120 cm, **R:** b, **D:** 2-3
70-75° F, 9 3/4", 47",

Gymnogeophagus meridionalis REIS & MALABARBA, 1988

Pearl-Striped Geophagus

Syn.: None.

Hab.: South America; south Brazil (Rio Grande do Sul), Uruguay and northwestern Argentina (Rio Uruguay, Parana).

F.I.: 1977 to Germany (GDR).

Sex: The species is sexually dichromatic. ♂♂ are much more colorful than ♀♀. It is also sexually dimorphic; the ♂♂ become markedly larger.

Soc. B.: Territorial, the species is peaceful and sedate but digs a lot (name!). The animals do not bother plants. Open spawner; nuclear family.

M: Provide a bottom of fine sand, some hiding places and caves made of stones and roots, and well-rooted, tough plants. Supply some stones as spawning substrates. No major demands are placed on water chemistry; the animals tolerate a hardness up to 30° dGH; pH 7.0-7.5. Associate with equally sedate and peaceful species.

B: 23-25° C (73-77° F); water values are of secondary importance. A detailed breeding report of this species was given by STAWIKOWSKI (1982) in the DCG-Informationen **13** (4): 74-80. Spawning occurs on a previously cleaned substrate after an extensive courtship. There is an average of 300, light brown to transparent whitish eggs. They are oval and have a maximum 1.2 mm (1/16") length (I-type). Both parents participate in the care of the spawn, whereby the ♀ is the more intense caretaker. The ♀ always remains in the immediate vicinity of the spawn, while the ♂, besides territorial defense, often distances itself from the spawn. The larvae hatch after roughly 48 hours at 23° C (73° F) and are deposited into a previously dug pit and transferred several times prior to being free-swimming, which occurs after 4-5 days. The young are guided by both parents. Feeding the tiny fry during the first days is problematic. Benthic microorganisms are eaten. After 1 week, *Artemia* nauplii are taken. The young are very slow growing.

F: O; nonproblematic omnivore: hardy live food of all kinds, beef heart, flake and tablet food.

S: The species can be identified by the following characteristics: 1. There are less than 11 divided rays on the dorsal fin (9-10). 2. Divided crossbands on the sides of the body are absent. 3. The black spot on the side of the body is located below the upper lateral line. 4. The caudal peduncle is wider than it is long.

T: 20-25° C, **L:** 15 cm, **A:** 120 cm, **R:** b, **D:** 2
68-77° F, 6", 47",

Gymnogeophagus gymnogenys ♂

Gymnogeophagus meridionalis ♂

Champsochromis spilorhynchus ♂, page 904

Hemitilapia oxyrhynchus ♂, page 918

Haplochromis obliquidens HILGENDORF, 1888

Syn.: *Chromis obliquidens, Ctenochromis obliquidens, Tilapia obliquidens, Clinodon bayoni, Hemitilapia bayoni.*

Hab.: Africa; Lake Victoria (endemic). The animals prefer to colonize the rocky littoral, but also occur above sandy substrates and in reeds.

F.I.: Uncertain; probably already before 1914.

Sex: Marked sexual dichromatism. ♂ is much more colorful and also larger. The anal fin has egg spots. ♀♀ are very plain. On a yellow-gray background, they display 8 or 9 dark crossbands.

Soc. B.: Territorial; the ♂♂ require large territories that they often defend very aggressively. The species does not bother plants. Agamic mouthbrooder; matriarch family.

M: Needs a fine sand substrate and rockwork with plenty of hiding places and shelters. Divide and delimit territories in the tank with dense plant groups of hardy species; leave a free swimming area. Always maintain one ♂ with several ♀♀. Combine with other species of the former megagenus *Haplochromis*.

B: 26-29° C (79-84° F); one ♂ with 2-3 ♀♀. Breeding can take place in a community tank. Courtship and spawning behavior follows other "*Haplochromis*" species of Lake Victoria. Fertilization is by the egg spot method. Brood care by the ♀ lasts about 3 weeks. The released fry are relatively large and are fed small *Daphnia* and ground flake food.

F: Omnivore which accepts all common foods without difficulty.

S: An exceptionally beautiful cichlid. One of the few species that remains in the genus *Haplochromis*.

T: 24-26° C, L: 12 cm, A: from 100 cm, R: b, m, D: 2
75-79° F, 4 3/4", from 39",

Hemichromis cristatus LOISELLE, 1979

Crown Jewel Cichlid

Syn.: None.

Hab.: Africa; Guinea, Ghana and Nigeria. The species inhabits small creeks with soft, acid water.

F.I.: 1981 (?).

Sex: Differentiation of the sexes is difficult and only recognizable by the larger circumference of the ♀. A certain separation of the sexes is only possible at spawning time. ♀♀ usually remain somewhat smaller.

Soc. B.: Similar to *Hemichromis letourneauxi. H. cristatus* is a peaceful species. Open spawner; nuclear family.

M: As with *H. letourneauxi.*

B: Similar to *Hemichromis bimaculatus* (Vol. 1, page 722).

F: C, O; live foods of all kinds; frozen food, freeze-dried food, shrimp; also flake and tablet foods.

S: *Hemichromis cristatus* is a representative of the *Hemichromis bimaculatus* group.

T: 23-26° C, **L:** 9 cm, **A:** 100 cm, **R:** b, **D:** 3
73-79° F, 3 ", 39",

Hemichromis elongatus (GUICHENOT, 1859)

Elongate Hemichromis

Syn.: *Chromichthys elongatus, Hemichromis auritus.*

Hab.: West Africa; from Guinea through the entire west African coastal region to Zaire, Angola and even Zambia.

F.I.: ?

Sex: When in normal coloration, the sexes cannot be differentiated.

Soc. B.: Territorial, forms pairs; *Hemichromis elongatus* belongs, as does *H. fasciatus*, to the most bellicose cichlids. The animals are marked predators. They dig a lot and molest the plants. Open spawner; nuclear family.

M: Tank with many hiding places, niches and caves constructed of stones and roots, substrate of fine sand, vegetation can be waived, perhaps floating plants. No high demands are placed on water quality (hardness up to 15° dGH, pH about 7). Since the animals also enter brackish water, sea salt can be added (1-2 teaspoons of salt per 10 l; 2.5 gal water). Only house with equal sized fishes of similar demands, or keep in a species tank.

B: 25-28° C (77-82° F); water as above. The animals are open spawners, usually spawning on stones. The spawning site is cleaned beforehand. The up to 800 eggs are guarded and cared for exemplarily by both parents. Egg development takes 50 hours at 28° C (82° F), and the fry are free-swimming after an additional 132-144 hours. The young are guided by their parents until they are 3 cm (1 ") long. Feed the young with micro foods and *Artemia* nauplii. Later, feed with hardy sieved live foods.

F: O; especially meat and hardy live foods (small crustacea, insects and insect larvae, *Tubifex*, Enchytraea, earthworms, small fish); frozen food; tablet food.

S: *Hemichromis elongatus* differs from *H. fasciatus* by having a longer caudal peduncle, more in the lower jaw, and a different coloration.

T: 23-25° C, **L:** 15 cm, **A:** 100 cm, **R:** b, **D:** 4 (predator)
73-77° F, 6", 39",

Hemichromis cristatus

Hemichromis elongatus

Hemichromis letourneauxi SAUVAGE, 1880
Letourneaux' Jewel Cichlid

Syn.: *Hemichromis exsul, H. rolandi, H. saharae.*

Hab.: Africa; Egypt, Algeria, Sudan, Guinea, Senegal, Chad, Ivory Coast, Ghana, Togo, Republic of Central Africa.

F.I.: 1981 (?).

Sex: It is very difficult to distinguish between the sexes. Large ♂♂ are said to have a slight frontal hump.

Soc. B.: A territorial species that forms pairs. Outside the spawning season, the species is not uncommonly aggressive. Housing them with animals that are of similar size is nonproblematic if the aquarium is sufficiently roomy. The species is a strong digger, particularly during spawning time. Open spawner; nuclear family with pronounced brood care.

T: 22-25° C, **L:** 15 cm, **A:** 100 cm, **R:** b, **D:** 3
72-77° F, 6", 39",

M: Needs a tank with many hiding places of stones and roots. The bottom should be of fine sand or gravel. Place stones and roots directly on the bottom (or risk collapse from digging). The fish are the most comfortable with rich vegetation. Water should be soft (about 5° dGH), acid (pH about 6.0), clean and oxygen-rich. Create a slight water movement with a power filter. Change the water regularly (every one to two weeks 1/3 of the tank volume).

B: Nothing is known about reproduction in an aquarium. Breeding is probably similar to other jewel cichlids (e.g., *Hemichromis bimaculatus* or *H. lifalili*).

F: C, O; live foods of all kinds, frozen food, freeze-dried food, flake and tablet foods.

S: *Hemichromis letourneauxi* is closely related to *Hemichromis lifalili*. They form the *Hemichromis letourneauxi* group.

Hemichromis paynei LOISELLE, 1979
Faded Jewel Cichlid

Syn.: None.

Hab.: Africa: Guinea, Sierra Leone and Liberia. The animals are at home in flood and rice growing regions, as well as small flowing waters of savannas and forests.

F.I.: 1981 (?).

Sex: Outside of spawning, the sexes are difficult to distinguish. During spawning, the ♂♂'s chin, throat and part of the stomach become fire red, and the head and sides of the body develop light blue iridescent dots.

Soc. B.: Similar to *Hemichromis letourneauxi.*

T: 23-25° C, **L:** 10 cm, **A:** 100 cm, **R:** b, **D:** 3
73-77° F, 4", 39",

M: As indicated for *H. letourneauxi.*

B: No reports are available about a successful aquarium spawn.

F: C, O; live foods of all kinds, frozen food, shrimp, beef heart, flake and tablet foods.

S: *Hemichromis paynei* belongs with *H. bimaculatus* GILL, 1862 and *H. cristatus* LOISELLE, 1979 in the *Hemichromis bimaculatus* group.

Hemichromis letourneauxi

Hemichromis paynei

Hemitilapia oxyrhynchus BOULENGER, 1902

Syn.: None.

Hab.: Africa; Lake Malawi (endemic). The species prefers to inhabit the sandy littoral zones that are vegetated with *Vallisneria*.

F.I.: At the beginning of the '70's.

Sex: Clear sexual dichromatism exists. ♂ is very colorful with a metallic turquoise body; ♀ is silver to yellow-gray and has 3 large black spots in the dorsal region which appear more or less pronounced, depending on the mood of the animal.

Soc. B.: Territorial, the ♂♂ are often rough towards the ♀♀ and pursue them strongly; otherwise, the animals are quite amiable despite their size. The species does not bother plants excessively. Mouthbrooder; matriarch family.

M: Best kept in a community tank. Furnish the aquarium with stone plates and rocks to create hiding places. The bottom area should be divided into several zones. Use a sandy substrate. Plant with large, robust species. Natural vegetation consists of *Vallisneria* or giant *Vallisneria*. If possible, do not maintain the fish in pairs, but always one ♂ with several ♀♀. The ♂♂ often pursue the ♀♀ strongly. Associate with *Cyrtocara* species or large mbuna species, such as *Petrotilapia tridentiger*.

B: 24-28° C (75-82° F); water values as indicated for *Cyrtocara* species of Lake Malawi. *H. oxyrhynchus* is also an agamic mouthbrooder. The care and rearing of the brood is the exclusive responsibility of the ♀. Development of the spawn in the buccal cavity of the mother is concluded after 18-21 days. They then leave the mother's mouth for the first time. Feed the young with small live foods and crumbled flake food.

F: Hardy live foods of all kinds (mosquito larvae, crustacea, *Tubifex*, small earthworms, etc.); chopped shrimp, flake food, tablet food.

S: *H. oxyrhynchus* has a remarkable way to procure food in its natural habitat. The animals feed on aufwuchs, grazing the algae and microorganisms from the leaves of *Vallisneria*. For this purpose, the fish lies on its side, takes one of the ribbon-shaped *Vallisneria* leaves into its mouth and rasps the nourishment that has colonized on it ("*Vallisneria* sucker").

T: 24-26° C, **L:** 20 cm, **A:** from 150 cm, **R:** b, m, **D:** 3
75-79° F, 8", from 59",

Iodotropheus sprengerae OLIVER & LOISELLE, 1972

Rusty Cichlid

Syn.: Trade name "*Melanochromis brevis*".

Hab.: Africa; Lake Malawi (endemic). The animals are inhabitants of the upper rock littoral and belong to the mbuna cichlids. They have only been captured around the islands of Boadzulu and Mumbo.

F.I.: 1958.

Sex: Well developed sexual dichromatism, the ♂ has a strong violet or bluish sheen on the sides or fins and distinct egg spots on the anal fin.

Soc. B.: Territorial; the species is relatively peaceful. It does not dig, and plants are left undisturbed. Agamic, ovophile mouthbrooder; matriarch family.

M: The background of the tank should have stone constructions with many caves, crevices and niches, reaching the water surface. Decorate with some roots, bottom of sand or gravel and perhaps plant with tough species. Water medium-hard to hard (12-20° dGH) and in the alkaline range (pH 7.5-8.5). Combine with other mbuna cichlids (*Pseudotropheus, Melanochromis* or *Labidochromis* species).

B: 25-28° C (77-82° F); the water should not be too soft, values as indicated above. Keep 1 ♂ and 3-4 ♀♀ together. *I. sprengerae* is a highly specialized mouthbrooder, similar in reproductive behavior to *Pseudotropheus* or *Cyrtocara*. The ♀ broods the eggs in a throat sac. The eggs are fertilized via the egg spot method. Raising the young poses no problems.

F: O; live foods of all types (especially small crustacea, mosquito larvae, *Tubifex*, Enchytraea), frozen and flake foods.

S: If the animals are not fed *Cyclops*, the beautiful red-brown coloration of *I. sprengerae* pales to a plain gray. The genus *Iodotropheus* is monotypic; it has only one species.

T: 24-26° C, **L:** 10 cm, **A:** 100 cm, **R:** m, b, **D:** 2
75-79° F, 4", 39",

Hemitilapia oxyrhynchus ♀, ♂ page 912

Iodotropheus sprengerae

Labidochromis caeruleus — FRYER, 1956
Blue-White Labido, Caeruleus

Syn.: None.

Hab.: Africa; Lake Malawi (endemic). The species occurs above rocky bottoms as well as in sections with *Vallisneria aethiopica*. They inhabit depths of 2-40 m (2.2-44 yd). Their distribution is limited to Nkata Bay.

F.I.: 1968 (?).

Sex: The ♂ is considerably more colorful at spawning time; they develop a bluish coloration and grow somewhat larger.

Soc. B.: *L. caeruleus* is not territorial. The fish live either singly or in pairs. They are one of most peaceful mbuna cichlids. Ovophile mouthbrooder; matriarch family.

M: As indicated for *Labidochromis vellicans*.

B: As indicated for *L. vellicans*. A detailed breeding report is given by SCHEUERMANN (1974); Das Aquarium **8**, 439-441. According to his report, the young leave the mouth of the mother for the first time after 40 days at a temperature of 23-24° C (73-75° F) or already after 25 days at 27-28° C (81-82° F). The mother continues to care for the young for about 1 week.

F: O; live foods of all kinds, freeze-dried, frozen, flake and tablet foods.

S: Two groups of *L. caeruleus* exist which differ because of their habitat: one group lives above the rocky bottoms, has less developed pharyngeal bones and feeds on lithophile (stone-loving) invertebrates. The other group has much more massive pharyngeal bones and feeds primarily on snails of the genus *Gabiella* in stands of *Vallisneria*.

T: 23-26° C, **L:** 8 cm, **A:** 80 cm, **R:** all, **D:** 2-3
73-79° F, 3", 31",

Labidochromis ianthinus — LEWIS, 1982

Syn.: None.

Hab.: Africa; Lake Malawi (endemic). The species has only been found at the Mbenji Islands. It inhabits rocks of the shallow regions.

F.I.: Probably after 1980.

Sex: ♂ is darker colored and has a more intensive light violet sheen on the sides; ♀ is paler with a less intense light violet sheen.

Soc. B.: As *Labidochromis vellicans*.

M: See *L. vellicans*.

B: No reports are yet available about successfully breeding this fish in an aquarium. Presumably it does not deviate from that of other *Labidochromis* species.

F: O; live foods of any kind, frozen food, also flake and tablet foods.

S: *Labidochromis ianthinus* is similar to *L. vellicans* but principally differs by having a more rounded snout and stronger pharyngeal bones.

T: 23-26° C, **L:** 9 cm, **A:** 80 cm, **R:** all, **D:** 2-3
73-79° F, 3 ", 31",

Labidochromis caeruleus

Labidochromis ianthinus ♂

Labidochromis vellicans TREWAVAS, 1935

Vellicans

Syn.: None.

Hab.: Africa; Lake Malawi (endemic). The species inhabits the rocky littoral zone.

F.I.: 1958 (?).

Sex: ♂ has metallic blue and orange-yellow shades which are usually absent in the ♀. The ♂ grows somewhat larger. The egg spots on the anal fin are equally intense in ♂♂ and ♀♀.

Soc. B.: Territorial, *L. vellicans* is one of the most peaceful mbuna cichlids. It does not touch other fishes or plants. Agamic, ovophile mouthbrooder; matriarch family.

M: The background should have rock formations extending to the water surface with numerous hiding places and a bottom of sand or small-grained gravel. Because the fish does not touch plants, decorative hiding places for brooding ♀♀ and young can be created with the aid of dense stands of plants. Breeding animals do not place high demands on water composition since they readily adapt. Nevertheless, medium-hard (about 12° dGH) and slightly alkaline (pH 7.5-8.5) water should be offered. Associate with other mbuna cichlids.

B: 25-28° C (77-82° F); follow the water values indicated under **M**. Use one ♂ and several ♀♀ for breeding. The animals are typical mouthbrooders for relatives of *Cyrtocara*. The eggs are taken by the ♀♀ into her throat sac and fertilized following the egg spot method. Up to 30 eggs are laid. Brooding takes about 18-21 days. The ♀ continues to care for the young for about 1 week after the first release. Raising the young is not complicated.

F: O; live foods of all kinds, frozen, freeze-dried, flake and tablet foods.

S: *Labidochromis vellicans* has developed a very specialized feeding form. The animals do not graze the aufwuchs but pick the small organisms out of the algae mat. For this, they use their pointed teeth of the first row of the upper and lower mandible in their terminal mouth.

T: 23-26° C, 73-79° F, **L:** 10 cm, 4", **A:** 80 cm, 31", **R:** all, **D:** 2-3

Neolamprologus brevis (BOULENGER, 1899)

Brevis Shelldweller

Syn.: *Lamprologus taeniurus, L. brevis.*

Hab.: Africa; Lake Tanganyika (endemic). The species inhabits muddy and sandy areas of the lake where large numbers of snails of the genus *Neothauma* can be found. The empty houses of these snails serve as hiding places and spawning caves for *L. brevis*. The species prefers great water depths (6-55 m; 6.5-60 yd).

F.I.: End of 1979.

Sex: Unequivocal differentiation of the sexes based on external characteristics is very difficult. ♂♂ grow larger and have a clearly pronounced orange fringe on the upper edge of the dorsal fin. This is absent in ♀♀.

Soc. B.: Territorial, it claims small territories (10-20 cm; 4"-8" in diameter). The animals are quite aggressive within the territory. Will not damage plants. Cave spawner, paternal-matriarch or matriarch family.

M: Substrate should be out of sand and roughly 5 cm (2") deep (free sand areas are necessary!). There the empty snail houses are laid. The animals not only accept houses of the Tanganyika snails (*Neothauma*) but also similar houses of escargot (*Helix pomatia*). Empty houses of this snail can either be collected in nature or bought frozen in a deli. The animals bury the snail shell at a particular angle up to its opening in the sand. Only when the angle is correct can they hide in the house lighting fast. Decorate the tank with some plants. House with small *Julidochromis* species (*J. ornatus, J. transcriptus*) and *Tropheus duboisi*.

Continued on page 924.

Labidochromis vellicans

Neolamprologus brevis ♂ and ♀

Neolamprologus brevis ♂

B: 24-27° C (75-81° F). Needs medium-hard (about 15° dGH) and slightly to moderately alkaline (pH 7.5-8.5) water. Provide some snail shells as spawning caves. The shells are buried until only the opening remains free. In front of it, the ♀ positions herself and guards her territory. When a ♂ approaches a ripe ♀, she quickly nudges the ♂ on the side and half disappears into the shell. Only the tail fin can be seen. The ♂ follows the ♀ to the shell, positions himself above the opening and ejects its semen while shivering lightly, fertilizing the eggs located in the interior of the house. After spawning, the ♂ is no longer tolerated in the proximity of the shell. Eggs seem to be few (15-30). Development takes about 24 hours at 26° C (79° F), and the young are free-swimming after about 6 days. The young are fed *Artemia* nauplii and crumbled flake food. The ♀ cares for the young for about 2 weeks.

F: Live foods (*Artemia, Daphnia, Cyclops, Tubifex*). The animals also accept flake food.

S: The method *N. brevis* uses to put its shell into the correct position is interesting. STAECK & LINKE (1982) describe 3 different techniques the fish uses: 1. They push the house directly by griping the edge with the mandibles and swimming against it. 2. They move it indirectly by removing the sand from beneath it. 3. They bury it by lying with the belly on the bottom and strongly beating their tail; thus larger quantities of sand are transported posteriorly and the shell sinks.

T: 23-25° C, L: ♂ 6 cm, ♀ 3.5 cm, A: 50 cm, R: b, D: 3-4 (C)
73-77° F, ♂ 2⅓", ♀ 1⅓", 20",

Neolamprologus sp. "*daffodil*"
Daffodil

Syn.: *Lamprologus* sp. "*daffodil*".

Hab.: Endemic to Lake Tanganyika, Africa.

F.I.: 1982/83.

Sex: The ♂♂ are somewhat more colorful than the ♀♀ and have more pointed fins.

Soc. B.: A very peaceful species which can hold its ground in a community tank, even against larger fishes.

M: Likes a densely planted, not too brightly lit tank. The animals are almost always in a plant thicket and are rarely in the open. Plants are not bothered. Water should have an unproblematic pH of 7.0-8.8; hardness 10-30° dGH.

T: 22-27° C, L: 7 cm, A: 60 cm, R: b, m, D: 1
72-81° F, 2³/₄", 24",

B: A species tank with a substrate of coarse pebbles (2-4 cm Ø) and a floating plant cover is recommended. This will allow some young to survive. Cave spawner, see Vol. 1, page 732.

F: C, O; flake food, frozen bloodworms.

S: One of the most adorable and beautiful small cichlids recently imported. It is either a color morph of the better known *N. brichardi* (previously *N. savoryi elongatus*) or a sub-species still to be described.

Altolamprologus calvus (POLL, 1978)

Pearly Lamprologus, Pearly Compressiceps

Syn.: *Lamprologus calvus.*

Hab.: Africa; Lake Tanganyika (endemic). The species has been found around Sumbu National Park (Zambia). The animals inhabit rocky littoral zones.

F.I.: Probably already in 1958 with *Altolamprologus compressiceps.*

Sex: Little pronounced; the ♂♂ grow larger, have longer pelvic fins and more pointed, elongated anal and dorsal fins.

Soc. B.: Territorial, the animals are very sedate, sometimes even shy. They do not dig and are plant friendly. Cave spawner; patriarch-matriarch family.

M: Needs roomy tanks with stone and rock structures to provide many crevices, niches and caves. Use dense vegetation of *Hygrophila corymbosa* and *Microsorium pteropus* at the edges and a sandy bottom. Full-grown *A. calvus* are sensitive to new water. Cover the tank well because the animals are precise jumpers. Water as for other inhabitants of Lake Tanganyika.

B: 25-27° C (77-81° F); SOMMER (1982): Aquarienmagazin **16** (9): 552-554 reports a successful spawn of *A. calvus.* The group involved consisted of 2 ♂♂ and 3 ♀♀ in the presence of *Cyprichromis leptosoma* and *C. microlepidotus.* The water was neutral to slightly alkaline (pH 7.0-7.5) and medium-hard (about 15° dGH). Breeding was preferably performed in crevices and caves. There were up to 200, 2 mm (1/16"), dirty yellow to greenish eggs. Spawns were guarded by the ♀. The larvae hatched after about 50 hours at 25° C (77° F); after an additional 8-10 days, they were free-swimming. Feed with *Artemia* nauplii. *Cyclops* nauplii were also readily taken.

F: C; live foods of all kinds. The animals are difficult to acclimate to flake food.

S: *Altolamprologus calvus* is very similar in appearance to *A. compressiceps* BOULENGER, 1898, to which it is closely related. *A. calvus* has a longer, shallower body and has no scales on the forehead between the eyes. Photo of a juvenile animal is shown on page 931.

T: 25-25° C, **L:** 14 cm, **A:** 90 cm, **R:** m, b, **D:** 3
73-77° F, 5 ", 35",

Lamprologus congoensis SCHILTHUIS, 1891

Congo Lamprologus

Syn.: None.

Hab.: Africa; Zaire, the animals occur in the rapids of the Congo River.

F.I.: 1957.

Sex: Clear sexual dimorphism. ♂♂ grow significantly larger, have numerous golden iridescent scales on the sides of the body and develop a frontal hump with age.

Soc. B.: Territorial; ♂♂ are polygamous and form a "harem". Keep one ♂ with several ♀♀. The animals are quite aggressive among themselves, but there are no losses in the presence of sufficient hiding places. Cave spawner; paternal-matriarch family.

M: Tank with large surface area, moderate water depth (30 cm; 12"), gravel or sand bottom, many hiding places and caves of stone, roots and tough plants as territorial delimiters. A moderate current should be produced with a pump. In accordance with their natural habits, *L. congoensis* is best kept in groups. Water chemistry is of secondary importance: medium-hard (up to 15° dGH) and slightly acid (pH around 6.5). Associate with other, non-cave spawning cichlids.

B: 25-27° C (77-81° F); water values as indicated above. The polygamous ♂ spawns in turn with the ♀♀. These all occupy different caves, limiting their territories among themselves. Pairing courtship and aggression constantly alternate. The ♀♀ try to lure the ♂ into their cave. The eggs are almost 2 mm (1/16") long and are usually placed on the ceiling of the cave or on a wall. The eggs adhere on their side (I-type); each spawn has up to 80 eggs. The larvae hatch after 54 hours at 26° C (79° F) and are spit into a pile on the floor of the cave by the brooding ♀. After an additional 8 days, the young are free-swimming. The ♀ guards the spawning cave with the young while the ♂ controls the entire harem area.

Continued on page 928.

Altolamprologus calvus

Lamprologus congoensis ♂

Continuation of *Lamprologus congoensis*:

F: O; live foods of all kinds, freeze-dried food, frozen food, shrimp, flake and tablet foods.

S: *Lamprologus congoensis* is well adapted to its life in rapids with its streamlined body, strong pectoral fins, large tail fin and reduced swim bladder.

T: 23-25° C, **L**: 15 cm, **A**: 100 cm, **R**: b, **D**: 2
73-77° F, 6", 39",

Lepidiolamprologus cunningtoni (BOULENGER, 1906)

Syn.: *Lamprologus cunningtoni*.

Hab.: Africa; Lake Tanganyika (endemic). The species belongs to the most common cichlids in the shore area of the lake. The animals prefer stony substrates, but also occur above sandy bottoms.

F.I.: 1971.

Sex: Not possible to determine based on external characteristics. Perhaps the ♂♂ have longer ventral fins.

Soc. B.: Territorial; the animals are said to be quite aggressive during the spawning period. Cave spawner; patriarch-matriarch family (?).

M: As indicated for *Lamprologus lemairii*.

B: There have been no reports dealing with a successful aquarium spawn.

F: C, O; predominantly live foods of all kinds; after adaptation the animals can also be feed other foods (shrimp, frozen food, flake food).

S: Until recently, *Lepidiolamprologus cunningtoni* was considered *Lepidiolamprologus attenuatus* in the aquarium literature. In an article which appeared in Cichlidae (BCV), Pierre BRICHARD exposed this error (Cichlidae/BCV **8**, 63-66, 1982).

T: 23-26° C, **L**: 15 cm, **A**: 100 cm, **R**: b, m, **D**: 3
73-79° F, 6", 39",

Lepidiolamprologus elongatus (BOULENGER, 1898)
Elongate Lamprologus

Syn.: *Lamprologus pleurostigma* DAVID, 1936, *L. elogatus*.

Hab.: Africa; Lake Tanganyika (endemic). The species inhabits the rocky coastal areas. Widely distributed throughout the lake.

F.I.: Probably already in 1958.

Sex: Monomorphic, very difficult to distinguish the sexes; ♂♂ grow somewhat larger.

Soc. B.: Territorial; the fish often show strong aggressions, especially towards conspecifics. *L. elongatus* is a predator which captures its prey similar to a pike. The species is plant friendly. Cave spawner; nuclear family with a lasting pair bond.

M: Needs a tank with rocky formations and roots with plenty of hiding places. Use small gravel as a substrate. Plants are absent in its natural biotope; leave free swimming space. Medium-hard (about 12° dGH) and alkaline (pH 8.0-9.0) water. However, the species can also be adapted to other values. Because of its predatory lifestyle, it should be maintain in a species tank or with larger relatives of *Lamprologus*.

B: 25-27° C (77-81° F); only possible in roomy tanks which offer many hiding places. Animals for the breeding set-up should come from a group of 4-8 young that form pairs at the onset of sexual maturity. Such pairs harmonize well in most cases. *L. elongatus* is a cave spawner who prefers roomy caves. The spawns are very large, often consisting of more that 500 eggs. These are adhered to a vertical cave wall and/or the ceiling of the cave. The larvae hatch after 2-3 days and are free-swimming after an additional 4. Both partners care for the eggs and young; however, the ♀ has priority. Feed the young with *Artemia* nauplii at first.

F: C; there may be some feeding problems. In nature the animals almost exclusively live off small fish. The species can be trained with some difficulty to accept substitute food (beef heart, mosquito larvae, or *Gammarus*). Flake food is not readily taken.

S: *L. elongatus* is a very large species. It is an ambush predator. Characteristics for ambush predators are a torpedo-shaped body and a well developed, triangular caudal fin which makes fast acceleration possible.

T: 23-25° C, **L**: 20 cm, **A**: 100 cm, **R**: b, m, **D**: 3-4 (C)
73-77° F, 8", 39",

Lepidiolamprologus cunningtoni

Lepidiolamprologus elongatus

Neolamprologus fasciatus (BOULENGER, 1898)
Barred Lamprologus

Syn.: *Lamprologus fasciatus.*

Hab.: Africa; Lake Tanganyika (endemic). The natural habitat of this cichlid is the rocky littoral zone where the animals inhabit depths between 2 and 5 m (2.2-5.5 yd).

F.I.: 1976.

Sex: Differentiation of the sexes based on external characteristics is not possible. At spawning time, the ♀♀ should appear fuller.

Soc. B.: The fish is territorial but quite sedate. It does not bother plants. Cave spawner, probably nuclear or paternal-matriarch family.

M: Needs stone structures with many crevices and caves as background decoration and territorial delimiters. Moderate planting with tough species (plants are absent in its natural biotope). Can be kept in a community tank. Do not associate with fish that are too lively; best kept together with other small *Neolamprologus* species as well as cichlids from the genera *Chalinochromis, Eretmodus, Julidochromis, Spathodus* and *Telmatochromis*, perhaps with *Tropheus.*

B: No successful spawning reports are yet available.

F: Hearty live foods (mosquito larvae, small crustacea, *Tubifex*, Enchytraea), finely cut shrimp, flake and tablet foods.

S: The turquoise iris is a characteristic of *Neolamprologus fasciatus.*

T: 23-25° C, L: 14 cm, A: 100 cm, R: b, m, D: 2-3
73-77° F, 5 ", 39",

Neolamprologus fasciatus

Neolamprologus fasciatus

Altolamprologus calvus, juv.

Neolamprologus furcifer (BOULENGER, 1898)

Fork-Tailed Lamprologus

Syn.: *Lamprologus furcifer.*

Hab.: Africa; Lake Tanganyika (endemic). The species is distributed throughout the lake. The animals live in the upper rocky littoral zone and are strongly bonded to caves and crevices.

F.I.: Probably already in 1958.

Sex: The sexes only exhibit slight exterior differences. The ♂♂ develop a buccal hump with age.

Soc. B.: Territorial; the animals are very aggressive among themselves. Only the breeding partner can share the territory. *N. furcifer* does not damage plants. Cave spawner; nuclear family.

M: Stone constructions with many crevices and caves are required for the well-being of *N. furcifer.* The animals like to swim belly-up along the ceiling of a cave. Its natural biotope is devoid of plants; nevertheless, the aquarium can be sparsely planted. Should be kept in a community tank since the intraspecific aggressions are strongly dampened by the presence of other fishes. Best associated with small *Julidochromis* and *Lamprologus* species.

B: 24-26° C (75-79° F); water values as for other *Lamprologus* species. *N. furcifer* is rarely bred. It is achieved with pairs in a biotope aquarium. The animals are specialized cave spawners which prefer to do so on a ceiling. Up to 50 greenish eggs are laid. Hatching time is almost a week. Both parents guard the eggs, larvae and fry. The fry are small and are fed *Artemia* nauplii and crumbled flake food.

F: Live foods of all kinds (*Daphnia*, mosquito larvae and other insect larvae, *Tubifex*). After a training period, the animals also eat flake food and minced fish and crustacean meat.

S: An obvious characteristic of *N. furcifer* is its golden yellow and sky blue iridescent iris and the deeply forked caudal fin (name!). The tail fin terminates in two long points in older animals. Of all the *Neolamprologus* species, *N. furcifer* is the most dependent on caves and rock crevices.

T: 23-25° C, **L:** 15 cm, **A:** from 100 cm, **R:** b, m, **D:** 3
73-77° F, 6", from 39",

Neolamprologus longior (STAECK, 1980)

Elongated Lemon Cichlid

Syn.: *Lamprologus leleupi longior.*

Hab.: Africa; Lake Tanganyika (endemic). The animals have been caught at the east shore of the lake between Kabogo Point and Kibwe Bay. The species lives in the mid to lower rocky littoral zone.

F.I.: 1975 by Dr. Wolfgang Staeck, Berlin, Germany.

Sex: Barely present, monomorphic. ♂♂ grow larger; in addition, the pelvic, dorsal and anal fins are elongated.

Soc. B.: Territorial; the species is relatively peaceful. Sometimes the ♂♂ are quite rough among themselves and towards superfluous ♀♀; plant-friendly fish. Monogamous cave spawner; patriarch-matriarch family.

M: Needs a tank with stone structures in the background, offering many caves, shelters and niches; decorate with some roots. Perhaps the edges of the tank should be planted; use a fine sandy bottom. Medium-hard to hard (10-20° dGH) and slightly alkaline (pH 7.5-8.5) water. Associate with other peaceful fishes of Lake Tanganyika.

B: 25-30° C (77-86° F); water values as indicated above. The animals preferentially spawn on the cave ceiling. Up to 200 eggs are laid. The ♀ guards the spawn and brood while the ♂ secures and defends the territory. The larvae are freed from their egg shells after about 3 days by the ♀ and deposited in a pit next to or within the spawning cave (made prior to spawning). After an additional six days, the young are free-swimming. Now, *Cyclops* and *Artemia* nauplii can be fed.

F: C; the species prefers to eat live food, but it can also be trained to accept frozen food, shrimp and flake food.

S: *Neolamprologus longior* differs from both former sub-species by its narrower, elongated body. In addition, the caudal peduncle is longer than it is wide.

T: 24-26° C, **L:** 10 cm, **A:** 80 cm, **R:** m, b, **D:** 3
75-79° F, 4", 31",

Neolamprologus furcifer

Neolamprologus longior

Continuation of *Neolamprologus* spec. "*magarae*":

S: In contrast to other shell-dwelling cichlids so far kept in the hobby, *N. "magarae"* does not bury its house. It lies open on the substrate and only its position is changed. The young do not exhibit a strong bond to the empty shell.

T: 24-26° C, L: ♂ 7 cm, ♀ 5 cm, A: 60 cm, R: b, D: 3
75-79° F, ♂ 2 3/4", ♀ 2", 24",

Lamprologus lemairii BOULENGER, 1899
Lemaire's Lamprologus

Syn.: None.

Hab.: Africa; Lake Tanganyika (endemic). The species inhabits the shores of the lake, but it is not limited to a particular biotope in its distribution. It can be found above rocky bottoms as well as sandy and muddy substrates.

F.I.: At the beginning of the '70's.

Sex: The sexes cannot be distinguished based on external characteristics.

Soc. B.: Territorial; this is a quite sedate, sluggish cichlid. The species is an ambush predator. Cave spawner; probably paternal-matriarch family.

M: Decorate with some stones and plant groups; hiding places should be available. Needs a sandy bottom or fine gravel. No major demands are placed on decor. Water should be slightly to moderately alkaline (pH 7.3-8.5) and medium-hard (10-18° dGH). Associate only other large cichlids (predator!), such as *Neolampro-logus tetracanthus* or *Lepidiolamprologus elongatus*.

B: Has not been successful in an aquarium.

F: Predominantly live foods of any kind; above a certain size, the animals feed exclusively on fish (other cichlids) in nature; therefore, feed them regularly with fish meat.

S: Compared to its size, *Lamprologus lemairii* has a relatively small space requirement. In Lake Tanganyika the animals can reach a weight of up to 150 g (1/3 lb).

T: 23-26° C, L: 24 cm, A: 80 cm, R: b, D: 3
73-79° F, 9 1/3", 31",

Neolamprologus meeli (POLL, 1948)
Meeli Shelldweller

Syn.: *Lamprologus meeli.*

Hab.: Africa; Lake Tanganyika (endemic).

F.I.: 1980 (?).

Sex: A sure determination of sex based on external characteristics is not possible. However, ♂♂ grow significantly larger.

Soc. B.: Similar to *Neolamprologus brevis* and *Lamprologus ocellatus.*

M: As for *L. brevis.*

B: *Neolamprologus meeli* has already been bred in an aquarium, but detailed breeding reports are still missing. Breeding is similar to *N. brevis* or *L. ocellatus.*

F: C; live foods of any kind (mosquito larvae, *Tubifex*, shrimp, other small crustacea, snails).

S: *Neolamprologus meeli* belongs to the shell-dwelling *Neolamprologus* species.

T: 23-25° C, L: ♂ 7 cm, ♀ 4.5 cm, A: 50 cm, R: b, D: 3
73-77° F, ♂ 2 3/4", ♀ 1 3/4", 20",

Lamprologus lemairii ♂

Neolamprologus meeli ♂

Neolamprologus sp. "*magarae*"

Syn.: None; the name *"magarae"* is only a trade name.

Hab.: Africa; Lake Tanganyika (endemic); Magara, Burundi. The species inhabits the sandy littoral zone where it can find empty *Neothauma* shells.

F.I.: 1983.

Sex: No definite external ones are known. ♂♂ grow somewhat larger.

Soc. B.: Territorial; the territory is defended quite energetically. Cave spawner; paternal-matriarch family.

M: This species can even be kept in small aquaria. Use a sandy substrate, perhaps sparse vegetation at the edges. Provide empty snail shells as hiding places and spawning caves. The species is dependent on hard aquarium water (from 15° dGH). Like all cichlids from the African rift lakes, *N. "magarae"* is also very sensitive to sudden temperature changes (e.g., during water exchanges). Keep in a species tank or together with other small *Neolamprologus* species.

B: 24-26° C (75-79° F); a sandy bottom and some snail shells as spawning caves. A dominant ♂ can breed with several ♀♀. The ripe ♀ is pushed by the ♂ into a free shell. The eggs are laid mainly in the second turn of the shell and posteriorly fertilized by fast fin movements by the ♂ who normally follows the ♀ into the first turn. Through the first 3 or 4 developmental stages, the ♀ has constant contact with the spawn and directs new water towards it through strong breathing and fanning movements. In all observed cases, the ♀ has moved back to the 1st chamber of the shell as soon as the larvae showed movement. After an average developmental period of 14 days, the 8-10 mm (5/16"-1/3") young are capable of abandoning the shell to feed on *Artemia* or similar small foods.

F: O; live foods of all kinds, flake food, tablet food.

Continued on page 934.

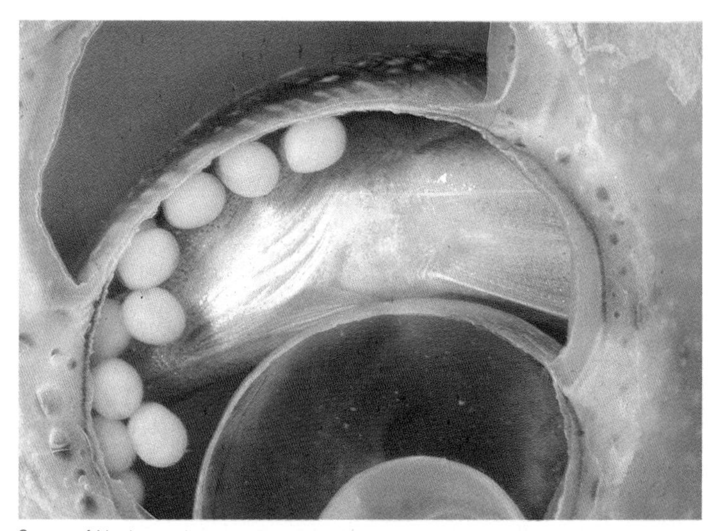

Spawn of *Neolamprologus* sp. *"magarae"* in a snail shell. The lower of head and throat of the ♀ are visible.

Left, "escargot" snail shell; to the right, a shell (genus *Neothauma*) from the biotope of *Neolamprologus*.

Neolamprologus modestus (BOULENGER, 1898)
Modest Lamprologus

Syn.: For a long time *Neolamprologus mondabu* BOULENGER, 1906 was considered a synonym of *N. modestus*. Only in 1978 did POLL determine that *N. mondabu* is a true species after all.

Hab.: Africa; Lake Tanganyika (endemic). The animals inhabit the upper rock zones. The pictured color morph originates from the southern part of the lake (Nkamba Bay in Zambia).

F.I.: Exact year is not known, probably not until 1958.

Sex: Sexual determination is difficult since ♂♂ and ♀♀ are exteriorly similar. ♂♂ are larger, and their dorsal and anal fins are somewhat more pointed and elongated.

Soc. B.: Territorial; the species is occasionally quite aggressive. *L. modestus* does not bother plants and will dig when no acceptable hiding places are offered. Cave spawner; nuclear family.

M: Needs stone structures with many caves, crevices and niches. Sparse vegetation in the aquarium is possible. Provide a sandy bottom. Combine with *Julidochromis*, other *Lamprologus* and *Telmatochromis* species, also *Cyprichromis* species are suitable.

B: 25-27° C (77-81° F); water values as indicated for other *Lamprologus* species. Breeding is best accomplished in a breeding tank with a single pair. The animals are cave spawners; eggs number 50-100 and develop in about 8-10 days. The fry are relatively small and do not lead the reclusive life of younger *Julidochromis*. They form a school which rises above the ground but always remains in the center of the parental territory. Both parents guard and care for the young. Feed the young with *Artemia* nauplii and crumbled flake food.

Continued on page 948.

Variabilichromis moorii (BOULENGER, 1898)
Moore's Lamprologus

Syn.: *Lamprologus moorii, Neochromis moorii.*

Hab.: Africa; in the southern half of Lake Tanganyika (endemic). The species inhabits near shore areas of the rocky zone down to roughly 3 m (3.3 yd).

F.I.: Probably around 1975.

Sex: Determination of the sexes is very difficult since *V. moorii* does not exhibit external differences. As a rule, in adult ♂♂ the pelvic fins are clearly longer; in addition, dorsal and anal fins are usually more elongated into a point than in ♀♀.

Soc. B.: Territorial; the animals are relatively peaceful, even at spawning time aggressions remain limited. Cave spawner; nuclear family a with relatively close bond between the partners.

M: Background decoration of rockwork to provide a number of caves and crevices. Plant species which fasten on stones (*Anubias* species, *Microsorium pteropus*). Keep free swimming space. Maintenance in a community aquarium is possible, but the decoration should reflect the natural biotope. It can be kept with the following cichlids: *Chalinochromis brichardi, Eretmodus cyanostictus, Julidochromis regani, Neolamprologus modestus, N. mustax, Spathodus* species, *Tanganicodus irsacae* and *Tropheus moorii.*

B: 25-28° C (77-82° F); water values as for other *Neolamprologus* species. Breeding in a community aquarium is possible, but a breeding aquarium is better to raise a large number of young. Keep animals in pairs. A strong bond develops between the partners. The animals spawn in caves and eggs number to 100. The young leave the cave for the first time after seven days at 26° C (79° F) and hover in a dense school a few centimeters above the bottom. STAECK made the same observation in its natural biotope. The young do not move about under the guidance of the adults. They always remain in close proximity of the breeding cave which is defended by the parents. Feed the young

Continued on page 940.

Neolamprologus modestus compare to the photo on page 949

Variabilichromis moorii juv

Continuation of *Variabilichromis moorii*:

with *Artemia* nauplii and crumbled flake food.

F: Live foods of all kinds. A. [illegible] a short acclimation period, all usual foods are accepted (flake food, frozen foods, etc.)

S: *V. moorii* belongs to the smaller representatives of the genus. The species is an exception in the genus because of its notorious, age dependent, color transformation (see photos).

T: 24-26° C, L: 10 cm, A: 100 cm, R: b, m, D: 2-3
75-79° F, 4", 39",

Variabilichromis moorii subadult

Variabilichromis moorii adult

Neolamprologus mustax (POLL, 1978)
Mustax

Syn.: *Lamprologus mustax.*

Hab.: Africa; in the southwestern part of Lake Tanganyika (endemic). The species is widely distributed throughout the lake.

F.I.: About 1975.

Sex: The ♂♂ grow larger and develop a slight cranial hump with age; the ♀♀ are fuller.

Soc. B.: Territorial; *N. mustax* is a very gregarious cichlid. The ♂♂ tolerate any other fishes, provided the tank is roomy enough and there are sufficient ♀♀ present (at least 2 ♀♀ per ♂). According to STAWIKOWSKI, *N. mustax* is very aggressive towards conspecifics. Cave spawner; patriarch-matriarch family.

M: Like *Neolamprologus longior.*

B: 25-28° C (77-82° F); keep one or two ♂♂ and several ♀♀ together. The animals spawn in caves, preferably on the ceiling. The white eggs number to 80. Both parents remain in the cave until the larvae have hatched (about 3 days). Only then the ♂ is chased away and the ♀ cares for the brood alone. She continues until they are free-swimming and abandon the cave (occurs after an additional week). Feed the young with infusoria, rotifers, *Artemia* and *Cyclops* nauplii.

F: C, O; live foods of any kind, frozen foods, freeze-dried food, flake food, FD-Menu.

S: *Neolamprologus mustax* is closely related to *Neolamprologus modestus* and *N. petricola*

T: 24-26° C, L: ♂ 10 cm, ♀ 7 cm, A: 70 cm, R: m, b, D: 2
75-79° F, ♂ 4", ♀ 2¾", 28",

Lepidiolamprologus nkambae (STAECK, 1978)

Syn.: *Lamprologus nkambae.*

Hab.: Africa; Lake Tanganyika (endemic). The animals inhabit the rocky littoral zone of Nkamba Bay in the southern part of the lake.

F.I.: 1975 by Dr. Wolfgang Staeck, Berlin, Germany.

Sex: No external ones are identifiable.

Soc. B.: Similar to *Lepidiolamprologus elongatus.*

M: As with *L. elongatus.*

B: No successful reports are available. It is probably similar to *L. elongatus.*

F: C; live foods of all kinds. The animals can be trained with difficulty to replacement foods (beef heart, meat).

S: *Lepidiolamprologus nkambae* is very similar to *Lepidiolamprologus elongatus* but differs from it by its notorious coloration. STAECK (1978) excludes the possibility that *L. elongatus* and *L. nkambae* represent 2 morphs of the same species in his species description. Deviating colors have not been observed in the well researched *L. elongatus.*

T: 23-25° C, **L:** 14 cm, **A:** 100 cm, **R:** b, m, **D:** 3-4 (C)
73-77° F, 5 ", 39",

Lamprologus ocellatus (STEINDACHNER, 1909)
Ocellated Shelldweller

Syn.: *Julidochromis ocellatus.*

Hab.: Africa; Lake Tanganyika (endemic). The species is widely distributed in the lake. The fish live above a soft, sandy bottom at a depth between 5 and 30 m (5.5-33 yd). There they inhabit empty shells of *Neothauma.*

F.I.: 1979.

Sex: A definite distinction of the sexes by external differences is not possible. ♂♂ grow significantly larger.

Soc. B.: Territorial; the small territories are furiously defended against even much larger fish. The species does not damage plants but will dig. Cave spawner; patriarch-matriarch family.

M: Like with *Neolamprologus brevis.*

B: Similar to *N. brevis.* Details are found there.

F: C; live foods of all kinds (snails, shrimp, other small crustacea, mosquito larvae, *Tubifex*).

S: *Lamprologus ocellatus* and *Neolamprologus brevis* appear very similar, but they differ significantly based on the following characteristics: the base coloration of *L. ocellatus* is brown, the sides are violet, the belly is whitish. The coloration of *N. brevis* is similar, but additionally, 9 blue iridescent vertical strips appear on the sides of the body (compare photo of *N. brevis*, page 924).

T: 23-25° C, **L:** ♂ 6 cm, ♀ 3.5, **A:** 50 cm, **R:** b, **D:** 3-4 (C)
73-77° F, ♂ 2 1/3", ♀ 1 1/3", 20",

Lepidiolamprologus nkambae

Lamprologus ocellatus ♂

Lamprologus ornatipinnis POLL, 1949

Syn.: None.

Hab.: Africa; Lake Tanganyika (endemic); Tanzania and Zaire (Kungwe, Tembwe, Moba, Kap Bwana Denge, Katibili). The species inhabits the sandy littoral zone where sufficient empty snail shells are at hand. *L. ornatipinnis* can be found along the shore as well as in deep zones to a depth of 100 meters (109 yd).

F.I.: 1981.

Sex: There are no external differences distinguishable. The ♂♂ grow larger than the ♀♀.

Soc. B.: Territorial; the animals defend their snail shell energetically against strangers. Cave spawner, paternal-matriarch family (?).

M: As indicated for *Neolamprologus brevis*, but the tank should have a volume of at least 100 l (26 gal).

B: 24-26° C (75-79° F); sufficiently large tanks are necessary for breeding. Reproduction is more difficult than in other "snail dwellers". A sufficient number of hiding places should be provided since the ♂♂ strongly pursue each other and the ♀♀. Fine sand is recommended as substrate. The offered shells should match the fish; full-grown ♂♂ require a shell diameter of 5 cm (2") and ♀♀, 3 cm (1 "). "Escargot" shells are suitable. The shells are slanted and totally buried in the sand so that only the opening is visible. Development and rearing of the young is the same as with *Neolamprologus "magarae"*.

F: O; live foods of all kinds, flake food, tablet food, freeze-dried food.

S: None.

T: 24-26° C, **L:** ♂ 8 cm, ♀ 5 cm, **A:** 80 cm, **R:** b, **D:** 4
73-77° F, ♂ 3", ♀ 2", 31",

Neolamprologus savoryi savoryi (POLL, 1949)

Syn.: *Lamprologus savoryi savoryi.*

Hab.: Africa, Lake Tanganyika (endemic). The species inhabits the near shore area of the rocky zone. There the animals lead a seclusive life.

F.I.: Probably in 1958 with *Neolamprologus brichardi.*

Sex: Based on exterior characteristics, determination of the sexes is impossible. According to SOMERMAYER (1980): Buntbarsche Bulletin no. 79, 9-10, the dorsal and anal fins are more elongated in the ♂.

Soc. B.: Territorial; towards conspecifics and other cichlids of the rocky littoral zone, they are usually agreeable. Only aggressive when spawning. The species does not bother plants. Cave spawner; nuclear family.

M: Needs stone structures with many crevices and caves. If kept in pairs, the tanks should have a length of 50 cm (20"). Use unobtrusive vegetation since the fish require free swimming space. Plants other than algae do not occur in its natural biotope. This cichlid can also be maintained in a community tank, but because of its relatively large territory, the aquarium as to be at least 120 cm (47") long. Associate with *Julidochromis, Lamprologus* and *Telmatochromis* species.

B: 24-26° C (75-79° F); water up to 18° dGH and a pH of 7.3 to 8.5. Breeding has been sporadic, attributed to the infrequent imports of *L. savoryi.* For this reason, finding suitable breeding pairs is difficult. JACH (1979): Das Aquarium **13**, 153-154 gives a detailed spawning report.

F: Omnivore; eats live foods of all kinds as well as flake food, fish and crustacean meat.

S: The species has the same deep black edges on the operculum that one finds on *Neolamprologus brichardi.*

T: 23-26° C, **L:** 9, **A:** 50 cm, **R:** b, m, **D:** 2
73-79° F, 3 ", 20",

Lamprologus ornatipinnis

Neolamprologus savoryi savoryi

Neolamprologus sexfasciatus (TREWAVAS & POLL, 1952)
Six-Bar Lamprologus, Sexfasciatus

Syn.: *Lamprologus sexfasciatus.*

Hab.: Africa; in the southern part of Lake Tanganyika (endemic). The species occurs in near shore areas of the rock littoral between 2 and 3 meters, to a maximum of 5 m (2.2-3.3 to a max. of 5.5 yd) depth.

F.I.: 1975 by a group of German aquarists.

Sex: The sexes are difficult to distinguish based on external characteristics. In its natural habitat, adult ♂♂ are always larger than ♀♀.

Soc. B.: Territorial; quite aggressive during spawning, but more peaceful at other times. The species does not harm or eat plants. Cave spawner; nuclear family.

M: Build stone structures along the back of the aquarium to provide caves, crevices and niches of varying sizes. In its natural biotope, plants other than algae are absent. Nevertheless, moderate planting with species that grow on stones is possible (*Anubias, Microsorium pteropus*). Preserve free swimming space. Bottom of sand or fine gravel. Associate with *Julidochromis*, other *Neolamprologus, Spathodus* and *Telmatochromis* species.

B: Has only sporadically been successful. It is the opinion of STAECK and LINKE that deficient nutrition, resulting from association with unsuitable species (= fast feeders, e.g., *Tropheus*), is the culprit. Sexually mature animals pair up and create a territory together which has the spawning cave as its center. The young are cared for and raised by both partners. The parents do not move about with their school but remain with their young in their established territory.

F: Hardy feeder that accepts any live food. Small snails are especially relished. After a certain adaptation period, the animals also accept flake food. Continue feeding with minced fish and crustacean meat (shrimp), beef heart, etc.

S: *N. sexfasciatus* is closely related to *Neolamprologus tretocephalus*. Both species have a similar coloration. The main difference between them is that *N. sexfasciatus* has 6 crossbands while *N. tretocephalus* has only 5. STAECK captured specimens of *N. sexfasciatus* in the vicinity of Kipili (southeast coast/Tanzania) which instead of the green-white base color, showed a lemon-yellow base coloration.

T: 23-26° C, **L:** 15 cm, **A:** 100 cm, **R:** b, m, **D:** 2-3
73-79° F, 6", 39",

Neolamprologus wauthioni (POLL, 1949)

Syn.: *Lamprologus wauthioni.*

Hab.: Africa; Lake Tanganyika (endemic). The animals are inhabitants of the sandy littoral zone where they depend on empty *Neothauma* shells. The capture sites of the species are located 1-8 km (0.6-5.0 mi) offshore. *N. wauthioni* is encountered at an average depth of 35 m (38 yd).

F.I.: 1984.

Sex: No external characteristics are known. The sexes only differ in their size.

Soc. B.: Territorial; the territories are defended against intruders. Cave spawner.

M: As with other snail dwelling species (*"magarae"*, *brevis, ornatipinnis*, etc.). The decoration of the aquarium is of secondary importance, but a 4-8 cm (1²/3"-3") layer of sand on the bottom is important to successfully breed *N. wauthioni.* In larger aquaria the species can be successfully housed with peaceful species.

B: 24-26° C (75-79° F); it is similar to other "snail dwellers". *Neolamprologus wauthioni* erects its snail house on a sand mountain.

F: O; live foods of all kinds (small crustacea, *Tubifex*, mosquito larvae), flake food, tablet food, freeze-dried and frozen food.

S: See under **B** (house on sand mountain).

T: 24-26° C, **L:** ♂ 7 cm, ♀ 4.5 cm, **A:** 60 cm, **R:** b, **D:** 3
75-79° F, ♂ 2³/4", ♀ 1³/4", 24",

Neolamprologus sexfasciatus

Neolamprologus wauthioni

Limnochromis auritus (BOULENGER, 1901)
Auritus

Syn.: *Paratilapia aurita, Pelmatochromis auritus.*

Hab.: Africa; Lake Tanganyika (endemic). The animals are inhabitants of the sublittoral benthic zone. They occur over sandy or muddy ground. Depths between 30 and 50 m (33-55 yd) are preferred. The maximum proven depth was over 100 m (109 yd).

F.I.: Probably already in 1958.

Sex: The species is monomorphic. ♂ and ♀ are difficult to distinguish from the exterior. Pelvic fins of the ♂♂ are said to be longer.

Soc. B.: Territorial. The animals are sedate and peaceful; at spawning time, however, intraspecific aggressions do occur. Specialized ovophile mouthbrooder; nuclear family.

M: Arrange the background of the tank with stone structures, forming some caves and other hiding places. Use roots as decoration. The sides of the tank can be planted; the bottom should be fine sand with a large open area. Regular partial water changes. Medium-hard (10-20° dGH) and alkaline (pH above 7.0) water. Do not associate with overly aggressive species.

B: 25-27° C (77-81° F); aquarium breeding has not been successful very often. Reliable reports are correspondingly sparse. The animals are specialized mouthbrooders. Both sexes brood the eggs in their mouth. Eggs and larvae are exchanged several times between the ♂ and ♀. Sometimes both parents care for part of the spawn simultaneously. Up to 300 eggs. A very detailed breeding report is given by VRIESMAN (1980) in the magazine "Cichlidae" **6**: 38-48. However, the article is written in Flemish.

F: C, O; live foods of all kinds, frozen food, freeze-dried food, shrimp, beef heart, flake food.

S: *Limnochomis auritus* is one of the big exceptions: a mouthbrooder that forms a nuclear family.

T: 24-26° C, **L:** 14 cm, **A:** 100 cm, **R:** b, m, **D:** 2
75-79° F, 5 ", 39",

Continuation of page 938:
Neolamprologus modestus

F: Live foods (insect larvae, *Daphnia*, *Artemia*, *Cyclops*), fish and crustacean meat (shrimp), flake and tablet foods.

S: Animals originating from the southern part of the lake have notoriously yellow colored pectoral fins. This coloration is lacking in animals from the northern part of the lake; their pectorals are transparent.

T: 23-25° C, **L:** 12, **A:** 100 cm, **R:** b, m, **D:** 2-3
73-77° F, 4 3/4", 39",

Limnochromis auritus

Neolamprologus modestus

Labidochromis cf. *pallidus*

Buccochromis lepturnus ♂ (without text)

Melanochromis chipokae (without photo) JOHNSON, 1975

Chipokae Mbuna

Syn.: *"Melanochromis chipoka"* (trade name!).

Hab.: Africa; Lake Malawi (endemic). Has only been found at the Chindunga Rocks, an underwater reef in the proximity of the town Chipoka (name!). The animals inhabitat the rocky littoral zones.

F.I.: At the beginning of the '70's.

Sex: Clear sexual dichromatism; ♂♂ are predominantly blue-black and have two light blue, longitudinal stripes on the upper half of the body; anal fin has clear egg spots. ♀♀ are sand- to gold-yellow and have 2 black longitudinal stripes.

Soc. B.: Territorial, ♂♂ are agamic; therefore, always keep one ♂ with several ♀♀. *M. chipokae* is especially aggressive in small aquaria. These aggressions are directed towards conspecific as well as heterospecific animals. The species does not eat plants or dig. Ovophile mouthbrooder; matriarch family.

M: Stone structures with many caves, crevices and niches that extend to the water surface, but leave plenty of free swimming space in the foreground. Plants in the tank are possible but not necessary, since there is no dense plant growth in its natural biotope. Bottom of sand or fine-grained gravel. House only with robust Malawi species from the rocky littoral zone (large *Melanochromis, Pseudotropheus, Petrotilapia tridentiger* or *Cyrtocara* species).

B: 25-28° C (77-82° F); water with 7-18° dGH and pH 7.3-8.5 is recommended. Always maintain 1 ♂ and several ♀♀. Propagation is easy. It can also be accomplished in a community tank; however, shortly before the completion of larval development, the ♀ should be transferred to a separate tank to allow it to conclude caring for the young without large losses. Courtship and egg-laying are as with other mbuna cichlids from Lake Malawi. Fertilization of the 20-40 eggs is by the egg spot method. Development of the eggs in the mouth of the ♀ takes about 20 days at 26° C (79° F). Only the mother cares for the young. The mother ceases care soon after the young abandon her buccal cavity. Feed with sieved small crustacea and crumbled flake food.

F: Live foods of all kinds (crustacea, insect larvae, *Tubifex*, etc.), fish and crustacean meat in small pieces, flake food.

S: None.

T: 24-26° C, L: 15 cm, A: 120 cm, R: all, D: 2-3
75-79° F, 6", 47",

Melanochromis loriae ♂ (trade name *M. chipokae)*

Melanochromis melanopterus TREWAVAS, 1935

Black Mbuna

Syn.: None.

Hab.: Africa; it has only been found in the southwestern part of Lake Malawi (endemic). The species inhabits the near shore area of the rocky habitat.

F.I.: Probably as by-catch already in 1958.

Sex: Marked sexual dichromatism; ♂ is predominantly black with a light blue longitudinal band and has an anal fin with pronounced egg spots; ♀ has a light background and two black longitudinal bands.

Soc. B.: Territorial; the animals show strong intraspecific aggressions and are quite rough towards heterospecifics. The species neither digs nor harms plants. Agamic, ovophile mouthbrooder; matriarch family.

M: As indicated for *Melanochromis chipokae*. It is best to keep them in a community tank with other robust mbuna cichlids and larger *"Haplochromis"* species.

B: 25-28° C (77-82° F); water values as for other *Melanochromis* species. Agamic mouthbrooder. Always keep 1 ♂ with several ♀♀. Courtship and spawning behavior is the same as other mouthbrooders of Lake Malawi. The up to 60 eggs are fertilized by the egg spot method. Development time of the eggs in the mother's mouth is about 3 weeks at 26° C (79° F). The released young are relatively large and can be fed small water fleas, *Cyclops*, and crumbled flake food. Brood care ends soon after the young leave the mother's mouth.

F: Live foods (*Daphnia*, *Artemia*, *Gammarus*, mosquito larvae, moderately *Tubifex* and Enchytraea, small earthworms), minced fish and crustacean meat (shrimp), flake food.

S: The ♂♂ of *Melanochromis melanopterus* exist in two color morphs. These differ by the coloration of the dorsal fin: in one morph it is blue and in the other orange-brown.

T: 24-26° C, **L:** 13 cm, **A:** 120 cm, **R:** all, **D:** 2-3
75-79° F, 5", 47",

Melanochromis parallelus BURGESS & AXELROD, 1976

Parallel-Striped Mbuna

Syn.: None.

Hab.: Africa; Lake Malawi (endemic).

F.I.: Not clear.

Sex: Clear sexual dichromatism. ♂♂ are blue and black striped; the ♀♀ are whitish-yellow and black striped. ♂♂ have distinct egg spots on the anal fin.

Soc. B.: Territorial, the animals are quite robust and aggressive. They do not dig or bother plants. Agamic, ovophile mouthbrooder; matriarch family.

M: As indicated for *Melanochromis chipokae*.

B: Similar to *M. chipokae* or *M. melanopterus*.

F: O; live foods of all kinds, small pieces of fish meat and crustacea, frozen food, flake food.

S: *Melanochromis parallelus* was called the black-white auratus in American reports until its scientific description (because of its similarity to *Melanochromis auratus*).

T: 24-26° C, **L:** 12, **A:** 100 cm, **R:** all, **D:** 2-3
75-79° F, 4 3/4", 39",

Melanochromis melanopterus ♂

Melanochromis parallelus ♂

Paranochromis caudifasciatus (BOULENGER, 1913)
Banded-Tail Nanochromis

Syn.: *Pelmatochromis caudifasciatus, Nanochromis caudifasciatus.*

Hab.: Africa; southern Cameroon, in the tributaries of the Nyong River.

F.I.: 1975 by Otto Gartner, Vienna, Austria.

Sex: Marked sexual dimorphism; the ♂♂ are larger and differently colored and have a metallic iridescent band in the hard-rayed part of the dorsal fin.

Soc. B.: Territorial, the species is relatively shy and peaceful. Only the ♂♂ are often very aggressive among themselves. The species does not bother plants. Cave spawner, patriarch-matriarch family.

M: A bottom of fine gravel, cave-like stone structures and coconut shells with a 3 cm (1 ") diameter hole are important pieces of decoration. Needs generous edge and background vegetation. The water should be clean, rich in oxygen and have a slight water movement; pH of about 6.0, hardness less than 2° dGH; regular water changes. It should be mentioned that the maintenance of *N. caudifasciatus* is problematic.

B: 24-26° C (75-79° F); soft acid water is required for successful breeding. A harmonizing pair claims a stone cave or coconut shell where they spawn after intense courtship. Over 100 eggs are usually laid on the ceiling of the cave. The ♀ cares for the spawn and remains alone in the cave while the ♂ controls the territory and defends the spawning site. At 25° C (77° F) the young leave the cave for the first time with their mother after 9-10 days. Now the ♂ will also actively participate in the care of the young. Feed the young with *Artemia* nauplii and pulverized flake food. With good food, the young grow quickly.

F: O; hardy live foods (mosquito larvae, small earthworms, *Tubifex*, mayfly larvae, *Daphnia*), shrimp; flake food is also readily eaten.

T: 23-25° C, L: ♂ 11 cm, ♀ 8 cm, A: 80 cm, R: b, D: 3-4 (C)
73-77° F, ♂ 4¹/₃", ♀ 3", 31",

Melanochromis parallelus ♀

Paranochromis caudifasciatus

Nanochromis transvestitus ♂

Limbochromis robertsi (THYS & LOISELLE, 1971)
Robert's Nanochromis

Syn.: *Nanochromis robertsi.*

Hab.: West Africa; according to LINKE & STAECK (1981), it probably exclusively inhabits the southwestern Kumasi region in west central Ghana. One biotope is the Birim River; its headwaters flow through secondary forests and plantations and fill a number of pools void of plants.

F.I.: 1975 one ♀ by Horst Linke, Berlin, Germany. ♂♂ have not yet been imported to Europe.

Sex: ♂♂ are larger and have a forked tail fin. They are more colorful and have more yellow in the fins and a pointed and conical genital papilla; ♀ is smaller, tail fin is slightly indented, less yellow in the fins, genital papillae longer and tube-shaped.

Soc. B.: Territorial, one ♂ tolerates 2 to 3 ♀♀ in his territory. Cave spawner, probably paternal-matriarch family.

M: Bottom of light sand or fine-grained gravel to 2 mm (1/16"); some large stones placed directly on the bottom of the aquarium; decorate with roots. Vegetation can be waived since it is absent in its natural habitat. In its natural biotope, the water course is overgrown with emerged short plants. Water should be very clean and clear, pH of about 6 and a hardness of around 5° dGH. In nature, *N. robertsi* is found with *Barbus walkeri, Epiplatys chaperi* and *Amphilius atesuensis.*

B: In the wild, ♂♂ claim large territories in which 2-3 large ♀♀ and several medium young are tolerated. Within the large territory of the ♂, several ♀♀ maintain breeding territories with corresponding spawning caves. Younger ♂♂ pretend to be ♀♀; thus they are tolerated in the territory of a dominate ♂.

F: Live foods of all kinds: mosquito larvae, *Daphnia*, *Cyclops*, *Artemia*, *Tubifex*, Enchytraea.

S: The tail fin of the ♂♂ is, as in some *Apistogramma* species, elongated into two wimples.

T: 22-25° C, L: ♂ 11 cm, ♀ 8 cm, A: 120 cm, R: b, D: 2-3
72-77° F, ♂ 4 1/3", ♀ 3", 47",

Nanochromis transvestitus STEWART & ROBERTS, 1984

Syn.: None.

Hab.: Africa; Zaire, only known from Lake Maji-ndombe (previously Lake Inonongo or Lake Leopold II).

F.I.: Probably 1985.

Sex: Pronounced sexual dimorphism is present. ♂♂ grow larger and are plain in color; ♀♀ are smaller and more beautifully colored (photo).

Soc. B.: Territorial, the species is relatively peaceful. Occasional quarrels occur between ♂♂. The animals are cave spawners; probably paternal-matriarch family.

M: Needs an aquarium with fine sand and plenty of edge and background vegetation. Build caves of stone structures and other cave-shaped hiding places. The water should be clean with a pH of 6.5-7, hardness to 10° dGH. Because of its small size, keep in a species tank or associate with other peaceful fishes.

B: No reports are presently available on a successful aquarium spawn.

F: O; not overly large live foods of all kinds, frozen food, freeze-dried food and also flake food.

S: *Nanochromis transvestitus* is one of the smallest known cichlids. The "traded" coloration is notorious. In this species, in contrast to all other representatives of the genus, the ♀♀ are more brightly and strikingly colored. The species name, *transvestitus,* makes reference to the reversed sexual dichromatism.

T: 24-26° C, L: ♂ 4 cm, ♀ 3.5 cm, A: 50 cm, R: b, D: 2-3
75-79° F, ♂ 1 2/3", ♀ 1 1/3", 20",

Limbochromis robertsi

Nanochromis transvestitus ♀; ♂ on previous photo page

Neetroplus nematopus GÜNTHER, 1866
Little Lake Cichlid

Syn.: *Neetroplus fluviatilis, N. nicaraguensis.*

Hab.: Central America; in rivers and lakes of the Central American drainage system, especially of Nicaragua and Costa Rica.

F.I.: 1976.

Sex: The ♂♂ grow larger and have strongly elongated dorsal and anal fins.

Soc. B.: Territorial, outside of the spawning season the animals are relatively amiable; during the reproductive period, they are very aggressive towards other tankmates. Cave spawner; nuclear family, both parents initially care for the spawn; then one animal takes over.

M: Needs aquaria with roomy caves in stone. Decorate with dense vegetation of tough species in sections. Some roots and round pebbles and a bottom of coarse sand should be added. Good filtration. No special demands are placed on water composition: hardness 10-20° dGH, pH 7.0-7.5.

B: 26-28° C (79-82° F); water values as indicated above. The aquarium should be as large as possible. During the three to four day courtship, the animals completely change their coloration. Out of the positive normal coloration (light body with dark band), a negative (dark body with light band) evolves which is maintained for the entire duration of brood care. Spawning occurs on a vertical or slightly overhanging site of the spawning cave. The 50-60 eggs are quite large and transparent, but not fastened on their pole. The larvae hatch after five or six days (!) and are free-swimming after an additional week. The offspring's bond to the parents is slight, but strongly developed to the immediate vicinity of the cave. According to SCHMETTKAMP (1978): DCG-Information 9 (2): Cichliden von A-Z, four different forms of brood care exist. Feed the young with *Artemia* nauplii and ground flake food.

F: O; live foods of any kind, scraped beef heart, flake food.

S: Since the revision by ROGERS (1981): Copeia no. 2, 286-296, the genus *Neetroplus* is monotypic. The previously valid species *N. fluviatilis* MEEK, 1912 and *N. panamensis* MEEK & HILDEBRAND, 1913 were repealed. *N. fluviatilis* is a synonym of *N. nematopus*, and *N. panamensis* is a synonym of *Cichlasoma panamensis*.

T: 24-26° C, **L:** ♂ 11 cm, ♀ 8 cm, **A:** 90 cm, **R:** b, **D:** 2
75-79° F, ♂ 4 1/3", ♀ 3", 35",

Neetroplus nematopus, normal coloration

Neetroplus nematopus, brood care coloration.

Neochromis nigricans (BOULENGER, 1906)

Syn.: *Tilapia nigricans, Haplochromis nigricans, Tilapia simotes.*

Hab.: Africa; Lake Victoria and Victoria Nile (endemic). The animals preferentially inhabit the rocky shores.

F.I.: About 1972.

Sex: Pronounced sexual dichromatism. Courting ♂♂ are darker and have a metallic blue-green sheen on the sides; the anal fin is red and has yellow egg spots. ♀♀ are olive-green with a yellowish anal fin and do not have egg spots.

Soc. B.: Nothing is known about the social behavior of *N. nigricans*. It is probably similar to that of other haplochromines from Lake Victoria. In all likelihood, the animals are mouthbrooders with a matriarch family.

M: As for *Haplochromis obliquidens.*

B: The species has not yet been bred in an aquarium. It is not likely to be difficult in appropriately decorated aquaria.

F: O; in the wild the animals feed on aufwuchs (biocover).In captivity they can become accustomed to ordinary cichlid foods; in addition, vegetable matter should be fed.

S: As an aufwuchs feeder, *N. nigricans* has a long and coiled intestine. *Neochromis nigricans* is closely related to *Neochromis serridens* (REGAN, 1925) from Lake Edward.

T: 24-26° C, **L:** 12 cm, **A:** 100 cm, **R:** b, m, **D:** 2-3
75-79° F, 4 3/4", 39",

Ophthalmotilapia nasuta (POLL & MATTHES, 1962)

Long-Nosed Gold-Tip Cichlid

Syn.: *Ophthalmochromis nasutus.*

Hab.: Africa; Lake Tanganyika (endemic). The species inhabits the near shore areas of the rocky littoral zone. It prefers depths between 2 and 5 m (2.2-5.5 yd).

F.I.: Probably 1972 or 1973.

Sex: Pronounced sexual dimorphism; ♂♂ have extremely elongated pelvic fins whose ends sport broadened yellow tips; the dorsal, anal and caudal fin tips are clearly elongated; the ♂♂ are darker. The ♀♀ are clearly a lighter color, do not have elongated ventral fins, and the rays of the unpaired fins are less elongated and pointed.

Soc. B.: Only territorial during spawning time; otherwise, the animals live together in a loose group. ♂♂ are agamic. Therefore, always keep 1 ♂ with several ♀♀. At spawning time, the animals are quarrelsome towards conspecific and heterospecific fishes and will dig. Ovophile mouthbrooder; matriarch family.

M: The animals can only be cared for in large aquaria with a lot of free swimming space. Provide rock structures with many caves and crevices as background and a bottom of sand or fine-grained gravel. Vegetation is not absolutely necessary, but it should only consist of low growing species, if provided. Plants that fasten to stones (*Anubias* species, *Microsorium pteropus*) are best. Combine with *Chalinochromis, Julidochromis* and medium-sized *Lamprologus* species.

B: EYSEL (1982) reports a successful spawn in DCG-Informationen **13** (5): 81-87. Details can be obtained from this informative article. The reproductive behavior of *O. nasuta* is very similar to that of *Ophthalmotilapia ventralis.*

F: O; omnivore which feeds primarily on insects, mollusks and plants. In nature, the species feeds on detritus. It is important that *O. nasutus* receives enough food. The animals also eat fish and crustacean meat, freeze-dried and flake foods.

S: *Ophthalmotilapia nasuta* can easily be distinguished from *O. ventralis* by a fleshy appendage which extends beyond the mouth. This proboscis is more developed in ♂♂ than in ♀♀. *O. ventralis* lacks such a proboscis.

T: 24-26° C, **L:** 18, **A:** 150 cm, **R:** b, m, **D:** 3-4
75-79° F, 7", 59",

Neochromis nigricans ♂

Ophthalmotilapia nasuta

Schwetzochromis stormsi (BOULENGER, 1902)

Syn.: *Orthochromis polyacanthus, Haplochromis polyacanthus, Tilapia stormsi, Haplochromis stormsi, Rheohaplochromis polyacanthus.*

Hab.: Africa; Lake Mweru, Zaire (Stanley Pool).

F.I.: Probably in 1982. First pictured in DATZ 10/1982.

Sex: No certain ones are known.

Soc. B.: The animals are territorial and expel conspecifics and heterospecifics from their resting places. ♂♂ are agamic; ♀♀ are mouthbrooders. Matriarch family.

M: Gravel or sandy bottom with stones, whereby the stones should form caves and other hiding places. Use shallow tanks with a large surface area; perhaps a current should be created with a pump (rheophilic fish). Medium-hard (up to 15° dGH) and slightly acid (pH 6.5) water is suggested. Association with other fishes is possible.

B: Bernd Rödling from Friedberg, Germany (written communication) reports a successful spawn in the aquarium. A 250 l (65 gal) tank was furnished with slate structures; the bottom consisted of coarse gravel and *Vallisneria*. Water temperature was 26-28° C (79-82° F). The water was medium-hard (12° dGH) and slightly alkaline (pH 7.5). Every 3 weeks 2/3 of the water was exchanged. After eggs were discovered in the ♀'s mouth, it was transferred into a smaller aquarium. After about 10 days the young were released from the mouth. 21 young survived which were 1.5 cm (2/3") long approximately 6 weeks after being free-swimming. Rear the young with usual foods.

F: O; live foods of all kinds, freeze-dried, frozen, flake and tablet foods.

S: None.

T: 22-27° C, **L:** 12 cm, **A:** 120 cm, **R:** b, **D:** 2-3
72-80° F, 5", 50",

Microgeophagus ramirezi ♂. This beautiful South American was also called *Papiliochromis ramirezi*.

Pelvicachromis humilis (BOULENGER, 1916)
Yellow Krib

Syn.: *Pelmatochromis humilis.*

Hab.: West Africa; Liberia, southeastern Guinea and Sierra Leone. The animals inhabit slow-flowing, oxygen-rich water ways which flow through forest and brush land as well as plantation regions.

F.I.: 1962 by Erhard Roloff, Karlsruhe, Germany.

Sex: ♂♂ have pointed pelvic fins and pointed, elongated dorsal and anal fins; ♀ has rounded ventral fins and slightly rounded dorsal and anal fins.

Soc. B.: Territorial, forms pairs; the animals are amiable, turning aggressive only at spawning time. They dig during this time. However, they do not bother plants. Cave spawner; patriarch-matriarch family.

M: Maintain the animals in roomy aquaria. The water level is of secondary importance (from 40 cm; 16"). Bottom of dark fine-grained gravel. Caves, niches and shelter of rounded stones. Gravel and stones must be free of calcium. Acid test: if the material foams when a drop of acid is placed on it, it contains calcium; if it does not foam, it is free of calcium. Decorate with bogroots. Dense side vegetation and partial vegetation between the stone structures, perhaps some floating plants to dim the light. Good filtration and strong water movement; substrate heater. Water soft (about 5° dGH) and slightly acid (pH 6.5-6.9). Every 1 to 2 weeks perform a water change of 1/3 the tank volume. Associate with other *Pelvicachromis* and *Chromidotilapia* species.

B: 26-28° C (79-82° F); dark substrate (up to 3 mm; 1/8" gravel), 1-2 stone caves filled with gravel. Substrate heater to inhibit fast proliferation of bacteria in the substrate. In addition to the spawning caves, additional hiding alternatives of stones, roots and vegetation should be offered so the ♀ can hide from the aggressive ♂. Breeding water should be very soft (1-2° dGH) and slightly acid (pH 6.0-6.5). Use one pair in the breeding set-up. As dither fishes and confidence builders, add some livebearers or labyrinth fishes. Breeding is not very easy. Prior to spawning, the gravel is dug out of a cave. The ♀ indicates her willingness to spawn by pronounced shivering of her strongly curved body. The ♂ "answers" through shaking movements and a slanted swimming position; afterwards, they spawn in the cave. The ♀ guards the eggs and larvae; after about 8 days, it leaves the cave for the first time with the young. The young are also guided and guarded by the ♂. Guiding by the parents lasts several weeks. Feed the young with *Artemia* nauplii and TetraMin Baby Food.

F: C, O; live foods of any kind: mosquito larvae, adult insects, Enchytraea, *Tubifex*, *Daphnia*, *Cyclops*; flake food and tablet food.

S: 7 color morphs are presently known of *Pelvicachromis humilis.*

T: 24-26° C, L: ♂ 12.5, ♀ 10 cm, A: 120 cm, R: b, D: 2-3
75-79° F, ♂ 5", ♀ 4", 47",

Pelvicachromis humilis, Kasewe color morph

Pelvicachromis humilis, Kenema color morph

Pelvicachromis roloffi (THYS, 1968)

Roloff's Kribensis

Syn.: *Pelmatochromis roloffi.*

Hab.: West Africa; eastern Guinea, Sierra Leone and western Liberia. The animals occur in small water accumulations and flowing waters of plantation regions, brush and forest areas. They stay close to shore among plants and roots.

F.I.: 1968 by Erhard Roloff, Karlsruhe, Germany.

Sex: ♂♂ are larger and their dorsal, anal and pelvic fins are extended and pointed. They have a dark longitudinal band from the head to the caudal peduncle. Adult ♀♀ have a round, violet stomach and almost black, rounded pelvic fins; dorsal and anal fins are not elongated into a point.

Soc. B.: Territorial, forms pairs; a relatively peaceful species, only quarrelsome at spawning time. The animals dig somewhat but leave plants alone. Cave spawner; patriarch-matriarch family.

M: Use fine-grained, calcium-free gravel as substrate. LINKE & STAECK (1981) recommend a substrate heater so that this bottom dwelling species has an oxygen-rich, bacteria-poor substrate. Furnish hiding places of stones and roots. A heavily planted tank is important for the well-being of the animals; perhaps some floating plants (*Pistia* species) should be added to the surface. Requires very soft (1-2° dGH), moderately acid to neutral (pH 5.9-7.0), clear and oxygen-rich water. However, maintenance is also possible in medium-hard water (up to 15° dGH). House with barbs and labyrinth fishes.

B: 25-26° C (77-79° F); water values as indicated above, though hardness should not be above 5° dGH to insure proper development of the eggs and larvae. Spawning is preceded by an extended courtship, whereby the ♀ is the most active partner. The spawning site is cleaned; spawning occurs in a cave. The ♀ guards the eggs and larvae while the ♂ defends the cave and surroundings. Spawns are never very large. After about 1 week, the ♀ leaves the cave for the first time with the young. The young are guided and defended by both parents. Feed the young with micro food, *Artemia* nauplii and TetraMin Baby Food.

F: Live foods: mosquito larvae, mayflies, flies, *Daphnia*, *Cyclops*, *Artemia, Tubifex*, Enchytraea; flake food and tablet food.

S: *P. roloffi* can be distinguished from other *Pelvicachromis* species by the numerous black dots on the base of the dorsal and tail fin. The white border of the dorsal fin, at least in ♀♀, is characteristic for this species.

T: 24-26° C, **L:** ♂ 8.5 cm, ♀ 6 cm, **A:** 100 cm, **R:** b, **D:** 3
75-79° F, ♂ 3 1/3", ♀ 2 1/3", 39",

Petenia splendida (GÜNTHER, 1862)

Red Snook

Syn.: *Astronotus splendida.*

Hab.: Central America; southeastern Mexico, Guatemala, Belize (British Honduras) and Nicaragua.

F.I.: To the USA in 1975.

Sex: Monomorphic; the sexes cannot be distinguished from the exterior.

Soc. B.: A territorial piscivore. Nevertheless, a sedate fish. Open spawner; nuclear family.

M: On the back wall of the aquarium, heavy rockwork with hiding places and shelter are arranged; bottom made of fine-grained gravel; roots provided as decoration. Water up to 15° dGH and neutral to slightly alkaline (pH 7.0-7.5). Because of its predatory nature, a species tank is recommended; otherwise, associate with equal sized cichlids.

B: It is probable that the species has not been bred in an aquarium.

F: C; live foods of all kinds. From a certain size on, fishes are especially relished.

S: Besides a silver-gray normal morph, there is also an orange morph of *Petenia splendida*. The animals can reach 3 kg (6.6 lb) and are a food fish in their home range.

T: 24-26° C, **L:** up to 50 cm, **A:** 150 cm, **R:** b, m, **D:** 4 (C)
75-79° F, up to 20", 59",

Pelvicachromis roloffi, ♂ front, ♀ back

Petenia splendida

Petrochromis famula

MATTHES & TREWAVAS, 1960

Syn.: None.

Hab.: Africa, Lake Tanganyika (endemic). The species has been found in the vicinity of Kigoma (Tanzania) and at the northwest coast of Zaire. The animals are inhabitants of the near shore rocky littoral zone and prefer shallow water.

F.I.: The exact date could not be determined.

Sex: There is relatively clear sexual dimorphism (dichromatism). The ♂♂ are more intensely colored; dorsal, anal and pelvic fins are more elongated; the anal fin has 3-4 egg spots. ♀♀ are clearly paler; dorsal, anal and pelvic fins are less elongated.

Soc. B.: Territorial, this species is strongly aggressive among themselves. These aggressions are somewhat dampened when they are placed with other fishes. The species eats tender plants and plant shoots. The animals are agamic. Ovophile mouthbrooder; matriarch family.

M: Because of its intraspecific aggressions, housing them in a community tank is best. Crevice- and cave-riddled structures built of rock pieces and stone plates are used to provide hiding places. Substrate of sand or fine gravel. If plants are desired, only use robust, tough-leaved specimens; leave plenty of free swimming space. House with lively and robust species from Lake Tanganyika (*Tropheus*) or Lake Malawi (*Melanochromis, Pseudotropheus*).

B: 25-27° C (77-81° F); medium-hard (7-18° dGH) and slightly to moderately alkaline (pH 7.5-8.5) water. Breeding in community aquaria is possible. Keep 1 ♂ and 2-3 ♀♀. Courtship and spawning behavior follows other mouthbrooders of Lake Tanganyika. The ♀ lays as many as 60 eggs which are taken into her mouth; there development takes about 4 weeks at 26° C (79° F). The young are already over 10 mm (1/3") long when first released from the mouth. Feed the young with sieved small crustacea and crumbled flake food.

F: In nature, a specialized aufwuchs feeder; therefore, feed fiber rich fare in the aquarium (*Daphnia*, *Cyclops*, *Artemia*, mosquito larvae). Flake food is also readily accepted. Feed *Tubifex* and Enchytraea as an exception (not enough fiber).

S: So far, five *Petrochromis* species have been described, but new species will be added in the near future. *Petrochromis* are the most specialized aufwuchs feeders of all cichlids.

T: 23-26° C, 73-79° F, **L**: 15 cm, 6", **A**: 100 cm, 39", **R**: b, m, **D**: 3

Petrochromis polyodon

Brown Petrochromis

BOULENGER, 1898

Syn.: *Petrochromis fasciolatus*.

Hab.: Africa; Lake Tanganyika (endemic). The animals are widely distributed throughout the lake. They are inhabitants of the rocky shore zone and prefer shallow water.

F.I.: Probably around 1970.

Sex: ♂ has egg spots on the anal fin.

Soc. B.: Territorial, the fish are very aggressive and bellicose towards conspecifics and heterospecifics; in tanks which are too small, they continue their aggressions to obliteration. *P. polyodon* chews plants. Agamic, ovophile mouthbrooder; matriarch family.

M: Likes large tanks with rockwork offering many caves, niches and hiding places. Maintenance in a community tank is recommended since it allows the fish to distribute their aggressions. Needs a bottom of sand or fine-grained gravel; use only tough vegetation, if at all; conserve free swimming space. Water should be medium-hard to hard (10-20° dGH) and in the alkaline range (pH 7.2-8.5). Only associate with robust fishes.

B: As with *Petrochromis trewavasae*.

F: O; an extreme aufwuchs feeder (biocover feeder) in the wild. Therefore, offer fiber-rich foods (all kinds of small crustacea, mosquito larvae, algae). Flake food, *Tubifex* and Enchytraea should only be fed sporadically because of their low fiber content.

S: None.

T: 23-26° C, 73-79° F, **L**: 21 cm, 8 1/3", **A**: 150 cm, 59", **R**: all, **D**: 3

Petrochromis famula

Petrochromis polyodon

Petrochromis trewavasae POLL, 1948

Syn.: None.

Hab.: Africa; Lake Tanganyika (endemic). To now, the animals have only been found at the southwestern shore in the border area of Zambia and Zaire. The animals inhabit the upper rocky littoral zone.

F.I.: Unknown.

Sex: Not very distinctly divergent. In old ♂♂, the anal and caudal fins are more elongated; the anal fin has egg spots.

Soc. B.: Territorial, the animals tolerate other species, but they are strongly aggressive towards heterospecifics. Agamic, ovophile mouthbrooder; matriarch family.

M: Provide a background of rockwork that extends to the water surface, creating many caves and niches. Demarcate territories with roots; use a sandy bottom; vegetation can be waived; leave free swimming space. Water should not be too soft (from 10° dGH) and nonacidic (pH 7.5-8.5). Associate with other Tanganyikan cichlids.

B: 25-27° C (77-81° F); water values as indicated above. Use one ♂ with several ♀♀. The animals are specialized mouthbrooders. After spawning, the ♀♀ take the relatively large 10-15 eggs into their mouth. At 27° C (81° F) development takes about 4 weeks. The ♀ feeds during that time. The young are roughly 2 cm (3/4") in length when they first leave the mouth of the ♀. Feed the young with sieved small crustacea.

F: O; live foods of all kinds, also frozen, freeze-dried and flake foods.

S: *Petrochromis trewavasae* is the only representative of the genus with a forked caudal fin. Confusion with other members of the genus is not possible. Characteristics of the genus are tricuspid teeth and the large number of hard rays in the dorsal fin.

T: 23-25° C, **L**: 18 cm, **A**: 100 cm, **R**: all, **D**: 2-3
73-77° F, 7", 39",

Pseudosimochromis curvifrons (POLL, 1942)
Thick-Headed Pseudosimochromis

Syn.: *Simochromis curvifrons.*

Hab.: Africa; Lake Tanganyika (endemic). The animals inhabit the rubble zone. They are aufwuchs feeders.

F.I.: Unknown.

Sex: There is a marked difference between ♂♂ and ♀♀. ♀♀ have strongly pronounced bands which are absent in the ♂♂; in addition, the ♂♂ are larger, have longer pelvic fins and a pointed dorsal and anal fin.

Soc. B.: Territorial, intraspecific aggressions are strongly developed. Plant eater. The species does not dig. Ovophile mouthbrooder; matriarch family.

M: Rockwork with many caves and crevices as hiding places; strong illumination from above to foment algae growth; maintain free swimming space; use gravel or sand for substrate; plants in the tank should be waived. Water medium-hard (about 15° dGH) and slightly alkaline (pH 7.5-9.0). Keep together with *Simochromis* and/or *Tropheus* species.

B: The species has been bred, and a report published by BRÜHLMEYER (1978): Aquarien Terrarien **25** (8): 268-269.

F: O, H; live foods of all kinds, algae, supplementary vegetable foods (blanched lettuce, spinach; rolled oats), Tetra Conditioning Food or similar foods.

S: *P. curvifrons* is sensitive to copious water additions.

T: 24-26° C, **L**: 14 cm, **A**: 100 cm, **R**: b, m, **D**: 3
75-79° F, 5", 39",

Petrochromis trewavasae

Pseudosimochromis curvifrons ♂

Pseudotropheus heteropictus STAECK, 1980

Syn.: None.

Hab.: Africa; Lake Malawi (endemic). The animals have only been found in the upper littoral zone of Tumbi Island.

F.I.: 1975.

Sex: Well developed sexual dichromatism. The ♂♂ are differently colored than the yellow ♀♀.

Soc. B.: Territorial, the animals are quite aggressive among themselves. They do not bother plants. Ovophile mouthbrooder; matriarch family.

M: As indicated for *Pseudotropheus lombardoi*.

B: As with *Ps. lombardoi*. The animals are specialized mouthbrooders. The ♀ carries the 25-30 eggs in her mouth. At 27° C (81° F), the eggs remain in the mouth for about 2 weeks and the young are guarded for an additional 2-3 days after being released.

F: O; live foods of all kinds, freeze-dried food, frozen food and flake food.

S: There is a certain similarity between the appearance of ♂ *P. heteropictus* and *Pseudotropheus socolofi*. However, in the latter species, the dark crossbands are missing and there is no sexual dichromatism.

T: 24-26° C, **L**: 10 cm, **A**: 100 cm, **R**: m, b, **D**: 2-3
75-79° F, 4", 39",

Pseudotropheus livingstonii (BOULENGER, 1899)
Livingstone's Mbuna

Syn.: *Tilapia livingstonii*.

Hab.: Africa; Lake Malawi (endemic). The species seems to inhabit the sandy regions of the coast.

F.I.: 1964 (?).

Sex: The distinct sexual dimorphism of other *Pseudotropheus* species is absent. The ♂♂ have egg spots on the anal fin, and they are somewhat larger and more intensely colored.

Soc. B.: Territorial, the species is less unsociable and quarrelsome than other *Pseudotropheus* species. The animals do not bother plants or dig. Agamic, ovophile mouthbrooders; matriarch family.

M: Best kept in a roomy community tank with rockwork. The structures can reach the water surface. The presence of numerous caves and crevices is important. Plant tough vegetation, but it can be waived. Needs a sandy bottom and some snail shells as additional shelter. The water should be medium-hard to hard (12-20° dGH) and medium alkaline to alkaline (pH 8.0-9.0). Keep mbuna cichlids as tankmates.

B: 25-28° C (77-82° F); water conditions as indicated under **M**. The set-up consists of one ♂ and several ♀♀. Mouthbrooder, the ♀ takes the up to 60 eggs into her mouth; fertilization is achieved by the egg spot method. Development takes about three weeks at 26° C (79° F). At this time the young are released for the first time from the mother's mouth. Care continues for about 8 days. Feed the young with small crustacea and crumbled flake food.

F: O; live foods of all kinds, vegetable fare, freeze-dried food, frozen and flake foods.

S: During danger, small *Pseudotropheus livingstonii* seek empty shells of the *Lanistes* snail that live in the sandy littoral of the lake.

T: 22-26° C, **L**: 15 cm, **A**: 100 cm, **R**: all, **D**: 2
72-79° F, 6", 39",

Pseudotropheus heteropictus ♂

Pseudotropheus livingstonii

Pseudotropheus lombardoi BURGESS, 1977

Syn.: *"Pseudotropheus lil(i)ancinius"*, *"Ps. ken(n)yi"* (trade name!).

Hab.: Africa, Lake Malawi (endemic). The species only occurs in the rocky shore zone of the Mbenji Islands. The fish are aufwuchs feeders.

F.I.: 1974.

Sex: Very pronounced sexual dichromatism; the ♂ has a luminous yellow anal fin with egg spots; ♀ has a sky-blue base coloration with 6 black crossbands.

Soc. B.: The animals show strong intraspecific aggressions, and the resulting quarrels can cause major damage. The ♂♂, but also the ♀♀, are aggressive. In aquaria which are too small, *Ps. lombardoi* is also quarrelsome towards other species. The animals sometimes eat tender plants shoots. Agamic, ovophile mouthbrooder; matriarch family.

M: Keep the species in a large community tank since the presence of other species somewhat distracts *Ps. lombardoi* from its intraspecific aggressions. The back wall of the aquarium should have extensive rockwork and outcroppings to provide numerous caves and crevices. These structures can ascend to just below the water surface. Tough vegetation is possible but not required. Only associate with robust cichlids (*Labeotropheus fuelleborni, Melanochromis chipokae, M. melanopterus, Pseudotropheus elongatus, Ps. zebra*).

B: 25-28° C (77-82° F); water chemistry as with other *Pseudotropheus* species (medium-hard to hard: 10-20° dGH and moderately alkaline (pH about 8)). The animals have no bond to the breeding partner, so always keep one ♂ and several ♀♀. Spawning occurs on a flat stone. Up to 50 eggs are laid and taken into the mouth by the ♀ and fertilized by the familiar egg spot method. Development takes about 20-25 days at 26° C (79° F). After this time, the shiny blue young are released for the first time from the mouth, are about 1 cm (1/3") long and can be fed small crustacea and crumbled flake food.

F: Nonproblematic feeder which, besides live foods of all kinds, readily accepts fish and crustacean meat as well as flake food. Regular feeding with carotene-containing foods maintains the luminous yellow color of the ♂.

S: The sexual dichromatism of *Ps. lombardoi* is in clear contrast to that of the remaining mbuna cichlids. In many *Melanochromis* and *Pseudotropheus* species, as well as both *Labeotropheus* species, the ♂♂ are blue and the ♀♀ are yellow or orange. In *Ps. lombardoi*, however, the ♂♂ are shiny yellow while the ♀♀ are blue. With age, some of the ♀♀ resemble ♂♂ in coloration.

T: 24-26° C, **L:** 15 cm, **A:** 150 cm, **R:** all, **D:** 2-3
75-79° F, 6", 59",

Pseudotropheus microstoma TREWAVAS, 1935

Small-Mouthed Tropheus

Syn.: None.

Hab.: Africa; Lake Malawi (endemic). The animals are inhabitants of the rocky shore.

F.I.: 1964.

Sex: Distinct sexual dichromatism; the ♂'s anal fin has egg spots and is much more iridescent and intensely colored; ♀♀ are a plain yellowish or brownish color.

Soc. B.: Territorial, the animals are aggressive and bellicose among themselves. Agamic, ovophile mouthbrooder; matriarch family.

M: As with *Pseudotropheus lombardoi*.

B: 26-28° C (79-82° F); easily possible. It is similar to other *Pseudotropheus* species. For details, see *Ps. lombardoi*. Fertilization of the eggs follows the egg spot method. Incubation is 17-20 days in the mother's mouth. Care of the young terminates a few days after their first release.

F: O; live foods of all kinds, fish and crustacean meat, frozen food, flake food.

S: *Pseudotropheus microstoma* occurs in two color morphs. The ♂♂ of one morph are a shining lemon yellow, while the ♂♂ of the other morph have an orange-yellow area between the eyes and the base of the pelvic fins. The head and the posterior half of the body are blue. FRYER's opinion is that *Ps. microstoma* is only a morph of *Pseudotropheus tropheops*.

T: 24-26° C, **L:** 13 cm, **A:** 100 cm, **R:** m, b, **D:** 2
75-79° F, 5", 39",

Pseudotropheus lombardoi ♂

Pseudotropheus lombardoi ♀

Pseudotropheus microstoma

Pseudotropheus socolofi JOHNSON, 1974

Eduard's Mbuna

Syn.: *"Pseudotropheus pindani"* (trade name!).

Hab.: Africa; at the east coast of Lake Malawi in Mozambique (endemic). Most capture sites are located near the Likoma Islands. The animals inhabit the upper zone of the rocky littoral. They are aufwuchs feeders.

F.I.: Beginning of the '70's.

Sex: There is no strongly developed sexual dimorphism (dichromatism). The ♂♂ are best separated from the ♀♀ by the 3-4 egg dummies on the anal fin and a distinctly longer pelvic fins.

Soc. B.: Territorial, *Ps. socolofi* is relatively peaceful and usually gets along with conspecific and heterospecific fishes when compared with other *Pseudotropheus* species. The species does not bother plants. Ovophile mouthbrooder; matriarch family.

M: As with *Pseudotropheus lombardoi*. It is important to offer the fish free swimming space. Keep together with *Pseudotropheus* and *Melanochromis* species that are not overly aggressive.

B: 25-28° C (77-82° F); the same water values as with other *Pseudotropheus* species. Breeding is also successful in a biotopically correct community aquarium. Maintain 1 ♂ and several ♀♀. Courtship and spawning behavior parallels other *Pseudotropheus*. The 20-50 eggs are taken into the mouth of the ♀; fertilization of the eggs is by the usual method. Only the ♀ cares for the brood; the young are released from her mouth after about 3 weeks at 26° C (79° F). Brood care now ceases rapidly because the young disappear in cracks and niches. Raise with sieved small crustacea and crumbled flake food. To avoid losses of young, transfer the ♀ after about 2 weeks of brood care to a rearing tank.

F: Live foods of all kinds, freeze-dried foods, frozen food and any kind of flake food.

S: *Pseudotropheus socolofi* differs from most mbuna cichlids by the absence of marked sexual dimorphism (dichromatism).

T: 24-26° C, **L:** 12 cm, **A:** 100 cm, **R:** b, m, t, **D:** 2-3
75-79° F, 4 3/4", 39",

Pterophyllum dumerilii (CASTELNAU, 1855)

Long-Nosed Angelfish

Syn.: *Plataxoides dumerilii, P. leopoldi.*

Hab.: South America; the species inhabits the Amazon region from the Atlantic coast (Belèm, Cacaul) to the Rio Solomoes. The species has also been found in Guyana.

F.I.: Not known.

Sex: There are no recognizable sexual differences outside the spawning season. At spawning time, the ♀♀ are somewhat fuller and have a rounded genital papilla. The genital papilla of the ♂ is pointed.

Soc. B.: Territorial, juveniles live in schools, while adults live in pairs. The species is peaceful and does not dig. Open spawner; nuclear family with pronounced pair bonding.

M: Keep in well-planted, relatively tall tanks; plant the edges and background with tough species (*Sagittaria, Vallisneria*, etc.); leave free swimming space. Decorate with some roots. Water should be soft (about 5° dGH) and slightly acid (pH 6.0). Keep with other *Pterophyllum* or in a species tank.

B: 28-31° C (82-88° F); water values as indicated above. The Swedish aquarist Jörgen ERLANDSSON has breed the species successfully and published the results in Swedish magazines. Breeding is not significantly different from *P. scalare*.

F: C, O; live foods of all kinds, freeze-dried food, flake food, supplemental vegetable fare (lettuce, spinach).

S: In *Pterophyllum dumerilii*, the ascending forehead-dorsal line originating from the snout, and the descending chest line (head profile) only form an angle of 66° to a maximum of 80°; therefore, the animals appear more elongated then *Pterophyllum altum* or *P. scalare*. The dark spot on the base of the dorsal fin is also a characteristic of the species.

T: 26-30° C, **L:** 10 cm, **A:** 80 cm, **H:** 50 cm, **R:** m, **D:** 2-3
79-86° F, 4", 31", 20",

Pseudotropheus socolofi ♂

Pterophyllum dumerilii

Oreochromis alcalicus grahami (BOULENGER, 1912)
Graham's Soda Tilapia

Syn.: *Tilapia grahami, Sarotherodon alcalicus grahami.*

Hab.: Africa; Kenya, in Lake Magadi (endemic). The species occurs in strongly soda containing and alkaline (pH 10.5!) waters of this lake.

F.I.: A few specimens were probably already imported in 1958.

Sex: The ♂♂ are usually larger and brighter colored than the ♀♀. The ♀♀ are smaller, paler, and they are recognizable by their drooping throat area with advanced age (mouthbrooder).

Soc. B.: Territorial, a very quiet and peaceful fish which is sometimes even timid. The animals dig some at spawning time. Ovophile mouthbrooder; matriarch family.

M: Needs a tank with a surface as large as possible and shallow water (about 30 cm; 12"). The tank should have a sandy bottom and perhaps offer some hiding places. These furnishings come quite close to its natural habitat. Through careful acclimation, wild caught specimens can be kept in water values found in other African lakes: 10-20° dGH and pH of 7.5-8.5. Maintenance is best accomplished in a species tank.

T: 24-32° C, **L:** 12 cm, **A:** 90 cm, **R:** b, **D:** 2-3
75-90° F, 4 3/4", 35",

B: 26-30° C (79-86° F); breeding is relatively easy with adapted animals; water values as above. The animals build small spawning pits in the sand, where the eggs are laid. The eggs are very small (1-1.5 mm; 1/16" in diameter), yellow and, according to SCHOLTZE (1981): Aquarien Terrarien **28**, 377, not very numerous. He only counted 20. The average number is probably higher, especially since the eggs are small for a mouthbrooder. The eggs are taken into the mouth of the ♀ and incubated for 23 days at 28° C (82° F). After the release of the young, brood care is terminated. Feed the young with *Artemia* nauplii.

F: O; live foods of all kinds, frozen foods, beef heart, flake food.

S: *Oreochromis alcalicus* has two subspecies: *O. alcalicus alcalicus* (HILGENDORF, 1905), which is found in Lake Natron (Tanzania), and *O. alcalicus grahami* (BOULENGER, 1912). Both sub-species are physiological "wonders". They are neither harmed by pH 10.5 water nor by temperatures above 40° C. Such a high pH value would cauterize the tender gills of most fishes.

Oreochromis aureus (STEINDACHNER, 1864)
Blue Tilapia

Syn.: *Chromis aureus, Sarotherodon aureum, Tilapia aurea, T. aurea exsul, T. kacherba, T. kashabi, T. lemassoni, T. monodi.*

Hab.: Northwest Africa and southwest Asia; Senegal, middle Niger, Chad, Benue, lower Nile and Jordan system.

F.I.: Not known.

Sex: The ♂♂ are more colorful.

Soc. B.: Territorial, these are lively and moderately aggressive (schooling?) fish. Ovophile mouthbrooder; matriarch family (?).

T: 17-24° C, **L:** 40 cm, **A:** 120 cm, **R:** b, m, D: 2
63-75° F, 16", 47",

M: As with *Oreochromis karomo.*

B: There are no reports of this species having been bred in an aquarium. Reproduction is probably not very difficult.

F: O; live foods of all kinds, freeze-dried food, frozen food, vegetable supplementary food, flake and tablet foods.

S: In the Nile delta, *Oreochromis aureus* enters brackish water. The species tolerates chloride values of 6-10 g Cl^-/l in some ponds!

Oreochromis alcalicus grahami

Oreochromis aureum

Oreochromis urolepis hornorum (TREWAVAS, 1966)

Syn.: *Tilapia hornorum, T. hornorum zanzibarica, T. adolfi* STEINDACHNER, 1916, not *T. adolfi* STEINDACHNER, 1909! *Sarotherodon hornorum.*

Hab.: Africa; Tanzania, in the Wami River and in the lakes and rivers of its drainage. The species was introduced into Zanzibar in 1918, as well as into numerous fish ponds throughout the tropics worldwide, especially in Asia.

F.I.: 1979 (?) by G. Eggers and L. Seegers.

Sex: The ♂♂ are more intense and darker colored.

Soc. B.: Territorial; this is a moderately aggressive species. Ovophile mouthbrooder; matriarch family (?)

M: As indicated for *Oreochromis karomo.*

B: No reports of a successful aquarium spawn are available.

F: O; live foods of all kinds, frozen food, plant fare, flake food.

S: *O. u. hornorum* was released in 1918 by the medic Dr. W. M. ADERS in Zanzibar to aid in mosquito control. Prior to 1918, the species was not found in Zanzibar.

T: 22-26° C, 72-79° F, **L:** 17 cm, 6¾", **A:** 100 cm, 39", **R:** b, m, **D:** 2

Oreochromis karomo (POLL, 1948)

Syn.: *Tilapia karomo, Sarotherodon karomo.*

Hab.: Africa; Tanzania, the species lives in the swamps of the Malagarasi, a tributary of Lake Tanganyika.

F.I.: Not known.

Sex: The ♂♂ are significantly more beautiful and darker colored with a strongly elongated (10-15 mm; 1/3"-2/3"), two-part genital papilla; the ♀♀ remain lighter and are recognized, specially during spawning time, by their fuller ventral area.

Soc. B.: Territorial; sometimes the animals are quite rough and bellicose. If sufficient hiding places are not available, fights can end in death of the weaker animal. Ovophile mouthbrooder; matriarch family.

M: Needs bottom of sand or gravel, some larger flat stones as spawning substrate and many hiding places and caves of stones and roots. Plants are not recommended because the animals constantly "redecorate" the aquarium. The animals do not place particular demands on water chemistry, but it should not be acidic. Best kept in pairs in a species tank.

B: RICHTER (1982): Das Aquarium **16**, 19-21 reports extensively on a successful spawn. A flat stone is placed in the aquarium as spawning substrate. For breeding, RICHTER adds one spoon of sea salt for every 10 l (2.5 gal) of water. After intense courtship, spawning occurs on a stone; up to 10 eggs are laid each time. These are yellowish, about 2 mm (1/16") in size and number up to 250. The ♂ brings its genital papilla above or into the vicinity of the eggs and probably fertilizes them at that time. Only then does the ♀ take the eggs into her mouth. The ♂ should be removed to avoid disturbances after spawning is complete. After about 20 days, the young are released from the mother's mouth.

F: O; live foods of all types, frozen food, freeze-dried food, plant fare, flake food.

S: *Oreochromis karomo* belongs to the "flagellum tilapias". In ♂♂, the genital papilla enlarges to a conspicuous two-part genital appendage. It reaches 10-15 mm (1/3"-2/3") in length, is semitransparent, and covered with orange nodules.

T: 22-28° C, 72-82° F, **L:** 30 cm, 12", **A:** 120 cm, 47", **R:** b, m, **D:** 2-3

Oreochromis urolepis hornorum

Oreochromis karomo

Oreochromis leucostictus ♂

Oreochromis leucostictus ♀

Oreochromis leucostictus (TREWAVAS, 1933)
Iridescent Tilapia

Syn.: *Tilapia leucosticta, Sarotherodon leucostictus.*

Hab.: Africa; Uganda: lakes Albert, Edward and George (endemic).

F.I.: 1967 (?).

Sex: Sexually active ♂♂ become black; otherwise, they are olive-gray to olive-green. ♀♀ are lighter.

Soc. B.: Territorial; ♂♂ are constantly courting, but are not excessively aggressive. The animals are active swimmers and like to eat plants. Ovophile mouthbrooder; matriarch family.

M: Needs a roomy tank with a sandy bottom. Provide some flat stones as spawning substrate and hiding places of rocks and roots. The species adapts well to various water compositions, but its water should not be too cold. Medium-hard (around 10° dGH) water with a pH of 7.0-7.5. Keep in a species tank or associate with not overly aggressive cichlids.

B: About 28° C (82° F); water chemistry as listed under M. The species is a mouthbrooder; all of the brood care is accomplished by the ♀. No true partner bond occurs. The ♂ digs a pit that does not serve exclusively as the spawning site. Spawning can also occur on a hard substrate. Spawning is preceded by intense courtship. About 100 eggs are taken into the mouth by the ♀, where they require about 23 days at 24° C (75° F) to develop. After this time, the young are released for the first time from the mouth of the mother. For several days, the young are readmitted into the mouth overnight and during potential danger.

F: O, H; the animals are voracious omnivores: live food, vegetable fare, frozen food, meat, shrimp, beef heart, and flake food.

S: *O. leucostictus* occurs, among other places, in the Mogedo, a water course of the Ruwenzori Falls in west Uganda. Due to hot springs, the otherwise 28° C (82° F) water has areas that reach 73-92° C (163-198° F). The fish traverse 70° C (158°F) areas quickly and can remain for minutes

Oreochromis leucostictus ♂

in areas of 40-50° C (104-122° F) (see WERNER, 1980: DEG-Informationen **11** (8): Cichliden von A-Z).

T: 26-28° C, **L**: 28 cm, **A**: 100 cm, **R**: b, m, **D**: 2
79-82° F, 11", 39",

Continuation of *Sarotherodon melagaster* from page 984:

F: O; live foods of all kinds, frozen food, freeze-dried food, plant fare (algae, lettuce), flake food.

S: Notoriously, the different division of duties between ♂ and ♀ is not absolutely set. Normally only the ♂ broods the eggs in his mouth. If for any reason the ♂ does not collect any or only a part of the eggs, the ♀ may take up the remainder in her mouth. However, ♀♀ are much less reliable brooders than the ♂♂.

T: 23-25° C, **L**: 20 cm, **A**: 100 cm, **R**: b, m, **D**: 2-3
73-77° F, 8", 39",

Sarotherodon melagaster (BLOCH, 1792)
Black-Throat Tilapia

Syn.: *Tilapia melanotheron, T. macrocephala, T. microcephala, T. heudelotii macrocephala, Chromis microcephalus, Melanogenes microcephalus, Sarotherodon melagaster.*

Hab.: West Africa; from the Ivory Coast to Cameroon. The animals primarily inhabit estuaries and coastal lagoons.

F.I.: 1907 by the Vereinigten Zierfischzüchtereien in Conradshöhe of Berlin, Germany.

Sex: ♂♂ grow larger than ♀♀.

Soc. B.: Territorial, during the spawning period, the animals are aggressive towards conspecifics and heterospecifics. They are more peaceful out of spawning season. The species infrequently digs and rarely bothers plants as long as vegetable fare is given. Ovophile mouthbrooder; patriarch family.

M: Give this species a bottom of sand or fine-grained gravel and dense edge and background vegetation with tough species and some hiding places of stones and roots. Good filtration. No major demands are placed on water composition. As the species also enters brackish water, the addition of sea salt is also recommended (1 tablespoon per 10 l; 2.5 gal of water). Maintain in a species tank or house with other west African tilapias.

B: 25-27° C (77-81° F); pair formation occurs during an extended courtship; ripe ♀♀ are clearly more active than ♂♂ at this time. As pair formation proceeds, the ♂ also courts more actively. His aggressions towards other fishes increase, and he helps the ♀ defend the spawning territory. ♀ and ♂ dig a simple pit to lay the eggs in. They are immediately fertilized by the ♂. The eggs have a diameter of 2-3 mm (1/16"-1/8") and are yellowish to greenish colored. In large ♀♀, they can number up to 150. The ♂ takes the spawn into his mouth after spawning. The larvae hatch in the mouth of the father after about 6 days and are released for the first time after about 2 weeks at 26° C (79° F). The fry are not readmitted. The young show no bonding behavior to the father. Feed the young sieved small crustacea.

Continued on page 983.

Simochromis babaulti PELLEGRIN, 1927
Babault's Mouthbrooder

Syn.: None.

Hab.: Africa; Lake Tanganyika (endemic). The animals inhabit the rocky littoral zone.

F.I.: Could not be determined.

Sex: Marked sexual dichromatism is present; ♂♂ have a black longitudinal band on the dorsal fin and egg spots on the anal fin.

Soc. B.: Territorial, the animals show strong aggressions which, in small aquaria, can lead to the death of the inferior tankmate. Mouthbrooder; matriarch family.

M: In the background of the aquarium there should be stone structures with many crevices, niches and caves; leave a lot of free swimming space. Only the toughest plants can be used, because *S. babaulti* eats plants. Water should be medium-hard to hard (10-20° dGH) and moderately alkaline (pH 7.5-8.5). Best kept in a species tank.

B: 26-28° C (79-82° F); water values as indicated above. Maintain one ♂ with at least three ♀♀. Reproduction is similar to *Tropheus* species. The animals are mouthbrooders. Spawning occurs on a previously cleaned hard substrate (i.e., flat stone). The eggs, up to 50, are taken into the mouth of the ♀ and fertilized by the "egg spot method". Incubation takes three weeks. The ♀ does not feed while brooding.

F: O; live foods of all kinds, plant fare (blanched lettuce or spinach), also flake food.

S: *Simochromis babaulti* is the only species of the *Simochromis-Tropheus* group which has marked sexual dimorphism.

T: 24-26° C, L: 11 cm, A: 120 cm, R: m, b, D: 2-3
75-79° F, 4 1/3", 47",

Sarotherodon melagaster ♂

Simochromis babaulti

Simochromis dardennii (BOULENGER, 1899)

Syn.: *Tilapia dardennii, Limotilapia dardennii.*

Hab.: Africa; Lake Tanganyika (endemic). The species is widely distributed in the lake. It inhabits the littoral zone and is said to occasionally venture into the open water.

F.I.: 1968 or later.

Sex: ♂ has egg dummies on the anal fin.

Soc. B.: Territorial, robust fish with average aggressivity. The species eats plants. Ovophile mouthbrooder; matriarch family.

M: Provide a background of rockwork with many caves and niches, some roots as decoration, and an open swimming area. A substrate of sand or fine gravel is suggested, but vegetation should be waived (herbivore!). Water should be medium-hard to hard (10-20° dGH) and neutral to moderately alkaline (pH 7.0-8.5). Can be kept in a species tank.

B: *Simochromis dardennii* has not yet been bred in an aquarium.

F: H, O; vegetable fare, live foods of all kinds, frozen and flake foods (Tetra Conditioning Food).

S: The genus *Limnotilapia* was dissolved in 1979 by GREENWOOD, and its species transferred into *Simochromis*. Only the taxonomic position of *"Limnotilapia" trematocephala* (BOULENGER, 1901) caused problems. A definite classification of this species will only be possible after additional studies are done on comparative material.

T: 23-26° C, **L:** 26 cm, **A:** 120 cm, **R:** b, m, **D:** 3
73-79° F, 10 ", 47",

Spathodus erythrodon BOULENGER, 1901
Blue Goby Cichlid

Syn.: None.

Hab.: Africa; Lake Tanganyika (endemic).

F.I.: Probably already in 1958 together with *Eretmodus cyanostictus.*

Sex: Cannot be determined with certainty from external characteristics (monomorphic). The ♂♂ probably grow somewhat larger and generally have longer pelvic fins than the ♀♀.

Soc. B.: Territorial, they are quarrelsome towards conspecifics. The species does not bother plants. Ovophile, monogamous mouthbrooder; nuclear family with close pair formation.

M: Keeping this species is easy since its natural biotope can easily be imitated in an aquarium. The bottom should be of light sand with many stones arranged like a rubble field. It is important that a lot of caves, niches and crevices result (hiding places for young). Vegetation can be omitted since it is also missing in its natural biotope. Provide stone-free areas and open swimming space. Best housed with representatives of the genera *Julidochromis, Lamprologus* and *Telmatochromis.*

B: 26-29° C (79-84° F); the water ought to be 10-20° dGH, pH 7.2-8.5. Breeding is not difficult, yet it will only succeed if the animals are offered correct living conditions. *S. erythrodon* should be kept in pairs. The species is a mouthbrooder, but shows uncommon brood care behavior for this group. Partner bonding begins several days prior to spawning; a horizontal or vertical stone surface serves as substrate. The eggs, up to 25, are immediately taken into the mouth of the ♀ and fertilized through the inhalation of sperm. In *S. erythrodon,* the bond between ♂ and ♀ remains after spawning. After barely 2 weeks, the young are released by the mother and transferred under specific rituals to the ♂. He now continues the brood care for an additional 8 days. The young are very slender (2 mm; 1/16") in relation to their length (10 mm; 1/3"). Feed the young with newly hatched *Artemia* nauplii.

Continued on page 988.

Simochromis dardennii

Spathodus erythrodon

Continuation of *Spathodus erythrodon*:

F: Live foods (*Daphnia*, *Cyclops*, *Artemia*, glassworms, bloodworms), minced crustacea meat and flake food.

S: Like other goby cichlids, *Spathodus erythrodon* has lost much of its swimming capability. Swimming would only be a dis advantage for the animals in the fast waters of the surge zone in such a large lake as Lake Tanganyika. They would have to expend too much energy to prevent themselves from being swept away. That is why their swim bladder is strongly reduced.

T: 25-27° C, L: 8 cm, A: 100 cm, R: b, D: 2-3
77-81° F, 3", 39",

Rubble zone in Lake Tanganyika.

Spathodus marlieri POLL, 1950
Plain Goby Cichlid

Syn.: None.

Hab.: Africa; Lake Tanganyika (endemic). The species has only been caught in the northern part of the lake.

F.I.: Around 1975.

Sex: Pronounced sexual dimorphism; the ♂♂ are distinctly larger with longer pelvic fins and pointed anal and tail fins. Old ♂♂ develop a cranial hump.

Soc. B.: Similar to *Spathodus erythrodon*. The animals are territorial, quarrelsome towards conspecifics and will not bother plants. Ovophile mouthbrooder; matriarch family.

M: As indicated for *Sp. erythrodon*. Do not keep the species in soft and/or acid water.

B: Breeding is similar to *Sp. erythrodon*. However, the animals only display remnants of a pair bond. Ovophile mouthbrooder, the ♀ cares for the brood alone (matriarch family). Feed the young with *Artemia* nauplii.

F: O; live foods (small crustacea, mosquito larvae, *Tubifex*), shrimp, flake food.

S: *Spathodus marlieri* differs from *Sp. erythrodon* in having fewer hard rays in its dorsal fin (21-22 instead of 23-25) and in its brood care (maternal family instead of a nuclear family).

T: 25-27° C, L: ♂ up to 9 cm, A: 100 cm, R: b, D: 3
77-81° F, ♂ up to 3 ", 39",

Steatocranus glaber ROBERTS & STEWART, 1976

False Mpozo Lionhead Cichlid

Syn.: None. The species was initially considered to be *Steatocranus mpzoensis.*

Hab.: Africa; Zaire, in the rapids of the Zaire River.

F.I.: End of 1981 or beginning of 1982.

Sex: ♂♂ grow larger than ♀♀.

Soc. B.: Territorial, *St. glaber* is a quite peaceful cichlid. The species does not bother plants. It is probably a cave brooding, substrate spawner.

M: A shallow, broad tank of 30 cm (11³/4") depth is sufficient. Rockwork, roots, etc., are needed to offer innumerable caves which, if possible, should be close to the bottom. The caves are used as the centers of territory, hiding places and spawning sites. The caves should be located at varying intervals. A strong water current, which the animals are exposed to in nature, can be waived. The animals do not place special demands on the chemical make-up of the water (hardness up to 20° dGH, pH 6.0-7.5). Only clean, oxygen-rich water (good filtration and aeration) is important. Associate with other rheophile (= current-loving) cichlids.

B: Breeding has not been successful in an aquarium, but it should not be more difficult than for *St. casuarius.*

F: O; live foods of all kinds, algae, flake and tablet foods. In nature, the species is probably a highly specialized aufwuchs feeder.

S: *Steatocranus glaber* differs from all other members of the genus by having large chisel-shaped teeth. *St. glaber* most resembles *St. gibbiceps* and *St. mpozoensis.* It differs from *gibbiceps* by its dentition and long coiled intestine and from *mpozensis* by its terminal mouth, the longer fins and fewer gill rakers.

T: 23-27° C, 73-81° F, **L:** 6 cm, 2¹/3", **A:** 60 cm, 24", **R:** b, **D:** 2

Steatocranus tinanti (POLL, 1939)

Slender Lionhead Cichlid

Syn.: *Gobiochromis tinanti, Leptotilapia tinanti.*

Hab.: Africa; region around Kinshasa in the Zaire River at the exit of Pool Malebo (previously Stanley Pool). The animals inhabit the rapids where they live on the bottom of depressions in the shallow waters of the shore region.

F.I.: Probably already in 1958; however, the date is uncertain.

Sex: ♂♂ have larger heads and a much elongated dorsal and anal fin. ♂♂ grow larger.

Soc. B.: Territorial. With suitable aquarium furnishings, hostilities do not become excessive, although other opinions have been expressed in aquaristic literature. Cave spawner; patriarch-matriarch family.

M: Offer aquaria with a large surface area (from 120 x 50 cm; 47" x 20"); the water does not have to be very deep (from 30 cm; 11³/4"). Build many hiding places of rocks. Use a fine-grained gravel bottom. Dense side and background vegetation creates additional hiding places. Water soft (5-8° dGH) and in the neutral range (pH 7). It should always be clear and clean. A strong, pump created current is recommended. Keep in a species tank or associate with fishes that have similar demands.

B: According to the aquarium literature, breeding can be problematic. The most important factor for a successful spawn is harmony between the partners. If two animals have paired, the ♀ usually enters the cave of the ♂ where spawning occurs. A spawn can be comprised of 100 eggs. These are relatively large and cared for and guarded by the ♀. Egg development takes about 5 days at 26° C (79° F). After an additional week, the young are free-swimming. After about 14 days, the young abandon the cave for the first time and are guarded and guided by both parents. Feed the young with *Artemia* nauplii and micro food.

F: Hardy live foods (mosquito larvae, freshwater isopods, *Gammarus*, Enchytraea, *Tubifex*, small earthworms); tablet food is also readily eaten.

Steatocranus sp. cf. *mpozoensis* or *S. glaber*?

Steatocranus tinanti

S: Because of its life in the rapids, the swim bladder has degenerated. *Steatocranus tinanti* has hereby, like other inhabitants of this biotope, lost the capability to hover in open water.

T: 25-27° C, L: 15 cm, A: 120 cm, R: b, D: 2-3
77-81° F, 6", 47",

Cross with *Symphysodon discus* HECKEL
The parents: according to the importer, Heiko Bleher, Kelsterbach/ Ffm., these fish came from the mouth of the Rio Branco in Brazil (natural Heckel cross?). Dr. Schmidt-Focke received some of these wild caught specimens. The center stripe was not as strongly pronounced in the wild caught specimens as it was in these crosses with turquoise discus.

Turquoise discus with red base coloration.
Dr. Schmidt-Focke obtained this color by crossing a red discus ♀ (refer to Mayland's book, page 213) with a royal blue ♂ in 5 generations of inbreeding and selection.

The discus is considered king of the aquarium fishes. This title was previously given to the angelfish, *Pterophyllum scalare*, when it was one of the most popular aquarium fishes.
It would follow that the discus would have to be elevated to the rank of an emperor, because it is without a doubt a majestic aquarium fish. But whether king or emperor, we still continue to call him just discus. In Vol. 1, pages 770-773 the four natural species and sub-species have already been presented. However, many aquarists want to know more about the discus. There are specialized books that exclusively deal with care and maintenance, e.g., J. Wattley " Discus for the perfectionist "; B. Degen " The Degen book of discus "; J. Wattley " Handbook of discus "; B. Degen " discus, how to breed them", all published by t.f.h.; see your pet dealer or book store.
Pictures of the following discus strains were made available to me by Dr. Schmidt-Focke, a successful and probably the best known discus breeder in Germany. Dr. Schmidt-Focke makes the following comments about the different strains.

1.
Bred form of a completely green discus. These intensely green animals result when green striped, wild caught specimens from the Rio Jourus are bred. When young, this color morph will often still have brown stripes and spots which disappear at sexual maturity.

2.
This is a totally striated "royal blue" (*Symphysodon aequifasciatus haraldi*) bred male from the lake areas of the Rio Manacapuru, Brazil.

3.
A rare, especially beautiful, striped bred male of *Symphysodon aequifasciatus aequifasciatus* (green discus). If iron was added to the breeding water, the red spots on the midline would be even more pronounced.

1.

2.

3.

Giant discus, juvenile of 10 months of age. Its predecessors were caught by Jack Wattley in the Rio Jurna, Brazil. The ♂♂ were striped pale blue and the ♀♀ looked like brown discus. By crossing with turquoise striped discus, color and shape were significantly improved.

Tanganicodus irsacae POLL, 1950
Speckled Goby Cichlid

Syn.: None.

Hab.: Africa; in the northern half of Lake Tanganyika (endemic). The species lives in the surge area in the extremely shallow regions of the rubble littoral zone (to 1 m; 1.1 yd in depth). The fish are aufwuchs feeders.

F.I.: 1975.

Sex: Sex determination by external characteristics is very difficult. Older ♂♂ are said to have somewhat elongated ventral fins.

Soc. B.: Territorial, they are very aggressive and quarrelsome among themselves. Monogamous (?) mouthbrooder; probably nuclear family.

M: As with *Spathodus erythrodon*.

T: 24-28° C, **L:** 7 cm, **A:** 100 cm, **R:** b, **D:** 3
75-82° F, 2¾", 39",

B: No detailed reports are available. *T. irsacae* is a mouthbrooder. The opinion exists that the ♂ participates in mouthbrooding (similar to *Eretmodus cyanostictus*).

F: Live foods of all kinds (small crustacea, mosquito larvae, *Tubifex*). After a certain adaptation period, the animals can be at least partially trained to flake food.

S: *Tanganicodus irsacae* can easily be distinguished from the other goby cichlids of the genera *Eretmodus* and *Spathodus* by its clearly inferior, much smaller and narrower mouth.

Telmatochromis temporalis BOULENGER, 1898

Temporalis Cichlid

Syn.: None.

Hab.: Africa; Lake Tanganyika (endemic). The species occurs in the rocky shore.

F.I.: 1958 (?).

Sex: With advanced age, the ♂♂ develop a frontal hump; the ♀♀ are usually smaller and show their ripeness.

Soc. B.: Territorial, normally this fish is peaceful. They are only very aggressive when defending their territory. Cave spawner with nuclear family.

M: Needs rockwork with many caves and other hiding places; plants are not necessary. Medium-hard to hard (10-20° dGH) and alkaline (pH 8.0-9.0) water.

T: 25-27° C, **L:** 10 cm, **A:** 80 cm, **R:** b, **D:** 2-3
77-81° F, 4", 31",

B: 26-28° C (79-82° F); water values as indicated above. The animals are cave spawners which usually lay their eggs on the ceiling. One spawn is comprised of about 60 eggs which are fanned by the ♀. The larvae hatch after 4-5 days and are free-swimming after an additional 7. The young are guarded by both parents.

F: O; live foods of all types, but also frozen, freeze-dried and flake food.

S: The monocuspid teeth of *Telmatochromis temporalis* are strong. They serve to crack the chitin shell of aquatic insects.

Thoracochromis wingatii (BOULENGER, 1902)

Syn.: *Paratilapia wingatii, Haplochromis wingatii.*

Hab.: East and central Africa, also in Lake Albert and Edward, in rivers and standing waters. Wild caught specimens; the species is only rarely offered in the trade.

F.I.: Not precisely known.

Sex: Marked sexual dichromatism. The ♂ is more brightly and intensely colored with egg dummies on the anal fin . The ♀ is plainer and lacks egg dummies.

Soc. B.: Territorial only at spawning time; otherwise, it is a schooling fish. At spawning time, the ♂♂ congregate in colonies of about 10. Every ♂'s territory consists of a central pit which has a diameter of at least 1 m (1.1 yd). The species is relatively peaceful but digs a lot; matriarch family.

T: 24-26° C, **L:** 12 cm, **A:** 100 cm, **R:** b, **D:** 2
75-79° F, 4 3/4", 39",

M: The aquarium needs to be long (from 100 cm (39") but not necessarily very tall. Give the aquarium a deep layer of fine-grained sand, sparse plant stands, some caves of stone, flat stones and roots, and free swimming space. Temperature of 24-26° C (75-79° F); the animals usually live in the lower water strata.

B: As with *Astatotilapia desfontainesii.*

F: C, O; live, frozen, flake foods.

S: *Thoracochromis wingatii* can be easily confused with *Astatotilapia burtoni.* The following differences exist between the two species: the forward most egg spot on the anal fin of *T. wingatii* begins at the 8th fin ray, on *A. burtoni* at the 5th fin ray. *T. wingatii*'s egg spots are always on the membranes between two fin rays.

Telmatochromis temporalis

Thoracochromis wingatii ♂

Thysochromis ansorgii (BOULENGER, 1901)

Five-Spot African Cichlid

Syn.: *Pelmatochromis ansorgii, P. arnoldi, Thysia ansorgii.*

Hab.: Africa; forested coastal areas of Nigeria, Ivory Coast, Ghana and Cameroon.

F.I.: 1913 by Christian Brüning and J. F. Arnold, Hamburg, Germany.

Sex: Distinct sexual dichromatism and dimorphism; ♂ is larger and has longer ventral fins. Posteriorly, the dorsal fin in the ♂ is pointed, and in the ♀, slightly rounded. ♂ has brown-red dots on the unpaired fins; these are absent in the ♀. Sexually mature ♀♀ have a red-brown stomach of variable intensity and a shiny white spot on both side of the anus.

Soc. B.: Territorial, very sedate and peaceful; the species digs at spawning time, but does not bother plants. First paternal-matriarch family, later nuclear family.

M: Likes an aquarium with gravel bottom, hiding places of stones and roots and dense vegetation in parts, leaving free swimming room. House with species of the genera *Pelvicachromis, Nanochromis* or *Chromidotilapia.* Regular water changes every 8-14 days, up to one third of the tank volume.

B: Around 25° C (77° F); water should be soft (around 5° dGH) and slightly acid (pH around 6.5). The animals are open spawners with a tendency towards cave spawning. Spawns are comprised of up to 500 eggs which are often eaten. ♀♀ guard the spawn while the ♂♂ dig pits. The embryos break the eggshells after about 3 days. The larvae are placed into the pit by the ♀, and in the course of the following days, she transfers them several times. Brood care is usually by the ♀ alone, and the ♂ defends the spawning territory. Contrary to this, the young are cared for by both parents.

F: Live foods of all kinds; but the animals also accept flake food and freeze-dried food. Vegetable fare should also be offered.

S: An additional *Thysochromis* species exists: *T. annectens* (BOULENGER, 1913), with the synonyms of *Pelmatochromis annectens* and *P. maculifer.* At present, both species are treated as "one".

T: 24-26° C, **L:** 13 cm, **A:** from 120 cm, **R:** m, b, **D:** 2
75-79° F, 5", from 47",

Tilapia busumana (GÜNTHER, 1902)

Syn.: *Chromis busumanus, Sarotherodon busumanum.*

Hab.: West Africa; in the Kumasi area of southern Ghana. The species occurs in water courses of the rain forest and plantations, inhabits the rivers Bia, Tano, Ofin, Birim and Pra, as well as the Volta reservoir, Lake Botsumtwe and other larger lake-like bodies of water.

F.I.: 1968 by Erhard Roloff, Karlsruhe, Germany.

Sex: Adult ♂♂ do not have the *Tilapia* spot on the dorsal fin, and their base coloration is somewhat lighter; ♀ has a *Tilapia* spot and a strong blue-green base coloration during courtship.

Soc. B.: Territorial; the species is relatively peaceful and does not bother plants very much; every once in a while, young shoots are eaten. Open spawner (substrate spawner); nuclear family (according to WHYTE 1975).

M: Provide a substrate of fine-grained gravel, hiding places of stones and roots and side and background vegetation of tough species. Water values as listed for *T. buttikoferi.* Maintain in a species tank or associate with fishes that place similar demands (e.g., other tilapines, large characins).

B: No reports are available dealing with successful aquarium breeding. Something on the reproductive biology in nature is reported by WHYTE (1975): J. Zool. (Lond.) 177: 25-56, on page 43. 10 cm (4") fishes of river populations lay about 400 eggs.

F: O; omnivore.

S: It has not been determined beyond a shadow of a doubt if specimens from Lake Botsumtwe are not mouthbrooders instead. The animals from the rain forest and plantation waters reach a maximum length of 10 cm (4"), yet specimens from large rivers and lakes can reach a length up to 20 cm (8").

T: 23-25° C, **L:** 20 cm, **A:** 120 cm, **R:** b, m, **D:** 2
73-77° F, 8", 47",

Thysochromis ansorgii ♀

Tilapia busumana

Tilapia buttikoferi (HUBRECHT, 1881)

Zebra Tilapia

Syn.: *Chromis buttikoferi.*

Hab.: West Africa; from Guinea-Bissau to west Liberia; the animals occur in rivers.

F.I.: 1969 by Erhard Roloff, Karlsruhe, Germany.

Sex: ♂♂ are larger.

Soc. B.: Territorial, young animals are peaceful but with age turn pugnacious and become predatory towards smaller fishes. *T. buttikoferi* digs, especially during spawning season. Offensive plants are either dug up or bitten off. Substrate spawner; nuclear family with intensive brood care.

M: The species should solely be kept in roomy tanks. Provide stones and roots as cover and a bottom of medium-sized gravel. Plant the tank with tough species (*Anubias* and *Bolbitis* species) since tender plants are eaten. Water soft to medium-hard (up to 15° dGH) and slightly acid to neutral (pH 6.5-7.0). Combine with similar sized fishes, or keep in a species tank.

B: Nothing is known concerning a successful aquarium spawn.

F: O; hardy foods of all kinds: mosquito larvae, adult insects, earthworms, crustacean meat (shrimp), minced meat; vegetable fare (important!), flake and tablet food.

S: *Tilapia buttikoferi* is a rare fish in its natural habitat; therefore, only a few specimens are captured.

T: 23-25° C, L: 25 cm, A: 120 cm, R: b, m, D: 2
73-77° F, 9¾", 47",

Tilapia joka THYS, 1969

Syn.: None.

Hab.: West Africa; Sierra Leone. The animals inhabit the water ways in the south of the country.

F.I.: 1968 by Erhard Roloff, Karlsruhe, Germany.

Sex: Definite external sexual differences are not known, but according to THYS (1969), the anal fin of the ♀ is longer.

Soc. B.: Territorial, the species is peaceful and plant friendly. Cave spawner; patriarch-matriarch family.

M: Needs a roomy tank with fine-grained gravel or sand as substrate. Hiding places among stones and some roots, and dense edge and background vegetation with *Anubias* and *Bolbitis* species should be added. Be sure the water is clean and rich in oxygen, pH 6.5-7.0 and up to 12° dGH. House with other west African species.

B: LINKE (1983): Tetra-Information **18** (62): 13-14 presents the first report of a successful aquarium spawn. Soft, acid water is necessary for breeding. *Tilapia joka* is a cave spawner. The ♀ deposits, after an extended courtship, the yellow-brown eggs on the previously cleaned ceiling of the cave. A spawn is about 200 eggs. The ♀ is clearly the more active partner in brood care. She cleans the cave, cares for the eggs and energetically defends the spawning site. The ♂ guards the spawning territory. About 4 days after fertilization, hatching begins. After an additional 4-6 days (at 26° C; 79° F), the young are free-swimming. Feed with newly hatched *Artemia* nauplii and TetraMin Baby Food.

F: O; vegetable fare is important. All types of live foods, crustacea and other fine cut meats, flake and tablet foods.

S: According to THYS (1969): Rev. Zool. Bot. afr. **80**: 157-165, the closest relative to *Tilapia joka* is *Tilapia mariae*. In comparison, *T. joka* has a smaller mouth and does not have micro gill rakers. *T. joka* lacks the *Tilapia* spot.

T: 23-25° C, L: 13 cm, A: 100 cm, R: b, m, D: 2
73-77° F, 5", 39",

Tilapia buttikoferi

Tilapia joka

Tropheus brichardi NELISSEN & THYS, 1975
Blue-Eyed Tropheus

Syn.: *Tropheus moorii* (brown morph).

Hab.: Africa; on the northern shore of Lake Tanganyika (endemic). The distribution of this species is limited to southern Burundi (Nyanza Lac). The animals inhabit the upper rocky shore between 2 and 5 m (2.2-5.5 yd).

F.I.: 1968 (?).

Sex: Sexes are not distinguishable by external characteristics.

Soc. B.: Territorial, *T. brichardi* probably does not live in tightly closed social groups. The animals are often aggressive among themselves but peaceful towards other fishes. In captivity the species also keeps its natural shyness.

M: Provide a large aquarium with rock constructions extending to the water surface, offering many caves, niches and passages. Preserve enough free swimming space. Provide strong overhead illumination to encourage algae growth (aufwuchs feeder). Associate with goby cichlids of the genera *Eretmodus*, *Spathodus* and *Tanganicodus* and also *Julidochromis* species.

B: 26-27° C (79-81° F); medium-hard (10-15° dGH) and neutral to moderately alkaline (pH 7-9) water is suggested. The animals are open spawning, highly specialized mouthbrooders. The eggs are yellow and up to 7 mm (") in diameter. Depending on temperature, the young are free-swimming in 28-33 days. Each cycle yields about 10 young.

F: Live foods of all kinds; the animals are specialized aufwuchs feeders; therefore, vegetable fare should also be offered (algae, lettuce, spinach, etc.). Foods low in fiber (e.g., *Tubifex* or Enchytraea) should be fed with caution.

S: MATTHES (1962) considered *Tropheus brichardi* a geographical color morph of *Tropheus moorii*. To aquarists, this species was already known prior to its classification as a true species by the name blue-eyed tropheus.

T: 24-26° C, L: 12 cm, A: 150 cm, R: m, b, D: 3-4
75-79° F, $4^3/_4$", 59",

Tropheus moorii

Tropheus moorii, rainbow morph

Tropheus moorii, striped morph

Tropheus moorii, orange morph

Tropheus moorii, green morph

Tropheus moorii, kaiser moorii

Tropheus moorii, double spot morph

Tropheus moorii, black-striped morph

Tropheus polli, yellow-rainbow morph

Tropheus polli, frontal-stripe morph

Tropheus polli, wimple morph

Tropheus polli, green-red morph

Xenotilapia boulengeri (POLL, 1942)

Boulenger's Xenotilapia

Syn.: *Enantiopus boulengeri.*

Hab.: Africa; Lake Tanganyika (endemic). The animals live in depths between 1 and 60 m (1-65 yd), primarily above sandy bottoms.

F.I.: Unknown.

Sex: The ♂'s anal fin has a distinct design and stronger coloration.

Soc. B.: Territorial, this is an extraordinarily peaceful cichlid. During the day, the animals are lively swimmers. Mouthbrooder with nuclear family.

M: Use a thick layer of sand on the bottom and perhaps some plants along the sides. The background should have some rocks and roots as hiding places and decoration. Water hardness to 20° dGH and moderately alkaline (pH 7.5-8.5). Keep in a species tank or with other *Xenotilapia* species.

B: A first, detailed breeding report of a *Xenotilapia* species in an aquarium, probably *X. boulengeri*, is given by V. PUTTBERG (1985) in Aquarium **19**, 623-628. The ♂♂ establish territories during spawning time that are defended against all conspecifics. The ♀ is tolerated in the territory and territorial defense becomes a mutual endeavor. The ♂ builds a spawning pit where the ♀ lays her cream colored, 2 mm (1/16") eggs. The eggs in the spawning pit are now fertilized by the ♂ and only then taken into the ♀'s mouth. The eggs number between 20 and 30. After about 12 days, the larvae are transferred from the ♀ to the ♂ who continues to care for them in his mouth. The fry are seen for the first time after 18-20 days. The young are then about 5 mm (3/16") long and are readmitted into the mouth of the ♂ in times of danger. Raising the young is not difficult. Feed crumbled dry food, *Artemia* nauplii and small frozen foods.

F: O; live food of all kinds (aquatic insects and their larvae, water fleas, *Cyclops, Artemia, Tubifex*), frozen, flake and tablet foods.

S: The appearance of *Xenotilapia boulengeri* is similar to that of *Xenotilapia sima*, but it differs from the latter by a flat looking forehead and a longer mouth.

T: 23-26° C, L: 15 cm, A: 100 cm, R: b, m, D: 3
73-79° F, 6", 39",

Ambassidae see under Chandidae

Fam.: Apogonidae (Cardinalfishes)

The family is not numerous and is chiefly comprised of small representatives. The largest species is about 20 cm (8") long. Most inhabit flood regions of tropical and subtropical seas. Few species live in freshwater. Cardinalfishes are mostly found in the Indo-Pacific, where they appear in schools in reef areas and represent an important food source for larger predators. Apogonidae have two dorsal fins; the first is made up entirely of hard rays. Most representatives only have two spines on the anal fin. Relatively large ctenoid scales are present. Many species care for their young. Eggs and fry are usually taken into the mouth of the ♂, but sometimes also by the ♀.

Fam.: Centropomidae (Giant Perches)

Previously, mainly the glassfishes belonged to this family. Today, only 4 genera remain in this family with about 20 species which are distributed from Africa through southeast Asia to Australia. Seven of the 20 species are freshwater fishes; the remaining species are marine. Fossil finds in Australia document the age of these fishes at approximately 55 million years. Similar finds in Africa are about 22 million years old.

In Australia, the giant perches are economically important. In 1978-1979, 3200 tons were captured commercially. Only 1800 tons were caught in 1980-1981. Australia gave overfishing and environmental degradation as reasons for the decline—as can be found almost anywhere in the world.

Fam.: Chandidae (Glassfishes)

The description of the family can be found in Vol. 1, page 788 (under Centropomidae). GREENWOOD established this new family and separated it from the old. Some authors still use the old family name Ambassidae.

Fam.: Kuhliidae

The Kuhliidae represent a small family with barely a dozen species. They are found in the Indo-Pacific region. Most Kuhliidae are salt water fishes; however, some species occur in brackish or even freshwater.

The body shape of Kuhliidae is similar to sunfishes (Centrarchidae). The Kuhliidae are usually slender with the body and head covered with medium size ctenoid scales. They have a divided dorsal fin. The anterior, hard-rayed part is not connected to the posterior, soft-rayed one. Best known genera are *Kuhlia* and *Nannoperca.*

Fam.: Serranidae (Sea Basses and Groupers)
The more than 400 species of the Serranidae are primarily tropical; some species are also found in temperate seas. Most species are marine. Some, however, are pure freshwater inhabitants. Almost all marine representatives remain close to the coast. Giants of over 300 kg (660 lb) as well as the smallest fishes, which only measure 2 cm (3/4") and weigh close to nothing, can be found among the Serranidae. In general, Serranidae are stoutly built and have large heads with spacious mouths. They have two dorsal fins; the first has strong spines. Many Serranidae are hermaphrodites. In some species, egg and sperm develop side by side in the same fish, but it is more common that the fish are ♀♀ when young and later transform into ♂♂ (protogynous hermaphrodites).

Fam.: Teraponidae (Grunters and Tigerperches)
The Theraponidae represent a small family of fishes widely distributed in the Indo-Pacific region. They are found from the east African coast and the Red Sea to Australia and some west Pacific islands. The majority of the species are medium large and live in the sea. Some species grow large enough to represent locally important food fishes. Many species occasionally enter freshwater, and a few live in it permanently. The Theraponidae differ from the Serranidae by their number of dorsal fin rays (11-14), the much smaller mouth and the numerous teeth which are tricuspid or serrated.

Fam.: Percichthyidae
Some genera of the family Serranidae differ in their appearance and way of life from the remaining Serranidae. For this reason, these genera are grouped by many ichthyologists into the separate family Percichthyidae.

Fam.: Lutjanidae (Snappers)

About 300 species are considered snappers. With the exception of the eastern Pacific, they are represented in all warm seas. Typical members of the family are easily recognized by their almost triangular head profile. The dorsal fin is not divided; the hard-rayed and soft-rayed segments are joined. The Lutjanidae differ from the Serranidae by the 10 hard rays in the first dorsal fin, the pointed pectoral fins and the tail fin, which is usually much more forked. Several important food fishes belong to the family. Some species in certain regions cause ciguatera, a form of fish poisoning. This is because some species feed on poisonous algae. Along the food chain, these toxins accumulate progressively, reaching their highest concentration in the snappers.

Elassoma okefenokee ♂, ♀ see page 1015

Badis Badis burmanicus, see page 1013

Glossamia aprion aprion (RICHARDSON, 1842)
Northern Queensland Mouthbrooder

Syn.: *Apogon aprion.*

Hab.: Australia; in northern rivers. The species only lives in freshwater.

F.I.: Could not be determined.

Sex: None known.

Soc. B.: A relatively peaceful fish that lives in schools. Mouthbrooder; patriarch family.

M: Offer roomy aquaria. Use fine sand for the bottom and some roots and stones as decoration. Plant the sides and background densely with Australian species, leaving sufficient swimming room. The water should be medium-hard to hard (12-20° dGH) and neutral to slightly alkaline (pH 7.0-7.5). Combining with rainbow fishes is possible.

B: Not yet bred in an aquarium. From observations in the wild, it is known that the ♂♂ take the eggs into their buccal cavity to brood them. The animals do not eat during that time.

F: C; live foods of all kinds: small crustacea, mosquito larvae, *Tubifex*; scraped meat and flake food.

S: Besides *Glossamia aprion aprion*, there is an additional sub-species, *G. aprion gilli*, the Queensland mouthbrooder. It inhabits regions further south. Both species can easily be distinguished by the number of scales along the lateral line: *G. a. aprion* has 37-41, *G. a. gilli* in contrast, only has 25-31.

T: 23-25° C, **L:** 12 cm, **A:** 100 cm, **R:** m, **D:** 2
73-77° F, $4^3/_4$", 39",

Badis badis burmanicus AHL, 1936

Burmese Badis

Syn.: None.

Hab.: Southeast Asia; Burma, in Lake Inlé.

F.I.: Around 1960.

Sex: ♂ has a concave ventral line and brighter colors; ♀ has a convex ventral line, less intense colors and is somewhat smaller.

Soc. B.: Peaceful fish, it is even less territorial than *Badis badis badis*. Cave spawner; patriarch family.

M: Needs a densely planted tank with a fine sand substrate and caves (e.g., halfved coconut shells, flower pots). Use roots and rocks to provide many hiding places. No special demands are placed on water chemistry; and slightly acid (pH around 6.5) and to 15° dGH. The aquarium should not be brightly lit since the animals do not appreciate too much light, use floating plants. Regular water exchanges are important.

B: 26-28° C (79-82° F); easily possible. Can be accomplished in very small tanks. Use water values listed above and maybe peat filtration for amber, slightly acid water. Spawning occurs in a cave; the ♂ cares for the spawn of up to 150 eggs. The young hatch after about 3 days and are cared for by the ♂ until the yolk sac is absorbed. Feed the young with crustacea nauplii.

F: C; live foods of all types, shrimp, scraped meat, liver. Flake food is only eaten in exceptional cases.

S: *Badis badis burmanicus* differs from the nominate form, *Badis badis badis* (HAMILTON, 1822), in its coloration and its different distribution area. *B. b. badis* is blue and occurs in India.

T: 24-26° C, **L:** 8 cm, **A:** 70 cm, **R:** m, b, **D:** 4 (C)
75-79° F, 3", 28",

Ambloplites rupestris (RAFINESQUE, 1817)
Rock Bass

Syn.: *Bodianus rupestris, Ambloplites aeneus, A. ictheloides, Centrarchus aënaeus, C. pentacanthus, Cichla aenea, Icthelis erythrops, Lepomis ictheloides.*

Hab.: North America; southern Canada (Great Lakes) to Louisiana (USA).

F.I.: 1887 by Max von dem Borne, Berneuchen.

Sex: The ♂ has a black, golden-edged opercular spot, blackish pectoral fins; the ♀ has a black opercular spot without a golden outline, brownish pectoral fins.

Soc. B.: A predatory, contentious fish that becomes asocial with age. The ♂♂ establish territories at spawning season. The species cares for its brood (patriarch family).

M: The fish should be kept in large tanks with sand or gravel bottoms and some hiding places of rocks and roots. Add thickets of coldwater plants. Clear, cold, not too soft (from 10° dGH) and neutral (pH 7.0) water is suggested. The animals are enduring and robust in large tanks but very sensitive in small tanks.

B: 16-20° C (61-68° F); the ♂♂ dig a palm-sized, shallow pit in the sand which is energetically defended against other ♂♂. Prior to spawning there is courtship. Spawning occurs in or above the pit, and the ♀ should be removed afterwards. The ♂ alone cares for the young. When the ♂ can no longer keep the young together, he should be removed before he begins to devour them. The young like to form loose schools.

F: Primarily live foods of all kinds, also fish. The rock bass can also be trained to accept meat and flake food.

S: *Ambioplites rupestris* is eaten and considered a good food fish in its natural range.

T: 10-20° C (coldwater fish), L: 25 cm, A: 100 cm, R: b, m, D: 1-2
50-68° F (coldwater fish), 9¾", 39",

Elassoma okefenokee BÖHLKE, 1956
Okefenokee Dwarf Sunfish

Syn.: None.

Hab.: North America; USA, in the Okefenokee Swamp of southwest Georgia (probably endemic).

F.I.: 1980 by Manfred Rogner, Aachen, Germany.

Sex: ♂♂ are darker in color and have courtship dress during spawning season; ♀ is lighter and ventrally fuller.

Soc. B.: Though territorial, it is still a quite peaceful species.

M: Densely plant the tank with fine-leaved coldwater species (*Myriophyllum brasiliense, Riccia fluitans*). Use a fine sandy bottom and some stones to demarcate territories, leaving some free swimming space. Soft (5° dGH) and acid (pH about 6) water. The animals are best kept in a species tank; otherwise, combine them with coldwater fishes that are just as small.

B: Has been bred in a species tank. ROGNER (1982): Das Aquarium **16** (158): 423-424, reports a successful spawn. The ♀♀ are lured by ♂♂ into the plant thicket where spawning occurs. The eggs hang on the plants by fine threads. According to ROGNER, the fish lay the eggs in groups of 10-30. The parents eat neither the spawn nor the young. Raising the young is accomplished with finest micro food. From the 10th day *Artemia* nauplii can be given.

F: Live foods of all kinds (crustacea such as *Daphnia*, *Cyclops*, *Artemia*; glass and blood worms, *Tubifex*, Enchytraea).

S: *Elassoma okefenokee* differs from *E. evergladei* by the absence of scales on the upper head and the darker dorsal fin of the ♂♂.

T: 4-30° C (coldwater fish), L: 4 cm, A: 50 cm, R: b, D: 2-3
39-86° F (coldwater fish), 1⅔", 20",

Ambloplites rupestris

Elassoma okefenokee ♀, ♂ see page 1010

Lepomis auritus solis (VALENCIENNES in CUVIER & VALENCIENNES, 1831)
Golden Sunfish

Syn.: *Labrus auritus, Apomotis albulus, Bryttus albulus, B. unicolor, Eupomotis euyorus, Ichthelis auritus, I. rubricauda, Lepidopomus miniatus, Lepomis appendix, L. miniatus, Pomotis elongatus, P. solis, Xenotis ophthalmicus, Xystroplites gilli.*

Hab.: North America; USA, from Maine to Virginia; in sandy bottomed, clear water creeks, rivers and lakes.

F.I.: 1895 by Paul Matte, Lankwitz, Germany.

Sex: ♂♂ are more beautiful and intensely colored.

Soc. B.: The animals are often belligerant and aggressive among themselves. The species practices brood care (patriarch family).

M: Give the aquarium a bottom of fine gravel; plant with fine-leaved coldwater species which should be in pots (the animals dig!). Leave a lot of free swimming room. Provide good aeration, creating a slight current simultaneously. A heater is not necessary. Medium-hard (up to 15° dGH) and neutral to slightly alkaline (pH 7.0-7.5) water.

B: 18-20° C (64-68° F); water not less than 10° dGH. The ♂ fans out a shallow pit about 30 cm (12") in diameter with its tail. The pit (nest) is energetically defended against conspecific ♂♂ and heterospecifics. Prior to spawning there is elaborate courtship with pseudopairings. Afterwards, the ♀ deposits her eggs in several passes. These can number over 1000 with large ♀♀. The ♀ then needs to be removed to prevent the ♂ from harassing her. Intense care and defense of the spawn and young is performed by the ♂. Guiding the young, as seen with cichlids, does not occur.

F: Hearty live foods of any kind; in time, the animals also adapt to flake food.

S: *Lepomis auritus* is divided into two subspecies: *L. auritus auritus* (LINNAEUS, 1758) and *L. auritus solis* (CUVIER & VALENCIENNES, 1831). The latter has a more southern distribution.

T: 4-22° C (coldwater fish), **L:** 20 cm, **A:** 80 cm, **R:** m, b, **D:** 2
39-72° F (coldwater fish), 8", 31",

Micropterus dolomieui LACÉPÈDE, 1802
Smallmouth Bass

Syn.: *Bodianus achigan, Calliurus punctulatus, C. fasciatus, Centrarchus obscurus, Cichla fasciata, C. minima, C. ohioensis, Dioplites variabilis, Etheostoma notata, Grystes nigricans, Lepomis flexuolaris, L. salmonea, L. trifasciata.*

Hab.: North America; from southern Canada to South Carolina and Arkansas. The species was released in Germany at the turn of the century, but it seems to have disappeared again.

F.I.: 1883.

Sex: ♂ is more slender and darker colored; ♀ is plumper and lighter in color. There are no other external differences known.

Soc. B.: The animals are territorial during the spawning season; in the center of the territory, a spawning pit is dug. The species is a greedy predator. Open spawner; nuclear family.

M: As indicated for *Micropterus salmoides*. Only juveniles are suitable for aquaria.

B: Not yet successful in an aquarium (size of the animals!). In the wild, reproduction is similar to *M. salmoides*. However, the spawning pit is not lined with leaves. The larvae are black, but they are gray in *M. salmoides*.

F: C; live foods, predominantly fishes. The animals have a large appetite.

S: *Micropterus dolomieui* differs from *M. salmoides* by a number of characteristics: tail fin 16 soft rays/18 soft rays; anal fin 10 soft rays/11-12 soft rays; pectoral fins 16-17 soft rays/13-14 soft rays; the scales on the interoperculum cover only the bone/ the whole bone; respectively

T: 10-18° C (coldwater fish), **L:** 50 cm, **A:** 100 cm, **R:** b, m, **D:** 2-3
50-64° F (coldwater fish), 20", 39",

Lepomis auritus solis

Micropterus dolomieui

Micropterus salmoides (LACÉPÈDE, 1802)
Largemouth Bass

Syn.: *Labrus salmoides, Aplites salmoides, Grystes salmoides, Huro nigricans.*

Hab.: North America; southern Canada to Mexico. Has been repeatedly released in Europe with some success. Was established in Lake Wörther and some Russian waters (e.g., Lake Abran).

F.I.: 1883.

Sex: ♂ is more slender and darker colored; no other differences are known.

Soc. B.: Greedy predator who establishes territories during the spawning season. The animals practice brood care (nuclear family).

M: Needs a tank with a large surface area, a thick layer of fine sand, some large rocks and dense vegetation along the edges with coldwater species; use well aerated, clean, clear water. Roots as hiding places and cover are suggested. Water should be medium-hard (from 10° dGH) and neutral to slightly alkaline (pH 7.0-7.5). Only young fish are suitable for normal aquaria.

B: Not yet successful in an aquarium (size!). In the wild, the animals build a shallow pit up to 1 m (1 yd) in diameter. These pits are meticulously cleaned and lined with leaves. They then spawn within them. The eggs are guarded alternately by the ♂ and ♀. The young hatch after 7-10 days. Brood care terminates with hatching.

F: Live foods, primarily fishes. Largemouth bass are marked predators with a large, very voracious appetite.

S: Representatives of the genus *Micropterus* differ from all other centrarchids by their elongated, relatively shallow body and the low dorsal fin which is almost divided into two by a central indention.

T: 10-18° C (coldwater fish), L: 60 cm, A: 100 cm, R: b, m, D: 4 (C)
50-64° F (coldwater fish), 24", 39",

Lates calcarifer (BLOCH, 1790)

Barramundi, Giant Perch

Syn.: *Holocentrus calcarifer, Pseudolates cavifrons.*

Hab.: Asia and Australia; distributed from the Persian Gulf eastward through China to the Indo-Australian Archipelago. The animals are found in fresh, brackish and salt water.

F.I.: The species has probably not been imported into Germany.

Sex: No external ones are known. The fish are said to go through a sexual transformation. Animals up to 50 cm (20") are almost always ♂♂; larger animals are usually ♀♀.

Soc. B.: The animals are quarrelsome among themselves. Smaller fishes are considered prey. The fish is a pronounced predator.

M: Only young are suitable for an aquarium. Larger specimens are reserved for public aquaria.

B: Has not yet been successful in an aquarium.

F: C; hardy live foods of all kinds, especially fish. However, substitute food in the form of frozen food or beef heart and meat is also eaten.

S: In their natural habitats, the fish are extremely appreciated food fish. *Lates calcarifer* should not be confused with *Scleropages leichhardti* which is also called Barramundi.

T: 15-28° C, L: 180 cm, A: from 150 cm, R: m, b, D: 3-4 (C)
59-82° F, 71", from 59",

Chanda agramma (GÜNTHER, 1867)

Syn.: *Ambassis agrammus.*

Hab.: Australia; Northern Territory and Queensland, in rivers that flow into the Gulf of Carpentaria. The species also occurs in the Fitzroy river system (western Australia).

F.I.: 1936 by W. Riemenschneider, Bremen, Germany.

Sex: ♂ is brighter colored with a posteriorly pointed swim bladder and a straight or slightly concave ventral line; ♀ is paler with a posteriorly round swim bladder and a convex ventral line.

Soc. B.: The animals school loosely. Peaceful towards heterospecifics, but slight confrontations can occur among themselves. The species likes to swim.

M: As recommended for *Chanda commersonii.* The addition of sea salt is suggested but not absolutely necessary for *Chanda agramma.*

B: No reports are available about a successful spawn in captivity. Reproduction is probably similar to *Chanda commersonii* or *Ch. ranga* (compare Vol. 1).

F: C; almost only live foods (any kind). Food must be very small.

S: The scales of *Chanda agramma* are relatively large. 26-28 scales are on the lateral line.

T: 20-28° C, L: 7 cm, A: 60 cm, R: m, t, D: 3
68-82° F, 2¾", 24",

Chanda commersonii (CUVIER & VALENCIENNES, 1828)
Commerson's Glassfish

Syn.: *Ambassis commersonii, A. safgha.*

Hab.: Africa, Asia and north Australia: the distribution area extends from the Red Sea and the east coast of Africa to north Australia and New Guinea. In some places the species enters freshwater.

F.I.: 1912.

Sex: The tip of the dorsal fin and the tips of the caudal fin are black on the ♂; ♀ lacks these black tips.

Soc. B.: Peaceful and sedate schooling fish. Whether or not *Chanda commersonii* claims territories is unknown.

M: A dark bottom of lava or basalt and dense vegetation of brackish water and/or sea water tolerant species is suggested. Needs hiding places of stones and roots. It is necessary to add sea salt (0.5-1%) for the well-being of this species. Associate with other *Chanda* species or maintain in a species tank.

B: 26-28° C (79-82° F); this species has been bred in an aquarium. To induce breeding, STERBA states that it is necessary to place the animals from time to time into full-strength sea water which is then slowly diluted over the course of days. Plant the tank densely with fine-leaved plant thickets for spawning. The eggs are small and are laid in large numbers. Raise the young with small crustacean nauplii.

F: C; predominately live foods of all kinds. Flake food is only taken exceptionally.

S: *Chanda commersonii* differs from *Chanda ranga* by its elongated body shape and fewer soft rays in the dorsal fin (9-10 to 12-15) and anal fin (9-10 to 13-15).

T: 22-26° C, L: 10 cm, A: 80 cm, R: m, D: 3-4
72-79° F, 4", 31",

Chanda agramma

Chanda commersonii

Chanda elongata (CASTELNAU, 1878)
Elongated Glassfish

Syn.: *Ambassis elongatus.*

Hab.: Australia; the species inhabits the freshwaters of north Australia.

F.I.: Has probably not yet been imported into Germany.

Sex: No definite ones are known; ♀♀ are said to be somewhat fuller.

Soc. B.: Peaceful, calm schooling fish.

M: As indicated for *Chanda macleayi.*

B: Not yet accomplished in captivity.

F: C; small live foods of all kinds; flake food is reluctantly accepted.

S: *Chanda elongatus* has a longer body than *Chanda macleayi.*

T: 20-32° C, L: 7.5 cm, A: 60 cm, R: m, D: 2
68-90° F, 3", 24",

Chanda macleayi (CASTELNAU, 1878)
Macleay's Glassfish

Syn.: *Pseudoambassis macleayi, Ambassis macleayi, Austrochanda macleayi.*

Hab.: Australia and New Guinea; Northern Territory, Queensland (drainage area of the Gulf of Carpentaria). West Australia (only in the Ord and Carson rivers) and southern New Guinea. The species inhabits freshwater.

F.I.: Probably has not been imported to Germany.

Sex: No certain differences are known for *Chanda macleayi.* ♀♀ might be somewhat fuller.

Soc. B.: Peaceful, calm schooling fish.

M: Needs a dark bottomed tank of lava or crushed basalt, densely planted edges and background, hiding places made of stone or roots and a free swimming area. The animals inhabit freshwater; therefore, salt should not be added as with other centropomids. Otherwise, no demands are made on the water. If possible, keep the animals in a group (from 6 specimens). Maintain in a species tank or with other chandids.

B: Not yet successful in an aquarium.

F: C; small live foods of any kind are readily eaten; the animals can also be trained to flake food.

S: *Chanda macleayi* is easily distinguished from other *Chanda* species by its net pattern, formed from black-edged scales.

T: 20-32° C, L: 10 cm, A: 80 cm, R: m, D: 2
68-90° F, 4", 31",

Chanda elongata

Chanda macleayi

Denariusa bandata WHITLEY, 1948
Penny Fish

Syn.: None.

Hab.: Australia; Northern Territory and Queensland. The animals inhabit weed choked waters.

F.I.: Probably not yet imported into Germany.

Sex: ♂♂ are more slender and somewhat larger; ♀♀ are fuller, especially during the spawning season.

Soc. B.: Peaceful, small schooling fish.

M: Prefers a bottom of fine dark sand or lava, dense edge and background vegetation and some cover made of stones and roots. Preserve some free swimming space. No special demands are make on water composition. Always keep a group (6 or more animals). Associate with other gentle fishes of similar size.

T: 22-32° C, **L:** 5 cm, **A:** 40 cm, **R:** m, **D:** 3
72-90° F, 2", 16",

B: Has not yet been successful in an aquarium.

F: C; small live foods of any kind. The animals are difficult to train to substitute foods. Without live food, they decline.

S: The lateral line of *Denariusa bandata* is greatly reduced.

Cattle Creek. Near the coast of central Queensland, Australia. Rainbow fishes, glassfishes and gobies can be found here.

Gymnochanda filamentosa FRASER-BRUNNER, 1954
Filament Glassfish

Syn.: *Gymnochanda filamentosa* (BOESEMAN, 1954).

Hab.: Southeast Asia, Malaysia (Province of Johore) and Singapore.

F.I.: 1955.

Sex: Anal fin and second dorsal fin of the ♂ have strongly elongated fin rays.

Soc. B.: Similar to *Chanda* species.

M: As with *Chanda commersonii*. *G. filamentosa* should be kept in brackish water.

B: Breeding the species has been sporadically successful. However, detailed reports are not available.

T: 23-26° C, L: 5 cm, A: 50 cm, R: m, D: 3-4
73-79° F, 2", 20",

F: C; predominately live foods of any kind. Flake and other foods are not readily taken.

S: The ♂♂ of *Gymnochanda filamentosa* can be easily distinguished from ♂♂ of *Chanda* species by their extremely elongated fin rays of the anal and second dorsal fin. According to STERBA, these elongated fin rays are much shorter in bred specimens.

Edelia obscura (KLUNZINGER, 1872)
Yarra Pygmy Perch

Syn.: *Nannoperca obscura.*

Hab.: Australia; Victoria, in creeks around Melbourne.

F.I.: Probably not yet imported into Germany.

Sex: ♂ is slimmer.

Soc. B.: A peaceful species which gets along well with conspecific and heterospecific fishes.

M: Provide the tank with a sandy or fine gravel bottom, dense edge and background vegetation and some places to hide. Good filtration of the tank is indicated. No special demands are placed on water values. Maintain in a species tank or keep with other dwarf perches or similar sized cichlids.

B: No details have been given. Breeding is probably similar to *Edelia vittata.*

F: C, O; small live foods of any kind, also flake food.

S: *Edelia obscura* differs from *Edelia vittata* CASTELNAU, 1873, by the third anal fin ray being longer than the second. •

T: 10-30° C, L: 7.5 cm, A: 60 cm, R: m, b, D: 2
50-86° F, 3", 24",

Edelia vittata — CASTELNAU, 1873

West Australian Pygmy Perch

Syn.: None (?).

Hab.: Australia; in coastal rivers, lakes and pools between Hopetown (Phillips River) and Moora (Moore River).

F.I.: Probably not yet imported into Germany.

Sex: ♂ has courtship coloration during the spawning season, slimmer; ♀ fuller. According to SHIPWAY, the ♂ can be recognized outside the spawning time by its darker fins.

Soc. B.: The animals are peaceful among themselves and towards heterospecific fishes.

M: Offer a well-planted tank with a fine, sandy bottom and constructions of rocks and/or roots for hiding places. Preserve some open swimming space. The fish do not have any other demands. Keep in a species tank or house with other Australian dwarf perches, cichlids or correspondingly sized centrarchids.

B: The animals breed in a species tank without intervention of the hobbyist. However, spawning can also be induced by a partial water exchange. There is no brood care. In nature, the animals spawn between July and January. The eggs are laid in groups of 60. They have a diameter of 1.2 mm (1/32"), sink to the bottom and are adhesive. At 16-22° C (61-72° F), the larvae hatch after 60-72 hours. The larval stage lasts another 2-3 weeks. The animals are sexually mature after 1 year.

F: C, O; small live foods of any kind, also flake food.

S: *Edelia vittata* is the most beautiful and hardy species among the Australian dwarf perches. In Australia, *E. vittata* is a popular aquarium fish.

T: 10-30° C, **L:** 7 cm, **A:** 60 cm, **R:** m, b, **D:** 2
50-86° F, 2 3/4, 24",

Kuhlia rupestris — (LACÉPÈDE, 1802)

Jungle Perch

Syn.: *Centropomus rupestris, Dules guamensis, Moronopsis rupestris.*

Hab.: Indo-Pacific coastal regions. The species inhabits salt and brackish water but also enters freshwater.

F.I.: Unknown.

Sex: No external ones known.

Soc. B.: Lively, fast swimmer with a predatory lifestyle. The animals are somewhat antagonistic among themselves.

M: Use a sand or gravel bottomed tank; vegetation can be waived; provide cover of stones and/or roots. The species can be kept in freshwater. Since the animals also enter fast flowing creeks in nature, a current should be provided with a strong pump; in addition, the tank should be well-filtered. Keep singly or in a small school; housing them with equal sized cichlids should be possible.

B: *Kuhlia rupestris* has not yet been bred in an aquarium.

F: C; only hardy live foods of any kind (fish, earthworms, insects). The species rarely takes substitute foods.

S: The lateral line of *Kuhlia rupestris* is comprised of 41-44 scales. Large specimens can reach 3 kg (6.6 lb).

T: 20-26° C, **L:** 45 cm, **A:** from 150 cm, **R:** m, t, **D:** 4
68-79° F, 18", from 59",

Edelia vittata

Kuhlia rupestris

Nannatherina balstoni REGAN, 1906
Balston's Perchlet

Syn.: None (?).

Hab.: Australia; the species inhabits soft, slightly acid waters of the southern coast of southwest Australia between Two People Bay and the Blackwood River.

F.I.: The species has probably not been imported into Germany.

Sex: The ♂ is more slender and colorful at spawning time.

Soc. B.: A peaceful dwarf perch which harmonizes well with conspecifics and heterospecific fishes.

M: The tank should have a bottom of sand or fine-grained gravel, edge vegetation and some hiding places of stones and roots. Keep some free swimming space. Fill with soft (5-10° dGH) and moderately acid (pH 6.0-6.5) water. Keep in a species tank, or combine with equal sized cichlids.

B: Nothing is known about successfully breeding this fish in an aquarium.

F: C; small live foods of all kinds, frozen and freeze-dried foods.

S: *Nannatherina balstoni* differs from the western dwarf perch, *Edelia vittata* CASTELNAU, 1873, by the much larger eye diameter and the larger mouth. In addition, the first dorsal fin is much shorter than the second; in *E. vittata*, the first dorsal fin is somewhat larger than the second.

T: 15-30° C, **L:** 8 cm, **A:** 60 cm, **R:** m, b, **D:** 2
59-86° F, 3", 24",

Nannoperca australis GÜNTHER, 1861
South Australian Pygmy Perch

Syn.: None (?).

Hab.: Australia; Murray river system, New South Wales, South Australia and northern Tasmania. The animals inhabit all types of waters.

F.I.: Probably has not been imported into Germany.

Sex: The ♂ is more slender and colorful at spawning time.

Soc. B.: The animals are peaceful and sociable among themselves and towards heterospecific fishes.

M: Keep in well-planted tanks with fine substrate, some hiding places and shelter of rocks and roots. Maintain some swimming space. *N. australis* can be kept in small tanks as long as there are enough hiding places. Otherwise, no demands are made. Keep in a species tank, or associate with other Australian dwarf perches.

B: The animals spawn in a species tank without major doings by the aquarist; however, spawning can be induced by partial water exchanges. *Nannoperca australis* does not care for its young.

F: C, O; small live foods (water fleas, *Cyclops*, *Tubifex*, mosquito larvae, etc.), but also flakes and freeze-dried foods.

S: *Nannoperca australis* differs from *N. oxleyana* in the following characteristics: 1. The second and third anal fin ray are of the same length (the third anal ray is longer), 2. The lateral row of scales have 28-31 scales (25 scales), 3. The length of the body is 3.5 (3.0) times the body depth.

T: 10-30° C, **L:** 8 cm, **A:** 60 cm, **R:** m, b, **D:** 2
50-86° F, 3", 24",

Nannatherina balstoni

Nannoperca australis

Nannoperca oxleyana WHITLEY, 1940
Northern Pygmy Perch

Syn.: None.

Hab.: Australia; southern Queensland and northern New South Wales. The animals inhabit coastal rivers with soft, acid water.

F.I.: Probably not yet imported into Germany.

Sex: The ♂ is more slender, smaller and is jet black during the spawning season; the ♀ is fuller and grows larger.

Soc. B.: As indicated for *Nannoperca australis*.

T: 16-30° C, L: 7.5 cm, A: 60 cm, R: m, b, D: 2
61-86° F, 3", 24",

M: See *N. australis*. However, *Nannoperca oxleyana* loves soft (5-10° dGH) and slightly acid (pH 6.0-6.5) water.

B: As for *N. australis*.

F: C, O; small live foods of all kinds, freeze-dried and flake foods.

S: Both *Nannoperca* species are popular aquarium fishes in Australia.

Lutjanus argentimaculatus (FORSKÅL, 1775)
Mangrove Jack

Syn.: *Sciaena argentimaculata, Mesoprion gembra, M. maus.*

Hab.: Tropical Indo-Pacific; from the Red Sea and east African coast to northern Australia and the islands of the west Pacific. The animals also enter freshwater.

F.I.: Probably after 1980.

Sex: No external ones known.

Soc. B.: The animals are pronounced predators. Even smaller juveniles have a distinct predatory lifestyle and are quarrelsome.

M: Only juveniles are suitable for aquaria. Larger specimens are jewels for show aquaria. Best kept singly. Decorate the tank as for large cichlids. Perhaps the animals should be kept in brackish or salt water.

B: Unknown.

F: C; hearty live foods of all kinds, frozen food (shrimp), beef heart and other meats.

S: After a certain acclimation period, the animals become quite tame. *L. argentimaculatus* is one of the few snappers that live in freshwater.

T: 16-30° C, L: 100 cm, A: from 150 cm, R: m, D: 3
61-86° F, 39", from 59",

Monodactylus sebae (CUVIER in CUVIER & VALENCIENNES, 1831)
Seba Mono

Syn.: *Psettus sebae, Chaetodon rhombeus.*

Hab.: West Africa; the coast from Senegal to Zaire. The animals are salt water fish that will sometimes enter the brackish waters at the mouth of rivers and may enter freshwater (very rarely).

F.I.: 1914.

Sex: None can be determined.

Soc. B.: Peaceful schooling fish. Often, the animals are timid and nervous in an aquarium. The species is predatory towards smaller fishes.

M: Offer crushed shell, or other calcium containing materials, such as dolomite, etc., as substrate. Plant with salt water species; use seawater-safe stone and root decorations; leave plenty of free swimming space. Keep only in salt or brackish water, since freshwater does not agree with the fish over the long term; provide good aeration and a protein skimmer. Combine with species having similar demands (other monos or scats).

B: The species has not yet been bred in an aquarium.

T: 24-28° C, L: 20 cm, A: 100 cm, R: m, t, D: 3-4
75-82° F, 8", 39",

Nandus nebulosus (GRAY, 1830)
Fog Nandus

Syn.: *Bedula nebulosus.*

Hab.: Southeast Asia; Thailand, Malay Peninsula, Indonesia (Greater Sunda Islands).

F.I.: 1934.

Sex: None known.

Soc. B.: Predatory, twilight-active fish which are predominantly loners.

M: Needs a bottom of gravel or sand, dense vegetation on the sides and the background of the tanks, and floating plants to dim the light. The tank should not be too brightly illuminated. Create hiding places of roots and/or stones. Clear, at least medium-hard water (from 10° dGH), pH about 7.0 is recommended; the addition of sea salt is not really necessary; provide good filtration. Do not associate with smaller fishes (predator!).

B: Possible, similar to *N. nandus* Vol. 1, page 806.

F: C; the species feeds almost exclusively on live foods (mosquito larvae, larvae of aquatic insects, *Tubifex*, earthworms, small fishes).

S: *Nandus nebulosus* only has 34 scales on the lateral line, while *Nandus nandus* (see Vol. 1) has 46 to 57.

T: 22-26° C, L: 12 cm, A: 80 cm, R: m, b, D: 2-3
72-79° F, 4 3/4", 31",

F: O; omnivore: live foods of all types, scraped meats, frozen food, flake food, plant fare (lettuce, spinach, algae).

S: *Monodactylus sebae* has a significantly higher back than *M. argenteus*; in addition, the design differs. In *M. sebae*, a dark band runs from the tip of the dorsal fin over the body to the tip of the anal fin (see photo).

Macquaria australasica CUVIER & VALENCIENNES, 1830

Macquerie Perch

Syn.: None.

Hab.: Australia; in cool waters of southeast Australia.

F.I.: Probably has not been imported into Germany.

Sex: No external ones known.

Soc. B.: A peaceful, calm species which gets along well with conspecifics and other tankmates that are not too small.

M: Use tanks that are not overly small and have good side and background vegetation. Some hiding places of stones and roots are recommended, so they can retreat when the surroundings become too hectic. No other special requirements are demanded. Do not associate with fishes that are too hectic and aggressive.

B: No reports are available dealing with successfully breeding this species. In the wild, the spawning season lasts from September to November. A two pound ♀ can lay up to 200,000 eggs.

F: C; live foods of all types, frozen food (e.g., shrimp), also beef heart and other meats.

S: In its natural range, the species is appreciated as a good sports fish.

T: 4-25° C, **L:** 35 cm, **A:** 120 cm, **R:** m, b, **D:** 3
39-77° F, 14", 47",

Plectoplites ambiguus (RICHARDSON, 1845)

Australian Golden Perch

Syn.: *Datnia ambigua, Macquaria ambigua.*

Hab.: Australia; in the Murray river system; Queensland, New South Wales, from Victoria to south and central Australia. The species has been introduced into West Australia and is cultured in reservoirs in Queensland.

F.I.: Probably not yet imported into Germany.

Sex: The ♂♂ are thinner than ♀♀.

Soc. B.: The species is very sedate, but since it has a predatory lifestyle, it should not be associated with smaller fishes. Among themselves, the animals are quite quarrelsome.

M: Only young are suitable for the normal aquarium. Older specimens remain subjects for large public aquaria. However, the species barely grows larger than 30 cm (12") in a normal aquarium. Maintenance should either be in a species tank or with equal sized, robust fishes.

B: Not yet accomplished in an aquarium. The animals have been bred in fish culture installations. In the wild, *P. ambiguus* spawns during the seasonal flooding, whereby the planktonic eggs are widely distributed by the flood.

F: C; hardy live foods of any kind.

S: The species is a good sports fish. Large specimens can reach weights of up to 25 kg (55 lb).

T: 10-30° C, **L:** 75 cm, **A:** 150 cm, **R:** m, b, **D:** 4
50-86° F, 30", 59",

Macquaria australasica

Plectoplites ambiguus

Maccullochella macquariensis (CUVIER & VALENCIENNES, 1829)
Trout Cod, Murray Cod

Syn.: *Grystes macquariensis*.

Hab.: Australia; in the Murray-Darling river system from south Queensland to South Australia and New South Wales. The species has also been introduced in other regions of Australia.

F.I.: Probably not yet imported into Germany.

Sex: No definite ones known.

Soc. B.: A relatively sedate perch species with a strong predatory lifestyle.

M: Only young are suitable for an average aquarium. Full-grown specimens are beautiful subjects for large show aquaria. Provide a bottom of fine gravel, background vegetation of robust species and some shelter and hiding places of roots and stones. Leave free swimming space. No special demands are placed on the water. Associate with robust fishes of at least the same size. Best kept in a species tank.

B: It is not possible in an aquarium due to lack of space, and to our knowledge, it has not been accomplished. In the wild, the animals spawn when the water temperature has reached 20° C (68° F) and flooding has occurred. The animals are substrate spawners which normally lay their adhesive, 2-3 mm (1/16"-1/8") eggs in hollow trunks and on leaves of fallen rubber trees. The average number of eggs is 20,000. Depending on temperature, the young hatch in 8-13 days.

F: C; hardy live foods of all kinds; the animals can also be trained to beef heart and other meats.

S: *M. macquariensis* is one of the largest and most important freshwater food fish in its natural habitat. According to WHITLEY, two varieties exist which differ in their coloration and pattern: *Maccullochella macquariensis* var. *macquariensis* (CUVIER & VALENCIENNES, 1829) (= trout cod) and *Macculllochella macquariensis* var. *peelii* MITCHELL, 1838 (= Murray cod, see bottom photo).

T: 18-28° C, L: 80 cm, A: from 150 cm, R: m, D: 3-4
64-82° F, 31", from 59",

Maccullochella macquariensis

Maccullochella macquariensis var. *peelii*

Amniataba percoides (GÜNTHER, 1864)
Black-Striped Grunter

Syn.: *Therapon percoides.*

Hab.: Australia; distributed in all freshwater systems of northern Australia.

F.I.: Probably not yet imported into Germany.

Sex: No external ones known.

Soc. B.: The animals are very bellicose; therefore, it is best to keep them singly or in a small school. The species has a predatory lifestyle.

M: Bottom should be of sand or fine gravel. Plant the edges with tough species. Provide hiding places and shelter of stones and roots. No demands are placed on water composition. Associate with robust fish (e.g., cichlids) or keep in a species tank.

B: Nothing is yet known about a successful spawn in an aquarium.

F: C; live food of all types, freeze-dried foods, beef heart and other meats.

S: Three sub-species of *Amniataba percoides* have been described.

T: 22-28° C, **L**: 20 cm, **A**: 100 cm, **R**: m, **D**: 3
72-82° F, 8", 39",

Bidyanus bidyanus (MITCHELL, 1838)
Australian Silver Perch

Syn.: *Therapon bidyana, Terapon bidyana.*

Hab.: Australia; Queensland, New South Wales, Victoria, South and Western Australia.

F.I.: Unknown, with some certainty, it can be said that it has not been imported into Germany.

Sex: No external ones known.

Soc. B.: The animals are very aggressive and pugnacious. Larger specimens have a predatory lifestyle.

M: Maintenance is only possible in the largest of tanks. The animals are otherwise undemanding. Juveniles can be kept in a school, but older specimens should be maintained alone.

B: Has not been successful in an aquarium. In aquaculture, it has been done. The spawning season lasts from September to October in the wild, sometimes also in March and April. Larger ♀♀ can lay 500,000 eggs. The pelagic eggs have a diameter of about one millimeter (1/32").

F: C, O; hearty live foods of all kinds, especially fish, but also beef heart and other meats.

S: The animals can produce sound. In their habitat they are an appreciated sport fish.

T: 10-30° C, **L**: 50 cm, **A**: 150 cm, **R**: m, b, **D**: 4
50-86° F, 20", 59",

Amniataba percoides

Bidyanus bidyanus

Hephaestus carbo (OGILBY & McCULLOCH, 1916)
Coal Grunter

Syn.: *Therapon carbo.*

Hab.: Australia; Arnhem Land and Cap York Peninsula.

F.I.: Probably not yet imported into Germany.

Sex: No external ones known.

Soc. B.: Although they are found in small groups in the wild, in small aquaria they are very quarrelsome among themselves. Larger specimens are predatory.

M: Use roomy tanks with densely planted edges and background; offer some hiding places (roots) and fine gravel as substrate. No special requirements are placed on the water. Up to a length of 10 cm (4"), *H. carbo* can be kept with rainbow fishes; larger specimens can be housed with robust cichlids.

B: Has not been successful in captivity.

F: C; live foods of all types, but also frozen and freeze-dried foods.

S: *Hephaestus carbo* is one of the most beautiful perches of Australia. The fish can become very tame in an aquarium.

T: 25-30° C, L: 33 cm, smaller in aquaria, A: 100 cm, R: m, D: 3
77-86° F, 13", smaller in aquaria, 39",

Hephaestus fuliginosus (MACLEAY, 1883)
Sooty Grunter

Syn.: *Therapon fuliginosus.*

Hab.: Australia; eastern Northern Territory and northern Queensland.

F.I.: Probably not yet imported into Germany.

Sex: Unknown.

Soc. B.: As indicated for *Hephaestus carbo.*

M: See *H. carbo.*

B: Has not been successful in captivity.

F: C; live foods of all kinds, frozen and freeze-dried foods.

S: The species is an appreciated food fish in its home range.

T: 25-30° C, L: 50 cm, A: 150 cm, R: m, D: 4
77-86° F, 20", 59",

Hephaestus carbo

Hephaestus fuliginosus

Leiopotherapon unicolor (GÜNTHER, 1859)
Jewel Perch

Syn.: *Therapon unicolor, Madigania unicolor.*

Hab.: Australia; the species widely distributed throughout northern Australia.

F.I.: Probably not yet imported into Germany.

Sex: No external ones known.

Soc. B.: Lively fish which are very quarrelsome. Still, the fish are best kept in a school.

M: Needs a tank with a sand or a fine gravel bottom and dense edge and background vegetation. The animals should be offered plenty of hiding places and shelter. No special demands are placed on water composition. Keep in a species tank or with cichlids.

B: Breeding has not been successful in an aquarium. In the wild the animals are fertile open spawners.

F: C; live foods of all types, beef heart and other meats, frozen food.

S: *L. unicolor* is an excellent jumper. The tanks, therefore, need to be covered very well.

T: 15-30° C, L: 15 cm, A: 80 cm, R: m, D: 2
59-86° F, 6", 31",

Scortum barcoo (McCULLOCH & WAITE, 1917)
Barcoo Grunter

Syn.: *Therapon barcoo.*

Hab.: Australia; in freshwaters of inner Australia.

F.I.: Unknown, probably not yet imported into Germany.

Sex: No external ones known.

Soc. B.: The animals are very bad-tempered among themselves. They are predators and should only be associated with same sized fishes.

M: Use a sandy or gravel substrate; plant with robust species; offer hiding places out of stones and roots; leave free swimming space. No demands are placed on water composition.

B: Has not yet been successful in captivity. In the wild the animals are open spawners. No other data are yet known.

F: C, O; live foods of all kinds, freeze-dried, frozen, tablet and flake foods.

S: The animals become very tame in an aquarium.

T: 10-30° C, L: 30 cm, A: 100 cm, R: m, D: 2
50-86° F, 12", 39",

Leiopotherapon unicolor

Scortum barcoo

Toxotes lorentzi (WEBER, 1911)
Primitive Archer Fish

Syn.: *Protoxotes lorentzi.*

Hab.: Australia and New Guinea. The species occurs in freshwater.

F.I.: Probably not yet imported into Germany.

Sex: No visible signs known.

Soc. B.: While the fish are peaceful to other species, they are somewhat antagonistic among themselves. Keep a small school to diminish aggressions. When kept like this, they will get along quite well.

M: Well-planted, large surface aquaria with plenty of free swimming room. The water does not need to be deep (30 cm, 12"). According to present observations, this species only lives in freshwater. No special demands are placed on water chemistry, but it needs to be warm. Best kept in a species tank.

B: Has not been successful in captivity, nor are there reports dealing with the reproductive biology of this species in the wild.

F: C; live foods of any kind. Especially relished are flying insects (flies, small grasshoppers, etc.). Only feeds on floating foods.

S: *Toxotes lorentzi*'s closest relative is *Toxotes microlepis.* The former differs from the latter by having smaller scales.

T: 24-32° C, **L:** 23 cm, usually much smaller, **A:** 80 cm, **R:** t, m, **D:** 3-4
75-90° F, 9", usually much smaler, 31",

Toxotes oligolepis BLEEKER, 1876
Few-Scaled Archerfish

Syn.: None.

Hab.: Southeast Asia, New Guinea and Australia.

F.I.: Probably not yet imported into Germany.

Sex: Unknown.

Soc. B.: As listed under *Toxotes lorentzi.*

M: See *Toxotes lorentzi.*

B: Has not been successful in an aquarium. Nothing is known about spawning in the wild either.

F: C; live foods of all kinds (chiefly insects). Feeds almost exclusively from the water surface.

S: *Toxotes oligolepis* is a rare species with an almost totally unknown biology.

T: 24-30° C, **L:** 15 cm, **A:** 80 cm, **R:** t, m, **D:** 3-4
75-86° F, 6", 31",

Toxotes lorentzi

Toxotes oligolepis

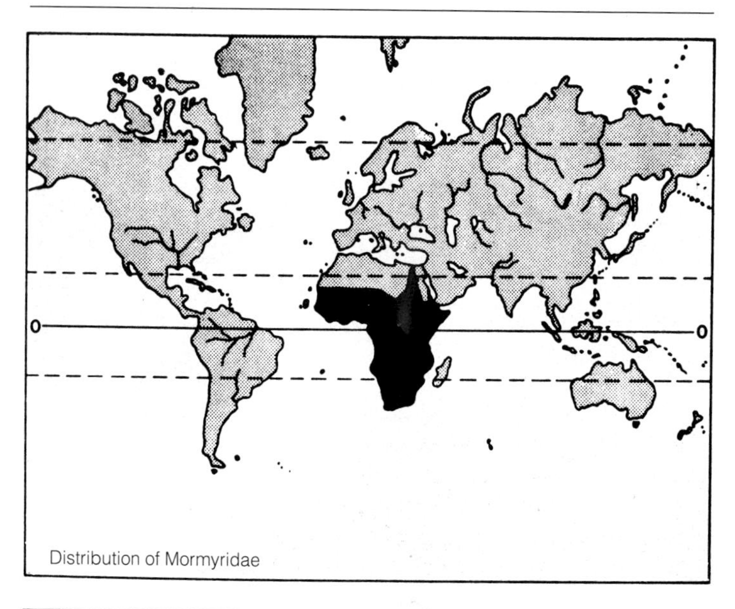

Distribution of Mormyridae

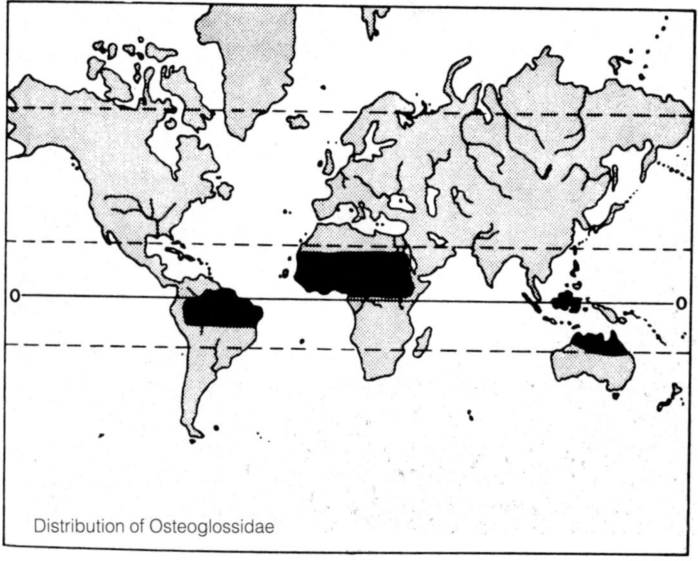

Distribution of Osteoglossidae

Hypseleotris compressa, one of the most beautiful Australian goby species. See page 1066.

Fam.: Aplochitonidae
All members of this family occur in temperate waters of the southern hemisphere. They inhabit rivers, sometimes lakes, but also coastal waters at the southern tip of South America, southern Australia, Tasmania and New Zealand. Many are migratory (andromous) fishes; that is, they live in the sea and spawn in freshwater. Most members are small (30 cm; 12" or less) and are similar to salmonids of the northern hemisphere. All Aplochitonidae have an adipose fin. Some species are naked while others are fully scaled.

Fam.: Bovichthyidae (Ice Fishes)
All Bovichthyidae inhabit the southern hemisphere, usually right at the border of the Antarctic area. Their distribution area extends through the southern tip of South America (Tierra del Fuego) and Australia to New Zealand and some Pacific islands. They are absent from the Antarctic region proper. The opercular membranes are free of the throat, and the animals have teeth on the palate.

Fam.: Clupeidae (Herrings)
The majority of the herrings live in tropical seas (about 150 species). Thirty additional species are confined to the temperate regions. The greatest species richness is reached in the west Indo-Pacific region. Some species are brackish water inhabitants, while others live in freshwater. The conus arteriosus (a part of the heart) is absent in herrings, the mucous channels on the head are well developed and the lateral line is nonexistent. Some species are migratory, most school. The animals are dark dorsally and light ventrally. The body is covered with fragile scales which easily fall off. Almost all herring are planktivores which grow little larger than 50 cm (20") in length (maximum size is about 1 m; 1 yd). Herrings are still the most important fishery on earth.

Fam.: Gadopsidae
Gadopsidae are freshwater fishes with a distribution area limited to southern Australia and, especially, Tasmania. The family is comprised of a single genus with a single species (*Gadopsis marmoratus*). The animals are quite slender, have a long dorsal fin and a scaled body. The pelvic fins are anterior to the pectoral fins and consist of only one single long ray.

Fam.: Galaxiidae
Representatives of this family are predominantly found in freshwaters of the southern hemisphere, occurring in southern South America, Australia, New Zealand, New Caledonia and South Africa. It is made up of naked, usually small fishes which spawn in freshwater. Some spe-

cies migrate and spend part of their life in the sea. All Galaxiidae have round dorsal and anal fins which are opposite to each other and located far to the posterior. They differ from their closest relatives, the Retropinnidae, by the absence of an adipose fin.

Fam.: Lepidogalaxiidae (Salamander Fishes)
The family Lepidogalaxiidae is very small. It consist of only one genus with only a single species (*Lepidogalaxias salamandroides* MEES, 1961). Its distribution is limited to the southern hemisphere. The animals occur in rivers and pools of southern Australia between Lake Powell and the Scott River. It seems to be the last representative of a very old family.

Fam.: Megalopidae (Tarpons)
This small family has the largest representatives of the herring-like fishes (Clupeiformes). The atlantic tarpon, *Megalops atlanticus*, reaches a length of almost 2 m and a weight of 50 kg (2.2 yd and 110 lb). The fishes of this family have a conus arteriosus with two rows of flaps, a long anal fin and the last dorsal fin ray extremely elongated. Pseudobranchials are absent. The development of Megalopidae includes a metamorphosis. From the genus *Megalops* exist two recent species which occur in the tropical waters of the Indo-Pacific (*M. cyprinoides*). Sometimes these fishes enter rivers.

Fam.: Retropinnidae
In appearance, Retropinnidae are similar to the Osmeridae. In contrast, the Retropinnidae are inhabitants of the southern hemisphere. Their distribution is limited to the waters around southern and eastern Australia, on Tasmania and New Zealand. Some species inhabit salt water but migrate into freshwater to spawn. The Retropinnidae differ from the Galaxiidae by the presence of an adipose fin and smaller scales.

Fam.: Scorpaenidae (Scorpion Fishes, Lionfishes)
Scorpion fishes are characterized by their perch-like body shape. The body is covered with scales; the head has more or less developed spines. The hard rays of the fins are well developed. The distribution of Scorpaenidae is worldwide with the exception of the Antarctic. All are marine; many occur in temperate and cool regions. A large number are bottom dwellers. About 300 species are known. Among the Scorpaenidae are some of the most poisonous fishes. Red is a typical color of many scorpion fishes.

Fam.: Soleidae (Flatfishes)

The flatfishes are characterized by an elongated body and eyes that are located on the right side of the body. The preoperculm does not have a free edge; it is totally covered with skin and scales. The flatfishes are bottom dwelling flat fishes with a worldwide distribution in tropical and temperate seas. Some species also enter freshwater or live therein permanently. The Soleidae have a planktonic, totally symmetrical larval stage. During development, one eye moves to the other side (right). Many flatfishes are appreciated food fish.

Fam.: Synbranchidae

These animals have an eel-like body shape. The unpaired fins are usually fused into one. The body is either covered with small scales or is naked. The right and left gill slit are fused to a slit-shaped gill opening in the center of the throat. The small eyes are covered with skin. The animals can breath atmospheric air through richly vascularized protrutions in the gill cavity or parts of the hind gut. Some species live amphibiously at the edge of water. The animals inhabit tropical areas of America, Africa, Asia and Australia.

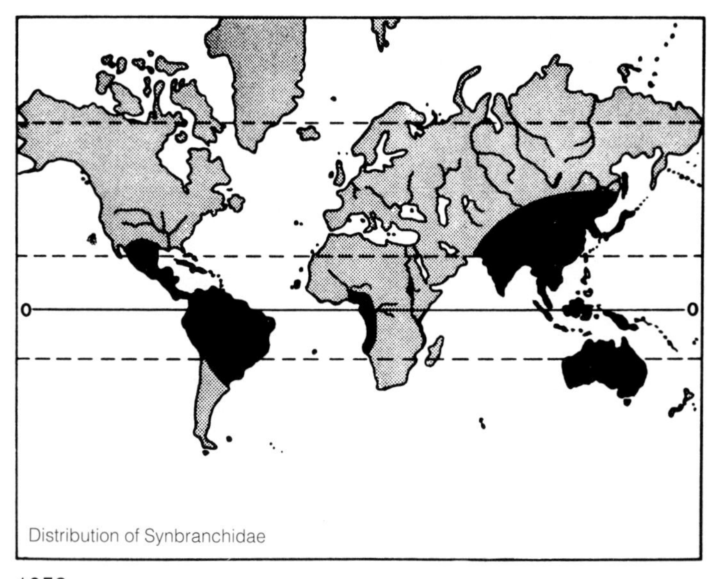

Distribution of Synbranchidae

Prototroctes maraena GÜNTHER, 1864

Grayling, Cucumber Herring

Syn.: None (?).

Hab.: Australia; in coastal rivers of New South Wales, Victoria and Tasmania.

F.I.: Probably not yet imported into Germany.

Sex: No definite external ones known; the ♂ is probably more slender.

Soc. B.: Very active, peaceful schooling fish.

M: Because of the active swimming pattern of the fish, it can only be kept in very roomy aquaria. Needs background vegetation which preserves a lot of swimming space; otherwise, the fish has no demands. Always keep a school (6 or more animals), and it is best kept in a species tank.

B: Nothing is known about a successful aquarium spawn. Very little is known about the reproductive biology of *P. maraena*. It is assumed that the species migrates and spawns in freshwater.

F: C, O; live foods of all types, freeze-dried, frozen and flake foods.

S: In the wild, *Prototroctes maraena* is in danger of extinction by various different factors (straightening of river courses, introduction of exotic species, overfishing, etc.).

T: 10-25° C, **L:** 30 cm, **A:** over 150 cm, **R:** m, b, **D:** 3
50-77° F, 12", over 59",

Craterocephalus eyresii (STEINDACHNER, 1884)

Syn.: *Atherinichthys eyresii.*

Hab.: Australia; South Australia and the Northern Territory.

F.I.: The species has probably not been kept in German aquaria.

Sex: None known.

Soc. B.: Active, very peaceful schooling fish.

M: As indicated for *Quirichthys stramineus.*

B: See *Craterocephalus stercusmuscarum.*

F: C, O; live foods of all kinds, frozen and flake foods.

S: The species is limited to rivers and lakes of central Australia.

T: 24-30° C, **L:** 10 cm, **A:** 70 cm, **R:** t, m, **D:** 2-3
75-86° F, 4", 28",

Craterocephalus marjoriae WHITLEY, 1948
Marjorie's Hardyhead, Straw Man

Syn.: None.

Hab.: Australia; in the coastal rivers of southern Queensland.

F.I.: Probably not yet imported into Germany.

Sex: No sure ones known.

Soc. B.: Extremely peaceful, lively and active schooling fish.

M: As with *Quirichthys stramineus.*

B: See *Craterocephalus stercusmuscarum.*

T: 24-30° C, **L:** 8 cm, **A:** 60 cm, **R:** t, m, **D:** 2
75-86° F, 3", 24",

F: C, O; small live foods of any kind, freeze-dried food, frozen and flake foods.

S: During the spawning season, the animals acquire a canary yellow breeding dress, indicated also by their Australian name (= straw man). *Craterocephalus marjoriae* has relatively large scales.

Craterocephalus eyresii

Craterocephalus marjoriae

Craterocephalus stercusmuscarum GÜNTHER, 1867
Fly-Speckled Hardyhead

Syn.: *Craterocephalus fluviatilis.*

Hab.: Australia; eastern coastal rivers in Queensland from Mackay to Brisbane.

F.I.: 1982 (?).

Sex: No definite ones known.

Soc. B.: Peaceful, actively swimming fish which is somewhat nervous.

M: Requires long aquaria with sparse vegetation and a lot of room to swim. Water should be soft (5-10° dGH) and slightly acid (pH 6.0-6.5). Always keep a school (6 or more specimens). Associate with rainbow fishes and/or other silversides, or maintain in a species tank.

B: *Craterocephalus* species have surely already been bred by Australian aquarists. European and American aquarium literature contain no reports as of yet.

F: O; the animals eat almost everything that is offered (live foods of all kinds, freeze-dried, frozen and flake foods)

S: *Craterocephalus stercusmuscarum* is a popular aquarium fish in Australia. Since the fish are excellent jumpers, the tanks must be well covered. All *Craterocephalus* species eat a lot of mosquito larvae; therefore, they are used in their control.

T: 24-30° C, **L:** 10 cm, **A:** 90 cm, **R:** t, m, **D:** 2
75-86° F, 4", 35",

Quirichthys stramineus (WHITLEY, 1950)
Straw Man

Syn.: *Quiris stramineus.*

Hab.: Australia; in Western Australia, only in the Ord river system. The species is numerous in Lake Kanunurra and Spillway Creek, north of Lake Argyle. The fish also occur in the Katherine River (Northern Territory) and some rivers which flow into the Gulf of Carpentaria (Queensland).

F.I.: Unknown, probably not yet imported into Germany.

Sex: No definite ones known.

Soc. B.: A very peaceful, lively schooling fish.

M: Similar to *Pseudomugil* species. Provide the tank with dense edge and background vegetation, fine substrate and sufficient room to swim. Water should not be too hard (up to 12° dGH) and in the neutral range (pH 7.0). Best kept in a species tank (always in a school) or housed with small rainbow fishes and other silversides (e.g., *Craterocephalus* species).

B: *Quirichthys stramineus* has surely already been successfully bred by Australian aquarists, but a detailed breeding report has not been found.

F: C, O; live foods of all types (insects and their aquatic larvae, small crustacea, snails), probably also water plants.

S: *Quirichthys stramineus* has no known relatives in New Guinea, but it does on Sulawesi (Celebes).

T: 25-30° C, **L:** 7 cm, **A:** 70 cm, **R:** m, t, **D:** 2-3
77-86° F, 2¾", 28",

Craterocephalus stercusmuscarum

Quirichthys stramineus

Pseudaphritis bursinus (CUVIER in CUVIER & VALENCIENNES, 1830)
Congolli, Tupong

Syn.: *Eleginus bursinus.*

Hab.: Australia; southeast Australia and Tasmania, the animals occur in seawater, brackish water and freshwater.

F.I.: Probably not yet imported into Germany.

Sex: No external ones known.

Soc. B.: Bottom fish with a predatory lifestyle. Its appearance and behavior reminds one of sleeper gobies.

M: Use a fine bottom, allowing the fish to burrow. Provide some rock shelters. The tank does not need to be planted. Keep the animals in fresh or brackish water (1 tablespoon of sea salt per 10 l; 2.5 gal). Overly warm aquaria, above 25° C (77° F) are detrimental to the animals. Keep in a species tank, or associate with sleeper gobies.

B: Has not been successful in an aquarium.

F: C; live foods of all kinds, also frozen and freeze-dried foods.

S: In nature the animals seem to migrate between sea and freshwater.
It is possible that the species presented here is *Pseudaphritis urvillii* (VALENCIENNES, 1831). Which of the two names is valid for the species pictured here could not be determined. We have decided to use the older name. The family Bovichthidae predominately occurs in the waters of the Antarctic (therefore, ice fish). Only one species migrates to Australia and enters freshwater there.

T: 5-20° C (coldwater fish), L: 20 cm, A: 100 cm, R: b, D: 3
41-68° F (coldwater fish), 8", 39",

Parachanna africana (STEINDACHNER, 1879)
African Snakehead

Syn.: *Channa africana, Ophicephalus africanus, Ophiocephalus africanus.*

Hab.: West Africa; Nigeria and Cameroon.

F.I.: 1908.

Sex: No definite ones known; the ♂♂ may have richer colors; the ♀♀ have a fuller ventral area.

Soc. B.: As with *Channa marulia*; patriarch family.

M: See *Channa marulia.*

B: Breeding sporadically successful (ARMBRUST, 1967: DATZ **20**, 367-368). 27-30° C (81° F); need large tanks with at least 150 l (39 gal); requires dense floating plant cover. Pairings occur close to the water surface and end with the ♂ turning the ♀ belly up. The eggs are lighter than water and float at the surface, but are light sensitive (floating plant cover!). The ♂ guards eggs and larvae. After the young are free-swimming, the parents should be removed.

F: Live foods of all kinds (fish, earthworms, snails, large aquatic insects).

S: *Channa africana* has, like all snakeheads, an accessory breathing organ that allows the animals complementary air breathing. This permits them to inhabit very polluted waters.

T: 25-28° C, L: 32 cm, A: from 100 cm, R: all, D: 1-2
77-82° F, 13", from 39",

Channa argus (CANTOR, 1842)
Spotted Snakehead

Syn.: *Ophicephalus argus, O. nigricans, O. pekinensis, Ophiocephalus argus.*

Hab.: China: Amur, Yunnan, Anhwei, Hokon, Kiangsi and border region to the former USSR (north of the Amur).

F.I.: 1956 into Czechoslovakia (from Moscow).

Sex: Not known; ripe ♀♀ are significantly fuller.

Soc. B.: Calm predator. Practices brood care; patriarch family.

M: Only one adult specimen should be kept in an average aquarium. If large show aquaria are used, combining with correspondingly large fishes is possible.

B: It is not likely, and it has not been done in home aquaria (size!).

F: C; juveniles eat earthworms; older animals eat fish but can be trained to meat strips.

S: SOIN (1960): Voprosy ichtiologii, page 127-137, reports that the sub-species *Channa argus warpachowskii* (BERG, 1909) builds a nest in the wild. In June/July the fish build a nest out of various plant parts floating on the water surface in densely vegetated shallow water (50-100 cm; 20"-39"). During pairing, the ♀ is embraced by the ♂ and turned on her back. One ♀ produces up to 50,000 eggs which are attentively guarded by the ♂. The eggs have a large oil drop which allows them to float on the water surface. At a temperature between 23-25° C (73-77° F) the larvae hatch after about 36 hours and are free-swimming after an additional 3-4 days. At this point, brood care by the ♂ is concluded.

T: 14-22° C, L: to 85 cm, A: 100 cm, R: all, D: 4, but only because of the food requirement.
57-72° F, to 33", 39",

Channa marulia (HAMILTON, 1822)

Syn.: *Ophiocephalus marulius, Ophicephalus marulius.*

Hab.: Asia; from India to southern China.

F.I.: 1906.

Sex: No external sexual differences are known. Presumably the ♂♂ are more intensely colored at spawning time, while the ♀♀ have a larger girth.

Soc. B.: The animals are usually loners. The species is predatory. Quite peaceful towards equal sized conspecifics.

M: Requires a fine substrate, dense vegetation and roots for decoration. The animals do not place any demands on water composition. Well covered tanks should be used since the fish are good jumpers. Only associate with same sized or larger fishes.

B: To our knowledge *Channa marulia* has not been bred in an aquarium.

F: Live food, primarily fishes. The animals can be trained to accept pieces of meat.

S: *Channa marulia* is an appreciated food fish in some areas. The fish can breath atmospheric air. For this purpose, they have an accessory breathing organ in the form of a open area connected to the gill cavity. All snakeheads are very sensitive to sea or table salt in the water.

T: 24-28° C, L: 120 cm, A: from 100 cm, R: m, b, D: 1-2
75-82° F, 47", from 39",

Channa argus

Channa marulia

Nematalosa erebi (GÜNTHER, 1868)
Bony Bream

Syn.: *Chatoessus erebi, Fluvialosa bulleri, F. paracome.*

Hab.: Australia and New Guinea; the species is widely distributed in Australia and also occurs in New Guinea.

F.I.: Has probably not been imported into Germany.

Sex: Outside the spawning season, the sexes cannot be distinguished. Within the spawning season, the ♂♂ look like giant rummy nose tetras: a blood red snout, golden back and silver sides with a pink sheen.

Soc. B.: Peaceful, active schooling fish.

M: Only possible in large aquaria. The bottom should have very fine sand since the animals like to search through it for food. Provide plenty of free swimming space; otherwise, the fish have no special demands. Keep a school in a large species tank.

B: Not known.

F: O; live foods of all kinds, flake food and also vegetable fare (bottom algae).

S: *Nematalosa erebi* are extremely prone to shock and usually die during capture. They are also sensitive to injury. *N. erebi* is the most common fish of Australia, often found in masses.

T: 15-25° C, L: 47 cm, A: 150 cm, R: m, b, D: 4
59-77° F, 19", 59",

Butis butis (HAMILTON, 1822)
Bony-Snouted Gudgeon

Syn.: *Cheilodipterus butis, Butis prismaticus, Eleotris butis, E. humeralis, E. melanopterus, E. prismatica.*

Hab.: Indo-Pacific species; from east Africa through southeast Asia to New Guinea and Australia. The animals occur in salt, brackish and freshwater.

F.I.: 1932 or 1933 by "Aquarium Hamburg".

Sex: No definite external ones are known.

Soc. B.: Territorial, these are predatory twilight and nocturnal active fish.

M: Needs a bottom of sand, gravel or coral sand and hiding places of rocks or seawater-safe roots. Vegetation in the tank can be waived, or brackish water resistant plants should be chosen. Though the animals can be acclimated to freshwater, the addition of sea salt (1-1.5%) is recommended. When maintained in freshwater, it should have a hardness to 18° dGH and be neutral to slightly alkaline (pH 7.0-7.8); provide good tank aeration. Best kept in a species tank.

B: Has not been successful in an aquarium.

F: C; live foods of any kind, small fishes are especially savored; fish, crustacean and beef meats. The animals are very voracious feeders.

S: It is a trait of *Butis butis* to float through the water belly up, as if dead. The reason for this behavior is unclear.

T: 22-28° C, L: 15 cm, A: 90 cm, R: b, (m), D: 3
72-82° F, 6", 35",

* The Eleotridae is now the Gobiidae. Some of the species belong to the sub-family Butiinae is still subsistent.

Gobiomorphus australis (KREFFT, 1863)
Stripe Gudgeon

Syn.: *Eleotris australis, Mogurnda australis.*

Hab.: Australia; eastern Queensland and New South Wales. The species inhabits fresh and brackish water.

F.I.: Unknown.

Sex: None known.

Soc. B.: Very calm fish which, however, is a dedicated predator. Associate only with equal sized fishes.

M: This fish does not have any special demands. The species can be maintained like *Hypseleotris compressa.*

B: Breeding has not been successful in an aquarium.

F: C; almost exclusively live food in any form.

S: *Gobiomorphus australis* has nine rays in the second dorsal fin.

T: 18-25° C, **L:** 22 cm, **A:** 90 cm, **R:** b, m, **D:** 2
64-77° F, 8³/₄", 35",

Hemieleotris latifasciata (MEEK & HILDEBRAND, 1912)

Syn.: *Eleotris latifasciatus.*

Hab.: America; Ecuador to Costa Rica; pacific drainage.

F.I.: 1977 (?).

Sex: ♂ has a bright spot on the first dorsal fin, wider iridescent stripes on the sides and a posteriorly elongated second dorsal and anal fin. ♂♂ are more slender.

Soc. B.: Very peaceful fish, calm swimmers.

M: Needs aquaria planted densely along the edge and back. The animals primarily live close to the bottom, sometimes hovering for longer periods of time in one spot. They often retreat to a plant thicket for the day. Leave free swimming space. No special demands are placed on water composition. Maintenance in a community aquarium is possible.

B: A breeding report is given HORSTHEMKE & EBERHARDT (1985) in Das Aquarium **19**, 566-567. Low or narrow caves are chosen as spawning sites. The eggs are small and develop rapidly. The larvae are incompletely developed.

F: C; live food is preferred (water fleas, *Cyclops*, mosquito larvae, *Tubifex*, Enchytraea), but flake food is also eaten.

S: None.

T: 22-26° C, **L:** 12 cm, **A:** 80 cm, **R:** b, m, **D:** 2
72-79° F, 4³/₄", 31",

Hemieleotris latifasciata, juv. ♀

Gobiomorphus australis

Hemieleotris latifasciata ♂

Hypseleotris compressa (KREFFT, 1864)
Empire Gudgeon

Syn.: *Eleotris compressus, Carassiops compressus.*

Hab.: Australia and New Guinea; western Australia (Pilbara and Kimberley rivers), from northern Australia to the east coast of Queensland, southern New Guinea.

F.I.: First in the '70's and then again in 1987 in greater numbers.

Sex: The ♂ is shiny red at spawning time. Even outside of spawning season, it is more colorful than the ♀.

Soc. B.: A peaceful goby species recommendable for the community tank. The ♂ practices brood care. Courting and brood caring ♂♂ establish and defend small territories.

M: Provide a bottom of sand or fine-grained gravel; offer some hiding places of stone. The aquarium can be planted if freshwater is used, but the choice of plants becomes problematic if the animals are kept in brackish or pure sea water. The species is nonproblematic and does not place special demands. Keep in a species tank or associate with other gobies.

B: Although it is occasionally possible to receive a spawning pair, breeding *Hypseleotris compressa* is problematic. Spawning occurs on stones, wood or sea shells. The ♂ guards the enormous spawn until the tiny larvae hatch after about 24 hours, immediately requiring their first feeding. Because of their small size, feeding proves difficult. Normal first foods, such as rotifers, infusoria, etc., are not accepted. One option may be to carefully feed algae water ("algae bloom"); no reports have been made about a totally successful rearing.

F: C, O; live foods of any kind, flake food, frozen food and freeze-dried foods.

S: The second dorsal fin of *H. compressa* has nine or ten rays; it has 24-25 vertebrae. Normal coloration is shown on page 1049.

T: 10-30° C, **L:** 11 cm, **A:** 70 cm, **R:** m, **D:** 2
50-86° F, 4 1/3", 28",

Hypseleotris galii (OGILBY, 1898)
Fire-Tailed Gudgeon

Syn.: *Carassiops galii.*

Hab.: Australia; southeastern Queensland and eastern New South Wales. This species inhabits freshwater.

F.I.: Probably has not been imported into Germany.

Sex: ♂ is more colorful with larger fins; ♀, especially at spawning time, is fuller, and the eggs are visible.

Soc. B.: Outside of spawning, this is a peaceful and calm goby species. The ♂♂ practice brood care and are aggressive at this time.

M: As with *Hypseleotris compressa.*

B: Similar to *H. compressa.* The ♀♀ are sexually mature at 3 cm (1 "); their bodies are so translucent that the large eggs can clearly be seen. The clutch is approximately 100 eggs which are deposited on a hard substrate (i.e., stones). The young hatch after about twelve days and are feed small live foods.

F: C, O; live foods of all kinds, frozen and freeze-dried food; flake food and tablet food are less readily accepted.

S: The second dorsal fin of *Hypseleotris galii* has, the same as *H. klunzingeri*, 11-14 rays.

T: 10-30° C, **L:** 8 cm, **A:** 80 cm, **R:** b, m, **D:** 2
50-86° F, 3", 31",

Hypseleotris compressa ♂, in spawning coloration

Hypseleotris galii

Hypseleotris klunzingeri (OGILBY, 1898)
Western Carp Gudgeon

Syn.: *Carassiops klunzingeri, Eleotris klunzingeri.*

Hab.: Australia; the species occurs in the Murray-Darling river system from Queensland to South Australia.

F.I.: Unknown.

Sex: ♂ is larger and has elongated fins. ♀ is very plump at spawning time; the egg mass is clearly recognizable.

Soc. B.: Calm, peaceful fish. The ♂ practices brood care.

M: As indicated for *Hypseleotris compressa*. *Hypseleotris klunzingeri* is an undemanding fish.

B: Very similar to *H. compressa*. In nature *H. klunzingeri* spawns in shallows of rivers, when the temperatures have risen above 22° C (72° F). The eggs are very small (less than 1 mm (1/32") in diameter) and are adhered to water plants at a depth of 5 to 25 cm (2"-10"). After 48 hours, the larvae hatch. The ♂ is very aggressive during brood care. Feed the young with smallest micro foods.

F: C, O; live foods of all kinds, flake and frozen foods.

S: Several true species seem to be hidden under the name *Hypseleotris klunzingeri*. This problem is currently being investigated. *H. klunzingeri* has 11-14 rays on the second dorsal fin.

T: 10-30° C, **L:** 6.5 cm, **A:** 50 cm, **R:** m, b, **D:** 1-2
50-86° F, 2 2/3", 20",

Hypseleotris guentheri (BLEEKER, 1875)

Syn.: *Eleotris guentheri.*

Hab.: Southeast Asia: Sulawesi (Celebes).

F.I.: 1936.

Sex: ♂♂ grow larger than ♀♀ and have significantly more colorful fins; the fins of the ♀♀ are transparent.

Soc. B.: A free-swimming goby with a certain home range. During courtship, minor quarrels occur between some animals but never lead to injury; otherwise, the fish are peaceful.

M: Easily kept goby. Furnish a bottom of fine sand with some stones and roots for decoration. There should be dense vegetation, but leaving free swimming space. Medium-hard (10-15° dGH) and neutral (pH 7.0) water.

B: Probably has already been repeatedly spawned in captivity. Successful rearing of these surely very small young has not been described.

F: C, O; live foods of all kinds, freeze-dried, frozen and flake foods.

S: *Hypseleotris guentheri* is very similar to *Hypseleotris cyprinoides* but differs from the latter by the presence of a dark longitudinal band on the body (see ALLEN & BOESEMAN, 1982: Records Western Australian Museum **10**, 67-103, on page 88).

T: 25-27° C, **L:** 7 cm, **A:** 70 cm, **R:** m, **D:** 1-2
77-81° F, 2 3/4", 28",

Hypseleotris klunzingeri ♂

Hypseleotris guentheri ♂

Mogurnda mogurnda (RICHARDSON, 1844)

Purple-Striped Gudgeon

Syn.: *Eleotris mogurnda.*

Hab.: Australia and New Guinea; inland and coastal rivers.

F.I.: 1932.

Sex: Adult ♂♂ are always smaller than ♀♀. Based on other external characteristics the sexes are barely distinguishable. The ventral area of the ♀♀ is somewhat lighter.

Soc. B.: Territorial, the animals are quite bellicose among themselves. Always keep several specimens to distribute aggressions. Cave spawner; patriarch family.

M: Water should be medium-hard to hard (10-20° dGH), pH around 7. The addition of salt can be waived. Decorate with bogwood, and create hiding places of rocks (some caves). Side and background vegetation along with a sand or fine gravel bottom. Best kept in a species tank.

B: Though breeding is possible, a species tank should be used. Behavior during spawning is comparable to cichlids. A successful spawn is reported by ZIEHM (1982) in DATZ **35** (6): 201-203. Normally, the ♂ claims a cave and entices a ♀ to spawn. The spawns are almost always adhered to the ceiling of a cave. There can be as many as 200 oval eggs. After spawning, the ♀ is chased away by the ♂. The ♂ alone tends the brood. Development of the eggs takes 2-3 days at 25° C (77° F). When the young are free-swimming, brood care ceases, and the ♂ should be removed. Rear the young with *Artemia* nauplii, later with *Daphnia* and chopped beef.

F: C, O; hardy live foods of all kinds, finely chopped meats, shrimp, flake food. However, live food is preferred.

S: Representatives of the Eleotridae (Sleeper Gobies) and Gobiidae (True Gobies) can be best distinguished by the pelvic fins. In the Eleotridae the pelvic fins are always separate; in the Gobiidae, they are more or less fused.

T: 24-26° C, **L:** 17 cm, usually smaller, **A:** 80 cm, **R:** b, **D:** 3
75-79° F, 6¾", usually smaller 31",

Batanga lebretonis (STEINDACHER, 1870)

Syn.: *Eleotris lebretonis, Eleotris omosema, Batanga lebretonis microphthalmus.*

Hab.: West Africa; from Senegal to southern Angola, in brackish estuaries and lagoons and in freshwater of lower river courses.

F.I.: 1905.

Sex: ♂♂ have longer posterior rays in D_2 and the anal fin and a very large, flat, pointed genital papilla; some ♂♂ develop a cephalic hump at spawning time.

Soc. B.: A peaceful species overall. ♂♂ are territorial at spawning time. In sparsely decorated tanks, the fish usually cling to the bottom; in well-planted aquaria, they swim at all water levels.

M: See species above.

B: In aquaria, the gobies spawn in roomy caves or on plants. Sometimes 2 or 3 ♀♀ pair simultaneously with one ♂. The tiny eggs hatch, producing still incompletely developed larvae.

F: O; omnivore: small live and frozen foods, flake food, boiled vegetables.

T: 25° C, **L:** 12 cm, **A:** 100 cm, **R:** all, **D:** 2-3
77° F, 4¾", 39",

Mogurnda mogurnda

Batanga lebretonis

Ophieleotris aporos (BLEEKER, 1854)
Snakehead Gudgeon

Syn.: *Ophiocara aporos, Eleotris aporus, E. macrocephalus.*

Hab.: Indo-Pacific region from Madagascar through southeast Asia to the Philippines and into Australia and New Guinea.

F.I.: 1935.

Sex: The ♂ is more colorful and often has green dots on the sides of the body; overall, the ♀ is more brown.

Soc. B.: Predatory living sleeper goby whose ♂♂ practice brood care.

M: Requires a roomy tank with fine sandy bottom, several flat stones, and rocks and roots to provide hiding places. Vegetation is not necessary. It is best to offer the animals brackish water (1 tablespoon per 10 l; 2.5 gal water) or salt water. An undemanding species. A cover for the aquarium is necessary since the animals are good jumpers. Maintain in a species tank or with other gobies.

B: Breeding in the aquarium has been achieved, but no detailed reports are available.

F: C; exclusively hardy live foods of all kinds.

S: Three color varieties exist of *Ophieleotris aporos*: *O. aporos* var. *aporos* (BLEEKER, 1854), *O. aporos* var. *hoedti* (BLEEKER, 1854) and *O. aporos* var. *guentheri* (KOUMANS, 1937).

T: 20-30° C, **L:** 40 cm, **A:** 150 cm, **R:** b, m, **D:** 2
68-86° F, 16", 59",

Ophiocara porocephala (VALENCIENNES, 1937)
Flat-Head Sleeper

Syn.: *Eleotris porocephala, E. ophicephalus, E. viridis, Ophiocara ophiocephala.*

Hab.: Indo-Pacific region; from Madagascar and the Seychelles through Burma, China and the Malaysian Archipelago to Australia, New Guinea and some islands of the South Sea.

F.I.: 1913 by Berta Kuhnt, Berlin, Germany.

Sex: No certain ones known.

Soc. B.: The animals have a predatory lifestyle. The ♂♂ practice brood care.

M: As indicated for *Ophieleotris aporos*. *Ophiocara porocephala* feels most comfortable in brackish water.

B: There are no available breeding reports.

F: C; consumes all types of hardy live foods almost exclusively. Usually losses are suffered when training the animals to substitute foods.

S: *Ophiocara porocephala* seems to have been imported several times as by-catch.

T: 20-30° C, **L:** 30 cm, **A:** 100 cm, **R:** b, m, **D:** 2
68-86° F, 12", 39",

Ophieleotris aporos

Ophiocara porocephala

Tateurndina ocellicauda NICHOLS, 1955

Peacock Goby, Eye-Spot Sleeper

Syn.: None.

Hab.: New Guinea; lowland rivers and ponds of east Papua. The animals are freshwater inhabitants.

F.I.: Probably in 1982.

Sex: ♂♂ have a straight ventral line and lighter colored anal and dorsal fins; ripe ♀♀ have a spherical, bright yellow ventral area and more yellow on the fringes of the anal and dorsal fins.

Soc. B.: Peaceful species that does not show firm bonds to a partner or a territory outside the spawning time.

M: As with *Mogurnda mogurnda*. The species obviously loves soft freshwater. It is ideal for well-planted small aquaria.

B: Easily possible; the ♂ courts a ripe ♀ by "fluttering". One or both partners clean a firm substrate; cramped hideaways are preferred spawning sites. The eggs are comparatively large and glassy transparent with a whitish sheen. After spawning, the ♂ chases the ♀ away, guarding and fanning the spawn alone. It will often press itself into the spawn. The ♀♀ occasionally try to steal the eggs. The fry do not hatch at the same time. At 26° C (79° F), (pH 7.0, 7° dGH) the young are free-swimming on the fourth to sixth day and can immediately feed on newly hatched *Artemia* larvae. Rearing the young poses no problems.

F: O; small live foods (pond food) and worms (grindal), but also any substitute foods are accepted.

S: *Tateurndina ocellicauda* is one of the smallest sleeper gobies and truly one of the most beautiful.

T: 22-26° C, L: 7.5 cm, A: 50 cm, R: b, D: 2
72-79° F, 3", 20",

Gadopsis marmoratus RICHARDSON, 1848

River Blackfish, Freshwater Cod

Syn.: None.

Hab.: Australia; in freshwaters of southeast Australia (southern Queensland, New South Wales, Victoria, South Australia) and in northern Tasmania.

F.I.: Probably has not been imported into Germany.

Sex: The ♀ grows larger and is fuller.

Soc. B.: The animals are mainly nocturnal. After an acclimation period, they will also become active during the day. The animals are predatory. They are compatible among themselves, as long as there are enough hiding places available.

M: Only young are suitable for aquaria. Bottom should consist of not overly coarse gravel; arrange hiding places of stone and roots. Planting robust coldwater species is possible. No special demands are placed on the water; however, the species does not tolerate high temperatures. Maintain in a species tank or combine with fishes of the same size (e.g., cichlids or sunfishes).

B: Has not been successful in an aquarium. *Gadopsis marmoratus* might be a cave spawner. The eggs are large, laid in small numbers, demersal (lie on the bottom) and adhesive.

F: C; hardy live foods of all kinds (fish, shrimp, earthworms), beef heart and other meats.

S: The young of *G. marmoratus* have beautiful red-black markings. The average size of the fish is about 30 cm (12") with a weight of 250-500 g (-1 lb). In exceptional cases the fish can reach up to 6 kg (13 lb).

T: 5-20° C (coldwater fish), **L:** up to 60 cm, **A:** from 100 cm, **R:** b, m, **D:** 3
41-68° F (coldwater fish), up to 24", from 39",

Brachygalaxias bullocki (REGAN, 1908)

Syn.: *Galaxias bullocki.*

Hab.: South America; southern Chile, south of the city of Temuco in the Valdivian Rain Forest.

F.I.: 1981 by Dr. K. Busse, Bonn, Germany.

Sex: The ♂♂ are brown and have a whitish, mother-of-peal spot behind the pectoral fin. ♀♀ are somewhat fuller and only have a hint of the shoulder spot.

Soc. B.: The animals live in loose groups. More precise social behavior has not been investigated.

M: An aquarium with a sandy bottom and very soft water is recommended. It is important that the temperature does not rise above 20° C (68° F). Cooling can be accomplished either with a refrigeration unit or with a thin hose wound through the aquarium, one end connected to the water line, and the other connected to the drain. The vegetation has to be in accordance to the low temperatures; *Elodea,* milfoils, *Hottonia* and other coldwater plants can be used.

B: Not yet successful.

F: C; live foods of all kinds, also larger pieces of food up to earthworms. Flake food is not really accepted.

S: When in danger, these fish will occasionally bury themselves in the bottom.

T: 15-20° C, also lower **L**: 5-6 cm, **A**: 50 cm, **R**: m, t, **D**: 4
59-68° F, also lower 2-2 1/3", 20",

Brachygalaxias gothei BUSSE, 1982

Syn.: None.

Hab.: South America: southern Chile, Fundo Porvenir at Talca.

F.I.: 1981 by Dr. K. Busse, Bonn, Germany.

Sex: ♂♂ are brown with a silver stomach. A red band extends from the pectoral fins to the caudal peduncle. Above it are iridescent rainbow-like colors of green and blue extending to approximately the lateral line. ♀♀ are paler, especially the red stripe is not as intense.

Soc. B.: As with *Brachygalaxias bullocki.*

M: As with *B. bullocki*, but it is not as sensitive, especially towards harder water and higher temperatures. Furnish the aquarium similar to *B. bullocki.* Can be kept in a moderately warm room without heating.

B: The animals need an annual cycle of temperatures with a cool winter (about 5° C; 41° F). Therefore, keeping them in the open until late fall is recommended. In the spring, spawning occurs after heavy pursuits, whereby several ♂♂ follow one ♀. The first spawn was largely coincidental. The young, after their discovery, were fed with *Cyclops* and *Artemia salina.* Finely crumbled flake food can be fed for additional nourishment. Later coarser food was given. The animals grow relatively slow.

F: C; all live foods which the fish can tackle. On average, smaller foods than what is appropriate for *B. bullocki,* since these animals have a smaller mouth.

S: None.

T: 15-22° C, **L**: 5 cm, **A**: 50 cm, **R**: m, b, **D**: 3-4
59-72° F, 2", 20",

Brachygalaxias bullocki

Brachygalaxias gothei

Galaxias auratus JOHNSTON, 1883
Golden Galaxias

Syn.: None (?).

Hab.: Australia; Tasmania, in the Sorell and Crescent lakes and their tributaries.

F.I.: Probably not yet imported into Germany.

Sex: None known.

Soc. B.: Actively swimming, peaceful schooling fish.

M: See indications for *Galaxias olidus*.

B: To our knowledge, *Galaxias auratus* has not been bred in an aquarium.

F: C, O; predominantly live foods of any kind; the animals do eat other foods (frozen and flake foods, etc.).

S: In the wild, *Galaxias auratus* is an important food for trout.

T: 10-28° C, **L:** 24 cm, **A:** 100 cm, **R:** m, **D:** 2-3
50-82° F, 9 1/3", 39",

Galaxias cleaveri SCOTT, 1934
Mud Galaxias

Syn.: *Galaxias anguilliformis, G. upcheri, Lixagasa cleaveri, Saxilaga anguilliformis, S. cleaveri.*

Hab.: Australia; in coastal waters of Tasmania, rare in Victoria.

F.I.: Probably has not been imported into Germany.

Sex: No external ones known.

Soc. B.: Contrary to most galaxids which, despite all their quarrels, prefer to live in schools, *Galaxias cleaveri* is chiefly a nocturnal loner.

M: Provide a bottom of fine-grained material; plant the sides and background densely; offer some hiding places; *G. cleaveri* does not have other demands. Best kept in a species tank.

B: Breeding procedures for this species are unknown.

F: C, O; live foods of all kinds. It is very hard to get the animals to accept substitute foods.

S: *Galaxias cleaveri* likes to bury itself into the substrate.

T: 10-20° C (coldwater fish), **L:** 14 cm, **A:** 90 cm, **R:** b, **D:** 4
50-68° F (coldwater fish), 5 ", 35",

Galaxias auratus

Galaxias cleaveri

Galaxias maculatus (JENYNS, 1842)
Common Jollitail

Syn.: *Mesistes maculatus, M. alpinus, M. attenuatus, M. gracillimus, Galaxias alpinus, G. attenuatus, G. coppingeri, G. gracillimus, G. minutus, G. punctulatus, G. titcombi, G. variegatus.*

Hab.: *Galaxias maculatus* is widely distributed in the southern hemisphere: southern and western Australia, New Zealand, Chantan Island, Chile, Argentina, Tierra del Fuego and Falkland Islands (Malvinas).

F.I.: Probably has not been imported into Germany.

Sex: No certain ones known.

Soc. B.: Peaceful schooling fish

M: Provide a bottom of sand, sufficient hideouts and open swimming areas. Keep a school (six or more specimens) in fresh or brackish water. Best kept in a species tank.

B: No reports are available. In New Zealand, *G. maculatus* spawns in brackish water. The eggs are released in shallows with dense sea grass. They are often beached when low tide comes. Larval development occurs in salt water, but the young migrate into freshwater, where they also reach sexual maturity.

F: C; live foods of all types; the animals are hard to train to substitute foods.

S: The marine larval phase seems to be missing in some west Australian populations, e.g., those of the Pallinup River.

T: 10-22° C (coldwater fish), L: 19 cm, A: 100 cm, R: m, b, D: 3
50-72° F (coldwater fish), 7 ", 39",

Galaxias olidus GÜNTHER, 1866
Mountain Galaxias

Syn.: *Galaxias bongbong, G. coxii, G. findlayi, G. fuscus, G. kayi, G. oconnori, G. ornatus, G. schomburgkii, Lyragalaxias oconneri.*

Hab.: Australia; Victoria. *G. olidus* is a numerous inland species which primarily inhabits mountain streams.

F.I.: Probably not yet imported into Germany.

Sex: None known.

Soc. B.: Peaceful, lively schooling fish.

M: KUITER (1982): DATZ **35** (11): 401-405 writes that most Australian aquarists are not interested in native fishes. This is why little is known about their care. Furthermore, KUITER writes that he himself has only been moderately successful so far. He still admits to problems, especially with the mountain species *Galaxias olidus*. His opinion is that the secret for their maintenance seems to be in their habitats (small, rocky rivers in a dense forest). In many cases, the water there appears dark brown due to rotted and rotting vegetation (leaves, twigs). Specimens of these rivers are the most difficult to maintain.

F: C, O; predominantly live foods of all kinds. They do accept other types of food (frozen, freeze-dried and flake foods).

S: In the wild, *Galaxias olidus* tolerates extreme temperatures, from the cold snow regions to the warmth of the lowlands, where temperatures can rise above 30° C (86° F).
The picture on the bottom right shows the mountain galaxias which until now had been presented under the synonym *G. fuscus*.

T: 4-30° C, L: 13.5 cm, A: 80 cm, R: m, b, D: 3-4
39-86° F, 5 1/3", 31",

Galaxias maculatus

Galaxias olidus

Galaxias "fuscus" olidus

Galaxias rostratus KLUNZINGER, 1872
Murray Jollitail

Syn.: *Galaxias planiceps, G. p. waitii, G. waitii.*

Hab.: Australia; in the Murray River.

F.I.: Probably not yet imported into Germany.

Sex: No external ones known.

Soc. B.: Peaceful, agile schooling fish.

M: Practically nothing is known about the maintenance requirements of this species. Refer to the annotations for *Galaxias olidus.*

B: Has not been bred in an aquarium.

F: C, O; the animals prefer to feed on live food, but other types of food are also accepted.

S: *Galaxias rostratus* is a very rare fish species which, up to now, has hardly been seen by anyone.

T: 10-26° C, L: 13 cm, A: 80 cm, R: m, D: 3-4
50-79° F, 5", 31",

Galaxias tanycephalus FULTON, 1978
Saddled Galaxias

Syn.: None.

Hab.: Australia; Tasmania, in lakes Arthur and Woods.

F.I.: Probably not yet imported into Germany.

Sex: No external ones known.

Soc. B.: Peaceful, lively schooling fish

M: Practically nothing is known about maintenance conditions needed for this species. Therefore, the aquarist who receives this fish into his care has an open experimental field.

B: Unknown.

F: C; almost exclusively all types of live food. The animals barely become accustomed to substitute foods.

S: None.

T: 10-26° C, L: 15 cm, A: 90 cm, R: m, b, D: 3
50-79° F, 6", 35",

Galaxias rostratus

Galaxias tanycephalus

Galaxias truttaceus (CUVIER, 1817)
Spotted Mountain Trout

Syn.: *Esox truttaceus, Galaxias forsteri, G. hesperius, G. ocellatus, G. scorpus, G. truttaceous, G. truttaceus hesperius, G. truttaceus scorpus.*

Hab.: Australia; in coastal waters close to Victoria and southwest Australia, on the islands of the Bass Strait and Tasmania

F.I.: Probably has not been imported into Germany.

Sex: No external differences are apparent.

Soc. B.: Peaceful schooling fish.

M: Prefers a tank with a bottom of fine sand, heavily planted sides and back, maybe some hiding places and some open swimming space. No special demands are placed on water composition. Keep in a species tank or associate with other representatives of the family. If possible, the animals should be kept in a school.

B: No reports of successfully reproducing the animals in an aquarium are available.

F: C; live foods of all kinds.

S: *Galaxias truttaceus* is the most common fish species of southwest Australia. Its coloration can be extremely variable.

T: 6-20° C (coldwater fish), **L**: 13 cm, **A**: 90 cm, **R**: m, b, **D**: 3
43-68° F (coldwater fish), 5", 35",

Galaxiella munda McDOWALL, 1978
Swamp Pygmy Galaxias

Syn.: None.

Hab.: Australia; in coastal rivers, swamps and pools of Western Australia between Albany and Ellen Brook.

F.I.: Probably has not been imported into Germany.

Sex: The ♂ is more intensely colored; the ♀ grows larger.

Soc. B.: Peaceful schooling fish.

M: As indicated for *Galaxiella pusilla*.

B: Not yet successful in an aquarium. Additionally, almost nothing is known about its reproductive biology in the wild.

F: C, O; small live foods, small flake food.

S: Although the species was known for many years to local scientists, only in 1978 was it described scientifically by McDOWALL. *Galaxiella munda* reportedly burrow into the mud during droughts.

T: 8-24° C, **L**: 5 cm, **A**: 50 cm, **R**: b, m, **D**: 2
46-75° F, 2", 20",

Galaxias truttaceus

Galaxiella munda

Galaxiella nigrostriata (SHIPWAY, 1953)
Black-Striped Dwarf Galaxias

Syn.: *Galaxias pusillus nigrostriatus, Brachygalaxias nigrostriatus, Galaxias nigrostriatus.*

Hab.: Australia; in coastal rivers, swamps and pools of Western Australia between Albany and Northcliffe.

F.I.: Probably not yet imported into Germany.

Sex: ♂ more slender and brighter colored.

Soc. B.: Very peaceful schooling fish.

M: As indicated for *Galaxiella pusilla. Galaxiella nigrostriata* should definitely be kept in a species tank because of its fragility.

B: Has not yet been bred in an aquarium.

F: C, O; smallest live foods, flake food.

S: *Galaxiella nigrostriata* is one of the smallest representatives of the genus. Not much is known about the biology of this tiny "dwarf". Only few specimens have been collected thus far.

T: 10-25° C, **L:** 3.5 cm, **A:** 40 cm, **R:** m, **D:** 3
50-77° F, 1 1/3", 16",

Galaxiella pusilla (MACK, 1936)
Eastern Dwarf Galaxias

Syn.: *Galaxias pusillus, Brachygalaxias pusillus, B. pusillus flindersiensis, B. pusillus tasmanensis.*

Hab.: Australia; in creeks and ditches of southern Victoria.

F.I.: Probably has not been imported into Germany.

Sex: The ♂ is smaller and more colorful.

Soc. B.: Peaceful, lively schooling fish.

M: *G. pusilla* should be kept in a species tank. Needs a bottom of fine sand with a 1 cm (1/3") mulm layer. Thick edge and background vegetation with fine-leaved plants. No special demands are placed on the water.

B: The species has been bred in an aquarium. In a species tank, it will follow without special stimuli. The eggs are adhered singly to plants, but are also laid on other substrates; nothing more is known to date.

F: C, O; small live foods of all kinds (*Cyclops*, water fleas, grindal worms), but also fine flake food.

S: None.

T: 10-30° C, **L:** ♂ 3 cm, ♀ 4.5 cm, **A:** 50 cm, **R:** m, **D:** 2
50-86° F, ♂ 1", ♀ 1 3/4", 20",

Paragalaxias mesotes McDOWALL & FULTON, 1978
Arthur's Paragalaxias

Syn.: None (?).

Hab.: Australia; the species only occurs in a few waters of Tasmania.

F.I.: *P. mesotes* has probably not been imported into Germany.

Sex: No external ones are known.

Soc. B.: Bottom dweller, it is peaceful towards other fish species; among themselves, the animals are somewhat contentious.

M: Make the bottom of fine sand; use coldwater plant species, form hiding places out of rocks and roots. As a coldwater fish, *P. mesotes* requires good filtration and aeration of the tank. Care is best accomplished in a species tank.

B: No reports are yet available on a successful spawn in captivity. Information on reproductive behavior in the wild is also lacking.

F: C; small live foods of all kinds (*Cyclops*, water fleas, grindal worms, small insect larvae). The animals only feed on live foods.

S: *Paragalaxias mesotes* reminds one more of a sleeper goby than a *Galaxiidae*.

T: 5-20° C (coldwater fish), **L:** 8 cm, **A:** 60 cm, **R:** b, **D:** 3
41-68° F (coldwater fish), 3", 24",

Galaxiella nigrostriata

Galaxiella pusilla

Paragalaxias mesotes

Redigobius balteatus (HERRE, 1935)
Balteata Goby

Syn.: *Vaimosa balteata, "Gobio vaimosa", Acentrogobius balteatus.*

Hab.: Southeast Asia; Maluku Island Waigeu, Kalimantan (Borneo), Malay Peninsula, Philippines, Vietnam, Sri Lanka (Ceylon). The animals inhabit brackish waters.

F.I.: Unknown.

Sex: The ♂'s second dorsal and anal fins are better developed; in addition, the mouth is deeper split and the head is blunter.

Soc. B.: Adult animals who are not sexually mature or are not ripe show no territorial behavior. In large aquaria they often form small, loose groups. In contrast, breeding ♂♂ are territorial. Shelter spawner with patriarch family.

M: Requires a tank with a layer of fine sand, sufficient caves and shelters out of rocks and resistant plants such as Java fern and hornwort. Brackish water (1 tablespoon of sea salt per 10 l; 2.5 gal of water) is suggested. Care for in a species tank since the animals are slow feeders, or it can be housed with other slow fishes.

B: Has been successfully accomplished in an aquarium. An exact breeding report is given by HORSTHEMKE in Aquarium 17 (167): 247-252, 1983. The ♂ claims a cave or a protected area open on top; he defends it against other ♂♂. ♀♀ are courted and chased away if they are unwilling to breed. Otherwise, the ♂ guides the ♀ to the spawning site, and after additional courtship, spawning occurs. Vertical walls are normally selected as sites to lay the several hundred eggs. Care of the young is solely the responsibility of the ♂. The larvae hatch after about 4 days, always in the dark. The larvae are about 2 mm (1/32") in length and are fed finest micro foods (infusoria, rotifers). Raising the young is very difficult since the larvae often die of inexplicable causes. Perhaps feeding marine plankton should be tried!

F: C; the species only takes small animal food (live and frozen food). Flake food is rejected.

S: HORSTHEMKE (1983): Das Aquarium 17, 247-252, observed that gobies kept in very soft, tap water (8° dGH) developed a goiter-like swelling in the throat region which was fatal for some specimens. These symptoms disappeared after the addition of sea salt.

T: 25-28° C, **L:** 5 cm, **A:** 60 cm, **R:** b, m, **D:** 3-4
77-82° F, 2", 24",

Boleophthalmus pectinirostris (LINNAEUS, 1758)

Syn.: *Gobius pectinirostris, Apocryptes pectinirostris, Boleophthalmus chinensis, B. inornatus.*

Hab.: Southeast Asia; from Japan and China through Malaysia to Thailand and Burma. The animals are coastal residents. They usually occur in marine and brackish waters, rarely in freshwater.

F.I.: 1909 by the Vereinigten Zierfischzüchtereien Conradshöhe, Berlin, Germany.

Sex: No certain ones known.

Soc. B.: Territorial, partially amphibious fish.

M: Keep in tanks with a large surface area. Create a shore zone with fine sand. The sand can be held with twigs and flat stones to imitate a mangrove swamp. The aquatic part of the tank is filled with brackish water (a 1-2 % addition of sea salt, pH 8-8.5). The tanks are provided with a tight cover to allow a high humidity. *B. pectinirostris* is an amphibious fish. The temperature of the air should be as high as that of the water. The animals can be gradually accustomed to freshwater. Keep in a species tank or maintain with other mud skippers.

B: Nothing is known about a successful spawn in captivity.

F: C; in the wild, rotifers and microorganisms, that is, detritus, is exclusively eaten. In aquaria, live foods are mainly eaten, especially worms (small earthworms, *Tubifex*, Enchytraea); flake food.

S: None.

T: 26-30° C, **L:** 20 cm, **A:** 100 cm, **R:** t and land, **D:** 4
79-86° F, 8", 39",

Redigobius balteatus

Boleophthalmus pectinirostris

Chlamydogobius eremius (ZIETZ, 1896)
Desert Goby

Syn.: *Gobius eremius*.

Hab.: Australia; the species inhabits permanent waters of central Australia and the springs of the Lake Eyre basin (South Australia).

F.I.: About 1984/85 through unnamed sources. However, bred animals are already in the trade (see DATZ 8/86).

Sex: The ♂ is larger and much more colorful; the ♀ is plain in coloration.

Soc. B.: The ♂♂ are territorial and very quarrelsome among themselves; the species is peaceful towards other fishes. Cave spawner with patriarch family.

M: Should be kept in shallow tanks with a large surface area, to permit several ♂♂ to claim small territories. Use fine sand as substrate; offer the animals as many hiding places of stones and roots as is possible. The water should be hard (from 12° dGH) and alkaline (pH 7.5-8.0).

B: Breeding is easy. The species is a cave spawner who often adheres large, oval eggs to the ceiling of the cave. The ♂♂ practice brood care. The larvae hatch after 5-7 days at 25° C (77° F) and immediately feed on *Artemia* nauplii. With good food, they are sexually mature after 6-8 months.

F: C, O; small live foods of all kinds, frozen and freeze-dried foods.

S: *Chlamydogobius eremius* is sensitive to temperature drops.

T: 10-35° C, L: 6 cm, A: 60 cm, R: b, D: 2
50-95° F, 2 1/3", 24",

Gobioides broussonnetii LACÉPÈDE, 1798
Violet Goby, Dragon Fish Sub-Fam.: Gobionellinae

Syn.: *Amblyopus brasiliensis, A. mexicanus, Gobioides barreto, Gobious oblongus, Ognichodes broussonnetii, Plecopodus broussonnetii.*

Hab.: America: northward to Georgia, USA; southward to Santa Catarina, Brazil.

F.I.: Unknown.

Sex: No definite ones known.

Soc. B.: A solitary inhabitant of bottom caves and tunnels; territorial; displays strong intraspecific aggressions in small aquaria.

M: Bottom of a thick sand layer since the animals bury themselves; offer hiding places of stones and roots. Brackish water (0.5-1 %). Best cared for in a species tank. *G. broussonnetii* is a fish for specialists.

B: Has not yet been successful in captivity.

F: Small benthic foods (*Tubifex*, mosquito larvae).

S: Representative of the genus *Gobioides* differ from other goby genera by their extremely elongated body.

T: 23-25° C, L: 63 cm, A: 120 cm, R: b, D: 4 (C)
73-77° F, 25", 47",

Chlamydogobius eremius

Gobioides broussonnetii

Gobiopterus chuno (HAMILTON, 1822)
Glass Goby

Syn.: *Gobius chuno, Gobiella pellucida, G.birtwistlei.*

Hab.: Southeast Asia: India, Bangladesh, Thailand, Singapore. The species inhabits freshwater.

F.I.: 1954.

Sex: No external ones are known.

Soc. B.: Very peaceful bottom dwelling fish.

M: Does best with a fine sand bottom, hiding places and loose edge vegetation. The species has been so rarely kept that no recommendations about water chemistry can be made.

T: 23-26° C, **L:** 2.5 cm, **A:** 40 cm, **R:** b, **D:** 4
73-79° F, 1", 16",

B: Has not yet been bred in an aquarium.

F: Smallest live foods of all kinds: *Cyclops*, water fleas, grindal worms.

S: *Gobiopterus chuno* has proven to be very delicate. Despite sufficient feeding and acceptance of food, the animals always died.

Oligolepis acutipennis (VALENCIENNES, 1837)

Syn.: *Gobius acutipennis, Aparrius acutipinnis, Ctenogobius acutipinnis, Acentrogobius acutipinnis, Gobius acutipinnis, G. melanostigma, G. pasuruensis, G. oligolepis, G. setosus, G. spilurus, G. temminckii, Rhinogobius melanostigma, Stenogobius acutipinnis, St. melanostigma.*

Hab.: South and southeast Asia; Singapore, Sumatra, Java, Nias, Madura, Bali, coastal areas of Natal, India, Sri Lanka (Ceylon), Penang, Riu Kiu Islands, Philippines, New Hebrides. The species occurs in marine and brackish waters, but it will also enter freshwater.

F.I.: Not known.

Sex: ♂ is larger, more elongated and has longer fins.

Soc. B.: Despite its large mouth, it is a peaceful species, even when ♂♂ are chasing each other. Otherwise, the animals are retiring and slightly sensitive.

T: 22-26° C, **L:** 12 cm, **A:** 60 cm, **R:** b, **D:** 3
72-79° F, 4³/₄", 24",

M: Keep tanks rich in hiding places with fine substrate; vegetation is possible; the addition of salt water is possible; the animals are pure bottom dwellers which like to sit up on their pelvic fins and only "hop" rather than swim. Food is taken from the bottom.

B: Cave spawner; the larvae, hatching from tiny eggs, float/drift pelagically in the open water. They have not been successfully reared.

F: O; frugal omnivores which like worms, mosquito larva and other small live foods.

S: In their natural habitat the animals live in tight tunnels with a soft bottom and two (hidden) exits. If danger threatens from one side, the animals flee through the other exit, simultaneously producing a cloud of mud which obscures the fish as well as its hiding place.

Gobiopterus chuno, greatly enlarged

Oligolepis acutipennis ♂

Padogobius martensii (GÜNTHER, 1861)

Syn.: *Gobius martensii.*

Hab.: Europe: northern Italy, Po, Etsch and tributaries of the Gulf of Venice, lakes Maggiore and Garda. The animals inhabit the clear waters of shore regions.

F.I.: Unknown.

Sex: ♂ is more slender and has a black spot on the first dorsal fin; ♀ has a more convex ventral line and does not have a black spot on the first dorsal fin.

Soc. B.: Stationary bottom fish which claims small territories.

M: Use sand or fine gravel as substrate; rockwork should form hiding places; vegetation can be waived. The clear, cool water should be moderately alkaline to neutral (pH 7-7.5) and medium-hard (about 10° dGH). Good aeration is essential since the animals are very oxygen requiring; perhaps a current produced with a power head would help.

B: In nature the animals spawn in the late spring. In the aquarium the eggs are always laid in the first morning hours. This process takes about 2 hours. The eggs are laid beneath stones or, if absent, on the aquarium glass. The young hatch at 20° C (68° F). From this moment on, brood care by the ♂ ceases. Rearing the young with *Artemia* is easy.

F: C; predominately live foods of all kinds. The animals are reluctant to accept flake food.

S: In nature, *Padogobius martensii* is a forage fish for trout.

T: 10-18° C (coldwater fish), **L:** 6 cm, **A:** 60 cm, **R:** b, **D:** 2-3
50-64° F (coldwater fish), 2 1/3", 24",

Pandaka pygmaea HERRE, 1927

Syn.: None.

Hab.: Southeast Asia; Philippines.

F.I.: 1958?

Sex: The ♂♂ remain smaller; especially at spawning time, they are much more slender.

Soc. B.: Very calm and peaceful fish which claim the smallest territories.

M: Needs a bottom of fine sand. Add many hiding places of stones, roots, etc. In the wild the animals live in brackish water; therefore, the addition of sea salt is recommended (1-2 tablespoons per 10 l; 2.5 gal of water); water should be hard (up to 30° dGH) with a neutral to alkaline (7.0-8.4) pH. Keep in a species tank or with other *Brachygobius* species that demand similar maintenance.

B: To our knowledge, breeding has not been accomplished in an aquarium.

F: C, O; smallest live foods of all kinds, rice bran (!), also flake food.

S: *Pandaka pygmaea* is not only the smallest fish, but the smallest of all vertebrates*. Specimens of the species have long been considered young of other species.

T: 24-30° C, **L:** ♂ 9 mm, ♀ 15 mm, **A:** 40 cm, **R:** b, **D:** 3
75-86° F, ♂ 1/3", ♀ 2/3", 16",

* Meanwhile this record was broken by *Trimmatom nanus,* a marine goby; 8.6 mm (5/16") for ♂♂, 8.9 mm for ♀♀! See TI 75 (June 1986).

Padogobius martensii

Pandaka pygmaea

Periophthalmus papilio BLOCH & SCHNEIDER, 1801
Butterfly Mudskipper

Syn.: None (?).

Hab.: Coast of west Africa. The animals come from estuaries and their mangrove swamps.

F.I.: Not determinable.

Sex: No definite ones are yet known.

Soc. B.: It is similar to *Boleophtalmus pectinirostris*.

M: As *B. pectinirostris*.

B: Not yet successful in an aquarium.

F: C; predominately live foods (all types of worms, insects and their larvae).

S: According to MUNRO (1955): Fishes of Ceylon, *Periophthalmus papilio* is not a true species, but a sub-species of *Periophthalmus koelreuteri*. However, JAYARAM (1981): The Freshwater Fishes of India, not only claims *P. papilio* is a valid species, but says it even represents the type species for the genus *Periophthalmus*.

T: 26-30° C, **L:** 25 cm, **A:** 100 cm, **R:** t and land, **D:** 4
79-86° F, 10", 39",

Proterorhinus marmoratus (PALLAS, 1811)
Amur Tube-Nose

Syn.: *Gobius marmoratus, G. blennioides, G. macropterus, G. nasalis, G. quadricapillus, G. rubromaculatus, G. semilunaris.*

Hab.: Europe and western Asia; in the Black and Caspian Sea. The species is widely distributed in brackish water and freshwater tributaries of the seas. One population exists in the Neusiedlersee (lake in Austria).

F.I.: Not known.

Sex: Purportedly, the ♂♂ become totally black with a red spot on the first dorsal fin at spawning time. Outside the spawning season, this spot is a pale yellow and barely distinguishable.

Soc. B.: Nothing is known about the social behavior of this goby.

M: This species likes rocks to create hiding places and a sand or fine-grained gravel bottom. Vegetation is not necessary. Medium-hard (around 10° dGH) and neutral to weakly alkaline (pH 7.0-7.5) water is recommended. Perhaps the slight addition of sea salt (1-2 teaspoons per 10 l; 2.5 gal of water) is beneficial. Keep in a species tank or with other bottom dwellers with similar requirements.

B: Probably not successful in an aquarium. The animals are bottom spawners.

F: C; live foods of all kinds (*Tubifex*, Enchytraea, *Gammarus*, mosquito larvae).

S: The anterior nasal openings are two 1 mm (1/32") long tubes.

T: 10-18° C (coldwater fish), **L:** 11 cm in the sea, 8.5 cm in freshwater, **A:** 80 cm, **R:** b, **D:** 2-3
50-64° F (coldwater fish), 4 1/3" in the sea, 3 1/3" in freshwater, 31",

Periophthalmus papilio

Proterorhinus marmoratus ♂

Rhinogobius brunneus lindbergi (TEMMINCK & SCHLEGEL, 1845)

Syn.: None.

Hab.: Asia; Soviet Union; Amur basin, Bidzhan River and Lake Khanka.

F.I.: Probably not yet imported into Germany.

Sex: Unknown.

Soc. B.: Unknown, it could be territorial like other gobies.

M: Supply a sandy bottom, some hiding places of stone and water with a hardness up to 20° dGH and a neutral pH (7.0).

T: 16-20° C, **L:** 4.5 cm, **A:** 50 cm, **R:** b, **D:** 3
61-68° F, 1¾", 20",

B: There are no reports dealing with a successful aquarium spawn. Reproductive biology in its natural habitat is also unknown.

F: C; live foods of all kinds.

S: The systematics of this sub-species is under discussion. For some authors, only the nominate form *Rhinogobius brunneus* (TEMMINCK & SCHLEGEL, 1845) exists.

Stiphodon elegans (STEINDACHNER, 1879)
Emerald River Goby

Syn.: *Sicydium elegans, Stipodon elegans.*

Hab.: Southeast Asia; Indonesia (Java, Sumatra, Flores, Nias, Celebes), Philippines, Pelew Island, Fidschi Island, New Caledoia and western New Guinea, Riukin Islands and Japan.

F.I.: 1974 by Edith Korthaus, Hagan (Dahl) Germany.

Sex: Without a doubt the coloration of the ♂♂ and ♀♀ differ, but up to now, it cannot be said with certainty which corresponds to the ♂ and which to the ♀.

Soc. B.: Despite its reduced swimming capability (rheophile fish), these are nimble, restless animals which claim small territories from which conspecifics are expelled.

M: Needs a bottom of sand and some stones which are used as hiding places and lookouts. The tank can be planted. Plant leaves are readily occupied to have a better overview. The animals can be kept in freshwater; however, they like clear, oxygen-rich, flowing water, exactly as it is in their natural habitat. A strong pump should be used. Housing with fishes that place similar demands is possible.

T: 24-28° C, **L:** 4.5 cm, **A:** 50 cm, **R:** b, **D:** 3
75-82° F, 1¾", 20",

B: P. BEYER (1985) in DATZ **38**, 445-448 and 491-494 reports the first partial breeding successes of *Stiphodon elegans.* This very interesting essay contains a richness of detail which is difficult to summarize. Therefore, reading this article is recommended for all hobbyists prior to any breeding attempts.

F: O; omnivore; in an aquarium the animals accept almost any common food. In nature the species seems to graze on algae lawns.

S: In *Stiphodon elegans,* like other gobies, the pelvic fins are fused to an attachment organ which works like a suction cup. It makes it possible for the animals to fasten themselves to smooth, even vertical, surfaces without falling off by their own weight or being carried away by the current. As a current-loving fish (rheophile), *Stiphodon elegans* is well adapted to its habitat: the swim bladder is not developed, the body is streamlined and the stabilizing pectoral fins are especially long and wide.

Rhinogobius brunneus lindbergi

Stiphodon elegans or *S. ornatus*?

Pseudogobius javanicus (BLEEKER, 1856)
Pug-Nose Goby

Syn.: *Vaimosa piapensis.*

Hab.: India to the Riukiu Islands and the tropical west Pacific.

F.I.: Not known.

Sex: The animals can only be distinguished by the genital papilla which is pointed in ♂♂ and thick and round in the ♀♀.

Soc. B.: Nothing is known.

M: Use a sand or fine-grained gravel substrate; plant the edges and back of the tank. Stone caves as hiding places and roots as decoration are recommended. Water should be about medium-hard (10-15° dGH) with a neutral pH (7.0). A species tank or combining with other fishes from the Philippines which prefer the middle and upper water strata is appropriate.

B: The eggs are deposited on the surface of a stone or a sea shell and cared for by the ♂ until hatching. The eggs are elliptical with a diameter of 0.5 mm (1/64"). The larvae hatch after 78 hours (temp. ?), 2 mm (1/16") length. They swim in the open water.

F: O; in the wild, diatoms, filamentous algae, copepods and other crustacea; algae dominate.

S: In *Pseudogobius* species, the curved snout extends over the mouth.

T: 23-25° C, **L**: 3 cm, **A**: 40 cm, **R**: b, **D**: 3
73-77° F, 1 ", 16",

Rhinogobius wui (LIU, 1940)
Sub-Fam.: Gobiinae

Syn.: *Ctenogobius wui, Tukugobius wui.*

Hab.: Asia: southern Chinese highlands, numerous in the New Territories of Hong Kong, in creeks.

F.I.: Not certain, about 1960.

Sex: The ♂♂ have distinct red spots and lines on the branchiostegal membranes. In addition, they have longer posterior rays in D_2 and A and a wider head than the ♀♀.

Soc. B.: Bottom-bound rheophile species. The ♂♂ are territorial at spawning time; they dig a shallow cave (for example, under stone plates) or occupy existing cavities (fragments of flower pots) and defend the surrounding territory. The ♂♂ impress and threaten by raising their head and showing their flared gill membranes, to display their prominent red markings.

M: Needs a freshwater aquarium; a strong water current may be beneficial. Place stone plates on the bottom to offer hiding places. A bottom of fine gravel is suggested. Best cared for in a species tank.

B: About 10 to 50 large eggs are laid on the ceiling of the cave and intensely guarded by the ♂. The species has direct development; at 24° C (75° F), 8 mm (5/16") long young hatch after 14-15 days, already with completely developed fins. One to two days after hatching, the yolk sac is absorbed and they immediately feed on *Artemia* nauplii; shortly thereafter, they are ready to accept chopped *Tubifex*. Raising them is easy.

F: C; small live and frozen foods, mosquito larvae, and aquatic insect larvae, *Tubifex*, etc.

S: *Rhinogobius wui* tolerates temperatures to slightly below 10° C (50° F). Cool overwintering at room temperature may stimulate them to breed in the spring. High temperatures for extended periods of time should be avoided.

T: 15-25° C, **L**: 4.5 cm, **A**: 50 cm, **R**: b, **D**: 2
59-77° F, 1¾", 20",

Pseudogobius javanicus

Rhinogobius wui

Dermogenys pusillus sumatranus (BLEEKER, 1853)
Sumatra Halfbeak

Syn.: *Hemirhamphus sumatranus.*

Hab.: Southeast Asia; Indonesia (Sumatra, Kalimantan = Borneo), Singapore. The species prefers to live in freshwater, but will sometimes enter brackish water.

F.I.: 1933 by the H. Stolz Co., Potsdam, Germany.

Sex: ♂♂ are usually smaller, and the anal fin is modified into a gonopodium.

Soc. B.: Lively surface fish which is often quite quarrelsome towards conspecifics. The ♂♂ engage in bitter fights which can sometimes even lead to injuries. The species is very shy and skittish, especially during acclimation.

M: Use a shallow tank (20 cm; 8") with a large surface area. Bottom of fine-grained gravel, loose vegetation around the edges and some floating plants to dim the lights are recommended; leave plenty of free swimming space. The animals need warmth. In contrast to *Dermogenys pusillus*, the addition of sea salt is not needed. Water should not too hard (up to 15° dGH) and in the neutral range (pH 7.0).

B: The species is a livebearer. Reproduction is occasionally very difficult since the ♀♀ can give birth to dead young. Copulation is preceded by intense courtship. The ♂ stands beneath the ♀ and dabs at her underside with its beak. During copulation, the ♂ presses laterally onto the ♀; insemination occurs with the andropodium of the ♂. Gestation is usually 6-8 weeks; the number of young is rarely more than 30.

F: C; almost exclusively live foods of all kinds (*Drosophila* and other flies, mosquito larvae, small crustacea, *Tubifex*). Flake food is usually not readily eaten.

S: Cover the aquarium well; *Dermogenys pusillus sumatranus* is a precise and able jumper.

T: 26-30° C, L: ♂ 5 cm, ♀ 6 cm, A: 70 cm, R: t, D: 3
79-86° F, ♂ 2", ♀ 2 1/3", 28",

Hemirhamphodon pogonognathus (BLEEKER, 1853)
Long-Snout Halfbeak

Syn.: *Dermogenys pogonognathus, Hemirhamphus pogonognathus.*

Hab.: Southeast Asia: Thailand, Malay Peninsula, Sumatra, Kalimantan (Borneo), Bangka, Belitung.

F.I.: 1936 by Wilhelm Schreitmüller, Frankfurt/M, Germany.

Sex: The ♂ is significantly larger, and the anal fin is modified into an andropodium. In contrast to *Dermogenys* and *Nomorhamphus, it is* the posterior section of the anal fin that is modified.

Soc. B.: Lively surface living schooling fish which is very bellicose towards conspecifics. ♂♂ are particularly merciless in attacking each other. Therefore, keep only one ♂ with several ♀♀. *H. pogonognathus* is not as skittish as *Dermogenys pusillus.*

M: Use a tank with a large surface and a low water level (20 cm; 8" is sufficient). Bottom of sand or fine-grained gravel, edge and background vegetation and floating plants to dim the light are suggested. Leave a lot of free swimming space. Good filtration, producing a current with a pump. The animals face into the current. The tanks need to be covered since the species is an excellent jumper. The water is best not overly soft (around 10° dGH) and neutral to slightly alkaline (pH 7.0-7.5). Adding sea salt is not recommended.

B: 26-28° C (79-82° F); *H. pogonognathus* is a livebearer. Fertilization is accomplished with the andropodium. The animals daily give birth to 1-5 young over a period of 2-3 weeks. 30-40 young are born per ♀. The young are about 12 mm (") long at birth and have strikingly large eyes. Feed with *Artemia* nauplii. When well fed, the young grow very fast. The parents do not pursue their young. Nevertheless, it is better to

Continued on page 1104.

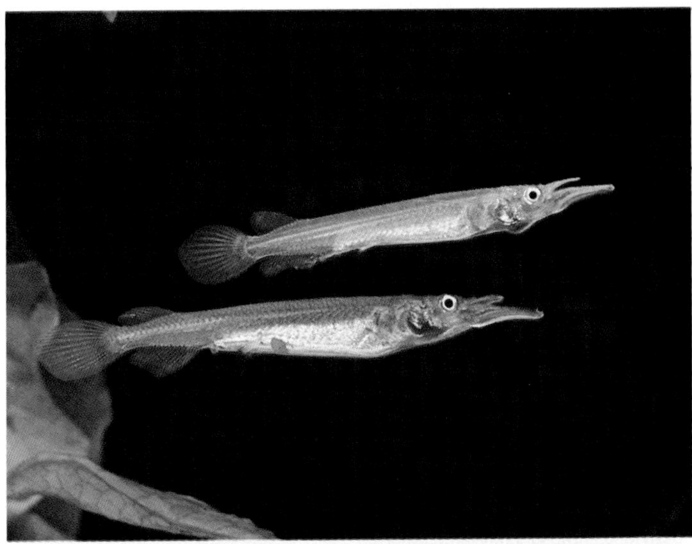

Dermogenys pusillus sumatranus

Hemirhamphodon pogonognathus

Continuation of *Hemirhamphodon pogonognathus*:

The parents do not pursue their young. raise them in a small rearing tank (from 12 cm; 4³/4" length).

F: C, O; live foods of all kinds (all kinds of flies, mosquito larvae, small crustacea); flake food is readily eaten. In nature, the species principally lives on food blown onto the water surface.

S: The genus *Hemirhamphodon* has small teeth all the way to the tip of the mandible, and the base of the dorsal fin is clearly in front of the base of the anal fin. *Dermogenys*, on the other hand, has a toothless mandible, and the base of the dorsal fin is above or slightly posterior to the base of the anal fin.

T: 22-28° C, L: ♂ 9 cm, ♀ 6 cm, A: 80 cm, R: u, D: 3
72-82° F, ♂ 3 ", ♀ 2¹/3", 31",

Lepidogalaxias salamandroides MEES, 1961
Salamander Mud Minnow

Syn.: None.

Hab.: Australia; in rivers and pools of the southern coast between Lake Powell (Albany District) and the Scott River.

F.I.: Presumably has not been imported into Germany.

Sex: The anal fin of the ♂ is surrounded by a flap of skin.

Soc. B.: A peaceful fish. We are almost totally ignorant about its social behavior. *L. salamandroides* reminds one of a loach.

M: Requires a soft, fine bottom, some hiding places, edge and/or background vegetation. Soft (around 5° dGH) and acid to neutral (pH 4.5-7) water. Should be cared for in a species tank.

B: Unsuccessful in an aquarium. Little is known about its reproductive biology in the wild.

F: C; the species requires small live foods. Difficult to train to anything else.

S: *Lepidogalaxias salamandroides* seems to be the last recent representative of a very old family.

T: 8-25° C, L: 6.5 cm, A: 50 cm, R: b, D: 3
46-77° F, 2²/3", 20",

Lepidogalaxias salamandroides

Afromastacembelus moorii (BOULENGER, 1898)
Mottled Spiny Eels

Syn.: *Mastacembelus christyi, M. moorii, M. moorii nigrofasciatus.*

Hab.: Africa; Lake Tanganyika.

F.I.: Unknown.

Sex: No definite sexual differences are known. Ripe ♀♀ are presumably plumper.

Soc. B.: Similar to the other *Mastacembelus* species (compare Vol. 1); a pronounced predator.

M: *M. moorii*'s requirements are similar to its southeast Asian relatives. Large tanks with soft bottom and numerous hiding places contribute to its well-being. No special demands are placed on water composition. Because of its predatory ways, keep singly, or house with tankmates of at least the same size.

B: Not yet bred in an aquarium.

F: C; hearty live foods of all kinds; fishes are especially relished.

S: A rarely imported species.

T: 25-28° C, L: 44 cm, A: 100 cm, R: b, m, D: 3-4 (C)
77-82° F, 18", 39",

Afromastacembelus plagiostomus (MATTHES, 1962)

Syn.: *Mastacembelus plagiostomus.*

Hab.: Africa; Lake Tanganyika.

F.I.: Unknown.

Sex: None known.

Soc. B.: No details about its social behavior are available. It is probably similar to other *Mastacembelus* species.

M: As indicated for *Mastacembelus moorii.*

B: Not successful.

F: C; hearty live foods of all kinds.

S: A characteristic is the notorious color pattern. Two additional, similarly patterned eels are known from Lake Tanganyika, but they have not been imported.

T: 25-28° C, **L**: 35 cm, **A**: 100 cm, **R**: b, m, **D**: 3-4 (C)
77-82° F, 14", 39",

Megalops cyprinoides (BROUSSONET, 1782)
Indopacific Tarpon

Syn.: *Clupea cyprinoides, Brisbania staigeri, Clupea setipinna, Cyprinodon cundinga, Elops cundinga, E. cyprinoides, Megalops curtifilis, M. filamentosus, M. indicus, M. kundinga, M. macrophthalmus, M. macropterus, M. oligolepis, M. setipinnis.*

Hab.: Indo-Pacific region from the east coast of Africa to Australia, Melanesia, Micronesia and Polynesia. The young live close to the coast; full-grown specimens leave the coastal areas. Animals are sometimes found over 100 km (62 mi) upriver.

F.I.: Could not be determined.

Sex: No definite external ones are known. ♀♀ are likely to be fuller during the spawning season.

Soc. B.: Pelagic fish which form small schools. The animals are avid swimmers.

M: Only the young are suitable for the aquarium. Offer large, roomy tanks with sand or gravel bottom. Corresponding to the natural biotope of the young, a mangrove swamp should be imitated. Leave enough room for swimming. The water should be at least brackish (1-1.5% addition of sea salt). In freshwater, they waste away. Keep in a species tank or with fishes that have similar requirements (e.g., *Monodactylus* species).

B: Because of its size, breeding in an aquarium is not possible. Almost nothing is known about the reproductive biology of this species in nature. Spawning occurs in the spring or the beginning of summer, apparently close to the bottom.

F: C; live foods, mainly small fish.

S: The larvae of *Megalops cyprinoides* are thin and transparent. They are very similar to larvae of eels but differ by their forked caudal fin.

T: 22-24° C, 72-75° F, L: up to 150 cm, up to 59", A: 150 cm, 59", R: m, t, D: 3-4

Cairnsichthys rhombosomoides (NICHOLS & RAVEN, 1928)
Cairns Rainbowfish

Syn.: *Rhadinocentrus rhombosomoides.*

Hab.: Australia; northern Queensland at Cairns. The species is limited to small rivers which drain the Bellenden Ker Range (a small mountain range). Recently, *Cairnsichthys* has also been found in a small river at Innisfails, 75 km (47 mi) south of Cairns.

F.I.: Has probably not been imported into Germany.

Sex: Sexual differences are minor. The ♂♂ are somewhat deeper bodied and tend to have yellow edges on the dorsal and anal fins.

Soc. B.: Peaceful, active swimming fish.

M: Use sand or fine gravel substrate; sparsely plant the tank; provide sufficient swimming space. *Cairnsichthys* is a delicate aquarium subject. The fish prefer water that is not too soft (from 10° dGH) and slightly alkaline (pH 7.2-7.6). Keep in a species tank or associate with *Melanotaenia maccullochi* and/or *M. splendida.*

B: The species is not known to the European hobby. Breeding has been accomplished by Australian aquarists. It is similar to *Melanotaenia* species.

F: C, O; mainly live foods of all kinds, but flake food is accepted after an acclimation period.

S: *Cairnsichthys* is a monotypic genus, that is, it consists of one species. The animals are not very long-lived; three years is about the maximum life span.

T: 21-25° C, **L:** ♂ 8 cm, ♀ 7 cm, **A:** 80 cm, **R:** m, t, **D:** 3-4
70-77° F, ♂ 3", ♀ 2¾", 31",

Chilatherina bleheri ALLEN, 1985
Bleher's Rainbowfish

Syn.: None.

Hab.: Danau Biru (Lake Holmes) Irian Jaya; New Guinea.

F.I.: 1983 by Heiko Bleher, Frankfurt, Germany.

Sex: The photo shows a ♂. ♀♀ are fuller and paler.

Soc. B.: A recommendable species for the community tank. A small school of about 5 individuals should be kept. These traverse the middle water strata in a lively fashion.

M: Place the shallow tank in a sunny location. Leave plenty of open swimming space. Water values are not problematic: pH between 7.0 and 9.2 (measured in nature). Strong filtration with water current is desirable. Sparse vegetation on the sides should provide some shelter.

B: Easily bred at a pH around 7; hardness 8-15° dGH. Breeders should be well conditioned with live foods.

F: C, O; insect larvae (bloodworms), flake food.

S: The fish grows very slowly and develops its full color after 12-18 months.

T: 23-27° C, **L:** 10 cm, **A:** 80 cm, **R:** m, b, **D:** 2
73-81° F, 4", 31",

Cairnsichthys rhombosomoides

Chilatherina bleheri

Chilatherina campsi (WHITLEY, 1956)
Highlands Rainbowfish

Syn.: *Anisocentrus campsi, Centratherina tenuis.*

Hab.: New Guinea; central highlands of Papua New Guinea in the Waligi Valley and Pima River, as well as in the Jimmi and Omsis rivers.

F.I.: Unknown, probably has not been imported into Germany.

Sex: ♂♂ are deeper-bodied. The sexes differ little in color, but ♂♂ are perhaps more brightly colored.

Soc. B.: Peaceful, active schooling fish.

M:Requires a tank with heavy vegetation along the edge and background; keep sufficient open swimming space; bottom made of sand or fine gravel; provide good filtration. The animals appreciate sunshine in the tank. The water should not be too soft (from 10° dGH) and have a slightly alkaline pH (7.5-7.8). Keep in a species tank or with *Melanotaenia* and/or *Glossolepis* species.

B: To our knowledge, *Chilatherina campsi* has not been bred in an aquarium. In the wild, the animals are continuous spawners which deposit several eggs every day. These adhere to water plants with thread-like filaments. At 22-24° C (72-75° F), the larvae hatch after about 15 days. They grow very fast and reach sexual maturity in less than a year.

F: C, O; live foods of all kinds; frozen, freeze-dried and flake foods; filamentous green algae.

S: In nature, *Chilatherina campsi* and *Melanotaenia affinis* can crossbreed. ALLEN collected two such hybrids (both ♀♀) in the Omsis River.

T: 21-26° C, **L**: ♂ 10 cm, ♀ 8 cm, **A**: 100 cm, **R**: m, **D**: 2-3
70-79° F, ♂ 4", ♀ 3", 39",

Chilatherina crassispinosa (WEBER, 1913)
Silver Rainbowfish

Syn.: *Rhombatractus crassispinosus, Centatherina bulolo, C. crassispinosa.*

Hab.: New Guinea; widely distributed throughout northern New Guinea, reaching from the Markham river system to the Mamberamo River in Irian Jaya

F.I.: Unknown, probably not yet imported into Germany.

Sex: ♂ has a higher back.

Soc. B.: Agile, peaceful schooling fish.

M: As indicated for *Chilatherina campsi.* However, *Chilatherina crassispinosa* requires warmer and more alkaline water (pH 7.7-8.5). Place with other members of the genus, or maintain in a species tank.

B: Unsuccessful in an aquarium.

F: C, O; all types of live foods, frozen and flake food; green algae (filamentous) are also eaten.

S: In contrast to other members of the genus, *Chilatherina crassispinosa* can occasionally be found in fast-flowing, small rivers with a strong gradient.

T: 25-30° C, **L**: 10 cm, **A**: 90 cm, **R**: m, **D**: 2-3
77-86° F, 4", 35",

Chilatherina campsi

Chilatherina crassispinosa

Chilatherina fasciata (WEBER, 1913)
Barred Rainbowfish

Syn.: *Rhombatractus fasciatus, Chilatherina lorentzi* (not WEBER).

Hab.: Lake Wanam, Papua New Guinea, waters of the rain forest in open places that receive plenty of sunlight.

F.I.: 1984.

Sex: The photo shows a ♂. ♀♀ are paler, smaller and can be dark gray to almost black.

Soc. B.: Nimble, peaceful schooling fish. In nature, *Chilatherina crassispinosa* and *Melanotaenia affinis* are found with this species.

M: Requires a brightly placed, shallow tank with a slight current created by a strong filter. Plants should be sparsely planted along the edges and tall enough to reach the surface. The species tolerates hard water (up to 30° dGH), but it can also be kept in softer water down to 8° dGH. The pH should be stable between 7.0 and 8.0 and not fluctuate. Regular water exchanges are indicated.

B: Very easy, like most large rainbows. Rearing of the young is possible with finest flake foods.

F: C, O; live foods of all types, frozen and flake foods.

S: It is likely that fishes imported under the name of *C. sentaniensis* are in reality this species.

T: 28-32° C, L: ♂ 11 cm, ♀ 10 cm, A: 120 cm, R: m, t, D: 2
82-90° F, ♂ 4 1/3", ♀ 4", 47",

Chilatherina sentaniensis (WEBER, 1908)
Sentani Rainbowfish

Syn.: *Rhombatractus sentaniensis.*

Hab.: New Guinea; the species is said to originate from Lake Sentani, located about 12 km (7 mi) from Jayapura in Irian Jaya, but in the last years, it could not be found there despite intensive searches.

F.I.: Probably has not been imported into Germany.

Sex: No definite ones known; the ♂♂ grow somewhat larger.

Soc. B.: Peaceful, active fish; it is not known whether or not they school.

M: As described for *Chilatherina campsi. Ch. sentaniensis* likes dense vegetation in its tank. Keep in a species tank or together with *Glossolepis incisus.*

B: Not known.

F: C, O; live foods of all kinds, frozen food, freeze-dried food, green algae and flake food.

S: *Chilatherina sentaniensis* is the only representative of the genus that exclusively inhabits lakes. Additional lake inhabiting populations of *Chilatherina fasciata* are known. Due to the uncertainties surrounding this species, the species in the photo cannot be named with certainty.

T: 24-28° C, L: ♂ 11.5 cm, ♀ 10 cm, A: 100 cm, R: m, D: 2-3
75-82° F, ♂ 4 ", ♀ 4", 39",

Chilatherina fasciata ♂

Chilatherina sentaniensis

Glossolepis maculosa ALLEN, 1981
Spotted Rainbowfish

Syn.: None.

Hab.: New Guinea; only known from the Omsis River and one of its small tributaries, 24 km (15 mi) west of Lae, Papua New Guinea.

F.I.: Probably by J. Clasen in 1985.

Sex: The ♂ is more intensely colored with a deeper body. In addition, the middle rays of the anal fin and the first dorsal fin are elongated.

Soc. B.: Very peaceful, active, schooling fish. The animals are somewhat skittish.

M: The tank should be moderately planted with medium-leaved species. Only planting the sides and the background is best. Preserve a lot of space for swimming; use a fine-grained bottom. The animals appreciate morning sun. Hard (from 12° dGH) and slightly alkaline (7.5-7.8) water is suggested. Keep in a species tank or associate with other rainbowfishes (*Glossolepis, Chilatherina* or *Melanotaenia* species).

B: Breeding of *Glossolepis* species is similar to breeding *Chilatherina* and *Melanotaenia* species. The breeding tank does not require a substrate. Use a bunch of Java moss as spawning substrate. Usually the animals spawn in the morning, laying a few eggs every day (continuous spawner). The eggs are very adhesive; their development takes about 7-10 days at 23-25° C (73-77° F). The brood should be fed fine live foods. They grow fast, reaching sexual maturity the first year of life.

F: C, O; live foods of all kinds (*Tubifex, Daphnia, Cyclops, Artemia*, mosquito larvae, etc.), freeze-dried and flake foods.

S: The characteristic spots along the sides appear in young specimens at a standard length of 18-25 mm (3/4"-1") or at an age of 2-3 months.

T: 23-27° C, **L:** 6 cm, **A:** 60 cm, **R:** m, t, **D:** 2
73-81° F, 2 1/3", 24",

Glossolepis multisquamata (WEBER & DE BEAUFORT, 1922)
Sepik Rainbowfish

Syn.: *Melanotaenia multisquamata, Lomanetia multisquamata, Melanotaenia kabia, M. rosacea, Nematocentris multisquamata.*

Hab.: New Guinea; in the lower Sepik River (Papua New Guinea), the Taritatu River (previously the Idenburg River) and in the Doorman River, a tributary of the Taritatu (both Irian Jaya).

F.I.: Probably has not been imported into Germany.

Sex: ♂♂ grow larger and somewhat deeper. The middle rays of the anal fin and first dorsal fin are elongated.

Soc. B.: As with *Glossolepis maculosa*.

M: See *G. maculosa*. In contrast, *Glossolepis multisquamata* likes slightly acid (pH 6.2-6.8) and softer water (about 8° dGH).

B: Similar to that of *G. maculosa*.

F: C, O; live foods of all kinds, frozen and flake foods.

S: *Glossolepis multisquamata*, together with *Glossolepis incisus* (see Vol. 1), are the largest representative of the genus. It differs from the latter by less gill rakers on the gill arch (19-23 vs. 26-32 in *G. incisus*) and the different coloration of the ♂♂ (not a bright red as *G. incisus*).

T: 26-30° C, **L:** ♂ 13 cm, ♀ 11 cm, **A:** 100 cm, **R:** m, t, **D:** 2
79-86° F, ♂ 5", ♀ 4 1/3", 39",

Glossolepis maculosa

Glossolepis multisquamata ♂

Glossolepis wanamensis ALLEN & KAILOLA, 1979
Lake Wanam Rainbowfish

Syn.: None.

Hab.: New Guinea; the species only occurs in Lake Wanam, Papua New Guinea.

F.I.: To Belgium in 1985.

Sex: The ♂♂ grow larger and are deeper-bodied. In addition, the central rays of the anal fin and the first dorsal fin are elongated.

Soc. B.: As *Glossolepis maculosa*.

M: As for *G. maculosa*. Water should not be too soft (from 10° dGH) and slightly alkaline (a pH of about 7.8). Keep in a species tank or associate with *Chilatherina fasciata*.

B: Follow recommendations for *G. maculosa*.

F: C, O; live foods of all kinds, freeze-dried, frozen and flake foods.

S: *Glossolepis wanamensis* is similar to *Glossolepis multisquamata*, but it remains smaller. In addition, the scales above the pectoral fins are irregularly placed, not like *G. multisquamata* whose scales are arranged in regular, parallel rows.

T: 26-30° C, **L**: ♂ 10 cm, ♀ 9 cm, **A**: 100 cm, **R**: m, t, **D**: 2
79-86° F, ♂ 4", ♀ 3 ", 39",

Iriatherina werneri MEINKEN, 1974
Thredfin Rainbowfish

Syn.: None.

Hab.: New Guinea and Australia; southern New Guinea between the Merauke and the Fly rivers; in Australia in the Jardine River at the tip of the Cap York Peninsula.

F.I.: 1973 by Mr. Werner, München, Germany.

Sex: Both dorsal fins of the ♂♂ have long, drawn out fin rays, especially the second. The anal and the caudal fins are also elongated.

Soc. B.: Peaceful, lively schooling fish.

M: Use a fine sandy bottom, moderate edge and background vegetation and leave open swimming space. The water should not be overly soft (from 10° dGH) and around neutral (pH 7.0). Weekly water exchanges are recommended (about of the tank volume). Associate with *Melanotaenia maccullochi* and/or *Pseudomugil gertrudae*, or maintain it in a species tank.

B: Breeding this fish requires some attention. The breeding tank is furnished with Java moss. After intense courtship by the ♂♂, whereby the full beauty of their finnage can be appreciated, spawning occurs in the Java moss. Well nourished animals spawn almost constantly but have certain phases of increased egg production. When enough eggs have accumulated in the moss, it is transferred to a small rearing tank without substrate. The young, depending on temperature, hatch after 8-12 days. They are very small and stay in the upper water strata. First food is rotifers, pulverized dry food, nettle dust or pulverized dry egg yolk. Paramecium are not suitable as rearing food. They seem to sting and injure the young.

F: C, O; fine live foods of all types, flake food.

S: Due to its notorious finnage, *Iriatherina werneri* cannot be confused with any other rainbowfishes. *Telmatherina ladigesi*'s fins are the most similar to this species.

T: 24-28° C, **L**: ♂ 5 cm, ♀ 3.5 cm, **A**: 60 cm, **R**: m, t, **D**: 2-3
75-82° F, ♂ 2", ♀ 1¹/₃", 24",

Glossolepis wanamensis ♂, "yawning"

Iriatherina werneri ♂ and ♀

Melanotaenia affinis (WEBER, 1908)
North New Guinea Rainbowfish

Syn.: *Rhombatractus affinis, Rhombosoma sepikensis.*

Hab.: New Guinea; in freshwaters of the north.

F.I.: Around 1983.

Sex: ♂♂ are larger, more colorful and have pointed dorsal and anal fins.

Soc. B.: Peaceful, active schooling fish.

M: Like *Melanotaenia goldiei.*

B: See *M. goldiei.*

F: C, O; predominately live foods of all kinds, but also freeze-dried and flake foods.

S: *Melanotaenia affinis* is closely related to *Melanotaenia goldiei*, but it has a less pronounced lateral stripe, and the anal fin and the second dorsal in adult ♂♂ are orange or pink.

T: 20-30° C, **L**: 12 cm, **A**: 90 cm, **R**: m, t, **D**: 2
68-86° F, 4 3/4", 35",

Melanotaenia boesemani ALLEN & CROSS, 1980
Boesemani Rainbow

Syn.: None.

Hab.: New Guinea; in the Ajamaru lakes of Irian Jaya.

F.I.: 1982 by H. Bleher, Frankfurt.

Sex: ♂♂ are larger and are deeper-bodied. ♂♂ have strong colors; ♀♀ have less color and no orange.

Soc. B.: Peaceful, active, schooling fish.

M: As with *Melanotaenia goldiei*; however, *M. boesemani* is somewhat more warmth requiring. Good jumpers; cover the tank well.

B: A continuous spawner that is very easy to breed with normal water conditions (pH 7, hardness 8-15° dGH). Water in its natural habitat has a pH of 9.2-9.5 and a hardness of 7-8° dGH. Continued on page 1120.

F: C, O; predominantly live foods of all kinds, freeze-dried and flake foods.

S: *Melanotaenia boesemani* is a rare rainbowfish in its natural habitat. The animals inhabit lakes. The picture on the right shows an animal with a gaping mouth which may be a type of "yawning" or a defense reaction. The animals develop their full, splendid coloration at an age of 12 months and more.

T: 27-30° C, **L**: ♂ 10 cm, ♀ 8 cm, **A**: 90 cm, **R**: m, t, **D**: 2
81-86° F, ♂ 4", ♀ 3", 35",

Melanotaenia boesemani, a fully colored ♂

Melanotaenia affinis

Melanotaenia boesemani

Continuation of *Melanotaenia boesemani*:

B: In DATZ 8/1986, EISELE revealed some interesting details about breeding: rearing, as usually practiced with infusoria, is rarely successful with this species since the larvae grow very slowly. EISELE feeds infusoria the first 4-5 days and then finest liver pieces rubbed through an *Artemia* net. For cleanup, some *Ampullaria* snails should be kept in the 60 l (16 gal) rearing tank.

Melanotaenia eachamensis — ALLEN, 1982

Lake Eacham Rainbowfish

Syn.: None.

Hab.: Australia; the species is only found in Lake Eacham, a small crater lake located in the Atherton Plateau, 40 km (25 mi) southwest of Cairns in Queensland.

F.I.: Probably not yet imported into Germany.

Sex: The ♂ is somewhat deeper-bodied and more colorful.

Soc. B.: Peaceful schooling fish.

M: As indicated for *Melanotaenia trifasciata*.

T: 24-30° C, L: 8 cm, A: 90 cm, R: m, D: 2
75-86° F, 3", 35",

B: No reports are available yet, but it probably does not deviate from other Australian *Melanotaenia* species.

F: C, O; live foods of all kinds, frozen food, but also flake food.

S: *Melanotaenia eachamensis* is closely related to *Melanotaenia splendida splendida*.

Melanotaenia exquisita — ALLEN, 1978

Syn.: None.

Hab.: Australia; Northern Territory, the species is only known from the Edith River and nearby Lake Malkyllumbo in Edith Falls National Park.

F.I.: Not known.

Sex: The ♂♂ are larger, deeper-bodied and more beautifully colored.

Soc. B.: Peaceful, active schooling fish.

M: As indicated for *Melanotaenia trifasciata*. In nature the animals prefer sites exposed to sunlight. This should be considered when choosing a place for the tank. Keep in a species tank, or maintain with other rainbows (i.e., *Melanotaenia splendida australis*).

B: Detailed breeding reports are not available. However, breeding should be similar to other Australian *Melanotaenia* species.

F: C, O; predominantly live foods of all kinds, also frozen and flake foods.

S: The orange to red spot on the operculum seems to be a distinctive characteristic for this species.

T: 24-30° C, L: ♂ 7 cm, ♀ 6 cm, A: 70 cm, R: m, D: 2
75-86° F, ♂ 2 3/4", ♀ 2 1/3", 28",

Melanotaenia eachamensis ♂

Melanotaenia exquisita

Melanotaenia goldiei (MACLEAY, 1883)
Goldie River Rainbowfish

Syn.: *Aristeus goldiei, Melanotaenia dumasi, Nematocentris novaeguineae, Rhombatractus kochii, R. senckenbergianus, R. weberi, Rhombosoma goldiei, R. novaeguineae.*

Hab.: New Guinea and Aru Islands. *M. goldiei* is one of the widest distributed rainbowfishes of New Guinea.

F.I.: Around 1985.

Sex: ♂♂ are more colorful and grow larger. They are usually deeper-bodied.

Soc. B.: Lively, peaceful schooling fish.

M: Needs a tank with dense edge and background vegetation and a sandy bottom; leave a sufficient area open for swimming. Prefers water that is neutral to slightly alkaline (pH 7.0-7.8) and not too soft (from 10° dGH). Keep in a species tank or associate with rainbowfishes of similar needs.

B: Breeding is not problematic; use water values listed above. *Melanotaenia goldiei* is, like many members of the genus, an open spawner. The eggs have short adhesive threads. At 25° C (77° F), the eggs need about 1 week to develop. *Artemia* and *Cyclops* nauplii are good starter foods. The parents must be well fed, or they eat the eggs and young.

F: C, O; predominately live food of all kinds. After an acclimation period, substitute foods are also accepted.

S: The black lateral band is commonly very wide (about 2-2 rows of scale) and jet black.

T: 25-28° C, **L:** 12 cm, **A:** 90 cm, **R:** m, t, **D:** 2
77-82° F, 4³/₄", 35",

Melanotaenia gracilis ALLEN, 1978
Slender Rainbowfish

Syn.: *Nematocentris species 2.*

Hab.: Australia; northern part of Western Australia.

F.I.: Unknown, probably has not been imported into Germany.

Sex: The ♂♂ grow larger and are deeper-bodied.

Soc. B.: Peaceful, lively schooling fish.

M: As for *Melanotaenia trifasciata.*

B: Breeding is probably not very difficult, but there are no detailed reports. Breeding will be comparable to other Australian *Melanotaenia* species.

F: C, O; moderately sized live foods, also frozen and flake foods.

S: *Melanotaenia gracilis* is sometimes found together with *Melanotaenia splendida australis*, but it can be easily distinguished by its coloration and more slender silhouette.

T: 22-28° C, **L:** ♂ 7.5 cm, ♀ 6 cm, **A:** 90 cm, **R:** m, t, **D:** 2
72-82° F, ♂ 3", ♀ 2¹/₃", 35",

Melanotaenia goldiei, ♂ bottom ♀ top

Melanotaenia gracilis

Melanotaenia herbertaxelrodi ALLEN, 1981
Lake Tebera Rainbowfish

Syn.: None.

Hab.: New Guinea; the species is only known from the Lake Tebera basin in the southern highlands of Papua New Guinea.

F.I.: 1979 or 1980 to the USA; 1984 or 1985 to Germany.

Sex: The ♂♂ are deeper bodied and more beautifully colored than the ♀♀.

Soc. B.: Lively, peaceful schooling fish.

M: Densely plant the sides and background, leaving the fish an open space for swimming; use fine sand for bottom. Water should have at least 10° dGH and be slightly alkaline (pH 7.5-7.8). Keep in a species tank or with other rainbowfishes.

B: Similar to other *Melanotaenia* species. The ♀♀ lays about 30 eggs a day on water plants. These hang by fine threads. The eggs are not guarded by the parents. At 22-24° C (72-75° F), the larvae hatch after about 1 week. The parents should be removed afterwards since they will pursue the young. The larvae are small; feed the smallest live foods (rotifers, *Artemia* nauplii).

F: C, O; live foods of all kinds, also frozen and flake foods.

S: *Melanotaenia herbertaxelrodi* is one of the most colorful *Melanotaenia* species of New Guinea.

T: 20-26° C, **L:** 9 cm, **A:** 90 cm, **R:** m, t, **D:** 2
68-79° F, 3 ", 35",

Melanotaenia nigrans (RICHARDSON, 1843)
Dark Australian Rainbowfish

Syn.: *Atherina nigrans, Atherinichthys nigrans, Nematocentris nigra, Rhombatractus archboldi, Zantecla pusilla.*

Hab.: Eastern Australia and coastal rivers of southwest Papua (New Guinea). The species lives in freshwater but also enters brackish water.

F.I.: It is probable that the fish imported under this name in 1927 were actually *Melanotaenia splendida fluviatilis*. The true *"nigrans"* was probably only imported into Germany at the end of the '70's.

Sex: The ♂♂ have brighter colors and larger dorsal and anal fins; both fins are edged in black. The ♀♀ are plainly colored and have smaller dorsal and anal fins without the black outline.

Soc. B.: Actively swimming, peaceful schooling fish.

M: Needs a fine substrate, moderate edge and background vegetation and a lot of free swimming space. The aquarium should receive some morning sun. The water should be medium-hard to hard (from 10° dGH). pH 5.2-5.6, temperature 24-30° C (75-86° F). The addition of sea salt is not absolutely necessary, but it can be added (1-2 teaspoons per 10 l; 2.5 gal of water).

B: 24-26° C (75-79° F); breeding is totally nonproblematic. It is important that the animals are offered roomy breeding aquaria. Pairing is initiated by heavy chasing. During courtship, the ♂♂ flare their fins and push the ♀♀ into the plant thicket to spawn. The animals spawn daily over a period of 1 to 2 weeks. The eggs are attached to the plants by tiny threads. Their development takes 8-11 days. After a few additional days, the larvae are free-swimming. Feed with micro food and crumbled flake food.

F: Live foods of all kinds, flake food is readily accepted.

S: *Melanotaenia nigrans* is sensitive to sudden drops in temperature. If ripe ♀♀ are kept without ♂♂, they will expel mature eggs from time to time.

T: 18-24° C, **L:** ♂ 7 cm, ♀ 6 cm, **A:** 100 cm, **R:** m, t, **D:** 1
64-75° F, ♂ 2¾", ♀ 2⅓", 39",

Melanotaenia herbertaxelrodi

Melanotaenia nigrans ♂

Melanotaenia papuae ALLEN, 1981
Papuan Rainbowfish

Syn.: None.

Hab.: New Guinea; in freshwaters around Port Moresby.

F.I.: Not known.

Sex: The ♂♂ grow larger and are more intensely colored.

Soc. B.: Actively swimming, peaceful schooling fish.

M: As for *Melanotaenia goldiei*. *M. papuae* also loves slightly alkaline water (pH 7.2-7.8) with a hardness over 10° dGH. Keep in a species tank or house with other rainbowfishes.

B: As for other representatives of the genus. Detailed breeding reports are not available.

F: C, O; predominately live food, but also flake food.

S: *Melanotaenia papuae* usually has 9-10, occasionally 11, or rarely 12, soft rays on the second dorsal fin.

T: 22-32° C, **L:** ♂ 6.5 cm, ♀ 6 cm, **A:** 70 cm, **R:** m, **D:** 2
72-90° F, ♂ 2²/₃", ♀ 2¹/₃", 28",

Melanotaenia parkinsoni ALLEN, 1980
Parkinson's Rainbowfish

Syn.: None.

Hab.: New Guinea; the species has only been found in two small tributaries of the Kamp Welsh River about 75 km (47 mi) southeast of Port Moresby.

F.I.: 1985.

Sex: The ♂♂ grow larger, are somewhat higher-bodied and have bright yellow to orange colored dorsal, tail and anal fins.

Soc. B.: Peaceful, active schooling fish.

M: Needs a fine substrate and dense vegetation. Leave sufficient free swimming space. Hardness should not be less than 8° dGH with a pH of 7.5-7.8. Combine with other rainbowfishes, or keep in a species tank.

B: Like most other *Melanotaenia* species, breeding is nonproblematic.

F: C, O; live foods of all kinds, frozen, freeze-dried and flake foods.

S: Other than *M. splendida rubrostriata*, *Melanotaenia parkinsoni* has the most soft anal fin rays (18-23, usually 20-21) of all *Melanotaenia* species from southern New Guinea.

T: 26-30° C, **L:** ♂ 12 cm, ♀ 10 cm, **A:** 100 cm, **R:** m, t, **D:** 2-3
79-86° F, ♂ 4³/₄", ♀ 4", 39",

Melanotaenia papuae ♂

Melanotaenia parkinsoni ♂

Melanotaenia splendida australis (CASTELNEAU, 1875)
Western Splendid Rainbowfish

Syn.: *Melanotaenia solata.*

Hab.: Swan River in Western Australia, Groote Eylandt in the Northern Territory, Australia.

F.I.: 1983 by Heiko Bleher, Kelsterbach, Germany.

Sex: Not known.

Soc. B.: Peaceful schooling fish; suitable for almost any community tank. At least 5-7 animals of the same species should be kept together.

M: A refreshingly easy species to care for. It accepts any water as long as it is clear and low in nitrates (up to 20 mg NO_3/l). Overstocking the tank should be avoided. Plant the background. Leave a lot of open swimming space. The aquarium can be put in a sunny place. Regular water changes every 2-3 weeks ( ) are recommended.

B: Use mosquito larvae to bring into condition. This species scatters its eggs among plant bunches. Every day for 14 days a few, relatively large eggs are laid. These have adhesive threads and stick to the plants. After 5-10 days, the larvae hatch and the parents should be removed. The newly hatched young are already quite well developed and accept standard rearing foods, such as, Liquifry, TetraMin Baby Food, etc., and, of course, any fine micro foods such as infusoria and protozoa. After a few days, newly hatched *Artemia* are eaten.

F: C, O; all types of flake foods, FD foods and live foods.

S: One of the most beautiful rainbows. However, at least 12 months are needed to develop full coloration. Young animals are quite plain initially. The life span is 4-8 years.

T: 22-28° C, **L:** ♂ up to 10 cm, ♀ 8 cm, **A:** 80 cm, **R:** m, t, **D:** 2
72-82° F, ♂ up to 4", ♀ 3", 31",

Melanotaenia splendida rubrostriata (RAMSAY & OGILBY, 1886)
Red-Striped Splendid Rainbowfish

Syn.: *Nematocentris rubrostriatus, Aristeus loriae, Melanotaenia maculata, Rhombatractus patoti.*

Hab.: New Guinea; between the Aramia River and Etus Bay (central Irian Jaya).

F.I.: End of the '70's by J. Clasen.

Sex: ♂♂ grow larger, are more colorful and usually have a deeper body.

Soc. B.: Peaceful, lively schooling fish.

M: As with other *Melanotaenia* species of New Guinea. The pH of the water in nature fluctuates between moderately acid and slightly alkaline (pH 5.6-7.4).

B: Similar to other *Melanotaenia* species of New Guinea (compare, for instance, with *M. goldiei*).

F: C, O; live foods of all types, frozen and flake foods.

S: Six sub-species of *Melanotaenia splendida* have been described. *Melanotaenia splendida rubrostriata* is closely related to *M. splendida inornata* (CASTELNEAU, 1875) of northern Australia, only differing in coloration.

T: 24-28° C, **L:** ♂ 13 cm, ♀ 10 cm, **A:** 100 cm, **R:** m, t, **D:** 2-3
75-82° F, ♂ 5", ♀ 4", 39",

Melanotaenia splendida australis

Melanotaenia splendida rubrostriata ♂

Harrey Creek, Australia. *Cairnsichthys, Melanotaenia maccullochi* and *Melanotaenia splendida splendida* can be found here.

Melanotaenia splendida australis ♂

Melanotaenia splendida australis ♂ + ♀

Melanotaenia splendida inornata

Melanotaenia splendida inornata, ♂ b. ♀ t.

Melanotaenia s. splendida, ♂ front ♀ back

Melanotaenia splendida rubrostriata ♂ ♂

Melanotaenia trifasciata ♂

Melanotaenia s. splendida, Harrey Creek

Melanotaenia trifasciata (RENDAHL, 1922)
Banded Rainbowfish

Syn.: *Rhombosoma trifasciata.*

Hab.: Australia; Northern Territory and Cap York Peninsula. Several color morphs are known.

F.I.: 1976 by J. Clasen.

Sex: The ♂ is more colorful, dorsal and anal fin are pointed, and in some morphs, the ♂ is deeper bodied.

Soc. B.: Peaceful, lively schooling fish.

M: Differs depending on the origin of the fish. Animals out of the Goyder River are most comfortable in hard, alkaline water; other morphs prefer soft water. The animals show their beautiful colors best in well-planted tanks with dark substrate (lava). Provide regular partial water changes. Keep in a species tank or associate with other rainbow species.

T: 25-30° C, 77-86° F, L: 12 cm, 4³/₄", A: 90 cm, 35", R: m, D: 2

B: Breeding is easy. The willingness to spawn can be enhanced by partial water exchanges. The animals are continuous spawners. As a number of other species, the ♂ has a bright golden to light blue "neon-band" (color depends on origin) during courtship; it extends from the upper lip to the first dorsal fin. The larvae hatch after 6-8 days at 25° C (77° F) and should be fed fine live foods.

F: C, O; all types of live foods, frozen and flake foods.

S: The morphs of *Melanotaenia trifasciata* are very different in color and body shape. For this reason, it is possible that we are dealing with several species with this fish. *Melanotaenia trifasciata* is closely related to *Melanotaenia goldiei* from southern New Guinea.

Melanotaenia trifasciata, Coen, Cape York Peninsula, NE Australia

Melanotaenia trifasciata ♂, Goyder River, Northern Territory, Australia

Melanotaenia trifasciata ♂, Giddy River, Arnhem Land, Australia

Pseudomugil connieae ALLEN, 1981
Podondetta Rainbowfish

Syn.: *Popondetta connieae, Popondichthys connieae.*

Hab.: New Guinea; in the vicinity of Popondetta, Papua New Guinea.

F.I.: 1983 by Heiko Bleher, Frankfurt, Germany.

Sex: The ♂♂ have more beautiful finnage and coloration. The first dorsal fin of the ♂♂ is elongated. Additionally, the ♂♂ are somewhat larger.

Soc. B.: Peaceful, active schooling fish. The ♂♂ can be quite aggressive at spawning time.

M: Needs an aquarium with a fine sand substrate. Plant well with Java moss and use floating plants (e.g., *Riccia*). Water should be slightly alkaline (pH 7.7-7.9) and not too soft (from 10° dGH). Put with other peaceful fish, such as *Pseudomugil gertrudae* or *Iriatherina werneri*. But best kept in a species tank.

B: A successful breeding set-up for *Pseudomugil* is described by ALLEN & CROSS (1982): Rainbow-fishes of Australia and Papua New Guinea, TFH Publications: a tank of 40 x 25 x 25 cm (16" x 10" x 10") is sufficient. The bottom should have a thin layer of sand, a clump of Java moss, two or three floating *Riccia* mats and a slow bubbling airstone. The animals can be set up in pairs as well as in groups. If the ♂ is too aggressive, 1-2 additional ♀♀ are added. A set-up with a school yields significantly better results than breeding with pairs. The animals usually spawn in the morning. Eggs have adhesive threads and stick to water plants. Development takes 15-20 days at 25° C (77° F). Remove the parents (spawn predators). Feed the young with infusoria and micro food.

F: C, O; predominately live foods of all kinds but also flake food.

T: 25-28° C, L: ♂ 5.5 cm, ♀ 4.5 cm, A: 60 cm, R: m, t, D: 2
77-82° F, ♂ 2", ♀ 1¾", 24",

Pseudomugil furcatus (NICHOLS, 1955)
Forked-Tail Rainbowfish

Syn.: *Popondetta furcata, Popondichthys furcatus.*

Hab.: New Guinea; coastal plains and adjacent lowlands between Dyke Ackland Bay and Collingwood Bay at the eastern end of New Guinea.

F.I.: In 1985 these appeared for the first time in German aquaria; however, sometimes only ♂♂ were available. Still a rare find.

Sex: The ♂♂ have a longer first dorsal fin; furthermore, they are somewhat larger and more intensely colored.

Soc. B.: Lively, peaceful schooling fish.

M: As suggested for *P. connieae*. *P. furcatus* loves heavily planted tanks.

B: Very similar to *P. connieae*. Details can be found there.

F: C, O; predominantly small live foods, freeze-dried food and flake food.

S: *P. furcatus* differs from *P. connieae* by the presence of usually 8-9 (rarely 7) segmented rays in the second dorsal fin (10-11, occasionally 9 rarely 12, in *P. connieae*) and by a black outline on the top and bottom of the caudal fin. ♂♂ of *P. furcatus* have a bright orange colored chest, while that of *P. connieae* is yellow.

T: 24-26° C, L: ♂ 5.5 cm, ♀ 4.5 cm, A: 60 cm, R: m, t, D: 2
75-79° F, ♂ 2", ♀ 1¾", 24",

Pseudomugil connieae ♂

Pseudomugil furcatus ♂ + ♀

Pseudomugil gertrudae — WEBER, 1911

Gertrud's Blue-Eye, Spotted Blue-Eye

Syn.: None.

Hab.: Australia, New Guinea and Aru Islands; northern Australia (Finiss River, Jardin River system, Cape York Peninsula, Murray swamps in Queensland), southern New Guinea (upper and mid Fly river system and Pahoturi river system).

F.I.: Imported in 1985 by West-Aquarium, Germany

Sex: ♂ more colorful and has more elongated fins.

Soc. B.: Active, very peaceful schooling fish.

M: Supply the tank with a fine bottom and vegetation along the periphery; leave sufficient open swimming space. Water should be soft (4-8° dGH) and slightly acid (pH around 6.5). Because of the fragile nature of the fish, it is best kept in a species tank.

B: Breeding *Pseudomugil gertrudae* is not easy. In a species tank, the animals breed on their own. They are continuous spawners. The eggs are large and can be stored in damp moss or peat for an extended period of time (4 weeks), as for killifishes.

F: C, O; small live foods and flake food.

S: Three forms are known from northern Australia. These differ in the coloration of the upper pectoral fin rays: 1. "Yellow-wing" (yellow; Jardine River), 2. "White-wing" (white; Cairns/Innisfail), 3. "Red-wing" (red; Arnhem Land and surroundings of Darwin, Northern Territory).

T: 25-30° C, **L**: 3 cm, **A**: 50 cm, **R**: m, t, **D**: 2
77-86° F, 1 ", 20",

Pseudomugil mellis — ALLEN, 1983

Honey Blue-Eye

Syn.: None.

Hab.: Australia; surroundings of Tin Can Bay (opposite to Fraser Island) south of Beerwah in Queensland.

F.I.: 1976 by J. Clasen.

Sex: ♂ is more colorful and has longer fins.

Soc. B.: Peaceful, very active schooling fish.

M: Best kept in a species tank. Despite its limited size, *Pseudomugil mellis* is a robust fish that likes soft (4-8° dGH) and slightly acid water (pH 6.0-6.5). However, the animals can also be cared for under different conditions. Plant densely; preserve sufficient swimming space; use fine-grained bottom material.

B: As indicated for *Pseudomugil gertrudae*. However, it is not known if the eggs can be stored.

F: C, O; small live foods of all kinds, also flake food and freeze-dried food.

S: The habitat of this species is only one hour in car from the city of Brisbane. The fish is known to Australian aquarists for at least 25 years as "honey blue-eye". Until the description by ALLEN, this species was considered a morph of *Pseudomugil signifer*.

T: 24-28° C, **L**: 3 cm, **A**: 60 cm, **R**: m, t, **D**: 2
75-82° F, 1 ", 24",

Pseudomugil gertrudae ♂

Pseudomugil mellis ♂ ♂

Pseudomugil signifer ("Cairns Form")
Southern Blue-Eye

KNER, 1864

Syn.: *Atherina signata, Pseudomugil signatus.*

Hab.: Australia; northeastern Queensland, the pictured animals have only been found in the tributaries of the Mulgarve and Russel rivers, located between the towns of Cairns and Innisfail.

F.I.: 1983 by Heiko Bleher (?), Frankfurt, Germany.

Sex: The ♂ is more colorful and has longer fins.

Soc. B.: The animals are active schooling fish. Peaceful towards heterospecifics. ♂♂ are territorial. Keep one ♂ with several ♀♀.

M: Needs a bottom of fine gravel and meager vegetation. The animals inhabit running waters in nature; therefore, a weak current with a pump may be helpful. Leave a lot of open swimming space. Water should be soft (4-8° dGH) and slightly acid (pH around 6.5). Can be kept in a community tank as long as the other fishes are not too rough.

B: Breeding is easy. Rearing of the young, however, can cause difficulties. Since the ♂ actively pursues the ♀, always keep one ♂ with several ♀♀. The animals are continuous spawners. The eggs are quite large. The young hatch after 7-10 days at 25° C (77° F). With dense vegetation, the breeders can remain in the tank; otherwise, they have to be removed (spawn predators!).

F: C, O; small live foods of any kind, frozen food, freeze-dried and flake foods.

S: The "Cairns form" of *Pseudomugil signifer* is probably a new species. The fish differ clearly from the "true" *Pseudomugil signifer* by their finnage and behavior.

T: 23-28° C, **L:** 4 cm, **A:** 60 cm, **R:** m, t, **D:** 2
73-82° F, 1 2/3", 24",

Pseudomugil tenellus
Delicate Blue-Eye

TAYLOR, 1964

Syn.: None.

Hab.: Australia; only known from the east Alligator river system in the Northern Territory.

F.I.: Probably not yet imported into Germany.

Sex: The ♂♂ are more intensely colored.

Soc. B.: Very peaceful, active schooling fish.

M: As for *Pseudomugil gertrudae*. In nature, *Pseudomugil tenellus, Melanotaenia nigrans* and *M. splendida inornata* are found together.

B: Similar to *P. gertrudae*. Exact breeding reports are not available.

F: C, O; small live foods; the animals also eat flake food.

S: *Pseudomugil tenellus* chiefly inhabits swampy pools (billabongs) and calm backwater of rivers with mud and gravel bottoms.

T: 28-35° C, **L:** 3 cm, **A:** 50 cm, **R:** m, t, **D:** 2
82-95° F, 1 ", 20",

Pseudomugil signifer ("Cairns form")

Pseudomugil tenellus

Rhadinocentrus ornatus REGAN, 1914
Southern Soft-Spined Rainbowfish

Syn.: None.

Hab.: Australia; between Coffs Harbour (northern New South Wales) and Maryborough (southern Queensland), on the sand islands Stradbroke, Moreton and Fraser in soft, acid water.

F.I.: In 1987 the blue form was first imported.

Sex: The ♂ is larger, more colorful and has pointed anal and second dorsal fins. Those of the ♀ are rounded.

Soc. B.: Peaceful, lively schooling fish.

M: Acclimated animals are undemanding; however, until the animals are acclimated, they may fall victims to inexplicable losses. Provide a fine sand bottom, side and background vegetation of fine-leaved plants, and sufficient free swimming space. Soft (4-8° dGH) and acid (pH 6.0-6.5) water is recommended. Keep in a species tank or house with rainbowfishes that have similar requirements.

B: Breeding is easy. In a species tank, the fish reproduce without special attention. They are continuous spawners. Development of the eggs takes seven to ten days at 25° C (77° F). Feed the young with fine live food.

F: C, O; small live foods of all types, also flake food.

S: *Rhadinocentrus ornatus* has proven extremely sensitive to transport. So far, four color morphs are known. One of the morphs is brick red posteriorly. The genus *Rhadinocentrus* is monotypic; that is, it only consists of one species.

T: 20-30° C, L: ♂ up to 7 cm, ♀ 4 cm, A: 70 cm, R: m, t, D: 2
68-86° F, ♂ up to 2 3/4", ♀ 1 2/3", 28",

Biotope of *Rhadinocentrus ornatus*.

Rhadinocentrus ornatus ♂, red form

Rhadinocentrus ornatus, blue form

Gnathonemus schilthuisiae BOULENGER, 1899
Schilthuis' Elephantnose

Syn.: None (?).

Hab.: Africa; middle Congo River.

F.I.: 1952.

Sex: None are known.

Soc. B.: A twilight and nocturnally active species; they are often gregarious with similar sized animals. Weaker conspecifics are often oppressed. The animals are territorial and, in most cases, peaceful towards heterospecifics.

M: Since the animals like to dig in search of their food, a soft sand substrate is suggested. Use thick vegetation to create dark areas, perhaps floating plants can be used to reduce the light. Caves and other hiding places should be built of roots and rocks. Up to medium-hard (5-15° dGH) water with a pH around 7.0; occasionally add new water with a good water conditioner.

B: Unsuccessful in an aquarium.

F: C, O; live foods of all kinds, freeze-dried food, frozen and flake food.

S: Especially in *G. schilthuisiae* a marked playfulness can be observed.

T: 24-28° C, **L:** 10 cm, **A:** 80 cm, **R:** b, **D:** 3
75-82° F, 4", 31",

Marcusenius brachyistius GILL, 1862

Syn.: *Mormyrus brachyistius.*

Hab.: West Africa; Sierra Leone, Liberia, Ivory Coast.

F.I.: 1935 by "Aquarium Hamburg", Germany.

Sex: No external ones known.

Soc. B.: Twilight- and night-active fish that possesses a weak electrical organ.

M: As indicated for *Marcusenius macrolepidotus*. Best kept in a species tank or singly. The animals disturb each other with their electrical organ when housed in the tanks that are too small.

B: *M. brachyistius* has not been bred in an aquarium.

F: C; all live foods of appropriate size.

S: None.

T: 25-28° C, **L:** 18 cm, **A:** 100 cm, **R:** b, m, **D:** 3
77-82° F, 7", 39",

Gnathonemus schilthuisiae

Marcusenius brachyistius

Marcusenius longianalis BOULENGER, 1901
Slender Elephantnose

Syn.: None.

Hab.: Africa; Nigeria and Cameroon. The animals inhabit the lower Niger River and the Kribi River. The species lives in freshwater.

F.I.: 1906 by Herrn Schoot, Hamburg, Germany.

Sex: No external differences are known.

Soc. B.: Very peaceful twilight- and night-active species. The species is very friendly towards heterospecific fish but bothers them with the slight electrical impulses it generates. *M. longianalis* can be bellicose towards conspecifics.

M: As indicated for *Marcusenius macrolepidotus*. Best kept in a species tank.

B: Reproduction in an aquarium has so far been unsuccessful.

F: C, O; live foods (small crustacea, mosquito larvae, all types of worms); algae and detritus.

S: *Marcusenius longianalis* is notoriously slender for a Mormyridae.

T: 25-30° C, **L:** 15 cm, **A:** 90 cm, **R:** b, m, **D:** 3
77-86° F, 6", 35",

Marcusenius macrolepidotus (PETERS, 1852)
Large-Scaled Elephantnose

Syn.: *Mormyrus macrolepidotus, Gnathonemus macrolepidotus.*

Hab.: Africa; the species inhabits southeast Africa. The animals are pronounced freshwater inhabitants.

F.I.: 1937 by the Scholze & Pötzschke Co., Germany.

Sex: Unknown.

Soc. B.: Twilight- and night-active species.

M: Water to medium-hard (10° dGH) and in the neutral range (pH 7.0).

B: The species has not been bred in an aquarium.

F: C; live foods of any kind are accepted as long as they are small enough.

S: *Marcusenius macrolepidotus* has a very small mouth and can only feed on the smallest food items.

T: 22-26° C, **L:** 25 cm, **A:** 100 cm, **R:** b, m, **D:** 3
72-79° F, 9 3/4", 39",

Marcusenius longianalis

Marcusenius macrolepidotus

Petrocephalus bovei (VALENCIENNES, 1846)

Syn.: *Mormyrus bovei.*

Hab.: Africa; the species inhabits the lower Nile, Senegal and Gambia rivers

F.I.: 1937.

Sex: None known.

Soc. B.: Peaceful toward heterospecifics but quite aggressive towards conspecifics; twilight- and night-active.

M: Needs a bottom of fine sand, hiding places of rocks and roots, and thick vegetation. Leave an open area for swimming. Occasional water exchanges are beneficial. Only keep one or two specimens per tank; the animals upset each other with the electric impulses they constantly generate. Therefore, the fish should be kept in a species tank.

B: Has rarely been successful so far. BIRKHOLZ succeeded in 1969. He discovered a complete nest with eggs and young in a dark corner of the aquarium. The nest was a ball-shaped bunch of algae and other plant parts. Among the algae, 28 eggs and young in different stages of development were located. The young were very photophobic. No parental brood care was observed. The yolk sac of the young was absorbed after ten to twelve days. *Artemia* nauplii proved too large at first, so infusoria and rotifers were initially fed.

F: C; live foods of all kinds: mosquito larvae, small crustacea, *Tubifex*, Enchytraea.

S: *Petrocephalus bovei* is quite sensitive and easily injured. The animals do not have an elephant nose.

T: 23-26° C, **L:** 12 cm, **A:** 80 cm, **R:** b, m, **D:** 4
73-79° F, 4 3/4", 31",

Petrocephalus catostomus (GÜNTHER, 1866)
Big-Nosed Whale

Syn.: *Mormyrus catostomus.*

Hab.: This species is widely distributed in the lakes of eastern and southern Africa. It can be found from the upper Victoria-Nile to Natal (South Africa).

F.I.: Unknown.

Sex: ♂♂ have longer fin rays than the ♀♀ and an anal fin with a wavy margin.

Soc. B.: The animals are active and lively schooling fish.

M: A bottom of fine sand, hiding places constructed of rocks and roots and dense side and background vegetation is recommended. Produce a slight current with a pump. The occasional addition of fresh water, together with a good water conditioner, is needed. Keep in a species tank.

B: Not yet successful in an aquarium. Observations from the wild are not available.

F: C; live foods: *Tubifex*, other small worms, water fleas, *Cyclops*, mosquito larvae.

S: The species rarely exceeds 9 cm (3 ") length in an aquarium.

T: 23-26° C, **L:** 13 cm, **A:** 80 cm, **R:** b, m, **D:** 3
73-79° F, 5", 31",

Petrocephalus bovei

Petrocephalus catostomus

Oryzias latipes (TEMMINCK & SCHLEGEL, 1850)
Japanese Rice Fish, Medaka
Sub-Fam.: Oryziinae

Syn.: *Poecilia latipes, Aplocheilus latipes, Haplochilus latipes, Aplocheilus latipes* var. *auratus*.

Hab.: East Asia: Japan, China, South Korea. The exact area of distribution is unknown.

F.I.: 1895 by various Hamburger hobbyists.

Sex: Not always easy to determine. As a rule, ♂♂ are more slender, and their anal fin is larger and ends more pointed. The coloration is more intense. In the white and orange morphs, the ♂♂ have numerous silver, shiny scales, specially on the posterior part of the body. These are not as numerous in ♀♀.

Soc. B.: Peaceful fish which like to school. The species is extremely peaceful towards tankmates.

M: *Oryzias latipes* is suitable for a well-planted community aquarium, but the tankmates should not be overly large. Water values are of secondary importance; most suitable is medium-hard (10-15° dGH) and neutral water. The fish like aeration with water movement and clean water. Therefore, a filter is indicated.

B: If a pair or a small school are placed into a breeding tank, the young can be skimmed from the surface 2-3 weeks later. One can also collect the eggs regularly and hatch them in a small brooding container. They hatch after 10-12 days. It is quite remarkable that the ♀♀ which usually spawn in the morning hours, continue to carry their eggs in a bundle hanging in front of the anal fin, until they are brushed off on plants, etc. This is possibly a first step towards brood care.

F: O, C; live foods of all kinds, also flake and freeze-dried foods.

S: The genus *Oryzias* has recently been reclassified (Amer. Mus. Nov., 2719), after already for some time it had not belonged to the killifishes. It is now part of the Adrianichthyoidei and is closer related to the half-beaks. In Japan, *O. latipes* is used as an experimental animal in genetic and physiology experiments. A number of different color mutations exist. However, little is known about behavior, biology and distribution.

T: 18-24° C, L: 3.5 cm, A: 50 cm, R: m, t, D: 2
64-75° F, 1 1/3", 20",

Oryzias latipes ♂

Oryzias latipes ♀ with egg cluster

Chitala ornata (GRAY, 1831)
Clown Knifefish

Syn.: *Notopterus chitala, N. ocellifer.*

Hab.: Southeast Asia: Thailand, Burma, Mekong.

F.I.: 1934.

Sex: No definite ones known.

Soc. B.: Twilight and nocturnally active fish. The animals are quarrelsome and waspish among themselves. With advancing age they become loners. The species practices brood care; patriarch family.

M: The periphery of the tank should be planted heavily, always keeping enough open space for swimming. Construct hideaways of stones and roots. Utilize floating plants to help dim the light. Water should be soft (around 5° dGH) and slightly acid (pH 6.0-6.5). Keep in a species tank, or very aggressive individuals should be housed singly.

B: Has been successful in captivity. Reproduction of *C. ornata* is similar to *N. notopterus*. The animals spawn on a hard substrate (stone, wood); the spawn is guarded and fanned by the ♂. In the wild, brood care is important for two reasons: 1. The eggs receive oxygen. 2. In the slowly flowing water, the eggs become covered with sediment. By fanning, the sediment is removed. The young hatch after barely one week and brood care by the ♂ continues for a few more days.

F: The animals are greedy predators. They eat live foods of all kinds (worms, insects and their larvae, mollusks, fish). Chopped meat and crustacean meat is also accepted.

S: *Chitala ornata* is the largest representative of the family. In exceptional cases, individuals can reach one meter in length. The animals are appreciated food fish in their native range.

T: 24-28° C, L: up to 100 cm, A: 120 cm, R: m, b, D: 3
75-82° F, up to 39", 47",

Arapaima gigas (CUVIER, 1829)

Paiche, Pirarucú, Arapaima

Syn.: *Sudis gigas, S. piracuru, Vastres agassizii, V. cuvieri, V. mapae.*

Hab.: South America: Amazon and its drainage area.

F.I.: 1960 by K. H. Lüling, Bonn, Germany.

Sex: The sexes are difficult to distinguish. During the spawning season the ♂♂ have a more intense coloration and an exceptionally dark head.

Soc. B.: Predatory species which is very aggressive towards conspecifics. Large arapaimas are usually loners. They claim a territory at spawning time. *A. gigas* practices brood care; patriarch family, later nuclear family.

M: This fish can only be kept in the largest of tanks. For normal aquaria, care is limited to young specimens which are very rarely imported. The aquarium should have a large surface area, a sandy bottom, dense side and background vegetation with *Panicum polystachium* and *Eichhornia azurea*, and part of the surface covered with floating plants (*Pistia stratioides* and/or *Neptunea oleracea*). Insure sufficient open swimming space. The species does not place any special demands on the chemistry of the water; nevertheless, keep water hardness 10° dGH and below and acidic (pH 6.0-6.5). Keep singly or in a large species tank.

B: Not possible in an aquarium because of its size. In the wild, the main spawning season is November, at the end of the dry season. From December on, the water begins to rise again. The animals spawn in shallow pits. The ♂ remains in the immediate proximity of the spawn, while the ♀'s likely responsibility is to keep larger fishes at some distance (10-15 m; 11-16 yd) from the spawning site. The hatched larvae and young are cared for by the ♂, also some by the ♀. Brood care lasts 10-14 weeks.

F: C; hardy live foods of all kinds.

Continued on page 1156.

Heterotis niloticus (EHRENBERG, 1829)
African Bony-Tongue

Syn.: *Sudis niloticus, Clupisudis niloticus.*

Hab.: West and central Africa.

F.I.: Unknown.

Sex: No external ones known.

Soc. B.: The species is eminently bellicose towards its own species. They are extremely waspish. *H. niloticus* is peaceful towards heterospecifics. This species can be combined with many other fishes; one only has to keep in mind that its active swimming and curiosity can bother many tankmates (written communication by Jürgen INGE, Langenselbold, Germany). During the spawning season the animals are territorial and build nests. Brood caring species; matriarch family.

M: As for *Scleropages formosus.* However, peat filtration can be waived. *H. niloticus* likes warmth. Proper maintenance of this species is only possible in large show aquaria.

B: Because of the size of the animals, they have not been bred in an aquarium. In the wild at the beginning of the rainy season, the ♂ and ♀ construct an almost round nest 1-1.5 m (1.1-1.6 yd) in size, out of bits of plants found in shallow, plant-rich, still waters. Construction time is 5-7 days. The bottom of the nest is smoothed and hollowed out slightly. The embankment of the nest lies 20 cm (8") above the water level. After it is finished, the water in the nest becomes clear and clean. The ♀ enters alone to spawn in the nest; it lays the eggs close to a wall. The ♀ abandons the nest, the ♂ then jumps into the nest and fertilizes the eggs. After fertilization, the spawn and the nest are guarded by the ♀. The orange eggs have a diameter of 2.5 mm (1/10"). The larvae hatch after about 24 hours. The young are guarded 3-4 weeks by the ♀.

F: C, O; they feed on plankton and coarse detritus in the wild.

S: To catch the inhaled detritus and plankton, *Heterotis niloticus* has dense gill rakers and a snail-like coiled organ under the roof of the mouth-throat cavity, the suprabranchial organ. There the fine food particles are concentrated and coated in mucus.

T: 25-30° C, **L:** 90 cm, **A:** 150 cm, **R:** t, m, **D:** 4 (feeding specialist)
77-86° F, 35", 59",

Scleropages formosus (MÜLLER & SCHLEGEL, 1844)
Asian Arowana

Syn.: *Osteoglossum formosum.*

Hab.: Australia and southeast Asia (Borneo, Sumatra, Bangka, Thailand, west Malaysia). The species inhabits calm, weed-choked creeks and rivers.

F.I.: 1932 by O. Winkelmann, Altona, Germany.

Sex: No certain ones known. The ♀♀ are probably thicker during the spawning season.

Soc. B.: Predatory living fish. The animals are very quarrelsome towards conspecifics. Only combine with equal sized or larger animals. The animals practice brood care; mouthbrooder, matriarch family.

M: Needs soft water with a slight peat content, loose vegetation with medium tough to tough plants, open swimming space in the upper and midwater column and fine sand or small gravel as substrate. For the hobbyist, only young *Scleropages formosus* are suitable. The species needs a lot of warmth.

B: Unsuccessful in an aquarium. *Scleropages formosus* is a mouthbrooder. The few, large eggs are incubated by the ♀.

F: Predominantly live foods of all kinds: fish, insect larvae and crustacea.

S: The scales of this fish are very large. The barbels of the lower jaw are significantly shorter in the genus *Scleropages* in contrast to those of the genus *Osteoglossum*. The species is protected under the Washington Species Protection Act and cannot be offered in the trade.

T: 24-30° C, **L:** 90 cm, **A:** from 100 cm, **R:** t, m, **D:** 2-3
75-86° F, 35", from 39",

Heterotis niloticus

Scleropages formosus

Scleropages leichardtii GÜNTHER, 1864

Spotted Barramundi

Syn.: None.

Hab.: Southern New Guinea and in northern, tropical Australia, the rivers of the Gulf of Carpentaria and waters of eastern Queensland south of the Dawson River.

F.I.: Unknown.

Sex: No certain ones known. The ♀♀ are likely to be fuller during the spawning season.

Soc. B.: Predatory living fish which is bellicose towards conspecifics. Mouthbrooder; patriarch family?

M: As indicated for *Scleropages formosus*. *S. leichardtii* also requires warm water.

B: Has not been successful in an aquarium due to its size. Very little is known about the reproductive and brooding biology of *S. leichardtii*. From animals shot with a rifle, it is known that the species is a mouthbrooder. Spawning time in the wild is in October. According to WHITLEY (1960): Native fresh water fishes of Australia, p. 18-19, the ♂ allegedly incubates the eggs until the larvae hatch. During this time, no food is taken.

F: C, live foods of all kinds: fish, crustacea, insects and their larvae.

S: Some ichthyologist differentiate between two Australian *Scleropages* species: *S. leichardtii*, which only occurs in the area of the Fitzroy River, and *S. jardini*, which inhabits some rivers of the Gulf of Carpentaria and is distributed in southern New Guinea. Until the final decision, the geographic morphs of both species (?) remain combined under *S. leichardtii*. *S. leichardtii*, like *S. formosus*, belongs to the endangered species, which means Washington—as well as the German Species Protection Act— forbids their importation.

T: 24-30° C, L: 80 cm, A: 150 cm, R: t, m, D: 3
75-86° F, 31", 59",

Scleropages leichardtii

Scleropages jardini

Notesthes robusta (GÜNTHER, 1860)
Bullrout

Syn.: *Centropogon robustus.*

Hab.: Australia; Queensland and New South Wales; the species occurs in brackish water and freshwater.

F.I.: Small numbers were imported in 1984 to the area of Aachen, Germany.

Sex: None known.

Soc. B.: Greedy predator which ambushes its prey and overpowers it.

M: Provide a bottom of sand or fine-grained gravel, dense vegetation along the sides and back, some hiding places out of roots and rocks. Preserve free swimming space. No other demands are made. Perhaps sea salt can be added to the water (one tablespoon per 10 l; 2.6 gal). Associate only with equal sized or larger fishes, or keep it in a species tank.

B: Has not been accomplished in captivity.

F: C; hearty live foods (fish, shrimp, earthworms, etc.), also frozen food, beef heart and other meats.

S: One has to be cautious in handling *Notesthes robusta* since the species is a scorpionfish and has poisonous spines.

T: 10-30° C, L: 35 cm, A: from 100 cm, R: b, m, D: 3
50-86° F, 14", from 39",

Continuation of *Arapaima gigas* from page 1151:
S: *Arapaima gigas*, with his 3 m (3.3 yd) length, is the largest **true** freshwater fish on earth; that means a fish which only lives in freshwater and not, for example, like the larger sturgeons who migrate between brackish water in the vicinity of the sea and freshwater. In its home, the fish is caught with big pieces of meat which are hung on large floating inflated inner tubes. Down river, the tubes are again collected. This is an endangered species and cannot be imported.

T: 25-29° C, L: up to 3 m, A: from 150 cm, R: t, D: 4 (C)
77-84° F, up to 118", from 59",

Synaptura salinarum OGILBY, 1911
Salt-Pan Sole

Syn.: *Trichobrachirus salinarum, Brachirus salinarum..*

Hab.: Australia; in fresh and brackish waters of rivers that flow into the Gulf of Carpentaria.

F.I.: Probably not yet imported into Germany.

Sex: No external ones known.

Soc. B.: *S. salinarum* is a bottom-dwelling flatfish that hides during the day, but is very active at night. Peaceful towards other fishes.

M: Use large, low aquaria. The water does not need to be deep (20-30 cm; 8"-12"). Use a fine sand bottom, permitting the animals to burrow. Place some flat stones into the tank. No special demands are placed on the water; the addition of sea salt (1 tablespoon per 10 l; 2.5 gal of water) could be beneficial. Either keep in a species tank or combine them with gobies (Gobiidae, Eleotridae). Feed after turning the lights off so that the nocturnal animals do not starve.

B: Presently, nothing is known about a successful aquarium spawn.

F: C, O; principally live foods, which can be eaten off the bottom (mosquito larvae, *Tubifex*, small fairy shrimp, etc.). However, flake and tablet foods are also eaten.

S: There is one additional Australian *Synaptura achirus* species which occurs in freshwater: *Synaptura selheimi* (MACLEAR, 1882). *S. salinarum* differ from *S. selheimi* by the number of scales along the lateral line (85 vs. 80) and the number of tail fin rays (12 vs. 15).

T: 22-30° C, L: 15 cm, A: 80 cm, R: b, D: 3-4
72-86° F, 6", 31",

Monopterus albus (ZIEUW, 1793)

Syn.: *Muraena alba, Fluta alba, Monopterus javanensis, M. javanicus.*

Hab.: Asia; from Japan and northern China through the Malaysian Archipelago to Thailand and Burma. The animals occur in rivers and ponds, as well as in swamps, irrigation channels and rice fields.

F.I.: 1905.

Sex: No certain ones known.

Soc. B.: Twilight and nocturnal predators. The species practices brood care and builds bubble nests; patriarch family(?).

M: As indicated for *Synbranchus marmoratus*. These predatory animals are best kept singly.

B: The species has not been reproduced in captivity. An ichthyologist from Thailand has made observations in the wild with respect to the reproductive behavior of this species. According to his report, the animals spawn in shallow water. The eggs are gathered, forming free floating bubble nests. Several hundred eggs develop.

F: C; live foods of all kinds, especially small fishes.

S: In much of its natural habitat, *Monopterus albus* is an appreciated and good tasting food fish.

T: 25-28° C, **L:** 90 cm, **A:** 100 cm, **R:** b, **D:** 3-4 (C)
77-82° F, 35", 39",

Synbranchus marmoratus BLOCH, 1795
American Marbled Eel

Syn.: *Unibranchapertura marmorata, Muraena lumbricus, Synbranchus fuliginosus, S. transversalis, Unibranchapertura grisea, U. immaculata, U. lineata.*

Hab.: Central and South America; from southern Mexico to southern Brazil. The species occurs in fresh and brackish water.

F.I.: 1905.

Sex: Unknown.

Soc. B.: Predatory, aggressive and contentious fish.

M: Long, low (20 cm; 8") tanks are the most appropriate. It is recommended, in addition, to construct a shore area. Needs a soft bottom which should be slightly muddy; add some hiding areas of rocks and roots. The species places no demands on water make-up. Since the animals are pronounced predators, solitary maintenance is recommended; otherwise, associate only with large species.

B: Has been unsuccessful in captivity. Almost nothing is known about the reproductive biology and development of this species.

F: C; meat and carrion eater. The animals are very voracious.

S: In *Synbranchus marmoratus*, the entire gill cavity serves as an additional breathing organ. The animals usually live amphibiously at the water edge in the wild. They can transverse large distances snaking over the land.

T: 20-22° C, **L:** 150 cm, **A:** from 100 cm, **R:** b, **D:** 3-4 (S)
68-72° F, 59", from 39",

Monopterus albus

Synbranchus marmoratus

Chelonodon patoca (HAMILTON, 1822)
Milk-Spotted Puffer

Syn.: *Tetrodon patoca, Chelonodon dumerilii.*

Hab.: Coastal waters from southeast Africa to southeast Asia, including the Malayan Archipelago, Australia and New Guinea.

F.I.: 1952.

Sex: None known.

Soc. B.: Usually peaceful towards conspecifics; however, some skirmishes can occur. Very peaceful towards other species.

M: Use sand or fine shell as substrate. Hiding places made out of stone or roots that resist brackish water. Brackish or seawater (pH slightly alkaline).

B: Not yet successful.

F: C; only feeds on live food; preferentially snails, but also *Tubifex*, Enchytraea, earthworms, mosquito larvae and meal worms.

S: *Ch. patoca* inflates itself with water, tripling its circumference without apparent reason. Initially the species is very easily frightened, but with time it gets to know its keeper and becomes friendly. The meat of this species is very poisonous.

T: 23-28° C, L: 25 cm, A: 100 cm, R: b, m, D: 3 (C)
73-82° F, 10", 39",

Colomesus psittacus (BLOCH & SCHNEIDER, 1801)
South American Puffer

Syn.: *Tetrodon psittacus, Tetraodon psittacus.*

Hab.: South America: Peru, Venezuela, Guyana, Brazil (Amazon and some tributaries). The species occurs predominantly in brackish waters, seldom in freshwater.

F.I.: 1924.

Sex: None definitely known.

Soc. B.: Peaceful, lively puffer species.

M: Use fine sand as bottom cover. The species is said to dig itself in! Closely spaced plants at the edges and the back; hiding places out of stones and roots; leave some free swimming space. Best to keep in medium-hard (10° dGH) and neutral (pH 7.0) freshwater. Can be kept with other fishes.

B: Has not been successful in the aquarium.

F: C; live food of any kind (snails, mosquito larvae, earthworms); shellfish and crab meat.

S: The differences between the genus *Colomesus* and the genus *Tetraodon* lie in the cranial morphology, especially in the narrower frontal.

T: 23-26° C, L: 25 cm, A: 100 cm, R: m, b, D: 3
73-79° F, 10", 39",

Chelonodon patoca

Colomesus psittacus

Tetraodon fahaka LINNAEUS, 1758
Nile Puffer

Syn.: *Crayracion fahaka, Tetraodon lineatus, Tetrodon fahaka, T. physa, T. strigosus.*

Hab.: Africa; Senegal, Gambia, Niger, Chad basin, Nile, Lake Rudolf. The species lives in freshwater.

F.I.: 1902.

Sex: No external ones are known.

Soc. B.: The animals are very quarrelsome and waspish.

M: Always keep *T. fahaka* in roomy tanks. Needs a bottom of sand or gravel, dense edge and background vegetation and an open swimming area. Some hiding places of stones and/or roots should be provided. The water should not be too soft (from 10° dGH) and around neutral (pH 7.0). Because of the aggressive behavior of the animals, maintenance in a community tank cannot be recommended.

B: To our knowledge, the species has not been bred in an aquarium. Breeding is only possible in very large tanks. The animals spawn at major depths in the wild.

F: C; live foods of all kinds (mollusks, worms); shrimp, shellfish meat.

S: Several sub-species of *Tetraodon fahaka* have been described. Of these, *T. fahaka rudolfianus* DERANIYAGALA, 1956 is especially well suited for aquaria since this sub-species only grows to a length of 6 cm (2 1/3").

T: 24-26° C, **L**: 45 cm, **A**: 120 cm, **R**: b, m, **D**: 3
75-79° F, 18", 47",

Tetraodon leiurus brevirostris BENL, 1957
Twin-Spot Puffer

Syn.: None.

Hab.: Southeast Asia: probably Thailand.

F.I.: 1955.

Sex: Very difficult to determine. During cleaning and egg laying, the dark dots on the ♀ turn light, and the normal light net pattern turns totally dark. In the ♂, there is no such transformation.

Soc. B.: The animals are extremely waspish and bellicose. *T. leiurus brevirostris* is less active than, for example, *T. fluviatilis* or *T. schoutedeni*. The species practices brood care; patriarch family.

M: Requires a bottom of coarse quartz sand and some pieces of lava. Plant the tank with cryptocorynes and *Limnophila*; dim the light with mats of *Riccia*. Add roots to make hiding places. Medium-hard (up to 12° dGH), neutral (pH 7.0) water is suggested. The species should always be kept alone.

B: 26-30° C (79-86° F); already successful. An exact report is given by GEISER (1958): DATZ **11**, 100-101. Prior to spawning, the animal begins to clean a stone. This procedure takes about 1 day. Spawning occurs spontaneously; the ♂ immediately fertilizes the eggs. The parents brush together with their belly over the eggs. In this manner, the spawn is smoothed some more. The eggs are clear and vary in number between 300 and 500. Afterwards, the ♀ is chased away and the ♂ alone practices brood care. It fans freshwater over the spawn. Brood care terminates after the young hatch. The young hatch after 4-5 days at 30° C (86° F) and immediately swim to the water surface. Feed with *Artemia* and *Cyclops* nauplii.

F: C; live food of all kinds, primarily snails, but also *Tubifex*, small earthworms, shrimp, shellfish and liver.

S: The nominal form *Tetraodon leiurus leiurus* BLEEKER, 1850 has not been imported. The snout of that sub-species is longer and more pointed than that of *T. leiurus brevirostris* (name!).

T: 24-28° C, **L**: 12 cm, **A**: 70 cm, **R**: b, m, **D**: 2
75-82° F, 4 3/4", 28",

Tetrodon fahaka

Tetrodon leiurus brevirostris

Tetraodon mbu BOULENGER, 1899
Giant Puffer

Syn.: None.

Hab.: Africa; in the middle and lower Congo River. The species only lives in freshwater.

F.I.: 1954 by the A. Werner Co., Munich, Germany.

Sex: None are known so far.

Soc. B.: The animals are extremely quarrelsome and waspish.

M: As indicated for *Tetrodon fahaka*. Best kept individually.

B: The species has not been bred in captivity. Reproduction is probably only possible in very large aquaria.

F: C; hearty live foods of all kinds, snails and shellfish are especially relished.

S: *Tetraodon mbu* is a very large puffer species. The animals supposedly reach a weight of 6.5 kg (14 lb).

T: 24-26° C, **L:** 75 cm, **A:** 120 cm, **R:** b, m, **D:** 4
75-79° F, 30", 47",

Tetraodon miurus BOULENGER, 1902
Congo Puffer

Syn.: None.

Hab.: Africa; Zaire, in the middle and lower parts of the Congo River. The species is a freshwater inhabitant.

F.I.: 1954 by the A. Werner Co., Munich, Germany.

Sex: None known.

Soc. B.: The animals are very quarrelsome and waspish. The species is predatory and eats smaller fishes.

M: As indicated for *Tetraodon fahaka*. Bottom of a thick layer of sand. Because of the nature of the animal, solitary maintenance is recommended.

B: Breeding *Tetraodon miurus* in an aquarium has not yet been successful.

F: C; live foods of all kinds, primarily fishes. Mosquito larvae, earthworms and *Tubifex* are also eaten. The animals do not like snails.

S: The animals bury themselves into the ground (fine sand), camouflaging themselves to ambush any passing prey. Only the eyes and the superior mouth are exposed. The upward eyes are characteristic for this species.

T: 24-28° C, **L:** 15 cm, **A:** 90 cm, **R:** b, **D:** 3
75-82° F, 6", 35",

Tetraodon mbu

Tetraodon miurus

Index

In our index the genus- and species-names are printed in *italics*.
The family-names and the sub-family-names are printed **bold**.
The **bold** printed page-numbers will show you, where you'll find the species description.
Normal printed page-numbers will show you it is a synonym.

Index

Index

Index

Index

Index

Index

Index

Index

Index

Index

Index

Index

Literature

This bibliography is intended as a supplement to the literature listed in Volume 1.

Allen, G. R. (1982): A field guide to inland fishes of Western Australia, Western Australia Museum, Perth, Australien.

Allen, G. R. & Cross, N. J. (1982): Rainbowfishes of Australia and Papua New Guinea. T.F.H. Publications, Neptune City, N. J., USA.

Arnold, Andreas (1990): Eingebürgerte Fischarten. Zur Biologie und Verbreitung allochtoner Wildfische in Europa. Wittenberg Lutherstadt.

Bannister, K. E. (1973): A revision of the large *Barbus* (Pisces, Cyprinidae) of East and Central Afrika. Studies on african Cyprinidae, part II. Bull. Br. Mus. (Nat.Hist.) Zool. **26**, 1-148. British Museum, London.

Bassleer, G. (1982): Bildatlas der Fischkrankheiten. Verlag J. Neumann, Melsungen.

Bless, R. (1978): Bestandsänderungen der Fischfauna in der Bundesrepublik Deutschland. Ursachen, Zustand und Schutzmaßnahmen. Kilda Verlag, Greven.

Boulenger, G. A. (1907): The fishes of the Nile. Hugh Rees, London.

Boulenger, G. A. (1909-1916): Catalogue of the fresh-water fishes of Africa, Vols. I-IV. British Museum, London.

Bruton, M. N., Jackson, P. B. N. & Skelton, P. H. (1982): Pocket guide to the freshwater fishes of Southern Africa. Centaur Publishers, Kapstadt, Südafrika.

Cross, F. B. (1967): Handbook of fishes of Kansas. Museum of Natural History, Lawrence, Kansas, USA.

Day, F. (1889): The fauna of British India including Ceylon and Burma. Fishes, vols. I + II. Taylor and Francis, London.

Degen, B. (1984): Das neue Diskusbuch - Erfolgreiche Diskuszucht - . Verlag Bernd Degen, Kollnburg.

Gosse, J.P. (1982): Das Aquarium - Tropische Süßwasserfische -. Benziger Verlag, Zürich und Köln.

Grant, E. M. (1972): Guide to fishes of Queensland. Department of Primary Industries, Brisbane, Queensland, Australien.

Greenwood, P. H. (1976): A review of the family Centropomidae (Pisces, Perciformes). Bull. Br. Mus. (Nat.Hist.) Zool. **29**, 1-81. British Museum, London.

Greenwood, P. H. (1981): The Haplochromine fishes of the East African Lakes. Kraus International Publications, München.

Hegemann, M. (1964): Der Hecht. Neue Brehm Bücherei Band 336. A. Ziemsen Verlag, Wittenberg.

Hoedeman, J. J. (1980): Zwergcichliden: Zuidgroep BV Uitgevers-Best, Holland.

Howes, G. J. (1980): The anatomy, phylogeny and classification of bariliine cyprinid fishes. Bull. Br. Mus. (Nat. Hist.) Zool.**37**, 129-198, British Museum, London.

Hunnam, P. (1983): Lebensraum Aquarium. Verlag Eugen Ulmer, Stuttgart.

Jayaram, K. C. (1981): The freshwater fishes of India, Pakistan, Bangladesh, Burma and Sri Lanka - A handbook. Zoological Survey of India, Kalkutta, Indien.

Jordan, D. S. (1917-1923): The genera of fishes and a classification of fishes. Stanford University Press, Stanford, USA.

Jordan, D. S. & Seale, A. (1907): Fishes of the islands of Luzon and Panay. Bull. Bureau of Fisheries **26**, 1-48. Government Printing Office, Washington, USA.

Kottelat, M. (1990): IndochineseNemacheilines. A revision of nemacheiline loaches (Pisces: Cypriniformes) of Thailand, Burma, Laos, Cambodia ans southern Viet Nam. München.

Kullander, S. O. (1983): A revision of the South American cichlid genus Cichlasoma (Teleostei: Cichlidae). The Swedish Museum of Natural History, Stockholm, Schweden.

Lampert, K. (1925): Das Leben der Binnengewässer, Verlag Tauchnitz, Leipzig.

Lüling, K.-H. (1979): Die Lungenfische und der Südamerikanische Kurzschwanzaal (Dipnoidea; Synbranchidae). A. Ziemsen Verlag, Wittenberg.

Maitland, P. S. (1977): Der Kosmos Fischführer - Die Süßwasserfische Europas in Farbe. Franckh'-sche Verlagshandlung, Stuttgart.

Maitland, P. S. (1978): Biology of fresh waters. Blackie & Son, Glasgow and London.

Mayland, H. J. (1980): Labyrinthfische - Artenbeschreibung, Pflege, Zuchtverhalten. Philler Verlag, Minden.

Mayland, H. J. (1982): Der Malawisee und seine Fische. Landbuch Verlag, Hannover.

Mayland, H. J. (1981): Diskusfische - Könige Amazoniens. Landbuch Verlag, Hannover.

Meyer, M. W., Wischnath, L. & Förster, W. (1978): Lebendgebärende Zierfische - Arten der Welt, Mergus Verlag für Natur- und Heimtierkunde, Melle.

Migdalski, E. C. & Fichter, G. S. (1978): Fische - Das große Buch der Süßwasser- und Meeresfische. Büchergilde Gutenberg, Frankfurt/Main.

Mihalik, J. (1982): Der Wels - Siluris glanis. A. Ziemsen Verlag, Wittenberg.

Misra, K. S. (1976): The fauna of India and the adjacent countries. Pisces, vol. III: Teleostomi; Cypriniformes; Siluri. Zoological Survey of India, Faridabad, Indien.

Mühlberg, H. (1980): Das große Buch der Wasserpflanzen. Verlag Werner Dausien, Hanau.

Müller, H. (1956): Die Forellen. Neue Brehm Bücherei Band 164. A. Ziemsen Verlag, Wittenberg.

Müller, H. (1975): Die Aale. Neue Brehm Bücherei Band 471. A. Ziemsen Verlag, Wittenberg.

Müller, H. (1983): Fische Europas. Ferdinand Enke Verlag, Stuttgart.

Neergaard, S. (1981): Mbuna-Cichliden, Alfred Kernen Verlag, Stuttgart.

Neergaard, S. (1982): Tanganjika-Cichliden, Alfred Kernen Verlag, Stuttgart.

Neumann, W. (1983): Die Hechtlinge. A. Ziemsen Verlag, Wittenberg.

Paepke, H.-J. (1983): Die Stichlinge - Gasteorsteidae. A. Ziemsen Verlag, Wittenberg.

Pullin, R. S. V. & Lowe-McConnell, R. H. (1982): The biology and culture of Tilapias. International Center for Living Aquatic Resources Management, Manila, Philippinen.

Ribbink, A. J. et. al. (1983): A preliminary survey of the cichlid fishes of rocky habitats in Lake Malawi. S. Afr. J. Zool. **18**, 149-310. Grahamstown, Südafrika.

Riehl, R. & Baensch, H. A. (1983/84): Mergus Aquarien Atlas, Band 1. 4. Auflg., Mergus Verlag für Natur- und Heimtierkunde, Melle.

Roberts, T. R. (1989): The freshwater fishes of Western Borneo (Kalimantan Barat, Indonesia). Mem. Calif. Acad. Sci. **14**, 1-210. 1989

Robins, C. R. et. al. (1980): A list of common and scientific names of fishes from the United States and Canada. American Fisheries Society, Special Publication No. 12, 4. Auflage; Bethesda, Maryland, USA.

Schmettkamp, W. (1982): Die Zwergcichliden Südamerikas. Landbuch Verlag, Hannover

Schmitz, S. (1977): BLV-Naturführer Aquarienfische. Die wichtigsten Arten für das Süßwasseraquarium, ihre Haltung und Pflege. BLV-Verlagsgesellschaft, München.

Staeck, W. (1982): Handbuch der Cichlidenkunde. Franckh'sche Verlagshandlung, Stuttgart.

Staeck, W. (1983): Cichliden - Entdeckungen und Neuimporte, Band 3. Engelbert Pfriem Verlag, Wuppertal.

Steffens, W. (1980): Der Karpfen - Cyprinus carpio. A. Ziemsen Verlag, Wittenberg.

Steiniger, F. (1972): Lebendes Wasser. Kilda Verlag, Greven.

Sterba, G. (1977): Süßwasserfische aus aller Welt, Verlag J. Neumann, Melsungen.

Stockell, G. (1955): Freshwater fishes of New Zealand. Simpson & Williams, Christchurch, Neuseeland.

Tesch, F. W. (1983): Der Aal - Biologie und Fischerei; 2. Auflage. Verlag Paul Parey, Hamburg und Berlin.

Trewavas, E. (1983): Tilapiine fishes of the genera *Sarotherodon*, *Oreochromis* and *Danakilia*. British Museum, London.

van Ramshorst, J. D., ed. (1977): Handbuch der Aquaristik. Nova Buch Verlags GmbH, München.

Vierke, J. (1982): Vierkes Aquarienkunde - Grundlagen der Süßwasseraquaristik. Franckh'sche Verlagshandlung, Stuttgart.

Wendt, A. (1952ff): Die Aquarienpflanzen in Wort und Bild. Alfred Kernen Verlag, Stuttgart und Essen.

Wesenberg-Lund, C. (1939): Biologie der Süßwassertiere, Reprint Otto Koeltz, Königstein.

Wesenberg-Lund, C. (1943): Biologie der Süßwasserinsekten. Reprint Otto Koeltz, Königstein.

Wheeler, A. (1977): Das große Buch der Fische. Verlag Eugen Ulmer, Stuttgart.

Wundsch, H. H. (1963): Barsch und Zander. Neue Brehm Bücherei Band 305. A. Ziemsen Verlag, Wittenberg.

Allen, Dr. Gerald R.: 1012, 1021 t, 1111 t, 1115 (2), 1121 b, 1125 t, 1127 b, 1129 b, 1132.
Allison, David: 369 t, 375 t, 407 t, 437 t, 451 t, 489, 493 b, 497 t, 509 t, 523, 567 t, 989, 1005 t.l., 1143 t.
Axelrod, Dr. Herbert R.: 351 b.
Baensch, Hans A.: 222, 236, 249 t, 259 (2), 265 t, 276, 279, 287, 291 t, 296 b, 297, 298, 314, 315, 317, 323, 333 b, 440, 444, 473 t, 476, 517 t, 520, 521, 522, 641 t, 782, 810, 877 b.
Bleher, Heiko: 515 b, 1118.
Böhm, Otto: 263 t, 268 b, 305 b, 341 t, 353 b, 437 b, 702, 713 (3), 717 t, 719 b, 721 t, 729b, 733 t, 740, 745 b, 748 b, 751 t, 753 t, 755 (2), 975 t, 1013, 1069 b, 1097 b.
Bohlen, Jörg: 1010.
Bork, Dieter: 831 b.
Brun, Sven: 784 b.
Dieckhoff, Horst: 839 b, 841, 933 t.
Dokoupil, Norbert: 723 t, 731 t.
Eliás, Jaroslav: 373 t, 377 t.
Evers, Hans-Georg: 461 t, 465 b, 467 b, 475 b.
Foersch, Dr. Walter: 397 (2), 439 b, 457 b, 475 t, 573 b, 667 t, 789 t, 793 (2), 795 b, 796, 805, 806, 809 (2).
Frank, Dr. Stanislav: 245 b, 278, 281 b, 322, 327 b, 367 t, 407 b, 635 t, 1103 t.
Franke, Dr. Hanns Joachim: 231 t.
Frickhinger, Karl Albert: 214.
Göbel, M.: 996.
Hansen, Hilmar: 204, 211 b, 213 t, 217 (2), 219, 221, 301 t, 353 t, 357 b, 365 b, 395 t, 399 b, 419t, 421 t, 487 t, 499 t, 505 b, 565 t, 813 b, 955 b, 957 t, 1107, 1145 t, 1147t, 1150, 1151 (Aquarium Berlin).
Hartl, Andreas: 232.
Herrmann, Hans J.: 969 t.
Hoffmann, Peter: 277 b.
Horsthemke, Hans: 1063 t.
Huwald, Kurt: 273 b.
Jung, Heinrich: 459 b, 463 b.
Kahl, Burkhard: 233, 241 b, 249 b, 275 (2), 283 b, 289 b, 305 t, 307 t, 313 b, 321 t, 361 t,, 387 b, 389 t, 403 b, 417 b, 423 b, 429 b, 431 t, 441 b, 445 t, 453 b, 471 t, 517 b, 519 b, 527, 551t, 561 t, 723 b, 819 b, 863 b, 887 t, 953 t, 975 b, 979 b, 983, 985 t, 987 t, 999 b, 1007, 1064, 1065 b, 1099 b.
Kochetov, Dr. Sergei M.: 345 b, 347 b, 351 t, 355 (2), 359 (2), 361 b, 405 b, 409 t, 891 t, 1099 t.
Konings, Dr. A.: 930, 949 b.
Koslowski, Ingo: 823 b, 825 t, 827 (2).
Kottelat, Dr. Maurice: 341 b, 351 m, 454, 579 b.
Linke, Horst: 727 b, 789 b, 791 t, 799 t, 801 t, 804, 807, 811, 825 b, 829 t, 855 b, 857 t, 913, 915 u, 917 (2), 939 b, 955 t, 957 b, 965 b, 1001 (2), 1003 (2).
Lamboj, Anton: 965 t, 967 t.
Hans J. Mayland: 837 (2), 839 t, 843 t.
Manfred K. Meyer: 705, 709 t, 739 b, 749 t + m, 759 t, 775 b, 777 (2), 836, 840 (2), 843 b, 925, 931 b, 936, 937 (2), 945 t, 947 b, 949 b, (843, 844) 4 .
Meyer, Manfred K./ Wischnath, Lothar: 707 b, 711 b, 714, 717 b, 719 t, 721 b, 733 b, 735 (2), 737t, 741 b, 743 (3), 745 t, 747 b, 751 b, 757 (2), 759 m+b, 761 (2), 763 (2), 766 (4), 767 (4), 769t, 771 (2), 772, 773 (2), 775 t, 776, 779 (2), 781 (2), 783 (2), 785.
Nieuwenhuizen, Arend van den: 218, 294, 371 b, 379 (2), 415, 513 b, 565 b, 801 b, 1143 b.
Norman, Aaron: 205, 211 t, 235 t, 237 t, 241 t, 243, 247 (2), 251, 253 t, 255 b, 257 t, 262, 271 t, 286, 291 b, 293 (2), 309 t, 311 t, 329 b, 331 t, 333 t, 337, 357 t, 385 t, 387 t + m, 393 b, 395 b, 399 t, 401 (2), 403 t, 411 t, 421 b, 425 t, 431 b, 439 t, 447 (2), 455, 469 b, 477, 493 t, 505 t, 507 t, 514, 531 b, 553 t, 555 t, 557 b, 563 b, 577 t, 739 t, 797 b, 853 t, 857b, 858, 861 b, 867 t, 877 t, 879 b, 883 b, 893 b, 897 (2), 929 b, 935 t, 947 t, 961 b, 975 m, 977 b, 985 b, 991 b, 1015 t, 1017 (2), 1018, 1021 b, 1033, 1034, 1059, 1089 b, 1091 b, 1093 t, 1095 b, 1097 t, 1101 (2), 1105, 1106, 1145 b, 1153 (2), 1159 b, 1161 t.
Ott, Gerhard: 339 t, 349 b, 381 b.
Paffrath, Kurt: 7-170 (alle).
Paysan, Klaus: 225 t, 311 b, 312, 343 (2), 429 t, 441 t, 545 b, 559 b, 575 t, 581 b, 1026, 1163 t.
Pieter, A.: 994.
Pürzl, Eduard: 704, 707 t, 709 b, 727 t, 729 t, 753 b.

Photo Credits

Reinhard, Hans: 201, 203, 207, 208 b, 225 b, 227 t, 229 (2), 242, 260, 271 b, 299, 335 (2), 336, 339 b, 345 t, 349 t, 363 t, 365 t, 381 t, 391 t, 432, 433, 435 t, 443 (2), 445 b, 449 b, 453 t, 479 t, 485 t, 487 b, 488, 491 b, 495 b, 497 b, 503 t, 515 t, 533 t, 537 b, 539 t, 541 b, 547 t, 549 t, 553 b, 557 t, 563 t, 581 t, 848, 853 b, 873 b, 896, 981 t, 1071 b, 1095 t, 1159 t, 1161 b, 1163 b, 1165 (2).

Reitz, Günter: 198, 892, 988.

Rham, Dr. Patrick de: 829 b.

Richter, Hans-Joachim: 215, 220, 223, 235 b, 237 b, 245 t, 253 b, 257 b, 258, 261, 263 b 265 b, 267 b, 268 t, 273 t, 277 t, 281 t, 283 t, 285 (2), 289 t, 295, 296 t, 301 b, 303, 307b, 319 (2), 321 b, 325 (2), 327 t, 329 t, 347 t, 375 b, 385 b, 405 t, 409 b, 411 b, 417 t, 423 t, 425 b, 461 b, 465t, 469 t, 471 b, 479 b, 481 b, 483 b, 495 t, 501 b, 503 b, 511 b, 513 t, 519 t, 525t, 526, 531 t, 533 b, 547 b, 551 b, 555 b, 561 b, 573 t, 579 t, 582, 661 t, 715, 787, 791 b, 802, 803, 827 m, 831 t, 833 b, 849 b, 851 b, 860, 901 b, 915 t, 907 t, 923 b, 931 t, 940 b, 943 (2), 959 b, 962, 967 b, 981 b, 999 t, 1004, 1006 t, 1011, 1109 b, 1113 t, 1117 b, 1119 b, 1129 t, 1131 b.l., 1135 b, 1139 t, 1149 b.

Römer, Uwe: 821 b, 823 m+b.

Rösler, Hans J.: 673 t, 1074.

Rogner, Manfred: 1015 b.

Sandford, Mike: 213 b, 239 (2), 309 b, 331 b, 383 b, 393 t, 413 (2), 419 b, 427 b, 459 t, 491t, 499 b, 509 b, 525 b, 535 t, 537 t, 543 t, 575 b, 577 b, 867 b, 875 b, 1113 b, 1155 t.

Sands, David D.: 457 t, 463 t, 473 b, 481 t, 483 t, 529 (2), 535 b, 539 b, 541 t, 545t, 549 b, 567 b.

Schmettkamp, Werner: 833 t.

Schmida, Gunther E.: 206, 208 t, 435 b, 569 (2), 571 (2), 963, 1019, 1023 (2), 1024, 1025, 1027, 1029 (2), 1031 (2), 1032, 1037 (2), 1039 (2), 1041 (2), 1043 (2), 1045 (2), 1047(2), 1049, 1053, 1055 (2), 1057 (2), 1058, 1062, 1065 t, 1067 (2), 1069 t, 1071 t, 1073 (2), 1075, 1079 (2), 1081 t, m, b, 1083 (2), 1085 (2), 1087 (3), 1091 t, 1104, 1109 t, 1111 b, 1117 t, 1121 t, 1123 (2), 1125 b, 1127 t, 1130, 1131 (7), 1133 (2), 1135 t, 1137 (2), 1139 b, 1141 (2), 1154, 1155 b, 1156, 1157.

Schmidt, Jürgen: 795 t, 797 t, 799 b, 1061.

Schmidt-Focke, Dr. Eduard: 992, 993, 995 (2).

Schraml, Erwin: 367 b, 835 b, 885 t, 961 t.

Schulz, Thomas: 911 t.

Seegers, Lothar: 255 t, 267 t, 269, 356, 369 b, 371 t, 373 b, 377 b, 451, 511 t, 543 b, 584, 585, 587 (2), 589 (2), 591 (2), 593 (2), 595 (2), 597 (2), 599 (2), 601 (3), 603 (2), 605 (2), 607 (2), 609 (2), 611 (3), 613 (2), 614, 615 (2), 617 (2), 619 (2), 621 (2), 623 (2), 625 (2), 627 (2), 629 (2), 631 (2), 633, 635 b, 637 (2), 639 (2), 641 b, 643 (2), 645 (2), 647 (2), 649 (2), 651 (2), 653 (2), 655 (2), 657 (2), 659 (2), 661 b, 663 (2), 665 (2), 667 b, 669 (2), 671 (2), 673 b, 675 (2), 677 (2), 679, 681 (2), 683 (2), 685 (2), 687 (2), 689 (2), 691 (2), 693 (2), 695 (2), 697 (2). 699 (2). 700, 703, 711 t, 731 b, 737 m+b, 741 t, 747 t, 1077 (2), 1089 t, 1103 b, 1147 b, 1149 t.

Seuss, Werner: 415 b, 467 t.

Sommer, Wolfgang: 302.

Spreinat, Andreas: 838, 865 t, 899 b, 903 (2), 912 (2), 921 (2), 923 t, 939 t, 941, 950 (2), 973 t.

Staeck, Dr. Wolfgang: 853 m, 895 t, 899 t, 919 b, 924, 927 t, 933 b, 940 t, 945 b, 951, 953 b, 954, 971 (2), 973 b, 977 t, 987 b, 997, 1005 (7), 1006 (3).

Stawikowski, Rainer: 813 t, 851 t, 863 t, 865 b, 868, 873 t, 875 t, 881 b, 883 t, 885 b, 889 b, 891 b, 893 t, 895 m+b, 899 t, 901 t, 905 m+b, 907 b, 909 (3), 911 b, 919 t, 929 t, 949 t, 969 b, 982 (2).

Vierke, Dr. Jörg: 559 t, 821 t, 1035, 1061 t.

Werner, Uwe: 507 b, 815 (2), 817 (2), 819 t, 835 t, 849 t, 855 t, 859, 861 t, 869, 870, 871, 874, 879 t, 881 t, 887 b, 889 t, 905 t, 927 b, 935 b, 959 t, 979 t, 991 t, 1093 b, 1119 t.

Wildekamp, Ruud: 227 b, 250, 383 t, 391 b, 427 t.

Wischnath, Lothar: 11, 149 b. r., 701, 748 t, 768, 769 b, 770, 784 t, 786 (2).

Zarske, Dr. Axel: 231 b, 363 b, 501 t.

Zukal, Rudolf: 313 t, 389 b, 485 b.

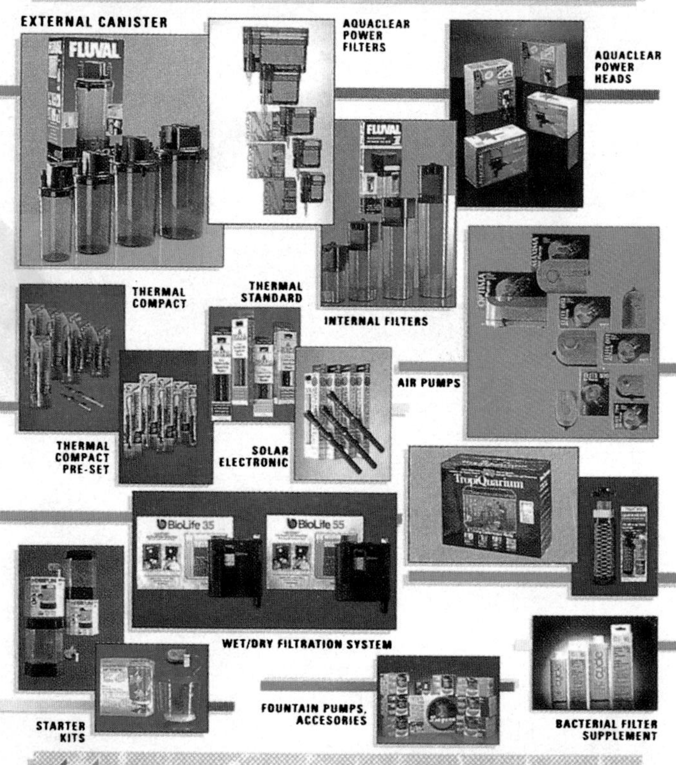
EXTERNAL CANISTER
FLUVAL
AQUACLEAR POWER FILTERS
AQUACLEAR POWER HEADS
FLUVAL
INTERNAL FILTERS
THERMAL COMPACT
THERMAL STANDARD
AIR PUMPS
THERMAL COMPACT PRE-SET
SOLAR ELECTRONIC
TropiQuarium
BioLife 35
BioLife 55
WET/DRY FILTRATION SYSTEM
STARTER KITS
FOUNTAIN PUMPS, ACCESORIES
BACTERIAL FILTER SUPPLEMENT